ISBN 978-0-266-03204-5
PIBN 10958091

This book is a reproduction of an important historical work. Forgotten Books uses
state-of-the-art technology to digitally reconstruct the work, preserving the original format
whilst repairing imperfections present in the aged copy. In rare cases, an imperfection in
the original, such as a blemish or missing page, may be replicated in our edition. We do,
however, repair the vast majority of imperfections successfully; any imperfections that
remain are intentionally left to preserve the state of such historical works.

1 MONTH OF
FREE
READING

at
www.ForgottenBooks.com

By purchasing this book you are eligible for one month membership to ForgottenBooks.com, giving you unlimited access to our entire collection of over 1,000,000 titles via our web site and mobile apps.

To claim your free month visit:
www.forgottenbooks.com/free958091

English
Français
Deutsche
Italiano
Español
Português

www.forgottenbooks.com

Mythology Photography **Fiction**
Fishing Christianity **Art** Cooking
Essays Buddhism Freemasonry
Medicine **Biology** Music **Ancient
Egypt** Evolution Carpentry Physics
Dance Geology **Mathematics** Fitness
Shakespeare **Folklore** Yoga Marketing
Confidence Immortality Biographies
Poetry **Psychology** Witchcraft
Electronics Chemistry History **Law**
Accounting **Philosophy** Anthropology
Alchemy Drama Quantum Mechanics
Atheism Sexual Health **Ancient History**
Entrepreneurship Languages Sport
Paleontology Needlework Islam
Metaphysics Investment Archaeology
Parenting Statistics Criminology
Motivational

CONDENSED

REPORTS OF CASES

IN THE

Superior Court of the Territory of Orleans,

AND IN THE

SUPREME COURT OF LOUISIANA;

CONTAINING

THE DECISIONS OF THOSE COURTS FROM THE AUTUMN TERM
1809, TO THE MARCH TERM, 1830, AND WHICH WERE
EMBRACED IN THE TWENTY VOLUMES OF
FR. XAVIER MARTIN'S REPORTS;

WITH

NOTES OF LOUISIANA CASES, WHEREIN THE DOCTRINES ARE
AFFIRMED, CONTRADICTED, OR EXTENDED, AND
OF THE SUBSEQUENT LEGISLATION.

EDITED

BY J. BURTON HARRISON,

COUNSELLOR AT LAW.

VOL. IV.

EMBRACING PART OF VOL 6, AND VOLS. 7 and 8, MARTIN'S REPORTS, NEW SERIES.

NEW ORLEANS:
E. JOHNS & Co., STATIONERS' HALL.

1840.

PRINTED BY T. K. & P. G. COLLINS, PHILADELPHIA.

TABLE OF CASES.

VOL. IV

TABLE OF CASES.

A*

TABLE OF CASES.

CASES

ARGUED AND DETERMINED

IN THE

Supreme Court of the State of Louisiana.

EASTERN DISTRICT, FEBRUARY TERM, 1828.

Mayor *et al. v.* Hennen.   VI, N. S. 428.

A claim for rent is barred by the prescription of five years.

PARISH Court of New Orleans.

PORTER, J., delivered the opinion of the court.

This is an action to recover of the defendant the ground rent of two lots belonging to the petitioners, which were purchased by the former in the year 1813 at sheriff's sale.

The defendant, among many other grounds of defence, pleaded, that he bought the lots as the agent of the petitioners, and if they refused to acknowledge his agency, he then offered, as an exception to all their demands except the last five years, the plea of prescription. Civil Code, 488, art. 78.

The court below sustained the exception, and condemned the defendant to pay the rent for the last five years. It also gave judgment against him for the price he had promised to pay for the lot when he purchased them at sheriff's sale, the petitioner being the plaintiff in the action in which the *fieri facias* had issued; though we do not see that any such demand was made in the petition.

The defendant has not complained of this and the appellants can not have the interest where there is no claim for the principal.

[Mayor *et al. v.* Hennen.]

It is, therefore, ordered, adjudged and decreed, that the judgment of the parish court be affirmed, with costs.

Moreau and *De Armas,* for the plaintiff.

Hennen, for the defendant.

Roulin v. Sabatier *et al.*, Syndics.   VI, N. S. 429.

An act *sous seing privé,* accompanied by possession, has effect against third persons.

PARISH Court of New Orleans.

PORTER, J., delivered the opinion of the court.

The husband of the petitioner made, in his lifetime, a conveyance to B. Grima, of the house of Sabatier & Grima, by which he sold to him for the sum of 5630 dollars, five slaves and a lot of ground situated in one of the suburbs of the city.

The property thus conveyed, remained, however, in the possession of the vendor—no delivery of it was made, and two days after, receiving the bill of sale, the vendee executed under *sous seing privé,* and delivered to him a counter letter; by which he acknowledged and declared, that the deed had been made merely in the view to enable the vendor to pass his property, after his death, to certain persons by him designated: that the price mentioned in the act had not been paid; and the vendee held the lot and slaves for the purposes already mentioned.

The only question in the cause is, whether the creditors are bound by an act under private signature. They contend they are not; that they had no notice of the counter letter; and that the property claimed by the petitioner, being vested in one of the insolvents by a public and authentic act, it makes a part of the estate surrendered.

The force and effect which should be given to acts *sous seing privé,* accompanied by possession, in opposition to the claims of creditors, has been most fully considered by this court in the cases of Doubrere *v.* Grillier's Syndics, 2 *N. S.* 171, and Martinez *v.* Layton, 4 *N. S.* 369. The principles there established govern this case, and we do not think it necessary to go into the question again. The subject is one of considerable difficulty, and has already occupied our attention, and exercised our judgment, as much as any other we have been called on to consider. When the date of acts under private sig-

[Roulin *v.* Sabatier *et al.,* Syndics.]

nature, is proved by evidence of facts *dehors* the instrument; when possession accompanies them, and the transaction is *bona fide;* we continue in our former impressions, that the law is best satisfied, and justice promoted, by giving to them the same effect against third persons, they would have against the party who executes them.

It is, therefore, ordered, adjudged and decreed, that the judgment of the parish court be affirmed, with costs.

Canon and *Trabuc,* for the plaintiff.

Mazureau, for the defendant.

Pignatel *v.* Drouet. VI, N. S. 432.

A *sous seing privé* not made double forms a commencement of proof in writing.

A commencement of proof in writing, is presented by every instrument which requires parol evidence to establish its reality.

And therefore, where the contract is for land, if the agreement has been reduced to writing, proof of its being signed by the parties, may be given by parol, though it was not made double.

A sale *sous seing privé* is obligatory, though in the agreement the parties promise to pass their contract before a notary, and although that promise is not complied with.

FIRST District.

PORTER, J., delivered the opinion of the court.

The plaintiff and defendant by act *sous seing privé,* of date the 5th March, 1827, entered into an agreement by which they stated, that the defendant had purchased five lots from the plaintiff such as they were, with the buildings thereon, situated in the fauxbourg La Fayette, Parish of Jefferson, for the price and sum of 3,200 dollars, and that the sale would be passed by public act, (*au greffe,*) as soon as the plaintiff would receive from one M'Dougald, of Baton Rouge, to whom he had previously sold, an act annulling the title vested in the latter; and if M'Dougald did not pass such an act, the defendant was to wait until the plaintiff could comply with the necessary formalities to enable the sheriff to make a title. The conditions were two notes, one payable in June, 1827, and the other in March, 1828.

The petition sets out this agreement, designates particularly the lots sold—states that a rescission of the sale to M'Dougald had been obtained from him; that he was willing and ready to pass to the defendant a clear and unincumbered title to the premises, but that the latter had refused to accept it or comply with his agreement.

It concludes by a prayer that the property mentioned should be decreed to belong to the defendant, and that he should be decreed to be the debtor of the petitioner in the sum of 1600 dollars payable in June, 1827, and 1600, payable in March, 1828.

The defendant pleaded, that if such an instrument of writing could be produced, as was stated in the plaintiff's petition, it still had no effect in law; and although the respondent had the intention to acquire the property in plaintiff's petition mentioned, yet as the plaintiff delayed to make a title, and was unable to do so, the respondent was compelled to purchase other property for the immediate use of his family.

And further, that the plaintiff was not the owner of the property mentioned in the petition; that he could make no title to the same; and moreover, that it was incumbered by mortgages.

The district court decreed, that the plaintiff should recover as he had prayed in the petition, but that he should not have the benefit of the judgment until he made to the defendant a clear and unincumbered title to the premises.

From this judgment the defendant has appealed, and in this court has relied on the following grounds for its reversal.

1. That the agreement was a synallagmatic one, executed under private signature, and that, as there was not as many originals as there were parties, it is not binding.

2. That the act on which suit is brought does not establish a sale, but contains a promise to sell, with the further clause that the sale is to be executed by an authentic act, and that until that is done either party may retract.

3. That the plaintiff did retract, and if he did not, there was such unreasonable delay in carrying into effect his agreement to pass a sale by public act, that the defendant was not obliged to accept it at the period it was tendered.

4. That the property was incumbered by mortgages: that this circumstance was unknown to the appellant at the time he entered into the agreement, and authorises him to refuse a compliance with his contract.

I. The agreement on which this suit is brought, was entered into since the passage of the amendments to the Civil Code, and since the publication of those amendments, and a portion of the old Code, under the title of " The Civil Code of Louisiana." The compilers of the last mentioned work have left out of it those articles in the old Code which contained provisions in relation to the perfection of synallagmatic agreements. But the defendant contends, that their failure to insert them does not repeal the former law, and he has relied on a decision of this court in the case of Flower v. Griffith, *ante* 89, by which we held, that the omission to reprint the last title of the first Civil Code, could not be considered as abrogating it.

[Pignatel v. Drouet.]

This court did so decide in the case alluded to. In that instance, however, there was nothing to show either in the law as printed, the amendments engrossed in the office of the secretary of state, nor in the report made to the legislature that there had been any thing done, from which a repeal or even an intention to repeal the omitted title could be inferred. In the case before us, it is seen from the report of the jurists appointed to draw up the amendments to the Code that they recommended the suppression of these articles as useless, and tending to promote the evils they were intended to guard against. Whether this recommendation, coupled with the knowledge we possess of the manner in which this report was acted on, and the fact of their not being reprinted, would authorise a court of justice to conclude, that there was a repeal of them, our opinion of the case, supposing it to be governed by the old Code, dispenses with the necessity of deciding.

It has been declared by this tribunal in more than one instance, that a failure to comply with the provisions of the Civil Code which required as many originals, as there were parties, for the validity of acts *sous seing privé*, evidencing synallagmatic agreements, did not render them null and void—that they were still good as a commencement of proof in writing. It is deemed unnecessary to go again into the reasons which brought us to that conclusion, or to advance others in support of it which the subject fruitfully suggests. 3 *N. S.* 81; 4 *N. S.* 200.

Its correctness has not indeed been impugned, but it has been strenuously contended that this case offers a complete exception to that principle, because the contract being for immovable property, the sale of which can not be proved by parol, it follows as a consequence, that the commencement of proof in writing can not be eked out, and made complete by oral testimony. That the prohibition in the law extends to the part, as well as the whole.

If the words *commencement of proof in writing* meant alone a proof, not of the whole matter that was alleged against the party to whom it was opposed, but of something which led to, or made a part of it, then this reasoning would be entitled to all the weight which the counsel seemed to consider due to it. But these expressions in our law have a much more extensive sense than that which this argument ascribes to them. They apply to every instrument which does not make proof in itself of its existence, and the truth of the facts therein set forth; to every act which parol evidence is required to establish—in one word, to all instruments that are not authentic. Without the sanction and command of positive authority, no writing would establish by itself the truth of what it contained, nor of the hand that traced its characters, nor of the time in which it was executed. The legislatures of most countries to avoid the difficulties this principle would produce in its application to the transactions of society, and to simplify the proof of contracts, have declared, that acts passed before public officers if clothed with certain formalities

1*

shall prove themselves. All instruments which do not come within
the provisions that confer this authenticity, remain within the operation of the doctrine just stated—they require other evidence to
establish their validity; they are therefore not proof, but a commencement of proof, as the modern French jurists call them; or in the
language of the Roman civilians, *semiplenam probationem.—Toullier, Droit Civil, vol. 9, chap. 6, no. 61; Mascardus de prb, vol. 1,
p. 38.*

It was necessarily in this understanding of these words that this
court said in the cases already cited, that a *sous seing privé* not made
double, formed a commencement of proof in writing, for the instruments on which those suits were brought, contained within themselves every thing necessary to show a legal contract. The evidence
required to make them complete, was not to prove that other matters
than those expressed in the act were agreed on: but that the writing
which was presented as the evidence of the agreement, was the act
of the parties whose signatures were affixed to it.

II. Being thus of opinion, that the instrument sued on was not
void, but on the contrary formed such a commencement of proof, as
enabled either party to establish its existence by parol evidence, there
is next to be considered the objection; that it was nothing more than
a promise to sell, with an agreement to reduce that sale to writing
by public act, and until that was done, either party might retract. In
support of that position, we have been referred to a passage in *Febrero,* which correctly states as the former law of this country, that a
sale may be made either by parol, or in writing, but that where it is
agreed there shall be a sale in writing, it is not perfect until the writing is executed, and either party may retract: the promise to sell being
one thing, and the other the completion of the contract. Whether
the provision in our Code which declares, that a promise to sell
amounts to a sale, has not in some measure changed this doctrine, in
relation to that species of property the alienation of which may be
proved by parol, need not be inquired into; because in this instance
the agreement was reduced to writing, and the authority quoted applies only to cases where the contract is verbal. Upon this ground,
therefore, the defendant had no right to retract, and he had none upon
the other position advanced in the argument, that this was a promise
to sell, and that acts were committed by the vendor which authorised him to refuse to make the contract complete. The instrument
which they signed was not a promise to sell, but a sale. This assertion requires no other, and can receive no greater, support, than that
which the act itself furnishes. It begins in these words: *"Nous somme
convenus entre Lazarre Pignatel et Jean Babtiste Drouet d'un
commun accor que le sieur Jean Babtiste Drouet a acheté au sieur
Lazarre Pignatel cinq terrains tels qu'ils se comportant avec toutes
les batisses qui se trouvent dessus,"* &c. &c.

These expressions although awkward and ungrammatical, leave
no doubt on the mind that there was a sale, and the further stipula

tion contained in the instrument, that a public act should be made of the contract, as soon as the vendor could obtain a rescission by suit, or otherwise, of the sale previously given to M'Dougal, does not turn it into a mere promise to sell. It is confounding two things entirely distinct, to assimilate a promise to sell, and that sale reduced to writing, to a sale *sous seing privé*, containing an agreement that there shall be hereafter a public act. In the latter, where, as in this instance, there is thing, price, consent, and words amounting to an alienation, the parties are as much bound by the act under private signature as they would be by one passed before a notary. The agreement to give their contract greater publicity, either by registering it, or by passing it in the form of an authentic act, does not change or alter the substance of the contract. Nor does the failure to do so unnul it. Hence *Portalis* in reporting the title of sale of the Napoleon Code, from which that of ours is principally taken says: " *On a jugé con-stamment qu'une vente sous seing privé etait obligitoire quoique dans l'acte on se fut reservé de faire rediger ses accords en acte public et que cette reserve n'eut jamais eté realisée. Code Civil avec les discours, rapports et opinions, vol.* 4, 258; *Cinq Codes, no.* 1582; Code Civil, note 2.

Being, therefore, of opinion there was a sale by the act under private signature, it is unnecessary to examine at length the other questions raised, as to the parties having retracted, and the length of time that elapsed before the vendor was ready to make the public act.

And as to the right to resist the execution of the contract because there were mortgages on the property given, both before and after the date of the *sous seing privé*: they do not form in themselves a ground of rescission, and the judge below has amply secured the defendant, by decreeing that the contract should not be enforced, until the property is liberated from these charges.

It is, therefore, ordered, adjudged and decreed, that the judgment of the distric court be affirmed, with costs.

Chapotin, for the plaintiff.

Preston, for the defendant.

Wooter *v.* Turner.   VI, N. S. 442.

The jurisdiction of an appellate court depends on the fact of a judgment being rendered in that of the inferior tribunal from which an appeal lies, and is not affected by the causes which produced that judgment.

Where the right of a legatee is disputed, he may bring suit to have the claim recognised, though judgment cannot be given for any specific amount, until the curator renders his account.

And a jury may be called to try the facts on which the legatee's claim is disputed.

The act of 1820, relative to the probate court, while it directed all suits cognisable therein to be tried without jury, did not destroy the duty of the district court, on appeals, to call a jury to try facts.

THIRD District.

Porter, J., delivered the opinion of the court.

This is an action against the defendant, curator of the estate of James Nolasco, deceased, in which the plaintiff, in her own right, and as tutrix to her minor children, demands payment of a legacy of 1000 dollars left her, and the residue of the testator's estate, by virtue of a bequest contained in the will, to these children, and to one John Rousso, who is since dead, and whose share belongs to them by right of survivorship.

The petition is rendered obscure, and the understanding of the case difficult, by the plaintiff's having crowded into it a mass of matter that would more properly have belonged to an opposition to the defendant's account when it was presented.

It appears, that two persons, called John Rousso and Antonio Nolasco, were in the habit of the closest intimacy with James Nolasco. Rousso died in the year 1811, and, by his will, gave a legacy to James Nolasco. Antonio Nolasco, who had been in partnership with Rousso, now formed a connection of the same kind with James Nolasco, and before his death in the year 1817, made his testament, and bequeathed his estate to the son of his former partner Rousso, and to James Nolasco. No separation of the estate ever took place, and the executors which they respectively appointed, having been discharged, the defendant was appointed curator to the three successions.

The petition sets out all these facts in detail, and avers, that the several legacies left to J. Nolasco, by Rousso, and Antonio Nolasco, are yet unpaid; and concludes with a prayer, that the defendant may render an account of the three estates; that he be condemned to pay the petitioner the sum of 1000 dollars, bequeathed to her by James Nolasco, with interest since the 1st January, 1818, and the residue of the estate, which she avers to be 2000 dollars.

[Wooter v. Turner.]

The defendant pleaded, first, that the suit could not be maintained, because it was against three successions, each having separate and distinct interests; secondly, that the facts alleged by the petitioner were untrue; and thirdly, and lastly, that the estate was insolvent.

If the suit were against the three estates, as the defendant alleges, then we should think the conclusion he has drawn correct. But it appears to us to be against that of James Nolasco alone, and to ask for judgment against the defendant in that character and no other. The prayer at the conclusion is expressly thus. The setting out in it, the different claims of James Nolasco's estate on that of Antonio Nolasco and Rousso, and the call on the defendant, to render an account as curator of these successions, was most probably the cause of the defendant's presenting the objection. But a reference to the situation of the estates, affords a more satisfactory explanation of the objects sought to be obtained by the insertion of these matters in the pleadings. No separation of the different successions has been made. James Nolasco was the last survivor of the three partners; the amount of his estate depended in a great measure on the sum it should receive from that of Rousso, and Antonio Nolasco, and the plaintiff deemed it necessary the defendant should render an account of these two successions before it could be ascertained how much she could recover as a legatee. That the insertion of the various facts in the petition, showing the claims of James Nolasco's estate on the two others, was for this object, and not to lay the basis of distinct claims against the defendant on which she expected judgment, is manifest from the following clause in the petition, in which, after setting out these claims, is stated, " that the legacies aforesaid, to him left, by the said John Rousso, under the name and denomination of Santiago Monovilio, and the legacy to him left, by the said Antonio Nolasco, *constitute a part of the said vacant estate or succession of the said James Nolasco.*"

These statements, therefore, can be considered in no other light, than as averments in the petition of the various things which constituted the succession of James Nolasco, and the call on the defendant to render an account, nothing more than a demand from him, who, as curator of the other estates, had a knowledge of their situation, to furnish that evidence which would enable the court to judge correctly of the amount of James Nolasco's estate. It would certainly have been more regular, and have greatly simplified the proceedings, to have taken no notice of these matters in the petition; and to have called on the defendant to furnish an account of James Nolasco's estate, without avowing in detail of what it was made up. On the account being presented, if the moneys coming to it from the other estates, had not been inserted, an opposition to the account of the curator would have brought these matters more regularly before the court. But the irregularity of setting them forth in the petition does not so vitiate the proceedings as to require us to nonsuit the plaintiff; though she has somewhat obstructed the road before her, it is still open and clear enough, to enable her to travel on to final judgment.

[Wooter v. Turner.]

This case was commenced in the probate court, at a time when an appeal lay from that tribunal to the district court. The plaintiff, failing to procure any, or sufficient evidence, to make out her case in the court where the action commenced, was nonsuited, and she appealed to the district court, where the cause was submitted to a jury who found a special verdict.

Before examining that verdict and the objections that have been made to it, it is necessary to notice a point relied on by the defendant in this court. She contends that, as the case related to matters appertaining to the jurisdiction of the court of probates, it was improperly submitted to a jury in the district court; that the plaintiff could not take an appeal from a judgment of nonsuit, rendered on a failure to produce any evidence in the former; that it was an evasion on her part, of the law which requires the probate court to take cognisance of the cause in the first instance, and was virtually giving that of the district, original jurisdiction.

The argument against the legality of submitting the case to a jury in the district court, is principally founded on inconvenience, and though it certainly derives some support from the nature of the transactions which are generally submitted to probate tribunals, yet it is not of sufficient weight to enable us to make an exception where the legislature has made none. Previous to the year 1820, parties had the right even in the parish court, which, as such, possessed probate jurisdiction, to have any contested fact arising between them, submitted to the country. The act passed in that year, fixing the jurisdiction, and regulating the form of proceedings, in the court of probates, directs, that all the causes cognisable by the said court shall be tried therein, without the intervention of a jury. The same act gives an appeal to the district court, and is silent as to any change in the mode of trial when the cause goes thither. The district court, previous to the act, had the power, as well as the probate court, to try all cases by a jury. The prohibition against trying them in that mode thereafter, is confined to the probate tribunal; hence, we conclude the form of proceeding remains the same in the district court as before. We have reason to believe, that the inconvenience of calling the citizens too often from their occupations to serve as jurors had as much weight with the legislature in causing this enactment, as the incompetency of the tribunal to investigate cases of the kind. But whether it had or not, on no sound rules of construction could the clause in the act changing the form of proceeding in one court, be held to apply to another, when in the same law, they provide for the case going before the latter, and are silent as to any change in the mode of trial when it arrives there.

The objection growing out of the fact of the plaintiff having submitted to a nonsuit in the court of the first instance, appears to be quite untenable. The jurisdiction of an appellate court depends on the fact of a judgment being rendered in that of the inferior, from which an appeal lies, not on what preceded that judgment, or the causes that led to it.

[Wooter v. Turner.]

The special verdict, as set forth in the record, finds a variety of facts in relation to the matters stated in the petition, the death of Rousso, Antonio Nolasco, and James Nolasco, their partnerships, and their wills; but it does not find any specific sum which the plaintiff should recover, and the defendant contends, that by reason of this defect, no judgment can be rendered on it in favor of the petitioner; of that opinion was the court below, and nonsuited her.

. When the claims of a residuary legatee are contested on the grounds which were presented by the answer, and put at issue in this cause, it is impossible for the court that tries it, to give judgment for any specific sum. What remains can only be known after the curator has rendered his account, and he, by disputing the will, and the right of the person claiming, forces a decision on these facts, before he can be compelled to show how he administered the estate and how much is in his hands. Two questions then occur: First, whether the legatee is disqualified to bring an action to have his claim recognised, before the curator renders an account? and Secondly, if he can, and does, whether the facts which are necessary to establish his right can be tried by a jury? and if they can, if the verdict establishing this right, but not finding any specific sum due, can be the basis of a judgment of the court? We have not a doubt that the suit may be brought the moment the right is disputed, and that on such a verdict the court may well pronounce judgment. We have already decided, that, in ordinary cases, a creditor may sue the representative of an estate, who refuses to recognise his demand, and is not obliged to wait until the tableau of distribution is filed.* We cannot distinguish the case of a legatee from that of any other person having claims against the succession. It may be as important to him as it is to a creditor, not to be obliged to wait until the curator is ready to pay, before he can have his demand established.

As has been already remarked, it is impossible to ascertain what is the residue of the estate, until the curator renders an account; the jury, therefore, cannot find any sum to be due, but they can find those facts on which the court is authorised to give a judgment that will establish the right of the plaintiff to whatever will remain. We know of no technical rule of our law which forbids it, and surely the ends of justice are promoted by sanctioning the course pursued in this cause. We cannot imagine an instance where those courts of our country, which have the power to bring juries before them, are required to decide on any facts, (whether those facts may authorise a judgment for a sum of money, or call for a special decree to meet the justice of the case,) that the parties are debarred from having the facts disputed, tried by a jury. There is no exception that we are aware of, unless in relation to long and intricate accounts, which the statute directs to be sent before referees.

In this instance the jury have found facts sufficient to enable the

* Baillio et al. v. Wilson et al. 5 N. S. 218.

court to decree that she and her children are entitled to the legacies left them by James Nolasco, if there be any sufficient funds to pay them. ' In order to ascertain this, the cause must be remanded to the court of probates, and the defendant be compelled to render his account as curator.

If, in rendering that account, he fails to insert to the credit of the estate, any moneys which belong to it, whether coming from the succession of John Rousso, Antonio Nolasco, or any other source, the plaintiff, by proper opposition, can bring the fact before the court; any decree respecting them at this stage of the cause, would be premature and illegal.

Nor can we examine now into the claim of survivorship set up in behalf of the children of plaintiff, to the portion left John Rousso, Jun., because the attorney for the absent heirs has not been made a party to the suit, and this claim must be decided contradictorily with him.

We had almost forgotten to notice the objection taken on the ground, that the estate is insolvent, and that the plaintiff has not shown there is any thing in the curator's hands. The appointment itself, to the office of curator, presupposes property; the inventory and sale show it, and the burthen of proving the estate insolvent devolves on the defendant.

The question as to costs must remain open until final judgment.

It is, therefore, ordered, adjudged and decreed, that the judgment of the district court be annulled, avoided and reversed; and it is further ordered, adjudged and decreed, that this cause be remanded to the court of probates, with directions to the judge thereof, to compel the defendant to render an account of his administration of the estate of J. Nolasco, according to law, and that on rendering said account, he pay to the petitioner the sum of 1000 dollars, if so much remain in his hands after discharging higher claims against the succession, if any such there be; and that he also pay over to the petitioner, as representative to her children, and as heir to one of them deceased, the one-half of the residue of said estate, after all debts due by it, and special bequests made by the will, are satisfied; and it is further ordered, that the appellee pay the costs of the appeal.

Commaux *v.* Barbin. VI, N. S. 454.

The grandfather has a right to the tutorship, after the father and mother, without being recommended by a family meeting, who are, however, to pass on the sureties he offers.

At such a meeting the under tutor should be present.

COURT of Probates, Parish of East Baton Rouge.

Martin, J., delivered the opinion of the court.

The minor being under the age of puberty, his grandfather prayed to be appointed his tutor, on a suggestion that the mother and tutrix had contracted a second marriage, without having applied for a family meeting for the purpose of determining whether she should be continued in the tutorship. The judge of probates ordered a family meeting to examine and report on the sureties he offered.

The meeting was ordered for the 12th of April.

On the 14th of May, the under tutor opposed the appointment of the grandfather as tutor on various grounds.

The grandfather prayed that the opposition be dismissed, on the ground of its having been filed too late. Of this opinion was the judge, and it was accordingly dismissed.

The under tutor took a bill of exceptions to the opinion of the court.

Afterwards, at a special court of probates, letters of tutorship were directed to issue to the grandfather, the court expressing again its opinion, that the opposition was too late, and stating that the under tutor did not apply for the tutorship himself, or for any other person—that the grandfather had a legal claim to the tutorship, and was recommended by the family meeting as a fit person. The under tutor appealed.

We do not see on what ground the opposition was rejected as tardy, and the record is extremely obscure on this head—the petition of the grandfather, the order for the family meeting, and the summons of its members, are without a rule. We collect from the summons, that the meeting was to be holden on the 12th of April.

The proceedings at this meeting make no part of the record.

The grandfather, as the nearest ascendant, (the father being dead, and the mother having forfeited the tutorship,) had a right to the tutorship, without the recommendation of the family meeting, but the assembly was to consider of the sureties he offered.

[Commaux *v.* Barbin.]

At the meeting for this purpose, the under tutor was to be present and the sheriff's return shows that he was not.

The proceedings of this meeting were irregular, and the under tutor had a right to complain of this—and we are ignorant of, and the grandfather has not shown, any provision of law, fixing any period after which delay is fatal.

The court ought not to have ordered letters to issue till surety was given according to law, *i. e.*, a bond with surety, approved by a family meeting, to which the under tutor was summoned.

It is, therefore, ordered, adjudged and decreed, that the judgment of the court of probates be annulled, avoided and reversed, and the case remanded, with directions to the court of probates to proceed therein according to law.

Eustis, for the under tutor.

Pritchard *v.* Hamilton.   VI, N. S. 456.

The notary's certificate should state in what post-office he put the notice.
The Supreme Court cannot give a judgment which the judge *a quo* could not give.
There cannot be a nonsuit after a general verdict.

THIRD District.

PORTER, J., delivered the opinion of the court.

The defendant is sued as endorser of a promissory note. On the trial, evidence of notice of protest was presented under the certificate of a notary. Many objections were made to its introduction, the court overruled them, and admitted the paper, but at the same time told the jury, that without further proof it was not sufficient evidence of notice. Of this opinion was the jury, and the court having rendered a judgment conformable to their verdict, the plaintiff appealed.

The certificate is defective in not stating the post office in which the letter was put. The point has been already decided in this court.

The plaintiff failing to give any other evidence, the jury did not err in the conclusion they drew from the proof before them, nor the court in rendering judgment thereon. Laporte *v.* Landry, 4 *N. S.* 125.

We have been pressed to give a judgment of nonsuit. But this

[Pritchard v. Hamilton.]

court can not on appeal give a judgment which the court below could not. It was settled in the cases of Chetodeau's Heirs v. Dominguez, and Abat v. Rion, that a judgment of nonsuit could not be pronounced after a general verdict. The Code of Practice has made no change in this jurisprudence. 7 *Martin*, 490, 567.

It is, therefore, ordered, adjudged and decreed, that the judgment of the district court be affirmed, with costs.

Eustis, for the plaintiff.

Hennen, for the defendant.

Thompson v. Chaveau et al. VI, N. S. 458.

An officer, sued as a trespasser, in a sale on a *fi. fa.* may cite the party by whose directions he acted, and who gave a bond of indemnity.

A case will not be remanded, because irrelevant testimony was received.

A witness is not to be rejected, because he is a creditor of the estate of the defendant's ancestor.

Nor because having a mortgage on a tract of land purchased by the plaintiff, he received from the latter part of the price, in payment of his debt, and released his right on the mortgage.

The defendant on a *fi. fa.* on which land was sold is not a good witness in a suit for the rescission of the sale.

The order of a court of probates for appointing a curator, is evidence of that appointment, between persons not parties thereto.

When a document is legal evidence of a fact, and not of another, and the trial is before the court, it must be read, and the party may afterwards make his objections.

He who claims under a sale on a *fi. fa.* is bound to produce the judgment and writ, but no other part of the record of the suit; and the certificate of the record from below, should simply be, that the copy is a true one.

PARISH Court of New Orleans.

MARTIN, J., delivered the opinion of the court.

The defendant, marshal of the city court of New Orleans, is sued for a trespass, committed by the illegal seizure and sale of the plaintiff's house and lot. He justified under several suits of *fieri facias*, and prayed that the plaintiffs in these suits, by whose order, and under whose bonds of indemnity he acted, might be cited to defend him; they accordingly were, and their answer justifies the seizure and sale, and avers that the plaintiff purchased the premises in fraud of their rights.

The plaintiff moved that so much of the answer of the original defendant as related to bringing in these new parties, should be stricken out. It was accordingly ordered, and he appealed from the order. The cause however, proceeded to judgment, which was for the plaintiff, and the defendant appealed.

The plaintiff now took a rule on Buckman, one of the intervening parties, and the purchaser of the premises, to show cause why a writ of possession should not issue against him on showing cause; the rule was discharged, and the plaintiff appealed.

Both parties have brought up the record, and the appeals are submitted together.

Our attention is first arrested on several bills of exceptions.

1. The first is taken by the defendants to the admission of Preval as a witness, on the ground of the irrelevancy of the testimony offered. The consequnce of the court's error, if it erred, was the loss of time in hearing immaterial testimony. It would be aggravated, if to correct the error the case was remanded, for we cannot comprehend how the absence of immaterial testimony would lead the inferior court to a different conclusion.

2. The next is taken by the defendant to the opinion of the court in rejecting Orr, offered as a witness, on the score of interest. This witness on his *voir dire* declared, he considered himself a creditor of the estate of M'Dermott, whose heirs were defendants in the suit in which the *fieri facias* had issued, but he thought he had no interest in the suit, because he believed the estate amply sufficient. We are of opinion he was improperly rejected. Hughes *v.* Lawes, 6 *Martin*, 502.

3. The third is taken by the plaintiff to the introduction of Clark and Grymes as witnesses on the score of interest.

To repel Clark, reference is made to the deed of sale by which the plaintiff purchased the premises from M'Dermott's daughter, the wife of Grymes. It thereby appears, that Grymes and wife acknowledged the receipt of part of the price, by a release of a mortgage of the premises which Clark had, he having received payment from the vendee, the present plaintiff.

We are of opinion the court did not err by admitting him.

The parties brought in by the original defendant, avail themselves of their being cited, by filing a petition of reconvention to demand the rescission of the sale under which the plaintiff claims. Grymes and wife are the parties defendant in the *fieri facias*, on which the sale took place. If the sale be set aside, the present plaintiff will have an action against Grymes's wife, and the judgment of rescission would be *prima facie* evidence against her: Grymes has therefore an interest in support of the plaintiff's title, and the court erred in admitting him.

4. The fourth bill is taken by the plaintiff to the admission in evidence of the proceedings in the court of probates on the appointment

[Thompson v. Chavean et al.]

of Gainie as curator of M'Dermot's daughter, Grymes's wife. The objection is stated to have been because these proceedings are *res inter alios acta.* This may be, but we cannot see what other legal evidence could be adduced of the appointment of a curator. We do not think the court erred.

5. A bill is taken by the plaintiff to the introduction of the defendant's bill of sale as marshal, to the plaintiff, of the premises, to prove any thing but the adjudication—on the ground that it was no evidence of title in the vendee because not duly registered.

This objection admits the legality of the evidence for a certain purpose. Had the case been before a jury, the party objecting to it on evidence for other purposes, ought to have requested the judge to charge the jury accordingly—but when the case is tried by the court, the deed must be read if it be evidence of any fact material to the issue, and the party may afterwards argue against it being used to establish other facts. We do not think the court erred in admitting the document in evidence.

6. The last bill was taken by the plaintiff to the introduction in evidence of the judgment of one of the intervening parties against the heir of M'Dermott, on the ground of its being as to the parties in the present suit *res inter alios acta.* This may be, but he who claims under a sale on a *fieri facias* may, indeed must, produce the judgment on which this writ issued, to justify the sale.

The judgment is also objected to on the ground that the certificate at the foot of the record does not state that it contains all the proceedings in the case. The objection is untenable: he who claims under a sale of a *fieri facias* is only bound to produce the judgment on which it issued. When a case comes up to this court after a trial, entirely on documental evidence, the certificate ought to certify that the record contains all of it—but in other cases, the certificate is only that the copy is a true one.

We do not think the court erred.

As legal evidence has been rejected, this prevents an examination of the case on the merits, and compels us to remand the case.

We think the court erred in directing that part of the original answer which related to the bringing in of the plaintiffs in the *fieri facias* to be stricken out. The marshal had a right to demand that they should defend him, and on their failing, judgment should be given against them. This case is in this respect perfectly analogous to that of Lafonta *v.* Poutz, determined at the last term.

It is therefore ordered, adjudged and decreed, that the judgment of the parish court be annulled, avoided and reversed, and the case remanded for trial, with directions to the parish judge to allow the part of the answer stricken out to be reinstated—not to reject the testimony of Orr on the score of interest, and not to admit that of Grymes; and it is ordered that the plaintiff pay costs in this court.

Nixon, for the plaintiff.
Canon, for the defendant.

2*

Williams *v.* Chew. VI, N. S. 463.

An appeal suspends all proceedings before the judge *a quo.*
Whether appeals or writs of error, by the United States as appellant, do not in every
case suspend executions ? *Quære.*

FIRST District.

MARTIN, J., delivered the opinion of the court.

The defendant, collector of the United States for the port of New Orleans, having received a sum of money from the marshal, as his portion of the proceeds of the sale of sundry goods of the plaintiff's, condemned in the district court of the United States for a breach of the revenue laws, is sued, in an action for money had and received, the decree of condemnation having been reversed in the Supreme Court of the United States.

The answer admits the seizure, condemnation and reversal of the judge of the district court, but avers that the Supreme Court sent back the case to the district court for an amendment of the pleadings and further proceedings on which the plaintiff had judgment, but an appeal was taken by the United States and is still undetermined and pending in the Supreme Court of the United States.

The court below gave judgment of nonsuit, being of opinion that the suit was prematurely brought, the appeal leaving the case and all the orders taken in it, in the state in which they were before the judgment. That the judgment being in abeyance by the appeal, every thing is suspended thereby, except the execution, which the plaintiff is at liberty by statute to take.

We concur in the opinion expressed by the judge *a quo*, except as to the right of the plaintiff to take execution, on which we express no opinion, the case not requiring one. It is true, in ordinary cases, appeals or writs of error do not prevent execution to issue when the appellant or plaintiff in error does not give a bond with sureties. Perhaps the United States enjoy an exception to the general rule; they pay no costs or damages, consequently give no security; and their appeal or writ of error perhaps suspends the execution in every case.

It is, therefore, ordered, adjudged and decreed, that the judgment of the district court be affirmed, with costs.

. *Hennen* and *Pierce*, for the plaintiff.

Smith, for the defendant.

Oldham *v.* Polk.   VI, N. S. 465.

A clause in an act, authorising any attorney to confess judgment, does not authorise the issue of a writ of seizure and sale, but is irreconcilable with the idea of an execution on the act without a previous confession of judgment in court.

SECOND District.

PORTER, J., delivered the opinion of the court.

The plaintiff obtained an order of seizure and sale on a mortgage by public act, which the defendant had executed in his favor. The instrument was in the usual form, with the exception of the following clause: " and the said George W. Oldham does hereby for himself and his heirs, in the event the said note be not paid at maturity, grant power to any attorney at law duly admitted to practise in the courts of this state, to appear, and for him, and in his name, confess judgment in due and legal form, in favor of said Samuel W. Polk, up to the amount of the said note," &c. &c.

Our Code provides, that where the title amounts to a confession of judgment (*emporte execution parée*) the creditor on making out that the debt is due, may obtain an order for the immediate seizure of the property mortgaged: and this court has decided, that an authentic act containing a mortgage, is such a title as amounts to a confession of judgment.

And so the instrument on which the order of seizure and sale was obtained in this case would be, were it not for the clause already set out. To give that part of the act any meaning, or suppose it inserted for any purpose, we must conclude the parties did not intend this instrument should *amount to a confession of judgment,* for if they had, they would not have provided for an attorney going before a court to *confess judgment.* The conferring such a power is irreconcilable with the idea, that execution was to issue on the act without judgment being previously confessed.

It is, therefore, ordered, adjudged and decreed, that the judgment of the district court be affirmed with costs.

Porter, for the plaintiff.

Zacharie v. Richards.   VI, N. S. 467.

The last residence of a person who has removed out of the state, is the house in which he lived, not that occupied after his departure, by the family with whom he lived.

FIRST District.

MATHEWS, J., delivered the opinion of the court.

This cause was heard in the court below, on exceptions taken by the counsel for the defendant in relation to the service of the citation, which was held to have been illegally made, and the suit was ordered to be dismissed. From the judgment of dismissal the plaintiff appealed.

It appears by the evidence in this case, that the defendant resided in New Orleans some time previous to the institution of this suit; and that he was a merchant, became bankrupt, and was not to be found in the city, when citation issued in the present action. While he remained here, he lived with one Charles Clark, as a boarder, in Jefferson Street. Clark removed to Conde Street after the defendant had left the city, and the citation was left at the house of the witness in his latter place of residence, where the defendant never lived with him.

The latter place was not at any time the domicil of the defendant, and the service of citation there was clearly illegal. If the defendant was ever domiciliated in New Orleans, his domicil must have been in that house where he eat and slept, or in that where he carried on his mercantile affairs. According to the provisions of the Louisiana Code, a change of domicil ought regularly to be declared by a person intending to make such change. See articles 43d and 44th: and in case this declaration is not made, the proof of the intention to change shall depend on circumstances, art. 45. Now it appears to us that circumstances more calculated to induce a person to change his domicil, could scarcely be imagined, than those in which the defendant found himself after his failure, which appears to have been entire and complete, accompanied by a charge of forgery made against him in relation to his bilan.

The circumstance of the defendant appearing before a commissioner in Philadelphia (who had been appointed to examine witnesses), and filing cross interrogatories, does not cure the illegality of service of the citation. No issue had been joined either express or tacit, the action had no foundation in consequence of the want of citation. See Code of Practice, art. 359. In truth the defendant never appeared

[Zacharie v. Richards.]

in court to plead to the merits of the case, and thereby join issue with the plaintiff, which perhaps alone could cure the defect in serving the citation.

It is, therefore, ordered, &c. that the judgment of the district court be affirmed, with costs.

Strawbridge, for the plaintiff.
Maybin, for the defendant.

Semple *et al. v.* Buhler.   VI, N. S. 469.

A plaintiff does not lose his claim on a sheriff who has taken a twelvemonths' bond without proper surety by receiving the bond and attempting to procure the money.
Nor by failing to oppose the rightful claim of a third party.

THIRD District.

MATHEWS, J., delivered the opinion of the court.

This suit is brought to recover from the defendant, reparation for damages which the plaintiffs allege that they have sustained, in consequence of his negligence and malfeasance, as sheriff of the parish of East Baton Rouge. Judgment was given for them in the court below, from which the defendant appealed.

The pleadings and facts of the case as exhibited on the record show, that the present plaintiffs had obtained a judgment against one Robert Lawes, on which a *fieri facias* issued and came into the hands of the defendant to be executed by him, in his capacity of sheriff aforesaid; that in virtue of the writ he seized certain slaves as being the property of Lawes, which were finally sold (in pursuance of law) on a credit of twelve months, and at the sale thus made the defendant in execution became the purchaser, and gave his wife as surety in the twelve months' bond, who was accepted by the sheriff. Subsequently the wife of Lawes obtained against her husband a decree of separation of goods, and judgment for the amount of her claims on his estate.

When the twelve months' bond taken as above stated, was about to be executed, and the property therein mortgaged was seized, Mrs. Lawes claimed it as her own, and obtained an injunction, prohibiting the sale thereof: in the suit for the injunction, the present plaintiffs were made defendants and cited, but did not appear or make any defence.

From these facts the counsel for the appellee induces four objections to the correctness of the judgment rendered by the district court.

1. That the plaintiffs ratified the act of the defendant in taking the security, by issuing execution on the twelvemonths' bond.

2. The damage (if any) arose out of their default, in not appearing to the suit of injunction.

3. No damage has been sustained, as Lawes was wholly insolvent when execution issued against him, and his property was covered by his wife's tacit mortgage.

4. Prescription against the plaintiffs' claim.

In relation to the last of these objections, it suffices to observe, that prescription has not been regularly pleaded; but if it had been, we believe that the prescription of one year relied on, could not be legally supported.

The first objection cannot avail the defendant. The real ground for the plaintiffs' action against the sheriff, is a failure on his part to take any security on the twelvemonths' bond. Receiving the wife of the purchaser as security was equivalent to taking none, as she by such an act could not be legally bound. The officer would, probably, have been immediately responsible to the plaintiffs in execution for that neglect of duty. Their indulgence to him in endeavoring to obtain satisfaction of the judgment, by issuing an execution on the bond imperfect as it was, cannot on any sound principles of justice, be made to prejudice their claim for remuneration in damages against the appellant on account of neglect of duty, for which he is legally held responsible.

If this reasoning in opposition to the first objection be correct, it refutes also the second; for the failure of the plaintiffs to appear and contest the right of property in the injunction case with Mrs. Lawes could not destroy their claim against the defendant, which rests on his neglect in not taking security in the twelvemonths' bond.

As to the third the evidence does not show that Robert Lawes was wholly insolvent at the time the execution against his property came into the hands of ths appellent. The case may be hard on the defendant; but we believe has been adjudged according to law by the court below.

It is, therefore, ordered, adjudged and decreed, that the judgment of the district court be affirmed, with costs.

Preston, for the plaintiff.

Watts, for the defendant.

Oddie *v.* His Creditors.   VI, N. S. 473.

A builder who does not record his contract, is not entitled to any privilege.
Even if he obtains judgment against the debtor, but the judgment be pronounced two
days after the cession, and remain unrecorded, yet is his situation not bettered.

PARISH Court of New Orleans.

MATHEWS, J., delivered the opinion of the court.

In this case the homologation of the tableau of distribution of the insolvent's estate, filed by his syndic in the court below, is opposed by the creditor Brand, in consequence of not assigning him a place of privilege and preference, as undertaker and builder of a house for the insolvent, to the amount of 1743 dollars, 60 cents, claimed by him as a privileged debt on said building. His opposition was set aside by a judgment of the parish court.

The facts necessary to be noticed in relation to the appellant's claim of privilege, are as follows:

The contract between the undertaker and the insolvent was not formally drawn up in writing, and signed by the parties; the only written evidence of it is an entry of it on a memorandum book of the latter on the 17th of March, 1823, containing the terms, according to which the work was to have been executed and paid for. In November 1823, Brand caused the building to be sequestered on his pretended privilege; and on the 14th of April, 1824, obtained a final judgment for the amount by him claimed, which was recorded, &c. on the same day. On the 12th of the same month Oddie made a surrender of his property for the benefit of his creditors, which from that period, has been administered by a syndic, who, on the 7th of April, 1827, filed the tableau of distribution, of which the appellee complains and to the homologation of which, he makes the opposition above stated.

The rights of the opposing creditors depend on a just interpretation of the 8th section of the act of the legislature passed in 1817, relative to the power of giving special mortgages in certain cases, and for other purposes. According to this law, no architect, undertaker, or other workman, has, with regard to third parties, any privilege or legal mortgage, on any immovable property, &c. on account of work building or repairs, unless he shall have entered into a written contract with the owner &c., and the said contract shall have been recorded, &c. By a second clause of this section of the act, architects, undertakers, workmen and carpenters, forfeit their right of action against purchasers of the immovable property, (on which they claim a lien or tacit mortgage,) to enforce payment of the claim, unless their contracts have been recorded as required by law. By a third clause, in case of failure of the person with whom they have contracted, they are placed on the footing of simple contract creditors, if their contract has not been recorded agreeably to the provisions of the act.

The contest in the present case is between creditors in relation to their rank and privileges; it is, therefore, useless to inquire into the effects of the privilege of an architect or undertaker, as it relates to his employer. So long as the latter is solvent, it is not easy to perceive what advantage the former can derive from such privilege or tacit mortgage.

The only question which the facts of the case, and the law which must govern it, present for solution, is, whether the appellant be entitled to a privilege and preference on the building proceeds, against other priveleged creditors or the whole mass of creditors. It is doubtful, from the evidence, whether any written contract was ever entered into between him and the insolvent, as required by law; but such as it appears, it was not recorded in pursuance of the requisitions of the act of the legislature; consequently, according to the third clause of the section cited, the appellant was properly placed on the tableau of distribution as a simple contract, or chirographic creditor. The circumstance of his having obtained judgment against the insolvent can not better his situation, for that judgment was not pronounced or recorded until two days after the *cessio bonorum;* neither, in our opinion, can the sequestration which preceded, admitting (as contended for by the counsel for the appellant) that it preserved the rights of all parties concerned; it is a *non sequitur*, that any were conferred which did not previously exist; and no lien, privilege, or tacit mortgage, did exist according to law in favor of the opposing creditor.

It is, therefore, ordered, adjudged and decreed, that the judgment of the parish court be affirmed, with costs.

Watts and *Lobdell*, for the plaintiff.
Eustis, for the defendant.

Wamack v. Kemp. VI, N. S. 477.

No action will lie for a charge of perjury made in the course of judicial proceedings.

EIGHTH District.

Martin, J., delivered the opinion of the court.

The petition in this case contains two distinct counts.

The first states, that the defendant falsely and maliciously charged the plaintiff, in a voluntary affidavit, with the crime of perjury, and at different times and places, told, in the hearing of many persons, that the plaintiff had been guilty of perjury—whereby he was injured in his good fame, and claims damages.

The second count states, that in consequence of such voluntary affidavit, the plaintiff was imprisoned, committed to, and detained in jail, till the sitting of the court, when, no proceedings being had, he was discharged—for which false imprisonment he claims damages.

The defendant demurred to the petition, as the two causes of action could not be cumulated; the demurrer being overruled, he pleaded the general issue.

There was a verdict of judgment against him, and he appealed.

This case displays the sad consequence of a village administration of justice. The plaintiff, for reasons which are not stated, made oath before a magistrate, he had never invaded the marital rights of the defendant, who made oath before the same magistrate, he had committed perjury in his affidavit; a warrant was thereupon issued, and the defendant having, in the opinion of the magistrate, administered such evidence, as established a probable ground, the plaintiff was committed to jail, in the words of the mittimus, "as the power to bail is not within the jurisdiction of a justice of the peace."

German deposed, that the plaintiff and the defendant's wife, left the house of the defendant, for the alleged purpose of looking for an animal that had strayed from the pen; they went out in the same direction, and returned together by the same path. In a conversation which ensued, the witness observed they varied in their account of the route they had taken; from which the witness drew the conclusion, equally illogical and uncharitable, that their excursion into the woods had a motive less honorable than the recovery of the stray beast. He added that, on another day he slept at the house of the defendant, who was then absent; after he went to bed, the plaintiff and the defendant's wife set up for some time, romping and playing together, after which, the plaintiff came to take part of the witness's bed, and a considerable time after, he got up and walked out of the room, and from the noise made and shaking of the bed he concluded the defendant's wife had mistaken the plaintiff for her husband.

John M'Allister deposed, that he was at the house of the defendant, who was then absent, and he saw the plaintiff take hold of the defendant's wife and retire with her; they were together nearly an hour, and from their behaviour he concluded they had not been idle.

Odin deposed he heard the defendant's wife say to him, that if she was with child by the plaintiff, the plaintiff was a white man and not a negro, and she could make him whip the defendant to death.

The defendant now offered Williams as a witness, to prove that the plaintiff admits that he had kept the defendant's wife as a mistress before he made the affidavit on which he was charged with perjury. The witness was rejected, on the ground that there was no plea of justification—and the defendant's counsel took a bill of exceptions.

The defendant made an unsuccessful attempt to obtain a new trial.

Notwithstanding the verdict of the jury, it appears to us no action can be sustained in this case. The charge of perjury was made in a legal proceeding, with the view of bringing the defendant to justice. It is true the plaintiff did take the oath, by which he was charged with perjury himself in a voluntary affidavit, neither taken nor intended to be used in a legal proceeding; but nothing shows malice in the defendant. The plaintiff suffered in consequence of the ignorance of the magistrate, who ought neither to have arrested or confined him.

We do not think that justice requires a remanding of this case.

It is, therefore, ordered, adjudged and decreed, that the judgment of the district court be annulled, avoided and reversed; and that there be judgment for the defendant with costs in both courts.

Preston, for the plaintiff.

Christy, for the defendant.

Stackpole *v.* Hennen. VI, N. S. 481.

Counsel are responsible for speaking maliciously on the trial of a cause.

Counsel are not responsible for statements made by them, if they are portinent to the cause, and instructed by their client to make them.

And if the client is present when the words are spoken, he will be presumed to have authorised them.

PARISH Court of New Orleans.

PORTER, J., delivered the opinion of the court.

This cause has called for great attention and reflection on the part of the court, not from the magnitude of the matter in dispute in a pecuniary point of view, nor from its importance to either of the parties, but from the great interest the public, and the profession of the law have in a correct decision of the legal principles it involves.

It is an action brought against the defendant, for having, on the trial of a cause where he was of counsel, charged the plaintiff who was examined as a witness, with being guilty of perjury, and of having come there with an intention of perjuring himself. The petition alleges the words to have been spoken falsely and maliciously, and with the intention of injuring the plaintiff.

The answer, after a general denial, avers, that the words were used in reply to observations, or questions, put to the defendant by the judge of the court while the defendant was acting as attorney and counsel. That in this capacity he was authorised to speak them, believing, as he then did, the case might justify the words spoken, and that they were necessary in the defence. That he was not actuated by any malice against the plaintiff.

The cause was submitted to a jury in the court of the first instance, who found a verdict in favor of the plaintiff, and assessed his damages at 500 dollars. No motion was made for a new trial, and the court having rendered judgment conformably to the finding of the jury, the defendant appealed.

The effect which should be given to this verdict in the appellate court has been much controverted in the argument. This tribunal it is true, is not like those courts of error at common law, where questions of fact cannot be examined and finally decided on. By the law organising the Supreme Court of this state, the power is conferred on it to inquire into the correctness of the judgment below, both as it relates to law and facts, and to reverse or affirm it as the case may be. The conferring this power, as counsel correctly argued, supposed on the part of those by whom it was granted, that it would be exercised, and we have certainly no more authority for declining to reverse a judgment where there is error in fact, than we would have where the mistake proceeds from an improper application of the law. But in the exercise of this power, it has been a matter of great solicitude with the members of this court, so to use it, as to carry into effect the object the legislature had in view when they conferred it. In their deliberations on this matter, they have been deeply impressed with the conviction, that with a few exceptions arising out of party violence, or prejudice the facts of a cause are in general better tried, and more correctly understood the nearer the investigation is carried on to the parties: and that at each remove from this vicinage, what is gained in the ascent to a higher tribunal, in its superior knowledge and freedom from extraneous influence, is more than counterbalanced by the intimate knowledge possessed by the lower court, and above all by the jury, of the character and conduct of the parties and witnesses. Hence a rule has been established in this tribunal and acted on for some years, not to refuse reversing a judgment where there is error in fact, but never to reverse it unless the error is so manifest, that the verdict can not be accounted for by any of these presumptions of greater advantages in the investigation to which we have just attended. This doctrine has received a more frequent application in cases where the truth depended on the weight to be attached to conflicting testimony, where fraud was at issue, or damages were to be assessed, than any others, because we have felt, that the species of knowledge which the juries possess, is peculiarly adapted to aid the reaching a correct conclusion in causes of this description: and that every difference of opinion on our part, would not authorise a reversal, when that difference perhaps proceeded from wanting the advantages in the investigation which the lower tribunal enjoyed.

But even in cases such as those stated, if matters of law are presented on the record which, notwithstanding the evidence, show the judgment to be erroneous, the verdict of the jury presents no obstacle to the reversal. The influence given to the finding, necessarily yields to the superior control which the law exercises over the case, when the conclusion drawn from the facts is contrary to that which the law sanctions.

With this explanation of the power we possess, and the principles which govern us in the exercise of it, we proceed to state; that it appears from the evidence given on the trial below, that the defendant, on cross examining the plaintiff, who was a witness in the case of Millar v. Morgan, was asked by the judge what object he had in view in putting certain questions. His answer was, I wish to show *the witness is perjured, and that he came here to perjure himself.* There is some contradiction in the testimony as to the answer of the plaintiff, which elicited these remarks from the defendant. But taking it in the most favorable point of view for the latter, we think the

[Stackpole *v.* Hennen.]

observation was rash and unnecessarily severe. The error of the witness was evidently unintentional, and a question by way of explanation would have enabled him to correct the mistake. It is now admitted on the record, that the plaintiff is a man of truth and fair character. It also appears the plaintiff was an entire stranger to the defendant at the time the words were spoken.

The question of law is one of considerable difficuly, and our jurisprudence and laws are by no means so full and explicit on the subject as could be desired. In Rome, while a generous freedom was inculcated on counsel in advocating the causes of their clients, the prohibition was express against profiting by this liberty, to speak untruths and utter slander. Spain, in her written laws, has repeated nearly *verbatim* the restraints imposed by the imperial Code. But we find nothing in either system which enables us to ascertain the extent to which counsel might carry their observations; what were the presumptions attached to their acts, or how far they were protected by them when called to answer for an alleged violation of the rights of others. The prohibition, however, contained in these Codes, establishes very clearly the existence of certain limits which could not be passed; a prohibition which, we may remark, must be supposed to exist in every civilised, and more particularly in every free country, independent of positive authority. The proposition, that any class of men under the pretence of aiding in the administration of justice, should say what they pleased of every individual who was a witness or a party, without incurringr esponsibility, is too revolting to require refutation. Equally unfounded do we consider a ground assumed in the defence of the present case, that counsel is not responsible even for speaking maliciously, if the matter was spoken during the trial, and relative to the cause in hand.

It can never be a correct discharge of duty to clients to act maliciously towards others. The privileges which counsel enjoy, are given for the benefit of society, and not to enable them to indulge angry passions with impunity.

It is difficult to draw the line in such a manner as that, on one side may be found the right of parties to have every thing pertinent in defence of their cause told; to have motives arraigned; conduct scrutinized, and to exercise that freedom of discussion which is so necessary to the discovery of truth: and on the other side, that protection from calumny and unfounded invective, which honest men have a right to expect, while standing before a court of justice as witnesses or parties. The best rule is, we think, to protect counsel for every thing they say which is pertinent to the cause, if they are instructed by their clients to say it; and to hold them responsible for every thing that is impertinent to the case, whether they are instructed or not. The last part of this rule is obviously just. The great latitude which the law allows in discussion has for its object the discovery of truth in the matters at issue, and that object can never be promoted by invective foreign to the subject under examination.

3*

The first part of the rule we think equally sustainable on principles of utility. The protection accorded by it, does not place suitors and witnesses at the mercy of their adversaries and counsel. It only fixes the responsibility on the client instead of the advocate. Counsel are bound to believe the information communicated to them by those whose interests they advocate. Parties have a right to present their case through their agents to the tribunal that tries it in such manner as to them may seem meet; and it would be a great impediment to the free and efficient administration of justice, if the attorney was obliged to make every statement the cause might require on his own responsibility. It is no doubt desirable that investigations in courts should be conducted with all the circumspection and delicacy which characterise the intercourse of social life. But this in too many instances would be inconsistent with the rigorous obligations imposed on those who administer justice. A great deal of litigation is produced by the knavery of men; hence the necessity of free and bold examination; vice frequently requires to be stripped of the mantle in which hypocrisy and cunning envelop it, and laid open to the animadversion of justice, and the indignation of mankind. But these important objects could not be accomplished, if the ministers, whom the law authorises parties to employ, were not protected in the discharge of their duty. In England the privileges of counsel extend as far as the rule just recognised will permit them to go in this country. In France the same limits are assigned, with this sole difference, that there, by positive legislation of a very recent date, the instructions must be in writing. 3 Blackstone's Com. 29; 1 Martin, 464.

The jury, in the case before us, have found a verdict against the defendant, and it must be enforced unless the law which governs the case shows their finding to have been contrary to the conclusions which it authorises on the evidence adduced on the trial.

The defendant contends it does, because the words spoken by him were pertinent to the cause in hand; and being so must, in the absence of proof to the contrary, be presumed to have been spoken under instructions from his client.

On the first branch of this subject, it has been contended by the counsel for the plaintiff, that the finding of the jury has established, the words spoken were not pertinent to the case, and that the court is concluded by the verdict. To this position we can by no means assent. The relevancy of observations made in the progress of a cause is a matter of law, not of fact. The words spoken were in answer to a question by the judge. They were pertinent therefore as to time: so they were as to matter, for it can never be impertinent to a case to show that one of the witnesses brought in to establish the adversary's case is perjured.

On the second branch, the defendant has relied on the presumption that counsellors at law acting as the agents of others, must be supposed to follow the instructions they have received, and he has quoted a case of ancient date from the English books, where it was

[Stackpole v. Hennen.]

decided, that if an advocate should speak slanderous words, it would be intended he spoke according to his instructions. 6 Bac. Ab. 225; Style's Rep. 462.

It is somewhat difficult to say whether such be still the rule in that country. The elementary writers are silent respecting it, and the late decision on this subject by the court of King's Bench, does not directly decide the point, though the reasoning of some of the judges would induce us to presume that they thought the doctrine correct, for they seemed to think it necessary express malice should be shown. 3 Black. Com. 29; Starkie on Slander, 207; 1 Barnwell & Alderson, 232.

However the rule may be in cases where the client is not present when the words complained of are spoken, we think such is the presumption of our law when, as in the present instance, he attended on the trial of the case, was present when the slanderous words were uttered, and did not disavow them. Nay more, we hold that, under such circumstances, the client is responsible, whether the injury inflicted was the result of previous instruction or not. This principle can be traced to the fountain head of our jurisprudence, and its correctness is recognised by one of the most modern and eminent writers of a country whose laws have the same source as our own.

There is a formal text of the Roman Code, which declares, that the allegations made by lawyers in the presence of those they are acting for, are considered as if made by the parties themselves. The 8th law of the 6th title of the third Partidas, is still more positive, and states, " *ca toda cosa que el abogado dixere in juicio, estando delante aque a quien pertenece el pleyto, si lo non contra dixesse, entendiola tanto vale, è asi deve ser cabida como si la dixesse por su boca misma el senor del pleyto.*" Merlin in his *Repertoire de Jurisprudence*, in treating of the responsibility of counsel for slanderous words, observes, "*Lorsqu'un avocat sort de lui meme des bornes que lui sont prescrites, il peut etre desavoué. Mais il faut que ce desaveu se forme verbalment sur le champ par la partie, ou par le procureur qu sont censés presens a l'audience sans quoi il est presumé n'avoi rien avancé que de leur aveu.* Merlin's Rep. de Juris., vol. 1, p. 464 *Code, liv. 2, tit. 10, l, 1 and 3.*

With these laws and principles controlling and guiding us, we ca not refuse to the defendant the benefit of the presumption he invokes We think it clearly results from them in the first place, that the advo cate is presumed to have spoken after the instructions of his client because his client by his silence gives his assent to what has bee said, and in the second, that the latter is responsible whether he ha so instructed him or not, because he makes the injury his own b ratifying what his agent does. Nor can we dismiss the case withou stating at the same time our entire approbation of the wisdom an utility of such a rule. Where express malice is not shown on th part of the attorney, it can hardly be supposed he is actuated b motives other than those of advancing the interests of his clients. the latter, who is to be benefitted by these observations, stands by an

acquiesces in them, and is willing to take all the advantages, which
the zeal and warmth of his advocate, whether justifiable or not, can
bestow, it is but strict justice he should be equally responsible for the
injury. *Qui sentit commodum, debet sentire et onus.*

It is, therefore, ordered, adjudged and decreed, that the judgment
of the parish court be annulled, avoided and reversed; and it is further ordered, adjudged and decreed, that there be judgment against
the plaintiff as in case of nonsuit, with costs in both cases.

Livermore, for the plaintiff.
Mazureau, for the defendant.

Penniman *v.* Barrymore.   VI, N. S. 494.

Surety on a sequestration bond, has no right to the discussion of his principal's property.
A bond dated the 9th may be shown to have been delivered the 10th.
The words *fourteen hundred and ten* may be understood to be *fourteen hundred and ten
dollars.*

PARISH Court of New Orleans.

PORTER, J., delivered the opinion of the court.

This action is brought on a bond given on taking out a writ of
sequestration in a suit in which the present plaintiff was defendant.
It is in the usual form, with the exception that fourteen hundred and
ten is written as the amount which the obligors promised to pay,
omitting the word dollars. The condition recites the issuing the
writ, and states, that should it appear to be wrongfully taken out, the
obligors will pay all damages the obligee may sustain therefrom.

The petition avers, the bond was made for 1400 dollars, conditioned to pay all damages the plaintiff might sustain, and prays
judgment for that sum. The answer of the defendant excepts to the
form of the suit, because he was but surety on the bond, and it is not
shown an action had been instituted against the principal—that he is
not liable on the obligation for the sum claimed, or any other sum as
demanded, and concludes by a prayer in reconvention.

The cause was submitted to a jury in the court below, who found
a verdict in favor of the plaintiff for 1000 dollars. The defendant
made an unsuccessful attempt to set it aside by a motion for a new
trial, and judgment being rendered thereon, he appealed.

The first question in the cause is, whether the defendant being surety can be pursued at law, before recovery is sought from the principal on the bond. We think he may, for the obligation he signed was one required by law in the course of a judicial proceeding, and the right to discussion in such cases is expressly denied by the positive provisions of our code. Louisiana Code, 3035.

The next is in relation to an alleged defect in the instrument, owing to the bond being dated the 9th January, and the petition in the cause wherein the writ of sequestration was obtained not being filed until the 10th. This circumstance is quite immaterial, provided the obligation was delivered on taking out the writ, and the evidence in the cause we think well justifies the conclusion the jury came to, that it was so delivered.

The most important question in the cause relates to the defect in the bond from the omission of the word dollars, or some other words after those of *fourteen hundred and ten*. There can be no doubt what the parties intended to do in this instance—there is as little, we think, that the omission of the word dollars proceeded from error or haste in transcribing the bond; and we are of opinion that the jury and the court below were authorised to supply the omission and act on the instrument, as if this word had been written in it. The laws of this state direct, that no writ of sequestration shall issue in a case such as that which the contest between these parties presented, without bond and security being given by the party applying for it. The judge's order in this instance, directed the plaintiff to furnish one in the sum of 1400 dollars. In compliance with the requisition of the law and the order of the judge, the obligation was given, and the omission to insert the word *dollars* can be considered in no other light but a clerical error, which may be corrected when there exists as high, or higher evidence that can be resorted to, to ascertain the meaning and intention of the parties.

Again, when there is doubt as to the sense in which words are used, they may be explained by reference to other words and phrases used in the same contract. Now, in looking into the condition of this bond, we find the obligors stating it to be, that if the writ was wrongfully sued out, and they paid all the damages arising therefrom, the obligation was to be null and void, otherwise it was to remain in full force and virtue. According to the construction contended for at present, the bond never had any force or virtue, therefore, that construction would lead us to a conclusion, that every thing inserted in the condition was useless and for no purpose. Courts of justice have decided in other countries, that words used in a contract which led to a manifest absurdity might be rejected, or understood, in a sense, by which the agreement would have some effect. As where a man acknowledged to owe a sum of money which he promised *never* to pay. Where an obligation was made for *threty ponds*, it was held to be one for thirty pounds, to answer the intention of the parties. Where the name of the party contracted with had been omitted by mistake, the omission was allowed to be supplied

by parol evidence. And even on an indictment for forgery, where
the bill, when produced, appeared to be for fifty, without the addition of the word *pounds*, it was held that the same sum in the margin preceded by the letter £ removed all doubts, and showed, the
word *fifty*, in the body of the note, was *intended* for pounds. So
here we think the order of the judge to give a bond for *fourteen
hundred and ten dollars* removes all doubt as to the meaning of
the words *fourteen hundred and ten*, inserted in that bond. It is
one of the rules of our jurisprudence, that neither the principal or
surety can escape from responsibility, by an error that arises in drawing up the act by which they contemplated binding themselves. *Si
librarius in transcribendis stipulationis verbis errassit: nihil no-
cere, quominus et reus et fidejussor tenentur. Dig. liv.* 50, *tit.*
17, *l.* 92; *Crojac*, 607; 10. *Co.* 133; 13. Mass. 161; 2 East, Pleas of
the Crown, 951.

But whether the conclusion we have just expressed be sound or
not, upon general principles, there cannot be a doubt of its correctness, when considered in relation to those rules which govern what
are termed, in law, judicial conventions. In regard to them, the
principle is perfectly established, that where any obscurity or doubt
is presented by the terms in which they are drawn up, they must be
interpreted by the sentence or order in pursuance of which they were
made. *Dig. liv.* 45, *tit.* 1, *law* 52; *Ibid., liv.* 46, *tit.* 5, *law* 9; *Domat,
liv.* 1, *tit.* 1, *sect.* 2, *no.* 24.

The counsel for the defendant has contended, that the slightest
defect in an instrument of this kind, or variance from an order of the
court, renders it null and of no effect. The argument confounds
the rights of the obligee and obligor. It is no doubt true, the former
has a right to exact from his adversary a strict compliance with all
the previous steps which may be required before process can issue.
But if the latter fails to comply with them, and, as in this instance,
furnishes an obligation which, though defective in point of form, substantially and really, contains an engagement on his part, it ill becomes him, or those who join him, to endeavor to shelter themselves
from responsibility, by pleading defects which proceeded either from
negligence or bad faith, and it would be a just reproach to the law
if it suffered such a defence.

On the whole, we can discover no error in the judgment below,
except that part which adds interest from judicial demand on the
amount found by the jury. The judge had no power either to add
to the verdict, or diminish it. This point was fully examined in the
case of Bedford *v.* Jacobs, 5 *N. S.*

It is, therefore, ordered, adjudged and decreed, that the judgment
of the parish court be annulled, avoided and reversed; and it is further ordered, adjudged and decreed, that the plaintiff recover from
the defendant the sum of one thousand dollars, with costs in the court
of the first instance, those of appeal to be borne by the appellee.

Morse, for the plaintiff.

Mercier and *Buchanan*, for the defendant.

Dreux v. His Creditors. VI, N. S. 502.

Pending an appeal from the homologation of a tableau of distribution, none of the creditors can compel payment of the sum for which they are placed on the tableau.
The wife by renouncing her mortgage on property sold by her husband, does not abandon her right on that previously alienated by him.

FIRST District.

Mathews, J., delivered the opinion of the court.

This case was before the Supreme Court in June term, 1826, on an appeal taken by two of the creditors, who opposed the homologation of a tableau of distribution, which had been filed by the syndics of the insolvent's estate. The appellees in that instance succeeded in their opposition, and the cause was remanded to the court below, with directions to that court to make a new tableau in such a manner as to secure to them the right of privilege and preference, which they claimed on certain specified property belonging to the estate of defendant. The executors of Mrs. Destrehan, obtained an order directing the syndics to pay over to them 2442 dollars,.an amount claimed as being due to the estate of their testatrix, on mortgage, according to the mode in which it was set down on the tableau of distribution.—This order was obtained at the instance of the coun sel for said executors, with the consent of the counsel, for one of the creditors who had appealed as above stated, and pending the appeal. The counsel for the syndics moved to have it set aside, and having failed in his motion, he now appeals on their behalf.

After the cause returned to the district court, and when a tableau, amended in pursuance of the directions given by the Supreme Court was about to be homologated, opposition was made to its homologa tion, by two other creditors, viz. Mrs. Dreux, and the executors of Mrs. Destrehan. The counsel of the former being satisfied with the man ner in which the court below ordered the homologation, took no appeal, as the rights of his client appear to have been recognised and secured.

An appeal having been taken on the part of the latter, and the syndics having appealed from the decree by which they were ordered to pay the sum above stated, to the executors of Mrs. Destrehan, the respective rights of these two parties in relation to the subjects presented by these several appeals, require investigation.

The order of which the syndics complain, we think was improperly made; it certainly was premature, for pending the appeal which was heretofore taken by some of the creditors, it could not be known in what degree the privilege of others might be affected by the judgment of the appellate court. The result shows, that Mrs. Dreux's right of preference may have been deteriorated, as by that judgment she was postponed to the appellants, in relation to part of the insolvent's estate, whom she outranked on the tableau, as homologated by the court below. This change of situation would render it necessary, in supporting the privilege, to lessen the privilege of other mortgage creditors, should the unincumbered part of the insolvent's property fail to make good his claim. The manner in which the decree of homologation of the last tableau is worded, would, perhaps, prevent any difficulty in the final distribution of the estate; but as the order requiring the syndics to pay over any part of it to the executors of Mrs. Destrehan, was improvidently made, previous to the final adjustment of the whole, we are of opinion that said order ought to be annulled.

The opposition made on the part of these executors in the present instance, and in relation to which an appeal is now taken, purports to be based on the rights secured to them by the first tableau which was homologated, and which they allege to be *res judicata,* as to the rights of the succession which they represent.

Two other grounds of opposition state, 1. That the executors allege themselves to be mortgagee creditors of the earliest date, and that therefore, the property on which they hold their mortgage ought not to be subjected to any of the expenses incurred in the administration of the insolvent's estate.

2. That as Madam Dreux has renounced her mortgage on her husband's property, subsequently hypothecated by him to other creditors she is barred from exercising any claim on the property which was specially mortgaged to Mrs. Destrehan.

It is doubtful, from the manner in which the judgment was given by this court when the cause was last before us, whether the decree of the court was reversed so entirely as to change the situation of any of the parties to the *concurso,* except the appellants, in that instance: but admitting that the others remained in the places assigned them on the tableau by the former judgment of the district court, the present appellants can derive no advantage from it, considered as *res judicata,* for their claim was postponed to that of Madam Dreux.

Allowing the case to be open to the opposition filed on the last trial in the district court, the grounds therein assumed are untenable, as has been already settled by decisions of the Supreme Court. See Delor v. Montegut's Syndics, 5 *Martin,* 468, and a case lately decided in relation to Madam Lanusse's claims on her husband's estate after his insolvency.

It is, therefore, ordered, adjudged and decreed, that the judgment of the district court be affirmed with costs, to be paid by the executors of Mrs. Destrehan, &c.

Seghers, for the plaintiff.

Canon, Denis and *Monroe,* for the defendants.

Louisiana State Bank *v.* Rowel *et al.*   VI, N. S. 506.

Where the endorser lives within three miles of the post-office, notice put there is not sufficient.

THIRD District.

Porter, J., delivered the opinion of the court.

This action is brought against one of the defendants, as endorser of promissory notes. Various grounds of defence have been set up by her, and, among others, a want of due and regular notice of non-payment by the maker.

It appears, in evidence, that the appellee resides near to the town of Baton Rouge, and that her residence is three miles from the village, nearer the post office than any other: that the morning after the protest was made, notice was put in the post office; that a servant from the house where the defendant resides, frequently calls before nine o'clock in the morning for letters; that they seldom remained as long as forty-eight hours in the box before being asked for, rarely seventy-two, and very rarely ninety-six.

The time at which the notice was thus deposited was previous to the passage of a late act of the legislature, in respect to giving notice of the protests of promissory notes and bills of exchange. The case must, therefore, be decided by the *lex mercatoria*, independent of positive legislation, and so considered, we have not a doubt of the correctness of the judgment below, in considering the notice insufficient to render the defendant responsible.

The case has been well argued, but the reasoning of the counsel, in our opinion, rested entirely on an incorrect view of the obligation contracted by an endorser of instruments of this kind. The obligation which such an act creates is strictly a conditional one, and that condition is, that he will pay the money in case the maker does not, provided, due notice is given to him of the default of the former. By the *lex mercatoria*, this fact must be proved, by establishing that knowledge of the failure of the principal to pay, was communicated personally to the endorser, or that information to that effect was left at his house. A relaxation of this rule has been introduced for the convenience of trade, when the endorsers live at such a distance, that their residence is nighe ranother post office than that where the holder lives; in such case, it is sufficient to send by mail a notice directed to the endorser. There has been another relaxation of the rule in large cities where there are establishments called the penny-post, by which letters are daily sent round to all persons residing within certain limits. These are the only exceptions we know of to the rule already stated. We have looked into all the elementary treatises on this subject, and have examined with care the reports of adjudged cases, and we have found nothing to support, in the slightest degree, the position taken by the appellants, that depositing a notice in a post-office when the party giving it resides in the same place with the endorser, or near to him, is a sufficient evidence of that notice having reached him in due time. But we have been told this is only going one step further than other countries have gone in relaxing this rule, and that for the convenience of trade we should take that step. We see no reason of public convenience to induce us to make such a change in the law merchant, if we had the power to do so. We find none in the equity of the case. The parties must be presumed to have contracted in relation to the law as it existed at the time the notes were executed and endorsed, not by the modifications which courts might afterwards introduce into it. In any case, evidence such as this, would be furnishing but presumption in place of proof. Here it is but a slight one, for it is proved letters remain sometimes seventy-two hours before they are sent for, and how can we know the notice did not remain for this length of time. We think the case most clearly with the defendant, but that the judgment should have been one of nonsuit, instead of being final. 2 *N. S.* 511.

It is, therefore, ordered, adjudged and decreed, that the judgment of the district court be annulled, avoided and reversed; that there be judgment for defendant as in case of nonsuit, with costs in the court below; those of appeal to be paid by the appellee.

Executors of Sprigg *v.* Herman.   VI, N. S. 510.

FIRST District.

In a petitory action, where fraud is not alleged, parol evidence cannot be given that a deed was dated at another day than that which it purports.

Where the mandate gives a power to sell, the opinion expressed by the principal, that the property should bring a certain sum, will not invalidate a sale by the agent for less.

Legendre *v.* M'Donough. VI, N. S. 513.

FIRST District.

The act of the legislature, which accepts the accession of territory, comprising East Baton Rouge, proffered by congress to the state, was approved by the governor on the 4th of August, 1812; consequently, on its promulgation, the state constitution was extended to the part annexed.

There was once a difference of opinion among the members of this tribunal, one of them holding, that judgments which contain no reasons are absolutely void. It is now settled that they are not so; and that the nullity must be pronounced on an appeal, or by judgment in the court which rendered the judgment.

When a defendant dies, a judgment rendered against him must be declared executory against his heirs or representatives, because property which has ceased to be his cannot be affected by a judgment to which the new owners are not made parties; but on the death of the plaintiff, nothing prevents his heir or representative from taking out execution.

M'Micken *v.* Fair. VI, N. S. 515.

When the witness who declares a fact which will render him incompetent, states at the same time facts to restore his competency, his evidence cannot be rejected.

THIRD District.

MARTIN, J., delivered the opinion of the court.

This case was remanded from this court at January term, 1826. 4 N. S. 172.

There was verdict and judgment against him, and the plaintiff appealed.

Our attention is drawn to several bills of exceptions taken by the plaintiff.

[M'Micken v. Fair.]

1. The first, to the refusal of the court to permit the reading of part of John Fair's deposition, on the ground, that it related to goods which had been charged in the plaintiff's books to the witness and his mother, the account presented him, and payment demanded; so that if he established the account against the present defendant, he would secure his discharge, and so he was interested in doing so. See the cause of Evans v. Gray, 1 *N. S.* 709.

The plaintiff's counsel urges, that, as this circumstance was disclosed by the deposition which established, also, that this was done through error, and the plaintiff had since corrected the entry, it appeared, upon the whole, that the plaintiff was not chargeable, and, therefore, was without interest.

We think the court erred in rejecting that part of the deposition.

2. The defendant read to the jury the cross examination of John Fair, to establish that he, John Fair, was charged with the goods, as stated in the first bill.

Afterwards the plaintiff contended he had a right to read the whole deposition, even the part rejected before.

If the court had been correct in the first bill, they would also be in this; for a part being once rejected properly, could not become admissible by the use of the unobjectionable part.

3. The last bill is to the opinion of the court in charging the plaintiff with costs, for want of an amicable demand.

Costs are adjudged by the final judgment, and neither to this, nor any part thereof, can a bill of exceptions be taken.

It is, therefore, ordered, adjudged and decreed, that the judgment of the district court be annulled, avoided and reversed, and the case remanded, with directions to the court to allow the reading of the part of the deposition objected to; and it is ordered that the defendant and appellee pay costs in this court.

Preston, for the plaintiff.

Stone *et al. v.* Vincent.　VI, N. S. 517.

The pendency of a suit in another state, cannot be pleaded in abatement of an action brought in this.

When a man gives two endorsers, the first is liable to the second and subsequent endorsers.

FIRST District.

MARTIN, J., delivered the opinion of the court.

This is an appeal from judgment against the payee and first endorser of a note, in favor of a subsequent endorser.

1. The appellant's counsel urges, that the court erred in overruling a plea in abatement of the pendency of a suit for the same cause of action between the same parties, in one of the courts of the state of Alabama.

2. That the court erred in giving judgment for the plaintiffs, because there is proof that they were fully satisfied by the sale of some property of the drawer, conveyed by him to Gordon, in trust for securing the payment of the note.

3. That the court erred in giving judgment against the defendant for the whole sum due on the note, because there is proof, that the plaintiff and he endorsed the note as co-sureties, to the bank of Mobile.

We do not think that the court erred in overruling the plea of abatement. The pendency of a suit between the same parties, and for the same action, does not deprive the courts of this state of their jurisdiction of the demand.

The drawer of the note had conveyed a lot and wharf in Mobile, to Gordon, in trust, for securing the payment of the note. After the protest, the trustee put up the premises at auction, and they were bid off by the plaintiff for 2600 dollars. No deed of sale was, however, executed, the trustee being told the sale was illegal. However, at the request of the plaintiffs, he advertised the premises for sale a second time, and they were purchased by McLoskey for 1300 dollars. The drawer of the note had requested the trustee not to execute the deed to the plaintiffs, as they had agreed to receive the amount due them, and he was making arrangements to raise it. On these facts, we think that the first sale was disagreed to by both debtor and creditor, and the trustee acted correctly in refraining to execute the deed of sale. Afterwards, when the debtor's attempts to raise the money proved useless, the land was rightfully sold a second time. For the price of the second sale, the district court has given credit.

4*

The last objection is obsolutely untenable.—When a man gives two endorsers, they are liable in a different manner; the first to the second and subsequent endorsers—the second, to the third and subsequent ones.

It is, therefore, ordered, &c. that the judgment of the district court be affirmed, with costs.

Denis, for the plaintiff.
Pierce, for the defendant.

Saunders *v.* Taylor.   VI, N. S. 519.

A bond given in a court of the United States, on taking out a writ of error, may be put in suit in a state court.

Suit may be brought against the heirs of a succession in the ordinary courts.

PARISH Court of New Orleans.

MATHEWS, J., delivered the opinion of the court.

This suit is founded on a bond given by G. M. Ogden, as principal, and P. V. Ogden and Thomas L. Harman as sureties; conditioned to be void, if the principal should prosecute to effect a writ of error, which he had obtained to the district court of the United States for the district of Louisiana, on a judgment rendered in said court in favor of the plaintiff.

All the obligors are dead, and the present action is commenced against the tutor of the minor children and heirs of Harman, the last signer on the bond.

The defendant pleads in his answer, two exceptions to the suit: first, to the jurisdiction of the court; and secondly, to the plaintiff's right to prosecute the action, being a non-resident of the state, &c.

The plea to its jurisdiction was sustained by the court below, and the plaintiff appealed.

The exception to the jurisdiction appears, from the argument of counsel, to be based on two grounds: 1. that as the suit is against a succession, the court of probates is the only tribunal which can legally take cognisance of it; 2. that as the bond relates to, and was given in consequence of, a judgment rendered by the district court of the United States, that court alone is competent to entertain any suit which

[Saunders v. Taylor.]

may be brought on it. The second exception, based on the want of residence, and also the last ground of opposition to the jurisdiction, was overruled by the parish court; and, in our opinion, correctly.

No objection has been made to the authority of the plaintiff's counsellor or attorney, and our courts have always been open to foreigners for the purpose of prosecuting their rights, when represented by attorneys at law. Perhaps a more summary remedy on the bond might have been obtained in the United States court, in relation to the jurisdiction of which it was given; but that circumstance ought not to preclude the obligee from attempting to enforce its obligations in the courts of the state.

The correctness of the opinion of the court below, on the first ground of exceptions to the jurisdiction of that court, depends on a proper construction or interpretation of articles 995 and 996 of the 5th section of the chapter of the Code of Practice, relating to the mode of proceeding in the courts of probate.

According to the general provisions found in this section, and others in the Louisiana Code, it would seem, that debts due from a succession should be liquidated, and their payment enforced by the court of probates of the place where the succession was opened. It is, however, contended for on the part of the plaintiff, that these general rules are limited by the articles of the Code of Practice above cited. The last of them having a direct reference to the first, they must be examined, as dependent on each other, in ascertaining the intention of the legislature, and the sense and meaning conveyed by the terms in which they are written. Art. 95 confines the application of the rules established in the previous prov s ons of the section, to estates administered by persons appointed by a court, or by testamentary executors.

According to the succeeding article, when estates are in the possession of heirs, either of full age, or minors, suits must be brought against the heirs, or their curators, (if the heirs be minors,) in the ordinary tribunals. The present action is against a tutor, who, according to law, holds and manages the estate of his wards under the age of puberty, in the same manner as a curator would the succession of minors above that age. There is some ambiguity in the two articles taken together; we are, however, of opinion, that a just construction of them, authorises the courts of ordinary jurisdiction to take cognisance of cases like the present.

It is, therefore, ordered, adjudged and decreed, that the judgment of the parish court be annulled, avoided and reversed; and it is further ordered, adjudged and decreed, that the cause be remanded to said court, to be tried on its merits, and that the appellee pay the costs, &c.

Strawbridge, for the plaintiff.

Grymes, for the defendant.

Pierce *v.* Morgan.   VI, N. S. 523.

The purchaser of three lots, who is disturbed in the possession of one of them, cannot suspend the payment of the price of the other two.

PARISH Court of New Orleans.

Mathews, J., delivered the opinion of the court.

In this case the plaintiff obtained an injunction, by which the sale of certain property, seized, in his possession, under an order granted at the instance of one Susanna Hepp, as hypothecary creditor, was suspended. On hearing the cause, the court below dissolved said injunction, and from the decree of dissolution the plaintiff appealed, &c.

The evidence of the case shows, that Mrs. Hepp became the proprietor of the debt on which this order of seizure was issued, by regular transfer under authentic act, and endorsement of the mortgage and notes which had been given by one Nichols, to secure the payment of the price of three lots of ground situated on the batture in front of fauxbourg Saulet, designated in a plan of the place by Nos. 19, 20 and 21. Nichols sold these lots to the plaintiff, who possesses them under this sale, and has commenced the erection of a steam saw-mill thereon. The first two, Nos. 19 and 20, were sold to Nichols by S. B. Bennet, and also, one-half of the lot No. 21; the other half being sold and conveyed by the widow and heirs of George Hunter; the act of sale was executed on the 25th of January, 1825, in which George H. Hunter appeared, and sold as one of these heirs, but had previously failed, and surrendered his estate, which was held by syndics, to be disposed of for the benefit of his creditors. In consequence of this surrender and proceedings in the *concurso*, the interest which the insolvent had in the lot No. 21 being one-tenth, has been sold at auction, and brought the price of 700 dollars. The injunction was obtained to prevent the injury which the last purchaser and third possessor of the property was liable to suffer from this claim of the creditors of George H. Hunter. Previous to the dissolution of said injunction an actual disturbance took place, by the sale of his interest, made by order of the syndic, and the amount of loss to the possessor ascertained to be 700 dollars.

According to this statement of the case, we are of opinion, that the parish court erred in dissolving the injunction *in toto*. Admitting that the cause must be determined by the law on this subject, as it existed, and had been interpreted, by decisions previous to the adop-

[Pierce v. Morgan.]

tion of the Louisiana Code, still the plaintiff ought to be relieved against an injury, not only probable in consequence of judicial proceedings having been commenced, calculated to affect a part of the property which he holds *bona fide*, but certain and fixed, as to amount, by actual sale under those proceedings.

As there is no incumbrance or disturbance shown in relation to the two lots Nos. 19 and 20, the sheriff should be permitted to proceed without injunction to sell them for the purpose of effecting payment of their price. The circumstance of the present proprietor and possessor having consolidated the three lots into a single tract or space of ground, to suit his own convenience, cannot affect the rights which the vendors retained on them separately to secure payment of the price for which they were sold. In the sale to be made under the seizure of lot No. 21, the present value of George H. Hunter's share, which appears to be lost to the plaintiff in the injunction, and is shown by public sale to amount to 700 dollars, should be deducted from the original price for which said lot was sold to Nichols, and by him mortgaged, &c.

It is, therefore, ordered, adjudged and decreed, that the judgment of the parish court be annulled, avoided and reversed, by which the injunction heretofore granted was entirely dissolved. And proceeding here to make such judgment and decree, as, in our opinion, ought to have been rendered in the court below, after hearing the cause on its merits; it is ordered and adjudged, that the injunction granted in the first instance by the parish court be entirely dissolved, so far as it stayed the sale of lots Nos. 19 and 20, which form a part of the matters in dispute; and it is further ordered and decreed, that it be made perpetual, to the extent of seven hundred dollars, on the amount claimed by the plaintiff, in execution, as the price of lot No. 21, and that said injunction be dissolved as to the balance of the price of said last mentioned lot, to satisfy which, the sheriff may legally proceed to sell: the appellee to pay costs of this appeal.

Lockett, for the plaintiff.

McCaleb, for the defendant.

EASTERN DISTRICT, MARCH TERM, 1828.

*

M'Caleb *v.* Maxwell.   VI, N. S. 527.

If the plaintiff be indulged with leave to perfect an irregular service, the bail will not thereby be precluded from availing himself of the irregularity.

THIRD District.

MARTIN, J., delivered the opinion of the court.

The defendant, sued as bail, urged that the plantiff was not entitled to recover, because no service of the petition and citation had been made in the French language. There was judgment against him, and he appealed.

The counsel for the appellee urges there was no irregularity in the service on the principal, and that, if there was, the bail can not avail himself of it.

The record shows that the petition and citation were served in the English language only; that the principal pleaded this in abatement; and the court was of opinion that the service ought to be in the French language also, but that the plaintiff was still in time to complete the service, by supplying the defect by copies in that language. Judgment was given against the principal, and it does not appear that he appealed.

The time of service in the French language, bears the date of the 4th of September, 1824, and the bail bond that of the 13th of April preceding.

[M'Caleb *v.* Maxwell.]

All these proceedings took place before the promulgation of the Code of Practice, while the law required service in the French language. The indulgence granted by the court to the plaintiff, in giving him time to perfect the service, ought not to prejudice the bail, who, perhaps, signed the bond, merely because he saw that the plea in abatement would avail, and to afford to the defendant the opportunity of availing himself of the irregularity in the service.

The plaintiff, it is true, obtained from the court below time to perfect the service, but this ought not to prejudice the bail, who had not the opportunity of resisting the application, and therefore must not suffer by it. ·

This case resembles that of Ryan *v.* Bradley, Taylor, 77, in which the superior court of South Carolina held that the bail was discharged, the nature of the action having been changed from debt to case. They held the bail could say with truth, *non in hæc fœdere venimus.*

In the present case, the original defendant being arrested on the service of a petition and citation, in a manner not supported by law, had the right of taking advantage of this, and could do so without going to jail. His friend would willingly bail him, on being shown that the suit must abate, on the illegality of the service being pleaded in abatement. If, afterwards, the plaintiff, on discovering this, procured time to perfect the service, the bail ought not to suffer, and, without his consent, be compelled to stand bound for the appearance of the defendant, on a process to the service of which no objection could be made.

It is, therefore, ordered, adjudged and decreed, that the judgment of the district court be annulled, avoided and reversed; and that our judgment be for the defendant, with costs in both courts. ·

Woodruff, for the defendant.

Vialet *v.* Lalande.   V, N. S. 530.

THIRD District.

The Supreme Court will not, without particular grounds, interfere with a verdict on matter of fact.

Planters' Bank of Georgia *v.* Proctor.   VI, N. S. 531.

FIRST District.
The third possessor may appeal from a judgment against the mortgagor.
The mere endorser of a note secured by mortgage, cannot obtain an order of seizure and sale out of court.

Quick *v.* Johnson.   VI, N. S. 532.

PARISH Court of New Orleans.
Held, confession must be taken together, but when extrajudicial, the weight of evidence by which they may be rebutted depends on all the circumstances of the case, as disclosed by the testimony.

Winter *v.* Donaldsonville.   VI, N. S. 534.

Where plaintiff swears positively that an absent witness will prove *all the facts alleged* in his petition, the court will hardly declare that his facts are irrelevant, and so refuse a continuance.

SECOND District.

PORTER, J., delivered the opinion of the court.
The contest between the parties to this suit, arises out of a claim

[Winter v. Donaldsonville.]

set up by the defendants, to tax a portion of the land which the plaintiff has inclosed within his plantation. They aver that it is a part of the town of Donaldsonville, and he contends it is without the incorporated limits. The judge who tried the cause in the court of the first instance, by his decree sustained the pretensions of the defendants, and the plaintiff appealed.

It appears that William Donaldson, in the year 1806, or 1807, being then owner of the land at the mouth of the La Fourche, on which the town of Donaldsonville is now situated, had a survey made of the rural estate thus possessed by him, divided it into lots, squares, and streets, and deposited the plan in the office of the parish judge. Immediately after making this survey, he sold lots according to the designation given them in the plat, and it does not appear in evidence that any change was afterwards made by him in regard to this property, or that he even attempted to use it as a plantation.

In the year 1816, the undertakers of roads and levees obtained a judgment against Donaldson, and, in virtue of said judgment, caused to be seized and sold a portion of the land which had been previoosly laid of as the town of Donaldsonville. In the sale of the sheriff to Gilbert, under whom the defendant holds, the property is described as follows: " one lot of twenty two arpents, one lot of twenty arpents and one of eight arpents, making in all fifty superficial arpents of land, more or less; bounded on the south side by lands belonging to Walker Gilbert, on the east by lands belonging to the widow Lessard, on the west by the Bayou La Fourche, and on the north by Claiborne street, according to the plan of the town of Donaldsonville." At the date of the sale, the land was covered with woods, and uninhabited, and a short time after Gilbert, the purchaser, inclosed nearly the whole of it, including, as well the streets as the lots, and it has remained in that situation up to the commencement of this action. Nor is jt shown the corporation have ever since assessed the said land as subject to the town taxes, or attempted to enforce the same, until they took these steps, which induced the plaintiff to apply for the injunction by which this suit has been commenced.

The plaintiff and appellant has, in this court, made the following points:

1. That a private individual cannot, by his own act or authority, confer the privileges of a town on his land.

2. That plaintiff's land is not included within the chartered limits of the town of Donaldsonville.

3. That, if he were, he is not bound by it: the legislature cannot, without the owner's consent, or in the mode prescribed,jaffect the rights of private property.

In addition to the points filed, counsel have relied, in argument, on an alleged error of the judge below, in refusing a continuance; the application for which was bottomed on an affidavit of the plaintiff, that he expected to prove by a witness who was absent, " all the matters alleged in his petition; that the land in his possession was not within the incorporated limits of the town of Donaldsonville, and was sold in block and not in lots; that it had been inclosed as a plantation since 1819, and was so in 1823, when the town of Donaldsonville was incorporated." The court was of opinion that all the facts set forth in the affidavit were irrelevant, except those in relation to the inclosure; and the counsel for the defendants having admitted the latter, no continuance could be granted.

It appears to us the court below erred, and that the continuance should have been granted. The plaintiff swore positively he expected to prove by the witness all the facts alleged in his petition. If he did, it is hard to come to the conclusion they were irrelevant, for it sets out matter sufficient to recover. The cause must, therefore, be remanded for a new trial.

It is, therefore, ordered, adjudged and decreed, that the judgment of the district court be annulled, avoided and reversed; that the case be remanded for a new trial, and that the appellee pay the costs of the appeal.

Watts, for the plaintiff.
Ripley, for the defendant.

Moore v. Stokes. VI, N. S. 538.

EIGHTH District.
When the only question is as to the weight the testimony is entitled to, the Supreme Court respects the conclusions of the jury.

Dunbar v. Skillman.   VI, N. S. 539.

THIRD District.

Parol evidence may be received of the disclosure to vendee, by the vendor, of a redhibitory vice in a slave, before the sale. Louisiana Code, art. 2498.

Tremoulet v. Cenas's Heirs.   VI, N. S. 541.

A sheriff who has received money on an execution, cannot invoke the prescription of five years.

The delay of a demand during seven years, and the circumstance of the plaintiff having, since the debt accrued, made a cession of his goods, without including the debt in the schedule, are not evidence of payment.

COURT of Probates of New Orleans.

Martin, J., delivered the opinion of the court.

The plaintiff claims from the heirs of a late sheriff, a sum of money which came to that officer's hands on an execution which the present plaintiff had put into his hands.   The pleas were prescription and payment.

There was judgment for the plaintiff, and the defendant appealed.

The case is perfectly similar to that of Delasize against the present defendants, determined in this court at June term, 1826, 4 *N. S.* 508.

To support the plea of prescription, the old Civil Code, 481, art. 78, is relied on.   By this article, the arrears of all sums of money, payable by the year, or at shorter periods, are prescribed by the lapse of five years.   The counsel urges that as the sheriff was bound to pay the money claimed immediately, the money was payable at a shorter period than one year; *ergo*, the prescription attaches.   It is clear that this article of the Code applies only to sums payable by

[Tremoulet *v.* Cenas's Heirs.]

annual, semiannual, quarterly, monthly, or daily rates; otherwise, it would apply to every debt at maturity.

The plea of payment is based on a presumption arising from two circumstances—the first is, that the money was received by the sheriff in 1809, and no claim appears to have been made till 1826; the second is, that in the meanwhile, the plaintiff offered a cession of his goods, and in the schedule annexed to the petition, no mention is made of the present claim.

To this it is urged that a plaintiff is not warned, by the plea of payment, of the necessity of establishing a demand anterior to the petition, and that the plaintiff was ignorant of his right against the present defendants, believing that their ancestors were discharged by the payment made under an *ex parte* order, and did not discover his error till after the decision of this court in Delasize's case.

We are of opinion that both pleas were correctly determined in favor of the plaintiff.

It is, therefore, ordered, adjudged and decreed, that the judgment of the court of probates be affirmed, with costs.

De Armas, for the plaintiff.
Christy, for the defendant.

Bayon *v.* Bayon.　VI, N. S. 543.

SECOND District.

A creditor by judgment rendered after the repeal of the act of 1813, by that of 1824, cannot resist the wife's claim to priority, on the ground that her marriage contract was not recorded, inasmuch as the rights of married women no longer depended on the registry of their marriage contract.

Hagan *et al. v.* Clark. VI, N. S. 545.

The creditor can put the debtor in *mora*, in no other manner than by a suit, writing, notarial protest, or a demand proved by the testimony of two witnesses.

FIRST District.

MATHEWS, J., delivered the opinion of the court.

This suit is brought on a promise to give merchandise to the amount of 800 dollars, for a note made by Eben Fiske, and endorsed by Hyde & Merrit, of which the plaintiffs were holders. The defendant resists their claim, on the ground that he has not been put *in mora*, by a tender to him of said note, and demand of merchandise. The cause was submitted to a jury in the court below, who found a verdict for the plaintiffs; and judgment being rendered in pursuance of said verdict, the defendant appealed.

In the course of the trial in the court below, the judge was required to instruct the jury that the proofs in the case would not authorise the plaintiffs to recover, according to art. 1905 Louisiana Code, which he refused, and a bill of exception was taken, &c.

Notwithstanding the numerous points made on the part of the appellant in this court, we believe that the decision of the cause rests solely on a proper construction of that article of our Code. It provides that a debtor may be put in default, by the terms of the contract, by the act of the creditor, or by the operation of law. The second mode of placing an obligor *in mora*, has alone relation to the present case. This is done by a demand on the part of the obligee, evidenced either by commencement of a suit, writing, protest of a notary, or testimony of two witnesses, made at or after the term stipulated for the fulfilment of the obligation. The appellant agreed that he would receive the note above described, in payment for merchandise of any kind, which he then had on hand, or might have previous to the term at which said note would become due. This agreement was made on the 17th of February, 1827, and the note was dated on the 13th of the same month, having six months to run from date.

The testimony of two of the clerks of the appellees, shows that they had each, at a different time, tendered the note to the defendant and demanded merchandise from him to its amount, which he refused to deliver, on various pretexts. The present suit was commenced within the period limited for the performance of the contract by its stipulations, and the prayer of the petition is in the alternative, either that the defendant be ordered to pay 800 dollars, or deliver to the plaintiffs merchandise to that amount. According to the article of

5*

[Hagan *et al v.* Clark.]

the Code on which the appellant relies, the commencement of this suit
is sufficient to put him in default; and if he had been willing to comply
with the stipulations of this agreement he might in his answer have
demanded that the note should be delivered over to him. Whether
the plaintiffs were bound to make a tender of the note in their petition, is a question which, in the present case, need not be settled; for
it is in proof that it had previously been twice tendered to him, and
as often refused, and a total unwillingness shown on his part to discharge the obligation of the contract.

It is, therefore, ordered, adjudged and decreed, that the judgment
of the district court be affirmed, with costs.

Carleton and *Lockett*, for the plaintiff.
Maybin, for the defendant.

Foucher *v.* Carraby *et al.*   VI, N. S. 548.

FIRST District.
This case involved the jurisdiction of the district courts.

The Court, MATHEWS, J., said:—We had occasion to examine the
subject which the suit now under consideration presents, in the case
of Tabor *v.* Johnson, 3 *N. S.* 674. The court then, after mature consideration, and under some apparent embarrassment, caused by
former decisions, came to the conclusion that the courts of ordinary
jurisdiction of the state, are not incompetent to entertain jurisdiction
of suits against tutors, curators, and testamentary executors, in relation to the administration of successions, *ratione materiæ;* but rather
ratione personæ. If the doctrine taught by that case be true, it follows as a necessary consequence, that judgments rendered by those
tribunals, against estates held and administered as above stated, are
not absolutely void; and that sales made in executing such judgments
give title to purchasers. So far from changing our opinion relative
to the principles established by the decision of the case referred to,
further reflection has fully confirmed us in a belief of their correctness.

Clamageran *v.* Banks *et al.*   VI, N. S. 551.

An abandonment rightfully made, reverts back to the time of the loss.

PARISH Court of New Orleans.

PORTER, J., delivered the opinion of the court.

The correctness of the judgment rendered in the court below, between the plaintiff and defendants, is not complained of, but the garnishees aver that there is an error in it, so far as it condemns them to the payment of moneys which are in their hands.

In answer to the interrogatories propounded to them, they stated that they had no knowledge of the defendants, but that they had insured, on the 7th of May, 1825, the schooner Samuel Smith for 2500 dollars, and her freight for 1400 dollars; that on the 13th of August, a demand had been made on them for 2929 dollars and 27 cents, in consequence of an averred total loss of the vessel; but that no part had been paid, as the sum insured was held subject to any lien which the respondents may have from having insured cargo in said schooner, to the amount of 3900 dollars.

The defendants have become indebted to the garnishees, by having received the amount which the property insured sold for at the port where the voyage was broken up. Whether they have a right to retain this sum as against the attaching creditor, is the only question in the cause.

It is contended they have not: First, because they did not accept the abandonment, and are yet contesting the claim of the assured, for which they now insist they have a right to retain the moneys attached: and Secondly, because they owed the money at the time the attachment was levied, and no subsequent act of the defendants, by which they became indebted to the garnishee, can affect the rights of the attaching creditor.

It appears from the case agreed on, that the abandonment was made on the 13th of August, 1825. On the 20th of the same month, the attachment issued by the plaintiff, was levied on the sum in the plaintiff's hands due to the defendants. At what time Banks and Hendricks received the proceeds of the sales of the cargo of the schooner Samuel Smith, is not conclusively shown, either by the case stated, or by any evidence appearing on record.

As to the objection to the garnishees holding this money in their hands, because they did not accept the abandonment, and are yet contesting the claim of the insured, it is removed by the decision just made in this tribunal, which declares that abandonment to have been rightfully made, and the garnishees in consequence responsible. There is no principle better settled in maritime law, than that an abandonment, rightfully made, reverts back to the time of the loss, and renders the insurer thenceforward the proprietor of the thing insured; and, whether the legality or correctness of this abandonment be ascertained by his acceptance of it, or by a decision of a court of justice, in opposition to his wishes, the result is the same. Phillips on Ins. 459.

But it is contended the insurers have no right to retain the money, because they were debtors to the defendants by the abandonment, and that the latter having since received money from them, cannot affect the right of the seizing creditor. In support of this position, the 2212th article of the Civil Code is relied on, which declares " that compensation cannot take place to the prejudice of the rights acquired by a third person; therefore, he, who, being a debtor, is become a creditor since the attachment made by a third person in his hands, cannot, in prejudice to the person seizing, oppose compensation." Whether this provision could apply to a case such as that before the court, where the receipt of the money after the attachment, was in virtue of an authority conferred before, we need not say, as the weight of evidence shows that the money was in fact received by the defendant previous to the time the seizure was made in the hands of the garnishees, so that they can properly offer it in compensation of the debt due by them.

The amount due on the two policies is 3822 dollars. From which must be deducted 2488 dollars, received by Banks and Hendricks. This will leave a balance of 1334 dollars, from which again must be taken the proceeds of the wreck, 206 dollars 73 cents, and 254 dollars, for which Zacharie has a lien; and the balance will be 874 dollars and 27 cents. If the captain is entitled to any commission under the circumstances of the case, which we doubt, it must be in a suit where he is a party.

It is, therefore, ordered, adjudged and decreed, that the judgment of the parish court be annulled, avoided and reversed; and it is further ordered, adjudged and decreed, that the plaintiff do receive from the garnishee 874 dollars and 27 cents; the costs of the appeal to be paid by the appellees.

Eustis, for the plaintiff.

Cuvillier, for the defendants.

Volant *v.* Lambert.   VI, N. S. 555.

The article in the constitution of the United States relative to fugitive slaves, does not apply to a case where a right of property is claimed in them by a citizen of the state where he is found.

Whether the vendor of a slave in this state, warrants a good title according to the laws of another state into which the slave is removed? *Quære.*

Warranty of title in a slave is not limited to title with possession, but extends to cases where possession is lost, and the vendee is compelled to bring suit for him.

FIRST District.

Porter, J., delivered the opinion of the court.

The petitioner states that, in the year 1820, he purchased a negro boy named Robert, from Julie Lambert; that in the year 1821, while he was in peaceable possession of this slave, he was suddenly and clandestinely taken from him and carried into the state of Mississippi; that he has there been found in the possession of one Richard Terrill, who refuses to give him up, and that the petitioner has been obliged to commence suit for him.

The petition concludes with a prayer, that the defendant may be notified to go and defend the suit in the state of Mississippi, and that, in case the plaintiff should fail in the same, she be condemned to pay the price she received for the slave, viz: 732 dollars, the costs of the suit, those of the present action, and all such other damages as may be suffered by the petitioner.

The defendant pleaded, that the disturbance complained of, was not yet such a one as the warranty in her act of sale made her responsible for. But that to guard against the consequence of a judgment in the state of Mississippi against her vendee, by which she might become liable, she prayed that Peter K. Wagner, from whom she purchased, might be cited to answer this action, and condemned to pay the petitioners the amount of any loss they might sustain by the eviction of said slave.

Before any proceeding was taken against Wagner on this demand in warranty, the cause was tried in the court, and judgment rendered against the defendant for the sum of 732 dollars, with interest from judicial demand, and 24 dollars 90 cents, the costs of the suit against the plaintiff in the state of Mississippi.

Subsequent to this decree, the defendant took a judgment by default against Wagner, which, on his motion, was set aside, and an answer filed by him, in which, after a general denial, he pleaded, that he purchased the slave in question from H. H. Gurley, for the price of ——dollars, and prayed, that said Gurley might be cited in warranty, and in case the defendant recovered of this respondent, that he should have judgment against his vendor for the purchase-money, with damages and costs.

• In a supplementary answer, he stated that he had committed an error in alleging that he purchased from Gurley, that on the contrary his vendor was one Jasper Lynch, whom he prayed might be cited, and against whom judgment might be rendered in case the defendant recovered from him.

Lynch appeared and answered, that he had bought from Gurley, whom he required to be called in warranty, to defend the right and title to the slave.

Gurley pleaded:

That Volant, the plaintiff, could not recover from Lambert, nor Lynch from the defendant, because he only warranted the slave against legal demands, when it appears by the allegations in the petition, that the slave was surreptitiously taken from Volant's possession and carried out of the state:

That he bound himself to assure a good and legal title to the slave and that he is prepared to do so, should a suit be brought against a proper person, but that he was not bound to defend the suit against Terrill.

That the petitioner lost the slave by his own neglect, and not for want of title; that if the property sold was feloniously taken out of his possession, he should have proceeded by a criminal prosecution, and have had the property brought back within the state.

And that he bought the slave from one Sarah Mason, now deceased, whose heirs he prayed might be cited in warranty, and be condemned to pay him whatever sum Lynch might recover.

The court below decreed, that the defendants should recover from Wagner the sum of 500 dollars, being the price paid by her for the slave; that Wagner should have judgment against Lynch for 800 dollars, being the amount the former paid to the latter, and that Gurley should pay Lynch the said sum, with costs. From this judgment Gurley has appealed.

In this court he has alleged several errors in it.

1. That judgment has been rendered against him for 800 dollars, when it appears he sold the slave to Lynch for 500 dollars. In this position he is certainly correct, and should we find on examining the other points in the case, that he is at all liable, this error must be corrected. 2 N. S. 466.

2. That the sale from Wagner to the defendant does not appear on the record: that the judgment against him is erroneous; and that there is no evidence to connect the sale made by the appellant, with the slave which was recovered by Terrill in the state of Mississippi.

Wagner, if he had appealed, might have complained of the correctness of the judgment rendered against him. The appellant has nothing to do with the defect in the proof, except as presenting the case without evidence to show, that the slave he sold, is the same of which the defendant was evicted. We think, however, the record exhibits sufficient proof of that fact under the pleadings. Lynch, who sold to Wagner, does not deny it; and the appellant himself does not put in issue.

The appellant's next position is, that the last vendee, who was plaintiff in the suit in Mississippi, lost the slave by his own neglect; that he should have reclaimed him as a fugitive, or as having been stolen.

There is no evidence to show the slave was stolen, or that Terrill got possession of him feloniously. But there is abundant proof to the contrary, in the judgment rendered by a court of competent jurisdiction, declaring the property to be in his possession. The article in the constitution of the United States does not apply to a case where the citizens of another state, whose laws recognise slavery, set up a title to a slave found within its limits.

The only question in the cause of any importance, is in relation to the effect of the judgment rendered in the state of Mississippi. The appellant contends he only warranted a good title, according to the laws of this state, and that the adjudication under the laws of another country does not falsify the warranty. If it were shown in evidence, that by the laws of Mississippi, a different rule prevailed there, in respect to the right and title to property of this kind, from that which governs it here, and that a title which had originated in Louisiana, was declared bad by those laws, when it would have been good in this state; this question might be one of very serious consideration, at least it would be so in the judgment of the member of the court who now delivers its opinion. But in the present case that is not shown, and even if it were, we are bound to presume and believe, that the district court of the United States did not apply those laws to this case improperly. If the facts showed Terrill's right to the slave to have been acquired in the state of Mississippi, anterior to any title having vested here, then the court did right to decide by these laws, for a court of Louisiana would have done the same thing. If on the contrary, it was derived from purchase, gift. or descent, in this state, then we presume, the court decided it by our laws, and, as it was a competent tribunal, its decision is conclusive, unless the vendor can show that, had he received notice of it, he could have given facts in evidence, which would have required a different judgment. That evidence has not been offered: and as to the objection that the vendee should have brought a possessory action, we do not know the laws of that state recognised or permitted such a proceeding; and if it did, we are of opinion the warranty of title to a slave is not limited to title with possession; but is a warranty against all mankind, whether they are plaintiffs or defendants. Again: every stipulation of the kind must be understood in relation to the subject matter in reference

[Volant *v.* Lambert.]

to which it is taken. Sellers of slaves know that they are liable to abscond, and that they may run into a state whose citizens may set up a title to them, and where, of course, the suits to recover them must be according to the modes of proceeding which the laws of that state sanction.

There is no error, therefore, in the judgment of the court below, except so far as it relates to the sum which the appellant is condemned to pay and in not giving judgment against his vendors.

It is, therefore, ordered, adjudged and decreed, that the judgment of the district court as between Lynch and Gurley be annulled, avoided and reversed; that the said Lynch do recover of the appellant the sum of five hundred and eighty dollars, with costs of the court below; and that Gurley do recover of the heirs of Sarah More, cited in warranty, the sum of five hundred dollars, with costs of the court of the first instance; those of appeal to be paid by Lynch, the appellee.

Mercier, for the plaintiff.

Canon, for the defendant.

Baune *v.* Thomassin. VI, N. S. 563.

PARISH Court of New Orleans.

Decided, that under the act of 1817, which limited process of attachment to cases of damages *ascertained and specific*, an action of slander could not begin with an attachment.* See Cross *v.* Richardson, 2 *N. S.* 323.

* It would seem to be *aliter* under the Code of Practice as amended.

Bowen v. Viel. VI, N. S. 565.

When the consideration of a note to bearer and the right of the holder are put at issue, he must show he came by it *bona fide.*

FOURTH District.

Porter, J., delivered the opinion of the court.

This action is brought on a note alleged to have been executed by the testator of the defendant in his lifetime, in favor of one Jacob Petit, *or bearer,* for 1500 dollars, and payable twelve months after date.

The answer denies the execution of the note; avers that the plaintiff holds it fraudulently, and in bad faith, and gave no value for the same; that if the signature to the note should be that of Goyer, it was obtained fraudulently, knavishly, and without consideration.

The case originated in the court of probates, where judgment was given for the plaintiff.—From that tribunal an appeal was taken to the district court, where the issue joined, was tried by a jury, who found for the defendant. The plaintiff was unsuccessful in an attempt to obtain a new trial, and appealed.

The evidence, in our opinion, does very fully support the verdict of the jury, and shows the signature of the deceased to have been obtained by the grossest fraud. There is no proof, indeed, the plaintiff participated in the transaction, though the evidence shows that he is now willing to profit by it, without any other interest in the transaction but that which arises *lucrum captando.* The note was payable to bearer, and, as both the consideration on which it was given, and the right and title of the petitioner, were put at issue by the answer, it was his duty to prove he came by it *bona fide,* and for a good consideration. This case presents one of the exceptions to the general rule, enumerated in the case of Bank *v.* Eastin, 2 *N. S.* 293; See also, 1 Camp. 100; 3 Burrows, 1516, 1517; 2 Show. 235; Taunton, 114; Chitty on Bills, 1821, 89.

It is, therefore, ordered, adjudged and decreed, that the judgment of the district court be affirmed, with costs.

Eustis, for the plaintiff.
Christy, for the defendant.

Glasgow *v.* Stevenson.   VI, N. S. 567.

A plaintiff, from whom the fact of the delivery of a bill is drawn by an interrogatory,
may prove its loss by the answers admitting the delivery.
Interest cannot be allowed on a contract made in Ireland on evidence, that it is customary, without showing that it is authorised by law.

FIRST District.

Mathews, J., delivered the opinion of the court.
This is an action on an open account, to recover the value of goods
alleged to have been sold to the defendant in the year 1817, whilst
both parties resided in Ireland, from whence the debtor absented
himself soon after the purchase.

The answer to the petition contains a general denial and plea of
prescription; and in a supplement, interrogatories are put to the
plaintiff, in relation to an acceptance or note of the defendant for the
amount now claimed from him on open account. These interrogatories were answered by acknowledging the existence of the bill of
exchange and acceptance, which the respondent declares to be lost,
and that it has never been paid, &c. After the return of the answers,
the plaintiff moved the district court for, and obtained leave to, amend
his petition, by alleging the existence and loss of the bill of exchange
which had been accepted in his favor by the defendant, and that it
had never been paid. On these pleadings, the cause went to trial in
the court below, where judgment was rendered in favor of the plaintiff, from which the defendant appealed.

The facts of the case show clearly, that goods were purchased by
the defendant from the plaintiff, to the amount claimed by the latter,
and that the former had accepted a bill of exchange drawn on him
for the price of said goods. The discovery of the existence of this
negotiable instrument, by which the appellant is bound, ought to
destroy, or at least, suspend, the plaintiff's right to recover on the
original contract of sale, unless the bill of exchange be satisfactorily
accounted for; and in order to effect this purpose, the amendment
to the petition, as above stated, was permitted by the court below,
on a construction of the 419th article of our Code of Practice, which
authorises amendments after issue joined, when they *do not* alter
the substance of the demand, &c.

There are many decisions of this court which fully establish the
principle, that a debtor, by giving his note for money owing by him,
on open account, or other contracts, does not novate the original debt;

and when the written evidence is lost, the creditor may recover on proof of the original contract or implied promise. A suggestion, by way of amendment to an original petition, of the loss of the written evidence, it is believed, would not so alter the substance of the primary demand, as to exclude a plaintiff from the benefit or privilege accorded by the article of the Code above cited.

In the present case a question of fact occurs in relation to the proof of loss. The only evidence to support it, is the testimony of the plaintiff, given on interrogatories put by the defendant. The object of these interrogatories seems to have been to establish the existence of a bill of exchange, accepted by the appellant. The answers acknowledge its existence, and proceed farther by stating its loss. By this mode of proceeding, adopted on the part of the defendant, he compelled the plaintiff to disclose facts injurious to the pursuit which he had commenced for the recovery of the price of his goods on the original contract of sale; and being thus made competent to prove the existence of the written promise to pay, we can discover no good reason why he should not be allowed to prove the loss also. His situation is analogous to that of a defendant, who is called on to acknowledge the existence of a debt, which he may also declare that he has paid.

An objection is raised to the plaintiff's right to recover, arising out of the situation in which the bill appears to have been placed prior to its loss, by the endorsement of the payee, as exhibited on the copy annexed to the protest which appears in evidence. As the suit is founded on the original contract, and not on the bill of exchange, we are of opinion that the cases cited in support of this objection, do not apply, and that it is not well founded in reason or law.

The court below gave interest on the principal demanded, assuming from the evidence, that the *lex loci contractus* authorised it; and security was not required from the plaintiff to protect the defendant against the effects of his acceptance, should it ever re-appear. In both these respects, we think the judgment of the district court to be erroneous.

The only evidence on the record with regard to interest is the testimony of one witness, who states, that it is customary among merchants in Ireland to charge interest on accounts at a certain rate. Now, we find the same thing practised by our merchants, but it is not authorised by law, and payment thereof cannot be enforced.

As to the prescription relied on by the appellant, it is clearly not supported by our laws, which, in relation to this part of his defence, must govern.

It is, therefore, ordered, adjudged and decreed, that the judgment of the district court, be avoided, reversed and annulled: and it is further ordered, adjudged and decreed, that the plaintiff and appellee do recover from the defendant and appellant, three hundred and sixty-nine dollars and twenty-three cents, with the costs of the court below; that the appellee pay the costs of this appeal; and that he shall not be permitted to take out execution on this judgment, until he shall have given security to the satisfaction of the district court to secure the defendant, harmless, from all injury or loss which might hereafter occur to him, in consequence of his acceptance of the bill of exchange, which seems to have been drawn on him for the amount of the account now sued on.

Watts and *Lobdell*, for the plaintiff.

Preston, for the defendant.

O'Connor *v.* Bernard. VI, N. S. 572.

The jury are not bound to say a debt is paid because a witness swears he thinks it is. Interest must now be allowed on a protested note, from the day of protest.

Where an attorney-at-law receives notes from a debtor, against whom he has claims for collection as collateral security with a promise to sue on them, he acts as agent of the debtor in the collection.

THIRD District.

PORTER, J., delivered the opinion of the court.

This is an action against the partner of a commercial firm, for the amount of a note executed in the name of the partnership. The defence set up in the answer is a debt due by the plaintiffs for goods sold, and an allegation, that notes to the amount of 3276 dollars and 47 cents were placed in the hands of one Colt, an attorney-at-law, and agent of the plaintiff, who was authorised to receive them, and that they have never been accounted for or returned.

The cause was tried by a jury, who found a verdict against the defendant for 450 dollars. The plaintiff appealed, and the defendant, in this court, has assigned errors in the judgment, which he prays to be relieved against.

The principal matter in dispute between the parties, grows out of the delivery of the notes and accounts to Colt. The appellant insists that she was not responsible for the collection of these papers, or the fidelity of the agent to whom they were entrusted. The defendant contends, that Colt, duly authorised by the plaintiff, received the notes; that there was laches in not collecting them, by reason of which, no recovery can be had on the note they were given to discharge; that large sums of moneys have been collected on them, which more than compensate the note sued on, and that, at all events, the plaintiff can not have judgment against him, without, at the same time, being decreed to deliver up the notes which her agent received as collateral security.

Colt was an attorney-at-law. It is also proved that he was agent for the plaintiff, in collecting moneys for her, and paying debts. The note on which the suit is brought, was in his hands for collection. The receipt he gave for the notes and accounts delivered to him by the defendant, is in the following words: "Received of Messrs. Crawford & Bernard, by the hands of Joseph Bernard, the above mentioned notes, in amount 3276 dollars and 47 cents, as collateral security on two endorsements—one of Jas. O'Connor for 800 dollars; one of James Flower for 1000 dollars, which, when collected, will go to discharge said endorsees; the balance, a debt due Wilkins & Linton, of about 5000 dollars; the notes in the hands of Woodruff are to be received. (Signed) J. D. Colt, acting for James O'Connor, James Flower, and Wilkins & Linton."

This case, with the exception of part of the money having been collected, presents almost the same features with that of Benson v. Shipp, reported 5 N. S. The attorney was the agent of both parties: of the plaintiff, to collect the debt due by the defendant, and to receive collateral security; of the defendant, to collect the debt so assigned, and pay over the moneys to those, for whose use they were placed in his hands. There is nothing proved in evidence, which shows the plaintiff enlarged the stipulation entered into by Colt, or that, in any respect, changes the responsibility created by the terms of the receipt. The defendant must, therefore, look to Colt, or his representatives, for the notes placed in his hands. 5 N. S. 154.

But, for the money collected by Colt, we think the jury did right to allow a credit. By the terms of Colt's agreement with the defendant, to which we think there is satisfactory evidence of the plaintiff's assent, the money when collected was to go in discharge of her claim. As soon, therefore, as it came into the agent's hands, its effect in discharging the debt can not be distinguished from a payment made in money to the attorney by the debtor.

The defendant complains there is an error in the verdict, in not allowing credit for all the moneys received on account of the notes. The draft of the plaintiff, and the sum paid by Bradford, are positively proved. The witness who deposed as to the collection of Guilbry, only swears he thinks it was paid. As the witness could not be certain of it, we do not see the jury can be considered in error for not allowing it in compensation.

But there is error in the verdict in not granting interest from the time the note fell due. It was protested; and by the act of 1821, bills of exchange and promissory notes carry legal interest from the day they are regularly protested for non-payment. Acts, 1821, 44.

The interest on the balance due on the note from the time it fell due, up to this time, is 119 dollars 75 cents, which added to 450 dollars,

[O'Connor v. Bernard.]

makes the whole amount to which the plaintiff is entitled, 563 dollars 75 cents.

It is, therefore, ordered, adjudged and decreed, that the judgment of the parish court be annulled, avoided and reversed: and it is further ordered, adjudged and decreed, that the plaintiff do recover of the defendant, the sum of five hundred and sixty-three dollars and seventy-five cents, with costs in both courts.

Thompson v. Linton et al.   VI, N. S. 576.

If, in a contract, certain advantages be stipulated in favor of a third person, in consideration of services to be by him performed, the parties may alter their minds, provided the third person be not injured in regard to services prior to the change.

FIRST District.

MATHEWS, J., delivered the opinion of the court.

This suit is brought against certain pilots, resident at the Balize, on a contract or agreement entered into amongst themselves, in relation to the employment of boats in their business of piloting; by which they stipulated that the boats or vessels employed should draw two-fifths of all money earned, and three-fifths the balance was to be shared by them, the pilots. In this contract they agree to make the plaintiff their agent, to collect debts for them, allowing a commission of 5 per cent. to him on collections, 2½ per cent. for money advanced, and 1¼ for all purchases made in produce for the boats, which were to be used as above stated. The plaintiff alleges that Mr. Linton and one Holman, purchased a schooner called the Eliza, in partnership, which was for some time used in the piloting business, but his partners had failed to account with him, or pay any of the profits which were derived from the use of the vessel, and prayed a dissolution of the partnership and final settlement of accounts. He afterwards dismissed his suit so far as it related to Holman.

In this mixed state of a suit, against the pilots to compel them to comply with the engagements they had entered into, (with each other,) for the benefit of the plaintiff, and also to compel Linton to pay over to him as part owner of the boat, his share of the two-fifths earned and to dissolve the partnership, the cause was submitted to a ury in the court below, who found a verdict for the plaintiff for 1500

[Thompson v. Linton et al.]

dollars an appeal was taken and the judgment of the district court was reversed, on account of the plaintiff having blended two distinct causes of action, against persons owing on different claims. The case was remanded for a new trial, and previous to entering thereon, the plaintiff discontinued so much of his petition, as prays for a dissolution of the partnership and sale of the schooner therein mentioned, and the cause seems to have been proceeded in exclusively in relation to his claim for damages occasioned by a breach of the contract made and entered into between the pilots themselves, in which they stipulated to employ him as their agent; and to recover his third part of the two-fifths which was earned by the Eliza, as being owner to that extent: also the amount advanced to and paid for the benefit of the defendants.

The plaintiff was not a party directly to the contract under which he claims the advantages which might have resulted from his services in collecting debts, advancing money and purchasing provisions. It was a stipulation made in his favor in consideration of services to have been by him performed; but in its origin wholly voluntary on the part of the defendants, who had a right to change their will in this respect, so as not to injure the person employed by them, in any thing which had been done by him previous to such change.

As a company, they are answerable to him for his proportion of the money earned by the use of the schooner Eliza, being one-third of two-fifths, and also for money advanced to them and articles furnished, &c.

In the last trial in the district court, the cause was submitted to a jury, who found a verdict for the defendants, on which judgment was rendered and the plaintiff appealed.

The decision of the case depends exclusively on questions of fact, as supported by the evidence. The appellant relies principally on the testimony, drawn from Brower, one of the defendants, by interrogatories, to show that the jury erred. In support of the verdict the appellees rely on that of Copping, a witness on their part. This witness swears that he paid to the plaintiff 154 dollars 50 cents; and that the sum thus paid, was in full for his share of the profits in the schooner Eliza, which had accrued up to the 7th of September, 1825.

Brower's testimony does not establish any certain amount, as owing by the defendants to the plaintiff; it is wholly indefinite both as to what may be due on account of the gains of the Eliza, and in consequence of purchases and advances made for the use of the appellees.

The record furnishes no evidence by which it can be clearly ascertained that the jury have erred in their conclusion on the facts of the case.

It is, therefore, ordered, adjudged and decreed, that the judgment of the district court be affirmed, with costs.

. *Pierce*, for the plaintiff.

Preston, for the defendants.

Peet *et al. v.* Morgan.   VI, N. S. 580.

A legislative declaration, Code of Practice, art. 400, that if the intervening party does
not give security, and the sheriff proceeds to sell, the latter shall be responsible for
damages, does not repeal all other parts of the law under which he was responsible
before.

For the rules of construction applicable to repealing statutes, see the repeated declarations
of the court, in 1 *N. S.* 158; *Ibid.* 73; 3 *N. S.* 190 and 236.

The exception attempted to be made, because this provision is found in the Code of
Practice, and not in an ordinary statute, is without any foundation. There is no repealing clause to it, except in relation to articles of the Civil Code to which it may be
repugnant; no rule presented for its construction which places it on different grounds
from other laws.

No delivery is necessary where the thing sold is already in the vendee's possession,
though in *autre droit.*

FIRST District.

Porter, J., delivered the opinion of the court.

This case has been already before the court, and by a judgment of
this tribunal of March term, 1827, it was remanded for a new trial.
Since its return to the district court the intervener discontinued by
leave of the court, and the case was tried between the original parties;
there was judgment against the defendant, and he appealed.

It is an action against the appellant for having, as sheriff, illegally
and forcibly taken possession of a certain quantity of merchandise,
of which the plaintiffs allege they are owners.

The defendant pleads that the trespass and injury complained of,
results from a seizure made by him in his official capacity in virtue
of a writ of attachment issued in a suit wherein T. W. Pratt was
plaintiff, and R. & B. W. Dewitt, were defendants, and that he took
the goods mentioned in the petition, by virtue of special instructions
from Pratt, in consequence of which he is not liable to an action at
the suit of the plaintiffs.

He further pleads that the goods were the property of the Dewitts,
and that the sale to the plaintiff, if any such there was, was false,
fraudulent, simulated and collusive.

This last ground of defence was disposed of when the case was
last before us. We there held, as we had repeatedly decided in other
cases quite similar to this, that frauds and collusion could not be
inquired into in an action arising on a seizure made by the sheriff;
that if the sale was fraudulent, a suit should be brought to set it aside,

and that the party could not, before a judgment was rendered, annulling the contract, treat the transaction as null and void, and seize the property as belonging to the vendors.

We then also expressed our opinion, if not at great length, at least after much reflection, that the first ground of defence was untenable. The counsel for the appellant has again gone fully into the subject, but after the best consideration we can give the question, our conclusions must be the same as before. The whole strength of the argument rests on the provision in the Code of Practice in relation to the opposition of third persons, whose property is seized by the sheriff, and particularly the 400th article, which declares, that if the third person, who has intervened to prevent the sale, does not furnish security to have it enjoined, the sheriff may sell; but that if he does, he shall be personally responsible to the intervener for all damages which the sale may occasion. The conclusion we draw from this provision, is directly opposite to that contended for by the appellant. He argues, because recourse is given in this instance, it is refused in all others; that this new provision is a repeal of our former law, by which the sheriff was responsible, if he seized property other than that of the defendant in execution. But we think that on no sound principle of construction, can the affirmative provision be considered a repeal of a former law, to which it is not contrary, nor even different; for previous to the passage of the Code of Practice, a third person, whose property was seized, might have endeavored to prevent the sale, and if the sheriff sold after the interference, he would have been responsible. But the responsibility, after judicial notification, is not irreconcilable with the rights of the owner to claim damages, though he does not interfere. They both stood together before the Code of Practice, and the re-enacting one of them, does not repeal the other. We have so often expressed our opinion in regard to the rules of construction applicable to repealing statutes, that it is deemed unnecessary to go into the subject at length. 1 *N. S.* 158; *Ibid.* 73; 3 *N. S.* 190 and 236.

The exception attempted to be made, because this provision is found in the Code of Practice, and not in an ordinary statute, is without any foundation. There is no repealing clause to it, except in relation to articles of the Civil Code to which it may be repugnant; no rule presented for its construction which places it on different grounds from other laws. Act of 1824, 178.

One of the points made by the appellee is, that the goods were delivered as a collateral security, and that there was no transfer of the property. The evidence, we think, shows that the securing of a debt due to the plaintiffs was the motive that induced the purchase; but the contract which intervened between them and their debtor, for the accomplishment of this object, was one of sale, and vested such a title to the goods in them, as prevented their seizure.

The cause was remanded to ascertain the date of the *sous seing privé* act, under which the plaintiffs claim. It appears by the evidence taken on the second trial, that it was executed the day prior to the seizure. The actual possession being in the plaintiffs, antecedent to, and at the time of the transfer, though not in their own right did not prevent possession following the title. No further delivery was necessary. None could have been made, unless the vendor first took them out of the hands of the purchaser, and then gave them back again, which would have been a vain ceremony the law does not require.

The judgment of the court below is complained of, as giving the plaintiffs a larger sum than they are entitled to: on this point the opinion of the court is with the appellant. As the goods have been sold by consent of both parties, since the inception of the suit, and as the amount of the sale will cover the price the plaintiff was to pay, we think the officer who acted in good faith, should not be responsible for more than the net amount produced by the sale at auction.

It is, therefore, ordered, adjudged and decreed, that the judgment of the district court be annulled, avoided and reversed; and it is further ordered, adjudged and decreed, that the plaintiff do recover of the defendant the sum of five thousand nine hundred and forty-three dollars and seventy-five cents, with costs in both courts.

Hennen, for the plaintiffs.
Watts, for the defendant.

Sabatier *et al. v.* Their Creditors. VI, N. S. 585.

Any legal evidence may be offered in support of the confession of an insolvent, that he owes one of the creditors in the *concurso.*

The obligation of a contract is that which the law in force at the time of the contract obliges the parties to do or not to do.

A law passed after a contract which would exempt all the property of the obligor from the payment of the debt, would be unconstitutional.

It would be equally so, if a portion was placed out of the reach of execution, provided the portion left was not sufficient to satisfy the debt.

The privilege on contracts of deposit entered into before the promulgation of the Louisiana Code, is not affected by its provisions.

PARISH Court of New Orleans.

PORTER, J., delivered the opinion of the court.
Brunetti, the appellant, complains of the judgment rendered in the

court below, which placed him on the tableau of distribution as a simple creditor; he contends that he is a privileged one.

The case presents two questions:

1. Whether he is a creditor to the amount claimed by him.

And 2. Whether he has a privity which authorises him to be paid in preference to chirographary creditors.

1. As the judgment of the court below recognised the debt, and the other creditors who oppose the appellant have not prayed for any amendment to it, that question would seem settled. But in this court it has been argued, that, though they have no objection to recognise him as a simple creditor, because they have no interest in contesting his claim on that ground, they are deeply concerned in disputing his claim to be paid in preference to others; and that in exercising the right to contest his privilege, they can put him on the proof of every fact necessary to establish it, among which the first and most important is, that he should show the existence of the debt claimed by him.

Perhaps they have: at all events, as our opinion accords with that of the lower court as to the justice and reality of the claim, we find it necessary to examine whether, under the state of the case, the question is open for examination. It is true, as contended for by the appellees, that on a contest between creditors in *juicio de concurso* the notes or obligations of the insolvent do not make, in themselves, proof of the debt apparently due to them. They must be supported by other evidence. What that other evidence must be, as was said by this court in the case of Menendez *v.* Larionda's Syndics, no author that we have been able to consult distinctly and positively states. But as the books declare they do make evidence, when supported by other circumstances (*otros adminiculos*), the conclusion come to in the case just stated, appears to us still to be a correct one, namely; it intends any legal evidence which will convince the minds of a court and jury of the fairness and justness of the claim. The evidence furnished in the case before us leaves not a doubt on our minds that the money was deposited as the appellant alleges, and we shall, therefore, proceed to examine whether he has a privilege for its payment. 3 *Martin*, 705; 12 *Ibid*: 157; *Febrero, p.* 2, *lib.* 3, *cap.* 3, *no.* 34.

II. This question is much more difficult than that just disposed of. At the time the money was placed in deposit, the provisions of our old Code regulated contracts of this description, and as, by them, no change was made in the ancient jurisprudence of the country, a privilege or right of preference existed on the irregular deposit. Since the contract was entered into, and before the failure of the insolvents, a change has been made in our law by which the privilege of the depositor is restrained to cases where the thing reclaimed is identically the same with that deposited: consequently, that arising from the irregular deposit, when the demand is not for the same thing, but for the same quantity of the thing placed in the hands of the depositary, is established: Louisiana Code, 2934, 3189; Durnford *v.* Seghers's Syndics, 9 *Martin*, 470.

By which of these laws should the right of the appellant be decided? that is the point presented for decision. If the privilege accorded by the law at the time of the contract, make a part of the rights flowing from the agreement, then the claim of privilege must be allowed. If, on the contrary, it is nothing but one of the remedies given to enforce the agreement, the control of them was within the legislative power, and the preference being abolished, the claimant must be put on the tableau as a simple creditor.

The distinction between rights and remedies is a subject of frequent discussion in courts, and the repeated contests they give rise to, is a sure proof how unsettled is the doctrine which governs them. The constitution of the United States prohibits any of the particular states from passing laws which will impair the obligation of a contract. As the obligation here spoken of is the legal, and not the moral obligation, it would seem to follow, that the obligation of a contract is that which the law in force at the time the contract is made, obliges the parties to do or not to do. If this be true, the right of each is, to obtain a performance of every obligation arising out of the agreement at the period it was entered into. The remedy is the means given by law to carry this right into effect. The question, then, in every case of this kind, is, what are the obligations of one of the parties, because the rights of the other are ever correspondent to, and co-extensive with, the duty imposed on the person with whom he stipulated.

Now, in the ordinary case of a promise to pay a certain sum of money on a particular day, the obligation of the contract is, that the debtor shall discharge the debt at the period fixed, or, that in default thereof, his property shall be responsible to satisfy his engagement. We are aware that a few have contended, that there is no implied obligation to make the property liable in a contract of the kind just mentioned, but we apprehend such a ground is quite untenable. Indeed, we do not see how it can be maintained without reducing the obligation from a legal to a moral one, since a right without a legal remedy ceases to be a legal right. If, by the contract, the property of the debtor did not become responsible, and was not, as between creditor and debtor, to be placed out of legislative control, there would be scarcely any thing left for the prohibition in the constitution of the United States to act on. It can not be believed the framers of it intended to guard against the states passing laws, which might add to, or take from, the amount to be paid, and change the time of performance, and leave them a power which would enable them to say, the debtor should be entirely released, both in person and property, from his engagement.

In the case of Sturges *v.* Crowninshield in the Supreme Court of the United States, it was admitted in argument, that all the present property of the debtor was responsible to the creditor; but it was urged that the obligation did not go so far as to make future acquisitions subject to it. The court, however, said, that both present and future were, and to release the latter from liability impaired the obligation. In the case of Green v. Biddle, they declared that any law introducing a deviation from the terms of the contract, by postponing or accelerating the period of performance, imposing conditions not expressed in the contract, or dispensing with those that were, violated its obligation. 4 Wheaton, 122; 8 Wheaton, 1.

We take it, therefore, as clear, that in the case put of an ordinary obligation to pay money, a law passed subsequent to the contract which would exempt all a man's property from the payment of the debt would be unconstitutional; and that it would be equally so if a part of it was placed out of the reach of execution, provided, the portion left liable was not sufficient to satisfy the debt.

If it be true, then, that on the implied obligation that the property is liable for the engagements of the debtor, the legislature cannot deprive the creditor of recourse on it, it would seem still clearer, that they cannot interfere with a special contract by which the debtor makes a part of his property liable in the first instance for it. Because, if the law sanctions at all such an agreement, the creditor acquires by the stipulation, a right to the thing, which no subsequent legislative act can take from him, without changing, or, in case of insolvency, weakening, and, perhaps, entirely destroying, his claim. Such would be the consequence in the common case of a conventional mortgage. The mortgagee lends his money because the law allows him to take security for his debt by obtaining a special lien on some part of the borrower's property. The security makes as much a part of the mortgagor's obligation and the mortgagee's right, as the promise to pay the money does, and future laws can no more deprive him of the one than of the other. If, instead of taking real security, he obtained personal, by getting another to join his debtor in the bond, it would not be pretended that a subsequent act of the legislature, by declaring that there should be no such contract, as that of security, enforced in our law, would discharge the co-obligor. And if the personal security could not be taken away, how can the real? They have both the same object; they are both permitted by the law; and they are both of equal importance to the creditor, who has trusted to them as a means of assuring the repayment of the money he lent on the faith of them.

In what respect the contract of deposit now before the court can be distinguished from that of mortgage in relation to the present question, we are unable to perceive; except, that in the former, the law gave a privilege to the depositor on all the property of the depositary, the moment the contract was made: in the latter, there required an express stipulation. But every principle that prevents legislative interference with the one forbids it with the other.

As to the argument, that creditors, subsequent to the repeal of the law, are not bound by the contracts made previously by their debtor, we understand it to be perfectly well established that they are bound by them. In many cases, the legislature have required, that acts

·which give a preference should be registered to make them have effect against third parties; but when this formality is not required, ·and the law declares the creditor shall have a privilege, it is as binding on others as on the debtor himself.

There have been some cases brought before the tribunals of France, which bear a close, if not a perfect analogy to that before the court, and they are more worthy of attention, because they were decided on general principles of law, without any special clause in the constitution of that country such as ours contains.

They arose on the 2161st article of the Napoleon Code, which declares, that when the debtor has given a general mortgage on his present and future property, and the objects hypothecated amount to more than was necessary to secure the debt, the debtor has an action to reduce the mortgage to such portion of the property as will be sufficient to secure and satisfy the sum due.

By the laws of France previous to the adoption of the Napoleon Code, no such power was vested in the mortgagor, and soon after its passage, a question was presented to their tribunals, whether a mortgage given under the ancient law could be reduced under the new. Two of the appellate tribunals to whom such a case was presented, decided in the negative: they held. that the right to make the whole .of the property responsible existed by the original contract, and that the new law could not change it without giving to that law a retroactive effect.

Two other courts of equal dignity held they might, but their decisions have not escaped severe animadversion. However, the principles on which they decided, strongly support the conclusion we have come to in the case. They considered, that so long as the law left enough of property hypothecated to secure the payment of the debt, it could, for public convenience, unlock the surplus from the lien imposed on it, and that, by such regulation, the right of the creditor was not touched; it was only a change made in the property on which it might be enforced: *Pothier's Traité des Hypoth. vol. 2, ed. 1809, p. 171 et 198; Questions Transitoires sur le Code Napoleon, 2 N. S. p. 47 to 59.*

The legislation of the 2118th article of the Code Napoleon, declares, that mortgages can be only given on immovable property and their accessories. By another article of the same work, (529,) rents of land were declared to be movable. The effect of these provisions was to abolish the right which had existed under their former law, of taking mortgages *sur des rentes foncieres.*

At the time this change was made in their law, there existed a great number of mortgages, which, previously to the adoption of the Napoleon Code, had been given on debts of this kind. Questions, we perceive, have been raised, whether it was not necessary these mortgages should be registered pursuant to the new law, but not a doubt is expressed as to their validity: *Questions Transitoires sur le Code Nap.* 68 et 73.

[Sabatier *et al. v.* Their Creditors.]

The question presented in this case renders it unnecessary to examine to what extent the legislative power to contract remedies may be carried. In many instances that power may impair the creditor's right. The terms of the courts may be placed at such a great interval of time, that before the creditor can obtain judgment, the debtor has wasted all his property. Execution may be required to be levied, on some description of goods before others can be seized, and the collection of the debt in this way delayed. The power of arrest on mesne process may be abolished, as may be that of imprisonment after judgment. But these are inconveniences incidental to the authority necessarily vested in the legislature to regulate the proceedings of court, and its constitutionality is undoubted. It is sufficient, in the present case, to say, that in the exercise of this power, they cannot turn a legal obligation into a moral one, nor change a privileged into a chirographary creditor.

It is, therefore, ordered, adjudged and decreed, that the judgment of the parish court be annulled, avoided and reversed—that the appellant be placed on the tableau of distribution as a privileged creditor, according to the rank he is entitled to, in reference to others holding privilege on the estate: and it is further ordered, that the appellee pay the costs of this appeal.

Workman, for the plaintiff.
Mazureau, for the defendant.

Plauche *et al v.* Gravier *et al.*   VI, N. S. 596.

THIRD District.
A mortgaged square may be sold in separate lots.
A defendant who did not appeal, cannot be heard in the court *ad quam.*

Chandler *et al. v.* Garnier.   VI, N. S. 599.

Lenders on bottomry and *respondentia* are liable to contribution on general average.

FIRST District.

Mathews, J., delivered the opinion of the court.
This suit is brought by the owners of a brig called the Samuel, to recover from the defendant an amount which they allege he is liable to pay on general average, in consequence of sacrifices made for the preservation of the vessel and cargo. He contends, in his answer, that the adjustment of average was incorrectly made, in two respects: 1. By enlarging the sacrifice or loss by the addition of pilotage and steamboat hire for towing the vessel from the Balize to New Orleans. 2. In exempting from contribution, the freight, to the amount of a bottomry bond, by which the brig and freight were hypothecated to certain lenders on marine interest, in the city of Bordeaux and kingdom of France.   A legal tender is made of the sum which the defendant acknowledges to be due; but is something less than that which was adjudged to the plaintiffs by the court below.   We find on the record what is there called, an " amended statement of average," in which the sum of 300 dollars, for the hire of the steamboat, and 8 dollars charged by the pilot for detention, are deducted from the amount sacrificed or necessarily lost according to the adjustment on which the action is founded.   Both parties were dissatisfied with the judgment of the district court, and both appealed.
The case presents two questions—one of fact—the other of law. That of fact arises out of the evidence which relates to the necessity of having the brig towed from the Balize to New Orleans, as a means of preservation from imminent danger of destruction of vessel and cargo.   From the testimony of the case, the court below seems to have been of opinion, that no absolute necessity of this kind did really exist, and consequently, the expense incurred should be borne by the owners, as is customary in ordinary occurrences.   With regard to this question in the case, after strict examination of the whole evidence, we do not find the facts therein disclosed, so conclusive in their nature, as to cause us to make deductions different from those which seem to have governed the judge *a quo* in rendering his judgment.
If the case were to be governed by the general law of merchants, unincumbered by decisions of the tribunals of England, apparently made in pursuance of the law in that country on the subject of bot-

[Chandler *et al. v.* Garnier.]

tomry and respondentia, and freed from some *obiter dicta,* to be found in the decisions of causes made by the courts of the United States, in relation to insurance, the legal question which it presents would be of easy solution. Vide M. Insur. Bac. 6; Park do. c. 21; Pell. do. 302; 2 Johns. Cases, 252.

It may be laid down as a general rule, recognised and established by all authors on the subject of commerce, that ship, freight and cargo are bound to contribute, in gross, or general average. In opposition to this general principle, an exception is claimed by the plaintiffs, as being supported by English and American decisions, which establish the doctrine, that lenders on bottomry and *respondentia* are free from contribution in case of general average. Now, if this doctrine be correct in any point of view, (which, in our opinion can hardly be admitted,) it can only be justly invoked for the protection of lenders; which can never be necessary, unless the value of the vessel and freight hypothecated, should prove inadequate to pay the money borrowed, after deducting the rateable contribution to be made, from said balance.

According to the evidence in the present case, it is clear that more than sufficient to pay off the bond would remain, of the value of the brig and freight, after deducting the amount which they are bound to contribute on gross average; this contribution should, therefore, be first made, and the bottomry bond be discharged from the remainder.

It is, therefore ordered, adjudged and decreed, that the judgment of the district court be avoided, reversed and annulled; and it is further ordered, adjudged and decreed, that the plaintiffs recover from the defendant the sum of eighty-one dollars and thirty three cents, and that the defendant pay all costs which accrued in the prosecution of the suit up to the time of the tender made; the plaintiffs to pay all subsequent costs, as well as those of appeal.

Pierce, for the plaintiff.
Strawbridge, for the defendant.

Millaudon *v*. Smith.   VI, N. S. 604.

THIRD District.
The copy of a plan certified to have been taken from the original,
by a surveyor not in possession of the original, is not legal evidence.
The court will remand a case for new evidence when they think
the justice of the case requires it.

Talmadge *et al. v.* Patterson.   VI, N. S. 604.

An administrator does not become personally liable, on his letter announcing the sale of
the property of the estate, and that the debt would be paid as soon as the money was
collected—even on proof of such collection.

PARISH Court of New Orleans.

MARTIN, J., delivered the opinion of the court.
The plaintiffs sued the defendant in his individual character, for a
debt due to them by the estate of William Dame, deceased, of whom
the defendant is administrator, on the ground that he has received
funds of the said estate, sufficient to pay said debt, and that he wrote
to the plaintiffs that their debtor was dead, that he (the defendant)
had been appointed administrator of the estate, that he had sold the
property at twelve months, and that they should have their money
as it is collected; and the defendant neglected to answer the plaintiffs
interrogatory, " Whether he had not received sufficient funds, belonging to the estate, to pay the plaintiffs' claim?"
The parish judge gave judgment for the defendant, being of opinion
that the plaintiffs had not shown a sufficient cause of action.
The defendant was appointed administrator to the estate of the
plaintiff's debtor in the territory of Arkansas, and wrote the letter
produced against him, to inform the plaintiffs of this circumstance
and announcing the sale of the property on a credit, and that the
debt would be paid as soon as funds were collected.

[Talmadge *et al.* *v.* Patterson.]

In doing so the defendant did his duty as administrator; and we think the parish judge acted correctly in declaring that he (the defendant) had not been made himself personally responsible, neither does his admission (resulting from the failure to answer the plaintiff's interrogatory) make him so; for, it at most shows, that assets came to his hands—but this does not make him liable in his individual capacity, nor does his letter which is evidently written in his capacity of administrator. Chitty on Contracts, 84.

It is, therefore, ordered, adjudged and decreed, that the judgment of the parish court be affirmed, with costs.

Christy and *Cenas*, for the plaintiffs.

Nixon, for the defendant.

Ory *v.* Winter. VI, N. S. 606.

(See 4 *N. S.* 277.)

SECOND District.

MATHEWS, J., delivered the opinion of the court.

This is the third time that this case has been before the appellate court. Once on a former appeal, a second on a rehearing, in consequence of which the cause was remanded to be tried *de novo;* and now by an appeal from the judgment rendered on the new trial.

This suit is brought by an endorsee of a promissory note, executed in the state of Mississippi, against the maker. The defendant pleads error and want of consideration for a large part of the whole amount for which the promise was made.

All the important principles of law which relate to the matters in dispute between the parties, were settled by a judgment of this court, pronounced on the last hearing: we have re-examined them in the present instance and believe that they have been correctly determined. 4 *N. S.* 277.

The judgment of the district court from which the present appeal is taken, allowed the defendant the entire deduction which he claimed from the amount of the note sued on, and from this judgment the plaintiff appealed.

The decision of the case as now presented to this court, depends principally on matters of fact, and the evidence of the cause seems to support the conclusions of the judge *a quo*, with two or three slight exceptions. These relate to the calculation and allowance of interest at 10 per cent. per annum, on the amount of an account, which the defendant claims to have deducted from the note; an item of 111 dollars, 16 cents, which Gilbert the payee of the note undertook to collect from one Jones; and another account of 25 dollars, 37 cents. With regard to the interest calculated on the account, there is no evidence on the record to show that, by the laws of Mississippi, interest is allowed on open accounts. It is agreed that, according to those laws, notes bear interest at the rate of eight per cent. per annum, after they become due. Mears's testimony, might induce a belief that Gilbert assented to the correctness of the charge of interest; but according to our laws, conventional interest is chargeable only when supported by an agreement in writing. In relation to the two sums which Gilbert undertook to collect, and pay over the amount; the breach of his contract has been passive only, and he is responsible from the time alone in which he may have been put in default; Louisiana Code, art 1927; and it does not appear that he has yet been placed in that situation. The interest on the whole of the account as calculated, and the last two items of said account, must therefore be deducted from the sum allowed in favor of the defendant by the judgment of the court below.

Objections by the plaintiff, are found on the record to the testimony of all the witnesses, Staunton, Mears and Gilbert. Those made to the testimony of the first, are clearly unfounded. And we deem it useless to inquire into the competency of the last two, because should they be rejected, there is still sufficient evidence to establish the error complained of by the defendant to the amount of his account current against Gilbert for the year 1821; which must be taken from the sum total of the note; and judgment rendered in favor of the plaintiff, for the balance, with interest at the rate of eight per cent. from the time at which it became due.

It is, therefore, ordered, adjudged and decreed, that the judgment of the district court be annulled, avoided and reversed; and it is further ordered, adjudged and decreed, that the plaintiff and appellant do recover from the defendant and appellee, eleven hundred and forty-four dollars and twenty-five cents, with interest at the rate of eight per cent. per annum, from the 1st day of April, 1823, until paid; and that the appellee pay the costs of both courts.

Ripley and *Conrad*, for the plaintiff.
Watts and *Lobdell*, for the defendant.

Parker *v*. Starkweather. VI, N. S. 609.

Reconvention may be pleaded in a supplemental petition, when the defendant has set up a reconventional demand, superior in amount to the sum claimed in the petition, and this does not conflict with the ancient law of this country, that *reconvention is not permitted.*

FIRST District.

Mathews, J., delivered the opinion of the court.

In this case the plaintiff claims from the defendant 850 dollars for rent of a house and blacksmith's shop. The defendant pleads in compensation a debt, due to him from the former for work and labor performed in his trade as a blacksmith, to an amount exceeding the sum demanded by the plaintiff, and asks judgment for the surplus. To this plea of compensation and reconvention the plaintiff replied by disputing the claim of the defendant, and pleading other claims against him in compensation.

On the trial of the cause in the court below, the judge refused to suffer the plaintiff to give any evidence in support of his replication or plea in compensation, and to the opinion by which this evidence was rejected, the counsel for the appellant took a bill of exceptions; which presents the only question in the case.

The compensation pleaded by the defendant being followed by a claim for a surplus remaining after full discharge of the plaintiff's demand, must be considered as a suit in reconvention. It is true that reconvention is one mode of claiming the benefit of compensation, and peculiarly so when any connection exists between the opposing claims of plaintiff and defendant. But when the party reconvening, demands more than sufficient to compensate the claim against him, his plea partakes much of the nature of an original suit, to which payment might certainly be pleaded; and compensation is a species of payment *solutionis vicem obtinet.* This is strictly true in cases where the opposing claims are liquidated and certain. If they be of the same nature and not of difficult liquidation, compensation as payment ought to be tolerated, and is authorised by law in defence.

The defendant relies on two principal grounds in support of the correctness of the opinion of the judge *a quo*, by which he rejected the evidence offered by the plaintiff on his plea of compensation. 1. That our Code of Practice does not authorise replications. 2. That the replication being a reconvention on the part of the plaintiff, against that pleaded by the defendant, it is not tolerated by law.

The 239th article of the Code of Practice provides that new facts alleged by a defendant in his answer, shall be considered as denied by the plaintiff, and therefore admits neither replication nor rejoinder. By the 377th article of the section which treats of demands in reconvention, a defendant may plead it either as an exception in his answer to the principal demand, or institute a distinct and separate demand, and the plaintiff is bound to answer.

Now in whatever form a defendant may choose to put his defence if he demand judgment against the plaintiff for a surplus, in his plea of compensation and reconvention, it is no longer a simple exception but beyond the extinction of the demand of the latter, it is the institution of a separate and distinct demand, to which the plaintiff is bound to answer, and cannot be rightfully prevented from using all legal means of defence, amongst which payment or compensation to the extent of payment alone may be used.

The doctrine on this subject carried thus far is in conformity with the ancient laws of the country, and does not conflict with the general rule that reconvention is not permitted; which rule itself suffers an exception, as explained by *Toullier, vol. 7, page* 495, *art.* 415. *See also Febrero Bt. 2d, book 3, chap.* 1, *no.* 256; *same part and book, chap. 2, no 212, and the Curia Phil. page* 75, *no* 8. In the present case, the amount pleaded in compensation (to the defendant's demand in reconvention) is equally easy to be liquidated, as the account set forth by the reconvenor. The reason of the rule which seems so much to eschew the danger of infinity in reconvention, will, we think, be sufficiently satisfied, by limiting the respondent to compensation alone, rejecting all claim for surplus.

It is, therefore, ordered, adjudged and decreed, that the judgment of the district court be avoided, reversed and annulled, and it is further ordered, adjudged and decreed, that the cause be remanded to said court to be tried *de novo*, with instructions to the judge *a quo* to admit the plaintiff to prove the amount which he offers as compensation to the defendant's demand in reconvention; the appellee to pay the costs of appeal.

Preston, for the plaintiff.

Hennen, for the defendants.

EASTERN DISTRICT, APRIL TERM, 1828.

Herbert's Heirs v. Babin et al. VI, N. S. 614.

Privileges on property seized do not form a good ground for suspending the sale.

SECOND District.

PORTER, J., delivered the opinion of the court.

The defendant obtained judgment against one Joseph Dugat, and proceeded to obtain satisfaction of it, by issuing an execution against his property. The plaintiffs applied for and obtained injunction, on the ground that they had a higher privilege on the property than that of the defendants. The district court, after hearing the parties was of opinion the plaintiffs had no right to prevent the sale, even admitting the facts set up by them to be true; that their remedy was on the proceeds. It therefore dissolved the injunction. The plaintiffs appealed.

We think the court below did not err. The plaintiffs have no right to the property. The judgment recovered by them against their stepfather for the price of the objects bought by him at the sale of their father's estate, is a ratification of the sale, and covers any irregularities the proceedings may present. They, can not, therefore, claim as owners. Their right is one of privilege; and as the law requires that property put up at auction by a sheriff, shall be sold, subject to all the privileges and hypothecations with which it is burthened, their position can not, in any respect, be altered by the sale, and, consequently, they have no authority to prevent it. This property may sell for more than will satisfy the plaintiffs' demand, and the defendants have, consequently, a right, even admitting their adversary's privilege is of a superior nature, to cause the thing subject to it to be sold, in order that they may get the overplus. Code of Practice, 679, 683.

The judgment of the district court is therefore affirmed, with costs.

Percy v. Millaudon.   VI, N. S. 616.

Joint owners must contribute rateably to useful expenses incurred on the property by a joint owner having the management of it, when no opposition on their part has been made to such expenses.

FIRST District.

Porter, J., delivered the opinion of the court.

The plaintiff and defendant were joint owners of a sugar plantation on the Mississippi. The former owning one-fourteenth, and the latter thirteen-fourteenths. The defendant has had the management and direction of the property, and has received the amount for which the crops have sold. This suit is to recover the plaintiff's proportion of the profits, and to compel the defendant to render an account of them.

The answer denies the existence of any profits, avers the expenses have exceeded the revenues, and prays judgment for the balance due to the defendant.

The court of the first instance gave judgment in favor of the defendant for 2519 dollars and 80 cents. The plaintiff appealed.

The greatest, if not the only difficulty in the cause, grows out of the different views which these joint owners seem to have entertained in relation to the most beneficial manner of managing the estate of which they were proprietors. The property in the situation it was placed when the parties became owners of it, was susceptible of being worked to conciderable advantage, and more revenue might have been made, had the defendant employed the means in his hands with a view to immediate profit. But as it was of great extent, and susceptible of being improved, so as to bring a large portion of it into cultivation, he directed his principal attention to preparing it for more extensive cultivation hereafter. In accom-

[Percy v. Millaudon.]

plishing this object, he placed a large number of negroes, belonging to himself, on the plantation, and erected valuable buildings. The plaintiff contends he is not responsible for these expenses, nor is he obliged to contribute to them; that the defendant must account for every thing which might have been made, had the estate been managed in regard to immediate profit.

The judge below was of opinion the plaintiff should pay his proportion of these improvements, and the hire of the slaves. The correctness of this opinion has been strenuously assailed: one of the grounds on which it is attacked is correct. As both the owners had an equal right to the control and direction of the property, the law supports the party who opposes any change. But the argument drawn from this right is pushed too far, when it is contended, that notwithstanding no opposition was made to the mode pursued by the defendant in managing the estate, the plaintiff shall profit by the increased value given to the land by the improvements, and yet not contribute his proportion of the expenses incurred in making them. It is urged this principle can not be applied to the parties before the court, because, during a great portion of the time, there was a suit pending between them, in which the plaintiff's right to the land was contested, and that until he was declared owner by a judgment of the court, he had no right to interfere with the management of the property. But this circumstance did not prevent him making opposition; nay the whole property might have been taken out of the defendant's hands, and sequestered, until the final termination of the suit, on a suggestion he was using it in such a way as to injure the right of the plaintiff. Code of Practice, 275. 3.

The fourth number of the 284 1st article of the Code has been relied on to show, that a purchaser can not dispose of, or make any change in real property belonging to the partnership, without the consent of his partners, even if that change should be advantageous to the partnership. This article does not apply to the parties now before the court, who were not partners: they were joint owners, and our Code has specially provided, that a community of property does not, of itself, create a partnership. But if they were partners, still, the circumstance of the improvements being made with the knowledge, and without the opposition of the plaintiff, would prevent him claiming the benefit of this provision. *Poth. Trait. de Soc. nos.* 87 and 88; *Domat, liv.* 1, *tit.* 8, *sect.* 4, *no.* 22; *Dig. liv.* 10, *tit.* 3, *law* 28.

The situation of the parties before the court bears a close analogy to that of an heir in a succession, who enters into possession of the whole estate, and contests the right of his coheir to any part of it. In case the latter finally succeeds in the suit, the former, in rendering an account, would be allowed credit for all the improvements he put on the property, though strictly speaking, he is, perhaps, a possessor in bad faith. *Pothier, Traite du Domaine de Propriété, nos.* 350, 345; *Dig. liv* 5, *tit.* 4, *law* 38, 39.

Our Code seems to have sanctioned the same doctrine; at least, the article in the Napoleon Code which is similar to it is so understood in France. Napoleon Code, 1381; Louisiana Code, 2292; *Toullier, Droit Civil, vol.* 11, *til.* 4, *no.* 111.

We have examined the various items of the account, and we see nothing erroneous in the judgment of the district court in relation to them. The charge for interest so much complained of was rejected below.

It is, therefore, ordered, adjudged and decreed, that the judgment of the district court be affirmed, with costs.

There being in the case an error in the calculation of the interest, it is agreed by the parties, that the former judgment of the court should be so modified that the judgment of the district court be reversed, and judgment rendered in favor of the defendant for 2674 dollars 10 cents, with interest from the date until paid, and costs in the court below, those of appeal to be paid by the appellees.

Denis, for the plaintiff.

Seghers and *Grymes,* for the defendant.

Johnson *v.* Rannels. VI, N. S. 621.

Foreign records must be proved according to the act of congress.
A will need not be probated in this state, when used merely as evidence of title.

EIGHTH District.

MARTIN, J., delivered the opinion of the court.

The defendant and appellant has first drawn our attention to a bill of exception taken to the opinion of the district judge, overruling an objection made to the introduction in evidence of a deed of gift, on the ground that the execution of it was not legally proved.

The original was produced, with an endorsement made thereon, and subscribed H. Sneed, clerk of the county court of Granville, North Carolina, certifying that the deed was proved in court and ordered to be recorded—another endorsement subscribed by R. D. Cooke, P. R., certifying that the deed was registered; and finally, the certificate of the clerk, attesting the official capacity of the person, who signed the second endorsement as registered.

The court erred in admitting the document. in evidence, because it lacks the attestation of the chief or presiding judge or magistrate of the court. Ingersoll, (1825,) 298, *verbo* Evidence.

Another bill was taken to the admission of the will of the donor in evidence. A copy was offered, certified by H. Sneed, the clerk of the county court of Granville, North Carolina, with his attestation that it was truly made from the original in his office. On the will, according to the copy, is one endorsement of the clerk attesting that the will was duly proved in open court, and ordered to be recorded. Next follows the certificate of the presiding magistrate, attesting the official character of the clerk, and that his attestation is in due form. The reading of the will was opposed by the defendant's counsel on the ground that the certificate was insufficient, and on the grounds that it did not appear that the will was proved in North Carolina, nor registered and ordered to be executed in Louisiana, nor proved and ordered to be executed according to the laws of Louisiana.

The court did not err—the question was examined in this court in Balfour *v.* Chew, 5 *N. S.* 517. There was no necessity for proving an order from any court of probates in this state for the execution of the will. This is only required when the will is to be carried into execution, by the executor suing for the property or the estate, not when the will is offered as evidence of title in the legatee against a party claiming title.

As the case was tried by a jury, and illegal evidence was admitted, the case must be remanded. It is contended that setting aside the deed of gift, the plaintiff had evidence of title in the will. This may be—but *non constat* that the jury did not ground their verdict on the right appearing to result from the deed. Besides, the will refers to the deed of sale—this deed must be therefore produced and proven, for it forms a link in the chain of plaintiff's will.

It is, therefore, ordered, adjudged and decreed that the judgment be annulled, avoided and reversed, the verdict set aside, and the case remanded, with directions to the inferior judge not to admit the deed of gift in evidence till clearly proved. It is ordered that the plaintiff and appellee pay costs in this court.

Llorente v. Gaitrie. VI, N. S. 623.

The obligor in a penal obligation, must be put in delay, in one of the modes prescribed
by the Code, before the penalty can be exacted.

THIRD District.

PORTER, J., delivered the opinion of the court.

The plaintiff agreed to sell to the defendant a house and lot for
2800 dollars, payable on the 1st of April, 1827, possession to be given
on that day. The contract contained a stipulation, that if either of
the parties failed to comply with his agreement, he should pay 500
dollars.

The plaintiff avers he was willing and ready to deliver the house,
but that the defendant refused to receive it. The petition prays judgment for the penalty, and 1000 dollars damages.

The answer states the plaintiff neglected or refused to comply with
his agreement; alleges the contract to be usurious, and prays judgment by way of reconvention for 500 dollars, the damages which the
defendant alleges he has sustained.

The case was tried by a jury in the court below, who found a verdict in favor of the plaintiff for 500 dollars. The court confirmed it,
and the defendant failing to obtain a new trial appealed.

In addition to the grounds of defence disclosed by the answer, the
appellant has contended the action must be dismissed because he was
not put in delay previous to its institution.

Our Code declares, that the penalty is forfeited only, when he who
has obligated himself, either to deliver, to take, or to do a certain
thing, is in delay. Louisiana Code, 2122.

And it further provides, that when, by the terms of the contract, or
the operation of law, the party is not in delay, he can only be put in
it by the act of the obligee, who must demand the performance of
the contract by the commencement of a suit, a demand in writing, a
protest by a notary public, or a verbal requisition in the presence of
two witnesses. Louisiana Code, 1905.

Now the evidence on the record does not show that the defendant
was put *en demeure* in any of the modes prescribed by the statute.
His letters which were read on the trial merely establish that after
the time for performance had elapsed, he wrote to the plaintiff thank-
ing him for his indulgence, and promising to comply with the contract according to his wishes. Such acknowledgments are neither
evidence of the demand which the law requires, nor a waiver of it,
and the placing of the defendant in delay being made an indispensable

APRIL TERM, 1828. 89

[Llorente v. Gaitrie.]

prerequisite to sustain an action of this kind, the plaintiff cannot recover. Code, 1906.

The counsel has contended that from the form which was given to the agreement the promise to pay the penalty was the principal obligation, and that no demand was necessary. The contract, after containing the stipulations of sale, price, &c., concludes thus: "and it is hereby agreed that if any of the contracting parties refuses to fulfil the contract as hereby agreed and understood, that the party refusing so to do, is to pay the other party the sum of 500 dollars."

We think on the contrary, that by the terms used, the penalty inserted was not the principal obligation, but a secondary one to enforce the primary obligation. This was evidently the intention of the parties, as it is clearly the legal interpretation of the contract. The articles 2116, 2117 and 2118 of the Code, which appear to have been taken from those passages in Toullier cited by plaintiff, satisfactorily, we think, sanction this view of the subject. Louisiana Code, 2116 2117, and 2118. *Toullier, vol. 6, liv. 3, tit. 3, sect. 6, 799 a 804.*

It is, therefore, ordered, adjudged and decreed that there be judgment against the plaintiff, as in case of nonsuit, with costs in both courts.

Walker v. Dunbar. VI, N. S. 627.

Plaintiff in an hypothecary action need not allege ownership in defendant: allegation of possession suffices.

EIGHTH District.

MATHEWS, J., delivered the opinion of the court.

This is an hypothecary action, in which the defendant is sued as a third possessor of a house and lot, which is alleged to be mortgaged to secure the payment of the money claimed by the suit. The defendant pleaded several exceptions to the manner of instituting the action: 1. That the petition contained no proper allegation that the person who lived in the house was a third possessor. 2. That an hypothecary action can not be maintained against a third possessor without an allegation of ownership in him, &c.

These exceptions were sustained by the district court and judgment of nonsuit pronounced, from which the plaintiff appealed.

8*

According to our Code of Practice, an hypothecary action is a real action—art. 61; and by the 41st article this species of action lies against a possessor of immovable property, where the plaintiff claims the ownership or the possession, or the exercise of some immovable right on property thus possessed. The right of mortgage is so strongly attached to the thing mortgaged, that it may as emphatically be considered an immovable right, as any other which can be imagined to exist on real property.*—We are, therefore, of opinion, that the second exception was erroneously sustained, nor do we believe the first should have been supported. The defendant, in one part of the petition, is described as living in the house as a merchant: in another place, there is an allegation that the note on which the suit is founded was given for the price of the house possessed by the defendant. Perhaps either of these clauses would be, in itself, sufficiently descriptive of the appellee as a third possessor, but taken together, they leave no doubt of the character in which he is sued.

It is, therefore, ordered, adjudged and decreed, that the judgment of the district court be avoided, reversed and annulled; and that the cause be remanded to said court to be tried on its merits, &c.; the appellee to pay costs.

Slidell and *Saunders,* for the plaintiff.

Shiff *v.* Louisiana State Insurance Company.
VI, N. S. 629.

The contract of insurance is to be construed with reference to the laws of the country where made.

Losses casual and inevitable are not a subject of general average.

FIRST District.

PORTER, J., delivered the opinion of the court.

This is an action on a policy of insurance. The plaintiff states he has sustained a loss from one of the perils insured against, to the amount of 770 dollars, and that the defendants refuse to pay it.

This loss has arisen, according to the statement in the petition,

---

* See Moore *v.* Allain, 11 *Lou. Rep.* 430.

from the goods which formed the object of the policy having been compelled to contribute in an adjustment of general average at the port of destination, for certain losses sustained by the ship on her voyage from New Orleans to Hamburg.

The evidence shows this loss proceeded from the vessel being obliged to carry a press of sail to avoid the dangers of a lee shore.

The protest of the captain and crew, given on her arrival in port, states, that immediately after escaping the danger they found the ship to leak very much, and that as soon as an opportunity was offered for examination, they discovered she had sustained damages that must be presumed to have arisen from the ship having been strained by the quantity of sail put on her.

The plaintiff has very clearly established, that by the *lex mercatoria* of the continent of Europe, such an injury as this to a vessel furnishes a claim for general average. *Nouveau Valin*, 607; *Pardessus, Droit Commercial, vol.* 3, 185; *Boulay Paty, Droit Commercial Maritime*, 4th, 445, 446; *Emerigon, vol.* 2, cap. 12, sect. 41; *Jacobson's Sea Laws, liv.* 4, cap. 2, 346.

But it is equally clear, that by the law merchant of the United States, and of Louisiana, it does not: Stevens on Average, 157 and 158; Parke on Ins. 173; 8 Mass. 468; 6 Taunton, 501; Phillips, 370. With us, all casual and inevitable damage and loss, as distinguished from that which is purposely incurred, is a subject of particular, not general average.

The question, therefore, presented for our decision in the case before us, is, whether the defendants are responsible for a loss which has arisen from the laws of the country where the goods were to be delivered subjecting them to general average, when those of the place where the contract was entered into did not?

The general rule is, that contracts are presumed to be entered into in relation to the law prevailing in the country where they are made, and that this law governs them. This principle is believed to be universal and unbending, subject only to these exceptions: when the parties agree to be governed by rules other than those existing in the place where the agreement was entered into, or where the contract is to be performed in another country.—The contract of assurance is as much within the control of these rules as any other: *Tout ce qui concerne la decision du fond*, (says Emerigon,) *est regi par la loi du lieu du contrat. On doit les interpreter*, (says Boulay Paty,) *en general suivant les régles, d'équité qui est l'ame du commerce, et suivant le style, les usages du lieu ou l'assurance a été faite. Emerigon, vol.* 1, 125; *Boulay de Paty, Cours de Droit Commercial Maritime, vol.* 3, 333; 4 East, 135; 1 Johns. Cas. 341.

The first exception noticed above is not presented here; there is nothing said in the contract from which we can infer the parties contemplated any other law but that of their own country. It is contended, however, the second is. The voyage, it was urged, is foreign in its inception, and in its termination.

Admitting it to be so, the question is still open, whether the contract which is the subject of this suit, was foreign, either in its commencement or its end.

It seems difficult to discover any ground on which it can be so considered. It was executed in New Orleans, and it was to be performed here: here the parties signed it, and here, in case the insurers became responsible, the payment was to be made. The performance of it was not, therefore, *in another country*, and, on that ground, there is no reason for taking the case out of the rules already stated.

It is true, many of the events on which the defendants would incur responsibility, might, nay, from the nature of the contract, must, take place out of the country where it was entered into. But this is a quite different case, from the contract being performed in another country. None of the writers on this most perplexing of all subjects, the conflict of laws, gives this as an exception to the rule: in reason, there is no foundation for making it one. Parties contracting in one country in relation to certain things which have occurred, or may occur, in another, cannot be presumed to have abandoned their own law, because they contract at home, and must perform at home. If a man were to become surety in New Orleans, that an agent sent from this place to London, would faithfully perform his duties, it would be understood the duties of agency imposed on him by the laws of Louisiana, not those of England, in case a difference should exist between them on this subject. Parties are always presumed to contract in relation to their own laws, unless the contrary is clearly shown. *La presomption* (says the author already cited) *est toujours que les parties ont entendu se conformer a la loi, s'il n'y a ete expressement deroge dans le police.* When the defendants agreed to become responsible to the plaintiff for *general average*, we believe they understood what was known to the laws of their own country as such, and that they are not responsible in this instance, as by these laws, the injury sustained was one of *particular average*. Boulay Paty, vol. 3, 333.

It was argued, the contract was one of indemnity, and that, by this doctrine, the agreement ceased to be one. To this, the answer given at the bar is satisfactory. The contract is not one of indemnity against *all perils*, but against *all covered by the policy of insurance;* this, of course, leaves the question open, whether that which produced the injury here was one of those insured against.

We have examined with attention the different authorities which were cited in the argument. Phillips, who gives a summary of them, we think, concludes very justly, " that they show the difficulty of the question, without seeming to present any principle on which it may be satisfactorily settled." Contradictory as they are, they offer nothing which can control the court in rendering that judgment, which, on the general principle stated in this opinion, it feels compelled to pronounce. Phillips on Ins. 369; Park, 630; 3 Johns. Cas. 178; 11 Johns. 323; 4 Maule & Selwyn, 141.

It is, therefore, ordered, adjudged and decreed, that the judgment of the district court be annulled, avoided and reversed; and it is further ordered, adjudged and decreed, that there be judgment for the defendants with costs in both courts.

Slidell, for the plaintiff.

Eustis, for the defendants.

Barrow v. Stewart.   VI, N. S. 635.

Where, from the time and manner of trying a suit, a party has had no opportunity of being heard, the cause will be remanded.

COURT of Probates, Parish of West Feliciana.

MARTIN, J., delivered the opinion of the court.

The defendant appeals from the judgment of the court of probates of the parish of West Feliciana, depriving her of the tutorship of her minor son under the age of puberty, and has relied on errors apparent on the face of the record.

The principal errors are that the judgment of destitution is illegal:

1. Because made at chambers, or at a special session, and not at a regular term of the court.

2. Because the cause was not fixed or set down for argument or trial, nor was any notice given to the defendant.

We think the court erred. The first principle of justice is that no one should be condemned unheard or without having had the opportunity of being heard. This necessarily implies that a cause should not be proceeded on without the parties being notified of the time and place by special notice, when a case is acted on, without being set down for argument, or at any other time and place than that established by law or the practice of the court.

It is, therefore, ordered, adjudged and decreed, that the judgment of the court of probates be annulled, avoided and reversed, and the case remanded over for further proceedings according to law. And it is ordered that the appellee pay costs in this court.

Abat *et al. v.* Nolte *et al.*, Syndics.   VI, N. S. 636.

The receipt of a draft *in payment*, extinguishes vendor's privilege on thing sold.

FIRST District.

MARTIN, J., delivered the opinion of the court.
The parties were before us at the last May term of this court, 5 *N. S.* 697. The defendants having since filed a tableau of distribution of the proceeds of the sale of the lot sold by the plaintiffs to the insolvents, they opposed its homologation, claiming payment of the price of the sale out of these proceeds by preference to all other crediitors, and on the rejection of this claim they appealed.

The case was submitted on the testimony on file in the former case. This testimony had been taken subject to all legal objections.

In the notarial act of sale, the plaintiffs, who were the vendors, acknowledged the receipt of the price, before the execution of the act. The testimony of witnesses was taken to show that the price had not been received before the execution of the act, but that the vendees gave the vendors a bill of exchange therefor soon after the execution of the act. Had therefore the counsel of the syndics insisted on it, this testimony could not have been received in the present case, because fraud is not alleged as it was in the former, and the testimony is offered against the contents of the act which is forbidden by the former Code, 310, art. 242, and by the new, 2234.

Admitting the fact, however, that payment was not made at the execution of the deed, the case shows that a bill of exchange was afterwards received in payment.

Millaudon, one of the plaintiffs' witnesses, deposes he knew the draft was given *in payment* for the lot, and the plaintiffs themselves in their original petition, in the former case, (the record of which is in evidence in the present,) expressly state they were prevailed on to receive the draft in payment of the lot. It appears to us from the documents and evidence, that the price of the sale was to be paid by a draft, that trusting in the honor of the vendees, the vendors acknowledged the receipt of the price in the act of sale and shortly after received the draft. After this they could not have any privilege, for the payment of the price was consummated according to the intention of the parties, and the form of the act shows the vendors had no idea of retaining a privilege.

But if even the original intention of the parties had not been that payment should be made by a draft, by receiving the draft in payment the vendors extinguished their original claim. See the case of Rama *et al. v.* Howe, 2 *N. S.* 144.

It is, therefore, ordered, adjudged and decreed, that the judgment of the district court be affirmed, with costs.

Denis, for the plaintiffs.
Pierce and *Eustis,* for the defendants.

Caldwell *v.* Townsend *et al.* VI, N. S. 638.

PARISH Court of New Orleans.

It has been repeatedly decreed by this court that nothing can be assigned as error apparent, which depends on the facts of a case, and might have been supplied by evidence or admissions, which cannot appear except by statement of facts, testimony taken down in writing, or bill of exceptions.

Beale *v.* Delancy *et al.* VI, N. S. 640.

A sale from a father to a minor child, paid for by the child's notes, the property remaining in the father's possession, will be presumed simulated, and the notes null, as regards drawer and his heirs.

COURT of Probates of New Orleans.

MARTIN, J., delivered the opinion of the court.

The plaintiff, widow of Thos. Beale, opposed the tableau of distribution filed by the curator of the estate of Thomas Beale, Jun., son of her late husband, in her own right, and as tutor of their minor children, claiming, as such, to be placed on the tableau for the sum of 124,400 dollars, the amount of sundry notes given by the son to the father as the price of immovable and movable property, purchased by the former from the latter, with a right of mortgage, according to the terms of the sale.

Her claim was opposed by the natural mother and beneficiary heir of Thomas Beale, Jun , and by the creditors of his estate.

By consent of the defendants, the curator was discharged on giving to the plaintiff a bill of sale for the property purchased by her at the vendue of the estate of Thomas Beale, Jun., on her executing her notes for the price, without endorser, but giving a mortgage according to law, the curator depositing said notes with the register of wills, and the right of the defendant Delancy as mother and beneficiary heir was recognised.

By a subsequent agreement, the claims against the estate placed by the curator on the tableau, were admitted and recognised to be due, according to ther respective order and privilege.

The court of probates declared the sale, for the consideration of which the notes, the amount of which is claimed by the plaintiff, were given, simulated and void, and consequently decreed the cancelling of the notes.

It decreed the moneys, titles and effects of the estate, and all the property in nature, and the proceeds of so much as may have been legally disposed of, to be sequestered and detained by the curator and register of wills, to be thereafter disposed of by the court, and respectively delivered as follows:

1. The estate of Thomas Beale, Jun., to the defendant Delancy, for liquidation and settlement.

2. The property attempted to be disposed of by the simulated sale, to the plaintiff, applicable, whenever separately prayed for, to the payment of the debts of Thomas Beale.

It was further decreed, that the creditors of Thomas Beale, Jun., should remain before the court *in statu quo*, as nonsuited, till other proceedings should take place for the settlement of the estates, and the creditors be respectively placed on new tableaux. From this judgment the plaintiff appealed.

We think the judge of probates did not err in considering the sale from the father to the son as simulated. This sale was made at the eve of the father's bankruptcy to an infant natural son, for a sum of upwards of 100,000 dollars, and consideration was received in the son's notes: the father remained in possession till his death.

The sale being set aside, it naturally follows, that the proceeds of the thing sold are not to be distributed, and the opposition of the plaintiff must be rejected.

The disposition of the property which the court below has made, appears to us correct; the property of Beale, Sen., is given to the plaintiff, who was common in goods with him, and is tutrix of his children; that of the son to his mother, acknowledged by all parties to be his beneficiary heir.

The creditors of either must prosecute the heirs of their debtors respectively.

It is, therefore, ordered, adjudged and decreed, that the judgment of the court of probates be affirmed, with costs.

Grymes, for the plaintiff.
McCaleb, for the defendants.

Reardon *v.* Zacharie. VI, N. S. 644.

The *onus probandi* lies upon the party which has the affirmative of a proposition.

FIRST District.

PORTER, J., delivered the opinion of the court.

This is an action to recover the freight of a certain quantity of fruit brought from the Havana to New Orleans. The defendant is the consignee to whom it was delivered. The intervenor was the owner of the property. The demand of the plaintiff is contested on the ground of the cargo being injured through his fault and negligence. The intervenor asserts he has sustained loss to a greater amount than the freight, and claims 1000 dollars damages.

The judge below was of opinion the injury sustained by the improper conduct of the plaintiff (who was captain of the vessel) was equal at least to the freight, and gave judgment accordingly. The plaintiff appealed. And the intervenor has complained there was error in not allowing him a larger sum in damages.

There is some contradiction in the testimony in relation to the contract entered into between the parties. But it is clearly established that the vessel was advertised to sail on a particular day, that the cargo was on board, or ready to be put on board, at or before the time of departure, that she did not sail for six days after—that fruit if kept long on board is very liable to spoil, and that in this instance it was so spoiled that a considerable portion of it was thrown over board.

The reasons given for delaying the departure of the vessel are, that on the Sunday on which she was to have sailed the weather was cloudy and blew a fresh gale from the north; that on the three following days the rain fell in such torrents the custom house was shut up; and that on Thursday a clearance could not be obtained in consequence of a new regulation making the captains of vessels responsible for the duties on goods they had imported.

VOL. IV.—9

[Reardon v. Zacharie.]

The principles of law which govern the case are clear and simple. Parties to a maritime contract, like all others, are subject to damages if they refuse, or delay to perform their agreement. In this case it made a part of the contract that the ship should sail on a particular day if the weather permitted, and the non-compliance with the agreement renders the plaintiff responsible in damages. The excuse set up by him cannot be admitted. It is not shown the new regulations spoken of by the witness were made after the cargo was shipped, and that they were not in force at the time it was announced the vessel would sail on a particular day. If they were it was the plaintiff's duty to establish the fact, for he had the affirmative of the issue. Jacobson's Sea Laws, book 2, cap. 1, page 98. *Boulay Paty, Droit Commercial*, vol. 2, sect. 7, 388 *a* 397.

The only difficulty in the case is whether the damage to the fruit was occasioned by the delay in the vessel's sailing at the appointed time. On such a question it is almost impossible to obtain positive evidence, but the weight of that given on the trial of this case inclines strongly to the belief that if the delay did not cause, it increased the damage, and on the whole, we think the conclusion to which the court below arrived is that which the testimony sanctioned.

It is, therefore, ordered, adjudged and decreed, that the judgment of the district court be affirmed, with costs.

Pierce, for the plaintiff.
Relf, for the defendant.

Clamageran v. Sacerdotte. VI, N. S. 647.

FIRST District.
Error of jury; case remanded.

Abat v. Tournillon. VI, N. S. 648.

FIRST District.

The names of the endorsers make no part of the bill unless they are necessary to trace a title to it in the plaintiff. Those which are subsequent to plaintiff need not be set out.

Poydras v. Hiriart. VI, N. S. 650.

A copy of a mortgage, not made by the proper officer, will not suffice in an action against a third possessor under the old Code.

FOURTH District.

PORTER, J., delivered the opinion of the court.

This is an hypothecary action in which the plaintiff prays for an order of seizure and sale of a certain slave, described in his petition, on which he claims a right of mortgage and seeks to enforce it on the property in the hands of the defendant, a third possessor. The court below gave judgment of nonsuit against the plaintiff, from which he appealed.

The proceedings in the case were commenced under the government of the late Civil Code, and have been conducted in reference to the rules therein prescribed in relation to actions of this kind. According to these rules a plaintiff who desires to have mortgaged property seized in the hands of a third possessor, must produce a copy in due form of the act of mortgage and a judgment against the principal debtor. See old Code, 460, art. 43.

In the present suit the plaintiff produces a record of the proceedings and judgment, by him obtained against the principal debtor, and amongst these proceedings is found a copy of the instrument of mortgage as transcribed by the clerk of the court before which said proceedings were carried on. This is clearly not a copy in due form as required by the Code. It is only the copy of a copy, and consequently

not directly certified by the officer intrusted to keep the register of
mortgages.

But to supply this defect, the counsel for the appellant insists on
the intervention of the present defendant, in the suit commenced and
carried on against the principal debtor. The object and the sole object of that intervention, as shown by the record of the proceedings
which took place in the case, was to obtain relief by the intervening
party against a sequestration, by virtue of which his slave had been
seized. We believe it to be a circumstance which does not change
his situation from that of an ordinary third possessor of mortgaged
property. The plaintiff failed to make out his case, by not producing
a copy of the mortgage in due form; and the judge *a quo* acted correctly in nonsuiting him.

It is, therefore, ordered, adjudged and decreed, that the judgment
of the district court be affirmed, with costs.

Avart v. His Creditors.   VI, N. S. 652.

Creditors may oppose the tableau of distribution at any time previous to the signing of
the judgment of homologation.

FIRST District.

MATHEWS, J., delivered the opinion of the court.

It appears by the record of this case that a tableau of distribution
of a part of the funds arising from the sale of the insolvent's estate
was filed by the syndics on the 20th of December, 1825, which, after
some amendments, was homologated by order of the court on the
6th of January, 1826. But this order or decree was not signed by
the judge until the 9th of July, 1827. On the 14th of April of the
year last mentioned, the counsel for the syndics filed an additional
tableau, by which it appears that a distribution of funds which came
into their hands subsequent to the first dividend, was about to be
made amongst the creditors, and to the homologation of this second
tableau, Michaud, the appellant, as one of them, made opposition,
purporting to be based on several and various grounds, having relation to matters contained in both tableaus, the most important of
which is the privilege and preference allowed to Delasize, one of the

syndics, as an hypothecary creditor, in which situation he is placed on each tableau.

The appellant was present, by the counsel who now represents him, at the filing and homologation of the first tableau, caused it to be amended, and made no opposition.

The appellees contend that as the opposing creditor made no objection to the manner of distribution within the ten days allowed by the act of 1817, but on the contrary assisted in its homologation, his opposition cannot now be permitted, on account of being too late in term, and waived by his presence when the decree was made for recording the tableau.

On the part of the appellant it is contended that the order of homologation is nothing more than an interlocutory decree, and does not form *res judicata*. But should it be considered in the light of a final judgment his opposition was filed in time, being before the judge signed said judgment.

It is somewhat doubtful whether such decrees partake more of the nature of interlocutory orders or final judgments. We are, however, inclined to the belief that so far as they settle the rank and privilege of creditors they ought to be held as final; and cannot be considered as having the force of *res judicata*, until they have the sanction of the judge's signature.

In relation to the right and privilege of appeal, the principle, that judgments rendered by the courts of the first instance are not absolutely final until they are signed, has been settled by many decisions of the Supreme Court, and we have not been able to discover any thing in our new codes which militates against the doctrine thus established. It is believed that a motion for a new trial would be in time before a judgment was signed, although a longer period should have elapsed than that within which it ought to have been completed by the judge's signature.

The ten days prescribed by the act of 1817, within which creditors are bound to make opposition, is analogous to the time given to defendants to file their answers in ordinary suits, which they may do before judgment by default, although a greater period may have passed than the law allows.

We are of opinion that the grounds of opposition stated by the opposing creditor are sufficient to require a reconsideration of the tableau of distribution filed by the syndics, and that said opposition has been made at a time when it may be legally tolerated.

It is, therefore, ordered, adjudged and decreed, that the judgment of the district court be avoided, reversed and annulled, and that the case be remanded, with instructions to said court to proceed to hear and determine on the opposition made by the appellant; and that the appellee pay costs.

Seghers, for the plaintiff.

De Armas, for the defendants.

9*

Leeds v. Holmes.   VI, N. S. 655.

The vendee of a partnership-stock and credits, cannot sue one of the partners (vendors) for charges against that partner on the books of the partnership.

FIRST District.

PORTER, J., delivered the opinion of the court.

The plaintiff purchased by two separate acts of sale, all the right, title and interest of C. C. Whitman & Co. to the Orleans Foundry, and all their right, title, interest and claim to the debts due to said firm.

On the books of that firm there appeared a debt due by one of the partners, Holmes, from whom the plaintiff had purchased. This debt the plaintiff contends, he bought with the others due to the partnership, and is entitled by the terms of the sale made him, to demand and receive the amount of it from the defendant.

It is difficult to believe that the debts due by the individual members of the firm, entered into the consideration of the contract. In any event, the plaintiff could only recover two-thirds of it, for Holmes, who is now sued, was one of the partners: one-third of it was his, and he could not sell a debt due by himself.

But the case need not, and cannot be, considered on that ground. The vendors could transfer no greater right than they had themselves. That right, as between themselves, was restricted to any balance that might be due on a general settlement of the partnership accounts. No particular debt due by one of the partners on the books could be selected and made the basis of a suit: they could not give the plaintiff a right they did not possess themselves.

It is, therefore, ordered, adjudged and decreed, that the judgment of the district court be affirmed, with costs.

Carleton and *Lockett*, for the plaintiff.
Mercier and *Buchanan*, for the defendant.

Marmiche *v.* Commagere *et al.* VI, N. S. 657.

PARISH Court of New Orleans.

Decided, that the opening of the argument in a case belongs to him who is emphatically the plaintiff; *i. e.,* to him who instituted the suit. This right does not belong to the intervenor, notwithstanding art. 392 of Code of Practice.

Also, *held,* that a bankrupt's books are evidence of fraud as against himself.

Raguet's Heirs *v.* Barron. VI, N. S. 659.

Co-heirs of a minor, under the pre-existing law, might be members of a family meeting.

COURT of Probates of New Orleans.

Porter, J., delivered the opinion of the court.

The defendant purchased immovable property at the sale of the estate of the ancestor of the plaintiffs. The terms of the sale were one and two years credit in notes satisfactorily endorsed, with special mortgage until final payment.

Having failed to comply with his agreement a rule was taken on him to show cause why he should not be compelled to perform it; to which he answered, that the family meeting, in virtue of whose deliberations the property had been directed to be sold, was composed of relations who had an interest in the matter on which they decided; that the sale was, consequently, made without the legal formalities, and the title to the respondent defective.

The court confirmed by its decree the correctness of the defence, and the plaintiffs appealed.

Before noticing the merits, an objection made by the plaintiffs must be disposed of. They contend the court of probates had no jurisdiction of the matter; that it was through error they went there; and, that the defect being one *ratione materiæ,* consent cannot cure it.

We think the plaintiffs were right in their first opinion on this subject, and wrong in their second. The court of probates has jurisdiction to compel purchasers to make their contract complete by affixing their signatures and giving their note. The plaintiffs have argued this point as if the defendant had accepted the title, given his obligations, and that this was an action to enforce their payment; when the application is merely to make the contract, which was inchoate by the bidding, complete by executing the writings necessary to render it so.

The court having power to order the sale, has, as a necessary incident, the power to make these sales in a legal manner.

The family meeting was composed, in part, of co-heirs of the minor; and it is contended, that as they were joint proprietors with her, they could not legally deliberate and decide on the propriety of selling the property.

This case arose previous to the late act of the legislature on this subject, and must be decided by the law as it then stood.

That law contained no positive provision which excluded the nearest relations who are joint owners with the minor. But the appellee contends there exists one in the reason of the thing; that those who have an interest in the property can not be impartial judges of the propriety of selling it, because their opinion must be more or less influenced by the consideration of the effect the sale will have on their own interests.

We were struck on the argument with the force of the objection, but our reflections since, have much weakened the influence we were at first disposed to give it. The law having declared that heirs either major, or minor, can not be compelled to remain owners in common, it follows they can not be influenced by the desire to retard or hasten the partition, for they have no power over it. In the manner in which the partition should be made they seem to be equally without an adverse interest to the minor, for if that property is to be divided in kind, whatever influence the division may have on a portion of the property partaken it will have on the other, more particularly as the lots must be drawn for, and chance decides to which of the heirs each lot must fall. If on the contrary it is to be sold together, all would share alike in the profit or the loss arising from the sale. There is then no conceivable interest in the heirs of full age giving false and pernicious advice except that suggested by counsel in the written argument, that being owners in part, they might be anxious to sell because they could buy to more advantage than strangers, who would be obliged to furnish the whole price of the property; while they would only have to pay that portion of which they were not owners. But the interest is so remote and uncertain, where the sale is to be made on credit, that we can not, on that ground, pronounce the incompetency of the co-heirs to form a family meeting.

The late act of the legislature, excluding persons such as those who formed the family meeting in this instance, strengthens this conclusion. If the law, previous to its passage, was as it is contended by the appellee, the act was vain and unnecessary. It is true that the introduction of a provision by statute in this country, is not, as has been properly urged, conclusive evidence that the law previous to the enactment, was otherwise, but in doubtful cases it creates a presumption it was so, and the weight which properly belongs to the presumption, cannot be disregarded by a court of justice.

It is, therefore, ordered, adjudged and decreed, that the judgment of the district court be annulled, avoided and reversed; and it is further ordered, adjudged and decreed, that the defendant do, within ten days from the rendition of this judgment, comply with the contract entered into by him in bidding for the property at the sale of the estate of the ancestors of the plaintiffs, or, that in default thereof, a writ of distringas issue to compel him thereto; and it is further ordered that he pay costs in both courts.

Seghers, for the plaintiffs.
Pierce, for the defendant.

EASTERN DISTRICT, MAY TERM, 1828.

Semple *v.* Buhler.   VI, N. S. 666.

An action against a sheriff, for taking an insufficient bond, is barred by the prescription of a year: negligence and malfeasance of public officers come within the definition of *quasi* offence.

THIRD District.

MATHEWS, J., delivered the opinion of the court.

This is an action against a sheriff, in which reparation is claimed from him on account of damages which the plaintiffs allege they have suffered in consequence of the negligence or malfeasance of the officer in relation to proceedings on an execution against one of their debtors. The case was before the court in February term, and by a decision then made all the points in the cause were settled, and we believe, all correctly, except one, viz. that relating to the prescription of one year, pleaded by the defendant for the first time in the appellate court. This plea was not placed amongst the papers when they were handed to the judges for examination, and was consequently neglected or very slightly investigated.

The right of defendants to avail themselves of pleas of prescription even on appeals, is clearly recognised by the art. 902 of our Code of Practice; and a plea of this kind having (as it now appears) been regularly filed in the present case, it only remains to test its legal form and validity.

The suit was commenced on the 25th of June, 1827. The malfeasance of the sheriff as alleged in the petition, is his conduct in taking the wife of the debtor as surety on a twelve months' bond, which happened on the 27th day of November in the year 1823. Execution was issued on the bond against the husband and wife, the latter as security, who obtained an injunction to stay all proceedings on the suit, and this injunction was made perpetual by a decree of the district court of the second judicial district, holden for the parish of Ascension, on the 19th of May, 1825. By this decree the plaintiffs were deprived of their recourse against the surety on the bond, the instrument being with regard to her void *ab initio.*

According to these facts, it is unnecessary to determine whether the liability of the officers commenced at the time of taking the bond, or the time when the surety availed herself of the protection accorded by law in favor of women; for more than one year had elapsed since the last period before the commencement of the present action.

Previous to the adoption of the Louisiana Code, it is believed that the short prescription of one year would not have barred a suit for remuneration on account of damages caused by malfeasance or neglect in a ministerial officer, by deviating from his duties as prescribed by law; although such conduct might come within the definition of *quasi* offence.

In relation to the time necessary to prescribe against actions, the first digest of our laws or Civil Code made few or no changes in the rules ordained by the Spanish laws. The Louisiana Code which was promulgated and obtained the force of law in the months of May or June 1825, fixes with considerable precision the duration of the different periods of time necessary to acquire or lose right by prescription. By the 3501st article, actions for damages resulting from offences or *quasi* offences are limited to one year from the time such damages were sustained. This rule must operate on all claims or causes of action which existed in favor of any person at the time the law was promulgated, as well as such as may have arisen in consequence of offences or *quasi* offences, when the party suffering injury or sustaining damage has neglected to institute a suit before the expiration of the year. According to the facts as extracted from the record, and above stated, it is clear that the present action was not commenced until more than one year had elapsed since the damage complained of had been sustained by the alleged negligence or misconduct of the sheriff; and this is the result, whether the time be computed from the day of taking the bond, or that on which the plaintiffs were finally enjoined from enforcing its obligation. The only question which remains to be examined is whether negligence and malfeasance of public officers come within the legal definition of a *quasi* offence. The definition of offences and *quasi* offences is found in the 2294th and 2295th articles of the Code; and it most clearly embraces the conduct attributed to the officer in the present instance, as coming under the latter term. On this head see also *Toul.* vol. 11, p. 156 and 157.

The law makes no distinction in this respect between public ministerial officers and private individuals; and we ought not to distinguish; and were we at liberty so to do, it would be difficult to find
any good reason for imposing a heavier responsibility on a public,
than on a private agent.

From this view of the case it is evident that the judgment of the
district court must be reversed and the plea of prescription for the
present be sustained.

It is not for us to question the wisdom of our law makers, but we
deem it not improper to express our opinion, that the law as it stood
in relation to actions for the recovery of reparation for damages
occasioned by *quasi* offences, as it regards prescription, was more consistent than the new regulations. Perhaps under the old law the
length of time was too great. But it is not easy to discover why a
loss occasioned to an individual by the negligence or malfeasance
of another should be prescribed against by a shorter period than that
which is allowed to enforce a promise to pay money or give some
specific article. What can be the difference to the sufferer, whether
he has lost by the negligence or unskilfulness of his fellow-citizen, or
failure of the latter to comply with some promise legally made by
which the former may be enriched *pro tanto.* Damages and losses
of the kind now under consideration would have been more properly
regulated by the new prescriptions of three or five years.

The law is, however, different, the indulgence granted by the
Code of Practice to plead prescription on the appeal (whether correct
or not we do not pretend to say) renders it obligatory on us to reverse
the judgment of the district court, and send the cause back for a new
trial, in order that the plaintiffs may avail themselves of any evidence
in their power to show an interruption of the prescription here pleaded
by the defendant.

Preston, for the plaintiff.
Watts and *Lobdell,* for the defendant.

Boyd v. Warfield. VI, N. S. 671.

Damages claimed, as growing out of proceedings originating in the same demand may be the object of reconvention, as in this case, damages suffered by the owners, through an attachment issued by the overseer of his plantation for the same cause of action as the present suit.

FIRST District.

PORTER, J., delivered the opinion of the court.

This is an action in which the plaintiff claims his wages for managing the plantation of the defendant. The general issue was pleaded; a plea that the plaintiff negligently discharged his duty, by reason whereof the defendant sustained damage to the amount of 500 dollars; and lastly, a demand in reconvention for damages sustained by the defendant in consequence of the plaintiff, previous to the commencement of this suit, illegally suing out a writ of attachment against him.

The plaintiff filed an exception to the action in reconvention, and the court sustained it.

The Code of Practice provides, that in order to entitle the defendant to institute a demand in reconvention, it is requisite such demand, though different from the main action, be necessarily connected with, and incident to the same. Art. 375.

If the writ of attachment was taken out for the same cause of action as that set forth in the petition filed in this cause, we think it would be necessarily connected with it, for the damages claimed grow out of a proceeding originating in the same demand.

The only difficulty, therefore, is, whether the language of the suit in reconvention being general, and not specifying particularly the cause of action for which the attachment was levied, the court could admit it. The true test in such cases, we think, is, could proof of it's being the same have been given under the pleadings, and we think there can be no doubt that under our liberal practice it might. If so, the court erred in rejecting the claim.

It is, therefore, ordered, adjudged and decreed, that the judgment of the district court be annulled, avoided and reversed; and it is further ordered, adjudged and decreed, that the cause be remanded to the district court, with directions to it, not to reject the demand in reconvention; and it is further ordered, that the appellee pay the costs in this appeal.

Watts and *Lobdell*, for the plaintiff.
Ripley and *Conrad*, for the defendant.

Vance v. Martin et al.   VI, N. S. 673. ·

PARISH Court of New Orleans.

If the surety on an attachment bond be needed as a witness by the plaintiff, it is proper to permit plaintiff to substitute another surety for him, provided no absolute and definitive right had been acquired by the defendants, resulting from the obligations imposed by the attachment bond. As long as their rights are merely contingent, any other solvent person ought to be accepted in his place. See 1 N. S. 674, and authorities there cited.

Daquin et al. v. Coiron et al.   VI, N. S. 527.

He who bids at an auction for, and in the name of another, has not the right of availing himself of the bid, in case that other disowns his authority, without the assent of the owners who were the vendors.

FIRST District.

PORTER, J., delivered the opinion of the court.

The plaintiffs state they are heirs of Thomas Daquin and François Daquin, who, in their lifetime, were owners of a tract of land in the Parish of Plaquemine, known by the name of *Chêne Vivant*, having forty-five arpents front, with the ordinary depth, and eighteen slaves.

That after the death of Francois Daquin, his daughter Marie Antoinette Daquin remained without any tutor legally appointed to her, although her uncle Thomas Daquin pretend to act as such.

That the said Thomas Daquin in his own name, and as tutor to his brother's daughter did, in the month of January, 1810, pray for an order of sale of the property which he held in common with her, but although the said sale was ordered it never was effected in any legal manner, nor indeed in any manner at all;—and that when Thomas Daquin died in September, 1810, the plantation and slaves were still his property, and that of his brother's daughter and heir.

The property since that time has passed through several hands, and the respective vendors are cited in warranty, and before the court. By the answers they have put in, the title of the plaintiffs is denied. They aver the land was legally sold, and that all the right of the petitioners is by that sale vested in them.

They further plead, that the property was sold to pay the debts of the plaintiffs' ancestors, and that if recovery is had in the present suit, this money must be repaid.

And finally, that the defendants are *bona fide* possessors and as such are entitled to retain the fruits they may have gathered on the property, and to be paid for any improvements they may have on it.

The title on which the defendants rely is derived from two sales, one made by the court of probates at the request of Thomas Daquin, the ancestor of one class of the heirs now before the court, and uncle to the other. The second was on a writ issuing from a court of ordinary jurisdiction at the suit of those who had originally sold to the ancestors of the plaintiffs.—The first requires the most particular attention, for on its validity, as will be hereafter seen, the legality of the second depends.

On the 19th of December, 1808, Whitten Evans, of Philadelphia, by his attorney in fact, sold to Thomas and Francois Daquin the plantation now sued for, and eighteen slaves, for the sum of 23,500 dollars, payable in six equal and annual instalments. This sale contains the pact of *non alienando,* and one Charles Borrome Dufau became surety that the purchasers would comply with the contract.

Shortly after the date of this sale Francois Daquin died, and by the request of the surviving partner and brother, Thomas Daquin, and the advice of a family meeting, the plantation and slaves were put up at auction, and adjudicated to one Charles Massicot, through his agent Dufau, the same who was surety in the contract between Evans and the Daquins. Massicot denied the authority, and refused to sanction the purchase. The plantation remained in the possession of Daquin's heirs for nearly two years, when Dufau applied to the parish judge, had himself declared the buyer in place of Massicot, and was put in possession.

The validity of this conveyance to Dufau has been assailed an various grounds:

1. That there was not such a family meeting deliberating in regard to the alienation of the minors' property as the law required.

2. That the minor heir of Francois Daquin was not assisted by a tutor.

3. That the property was sold for less than the price of estimation.

4. That it was stricken off to Massicot, not to Dufau, and that the latter had no right to take the purchase for himself.

5. That the property never was sold; the signature of the parish judge, the tutor of the minor, and that of the surviving partner being wanting to the act of adjudication.

[Daquin *et al* v. Coiron *et al.*]

We are strongly inclined to the opinion that all those objections are well taken, and supported by the evidence before us; but we deem it unnecessary to examine any but the last two.

In the process verbal of the sale which took place on the 6th of January, 1810, it is stated that the property was adjudged to Chs. Borrome Dufau, for and on account of Charles Massicot, on the same credit the vendors obtained from Evans, for 23,260 dollars.

Two years after, viz: on the 26th of March, 1812, a memorandum is inserted in the process verbal of the sale, stating that Massicot having renounced the purchase made by him, the judge considered C. B. Dufau as the purchaser, and had put him in possession.

It appears to us the parish judge had no authority to do this, and that such an act on his part did not transfer the property to Dufau.— We leave untouched the question whether Dufau having bought, without authority, could not be compelled to take the property at the demand of the owners or their representatives: but admitting that he could, there certainly existed no right in him without their assent to be considered as the buyer. No contract had intervened between them. The land was not adjudicated to him. The process verbal of the sale declared it had been bought by another. It is most clear then, that without their consent no title to it could pass to him, and as they were minors that consent could be given only in the manner which the law has prescribed for the alienation of their property.

It does not appear to have been ever given, and admitting this objection could be got over, the other appears to us insurmountable. The process verbal of the sale is neither signed by the vendor, nor the tutor, nor by Thomas Daquin, then alive.

The sale therefore was inchoate, as wanting the signature of the parties, and the judge who acted as auctioneer. The title yet remains in the vendors. The objection that might perhaps be made under other circumstances, to the representatives of Thomas Daquin, that he acquiesced in the sale while alive, is destroyed by the fact that he too died before Dufau obtained an order from the parish judge to be put in possession, and that he never assented to the change of purchasers.—No implied assent arising from any act of the plaintiffs, or their silence during their minority could give validity to these proceedings. 5 *Martin*, 372; 8 *Ibid.* 222; 11 *Ibid.* 709; 12 *Ibid.* 347.

Dufau, soon after he was put in possession, sold the property to Montegut and Hebert. To this act of sale, Evans, the original vendor, became a party, and accepted their engagement to pay him. Failing to comply with their promise, an order of seizure and sale was taken out, and the premises and slaves now in dispute, sold. It is unnecessary to inquire into the regularity of these proceedings, for conceding they were perfectly so, they could only transfer the right which Montegut and Hebert had from Dufau, and the invalidity of Dufau's title has been already explained.

The same observations apply to the defence set up that this was a partition, not a sale.—Considering it as a licitation, the want of the signatures of the vendors, and the party under whom the defendant claims not being the purchaser, is equally fatal to his title.

The most important question in the cause arises out of the claim set up by the defendants to be paid for the improvements, and not to be responsible for the fruits they have gathered. By an agreement on record, the parties have consented to waive all questions respecting the amount of the improvements until after the decision of the court on the titles. But we have been pressed in the argument to express our opinion on the principles which should govern the court below in adjusting the claims growing out of this part of the case.

The plaintiffs admit the defendants were possessors in good faith, and the question is, what are the rights of such a possessor, in case of eviction by the real owner?

It is deemed unnecessary to inquire how the question stood in Spain, or how it would be decided by the laws of that country, believing, as we do, that our Code has introduced provisions on this subject incompatible with any other previously existing.

This case must be governed by the provisions of the old Code, and we cite from it:

Page 102, art. 1, it is declared "the produce of the thing does not belong to the simple possessor, and must be returned with the thing to the owner, who claims the same, except in case of the detainer having possession *bona fide.*"

Page 104, art. 12, it is again provided, "nevertheless, if the plantations, edifices, or works, may have been done by a third person, evicted, but not sentenced to make restitution of the fruits, because said person possessed *bona fide*, the owner shall not have a right to demand the suppression of the said works, plantations, or edifices, but he shall have his choice either to reimburse the value of the materials and the price of workmanship—or to reimburse a sum equal to the enhanced value of the soil."

Page 480, art. 30, there is a further provision, "that the possession of him who possesses with a good conscience has also this effect, that while he is ignorant of a better right to the thing than his own, he enjoys and makes his own the fruits which he gathers, and not only those which he reaps from the ground by his own industry, but likewise those which the ground produces without culture; and if it happens that the thing is evicted from him, he shall restore no part of what he enjoyed before the demand, but he will be obliged to restore the fruits which he reaped after the demand."

It would be difficult by positive legislation to provide more clearly for the case now before us, than the enactments just cited, do. They expressly declare that the *bona fide* possessor makes the fruits his own and they as expressly declare that in case of eviction the owner must reimburse him the value of improvements. There is no ground therefore for this court to say the one must be compensated by the other—if we did, we should certainly violate the commands of the law—for the possessor would not make the fruits his own if we de-

10*

[Daquin *et al. v.* Coiron *et al.*]

creed he should pay for them; and where would be the difference between his paying for them in money at the time of eviction, or in paying for them in improvements by which the estate is benefitted, we are unable to perceive.

These provisions also settle another question much debated among the civilians, whether the owner was obliged to reimburse the value of the materials and workmanship, or merely the enhanced value of the land. They give the choice to the owner.

The judge below was of opinion the plaintiffs should recover the property. In that opinion we concur—as we do also in the view he took with regard to the ameliorations; but we cannot agree with him in regard to the defendants cited in warranty, not being paid the amount of the purchase-money before the plaintiffs are put in possession. He seems to think they had no right to stop the entry of the petitioners until the money is paid. It is now the settled jurisprudence of the court, that when the property of minors is sold, to pay the debts of their ancestors, from whom that property is derived, they cannot recover the property on the ground of the proceedings being informal, without repaying the money which has been applied to their benefit. In the present case the several vendors being cited in warranty, the parties stand before us in the same situation as if the first purchaser was in possession, and the suit had been instituted against him.

In the present instance the right of the several vendors cited in warranty has not been passed on in the court below; nor is there any evidence before us of the value of the improvements; the case therefore cannot be finally decided on—it must be remanded for investigation on these points, and the facts once ascertained, one judgment can settle the rights of all the parties before us.

It is, therefore, ordered, adjudged and decreed, that the judgment of the district court be annulled, avoided and reversed; that the case be remanded for a new trial, and that the appellees pay the costs of this appeal.

Derbigny, for the plaintiffs.
Mazureau and *Grymes*, for the defendants.

Overton v. Gervais. VI, N. S. 685.

A creditor, who has compelled his debtor to give surety before the debt was payable, must afterwards proceed against him by suit in the ordinary way.

FIRST District.

Martin, J., delivered the opinion of the court.

The plaintiff having had judgment in this court for the first instalment of the price of a number of slaves he had sold to the defendant, (after having attached the property of the latter, before any instalment had become due,) 5 *N. S.* 682, now offered a supplemental petition, in the court of the first district from which the attachment had issued, praying for judgment for the second and third instalments which were now due.

The court refused to permit the petition to be filed, because judgment had already been given in the case, and because a supplemental petition, relates back and makes part of the original one, and no judgment can be rendered now or hereafter on the matter set forth but what might have been rendered had it existed at the time of the judgment already rendered.

The plaintiffs counsel took a bill of exceptions and appealed.

We think the district court did not err. A creditor whose debt is not yet payable may in certain cases compel his debtor to give him security or attach his property. When this is done, if the debtor fails to pay, the creditor must proceed against him by suit, notwithstanding the security he has by bond or attachments; for judgment cannot be taken by default for a debt the non-payment of which cannot be presumed, and which the defendant is not bound to deny, because it is not averred.

In the present case the defendant appeared by his attorney, contested the plaintiff's claim on the first instalment, failed in establishing his pretensions, and judgment was given against him. If his failure to pay posterior instalments compelled the plaintiff to such a remedy by suit, he must allege the non-payment of the instalments, and give the defendant an opportunity to rebut the allegation, by a citation.

The first principle of justice is that no one should be condemned unheard, or without being cited to be heard. The attachment of one's property is not in our law considered as a citation—for the sheriff is required to cite the party by advertisements. Now, a citation necessarily relates to a complaint previously made, and the complaint must follow, not precede the injury to be redressed.

[Overton *v.* Gervais.]

At the time judgment was given for the first instalment, no complaint had been made that the two following were unpaid, the defendant was therefore no longer in court, though some of his property might be in the custody of the sheriff, this property he was at liberty to regain by giving bond. A creditor who has surety or security for his debt cannot obtain judgment, without giving his debtor, by a citation, the opportunity of contesting it, or proving payment.

It is therefore, ordered, adjudged and decreed, that the judgment of the district court be affirmed, with costs.

Ripley and *Conrad*, for the plaintiff.

Duncan, for the defendant.

Orleans Navigation Company *v.* Bingay.
VI, N. S. 688.

He who reconvenes is considered as a plaintiff, and a finding in his favor, without limitation must be viewed as embracing his whole claim.

FIRST District.

MATHEWS, J., delivered the opinion of the court.

This suit is brought to recover from the defendant the sum of 324 dollars arrearage of rent, or interest stipulated to be paid by him annually and perpetually on the price of a lot of ground purchased from the plaint.ffs. The answer contains two exceptions to the action. 1. That no such body corporate as the Navigation Company exists. 2. If it does legally exist, according to the terms of its charter it has no right to acquire or hold property situated as that is which was sold to the defendant. These exceptions were overruled by the court below, and we think correctly.

The pleas to the action in relation to its merits are a general denial and compensation to the amount of 201 dollars. The case was submitted to a jury, who found for the plaintiffs the full amount of their claim, and judgment being rendered in pursuance of the verdict, the defendant appealed.

Some time previous to the commencement of the present suit, the plaintiffs had instituted one to recover arrearages which were then

due, to which the defendant pleaded in compensation and reconvention, an amount as due and owing by them to him, which exceeded their claim by the sum of 201 dollars, now pleaded in compensation. The former cause was also submitted to a jury, who
found for the defendant, without stating any amount, and judgment
was pronounced conformably to the verdict, from which an appeal
was taken, and the judgment was affirmed by the Supreme Court.

The defendant in the cause now under consideration relied on the
former judgment, as *res judicata* in his favor, for the surplus which
he then claimed by way of reconvention, and requested the judge *a
quo* to instruct the jury to this effect, which was refused, and he took
a bill of exceptions. Notwithstanding the able argument of the
counsel for the appellees, made before this court in support of the
district judge's opinion, we think that on this point he erred.

In relation to the surplus which the appellant claimed in the former
action against him, by his petition in reconvention, he can be viewed
in no other light than a plaintiff, and the finding in his favor without
limitation or restriction, must, according to several decisions of this
court, be considered as embracing the whole amount of his claim,
subject, however, to a deduction of the sum claimed by the plaintiffs
in their original petition. See 4 *Martin*, 311; 5 *Ibid.* 451; and 3 *N.
S.* 7.

By allowing the amount offered in compensation of the sum
claimed by the plaintiffs in this suit, there remains a balance due to
the latter of 123 dollars, for which alone, in our opinion, they are
entitled to have judgment.

It is, therefore, ordered, adjudged and decreed, that the judgment
of the parish court, be avoided, reversed and annulled: and it is further ordered, adjudged and decreed, that the plaintiffs and appellees
do recover from the defendant and appellant, one hundred and twenty-
three dollars; the appellees to pay the costs of appeal, and the appellant those of the district court.

Workman and *Duncan*, for the plaintiffs.
Mercier and *Buchanan*, for the defendant.

Fisk *v.* Browder *et al.* VI, N. S. 691.

THIRD District.

Whether two sheriffs may be sued together for illegal returns, on different writs in the same suit?

The action for an illegal return, is prescribed by one year.

MATHEWS, J., said:—The Louisiana Code obtained the force of law in the city of New Orleans on the 20th of May, 1825; it was most probably received in the parish of West Feliciana before the month of November of that year.

Gayles' Heirs *v.* Gray. VI, N. S. 693.

A grant in the usual form, and signed by an officer authorised to grant land under the Spanish government, is legal evidence to go to the jury.

Whether the land was the proper subject of a grant, or political circumstances prevented a title passing, are questions as to the *effect*, not the *legality* of the grant.

THIRD District.

PORTER, J., delivered the opinion of the court.

This is a petitory action. On the trial in the court below, the plaintiffs, in support of their title, offered in evidence a grant from the Spanish government. Several objections were made to it, and over-ruled, and it was read to the jury. As soon as the reading was gone through, we are informed by a bill of exceptions, the defendant's counsel objected, "that the said patent could not be considered as legal evidence under the issue, in this case, because it appeared on the face of it to have been executed by an authority having no right to grant titles to lands in Louisiana at the time it was dated." The court was of this opinion, and withdrew the paper from the jury.

It appears to us the court below erred. The grant was in the usual form, and clothed with the signature of an officer authorised to issue grants for lands by the Spanish government. Such instruments, it has been frequently decided, are legal evidence, and we see no reason to take that which was offered in this case out of the general rule. Whether the land in dispute was, at that time, a proper subject for a grant by this officer—whether, from political changes, his power to make a concession of it had not ceased, was certainly a grave question. But it was one as to the *effect* of the instrument, and presented no legal obstacle to its introduction as proof in the cause. Whenever an instrument of writing is legally proved and relevant to the matter at issue, it should be received in evidence. The influence it should obtain in deciding the rights of the parties can only be ascertained when, after all the evidence is received, the cause is examined on its merits.

It is therefore, ordered, adjudged and decreed, that the judgment of the district court be annulled, avoided and reversed; that the cause be remanded to the said court, with directions not to refuse permission to the plaintiff to read in evidence the grant to their ancestor; and it is further ordered and decreed, that the appellee pay the costs of this appeal.

McCaleb, for the plaintiff.
Hennen, for the defendant.

Arsenaux *v.* Michel.   VI, N. S. 695.

COURT of Probates Parish of St. James.

A curator cannot be allowed credit for higher than legal fees paid by him to the parish judge. The fees of the parish judge are fixed by law; of this law no one can plead ignorance; if the curator paid higher fees he did so in his own wrong, and it is no justification that they were demanded of him.

He must suffer by the neglect of a person whom he entrusts with the collection of a note of the estate.

Bourgignon *v.* Boudousquie.   VI, N. S. 697.

On a sale of a tract of so many arpents in front, with the usual depth, the side lines will be presumed to be parallel, and fall perpendicularly at right angles on the front, unless expressions in the deed control the legal intendment.

FIRST District.   '

PORTER, J., delivered the opinion of the court.

The plaintiff states in the petition that this is an action of *bornage,* and avers that a boundary post was placed in the year 1792 between her land and that now occupied by the defendant, which boundary was renewed in the year 1821 by the person under whom the defendant claims.

She prays for a survey; for a definitive settlement of the boundaries: that she may be put in possession of the part belonging to her, now occupied by the defendant, and that he may be condemned to pay damages.

The defendant answers that all the allegations in the petition are untrue, except that which avers he purchased the premises from Destrehan, that the questions respecting the titles to said lands and the boundary lines have long since been settled in the case of Fleming *v.* Bourguignon.   He concludes by citing his vendor in warranty, and prays that he may be compelled to make the title good to the premises sold and conveyed by him.

To this defence set up by the defendant, Destrehan, the vendor called in warranty, added, that the plaintiff was barred by prescription for demanding damages; and that for the same reason the boundaries could not be changed, because the respondent and those under whom he claims have held the *locus in quo* for ten years under a just title, and with good faith.   And latterly, that there was a partition by which the new boundaries now contended for by the respondent, were definitively fixed.

The cause has been once before the court, and has been tried three times in the court below.   At the first trial there was a verdict for the defendant which on appeal to this court was set aside.   On the second, the jury could not agree—the third trial terminated by a verdict similar to the first, and from the judgment rendered on it, this appeal has been taken.

A statement of all the evidence, oral and written, introduced in the court below, would confuse the case, which if stripped of irrelevant matter does not present much difficulty.

No original grant is produced by either party. From the length of time the land has been possessed one may be presumed. For upwards of forty years the country around the premises in dispute seems to have been occupied by several proprietors in small portions. In the year 1786 one of them named Andre Friche, who owned four arpents, procured a survey to be made by Carlos Trudeau, then royal surveyor of the province of Louisiana. This survey has been produced, and it is of great importance in the cause, because the title under which the parties claim call for it as a boundary.

It is unnecessary to trace the many conveyances farther back than the year 1800, at which time we find that one Pierre Caillaud became the purchaser, from a certain John Hutchins, of one arpent and a half in front, and that the same day he acquired it, he sold it to Antoine Cambre. In these conveyances the land is designated, as being bounded, above, by that of Friche.

From this Cambre, both the parties before us derived title; the plaintiff for the upper half, or three-fourths of an arpent front; the defendant for the other moiety. The plaintiff or those under whom she claims were the first purchasers. In the act of sale the land is designated as containing three-fourths of an arpent front, being the half of that which the vendor acquired from Pierre Gaillant, bounded above by the lands of Andre Friche, and below by that of the seller.

It is a well settled principle of law that when a man sells so many arpents of land on a water course with the ordinary depth of forty, he is understood to convey the superficial quantity which results from multiplying the depth by the front, or, in other words, that the said lines must be run at right angles from the front, unless the lines are stated to close, or open, or other expressions used, by which the legal intendment of the terms so much front and depth is controlled.

It is equally clear and well settled that if the owner of a tract of land sells it out by separate portions at different times, and there is not enough for all the purchasers, that he who has first acquired gets the whole quantity he has bought, and the second, or other buyer, only takes what remains, after satisfying the prior sales. Louisiana Code, 843.

Let us apply these principles to this case. Cambre being the owner of one arpent and a half of land in front, sold to the person under whom the plaintiff claims, three-fourths of an arpent front, with the ordinary depth, without words restrictive of the quantity these expressions convey. The purchaser, therefore, acquired 30 superficial arpents, and the lines must run so as to give that quantity. If there is not a sufficient portion of the land owned by the vendor, to satisfy the purchase of those under whom the defendant holds, it confers no right on him to make up the deficiency, by taking a part of that which had been previously conveyed to others.

We are, therefore, perfectly satisfied the plaintiff has shown a good title to thirty superficial arpents, and that the defendant has no right, under the terms of the conveyance, to run his lines in such a manner as will diminish that quantity. It only remains to consider whether any thing has been done since, by the parties, which goes to destroy the just pretensions of the plaintiff under the act of sale.

On this part of the subject much has been said, and many objections stated, which, although highly creditable to the ingenuity of counsel, cannot receive the sanction of this court.

It appears that the fence which divides the two plantations, has stood for several years on the line contended for by the defendant. How this error originated, the evidence does not inform us, nor is it important to inquire. Though acquiesced in for some years, it appears, from proceedings had at different times in court, to have given great uneasiness to the plaintiff. The defendant contends this fence was placed there by virtue of a partition made between the proprietors of the respective tracts. We are unable to find any evidence to satisfy us such a division was made by mutual consent; and if it had it would clearly have been in error of the rights of the owner of the upper half, and would consequently fall within the principle on which in a case similarly circumstanced, we held that a mistake of this kind neither destroyed title, nor conferred it. See the case of Broussard v. Duhamel, 3 N. S. 11.

The defendant next urges, that the division fence has stood there for such a length of time as enables him to plead the prescription of thirty years. Here again the facts fail to sustain him. And if such a division fence had been erected previous to the time Cambre became the purchaser and proprietor of the two tracts, the union of both in his person, and the sales made by him giving different boundaries, would destroy any right in subsequent purchasers to claim under ancient limits. This very case is put in the Roman Digest, liv. 10, tit. 1, law 12. And the framers of our Code have adopted the principle, and it now makes a part of the positive regulations of the state. Louisiana Code, 840.

The evidence shows the defendant has possessed ten years under the line formed by the fences now standing on the land. If the case were to be decided by the new Code, this would be sufficient; but by the law as it stood previous to the adoption of the amendments to the old Code, thirty years were required to enable him who possessed under an erroneous decision to plead prescription. *Toullier, liv. 2, tit. 2, cap. 3, no. 177, 811; Code, liv. 3, tit. 39, law 6.*

The plea of *res judicata* is not supported. The parties were not the same in the former suit, and the cause did not proceed to final judgment.

Some objections were made to the form of the action. But it appears to us they are not well founded. Nothing in the proof adduced shows any such settlement of boundaries as precluded either of the parties from resorting to this action.

And as to the objection that the plaintiff averred in his petition that a line had been established in 1792 of which there is no proof, we have only to observe that the defect in evidence as to that allegation

[Bourguignon v. Boudousquie.]

does not prevent the appellant from enjoying the benefit of the other facts which he has established.

On the whole we are of opinion the plaintiff must recover. The verdict of the juries would have great weight with us if this case depended on matters of fact. But being one in which the contest is more of law than of fact, our conclusions can be more relied on than those of the jury.

The evidence does not enable us to say whether any damages are due, and if it did, we could not settle the amount. The case must therefore be remanded on that point.

It is, therefore, ordered, adjudged and decreed, that the judgment of the district court be annulled, avoided and reversed; and it is further ordered, adjudged and decreed, that the plaintiff do recover from the defendant and be put in possession of three-fourths of an arpent of front land, with the ordinary depth of forty, as claimed by her in her petition, giving to the front and side lines the same course and direction as the lower line of Andre Friche, according to a survey made by Carlos Trudeau, in the year 1785, filed in evidence in this cause. It is further ordered that the cause be remanded for inquiry into the damages sustained by the plaintiff, the appellee paying costs in this court.

Ripley and *Conrad*, for the plaintiff.
Hennen, for the defendant.

Nichols v. Pierce.   VI, N. S. 705.

A party interrogated whether he did not agree to erect a saw-mill for defendant, may well answer that he agreed to put up one in partnership with him, but that he, the defendant, failed to comply with his part of the contract, whereupon they had rescinded the contract.

FIRST District.

On this head PORTER, J., said:—The appellant complains of this answer, inasmuch as it states matters wholly irrelevant to the question put. But, in our opinion, the judge did not err in permitting it to be read in evidence. The Code of Practice permits the party interrogated to state other facts than those contained in the interrogatories, provided they be closely linked to the fact on which he has been

[Nichols *v.* Pierce.]

-questioned. In this instance, the connection is manifest, between the agreement asked about—and the nature of that agreement—the cause which led to it—and the facts which produced its dissolution. If the knowledge of the dissolution of the partnership, or rather the joint consent not to carry into effect that which they had contemplated entering into, was confined to the parties, and no witnesses were present when such an understanding took place between them, we have just such a case as we must suppose was in the mind of the legislature, when they extended the right of reply beyond a categorical answer to the question propounded. Code of Practice, 353.

It is, therefore, ordered, adjudged and decreed, that the judgment of the district court be affirmed, with costs.

M'Caleb, for the plaintiff.
Hennen, for the defendant.

Balfour *v.* Browder.   VI, N. S. 708.

The prescription of the action of a party, injured by a false return, runs from the return.

THIRD District.

PORTER, J., delivered the opinion of the court.

This is an action against the sheriff of the parish of West Feliciana for making a false return on an execution issued under an order of seizure and sale. The facts out of which the contest arises, are stated somewhat at length in the case of Balfour *v.* Chew, 4 *N. S.* 154.

Among other defences offered by the pleadings is that of the prescription of one year.

It has lately been decided in this court that the prescription established by the 3501st article of the Louisiana Code applies to the acts of a sheriff who makes a false return on a writ placed in his hands for execution. The return complained of in this case was made in May, 1824, and the present action was not commenced until August, 1826; more than a year had therefore elapsed.

But it is contended the prescription relied on does not run from the day of the return of the writ, but from the day the damage was sustained, and that in this case it was not until after the decision of the Supreme Court in the case of Balfour *v.* Chew, and the resale of the property first seized, in consequence of the untrue return of the first execution, that any damage was sustained by the plaintiff.

[Balfour. v. Chew.]

If the facts alleged in the petition be true, and they must be so considered in the examination of the question, the damage was sustained the moment the false return was made. The complaint of the petitioner is, that the land was in fact sold for 9450 dollars, and that the defendant returned that it was sold for 3450 dollars.—The injury therefore was committed the moment the execution was returned into court, for by it the defendant was deprived of a credit of 6000 dollars to which he was entitled. The clause contained in the 3502d article of the Code which makes the prescription run from the day the damage is sustained, may perhaps give rise hereafter to difficult questions, though it does not present such in the present case. As at present advised, we conceive it to apply to cases, where the act itself would not furnish ground for an action, but where as a consequence of that act damage was sustained.—Where the injury is consequential rather than direct; of which an example may be given from another system of jurisprudence where words, not actionable in themselves when spoken, may become so if they produce injury; or if a man were to erect a nuisance on the highway, by which one of his fellow-citizens sustained damage—in these, and similar cases, the prescription would not run from the day the act was committed, but from the day that the injury was suffered. The reason is obvious, because no right of action existing until the damage is sustained, the plaintiff cannot be barred by not bringing suit before he had a right to do so. But where, as in the present instance, the injury was the direct and immediate result of the act of the defendant, and the right of action existed the moment the false return was made, the prescription was from the time the act was committed; because then in truth, to use the language of our Code, the damage was sustained. It is not in our judgment a satisfactory answer to this doctrine to say, that if the land had risen in value it might have produced more on the second sale than the first, and that no loss would have been suffered by the plaintiff. If it did produce more, this might have been offered in mitigation of the damages which the plaintiff could have claimed in an action on the false return, but certainly would not have defeated it.

As to the argument urged in the court below and to the overruling of which by the judge in his charge, a bill of exceptions was taken that prescription could not run until after the decision of this court, because the plaintiff could not know until then, what would be the effect of the return made by the defendant, it has with great propriety not been pressed here. It is as novel as unsound; the plaintiff might with just as much propriety and correctness argue, he did not know the prescription was of one year.

It is, therefore, ordered, adjudged and decreed, that the judgment of the district court be affirmed, with costs.

11*

Higgins *v.* M'Micken.   VI, N. S. 711.

No appeal lies from the refusal of a court of this state to transfer a suit to the federal
court.

THIRD District.

MATHEWS, J., delivered the opinion of the court.

This appeal is taken from a judgment of the court below, by which that court retained jurisdiction of the cause, contrary to the right of the defendant, as alleged, to have it removed into the district court of the United States for the eastern district of the state of Louisiana.

This court has, in several instances, entertained jurisdiction of causes on appeals, wherein similar applications for removal had been made, and the decisions were in favor of the claims of the applicants. Such decisions or judgments were properly considered as final, in consequence of sustaining the petitions for removal. A request to change the jurisdiction of a suit from a state court to one of the United States, under the law of congress, is analogous to a plea on the part of the defendant, to the jurisdiction of the court in which proceedings commenced; and when a removal is ordered, the plaintiff would be without remedy against such order, however illegal it might be, unless by appeal.

The case is entirely different when the inferior court retains jurisdiction. The order is then a mere interlocutory decree, which has not the effect of doing an irreparable injury to the party against whom it is pronounced. If such decree be erroneous, the error may be corrected on an appeal from a final judgment rendered in the cause. The plea in abatement, or application to remove, will then be subject to examination.

It is, therefore, ordered, adjudged and decreed, that the appeal be dismissed, with costs.

Preston, for the appellant.

Parker v. Walden. VI, N. S. 713.

No interest can be allowed on an unliquidated claim.

A claim cannot be liquidated without the concurrence of both parties.

When the contract states a privilege existing on the thing sold, and the vendee discharges the vendor from the consequences, he cannot resist the privilege on the ground that the act from which it results was not duly registered.

PARISH Court of New Orleans.

MATHEWS, J., delivered the opinion of the court.

This suit is brought on a contract between the mayor and the plaintiff in pursuance of an adjudication publicly made to the latter as the lowest bidder, to fill up certain lots and streets on the batture. The undertaking was a sequence of an ordinance passed by the city counsel, which required the work to be done at the expense of the owners of the lots in that part of the city, on their neglect or refusal to cause it to be executed after a certain time prescribed. The present claim is against the defendant as one of these owners; and judgment being rendered in favor of the plaintiff with a right of lien or privilege on the lots which were filled up, the defendant appealed.

In opposition to the correctness of this judgment the counsel for the appellant has filed many points. Some of them relate to the manner in which the work was adjudicated, suggesting informalities in the proceedings. These we deem it unnecessary to examine, as the evidence of the case abundantly proves that the lots were filled up by the plaintiff, and that they were increased in value to the amount claimed by him, for his work and labor, and this to the advantage of the present proprietors; any question which might arise on these points has already been settled in the case of the Police Jury v. Hampton, 5 N. S. 392.

There are are three grounds of objection to the correctness of the judgment of the court below which might be noticed. 1. The allowance of interest. 2. The loss of privilege of lien on the real estate which was improved, in consequence of the failure of the contractor for the work to have the evidence of his contract recorded before the sale of the lot from Gravier's heirs to the defendant. 3. The declared intention of the owner to cause the work to be done under his own contract with M'Donough, and forbidding the plaintiff to proceed in its execution.

According to the Code of Practice, art. 554, interest cannot be legally allowed on accounts, or unliquidated claims.* A question

* This prohibition has been repealed by act of 1839.

here arises whether the claim of the plaintiff be unliquidated. By the contract, the price which he was to receive for his labor is fixed and certain as to the quantum for each cubic yard of earth he should put on the lots; but the whole amount which may be exacted from the owners individually, depends on measurement, and in this respect requires liquidation between the parties, in order to place the claim on the footing of those which in the legal acceptation of the word may be considered as liquidated or certain. No act of one of the parties alone is sufficient to liquidate a claim which is in any manner uncertain as to amount. To effect this would require the concurrence of both. The sum claimed by the plaintiff is rendered certain, but this has been done by *ex parte* admeasurement and proof of the result; we think that interest ought not to have been allowed.

Whatever might have been the effect of the want of registry of the contract in pursuance of which the plaintiff proceeded to do the work undertaken by him, to defeat his claim of privilege under other circumstances than those in which the present cause is situated, we believe that the defendant cannot profit by the alleged defect of recording according to the actual state of this case.

There is a clause in the act of sale from Gravier's heirs to him, which gave notice that the privilege or lien now claimed to be enforced on the property then sold existed at the time of sale—by this clause he relieves the vendors from all responsibility on account of any sum of money that might be recovered against him for the amelioration of the lot transferred by the act of sale; and it seems to us to follow as a corollary that he took this risk on himself.

The plaintiff obtained the contract for filling up the batture previous to the private agreement entered into between the defendant and McDonough. No attempt was ever made to carry this agreement into effect by commencing the work.

The present claimant pursued his labor without interruption or interference from either of the parties to the private agreement. He has fulfilled the obligations of his contract, and is justly entitled to the value of his labor as fixed by the judge of the court below.

But as this judgment allows interest it must be reversed, which is hereby ordered, adjudged and decreed; and it is further ordered, adjudged and decreed, that the plaintiff and appellee do recover from the defendant and appellant, the sum of two thousand and forty-seven dollars and thirty-nine cents; and on his refusal to comply with this judgment, that the lots filled up, be seized to satisfy said sum; and it is further ordered that the appellee pay the costs of the appeal, and the appellant those of the court below.

Mercier and *Buchanan*, for the plaintiff.
Hoffman, for the defendant.

Perillat *v.* Pueche.   VI, N. S. 717.

Parol evidence may be received to show that the contract sued on is not what it appears to be, but a cover to an usurious transaction.

PARISH Court of New Orleans.

MATHEWS, J., delivered the opinion of the court.

In this case the plaintiff claims from the defendant a large portion of the rents and profits of a certain house and lot which he sold to the latter under a *pact a remére,* for the sum of 1200 dollars; alleging that the sale was made in consequence of an usurious contract, by which it was verbally stipulated that the purchaser should receive interest at the rate of eighteen per cent. per annum on the price. The petition does not contain any precise and formal allegation that the contract was simulated and made in fraud of the laws against usury. It is indeed very vague and indefinite; but from the whole context it may be gathered that the object of the plaintiff is to be relieved against the effects of the sale, as having been made with a direct intention to cover usury. The court below refused to admit the oral testimony offered to prove the real contract between the parties as being contrary to that contained in the act of sale, and gave judgment for the defendant, from which the plaintiff appealed.

The decision of the cause in its present state depends on the bill of exceptions which was taken to the opinion of the judge *a quo,* by which he rejected the testimony offered.

The general principle of law, that oral testimony cannot be received to vary or contradict written agreements or contracts, has been long established, and has received the sanction of our Code to the fullest extent. Louisiana Code, art. 2256. This rule of evidence is however, not so stern or unbending as to admit of no exceptions. When a written act is attacked on the ground of fraud, or simulation, oral testimony is admissible to establish the existence of those facts which when legally established operate a defeasance of such act. This exception to the general rule is clearly recognised in the decision of the case of Crozet's Heirs *v.* Gaudet, 6 *Martin,* 524.

Although in the present case no direct or pointed charge of fraud or simulation is made against the *vente a remére* as a cloak to the usurious contract which really took place between the parties, yet that such attack was intended, may be well ascertained from the reiterated allegations in the petition of usury in the transaction.

It is true that a *bona fide* sale which grants to the vendor the right

[Perillat *v.* Puccbe.]

of redemption, although the property may have been sold for a price less than its value, authorises the vendee to receive the fruits as his own during the existence of the contract. But if the seller is in the habit of paying usurious interest, or other circumstances attend the transaction, calculated to raise a suspicion against its genuineness, it may be lawfully assailed on account of usury. *Curia Phil. verbo Usura, no.* 26.

From this view of the case we are brought to the conclusion that the judge below erred in rejecting the oral testimony offered on the part of the plaintiff to show that the act of sale relied on by the defendant is only a pretext to cover an usurious contract.

It is, therefore, ordered, adjudged and decreed, that the judgment of the parish court be avoided, reversed and annulled; and it is further ordered that the cause be remanded to be tried *de novo*, with instructions to the judge *a quo*, to admit the testimony of witnesses to show that the pretended *vente a reméré* is fictitious and simulated, and was entered into in fraud of the laws against usury; and that the appellee pay the costs of this appeal.

Young, for the plaintiff.

Derbigny, for the defendant.

Mayor *et al. v.* Morgan. VII, N. S. 1.

The city council are, by law, judges of the election of their members.

No *mandamus* lies to compel them to admit a member whom they do not think duly elected.

And the sheriff who executes a writ of *distringas*, to compel obedience to a *mandamus* in such a case, is a trespasser.

The Constitution, art. 6, sect. 23, speaks of the powers of the state government only: the legislature, in establishing corporations may enable them to exercise subordinate legislation, within a particular district, over their members, and *in regard to their rights and duties as corporators;* and the exercise of this legislative power in the city council is not inconsistent with the exercise of judicial power under the authority of the state.

PARISH Court of New Orleans.

MARTIN, J., delivered the opinion of the court.

Obedience having been refused by the city council to the peremptory *mandamus*, issued by the court of the first district, commanding them to admit to a seat a person whom they had refused to receive, a writ of *distringas* was placed in the hands of the defendant, sheriff of the parish, who seized the revenues of the city. Whereupon the present action was commenced for an alleged trespass. He justified under the authority of the writ. The plaintiffs were nonsuited, and appealed.

[Mayor *et al. v.* Morgan.]

Their counsel has assigned as errors in the judgment of the parish court.

1. That the appellee is liable in damages, because he was not bound to execute the writ, and could dispute the authority of the district court.

2. That the parish court had jurisdiction to inquire into it.

There is not any doubt with us that a sheriff is bound to inquire into the authority of a court whose writ is put into his hands for execution, and that he is liable in damages for any injury resulting from his executing a writ issued by a court who has no jurisdiction of the case in which it issued.

Hence it follows that the court before whom a remedy is sought for such an injury, must necessarily inquire into the jurisdiction of the court from which the writ issued.

The success of the appellants before us, depends on their ability to show that the district court was without jurisdiction.

Their counsel has referred us to the constitution, which provides that the citizens of the town of New Orleans have the right of appointing the several public officers necessary for the administration and police of the said city, pursuant to the mode of election which shall be prescribed by the legislature. Art. 6, sect. 23.

To the sixth section of the thirty-fourth chapter of the acts of 1816, 1 *Mart. Dig.* 331, n. 38, which declares that the city council shall be judge of the elections of the mayor and recorder, and of its members.

And to the 873d article of the Code of Practice, by which it is enacted that when the legislature has granted to a corporation the right to determine the validity of the elections of its members or officers, courts of justice shall not issue mandates to inquire into that fact.

So the district court was ousted of all jurisdiction, if the legislature had the constitutional power of rendering the city council judge of the elections of its members—and the only question for our solution is, whether the sixth section of the act of 1816, be contrary to the constitution. If it be, it is void.

We are ready to admit that we have found this case one of considerable difficulty; and we at first concluded that the law was unconstitutional; because to inquire into, and finally determine on the rights of a party claiming a seat in the council, is the exercise of judicial power. To judge, is to determine the rights of parties, and nothing else.

We thought that the right, created by law, to take a seat in the body of which the applicant for a *mandamus* asserted he was a member, could not be distinguished from any other right created by law— as the right of a child to a parent's succession, or any other which positive legislation confers. And we concluded that, as the constitution has declared the judicial power shall be vested in a Supreme and inferior courts, the judges of which must hold their officers during good behaviour, and be appointed by the governor, with the advice

[Mayor et al. v. Morgan.]

and consent of the senate, the city council, being composed of members appointed for a term of years, and elected by the people of their respective wards, is not a body in whom judicial power could be constitutionally vested.

But this reasoning presupposed that the legislative, executive, and judicial powers, of which the constitution speaks, are not merely the legislative, executive, and judicial powers of the state, exercised over every part of it, and over every individual, dwelling, sojourning, or accidentally being within its geographical limits, but included those which may be exercised by corporations, within certain divisions of the state, and over their respective members.

If it were true, that judicial power cannot be vested in the city council, because, according to the constitution, judicial power must be vested in a supreme or inferior court, it would follow that the council could not exercise legislative powers, and pass ordinances, because the constitution has declared that the legislative power is vested in a senate, house of representatives, and governor.

We think the constitution speaks of the powers of the state government only; that the legislature, in establishing corporations, may enable them to exercise subordinate legislation, within a particular district, over their members, and in regard to their rights and duties as corporators—that the exercise of this legislative power in the city council is not inconsistent with the exercise of judicial power under the authority of the state—that the legislature had constitutional power to enable the council to legislate on matters within the scope of the charter, notwithstanding the constitution has declared the legislative power shall be vested in a senate, house of representatives, and governor.

Likewise, as the council could not well proceed to business without ascertaining the rights of its members to their seats, the legislature had power to render it judge of the validity of their elections, and prohibit courts of justice from interfering with its decisions. There is no greater incongruity in the council exercising in this respect, within the city of New Orleans, a kind of judicial power, than in exercising legislative powers, which it is universally admitted they may exercise, in matters which are the object of the charter of the city.

The constitution itself contains a clause that supports the position, that the powers it speaks of, are state powers only. It disqualifies the mayor of New Orleans from sitting in the state legislature.

Now, in construing an instrument, it is a good rule to give effect to every clause, nay every word of it.

If the executive powers, of which the constitution speaks, be not state powers only, the mayor, who exercises executive power in the city, was excluded by the clause which forbids any person from exercising both legislative and executive powers, and the clause which excludes him from the state legislature, was absolutely useless. Its

[Mayor *et al. v.* Morgan.]

insertion favors the idea that the convention contemplated merely state powers.

This reasoning has satisfied our minds. If it were not absolutely conclusive, it would create such a doubt as would forbid us to declare an act of the legislature unconstitutional.

This court, and every court in this state, not only possesses the right, but is in duty bound, to declare void every act of the legislature which is contrary to the constitution. The due exercise of this power is of the utmost importance to the people, and if it did not exist their rights would be shadows, their laws delusions, and their liberty a dream; but it should be exerted with the utmost caution, and when great and serious doubts exist, this tribunal should give to the people the example of obedience to the will of the legislator.

It is desirable that, for every wrong, there should be a legal remedy in a court of justice. But in Louisiana, the constitution has left every judicial power in abeyance with the exception of that vested in this court, liable to be called into action, suspended or recalled at the discretion of the legislature. The supreme court, with one single exception, has no original jurisdiction, and the other courts have only that which the legislature has given them.

We can justly boast of the goodness of our institutions, but they are human, and consequently imperfect. In the present case, the error of the city council, if it be one, in rejecting the claim of the applicant, cannot be corrected in a court of justice. This is unfortunate, but the legislature has willed it, and it is not perhaps the only case in which a citizen seeking relief in the temple of the justice of his country, may find the divinity turning a deaf ear to his complaints, and her ministers powerless.

We conclude that the act of the legislature of 1816, did not violate the constitution; that the court of the first district was consequently without jurisdiction, that its proceedings were *coram non judice:* that the appellee derived no authority from the writ of *distringas,* and was guilty of a trespass in seizing the revenues of the appellants.

It is, therefore, ordered, adjudged and decreed, that the judgment of the parish court be annulled, avoided and reversed. That there be judgment for the plaintiffs; and that the case be remanded, with directions to the judge to ascertain the damages sustained by them in the premises, and that the appellee pay costs in this court.

Moreau, for the plaintiffs.

Livermore, for the defendants.

Nolte *et al. v.* Their Creditors. VII, N. S. 9.

The endorser of an accommodation note, is merely a surety, and can recover no more than he has paid.

The holder of a note, who discharges or grants a respite to the payee, thereby releases other parties.

A positive right conferred by law on the doing of a certain act, cannot be destroyed by speculations as to what would have been the situation of the parties, if that act had not been done.

FIRST District.

PORTER, J., delivered the opinion of the court.

The appellants opposed the homologation of the tableau of distribution filed, by the syndics, and alleged as the ground of their opposition, that they were not placed thereon as creditors for the damages on certain foreign bills of exchange, which were drawn by the insolvents, and returned protested. The court rejected their opposition, and they appealed.

From the statement agreed on by the parties, it appears that the appellees were endorsers on drafts of Nolte & Co., to a large amount. Their endorsements were not on real transactions, but made for the accommodation of the drawers, and the bills were by them negotiated at the branch bank of the United States in this city. When the failure of the drawers took place, the appellants entered into arrangements with the bank, by which they gave security, and obtained time for the payment. It made a part of the agreement that they should be released from the damages; and the principal question for our consideration is, whether not having paid damages, they are entitled to recover them from the drawers.

The act of our legislature on this subject, provides that on the return of any foreign bill of exchange unpaid, with legal protest, the drawer thereof, and all others concerned, shall pay and discharge the contents of said bill, with twenty per cent. advance for the damage thereof. *Mart. Dig. vol.* 1, 596.

The counsel have gone very fully into the question, whether the endorsee of bills, who does not pay damages, has a right to recover them from previous parties on the instrument. We do not find it necessary, however, to express any opinion on this point, as the case must be decided on particular grounds, which take it out of the general rule, conceding that rule to be what the appellants contend it is.

It is admitted the appellants did not take the bills in the usual course of trade; that they gave no consideration, but that they lent

their names to the drawers for their accommodation. It is also admit
ted the appellant did not transfer the notes, but that they were negotiated by Nolte & Co. for their own use and benefit.

It was not made a question at the bar; and if it had been, there
can be no doubt the court may look beyond the form in which this
contract is clothed, and examine into its real character. In doing so,
it is at once seen that though it possesses the features of a commercial transaction, evidenced by bills in a negotiable form and endorsed,
yet that in point of fact it is not so. The drafts never were in the
possession of the appellants; they had no interest in them, and they
did not transfer them. They were, therefore, in reality, the sureties
of the drawers, to enable them to raise money in market. Their
obligations and their rights must be ascertained by a reference to the
general law, not that of bills of exchange. We understand it to be
well settled, in respect to accommodation notes or drafts, that although,
as to subsequent parties to the endorser, the rules applicable to negotiable paper apply in full force, yet in regard to those who agree to
accommodate each other by the use of their names, these obligations
must be tested by the ordinary rules of law. The *lex mercatoria*
recognises no such contracts. Bayley on Bills, 224, 302; Chitty on
Bills, (ed. 1821,) 381.

Viewing the transaction in this light, we agree in opinion with the
district judge. The appellants, as sureties of the drawers, can recover
from them no more than was paid on their account.

The appellees have assigned, as error in the judgment below, the
placing the appellants on the tableau as creditors for the balance due
on a note of Cromelien, Davis & Co., of which the insolvents were
endorsers. The objection made to the decision of the judge *a quo*, is,
that the appellants attended a meeting of the creditors of the makers,
called for the purpose of deliberating on the propriety of according
them a *respite*, and that they (the appellants) voted in favor of it.

We think the objection well taken, and that the court below erred.
There is no rule more clearly or firmly established in relation to negotiable paper, than that discharging or giving time to any of the
parties, is a discharge of every other party who, on paying the bill or
note, would be entitled to sue the party to whom such discharge or
time has been given. The court below seems to have considered the
endorsers were not injured by the indulgence: that whether the appellants had consented or not, the respite would have been granted.
We do not think we are permitted to go into that question. What
would have been the effect of the appellants refusing the indulgence,
we do not know. What influence their example, either in rejecting
or acceding to the prayer of the petitioners, might have had on the
other creditors, cannot now be ascertained; and a positive right, conferred by law on the doing of a certain act, cannot be destroyed by
speculations as to what would have been the situation of the parties,
if that act had not been done.

It is, therefore, ordered, adjudged and decreed, that the judgment of the district court be annulled, avoided and reversed; and it is further ordered, adjudged, and decreed, that the case be remanded to the said court, with directions to amend the tableau by rejecting the claim of the appellants as endorsers of the note of Vincent Nolte & Co; And it is further ordered, adjudged, and decreed, that the appellants pay the costs of this appeal.

Grymes, for the appellants.

Pierce and *Eustis,* for the appellees.

Saunders *v.* Taylor. VII, N. S. 14.

PARISH Court of New Orleans.

By MATHEWS, J.—We have searched in vain for any law, either of the United States, or of this state, ancient or modern, which gives interest on judgments as a legal right. According to the 23d section of the judiciary act of congress, passed in 1789, the Supreme Court is authorised, on an affirmance of a judgment, to decree to the respondent in error just damages for his delay, &c. In the case of Saunders *v.* Ogden, the judgment was affirmed without damages; and as there is no law which declares that judgments shall bear interest, we cannot, in this respect, perceive any error in the judgment of the parish court.

Nolte *et al. v.* Their Creditors. VII, N. S. 16.

FIRST District.

In the case of a *concurso,* an appeal lies from the refusal to issue a commission to take testimony.

M'Nair *v.* Richardson *et al.*　VII, N. S. 17.

FIRST District.

A contractor employed to improve a lot of ground acquires a privilege for the value of the amelioration.　See Louisiana Code; art. 3216; Parker *v.* Walden, 6 *N. S.* 713.

Austin *et al. v.* Palmer.　VII, N. S. 20.

If a parent make a feigned sale to a child, the property will be ordered to be collated.
But the child will retain the part of it which is equal to the disposable portion.

COURT of Probates, West Feliciana.

Martin, J., delivered the opinion of the court.

The appellant complains that the court of probates decreed the collation of a sum of money, which he owed to his mother, now deceased, of whose succession a portion is demanded.

He contends the court erred, because he showed, by a notarial act, the receipt, acquittal, and discharge of said debt, by his mother; and because, admitting that he did not pay the said sum to her, the notarial act is evidence of a release of the debt, unless it exceeds the part of the deceased's estate which she was by law authorised to dispose of.

On a close examination of the evidence we think it sufficiently strong to prevent our interference with the decision of the inferior judge on the question of fact; and conclude that it is established that the debt was not paid, and the receipt, acquittance, and discharge, were given with a view to afford to this party an advantage over his brothers and sisters.

But we are of opinion the court of probates erred in decreeing an absolute collation of the whole debt. The release is good for the portion of her estate which the law leaves at the disposal of a parent.

[Austin *et al. v.* Palmer.]

The disposable part may be given either directly or indirectly, and if a donation be of more than the disposable part, it is not therefore void, but reducible. 4 *Toullier,* 471-5. Even when the donation assumes the shape of an onerous contract, or is disguised under another form. *Ibid.* 479, 485.

Considering the receipt given at an advantage to a child, it is a direct advantage and includes a donation, which is good, if it does not exceed one-third of the donor's liquid estate. If it does, it must be reduced to the said third.

It is, therefore, ordered, adjudged and decreed, that the judgment of the court of probates be annulled, avoided, and reversed, and the case remanded, with directions to the judge to proceed to a new partition, without requiring the appellant to collate any part of the debt he owed to his mother, if it does not exceed the one-third part of her net estate; and, in case it does, requiring him to collate the excess between the debt and the one-third of the estate; and it is ordered that the appellee pay costs in this court.

Watts, for the defendant.

Williams *et al. v.* Winchester.   VII, N. S. 22.

PARISH Court of New Orleans.

When goods are sold to an agent for an unknown principal, the latter is suable when discovered, although no inquiry was made by the vendor; unless the latter let the day of payment go by without demand on the principal, who afterwards pays the agent. 1 Camp. N. P. 85; 4 Taunt. 576; 15 East, 65; 2 Livermore on Agency, 199, 200.

Durnford *v.* Parker *et al.*　VII, N. S. 25.

FIRST District.

If the vendor promised to procure a ratification of the vendee's title from a third person, it is no defence that the title is perfect and requires no ratification.

Admitting the plaintiff's title, such as it is, to be perfectly good, yet, as he stipulated for, and the defendants agreed to refund him his purchase money, on his assigning all his rights in the lots to them, in case Livingston did not ratify his agent's act within nine months—as this ratification has not been obtained before the expiration of the time, nor since, the plaintiff is entitled to receive back his money, on assigning to the defendants all his rights in the lot.

Desboulets *v.* Gravier.　VII, N. S. 27.

Judgment on a suit for the price of a vessel, forms no *res judicata* as to a suit for damages occasioned by the illegal detention.

PARISH Court of New Orleans.

By PORTER, J.—We do not think the plea of *res judicata* sustained. In the first suit the demand was for the price of a vessel. Here, so far as we can gather any thing from the petition, the claim set up is for the detention of the vessel. If the defendant, in his answer, had acknowledged all the facts in the petition, and averred that by law they furnished no cause of action, we are inclined to think judgment must have been rendered in his favor, that he chose to join issue on the merits, and admit the plaintiff's testimony without opposition; the case must, therefore, be decided on the proof adduced.

Robeson *et al.'s* Syndics *v.* Carpenter.   VII, N. S. 30.

Judgment against a garnishee does not prevent his creditor from showing that a larger sum is due.

When the plaintiff in attachment releases the garnishee against whom he has judgment, the claim of the defendant in attachment is revived.

But the latter cannot issue execution till the satisfaction be entered on the judgment of the plaintiff in attachment.

PARISH Court of New Orleans.

PORTER, J., delivered the opinion of the court.

This action is on an open account, and was commenced by attachment. The court below gave judgment in favor of the plaintiffs, and the defendant appealed.

The most important questions in the cause grow out of proceedings which have taken place in the state of Mississippi against the defendant, who has been cited and condemned there as garnishee of the insolvents. He contends the judge erred: first, in not considering this judgment as *res judicata,* which precluded the plaintiffs from claiming more in the present action than he was considered to owe in that suit: and secondly, in including the sum for which he was condemned as garnishee in the decree now appealed from.

On the first point, we are of opinion that such a judgment does not preclude the defendant in attachment from showing that his debtor, who was summoned as garnishee, owes more than he was ordered to pay in that quality. To give to a judgment the authority of *res judicata,* it is among other things necessary that the demand must have been made between the same parties, and formed by them, against each other, in the same capacity. The present plaintiffs were defendants in the former suit, and were no way interested in establishing that funds of theirs were in the garnishee's hands. The *contestatio litis* was not formed between them on that point, nor on any other.

On the trial the plaintiffs agreed they would not put the judgment they expected to obtain in execution, until the defendant was written to, at his residence in the state of Mississippi, to ascertain from him whether he would be safe in paying here the amount for which he had been condemned as garnishee; and that if he decided he was not, they would not exact the same under the judgment. They further introduced a release from the plaintiffs in attachment in Mississippi, by which they discharged him from the payment of the judgment in their favor, and promised they would execute any other acquittance he might require. They further stipulated that payment to the syndics should be a complete bar to their demand.

The case of a defendant who has been sued in another country, as garnishee of his creditor, and against whom judgment has been rendered in that capacity, is *sui generis.* Although it does not, for the reasons already mentioned in the first point, authorise the plea of *res judicata,* it offers such strong and equitable claims to protection, that it has been held by courts in other countries it might be pleaded in a subsequent action brought by the creditor. We have, in a former case, recognised the correctness of this doctrine, and we are satisfied the debtor in such cases should be protected. 5 Johns. Rep. 102; 8 Mass. Rep. 458; 10 *Martin,* 628.

But as the defence is an equitable one, we do not think the court erred, under all the circumstances of the case, in giving judgment for the plaintiffs. When the creditors who had obtained judgment in the attachment suit, released the defendant from all responsibility, the right of the original creditors is revived. The court, however, should have directed that execution should not issue, until the plaintiff in the attachment in Mississippi entered satisfaction on record there, of the judgment against the garnishee. The release here was *sous seing privé,* and the defendant ought not to be compelled to prove it in Mississippi, and obtain a discharge on record in that state. The plaintiff should place him in the same situation as if that suit had not been brought.

We think the court below acted correctly in rejecting the claim for extra freight. But we are of opinion it erred in giving judgment for the one per cent. commission for accepting the drafts of the defendants. The witnesses sworn on the trial (and they were all commission merchants) declared, after an inspection of the account, that they would not make such a charge. The judge below was of opinion that as they said they would make other charges which would be equivalent, this should be allowed. But those charges appear to us still less susceptible of legal sanction than that made in this case.

It is, therefore, ordered, adjudged and decreed, that the judgment of the parish court be annulled, avoided and reversed; and it is further ordered and decreed, that the plaintiff do recover of the defendant the sum of two hundred and seven dollars and seventy-four cents, with interest from judicial demand, and costs in the court of the first instance. But that they shall not take out execution, until they file in the office of the clerk of the parish court, a copy (duly authenticated by the clerk of the court in the state of Mississippi, where judgment had been rendered against the defendants as garnishees of the insolvent) of the satisfaction entered on record, by the plaintiff in that suit, of the judgment so obtained by them as aforesaid. It is further ordered that the appellees pay the costs of this appeal.

M'Caleb, for the plaintiffs.

Watts and *Lobdell,* for the defendant.

Millaudon *v.* M'Micken. VII, N. S. 34.

An attorney has no power to release a debt.
But he may in certain cases grant a stay of execution.
Agents with general powers are not bound to exercise more than ordinary diligence, and such as is customary in similar undertakings.

THIRD District.

MATHEWS, J., delivered the opinion of the court.

This suit is brought on an instrument in writing, by which the defendant bound himself to pay to the plaintiff the amount of certain notes and other obligations, which the former had transferred to the latter, in the event of his inability to collect or recover, by due course of law, the several sums of money which had been transferred from the debtors in said notes and obligations. Proceedings at law were to be carried on by the transferee against the debtors, to a return of *nulla bona* upon the *fieri facias* in each case. The sum claimed in the present action, is the aggregated amount of judgments, and the costs thereon, on which executions were issued, and returns made that no property could be found. The transfer of the debts above stated, was made to secure the payment of a previous debt owing and due from the defendant to the plaintiff. The cause was submitted to a jury in the court below, who found a verdict in favor of the plaintiff for 2043 dollars and 44 cents; and judgment being rendered in pursuance thereof, the defendant appealed.

The appellant seems to rest his defence on three principal grounds. 1. A subsequent agreement entered into between him and J. D. Colt, who acted as attorney and counsellor for the plaintiff, by which he was released from all responsibility, in any event, to pay the whole or any part of the debts which he had transferred. 2. A verdict of a jury, on a former trial, in his favor, obtained in the court below. 3. Negligence of the transferror, by his attorney, in the pursuit of the debtors on whom the claims had been transferred.

The second agreement relied on by the defendant, as a release from all the obligations imposed on him by the first, is evidenced solely by an endorsement made on a note which was transferred to the attorney of the plaintiff, subsequent to the contract on which the present action is founded. The attorney had no power to make such an arrangement: it never received the sanction or confirmation of the appellee, and therefore, as to him, it is without force or effect.

In what way, or according to what principles of law, the appellant may profit by the verdict returned in his favor on the first trial of the cause, cannot be easily perceived. We are ignorant of any law, or sound rule of equity, which requires that parties to a suit, in the event of two contradictory verdicts, should submit their cause to the chance of a third. Independent of legal scrutiny, probabilities are in favor of the conclusions of the last, as being rendered under a stricter examination of the cause; but the first is entirely annulled by the grant of a new trial, made in the exercise of legal discretion by the judge *a quo*.

The ground of defence assumed as a consequence of the fault and negligence of the plaintiff's attorney, in the prosecution of suits instituted on the claims which were transferred to him, is worthy of serious investigation. The act of transfer, according to which pursuit was made, does not stipulate for any extraordinary promptitude and diligence to be exercised on the part of the transferee. As to the time within which judgments were obtained, it appears to us that no just complaint can be made; but in several instances, indulgence was granted by a stay of execution after judgment. The proceedings in this respect, against M'Gaher, one of the largest debtors, are much complained of; and we will examine that case (as being one of the strongest in favor of the pretensions of the defendant) in order to solve the difficulties which belong to others similarly situated. Exclusive of the delay granted after judgment, in issuing execution, it is contended, on the part of the defendant, that the plaintiff has lost all recourse against him for this debt, on account of the neglect of the latter to prosecute the claim against M'Gaher to judgment, in the state of Mississippi, where the debtor resided. This claim was secured by mortgage on some property in the parish of Feliciana, and had been transferred from the original payee of the note to the appellant. The maker was sued and held to bail in this state, and judgment was obtained against him in October 1822, on which execution was issued, after the stay which had been allowed until January, 1823; on which there was a return of no property to be found. By the suit thus prosecuted on the part of the plaintiff, it is believed that he has discharged the obligation imposed on him by the contract of transfer, so far as it compelled him to pursue the debtors to judgment. Whether the indulgence, by stay of execution, has produced a forfeiture of his right to be paid by the present defendant, remains to be ascertained.

The general principle of the contract of mandate, that the agent, or attorney, takes all risks, and subjects himself to all losses which occur in consequence of acts done by him, beyond the legal limits of his power, is fully established by every system of jurisprudence. An authority given to collect money, will not confer a right on the agent to prorogue the time of payment, and he would be responsible for the injury which his constituent might suffer from such conduct. Agents constituted with general powers to transact any business, are not bound to exercise more than ordinary diligence, and such as is customary in similar undertakings. *See Stracca De Contractibus Mercatoriis, til. Mandata, nos.* 29 and 41.

According to the Spanish laws, those who undertake the management of suits for others, are bound to exercise diligence, industry, and skill. *Part. 3, tit. 5, law 25* and *26.*

In bringing the conduct of the attorney who prosecuted the suits commenced by the plaintiff, on the claims which had been transferred to him, to the test of these rules, we find some difficulty in coming to a conclusion entirely satisfactory to our own minds. The grant of a stay of execution on a judgment, is certainly a species of prorogation of the time within which payment might possibly have been enforced; but where such indulgence is moderate in delay, and may have been used as a means of obtaining judgment with greater facility, and more speedily than could otherwise have been effected, we believe that it is in accordance with the general practice of attorneys at law, who are employed to collect debts in the country, where the terms of the court are semi-annual. Their conduct, in this respect, must be left to the government of a sound discretion to be by them exercised; and they ought not to be held responsible, unless for fraud, gross negligence (*lata culpa*), or proof that their clients have suffered a loss by the indulgence granted. The evidence in the present case, would not subject the attorney who pursued M'Gaher to refund to his employer for a loss as necessarily resulting from a fault in the management of that suit: neither ought the rights of the latter, under the act of transfer, to be affected by the conduct of his agent.

It is, therefore, ordered, adjudged and decreed, that the judgment of the district court be affirmed, with costs against the defendant and appellant in both courts.

EASTERN DISTRICT, JUNE TERM, 1828.

Cole's Widow *v.* His Executors.   VII, N. S. 41.

In the case of Saul *v.* His Creditors, the statute which regulates the rights of husband and wife, was decided to be *real*, not *personal*, and hence, property found in this state at the dissolution of the marriage was declared to be subject to distribution according to the laws of Louisiana, without regard to the fact that the marriage had been contracted, and that either or both spouses had always resided elsewhere.

The law of the *Fuero Real*, viz.: "every thing which the husband and wife acquire while together, shall be equally divided between them," is not repealed by the 2370th article of the Louisiana Code; which declares, that "a marriage contracted out of the state, between persons who afterwards come to live here, is also subjected to the community of acquests and gains with respect to such property as is acquired after their arrival;" but the latter is a positive statutory provision covering only part of the ground of the original principle.

Nor does the 3521st article of the Louisiana Code repeal that provision of the *Fuero Real*, for it only forbids the invoking of the former laws of Louisiana, where their objects are specially provided for by actual legislation. Now, the case of one of the married couple moving into this state, is not specially provided for: the former law, therefore, in relation to it, is not repealed by this general provision.

COURT of Probates of New Orleans.

PORTER, J., delivered the opinion of the court.
The widow of the testator claims from the executors the one half of the property, real and personal, of which he died possessed; on the ground that it was acquests and gains made during coverture.

The executors resist the action on two grounds; 1, that the court of probates had no jurisdiction of the case: and 2, that the plaintiff has no legal right to any portion of the property acquired during marriage.

The testator was married to the plaintiff, in the state of New York, in the year 1810. He was then about 24 years of age, and she 63. After their marriage, they lived some time together, when the husband came to New Orleans. After a year's residence here, he returned to New York, and there remained with his wife for the space of three years; at the expiration of which time he again removed to New Orleans, where he resided until his death in 1827, and where he acquired the property which is the subject of the present contest. The plaintiff remained in New York, and never was in this state. The deceased made a will, by which he bequeathed to a brother living in Ireland, nearly the whole of the property of which he died possessed.

The first question relates to the jurisdiction of the court of probates, and we think the judge below did not err in taking cognisance of the case. That court having exclusive jurisdiction of the settlement of all claims against an estate represented by an executor, and its liquidation and final settlement, it follows that it is before that tribunal a claim must be made, the rejection or admission of which is necessary to enable the succession to be closed. The other construction supposes the court not clothed with sufficient powers to carry its undoubted jurisdiction into effect. It sometimes, indeed, happens, that tribunals are so defectively organised, that one is compelled to act as the assistant of the other; but it requires a very clear expression of legislative will to authorise such a conclusion; the general rule being, that where the end is conceded, the means of arriving at it are granted.

The next, and more important question, relates to the right of the wife in the acquests and gains.

In the case of Saul v. His Creditors, which lately underwent so much discussion in this court, principles were established, which greatly facilitate the investigation of the rights of the parties now before us. It is true in that case, husband and wife had both resided in this state; and in the present instance, the husband alone lived in Louisiana. But we then determined that the law, or, to adopt the language of the jurisprudence of the continent of Europe, the statute, which regulated the rights of husband and wife, was *real*, not *personal;* that it regulated things, and subjected them to the laws of the country within which they were found. It follows, then, as a consequence, that property within the limits of this state, must, on the dissolution of the marriage, be distributed according to the laws of Louisiana, no matter where the parties reside; because, viewing the statute as *real*, it is the thing on which it operates that gives it application, not the residence of the person who may profit by the rule it contains. *Quando verba consuetudinis, vel statuti, disponunt circa rem, tunc de bonis judicandum est secundum con-*

suetudinem loci, ubi res sunt situatæ: quia consuetudo afficit res ipsas, sive possideantur a cive, sive a forensi. Greg. Lopez, Gloss. 2, *Par.* 4, *tit.* 11, *l.* 24; *Matienso, lib.* 5, *tit.* 9, *b.* 2, *gl.* 1, *n.* 75.— This doctrine has not, indeed, been much contested in the argument; and both parties seemed to concede, that the case must be governed by our law. But the counsel for the appellants have contended that even by it the claim of the wife can not be maintained. Their principal grounds of objection, are: first, the positive legislation of the state; and, secondly, the separation of the husband and wife during the whole of the time the property was acquired.

The law of the *Fuero Real,* so often quoted in this court, declares that "every thing which the husband and wife acquire while together, shall be equally divided between them." It is argued this law does not provide for such a case as is now before the court; and that if it did, it is repealed by the 2370th article of the Louisiana Code, which declares that a marriage contracted out of the state, between persons who afterwards come to live here, is also subjected to the community of acquests and gains, with respect to such property as is acquired after their arrival. The phraseology here used, it is said, indicates clearly the intention to exclude such a case as this. The statute refers to persons coming to reside here, not to one individual: it speaks not of *his,* or *her,* but their arrival.

The effect which the provisions in the late amendments to our Code have in repealing former laws, depends on the general disposition contained in them, which declares what influence shall be given to them in this respect; and to their operation, according to the general rules of construction.

The case of the appellants can receive no support on the first ground. It is provided by the 3521st article of the Louisiana Code, that the former laws of the country are repealed in every case for which it has been specially provided in this Code; and they shall not be invoked as laws, even under the pretence that their provisions are not contrary or repugnant to those of this Code. Now the case of one of the married couple moving into this state, is not specially provided for: the former law, therefore, in relation to it, is not repealed by this general provision.* Whether, on the general rules of construction, the article already cited can be considered as abrogating a former law which, although different, is not contrary, little need be now said. The vast quantity of positive legislation which has been given to the people of Louisiana since the change of government, has called the attention of our courts repeatedly to this subject, and

---

* But the general repealing law of 1828 has done this business effectually, though doubtless through pure inadvertence of the legislature. There is now no statutory provision supplying the place of that law of the *Fuero Real,* and hence, unless the spouses remove to, or reside in Louisiana, it would seem unquestionable that there will be no community of acquests and gains between them, as to the property found here at the dissolution of the marriage. Dixon *v.* Dixon's Executors, 4 *Lou. Rep.* 190, 191.

the principles which forbid such a conclusion have been again and again stated by this tribunal. The remarks, however, made in the case of Saul *v.* His Creditors, showing that the provisions in the old Code which gave a community of acquests and gains in marriages contracted within this state, did not repeal a former law which gave them in marriages contracted out of the state, when the parties afterwards removed into Louisiana, are so perfectly applicable to the instance before us, that we refer to them to show why a provision in relation to husband and wife coming to reside in this country, can not affect rules in relation to the removal of one of them.

The law of the *Fuero Real*, it is true, does not speak of one of the spouses coming into the country, nor does it provide for the case where both live under another government, at the dissolution of the marriage; but it is a necessary consequence of the statute being real, that the property acquired within the limits of the state, and found there on the marriage being dissolved, should be governed by its provisions, no matter where the parties reside.

Whether the separation, and the failure of the wife to contribute her portion of care and industry to the acquisition, will defeat her right, is the next question to be examined.—And finding, on this head, nothing in the law, its commentators, nor, in our judgment, in the reason of the thing, which makes the living apart, in different states, a greater objection than a separation would be in the country where the statute was in force, we shall examine what effect different residences would have, if both had lived within the state of Louisiana.

On the argument, counsel went at some length into the principles on which the community of acquests and gains was established; and taking for the basis of such a rule the care and industry of both the spouses, they drew the conclusion that when it was established in evidence that one of them had not, or could not have, assisted in the acquisitions, the one so failing to contribute, could not rightfully claim any portion of them.

The doctrine of the community of acquests and gains, was unknown to the Roman law; and, although now common, we believe, to the greater number of the European nations, its origin can not be satisfactorily traced. The best opinion appears to be that it took its rise with the Germans, among whom at a very early period of their history, the wife took, by positive law, the one-third of all the gains made during coverture. It is very probable that it was the real, or presumed, care and industry of the wife, which first produced this legislation; and, in an early state of society, the facts most probably fully justified such a rule. But, in this, as in many other instances, legislation survives long after the causes which occasioned it, have ceased to exist, and the non-existence of these causes will not authorise courts of justice to refuse giving effect to the law. There are few, we believe, who think, at the present stage of society, that the wife contributes equally with the husband to the acquisition of property. If such cases exist, they are exceptions to the general rule. And yet, in this state, neither idleness, wasteful habits, nor moral or physical incapacity, would deprive the wife of an equal share in the acquests and gains; for our Code declares that every marriage, in Louisiana, superinduces, of right, partnership, or community, in all acquisitions. Such, also, was the rule in Spain. *La. Code*, 2369. *Merlin's Rep. verbo Communauté, vol.* 2, *p.* 548; *Febrero, p.* 2, *lib.* 1, *cap.* 4, *p.* 1, *n.* 3.

The writers, who treat on this subject, make no such exceptions as are here contended for. On the contrary, they state that the residence of the parties in different places will not prevent the community from existing. In Spain, indeed, if the wife never went to cohabit with her husband, the community did not commence: *sin haber ida cohabitar con su marido,* is the case put by *Febrero,* in the passage relied on by appellant's counsel. As in the ancient customs of France, it began not from the day of the marriage, but from its consummation. The separation spoken of by the same author, is a legal one. It required the judgment of an ecclesiastical court, and although such jurisdiction is unknown to us, still a judicial sentence is necessary to destroy the community. It was so in France: it is so under our Code. The law wisely refuses any legal effect to a voluntary separation of those who are bound by the most solemn of obligations to live together. *Pothier, Traite de Com. Par.* 1, *n.* 22; *Ibid. Par.* 3, *no.* 494; *Febrero, Par.* 2, *lib.* 1, *cap.* 4, *nos.* 1, 2, 46 and 50.

On the particular circumstance of the case on which so much has been said at the bar, few remarks are required from the court. The match most probably originated (as such connections generally do, where there is so great a disparity of age) in cupidity on the one side, and folly on the other. He who sacrifices to avarice, has the less cause of complaint if the bargain turns out a hard one. The separation most probably was voluntary. The husband, at least, could not (if living) have urged it was not, for if he had desired his wife to live with him, it was his duty to have required her so to do.

We cannot take into our consideration the property in New York. Our statute is real, and where the parties are not married here, can only act on the property found in Louisiana. That which is in our sister state, will follow its laws.

It is, therefore, ordered, adjudged and decreed, that the judgment of the probate court be affirmed, with costs.

Smith and *Workman,* for the plaintiff.

Preston and *Strawbridge,* for the defendants.

Harang *v.* Harang *et al.* VII, N. S. 51.

If a parish be divided into two, proceedings on the *mortuaria* are to be commenced in the new parish, if the domicil of the deceased makes part of it, although he died before the division.

PARISH Court of New Orleans.

MARTIN, J., delivered the opinion of the court.

The appellant complains that the judge *a quo* dismissed his petition, praying that an inventory might be made, and proceedings had on the *mortuaire* of his late wife, who died before the division of the parish of Orleans from that part of it which now constitutes the parish of Jefferson: the judge being of opinion that the proceedings in this case should be had in the court of probates of the said parish.

The appellant contends that, by the death of the petitioner's wife, her succession was opened in the parish of Orleans, the court of probates of which was not ousted of its jurisdiction by the division of the parish.

Good order and convenience require that proceedings *mortuaire* should take place in the court of probates of the parish in which the deceased dwelt. Thus, the property of the estate, which is supposed generally to be at or near the domicil of the party, is better protected, and the creditors of the estate have a greater facility to attend to the recovery of their debts—the court of the parish being supposed the nearest. If proceedings, however, are delayed, as they were in the present case, until after the division of the parish, the same reasons operate to give jurisdiction to the court within whose district was the domicil of the deceased, in preventing the inhabitants of the new parish from being compelled to travel to the old, to answer in personal actions. The ground on which the petitioner claims the right of instituting proceedings in the old parish, is a mere technical one, which would occasion great inconvenience.

It is, therefore, ordered, adjudged and decreed, that the judgment of the court of probates be affirmed, with costs.

Derbigny, for the plaintiff.
Pitot, for the defendant.

Kenner *v.* Young. VII, N. S. 53.

No appeal lies from an order directing a purchaser to bring into court the price of the premises, to await the decision of the court on the claim of a mortgagee.

FIRST District.

By PORTER, J.—We think, with the judge, this is not such an order as will authorise an appeal. There is no suggestion that the property bought is not in the possession of the applicant. He is in no worse situation than if the sale had been a good one. If any subsequent order should place the funds out of the control of the court before the validity of the sale is decided on, another question would be presented.

The rule is, therefore, discharged.

Sterling *v.* Carruthers. VII, N. S. 55.

When it is necessary to explain or rebut the testimony of the defendant, the court has power to permit the plaintiff to do so.

THIRD District.

By PORTER, J.—We do not think that the court erred in permitting the plaintiff to examine a witness after the defendants had closed their testimony. The general rule is certainly opposed to such indulgence being extended; but when it becomes necessary to explain or rebut testimony, it is within the discretion and power of the court to permit either of the parties to do so. The 484th article of the Code of Practice does not appear to us opposed to this doctrine; the prohibition there spoken of, is in relation to testimony offered after the argument has commenced.

Dismukes *et al. v.* Musgrove.   VII, N. S. 58.

Proof of the signature of the witness to an instrument does not establish that of the obligor.

The witness's signature may be genuine, yet that of the party whose act it attests may be not so. He who offers the instrument must establish the fact itself, and not leave it a matter of inference from another fact with which it is probably, not necessarily connected, as in the case of proving the witness's signature.

EIGHTH District.

PORTER, J., delivered the opinion of the court.

The petitioners claim from the defendant certain slaves in her possession, to which they assert title in virtue of a deed of trust, executed by their father in the year 1811, by which a certain Champness Terry was created trustee, on condition of delivering the slaves and their increase to the petitioners when they came of age or married. Damages are also claimed by a supplemental petition for the defendant's having illegally entered into possession of the estate of Champness Terry, and intermeddled with it, and for the use of the slaves since they came into her possession.

The defendant pleaded that a judgment was rendered in the state of Mississippi, against the estate of Champness Terry, the trustee, for the negroes claimed in this suit; that on said judgment an order of seizure was granted, by the judge of the eighth district, in favor of Andrew Dismukes, the assignee thereof; that after said judgment, a transaction was entered into with the assignee and respondent, by which a final settlement was made of all matters arising in the present action.

She further pleaded, that the judgment in the state of Mississippi operates as *res judicata,* and that the plaintiffs are precluded by it from maintaining the present suit.

To her defence she added the general issue, and an exception to the jurisdiction of the court.

To the supplemental petitions, the defendant pleaded various dilatory exceptions, which were afterwards stricken out of the court, as being filed too late; and further averred that she held part of the negroes in her own right, and part under Robert Singleton, who was the legal proprietor thereof.

The answer closes by an allegation, that in consequence of the illegal sequestration sued out in this case by the plaintiffs, she has sustained damage to the amount of 5000 dollars, for which she claims judgment in reconvention.

The cause was submitted to a jury in the court below, who found a verdict in favor of the defendant. The court confirmed it, and the plaintiffs appealed.

The defendant offered in evidence a paper purporting to be an assignment from Ephraim Dismukes to Andrew U. Dismukes, before a person who styled himself Thomas Batchelor, notary public in the county of Amite, state of Mississippi, which was opposed on the ground that the defendant offered no proof of the handwriting of Dismukes, and that proof of the handwriting of Batchelor was not the best the nature of the case admitted of. The court admitted the evidence, and the plaintiffs excepted.

This exception brings before the court for the first time, the question whether proof of the handwriting of a witness be sufficient, when he is dead or absent, without proof of the signature of the party to the instrument to which the witness's name is affixed.

We have looked into the books to see how the law stands on this subject in England and our sister states, and we think the weight of authority, in the common law, is rather in favor of the opinion of the judge *a quo.*

But the rule is by no means perfectly settled. Starkie says, that when the absence of the subscribing witness is satisfactorily accounted for, the proper proof is by giving evidence of the handwriting of the attesting witness: and it is usual, in such cases to give evidence also of the handwriting of the obligor. Starkie on Evidence, Part 2, 344.

In a note, however, to the work, he adds, it has been decided that, if the witness be alive, proof must be given of the handwriting of the obligor. The case appears to be a very modern one.—3 Maddocks, 370.

In our sister states, the decisions are contradictory. In New York, Pennsylvania, Maryland, and North Carolina, proof of handwriting is sufficient. In New York, the rule is firmly established. In Pennsylvania, the first time the question came before their Supreme Court, they decided that proof might be made of the handwriting of the witness, but left it unsettled whether proof of that of the obligor should not also be furnished; intimating, however, clearly, their opinion that establishing the latter would be the best evidence. When the question came again before them, they concluded that proof of the witness's handwriting was sufficient, on the ground that it had been long the practice in that state to receive it. 1 Johns. Cases, 230; 4 Johns. 461; 3 Burney, 192; 6 *Ibid.* 45: 1 Har. and I. 337; 1 Haywood, 238; 2 Hay. 27, 404.

But in South Carolina, they require proof of the writing of the obligor as well as the witness. 1 Bay. 255; 2 Bay. 187.

And in the Supreme Court of the United States, on an objection being taken that the subscribing witness had not been produced, the court said, " The proof offered was such as is required, where a party to a deed, and the subscribing witness, are dead, the handwriting of both was proved. 8 Wheaton, 283.

[Dismukes et al. v. Musgrove.]

The doctrine, therefore, is not so well settled as to prevent this court from applying to the case those principles of law which, in their judgment, should govern it.

The rule is, that the best evidence the case is susceptible of should be produced. When the subscribing witness is alive, or within the process of the court, his testimony is the highest and should be offered. When he is dead or absent, proof of his handwriting is not the best the case admits of, because such proof is presumptive evidence only. The instrument was signed by the obligor. The witness's signature may be genuine, and yet that of the party it attests, not so. In such case, it is the duty of him who offers the instrument, to prove the handwriting of the obligor. Establishing it, establishes the fact to be proved, and does not leave it (as in the case of proving the witness' signature) a matter of inference from another fact, with which it is probably, but not necessarily connected.

The only case that can readily be imagined where this rule would produce hardships, is that of a stranger, whose handwriting was little known, coming into the country and exacting obligations before witnesses who, after his departure, died. No general rule can be laid down, that will not do injury in some particular cases. But that just spoken of, in our judgment, is nothing, in comparison with the danger that might result from sanctioning the other doctrine. The facility of proving any instrument under it is obvious. Whether forged or not, nothing more is necessary than to procure a nonresident of the state to put his name to it as a witness; and thus, a paper false in itself, might be established by proving nothing but the truth in a court of justice. If, to these considerations, we add that drawn from the 2241st article of our Code, which most plainly indicates the necessity of proving the handwriting of the obligor, no doubt can exist of the conclusion to which we are compelled to come.

It is, therefore, ordered, adjudged and decreed, that the judgment of the district court be annulled, avoided and reversed; and it is further decreed, that this cause be remanded for a new trial, with directions to the judge, not to admit a paper signed Ephraim Dismukes, on the proof of the handwriting of Thomas Batchelor; and it is further ordered, that the appellee pay the costs of the appeal.

Hennen, for the plaintiffs.

Brandegee *v.* Kerr and Wife.   VII, N. S. 64.

The circumstance of the wife having had a separate advantage in a contract, joint and several of husband and wife, being of the essence of her obligation, must be proved by some other evidence than proof that she touched the money.

FIRST District.

MARTIN, J., delivered the opinion of the court.

This is an action on the note of the wife, endorsed by the husband, alleged to have been received from the wife, on a loan made to her by a check delivered to her, and by her received to her proper use and benefit. The general issue was pleaded, and the wife denied having received any consideration. The plaintiff had judgment, and the defendants appealed.

According to the plaintiff's own showing, the note sued on is not the evidence of a contract by which the wife promised to pay a sum of money to the husband, but a mere accommodation paper, in which the husband intervened for no other purpose than to give it credit, and perhaps to manifest his assent to the act of the wife. We can not distinguish this paper from a note, joint and several, of husband and wife—for they are bound jointly and severally—and the plaintiff has prayed for a judgment joint and several. The only difference is in the form, which, as to the husband, perhaps created the necessity of a protest and notice. We say, perhaps, because we are not ready to say the husband is not bound by a note given by the wife with his assent as the evidence of a debt of the community.

Viewing, then, the contract as the joint and several one of the husband and wife, and the wife having pleaded the general issue, *i. e.*, denied all the facts alleged; and among others, that the consideration of the contract was received to her own use and benefit, we have sought in vain for any evidence of this circumstance—for in such a contract the wife is not bound, if the consideration of the contract be not for her separate advantage, and not something which the husband was bound to furnish her with.

The plaintiff's counsel presents this evidence in the circumstance of the wife having received the check and endorsed it, and the check having been paid in bank.

To give the plaintiff all the benefit of the verdict, we have considered it proved that the wife actually received the money. Is this evidence of the consideration of the contract having turned to her separate advantage?

Such is the influence which marital power gives to the husband over the wife, that the law has deemed protection necessary, from its improper exercise, and therefore freed the wife from every obligation resulting from any contract, joint and several, into which she enters with her husband, unless it be proved that its object was her separate advantage. It would be to render this privilege absolutely unavailable, if the circumstance of the money having passed through her hands, rendered the contract binding on her, without due proof of its having turned to her separate advantage. Whenever a husband could influence his wife to contract jointly and severally with him, he would have influence enough to induce her to receive the money or endorse the check.

We, therefore, conclude that the circumstance of the wife having a separate advantage in the contract, being of the essence of her obligation, must be proved by some other evidence than proof of her having touched the money. For, after receiving it, she may have handed it over to her husband, applied it to the wants of the family, employed it in relieving her husband from debts contracted for its support, or even for other purposes.

Her employing it in this manner is quite as probable as her using it in the payment of her debts, or in the repairs of the houses of her separate estate.

Being of opinion that there is no fact in evidence, from which it is possible to infer that the plaintiff's money was employed for the separate use of the wife, in something which the husband was not obliged to furnish her with, we conclude that the wife is not bound. Durnford *v.* Gross and Wife, 7 *Martin*, 465.

It is, therefore, ordered, adjudged and decreed, that the judgment, so far as it regards the wife, be annulled, avoided and reversed, and as far as it concerns the husband affirmed; and that there be judgment for the wife; the plaintiff and apppellee paying costs in this court.

Hennen, for the plaintiff.
Workman, for the defendants.

M'Donough v. Tregre et al.   VII, N. S. 68.

When the wife renounces the community, she has a mortgage on property bought by the husband.

FIRST District.

Porter, J., delivered the opinion of the court.

The plaintiff issued *fieri facias*, in virtue of a judgment he had obtained against the defendant, and an the 22d of December, 1827, sold, in virtue of this execution, a slave called Jean Denis.

On the 9th of January, 1828, the intervenor, who is wife of the defendant, had judgment against him of separation, and recovered at the same time the amount which he had received of her proper effects, from the date of her marriage up to that of separation. On that judgment she has collected, as is ¦shown by the sheriff's return, 257 dollars.

She claims the proceeds of the slave, averring that her mortgage is higher than that of the plaintiff—he resists the demand, on the ground that the property seized was acquired during marriage, and that it is first responsible for community debts.

So that the only question of any importance in the case is, whether the wife has a mortgage on the property purchased during coverture, which takes precedence of the ordinary creditors of the husband.

We have no doubt that she has. Some of the jurists of France have lately agitated this question, and expressed their opinions against the claim of the wife. But one of them, in the last edition of his works, acknowledges that the court of cassation has settled the question in opposition to his views of the law, and that he is bound to conclude those views were erroneons. One of the principal grounds of these writers, is, that the Code gives a mortgage on the property of the husband, and that the property acquired during marriage belongs, not to him, but to the community. This argument proceeds on the idea, that during marriage, the wife, by the effect of the law, is a partner in all the acquisitions made by the husband. But she is only so, in our judgment, when she accepts the community. From the moment she renounces, as she did in this case, every thing done during coverture, in regard to the purchase or alienation of property concerns the husband alone; and as such, her mortgage attaches as completely on the effects purchased by him, as those he possessed before marriage. The arguments on both sides of this question, are

[M'Donough *v.* Tregro *et al.*]

given at length in a note by *Paillet*, 2121st article of the Napoleon Code. *Persil, Regime Hypothecaire,* 2 edit. *vol.* 1, *p.* 268; *Delvincourt, Cours de Droit Civil, vol.* 2, 654; *Manual de Droit Français,* 5 *ed. p.* 641.

We think there is sufficient evidence on record to show that the husband did receive of the wife's property an amount larger than the proceeds of the sale of the slaves now claimed by her; and the objection of the lien not being recorded, cannot avail the plaintiff, for there does not appear to have been any written instrument ever given by him which could have been registered.

It is, therefore, ordered, adjudged and decreed, that the judgment of the district court be affirmed, with costs.

Mc Caleb, for the plaintiff,
Cuvillier, for the defendants.

NOTE.—At page 71, 7 *N. S.* of Judge Martin's Reports, the case of Cole's Widow *v.* His Executors, was, by mistake, repeated, *verbatim* from p. 41, *ante.*

Packwood *v.* Walden. VII, N. S. 81.

By the formation of the batture of the fauxbourg St. Mary, the place it occupied ceased to be a part of the port.

After the change, it became the property of the city.

FIRST District.

MATHEWS, J., delivered the opinion of the court.

According to the tenor and conclusion of the petition, this action appears to have been instituted for the purpose of causing the defendant to be dispossessed of certain lots of land which he holds on the batture or alluvion, in front of the fauxbourg St. Mary: and to compel him to abate, as nuisances, certain buildings and inclosures which he has lately erected thereon: also, to obtain a decree, declaring that a part of said alluvion which lies in front of a lot on   street, owned by the plaintiff, to be public property, free and open to the use of all, &c.

The petition contains a history of the establishment of the fauxbourg, by the person who last owned the plantation, or farm, on the front of which it was founded; with allegations that no batture or alluvion existed at the time the front of said plantation was changed into a fauxbourg; that the river, at high water, flowed up to, and washed, the levee adjoining the front street of said fauxbourg, to which boats and other craft used in navigation, made fast, &c. That in truth the space now occupied by the alluvion, was then a part of the port of New Orleans; was public property, and still continues to be such, notwithstanding the present extent and elevation of the new made land. The petitioner claims no right of property in the disputed premises, but seems to insist on one of servitude—a right of way direct to the river.

The defendant, in his answer, sets up title to the property, and obtained a judgment in his favor in the court below, from which the plaintiff appealed.

The batture, or alluvion, concerning which the present dispute was raised, has been a most fruitful source of litigation during the last twenty-four years. The questions in relation to it have heretofore assumed various shapes, according to the pretensions of the different parties who claimed it for themselves. This is the first time it has been claimed for the public; that is, as public property, the use of which belongs to all, the right of soil to none, either individuals or bodies politic.

The first title under which this property was claimed, is that supported in favor of the heirs of Bertrand Gravier, by a judgment of the Superior Court of the late territorial government. The decision in that case, so far as relates to facts, is based on evidence which proves that a batture in front of their ancestor's plantation, existed to the whole extent of said front, capable of being reclaimed from the river, and was a proper subject for private ownership at the time he established the fauxbourg St. Mary.

The next case in which the rights and titles of individuals were brought in question relative to this batture, is that of Morgan v. Livingston. The controversy was between the proprietor of a front lot, who claimed by right of alluvion, and a purchaser from the heirs of B. Gravier. Testimony was introduced which showed that no alluvion existed at the time of the sale from the original owner to his immediate vendee. Nothing in the evidence established the period when the alluvion might have been considered of sufficient elevation and extent to become private property. The cause was decided on principles applicable to rural estates; and the plaintiff succeeded.

A case occurred between Herman and the claimants under B. Gravier's heirs. This was submitted to a jury on special facts; and their finding proved that the claimant was not a riparious proprietor; and consequently he failed in his pursuit.

In these decisions there is an apparent contradiction. This is a consequence of the evidence which varied in each case. One among the greatest difficulties which occurs in the administration of justice, arises frequently from the incorrectness of witnesses, caused by for-

[Packwood v. Walden.]

getfulness, prejudice, and perhaps too often by motives more corrupt.

The present case presents no question of title personal to the plaintiff; a circumstance which relieves us in a great degree from weighing the immense mass of testimony offered on his part. In this respect it differs from all those already adjudged relating to the same subject; consequently none of the former judgments can be effectually opposed to it as *res judicata*.

The numerous points filed by the counsel for the appellee, may be fairly comprised in one or two questions of law.

1. By the formation of the batture, did the place which it occupied, cease to be a part of the port of New Orleans?

2. If so, after the change did it still continue to be public property, unalienable and unalterable in its destination, by any power except that of the state, or of the United States?

The claim made by the plaintiff, of a servitude, proposes a third question, as to his right in this respect, which will be also considered. The positive titles or rights to the property in relation to the city, the front proprietors, and the representatives of B. Gravier, will be left out of view so far as they might conflict; for if the batture was acquired under legal claims by all or one of these parties, the plaintiff must fail in the present suit.

Previous to entering into the solution of these questions, it is proper that we should put at rest a difficulty arising from acts of the legislative power of the state—one passed in 1808, the other in 1813, which seem to conflict. The first of these laws contains a prohibition to all the inhabitants of the state, preventing them, under certain penalties, from making *levees* or dykes in front of those which existed at the time of passing the act; unless by authorisation of a jury of twelve inhabitants, proprietors of plantations situate on the banks of the Mississippi. The law of 1813, contains general rules for the administration of parochial affairs in all the parishes of the state, under the superintendance of the judges of the different parishes, and police juries to be appointed as directed by the act. Among the powers granted to these political bodies, is that by which they have the entire regulation of roads and levees within their respective districts, both in relation to original creation and reparation of those already existing. The 7th section of this act excludes the city from the authority of the police jury of New Orleans, and makes it the duty of the corporation to exercise (within its limits) the functions committed by law to police juries.

We are of opinion that the act of 1808, which required the permission of a special jury to authorise the erection of new levees, is abrogated by that of 1813, whether the last law be considered as affecting the levees in the country or city. Police juries are empowered to legislate upon roads and levees, both in making and repairing. A power to make is distinguishable from one to repair, by the authority which it confers to create *de novo.*—The power granted,

14*

by the first law, to special juries, to permit the creation of new levees is similar, in all respects, to that granted by the last to police juries. These powers are equal and opposite, and must destroy each other, unless one of them can be made to yield; which may be done by a common and well established rule for the interpretation of the laws; *leges posteriores abrogant priores.*—The right of special juries to interfere in the creation of new levees being thus annulled and transferred to the police juries throughout the state, it follows, as a necessary consequence, that the city council now possess all powers proper to be used, in the exercise of a just police, relative to streets, levees, and all other public places belonging to its community. The powers of the corporation have, under the act of 1813, enabled its representatives to make the compromise which took place between them and the different claimants of the batture, by which the embankment or levee of the river received the direction which it now has.

We will now investigate the matters on which depends a correct solution of the questions proposed. And here it may be said, without impropriety, that the statement itself of the first proposition, seems to involve an absurdity. Land, according to any definition, can never be considered as making a part of a port. A bank, quay, or wharf, is a necessary appendage to it; and, according to the jurisprudence of this state, is always public and destined to the use of all, as well as the port itself. But this public use can not legally be extended farther than the bank or wharf, which is always distinct from alluvion fully formed, and subjected by law to the ownership of private individuals or public bodies.

By the Roman law, a port is defined to be *locus conclusus, quo importantur merces, et unde exportantur.* D. 50, 16, 59.

The definition in the 8th law, tit. 33, Part. 7, is nearly similar to the Roman Digest.

That found in the *Curia Philippica,* page 456, no. 35, states a port to be a place either on the seacoast or on a river, where ships stop for the purpose of loading and unloading, from whence they depart, and where they finish their voyages.

It is clear, from these definitions, that the place now occupied by the alluvion in front of the fauxbourg St. Mary, although formerly a part of the port of New Orleans, has long since ceased to be such. It is nearer to the port than other squares of the city situated farther from the river, but makes no more a part of it than they do. Reliance was had on the plan of the fauxbourg made by B. Gravier, to prove that the batture in front was destined for public use; in other words that it was designated as a public place. That such was not the intention of the founder, is evident from his having sold his right to a part of the alluvion to one or two of the purchasers of lots from him. The manner in which this place is marked out on the plan, indicates that it was done rather to show the peculiar localities which were about to be changed into a town, than for any other purpose.

[Packwood *v.* Walden.]

The second question is one of greater difficulty. Doubts may be fairly entertained whether the change of the limits of the port, effected by alluvion and accretion, did not leave the land thus raised public property in the most extensive sense of the terms—subject to have its destination altered only by the supreme legislative power of the state, or that of the United States.

In order to arrive at a correct decision relative to these doubts, we are compelled to examine the doctrine of alluvion, so far as it affects the rights of cities. We have not been able to find any law very explicit on the subject. According to the law of the Roman Digest *in agris limitatis,* although the right of alluvion is denied to fields of this description, yet it is granted to land on which a city is founded.

The 6th law of the 28th tit. Part. 3, declares that rivers, ports, public roads and places, belong to all men in common; and that the use of the banks of rivers is common to all, although the right of property may be vested in particular owners. The law 9th, same title and part, recognises battures on the banks of rivers, *arenales que son en las riberas de los rios,* as common property of the cities or towns to which they become attached.

Things destined and appropriated absolutely for public and general use, whether they appertain to a state at large, or to a subordinate community, such as a city or town, cannot be legally sold, alienated, or applied to private purposes. These are rivers, fountains, roads, public places, and similar objects. Perhaps this general use might be changed or restricted in some instances by the sovereign power of the state. See *Part. 5, tit. 5, law* 15.

But those things which are the common property of a city, *illa quæ sunt propria civitatis, et quæ non sunt in usu publico, vendere potest civitas, &c.* Second note of Lopez on the last law cited.

In conformity with the provisions of the law first invoked, it must be inferred that a city can acquire *jure alluvionis;* and land thus added becomes the property of the whole community; it is *propria civitatis,* and may be sold, alienated, and destined to private uses, by the legal authorities of the city.

According to this examination of the cause it is readily seen that if the city did really acquire the alluvion in question, the mayor and common council had power to lay it out into squares and lots, to order streets to be made, &c. and to sell the land, as they continue to do in relation to the commons in the rear of the city. Having power to sell, they could lawfully transact and compromise with other claimants of the same property; which has been done as above stated, and by which a new bank or levee has been made on the river, forming the quay or wharf of the port, the use of which is public and common to all. The second question must therefore be decided against the pretensions of the plaintiff on the batture as public property, and such as is *hors de commerce.*

As to his claim of a servitude—a right of way direct to the river and port: as the latter is now situated, we believe it to be wholly without legal foundation. Admitting the alluvion (as alleged in the petition) to have been entirely formed since the time when B. Gravier laid out the fauxbourg, it has been acquired either by the city or by the proprietors of the front lots. If by the latter, then the plaintiff, as owner of that part of it immediately in front of his lot, can have no servitude on it; for in order to constitute a servitude, it must have relation to two estates held by different owners—the *prædium dominans* and *prædium serviens*. If by the former, then it was acquired as common to all the inhabitants of the city, and no individual could in any manner obtain on it a right of servitude. While it remained common property, it was subjected to the use and service of all the citizens, which is wholly incompatible with the acquisition or existence of a particular servitude due to any individual of the corporation. Before the period when the alluvion was formed, no right of servitude could have been acquired; and by the allegations of the petition, which, so far as they affect the claims of the plaintiff prejudicially, must be taken to be true, no batture was in existence at the time when Bertrand Gravier sold the lots laid out on the front of his plantation: consequently, by those sales, no right of servitude could have been acquired by the purchasers as incidental to the property sold. We have shown that he could not have acquired any such right since that period. He must be contented with the ordinary ways to the river—the streets which are common to all.

It is, therefore, ordered, adjudged and decreed, that the judgment of the district court be affirmed, with costs.

Hennen, for the plaintiff.

Hoffman and *Livermore,* for the defendant.

•

Denis *v.* Clague's Syndics.   VII, N. S. 93.

The buyer who discovers a defect in his title, has not the right of requiring a rescission of the sale, but only a suspension of payment till security be given him.

PARISH Court of New Orleans.

PORTER, J., delivered the opinion of the court.

The petitioner states that he bought property at the sale of the insolvent's estate, and gave his notes for it, payable in several instalments; and that since the purchase he has discovered defect in the title of the vendors. He prays that the sale be rescinded, unless the defendants give security he shall not be disturbed, and for such other relief as his case may entitle him to. He also prays judgment for 600 dollars expenses by him incurred in keeping the property.

The answer denies the existence of any cause, which can authorise the plaintiff to refuse payment of his notes, or to have the sale made to him cancelled.

The defect in the title proceeds from the act of the vendor of the insolvent. The property was purchased by him during the life of his wife, and made, of course a part of the community estate. After her death he sold it as belonging to himself. The plaintiff insists the one half was owned by his minor children, and the sale by the father without the formalities of law for the alienation of minors' property being pursued, did not transfer their title.

These facts and the irregularity of the sale were not much controverted in argument; but it was contended, that West, the vendor of Clague, was also insolvent; that the community property was not sufficient to pay the community debts; and that the fears of the plaintiff were not well founded.

The 2535th article of the Louisiana Code provides that, if the buyer is disquieted in his possession, or has just reason to fear that he will be disquieted, he may suspend payment of the price, until the seller has restored to him possession, or prefers to give him security.

We think the buyer has just reason to fear being disquieted, when he has acquired by a defective title, which does not vest in him a legal right to the property purchased; and that when the title is clearly defective, he has nothing to do with the considerations that may or may not induce others to sue him. No man would wish to acquire property, or hold it, under such contingencies. It is sufficient for the buyer to claim the protection of the law that he holds at the will of others. It was urged that West was insolvent at the death of his wife, and that the children could not hereafter claim the land without becoming responsible for their mother's share of the debts. Admitting this to be true, who can tell what value the property may acquire before the time of prescription will run against the children? We should think there would be much less risk if West were perfectly solvent; for then his children could not accept his succession without becoming responsible for the warranty he gave when he sold to Clague.

Notwithstanding the right of the plaintiff to be relieved, the principal difficulty in the case is, the nature of the relief to which he is entitled.

The court below ordered the sale to be rescinded, and the notes to be given up, unless the defendants give security.

To this judgment we cannot assent. The provisions in that chapter of the Code under which this action was brought, recognise no such right in the buyer though they do in the seller, if the former re-

family meeting should approve? The power once admitted, the only question which could remain would be that of expediency.

An examination of the acts of the general assembly, subsequent to that just quoted, has convinced us that the legislature never contemplated the exercise of such power by the family meeting and the judge of probates.

In the year 1817, it was enacted that the family meeting who authorise the adjudication to the surviving father, or mother, may determine what part of the property shall be mortgaged. But it neither speaks of, nor contemplates, the case of removing the special mortgage when once acquired. Acts of 1817, 122.

Again: In the year 1824, we find a law authorising the husband to raise the legal mortgage in favor of his minor wife, by giving a special one. The law which gave that general mortgage, was not more positive than that which confers on the children a special one on their property purchased by their father or mother: and if positive law were required to do away the effect of the former, we have sought in vain for any reason why it is not equally necessary in the latter.

Still farther, and more conclusively, we see that, by an act passed in the year 1826, it was deemed necessary to provide, that in case one of the children came of age, and could not be paid but by a sale of part of the property adjudicated, so much thereof as was necessary to effectuate this object might be sold; and on this portion of the mortgage of the other children should not attach, provided other property was substituted in its place sufficient to secure them. If the mode now attempted of removing mortgages in favor of the minor be correct, the law was unnecessary; for, if the claim of all the minors can be transferred from one object to another by the advice of a family meeting, it might without the authority of this statute have been changed in respect to any one of them.

We think the judgment of the court below erroneous; that the opposition of the under tutor should have been sustained.

It is, therefore, ordered, adjudged and decreed, that the judgment of the court of probates be annulled, avoided and reversed; and it is further ordered, that the opposition to the homologation of the proceedings be sustained, and that the appellee pay costs in both courts.

Howard v. Cox. VII, N. S. 102.

FIRST District.

No appeal lies from a judgment overruling a plea in the jurisdiction, and an exception to the right of the plaintiff to sue the defendant, without making his other partners parties.

Richardson v. Nolan et al. VII, N. S. 103.

A party relieved, on appeal, from the denial of a continuance, it appearing to the Supreme Court he used sufficient diligence.

What is sufficient cause, shown by this example.

THIRD District.

MARTIN, J., delivered the opinion of the court.

The plaintiff and appellant complains that the district court improperly denied him a continuance.

The affidavit on which he prayed it, states the materiality of the testimony relied on, and its absence without his fault or neglect.

He swears that, in June, he gave a memorandum and directions to his attorney to procure and forward a commission for obtaining the testimony; that soon after, the attorney fell sick, and, a few months after, died; that in the meanwhile, having discovered that the commission had not yet issued, he procured one, and forwarded it by mail to Mobile, in the state of Alabama, where the witness resides; the latter's name, and the facts expected to be proved, are stated, and the other usual statements made.

The continuance was opposed on the ground that the petition had issued in January, and the application in October for time to procure testimony was too late: that the plaintiff urged he had not seen the account of the defendants till October, when it had been on file since June.

We think the continuance ought to have been granted. It is true the petition was filed in January, but the answer was not filed until the middle of June, and the plaintiff could not tell what part of the petition was to be supported by testimony.

It appears he directed a commission to issue as soon as the answer was filed; his counsel fell sick, lingered, and died; before his death he had employed another attorney, and forwarded the commission.

Although the defendant's account may have been filed in June, we can not, without injustice, disbelieve the plaintiff when he swears he did not see it till October. As he had employed counsel, he might have refrained from examining the papers filed in the suit.

It is, therefore, ordered, adjudged and decreed, that the judgment of the district court be annulled, avoided and reversed, the verdict set aside, and the case be remanded for further proceedings, according to law, and that the defendants and appellees pay costs in this court.

Ripley and *Conrad,* for the plaintiff.

Preston, for the defendants.

Balsineur *v.* Bills.   VII, N. S. 105.

The court of probates has alone jurisdiction of a suit against a curator to compel him to account.

The law disqualifying judges of probates from sitting in cases where they were witnesses was repealed by the act of 1828, p. 152, sect. 6.

THIRD District.

PORTER, J., delivered the opinion of the court.

This action is against the curator of a minor, to render an account and pay over the balance in his hands. It was commenced in the court of probates; but the judge of that court having a knowledge of the facts which required his testimony as a witness, he recused himself; and the case, by consent of parties, was transferred to the district court.

After trial there, and verdict, the defendant filed a plea to the jurisdiction of the court, which the judge sustained, and ordered the case to be dismissed.

This case has been argued before us as presenting the same question with several others heretofore decided in this court, on the pro-

[Balsineur v. Bills.]

visions of our old Code; and under which we held, that where the parties permitted judgment to be rendered in the district court, and execution to issue on them, the proceedings were not void. These decisions were predicated upon the fact that the district court did not want jurisdiction *ratione materiæ*, but from the situation or condition of the parties representing the succession, and that such defect of power could be cured by consent.

But by the provisions of our Code of Practice it is expressly declared, that the court of probates shall alone have the power to try causes such as that before us. The expressions being negative of the authority of any other tribunal, we are of opinion that the consent of the parties cannot confer it. Code of Practice, 997, 998, 999.

We think, however, the judge erred in dismissing the cause. It was well brought in the first instance, and should have been sent back to the tribunal from whence it came. The law which disqualified the judge of probates because he has a witness, has been repealed at the last session of the legislature, and the case can now be tried in the court where it originated. Acts of 1828, p. 152, sect. 5.

It is, therefore, ordered, adjudged and decreed, that the judgment of the district court be annulled, avoided and reversed; and it is further ordered, adjudged and decreed, that the cause be remanded to the district court, with directions to the judge to transfer the same to the court of probates of East Baton Rouge; and that the appellee pay the costs of this appeal.

Preston, for the plaintiff.

Union Cotton Manufactory *v.* Lobdell.
VII, N. S. 108.

The *lex fori* regulates the plea of prescription.

THIRD District.

MATHEWS, J., delivered the opinion of the court.

This suit is brought to recover a balance due on a promissory note, which appears to have been made in the state of New York by the defendant, together with one Isaac Lobdell, Jun. The note is alleged to have been executed by partners, (merchants,) and consequently created an obligation joint and several on the promissors. The answer contains a general denial, and a plea of prescription, founded on the laws of New York, and also on the laws of this state. The court below gave a judgment for the plaintiffs, from which the defendants appealed.

The only question in the cause, worthy of notice, arises out of the defence based on prescription. The laws of the place of contract, in relation to limitation or prescription, must be left out of view. The doctrine appears to be fully established, that the *lex fori* alone governs in respect to such matters. The law invoked to support the plea of prescription in the present case, on which the defendant mainly relies, is found in the 3505th article of the Louisiana Code. It prescribes actions founded on instruments similar to that on which this suit is instituted, by the lapse of five years, to be reckoned from the day when they were payable. Previous to the promulgation of the Code, the prescription or limitation of actions like the present was thirty years. The arguments used by the counsel for the defendant in favor of this peremptory exception, have for their foundation the differences between the force and effect of laws relating to legal remedies and those which relate to rights; and a supposed distinction which should be recognised in the application of the former class to contracts made under the operation of foreign laws. It is difficult to perceive any substantial difference between a law which should attempt to destroy a right by taking away entirely the remedy by which it might have been enforced, and one which should attack directly the right itself. They would in our opinion be equally unjust, and violate in the same degree the rule of interpretation, which denies to all laws a retroactive effect, to the prejudice of rights previously acquired.

The maxim of jurisprudence, which prevents from doing indirectly that which cannot be rightfully done directly, we believe to be sound.

This is the first time the court has been called on to interpret new rules of prescription established by the Louisiana Code. The change of limitation for actions from thirty years to five, is very great: and certainly it was not in the contemplation of law-makers, that it should operate instantaneously on contracts and promises, wherein few years had elapsed after the time at which they were to have been performed. Such a construction of the law would indeed have the effect to give it a most iniquitous retroactive influence on the rights of our citizens; and can on no principle of justice, or any fair rule of interpretation, be maintained.

The article of the Code relied on by the defendants, as it relates to the inhabitants of this state, can be only prospective in its operation and effect on the contracts and rights which existed at the time of its enactment. And we are unable to discover any good reason why it should operate differently on the contracts and rights of foreigners who claim the interference of our courts of justice to enforce their claims. The plaintiffs had a right of action against the defendant on the contract which is the foundation of the present suit, up to the period of the promulgation of the Code: it was vested in them, and

[Union Cotton Manufactory *v.* Lobdell.]

would have continued to exist much longer under the old law than the time allowed by the new regulation. Independent of any laws restrictive on the subject, the appellant might be forced by legal pursuit to comply with his promise, without regard to limitation of time. The right of the plaintiffs to make this pursuit was thirty years, by our laws, from the period when the debt to them became due. They failed to sue before the new law, in relation to the remedy, was changed; and their claim must now be regulated by the new law. The remedy has been modified, and must be used in pursuance of this new modification, according to the time therein prescribed, considered prospectively from the date of the last law, whether suits be brought on contracts made under the government of foreign laws or those of our own state. The same rights and privileges, the same restrictions and impediments, in relation to the remedies granted by the *leges fori*, are applicable to them, whether foreign or domestic.

It is therefore, ordered, adjudged and decreed, that the judgment of the district court be affirmed, with costs.

Hennen, for the plaintiffs.
Watts, for the defendant.

Donaldson *et al. v.* Hull.   VII, N. S. 112.

The possessor without a just title, owes the fruits from the beginning of his possession.

PARISH Court of New Orleans.

MARTIN, J., delivered the opinion of the court.

The defendant, in August, 1817, purchased by a notarial act, from West, attorney in fact of two ladies of Baltimore, who styled themselves executors of Mrs. Van Pradelle, their sister, mother of the plaintiffs, a negro woman, her two daughters, and her son. The sale was made without any order of court, and by public auction.

There having been no actual proof of Mrs. Van Pradelle's death, the plaintiffs, on a suggestion that she went to sea in 1813, and has never been heard of, procured themselves to be put in possession of her property and brought the present suit to recover the slaves purchased by the defendant, with their hire from the day of the sale. The parish judge thought the wages due from the institution of the

15*

suit, and allowed 1282 dollars therefor, from which he deducted 570 dollars paid by the defendant, and gave judgment for 712 dollars.

. From the judgment both parties appealed. The plaintiffs complain that the defendant being without a just title, *i. e.*, a title apparently transferring property, he is, though not morally, technically a possessor in bad faith. The title is said to be absolutely void, because it purports to be the evidence of a sale by executors; and such persons can only sell after an order of court, and by public auction; whereas, here there was no order of court; and the sale is, not by auction, but by private contract.

The defendant then is bound to restore the slaves and the value of their services; and we think the parish court erred in confining its judgment to the period that elapsed between the demand and decision of the suit.

The case appears peculiarly a hard one, as the defendant bought in moral good faith, with the knowledge of the only one of the plaintiffs who was of age, and from the aunts of all of them, who had been selected by their mother to protect their interests after her death, and as the plaintiff who was of age received from him her part of the price.

It is to be lamented that the law imposes on courts of justice the obligation of decreeing the restoration of the value of the services of slaves against a possessor who has fairly paid a full price for them, while it authorises them to do no more in the case of a dishonest holder, who has taken them in possession without paying any thing for them.

But on assessing the value of the services which a defendant is to be decreed to restore, we think the same rule ought not to prevail. In assessing damages for their detention, the good faith or dishonest conduct of a defendant should influence us; and if justice demands vindictive damages in the latter case, it prescribes a just moderation in the former. The plaintiff must not receive more than he would if he had been in possession.

The defendant bought a woman thirty-two years of age, who had two daughters, the one eleven and the other seven years of age, and a boy eighteen months old.

Her services, had she been hired by the month, would not have averaged 10 dollars a month or 120 dollars a year, from which a deduction of two months may be made for time lost by sickness, or the impossibility to find a person willing to hire her; and her wages must then be reduced to 100 dollars a year. Her taxes, clothing, medical attendance, and medicines, may be valued at 20 dollars a year, and thus reduce the sum earned to 80 dollars a year net, which would pay the ordinary price of such a woman's purchase in five years.

The services of the daughters, one eleven and the other seven, we have considered on an average as equalling, for both, the services of the mother, or 80 dollars a year: now from the date of the sale to the present date are ten years and ten months, which at 160 dollars a year, make 1728 dollars.

[Donaldson *et al.* *v.* Hull.]

We have considered the boy, who was but eighteen months old, a burthen. He required food, raiment, attendance from the mother, medical attendance, medicines; taxes were paid for him. For this we think 25 dollars a year, less than 50 cents a month, not an extravagant charge for ten years and ten months, make 271 dollars.

Two children were born during defendant's possession. This necessarily induced a loss of the mother's services for a while, some expenses on her lying in, some time lost in nursing, some food, &c. For this we have allowed, for both children, 250 dollars.

But of the defendant's money 570 dollars have actually come to the possession of one of the plaintiffs. If the sale be rescinded, and he charged with full hire from the day of sale, the plaintiffs should allow him the value of the use of his money which actually came to their hands. A jury would certainly consider this in the assessment of damages, and we have deemed it our duty so to do, and have taken five per centum., the legal rate of interest, for the value of the use of the money: thus, during nine years and ten months, this value on 570 dollars, is 208 dollars 57 cents. This, with the sum received, and the last two sums, make 1283 dollars 57 cents, which, deducted from 1728 dollars, leaves a balance due to the plaintiffs of 445 dollars 43 cents.

It is, therefore, ordered, adjudged and decreed, that the judgment of the parish court be annulled, avoided and reversed; and it is further ordered, &c. that the plaintiffs recover from the defendant the slaves mentioned in the petition, and the sum of four hundred and forty five dollars and forty three cents for the value of their services; and it is ordered that the plaintiffs pay costs in this court, and the defendant below.

M'Caleb, for the plaintiffs.

Morse, for the defendant.

Henderson *v.* St. Charles Church.   VII, N. S. 117.

A grant of twenty arpents in front with a depth of forty, passes a superficies of eight
hundred. If the contrary do not appear, the sides will be held to be parallel.

FIRST District.

MATHEWS, J., delivered the opinion of the court.

This action was commenced by the late J. N. Destrehan, and since his death has been prosecuted by the present plaintiff, who has acquired the title to the property in dispute, under which it was held by its former proprietor.

The object of the suit is to settle the upper limit of the plantation now owned by the plaintiff, which separates the ground from that held by the defendants as belonging to the church. The claim set up on the part of the former is for twenty-eight arpents front on the Mississippi, with all the depth of land existing between the river and lake Pontchartain, to be embraced by parallel lines. The latter claim by virtue of the prescription of thirty years; and having obtained judgment in their favor in the court below, the plaintiff appealed.

This action is strictly one of *Bornage.* The principal, if not the sole purpose for which it was instituted, being to determine the course of the line disputed between the parties. It is true, there is an apparent diminution of the extent of front claimed by the plaintiff, according to the plan of survey made, which has been received in evidence. This appears to be occasioned by a change given to the course of the side lines, by running them in a parallel direction, instead of allowing to the upper limit a small inclination, as contended for by the defendants. This incident in the cause needs no farther notice; for the whole evidence fixes the point designated by the letter A, on the plan made by the surveyor general Bringier, under the order of the district court, as that which has been the limit in front, between the plantation of the appellant and the land of the church, for more than thirty years previous to the commencement of the present suit.

The original grants are not in evidence, or any plans of survey purporting to have been made by proper authority at the time of the concessions under which the present parties claim title. According to the date of some of the mesne conveyances, it appears that the grant to the immediate grantee of the government, from which the plaintiff's title is presumed to have been derived, is older than that by virtue of which the defendants have obtained title.

This fact admitted, general principles of law and many decisions of the Supreme Court have been invoked to show that the appellant is entitled to have the whole front claimed by him, together with the quantity of land that may be included between parallel lines running to the extent of his grant: in other words, to the lake.

A concession of a certain number of arpents front on a water course or other object, with what is called in this country the ordinary depth or depth of forty arpents, will give to the grantee such superficies as results from a multiplication of 40 by the number granted in front. The side lines of the tract will be held to be parallel, if no legal impediment be shown to prevent them from taking that course; such as conflicting title of superior legal force, &c.

In actions of bornage, the prescription of 30 years prevailed previous to the Louisiana Code. See the case of Bourguignon v. Boudousquie, lately decided. A limit acquiesced in by a joining proprietor could not, after the lapse of that period, be changed, even by a claimant under a title which was older and better originally than that acquired by prescription. This is true to the fullest extent when uninterrupted possession is shown on the part of the person claiming by prescription, for all the land which he has actually possessed by inclosures, &c. The naked possession, *pro suo*, unsupported by any title, gives right.

The evidence of the present case establishes, free from doubt, that the church had possessed the land which its officers now claim by prescription, above a point fixed and certain, and included by a line of separation between them and the plaintiff, having the course for which they contend, for more than thirty years previous to the commencement of this suit. The direction of the line is ascertained by ditches and a fence between them, running back at different periods or according to the testimony of different witnesses, from three to ten arpents.

It cannot be denied, with the least semblance of truth, that by this possession the defendants have acquired a legal title to all the space actually inclosed, according to the extent and direction of the fence between their land and the plaintiff's plantation. So far it is the unalterable limit between the parties litigant. The only difficulty which the cause presents relates to the continuation of the division line towards the ultimate limits in the rear of the disputed premises.

Neither party, plaintiff or defendant, has shown the course which the lines of the respective tracts ought to take, in pursuance of any authentic document. The grants or concessions from the public under which they claim are both presumed. On this presumption neither of them is without title. But that of the plaintiff is the eldest.

The prescription *longissimi temporis,* as to general principles, is regulated, in most respects, like those which are of short duration. The possession by which it creates title, is under the influence of the 10 and 20 years. See *Pothier, Traite de Possession,* no. 170. Possession is acquired, *corpore et animo,* and the person who enters on a farm, acquires possession of the whole, though he can only occupy a particular spot. See same author, No. 41, and the law of the Roman Digest therein quoted.

The lands of the church, being held under a title derived from the sovereign power of the country which ruled at the time of the grant, it cannot be believed that possession was in any manner usurped without right or authority, by that religious community. By possessing a part of this tract, thus granted, they must be considered as legal possessors of the whole; and if they had shown any plan of survey made by proper authority, which represented the line to be then there, and the appellant's as having the direction for which they contend, the decision of the case would have been freed from all embarrassment. Although no boundary should have been placed (except that of the beginning on the river) nor a single tree marked, if the magnetic course of the line alone had been given, the possessors of the land *pro suo*, would have acquired title to the whole tract *jure prescriptionis*.

The want of direction to the line from any written evidence of title, may, in our opinion, be supplied by the testimony of the witnesses, who prove the course given to the ditches and fence, which form, and have formed, for thirty years at least, to a considerable extent, the common barrier between the plantation of the plaintiff and the land of the church. The latter obtained a concession of 40 arpents in depth, with a front of 10, and the line between this community and their immediate neighbor, sanctioned by prescription, has assumed a certain direction towards the lake or back lands, which must be continued in the same course and direction to the extent of their claim, without distinction in regard to the second concession.

The course given by the direction of the fence establishes the right of appellees to pursue it, (at least to the distance of 40 arpents,) as explicitly as a magnetic course, ascertained by a surveyor and laid down on his plan, could have done. It is true that the second concession made to the person under whom the appellant claims, bears date some time prior to that obtained in favor of the church; but the lateral lines by which it is embraced, according to the request and grant, must have the same direction *aire de vent*, as those which enclosed the plantation immediately on the river: and we have already shown that, in relation to the division line between it and the property claimed by the church, the course of this line is rightfully such as is insisted on by the defendants.

It is, therefore, ordered, adjudged and decreed, that the judgment of the district court be affirmed, with costs.

Seghers, for the plaintiff.

Mazureau, for the defendants.

Sorbé v. Salavignac. VII, N. S. 124.

FIRST District.
An affidavit to obtain a new trial, on the ground that part of a letter, on a different sheet, was not read, should state the contents of that part.

Byrne v. Louisiana State Insurance Company. VII, N. S. 126.

Nothing but necessity justifies a deviation. The necessity is not to be tested by the event, but by all the circumstances attending the case.

FIRST District.

PORTER, J., delivered the opinion of the court.
This is an action on a policy of insurance. The execution of the policy, the interest of the plaintiff in the vessel, her sailing on the voyage insured, and the loss by one of the perils covered by the policy, are all established. The only question, therefore, for our decision, is, whether there was such a deviation from the voyage as discharges the insurers?

From the evidence in the case, it appears that the vessel sailed from New Orleans in the month of January last, on a voyage to Clark's landing on the Rio Brassos. The captain swears that, on the 5th of February last, she arrived off the mouth of the river, and, and on the 7th, succeeded in taking a pilot on board; that under his directions she attempted to enter the river, and, in doing so, grounded; that on trying the pumps after she was afloat, she was found to make considerable water; that the captain and pilot then sounded the bar, to ascertain whether or not there was sufficient water to afford an entrance to the schooner, but were unable to find enough to enable her to pass; that on a survey the next day, they were still more unsuc-

[Byrne v. Louisiana State Insurance Company.]

cessful, not being able to get as much water as they did the day before; that after these examinations were made, it was the decided opinion of them both, that it was not possible for the vessel to enter the river with her cargo on board; that no lighters could be obtained, and that she could not remain in the situation she was in without the greatest risk of being lost, as the current set strong on shore to the west of the river, and if overtaken by a gale of wind from the south, shipwreck was inevitable; that a consultation was then had, and it was the opinion of the pilot and deponent, and of all on board, that the want of sufficient water to enter the river, the leaking condition of the vessel and the danger of remaining on the coast, made it necessary and highly expedient to put into some other port; that in coming to this determination, the deponent was influenced by no other considerations than those of necessity, and the welfare of all concerned; that the vessel accordingly sailed for Galveston bay, which was the nearest port, and one in which the cargo could be landed nearest the port of destination.

The other testimony in the cause strongly corroborates this evidence. The pilot swears that if they had not gone to Galveston, the vessel must have returned to New Orleans, as there was no means in their power to lighten the vessel so as to get her over the bar; that the river was up when the vessel was there; and that she could not have remained off the mouth of the Brassos without being in great danger.

The law which governs the case is well settled. To authorise a deviation there must be a necessity; and this necessity is not, in all cases, to be tested by the event; but more properly by the inquiry whether, under all the circumstances of the case, there was just and reasonable ground for the captain to believe necessity to exist.

In this case it has been contended, on the part of the insurers, that the vessel should have waited a reasonable time at the mouth of the Rio Brassos, to see whether the waters would not rise. But this objection is destroyed by the evidence, which shows she could not have done so without being exposed to great danger. Again: It has been urged she should have remained in the outer part of Galveston harbor, and returned to the Brassos when favorable winds would have raised the waters. There is no evidence before us, which would enable us to say, that she could have got in at any stage of the waters. On the contrary, the pilot swears, she must have returned to New Orleans unless she put into some other port. From aught therefore which appears, the captain would not have been authorised to return to a place which he had already tried, and could not enter, and off which he could not lie without great danger. See Philips on Ins. 192, 196; 11 Johns. 352.

As to the other point in the case, we do not think there was such an unnecessary delay in the port of Galveston as will discharge the defendants.

It is, therefore, ordered, adjudged and decreed, that the judgment of the district court be affirmed, with costs.

Workman and *Hoffman*, for the plaintiff.

Eustis, for the defendants.

Kirkland *v.* His Creditors. VII, N. S. 130.

When a creditor lays claim to a better place on the tableau, it may be opposed by any
• other thereafter, who deems it expedient and he cannot be said to be *in mora*, where
he received notice of this claim. He who pays the note of another, cannot avail himself of the mortgage the latter had given for the benefit of his endorser, unless the
mortgage be assigned him.

THIRD District.

MATHEWS, J., delivered the opinion of the court.

Ingram, who was placed on the tableau of distribution as a chiro-graphary creditor, opposed the homologation, and prayed to be placed as a mortgagee or privileged creditor. His opposition was dismissed, and he appealed.

His counsel has first called our attention to a bill of exceptions.

It appears, that when the application of this opposing creditor was heard, three other creditors of the insolvent filed their opposition to his pretensions to the rank of mortgagee creditor. He resisted the filing of their opposition on the following grounds:

1. All opposition to the tableau of the syndic, and the claims or opposition of creditors to each other, must be filed within ten days from the notification of the filing of the tableau of distribution. 2. Because the appellant had come into court to prove his claim and his right to a higher rank, and had no warning to come prepared to disprove the allegations in the opposition now made to his pretensions by these creditors, except by an oral communication from their coun sel, and therefore he was taken by surprise.

The district court overruled these objections and he excepted to its opinion.

It does not appear to us the district court erred. In a *concurso*, all the insolvent's creditors are plaintiffs and defendants: and any one who thinks he or any other creditor is improperly placed on the tab-leau, must file his claim or his opposition within ten days. But when a claim to a better place is set up within ten days, it may thereafter be opposed by any creditor who deems it urgent, and he can not be said to be *in mora*, because no notice was given of the claim he opposes.

If the appellant was taken by surprise, and wanted evidence to disprove the facts alleged in opposition to his pretensions, he ought to have made his affidavit and claimed a continuance; but he had no right to oppose the filing of the opposition.

The appellant claimed to be ranked as a mortgagee creditor, as assignee of a mortgage given on the 14th of September, 1825, by the insolvent to Browder and others, endorsers of a note of his, which became payable on the 30th of May, 1826. to indemnify from the consequences of their liability. The mortgagees having declined to aid the insolvent in the renewal of the note, the appellant furnished his check payable to the insolvent, with which the note was paid, the 30th of April, 1826.

On the 5th of January, 1827, Browder and others assigned the mortgage the insolvent had given them to the appellant and Croft, "for and in consideration of their having taken up a note of the insolvent on which they (Browder and others) were endorsers."

We do not see that the district court erred. Nothing shows, that previous to the appellant's relieving the insolvent, any agreement took place by which an assignment of the note was stipulated. The endorsers were discharged by the payment of the note if it was made by the insolvent, or by the expiration of the time during which it might have been usefully protested, if purchased by a third person before its maturity, if no protest took place; and their discharge destroyed the effect of the mortgage.

It is, therefore, ordered, adjudged and decreed, that the judgment of the district court be affirmed, with costs.

Watts, for the appellant.

Pradere *v.* Berthelot. VII, N. S. 133.

The appellant cannot be relieved, unless there be a judgment which the Supreme Court may reverse.

PARISH Court of New Orleans.

MARTIN, J., delivered the opinion of the court.

The proceedings in this case began by a petition, in which the plaintiff stated that Carrier owed him 800 dollars on a note secured by a mortgage, which Berthelot, who is said to be the defendant, and who was the payee, endorsed to the plaintiff, who has been subrogated to the rights of Berthelot by a judgment. A writ of seizure and sale was prayed.

No order of the judge for the writ appears; but the writ was issued by the clerk on the 17th of April, 1827, and on the same day the sheriff served a copy of the petition and of a citation on Berthelot. A slave was seized and sold.

Carrier now intervened and prayed an appeal, alleging he had an interest in the suit, and was therefore entitled to appeal. He urged as grounds on which he hoped for success above, that Berthelot's native language and his own was the French and that the plaintiff's petiton was filed in the English language only, and *he* had not been cited. The appeal was granted.

The appellant may have been injured, but the mode of relief has been mistaken. We find no judgment, which we may revise, in the record he has brought.

It is, therefore, ordered, adjudged and decreed, that the appeal be dismissed, with costs.

Chapotin, for the plaintiff.
Cuvillier, for the appellant.

Hewes *v.* Barron.   VII, N. S. 134.

A judge ought not to state what conclusions he draws from the evidence. But if he do' and the verdict appear according to the merits of the case, it will not be remanded.

FIRST District.

PORTER, J., delivered the opinion of the court.

This is an action to rescind a contract for slaves, on the ground that the mother was afflicted with redhibitory vices. The defect complained of is a swelling or large tumor on the leg.

The petition asserts tnat in the act of the sale there is the following clause:—" The parties hereby acknowledging that the said slave Phillis, has a swelling or tumor in one of her legs, which was occasioned by a rheumatism, for which disease the said purchaser renounces all claims whatever against the vendor or his heirs." But it alleges that this renunciation was made in consequence of the fraud practised on the plaintiff by the defendant, in concealing from him the real situation of the slave, and in making him false statements respecting her.

The answer denies generally the allegations in the petition. A supplemental petition was afterwards filed, charging the defendant with having represented the slave as an excellent cook, washer and ironer; of a quiet and mild disposition, and perfectly healthy; while each and all of these representations were false. To this petition a general denial was also put in. The cause was tried by a jury, who found a verdict for the defendant. A new trial was moved for, and refused; and the plaintiff appealed.

The court charged the jury, that there was no evidence of a concealment of the disease of the slave Phillis on the part of the defendant; that the disease was pointed out by the defendant to the plaintiff at the time of the sale: that the defendant, for aught that appeared in proof, had no other reason for knowing the cause of the disease than the plaintiff: but that, if the jury thought she was sold for a first rate cook, washer and ironer, and the evidence proved she was not so, they might reduce the price. The judge closed the charge by instructing the jury they were judges of the fraud alleged.

The plaintiff excepted to the charge, and it is very doubtful to us whether it can be reconciled with the 516th article of the Code of Practice, which inhibits a judge *from saying any thing about the facts,* but as we have been pressed to decide on the merits, and not remand the case, it is unnecessary to express a decided opinion respecting the question which the exception presents.

[Hewes v. Barron.]

But, though it may have been incorrect in the judge to have stated to the jury the conclusion he drew from the evidence, we see no error in those conclusions. A perusal of the evidence induces us to think the view taken by the court below correct; and the finding of the jury under the charge being made on evidence, doubtful, and in some instances contradictory, cannot be disturbed in this court.

It is, therefore, ordered, adjudged and decreed, that the judgment of the district court be affirmed, with costs.

Maybin, for the plaintiff.

Waggaman, for the defendant.

Babcock *v.* Malbie.   VII, N. S. 137.

Creditors can no longer attach the property of the debtor, when he has lost all control over it, and cannot change its destination.

FIRST District.

Porter, J., delivered the opinion of the court.

The petitioner states that the defendant, by a letter dated in Alabama, March 19, 1825, delivered to E. P. Anderson, one of the firm of Farris & Anderson, !who was then setting out for New Orleans, requested Banks, Miller & Kincaid to become responsible for the bearer, promising to guarantee them for any commitments they might make to the extent of 1500 dollars. That the said Anderson afterwards arrived in New Orleans, purchased goods from the petitioner, and delivered him a bill of exchange on Banks, Miller & Kincaid, which they accepted, but failed to pay. By reason whereof the defendant has become responsible to the petitioner.

The general issue was pleaded. The action was commenced by attachment, and third parties intervened, claiming the property as theirs. The court was of opinion the claim was well supported, and gave judgment the suit should be dismissed.

If the court was right in its judgment, it is unnecessary to examine whether the plaintiffs have or not a good cause of action. If the defendant was not properly before the court, there can be no inquiry into his responsibility.

The defendant, a resident of Alabama, was indebted to a house in

16*

[Babcock v. Malbie.]

New York, who forwarded their claim to an agent there for collection. He received an obligation from defendant of one Tucker for 2400 dollars, to be collected and applied to the payment of the claim. By the terms of this obligation, it might be discharged in .cotton at 7 cents per lb. The agent not having at that time any authortty to receive cotton for his principal, agreed with defendant that, if Tucker would pay a part or the whole of his obligation in cotton, it should be shipped to New Orleans or New York at the option of Sheller & King, at the risk of Malbie.

Malbie, some months afterwards, informed the agent that Tucker was ready to deliver cotton, which Malbie by the instruction of the agent received, and took a bill of lading in his name for the delivery of the cotton to B. Story of New Orleans. The agent forwarded the bill of lading to Story, with directions to hold the goods subject to the order of Sheller & King. Story received the bill of lading and the cotton before the service of the attachment, and insured it; but before he could find an opportunity of shipping it, the attachment was laid.

The authority of the agent to enter into an agreement to receive cotton on account of his principals in New York has been contested. But though that authority did not exist when the contract was made, it appears to have been given before the cotton was delivered, and that is sufficient.

The case then is almost precisely that of Canfield v. McLaughlin, reported in 9 *Martin*, except that in this instance the cotton was actually delivered to the persons to whom it was shipped, or to their agent which is the same thing, before the attachment was levied. The interveners were the agents of the owner to sell the cotton, and apply the proceeds to his credit. As such they had a lien on it for their advances, and the balance of the general account. The owner could not have taken it out of their hands, and his creditors can not. We think the rule on this subject was correctly laid down in Armory v. Cockburn, that where the owner of the property has lost all power over it, and can not change its destination, the creditors can not attach. 4 *N. S.* 669; 9 *Mart.* 316.

It is, therefore, ordered, adjudged and decreed, that the judgment of the district court be affirmed, with costs.

Smith, for the plaintiff.

Morse, for the intervening claimant.

Flower *et al. v.* Jones & Gilmore. VII, N. S. 140.

If a paper, rejected when offered as evidence, be accidentally put with the [rest, and taken out with the jury, this circumstance will not necessarily require a new trial.

The principal must relieve the agent from any responsibility properly incurred.

The agent can maintain a suit against the principal not merely for repayment but for indemnity, and the latter can only be released by producing an act by which the creditor accepts him in the place of the agent, or by paying the debt.

EIGHTH District.

Porter, J., delivered the opinion of the court.

The petitioners state that they formerly transacted business in New Orleans as commission merchants, and in that capacity acted on behalf of the defendants, in shipping on their account, to one Henry Thompson of Baltimore, 74 bales of cotton. That Thompson sold 35 bales of this cotton to one Barry, Jun., for 3250 dollars 44 cents; and that the petitioners erroneously supposing that Barry would pay for the same, gave the defendant credit for the net proceeds of the sale, and drew on Thompson a bill of exchange for the amount. That Barry and his endorser both failing, Thompson drew on the petitioners for the sum he had advanced them on the sale of the cotton. That they resisted the demand, but were compelled by a judgment of court to pay it; and that they have expended 400 dollars in defending the suit which Thompson brought against them. The petition concludes by praying judgment against the defendants for these sums, and interest and costs.

The defendants pleaded the general issue. The cause was submitted to a jury in the court below, who found a verdict in favor of the plaintiffs for 3220 dollars 44 cents. An application was made for a new trial, and overruled; and judgment was rendered conformably to the verdict. The defendants appealed.

The correctness of the opinion of the judge in refusing a new trial will be examined after the merits are inquired into, as it mainly depends on the weight which should be given to the evidence the plaintiffs introduced.

The plaintiffs, it appears, were commission merchants in New Orleans, and transacted business for the defendants as general agents. In the year 1818, the latter sent them some cotton, which they shipped, with the approbation and consent of the appellants, to one Thompson, of Baltimore, to be by him sold on their account and risk. This shipment was made on the 31st of December, 1818. The agency of the plaintiffs up to that time, and the correctness of the course they pursued, have not been disputed; but it is urged that all the ulterior proceedings on their part were irregular, and that they have made the transaction their own by the manner in which they acted in drawing the funds out of Thompson's hands, and in failing to give regular notice to the defendants.

In examining this ground of defence, we may take, as admitted, the principles of law which were forcibly urged by the counsel of the appellants in the argument. It may be true, that, the moment Flower communicated to Thompson the names of the persons for whom the cotton was shipped, Thompson became the factor of the principal; that Flower ceased to be the general and became the special agent of the defendants. But whether any or all of the propositions be true, if the defendants have ratified and confirmed the conduct of the plaintiffs in regard to this transaction, it matters not in what capacity they acted.

No express ratification is shown, but one equally strong is derived from the various communications made from time to time to the appellants, and their failure to communicate any disapprobation of it. The contract of mandate may be formed, tacitly as well as expressly. *Semper qui non prohibit pro se intervenire, mandare creditur,* was a maxim of the Roman law. Merlin, in the *Questions de Droit,* gives a number of instances, much stronger than that now before us, where silence by the principal, on the receipt of letters, was deemed in every respect equal to an explicit and positive ratification of the acts of the agent. *Merlin, Questions de Droit, verbo Compte Courant, vol.* 1, *p.* 482; *Manuel, de Droit Français par Paillet,* note on 1985th article of *Nap. Code.*

The assent which the law raises from the failure of the defendants to make any objection to the conduct of the plaintiffs, is proved by the following evidence:

On the 24th April, 1819, they forwarded an account current to the defendants, at the bottom of which it is stated, by way of note or memorandum, that 74 bales of cotton belonging to them had been shipped on their account and risk to Henry Thompson for sale.

On the 31st of July of the same year, in another account, they give the appellants credit for the amount of the cotton shipped to Thompson, and for sale by him.

In a third account, furnished June 1, 1820, the defendants are charged with 1200 dollars, paid by the plaintiffs, on their account, to Thompson, and the balance of 2320 dollars and 44 cents being unsettled by Thompson, is inserted in the body of the account, by way of memorandum, but not carried into the columns.

And on the 31st of July, 1821, in another account, the defendants are credited with 577 dollars and 65 cents, a part of the sum of 1200 dollars, which had been formerly charged them, as paid to Thompson, it being the proportion due by other persons, whose cotton was shipped by the plaintiffs at the same time as the defendants, and sold to the same persons by Thompson.

[Flower *et al. v.* Jones & Gilmore.]

The reception **of** these various accounts, without any opposition being made on the part of the defendants, up to the commencement of this suit, a period of six years, is in law a ratification of the conduct of the plaintiffs in shipping this cotton, in receiving the proceeds, and is an acknowledgment of the liability of the defendants for the balance due, when Thompson's claim against the plaintiffs was settled.

In addition to this, we have it in evidence that when the plaintiffs were sued by Thompson, one of the defendants went in company with W. Flower to the counsel who was engaged to defend it, and stated to him that he was interested in the suit.

It is now contended, the plaintiffs did not communicate as quickly as they ought to have done, intelligence of the dishonor of the bill taken by Thompson; and a good deal was said of the propriety of admitting evidence of the copy of a letter written by the plaintiffs in October, 1819, the receipt of which is denied by the defendants.— Whether the testimony was sufficient or not, we need not inquire; being of opinion that after the assent given by the defendants to a charge against them, in various and subsequent accounts current, for moneys paid on account of the non-payment of Barry's note, there was such a ratification of the acts of the plaintiffs, as discharges them from the responsibility they may have incurred by the alleged improper management of the business entrusted to them. Acts of the principal should be construed liberally in favor of an adoption of the acts of the agent; and an implied assent has the same effect in waiving a right of action for misconduct that an express one would. See Livermore on Agency, vol. 1, p. 50 and 338, 392, 396, and the authorities and cases there cited.

It is again urged that Thompson, by blending the sale of the defendants' cotton with his own in Baltimore, made the debt his. Supposing this position to be correct, on which we express no opinion, the plaintiffs are not responsible for Thompson's misconduct. They were used as the medium of communication between the principal and the foreign factor, and through them the funds proceeding from the sale were to be transmitted. So far as they have failed in that duty, they are responsible; but they are not answerable for the misconduct of the factor in Baltimore.

But it is said they have made themselves so: First, by accepting the bill Thompson drew to replace the advances he had made on the cotton; and, Secondly, by not using the legal means they might have urged in defence of the action Thompson instituted on this bill.

The acceptance did no injury to the defendants, for the plaintiffs afterwards refused to pay it, and compelled Thompson to bring suit on it, where every matter of defence was open that would have been on the original transaction. The defendants had notice of the action brought by Thompson, and they chose to trust it to the plaintiffs, who appear to have honestly used all the means in their power to prevent judgment being rendered against them. The additional proof now produced does not appear to us to vary the case.

[Flower *et al. v.* Jones & Gilmore.]

A question has been made, whether the plaintiffs had a right to bring this action before they paid Thompson the amount of the judgment against them. There is no doubt they have that right. The agent can maintain a suit against the principal, not merely for repayment, but for indemnity; and the latter can only be released by producing an act by which the creditor accepts him in place of the agent, or by paying the debt. The reason of such a rule is obvious. As the agent is obliged to transfer to the principal all rights which he might have acquired under the power of attorney, the latter must release him from any obligation he might incur in the performance of it. *Dig. Liv. tit.* 17, *law.* 45; *Pothier, Contrat de Mandat, no.* 80.

There remains for consideration the motion made for a new trial. A paper was presented in evidence, and rejected by the court.— Through mistake of the clerk, it was put up among the documents and carried out by the jury. Whether it was read by them or not we do not know. The defendants insist it may have materially influenced their judgment. The plaintiffs contend that if they did notice it, they must have recalled its rejection by the court, and have given it no weight in making up their verdict.

A case has been read from the reports of Massachusetts, where, under precisely similar circumstances, a verdict was set aside; and the opinion of that court would have great weight with us, if we were not placed in an entirely different situation. In that country, if we mistake not, all the facts of a case are tried and settled by a jury. Here we sit, not merely as a court for the correction of errors in law, but with the power to revise the conclusion drawn by the inferior tribunal from the facts. The court in Massachusetts being therefore bound to take the facts from the jury, did right not to receive them, if any irregularity occurred in the proceedings, because it could not know what influence that irregularity had on their finding. Here the whole of the evidence comes up, and is spread before us for our judgment. We are therefore enabled to know whether the mistake had or not an influence on the minds of the jury. In the present instance, the facts proved lead us irresistibly to the conclusion that, without this paper, the jury could have found no other verdict. If they had, our duty would have compelled us to reverse it, for the case depends not on the weight to be given to evidence, but on questions of law.

We cannot therefore turn the parties over to a re-investigation, which must end, as it is now about to do, by our judgment. If the case were a doubtful one, we would remand it. If improper evidence had been admitted to go to the jury, we would, as we have heretofore, send it back. But here, in the uncertainty we are, whether they perused the paper or not, the presumption that, if they did, they remembered the decision of the court that it was not evidence, and the certainty that there is ample evidence to sustain the verd.ct without it, the judgment of the court below must be confirmèd.

[Flower *et al. v.* Jones & Gilmore.]
It is, therefore, ordered, adjudged and decreed, that the judgment
of the district court be affirmed, with costs.
Hennen, for the plaintiffs.
Ripley and *Mc Caleb,* for the defendants.

Parker *v.* Starkweather.   VII, N. S. 150.

The defendant can only offer in compensation what the plaintiff owes him.
The plaintiff does not owe to the defendant the sum offered in compensation, when the
defendant owes him on another account a larger sum, which extinguishes it.

FIRST District.

PORTER, J. delivered the opinion of the court.
The plaintiff sued the defendant, claiming 850 dollars, for the rent
of a house and blacksmith's shop.
The defendant pleaded that he owed the plaintiff but 300 dollars,
for rent, and that the plaintiff was indebted to him in a larger amount
viz. the sum of 1094 dollars, for the balance of which he prayed
judgment.
To this, the plaintiff filed an answer, in which he alleged the defendant to be indebted to him for other matters than those set forth
in the petition, in the sum of 851 dollars and 95 cents.
The judge below refused leave to the plaintiff to give any evidence
in support of the matters set out in the plea in compensation. On
the cause coming here on appeal, the case was remanded with directions to the judge to admit the plaintiff to prove the account which
he offers as compensation to the defendant's demand in reconvention.
When the cause was on trial the second time, the defendant requested the court to charge the jury, that the plaintiff could not compensate his account filed to the reconvention of the defendant, to any
other or greater amount than for the balance claimed by Starkweather. The judge refused to give such a charge, and the defendant
appealed.
The effect of the charge asked for, would be, that instead of the
plaintiff being able to set up the whole of his demand against that of
the defendant, viz. the 850 dollars claimed in his petition, and the
851 dollars claimed by him in his answer to the defendant's demand

[Parker v. Starkweather.]

in reconvention and plea in compensation, he could only oppose a
sum sufficient to extinguish the balance the defendant averred to be
due him.   The case would then stand thus: The plaintiff claims
850 dollars.   Defendant avers the plaintiff owes him 1094 dollars.—
The plaintiff replies the defendant is indebted to him 851 dollars;
but as the balance due the defendant, by petition and answer, is only
244 dollars the plaintiff can only compensate that amount, and must
suffer the debt set forth in the petition, to be extinguished, although
the defendant owe him 606 dollars more.   This argument overlooks
the fact that the defendant can only rightfully compensate the demand
made in the petition by what is really due to him, and that the plaintiff does not owe the defendant the amount offered in compensation
by the answer, when the defendant is indebted to the plaintiff in another sum which extinguishes that set up by the defendant in his answer.   The whole matter must be tried together.   The attempt made
here is very novel and ingenious but it is quite incorrect, and the
judgment of the court below must be affirmed, with costs.

  Preston, for the plaintiff.
  Hennen, for the defendant.

EASTERN DISTRICT, JULY TERM, 1828.

Adams *v.* Lewis. VII, N. S. 153.

FOURTH District.

A privileged creditor has a right to a provisional seizure.

The seizure accorded by articles 284 and 285, Code of Practice, is not limited to cases in which the pledge was in possession of the creditor.

Bourguignon *v.* Boudousquie. VII, N. S. 156.

FIRST District.

Execution may issue on a judgment, which does not settle every claim of the parties: as for example, when there is a decree that plaintiff be put into possession of the land, but the cause to be remanded for inquiring into damages.

Singletary *et al. v.* Singletary.   VII, N. S. 158.

EIGHTH District.

An executor who qualified in another state, and removes to this state the property of the estate, is suable in the district court.

He never was an executor here, but one who has been executor elsewhere. The property which is claimed from him was not the testator's when it was brought into this state, but that of the heirs.

Love *v.* Dickson.   VII, N. S. 160.

EIGHTH District.

In the 254th article of the Code of Practice, the word "garnishee" was, by a clerical error, employed for "defendant."

Abat *v.* Whitman.   VII, N. S. 162.

The use of a common law denomination of a process does not necessarily introduce the English practice, such as *capias ad satisfaciendum.*

FIRST District.

PORTER, J., delivered the opinion of the court.

The only question in this cause is, whether a debtor who has been arrested on a writ of *capias ad satisfaciendum*, and discharged out of custody by the consent of the plaintiff, is not discharged of the debt, and whether this discharge does not operate in favor of those who were bound jointly and severally with him.

By the laws in force in Louisiana antecedent to the change of government, no such consequence followed the discharge of a debtor from imprisonment. By the common law of England it did. No statute of the state, or the former territory of Orleans, has repealed in express terms the rules previously in force. If, therefore, our former law is repealed, it must be from the use of the words *capias ad satisfaciendum*, in the act of the legislative council.

The repeal of laws is never presumed; and if the new and old laws can stand together, they should be so construed. It would be going far, to hold that the special enactment of a remedy which previously existed, should introduce the consequences that attended that remedy in another system of jurisprudence. In this respect there is a material difference between this case and that construction which should be given to our laws introducing *jury trial*, and the writ of *habeas corpus;* for they being unknown to our jurisprudence, the understanding of them was *ex necessitate*, to be sought somewhere else. The use of common law terms is easily accounted for, in the desire of the legislature to use those words which would convey in the most clear and concise manner, to persons acquainted with the English language alone, the remedies defined. And though the terms *capias ad satisfaciendum* is not English, yet it is well known that in those countries where the common law prevails, its meaning is as well understood as any word of their vernacular tongue which is used in law proceedings. So early as the year 1813, this court said that common law terms ought to be considered rather as a translation of the names formerly used than as emanating from the English jurisprudence. That their adoption as words can by no rule of law be considered as having introduced the English practice. 3 *Martin,* 185.

It is, therefore, ordered, adjudged and decreed, that the judgment of the district court be annulled, avoided, and reversed; that the cause be remanded, to be proceeded in according to law; and that the appellee pay the costs of the appeal.

Seghers, for the plaintiff.
Eustis, for the defendant.

Landry *et al. v.* Peytavin.   VII, N. S. 165,

FIRST District.

This was the case of a contract to build the state house at Donald-sonville.

The court, MARTIN, J., said:—From the evidence before us, it results, that the contractor, at the inception, had delayed the completion of the work he had engaged to perform, about four months and a half.

That the state had become indebted to him, and he had received cash and warrants for 20,250 dollars, 8050 of which had been punctually paid; and that in the payment of the remaining 12,200 dollars, he had been delayed for an averaged period of some three to six months, (one-third of the time he had taken to complete the work.) The warrant of 4000 dollars having been delayed six months; that of 5200 from eight to twelve months; and the last two, for 3000, six months; during which, more than one half of the funds he was entitled to receive, were kept back.

It is urged that the contract spoke of payments to be made in cash, and others in warrants on the treasury; and the contractor, as to the warrants, took his chance in regard to the state of the treasury. To this it is replied that the cash payments were only 900 dollars, not four per cent. on the price; that the payments stipulated for during the progress of the work, were evidently intended to enable the contractor to procure materials and pay his hands; and on stipulating that warrants on the state treasury should be delivered him, he must be understood to have stipulated that such warrants must be paid.

The commissioners have at least manifested their zeal for the interest of the state. Ours is the more august function of displaying her justice, and extending her protection to the humblest individual prosecuted by her officers, when their zeal leads them beyond the bounds of moderation.

We think the contractor has clearly shown that his activity has been checked, and his progress arrested, by the detention of the means he had calculated upon for the performance of his contract. In such a case the law is, that as the creditor has, by his own failure, prevented the debtor from complying with his engagement, the penalty is not recoverable. *ff.* 1, 45. 122, *s.* 3; *Hulot*, 52; 9 *Merlin's Repertory*, 228, 229; *Yerby, Peine Contractuelle.* If any proper delay should thereafter occur in the completion of the work, the defendant, though free from the penalty, will be responsible for the damages.

It is, therefore, ordered, adjudged and decreed that the judgment of the district court be annulled, avoided and reversed; and that ours be for the defendant.

Porter, for the appellees.
Moreau, for the appellant.

Kernion *v.* Guenon.   VII, N. S. 171.

PARISH Court of New Orleans.
The plaintiff cannot be nonsuited against his will.
A trespasser cannot allege that the plaintiff has a title which is voidable.

An objection has been made to the plaintiff's title because the act under which he claims the land is a private instrument, without a price, or which is the same thing, without a serious price, the consideration expressed in it being *one dollar.* But this objection cannot be received on the part of a trespasser. The nullity set up is not absolute, but relative, and no one can take advantage of it but the vendor or his heirs.

Powell *v.* Chappell.   VII, N. S. 172.

A register of the land office cannot be compelled by a writ of *mandamus,* in a suit to which he is not a party, to grant a certificate.

EIGHTH District.

MARTIN, J., delivered the opinion of the court.
The plaintiff claimed a tract of land in the possession of the defendant. The general issue was pleaded.

[Powell v. Chappell.]

The plaintiff prayed for a mandamus to the register and receiver of the land office of the United States at St. Helena court house, directing them to grant him a certificate of confirmation of the land sued for. The mandamus was refused, and he appealed.

It appears the mandamus was prayed for in the appellant's affidavit; that the certificate was necessary to him in the prosecution of his suit; that he had applied for it, and it had been refused; and he was legally entitled to it.

Admitting the right of the appellant to the certificate, the consequent obligation of the register and receiver to grant it, and the authority of the district court to interpose in favor of the appellant against them, he must seek his remedy in a distinct suit against them, at their domicil; and if we are to be called upon to express an opinion against or in favor of either, it must be in a suit in which they are a party.

Any court may compel the production of evidence in the possession of any person not a party to the suit, by the delivery of a copy as the production of an original paper; but where the evidence is to be exacted, which the party from whom it is required contends he is not bound to grant, the right of the applicant must be acted on contradictorily, with the person who refuses, but not incidentally as a suit in which he has no interest, and in a distant parish, to suit the convenience of the appellant.

It is, therefore, ordered, adjudged and decreed, that the appeal be dismissed, with costs.

Ripley and *Conrad*, for the appellant.
Hennen, for the appellee.

Randolph *v.* Daunoy.　VII, N. S. 174.

Held, the existence of a servitude must be established by proof positive, or otherwise irresistible.

FIRST District.

MARTIN, J., delivered the opinion of the court.

The petition states that the defendant's land, contiguous to the plaintiff's, is burdened with a servitude whereby the water that falls on the latter has its way through the former, and the defendant has

[Randolph *v.* Daunoy.]

stopped up the passage of the water through her lot, to the injury of the plaintiff. It concludes with a prayer that she be enjoined from preventing or obstructing the passage of the water from the plaintiff's lot through hers, &c.

The existence of the servitude was denied; the defendant had judgment, and the plaintiff appealed.

The statement of facts shows that the vendor of both parties built two houses in a block, which covered the whole lot on which they stand, so that the water which falls into the yard of the upper house, purchased by the plaintiff, can have no passage but over the yard of the house purchased by the defendant, or by a gutter to be made through the corridor or entry of the former house. There is now, and there has been for some time, a hole of the size of a hat, in the wall which separates both yards, through which the water passes from the plaintiff's yard into that of the defendant. It is not proved that this hole was left in the wall when it was erected, though one witness deposed he believed it was; but two others depose it has the appearance of having been made, by taking out a few bricks from the wall. It existed while the two houses belonged to the vendor of the parties, and he had noticed it. It was at times closed by the tenant of the lower house; but when she was requested to leave it open to avoid an inconvenience to the owner, she consented. It would cost about fifty dollars to have a gutter made through the entry or passage, to lead the water from the yard to the street.

On the facts, we think the district judge did not err in concluding that the plaintiff had failed to establish the existence of the servitude. It is not proved that the hole was left in the wall; and the witness who expresses his belief that it was, speaks only from the appearance of the bricks. Two others think differently.

The servitude not being proved, we think judgment was properly given for the defendant.

It is, therefore, ordered, adjudged and decreed, that the judgment of the district court be affirmed, with costs.

Maybin, for the appellant.

P. Derbigny, for the appellee.

WESTERN DISTRICT, SEPT. TERM, 1828.

Cormier *et al. v.* Richard *et al.*   VII, N. S. 177.

An attorney does not disclose professional secrets when he deposes to the plea he was directed to file in court.

FIFTH District, Judge of the Seventh presiding.

Martin, J., delivered the opinion of the court.

The petition states that L. Richard bought a tract of land from Gerard and wife, for 2500 dollars, payable in two equal instalments, in May, 1823 and 1824, with the privilege of postponing payment during three years, on paying interest at the rate of ten per cent. a year; and on the same day he and the other defendants executed their joint and several notes to Gerard for that sum, payable by two equal instalments on the same days; and no part thereof being paid on the last day of May, 1824, Gerard brought suit against the defendants, who availed themselves of the stipulation made in the act of sale in favor of the vendees, and Gerard dismissed his suit. Afterwards, Gerard and wife transferred the notes to the present plaintiffs, who now prayed for judgment against the defendants, with legal interest from the judicial demand; and farther, against L. Richard, interest at ten per cent. on each instalment, from the time it became due, until the judicial demand, and then at five per cent.

The general issue was pleaded; but the execution of the notes was admitted. There was judgment for the plaintiff, with interest at five per cent. They appealed.

As to L. Richard, the only question is, whether the notes created a novation of the debt, resulting from the act of sale. We think they did not. The debtor was not discharged; because such discharge must be express, and is not to be implied.

The judge *a quo* has thought there was no evidence connecting the debt resulting from the notes with that resulting from the act of sale. It is in evidence that when these three defendants were sued on their notes, they employed an attorney to resist the claim, on the ground that the amount of the notes was the consideration of the sale, and the vendee had the faculty of postponing payment during three years, on paying interest at the rate of ten per cent.

To the testimony of the witness who deposed to the fact (the attorney) there is a bill of exceptions. It was objected that the attorney came to disclose professional secrets. We think the district court did not err in overruling this objection. The direction to resist the claim on the ground stated, was not a secret confided to the attorney, since he was to spread the opposition on the record.

The testimony leaves no doubt on our minds that the allegation in the petition, that the notes were given for the price of the land, is duly proved. The defendant, L. Richard, was therefore bound to pay interest at ten per cent.; but as an interest at five per cent. has been allowed, he owes only an additional interest at five per cent. from the original days of payment until the judicial demand, as prayed for.

As to the other two defendants, the judgment is according to the prayer of the petition.

It is, therefore, ordered, adjudged and decreed, that the judgment of the district court be annulled, avoided and reversed, and that the plaintiffs recover from the defendants two thousand three hundred and ninety-four dollars; a credit of one hundred and six dollars being admitted, with legal interest from the judicial demand; and further, from the defendant, L. Richards, an additional interest of five per cent. on eleven hundred and forty-four dollars, from the last day of May, 1823, and on twelve hundred dollars, from the last day of May, 1824, up to the judicial demand; the defendants paying costs in both courts.

Lesassier and *Bowen*, for the plaintiffs.
Brownson, for the defendants.

Mayfield *v.* Comeau.   VII, N. S. 180.

Three creditors are necessary to form a *concurso*, but three are not necessary to form a meeting.

The creditor of an insolvent who is put on the *bilan*, cannot object to the regularity of the proceedings in a case where the effect of them is collaterally involved.

The sale of an insolvent's estate must be made on the same terms, and under the same formalities, as property seized in execution.

It is an essential pre-requisite of sales under execution, that public notice should be given of the time and place at which they are to be made. A purchaser under a forced sale does not acquire a good title when the formalities of law have not been pursued.

FIFTH District, Judge of the Seventh presiding.

Porter, J., delivered the opinion of the court.

This is an action to recover possession from the defendant, of a tract of land which the plaintiff purchased at the sale of an insolvent's estate.

The defendant was insolvent whose estate was sold by auction, and in his answer he has set forth several grounds of defence to the demand contained in the petition. They principally relate to irregularities in the sale, and the proceedings previous thereto. As an insolvent debtor has no right to call in question the legality of the measures pursued by his creditors after his cession is accepted, and a syndic appointed, we are freed from the necessity of examining any of the objections raised, except these, which deny that the cession was accepted, or a syndic duly appointed.

We are, however, of opinion that both these objections are untenable. Three creditors may be necessary to form a *concurso*, but the presence of three is not required to form a meeting. This point has been already decided in the case of Turcas *v.* L'Eglise. The proceedings of the two creditors who appeared before the notary, accepted the cession, and voted for a syndic appear to us free from any objection, and to have been conducted according to law. 4 *N. S.* 462.

One of the creditors who was placed on the *bilan*, and who failed to appear in the judgment of *concurso*, though duly cited so to do, has intervened in this cause, and in his petition of intervention has stated various matters why the possession claimed should be refused, and the sale to the plaintiff annulled.

These matters may be resolved into the following points.

1. That the creditors were never called to deliberate on the terms

of the sale; and that no notice of such meeting was ever given to the interpleader.

2. That if there was such a meeting, a sufficient number of creditors did not attend.

3. That the proceedings were not homologated before the 2d day of December, 1826, and that the property surrendered could not be disposed of previous to the homologation.

4. That the sale was illegally made for cash, when there was no special mortgage on the property.

5. That the sale was not advertised according to law.

All these objections, except that which relates to the advertisement of the property, may be considered and disposed of together. The interpleader was put on the bilan of the insolvent, and duly cited. Being thus a party to the suit in *concurso*, the judgment of homologation forms *res judicata* against him, and until that judgment be reversed, on appeal or otherwise, he is concluded by all the matters embraced by it. It would be an intolerable abuse to permit the various creditors of an insolvent, after all the proceedings had gone through without objection, to drop in one by one, and try them over again in suits in which the regularity of these proceedings was collaterally involved. This point was decided in this court so far back as the year 1816 in the case of Dussau's Syndics *v.* Bedaux, 4 *Martin*, 450.

But the interpleader contends, this homologation does not cure any defects in the sale, because the judgment of the court is prospective; authorising the property ceded to be sold; whereas at the time this judgment was rendered, the land in question had already been disposed of by the syndics. The judgment of homologation is of date the 2d of December. The sale is of the 9th of October, in pursuance of an order of court of the 23d of August preceding.

This irregularity most probably arose from inattention, at the time the judgment was drawn up, to what had been already done in the case. But as the syndic proceeded in strict conformity to law, by applying to the court for, and obtaining, an authorisation to sell the property, we are unable to see any thing which can prevent the court below confirming the sale, when the homologation of the tableau of distribution is there applied for.

It is still, however, contended, on the part of the plaintiff in intervention, that had the evidence which he offered in the court below been received, much would have been shown to have prevented the sale receiving the sanction of the court.

The act of 1817 directs that the syndics of an insolvent's estate shall, after obtaining an order of the judge, sell the property surrendered by public auction. No length of time is prescribed, by the statute, for the sale to be advertised. But a provision in the late amendments to our Code, has taken away all doubt on the subject by directing the sale of insolvent's property to be made on the same terms, and under the same formalities, as property seized on execu-

[Mayfield v. Comeau.]

tion. The act of 1826, indeed, authorises the creditors to vary the terms and conditions, but does not confer on them the power to dispense with the formalities which the Code prescribes; and if it had, as was contended, our conclusion in this case must be the same, for the creditors recommended the property to be sold "upon such notice of the time and place of the sale as may be required by law." Louisiana Code, 2180; Acts of 1826, 138, sect. 3.

It is an essential prerequisite of sales under execution, that public notice should be given of the time and place at which they are to be made. The bill of intervention avers, that in the instance before us, there was not any public notice given of the time and place of making the sale, and the bill of exceptions states, that evidence to prove the allegations in the petition, was rejected by the judge. In rejecting such proof, we think he erred. It has been already more than once decided in this court, on authorities which need not be now referred to, that a purchaser under a forced sale does not acquire a good title, where the formalities prescribed by law for the alienation have not been pursued. 4 *Martin*, 573; 11 *Ibid.* 610.

It is, therefore, ordered, adjudged and decreed, that the judgment of the district court be annulled, avoided and reversed; and it is further ordered, adjudged and decreed, that the cause be remanded, with directions to the judge *a quo* not to reject evidence on the part of the petitioner in intervention, that the property claimed by the plaintiff had not been advertised according to law; and it is further ordered that the appellee pay the costs of this appeal.

Brownson, for the plaintiff.
Simon, for the defendant.

Barbineau's Heirs *v.* Castille *et al.*   VII, N. S. 186.

Creditors of a succession cannot sue the heirs, while an action in which the same matters are involved, is pending between the curator and the defendants.

The curator of an estate is not a good witness where the legality of his conduct is at issue.

A party who refuses to bring in testimony unless his adversary will waive the right of commenting on its effect, cannot have the cause remanded to procure that testimony. Until the curator of a succession makes a demand of the heirs of the effects belonging to it, they are not in fault in retaining them.

FIFTH District, Judge of the Seventh presiding.

[Barbineau's Heirs v. Castille et al.]

Porter, J., delivered the opinion of the court.

The plaintiffs, who are mortgage creditors of one Augustin Bijeau, deceased, seek by this action to make the defendants, his widow, and her son by a former marriage, responsible in their private capacity for the debts due by the estate of the deceased. The petition charges, that notwithstanding the defendants had renounced all claims to his succession, they had lost the benefit of their renunciation: the widow, by taking an active concern in the community; by appropriating the effects belonging thereto to her own use—by concealing part of them, and not putting them on the inventory—by keeping in her possession the land sold by the petitioners to her husband, which was mortgaged to them, and by bringing suit against the succession for a sum of money.

The grounds of action against the son, who was testamentary heir of the deceased, are nearly the same as those alleged against the mother, with the addition of his not acknowledging himself debtor of a large sum which he owed his step-father; as also his working the slaves of the estate for his use and benefit.

The answer of the defendants, after denying all the allegations in the petition, except that Bijeau signed the note on which the suit is brought, and that the defendants had renounced; proceeds to state, that Bijeau died largely indebted to them, that they renounced his succession, and that a curator had been appointed to it. That this curator had advertised property of theirs for sale as belonging to the estate of Bijeau; that they had applied for and obtained an injunction to prevent his selling this property; and that as they were privileged creditors to a large amount, and apprehended a great sacrifice would be made of the other property of the estate in the manner it was announced for sale, they had obtained an injunction to prevent him disposing of it.

On this issue, testimony, oral and written, was taken in the court below, and the judge rendered judgment of nonsuit against the plaintiffs, being of opinion that the plaintiffs should have brought their action against the curator appointed for the vacant estate of Bijeau, and discussed the property mortgaged before they instituted this action. That in any event it could only lie against the defendants for the balance.

It is stated in the petition, that the defendants had commenced suits against the curator of the succession, for property belonging to it, to which they set up title; and that in these actions they had enjoined the sale of the remaining portion of the effects appertaining to the estate. The answer echos these facts, and avers the correctness and legality of the suits. The records of both actions have been made a part of the evidence in this case, and it appears that they are yet pending and undecided.

One of the most serious inquiries which the case presents, is, whether the pendency of these suits does not preclude us from an examination of many of the most important matters set out in the petition, and it appears to us that they do. In every thing claimed in this action, which relates to the property contested for with the curator, both as to title, and right to enjoin the sale, we must await the decision of the suits in which these questions have been first put at issue. That the same matters form the *litis contestatio* in these actions, though presented in a different form of action, we think will appear manifest, by supposing judgment to be rendered in the suit between the curator and the defendants; and then inquiring into its effect. If it should, peradventure, be decided that the latter had a good title to those very effects, the detention of which is now charged on them as a ground for their being responsible as heirs pure and simple; and in addition to a right to this portion of the objects claimed as making a part of the succession, that they were also in the exercise of their legal rights in inhibiting the sale of the remainder; most certainly, that judgment would be a bar to the present action, in every thing relating to the detention and use of that property.

If the averments in the petition were, therefore, confined to charging the defendants with detaining and administering the slaves and other effects claimed by the defendants, we should be of opinion that the suit ought to be dismissed.

But the allegations of the plaintiffs go further, and cover more ground, than the mere detention of the land and slaves to which the defendants set up a claim. They charge the defendants with concealing effects belonging to the deceased, and failing to put them on the inventory. They also accuse them with retaining other property of the succession in their hands contrary to law, and using it for their own benefit. The issue joined on these matters compels us to examine this branch of the case on its merits.

In the view we have taken of them, we are saved the necessity of inquiring whether the opinion of the district court rests on solid and legal grounds, as on other reasons we are brought to the conclusion that the judgment given below must be confirmed here.

Two bills of exceptions appear on record. The first is to an opinion of the judge refusing permission to the curator of the estate to testify in the present suit. The reasons given by the judge for rejecting him, were "that the petition charges the defendants with keeping back part of the property mentioned in the inventory, and not delivering it to the curator. They answer it was by his consent. If by his consent, it discharges them, and may go to charge him, for not taking it into possession." In this reasoning, and conclusion, we concur. The case does not fall within the rule which makes servants and agents witnesses *ex necessitate*. The curator had the authority and the means to have made the demand in presence of witnesses, and to have taken legal steps to enforce a delivery of the property.

The second is to the rejection of a number of witnesses who were offered to prove the possession of the effects belonging to the estate by the defendants, and of their having used them. This testimony was objected to, on the ground that if they did use it, they committed a trespass; but that such proof furnished no reason for charging them as heirs. Whether this position be true or not, we need not inquire; for, admitting it to be correct, the objection went to the effect of the testimony. It furnished no reason for rejecting the evidence, and the court greatly erred in sustaining such an opposition. The counsel for the defendants, after they had succeeded in excluding the testimony, offered to admit it, reserving all objections as to its effect. This reservation need not have been made, for all evidence is open to observation as to its effect; or in other words, to what it proves; and the offer was in truth the same as an unconditional consent to admit it. The plaintiff's counsel, however, would not accede to the proposition; and why, we are totally at a loss to conceive. He certainly could not expect the opposite parties to abandon their right of commenting on the influence and effect of the proof which their adversary presented; and after a refusal of this kind, so unreasonable in itself, and so contrary to law, we cannot in justice to the opposite party remand the cause to enable the evidence to be procured.

We come the more readily to this conclusion, because the testimony of the very witnesses, whose names appear on the bill of exceptions, is afterwards spread on the record. How it came there we can not tell; the parties differ in their explanation, and we must take it as legally there. We have perused it with attention, and far from proving a concealment of the effects of the succession, it has produced on our minds an impression of the fairness of the defendants' conduct, in disclosing to the judge every thing which they conceived belonged to the estate. There is no evidence the curator ever made a demand of them, to deliver up the effects of the succession; and until he did, they were not in fault in retaining them.

It is, therefore, ordered, adjudged and decreed, that the judgment of the district court be affirmed, with costs.

Simon, for the plaintiffs.
Brownson, for the defendants.

Dejean's Syndics *v.* Martin's Heirs.　VII, N. S. 194.

FIFTH District.

The surety on a twelvemonths' bond cannot compel the obligor to proceed against the land sold, if the obligee's wife has obtained an injunction, which he unsuccessfully attempted to have dissolved. Louisiana Code, art. 3016.

Pierre *et al. v.* Massey *et al.*　VII, N. S. 196.

FIFTH District, Judge of the Seventh presiding.

A party who wishes to interplead must show that the decision of the case is to affect his rights,

It is not enough that he shows that he has claims to enforce against either of the parties.

Sterling *v.* Luckett.　VII, N. S. 198.

FIFTH District, Judge of the Seventh presiding.

The court may reject evidence which it deems immaterial.

Delahoussaye *v.* Delahoussaye *et al.* VII, N. S. 199.

A privileged or mortgagee creditor, is not obliged to discuss the undivided property of a succession.
Third parties are not bound by the recitals in an act of sale.

. FIFTH District, Judge of the Seventh presiding.

. MATHEWS, J., delivered the opinion of the court.
The plaintiff in this case, after having obtained judgment against his tutor, for the amount or value of his property, which the latter had administered and wasted in his capacity as tutor aforesaid, commenced the present action to obtain a decree of the court below, which should authorise him to enforce his tacit mortgage against the property, now in the possession of several persons, made defendants to this suit, as having been acquired from his tutor, and on which he has a lien to secure the payment of the judgment by him obtained as aforesaid. These latter defendants appeared in court, and one of them pleaded in opposition to the plaintiff's claim on property by him held and and possessed as a purchaser from the tutor, his right to require of said plaintiff to discuss the property still in the possession of Balthazar Delahoussaye; and also such as had been sold by the latter subsequent to the sale made to him this defendant. He pointed out, by enumeration, a variety of articles of property, to the number of nineteen, still held by the principal defendant and other persons who derived title from the latter, which, he alleged, ought, according to law, to be discussed, before that which he held could be subjected to the influence of the plaintiff's lien. The judgment of the district court ordered only three of the articles of property designated in the answer to be discussed, viz: those pointed out in Nos. 1, 6 and 12; and the defendant Raymond François being dissatisfied with the decree thus rendered, appealed. The answer of the plaintiff on the appeal, admits the correctness of the judgment rendered in the court below, so far as it relates to the first and last of the numbers above cited, but complains of error in it in relation to the 6th number, according to the order in which they are placed by the answer of the defendant.
The principal questions in the cause arise out of the situation of the property designated in Nos. 6, 9 and 13. That shown by No. 6, is an undivided portion of a tract of land owned and possessed by the defendant Balthazar Delahoussaye, in common with his co-heirs, to the successor of his father. The plaintiff relies on the last art.
18*

but one of the old Code, to free him from the trouble and delay
which the discussion of the property suggested by this number,
would occasion. The law relied on denies to a plaintiff in execution the right of seizing an undivided portion of a succession belonging to his debtor; but authorises a judgment creditor to cause the
estate to be divided, &c. To effect such division, legal proceedings
would most probably be required on the part of the creditor. In
cases where property is thus situated, we are of opinion that a privileged or mortgagee creditor, is not obliged to discuss it. See *Pothier, Recueil de Deux Traités sur les Hypothèques, p.* 32.

According to this view of the question, which relates to the situation of the property designated in No. 6, we conclude that the judge
a quo erred in decreeing that the plaintiff should be compelled to discuss it, &c.

The difficulty in which the property designated by no. 9 is involved,
relative to the different rights and claims of the parties now before
the court, is suggested by a bill of exceptions to the introduction of
oral testimony with regard to the manner in which it was acquired
by the present proprietor and possessor. The act of sale is subsequent to that under which the appellant holds the property by him
purchased from B. Delahoussaye: but the person on whom the discussion is required to operate, seeks to release himself from its
effects by showing that he received it as a *dation en paiement*, in
discharge of a privileged debt which the vendor owed to a person
whom the purchaser represented; and for this purpose he offered
testimonial proof, which was received by the court below, and to
which reception the defendant made his exception in due form. The
deed purports to have been given in consequence of a sale; and the
price paid proves the execution of the act. The appellant contends
that the evidence of the witness offered and admitted, to show that
the contract evidenced by the written instrument was any thing else
than a sale as it purports to be, was in violation of the well known rule
of evidence, which prohibits oral testimony to be received in support of facts alleged contrary to the contents of contracts and agreements, reduced to writing, &c. This rule is perhaps without exception, so far as it relates to the rights and claims of the parties themselves to the instruments in writing. But it is not so unrelenting in
relation to the rights of third persons; and in this situation the plaintiff in the present case must be viewed. We are therefore of opinion
that the judge *a quo* did not err in receiving the testimony offered;
neither did he err in the effect which, by his final judgment, he seems
to have allowed to it.

The slaves pointed out in No. 13, as objects of discussion, are
nearly in the same situation as the land proposed by No. 9, just examined. They appear to have been given and received in discharge
of a debt due to the vendees, from their tutor, in his capacity as such,
and consequently privileged, &c.

In consequence of the error of the court below, in relation to the

[Delahoussaye v. Delahoussaye et al.]

property designated by No. 6, we are compelled to reverse the judgment of that court.

It is, therefore, ordered, adjudged and decreed, that the judgment of the district court be avoided, reversed and annulled; and it is further ordered, and we do hereby order, adjudge and decree, that the plaintiff and appellee be compelled to discuss the property designated in the plea of the appellant and defendant by Nos. 1 and 12 alone; that is to say, a tract of land of two arpents front with the ordinary depth, situated in the Parish of St. Martin, on the east bank of the bayou Teche, and the mulatto man named Louis, &c. The appellant to pay the costs of this appeal.

Brownson, for the plaintiff.

Simon, for the defendants.

Ponsony v. Debaillon et al. VII, N. S. 204.

FIFTH District.

An appeal cannot be taken from a decision overruling the exception of *litis pendentia.*

Williams v. Brent. VII, N. S. 205.

Plaintiff who takes a twelvemonths' bond and sues on it,' is not estopped from denying that he took it in discharge of his debt.

The return of the sheriff that a debt is satisfied, does not conclude the creditor.

There is no difference in the effect of a sale made to a stranger, and that made to the defendant in execution.

Judgment against one debtor *in solido,* is no bar to recovery against a co-debtor.

A twelvemonths' bond is not a payment of the debt on which execution issued.

Nor does it operate a novation.

FIFTH District, Judge of the Seventh presiding.

PORTER, J., delivered the opinion of the court.

This action is instituted on a note by which the defendant bound himself, jointly and severally with three other persons, to pay Samuel Richardson, 2833 dollars and 33 cents.

The plaintiffs, who are the representatives of Richardson, aver that the defendant yet owes 879 dollars and 17 cents, with interest at ten per cent. from the 1st of February, 1815, the time the note fell due, until paid.

The defendant pleads:

1. That although he executed the note *in solido*, he was, in truth and fact, but surety for Terrill, one of his co-obligors, and that he is entitled to every privilege sureties can claim.

2. That a judgment was obtained by Richardson, in his lifetime, against Terrill, the principal debtor, on which judgment property was seized and sold, to satisfy the debt, on twelve months' credit. That, owing to the sureties not being good, and the slaves being run off, the judgment was not paid. But that, notwithstanding, the respondent is discharged, as the sheriff and his sureties are responsible.

The court below was of opinion, that the sale of the property on twelve months' credit, was a complete satisfaction of the judgment rendered against Terrill; and that the satisfaction of this judgment discharged the defendant from all liability.

The execution which issued on the judgment, was in the usual form, and the return on it is as follows: "satisfied by the sale of the adjoining described property, at one year's credit, for the sum of 1500 dollars.

It is shown that Terrill was the principal debtor, and that although, as to the obligee, the respondent and his co-obligors were bound *in solido*, yet, as between them and Terrill, they were but sureties.

It appears from the evidence appearing on the record, that the property sold by the sheriff did not belong to Terrill, the defendant, but to Brown, one of the co-obligors, by whom it was voluntarily surrendered for that purpose.

On these facts, a question of considerable importance is presented. The case has been elaborately and ably argued, and it has been intensely considered by us. The judgment we are about to pronounce is the result of our best deliberations on the subject. It would be uncandid in us, if we did not state that the conclusion to which we have come, is not free even in our own minds, from objections; but we see much less difficulty on that side of the question, than we do on the other.

Before we approach the main point in the cause, it will be proper to clear from around it every thing which prevents the real question in dispute from being nakedly and distinctly considered.

We go along with the counsel for the appellant, in a concession, which follows from the whole tenor of the argument he addressed to the court; that the act of the legislature providing for the sale of property on twelve months' credit, considered merely as an extension of time, and as a means of enforcing the obligation of the debtor, is not unconstitutional. And if we were of a different opinion, this case would not present that question, for the plaintiffs having accepted the bond and received part of the debt due to them from a sale made under it, have waived the objection. We also concur with him in his position, that if the act be constitutional, so far as it extends a remedy, and unconstitutional in substituting one debt for another, that their acceptance cannot be considered as an abandonment of the latter objection. They must be presumed to have taken the bond for the purposes for which they could have been legally compelled to receive it.

We also agree with him in the soundness of the proposition, that the return made by the sheriff in the suit of Richardson v. Terrill, of the judgment being satisfied, cannot enlarge or diminish the rights of the parties; because he has returned how it was satisfied: and if that which he considered a satisfaction, be not in truth a discharge of the judgment, then most certainly his conclusions cannot render it so. For that would be to make him a judicial, not a ministerial officer, and to substitute his opinions, for the commands and the wisdom of the law.

It is also true as contended by the appellants, that though the sheriff is the agent of the plaintiff, he is also the agent of the law, and that he had no choice in his selection. But it is equally true, as urged by the appellee, that the act of that officer, in taking out execution on the twelve months' bond, and seizing property under it, must be considered as the act of the plantiff in execution; because the law has not authorised its officers to take out execution unless requested so to do, by those in whose favor judgment is rendered.—The appellee, therefore, has every advantage from this act of the sheriff, that he would have had, if it had been done by the appellant.

But we cannot assent to the proposition of the appellant, that the circumstance of the property sold, having belonged to one of the co-obligors, and not to the defendant in execution, and having been bought by the owner, can make any difference in the effects of the sale. If a sale for a twelve months' bond extinguishes the judgment and debt, then we are unable to recognise any difference between a sale to a stranger a co-debtor *in solido*—or to the defendant in execution. The principle on which such a consequence can be deduced, rejects all arguments drawn from the person to whom the sale is made; and though it may be true, that on an execution the sheriff is not authorised to seize the property of a stranger, even by his consent, the acceptance of the bond in this case given by the plaintiffs, waives all objection growing out of that circumstance.

It has been contended for by the appellee, that the debt of Terrill on the bond merged in the judgment. This argument has been repelled by the other side, as resting on principles peculiar to the common law, and unknown to our jurisprudence. Whether a debt at common law is not considered, for certain purposes, as merging in a judgment, it is of course immaterial for us in this country to inquire. It is equally immaterial, whether the same consequence does not follow the same proceeding here by our own law. This is an action against one of the several debtors bound *in solido*, or jointly and severally; and in regard to persons so bound, it is a well settled principle in our jurisprudence, that judgment against one, is no bar to recovery against another. That nothing but actual satisfaction from any of the creditors, will prevent judgment and execution against the person legally bound with him. Rev. Code, lib. 8, tit. 41, law 28; *Pothier on Obligations*, 270, 271, 272; Civil Code, 278, 103, 104.

We give an entire assent to the proposition of the appellant that the bond cannot be considered as *a payment*. Although it is true, that the obligation for the payment of one thing, may be discharged or paid by another, when the parties so agree; this principle suffers an exception, when the thing so given and received, is the obligation of another *to pay;* in that case the extinction of the first obligation is produced by novation; and this brings us to the important question in this cause, whether there was not a novation of the original debt due by Terrill. If there was, it is extinguished to his creditors *in solido.* 2 *N. S.* 144; Civil Code 296, art. 182.

Among the different modes prescribed by our law, by which novation is produced, is that "where a new debtor is substituted to the old one, who is discharged." The appellee contends, that the sale of the defendant's property in execution, for the price of which a bond at twelve months is taken, comes within the provision just cited. A new debtor is substituted. The law, he urges, contemplates it shall be a discharge; and the creditor's assent to its being so, is shown as completely, as if it made expressly a part of his agreement that he would take a bond at twelve months, if the debtor's property would would not sell at two thirds of its appraised value. The law was in force at the time of the contract and the parties must be presumed to have contracted in relation to it. He further insists, that if this implied assent is not strong enough to charge the plaintiffs, there is still stronger evidence in the case before us—their acceptance of the bond, and their attempt to enforce it.

To this reasoning the appellants have replied: That the law did not contemplate there should be an extinction of the original obligation. It merely intended it as one of the means of satisfying the creditor. If it meant any thing more, it would be unconstitutional: *First*, in making something else than gold and silver a payment of a debt in money: *Secondly*, in violating the obligation of a contract: That their consent was never given to any such change—neither impliedly, nor expressly: for the agreement was entered into in 1813;

[Williams v. Brent.]

and the act of assembly which, it is said, produces novation, was not passed until the year 1817.

The contract on which this suit was brought, was, it is true, made in the year 1813, and the act relied on became a law in the year 1817. But at the time the agreement was entered into, an act of the legislature was in force, which required property that did not bring two thirds of its appraised value, to be sold on twelve months' credit, the purchaser giving bond and security as provided by the act of 1817. The only change which this last law has introduced, is the salutary one, that instead of selling the property seized under execution, for the payment of the bond under appraisement, and at a credit, it must be sold for cash. This modification is favorable to the creditor; it enlarges, instead of restraining, his rights, and consequently deprives him of the protection which the constitution might afford, if the statute was subsequent to the contract, and impaired it.

We have then, on the constitutionality of the law presented to us the very same point which lately exercised the learning and the wisdom of the Supreme Court of the United States, aided by as full and able argument as any legal question ever received since the establishment of our government. A majority of that court were of opinion, that a law in force at the time a contract was made, could not be considered as impairing its obligation.

We could not add to the reasoning on which that conclusion was obtained: it would be useless to repeat it. It is certainly not free from difficulty; but it appears to us freer from it, than the other interpretation. It has our assent; and we may briefly remark—that, as the prohibition in the constitution of the United States against the states passing any law impairing the obligation of a contract, is conceded to mean the *legal* obligation; it would seem to follow, the legal obligation of a contract is, whatever the law in force at the time of making it, compels the parties to do, or not to do; and that consequently it cannot be correctly said that such a law impairs the obligation of the contract. That the laws of every country, in giving the right to enforce agreements, may state to what extent they will permit them, and that the whole legal obligation is to be sought, as well in the law which limits the right expressed on the face of the contract, as that which authorises it to be at all enforced.

The plaintiffs, therefore, cannot, in our judgment, successfully contend that the law is unconstitutional. Their ancestor knew at the time he made the agreement, that if the obligor did not comply with it, his property must be sold at twelve months' credit, if it would not bring two-thirds of its appraised value. He knew, too, that law required he should accept the bond, and try to enforce it. If this law relates alone to the remedy, no question can arise as to its constitutionality. If it is to be regarded as a modification of the contract as expressed by the parties, they must be understood to have contracted in relation to such modification, and must be bound by it.

If, therefore, the statute had declared, that a bond taken in pursuance of its provisions, should discharge the judgment and the original debt, we are unable to say that such a law would be unconstitutional in regard to any debts contracted after its passage.

But has it done so? This is the main difficulty in the cause. The statutory provisions directly applicable to the point, will be found in 2 *Martin's Digest*, 164, 11; and in the act of 1817, p. 36, sect. 15. The last directs that the sheriff shall return the manner he has executed the writ of *fieri facias*. The first contemplates, that satisfaction may be entered on the docket of judgment, and provides for it being done, whenever it shall appear by the sheriff's return, or the acknowledgment of the creditor or his attorney, that it is discharged. In neither of these laws, nor in any other of our statutes, is it declared that such shall be the effect of a sale at twelve months' credit, though it is true that no difference is expressly made between such a sale and one for cash.

But does not a distinction exist in the different results produced by the sale for cash, and one on a credit, which it required no positive law to point out. When made for the first, the creditor has obtained that which he contracted for. He has, of course, obtained satisfaction as far as it is possible the law or the debtor could furnish it. No express declaration was therefore necessary to make it such: it is the necessary consequence of the creditor receiving that which he stipulated for. But when the thing given to the creditor is not that which he stipulated for, although the law might make it a satisfaction, it can never be presumed it intended to do so. Because it is interfering without any just necessity in the contracts of individuals, and discharging the obligation by something different from that for which the parties contracted.

These observations as to there being no necessity for any declaration on the part of the law-maker, that the receipt of the thing promised should dischage the obligation; and that such an express declaration is required where something else is given, derives great, (and if the subject were not one on which such a difference of opinion is said to exist in the profession,) we would almost say unanswerable force, from the analogies furnished by the principles of our law in relation to the extinguishment of obligations by agreement between the parties. It is a well understood principle of our jurisprudence, that the discharge of an obligation is never presumed to be made in any other manner, than by the giving of that which the debtor has promised; and we have an article of our Code which explicitly declares, that the obligation by which a debtor gives to his creditor another debtor, does not discharge him who was originally bound, unless the creditor has expressly declared that he intends to discharge him. If then an express declaration be necessary on the part of the creditor to effect novation in the case just put; if it cannot be presumed, does not the same principle forbid us to presume the legislature intended it? Does not every reason which forbids it being inferred, exist in the one case, as well as the other? If there be a dif-

[Williams v. Brent.]

ference, we are unable to perceive it. We have already said the law was not unconstitutional, because being in force at the time of the contract, the creditor must be presumed to have assented to it, or in other words, that the contract must receive the same construction as if the provisions of the law had been incorporated into, and made a part of it. Now suppose it had been inserted in this contract that if the debtor's property did not sell on execution, for two-thirds of its appraised value, it should be sold at twelve months' credit; and that the bond of the purchaser should be delivered to the creditor; such a stipulation would not have novated the original debt, nor discharged the debtor. If it would not, the implied consent of the creditor to a law containing these stipulations, cannot have a greater effect.

We conclude, therefore, on this branch of the subject, by saying, that as the legislature have not declared that a twelve months' bond shall be a discharge of a debt, that the creditor, in case he is unable to make the money on the bond, may resort to his original judgment.

In this particular case, the decision works no injustice and violates no equity. One of the co-sureties voluntarily presented his property to be sold for the satisfaction of a judgment rendered against his principal. This property he bought in, and then, in the language of the testimony taken on the trial, ran it off. No injury, therefore, has been sustained by the person whose property was sold, and the defendant's equity must depend on his. But, although this case offers no proof of loss sustained; we are aware that under the operation of the principles we have established, other contests may arise on the consequences which may follow a sale made to a stranger. Whenever they do come up for decision, unless one or other of the parties has violated the law, or neglected its provisions, the case will not present the equitable claims of the debtor alone; those of the creditor will require an equal share of attention. When the debtor shall urge: "I contracted at a time when I had reason to believe I could perform my engagement. Circumstances beyond my control prevented me doing so. I did every thing in my power to repair the injury. I surrendered my property in execution. It has been sold to an amount sufficient to pay the debt. If it has failed to do so, the fault is not mine, but my creditor's, who resorted to a remedy that he knew might terminate, not in a sale for cash, but on a credit. If I am responsible for the insolvency of the purchaser, I may be made so again on the next sale, and thus the whole of my property may be wrested from me.'' May it not be answered, with equal truth, and greater strength on the part of the creditor: " I contracted with you in the firm belief you would comply with your engagement. On the faith of it, I have become bound myself to others. I gave you property to the full value of the money you promised to pay me; and now, because you have violated your contract, you wish to discharge it by that which yields me nothing. Thus I am to be the sufferer, without any fault of mine, excepting my confiding in your good faith. The consequences you deprecate, as to the constantly

[Williams v. Brent.]

recurring sales of your property, might be obviated by either permitting a portion of it to be sold for cash, or by buying it in yourself; as you take the benefit of an extension of credit, you ought to bear the burthen, and run the risks attendant on it." We know not how those conflicting appeals to equity might strike the minds of others, to us it appears the weight of them is decidedly with the creditor, and for this main reason—that all the misfortunes of the debtor have proceeded from his own act, and that he who is the cause of a state of things by which one or the other must lose, has no reason to complain if the loss is fixed on him with whom it originated.

It has been used as an argument against the construction we have adopted, that the law has pointed out no means of enforcing the original judgment, after the sheriff has endorsed the execution satisfied by a twelve months' bond. But this difficulty arises solely from the sheriff giving a greater effect to the sale, by his return, than it is entitled to in law. He should, in obedience to the act of 1817, when he sells for any thing but cash, state in what manner he has executed the writ, without stating what consequence follows it.

One or two minor questions remain.

The answer avers the responsibility of the sheriff for taking defective security, and that he should be pursued before recourse is had on the defendant. Admitting this objection to be sound, on which we do not express an opinion, there is no evidence on record that establishes the insolvency of the surety at the time he was received by the sheriff.

It has been further urged, that whatever may be the general principle, this case presents an exception, because no proof has been given that the money might not be made from the principal and surety on the twelve months' bond; and that this property must be exhausted, before the original debtor is resorted to. This is, perhaps, true; but the answer does not plead the exception; but acknowledges their insolvency, and of course dispensed with the creditor proving it.

It is, therefore, ordered, adjudged and decreed, that the judgment of the district court be annulled, avoided and reversed: and proceeding here to give such judgment as ought to have been given in the court below—it is ordered, adjudged and decreed, that the plaintiffs do recover of the defendant the sum of eight hundred and seventy-nine dollars and seventeen cents, with interest at ten per cent. from 1st February, 1815, until paid; and costs in both courts.

Brownson, for the plaintiff.

Simon, for the defendant.

WESTERN DISTRICT, OCTOBER TERM, 1828.

Dale *v.* Downs. VII, N. S. 223.

SEVENTH District, Judge of the Fifth presiding.
The jury may seal their verdict, and return it into court. Interest cannot be added by the court, to the verdict.

Hughes *v.* Harrison. VII, N. S. 227.

SEVENTH District, Judge of the Fifth presiding.
In a sale on a *fi. fa.* the property passes by the adjudication.
If there be a variance between the date of the deed annexed to the petition, and that stated in it, the former corrects the latter.
Code of Practice, art. 690, 694.

Green v. Boudurant. VII, N. S. 229.

If the debtor has a right to postpone payment on several notes given to the plaintiff, he cannot avail himself of an error in making payment to the assignees of these notes to prevent a recovery on one which remained in the hands of the assignor. A jury must be prayed for in time to prevent the cause being delayed a term.

SEVENTH District, Judge of the Fifth presiding.

PORTER, J., delivered the opinion of the court.

The defendant executed, in favor of the plaintiff, his three several notes, due in January, 1824, 1825 and 1826. They were given in payment of a tract of land, and a condition was annexed to them, that in case the land was overflowed, and a crop lost by high water, payment was to be postponed for one year, without interest.

There was an overflow in the years 1823 and 1826, and a partial one in 1824, which diminished the crop of that year.

This action is brought on the note which first fell due, and as a crop was made in 1825, there can be no doubt the plaintiff is entitled to recover, unless the defence of payment, set up in the answer, has been sustained.

The defendant paid the note which became due in 1825. He insists this payment was made in error, and should be imputed to the note then due, viz: that on which this suit is brought. This defence might, perhaps, avail him, if the payment had been made to the plaintiff; but it appears he paid his endorsers, to whom the note had been transferred for a valuable consideration. The error, therefore, is not one for which the plaintiff is responsible. He can not be prevented from recovering what is due to him, because the defendant has paid to others what was not due to them.

There is a bill of exceptions to the judge's refusal to grant a jury. The prayer was made after the jury was discharged; and though a portion of them were then out in a criminal case, and confined because they could not agree, the judge acted correctly in refusing the application. He could not know that the jury then in deliberation, would give a verdict before the end of the term, and the trial of the cause might have been postponed.

We do not think this a case in which damages should be given for the appeal being frivolous.

It is, therefore, ordered, adjudged and decreed, that the judgment of the district court be affirmed, with costs.

Johnston, for the plaintiff.
Patterson, for the defendant.

Walsh *v.* Texada's Syndic. VII, N. S. 231.

Parol evidence cannot be admitted to contradict written.

SEVENTH District, Judge of the Fifth presiding.

Porter, J., delivered the opinion of the court.

The plaintiff seeks to make the estate of one Texada, deceased, responsible to him as joint purchaser of a tract of land which he acquired from M. Collins. The defendant denies any share of his intestate in the original contract, but contends the intestate bought, during his lifetime, the one-half of the tract from the plaintiff. This difference between the parties, in relation to the manner in which the property was acquired, does not appear to arise so much from any contest between them as to the principal sum due, as from different stipulations in the contracts with regard to interest. In the deed by which the plaintiff acquired, he promised to pay at the rate of ten per cent. The sale to the deceased is silent on the subject.

The petition states the fact of the plaintiff's purchase—Texada's participation in it—his failure to comply with his engagement—and the large sum in interest and costs which the petitioner had been compelled to pay. The balance, after deducting two payments acknowledged to be made, is stated to be 3200 dollars.

The answer consists of a general denial.

On the trial the plaintiffs offered parol evidence to establish the partnership in the purchase of the land. The testimony, although objected to, was admitted: and in our opinion erroneously, for two obvious reasons: First, because it was contradicting the written act of the plaintiff, by which, as owner of the whole tract, he sold one half to the deceased; and Secondly, because it was giving parol evidence of the alienation of immovable property.

But though the judge admitted the evidence he refused to sanction the conclusions which the plaintiff endeavored to draw from it. Judgment was given for 2100 dollars, with interest at 5 per cent.

It is unnecessary for us to examine the correctness of the opinion given below, on the evidence there admitted. Rejecting it, as we are clear we must do, the judgment was correct. The amount of the purchase money was 3000 dollars—900 dollars is proved to have been paid, and the property being susceptible of producing fruits, interest was correctly charged at five per cent.

19*

It is, therefore, ordered, adjudged and decreed, that the judgment of the court of probates be affirmed, with costs.

Flint, for the plaintiff.

Scott, for the defendants.

Weathersby *v.* Hughes.   VII, N. S. 233.

The appellant cannot assign as an error, that the judgment was signed too soon.

SEVENTH District, Judge of the Fifth presiding.

By Martin, J.—By appealing, the defendant 'has chosen to consider the judgment as final, and it is now too late for him to pray to have his appeal dismissed, or assign as an error that the judgment was signed before the three days which were allowed him to move for a new trial had expired. Every one may waive what is introduced for his benefit alone. By signing the judgment, the district judge did not deprive the defendant from moving for a new trial. We held so in Gardere *v.* Murray, 5 *N. S.* 244. He might have done so at the following term, and if an execution had issued, he might have prevented proceedings on it by an injunction.

His interest might prompt him to consider the judgment as final. He did so by appealing. The appellee might then have said the appeal was premature; but the appellant cannot say so, and demand the dismissal of his own appeal. Neither can he assign as error, that the judgment was signed on the day it was given, because by appealing, he has recognised the judgment as final, or, in other words, as signed in proper time. See the case cited.

It is, therefore, ordered, adjudged and decreed, that the judgment of the district court be affirmed, with costs.

Downs, for the plaintiff.

Winn, for the defendant.

Brown *et al. v.* Reves *et al.*   VII, N. S. 235.

A buyer while in the peaceable and undisturbed possession of the thing sold, cannot, by law, withhold the price, simply on a plea of want of title in the vendor. The negation of right in a buyer, who purchased under the old Code, to suspend payment of the price when he dreads eviction, is not modified, as relates to such buyer by the provisions of the Louisiana Code.

SIXTH District.

Martin, J., delivered the opinion of the court.

The plaintiffs claim the amount of two promissory notes, with interest, given for the price of a tract of land, purchased by the defendant Reves, and by him sold to his co-defendants; and pray that on the failure of Reves to pay, the premises in the hands of the latter may be sold, under the mortgage in the deed of sale.

The claim was resisted, on the ground of the absence of any title to the premises in the vendors, at the time of the sale or since. There was a claim by way of intervention, for damages, and the value of improvements.

The district court, after a verdict for the plaintiffs, gave judgment against Reves for the amount of the notes, and interest at five per cent. and that the premises may be sold.

From this judgment, the defendant, Reves, appealed.

It is clear the court did not err, the defendants made no legal defence. The sale took place before the promulgation of the new Code and the law was decided by this court. 7 *Martin*, 223; 6*N. S.* 523. The vendee could not refuse the claim of the vendor for the price, on the ground that he had not a title to the premises, and therefore the vendee did not acquire any, unless the latter was actually disturbed by a suit.

There is, however, a bill of exceptions to the charge of the court, who instructed the jury that,

1. A buyer, while in the peaceable and undisturbed possession of the thing sold, cannot, by law, withhold the price, simply on a plea of want of title in the vendor.

2. In a suit for the price, the vendor is not bound to show a complete chain of conveyances to him, and a better title in himself than in the whole record.

3. If the jury were of opinion, from the evidence, that the plaintiff had fraudulently sold the property of another, and the consideration of the sale had entirely failed, they might for the defendant.

4. The vendee having accepted a conveyance of the vendor, with

[Brown *et al. v.* Reves *et al.*]

a warranty, could not require security, unless a suit was instituted against the former.

The first, second and last of these propositions are in perfect accordance with the decisions of this tribunal. See the cases already cited.

The third might have, perhaps, been objected to by the plaintiffs, as irrelevant, there being no allegation of fraud. Certainly it was more favorable than injurious to the defendants. But their counsel urges it was of the latter cast, being an affirmative pregnant with the negative that, unless there was fraud, the jury could not find for the defendants. Admit this, the negative proposition would be in accordance with the three of which we have expressed our approbation.

It is, therefore, ordered, adjudged and decreed, that the judgment of the district court be affirmed, with costs.

Scott and *Patterson*, for the plaintiffs.
Thomas, for the defendants.

Pirot *v.* Beard.   VII, N. S. 237.

SIXTH District.
Appeal dismissed for want of a statement, &c.

Green *v.* Davis *et al.*   VII, N. S. 238.

A purchaser of the property of a succession, cannot offer in compensation a note of the testator.

SEVENTH District.

MATHEWS, J., delivered the opinion of the court.

This suit is founded on a promissory note, by which it appears that the defendants agreed to pay to the plaintiff, in his capacity of executor, the sum of 650 dollars.—Their answer does not deny the execution of the note, or justice of the claim made on the part of the plaintiff; but contains a plea of compensation, in support of which they allege several sums of money to be due to them from the testator and his executor. The principal item in support of the plea of compensation was rejected by the court below; and the defendants, dissatisfied with the judgment which was rendered, appealed.

The evidence and documents of the case, show the items of set-off, or compensation, to be four in number; three of which appear to have been settled by a judgment of the court of probates for the parish of Concordia, in a proceeding which took place between the present appellee, and one of the appellants, viz. Davis. The judgment rendered by the court of probates appears to us to have been given according to the true spirit and meaning of our laws relating to the administration of inheritances. It orders a concurrent and *pro rata* payment of debts, due from the testator to various creditors who presented their claims to the court; amongst whom, Davis, one of the defendants to the present suit, seems to have appeared. This judgment, on the face of it, exhibits an adjustment and decree only in favor of one of the persons defendants to the present action; and, perhaps, on this ground alone, might have been legally rejected as evidence of compensation. But the sums claimed as set-offs, are in our opinion so clearly inadmissible, without doing violence to our system of jurisprudence established for the administration of the estates of deceased persons, that it is deemed unnecessary to decide any thing positively in relation to the discrepancy between the party defendants to this suit, and that in whose name the debt proposed as a set-off, appears to stand.

According to the judgment of the court of probates above cited, the appellee could not have paid, with propriety, the whole debt due to the appellant, Davis. The latter was bound to await a just and full administration of the estate managed by the former in his capacity of executor, and receive payment from him according to a legal distribution of the funds in his possession.

[Green *v.* Davis *et al.*]

To give effect to the compensation thus offered, would be contrary to the very evidence which establishes the debt due from the succession of the testator to one of the defendants; and in violation of the justice and equity inculcated by our laws on the subject of successions.

The note of the testator, dated in 1823, and transferred by endorsement to Davis, ought not to have been admitted in compensation. The present suit is brought on a promise made to the executor, in consideration of property purchased by the defendants at the sale of Dunlap's succession. If creditors of an estate were to be admitted to compensate in this manner debts contracted by them on account of property adjudicated under probate sales, the intention of the law to distribute the effects of the deceased among persons having just claims on his succession, according to the rank and privilege of their credits, might be entirely defeated; and the whole estate swallowed up by debts of inferior dignity; contradictory to the rights of the vigilant, which, on general principles of law, should be aided, and against every fair claim of privilege and preference.

It is, therefore, ordered, adjudged and decreed, that the judgment of the district court be avoided, reversed and annulled; and it is further ordered, adjudged and decreed, that the plaintiff and appellee do recover from the defendants and appellants six hundred and fifty dollars, with interest at the rate of five per cent. per annum from the judicial demand until paid, and costs in both courts.

Johnston, for the plaintiff.

Ogden, for the defendants.

Mead *v.* Tippet.   VII, N. S. 242.

SEVENTH District.

If the appellant fail to bring up the record, the appellee may do so, and claim an affirmance of the judgment and damages.

Broulette v. Lewis. VII, N. S. 243.

SEVENTH District, Judge of the Fifth presiding.
The appeal will be dismissed, if not taken within the time prescribed by law.

Adams v. Gainard. VII, N. S. 244.

SEVENTH District, Judge of the Fifth presiding.
Under a general power, an agent cannot sell a slave. The sale is
void until ratified by the owner: the receipt of the price by him
would be a ratification.

Gorton v. Barbin. VII, N. S. 248.

When the whole matter does not appear, the presumption is that the judge's charge was
correct.

SEVENTH District, Judge of the Fifth presiding.

PORTER, J., delivered the opinion of the court.
The plaintiff claims 5000 dollars damages from the defendant in
consequence of the latter stating in an affidavit made before a justice
of the peace, that a robbery had been committed of his property by a

negro, and "that the effects stolen were kept and could be found at Mr. Lewis Gorton's, the said Lewis Gorton knowing them to be stolen."

The plaintiff's grounds of complaint are set out in a petition and amended petition. They are not perhaps stated with all the clearness of which his case is susceptible, but we think it results from the whole, that the plaintiff intended to charge, and did charge the defendant on two grounds—*first*, for having libelled and slandered him —and *secondly*, for a malicious prosecution.

Whether the case was put on both grounds to the jury, the record does not inform us. There was a verdict for the defendant, and the plaintiff appealed.

During the trial a bill of exceptions was taken on which arises the only question that has been presented for our consideration.

The court charged the jury " that the affidavit contains no charge of a criminal nature; that it was not charged the plaintiff had received the stolen goods; that the affidavit only charges, that the defendant verily believes that the robbery was committed by a negro man Jack, and that the effects are kept and can be found at Mr. Lewis Gorton's—the said Gorton knowing them to be stolen; that the goods might be kept at the house of said Gorton and he be innocent; that if the warrant which issued on the affidavit contained any thing more than was set forth in the affidavit, the defendant was not responsible, but the justice."

In this opinion we concur. The affidavit did not contain a criminal accusation, and the justice of the peace acted incorrectly in issuing a warrant on it. There is no charge, the plaintiff received the effects, knowing them to be stolen, nor any that he concealed them. The allegation is nothing more than he knew stolen goods were at his house.

But though strictly and technically considered, the affidavit did not charge the plaintiff with any offence punishable by the laws of his country, it can not be denied that to ordinary understandings it conveyed an imputation which had a tendency to injure him, and the judge should have charged the jury that if they believed the expressions were used for the purpose of defaming him, the defendant was responsible. Whether he did so or not, we can not say. The whole charge does not come up. We can only pass on what was before us. We are bound to presume in the absence of any thing to the contrary appearing, that the judge stated the law correctly to the jury, on all points of the case. The defendant before this court, has disclaimed all intention of accusing the plaintiff with criminality, or improperly having, or concealing the goods, and it was we presume on these grounds the verdict below was rendered.

It is, therefore, ordered, adjudged and decreed, that the judgment of the district court be affirmed, with costs.

Scott and *Gorton*, for the plaintiff.

Thomas, for the defendant.

Hughes v. Harrison.   VII, N. S. 251.

Married women cannot, under any circumstances, become sureties for their husbands.

SEVENTH District, Judge of the Fifth presiding.

PORTER, J., delivered the opinion of the court.

The appellant assigns as error of law apparent on the face of the record:—a judgment against her for the whole amount of a note executed by her jointly and severally with her husband, the consideration of said note as expressed on the face of it., "being the amount of articles furnished them, for their and plantation use, as per account rendered."

The plaintiff contends, this error might have been corrected by evidence introduced on the trial; it was open to him to prove the whole of the note was for the benefit of the wife.

Married women can not under any circumstances become sureties for their husbands. It is alleged in the petition that part of the consideration of the obligation was a debt of the husband's, for so we understand the expression, *for their and plantation use*. No evidence could have been legally received to contradict this allegation of the plaintiff's. The apparent error therefore could not have been corrected by proof.

The case must be remanded in order that it may be ascertained what part of the consideration of the note was received by the wife.

At the close of the argument an objection was raised that there was nothing appearing on record which established the appellant, to be married to the person with whom she signed the note—all the papers in the case are entitled "Harrison and Wife." The citation is directed to Mrs. Harrison. The plaintiff in his petition states her to have signed the note with the consent and approbation of Benjamin Harrison. From all these facts and circumstances, we can not resist the conviction, that she is the wife of her co-obligor, and we yield our assent to this impression the more readily, because as we remand the case, an error on that side will only delay the plaintiff; a mistake on the other would forever deprive the appellant of the protection the law affords her.

It is, therefore, ordered, adjudged and decreed, that the judgment of the district court be annulled, avoided and reversed; and it is further ordered, adjudged and decreed, that the case be remanded to

[Hughes *v.* Harrison.]

the district court to be proceeded in according to law.   The appellee paying the costs of this appeal.
Scott and *Winn*, for the plaintiff.
Downs and *Flint*, for the defendant.

Sprigg *v.* Cuny's Heirs.   VII, N. S. 253.

Repossession of a note once specially transferred by the endorser, is not evidence of title but it is if the transfer was in blank.
The holder of a negotiable note, by blank endorsement, may maintain suit on it, without filling up the same to himself.

SIXTH District.

MATHEWS, J., delivered the opinion of the court.
This suit is brought on two negotiable notes, the amount of which the plaintiff claims from the defendants, as representatives of the first endorser, who is dead.   He obtained judgment against them in the court below from which they appealed.
The pleadings and evidence of the cause show that the notes in question had been regularly endorsed, in full from the payee down to the present claimant, who endorsed them in blank, which endorsement was never filled up to any person.   They passed into other hands, under the blank endorsement, who caused them to be protested for non-payment, and notice to be given to the endorsers.   No re-transfer from the last holder to the present plaintiff, appears to have been made in writing; but after he had obtained possession of the notes, he filled up his own blank endorsement to himself.
The act, as it appears to us, cannot better the situation of the appellee.   He could by it create no more title in himself, than that which he had by the re-delivery of the notes, and possession acquired under it, as a *bona fide* holder.   According to several decisions of this court, the drawer of a bill of exchange, accepted in favor of the payee, and endorser of a note of hand, when the endorsement has been filled up to the endorsee, cannot maintain actions on such instruments without proving a re-transfer of the title and interest thus transferred and acquired by the latter.   In those cases, the mere possession of the bill or note, unaided by any proof of the extinguishment of the rights acquired by the holders or the transferors, was

considered not even as *prima facie* evidence of title in the latter.—See 1 *N. S.* 301 and 273.

It has also been decided by this court, that the holder of a negotiable note, under a blank endorsement, may maintain a suit without filling up the same to himself. He is considered as having obtained a full and complete title to the instrument by delivery, when supported on regular endorsements. And it is immaterial through how many hands it may have passed in pursuance of this simple mode of transfer.

According to these decisions, the plaintiff must fail in the present action, unless a just and reasonable distinction can be drawn between the situation of an endorser in blank, and one who has made a full and complete transfer expressed in writing. This distinction, we are of opinion, may be fairly made when a note is handed over from one holder to another. Under a blank endorsement, possession alone is evidence of title, at least *prima facie.*[*] If it should return in the same manner to the last endorser in blank (whose endorsement, it is true, has transferred his right to all and every person who may become its holder, and remains transferable, by simple delivery, to all the world) what reason can be adduced to prove that the last endorser may not, in this manner, be revested with his original rights?—Until the re-delivery, he had no title, because that was transferred by his endorsement. But this being in blank, the signature of no other person was necessary to keep the paper in circulation; whereas, when an endorsement is full and perfect, the signature of the endorser is absolutely necessary to transfer right and title to any other person; and would be necessary in a re-transfer to the endorsee, or proof of payment under protest; but ought not to be required in cases of blank endorsement.

It is, therefore, ordered, adjudged and decreed, that the judgment of the district court be affirmed, with costs.

Thomas, for the plaintiff.

Johnston, for the defendant.

---

[*] The possession of a promissory note endorsed in blank is *prima facie* evidence of property, sufficient to throw the burthen of proof on the defendant: and when the signature is not denied, the plaintiff is not bound to make proof of it. 13 *Lou. Rep.* 12.

Fulton's Heirs *v.* Welsh *et al.*   VII, N. S. 256.

A judgment without reasons is voidable, not void.

SIXTH District.

MATHEWS, J., delivered the opinion of the court.

In this case the plaintiffs claim title to a certain tract of land described in the petition. The defendants pleaded as *res judicata*, a judgment obtained against the ancestor of the former, by Collins, who was cited in warranty. This plea was supported by the court below, and judgment rendered in favor of said defendants, from which the plaintiffs appealed.

This judgment is objected to, as being based on one absolutely void, on account of not having been supported by reasons adduced by the judge, who rendered it.

The appellate court has already settled the question relating to judgments thus situated, by determining that they are subjected to relative nullity only; in other words, that they are not absolutely null and void, but can only be avoided and annulled for cause shown on an appeal, or in some other legal way. The judgment which was pleaded as *res judicata*, remains unassailed by any legal proceedings and is in full force, and was properly recognised as such by the court below.

It is, therefore, ordered, adjudged and decreed, that the judgment of the district court be affirmed, with costs.

Thomas, for the plaintiff.

Baldwin, for the defendant.

Dean v. Carnahan. VII, N. S. 258.

A copy cannot be given in evidence, when the opposite party has produced the original under notice.

A payment made under the provisions of the old Code, to the holder of the obligation, is valid, although the possessor be afterwards evicted of it.

All laws except those in relation to remedies, are presumed to be made for cases which are subsequent to them.

SIXTH District, Judge of the Fifth presiding.

PORTER, J., delivered the opinion of the court.

A twelve months' bond was taken by the sheriff at Natchitoches in virtue of an execution issuing out of the district court of the parish of Rapides. The sheriff returned the bond into the office of the parish for which he was appointed, and the obligor finding his bond in the hands of the clerk, paid it to him. The main question in the case is the validity of this payment.

But before that question can be examined, one arising on a bill of exceptions must be disposed of. The plaintiff offered in evidence, a copy of the bond; its introduction was opposed by the defendant, and the court rejected it. We think this decision correct, because the defendant had already produced the original, under a notice from the plaintiff to do so. The copy was therefore secondary and inferior evidence.

We also concur with the judge below on the merits. If the case were to be decided by the amendments lately introduced in our Code, the conclusion he came to would be erroneous. But the bond was given at the time the old Code was in force, and by the 140th article of the 5th chapter of that work, page 288, it is provided that payment made *bona fide* to him who is in possession of the maker of the credit is valid although the possessor be afterwards evicted.

The argument at the bar turned principally on the question, which of the laws already alluded to, should govern the case. The bond was given under the old law, the payment made under the new. Perhaps an act of the legislature, such as this, could not be considered unconstitutional, if it were expressly made for contracts entered into before its passage, or if it resulted clearly from the whole context that the law maker intended to apply it to previous agreements. But it is a sound rule of construction to consider all laws, except those which relate to remedies, as applicable only to contracts entered into after their enactment. We have applied that doctrine to several cases which can not on principle be distinguished from this, more particu-

20*

[Dean v. Carnahan.]

larly that of Miller *v.* Reynolds *et al.*, 5 *N. S. 555;* 3 *N. S.* 17; 6 *Ibid.* 586.

It is, therefore, ordered, adjudged and decreed, that the judgment of the district court be affirmed, with costs.

Johnson, for the plaintiff.

Thomas, for the defendant.

Deblieux *v.* Case.   VII, N. S. 260.

There cannot be a variance between the instrument sued on and that given in evidence, when it is made a part of the petition.

SIXTH District, Judge of the Fifth presiding.

PORTER, J., delivered the opinion of the court.

The plaintiff was nonsuited in the court below, and he appealed. An examination of the case induces us to believe the judge erred. We can discover no variance between the note set out in the petition and that read in evidence. Indeed we do not see how such a question could have arisen, for the note itself, " was annexed to, and made a part of the petition."

But, on looking into the record, to see what judgment we ought to pronounce, we find the case so placed before us, that the merits cannot be inquired into. An important document, viz. the decree of separation between the defendant and her husband, is wanting. Two years ago, the appellant applied for and obtained a *certiorari,* to supply the diminution of the record. The return to it shows the document just spoken of, to have been read in evidence, but does not annex it.

It is, therefore, ordered, adjudged and decreed, that the appeal be dismissed, with costs.

Deblieux, for the plaintiff.

Rost, for the defendant.

Toten v. Case.   VII, N. S. 261.

A sale by a legatee, who holds under a will giving the whole of the estate, while there exists a *forced heir*, is not void, but voidable.

SIXTH District, Judge of the Fifth presiding.

MARTIN, J., delivered the opinion of the court.

The plaintiff, as forced heir of her grandmother, claims certain slaves in the possession of the defendant. The general issue, a release and prescription, were pleaded.

There was judgment for the defendant, and the plaintiff appealed.

It is admitted that the defendant is in possession of the slaves since the first of February, 1803, and the plaintiff became a widow in 1808. The present suit was instituted on the 19th of December, 1825, so that the defendant has possessed during upwards of twenty-two years; and if, as is contended, she can not avail herself of her possession during the plaintiff's coverture, she has possessed during seventeen years since the widowhood.

A claim of slaves is prescribed by the lapse of fifteen years, even where the possession is in bad faith.   Civil Code, 486, art. 66; *Ibid.* 488, art. 74.

But it is said the defendant possesses under the will of a person who had no right to transfer the whole property in said negroes from her forced heir, the plaintiff; and consequently the defendant, holds as co-tenant with the plaintiff, and can not prescribe.

The donation *causa mortis* of the whole estate of a person who is forced heir, is not void; the donation is good, but reducible; *Ibid.* 214, art. 26; and this reduction can only be claimed by the forced heir, art. 28—so the legatee's possession is in her own right.

It is, therefore, ordered, adjudged and decreed, that the judgment of the district court be affirmed, with costs.

Deblieux, for the plaintiff.

Morris, for the defendant.

Chain *v.* Kelso.   VII, N. S. 263.

SIXTH District, Judge of the Fifth presiding.
The letters of third persons are not evidence.
Interest cannot be given on a verdict, where the jury have not found any.

Mead *v.* Oakley.   VII, N. S. 264.

An answer praying for damages cannot be filed the day the cause is set for argument.
The plaintiff must pay costs, if no amicable demand is proved.

SIXTH District, Judge of the Fifth presiding.

MARTIN, J., delivered the opinion of the court.

In this case the appellee did not file his answer until on the day the cause was argued, and the appellant urged that it could not be received, as it prays for damages.

We think it can not: the Code of Practice, 890, has an express provision to that effect.

The only question the case presents, is one of costs—they were given below, although amicable demand was not proved; the defendant having expressly denied any was made.

The plaintiff and appellee relies on the Code of Practice, 549. In every case the costs shall be paid by the party, except in case of compensation or real tender.

The court law of 1813 sect. 31, requires an amicable demand, *verbally*, or in writing, before the institution of suit, and declares that without it, the plaintiff shall pay costs. This section might be said to be repealed by the 549th article of the Code of Practice, if the 169th article had not provided that it is not necessary previous to bringing a suit, to make an amicable demand in writing. This is a

[Mead v. Oakley.]

negative, pregnant with the affirmative, that the verbal one is still so, and the provision of the act of 1813 is not repealed.*

The district judge erred in giving costs to the plaintiff.

It is, therefore, ordered, adjudged and decreed, that the judgment of the district court be annulled, avoided and reversed; and that there be judgment for the plaintiff, for six hundred and ninety dollars, with interest at ten per cent. from the sixth day of September 1825, until paid.

Flint, for the plaintiff.

Oakley, for the defendant.

Miller v. Russell.   VII, N. S. 266.

SIXTH District.

Where a witness is ill, and cannot be brought into court, his evidence taken down on a former trial in the cause, may be read in evidence.   See Starkie, p. 2, 261.

* The 549th and 169th articles of the Code of Practice, are now (Amory *et al. v.* Black, 13 *Lou. Rep.* 564,) interpreted to charge the plaintiff, on his neglect to make amicable demand, with costs only up to the putting in of a defence by defendant. If defendant, by putting in a defence shows he would not have paid on previous request, he is rightly condemned to pay costs from that moment, whenever judgment goes against him on the merits. This would seem an equitable repartition of the expense of litigation. Some jurists reject the idea of the " negative pregnant" started from its burrow in the present case, on the ground that the act of 1828, section 25, abolished the necessity of verbal demands, by its general clause, previous demands in writing being imposed by the practice-law of 1817, or say by the Spanish Codes, and not saved, but abolished, by the Code of Practice. Any dregs of obligation to make other demand than that by suit, they think plainly abolished by a general repeal of all rules of practice, and not to be harbored under the outlaw logic of " negative pregnants."

Fisk *v.* Bynum. VII, N. S. 268.

SIXTH District.

It is not necessary for a defendant to swear that the answer of the plaintiff to his interrogatories is *material,* if he swear they will assist him in his defence.

Murray *v.* Bacon. VII, N. S. 271.

Under a promise to save the vendee harmless from a mortgage, judgment against the principal debtor will not enable the purchaser to resist the payment of the price.

SIXTH District, Judge of Rapides presiding.

Porter, J., delivered the opinion of the court.

The appellee has moved to dismiss the appeal, on an allegation of irregularities in the manner of bringing it up. This motion comes too late. The Code of Practice excludes all other answers, except those which pray for a confirmation of a judgment, if not put in within three days after the record is filed in this court.

On the merits the case presents the following facts. The plaintiff sold to the husband of the defendant, in his lifetime, a house and lot, for the sum of 12,000 dollars, payable in three instalments. At the sale of this property by the widow, he bought it in for 7000 dollars. Sued by her for the price, he pleaded in compensation, the last note of 400 dollars due to him with interest, and judgment was rendered against him for 1961 dollars, conditioned, however, that execution should not issue, unless the plaintiff give him security to save him harmless from a mortgage in favor of Ferguson & Rich.

The mortgage in favor of Ferguson & Rich was created by a note due on the second instalment, for the house sold by the plaintiffs, which note he had transferred to these persons. The petition states, the property purchased by him at the sale already mentioned, was

[Murray v. Bacon.]

not secured to him, as by the terms of the decree it should have been, but that he had been divested of it by a sale on an execution issuing in virtue of a judgment rendered in favor of Ferguson & Rich.

Admitting that on this eviction, the plaintiff was discharged from the judgment against him, and that a right vested in him, to sue on the note, pleaded in compensation in that suit. We are clearly of opinion that such right could only arise on the facts stated in the petition, namely; eviction of the premises sold to him. Now the record contains no proof of this fact. We have, it is true, in evidence, the record of Ferguson & Rich v. Bacon, showing judgment to have been obtained against the defendant, but there is nothing which establishes it was satisfied by the sale of the premises purchased in by the petitioner.

It is, therefore, ordered, adjudged and decreed, that the judgment, of the district court be annulled, avoided and reversed, and it is further ordered, adjudged and decreed, that there be judgment against the plaintiff as in case of nonsuit, with costs in both courts.

Scott, for the plaintiff.
Wilson, for the defendant.

Crane *v.* Baillio.   VII, N. S. 273.

The right of the assignee must be established by matter of record, before he claim a writ of seizure and sale.

A partner cannot offer a partnership debt, in compensation of a debt of his, in his individual capacity.

SIXTH District, Judge of the Fifth presiding.

MARTIN, J., delivered the opinion of the court.

The petitioner, as third possessor, obtained an injunction to prevent the execution of a writ of seizure and sale obtained by Baillio, as syndic of the creditors of the estate of J. H. Gordon, on a mortgage given by the petitioner's vendor to secure the payment of two notes due to Maria C. Wilson, for her benefit and that of her minor children—on the affidavit of Baillio that the notes were given for a debt of Gordon's estate, at the time it was administered by Mrs. Wilson, were surrendered by her to the court of probates and came to his possession as syndic of the estate.

[Crane v. Baillio.]

The injunction was dissolved and the petitioner appealed.

His counsel urges that the injunction issued improperly, as none of the facts to be established by the applicant, except the creation of the debt and mortgage, were established by authentic acts; but merely by the affidavit of the applicant. He relies on Wray v. Henry, 10 *Martin*, 222.

We held in this case that a writ of seizure and sale could not be obtained by an endorsee, who did not establish his right by an authentic act; it is not necessary that the applicant for a writ of seizure and sale should produce an authentic act, by which the debtor became bound to him—it is sufficient, after having produced the authentic act by which the debtor is bound, that he should show he has succeeded to the rights of the creditor: but this he must do by legal proof, and one's own oath is no legal proof, except in cases, in which the law for particular purposes made it receivable. *El que pide execucion ha de legitimar su persona. Cur. Phil. Executante 12, El heredero ha de legitimar su persona en principio de illa litis, o en lo menos, en el termino de illa oppocicion, id. n. 6.*

The reason of this difference, as to the heir, is that his heirship is often, without any fault on his part, not susceptible of proof by authentic act, as when, being of full age and only heir, he succeeds to his ancestor; while he, who succeeds to the rights of the creditors by contract, has it always in his power to produce authentic evidence of the transfer.

Having held, in the case from 10 *Martin*, that the endorser of a note, the payment of which is secured by mortgage, cannot establish the endorsement, at the judge's chambers, by witnesses and consequently by his own oath; it follows that Baillio could not establish his right under Mrs. Wilson, by his own affidavit.

But, in the present case the evidence spread on the record in the district court establishes by authentic documents that Baillio is the syndic of the creditors of the estate; that the notes were received by Mrs. Wilson while she administered the estate; that she surrendered them into the court of probates in the settlement of her accounts, as evidence of uncollected debts due to the estate. On this evidence at chambers, a writ of seizure and sale ought to have issued, and if the district court had made the injunction perpetual, the creditor might have instantly prayed for a new writ of seizure and sale; this justified the district court in dissolving the injunction.

An injunction, which has issued unadvisedly, will not be dissolved, if it appears from the evidence that the party will be instantly entitled to a new one. Bushnell v. Broom's Heirs, 4 *N. S.* 499. Exnicios v. Weiss, 3 *N. S.* 480.

The petitioner has offered in compensation a debt due by the estate to the firm of Kay & Shiff, of which his vendor, the maker of the note, is a member; this was properly rejected as a partner cannot apply a debt due to the partnership in compensation of what he owes in his individual capacity.

[Cranē v. Baillio.]

The petitioner had a right to complain of the issuing of the writ of seizure and sale, before due proof was exhibited of all material facts; he had a right to suspend the execution of it, and cannot be mulcted with costs for having done so.

It is, therefore, ordered, adjudged and decreed, that the judgment of the district court be annulled, avoided and reversed, and that the injunction be dissolved; the defendant and appellee paying costs in both courts.

Rigg and *Winn*, for the plaintiff.
Flint, for the defendant.

Casson *v.* Louisiana State Bank.   VII, N. S. 277.

Louisiana State Bank *v.* Casson.

If an absolute sale be made to a surety, for his indemnification, the legal title is in him, until he be relieved from the suretyship. A court cannot, by anticipation, act on questions of law.

He who has a superior privilege, cannot prevent a sale, but must exercise his privilege on the proceeds.

SIXTH District.

PORTER, J., delivered the opinion of the court.

In both these actions the plaintiffs have been seeking to enforce mortgage claims against the estate of John Casson deceased, on property in the possession of third persons, and each has obtained an injunction against the proceedings of the other.

Before inquiring into the regularity and legality of the action thus instituted, and the respective right of the parties in reference to each other, it becomes necessary to examine and decide whether the property which they attempted to seize and sell, did not actually form a portion of the estate of Casson.

Sprigg and Scott were endorsers on certain notes held by the Louisiana State Bank. To secure them against the effects of these endorsements, he made them an absolute conveyance of a tract of land owned by him in the parish of Rapides, and they on their part executed in his favor, a certain letter, in which they state, that "the conveyance so made to them, was for the sole purpose of securing the said Sprigg and Scott against endorsements—and that whenever the said Casson shall pay and release them from such endorsements, without their having recourse to the said conveyed property, then they would re-convey the same to him for his own use." It is proved in evidence that the vendors are yet responsible on endorsements to the amount of 1000 dollars.

On these facts, we are of opinion, that the legal title is vested in Scott and Sprigg, and that the land so conveyed cannot be considered as making a part of the estate. Taking the act of sale, and the counter letter together, we have in truth presented to us the contract known in law as the *vente a remèré*. The condition annexed to the conveyance is dissolving, not suspensive. If Scott and Sprigg are not paid or released from their indorsements, the land is theirs, and until that event takes place, it is of course no part of the estate of Casson.

These cases have been consolidated in the court below, but we find nothing on an examination of the record which presents any matter for our decision. The bank attempted to enforce their lien by an order of seizure and sale. The widow did not approve this proceeding, but prayed that the proceeds of the sale might be enjoined in the hands of the sheriff, until her right of preference could be settled. Previous to the service of the injunction on the bank, they directed a stay of proceedings, and no sale has since taken place of the premises. There is consequently no matter presented, on which an issue could be joined. The *contestatio litis* can only arise on the moneys coming into the hands of the sheriff, under a sale made at the demand of the bank, and without it there is nothing for this court to try.

It is true the bank has put in an answer to this petition, in which they deny the widow's right to interfere; the justice and legality of her claims, &c. But they had no right to do this, until the event occurred upon which her claim and theirs would come in contact. Certainly parties can not call upon the court to try by anticipation, questions of law which may arise on events, that may or may not take place hereafter. Were we now to decide the point presented by this answer, we might be settling matters which may never be contested between the parties, for *non constat*, that the defendant in injunction will ever execute the order of seizure and sale, or that the moneys in which the plaintiff claims a preference will ever come into the hands of the sheriff.

Dismissing therefore from our consideration all the matters growing out of the injunction obtained by the widow against the bank, we proceed to examine that, in which the relative position of the parties was changed, the bank becoming the petitioners in injunction, and the widow defendant.

In their petition they state the fact of the defendant having taken out an execution on a judgment obtained against her husband in his lifetime. They complain of the irregularity and illegality of doing so, without reviving it against the estate. They assert that there is other property to which she should resort before selling this, and they pray that further proceedings on her part be enjoined.

To this petition the defendant, among many other things, answered, that the plaintiff has no right to interfere—that their lien if superior to hers, was on the proceeds, but furnished no authority to stay her execution.

In this position we fully concur. The point has been lately decided in this court. The law requires that property exposed to sale by a sheriff, shall be sold subject to all the privileges and mortgages with which it is burthened. The right of the plaintiffs could not therefore be impaired by the sale. Admitting their lien to be of a higher nature than the defendants, she has still a right to have the property sold, for it may bring more than will pay their debt, and her claim to the overplus is undisputed. See 6 *N. S.* 615; Code of Prac. 679, 683.

Therefore we think the court below erred in making the injunction perpetual against the defendant Casson. It should have been dissolved. As to that granted in her favor, as it can not affect the bank until a sale takes place at their instance, and the proceeds come into the officer's hands, no judgment can be pronounced upon it.

It is, therefore, ordered, adjudged and decreed, that the judgment of the district court be annulled, avoided and reversed; and it is further ordered, adjudged and decreed, that the injunction granted at the suit of the Louisiana State Bank *v.* Casson, be dissolved, the bank paying costs in both cases.

Thomas, for the plaintiff.

Scott and *Boyce,* for the defendants.

Noble *v.* Martin *et al.*   VII, N. S. 282.

It is a good ground for the dismissal of an overseer, that he uses grossly abusive language to his employer.

If the deputy sheriff be absent from court on official duty, his testimony taken down on a former trial between the same parties may be given in evidence.

On the plea of the general issue, the defendant may avail himself of the defence, that the parties were partners.

A plea, that the time when the debt sued on became due, was subsequent to the commencement of the action, is a dilatory exception, and cannot be put in after an answer on the merits.

SIXTH District, Judge of the Fifth presiding.

MARTIN, J., delivered the opinion of the court.

The plaintiff claims 1000 dollars for his wages as overseer of the defendants for the year 1827, and a part of the crop for the labor of three slaves of his, on a special contract, the defendants having drove him and his slaves from the plantation without any just cause.

The answer denies every thing and avers the plaintiff and his slaves did not come to the plantation till the middle of January, and left it in that of April.

The plaintiff had a verdict for 950 dollars, for which the court gave judgment *in solido,* with interest, from the judicial demand; the defendants appealed.

The evidence shows that the plaintiff was not dismissed without cause; he was therefore entitled to his wages and the hire of his negroes during the period he staid, the cause of dismissal not being any neglect in the discharge of his duties, but gross abuse of one of the defendants, which rendered it insupportable that he should remain.

There are two bills of exception taken by the appellants.

The first is to the reading of the testimony taken down by the clerk at a preceding trial, the witness having been subpœnaed and not attending, being engaged elsewhere, in the discharge of his duties as deputy sheriff. We think the testimony was properly read. See Starkie on Evidence, Part 2, 262, where it is said the deposition of a witness will be read, if he fall sick on his way or be abroad.

The other bill is to the opinion of the court in refusing leave to the defendants to file an amended answer. This new answer averred that the parties to the suit were partners, and as the negroes of the defendants and some of the plaintiff's were working together, so the plaintiff could not maintain a suit, except for the balance that might appear due on a settlement, and had no right to sue till it took place. Further, that the plaintiff's wages could not be payable, even if dismissed without cause, till the end of the year, so the suit was premature.

We think the court did not err; the defendants might avail themselves of the first part of the amended answer, on the plea of the general issue, and the latter part was a dilatory exception which came too late.

On the merits, we think the evidence does not authorise a verdict to the amount given, and that justice requires that the defendants should have the benefit of a new trial.

It is, therefore, ordered, adjudged and decreed, that the judgment of the district court be annulled, avoided and reversed, the verdict set aside, and the case remanded for a new trial; the appellees paying costs in this court.

Thomas and *Johnston*, for the plaintiff.

Winn, for the defendants.

Beatty *v.* Wright's Estate.   VII, N. S. 285.

COURT of Probates, Parish of Rapides.

If a creditor's claim depends on a condition precedent, he has no right to interfere with the proceedings of the other creditors in relation to the sale of the estate.

No examination of the merits of a case can take place until issue be joined.

The *contestatio litis* in the language of the Code of Practice is the foundation of the suit. The Spanish law considered it the *raiz piedra angular, y fundamento del juicio*, and that no judgment was valid in which it was omitted. *Curia Phillip., p.* 1, *sect.* 14, *nos.* 1 and 4; *Partida* 3, *tit.* 10, *l.* 8; Code of Practice, 359.

Montgomery *v.* Russell.   VII, N. S. 288.

SIXTH District.

An unliquidated demand cannot be pleaded in compensation, but may in reconvention.

This was decided in Agaisse *et al. v.* Guedron *et al.*, 2 *N. S.* 73.

By Code of Practice, art. 374–377, demands in reconvention are required to be connected with the original demand.

A party propounding interrogatories, is not guilty of negligence in not procuring testimony to contradict the answers, before the answers are filed in court.

Rison *v.* Young & Turnbull.   VII, N. S. 294.

Any thing may be accepted in payment.

Giving credit on account is evidence of the thing credited being accepted in payment.

SIXTH District, Judge of the Fifth presiding.

MATHEWS, J., delivered the opinion of the court.

This suit is brought by the heirs of Jarret Rison, (whose succession was administered as being vacant,) against the sureties of a certain C. K. Blanchard, who appears (according to the bond on which the plaintiff relies for a recovery) to have been appointed curator to the vacant succession on the 27th of November, 1816. The court below gave judgment in favor of the plaintiff, for 4376 dollars and 90 cents, from which the defendants appealed.

The evidence of the case shows: that Blanchard gave his bond as curator of J. Rison's estate, with J. Dill, the ancestor of Mrs. Young, and W. Turnbull sureties, that he should faithfully perform the duties required of him by law, in his administration of the success committed to his charge as curator aforesaid, and that in his capacity as such, he received from the parish judge a large amount of notes and other orders of debts due to the estate of the intestate, to be by him collected for the benefit thereof. No account appears to have been rendered by him to the judge of probates, as required by law, but several of the claims which he had to collect, seem to be satisfactorily accounted for by the documents received in evidence in this suit which were offered on the part of the defendants: the judgment of the district court being only for the balance of the whole amount of claims placed in the hands of the curator for collection as above stated, after deducting the sums thus accounted for.

The appellants deny that they are in any manner responsible to the appellee, because the curator was guilty of no neglect of duty or *malfeasance* in office, during the period for which they bound themselves to answer for his faithful administration. Should it however be considered that they are responsible for the conduct of Blanchard, as curator, this responsibility ceased on the appointment of a new curator to the estate of Rison, which took place in the person of the said Blanchard on the 5th of March, 1818, and that up to that period, from the time he received the claims of the successor to collect, no part thereof could have been legally collected.

From this statement of the case, it is evident that the legal obligations of the defendants must be tested by the provisions of the old Civil Code, on the subject of vacant estates.

They are to be administered by curators appointed for that purpose, who are bound to give security for the faithful discharge of their duty, and the restitution of all sums which they may receive during their administration. See old Code, p. 176, art. 134. They were also bound to render an account to the parish judge by whom they were appointed, of their administration at the expiration of one year and one day, from the appointment, which term might be extended three months longer. See same art. p. 180, art. 144. Their functions ceased on the rendition of such account. See preceding art. same page.

We have already stated, that Blanchard received his first appointment on the 27th of November, 1816. On the 2d of May and 9th of November of the year 1817, (as appears by his receipt of those dates,) he received the notes, bonds, &c., to collect for the benefit of the succession which he then administered. The greater part of the sums which the curator was bound to collect, did not become due until the 1st of March, 1818, and 1819, long after the expiration of the time of office fixed by law for the duration of the administration of vacant successions by curators. On the 5th of March, 1818, it appears by the evidence of a bond, which was held by this court to be incomplete, and not binding on the sureties, (in the case of Wills *v.* Dill, reported in 1 *N. S.* p. 592,) that Blanchard was re-appointed curator of Rison's succession. It is objected that this instrument being imperfect, and without force against the sureties therein named, affords no proof of the re-appointment. The only evidence which appears on the record of the first appointment of Blanchard, is the bond on which the plaintiff relies. The last bond although incomplete, we are of opinion, proves the re-appointment as effectually as the first did that which took place in 1816, for both must have preceded the execution of the bonds.

The whole amount of debts which the curator had to collect according to his receipt of the 2d of May, 1817, did not become due until the 1st of March, 1818. His power to enforce payment as curator had ceased by limitation of law, on the 29th of November, of the year preceding. A violent presumption therefore arises that he did not collect any part of the debts thus intrusted to him. It is true perhaps that he ought to have returned the evidences of them to the parish judge from whom they had been received, and to have rendered an account of his administration within the time prescribed by law. In that event they would have been handed over to a new curator: but he obtained this office for himself and consequently held them under the new appointment and under that alone would have been responsible to J. Rison's heirs for any amount collected; or the return of the evidences which showed the debts due to the succession of the intestate. The curator was by law bound to render an account of his administration at the expiration of his first term of office; but it appears to us that his neglect in this respect, has not produced any injury to the plaintiff resulting from his management of the vacant succession, considered in reference to the sums which he ought to have collected in pursuance of his receipt of the 2d of May, 1817, because under his first appointment he had not time to enforce their payment. The sureties to the bond may well have imagined that they were entering into responsibility only for the acts which the curator had legal power to do during the period of one year and one day—within that period it is impossible that he could have enforced the payment of the debts specified in his first receipt to the parish judge, and as to them his sureties ought not to be held liable.

The amount of claims expressed in the receipt of November, 1817, must be presumed to have been due when the curator received them for collection, and as he has not accounted for them, the sureties are answerable to the plaintiff for the amount of those claims.

It is, therefore, ordered, adjudged and decreed, that the judgment of the district court be avoided, reversed and annulled; and it is further ordered, adjudged and decreed, that the plaintiff and appellee do recover from the appellants and defendants, (in solidio,) the sum of six hundred and thirty-two dollars, and eighty-one cents, and that the appellee pay the costs of this appeal, those of the court below to be borne by the appellants.

Thomas and Winn, for the plaintiff.
Oakley, Scott and Wilson, for the defendants.

Allen *v.* Martin. VII, N. S. 300.

SIXTH District.

By MARTIN, J.—Our attention is drawn by the appellant to a bill of exceptions taken by his counsel below to the opinion of the court, refusing him leave to examine a witness as to the value of the plaintiff's services. Leave was refused on the ground of the plaintiff's having declared on a special agreement, which precluded the necessity, and rendered it useless to inquire into the value of the services. We think the district court did not err.

Cox *v.* Williams. VII, N. S. 301.

By MATHEWS, J.—Proof which shows that credit has been given on account with the original debtor, in consideration of a delegation made by him to his creditor, is evidence that the latter accepted the debt thus delegated in payment.

By MARTIN, J.—There cannot be better evidence of the partial or entire payment of a debt than the express acknowledgment of the creditor evidenced by his giving credit to his debtor.

By PORTER, J., dissenting.—I cannot assent to the proposition contained in the opinion just delivered by the presiding judge of the court, " proof which," &c. In my mind—if the act of the creditor can be explained in any other way but that of discharging the debtor, the provisions of our Code prohibit such a construction being put on his act. Cases of Barron *v.* How, 2 *N. S.* 144, and Gordon *et al. v.* M'Carty, 9 *Martin,* 288, reviewed.

Sureties of a curator are not responsible for debts of the estate of which the curator could not enforce payment.

SIXTH District, Judge of the Fifth presiding.

MATHEWS, J., delivered the following opinion.
This suit is brought by the endorser of a negotiable note for the

sum of 1950 dollars, which was made payable to Isaac Baldwin. The defendant in his answer pleaded want of consideration or rather failure of the consideration, in consequence of which he made the promise to the payer of the note; and that it is subject to all objections in the hands of the plaintiff, to which it would have been liable in those of the original holder and payee.

The court below gave judgment in favor of the defendant, from which the plaintiff appealed.

This case was formerly before the appellate court; and was remanded on a bill of exceptions taken to the introduction of Baldwin as a witness, to prove that Cox, the present plaintiff, although he appears in the shape of an endorser, was the real payee of the note in question, which was obtained through the agency of the witness. This fact is now fully established by the testimony of Baldwin, and the case must be examined as if pending between the original parties to the instrument.

In proceeding thus to investigate it, a concise history of the transactions which led to the execution of the note becomes necessary.

The appellant had a claim against one L. H. Gardner, which he placed in the hands of Baldwin, as attorney, to collect. This claim was in the hands of the agent at the time of the death of Gardner. The estate of the latter was sold at probate sale, and the widow of the intestate became the purchaser of a family of negroes, which made a part of the succession, for the price of 2450 dollars, and to secure payment, the present defendant bound himself as her surety. Afterwards he was dissatisfied with the conduct of Mrs. Gardner, in relation to the management of her pecuniary concerns, and took the negroes which she had bought under a sale from the court of probates at the same price she was to have given for them, and gave his own note to Cox, the creditor of L. H. Gardner's estate, for that amount. On the receipt of this note. Baldwin, the agent of Cox, credited the estate of Gardner with the amount thereof, in an account which he filed in the office of the parish judge of Rapides. Subsequent to these proceedings, Jackson and Reynolds enforced a judicial mortgage which they had on the property of L. H. Gardner to the amount of 1300 dollars, and subjected the negroes in the possession of Williams to its payment. The record of a suit heretofore decided by this court, is made evidence in the present action. In the former case, Baldwin sued for the use of Cox on a note similarly situated with that now under consideration. The answers of the nominal plaintiff in that suit, proved a discharge given to the estate of Gardner, Cox's original debtor. His testimony in the present case proves the same fact, but it is here accompanied by a statement of an account between the witness, as agent for the appellant, and the succession of Gardner, wherein the latter is credited (amongst other matters) with the amount of the notes given by the appellee and made payable to the agent of Cox, the original creditor. This additional evidence, (which the witness now says is the only acquittance he ever gave in favor of

Gardner's estate,) it is contended on the part of the appellee, disproves his answers to the interrogatories in the former suit; upon the evidence of which this court then held that the acceptance of Williams's notes and discharge of the original debtor operated a novation.

We are, however, of opinion, that the introduction of this document, has no tendency to distinguish the present from the former case. It was made out before witnesses and deposited in the office of the judge of probates, as evidence of payment, or a release of the obligation, to the succession of the deceased, in consideration of having accepted a new debtor in pursuance of the true spirit and meaning of our laws on the subject of delegation. In the case of Barron v. How, reported in 2 *N. S*, 144, this court held that an acknowledgment of a receipt of the promissory notes of the person delegated, as payment, produced novation. This was nothing more than a credit given by the creditor to the original debtor in discharge of his obligation, in nature of a payment by delegation. A receipt is evidence of payment, but payment may be established by other evidence; and whenever such evidence shows that any thing has been accepted as payment, the debt is extinguished, whether it be by a transfer of obligations on other persons, a payment in money, or a *dation en paiement*. Proof which shows that credit has been given on account with the original debtor in consideration of a delegation made by him to his creditor, is evidence that the latter accepted the debt thus delegated in payment; and on failure of the person delegated to pay, he would not be permitted to annul the credit thereby given to his original debtor, and pursue the latter on his original obligation. A debt once extinguished by novation cannot be again revived, unless by the consent of both parties to the original contract. From this view of the case it may be easily perceived, that we are of opinion that the production of the document in question does not weaken the evidence procured from Baldwin on interrogatories in the former case, nor does it in any manner invalidate his testimony in the present; wherein he explicitly declares that his intention was to discharge the estate of Gardner from all liability to Cox, his constituent, and to receive the appellee as substituted in the place of that estate.

MARTIN, J.,—I assent to the opinion just pronounced; but as there is a difference of opinion amongst the members of the court, in regard to a part of it, the law requires I should express mine.

I think that there cannot be better evidence of the partial or entire payment of a debt, than the express acknowledgment of the creditor evidenced by his giving credit to his debtor.

If a planter send to his commission merchant a quantity of cotton to sell and a draft to receive, in order to discharge what he owes him for supplies on his farm, the merchant does not credit him with the proceeds of the cotton or draft, till they be actually received, or he means to take the cotton or draft on his own account. I think this is the universal practice. Till the cotton be sold and the amount received or the draft paid, the planter is not a creditor of the merchant and nothing makes him so but the money coming to the hands of the latter, by the sale of the cotton or the payment of the draft, and there cannot be a better evidence of this circumstance than credit given on the books of the merchant in the account of the planter.

In the case of Levy v. The Bank United States, 1 Dallas, 234, the Supreme Court of Pennsylvania held that credit given by the bank in the plaintiff's books, precluded the bank from saying that the check, the amount of which was credited, was a forged one, and that therefore the credit ought to be stricken out. When banks or merchants receive a draft or property on account of a customer, the amount is never carried out to the outer column, but inserted in an inner one. I consider credit given in the ledger as express evidence of a payment; as a receipt in full. On an account current, nothing but the balance is due, and the maker is bound by every item with which he has credited his customer, unless errors be proved.

This case differs from that of Gordon *et al. v.* Macarty. There a receipt was given for a note; here credit is given for the amount. The receipt was evidence of a liability to account: the credit of a payment.

PORTER, J.,—I agree in the conclusion to which the majority of the court have arrived. The agent swears positively that the notes of the defendant were received from Mrs. Gardner, in full discharge of the claims held by him, against her, and her husband's estate. The receipt on account now produced, which it appears was the only written instrument that passed between them, does not by any means contradict this statement. It on the contrary supports it.

But I cannot assent to the proposition contained in the opinion just delivered by the presiding judge of the court, " that proof which shows that credit has been given, on an account with the original debtor in consideration of a delegation made by him to his creditors, is evidence that the latter accepted the debt thus delegated in payment." Our Code requires that the discharge should be express. It is true, it is immaterial in what words that discharge is given, so that is clearly expressed. But in my mind the mere act of giving credit on account for the debt of another, remitted by the debtor, does not necessarily create an extinction of the original obligation, if the creditor retains that first given to him, and does not give up the one, when he receives the other. A strong presumption is, it is true, created of the fact, but that is not sufficient. If the act of the creditor can be explained in any other way but that of discharging the debtor, the provisions of our Code prohibit such a construction being put on his act. Merchants, I believe, are in the habit of entering credits on their books of all notes or bills remitted to them, and their usual course is to charge those bills and notes again to the correspondent if at maturity they should be unpaid. In the case of Gordon, Grant & Co. *v.* M'Carty we held, that when the creditor gave a receipt in which he acknowledged he had received another note on account, that such acknowledgment

[Cox v. Williams.]

did not produce novation. That was as strong a case as this; as
that which he received on account, it is presumed he credited on his
books.

It is, therefore, ordered, adjudged and decreed, that the judgment
of the district court be avoided, reversed and annulled; and it is further ordered, adjudged and decreed, that the plaintiff and appellaut
do recover from the defendant and appellee the sum of nineteen hundred and fifty dollars, with interest thereon at the rate of ten per cent.
per annum, from the first day of April 1821, until paid, with costs in
both courts.

Boyce, for the plaintiff.

Thomas, Scott and *Winn,* for the defendant.

Weathersby v. Latham. VII, N. S. 310.

SIXTH District, Judge of the Fifth presiding.
If the jury find contrary to the weight of evidence, the case will
be remanded.

Walsh v. M'Nutt's Syndics. VII, N. S. 311.

COURT of Probates, Parish of Rapides.
Under the old Code, the heirs in partition had a tacit mortgage,
for the execution of all the engagements therein contained. Civil
Code, 200, art. 246. By the new Code a special mortgage is required
in such case.

Oakley *et al. v.* Phillips *et al.*   VII, N. S. 313.

COURT of Probates, Parish of Rapides.

The interest of the appellants, a third party, in the matter in dispute being denied, this court directed a mandate to the court of probates to ascertain whether the appellants really had the interest therein on which they grounded their right of appeal.

Maes *v.* Gillard's Heirs *et al.*   VII, N. S. 314.

Indian tribes were entitled by settlement under the Spanish government to the quantity of land contained in a square league.

Testimony taken under the act for perpetuating it, if it be reduced to writing by the attorney of the party applying for it, will be rejected.

Those who hold without title, cannot plead less than thirty years actual possession.

SIXTH District, Judge of the Fifth presiding.

PORTER, J., delivered the opinion of the court.

This is a suit in jactitation, or slander of title. The plaintiff avers himself to be the owner of a large portion of land on Red River, in the possession and right of whichhe is distur bed by the defendants publicly asserting that he has no title to the premises, but that they are the owners thereof.

To this petition the defendants have answered by denying the plaintiff's title, and setting up one in themselves.

The principles of law which govern suits of this kind were gone into so fully in the case of Livingston *v.* Hermann, that it is deemed unnecessary to notice them particularly in the present instance. The defendants might if they had chosen, have admitted the assertions of which they were accused, and averred their readiness to bring suit. But as they have thought proper to pay up their title, the dignity and relative strength of their claims can be passed on and finally decided in this action. *9 Martin,* 656.

The plaintiff claims in his petition forty arpents in front on each side of the river, and immediately below these lands a tract of 640 acres, also lying on each side of the river.

The upper part of these forty arpents is demanded in virtue of an order of survey from the Baron de Carondelet, of date the 14th of May, 1794, in favor of one Dorothea, a free woman of color, which ripened into a complete grant the 25th of November, 1796. The grantee sold to the petitioner on the 7th of April, 1796. The next ten arpents front in descending, in virtue of an order of survey in favor of the petitioner, of date the 15th of March, 1797.

And the remainder, twenty arpents, under an order of survey of date the 18th of May, 1796, in favor of one Francois Boissier, who sold to the plaintiff all the land embraced by his title on the 1st of September, 1804.

The 640 acres which form the inferior portion of the petitioner's claims, was what is called a settlement right confirmed in favor of Felix Trudeau on the 5th of October, 1818.

The complete grant to Dorothea, f. w. c. and the other orders of survey in favor of the petitioner and Boissier, have been confirmed by the board of commissioners of the United States for the western district.

The defendants claim the land covered by these titles or a great portion of it, in virtue of a purchase from the Pascagoula Indians by Colin La Cour on the 9th of April, 1795, and an order of survey in favor of Joseph De Blanc of date the 6th of May, 1795, calling to bound on the lands of La Cour below, and above by the domain of his majesty.

The court of the first instance gave judgment in favor of the petitioner for all the land claimed by him, and expressed their opinion that the title of the defendants under the Indians, together with that claimed by them under the purchase from De Blanc, did not in fixing the lower boundary at the bayou St. Philip, embrace the premises covered by the plaintiff's titles. From that judgment the defendants appealed.

The titles of the plaintiff are such as give a good right to the land covered by them, and they appear to be properly located. The main questions in the cause, therefore, depend on the title set up by the defendants, under a purchase from the Pascagoula nation of Indians.

The plaintiff has assailed it on three grounds.

1. That the Indians had no right in the soil.

2. That they never sold.

3. That the quantity sold by them is not of sufficient extent to embrace the lands claimed by him.

I. The first can not be considered an open question in this court. To those who are desirous of knowing whether all the highest Spanish authorities in Louisiana, for the space of thirty-four years, were ignorant of their own laws, and violated them in sanctioning sales of land by the Indians; and whether this court has in various instances, misunderstood the laws of the Recopilacion, we refer them to the 24th chapter of the 20th book of *Soberano's Politica Indiana,* where the right of the Indians to sell, and the fact of their not losing their right in one *pueblo,* or *reduccion,* by being moved to another, is, in our opinion, clearly recognised.

II. The second question is, did they sell to those under whom the defendants claim?

The first proof offered in support of the purchase is contained in a certificate of the commandant of Natchitoches, dated the 9th April, 1795, in which he states, "that in virtue of the power which had been conferred on him by Mr. Colin La Cour of Pointe Coupée, of having bought the establishment and cultivable lands of the village of the Pascagoula Indians, bounded by the bayou L'Ecor, where the chief was established, and below by another bayou situated on the left bank in descending, which said sale and cession thus made by the said nation, of their proper will, and entire movement, for the price of two hundred and fifty dollars, which I have paid them in cash in the presence of Edward Murphy, Louis Lambre, Antoine Plauché and Jean Varangue, interpreter, besides the crews of two boats. In faith of which I deliver the present to serve as a title to Mr. La Cour, that he may apply to the governor-general for a title in form." This instrument is signed by the writer and two witnesses. At the bottom of it is the following: V. B. El Baron de Carondelet.

This court is fully aware of the loose manner in which business was transacted, and acts passed, under the former government of this country, and we have felt every desire to disregard the forms of the instruments of those times, and give them effect, according to the intention of the parties. But there must be some limit to this favorable view, and we think this case presents one. The act is not only devoid of form, but it essentially wants substance. The parties who are said to have sold their land never signed or put their marks to it.

It does not appear they were present when it was drawn up. Or if they were, that it was read over to them, and that they assented to its contents. It is not an authentic act. It is not under oath, and it is *ex parte.* It comes too from the agent of the vendee, a circumstance well calculated to weaken any confidence in it.

It may perhaps strengthen the other evidence in the cause, so far as it corroborates that evidence, but as to those facts of which there is no other proof it is not entitled to the least consideration.

The proof given on the trial in support of the sale is as follows:

The evidence shows that the Indians moved off from their settlement on Red River about the time mentioned in the commandant's certificate. St. André says he has heard of La Cour's purchase from the Indians. Ganché states in his evidence, that the chief who sold the land to La Cour, lived at Gaillard's place. Huit believes that La Cour bought the whole of the Indian land; Hoffman swears also, that he believes it.

- In addition to this parol evidence given in court, the testimony of witnesses taken before the board of commissioners, was read on the trial without objection. Three of these witnesses positively swear to a sale; one of them states he was the agent for Indian affairs; that he was the interpreter when the bargain was made between La Cour and the Indians. Two others swear that they had much conversation with many of the Indians at the period of their removal to Bayou Bœuf, and that they said they had sold their lands on Red River to La Cour.

In the case of Sanchez v. Gonzales, this court decided that under the former government of Louisiana, a verbal sale of immovables was valid: the evidence in this case coupled with the uninterrupted possession of the vendee and his successors for nearly thirty years previous to the commencement of this suit, satisfies us that La Cour did purchase as the defendants allege. 4 *Martin.*

III. The next point in the cause is, how much land did the Indians sell?

As the certificate of the vendees' agent does not, in our opinion, establish any fact, and as the testimony of Varangue, taken under the law for perpetuating evidence, must be rejected as written by the attorney of the party whose interest it was to preserve it, we lay out of view the boundary of the *Bayou des Ecors*, the proper location of which was the subject of so much testimony in the court below.— The parol evidence which establishes the sale gives no boundary.— It merely proves the Indians sold their land on Red River. All the evidence goes to show that their principal village was at the place where the defendants now live. 10 *Martin.*

The quantity of land to which tribes of Indians were entitled under the Spanish government, has been contested in this instance, as it has been in every case of this description that has come before the court. One party urges that it was a league round of the village in every direction. The other contends it was but a league square.

In the case of Reboul v. Nero, this tribunal declared that Indians were entitled by law to a league in extent round their village; whether that opinion was required for the decision of the case, does not clearly appear from the report of it. In the case of Martin v. Johnston, the court referring to that decision, said it was unnecessary to determine the question, for allowing the Indians much less, the titles of those who claimed under them in that action, would embrace the property in dispute. In Spencer's Heirs v. Grimball, the case was decided on the confirmation by congress, and an opinion on this point expressly waived. 5 *Martin*, 490, 655—6, 355.

The only law we can find which defines the extent of Indian settlements, and the quantity of land to which they have a right in virtue of them, is found in the 6th book of the Recopilacion, and is the 8th law of the 3d title of that book.

The translation of it, as given in the case of Martin v. Johnston, is substantially correct. It is in these words: " The seats on which the villages of Indians shall be placed, shall be such, as are all well provided with water, arable land, and woods, and to which there may be easy access, and they shall have a common of one league in extent, where their cattle may graze without being mixed with those of the Spaniards.

These expressions of "a common of one league in extent," are given in Spanish by the following: *un exido de una legua de largo*, and though the true meaning is not quite free from doubt, it does not appear to us, that they support the construction of a league in extent, round the village in every direction. Nothing of there being a league round the village, is said in the law. The common is to be of a league in extent. And by giving a league in every direction, there would be a common of two leagues in extent at every point of the compass.

This construction is somewhat opposed to the reasons given in the law for granting land to the Indians. The avowed object is, to prevent their flocks mixing with those of the Spaniards. And that object would certainly be better attained by granting them a league in every direction from their village. But other provisions of the laws of Indians deprive this argument of a great deal, if not all of its force. By them Spaniards are prohibited from placing their flocks of large animals (*ganado mayor*) within a league and a half of the ancient Indian settlements, and their flocks of smaller animals (*ganado menor*) within half a league. In regard to the new settlements, the prohibition extends to double this distance. These restrictions rendered it unnecessary to give the Indians the extent of a league in every direction round their villages for their cattle. The appellants have, however, relied on these laws, to show that the Indians were entitled to all the lands on which the Spaniards could not pasture their flocks. But nothing in our judgment can be more unfounded than this pretension, for it would make the quantity of soil which it is supposed was given to the Indians when they were settled by the government, depend on the kind of cattle, the white men approached them with. If it was a *ganado mayor* they had a league and a half in extent around them; but if a *ganado menor* was brought near them, their right diminished to half a league from their village. These laws were evidently political regulations, for the better preserving harmony among the different races of men who formed the population of these colonies, and for the protection of that race, on which they had inflicted so much injury, when they first discovered and settled the country. *Recopilacion de las Indias, liv.* 4, *tit.* 12, *law* 12; *Ibid. liv.* 6, *tit.* 3, *law* 20.

The government of the United States have so understood these laws in limiting their confirmation of the title to the quantity contained within a league square; and admitting with one of the counsel for the appellants, that by an ordinance passed in 1754, viceroys and governors were not limited to the quantity of a league, if a larger portion of soil was necessary for the use of the Indians, there is no evidence before us of the numbers of this tribe which would authorise us to conclude that a greater quantity of land, than that embraced by a league square was necessary for them. The grant of the governor does not establish it, for it places them on the hills near the Bayou Rigolet de Bon Dieu, in descending. If they afterwards scattered along the banks of the river so as to cover a much larger space of ground, and for their own convenience fixed their lower boundary out of the league; nothing in the evidence induces us to believe that the Spanish authorities ever consented to this extension of the limit below, on any other consideration, than that it should be proportionably contracted above.

The next question is, how should this league be located? The appellants seemed to concede on the argument, that if their claim was reduced to the quantity of a league square, they preferred taking it from their lower boundary. This conclusion is that to which this court would have come, because the lower boundary is established beyond all contradiction, and the upper is doubtful.

The appellee assuming it to be a fact, that the lower bluff where the heirs of Gillard are settled, had been the upper boundary by which the Indians sold; insists that the claim of the appellants must be limited to that place, and that if in running down to the Bayou St. Philip, a sufficient quantity is not found to give them the number of acres contained within a league square by laying off the land on the river, with the ordinary depth of forty, that the side lines must be extended, so as to embrace the whole superficies covered by the title, and that the upper limit could not be extended beyond the boundary given by the sale.

Under the view we have already given of the evidence, it is not proved that the *Bayou des Ecors*, was the boundary above. It is only spoken of in the commandant's certificate and Varang's testimony.—The last has been excluded, and the first does not prove the fact.

The course and direction of the side lines next require consideration. All the witnesses prove that the Bayou St. Philip or Bayou La Bourne, was the dividing line between the Pascagoulas and Apalachia tribes of Indians; as this was a natural boundary we think it must form the lower limit on one side of the river, and that the line of the upper boundary on the same side should be extended to correspond with the general course of the bayou. We are also of opinion that the direction of the side lines on the opposite side of the river must be conformable to these. This is the mode in which the commissioners of the United States contemplated the land should be located.

Giving therefore to the defendants the quantity contained within a square league, and laying it off conformable to the universal usage prevailing at the time the lands were settled by the Indians, by so many arpents in front, with the depth of forty on each side of the river, as will embrace the quantity called for by the title; we have next to decide on the conflict produced by the upper tract of the defendants lying immediately above and adjoining the Indian title, which they derive from a conveyance by De Blanc, the grantee; and the lower tract of the plaintiff which he acquired from Trudeau. We think the defendants' is a superior title and must prevail. It is an order of survey, dated in 1795. That opposed to it, is a settlement right, confirmed in 1818.

As to the plea of prescription, the defendants had no title beyond the quantity contained in a league square, they therefore required thirty years actual possession to enable them to hold under this title, and that is not shown here.

It is, therefore, ordered, adjudged and decreed, that the judgment of the district court be annulled, avoided and reversed; and it is further ordered, adjudged and decreed, that the defendants be quieted in their title and possession to the quantity of land contained within a league square, according to the following notes and bounds: Beginning at the mouth of the Bayou La Bourne at the point marked F. on the plat of survey filed in this cause—thence along a line drawn at right angles, from the general course of said bayou for forty arpents back from the river, such a distance as by measuring forty arpents on each side of said line, will contain the superficies embraced by a square league. The said lines on the opposite side of the river from the Bayou La Bourne on the lower boundary; and the side lines on both sides of the river on the upper boundary, to be in conformity with the generel course of said bayou from its mouth to the distance of forty arpents back.

And it is further ordered, adjudged and decreed, that the defendants be quieted in their title and possession, to a tract of land of twenty arpents front with the ordinary depth, lying above and adjoining the square league acquired from the Indians, the side lines having the same course and direction as those of said league; and that the plaintiff be perpetually enjoined from asserting any title to the same by virtue of any title acquired by him previous to this time; and it is further ordered, adjudged and decreed that he pay costs in both courts.

EASTERN DISTRICT, JANUARY TERM, 1829.

₊ Mathews, J., was prevented by indisposition from attending the Eastern District this year.

Thompson v. Chauveau.   VII, N. S. 331.

An execution from the city court, to seize goods and chattels does not authorise the marshal to seize and sell real estate.

When the principal appears in court to support the act of the agent, whatever is evidence against the latter, is evidence against the former.

When the purchaser at sheriff's sale intervenes to maintain the validity of it, the court may order him to restore possession.

PARISH Court of New Orleans.

Porter, J., delivered the opinion of the court.

The defendant, who is city marshal, seized, under execution against Grymes and wife, a lot which the petitioner had acquired by authentic

[Thompson v. Chauveau.]

act, and of which he was in possession. The plaintiffs in execution have appeared in the action, and alleged various grounds why the sale to the plaintiff was null and void, as it respects creditors.|

We are strongly inclined to think that none of these grounds are sustainable, in the situation the parties now present themselves. The plaintiffs were not authorised perhaps to treat the alienation as void, and seize the property in the hands of a third party. They ought to have brought an action to have it set aside. But supposing they were authorised to proceed in the manner they did, we are clear the language of the execution did not authorise the seizure of real estate and the marshal is responsible.

The writ issued by the justice of the peace, directed him to seize the *goods and chattels* of the defendants in execution. Neither in the technical understanding of these words as used in our law, nor in the ordinary meaning given to them by common use, and the authority of the best philologists, can they be considered as embracing real estate. The act of 1805, which gives the form of the writ of *fieri facias*, uses the expressions " goods and chattels, lands and tenements." If the terms *goods and chattels* comprehend lands and tenements, the latter words were useless, and placed there for no purpose. This of course we can not presume in an act of the legislature. More particularly, when in the French text of the law, which at that time was of equal authority with the English, we find " goods and chattels," rendered by *effets, meubles.* Johnson, in his dictionary, states *goods* to mean personal property, *chattels* any movable possession. The popular understanding of these words, it is unnecessary for us to remark, is in conformity with these definitions.

Several bills of exceptions were taken on the trial, to the introduction on the part of the plaintiff, of proceedings had by him against the defendant, Chauveau, before the justice of the peace. They were objected to on the ground that they were irrelevant, and not evidence against the plaintiffs in execution, who had appeared in this cause to support the proceedings of the marshal. They were not perhaps necessary to enable the plaintiff to maintain this action, but not being able to perceive any injury they could have done the defendants, we do not think the cause should be remanded on that account. As to their being *res enter alios acta,* and therefore not evidence against the intervenors, we are of opinion there is no weight in the objection. Parties who voluntarily appear in court to vindicate and justify the acts of their agent, can not, in any respect, deprive those who complain of those acts of the use of any evidence which could have been legally offered against him.

The appellee has complained of the judgment of the court below, in not directing one of the intervenors in the suit, who purchased the property at sheriff's sale, to give up possession of the premises; and the complaint we think well founded. The purchaser having declared that the acts of the marshal were done by his authority, and joined issue on the validity of his proceedings, of which the sale to

[Thompson v. Chauveau.]

himself made a part, the decree of the court would not reach the merits of the case, if he were not compelled to restore the possession.

It is, therefore, ordered, adjudged and decreed that the judgment of the parish court be annulled, avoided and reversed; and it is further ordered, adjudged and decreed, that the plaintiff do recover possession of the lot in question from H. Buckman, or of the intervenors in this cause; that he also recover from the defendant, Louis Chauveau, the sum of one hundred and fifty dollars, with costs in both courts; and that the said Louis Chauveau do recover from Norman, M'Cleod & Campbell, Henry Buckman, George Singleton, G. R. Baumgard and Hiram Houghton, the said sum of one hundred and fifty dollars, with costs in both courts.

Nixon, for the plaintiff.

Canon and *M'Caleb*, for the defendant.

Ratcliff *et al. v.* Ratcliff *et al.*   VII, N? S. 355.

COURT of Probates, Parish of West Feliciana.

Representation for the purpose of inheritance, does not extend to the children of cousins of the deceased. Civil Code, 893.

Parker *v.* Starkweather. VII, N. S. 337.

Artisans have no right to protect more tools from seizure on a *fi. fa.* than those which are necessary to their livelihood.
The landlord has a privilege on the tools of a tradesman found on the premises, for the payment of rent.

FIRST District.

PORTER, J., delivered the opinion of the court.

The defendant took a rule on the sheriff to show cause why he should not surrender up a quantity of blacksmith's tools and utensils which he had seized under an execution issued in this case. The court, after hearing the parties, made the rule absolute, and the plaintiff appealed.

The appellant has urged in this court, that the judge below erred in releasing the articles seized from seizure, without any evidence to show that they were necessary to the livelihood of the defendant, and he has urged from the great number of articles contained in the inventory returned by the sheriff, that they could not be all required to enable the defendant to carry on his trade.

We are inclined to think the construction contended for by the plaintiff is correct, and that such evidence should be given. The object of the law was to secure to citizens and others, the means of laboring at their trade or profession, and they cannot avail themselves of this provision to put more property than is necessary for that purpose out of the reach of their creditors.

But in this case we are unable to reverse the judgment of the inferior court on that ground, for there is no statement on what evidence the rule was decided.

The plaintiff, however, urges errors of law apparent on the face of the record, which could not have been cured by any evidence given below. The judgment was rendered for rent, and the law, he contends, authorises the seizure of tools and utensils to satisfy a debt of this description.

The Code of Practice, on which the exemption is claimed, is in these words: " The sheriff cannot seize———the tools and instruments necessary for the exercise of the trade or profession by which the debtor gains a living." Code of Practice, 644.

Those of the Civil Code on which the plaintiff relies, are as follow: " The lessor has for the payment of his rent and other obligations of the lease, a right of pledge on the movable effects of the lessee which are found on the property leased." Louisiana Code, 2675.

This right of pledge the plaintiff contends, is the right to retain the article pledged until payment is made of the debt; and as the objects are in the hands of the debtor, that right must be as effective as if they had been delivered into the possession of the creditor.

The question which these articles of our Code present, is by no means free from difficulty. The tenth section of the act, entitled "An act to provide for the printing and promulgation of the amendments made to the Civil Code of the State of Louisiana," passed April 12th, 1824, provides "that in case the Code of Practice should contain any provision contrary or repugnant to those of the Civil Code,* the latter shall be considered as virtually repealed or thereby amended in that respect." Acts of 1824, p. 178.

Is the provision of the Code of Practice contrary to, and repugnant to that of the Civil Code? We are of opinion it is not. The rules prescribed for the execution of a *fieri facias*, are for ordinary cases of debt, where no special privilege existed independent of the judgment. If the debtor had pledged his tools for a sum of money, we suppose there can be no doubt of his being unable to get them back until he paid the money he had borrowed on them. The right of pledge conferred by law in favor of the lessor, must have the same effect, or the words have no meaning.

The correctness of this construction will, we think be strengthened by recurring to two other articles of our Code. The 2677th art. of the Louisiana Code, declares that the movables belonging to *third persons*, found on the premises, are subject to the pledge of the lessor. The Code of Practice only authorises the seizure of the property of *the debtor*, under a *fieri facias* for debt in an ordinary suit. We do not suppose it could be contended that this provision deprived the lessor of his privilege, and if it does not, we do not see how the article relied on by the appellee can have that effect in relation to tools, &c.

It is necessary to remark that in this instance, the seizure was made under a writ of *fieri facias*, but the suit in which the judgment was rendered was for rent, and we are of opinion, that the privilege of the lessor was not lost by the form of execution in which he sought to enforce it.

It is, therefore, ordered, adjudged and decreed, that the judgment of the district court be annulled, avoided and reversed, and that the

* Observe, Civil Code here means the amended Code, or what ought scrupulously to be called the Louisiana Code. Both the amendments to the Civil Code and the Code of Practice received legislative sanction (Mayor *et al. v.* Ripley *et al.* 2 *Lou. Rep.* 345) on the 12th of April, 1824, but the new Code took the force of law at New Orleans on the 25th of May, 1825, (Fisk *v.* Browder, 6 *N. S.* 692) and the Code of Practice went into operation in September, 1825. "By Martin, J." Skillman *v.* Leverich *et al.* 11 *Lou. Rep.* 517. The sections 25 and 20, of the act of the 25th of March, 1828, are thought by some jurists to have first given the *vigorem legis* to this Code. *Ibid,* 516.

rule granted in this case be discharged at the cost of the appellee in both courts.

Preston, for the plaintiff.
Hennen, for the defendant.

Louisiana State Bank *v.* Rowell.   VII, N. S. 341.

A woman could not previous to the passage of the Louisiana Code, bind herself as surety, though she gave to her engagement the form of an endorsement on a note.
And she may give parol evidence that she was in fact surety though the instrument on the face of it creates a higher obligation.

THIRD District.

PORTER, J., delivered the opinion of the court.

This is an action against the defendant as endorser of a promissory note. The petition charges the responsibility in the usual mode.

The answer consists of a general denial, and a plea that the defendant signed her name as surety, and that by law she could not enter into such an engagement.

There was judgment against her in the court of the first instance, and she appealed.

The note is in the following words:—" In three years after date, I promise to pay to Mrs. Sarah Rowell, or order, at the office of discount and deposit of the bank of Louisiana at Baton Rouge, the sum of four hundred and ninety dollars, with interest at the rate of seven per cent. but if not punctually paid, to bear an interest of ten per cent. per annum, from date, agreeably to an act of the general assembly, approved the 24th of January, 1825, value received in the liquidation of a debt to the Louisiana State Bank—this being the third instalment.   Baton Rouge, March 12th, 1825.

(Signed)   " SAMUEL STEER."

(Endorsed) Pay to the order of the Louisiana State Bank, for Sarah Rowell, Samuel Steer per proc.

We decided in the case of Lacroix *v.* Coquet, that a woman could in no case bind herself as surety. That decision was made on a positive law of the Partidas, which on no principle of construction could be considered as repealed by our old Civil Code. The amend-

[Louisiana State Bank v. Rowell.]

ments to that work it is said have produced that effect. This may be so, but as this engagement was entered into previous to the promulgation of these amendments, the case must be decided by the law as it stood anterior to their enactment.

Before the merits of the case can be inquired into, it is necessary to examine the opinion of the judge *a quo*, in relation to the admission of the maker of the note as a witness. He was, as the bill of exception states, called and sworn as a witness on the part of the plaintiffs, and the defendant asking him on the cross-examination, "did not the defendant endorse the note, on which this action is instituted, as surety for a debt due by you to the State Bank of Louisiana;" the question was objected to, and the objection was sustained by the court.

On the argument here, the competency of the witness has been denied on the provisions of the act of 1823, page 76, which provides "that the drawer of a note, bill of exchange, or other negotiable paper, shall never in any case be admitted as a witness in any civil cause, or suit brought by the holder of any such note, order, bill of exchange, or other negotiable paper, against any of the endorsers of said note," &c. The terms of this enactment do certainly exclude the witness offered in this case, but the plaintiffs, by examining him as a witness in chief, waived the objection, and conferred on the defendant the right, in the cross-examination, to put to him any legal question.

The legality of the question put to the witness, in this instance, cannot be doubted. If the defendant instead of having passed the note to the plaintiffs for value received by her, was in truth the surety of another for a debt due by him, she had a right to show it. When the law incapacitates persons from making contracts of a particular kind, its provisions cannot be evaded by giving to these contracts a different form from that forbidden by law, when in substance the contract is that prohibited. To sanction such agreements, would be permitting that to be done indirectly, which the law will not permit to be done directly. Thus we have often decided, that the law which renders wives incapable of becoming sureties for their husbands, could not be evaded by giving to the contract the form of an engagement *in solido*.

It is, therefore, ordered, adjudged and decreed, that the judgment of the district court be annulled, avoided and reversed; and it is further ordered, adjudged and decreed, that this cause be remanded to the district court, to be proceeded in according to law, the appellee paying the costs of this appeal.

Denis, for the plaintiff.
Watts, for the defendant.

Lacroix v. Menard et al.   VII, N. S. 345.

When there has been an appeal and judgment in the appellate court, third parties cannot have the case again examined on appeal.

FIRST District.

Porter, J., delivered the opinion of the court.

The minor heirs of one Dalon, prayed an appeal in the court of the first instance from a judgment rendered in said court, which had been already appealed from by the parties thereto, and confirmed in this tribunal. In the petition addressed to the court below, it is stated that the object of the appeal is to have the judgment rendered here amended in certain matters which materially affect the interest of the minors.

Notice of this demand was given to the plaintiffs, but they failed to appear or make any objection to it. The court however considered the mode of proceeding irregular, and refused the appeal. From that decision this appeal is taken.

The court has already decided, that when persons, not parties to a judgment, appealed from it, they must allege and prove in the court of the first instance their right to do so; that is, that they were aggrieved by it. The correctness of this mode of carrying the 57th article of the Code of Practice into effect has been strongly contested in argument. But after much reflection we do not see what other course can be adopted. The fact, of a party being aggrieved by a judgment rendered between others, is an indispensable condition to his right of appealing. That right must be established somewhere, before the correctness of the judgment complained of, can be examined into. It cannot be tried in this court, and it must be in that below, or the statute would become a dead letter.

There is nothing in this doctrine which in the least degree clashes with the provisions of the 904th article of the Code of Practice, for if it appears on trying the party's right to appeal in the court below, that he is a creditor who did not prove his debt in the first instance, his appeal in behalf of the debtor will be rejected.

But the present case is different from any other yet presented to this court under the provision of the Code of Practice, for there has already been an appeal by the parties to the suit, and final judgment rendered between them in this tribunal. We do not believe the legislature intended to give more than one appeal from the judgments of inferior courts. The provisions of the 571st article, are understood

[Lacroix *v.* Menard *et al.*]

by us to apply to cases, where the parties to the suit choose to acquiesce in a judgment by which other persons may be injured, and to protect these persons, by enabling them to obtain the revision of such judgment in the appellate tribunal. This application in truth, is to obtain an appeal from our judgment, not from that of the court which decided the cause in the first instance. A decree of an inferior court if opened by an appeal, remains so during its pendency; and unless the appeal be dismissed is never restored to its vigor. If reversed, the judgment rendered in the appellate tribunal could not be called the judgment of the court below. Nor could it be confirmed. In either case, the execution would be that of the court of the last instance, as is expressly provided by the Code of Practice. We are of opinion we have no power to reverse our judgments in the way attempted here; and that the judgment of the district court must be affirmed, with costs. Code of Practice, 618, 623, 629.

It is, therefore, ordered and decreed, that the judgment of the district court be affirmed, with costs.

Seghers, for the plaintiff.
Denis, for the defendant.

Percy's Syndic *v.* Percy *et al.*   VII, N. S. 348.

COURT of Probates of New Orleans.

When the court of probates orders a syndic to account with a creditor according to his rank, the rights of the parties in relation to particular demands which may form a portion of that account can not be inquired into until it is rendered.

Dorothée v. Cequillon et al.   VII, N. S. 350.

A *statu liber* has no action for relief for ill treatment.

PARISH Court of New Orleans.

MARTIN, J., delivered the opinion of the court.

The plaintiff, a free woman of color, complains that her child was directed to be emancipated at the age of twenty-one, by the will of her mistress, who bequeathed her services in the meanwhile to the defendant's daughter, who is still a minor—that the will requires that the child be educated in such a manner as may enable her to earn her livelihood, when free—that no care of her education is taken and she is treated cruelly. The prayer of the petition is, that the child be declared free at twenty-one, and in the meantime hired out by the sheriff.

The answer denies the plaintiff's capacity to sue—that she has any cause of action, and the general issue is pleaded.

The petition was dismissed, and the plaintiff appealed.

The plaintiff can not sue for her minor daughter, in a case in which the latter could not sue were she of age.

The daugeter is a *statu liber*, and as such a slave till she reaches her twenty-first year. *Clef des Loix Romaines, verbo Statu Liber.*— As a slave she can have no action, except to claim or prove her liberty. Civil Code, 177.

Her right to her freedom will not begin till she is twenty-one; if in the meanwhile the legatee fails to perform the conditions of the bequest, and the heir of the testatrix have the legacy annulled therefor, the *statu liber* must continue a slave in the meanwhile, and her services be enjoyed by the heir, so that the object of the suit, as far as it concerns her, is relief from ill treatment, which a slave can not sue for. The plaintiff is without a right of action.

It is, therefore, ordered, adjudged and decreed, that the judgment be affirmed, with costs.

Seghers, for the plaintiff.
Denis, for the defendants.

Millaudon *v.* Percy's Syndic. VII, N. S. 352.

An appeal from a judgment of partition, where the property is in the actual possession of the appellee, is suspensive, although security was only given for costs.

FIRST District.

MARTIN, J., delivered the opinion of the court.
This case was remanded from this court in April, 1827. *5 N. S.* 551.

On the return of it in the district court the plaintiff filed a petition, stating that the property, the division of which, through a sale, had been decreed by the judgment appealed from, had been legally sold, and nothing now remained but payment of the defendant's share which was in court. The defendant's syndic he having failed, denies that a legal sale had taken place. The court considered it had, and gave judgment accordingly. The syndic appealed.

The record shows the defendant gave security for costs only, on his appeal here; the plaintiff contends it was not suspensive. The syndic urges it was suspensive, notwithstanding security was given for no more than costs. So the question is on the character of the appeal.

Every timely appeal is suspensive unless security be not given for the performance of the judgment, in a case on which it is required. Code of Prac. 575.

It is not contended that the appeal was untimely, but it is averred that the judgment decreeing the delivery of slaves and real property, security was required. *Ibid.* 576, 277.

The judgment directs the plantation and slaves held in common by the parties to be sold in order to effect a partition by a division of the premises.

The plaintiff contends that this is a judgment decreeing a delivery, because the sale can not take place unless the things to be sold, be delivered.

The appellees urge that the Code of Practice speaks only of judgments decreeing the delivery of slaves or land unjustly withheld—that in the present case the plantation and slaves appear by the record to be in the actual possession of the plaintiff.

Admitting that the decree be for the delivery of the plantation and slaves, it secures such a delivery by the party being in possession and he can not expect security for the performance of an act to be performed by himself. It is true, death may lessen the number of the slaves, and the Mississippi carry off a part of the plantation—children may be born and the river may add a batture to the plantation; some kind of property is liable to increase or diminish in value, but the law requires an appellant to give security that he will perform as much of a judgment as he is directed to perform, and for nothing else.

We conclude that the district court erred in considering the appeal as devolutive only, and the sale legal.

It is, therefore, ordered, adjudged and decreed, that the judgment of the district court be annulled, avoided and reversed; and the case remanded for further proceedings, the plaintiff and appellee paying costs in the courts.

Seghers, for the plaintiff.
Davis, for the defendant.

Tracy v. Tuyes *et al.*   VII, N. S. 354.

FIRST District.

When communication is made to a party months before trial, that a document will be introduced and relied on in defence—he cannot object that he was surprised by its introduction. 6 *Martin,* 649; 4 *N. S.* 277.

Balfour *v.* Chinn.   VII, N. S. 358.

When a demand is in the alternative, for a slave, or his value, the jury may find a verdict in favor of the plaintiff for the slave, and at the same time assess his value.

A possessor in good faith is only responsible for the fruits from judicial demand.

THIRD District.

PORTER, J., delivered the opinion of the court.

The petitioner sues for a slave in the possession of the defendant, which she avers to be her property.

He pleads that he bought the property at a sheriff's sale, in pursuance of an execution issued at the suit of Dicks, Booker & Co., against Wm. Balfour, who now resides permanently out of the state of Louisiana. He further denies all the allegations in the petition, and prays that Dicks, Booker & Co. may be cited in warranty.

They were cited, appeared in warranty, and pleaded the general issue.

The cause was submitted to a jury in the court of the first instance, who found a verdict in favor of the plaintiff for the slave, or in case of his failure to deliver him, for 500 dollars, and 100 dollars a year for his hire, from the time he came into the possession of the defendant until delivered.

The court rendered judgment in conformity with the verdict, and the defendant and interpleaders appealed.

The first question in the cause is, as to the propriety of admitting in evidence, the copy of the record and judgment in a suit between the plaintiff and defendant for the slave now sued for. It is urged that, although this evidence was correctly received as between the original parties, it could not affect Dicks, Booker & Co., the warrantors. Admitting it could not, it was properly received as between plaintiff and defendant, and the correctness of the decree, as between them, is alone presented for our decision. No judgment, over against the warrantors, was given in the court below.

It is objected in the points filed, that the jury erred in finding the value of the slave; but we are unacquainted with any rule of our law which forbids them doing so, when the suit is in the alternative for the property, or its value. It is unnecessary to examine whether the pleadings, in this instance, authorised the verdict, as the point was abandoned on the argument before this court.

The jury found a verdict for the hire of the slave from the time he came into the possession of the defendant, and in this we think they

[Balfour v. Chinn.]

erred. He bought at sheriff's sale, previous to the decree of the court introduced in evidence in this cause, and like other possessors in good faith he is only responsible for the fruits of the thing sued for, from judicial demand.

It is, therefore, ordered, adjudged and decreed, that the judgment of the district court be annulled, avoided and reversed; and it is further ordered, adjudged and decreed, that the plaintiff do recover from the defendant the slave mentioned in the petition, and that, on failure of his delivering the same, he pay to the said plaintiff the sum of five hundred dollars. It is further ordered and decreed, that the plaintiff do recover from the defendant one hundred dollars a year, from the 12th of July, 1827, until the date of the delivery of the negro, or the payment of five hundred dollars, his value; the defendant to pay the costs of the court of the first instance, and the plaintiff those of appeal.

Pierce, for the defendant.

Dicks *et al.* *v.* Cash *et al.*   VII, N. S. 361.

THIRD District, Judge of the Fourth presiding.

If the jury give more than legal interest, the plaintiff may release the overplus and have judgment.

Dicks *et al. v.* Cash *et al.* VII, N. S. 362.

If the jury give more than legal interest, the plaintiff may release the overplus and have judgment.

Before the arguments on the merits new evidence may be received.

The plaintiff may prove, without having pleaded it, that he had endorsed the note to an agent for collection.

A judgment of nonsuit cannot be pleaded as *res judicata*, even after payment of costs.

THIRD District.

Porter, J., delivered the opinion of the court.

The defendants were sued as makers of a promissory note. They pleaded as exceptions: *First*, a final judgment of nonsuit in their favor in a former action on the same note, and between the same parties, which was a bar to this: and *Secondly*, the pendency of another suit, for the same causes, alleged in the petition.

The court below overruled these exceptions, and an answer was put in on the merits. It contained an assertion that admitting all the allegations in the petition, and the documents thereto annexed, the defendants were not bound in law to pay the money claimed of them.

The cause was submitted to a jury; who found a verdict for the plaintiffs with six per cent. interest, from the date of the protest of the note. The plaintiffs entered a *remittitur* on the record for one per cent. and the court after overruling a motion for a new trial, gave judgment against the defendants for the amount of the obligation sued on, with five per cent interest.

On the trial, as it is called in the record, of the exceptions, after the argument had commenced on the part of the defendants, the counsel for the plaintiffs offered evidence to show he had paid the costs of the first action in which he had been nonsuited. This evidence was objected to on the ground that it came too late, but the court admitted it. The defendants excepted.

The provisions in the Code of Practice, article 484, under which we presume the objection was made, are understood by this court to apply to a trial on the merits, and do not govern arguments or exceptions, and other incidental questions which may arise in the progress of the cause.

But admitting they did, and supposing the proof was rejected, we do not think the defendants plea of *res judicata* sustained. The evidence introduced by them, merely shows that a judgment of nonsuit was rendered. Now, though it is true, the Code of Practice (article

536) provides, that such judgment cannot be pleaded as *res judicata,*
or in bar of another suit for the same cause of action, provided the
plaintiff shows he has paid the costs of the first suit—it by no means
follows that a judgment of this description can be pleaded as *res judicata,* when the costs of the suit are paid. We have had occasion
more than once to notice the effect which should be given to this
argument *contrario sensu;* and though it is frequently true in the
interpretation of laws, it is by no means conclusive. When an examination of the whole subject leads to a conclusion, that such was not
the intention of the law maker, these negative expressions cannot be
considered as binding in the same manner as a positive enactment
that a judgment of nonsuit could be pleaded as *res judicata.* There
is no one who will peruse the whole of this article, and compare it
with the French part of the law, (to which in cases of ambiguity, we
are bound to look,) who can doubt for one moment that its only
object was to afford protection by a dilatory exception against the
plaintiff harassing the defendant with repeated actions for the same
cause, without paying the costs of those which had been previously
dismissed. To carry it any further would lead to the most absurd
consequences. It would be making a judgment, which was rendered
because nothing could be adjudged on the merits, final and conclusive between the parties; and making that which the law contemplated to be final, and a bar to another suit, cease to be so on the
payment of costs.

As a plea therefore of *res judicata,* the defence set up by the defendant could not be sustained, and the court did not err in overruling it: as a dilatory exception it was defectively pleaded, for there
was no averment of the fact which could alone make it so; the non-
payment of costs by the plaintiffs.

In regard to the exception taken to the introduction of the decree
of the Supreme Court, it was quite surplusage in the plaintiffs offering such evidence. The proof introduced on the part of the defendants did not show any appeal to be pending. The decree of the
court below showed that the plaintiffs had been nonsuited.

We deem it unnecessary to notice particularly a bill of exceptions
taken by the defendants, not to a decision of the court in setting aside
the judgment by default—but to the reasons on which that decision
was founded. If the defendants had the benefit of their motion as
they had in this instance, it is useless to inquire into the course of
reasoning by which the judge below arrived at his conclusions.

On the trial of the merits, the plaintiffs introduced as a witness, the
endorsee, to whom they had passed the note in order to prove that it
had been endorsed to him as their agent, and that he had not any
interest in it. His testimony was objected to, because no such allegation was contained in the petition. We do not think there existed
any necessity for such an allegation   The petitioners state themselves
to be endorsers of the note. The proof introduced corresponds with
this averment. The objection that they had parted with their title,

[Dicks *et al. v.* Cash *et al.*]

was matter of defence, which was to come from the defendants, and whether that defence was suggested by the instrument introduced or not, cannot vary the plaintiffs' right to introduce evidence to destroy it, nor increase their obligation to set it our specially.

The jury found a verdict with six per cent. interest from the date of the protest. This was erroneous, and the plaintiffs immediately entered on the record a *remittitur* of one per cent.; a new trial was moved for on the ground, that the jury had erred, and that the plaintiffs had no right to correct the error. We agree with the court below, that the plaintiffs had a right to remove the objection to the verdict by a *remittitur*, and that judgment was correctly entered up for the principal of the note with five per cent. interest.

We have been requested to confirm the judgment of the court below, with ten per cent. damages, but we cannot accede to the demand. The case on the part of the defendants, it is true, comes before us without a shadow of defence on the merits, but it has been most ingeniously contested on technical grounds, which from the previous part of this opinion, are seen not to be free from difficulty, and the appellants may have honestly believed that some of those grounds might avail them before this tribunal.

It is, therefore, ordered, adjudged and decreed, that the judgment of the district court be affirmed, with costs.

Pierce, for the plaintiffs.

Turner, for the defendants.

Weir *et al. v.* Cox. VII, N. S. 368.

An endorsee of a bill of exchange, who has no interest in the bill, but endorses it to facilitate its discount, is not always to be considered merely as a surety.

As between the drawer and the payees who had agreed to endorse for his accommodation, the contract of suretyship was formed; as has already been decided in this court in the case of Nolte *et al. v.* Their Creditors. So also the payees and endorsers became sureties to all persons who might take the bill in the due course of trade. But the engagement of the acceptor was absolute to pay to *them*, and there is nothing in the terms of the obligation, nor we believe in the understanding of the parties, at the time they endorsed it, which creates the slightest presumption they intended to become sureties to the acceptor, or that he honored the draft on their responsibility; or that they were to be bound not only to the persons to whom the bill was to be paid, but also to the person who promised to pay it.

FIRST District.

Porter, J., delivered the opinion of the court.

This is an action by the payee of a bill of exchange against the acceptor. The liability of the defendant is set forth in the petition in the usual manner. The answer admits the acceptance, but avers that the bill has long since been paid: that the claim is barred by prescription: and finally, that the plaintiffs have deprived the defendant by their negligence of any recourse against the drawer, or his property, the bill being accepted merely for his accommodation.

The case was submitted to a jury in the inferior court, who found a verdict for the plaintiffs. The court confirmed it, and the defendant appealed.

Several bills of exceptions were taken, on the trial, to the opinions of the judge refusing the defendant permission to give in evidence, letters of one of the plaintiffs, letters of the drawer, and the proceedings of the defendant against his creditors for a respite. They were rejected on the ground of irrelevancy, and not being within the pleadings. In those cases where the proof was excluded, because it varied from the defence pleaded, the court was clearly correct; and an attentive perusal of the evidence considered to be irrelevant, has satisfied us that no error was committed in preventing it also, from going to the jury.

The defendant requested the judge to charge the jury, "that when the endorser of a bill of exchange has paid no value for it, nor been in reality the owner, but has merely endorsed it to accommodate the drawer, and enable him to raise money on it, such endorser, though he should pay the bill after protest, is to be considered as surety of the drawer, and his rights are to be regulated as such." The judge refused to give the opinion to the jury, and the defendant excepted.

We are of opinion the judge did not err in refusing to give such a charge to the jury. As between the drawer and the payees who had agreed to endorse for his accommodation, the contract of suretyship was formed; as has already been decided in this court in the case of Nolte *et al. v.* Their Creditors. So also the payees and endorsers became sureties to all persons who might take the bill in the due course of trade. But the engagement of the acceptor was absolute to pay to them, and there is nothing in the terms of the obligation, nor we believe in the understanding of the parties, at the time they endorsed it, which creates the slightest presumption they intended to become sureties to the acceptor, or that he honored the draft on their responsibility; or that they were to be bound not only to the persons to whom the bill was to be paid, but also to the person who promised to pay it. When an attempt is made not only to take a negotiable instrument out of the law merchant, but to give to it a construction directly opposite to its literal meaning, a clear case should be made out of the intention and understanding of the parties. So far from

[Weir *et al. v.* Cox.]

that being the case, we do not believe it ever entered into the thoughts of the plaintiffs, that they were to be sureties to the acceptor.— Nothing at least of that kind has been proved, and we are bound to conclude that the understanding of the parties was conformable to the terms of the contract.

ı This defence we presume has been suggested, as it appears to be sanctioned, by the opinions of a late eminent judge in England sitting at *nisi prius.* But these opinions have been since overruled. Certainly until these decisions of Lord Ellenborough, it never was suggested that the engagement of the acceptor was not absolute to all the previous parties, and that nothing could discharge him but payment, or release. The law merchant of the United States is decidedly against the doctrine on which the appellant has relied, and so also, we are satisfied, is the reason of the thing. Bayley on Bills, 121; 2 Camp. N. P. C. 185; 3 *Ibid.* 362; 4 Taunton, 730; 5 *Ibid.* 192; 2 Starkie, 531; 6 Cowen, 484; 9 Serg. & Rawle, 229; 3 Kent's Comm. 57.

It is, therefore, ordered, adjudged and decreed, that the judgment of the district court be affirmed, with costs.

Hawes and *Maybin,* for the plaintiffs.

Strawbridge, for the defendant.

Lane *et al. v.* De Peyster. VII, N. S. 372.

PARISH Court of New Orleans.

An agent is a competent witness without a release.

A surety on a bond given to release property from sequestration, is not a competent witness. See United States Bank *v.* Johnson, 5 *N. S.* 210.

Burroughs *v.* Jayne *et al.*   VII, N. S. 374.

FIRST District.

The ratification of a void contract, cannot affect the interest of third parties.

By PORTER, J.—The authorities cited by plaintiff's counsel are decisive, we think, in sustaining this position. Louisiana Code, 1789; *Ibid.* 2252; *Toullier, vol.* 8, *no.* 553; Merlin, Questions, *verbo* Ratification.

Donaldson *et al. v.* Dorsey's Syndic.   VII, N. S. 376.

The district court was not without jurisdiction *ratione materiæ* in suits against an estate administered by an executor.

And a possessor under a sale made in virtue ·of a judgment of that court, is not *mala fide.*

FIRST District.

MARTIN, J., delivered the opinion of the court.

This case was remanded from this court, in order to have the value of the improvements made, and the profits received by the insolvent, ascertained; it having been decided that he was without title to the house and lot, which is the principal object of the present suit. 5 *N. S.*

From the last judgment of the district court the plaintiffs have appealed, and they complain that the court erred in considering the insolvent in bad faith, only from the period at which this court declared he had no title; they complain also, that the improvements are overvalued and the profits undervalued.

Their counsel has made the following points:

1. The insolvent bought in bad faith.

2. If he did not, his bad faith began at the institution of the suit for the recovery of the premises.

3. Or on the institution of a previous suit, which was discontinued;

4. Or on the institution of the plaintiffs' suit for the provisional possession.

5. The evidence established a different value of the improvements and profits.

I. The insolvent purchased at a sale under a judgment of the district court, at the instance of a person who styled himself agent of the executrixes of C. Van Pradelle, the plaintiffs' mother.

And it is urged the sale is a nullity, being ordered by a court without jurisdiction, and the objections made by these plaintiffs in a suit lately determined, in which the present plaintiffs recovered sundry slaves from Hull, a purchaser under circumstances not absolutely the same as the insolvent, but in many points similar.

If the district court was absolutely without jurisdiction, *i. e.*, if they were so, *ratione materiæ,* the objection would prevail—but the point is now settled that district courts are not without jurisdiction *ratione materiæ,* in cases of vacant estates, or of estates administered by executors.   Tabor *v.* Johnson, 3 *N. S.* 674.

The striking difference between the present case and that in which the plaintiffs recovered from Hull, the existence of a judgment decreeing the sale, distinguishes the cases; and the insolvent bought at a sale, which would have transferred the property to him, if the person mentioned there, held as the testatrix had been really dead; the estate would have passed, unless the minority of the heirs would have prevented it; but this circumstance would have rendered the sale voidable not void; the nullity, if any, would be a relative one.

The absence of proof of the testatrix's death, makes her living to be presumed, and then the insolvent's title fails, because his vendors, the plaintiffs in the suit, had no title.

On the first point we think the district court did not err, in considering the insolvent as a *bona fide* purchaser.

II, III, and IV. On the three following points the appellee's principal reliance is in the provisions of the new Civil Code, 495, 3416. The sale under consideration is anterior to the Code and the rights to which it gave rise must be regulated by the laws in vigor at the time.   So the court is not precluded from the inquiry whether the purchaser knew, before judgment, that he was without title.   His title depended on the circumstance of the plaintiff's mother having died before the letters testamentary were granted to the persons named in her will, as executrixes.   The moral presumption. in every part of the world, where a vessel on a coasting voyage does not arrive within the year after her departure, and is not heard of, is that she foundered within that period.   In Louisiana the legal presumption does not arise perhaps, till the person, if living, would be one hundred years old.   The executrixes residing in Maryland, and having sent their powers from thence, and the suit being in their capacity of executrixes, the insolvent, we presume, might have believed either that direct proof was made of her death, or such circumstances established, which authorised the grant of the letters. He might possibly believe that the plaintiffs' mother was dead. His error would then be an error of fact. He knew that he had never heard of her death, but he could not know that no one else had, and the suit in which the house and lot were sold, would induce an honest man to believe not only that she was dead, but that her death was known.

We conclude that the insolvent's possession before the judgment declaring he had no title, was not in bad faith.

V. The last point relates to a question of evidence. We have examined the testimony. In such cases the weight the judge *a quo* gives it, generally influences our judgment.

In the absolute absence of moral bad faith, the party who relies on the technical, must make his case perfectly clear.

It is, therefore, ordered, adjudged and decreed, that the judgment of the district court be affirmed, with costs.

M' Caleb, for the plaintiffs.

Hennen, for the defendant.

Mounot *v.* Williamson. VII, N. S. 381.

When 'a property is sold by the sheriff, subject to a mortgage, and not subject to the *payment* of the mortgage, the purchaser is not responsible for the lien.

And if the property sold does not amount to the mortgage, there is no sale.

It is sufficient notice of such mortgage, that it is mentioned in the act of sale.

SECOND District, Judge of the Eighth presiding.

MARTIN, J., delivered the opinion of the court.

The petitioner states that he was possessor of a slave, on which his vendor held a mortgage for 400 dollars, and had obtained a writ of seizure and sale, and the defendant purchased her at a sheriff's sale, under an execution against him, the present plaintiff,. for the sum of 150 dollars, which was less than the sum she was mortgaged for. The petition concludes with a prayer that the sale be set aside, and that he may have judgment for the slave or her value.

The defendant averred himself the legal owner of the slave, and that if any writ of seizure and sale issued, it was illegally and improvidently issued.   He denied all the other allegations. I

The defendant had judgment, and the plaintiff appealed.

The statement of facts shows that the following documents were introduced:

The sheriff's sale to the defendant, May 16, 1824.

The execution issued in favor of Dufilho against the plaintiff.

The parish judge's certificate of his mortgage.

The writ of seizure and sale in favor of Arbonneaux, the plaintiff's vendor, April 16, 1824.

Parol evidence of the slave being in the defendant's possession.

The appellant's counsel contends that,

1. The sale is illegal as the price is not equal to the amount of the mortgage.

2. The registry of the vendor's lien was not a necessary guard to the appellee, whose title shows he had notice.

3. The sheriff should have sold subject to the payment of the mortgage, and not subject to the mortgage.

The appellee contends that,

1. There is no privity of contract between him and the appellant, nor any proof that the former profited by any injury sustained by the latter.

2. The act of 1817 requires only that the sheriff should sell subject to such mortgages as may exist—the clause inserted that the sale was subject to the order of seizure, is a mere surplusage.

3. The order of seizure in the present case illegally and improvidently issued, being claimed on no authentic act, but on one signed by a notary only, and not by two witnesses.

4. The order of seizure, even if legal, could give no right to any but to Arbonneaux.

5. The certificate of the parish judge, produced by the sheriff, repels any presumption of notice arising from any part of the sheriff's deeds.

6. The appellee, were he to pay the price to the appellant, would be still liable to Arbonneaux.

We are of opinion that the appellee, although he bought a slave subject to a mortgage of 400 dollars, for 150 dollars, did not bid 550 dollars, but 150 dollars for the slave, i. e., less than the sum she was mortgaged for; and therefore there was no legal sale.   Landreaux v. Hazzelton, 1 N. S. 600; De Armas v. Morgan, 3 N. S. 604; Balfour v. Chew, 4 N. S. 154.

We also think that the express mention in the bill of sale, is evidence of the existence of the mortgage, notwithstanding the certificate of the parish judge; for the certificate goes only as to mortgages recorded in his office, not as to those that may exist without a record there, or on record any where else.

So that the appellant ought to have recovered, unless there be something in the possession of the appellee that prevents it.

I. The absence of any privity of contract between the appellant and appellee is alleged. We are not prepared to admit that there is no privity, for were the appellee evicted by any but the appellant's vendor, he would have a right to demand from the appellant the amount of the debt paid to the creditor, on the *fieri facias*, and perhaps this right would exist if evicted by the vendor. It is true, there is no evidence of the appellee having been benefitted by any injury sustained by the appellant. But should the appellant be compelled to pay his vendor, in the absence of a personal obligation of the appellee to pay any more than his bid, he might suffer and the appellee be benefitted thereby.

II. The statute says the property shall be sold subject to the payment, by the purchaser, of the previous mortgages or privileges.

III. It is true the writ of seizure and sale issued illegally and improvidently, on a mortgage *sous seing privé*. Of this the mortgagee might have complained, and the writ would have been set aside. The creditor on the *fieri facias*, might, perhaps, have directed the sheriff not to regard the mortgage, but neither did so, and the sheriff's sale must be taken *pro est sonat:* a sale to which the creditor and debtor in the execution are, by their silence, presumed to have assented, and to which the appellee must be bound, because he willingly became a party thereto.

The appellant, had he demanded then the writ of seizure and sale, would *in foro conscientiæ* have done an injury to his vendor—the creditor in the *fieri facias*, was perhaps bound *in foro conscientiæ* not to resist the execution of the order of seizure and sale, if it did not retard or jeopardise his payment. Their consent must be presumed from their silence. The appellee having become a party, for his own benefit, to a contract which left the purchased property bound for the appellant's debt, without undergoing the personal obligation of paying it, did not bid a sum exceeding the amount of the mortgage. In such a case we have said there is no sale. As to him, the order of seizure and sale is as binding as if the mortgage resulted from an authentic act.

IV. The appellant's right, now insisted on, results from the illegality of the sale, and not from the order of seizure, which, it is true, gave no right to any but the vendor.

V. The consequences of the certificate have been examined.

VI. We have said the appellee is not personally bound to pay the mortgage: by surrendering the mortgaged slave, he will be discharged from any liability.

It is, therefore, ordered, adjudged and decreed, that the judgment of the district court be annulled, avoided and reversed; the sale set aside; and that the appellant recover the slave mentioned in the petition, with the value of her labor, while in the appellee's possession, to be assessed in the district court; he reimbursing thereout, or otherwise to the appellee, the sum mentioned in the sheriff's bill of sale, as

the consideration of it, with interest at five per cent.; the appellee paying costs in both courts.
Morse, for the plaintiff.
Eustis, for the defendant.

Acosta v. Robin.   VII, N. S. 387.

The natural father cannot compel the mother of a natural child to give up to him the possession of such child.
There is no tutorship until the death of the father or mother.

PARISH Court of New Orleans.

PORTER, J., delivered the opinion of the court.

The contest in this case arises out of the conflicting pretensions of the father and mother of a natural child; each claims the right of having the possession and care of it. The parish judge decided against the petitioner, and he appealed.

The evidence shows that the child was acknowledged by the father, who was a party to the act of baptism, in which he is stated to be such. It is also shown, that the parties lived for years in a state of concubinage. The defendant has urged that the acknowledgment of the father does not make proof against her. This is true, but taking the whole proof in the case, there is little doubt left in our minds, that the petitioner is the father of the child claimed in the petition. Civil Code, 48, art. 27.

Considering him such, the next question is, has he the right in law to the care of his natural child, in opposition to the mother? This is the first time in our experience that the question has been presented to our courts, but it is not a novel one in our jurisprudence. It has been long settled there.

In support of the pretensions of the appellant it has been urged that the father is the natural tutor of his child. But in our judgment there can be no tutor to a child while the father and mother are alive. The first law of the 16th title of the 6th *Partida* declares *tutela,* in Latin, to be that guardianship which is given over minor orphan children, not minors alone, as stated in Moreau & Carleton's translation of the law. The words are *tutela tanto quiére dicer en latin como guarda en romance, que es dada é otorgada al huerfano libre, me-*

nor de catorce anos. The commentators on this law, understand it
as conferred only for children, who have lost father, or mother, or
both. Our Code declares tutorship by nature to be the right of the
surviving father, or mother, on the dissolution of the marriage by
the death of one of them, to be tutor of the children. It contemplates
the father to act in another character during the marriage, and calls
him the administrator of the estate of his minor children. The opinion of the French commentators on the articles of the Napoleon Code,
which are the same as ours on this subject, is that there is no tutorship until the death of the father or mother. Civil Code, 58, art. 5
and 6; *Paillet* on the *Code Napoleon,* art. 389; *Toullier, vol. 2, liv.*
1, *tit.* 10, *no.* 1090.

The right therefore set up in this instance in behalf of the father,
can derive no support from the laws relating to tutorship; if it exist
at all, it must be found in that which treats of the paternal power, *la
patria potestad.*

But we are satisfied that it does not confer any such power on the
father of bastard children even when acknowledged by them. It did
not do so in Rome, where the authority of parents was carried further than in any other civilised country. The institutes of Justinian
declare, that the children whom we have under our power are those
which are born in legitimate marriage. The Digest has an express
provision that natural children can not be brought under the paternal authority; (*patriam potestatem*) The second law of the 17th
title of the 4th *Partida,* provides, that natural children are not in the
power of the father as legitimate children are, and the Spanish commentators state their law to be in conformity with this provision.
Partidas 4, *tit.* 17, *law* 2; *Febrero, p.* 1, *cap.* 12, *sect.* 3, *no.* 17;
Institutes, lib. 1, *tit.* 9; *Digest, lib.* 1, *tit.* 6, *no.* 11; *Merlin, Repertoire, verbo Puissance Paternelle,* 343.

The case was argued before us on the provisions of our Code alone.
we have gone into the examination of the law as it previously stood,
to show more clearly the construction we should put on that provision of our Code which declares " that bastards are not submitted to
paternal authority, even where they have been legally acknowledged;"
and believing as we do, that this provision (which is not founded in
the Napoleon Code) was taken from the laws of Spain, and introduced in conformity with the doctrine established there, we think
there can not be a doubt that it repels the demand made by the petitioner. Code, 56, 59.

Toullier, in commenting on the Napoleon Code which repealed the
civil law, and contains no provision such as that first cited from ours,
seems to consider that in tender age the child should be confided to
the mother, but that as it advances in life the reasons in favor of her
having the possession are not so conclusive. He considers it a question left to the prudence of the magistrate under all the circumstances
of the case, and that the right should be conferred on either father or
mother, as the interest of the minor may dictate. If we had such a
discretion, the facts of this case would induce us to prefer the mother.

[Acosta *v.* Robin.]

There is a claim in the petition for one thousand dollars, in case the father can not get the child: we doubt much whether two such demands can be joined; but admitting they could, the evidence does not authorise judgment in his favor.

It is, therefore, ordered, adjudged and decreed, that the judgment of the parish court be affirmed, with costs.

Rodriguez, for the plaintiff.

Moreau, for tho defendant.

EASTERN DISTRICT, FEBRUARY TERM, 1829.

———

M'Micken v. Riley et al., Administrators.
VII, N. S. 393.

When the appellee is absent, and has two attorneys on record, the citation may be served on either.

When the judge certifies, the presumption is that the counsel did not agree on the statement.

The law has not fixed the period during which the judge may certify.

THIRD District.

Porter, J., delivered the opinion of the court.

The defendants are stated in the petition, to have been appointed administrators in the state of Mississippi of a debtor of the petitioners, named Samuel Riley. The petition sets out the cause of action to be a debt due by the intestate in his lifetime; and avers that the defendants have taken into their possession the whole of his estate, and by doing so, have made themselves responsible by the laws of Mississippi for the debt due the plaintiff. It concludes with a prayer that an attachment may issue against the goods and chattels, &c., of the defendants. "And that it be ordered, adjudged and decreed, that the said John Y. Riley. and the said Henry Cage pay to your petitioner, the said sum of 923 dollars, with interest and costs."

The defendants pleaded as exceptions to the action,

1. That there was no cause of action set forth in the petition against them.

[M'Micken v. Riley et al., Administrators.]

2. That they were only administrators of the estate, and not liable individually.

3. Sundry errors apparent on the face of the proceedings.

4. The insufficiency of the affidavit.

5. The pendency of another suit for the same cause of action, in the state of Mississippi, as administrators.

6. Because the property of the defendants is not liable or bound for the payment of another person's debt.

In addition to these exceptions an answer was put in containing the general issue; a repetition of the allegations already set forth in the exceptions, that a suit for the same cause, and between the same parties, was pending in the state of Mississippi, and a prayer in reconvention.

The exceptions were overruled, and the case tried on its merits by a jury, who found for the plaintiff. The court confirmed the verdict, and the defendants appealed.

The appellee has moved in this court to dismiss the appeal on three several grounds.

1. Because there has been no sufficient legal service of the citation of appeal, nor any legal return to show the service.

2. Because there is no statement of facts, nor any thing answering in a sufficient legal form to supply the defect.

3. Because there is not a legal and proper certificate of the judge a quo, that the record contains all the facts on which the cause was tried.

I. The return of the sheriff is in the following words: "Served 16th September, 1828, a copy of this citation of appeal on Isaac Johnson, Esq. one of the attorneys for Charles McMicken, who is at present residing out of the state of Louisiana; also a certified copy of appellant's petition of appeal in the town of St. Francisville." The 582d article of the Code of Practice, states that "the sheriff shall serve the petition and citation on the appellee if he reside within the state, or his advocate, if he do not, by delivering a copy of the same to such appellee or his advocate, or by leaving it at the place of their usual domicil."

Where there are two attorneys on record, as was the case here, we think a service on one of them, is a compliance with both the letter and spirit of the law. The return of the officers states the appellee to be a non-resident of the state at the time of the service, and this appears to us sufficient under the Code of Practice. By the law as it stood previous to that Code being adopted, the absence of the party, and the authority of the attorney, must have been shown by a special affidavit. But these seem to be no longer required.

II. The judgment was rendered the 7th of May, 1828. The certificate of the judge is of the 20th of November of the same year, and is in the following words: "I certify that the record in this case contains all the evidence adduced by the parties on the trial thereof."

The first objection made to this certificate is, that by the provision of the Code of Practice, the judge is not permitted to give a certificate except when the parties disagree, and that there is no evidence here that the event had occurred which authorised him to act. This objection was taken in the case of Gayoso v. Garcia, 1 N. S. 324, on provisions of law similar to those contained in the Code of Practice; we were then of opinion, that the judge must be presumed to have given his certificate on the occurrence of those events which empowered him to make it, and that if the fact were otherwise, it was the duty of the appellee to establish it. Officers of such high station, in whom the law reposes so much confidence, cannot be presumed to have volunteered their services in cases where the law did not enable them to act. 1 N. S. 324. See also Trepagnier's Heirs v. Butler, 12 Martin, 534.

The next objection made to the certificate is the time at which it was made out. It appears to have been given six months and more after the judgment was signed.

The act of the legislature which first provided the mode of enabling this court to revise the decisions of inferior tribunals on questions of fact, after prescribing the different modes by which a statement could be made, contained a clause to this effect, "which statement may be made at any time before judgment at the request of one of the parties."

A case soon arose under this enactment, and was brought before the court, who were of opinion that a statement made after judgment could not enable the appellant to have the decision of the inferior tribunal examined. The reasons in favor of the policy and wisdom of such a rule, and those which showed the construction to be the true legal interpretation of the act, are given at length in the case as reported, and they appear to us still correct. 3 Martin, 201.

In the year 1817, the legislature declared that whenever all the facts proved in a suit shall appear on the record by the written documents filed in the same, it shall be sufficient that the judge below do certify that the record contains all the matters on which the case was tried in the first instance. Acts of 1817, p. 34, sect. 13.

The act not having specified any time at which the judge might give this certificate, it was held by this court he might do it at any time, when the cause was tried on written documents.

The 586th article of the Code of Practice is in these words. "If the testimony produced in the cause have been taken in writing, and if the record contain all the evidence produced in the suit, the judge shall certify at the foot of the records, that they contain all the evidence adduced by the parties, otherwise he must make a statement of facts in the manner hereinafter provided."

The expressions of the article in relation to the certificate of the judge are the same as those contained in the act of 1817. No time is prescribed at which he shall give it. The only difference in the enactment is, that now he may certify when the parol evidence is reduced to writing, formerly he could not do so, unless the cause was tried on written documents.

[M'Micken v. Riley et al., Administrators.]

As, therefore, no limitation is fixed to the time in which this certi-ficate may be given, this court cannot make one. With the wisdom of the rule, we have nothing to do. We must obey it in the sense in which we understand the legislature to have passed it.

It appears to us that on the merits there is no cause of action against the defendants in their individual capacity. The petition states they were appointed administrators in the state of Mississippi. No law of that state has been produced in evidence which makes the acceptance and acting in such an office a ground of personal respon-sibility. Nothing is averred or proved, which would make them responsible by the laws of our state.

It is, therefore, ordered, adjudged and decreed, that the judgment of the district court be annulled, avoided and reversed; that there be judgment for the defendants as in case of nonsuit, with costs in both courts.

Turner, for the plaintiff.
Watts, for the defendants.

Adams *v.* Lewis.   VII, N. S. 400.

It is not necessary after stating the residence of the defendant to be in *such a county*, to add the words state of Louisiana.

If the plaintiff bring inconsistent demands in different actions he may renounce all benefit to be derived from the first, in the court where the second is pending, and proceed with the last instituted.

If there be a demand in reconvention, plaintiff cannot dismiss the suit, so as to prevent the defendant having judgment against him, but he may waive benefit to be derived from it.

FOURTH District, Judge of the Third presiding.

Porter, J., delivered the opinion of the court.

The object of this suit is the rescission of the sale of a plantation and slaves, with damages, the vendee having failed to comply with his part of the contract.

The defendant filed various exceptions to the petition.

1. To the jurisdiction of the court; that it does not appear that the court before which the suit is brought is one of the courts of the state of Louisiana.

2. The residence of the plaintiff not sufficiently shown.

3. Nor that of the defendant.

4. The plantation and slaves are not shown to be within the state.

5. A suit pending for the consideration of the sale.

6. Another suit for the same property.

There is a prayer for setting aside the writ of sequestration because it improperly issued.

The court dismissed the petition, and the plaintiff appealed. The 1st, 2d, 3d and 4th exceptions are all bottomed on the absence of averments in the petition—that the parish in which suit is brought, the court to which the petition is addressed, or the parish wherein the parties are stated to live and the property to be situated, are within the state of Louisiana.

The petition is addressed "to the judge of the fourth district, sitting in and for the parish of Iberville." The petitioner avers himself to be of the parish of Iberville. The defendant is described as of the same parish, and the property is averred to be situated therein.

This in our opinion was sufficient without the words state of Louisiana. Courts of justice take notice, and are presumed to know the territorial and judicial divisions of the state or kingdom to which they belong. The objection made in this instance would be too technical if offered against an indictment at common law. For it is not required or necessary in that instrument, to aver that the county in which the offence was committed was in England.

The only question in the case which presents the slightest difficulty, is in relation to the plea which discloses the pendency of another suit growing out of this contract.

On the first instalment becoming due, the plaintiff commenced an action to enforce the payment of it. The suit was yet pending in the Supreme Court, when that now before us was instituted.

The defendant rests his objection on two distinct grounds. First, that the plaintiff can not maintain two actions at the same time, for the thing, and the price of the thing; and, secondly, because there is another suit pending for the same object, and growing out of the same cause of action.

The last ground may be dismissed from our consideration, for the evidence is that the suit pending is not for the same object. The first ground requires more attention.

The Code of Practice, art. 149, provides, that the plaintiff is not allowed to cumulate several demands in the same action, when one of them is contrary to, and precludes another. A vendor can not demand at the same time the rescission of the sale he had made, and the price for which it was made. He must decide for one or other of the two causes of action, as the one precludes the other.

This prohibition is confined in terms, to a cumulation in the same action. But in its spirit we think with the counsel of the appellee, that it prohibits the inconsistent demands in two distinct actions.

The plaintiff however contends, that he too complied with the spirit of it, in entering a waiver on record of all claim or advantage under

[Adams v. Lewis.]

the first suit, and electing to proceed on the second: that this act on his part brings him within the concluding clause of the article cited, which declares that in cases of this kind the petitioner must decide which of the two he will proceed on.

We think it did, and the court below erred in dismissing the petition. It was to all intents and purposes an election on his part which of the remedies he would pursue. It would have been sufficient had both demands been in the same action, and it cannot make him in any worse situation that they were in two separate actions.

In support of the decision of the court below, and consequently in opposition to the opinion just announced, several grounds have been taken. First, it is said that the suit being pending in another court he had no longer any control over it, and could not dismiss it. But though he could not dismiss the suit, he might renounce all advantages under it. The place where he made the inconsistent demands, can not affect his right of deciding between them It is sufficient if he does so before the court where one of the causes is pending, to enable that court to proceed with the claim to which he gives a preference. All that it should require is, that the election be made in such a manner, as would prevent the plaintiff taking advantage of the contrary demand. That put on record here, was an ample security against the other suit. The Code of Practice does not exact from a party who has cumulated two demands in the same petition, that he shall formally dismiss one of them. It requires him to choose between them. If the rules in the Code of Practice in relation to two contrary demands in the same action, be extended, as we think they ought, to the same kind of demands in separate actions for the protection of the defendant; we see no reason why the same means of getting rid of them should not be afforded to the plaintiff in both. A contrary rule would be extending the equity of the statute for the benefit of the defendant, and contracting it to the prejudice of the plaintiff.

Next it was said, there was a plea of reconvention, and that the plaintiff could not dismiss. He certainly can not, but he may well determine not to prosecute his claim in that suit, though he can not by a mere abandonment on his part, defeat any legal rights the defendant may have acquired under the demand in reconvention to have judgment against him. Then the question is reduced to an inquiry whether a suit pending by the vendee against the vendor is a bar to the latter's suing to annul the contract, and it is very clear that it is not.

As to the argument, that the waiver came too late, because the sequestration had issued before it was made, there is in our judgment no force in it. It would not be a good exception in case both demands were cumulated in the same petition. The only penalty affixed by law on the plaintiff for bringing two contrary demands is the dismissal of his petition unless he determines for one or other. It is not said in the law, nor can it be inferred from any of its provisions, that

25*

the suit is bad from the commencement. On the contrary, the permission to continue it, and to compel the defendant to answer after the plaintiff has made choice, negatives the idea that all the anterior proceedings are null and of no effect. If the sequestration was bad, so was the service of the petition, and every other incident in the cause prior to the plaintiff's decision. Again, it has been more than once decided in this court, that writs of this description would not be set aside, if the case showed sufficient grounds for immediately reinstating them. 2 *N. S.* 480, and *Ibid.* 499. But it is urged the case shows not sufficient ground for granting the writ of sequestration. We think it does. The suit is for the possession and property of land and slaves, which it is alleged the defendant sets up title to, under a contract with the plaintiff. That contract is alleged to be void and of no effect, because the vendee has failed to comply with his engagement, and the petitioner charges that the defendant is about to waste the fruits. These allegations bring the case within the 275th article of the Code of Practice.

The objections taken to the oath made on obtaining the sequestration; the return of the writ by the sheriff; and a want of a copy of the bond being given to the defendant, appear to us wholly untenable. The affidavit is in the usual form, and avers the truth of the allegations in the petition. In whatever form a man binds himself he is bound, as this court has repeatedly decided, on a law of the Recopilacion; and it was the duty of the sheriff to return the bond into court, which duty it appears he performed in this instance.

It is, therefore, ordered, adjudged and decreed, that the judgment of the district court be avoided and reversed; and it is further ordered that the exceptions filed in the case be overruled, and that the case be remanded to be proceeded in according to law, the appellee paying the costs of this appeal.

Porter, for the plaintiff.
Davezac and *Hiriart*, for the defendant.

Astor *v.* Price *et al.* VII, N. S. 408.

If the lender gives bank shares at a higher price than that of the market, the contract is usurious.

FIRST District.

Martin, J., delivered the opinion of the court. ⟨

The defendants, sued as indorsers of Morgan & Saul, pleaded the statute of usury of the state of New York—averred that Morgan the drawer of one of the notes and Saul the first endorser, and Saul the drawer and Morgan the first endorser of the other, gave both these notes, after they had been endorsed by the defendants, as second endorsers to the plaintiffs, in the city of New York, in consequence of an usurious loan made to them by the plaintiff. The loan purporting to be 64,000 dollars, while in reality the plaintiff disbursed 58,857 dollars and 26 cents only, and charged interest on 64,000 dollars—paying only 8,850 dollars in cash and transferring 564 shares of the United States Bank, which the borrowers were compelled to take, instead of 59,431 dollars and 50 cents, *i. e.*, at the rate of 105 3-8 per share, when they were worth a great deal less, viz: 104 1-8, or thereabouts, according to the market price.

There was judgment for the defendants, and the plaintiff appealed.

The counsel of the appellee relied on the statute of usury of the state of New York, which declares null and void all notes given on a contract in which interest is taken or stipulated at a higher than the legal interest, which is seven per cent.

The testimony offered by the defendants fully establishes the facts pleaded, and is uncontradicted.

It is therefore clear that the plaintiff received the notes sued on, on a contract reprobated by the law of the country in which he made the loan, and consequently he acquired no right thereby, the consideration of the contract being illegal. A contract void in the country where it is made and giving no right there, cannot give any elsewhere.

It is, therefore, ordered, adjudged and decreed, that the judgment of the district court be affirmed, with costs.

Grymes, for the plaintiff.

Hennen, for the defendants.

Morgan's Syndics *v.* Fiveash.   VII, N. S. 410.

The Supreme Court will not increase the damages assessed by a verdict.

Although a party be a resident, an agent may swear for him if he be absent.

In an affidavit to hold to bail the agent need not state he swears from his personal and direct knowledge.

A planter who occasionally permits his slaves to earn money by cordelling, cannot complain of those who hire them for that purpose.

THIRD District.

MARTIN, J., delivered the opinion of the court.

The defendant is sued for the value of a slave, drowned in cordelling a vessel of which the former was master, without the consent of the plaintiffs, owners of said slave, or any person having care of him. The general issue was pleaded: there was a verdict and judgment against the defendant, who appealed after an unsuccessful attempt to obtain a new trial.

The plaintiffs and appellees here, prayed to be relieved from an error in the verdict, by which 600 dollars are allowed as the value of the slave, while the petition states the value to be 1000 dollars, and the testimony 1500 dollars. We think that a party who has prayed for judgment on a verdict and refuted his adversary's claim to a new trial, demands with ill grace from us that we should send the case back for the decision of another jury. For it does not belong to us to increase the damages assessed by a jury.

The defendant has complained that the court erred in overruling his motion to have the bail bond cancelled. He complained of the insufficiency of the affidavit, because it was made by an agent, while the petition shows that the plaintiffs reside in the city, and the agent swears, without stating he does so on his personal and direct knowledge.

We think there is not any strength in either objection. The justice ought not to receive the agent's affidavit, unless in the absence of the principal: we must presume he did his duty, unless the contrary appear. Now the circumstance of the plaintiffs' residence in the city, does not preclude the possibility or probability of an occasional absence. Nobody can or ought to swear except as to his personal and direct knowledge.

There is a bill of exceptions to the admission of the record of the insolvent's *concurso* in evidence. We think the court did not err. The general issue was pleaded—the cession was therefore to be proved, and of this the record was the best evidence.

On the merits, the defendant and appellee's counsel show, that from the testimony of the plaintiff's own witness, it appears the slaves of the plantation to which the deceased belonged were permitted to earn money, by cordelling vessels; that the plaintiffs expressly state as a ground of their claim that the deceased was so employed without the knowledge or consent of the plaintiffs, or any person having care of him. The general issue has put this allegation of the petition at issue, and the jury should have found it for the defendants.

Fisher swears that sometimes the slaves were permitted to cordell vessels through the turn; witness has seen them do it and not forbidden. The negroes have been forbidden at all times during high water, and been punished for so doing at that time. On Sunday afternoon particularly, when the weather was fair, and during low water.

Kinsey, a witness of the defendant, swears that a white person (who is supposed to be the preceding witness) came on board, on the day after the accident, to inquire about the negro, who being asked why he permitted his people to track vessels at night, answered, it was the only time they had to make any thing for themselves, as they worked all day, and it was hard to be too strict with them.

Fisher being recalled, declared that he did not make the declarations attributed to him by Kensey, He admitted he was sent on board by the overseer, and repeated that sometimes the slaves were permitted to cordell.

We have a strong doubt, whether a planter who occasionally permits his slaves to earn money by cordelling vessels may complain of their being hired for that purpose. If I at times send my servant to market without money and on being called on pay for what he purchased, I am bound if he purchases on another day on credit, even if I gave him money so to do. So, if the insolvent slaves were during part of the year permitted to cordell vessels for money, the person who hired them during a season may well say, that permission being frequently allowed he might conclude it was always so, and the restriction ought not to affect him.

As the jury have found a verdict against the defendant, we cannot in opposition to their finding discharge him; the case must therefore be remanded.

It is, therefore, ordered, adjudged and decreed, that the judgment of the district court be annulled, avoided and reversed, the verdict set aside, and the case remanded for a new trial; the plaintiff appellee paying costs of the court.

Hennen and *Eustis*, for the plaintiff.
Maybin, for the defendant.

Heirs of Cole *et al. v.* Cole's Executors.
VII, N. S. 414.

In cases of doubt whether a will presents a substitution or not, it should be maintained
When the deceased leaves a father or mother, he or she is forced heir for the one-fourth
of the estate.   And the child may dispose of three-fourths by last will and testament.
Donations *inter vivos* cannot be made in the form of onerous contracts.

COURT of Probates of New Orleans.

PORTER, J., delivered the opinion of the court.

Two questions are presented on the *mortuaria* in this case.   The
first arises under the following disposition in the last will and testament of the deceased.

"I leave and bequeath unto my said brother, James Cole, all the
residue of the property and effects of which I may die possessed, after
the payment of my just debts, for and during his natural life; and at
his decease it is my will that the same descend to all his children,
share and share alike, without regard to the laws of primogeniture
existing in that country (Ireland.)"

"The foregoing disposition of my property may not be conformable to the laws of the state; nevertheless I make this my last and
solemn request, that the residue of my property after the legacies
be disposed of in the above manner, inasmuch as my said mother is
very old and has already been sufficiently provided for, and that my
said brother is a married man, and has a large and helpless family.
And in case of the foregoing disposition in favor of my brother being
disturbed, then I leave and bequeath unto my said brother James,
for him and his children as aforesaid, such part and portion of my
estate as by law I may and can."

The court below was of opinion that the legacy was good, except
so far as it affected the *legitime* of the mother, who was a forced
heir.   The judgment of that tribunal gave the one-fourth to the
mother, and the balance to the appellee.

The case has been very elaborately argued.   The abolishing of
substitution and *fidei commissa* appears not to have destroyed the
litigation of which they were such a fruitful source under the Roman
law.   It seems as if we were destined to have as many subtle and
perplexing questions about what is, or is not, a substitution, as were
formerly presented in relation to the application of the doctrine to
particular cases.   In the present instance however, the conclusions
to which our reflections have brought us, render it unnecessary to

decide, whether the clause in the will which has been the subject of so much discussion at the bar, does or does not present a substitution.

It is necessary to check the power of the citizen over his property after his decease; for the strong desire in mankind to perpetuate their authority over what they have acquired, would otherwise induce them to place it for a length of time, and for ever if they could, out of the reach of alienation. But nothwithstanding the authority of the law to restrain dispositions of testators contrary to public good, such is the respect paid to the wishes of the owner, that we believe it may be safely stated to be the spirit of the jurisprudence of every civilised country, to carry into effect his will, unless it clearly violates the prohibition which the legislature has established. The source of this doctrine is found in the heart of every man, and it promotes under proper limitation a great purpose of public policy: for one of the strongest motives to industry and economy; one of the highest excite. ments to the exercise of those duties which make a valuable citizen, is a conviction that the acquisitions of his frugality and enterprise, will be transmitted as he may direct at his death, to promote the happiness of those who were dear to him in life.

In all cases of doubt then the testament should be maintained. Thus in France, on provisions the same as ours, it is a well esta. blished principle of their jurisprudence never to annul a testamentary disposition unless it necessarily presents a substitution, and can not be sustained in any other manner. *Toullier, liv. 3, tit. 2, chap.* 1, *nos.* 44 and 46.

It is clear to us that the object of the testator, from the whole of the testament, was to give the mass of his property to his brother, and to the children of that brother. After leaving it to him for life, he directs that at his death it shall belong to his children: and appre. hensive that such a disposition of his property might be forbidden by law, he declares that in the event of it being so, " I leave to my said brother James and his children, such part and portion of my estate, as by law I may or can."

The portion of his estate which by law he might have given to his brother and children, was the remainder left after deducting the *legi. time* of the forced heir, the mo.her; and to that remainder, except so far as parts of it may have been given to others by particular lega. cies, we think the appellees are entitled.

It might perhaps be made a question, whether the father and children were not to take share and share alike under the will, or whether the father should not take a usufruct for life, with the re. mainder over to his children. The latter construction would perhaps come nearer satisfying the particular intent of the testator. But this question it is unnecessary we should decide. There is no contest between the father and his children, and it is sufficient for us, and the decision of the case, that by the will they can legally take the portion left them in any right, to the exclusion of the other collateral relations. Louisiana Code, 1509.

Error has been alleged in the amount given by the decree of the, court of probates, to the forced heir, the mother. By its judgment she was declared to be entitled to the one-fourth.

The doubt in relation to the correctness of that judgment arises from three articles in our Code.

The 1481st art. declares: " Donations *inter vivos*, or *mortis causa*, can not exceed two thirds of the property, if the disposers having no children leave a father, mother, or both."

The 899th art. is in the following words: " If any one dies leaving no descendants, but a father and mother, and brothers and sisters, or descendants of these last, the succession is divided into two equal portions; one of which goes to the father and mother, who divide it equally between them, the other to the brothers and sisters, or their descendants, as is prescribed in the following section."

Art. 900. " If the father or mother of the person who had died without issue, has died before him, the portion which would have been inherited by such deceased parent, according to the terms of the preceding article, will go to the brothers and sisters of the deceased, or to their descendants, in the manner directed by the following sections."

The first of these articles impliedly gives to the father and mother, as forced heirs, one-third of the estate, for it prohibits the child to dispose of more than two-thirds, if either of the parents survive him. But the third, by positive enactment, only gives to the father or mother the one fourth; the construction therefore just alluded to of the 1487th article, is irreconcilable with the direct and positive commands of the legislature in the 899th and 900th.

The 1481st, however, contains negative expressions prohibiting the descendant to give more than two-thirds by donation *inter vivos*, or *mortis causa*, when he leaves either father or mother. As the father or mother can only take the one-fourth, the question is, what becomes of the difference between the one-third which the ancestor can not take, and the one-fourth which he may inherit; are the next in order of succession forced heirs for the difference?

We at first thought so, but we have been estopped from coming to that conclusion, by the 1482d article, which declares the ascendants and descendants to be forced heirs. With these contradictions in the express commands of the legislature, we have been no little perplexed what conclusion to come to. None of the ordinary rules of interpretation afford us the least aid in solving the difficulty. If we say the descendant can give more than two-thirds when father or mother survives, we violate the 1481st article. If we decide that he can not, we are equally in opposition with the 1482d art.; and we make the brothers or sisters forced heirs between the difference which the parent can take, and that which the descendants may will away.

On reference to the report made to the legislature by the *jurisconsults*, who prepared the amendments to our late Code, we find them state, that their object in the change was to increase the disposable portion. Had the 899th article stood without that which follows it, the interpretation would have been easy. By it, father and mother take one-half. The construction would have been, that this was their right in case there was no will, but that· the testator might abridge it by a disposition *mortis causa.*

But the 900th article, by making the portion which the parent can take, less than the part which the testator is prohibited to dispose of, deprives us of all aid from that supposed intention in the law-maker. We cannot untie the knot: we must cut it. And ,we believe the intention of the legislature was to give full and entire disposition to the owner, of all property of which he died possessed, except that part reserved to the descendants or ascendants; that the collaterals are not forced heirs when there is neither father, nor mother, and that they are not so, when either survives.

It is, therefore, ordered, adjudged and decreed, that the judgment of the court of probates in the appeal taken by the coheirs of James Cole be affirmed, with costs.

The next question arises on the claim of Sarah Lee, a free woman of color. The executors resist the payment of a note of the deceased, in her favor, dated the 21st of July, 1826, for 3000 dollars, and payable on his return from Europe.

The defendants denied the consideration, and the court below being of opinion, that none had passed between the parties, gave judgment against the petitioner; from which judgment she appealed.

On the trial below, the defendants asked several witnesses whether the plaintiff was not the concubine of the deceased. These questions were objected to, on the ground that no defence of that kind had been set up in the pleadings. The court admitted the evidence and we think correctly. When the plaintiff produced witnesses to prove the value of her services in the house of the deceased, it was open to the defendants to show what the nature of these services were, and in what capacity they were rendered.

On the want of consideration, the evidence has brought our minds to the same conclusion as that to which the judge of probates arrived. We think the notes were not given for value received, but as a disguised donation. A great deal of ingenuity has been displayed in remarking on the evidence, and calculations have been offered, showing that the plaintiff might have made this money by her industry and care and lent it to the deceased. , We could not, within the limits of an opinion, detail all the proof, nor explain the various circumstances which have produced the conviction just expressed.

It has been contended this was a remunatory donation, not subject to the rules which apply to donations strictly such. Admitting the law to be as stated, the donee should prove the value of the services. *Toullier, liv.* 3, *tit.* 2, *chap.* 4, *no.* 186.

Now has this been done? She was the testator's slave in 1818; on the 3d of August of that year, she was emancipated. In eight years after, we find her owning seven slaves. If her services were given in the house of the testator during all that time and for his benefit, we think the money by which seven slaves were acquired, shows that she must have been paid for these services. In addition to this, a legacy of 100 dollars is given her by the will.

The note can be considered in no other light than an attempt to disguise under the form of an onerous contract a liberality to the plaintiff, and is null for want of the formalities prescribed by law for donations *inter vivos.*

It is, therefore, ordered, adjudged and decreed, that the judgment of the court of probates be affirmed, with costs.

Seghers and *Pierce,* for the plaintiffs.

Preston, Smith and *Strawbridge,* for the defendants.

Saul *v.* His Creditors.*　　VII, N. S. 425.

The authority of the thing judged does not depend on the points raised in argument, but on the matters put in issue by the pleadings.

When the syndics are suffered to litigate the claim of a creditor without any interference or opposition of the other creditors, the judgment rendered has the force of *res judicata* against all the parties to the *concurso.*

Whether a judgment rendered between two of the creditors would have that effect, *quære.*

Interest does not run on a judgment.

If interest be demanded in the petition, and the judgment be silent on it, a subsequent demand can not be made for interest.

When a judgment is set up as the basis of a demand, the party to whom it is opposed may avail himself of any limitation in his favor without pleading it.

Syndics have no control over the suits which the individual creditors may raise with each other in the *concurso.*

Where a meeting takes place before a notary by order of court, to deliberate on the mode of selling the estate, and the creditors differ as to the terms of payment, the privileged creditors cannot by an *ex parte* proceeding obtain an order of court to sell the property for cash.

And if they do, and a sale takes place at which the privileged creditor who obtains the order buys the property himself, the sale will be set aside.

General rules which govern a *concurso.*

FIRST District.

PORTER, J., delivered the opinion of the court.

The children of the insolvent were placed on the tableau of distri-

---

* Result of judgment in the great case of this title, 5 *N. S.* 569.

bution by the syndics, as privileged creditors, for the following sums:

1. Amount inherited by the surviving heirs of Mary
Saul, by the death of their brother, John D. Saul, and
the second marriage of their father; which amount is
not subject to execution or the payment of debts, but
is to be held by the father with the privilege of the usufruct during his life, $9015 34

Interest on do. at 5 per cent. per annum from the date of
the cession of his property, say 6th March, 1826, to 3d
March, 1828,   897 81

To a judgment rendered by district court and confirmed
by the Supreme Court in favor of the heirs of Mary
Saul, on the 3d of May, 1827, with interest, $77,756 94

Interest from 3d of May to 20th September, 1820, on
$54,092,   1,032 32

                                                                78,787 26
By payment as cash,   39,000 00

                                                                39,787 26
Interest on $39,787 26, from 20th Sept. to 1st March, 162
days,   822 78

                                                                $40,670 04

To this tableau, several creditors filed opposition; among these, the
Bank of the United States, the Bank of Louisiana, the State Bank
and the Bank of Orleans, offered the following:

The heirs of Mrs. Mary Saul are put down as creditors for the
sum of 86,722 dollars 28 cents, whereas by their own showing they
are only entitled to be placed as creditors for the sum of 54,092 dollars 24 cents.

2. That interest is allowed to the said heirs, to which they are not
entitled.

3. That a large sum of money, the proceeds of the sale of bank
stock, and other movables, has been illegally paid to the said heirs,
and that they are classed as privileged creditors, although in fact
they have no privilege.

4. That the sums charged for the plantation expenses are highly
extravagant, and particularly, they object to all the sums charged as
having been paid to Thomas H. Saul, for his services.

5. That the sale of the plantation in the parish of Plaquemine, is
wholly null and void, and ought to be set aside, because the same
was not made at the time, nor upon the terms directed by the creditors, but in pursuance of an *ex parte* order of court, and that the
same was not made at the seat of justice of the parish of Plaquemines,
but at New Orleans.

6. That the sale of the plantation in the parish of West Baton

Rouge is void, because not made at the seat of justice of that parish, and not in pursuance of the direction of the creditors.

7. That it was the duty of the syndics to have received the crop of the plantation in the parish of Plaquemines, and to have accounted for the same in their tableau of distribution, and that they are responsible for all damages which may result from such neglect, amounting to a large sum of money, viz: the sum of thirty thousand dollars.

8. That the charge of 396 dollars 87 cents, for negro board ought not to be allowed, the same being much more than compensated by the services of said negroes.

To these grounds of opposition the heirs replied: That the amount for which they had been placed on the tableau of distribution, as well as their rank thereon, had been fixed by a judgment which had the force of *res judicata*, and that it was otherwise well founded in law: that the sales objected to, were made in pursuance of law, and that the respondents being the *bona fide* purchasers, the fruits gathered by them are and ought to be their own.

They further prayed, that the suits which the opposing creditors had brought to have the sales set aside, might be cumulated with their proceedings, and that should they be evicted, inquiry might be had into the value of the improvements placed by them on the premises.

The court of the first instance overruled the opposition, and confirmed the tableau. The Bank of Louisiana, the Bank of Orleans, and the Bank of the United States appealed.

The three principal questions in the cause, are: 1. The right of the minor children to be placed on the tableau of distribution as privileged creditors. 2. Their claim for interest. 3. The regularity of the sales made for cash. We shall examine them in this order, in preference to that in which they are stated in the opposition, and then pass on the minor questions which may be necessary to a decision of the case.

I. The right of privilege is supported on two grounds: first, a judgment of a court of competent jurisdiction having the force of *res judicata*, and secondly, on principles of law, independent of any former decision between the parties.

To understand correctly what force should be given to the plea of *res judicata*, recurrence must be had to the pleadings in the other case, as well as to the judgment therein rendered.

On the first tableau of distribution, the heirs of Mary Saul were entirely omitted. To the homologation of that tableau they filed an opposition, in which, after stating that they were legitimate heirs of Mary Saul, the wife of the insolvent, who had died in Louisiana, leaving a large estate in community with her husband, their father, they aver, that the portion of each was 9015 dollars and 34 cents: that the insolvent Joseph Saul, became their tutor, " and on the 3d of August, 1819, took possession of and administered the property inherited as aforesaid, whereby all the property of the said Joseph

Saul became tacitly mortgaged for the payment of the said sum of money, with interest at five per cent. per annum, from the 3d day of August, 1819: which said sums, with interest as aforesaid, the said Joseph Saul heretofore acknowledged to be due, and promised to pay."

They conclude by praying "that the tableau of distribution filed by the syndics may be annulled, and that they may be placed on the said tableau as general mortgage creditors, each of them for the sum of 9015 dollars and 34 cents, with interest at the rate of five per cent. per annum on each sum, from the 3d of August, 1819, and that the said syndic be ordered to pay to each of them, in preference to every other creditor, or creditors, the said sum of money," &c.

The judgment of the court, on this opposition, and some others of minor consequence, not necessary to be specially set out, (after declaring certain law charges to be privileges of the highest nature,) directs them to be paid, and proceeds as follows:—" Next are to be ranked the claims of the children of Joseph Saul to their respective proportion of their mother's succession: their opposition is therefore sustained to the amount of one half of the community at the time of her death, by virtue of a tacit and general mortgage.

On appeal to this court, the judgment just set out was confirmed.

It has been urged on the court that the questions as to the amount due the minor heirs, and the rank of their privileged mortgage, were not brought into view nor discussed before this tribunal, when the judgment of the parish court was confirmed. This is true: nothing was said of them. The whole attention and argument of counsel were directed to the great question, whether there existed a community between the father and mother: and the court took no notice of matters which from the silence of the parties they presumed each assented to. But admitting these facts, the consequence to be drawn from them is not what the appellants contend—namely, that the judgment has not the authority of the thing judged. It is obvious that when the plea of *res judicata* is presented to a court for examination, it is not to be decided by the points which the parties may have raised in argument, but by the matters put at issue by the pleadings. The judgment has as much effect on those things embraced by it, which were not disputed, as it has on those which were.

Recurring therefore to the pleadings and the judgment, we find, that the heirs claimed to be paid by virtue of their tacit and general mortgage, in preference to every one. The judgment of the court directs them to be paid in preference to every one, except law charges, by virtue of their general and tacit mortgage. We think this judgment forms *res judicata* of all the parties to it at the time it was rendered, and that it is now too late to call the correctness of that judgment in question.

The matters therefore being the same in this suit with that already decided, we have only to inquire whether the parties are the same. The parties in the former suit were the syndics of the estate who refused to put the heirs on the tableau, and the heirs who filed an opposition on the failure to do so. In that suit the syndics represented all the creditors of the estate. It is true that in a *concurso* all are plaintiffs and defendants, and each may contest the claim of the other, if the syndics refuse to do so. A judgment between two creditors on such opposition would not perhaps form *res judicata*, except as between them. But where the individual creditors stand by, and suffer the syndics to litigate the demand of any person claiming to be paid out of the estate, the judgment is as binding on them as if given contradictorily with themselves. The syndics are their agents, and any other construction would introduce the extraordinary consequence, that no judgment homologating a tableau of distribution would have the authority of the thing judged on any claim placed thereon, unless each of the creditors on the tableau, had contested it, and joined issue on its validity.

This opinion renders it unnecessary to examine the other point whether, independent of the judgment, the minor heirs had not under our old Code a privilege on all the movables as well as immovables of their tutor. There is no doubt they possessed it by the Spanish law, and we may notice before we dismiss the point from our con sideration that it seems very difficult, if not impossible to distinguish this case from a variety of others, so often decided in this court; where we have held, that subsequent laws do not repeal former ones, by containing different provisions—that they must be contrary, to produce that effect.

The next important question in the cause, is in relation to the interest. On the tableau of distribution the heirs are placed as privileged creditors for the sum of 77,756 dollars 94 cents, in virtue "of a judgment rendered by the district court, and confirmed by the Supreme Court, in favor of the heirs of Mary Saul, on the 3d of May, 1827, with interest."

The opposition of the creditors states that by their own showing they are only entitled to be placed on the tableau for 54,092 dollars 24 cents.

It becomes therefore necessary to examine the pleadings and the judgment to see which of these sums they are entitled to. The difference is produced by the interest. One of the parties asserts, it was accorded by the judgment of the district court, confirmed in this tribunal. The other avers that by the terms of the judgment the interest was denied.

The opposition of the first tableau of distribution was made by six of the heirs of Mary Saul; the same individuals who are now placed on the tableau of distribution. Two of these who were majors presented their claims separately, and the minors, who were assisted by a curator *ad lites*, offered theirs in two several oppositions.

The language of all in relation to the matter now under consideration is the same. After stating their heirship; the marriage of their mother; her community in property with their father, the insolvent

[Saul v. His Creditors.]

·and her decease; they proceed to state, that their father was by law their tutor, and on the 3d day of August, 1819, took possession of and administered " the property inherited as aforesaid; whereby all the property of the said Joseph Saul, became tacitly mortgaged for the payment of the said sum of money, 9015 dollars 34 cents for each heir, with interest at five per cent. per annum, from the third of August, 1819, which said sum, with interest as aforesaid, the said Joseph Saul heretofore acknowledged to be due, and promised to pay."

The oppositions conclude with a prayer, that the heirs may be placed on the tableau as general mortgage creditors, each of them for the sum of 9015 dollars 34 cents, with interest as aforesaid, and that the syndics may be ordered to pay each of them the said sum of money, with interest as aforesaid, or so much interest as the court may consider due.

The judgment of the court sustains the claim of the children " to their respective proportions of their mother's succession; their opposition is therefore sustained (says the judgment) to the amount of one half of the community at the time of her death, by virtue of a tacit and general mortgage."

It is clear to us the claim for interest cannot be sustained under this judgment. Interest is, it is true, demanded by ͺthe opposition, but the judgment is entirely silent about it: or to speak more correctly, by its terms, excludes and rejects the claim: for it confines the recovery of the children to the one half of the community at the death of their mother. The one-half of the community at her death, is an entirely different thing, from the one-half of that community eight years after, with interest thereon at five per cent. for that space of time.

There cannot, therefore, we think, be a doubt, that the interest was not given by the judgment. It is silent about it, and we are ignorant of any law which makes the interest follow as a consequence of giving judgment for a debt which would bear it; even if the terms conveyed less strongly than they do in the decree of the district court in this instance the idea that it was excluded. By the third law of the 22d title of the 3d *Partida*, it is enacted, that if a judgment in rendering a final judgment concerning the principal thing in dispute, has omitted to mention its fruits or rents, or had not condemned the party cast to pay the costs, he might amend and rectify his judgment, if done on the same day the decree was given. Such a provision as to the necessity of an amendment, conveys most strongly the idea, that without it the fruits or rents would not follow the judgment as a consequence, and this positive rule is certainly in conformity with the general understanding on the matter, as it is with the decision of this court, in the case of Saunders v. Taylor, 7 *N. S.* 44.

But does the failure to give interest in the judgment, enable the defendants to set up the decree as *res judicata* against a second demand for that interest? This is a question of by no means such easy solution as that just disposed of. Had the judgment in express terms rejected interest, there would have been no room for argument, that it furnished to the parties opposing the claim, the plea of *res judicata* against a second demand. We think, there is equally a rejection of the claim, when both principal and interest are demanded, and the former alone is given by the decree. Both were asked for in the petition: both put at issue by the pleadings: evidence in support of both is found in the record, and the judgment of the court must consequently be presumed to have taken both into consideration, unless an express reservation was made in it of one of them. The Roman jurists, in obedience to the maxim that the whole includes a part, held, that the exception *rei judicatæ*, applied to any one of the things which formed the object of the previous demand. *Si quis cum totum petiisset partem petat, exceptio rei judicatæ nocet.* The same rule prevailed when several distinct things were demanded. This case can not after the severest attention we have been able to bestow on it, be distinguished from others, in which the soundness of the doctrine just stated would appear incontrovertible. If a suitor ask for 1000 dollars from the parties against whom the action is brought, on a particular cause, or many causes, and a judgment be given generally for 700 dollars, the balance claimed is necessarily excluded. So it would be if he demanded ten acres, part of a certain tract of land, and only recovered five. Why it should be otherwise when he claims money and interest, and only gets the money, it is difficult to conceive. The Supreme Court of New York state, that when the demand of a party is submitted to a jury, and they see fit to disallow it, either want of proof, or for any other cause, a verdict and judgment thereon is conclusive, and the same demand is barred for ever. In the case of Delahaye v. Pellerin, decided in this state, it was held that where the plaintiff had claimed a slave and damages for his detention, a judgment for the slave, without saying any thing of the damages, excluded a claim in a second action for the damages. In the case of Faurie v. Pitot, it was decided that interest can not be sued for in a separate action, and that when judgment had been obtained for the principal, the interest which was an accessory was lost. This decision is in strict conformity with a text of the Roman law. *Non enim duæ sunt actiones, alia sortis, alia usurarum, sed una: ex qua condemnatione facta, iterata actio, rei judicatæ exceptione repellitur.* 2 *Martin's Rep.* 82; *Code, liv.* 4, *tit.* 34, *no.* 4; *Dig.* 44, *tit.* 2, *law* 7; 16 *Johnson*, 138; 2 *Martin*, 142.

If we felt the force of these principles less strongly than we are compelled to do, and thought that we might examine the question of interest again, if in point of fact it was not acted on in the previous judgment, we should entertain strong doubts whether it did not enter into the consideration of the judge of the first instance, and was by him excluded. In endeavoring to satisfy our minds on this point, we leave out of view the confirmation of that judgment here. In this court, the question of interest was never, that we can recollect, once agitated, and no complaint was made that it had not been granted by the judgment in the first instance. But we can hardly believe that the judge below, when the interest was demanded and proof offered in support of it, never took that demand or proof into consideration in fixing the amount which the heirs should recover. Certainly every legal presumption is against such a conclusion; more particularly when from the terms of the decree, he limits their recovery by express terms to the amount of the community at the death of the mother. He may at least have equitably thought (and whether he might not have legally too so concluded we are not now permitted to inquire) that the support and education of the minors were fully equivalent to the interest of their money. Nor is this view of the intention of the judge the least weakened in our minds by the circumstance of the decree not making any mention of it. It not being the practice in this state to express in the decretal part of a judgment rendered in favor of a plaintiff, what portion of his claim can not be allowed, though it is frequently done in the reasons by which final judgments are prefaced.

There remains one consideration on this part of the case, and that is, whether the appellants can claim under the pleadings the benefit of the judgment. They do not specially set it up in bar to the claim of the heirs, though we think they have substantially done so. On the tableau of distribution the heirs are stated to be placed there for a certain sum, in virtue of a judgment with interest. The opposition avers, that the heirs by their own showing are only entitled to a sum, which appears on reference to the decree first given, to be the principal, without interest. When a judgment is presented as the basis of a demand, it would seem to follow as a necessary consequence of admitting it in evidence, that the party to whom it is opposed may avail himself of any limitations it contains which are favorable to him.

This brings us to the last question in the cause which materially affects the interests of the parties, and that is the validity of the first sale made by the syndics. The heirs were the purchasers, and bought a sugar plantation on the river Mississippi, having 40 arpents front by 40 deep, together with all the improvements, and sixty-six slaves, for 35,000 dollars. They also bought at the same time for 4500 dollars, a tract of land, with the improvements, in the parish of West Baton Rouge. It was complained that this sale was illegally ordered; irregularly executed; and that a great sacrifice of the property took place.

First, as to the legality of the order.

At a meeting of the creditors, before a notary, on the 10th of July, 1827, a majority of them decided on selling the property at one, two and three years' credit. The appellees, however, and some other creditors, voted that a sufficient portion of it should be disposed of for cash to pay the privileged claims. These proceedings were returned into court on the 17th of the same month, and on the 26th the following order was made.

"On motion of A. Hennen and E Mazureau. Esquires, of counsel
for Julia D. Saul, and others, children of the said Joseph Saul, it is
ordered by the court, that the syndics of the creditors of the said
Joseph Saul do proceed forthwith to sell for cash, after the advertisements required by law, so much of the property ceded by the said
Joseph Saul, on which the children have a special and legal mortgage, as will be sufficient to pay and satisfy the amount of their
claims; viz: the sum of 77,756 dollars 94 cents, with legal interest on
the said sum since the judgment in their favor."

On the same day this order was obtained, on the 26th of July, a
copy of it was delivered to the sheriff, by whom service was made
on the syndics on the 28th and 30th of the same month.

By an acknowledgment on record, signed by the counsel of one of
the opposing creditors, it is admitted that verbal notification of this
motion was given to two of the syndics, and it appears that while
the property was advertised for sale according to the order of the
court, they filed a petition for the appointment of appraisers, and that
appraisement was duly made.

It makes a part of the case, according to the record, that all judgments and decrees of the district court, since the cause was sent back
from this tribunal, shall be considered as directly appealed from.

On the part of the appellants, it has been urged, this order was *ex
parte*, and is not binding on the creditors. The appellees contend,
that the rule of law being peremptory that a sale should be made for
cash, notice was unnecessary: that if it was, the syndics were substantially informed of it, and that they acquiesced in the decree of the
court by praying for an appraisement of the estate.

It is to be regretted, that the legislature have not furnished any
rules for conducting the suit of *concurso*. The proceedings in it are
so materially different from ordinary actions, that the regulations
furnished for the one have little or no application to the other. But
there are certain fundamental principles which control all causes, in
every court, and in every country, where justice is not a mockery,
and law is not used as a cloak for oppression. Parties must be cited
and after being cited an opportunity must be afforded them to make
defence before they are condemned. We had occasion to express
our opinions fully on this subject, in the case of Ludeling v. His
Creditors, and further reflection has confirmed us in the correctness
of the views we then entertained. In that case, the court, without
any written opposition being filed to the tableau of distribution, permitted objections to be made to it orally, on the day it was called up
for homologation, and by the judgment rendered, changed the relative situation of the creditors. We considered the proceeding irregular, and reversed the judgment of the inferior court, because the
creditors who had already their rank assigned them, could not know
without being warned by the pleading that it was necessary for them
to appear in court, and support their pretensions. 4 *N. S.* 601.

A good deal of embarrassment is created in the conducting of cases

In *concurso*, from contradictory, and we think indistinct, views that are taken in relation to the powers of the syndics. An authority has been read to us, that they are the representatives of the mass, but not of particular portions of the creditors when they oppose each other. This we think true; for in this action all are plaintiffs and defendants, and each may, if they think proper, contest and put at issue, the claims of others, both as it regards the existence of the debt and its rank. And yet this rule must be understood and taken with limitations. If the syndics resist the claim of an individual creditor, put it at issue, and a trial be had, and judgment thereon, that judgment, as we are at present advised, would prevent a particular creditor from objecting to the claim at any subsequent stage of the proceedings. The syndics being suffered to contest the claim on behalf of all, without intervention on their part, can be considered in no other light but their representatives, and it would be intolerable when collusion was not alleged, that the case should be tried over and over again, on the opposition of every individual creditor. The consequence however which we attach to a judgment so rendered is founded in the presumed acquiescence in all to the proceedings, and we are far from thinking that an acknowledgment on the part of the syndics, prevents any person who has an interest in contesting a claim against the estate, from making opposition to it.

But it is certain that the syndics cannot control the suits which individual creditors may raise with each other. This results as well from the authorities on this subject, who all state that every creditor is at once plaintiff and defendant, as from the nature of the case and the duties which syndics have to perform. Appointed to sell the estate, collect the debts, and pay the creditors their respective proportions, it is in many instances a matter of complete indifference to them whom they are to pay or in what rank the particular creditors are marshalled on the tableau. Or if they have any interest as creditors, it may not unfrequently happen that it is favorable to a particular class of claims, whose privilege or mortgage others may wish to exclude or reduce. The law therefore has wisely not confined to them alone the assertion of rights, and the settling of questions, to which they may be indifferent but which to others are of primary importance. It has reserved to the parties really interested the power to watch over their own interests, and protect themselves in their individual capacity. The contrary doctrine would at once establish an authority in the syndics to settle the estate as they chose, and would render the privilege of each creditor to contest the claim of another a mere illusion.

With this expression of our understanding of the law, we proceed to examine the particular circumstances of this case. The syndics had contested the claim of the appellees on behalf of the other creditors, by refusing to put them on the tableau, a judgment was rendered on the issue thus joined, and that judgment we consider binding and conclusive on all parties to the *concurso*. After this judgment was rendered, the syndics applied to the court, and obtained an order that a meeting of the creditors should take place before a notary, to determine on the mode of disposing of the ceded property. At that meeting a contest arose, in relation to the manner the effects of the insolvent should be sold. Several creditors appeared and voted for its being disposed of on a credit. Others, among whom were the appellees, required a sale for cash, to satisfy the privilege claims.— The notary made a *process verbal* of the wishes and demands of each, and returned it into court. These conflicting pretensions produced a new contest between the creditors, and the moment it was commenced the syndics in our judgment could do no act on their part, either to weaken the rights of one party or strengthen those of the other. The control of it was in the hands of those who had chosen to litigate it in their own behalf, and no sale could be made until the conflicting pretensions of the creditors were decided on. Before the court decided, it was bound to hear the parties. We see no other conclusion to which we can possibly come, if the creditors had a right to make the opposition. For if they had a right to make it, they had a right to be heard on it. It is not either the smallness of a claim, nor its weakness in point of fact, or law, that can deprive a suitor in our courts of the privilege of presenting his proof, and his reasons before a decision is made against him. In this case, without a hearing of the parties interested, and without giving them an opportunity of being heard, a judgment overruling their pretensions, and materially affecting their interests was rendered.

But several grounds have been urged to take this case out of principles we have just been noticing.

Verbal notice it is said was given to the syndics, and they made no opposition. We have already said, it was not with them, but with the individual creditors, the suit should have been carried on. But admitting that it might be contested with them, as the representatives of the creditors who demanded a sale on a credit, they had no authority to give a verbal consent out of court; so as to deprive the proceedings of that publicity which would enable the parties really interested to protect themselves. Their authority in the most favored view that can be taken of it, did not extend so far: far less did it authorise them, after the portion of the creditors they represented had contested the claim to sell for cash, to acquiesce in that claim without opposition. And as if the case had been destined to exhibit every kind of irregularity, notice was only given to two of the syndics, one of them the father and forced heir of the appellees. The third received no notification. Were then the syndics the persons with whom the claim should have been contested, we would be of opinion that the proceedings had been contrary to law.

It has been forcibly urged, that the right of the privileged creditors to have a sale made for cash was peremptory, that no successful opposition could have been made to it. Admitting it to be peremptory, does it follow that no notice is to be given to those who are to be affected by this positive right, and that no opposition can be made to it? Is the right of the privileged creditor to have a sufficient portion of the insolvent's estate sold for cash to pay his claim, stronger than that of the payee of a bond to recover the amount from the maker? Is it conferred more expressly, or by higher evidence than that of the mortgage creditor, to seize the property on which he has a lien, in the hands of a third person? and could these rights be exercised without giving the debtor in the one instance, and the third possessor in the other, an opportunity to show what cause they had to urge against the apparent claim of the creditor? There are more things to be settled in all cases of this kind than the mere right of selling for cash. It must be first ascertained whether the party making the demand is a privileged creditor, and next the amount due to him, and neither of these are the result of a peremptory rule of law, but depend on the proof offered. If another case had been presented for our decision, the imagination could not have suggested any thing by way of illustration which would have more strikingly shown the necessity of hearing parties before making such an order, than the instance now before the court. On a judgment which only gave to the creditors, in favor of whom it was rendered, 54,000 and some dollars, an order was made to sell property to satisfy one of 77,000 dollars.

We have inquired whether this proceeding might not be supported on the ground, that after the return of the proceedings before the notary into court, the parties to the *concurso* must be supposed to have been then, ready to meet any motion that was made affecting their interests. But neither the law nor the practice of the court will, we apprehend, justify this position. It is not in the power of either plaintiff or defendant to call up an ordinary case at any moment he pleases, and try it in the absence of his adversary. It must be put on the docket, and a day fixed for its trial. It is of more importance to require a strict observance of this rule in the *juicio de concurso*, than any other; for from the number of parties litigating, and the variety of suits carrying on at once, an opportunity might be afforded of materially affecting the interests of litigants by *ex parte* proceedings. It surely cannot be the law of this country, that the creditors must keep a counsel standing as a sentinel for years in court, from the moment it opens until it closes each day, to guard against his adversary getting an order on his showing alone. If it be the law, then the necessity of a citation might as well be dispensed with entirely.

It was asked, who were the privileged creditors to give notice to? We answer, to those opposed to them. We see no difficulty in this. When a tableau of distribution is filed, notice is given to all parties by publication in the newspapers to oppose it if they think fit. Nothing prevented the same kind of notice, calling on those interested to show cause why the proceedings before the notary should not be homologated. It is said there is no law for this. There is no statutory provision it is true, but the act of 1817, by declaring that it shall no longer be necessary to homologate the proceedings for the appointment of syndics, strongly countenances the idea, that all other proceedings before a notary require as formerly to be acted on by the court after calling in the parties by public advertisement. But if there be no law for bringing the creditors in by publication, a rule could have been taken on them to show cause why the demand of the appellees should not be granted.

It makes a part of the statement of facts, that one of the counsel who appeared on the argument of this case on behalf of the appellants, was in court, and made no opposition, when this order was granted: admitting his silence to bind his clients, he was not the representative of the other creditors.

On the whole, after bestowing on the case the most serious attention, we are of opinion that the order of the court rendered *ex parte* without hearing the parties, or citing them to be heard, was illegal, and that the sales made in virtue of it, to those by whom it was obtained, must be set aside.

The legality of the order for selling the bank stock is not put at issue by the opposition, and no evidence before us shows the sale to have been made contrary to law.

The appellees have claimed the value of their improvements as *bona fide* possessors. There has been no evidence or argument on this point. That question, therefore, and others arising out of the fruits of the property, can be more properly determined when a new sale takes place, and the tableau is amended conformably thereto.

It is, therefore, ordered, adjudged and decreed, that the judgment of the district court be annulled, avoided and reversed; that the opposition filed thereto, so far as it relates to the amount for which the heirs of said Mary Saul are placed on the tableau be sustained, and that they be placed thereon for the amount recovered by them in the former action. It is further ordered, that the said opposition, so far as it relates to the sale of the bank stock and furniture, be overruled.

It is further ordered, adjudged and decreed, that the sale of the plantation and slaves in the parish of Plaquemines, and the land in the parish of West Baton Rouge be annulled and made void; that the case be remanded to be proceeded in according to law, the appellees paying the costs of the appeal.

The decree being made without prejudice to the claim of the creditors for the fruits of the plantation, or that of the purchasers for the improvements placed thereon.

Livermore, for the plaintiffs.
Hennen and *Mazureau*, for the defendants.

Delancy v. Grymes *et al.* VII, N. S. 457.

COURT of Probates of New Orleans.
No appeal lies from a judgment on a rule to pay money into court.
See same point and decree in Kenner v. Young, *ante*, 252.

Buisson v. Thompson. VI, N. S. 460.

The wife must, against creditors, produce other proof of the payment of the *dot*, than the husband's confession in the marriage contract.

PARISH Court of New Orleans.

MARTIN, J., delivered the opinion of the court.
The plaintiff seeks to enforce on her husband's vendee, a legal mortgage for the recovery of her dotal rights. The latter obtained an injunction. There was a judgment of nonsuit and she appealed.
Her counsel contends, that
The appellant's marriage contract being duly recorded, she has a legal mortgage. Old Civil Code, 454, art. 17; Civil Code, 3287.
The defendant's right being posterior to the record of the contract, can not contest the mortgage, nor the grounds, in consideration of which it results.
The appellee contends that the plaintiff ought to have proved the payment of the dot, and her contract forms no proof against third parties.
By the marriage contract, the wife constitutes to herself and brings in marriage, a dot of 2100 dollars, consisting of 1500 dollars the value of her clothes, jewels, plate and furniture, and 600 dollars in cash, the produce of her economy and savings. The husband declares he well knows all these things, and declares that on the celebration of the marriage, he will *ipso facto* be possessed of the dot, and be accountable for its value as stated.

[Buisson *v.* Thompson.]

Febrero says that the real dot is constituted not by writing, but by numeration. *Lo que constituye la verdadera dote es su numeracion no la escritura. Doti numeratio, non scriptum dotalis instrumenti facit. Ideo non ignoras demum te ad petitionem doti admitti posse si dotem a te re ipsa datam probatura est.* Febrero—*Nada aprovechara la (muger) la confession: y por consiguiente necesitara probar su numeracion y entrega. Lib.* 3, *cap.* 3, *sect.* 2, *no.* 138. *El privilegio de la dote verdadera no se estiende a la putativa.*

When the wife proceeds against her husband, or his heirs, or hers against him, slight proof will suffice, says Febrero; but when she concurs with his creditors and insists on a privilege over them, the proof must be conclusive: *es indispensable que las pruebas sean concluyentes. Ibid. n.* 136.

The appellant's counsel has not produced any authority in support of his position, that creditors, who became so after the marriage, are bound by the husband's confession, and we have not discovered any.

The wife having administered no other proof of the payment of the dot, than the husband's confession in the contract of marriage, we conclude that the parish judge correctly disallowed her pretension.

It is, therefore, ordered, adjudged and decreed, that the judgment of the parish court be affirmed, with costs.

Chapotin, for the plaintiff.
Pierce, for the defendant.

Walden *v.* Duralde. VII, N. S. 462.

The recorder of mortgages is bound to record, on the order of the judge, proceedings by *scire facias* to revive a judgment in a court of the United States in another district, and to state such a record on his certificate.

FIRST District.

MARTIN, J., delivered the opinion of the court.

The petitioner states he is the mediate and intermediate purchaser of several lots, which were sold on execution, as the property of Livingston, and being desirous of disposing of them, he applied to the defendant, the recorder of mortgages, for a certificate, and he instead of confining himself to a statement of the mortgages really existing on said lots, or stating that no mortgage existed on his books, obstinately refused, stating that the premises were encumbered by a pretended mortgage resulting from a judgment of the United States against said Livingston for 100,000 dollars and costs.

The petition concludes with a prayer that the pretended mortgage be declared null and of no effect against the petitioner, that the defendant may be prohibited from stating it in his certificate and pay damages.

The defendant denied the plaintiff's right to sue him, as he was without interest in the suit, and the United States were the only party concerned.   He denied he had stated any mortgage, on his certificate, not actually existing on his books, against the principal, and to the rest of the petition the general issue was pleaded.

There was judgment for the defendant, and the plaintiff appealed. His counsel urges, that

1. The pretended mortgage was not registered according to law.

2. The execution of the judgment of the United States was not ordered by one of the judges of this state.

3. No authentic copy of the judgment was given to the defendant to be recorded.

4. Nothing was offered for record or recorded but a *fieri facias*.

It appears that the attorney of the United States for this district on the fifteenth of July, 1822, presented a petition to the judge of the first district of this state, stating that the United States, in December 1803, had obtained the judgment stated in the petition, and in the district court of the United States for the district of New York, which was received by a writ of *scire facias* in May, 1822, whereupon he prayed an order for the record of the judgment in the books of the recorder of mortgages.   To this petition was annexed an authentic copy of the *scire facias*, the return of it, and the order and judgment of the court for the revival of the original judgments.   The district judge ordered the registry accordingly.

It is clear that on the prayer of the petition, as far as it goes, to the court, declaring that there exists no mortgage, and prohibiting the defendant to state any in his certificate, nothing could be done in a suit to which the United States are not a party.   They ought to be heard before any judgment affecting any right of theirs be given.

So that our only inquiry is, whether the plaintiff be entitled to damages from the defendant?

The appellant's counsel erroneously considered the judgment in favor of the United States, in one of their courts, as a judgment to be executed by one of the ministerial officers of this state, and consequently requiring the fiat of one of its judges.   In such judgments, the individual states, though independent, are mere judicial districts of the Union, and stand to each other in the same relation as one of the parishes of the state to any other.   The marshal of the United

[Walden v. Duralde.]

States for the Louisiana district derived his authority from the court of the United States in New York.

The decision of that court on the motion of the United States, after notice to Livingston in due form, asking the revival of the original judgment, was recorded as a judgment by the attorney of the United States, after obtaining an order for that purpose from a state judge.

The counsel also erred in considering the *scire facias* and proceedings upon it as a writ of execution or *fieri facias*.

The defendant acted correctly in recording the document presented, and would have acted otherwise in forbearing to state what was on his books in the certificate he delivered to the plaintiff.

It is, therefore, ordered, adjudged and decreed, that the judgment be affirmed, with costs.

Seghers, for the plaintiff.
Denis, for the defendant.

Carraby *v.* Carraby.   VII, N. S. 466.

A woman cannot be curatrix to an absentee.

Semble, a wife, to be preferred to the presumptive heir, under article 50, Civil Code, must have the qualification of the masculine gender?

The legislative construction of the constitution as to jurisdiction of this court, in article 876, Code of Practice, is to be respected.

COURT of Probates of New Orleans.

MARTIN, J., delivered the opinion of the court.

The appellant complains that his claim to the curatorship of the estate of his nephew, an absentee, was disregarded, and the absentee's sister preferred.

He opposed the appellee's claim on account of her sex, and the only question presented to us is, whether a woman may have the curatorship of an absentee's estate of whom she is the presumptive heir?

The Code, article 50, requires that, in the appointment of the curator of an absentee's estate—the wife be preferred to the presumptive heir—he to other relations—they to creditors, and these to strangers. Provided, however, that such a person be possessed of the necessary qualifications; *ayent les qualités requises.*

The qualifications, or *qualités*, spoken of in the proviso we take to be, the masculine sex and the age of majority; we can hardly think of any other.

Women cannot perform any civil function, except those which the law especially declares them capable of exercising. *Ibid.* 25.

They may be tutrixes of their minor children or grandchildren; they may be executrixes; curatrixes of their absent husband's estate.

The exercise of a right or power over the property of another, not conferred by him but by the law, we take to be a civil function.

By the Roman law, *Fæminæ ab omnibus officiis publicis vel civilibus remotæ sunt. L. 2 ff. de Reg. Jur.*

It is true the presumptive heir has an interest in the good management of the estate, and the appellee's counsel has concluded, that as she may manage her estate, she may manage one in which she has an interest. She has no vested right in the estate during the life of the absentee, except the share of the profits which the heir may have when sent into possession in the absence of the latter—the curator of the absentee's estate manages an estate not his own.

It is objected that women may be sent into provisional possession of an estate. This is an exception to the general rule, for they exercise a power on an estate not their own, which the owner did not give, but the law confers. But the law presumes the absentee, in some manner, to be dead; his will is to be opened; his instituted, repels the presumptive heir, if not a forced one. The heir sent in possession has a vested interest in a part of the profits at first, which gradually increases, and finally absorbs them all. The Civil Code requires the curator of the estate of an absentee to possess, besides the qualifications which entitle him to a preference, those which enable him to exercise the office.

A doubt has been suggested as to the jurisdiction of this court, the estate being of the value of 1500 dollars and the profits or interest of the parties, the commission, are below 300 dollars. But we have deemed it our duty to respect the legislative construction of the constitution, in the 876th article of the Code of Practice.

It is, therefore, ordered, adjudged and decreed, that the judgment of the court of probates be annulled, avoided and reversed, and that Etienne Carraby be appointed curator of Leufroy Carraby, the absentee; the appellee paying costs in both courts.

D. Seghers, for the plaintiff.

H. R. Denis, for the defendant.

Gosselin *et al.* *v.* Gosselin. VII, N. S. 469.

An act of the legislature, the execution of which is suspended by one of its clauses, or by a delay of its promulgation may in the meanwhile be modified or repealed by a posterior act.

PARISH Court of New Orleans.

MARTIN, J., delivered the opinion of the court.

The petitioners, children of the defendant, aver that their deceased father left a considerable property in land, slaves and movable property, which came to the defendant's possession. They pray for an account of the profits, and a partition of the property.

The defendant pleaded in abatement, a suit instituted by her in the district court for the partition of the estate, in which they were duly cited.

The court of probates sustained the plea and dismissed the petition. The plaintiffs appealed.

By the Code of Practice, 924, sect. 14, the court of probates has exclusive jurisdiction of partitions.

This Code was approved in 1824, and after its approbation, but before its promulgation, the legislature by an act of 1825, p. 122, sect. 3, gave to the district court jurisdiction in cases of suits for partition.

By an act passed in 1828, p. 156, sect. 13, amendatory of the Code of Practice, it is provided that in any case where the partition of a succession has been or may be made, &c., all the real and personal actions and others shall be brought in the district court.

There cannot be any doubt that an act of the legislature, the execution of which is postponed, either by a limiting clause, or a delay of its promulgation may be affected by an intermediate declaration of the legislative will modifying or repealing it. Thus the jurisdiction of the court of probates, which was exclusive in cases of partition, by the Code of Practice, was rendered concurrent only by the act of 1825, posterior to the approbation of the Code of Practice, by the governor though anterior to its promulgation. We do not wish to be understood now to speak of the exclusive jurisdiction of the court of probates in special cases, viz: those of minors, interdicted persons, &c.

It is, therefore, ordered and adjudged that the judgment of the court of probates be affirmed, with costs.

C. *Derbigny* and *Denis,* for the plaintiffs.

D. *Seghers,* for the defendant.

Ayraud *v.* Babin's Heirs. VII, N. S. 471.

A judicial sale to enforce the payment of the first instalment is necessary to protect the vendee against the vendor's privilege for subsequent ones.
Prescription does not run against one who cannot sell.

COURT of Probates, Parish of Ascension.

Porter, J., delivered the opinion of the court.

The petitioner bought of the defendants an arpent of land, front on the Bayou La Fourche, from which he was evicted by a sale under a mortgage in favor of Nicholas L'Aine and others. He brings this action to be reimbursed in the value of the land sold to him, and for the damages he has sustained by the eviction. The defendants cited in Winchester who sold to them, and he has called in warranty the curator of one Moncerratt, from whom in his lifetime he alleges to have purchased.

The court of probates, after hearing the parties, gave judgment against the defendant in the sum of 1200 dollars, the value of the land, rejecting the claim for damages, and at the same time decreed that the defendants should recover the same sum from Winchester, and that Winchester should have judgment in the same amount against the estate of Moncerratt.

The plaintiff and Winchester, who is cited in warranty, both moved for a new trial in the court below. The application of the latter was rejected, and that of the former granted, so far as to make the judgment extend to the administrator of the estate of Babin, as well as to the heirs.

From the judgment rendered against Winchester, he appealed.

The facts in this case are numerous, and many points of law have been raised in argument. To understand them correctly, it is necessary to give a statement of the case from the time when the right of mortgage was acquired under which the eviction took place.

The opinion of the court of probates contains a very ample detail of the facts, and we adopt it with some limitations and additions, as being conformable to our views of them as they appear on the record.

On the 27th of April, 1813, a tract of land containing four arpents front on the Bayou La Fourche with a depth of forty arpents, was sold at public auction by the judge of the Parish of Ascension, at the request of Rose Florence, widow of Etienne Herbert, and of François, and Margueritte Doucet, the latter represented by Baptiste Doucet, her curator. At the sale, one Estevan Hernandez became the purchaser for the price of 3000 dollars in one and two years from the day of sale, and furnished his two notes for 1500 dollars each, the first payable on the 25th of April, 1814, and the other on the 25th of April, 1815, endorsed by Moncerratt.

Two days after, Hernandez sold the premises to Moncerratt, who had become his endorser on the note given to the estate of Daublin. In this act, Moncerratt promised to pay the notes which Hernandez had given.

On the 30th day of March, 1816, the land was sold by the sheriff of the Parish of Ascension, at the suit of J. B. Doucet v. Moncerratt, and Winchester became the purchaser thereof.

On the 9th of April, 1818, Winchester conveyed the land to Charles Babin (the ancestor of the defendants) for 2500 dollars cash.

On the 1st of April, 1820, Babin sold one arpent front of this same tract to Ayraud (the plaintiff) for 1200 dollars, who on the 7th of January following conveyed it to Joseph Hidalgo.

On the 6th of December, 1824, an order of seizure and sale was obtained against Babin & Hidalgo, as third possessors of the tract originally sold to Hernandez. This order was granted on the petition of the heirs of Daublin as payees of the second note given by Hernandez at the time of the purchase. Babin & Hidalgo having failed to pay and discharge the debt, the land was seized by the sheriff on the 20th of December, 1824, and advertised to be sold on the 19th of January, 1825.

On the 27th of January, 1825, Winchester applied for and obtained an injunction to stay the executory proceeding, and on the 25th of June he took a nonsuit with the right of reproducing the same matters in defence, in case he should be called in warranty by his vendee.

On the 30th of July, 1825, Babin & Hidalgo obtained another injunction against the proceedings of the petitioners for an order of seizure, and prayed that Winchester and Ayraud, their vendors, might be called in to maintain their title to the premises. They appeared in the month of August following, and filed their answers. These injunctions were however dissolved by the court of the first instance, and on an appeal to this tribunal the judgment of dissolution was confirmed, principally on the ground that the defendants had not made opposition to the order of seizure within ten days after its notification.

The premises were afterwards sold by the sheriff; and Ayraud, Winchester's vendee, and vendor and warrantor to Hidalgo, became the purchaser, for the price of 2500 dollars, payable in one year.

The purchase which Ayraud then made of the land he had acquired from Babin is the ground alleged by him in his petition for this action. The answer of the heirs of Babin does not require to be specially set out. That of Winchester, who is cited by them in warranty, sets up the following grounds of defence.

1. That he bought the land at a sale made under an execution

issued at the suit of J. B. Doucet v. Joseph Moncerratt for the sum of 2206 dollars, at 12 months' credit, which money he has paid, and that at the time of the purchase he was ignorant of any mortgage on the premises.

2. That it was the duty of Babin, when notice of the intended seizure of the premises was given to him, to have notified the respondent, and legally called in warranty.

3. That if he had been called in warranty, he could have shown, that the judgment on which the order of seizure and sale had issued was fraudulent, and obtained by connivance: that it was not legally recorded; that it was null and void, as not containing any reasons: that no evidence was given on the trial of the land seized being the consideration of the property sold to Hernandez.

4. That the sheriff's sale at which the respondent purchased, was for the balance due on one of the notes given as the consideration of the land purchased by Hernandez, and that the respondent took the premises free from any incumbrance created by the other obligations given for the purchase-money.

5. Prescription.

The answer concludes by praying that Moncerratt, for whose debt the sale was made at which the respondent purchased, may be cited in warranty.

On the trial of the cause, the appellant offered in evidence the record of the proceedings, in the case of Doucet v. Moncerratt, for the purpose of showing that the note sued on in that case was given for the balance due by Hernandez on the first instalment of the land, and that it was in satisfaction of the judgment rendered for part of the original purchase-money, that the appellant had bought at sheriff's sale. Admitting the court to have erred in rejecting the testimony, it comes up on record and we do not see that, giving it all the effect which is claimed for it, it can sustain the defence of the appellant.— It shows indeed pretty clearly that the note of Moncerratt, on which Doucet, the curator of one of the heirs, brought suit, was given in part payment of the note which Hernandez owed to the succession of Daublin. Conceding that the curator of one of the heirs had a right to novate the debt due to all of them, or that if he had not that right he possessed the power to novate that portion which was due to the minor he represented, the consequence contended for by the appellant does not follow. The case shows nothing more than that the representative had converted a debt secured by mortgage against the original vendee into a personal one of the endorsers; consequently a sale to enforce this personal obligation cannot be considered as a sale under the mortgage debt for which it was substituted. The arguments by which the appellant can alone make the record of these proceedings evidence against the plaintiff, namely that it was a novation of the original obligation, necessarily destroys every consequence that would have followed a judicial enforcement of that obligation.

This position is susceptible of farther illustration. The defence of the appellant is that, at a judicial sale made to discharge the first instalment, he bought the property, and consequently took it free from any mortgage that might exist for any other portion of the same debt due on a second instalment. However true this may be in regard to the vendee at a judicial sale, it cannot apply to a purchaser by private contract, for if his vendor owed only a portion of the price for which he bought, the mortgage would follow the property in the hands of the third person. Had therefore the indorser voluntarily paid the whole of the first instalment in this instance, it would not have destroyed the vendor's privilege on the second. Payment of part of the first instalment, and giving his note for the balance must have the same effect. It requires a judicial sale to enforce the first instalment to enable the purchaser to get clear of the incumbrances existing in virtue of the second. In this instance the note which first fell due was extinguished by payment and by substituting a new debt, in which the creditor did not expressly reserve the privileges and mortgages conferred by the old. The sale here was not made to inforce the first instalment, but the debt that was substituted for it. If the note of the indorser is not considered as operating novation, but as collateral security, there would be still less reason for saying that a sale under judgment to enforce its payment could destroy the mortgages attached to the future instalments of the debt it was intended to secure. Another test may be applied which will show the correctness of these principles. If the endorser, previous to the judgment obtained against him by the curator on his personal obligation, had sold this land to a third person, and the curator had sought by an action of mortgage to have had the premises seized and sold, the purchaser could have successfully urged that the money paid by the endorser, and his note for the balance had extinguished the debt due by the original vendee. If then the creditor could not have enforced the hypothecary right against a third person, how can a sale of the property in the possession of the indorser be considered as tranferring that right to the purchaser at sheriff's sale.

This opinion disposes of the first two points made by the appellant.

There is no evidence before us that the judgment was obtained by fraud or connivance. And the objection that the judgment against the principal debtor does not contain any reasons cannot avail the appellant, for that merely rendered it voidable, and until set aside by the party interested it had all the effect of a judgment regularly rendered. Whether evidence was given on the trial against the debtor that this land was mortgaged for the payment of the debt is immaterial, provided it appear now clearly, as it does, that the premises sold were in point of fact subject to the lien. The law requires the creditor who is desirous of enforcing his mortgage on property in the hands of a third person to produce the judgment against the debtor together with the act of mortgage, and by this provision clearly conveys the idea that the existence of the debt is to be settled with the party that owed the money; and the existence of the lien created by

[Ayraud v. Babin's Heirs.]

that debt, with the third possessor who holds the property subject to the mortgage.

The plea of prescription cannot be sustained: for it is shown that for a length of time there was no authority to which the plaintiff could have applied for an order of seizure. *Contra non valentem agere non currit prescriptio.* The appellant was the judge of the district, and it was not until 1824 that provision was made by law for another judge to grant orders of this description. Acts of 1824, page 10.

These are all the grounds of defence set up in the answer of the appellant, but in this court he has made another. That the act of sale on which the seizure was made was neither a public nor private act. The appellees have objected to an inquiry on this ground, because no such allegation being made in the pleadings in the court of the first instance, an opportunity was not offered to them of meeting and disproving it there.

On reference to the petition, we find the plaintiff avers that he was evicted of the premises by an order of seizure founded on a mortgage or privilege existing on the land prior to the 1st of April, 1820. The answer of the appellant contains no general denial, nor special denial of the fact; it negatives the recording of the judgment, but it is silent as to the recording of the original contract of sale, and it is without any averment that the instrument on which the order of seizure issued was not an act of mortgage. Under this state of the pleadings, the party cannot put at issue here a fact on which the *contestatio litis* was not formed below. Every allegation in the petition which is not denied by the answer is admitted by it.

The act itself comes up with the record of the proceedings on which the eviction took place, and it appears to want the signature of the parish judge. Whether the defect exists in the original instrument, or proceeds from an error in making out the transcript, we cannot say. But admitting it to be such as the appellant contends, as no issue was joined on that ground below, it cannot be examined here.

It is, therefore, ordered, adjudged and decreed, that the judgment of the court of probates be affirmed with costs.

Davezac, for the plaintiff.
Mitchell, for the defendant.

Willard v. Parker.   VII, N. S. 483.

FIRST District.
A resale and delivery by a purchaser destroys the privilege of his
vendor on the property so resold.

Gayoso v. Wikoff.   VII, N. S. 486.

The defendant cannot plead title in himself to a possessory action.
Parties have no right to interrogate the judge.

THIRD District.

Porter, J., delivered the opinion of the court.
The petitioner states that, for the last six years he has been the
owner and possessor of a negro slave named Henney, during which
time he has always possessed her as owner; that the defendant
fraudulently and without the consent of the petitioner, has taken the
slave into his possession and refused to deliver her up.   The petition
concludes by a prayer that the defendant may be ordered to restore
possession of the slave, and pay 200 dollars damages for her detention—that possession of the property sued may be decreed to be in
the plaintiff until the decision of the cause, and that she be sequestered and put in the hands of the sheriff.
The defendant by his answer denied that the slave sued for had
ever been the plaintiff's, or in his possession as owner.   That on the
contrary she belonged to the respondent, and he prayed that she
might be decreed by the court to be such.
This answer was filed on the 6th of June, 1826.   In January,
1828, the defendant offered an amended answer; by which he set up
title to the property by a demand in reconvention, and averred that
the only possession the plaintiff ever had of the slave was as depositary of the defendant.

[Gayoso *v.* Wikoff.]

The judge of the fourth district, who presided at the term of the court at which the answer was presented, refused leave to file it, grounding his refusal on the 53d article of the Code of Practice which declares, that the possessory action excludes any testimony relative to the property. The court in its opinion declared that it seemed to be a conclusion from this provision, that a plea could not be received in relation to matters, of which the law prohibited any proof to be given.

To this refusal of the judge to permit the annexed answer to be filed, the defendant took a bill of exceptions.

It appears to this court, that the judge below did not err in refusing the defendant permission to set up title to the property. The provision of the Code of Practice is peremptory in excluding all such matters in possessory actions. The allegation in the petition that the plaintiff had possessed as owner does not make the suit a petitory one. It is an averment of the manner in which he had possessed. The prayer in the petition is for possession alone. Neither can the circumstance of the demand being set up in reconvention aid the defendant, for however strong the right might be in general principles of law, the Code of Practice by the 55th article forbids it. The provision is in these words: " he who is sued in a possessory action can not bring a petitory action until after a judgment shall have been rendered in the possessory action, and until, if he has been condemned, he shall have satisfied the judgment given against him." A demand in reconvention is in law a new suit, and the prohibition applies as well to this mode of bringing it as any other. See the case of Lanusse's Syndics *v.* Pimpinella, 4 *N. S.* 439.

The other branch of the answer was unnecessary, as the defendant could under the original one have given evidence to show that the possession of the plaintiff was as the depositary of the defendant.

The cause was not tried at the term the amended answer was proposed and rejected, and at the next term, when another judge presided, the defendant renewed his application to place the answer on the files of the court. The judge refused him permission to do so, declaring that, as the same answer had been rejected by another judge, he could not admit it, not having the power to revise his judgments. In this opinion we are not sure whether the judge was correct, for he perhaps had the same authority to consider this application, as if the decision had been made by himself at the former term. But we have no opinion formed on this point, for it is not necessary to the decision of the case. The judge did not err in rejecting it, from the considerations we have already expressed, and we do not sit here to reverse his reasons, but to correct his judgments.

As soon as the plaintiff had read his petition the defendant propounded the following question as the bill of exception states, to the judge. " Inasmuch as the plaintiff in his petition sets forth that he has been for six years owner and possessor of the slave sued for, is

[Gayoso v. Wikoff.]

this a petitory or possessory action?" The judge considering the point as already decided by the judge of the fourth district when he excluded the amended answer, refused to give any reply to the question. We are unacquainted with any rule of law or practice which authorises counsel, or parties, on the opening of a case, to propound interrogatories in this way to judges, and the learned person who presided in the court might well have declined giving any reply, until the appearing of evidence required of him to declare his opinion, or until a decision on the merits rendered it necessary for him to do so. We certainly do not think the decision of his brother judge excluding the answer prevented him from deciding any point afterwards arising in the case, as his judgment of the law might require him to do; for a decision on an interlocutory question during the pendency of a cause does not preclude a decision on other interlocutory matters in which the same principle of law may be involved. But as a direct answer to the question, if it had been put at a proper time, must have been unfavorable to the defendant, we can not send the cause back on that ground. More especially as we perceive by another bill of exceptions, that the silence of the judge did not prevent the appellant from requiring and obtaining his opinion on this point, at another stage of the cause when the defendant offered evidence of title. That evidence was rejected, and in our opinion correctly, as the suit was a possessory one.

On the merits we can discover no error in the judgment of the court below, and it is, therefore, ordered, adjudged and decreed that it be affirmed, with costs.

Hennen, for the plaintiff.
Morse, for the defendant.

Pritchard *v.* Scott. VII, N. S. 493.

THIRD District.
Since the act of assembly of 1823, the post-office is, in certain cases, a proper place of deposit for notices to endorsers. Before that time, *alias.*

Perez *et al* v. Miranda. VII, N. S. 493.

A merchant who has funds of another in his hands, and is compelled by political events to send them away, must as much as possible retain a control over them, and as soon as the cause which induced him to part with them ceases, must dispose of them according to orders.

FIRST District.

MARTIN, J., delivered the opinion of the court.

The defendant, a merchant of Tampico, resists the claim of the plaintiffs, merchants of Gibraltar, for the proceeds of a quantity of brandy, and other goods, which he sold for them in May, 1827, on the ground that, in the following winter, all European Spaniards were ordered to leave the republic of Mexico, and were so much alarmed at the proceedings of government that most of them removed their property to Havana, and other places of safety; that he and the plaintiffs are European Spaniards, and he thought it best for the interest of the plaintiffs, and a measure which the disturbed state of the country rendered indispensable, to disregard the plaintiffs' order to transmit their funds to Vera Cruz, and sent them to Havana, to a commercial house, whom he directed to hold them at the plaintiffs' disposal.

The district court sustained the defence, and gave judgment for the defendant. The plaintiffs appealed.

There is not any dispute about the plaintiffs' claim to a balance in the defendant's hands, nor as to its amount. The only question is as to the validity of the matter set up in discharge of the defendant.

The brandy was sold in May, on a credit—the plaintiffs, on being informed of this, expressed no dissatisfaction at it, and their consent may perhaps be presumed. But it remains for the defendant to show that it was not owing to any cause of his that the funds were not received and sent to Vera Cruz, before the order which excited alarm among the European Spaniards. This might have been done by showing the period of credit given. Are we to suppose then it was six months? Suppose it was three, there would have probably been sufficient time to collect and send the funds according to order.

We admit with his counsel, that if there was really a cause of alarm which induced the sending the funds to Havana, instead of Vera Cruz; necessity justified the act it induced, and we are willing to consider that necessity as proved by witnesses to whom the inferior judge has given credit.

. But nothing shows that the defendant could not, after the funds

28*

reached Havana, have preserved over those funds that control, which he was bound to resume as soon as the necessity which had compelled him to abandon it ceased. He was bound that they should be transmitted to the plaintiffs' correspondents as soon as possible, or kept at the latter's disposal. Nothing justified, because nothing compelled, the defendant to place the funds out of his reach or control. He ought to have kept such a command over them, as to have remained able to answer the plaintiffs' call at any time.

Neither is it very satisfactorily shown that the plaintiffs' funds were sent to Havana. It is indeed in evidence that the defendant sent a larger sum than that he owed the plaintiffs, to Havana, and that he afterwards directed his correspondent there to keep the sum due the plaintiffs at their disposal. Their counsel has seen nothing in this but a voluntary appropriation by the defendant of funds of his in Havana, to the discharge of what he owed to the plaintiffs; an appropriation which, as it had no other effect than to give them a new debtor, without their approbation, instead of the one in which they had placed their trust, could not release the latter.

There is another circumstance which militates against the defendant—his order to his Havana correspondent to hold the plaintiffs' funds at their disposal was clogged with the condition "that they should be reinstated in the management of their affairs."

After the shipment of the brandy, the plaintiffs informed the defendant that they had been compelled to stop payment, and desired him to suspend the execution of their anterior orders; that he should hold their funds at the disposal of the syndics that were to be appointed. They afterwards informed him that amicable arrangements being made with their creditors, they had resumed the management of their affairs, and gave him new directions about their funds. The defendant in reply, observed it would have been more according to mercantile usage if the syndics had communicated the information, but denied any want of confidence in the assertion of the plaintiffs, and expressed no desire to receive any communication from the syndics. The fact is that no syndics were appointed, the arrangements taken having precluded the necessity of any.

Thus the defendant added to the delay, unnecessarily created by placing the funds in Havana, at the plaintiff's disposal, instead of sending or keeping them at the disposal of their correspondent at Vera Cruz, a place nearer, and with which Havana has more frequent communication than Gibraltar, besides subjecting the plaintiffs to unnecessary delay and trouble, in establishing to the satisfaction of the defendant's correspondent the fact of their being legally reinstated in the management of their affairs.

We conclude then, admitting that the defendant was guilty of no laches in collecting and transmitting the plaintiff's funds to Vera Cruz, and that necessity justified (as the district judge has concluded) the sending of the money to Vera Cruz; nothing authorises the defendant in leaving them there out of his control, so as to disable himself from

[Perez et al. v. Miranda.]

effectually answering the plaintiffs' first call on him, or from sending them to Vera Cruz if an opportunity offered. As he parted illegally with the funds, his liability to produce them is not thereby affected.

It is, therefore, ordered, adjudged and decreed that the judgment of the district court be annulled, avoided and reversed, and proceeding to give such judgment as in our opinion the judge *a quo* ought to have given, it is ordered, adjudged and decreed, that the appellant recover from the appellee the sum of seven thousand three hundred and twenty-three dollars, thirty-seven and a half cents, with legal interest till paid, with costs in both courts.

Duncan, for the plaintiff.

Strawbridge, for the defendant.

Dorsey *et al. v.* Their Creditors.   VII, N. S. 498.

A party who endorses a bill for the accommodation of the drawer, is not entitled to receive damages from the latter beyond what he has actually paid.

FIRST District.

PORTER, J., delivered the opinion of the court.

The appellant contends there is an error in the tableau of distribution, because he was not placed thereon, for the damages on certain bills of exchange protested for non-payment, on which he was endorser.

The evidence on record shows the endorsement to have been made for the accommodation of the drawers. The case therefore differs in no important circumstance from that decided last summer in this court, in the suit of Nolte & Co. *v.* Their Creditors, except that in this instance the endorsement was made in the state of Pennsylvania. *Ante*, 135.

The court of the first instance rejected the claim for damages. Here it has been contended that decision should be reversed and a different one rendered, from that given in the case just cited. *First*, because the statute of Pennsylvania differs from ours—and, *Secondly*, because in that case, the conclusions to which the court came were incorrect, and unsupported by law.

I. We have been unable to discover any material distinction between the legislative provisions of our own, and our sister state on the subject.

The act of this state declares: " That if any person shall draw or endorse any bill or bills of exchange upon any persons living out of this state (territory) but within the limits of the United States of America, and the same be returned unpaid with a legal protest, the drawer thereof, and all others concerned in making and endorsing such bill or bills shall pay and discharge," &c. &c.

The Pennsylvania statute provides " That whenever any bill of exchange hereafter to be drawn or endorsed within this commonwealth upon any person or persons, or body corporate, of, or in any other state, territory, or place, shall be returned unpaid, with a legal protest, the person or persons to whom the same shall or may be payable shall be entitled to recover and receive of and from," &c. &c.

The terms used appear to us equally comprehensive in each of the enactments:—the language is broad enough in both to cover the case of the appellant, and we are unable to think of a single argument deducible from the literal terms of the law, that does not apply with the same force to the one act, as to the other.

No decision of the courts of Pennsylvania putting a construction on their statute, in a case such as that before us, has been shown, nor have our own researches furnished us with any. We are therefore bound to decide the case by those principles of law which would govern us, if the transaction had taken place here, and the statute been passed in Louisiana.

If the decision in the case of Nolte & Co. be correct, it settles the rights of the parties before us. We feel gratified that the zeal of the counsel for the appellant has enabled us to examine again attentively the doctrine there established, and though we are far from thinking the case free from difficulty, we believe the weight of authority, and of reason too, in favor of the principles which guided us in its decision. Looking beyond the form in which this contract is clothed, and considering it on the evidence adduced, and the admissions made on record, we have presented to us the case of an endorser of a bill of exchange who put his name on it for the accommodation of the previous parties, and to enable them to raise money on it. He has done so without paying damages, and yet requires the parties to whom he lent his name, should pay them to him. We can discover no equity at least in this demand, and if he has such a right it must be derived from positive law.

Were the appellant the holder of a bill of exchange taken in the due course of trade, and negotiated by him, we believe it would not be necessary for him to show that he had paid the damages, the law merchant considering the liability to pay them sufficient to enable the holder of a bill to recover them from previous parties.

But we considered in the former case that he was not the holder of a bill of exchange in the sense in which that term is used in the law merchant: and though as to all parties who came after him on the bill, the *lex mercatoria* applied in full force, and made him responsible under its rules, yet that as between him and those he engaged to accomodate with the use of his name, the contract was an ordinary one of suretyship.

The correctness of our former decision depends on the accuracy of considering the endorser as surety. To support that view we are aware that it is necessary we should be authorised to look beyond the form in which the contract is clothed. The propriety of our doing so, did not strike us to be contested in argument. If it had, the consideration of a supposed case will at once show the obligation of the court to do so. Should, for example, the drawer of a bill of exchange have given it for the accommodation of the payee, and the latter have taken it up on protest, most certainly in a suit by him against the person who had accommodated him, it would be open to the drawer to show that the bill had been given for the mere accommodation of the plaintiff. This case shows further, that in an action on a bill, a party might be completely within the letter of the statute giving damages on bills of exchange; and yet there can not be a doubt that the payee for whose accommodation it was given, could not recover them, nor the principal, for the payment of which, by the mere inspection of the bill, the drawer would appear to be responsible.

If then we are correct in concluding that the court are not bound by the terms in which parties on a bill of exchange have clothed their contract, and that we may look into the real nature of the transaction, to ascertain the extent of their rights and obligations: let us see what contract was formed between the appellant and those for whom he endorsed. It makes a part of the admissions on record as already stated, that he put his name on the bills to enable the previous parties to raise money on them, or in other words, that he made himself responsible to any person they might thereafter pass the bill to. Test this engagement by the definition of our Code, which declares suretyship to be "an accessary promise by which a person binds himself for another already bound, and agrees with the creditor to satisfy the obligation of the debtor if he does not," and we are totally at a loss to discover into what other class of contracts the engagement can fall. Louisiana Code, 2004.

In opposition to this, it was contended, the endorser could not be considered as surety, because he was liable in the first instance on the bill, to the holder, and that he could not, as sureties can, claim the right of discussion. But we understand it to be an elementary, as it certainly is a familiar doctrine of our law, that the contract of suretyship may exist between the principal and surety, although as to other parties, they should be bound *in solido.* Civil Code, 428, 7; Louisiana Code, 3014; *Pothier, Traité des Obligations, no.* 264.

Having thus seen that the contract was one of suretyship, let us next consider whether that of a change was also formed between the parties. In making this inquiry we have been unable to find a single feature of the latter, unless in the form of the contract. The bills in question never were passed to the appellant: they were not received by him in course of trade, they were not negotiated by him. He merely lent his name to enable the previous parties to put them into circulation. In no part of the *lex mercatoria* can we find any thing which will authorise us to say, that a person who thus becomes a party to a bill, is entitled to the rights of a holder who has taken and negotiated it for the purposes for which this contract was first introduced among men, and subsequently recognised and sanctioned by law. It cannot be contended that the form of the contract is to control the substance of it; if it did, the agent to whom a bill was passed for collection might with equal success, urge that the endorser's rights and obligations were to be settled by the rules which govern the transfer of bills of exchange, instead of the law of mandate.

It is said the authorities in the commercial law do not sustain us in the position assumed. It is certainly true that the point is nowhere expressly decided, and it is equally true, that there have not been many cases which furnish analogies on which the court can sustain the doctrine it believes correct; but those which come nearest to it in principle, do in our judgment completely support the position assumed.

Bayley, in his Treatise on Bills, in speaking of the remedy by an accommodation party, states "if the bankrupt were the person to whom the instrument was lent, in which case the endorser is a mere surety, he will be entitled, under 49 Geo. 3, on taking up the bill or note, to stand in place of the holder, if he had proved under the commission, and to prove himself if the holder had not. Bayley on Bills, 296.

Again, on the authority of a case in 4 Vesey, the author states, that mere reciprocal accommodation without any specific exchange of bills or notes, will not create a debt on either side. Each party in such case becomes surety for the other, and until obliged to pay bills or notes negotiated by the other, acquires no right to sue the other, or in the event of his bankruptcy, to prove under his commission.— *Ibid.* 302.

Eden, in his work on bankruptcy, states, "whatever be the situation on the bill of the person lending his name, whether he be acceptor, drawer, or endorser, he is substantially a surety for the person who has received consideration for it, and as such, is entitled to be indemnified by the estate of the principal. Page 149.

These authorities we think clearly establish, that in England the party who lends his name is considered as surety; and that his right to recover does not depend on the mere fact of his holding the bill, but his having paid it. If then his right to recover depends on paying that right must be limited to the sum he has paid. The obligations of the principal, cannot be extended beyond the injury the surety has sustained.

The strongest authority against this opinion is contained in the late Commentaries of Chancellor Kent, in which it is stated "accommodation paper is now governed by the same rules as other paper. This is the latest and best doctrine, both in England and in this country." In support of this opinion he cites 5 Taunton, 192; 6 Dow's Par. Cas. 224; 9 Serg. & Rawle, 229; 6 Cowen, 484.

The opinions of this eminent jurist and judge, are entitled to great respect, and when found different from our conclusions on a legal question, they well authorise further reflection before a decision is pronounced. In this instance, however, we do not believe that learned person had any such case in contemplation as that before us. Immediately before the sentence quoted, he is treating of the obligations of the acceptor, and in opposition to a novel doctrine first enounced by Lord Ellenborough, some years since, that the acceptor was not liable to the endorser, he continues to say, " He is bound though he accepted without consideration, and for the sole accommodation of the drawer; accommodation paper is now governed by the same rules as other paper." It is clear to us that the obligations of the acceptor to the other parties to the bill, were alone contemplated by the author. If he intended to say, that as between the party lending his name, and him to whom the name was lent, all the rules of mercantile paper apply, the cases quoted do not sustain the opinion to that extent. They all relate to the obligations of acceptors of bills, or makers of notes, to parties to the instrument other than those to whom they lent their names; and upon these principles, and in conformity therewith, the case of Postlethwaite *v.* Cox was decided a few days since in this court.*

As to the observations which fell from the court in the case of Harrod *v.* Lafarge, 12 *Martin*, 21, they are nothing more than the enunciation of the general principle, and as to all other parties to the bill but the person for whom the accomodation was made, they are correct, and still express the opinion of this court. The case before the court is quite different from that, and our decision now, does not in any respect conflict with it.

But the appellant claims interest on the drafts which were duly protested, and which were not given by the judgment of the district court—this must be altered.

It is, therefore, ordered, adjudged and decreed, that the judgment of the district court be annulled, avoided and reversed, and that the appellant be placed on the respective tableaux of Morgan Dorsey & Co., Benjamin Morgan and Greenbury Dorsey, for the sum of 31,704 dollars 71 cents, with interest, on 10,000 dollars from the 22d December, 1825, on 10,000 dollars from the 6th January, 1826, on 10,000 dollars from the 21st January, 1826, on 1700 dollars 71 cents from the 11th January, 1826, to the dates of filing the several bilans by said insolvents, and that the appellees pay the costs in both courts.

Slidell, for the opposing creditor.

Eustis, for the syndics.

* The title of this case is Weir *et al. v.* Cox, *ante,* 277.

EASTERN DISTRICT, MARCH TERM, 1829.

Kirkland *v*. His Creditors.   VII, N. S. 511.

THIRD District.

An opposition filed to a tableau of distribution of insolvent's property cannot be amended without leave.

Rowlett *v*. Shepherd.   VII, N. S. 513.

The notice in the 735th and 736th articles of the Code of Practice, is that which the
sheriff is to give to the defendant, before seizure.*

The act of 1828 has repealed those parts of the former laws which required an assignee
to prove the consideration of the assignment before he obtained a writ of seizure.

The authority of a sworn attorney is always presumed.

The demand which must precede the seizure, is the only notice required before payment
be enforced by a writ of seizure, by an assignee.

That part of the old Code, which required the plaintiff's oath before a writ of seizure
issued, is repealed.

* On notice of ten days.

FIRST District.

Martin, J., delivered the opinion of the court.

The plaintiff appealed from an order for setting aside a writ of seizure and sale.

The counsel for the defendant and appellee urges that the writ was properly set aside—because,

1. Issued without any previous notice to the defendant.

2. The plaintiff was an assignee, and had no right to the writ, as he did not prove he had given any consideration to the assignor.

3. The authority of the plaintiff's agent was not shown.

4. No notice of the assignment had been given to the debtor.

5. The oath was not taken by the party, but by his agent.

I. On the first point, the Code of Practice, 735 and 736, is relied on. We think the notice there spoken of, is that which the sheriff is to give before a seizure. For the Code requires, that besides the ordinary delay, the defendant should have further time, in proportion to the distance of the residence of the judge to whom the petition is presented.

II. On the second, the counsel relies on Nichols v. De Ende, vol. 3, 310; Wray v. King, 10 Martin 220; Cur. Phil. Executante, N. 18.

In the first case, we held that when the plaintiff is not the defendant's original creditor, he must produce authentic evidence of his own title to the debt; and on the other, that a writ of seizure and sale could not issue in favor of an endorser on parol proof of the endorsement. The Curia Philipica, indeed, requires that the plaintiff, before he obtains the writ, should prove the amount he paid to the assignor, in some other manner than the confession of the assignor. This we take to be a rule of practice which is now repealed by the act of 1828.

III. The same book requires the judge, before he grants a writ of seizure and sale, to consider si la execucion se pide, en virtud de poder del acreedor. Pedimiento, n. 13. In the present case the petition is signed by a sworn attorney, who, till the contrary be proved, is always presumed not to act without being employed. Hayes v. Cuny, 9 Martin, 87.

IV The notice required by the Civil Code 613 to the debtor, of the assignment of the debt, has for its object, to prevent his paying it to the assignor, or the creditors of the latter from seizing it. The demand which must precede the seizure is the only notice required before enforcing payment by the assignee.

V. That part of the Civil Code 3361, which required an oath from the plaintiff, is repealed by the Code of Practice, 734, which provides that he may obtain a writ of seizure and sale on a simple petition.

We think the writ in the present case ought not to have been set aside.

It is, therefore, ordered, adjudged and decreed, that the judgment

be annulled, avoided and reversed, the writ of seizure and sale reinstated, and the case remanded for further proceedings according to
law, the appellee paying costs in both courts.

Grymes, for the plaintiff.
Slidell, for the defendant.

Lacoste v. Bordere et al.　VII, N. S. 516.

PARISH Court of New Orleans.
A debt offered as compensation, must be as liquidated as the plaintiff's.　Louisiana Code, 2205; 7 *Toullier*, 444.
Reconvention must be, on matter necessarily connected with his
claim.　Code of Practice, 375.

Plauche et al. v. Gravier et al.　VII, N. S. 518.

(See 5 *N. S.* 597.)

FIRST District.
The prescription of ten years must be on a just title.

Russell *et al. v.* Ferguson.   VII, N. S. 519.

FIRST District.

A party is not obliged to accept several drafts for one debt.

The pleas filed by the defendant's counsel are supposed to be so with the assent of the client.

The general issue denies all the facts in the petition, and the legal inferences resulting therefrom.   See King *v.* Havard, 5 *N. S.* 193; 5 Wheaton, 277.

John K. Ferguson *v.* Wm. L. Foster.   VII, N. S. 521.

Plaintiff can not arrest the person of his debtor, and attach his property unless both remedies are necessary to insure the execution of the judgment.

A rule to show cause why an order of arrest should not be set aside does not put the truth of the allegations contained in the affidavit at issue.

FIRST District.

Porter, J., delivered the opinion of the court.

On the petition filed in this case, a writ of attachment was taken out and levied on a steamboat. The boat, by agreement between the parties, was to run during the pendency of suit, and the profits to be applied to the extinguishment of the debt. After two trips had been made, the plaintiff filed a supplemental petition, stating that instead of any profit having accrued from this agrement, the boat had lost on each voyage; and a further sum of 185 dollars 69 cents is demanded. Tho plaintiff also averred that the steamboat was incumbered by a heavy mortgage, and that he feared he would be deprived of the benefit of his attachment. He prayed that the defendant might be held to bail.

An order of court was given; the person of the defendant taken; and the question presented to our consideration is, whether under the

[John K. Ferguson *v.* Wm. L. Foster.]

circumstances just stated the plaintiff has a right to use both these remedies. On the hearing of a rule taken by the defendant to have the order of bail set aside, the court below sustained the objection to the correctness and legality of the steps taken by the plaintiff, and made the rule absolute. From that decision the present appeal was taken.

The rules of practice furnished by the legislature give us no positive provision on this subject. The 208th article of the Code of Practice in speaking of the conservatory acts which the plaintiff may resort to, in order to give effect to the suit he is about to institute, states that they may be used either against the person or the property. The defendant has urged, from this enactment being in the disjunctive, that it was not the intention of the legislature that both should be exercised in the same action. But it appears to us that this provision was rather intended to mark the extent of the remedy, by giving it against person and property, than to provide for the manner in which it should be used, and that little aid can be derived from it in deciding the point before us.

The question then is to be decided on general principles, and the best rule we can adopt is that which will carry into effect the object for which the right was conferred.

It was given for the purpose of enabling the plaintiff to insure the execution of the judgment he hoped to obtain, and whenever that can be secured by a resort to one of the remedies, the plaintiff should not be permitted to avail himself of both; because the making use of arrest and attachment would in such a case be oppressive to the defendant, without being useful to the plaintiff.

Laws which deprive men of the use of their property and their personal liberty, on the mere allegations of their adversary, supported alone by his oath, should be strictly construed, and he who claims the benefit of them should clearly establish his right to so severe a remedy. This rule increases in force, when he has already resorted to one means of giving effect to the future decree of the court; because the presumption of the necessity for further conservatory acts, is weakened by the security already obtained.

In the instance before us, the attachment was levied on a steam boat; if she afforded sufficient means of insuring the execution of the judgment, the plaintiff had no right to arrest the person of the debtor. That she was of sufficient value to do so has not been denied, and the oath of the plaintiff to hold the defendant to bail, alleging solely as the ground for it, that she was incumbered with a mortgage, furnishes strong presumption that without this incumbrance she would have been sufficient.

The case then is narrowed down to an inquiry whether legal and adequate proof of the failure of the first remedy was offered. In ordinary cases it is enough for obtaining a writ of attachment, or an order for arresting the person of the debtor, that the plaintiff makes oath of the facts, and the defendant if he wishes to have the order set aside must disprove them. Code of Practice, 218.

[John K. Ferguson v. Wm. L. Foster.]

But whether in a case such as this, where the plaintiff demands a double remedy, and is entitled to it only on special grounds, the defendant might not have put him on the proof of those facts which would authorise the issuing the order for arrest, after an attachment has been granted, may be well doubted. The pleadings in the inferior court however do not permit us to examine it. The affidavit of the plaintiff was sufficient in the first instance, and the rule taken did not put the verity of the allegations contained in it at issue. A call on the plaintiff to show cause why the order granted should not be set aside, put the legality of the steps taken by the plaintiff on his own showing alone at issue, and afforded him no notice to come prepared with proof to support them.

Assuming it therefore as a fact, that the property on which the attachment was levied, being incumbered with a mortgage, did not afford security for carrying into effect the judgment which the plaintiff expected to obtain, we think the court below erred in setting aside the order to arrest the person of the debtor.

It is, therefore, ordered, adjudged and decreed, that the judgment of the district court be annulled, avoided and reversed; and it is further ordered, adjudged and decreed, that the case be remanded, to be proceeded in according to law, the appellee paying the costs of this appeal.

Hawes, for the plaintiff.

Christy, for the defendant.

Gabaroche *v.* Hebert *et al.*   VII, N. S. 526.

FOURTH District.

The answer of the plaintiff to interrogatories may be taken under a general commission to examine all witnesses.

An answer to interrogatories must be categorical, but it is immaterial in what words the answer is made, provided an affirmance or denial result.

An endorsement in blank does not prevent the endorsee from suing on it and recovering.

Although it is not alleged in the petition that demand was made at the place where the note was payable, yet if the certificate of protest be annexed to it, and be given in evidence on trial, it cannot be said that petition was defective.

29*

Chew *v.* Chinn.　VII, N. S. 532.

If a suit be irregularly commenced in the *juicio executivo* and afterwards turned into the *juicio ordinario,* the plaintiff, though he should succeed, must pay the costs of the executory proceedings.

Parol evidence is admissible to show that a payment was made, *in a note,* where the receipt in writing expressed generally that the debt had been paid.

When a debt is assigned as collateral security, the holder becomes agent for the collection, and the net amount after deducting costs and other charges should be credited.

If counsel make a personal contract for their fee with the assignor of a debt they can not claim payment from the assignee.

An assignment of a mortgage debt does not carry with it a promise to pay ten per cent. to the transferee for an extension of credit which had expired at the time of the transfer.

THIRD District.

Porter, J., delivered the opinion of the court.

The plaintiff commenced this action by an injunction praying to arrest an order of seizure and sale which the defendant had obtained against him. The grounds laid in the petition are; various informalities in the proceedings, and the sum due being less than that for which the order issued.

There is only one of these objections which require particular notice from the court.

The defendant owed the sum of 18,000 dollars, payable in three equal instalments. The first two were settled and discharged by payment and a note of the defendant's for 1741 dollars 75 cents. This note, together with the last instalment of the 18,000 dollars, were transferred to the plaintiff, and the order of seizure and sale was granted by the court for the balance alleged to be due on the obligation for 6000 dollars secured by authentic act, and the note of 1741 dollars 75 cents *sous seing privé.* In this we think there was error. The note last mentioned, given and accepted in discharge of the balance due on the second instalment, was a personal not an hypothecary obligation, and did not enable the holder to enforce it by the executory process.

The defendant however urges that these irregularities are no longer a subject of examination, because the parties have joined issue on the allegations contained in the petition for an injunction: the suit has been turned from the *juicio executivo* into the *juicio ordinario;* there has been a trial on the merits, and judgment.

This position is correct so far as to prevent the subsequent proceedings in the *juicio ordinario* from being irregular, in consequence

[Chew v. Chinn.]

of the illegal manner in which the *juicio executivo* commenced. But it would be unjust and contrary to law to make the plaintiff responsible for the costs occasioned by the defendant taking out an order of seizure and sale where he was not entitled to it. They must be borne by the party through whose fault they were occasioned.

On the trial of the merits, the court below gave judgment against the plaintiff in injunction for the sum of 2977 dollars 5 cents, with interest thereon from the 3d of July, 1827, until paid, rejecting the note of 1741 dollars 75 cents. With this judgment both parties appear to be dissatisfied. The plaintiff has appealed from it; and the defendant has prayed that it may be so amended, as to include the note still due for the balance of the second instalment.

A bill of exceptions was taken by the defendant to the rejection of a witness to prove that the note of the plaintiff for 1741 dollars 75 cents grew out of the mortgage transaction, and was in part payment of the second instalment. The court would not admit the evidence, because it contradicted the receipt of the former holders of the obligation that it had been paid. That receipt on referring to it does not state in what manner the payment had been made, and though strictly speaking the acceptance of a new debt for the old was rather a novation, than a payment, yet we know that, in common understanding, where a note is given for another debt which by agreement of parties is to be extinguished by it, this extinguishment is considered by them as a payment, and called such. We therefore think the court erred in rejecting the witness. His testimony was not offered to prove that no payment had been made, but the manner in which that payment had been effected. It did not in any manner contradict the receipt, nor impair its legal effect. As it did not, it is unnecessary to remand the cause to procure the proof; for had it been received, the legal rights of the parties would have been the same, as they are now presented without it.

The principal questions in the cause, relate first to the alleged error of the court in not giving judgment for this note, and second in not allowing sufficient credit to the plaintiff in injunction on the payments made by him.

As the latter form the ground of complaint of the appellant, they will be first examined.

The plaintiff previous to the assignment of his obligation to the defendant, had placed in the hands of Johnson the assignor, as collateral security a debt of one Balfour, secured by mortgage. The collection of this debt was attended with considerable difficulty, and suits of different kinds grew out of the attempt to enforce its payment. The defendant in giving credit for the moneys made has deducted the costs of court, and the fees paid to counsel for advice, and other professional services attending the collection. Of this the plaintiff complains. He insists that the whole amount received should be credited to the obligation due by him, and that the sums

expended in collection should be considered as a personal obligation
on his part. On general principles this demand is certainly unfounded.
When a debt is assigned as collateral security, the holder becomes
agent for the collection, and the net, not the gross, sum should be
credited, as was decided in the case of Johnson *et al. v.* Sterling, 3
N. S. 486.

But in this instance part of the fees deducted stand on particular
grounds. One of them, that to Turner, never has been paid. The
assignor of the debt, Johnston, swears that when he employed him
he told him the plaintiff in this suit would pay him, and that if he
did not he, Johnson, would. There is no ground then for deducting
the amount due Turner. It is either a debt of the plaintiff's or
Johnson's; nothing shows the defendant to be responsible for it.
Another deduction made for the fee paid to Woodruff is also specially
circumstanced. He swears that he was employed by the plaintiff.
Now if counsel make a personal engagement with a party interested
in a suit, and on his request appear in it, they have no right to
demand payment for their services from another party to the action
who may be benefitted by them. The promise therefore by the
defendant to pay the counsel after he had been engaged by the plaintiff, and the subsequent payment, were entirely gratuitous, and though
they may furnish him with a claim for reimbursement from plaintiff
for money paid and expended for his use, the sum thus paid does not
form a portion of the expenses necessarily incurred in the collection,
and did not authorise him to divert the application of the funds in
his hands from the extinction of a debt which the plaintiff had a
greater interest to discharge. With regard to the other fees and
expenses, the evidence does not show any thing which takes them
out of the general rule, and they were therefore properly deducted
in the court of the first instance. Civil Code, 2153.

The next question in the cause is the right of the appellee to have
the judgment below so amended as to give him a judgment for the
note of 1741 dollars and 75 cents.

We think it ought. The note it is true is only put at issue for the
purpose of ascertaining whether the order of seizure and sale properly issued. But as the proceedings were afterwards turned into
the *juicio ordinario,* judgment should be given for the creditor in
that right in which the evidence shows the money to be due. The
proof established that the note is due and unpaid.

The plaintiff requires interest at ten per cent. in consequence of an
engagement entered into by the plaintiff with Charles G. Johnson,
in 1821, in which he promised that in case the credit of the three
notes then due by him were extended one year he would in lieu of
6000 dollars pay at the end of each annual instalment the sum of
6600 dollars. In the contract there is a clause "that nothing therein
contained shall in any manner interfere with, invalidate, or prejudice
the mortgage with which the full and final payment of the said sums
is secured."

[Chew v. Chinn.]

The assignment to the defendant acknowledges the receipt of 6000 dollars, and transfers to him all the assignor's interest in the mortgage. We do not think that by this contract, the obligation to pay 600 dollars for indulgence which had expired before the assignment, conveyed to the defendant the transferror's interest in a personal debt.

We can discover no error in the judgment of the court below in relation to credits, or calculation, except in the deduction of the fees of Turner & Woodruff, which appear to be 330 dollars 10 cents.

It is therefore ordered adjudged and decreed, that the judgment of the district court be annulled, avoided and reversed; and it is further ordered, adjudged and decreed, that the defendant do recover from the plaintiff the sum of two thousand six hundred and forty six dollars ninety four cents, the balance due on a note of Samuel Chew in favor of Charles G. Johnson, dated the 7th of November 1818, and payable on the first day of February, 1822, for 6000 dollars, secured by mortgage of date the 7th of November, 1818; and it is further ordered that the premises hypothecated to secure the payment of said note be seized and sold to satisfy this judgment.

It is further adjudged and decreed, that the defendant do recover of the plaintiff another sum of seventeen hundred and forty-one dollars seventy-five cents, with interest from judicial demand; the [costs incurred by the taking out the order of seizure and sale, and those of appeal, to be paid by the appellee. The other costs in the cause to be paid by the appellant.

Turner, for the plaintiff.
Watts, for the defendant.

Kenner *et al.* *v.* Their Creditors. VII, N. S. 541.

A bill at sixty days sight, accepted payable sixty-three days from the date of the acceptance, is accepted according to its tenor and is to be protested on the sixty-third day.

PARISH Court of New Orleans.

Martin, J., delivered the opinion of the court.

Hicks, Lawrence & Co. opposed the homologation of the tableau of distribution, on the ground that they were not placed thereon, as creditors for the amount of a protested bill of exchange, drawn by the insolvents. The opposition was overruled, and the opposing party appealed.

The bill, which was at sixty days' sight, was accepted on the twelfth* of September 1825, payable on the fourteenth of November following and protested on the latter day.

The appellees' counsel urge that the appellants lost their recourse on the drawer: because

1. The acceptance was contrary to the tenor of the bill, being for payment on the sixty-third instead of the sixtieth, day after sight.

2. The protest was made on the day of payment, instead of the last of the days of grace.

Both of the objections will be disposed of by the solution of the question, was the fourteenth of November (the day stated in the acceptance) the peremptory day of payment, or that from which the days of grace were to be reckoned? or, in other words, were the days of grace included between the day of acceptance and the fourteenth of November?

If that day was the peremptory one, and those of grace were included, then was the acceptance according to the tenor of the bill?

Then, was the protest timely?

Both parties admit, that all questions relative to the acceptance and protest of a bill of exchange are to be determined according to the law of the country in which it is accepted and protested.

In the present case, the bill was accepted and protested in England, and the laws of that country afford the only legitimate rule of decision.

These laws being here foreign laws, must be proved as facts, by testimony or documents.

For these purposes, the appellants have introduced the depositions of nine witnesses, conversant in banking business, at the place on which the bill was drawn.

1. Hall, the first of these, deposes, that a bill at sixty days' sight, and accepted in the following form, " accepted, payable on the tenth of September, Liverpool, July 12, 1825," can be protested, according to commercial usage, on the thirteenth of September. He would reckon sixty-three days from the twelfth of July, the day of acceptance.

2, 3. Henderson and Orford testify, the bill the first witness speaks of would be irregularly accepted. According to commercial usage, it should be protested on the thirteenth of September.

4. Gordon says, such an acceptance would be irregular and contrary to commercial usage. If he had a bill thus accepted, he would present it on the tenth, and again on the thirteenth, and protest it on the latter day.

5. 6. Anderson and Luke deposed as the first witness.

---

* The date of this acceptance was the 12th of September, and not the 14th as it was printed in the original; this correction was made by Judge MARTIN in a note to 8 *N. S.* 67.

7. Binns thinks the bill should be protested according to commercial usage on the 13th.

8. Ireland testified to the same purpose, adding, the words, "payable on the 10th of September," was surplusage.

9. Highfield viewed them likewise as surplusage.

These gentlemen may well consider the words "payable on the 10th of September," as useless or superfluous, for the acceptance would have precisely the same meaning and effect if .they were omitted. The drawee is required to pay sixty days after sight; the bill is presented on the twelfth of July, and he accepts to pay on the 10th of September, *i. e.*, as he is required, on the sixtieth day after presentation. But surplusage does not vitiate an act; *utile per inutile non vitiatur;* and authorities have been cited, which have not been contradicted, that there is no form of acceptance established or required by the law of England.

We conclude from the examination of the appellees' own witnesses on this point that it does not result therefrom that a dated acceptance is vitiated by the express designation of a day of payment, when that day is designated according to the tenor of the bill.

We cannot comprehend what Gordon, the fourth witness, means by saying he would present the bill on the tenth, and again on the thirteenth, and protest it on the latter day. We cannot see of what use the presentation on the tenth could be, when not followed immediately by a protest.

The same witnesses have been next examined, by the appellants, in regard to a bill at sixty days' sight, accepted on the ninth of July, payable on the tenth of September. The difference between the bill in regard to which the witnesses were first examined and that now to be considered is, that in the former the day expressly designated in the acceptance was the sixtieth, and the other the sixty-third; in the one case the nominal, in the other the peremptory day of payment.

1, 2, 3, 4, 5, 6. Six of the appellees' witnesses, Hall, Gordon, Anderson, Binn, Luke and Highfield, suppose the latter bill ought to be protested on the tenth day of September, the day designated in the acceptance.

7. Henderson thinks it should, if the days of grace were included.

8. Ireland deposes he would consider the words, "payable on the tenth of September," as surplusage, and would protest on that day.

9. Orford deems the acceptance irregular, and should think the acceptor had included the days of grace, and would protest on that day.

Thus, from the unanimous opinion of the nine witnesses introduced by the appellees, with the exception of the seventh, Henderson, who speaks hypothetically, it follows from a comparison of the tenor of the bill, the date of the acceptance and the day designated for payment, the latter is the third after the expiration of the days after sight: the day thus designated is the peremptory day of payment.

In such a case the acceptance is according to the tenor of the bill, and the protest made on the day expressly designated is timely.

Our attention has, however, been drawn by the counsel of the appellees to a vast number of British, American and French authorities, from a careful examination of which it appears to us that the counsel are correct in their assertion that there is no express form, established or prescribed by the English laws; but the proposition that the words "payable on the — day of ———," added between the words "accepted" and the acceptor's signature or date, are to be rejected as surplusage, must be confined to cases in which the day designated appears to be the nominal day of payment—because their insertion has then no effect—that when that day, from a like comparison, appears to be the peremptory day of payment, they have the effect of showing that the days of grace have been included; and thus when the day thus designated does not appear to be either of these days, as when in a bill at sixty days' sight, another than the sixtieth or sixty-third day is stated, the words "payable," &c., have the effect of controlling the acceptance, by showing that it is not the intention of the drawee to accept it according to its tenor.

When the contrary does not clearly appear, parties must be viewed as having done *id quod plurimum fit*, and an instrument must be construed, if circumstances do not demand a contrary construction, *ut res magis valeat quam pereat*, and if the expressions used be susceptible of two meanings, the construction must be against the party who used them. *Verba fortius accipiuntur contra proferentem.*

We conclude that the holders of the bill did not discharge the drawers by receiving the drawees' acceptance, because it was according to the tenor of the bill, which was protested in due time.

We think the parish judge erred in disallowing the appellants' opposition to the tableau.

Judge Mathews, whose indisposition has deprived us of his presence in court for some time past, attended the conference of the judges in this case, and authorises us to say that he concurs in this opinion.

It is, therefore, ordered, adjudged and decreed, that the judgment of the parish court be annulled, avoided and reversed; and proceeding to pronounce the judgment, which in our opinion ought to have been given in the parish court, it is ordered, adjudged and decreed, that the appellants' opposition be sustained and that they be placed on the tableau as creditors for the amount of the bill and charges consequent on the protest, the appellees paying costs in this court.

Hennen, for the plaintiffs

Livermore, Morse and *Smith,* for the defendants.

Tate *v.* Penne.   VII, N. S. 548.

When the original has not been in possession of the party offering the copy, the proof of loss which will authorise the introduction of the latter as evidence, must depend on the particular circumstances of the case.

The law presumes the husband the father of the children born during marriage.

In case of voluntary separation access is always presumed unless cohabitation has been physically impossible.

The condition of a child born during marriage cannot be affected by the declaration of one or both the spouses.

EIGHTH District, Judge of the Third presiding.

PORTER, J., delivered the opinion of the court.

This is an action by a mother against her daughter. The petitioner claims a slave and five children, which she alleges she purchased in the year 1812, and possessed them for a long time after: that the defendant has taken them into possession and refuses to deliver them up.

The defendant pleads the general issue; avers that she had a good title to the property sued for; that the slaves were purchased in trust for her; and finally that she has held them five years previous to the institution of this suit, in virtue of a just title, and with good faith.

The cause was submitted to a jury in the court of the first instance, who found for the defendant; judgment of nonsuit was rendered against the plaintiff, after overruling a motion for a new trial, and she appealed.

The plaintiff appears to have been married three times. After living one or two years with her first husband, Sims, a voluntary separation took place between them, and he removed from that part of the country in which they had resided. Subsequent to this removal the defendant was born, the alleged fruit of an illegitimate connection of the plaintiff with one Laurens. They lived together and cohabited until ten years had elapsed from the time Sims was heard of, when they were married. This marriage was preceded by a contract, in which among many other stipulations, it is stated, that the slaves which form the object of this suit should be secured to the petitioner; after which follows that clause in the contract under which the defendant sets up title to them, " which said mulattress named Sally, with her three children and their issue, the said parties agree respectively to secure to their natural daughter, named Delphine, her heirs and assigns forever." This contract was dated in 1816. In 1825, the

[Tate *v.* Penne.]

defendant intermarried with A. Penne, and the slaves were sent or permitted to be removed to the house of the plaintiff.

On the trial below an objection was made to reading in evidence the copy offered of the contract of marriage, in which the clause just set out is found. It appears from testimony taken on this objection, that a very irregular practice has prevailed in the parish of St Tammany of recording all original acts in a book of record, and after recording them to hand back the originals to the parties. The witnesses mentioned in the copy were called into court, and they deposed, that they had attested a contract of marriage between the plaintiff and Laurens which was passed, or acknowledged before the parish judge. Notice was given to the plaintiff to produce the instrument.

The defendant's husband swore that the contract was not in his possession nor in that of his wife; that he did not know where it was —that it was not in any of the public offices of the parish, and that he believed it lost. That he had been diligently searching for it for a year back, but without success. The parish judge testified it was not in his office, and had not been there since he took possession of it. One of the heirs of Laurens swore it was not in his, nor did he ever see it in the hands of any of the family. The person who recorded it in the notarial record deposed that the copy produced in court was a correct copy.

We think that under the circumstances of the case the court below did not err in admitting the copy in evidence. The book, in which the original had been recorded being produced in court, it was not the copy of a copy, but the copy of the original that was offered.— The instrument never had been in possession of the defendant. She appears to have taken all means in her power to procure it. The proof of loss which will authorise the introduction of inferior evidence must depend on the particular circumstance of each case.

The next question is in relation to the validity of the act. The appellant contends that it is an instrument *sous seing privé*, and as such could not be the evidence of a matrimonial agreement. The commencement of the act does not state, as is usually the case, that the parties came before the judge or notary. It begins with these words: " Articles of agreement made and concluded," &c.; and it terminates by declaring, that the parties affixed their names to it in the presence of the subscribing witness. After, and immediately following which declaration are these words: " Done and executed before me, the date above written, James Tate, parish judge.

The only objection which we conceive can be fairly made to this not being a public act, is the deviation from the ordinary form of commencing instruments of that description. But this objection is removed by the conclusion, in which it is stated the act was made and executed before the parish judge. This declaration at the close of the instrument is entitled to as much weight, and furnishes as strong evidence of its being executed before the notary, as if the same allegations were contained in several other parts of it.

[Tate v. Penne.]

But the allegations of the plaintiff go farther than the form in which the act was clothed. She contends that the stipulations in it, in favor of the defendant, were null and void.

If the defendant was capable of taking from the parties, we see nothing illegal in that clause of the marriage contract by which the slaves in question were secured to the defendant. The title, it is true, was in the mother, but the father, as he styles himself, also settled property at the same time on the defendant, and he gave to the plaintiff by the contract, 1500 dollars if she survived him.

The plaintiff, however, has resorted to a most extraordinary ground for annulling this conveyance to her child. She insists that her first husband Sims being alive at the time of the birth of the defendant, the latter was an adulterous bastard and incapable of taking from her by donation—that the agreement disturbed the legal order of succession.

We are satisfied this ground for annulling the contract cannot avail the plaintiff: for, admitting she was legally married to Sims at the time defendant was born, the consequence would be that the defendant would be the daughter of Sims, not of Laurens, and as such did not lie under any incapacity to receive a donation from the parties to the contract. The law (said our Code at the time of the birth of the defendant) considers the husband of the mother as the father of all the children conceived during marriage. In case of voluntary separation, access is always presumed unless the contrary be proved: the presumption of paternity is at an end, when the remoteness of the husband from the wife has been such that cohabitation has been physically impossible. Civil Code, p. 45, art. 7, 10 and 11.

The evidence establishes the marriage of the parties in 1806. The defendant was born in 1809. Cooper swears they lived together a year and then parted. Lanier testifies, he has not seen Sims since a year after his marriage. Edwards states he saw him in 1808 in New Orleans, and never saw him on the east side of the lake since he went over there. Woods swears they separated in 1807, that he saw Sims for a week after and never saw him since. Lanier says the plaintiff was in New Orleans in 1807.

This is all the evidence. It creates a presumption of absence and non-access: but that will not do in cases like this. The legal presumption of the husband being the father, and of access being presumed in cases of voluntary separation, can only be destroyed by evidence bringing the parties within the exception the law has created to the rule, namely, the physical impossibility of connection—moral will not do.

Now that physical impossibility can only be shown, by proving the residence of the husband and wife to be so remote from each other that access was impossible. The proof here wholly fails in establishing it. The evidence of the husband's residence is only negative. He was not on the east side of the lake. Where the wife was, the proof is silent. How can we tell from the evidence that they did not meet and cohabit.

[Tate v. Penne.]

We have left out of view in coming to this conclusion the fact of the mother and Laurens having declared the defendant to be their child, and of their having treated her as such. It being a perfectly well established principle in cases of this kind, that a child born during marriage can not have its condition affected by the declaration of one or both of the spouses. *Toullier, vol. 2, lib. 1, chap. 2, no.* 859.

We conclude therefore that the mother has failed to establish that her child was an adulterous bastard, and as such incapable of receiving the donation given to her by the marriage contract. Even if she had, we have strong doubts whether such a plea could be received from her, but we do not find it necessary to decide the question.

It is, therefore, ordered, adjudged and decreed, that the judgment of the district court be affirmed, with costs.

Waggaman, for the plaintiff.
Hennen, for the defendant.

Millar v. Coffman.   VII, N. S. 556.

FIRST District.

Decided, that the 2522d article of the Louisiana Code places the causes which justify a reduction of price (the action *quanti minoris*) on the same ground as those of redhibition; and concluded that, as in the latter action, the contract could not be set aside unless the slave was afflicted with some vice or defect which rendered him absolutely useless, or his use so inconvenient and imperfect that it must be supposed the buyer would not have purchased him had he known of his imperfections; the plaintiff could not demand any reduction for a defect which did not fall within either of the causes that furnish ground for redhibition.

Lawrence v. M'Farlane. VII, N. S. 558.

The causes for which a reduction in the price of a slave can be claimed are the same as those for which the rescission of the sale may be demanded.

Inquisition, whether a chronic rheumatism, under certain circumstances be a redhibitory vice?

PARISH Court of New Orleans.

MARTIN, J., delivered the opinion of the court.

This is a redhibitory action on the sale of a slave, stated to be affected with a rheumatism to such a degree as to render her perfectly useless and incurable at the time of the sale.

The defendant pleaded the general issue, and that the plaintiff, at the time of the sale, knew the slave to be old and afflicted with the diseases attendant on her age, which were increased by a prevalent epidemic.

The plaintiff had judgment, and the defendant appealed.

Bein, a witness for the plaintiff, deposed, he sold the slave to the defendant for 250 dollars, (the price paid by the plaintiff for her)—she was sick at the time for about a week, and the defendant attended her. She complained of rheumatism, but he thought she was more lazy than sick. He owned her during two or three years. She complained every third or fourth month, but never laid by, till her last sickness. She did not then complain of rheumatism, and the witness thinks she had the venereal. She was able to do a good deal then, and went to market daily, washed for the children and cooked.

On his cross-examination he added he saw her after he sold her. She appeared in better health than he ever saw her; he had paid 350 dollars for her.

Boyd, an auctioneer, called by the plaintiff, deposed, he sold the slave for the defendant. She appeared old and decrepid, and walked badly. He thinks she had been offered for sale several times before. He sold her under a full guarantee, by order of the defendant, who told him she complained of being sick, but was able to do the house work. The witness thinks that, for a woman of her age, she brought as much as if she had been healthy.

Vance, a witness of the plaintiff, deposed, he owned the slave for a year, and sold her to Bein. Her general health was not very good. She frequently complained of rheumatism; but he thought her more lazy than sick. He bought and sold her with warranty.

Dr. Davidson, deposed he owned the slave during the years 1819

30*

and 1820. He sold her because she smoked a great deal, and was dirty in her kitchen, but was sound and healthy. He does not think he ever gave her a dose of medicine. In the summer of 1828, a rheumatic fever prevailed in New Orleans, which was most generally epidemic, affecting persons of all ages, sexes and colors, especially the old and those who previously had rheumatic complaints. She drank freely, but was not a drunkard; she never complained of rheumatism while he owned her.

Short deposed, he saw the slave soon after the plaintiff purchased her, and has since seen her often. She has been lame all the time, and during the greatest part of it very lame; her ankles are much swollen, and she has not been able to do any work of consequence. The plaintiff has been compelled to hire another person to do the work he expected from her. She, at times, is unable to walk without a cane. She complained much of the rheumatic fever during the late epidemic, but not more than before.

Dr. Dehow, deposes that, in April or May last, he was called by the plaintiff to the slave, and found her affected with a chronic rheumatism, under which he thinks she has labored for some time. Her case appeared of a bad character, and her disease may become incurable in aged persons who have labored under it for a considerable time. He visited her several times, and found her by no means improved. Her limbs are much swollen, and he believes she has not been able to do the house work since he saw her.

On the cross-examination he added, he told the plaintiff she might be cured by a course of medicine, which might take a month. In a woman of her age, a rheumatism such as that which she had might come on within a month or two. The epidemic that prevailed last summer aggravated a case like hers very much. He does not recollect doing any thing for her, but external applications. He does not think he observed much swelling in her limbs when he first saw her; it has occurred principally since the late epidemic. He has known a few cases in which the epidemic, when there was previous disease has left as much swelling as there was in this slave, but the patients were not disabled from their business. He thinks the slave had a rheumatic complaint from the first time he saw her.

It does not appear to us that the facts in evidence state a redhibitory case. The disease according to the testimony of the plaintiff's own witness, is such as would yield to a course of medicine, within a month. We have the testimony of most of the persons who have owned the slave since the year 1819. None of them considered her as prevented from rendering services to them as other slaves, on account of her rheumatic complaint, except the last but one, who sold her for 100 dollars less than he had paid for her; and he swears he saw her in the hands of the defendant in a very good state of health. Slaves being human beings are necessarily liable to disease, and in old age to rheumatic affections particularly. The plaintiff bought this woman in February, and although some of his witnesses depose she was almost immediately taken with a swelling in her limbs, and thus disabled from labor, yet he called for no medical aid till April or May, and then did not accept the offer made him of a cure by a course of medicine that would have lasted one month. In the mean while a violent epidemic raged which brought a rheumatic fever on the healthy and considerably aggravated those of the afflicted. It is not extraordinary that a decrepid old woman, sold for 250 dollars, whose owner contented himself with a few external applications, while the physician he had called recommended a course of medicine that would cure her, should be disabled by her disease, long left to itself, from labor, and smart severely under the late epidemic.

The appellee's counsel has urged that, admitting the case is not a redhibitory one, he may have damages by a reduction of the price on an action *quanti minoris*, as the petition concludes with a prayer for a general relief. In the case of Millar *v.* Coffman, *ante* 352, we lately determined that the Civil Code, 2522, having provided that the action for the reduction of the price was subject to the same rules and limitations as the redhibitory, the plaintiff in the former was bound to establish every fact which was necessary to support the latter. It follows then, as it appears, that the disease with which the slave was afflicted was casual, and it is not shown that at the time of the sale she was so sick as to render her services absolutely useless, or so much so that the vendee, had he known the state of her health, would not have bought her, he cannot complain and demand a reduction of of the price.

It is, therefore, ordered, adjudged and decreed, that the judgment of the parish court be annulled, avoided and reversed, and judgment entered against the plaintiff as in a case of nonsuit, with costs in both courts.

Christy and *Cenas*, for the plaintiff.
Preston, for the defendant.

White *et al. v.* Lobre.　VII, N. S. 564.

A creditor who is put on the bilan of an insolvent for part of a debt due to him, cannot afterwards sue for that part which was omitted.

More especially, if it was put down in the name of another person, and the proceedings were suffered to be confirmed without opposition on the part of the real creditor.

FIRST District.

PORTER, J., delivered the opinion of the court.

The plaintiffs demanded payment of two notes of the defendant executed by him previous to his having obtained the benefit of a *cessio bonorum*, on the ground that they were not placed on the bilan as creditors for these notes.

One of the notes was put on the bilan in the name of the payee. The fact of its having come into the hands of the plaintiff by endorsement does not appear to have been known to the defendant at the time he filed the schedule of his affairs. The other note, which is for 237 dollars 58 cents, was put down on the bilan for 237 dollars in the name of the plaintiffs.

We think the court below did not err in giving judgment for the defendant. As to the note for 237 dollars 58 cents, on which recovery is demanded because an error of 58 cents was committed in designating it, no observations are required from us. That however for 1000 dollars which was put down on the bilan in the name of the payee requires some. The plaintiff has relied on the cases of Bainbridge *v.* Clay, and Herring *v.* Levy. It is true, that in these cases the court decided that where the insolvent issued negotiable paper he must take the risk of ascertaining in whose hands it was at the time of failure, and that if he failed to place the holder on the bilan, he could not set up the proceedings as a bar to an action by the person who had acquired a right to the paper by transfer and endorsement. These decisions, however severe they might have been as to the duty which they impose on the insolvent, we still think correct. They were founded on the elementary doctrine, that no man can be bound by judicial proceedings to which he is not a party, or privy, a doctrine to which we are not aware there is any exception. 3 *N. S.* 262; 4 *Ibid.* 383.

But in neither of these cases had the party who claimed to enforce the obligations he had acquired by assignment been put on the bilan, nor did it appear he had any notice whatever of the proceedings carried on by the debtor against his creditors. In this respect the case before us presents an entirely different feature. The plaintiffs were put on the bilan and were cited as creditors. The objection therefore, is not, that they were not parties to the judgment in *concurso*, but that the claim they now make never had been litigated in that suit; comparing it to an ordinary action where the judgment only applies to and protects the party against a second demand for the same thing. We do not think the principle advanced can apply to cases of this kind. When a creditor is called in, it is his duty to make known the whole amount of his claim against the insolvent. On another ground, however, these proceedings have the authority of *res judicata*, against the present demand, considering the case in the strictest and most technical point of view of which it is susceptible of being examined. The note of which they were the endorsees was put on the schedule in the name of the payees, and they permitted judgment to be rendered declaring the payees to be the holders and *bona fide* owners of it. In a *concurso* all the creditors are plaintiffs and defendants: plaintiffs for the amount claimed by them—defendants against the demand of the insolvent: and against the claim of each and all the other creditors. A judgment therefore recognising other parties *to* have the property of the note, without any opposition on the part of the plaintiffs, bars them from setting up a subseduent claim, that it belonged to them.

It has been said, the evidence does not show this note was put down in the name of the payees. Several notes to the amount of 3000 dollars are placed on the bilan in their name, and we think the court below did not err in concluding that this formed a part of them: and as to the objection that it is not proved that at the time of filing the bilan the plaintiffs were the holders of the note, it is only necessary to remark that if true there was still stronger ground for holding the proceedings in *concurso* binding on the plaintiffs, for they could not have acquired any right to the note from the payees since the insolvency, which would authorise the institution of this suit.

It is, therefore, ordered, adjudged and decreed, that the judgment of the district court be affirmed, with costs.

Maybin, for the plaintiff.

Waggaman, for the defendant.

M'Micken *v.* Turner.   VII, N. S. 568.

THIRD District.

By PORTER, J.—Whether there was an assignment of the debt or
not is in this case a question of fact.   There is no direct or positive
evidence of a transfer.   The proof adduced admits of some inferences in favor of there being one; but of more against it.   The conviction produced on our minds is the same as that of the jury, and
the court of the first instance.   We do not believe the debt ever was
assigned to the plaintiff—we think he acted as the agent of Fluker
in putting it into suit and collecting it in the hope and belief that
the collection of his debt would be promoted by the step he took.

Hyde & Merritt *v.* Groce.   VII, N. S. 572.

FIRST District.

When a note is produced on which the plaintiff's endorsement
exists, he may prove the endorsee was his agent, although there be
no such averment in the petition.   See Dicks, Booker & Co. *v.* Cash,
7 *N. S.* 362.

There were besides some particulars in this case which induced
the court to declare it could not be distinguished from Bynum *v.*
Armstrong, 5 *N. S.* 159.

Herman *v.* Smith *et al.* VII, N. S. 575.

When a third party wishes to appeal from a judgment rendered between others he must
show that he is aggrieved by it.

FIRST District.

Porter, J., delivered the opinion of the court.

The party who styles himself an intervener in this case, stated that he was aggrieved by the judgment rendered between the parties to the suit, and prayed an appeal from it. In this court his right to appeal was denied, as having no interest in the case. The cause was remanded to enable him to establish his authority to have the judgment of the court below between other parties revised at his instance. He offered proof, and the judge of the first instance decided that he was the *bona fide* holder of the promissory note annexed to his petition of appeal, and that so far as his interest may be affected by the judgment appealed from he is aggrieved, and if so by the Code of Practice has a right to appeal.

The Code of Practice gives the right to appeal to all parties aggrieved by a judgment between others. A man cannot be aggrieved by a right judgment, no matter what interest he may have in it. If the terms used in the Code were therefore taken literally, in remanding a cause to ascertain the right to appeal, the inferior court would be compelled to examine whether the judgment it had rendered was correct. It is clear that the only inquiry when a case is remanded as this was, is, has the party applying for an appeal such an interest in the case as will cause him to sustain injury in case the judgment complained of should be erroneous? That interest appears to be recognised here so far as to enable La Porte to appeal from the judgment rendered between Herman and Smith, and seeing no ground for this appeal, it must be dismissed at his costs.

Denis, for the plaintiff.

Seghers, for the intervening party.

Sinnott *v.* Michel.   VII, N. S. 577.

FIRST District.

An order of seizure and sale cannot issue on property in the hands of a third person unless on the production of an act of mortgage duly recorded.

M'Micken *v.* Sims.   VII, N. S. 579.

THIRD District, Judge of the Second presiding.

Land sold *sous seing privé* where the sale is not followed by actual delivery may be attached by a creditor of the vendors.   See 5 *N. S.* 423.

That constructive possession which the law presumes to follow the deed, will not protect the buyer against his neglect to register the act.

Loiseau *v.* Laizer *et al.*   VII, N. S. 580.

PARISH Court of New Orleans.

After two verdicts, the court in case of doubt will not interfere with the finding of the jury.

Canonge *v.* Louisiana State Bank. VII, N. S. 583.

FIRST District.
If an agent for collection of a note does not know the residence of the endorser on the day after protest, but acquires a knowledge of it afterwards, it is his duty to give notice.

By MARTIN, J.—In the present case, the notary appears to have been aware of this, for as soon as he discovered the endorser's residence he immediately sent notice there; but his duty was to *give* not to *send* notice only—the appellant must show that notice was *received,* for till then it is not *given.*

◆

Walker *v.* Dunbar. Dicks, Booker & Co. Intervenors. VII, N. S. 586.

An intervenor cannot retard the trial of a cause in which he interpleads.

THIRD District.

PORTER, J., delivered the opinion of the court.
This is an hypothecary action. The defendant pleaded that he was only a tenant at the time of the institution of the suit, and that he had given it up to another possessor. He further averred that the house of Dicks, Booker & Co. were the owners of the property, and he prayed that they might be cited in warranty to defend the suit. This answer was filed on the 12th of May, 1828.

The application to cite Dicks, Booker & Co. in warranty was opposed, and it is stated in the record that after argument the court took time to advise. No decision appears to have been made on it; but at the following term these parties appeared, prayed leave to file their claim in intervention, and were allowed to do so.
VOL. IV.—31

[Walker v. Dunbar.   Dicks, Booker & Co. Intervenors.]

In the answer, as it is called in this record, which the interpleaders filed, they require their vendors to be cited in warranty; and they afterwards moved that the cause might be continued, to enable them to have their warrantors cited.   The court overruled the application and it is assigned as error that the judge erred in doing so.

The appellants rely on the 380th, 381st, 382d and 383d articles of the Code of Practice, which confer the right on a party sued to have a continuance to enable him to cite in his warrantor.

The appellee contends that the appellants were not called in as warrantors—that they can not be considered as defendants—that they voluntarily intervened in the suit—and that by the 391st article of the Code of Practice, intervenors can not retard the trial of the suit in which they interplead.

We think as the appellants voluntarily appeared in the cause as intervenors, and not in pursuance of a citation in warranty, they must take all the responsibility which the law attaches to the character in which they thought proper to present themselves, and that the court below did not err in refusing them permission to continue the case.

It is, therefore, ordered, adjudged and decreed, that the judgment of the district court be affirmed, with costs.

Pierce, for the defendants.

———————————

Representatives of Dickey v. Rogers.   VII, N. S. 588.

Where there are several joint debtors, the surety has a right to call on each of them for the whole amount of his obligation.

THIRD District, Judge of the Second presiding.

PORTER, J., delivered the opinion of the court.

This action commenced by attachment.   The petitioner declares that he is surety for the defendant, and liable to pay the notes he has signed as such.   He prays for a judgment against the garnishee for any money he may owe the defendant; and he also prays that any property in the garnishee's hands may be surrendered up to discharge the notes and obligations for which the plaintiff is responsible.

The attorney appointed to defend the rights of the absent debtor, pleaded as a peremptory exception that from the showing in the petition the plaintiff was surety for three other obligors, and that there is no allegation they are insolvent—and the responsibility of the plaintiff was too remote and contingent to authorise the institution of a suit.

This exception was overruled. Whereupon the attorney filed another: that from the exhibition of the obligation declared on, it appears to have been signed by the plaintiff as principal co-obligor, and that he could not maintain this action without showing that he had paid the debt.

When the cause came on for trial, the petitioner offered in evidence the notes on which the suit had been instituted. They were objected to because they did not correspond with the allegations of the petition, which averred that the plaintiff had signed the notes as surety, when on their face they appeared to have been executed jointly and severally. The objection was sustained by the court: judgment as of nonsuit in favor of the defendant was given, and the petitioner appealed.

We think the court below did not err in overruling the first exception filed by the defendant. The provision of our law which gives to the surety the right to sue the principal for indemnification when the debt is due, and unpaid; contains no exception, such as that contended for. Where there are several joint debtors, the surety has a right to call on each of them for the whole amount of his obligation. Louisiana Code, art. 2026 and 3023.

The court erred in rejecting the evidence. The general issue was not pleaded. The exception admitted (for it did not deny) that the contract, as between the parties to this suit, was one of suretyship. The contract being *in solido*, did not contradict the allegation in the petition. It often happens that the several obligors are bound *in solido* to the obligee, though the contract of suretyship exists between them.

It is, therefore, ordered, adjudged and decreed, that the judgment of the district court be annulled, avoided and reversed; and it is further ordered, adjudged and decreed, that the cause be remanded to the district court, with directions to the judge not to reject the notes set out in the bill of exceptions, on the ground that they were contrary to the allegations in the petition: and it is further ordered that the appellee pay the costs of the appeal.

Turner, for the plaintiffs.

Cornie *v.* Leblanc. VII, N. S. 591.

FIRST District.
An agent while acting within the scope of his authority is a good witness without a release. See 5 *N. S.* 310.

Patin *v.* Poydras. VII, N. S. 593.

FOURTH District, Judge of the Third presiding.
The absence of an attorney in the service of the state, and having his client's papers too in possession, is a good reason for a continuance.

Saul *v.* His Creditors, on the opposition of the Syndics of B. Morgan. VII, N. S. 594.

In case of exchange, if one of the parties loses that which he was to receive, he has a right to get back the object he gave in lieu of it, although the person with whom he contracts is insolvent.

FIRST District.

PORTER, J., delivered the opinion of the court.
The creditors of Benjamin Morgan opposed the tableau of distri-

bution filed by the syndics, claiming a privilege on certain shares of bank stock.

The facts which have given rise to the contest are as follows:

On the 8th day of November, 1822, Saul borrowed from John Jacob Astor, of New York, 64,000 dollars, 30,000 dollars of which were for his own use, and 34,000 dollars for the use and account of Benjamin Morgan. In security for the payment of this money, Saul pledged stock of the Bank of Orleans, to the amount of 64,000 dollars, 40,000 dollars of which stood in his own name, and 24,000 dollars in the name of Morgan. Morgan having thus become the debtor of Saul, transferred to him in the month of January then ensuing, stock to the amount of 10,000 dollars, to replace the same quantity of Saul's which he had pledged on account of Morgan.

On the 30th of January, 1824, Saul, by act *sous seing privé*, after reciting the facts above stated, declared that "I do assign, transfer and set over to the said Benjamin Morgan, in lieu of a part of the said 10,000 dollars of stock so transferred by him to me, all my right, title and interest in two certificates lodged with the said Astor, viz: No. 36, dated the 21st of January, 1822, for eighty-three shares of stock, and No. 826, dated the 8th of January, 1818, for three-hundred and five shares of stock; on all of which only twenty-five dollars a share has been paid, amounting together to 9700 dollars, with full power to claim all dividends arising on the said 9700 dollars of stock and with right to demand the said certificates from the said Astor, at the fulfilment of the agreement entered into by the said Saul and Morgan with him, and with the full power to transfer the same to himself, or any person or persons, relinquishing as I hereby do all right to ownership whatever in the said stock to the said Morgan, his heirs and assigns, having settled with the said Morgan for the difference between 9700 dollars, and 10,000 dollars by a separate transfer of stock, viz: twelve shares, on which is paid twenty-five dollars, say 300 dollars."

On the failure of Saul, Astor attempted to enforce his lien on the bank stock which had been pledged to him, but judgment was rendered against him in this tribunal, on the ground that his contract being one of pledge, it had no force or effect against creditors, unless recorded according to the laws of Louisiana. On this judgment the Bank of Orleans granted new certificates of the stock, and it was sold by the syndics of Saul's estate as making a part thereof.

The syndics of Morgan state in their petition that his estate has a privilege on the stock transferred by him to Saul, no price or consideration having been paid therefor, or that it belongs to them; or if this pretension cannot be supported in law, that then the stock transferred by Saul which was in the hands of Astor belongs of right to the creditors of Morgan, and that they are entitled to the same by right of property or privilege. Both these claims are denied by the representatives of Saul's estate, and they further demand by way of reconvention, the sum of 500 dollars, being the amount of the divi-

31*

dends on the stock referred to in the opposition paid by error on the 4th of October, 1826, and 9th of January, 1827, to B. Morgan, agent for the syndics of his estate.

The court of the first instance sustained the opposition; being of opinion that the estate of Morgan could not be considered as creditors, that their claim was that of a vendor who reclaims the thing sold when the price has not been paid.

From this judgment the syndics of Saul have appealed; and demand a reversal of it, on the following grounds.

1. The appellees have no privilege as vendors of the stock transferred to Joseph Saul on the 10th of January, 1824, because this was not in fact a sale made at the period of transfer but simply a replacement of so much stock which Saul had pledged, belonging to himself, for the use of Morgan, and for which Morgan had already received the value in the loan from Astor.

2. If said transfer can be considered as a sale, then the price had already been paid by Saul and received by Morgan in the loan from Astor.

3. The agreement of the 31st of January, 1824, is not a transfer by sale of three hundred and eighty-eight shares of bank stock, but merely an unexecuted agreement to transfer, which was never consummated, and can have no effect as regards creditors and third persons. Because there was no legal delivery, the titles, viz, the certificates, were with Astor, and no use was made by Morgan of the stock, as proprietor; it still continues to stand in Saul's name, he receiving the dividends up to the time of his failure. Civil Code, 350, art. 81; 306, arts. 228, 229; Louisiana Code, 2457.

4. It is not a *dation en paiement*, delivery being of the essence of this contract. Louisiana Code, 2626, 2627, 2628; *Pothier, Contrat de Vente*, no. 601.

5. It cannot operate as an assignment, because nothing has been done by Morgan to give it effect. No notice has been given to Astor who had in his possession the certificates of the Bank of Orleans, while Saul continued to exercise acts of ownership, and receive the dividends. Civil Code, 368, art. 121 and 122; Louisiana Code, 1917, 4 *N. S.* 51; 5 *Ibid.* 180.

6. The agreement can not have the effect of a pledge, there being no delivery of the certificate of stock, and not having been registered, in conformity with the provisions of the Civil Code, 446, arts. 6 and 7; 5 *N. S.* 609.

7. The agreement to transfer being under private signature unaccompanied by delivery, has no date against third persons, and parol proof can not be admitted to establish its date. Civil Code, 306, arts. 228, 229; 2 *N. S.* 171; 4 *Ibid.* 368, 5 tit. 423.

The counsel for the appellee has declined controverting the truth of these propositions, but has contended, that the contract was one of exchange, and that Morgan not having received what he was to obtain, in lieu of that which he delivered, has a lien on the property if yet in the hands of the syndics of Saul, or on the proceeds if sold.

[Saul *v.* His Creditors.]

The counsel on the part of the appellant urges, that this was not a contract of exchange, because that is the giving of one thing for another. That in this instance no such contract was contemplated when Saul pledged the stock for Morgan, and that the subsequent act of Morgan's replacing it did not make it an exchange. In support of this doctrine he has relied on Louisiana Code, 2630; *Pothier, Traité de Vente*, 617; *Domat, liv.* 1, *tit* 3; *Par.* 5, *tit.* 6, 4.

These authorities, with the exception of *Pothier,* all concur in their definition of the contract of exchange, and nearly in the same language. They state it to be an agreement between the parties to give one thing for another, except it be money. *Pothier* states it to be a contract where they oblige themselves to give immediately one thing for another, and he lays a particular stress on the word *immediately* in the sentence next following the definition, by observing that if we agree that I will give you one thing for a certain price, in payment of which you will give me on your side another thing, the agreement is not a contract of exchange but of sale. It embraces a sale which I make of a thing belonging to me, and a *dation en paiement* on yours.

If a contract had been proved in this instance by which one of the parties agreed to give a thing for a certain price, and receive in payment for it another, as in the case put by the author, then clearly there would not have been a contract of exchange. So if any other contract had been shown to have been in contemplation of the parties at the time Saul advanced the stock, Morgan replaced it, and Saul again conveyed stock to Morgan, we should have given to that contract its legal effect. But in the absence of any proof to the contrary, we must conclude that the acts of the parties conformed to their previous understanding, and that was done which had been contemplated to be done. The act of Saul in advancing the stock was in nothing inconsistent with the idea of exchange, and did not necessarily throw the transaction into another class of contracts. In this view of the case there was an exchange of the one parcel of bank stock for the other, and the stock given to Morgan having been taken by the syndics of Saul, Morgan's estate has a right to get back that which was given in lieu of it, or its value. Louisiana Code, 2637, 3194.

It is, therefore, ordered, adjudged and decreed, that the judgment of the district court be affirmed, with costs.

Slidell, for the syndics of Saul.

Eustis, for the syndics of Morgan.

Nolte & Co. *v.* Their Creditors. VII, N. S. 602.

(Remanded, 6 *N. S.* 168, to amend the tableau.)

FIRST District.

By MARTIN, J.—We are ignorant of any law which gives to the party who furnishes money for the payment of a debt the rights of the creditor who is thus paid. The legal claim alone belongs not to all who pay a debt, but only to him who being bound for it discharges it. The appellant cannot therefore claim the benefit of a legal subrogation if he has shown no conventional one, the rights of the creditor paid with his money are therefore absolutely extinguished, and no part of them can be exercised by the appellant.

The document relied on shows indeed that he consented that his claims should be preferred to those then enumerated, but not that the party with whose money they might be discharged, could claim any privilege on the tableau.

Stewart *v.* His Creditors. VII, N. S. 604.

THIRD District, Judge of the Second presiding.

An imprisoned debtor who applies for the benefit of a *cessio bonorum*, cannot have his creditors called before a notary: but into open court, or before the judge. See act of assembly, 2 *Martin's Digest*, 442.

Beauchamp *v.* M'Micken.   VII, N. S. 387.

THIRD District.

By MARTIN, J.—The action of nullity is given by the Code of Practice, 507, when the plaintiff obtains judgment on the production of forged documents, or other ill practices. In the present case the document was not literally forged—but it was a *false* one. Whether the plaintiff availed himself of a false document, designedly alleging the loss of the original and knowingly giving an untrue recital of its contents—or having really mislaid it erroneously stated its contents— the injury to the defendant is the same. The court who gave judgment was equally deceived in either case, by the act of the plaintiff, beyond the control of the defendant. Truth must be the basis of all judgments, and where one is obtained on false documents, made by the party in whose favor it is rendered, the detection of the falsity must entitle the opposite party to relief, even where there is no malice, in that who is in possession of the judgment. The absence of malice ought not to have any other effect than to protect the party from punishment.

Nichols *v.* Peytavin.   VII, N. S. 608.

SECOND District, Judge of the Eighth presiding.
Appeal taken for delay—judgment affirmed with damages.

Bergh *et al. v.* Jayne.   VII, N. S. 609.

FIRST District.

The Code of Practice, art. 244, requires the agent, wishing to take out process of attachment, to swear on his knowledge; the act of 1826, p. 170, that he should swear to the best of his knowledge and belief. In the present case agent swore to the debt *as he believes:* this is bad.

By MARTIN, J.—We think with the appellant's counsel, that we are to be ruled by the intent of the legislature, and that "nullity is not necessarily to follow the omission of any redundancy with which legislative and judicial proceedings abound;" but the intent of the law cannot be disregarded. Accordingly, in Brides *v.* Williams, 1 *N. S.* 98, we held the affidavit of an agent, *to the best of his knowledge,* sufficient. Knowledge *includes* belief, but not *vice versa.* We believe the arrival of a friend when we see it announced in the gazette—we know it when we see him. The agent believes the debt is due, when the plaintiff whom he respects tells him so—he knows it when the defendant admits it and promises payment.

EASTERN DISTRICT, APRIL TERM, 1829.

Gravier *v.* Lafon *et al.* VII, N. S. 612.

COURT of Probates of New Orleans.

A party who has no share in the money to be distributed cannot oppose the homologation of the tableau of distribution.

Corcoran *v.* Hatch and Wife. VII, N. S. 614.

FOURTH District, Judge of the Eighth presiding.

Husband and wife being sued for the price of repairs to a house, and judgment by default against them: husband set it aside by pleading, but wife did not: there was judgment finally against husband, while the default against the wife remained definitive.

By MARTIN, J.—It is clear that as the wife did not answer, and there is no evidence of the *quantum* of her interest in the house, nor of the nature of her estate, judgment was irregularly given against her.

Babin v. D'Astugue. VII, N. S. 615.

A co-executor may appear in a suit when a person prays to be admitted as heir, and the
admissions of his co-executor, and the attorney for the absent heirs will not prevent
him insisting on strict and legal proof.

Though the time for which executors were appointed have expired they may contest the
right of a party claiming the estate as heir.

COURT of Probates of New Orleans.

PORTER, J., delivered the opinion of the court.

Jean Babin, who styles himself a resident of the district of Genozac in France, filed his petition in the court of probates, in which he stated that he was the sole heir of Jean Phillipon, who died at the Bay of St. Louis, in the year 1827, and prayed that D'Astugue, the acting executor of the last will and testament of the deceased, and Moreau Lislet, the attorney for the absent heirs, might be cited to show cause why the petitioner should not be put in possession of the estate.

The answer of the defendant D'Astugue, put the plaintiff on the strict and legal proof of all the allegations contained in his petition. And the attorney for the absent heirs did the same, by stating at the foot of the answer that he joined in it.

A. Carraby, the co-executor, who at the time of filing the answer is stated to be in France, and who is still there, appeared by his attorney in fact, Etienne Carraby, and filed an answer, in which he denied the petitioner was the heir of the deceased.

The court of the first instance gave judgment in favor of the petitioner, and Carraby appealed.

The first questions in the cause are, the right of the co-executor, Carraby, to file an answer, and the authority of the attorney in fact to bring this action for him, in his name?

And both of them we think must be answered in the affirmative. As co-executor he is responsible in solido, and being so, had a right to see that the funds were paid over to the person legally authorised to receive them. The power of attorney shows that the agent was authorised to represent the executor, as well in court as out of it, in relation to all matters connected with the liquidation and settlement of the estate.

On the trial of the cause, the plaintiff offered in evidence a document which he called an acte de notoriété executed before a notary public at Pons, in France, and dated the 4th of March, 1828. To the introduction of this proof Carraby objected, on the ground, 1. That it was *ex parte* evidence. 2. That it was not executed by the pro-officers. 3d, That the witness had been dispensed with the solemnity of an oath. The court overruled these objections, and admitted the document in evidence. To this decision a bill of exceptions was taken.

This evidence upon strict principles of law was clearly inadmissible, but in support of the judgment of the court below, it has been contended that the co-executor D'Astugue and the attorney for the absent heirs made no opposition to the legality of the proof, and consequently Carraby could not. To this position we cannot give our assent. Carraby, as co-executor, had an interest to see, that no person but the heir should receive the succession; for if he or his co-executor handed it over to any other, he would be responsible to those who had a legal claim to the effects of the estate, should they afterwards appear. His right to insist on strict and legal proof, controlled that of the co-executor and the attorney for the absent heirs, to admit evidence which was not so; for his act could not prejudice them, and theirs might work an injury to him.

Again, it has been urged that the letters written by D'Astugue to the heirs in France to send forward the evidence of their claims sanctioned the introduction of the document.—We have perused these letters, and find nothing in them which could be construed into a waiver to call for legal proof. And if they did authorise such an inference, the right of Carraby to object to them would still remain in full force.

It is further urged that the functions of the executors having expired they had no right to make the objection. But this circumstance in our judgment did not deprive them of the right of doing so. The termination of their authority deprived them of all powers of further administration, but did not authorise them to hand over the estate to any other person than the heir; and *de non apparentibus, et non existentibus, eadem est lex.*

The 1654th article of the Louisiana Code has been relied on to show, that the attorney for the absent heirs has alone the power to make opposition to any thing which may affect the interest of the absent heirs. This law certainly confers on him such power, but it is not exclusive in its expressions. The executors are not permitted to give up the estate to any person but the heir, and there is nothing in the law which would authorise us to say that the opinion of the attorney for the absent heirs can control their opinion as to the capacity of the person presenting himself as such. The attorney for the heirs who are absent could not demand the money for himself, and there is little or no difference between his doing so, and conferring on him the authority to point out who is to receive it.

It is, therefore, ordered, adjudged and decreed, that the judgment of the court of probates be annulled, avoided and reversed; and it is further ordered, adjudged and decreed, that the cause be remanded

[Babin v. D'Astugue.]

to the said judge, with directions not to receive in evidence the
document marked R: and it is further ordered that the appellee pay
the costs of this appeal.

C. Derbigny, for the plaintiff.

D. Seghers, for the defendant.

Saul v. His Creditors.　VII, N. S. 620.

If creditors of an insolvent direct his property to be sold at one, two and three years'
credit from a particular day, it cannot be sold on this credit after that day.

FIRST District.

PORTER, J., delivered the opinion of the court.

A meeting of the creditors of the insolvent took place before a
notary on the 17th of July, 1827, at which some of them required a sale
for cash; others, and they were the majority, demanded that the property should be sold at one, two and three years' credit—the sale to
take place at the Exchange Coffee House, on the 7th day of January
then next ensuing.

A sale was made of a considerable part of the effects for cash, on
an *ex parte* order obtained by some of the privileged creditors. That
sale has been set aside and annulled by this court, and a question
has arisen whether the syndics should now proceed under the deliberation of the creditors already mentioned; or whether the property
should not be sold according to law without any regard being paid
to the opinions expressed at the meeting.

The district judge thought the sale must be made according to law,
without attending to what had been deliberated on by the creditors.
We think with him. The day fixed by them for the sale, viz: the
7th of January, 1828, makes as much a part of their assent as the
period of one, two or three years. They wished the property sold at
one, two and three years from that time, not from any other. It
being impossible for the court to give effect to the whole of their
agreement, it cannot be executed in part.

It is, therefore, ordered, adjudged and decreed, that the judgment
of the district court be affirmed, with costs.

Cochran *et al. v.* Fort *et al.* VII, N. S. 622.

The principle established in the case of Livingston *v.* Herman—*that* a sale of so many feet, *front to the river Mississippi, conformably to a plan*, which plan exhibits the front line of the lot in question not extending to the river, but passing within the levee, does not pass the alluvion, provided any alluvion of sufficient height and magnitude was formed at the time said sale took place, but *that* the said alluvion remained the property of the vendor—*re-affirmed* very emphatically by the court.

The court decide that the weight of evidence is clearly in favor of the affirmative of the proposition of fact, that there did exist alluvion, opposite the lot now in question, of sufficient height and magnitude to be susceptible of ownership. Out of sixteen witnesses, nine depose to its existence from 1793 to 1803.

It seems that, in the last mentioned year, it was only covered at high water to the depth of five feet. There is no positive evidence at what height batture may be reclaimed, from the river and applied to private use.

But supposing, contrary to the conclusion of the court, that no batture susceptible of ownership existed in February, 1803, the plaintiff's case would still labor under a difficulty from a new quarter.

The fauxbourg was incorporated two years after. To enable them, therefore, to recover in this action, they must show a batture created between the day of their purchase, and the date of the act of incorporation, which was susceptible of ownership; for if the alluvion was formed afterwards it became the property of the city and not of the front proprietors.

FIRST District.

PORTER, J., delivered the opinion of the court.

The petitioners state that Bertrand Gravier, of the late Spanish province of Louisiana, being the owner of part of a plantation formerly belonging to the Jesuits, near the city of New Orleans, sold to a certain Joseph D. Hevia, then of the same place, a portion of said land adjoining the city having sixty feet in front, with the depth of three hundred and thirteen; and that the said Hevia afterwards sold the same to the petitioners.

That it was the intention of Gravier to sell, and of Hevia to acquire along with the said land the right of alluvion, as the same belonged to the vendor: and that by the deed of sale the vendee did acquire this right.

That since the sale of the land to Hevia, a valuable margin of soil has been formed in front of it, and incorporated therewith by alluvion, which is the property of the petitioners.

That notwithstanding their legal right to this alluvion the defendants have illegally entered thereon, pretending to be the owners, and detain the same.

The petition concludes with a prayer, for possession, damages for the detention, and general relief.

The defendants plead the general issue. Set up title under four persons, who they aver purchased the premises, at a sale made in virtue of an execution issuing from the district court to satisfy a judgment obtained against the heirs of B. Gravier. That this judgment was rendered for the amount due by Gravier's heirs, for making a levee, and other indispensable works and repairs on the lot; which work and labor gave a privilege or lien in it. The pleas of prescription, of ten, and of thirty years, are also contained in the answer.

There was judgment in the court of the first instance for the plaintiffs, and the defendants appealed.

The case made for this court consists not only of the evidence actually given on the trial, but by consent of parties embraces all the testimony taken in the cases of Gravier *v.* The Aldermen and Inhabitants of New Orleans; Morgan *v.* Livingston; Gravier and Others *v.* Livingston; Hawkins *'v.* Livingston; Gravier and Others; and Fort & Story *v.* The Syndics of B. Morgan. In a word, of. all the conflicting evidence, which this seemingly never failing source of litigation has produced for the last twenty-five years.

The argument, as heretofore, in all the other causes which have grown out of claims to the batture, has been able and elaborate, and several important questions of law have been raised and discussed: but the view we have taken of the case does not require us to examine several of the points to which counsel have devoted their attention.

By the pleadings, the plaintiffs are placed within the operation of the well established rule in petitory actions: that they must recover on the strength of their own title, not on the weakness of their adversaries.

The first question, therefore, for our inquiry is, have they shown a title to the property claimed in the petition?

They contend they have, by presenting, in the first place, a sale from Bertrand Gravier to Hevia. In this sale Gravier describes the premises as having sixty feet in front to the river Mississippi, with 313 in depth, conformably to the plan made by Don Carlos Laveau Trideau. This plan has been produced to the court, and it shows the premises to be one of the front lots, but the lines marked on it do not extend to the river.

They offer in the second place, the sale from Hevia to them. In this deed of conveyance the property is described in the same manner as in that from Gravier to Hevia.

And they urge that in virtue of these titles they have a right to all the batture that has been formed in front of them since the period of the purchase from Gravier.

Whether such a right does follow as a consequence of the sale thus made to them, depends on a question of fact: namely, whether any alluvion of sufficient height and magnitude was formed at the time these conveyances were made to them, to be susceptible of private ownership. If it was so formed, it remained the property of the vendor, and did not pass to the vendee.

This principle was established in the case of Livingston *v.* Herman, and it entered materially into the motives of the decision in the case of Morgan *v.* Livingston. Its correctness has not been impugned in argument, and a review of the reasons on which it was founded, has satisfied us still more of its correctness. 6 *Martin,* 19; 9 *Ibid.* 656.

The purchasers of the front lots being in this case the plaintiffs, they are required, in order to enable them to recover, not only to show a title in Hevia, but also the transmission of that title to them. It matters little in the decision of the cause, whether the batture was formed or not, at the period he acquired from Gravier. Admitting it was not, and that the alluvion afterwards added to the lot, belonged to him, it behoves the petitioners to show they have acquired it. Now, the sale from Hevia to them does not expressly convey the batture. If, therefore, it passes any right to the alluvion, in front of the lot sold, it can only do so under the principles already recognised by the court, viz: that there was not at the date of the conveyance any batture formed of sufficient height and magnitude to be susceptible of ownership. If such batture did exist, it was retained by Hevia, and did not pass to the plaintiffs. Our examination of the evidence has therefore been directed to an inquiry into the existence or non-existence of the alluvion on the 28th of February, 1803, the day of the sale from Hevia to Cochran & Rhea.

We have perused with attention the voluminous mass of evidence laid before us, and we have extracted what follows from it, as bearing materially on the matter in inquiry.

Trudeau, the former surveyor-general of the province, swears, that at the time he made the plan of the fauxbourg St. Marie, and divided it into lots, at the request of Bertrand Gravier, a batture existed along the whole front of it.

Two depositions of Girod have been produced. In that taken on the trial of this cause he states, that he arrived in New Orleans in 1788. In 1793, the batture began to be apparent from Julie street up to Madame Delor's. Below there was no batture. In 1803, he deposited cannon on the place where now stands the house of the defendants. In 1805, they were covered eight feet deep with alluvion. In August, 1803, a vessel belonging to him of 300 tons, moored within fifteen feet of the levee. In 1807, there was about twenty or thirty feet in space from the levee to the river at low water, and no more. In 1810 or 1811, the batture began to form considerably.

In the testimony given by the witness in the case of Fort & Story *v.* Syndics of B. Morgan, he stated, that in 1793 the batture opposite the property of Madame Delor was high, from thence it diminished gradually in breadth till opposite a small fort near the upper line of the city. That in the year 1803, he anchored one of his vessels opposite Hevia's house, and that she was not more than two hundred yards distance from the house. The witness was 77 years of age.

Flower states his recollection of the formation of the batture to be very imperfect. In 1807, there was a small portion of batture discoverable. At high water it was always covered. In 1817, there was about twenty or thirty feet in space from the levee, to the river.

Eves swears there was three feet water on the batture in the year 1809, when the river was at its highest point of elevation.

· Morgan states that in 1793, the river at low water came within fifty feet of the levee. Batture in front of the lots increased considerably from 1793 to 1803 and 1804.

Arnauld deposes that in the year 1793, a batture existed between Girod street and the city, which was dry when the river was low, and which was covered to the depth of two or three feet when it was high. That in the same year Hevia, and two other persons, Bailly and Trudeau, erected cabins on the batture outside of the levee, in the front of their lots, and that these cabins were demolished by order of the Spanish government.

Mayronne testifies to the erection of cabins on the batture, and knew that they were thrown down by orders of the government. Whether these were the same cabins spoken of by Arnauld can not be gathered from the evidence.

De Londe swears, that several persons established themselves in flat boats opposite the fauxbourg St. Mary, on the batture, from 1796 to 1803, but that they were removed therefrom by the government. That during the same space of time, when the river was high, there was enough of water from Girod street to the city, to enable flat boats to unload with facility.

Jorda states that there was for the last forty-three years a batture in front of what is now called fauxbourg St. Mary; that opposite the house of Hevia it was small; that the people coming down the river made use of the batture for unloading and loading their boats.

Percy testifies that the batture began to have a certain existence about the years 1790 and 1791 from the city up to Girod street, but it was unequal in height in different parts. That the batture decreased downwards in breadth and ended in a point near the city. In 1803, the batture opposite Gravier street was covered to the height of five feet.

Lauve states that thirty-six or forty years ago there was a batture in existence, commencing opposite the property of Madame Delor, and continuing to the gate of the city.

Wilkinson swears that he descended the river in the year 1789, with 13 flat boats, and that he saw no batture below the house of Madame Delor. It is not stated at what season of the year the witness arrived in the city. He left it in that year and did not return until 1799.

Morris deposes that from 1796 to 1804 flat boats and barges

approached the levee from Girod street to the city with ease, but that when the water fell, the boats were obliged to haul off.

Davezac states there was a batture susceptible of ownership in the year 1807, but that at high water it was covered.

Fortier testifies, that in 1793 or 1794 there was a batture opposite the property of D'Hevia, but not so large as at present.

Delasisse declares, that in 1794 the batture commenced about half an arpent above a small fort or battery on the river, which was about 100 toises below the fanxbourg St. Mary. It was not high at this point, but entirely uncovered at low water, and the soil firm. D'Hevia built a cabin on it in front of his lot in the year 1794.

There is some contradiction in this evidence. We think the weight of it decidedly in favor of the assertion of the defendants:—that at the time the petitioners bought from Hevia there did exist alluvion opposite the lot of sufficient height and magnitude to be susceptible of ownership. Out of the sixteen witnesses, nine of them depose to its existence from the year 1793 up to the year 1803. Only one of the others contradicts them, and his evidence taken on the different trials can not be reconciled. The error no doubt proceeding from the witness becoming old, and his memory waning.—Flower declares his recollection of the formation of the batture to be imperfect. Wilkinson deposes to its situation in 1789; does not state whether it was at high or low water he arrived with his flat boats in that year. Left the city the same season, and did not return until ten years after.

Whether it was of sufficient height to be susceptible of ownership at the period of the sale from Hevia, is the next question. And here too we think the proof preponderates in favor of the defendants. There is no positive evidence before us at what height batture may be reclaimed from the river, and appropriated to private use. It is not perhaps susceptible of direct proof, much depending on the position of the alluvion, the force of the stream where it is formed, and other circumstances. It is proved beyond doubt that so far back as 1793, the batture opposite Hevia's lot was of sufficient height to enable him to erect a cabin· on it: that it continued to increase in extent and height from that time up to 1803. That in the last mentioned year it was only covered at high water to the depth of five feet. With this elevation, a levee of less size than many found on the Mississippi would have enabled the proprietor to have excluded the river, and convert the soil to such purposes as he might have thought proper, or found profitable. We have been unable to discover in all the evidence any reason for saying this batture was not susceptible of ownership, except it being covered during the annual inundation of the river by the water. But this circumstance does not authorise the court to conclude that the alluvion was not susceptible of ownership. Such a principle would shake the titles to a large portion of the most valuable property in Louisiana. There is little or no land on the banks of the river, within the limits of this state, if we except an inconsiderable quantity in the neighborhood of and above Baton Rouge, which would not be covered with the waters of the Mississippi in the spring months, were it not for the artificial embankment which the industry of man has raised to exclude them.

Supposing, however, this view of the subject incorrect, and that we were to conclude with the plaintiffs, that no batture susceptible of ownership existed in February, 1803; their case could not be made much stronger. The fauxbourg was incorporated two years after. To enable them, therefore, to recover in this action, they must show a batture created between the day of their purchase, and the date of the act of incorporation, which was susceptible of ownership; for if the alluvion was formed afterwards it became the property of the city and not of the front proprietors. Now, every consideration, both of fact and law, which could authorise us to say it was not susceptible of being converted to private property in 1803, would prohibit us from concluding it was so two years after. The evidence does not establish any such change within that space of time as to enable us satisfactorily to distinguish, and say it was susceptible of ownership at one period, and it was not at the other. From the year 1803 to the year 1819, there was only a difference in the depth of water on the batture of two feet when the river was at its highest stage, according to the testimony of Eves and of Percy. *Partida 3, tit.* 28, *ley* 9; 7 *N. S.* 81.*

It is, therefore, ordered, adjudged and decreed that the judgment of the parish court be annulled, avoided and reversed, and that there be judgment here for the defendants, with costs in both courts.

Pierce and *Hennen,* for the plaintiffs.
Livermore and *Morse,* for the defendants.

---

* See Morgan *v.* Livingston, 6 *Martin,* 19, with a brief view of the batture questions in a note.

Dreux *v.* His Creditors. VII, N. S. 635.

FIRST District.

The wife should exercise her lien on movable property not subject to any special lien, before she has recourse to immovable property
not mortgaged to a third person.

Previous to the passage of the Louisiana Code, the mortgage
creditors in case of insolvency contributed rateably to the costs. See
Civil Code, 468, 470, arts. 76, 77; Louisiana Code, 3236. See Montegut *ads.* Delor, 5 *Martin,* 468, for a case on the old doctrine.

Nolte *et al. v.* Their Creditors. VII, N. S. 641.

If a cause be remanded, with directions to amend the tableau according to the principles
laid down by the Supreme Court, the district court has no authority to touch the
tableau in other parts.

FIRST District.

Martin, J., delivered the opinion of the court.

The syndics having filed an amended tableau of distribution of the
proceeds of a cotton press establishment, Beckman opposed its homologation, urging that over and above the sum for which he is therein
placed, he is a creditor of the insolvent for 1307 dollars 50 cents, for
which he has a privilege on the proceeds of the sale of said establishment; being the amount allowed him for employing an engineer to
go to New York (after the failure) and bringing and fixing an engine.
And also, because the dwelling house was not completed until nine
months after the commencement of the lease given by the insolvents,
and part of the sheds and warehouses were not completed during the
same period, and by a compromise with the syndics, the lease for
three years, at 5000 dollars per year, (by which he was entitled to
deduct his claim out of the first year's rent,) was changed into a lease

for two years, at 7500 dollars a year, whereby the establishment was sold for a higher price. Further, that the said sum of 1307 dollars 50 cents was allowed to him on the original tableau, which cannot be amended or altered.

The district court was of opinion that the sum now claimed was to be deducted from the first year's rent of the cotton press establishment; but as this first year's rent was by the consent of the opposing creditor merged in those of the second and third years, and the privilege lost by novation, the opposition was therefore dismissed. Beckman appealed.

His counsel urges that the claim for 1307 dollars 50 cents placed, on the original tableau, has passed *in rem judicatam*, as it was admitted by the syndics, and not touched by the judgment of the district court or ours. That our judgment having directed the original tableau to be modified according to the principles laid down in this court, the judge *a quo* was without authority to modify it in any part to which these principles were inapplicable.

In the case of Saul *v.* His Creditors, *ante*, 302, we held that when an opposition was made, and the opposing creditor claimed a certain sum, with interest, and was allowed the principal, without speaking of the interest, the latter was rejected—in other words, what was not admitted was disallowed.

In the present case, the appellant was placed on the tableau as a creditor for 1307 dollars 50 cents. An opposition was made, but not sustained. No appeal was taken, and the tableau was homologated. From this judgment of homologation an appeal was taken by opposing creditors, whose claims were wholly or partially disallowed, or who contested other claims. We were of opinion that some of these oppositions were improperly disallowed, and with a view to correct the errors of the inferior court, we reversed the judgment, and sent back the case, with directions to the district court, to amend the tableau according to the principles we had established, in order that justice might be done to the appellants on the points they complained of.

As to the parts of the tableau which we did not notice, and which are unaffected by the amendments we directed, the judgment of the district court was affirmed, and now forms *rem judicatam*, and the district court was without authority to amend.

It is, therefore, ordered, adjudged and decreed, that the judgment of the district court be annulled, avoided and reversed, and the case remanded, with directions to the judge to correct the amended tableau, so as to allow the appellant a place therein as a creditor of the sum of 1307 dollars 50 cents, which he occupied in the original tableau. The appellees paying costs in this court.

Pierce, Eustis and *Morse*, for the plaintiffs.
Lockett, Preston and *Seghers*, for the defendants.

Ursuline Nuns v. Depassau. VII, N. S. 645.

If a writ of seizure and sale be set aside, the plaintiff may amend his petition, without giving the debtor notice of the motion to amend or serving him with a copy of the amendment.

The person who makes an affidavit for a corporation need not prove his authority till it be denied.

The law requires a demand or notice before a writ of seizure and sale issues.

A court takes notice of the authority of the officer to whom it issues a writ.

FIRST District.

MARTIN, J., delivered the opinion of the court.

The plaintiffs having procured an order of seizure and sale, as vendors of a lot of ground, sold to the defendant, he procured it to be set aside. They now obtained leave to amend the petition, and having done so, prayed for and obtained a new order.

The defendant now moved that this second order might be set aside, on the following grounds:

1. By setting aside the first order, the parties were out of court, and no amendment could take place.

2. No notice of the intended motion to amend was given, nor copy of the amendment served on the defendant.

3. The affidavit was insufficient: inasmuch as it was made by an agent—his authority was not proved, and it stated no demand.

4. The order of seizure improperly issued; there being no notice to, or demand from, the mortgagor.

5. The person who executed it was not a coroner as he states himself to be.

These exceptions were overruled, and the defendant appealed.

The first two exceptions would have been correctly taken, in a regular suit, where the party must be cited to answer: for there, when he is once dismissed, he cannot be called on to answer anew, without a second petition and citation. There an amendment of the petition being as a supplemental one, a copy of it must be served, as a copy of the original petition. But on summary proceedings *ex parte*, no notice of a motion to amend is to be given, because the adverse party is not in court; and no copy of the amendments is to be served on him, because none of the petition itself is required.

The setting aside of the order of seizure did not affect the petition; neither did it dismiss the defendant, because he had not been brought in, but came voluntarily. If the order was dismissed on account of the insufficiency of the affidavit, nothing was wanted to obtain a second order, but the annexation of a sufficient affidavit: to copy the petition and introduce it anew, would be a vain and unnecessary act, which the law does not require. *Lex neminem cogit ad vana.* If the order was set aside because a copy of the authentic act was not annexed, a like remedy would cure the defect. Likewise if the writ was set aside on account of the absence of a necessary averment—an amendment of the petition must enable it to support a new order.

The plaintiffs sue as a corporation: the oath must necessarily be taken by the proper officer. The person who took it states herself to be the superior of the nuns. It is not complained that she had no authority, but that she did not prove that she had. We think that was useless, till her authority was denied. No law requires a demand or notice to be sworn to or made.

The court below was bound to know the character of the officer to which it directed its order for execution. Had it erred, the circumstance might have authorised some other remedy than setting aside the order.

It has been urged in argument by the appellant that the appellees are not a legal corporation. This was not urged below—they cannot be expected to be prepared with their charter.

It is, therefore, ordered, adjudged and decreed, that the judgment of the district court be affirmed, with costs.

Seghers, for the plaintiffs.
Wuggaman, for the defendant.

Pilié v. Lallande *et al.*   VII, N. S. 648.

FIRST District.

In a redhibitory action, the plaintiff may prove that the slave ran away after he was purchased, as showing the continuance of the habit of running away. 7 *Martin*, 43; 10 *Martin*, 659.

The presumption of slavery arising from color is confined to blacks.

Gracie v. Gayoso. VII, N. S. 650.

The failure of a defendant in a petitory action to demand the value of his improvements, does not prevent his suing for them after eviction.

If the judge admits illegal evidence to go to the jury but afterwards charges them not to consider it in making up a verdict, the cause will not be remanded.

THIRD District, Judge of the Second presiding.

PORTER, J., delivered the opinion of the court.

This suit has grown out of a decree of this court, in the case of Gayoso v. Gracie, by which the present plaintiff was condemned to deliver up to the defendants a tract of land, which the latter had inherited from their ancestors. 1. N. S. 320.

The petition avers that the money paid for the land by the person under whom the plaintiff claimed title, was applied to the discharge of a debt due by the father of the defendants, and that the sale by his executor, which this court annulled because it was not executed in the form prescribed by law, was made expressly to discharge that debt. It also avers that the plaintiff made extensive improvements on the property in good faith, for which he has a right to be reimbursed; and that there was a valuable crop growing on it at the time of eviction, for which the plaintiff is entitled to be paid.

The answer denies that the defendants are responsible to the person who bought from their father's executor, and avers that if they were, the present plaintiff is not subrogated in his right. It sets up the plea of *res judicata*, asserts that the plaintiff was a possessor in bad faith, and has no right to claim the value of the improvements made by him, and denies there was any crop growing on the premises at the time of eviction.

The first question for our consideration is that presented by the plea of *res judicata*, for if found correct, it precludes an examination of other points arising in the cause.

A reference however to the record, in the case of Gayoso v. Gracie has satisfied us that this defence cannot be sustained. The question as to the right of the defendant to claim the purchase-money is excluded in express terms by the opinion and judgment there rendered. The court in this opinion says: " We cannot in this suit examine the rights of the parties growing out of that contract"—that is the contract by which the defendant acquired the land from the vendee of the executor. No claim was made for the value of the improvements in that suit. Consequently they were not passed on. We have already decided in the case of Richardson v. Packwood, that the failure of a defendant to demand them, did not prevent him claiming them in another action. 1 *N. S.* 324 and 299.

The judge charged the jury that the plaintiff was entitled to claim from the defendants the money paid by the person under whom they held. To this opinion the plaintiff excepted; but as they have not joined in the appeal, nor prayed that the judgment may be amended it is unnecessary to examine whether the judge was correct or not. We notice it for the purpose of showing that this direction to the jury dispenses with the necessity of our deciding the question raised by the defendants as to the admissibility of the document D, in relation to the judgment obtained against the executor. The evidence applied solely to the point excluded from the consideration of the jury, and though we are inclined to think the judge did not err, a positive opinion is not required from us, for the decision of the cause, as it stands before the court.

The principal question in the case, and that which has been most argued before us, is the right of the plaintiffs to be paid for improvements made after the commencement of the suit. We have already expressed fully our opinion of the law on the subject in the case of Richardson *v.* Packwood, 1 *N. S.* 299, and that of the Heirs of Vanpradelle *v.* Donaldson *et al.,* lately decided in this court. Our opinion was, that under the provisions of the old Code, the good faith of the party in possession did not necessarily cease with the commencement of the suit. The decision of the court is not free from difficulty but the argument has not produced a conviction on our minds that our former impressions were incorrect.

But in the instance before us, the appellants contend the plaintiff was in bad faith after the commencement of the suit, because he has acknowledged in his petition he was in good faith previous thereto. We agree with the jury and court below, that these expressions did not necessarily contain an acknowledgment of his bad faith subsequent to the institution of the suit. From all the circumstances of case, we believe he considered himself the *bona fide* owner of the the property at the commencement of the suit; that he was confirmed in this persuasion after he obtained a decision of the inferior court in his favor, and that he continued in this belief up to the time judgment was rendered against him in this tribunal.

It is, therefore, ordered, adjudged and decreed, that the judgment of the district court be affirmed, with costs.

Workman, for the defendant.

Ramsay *v.* Littlejohn.   VII, N. S. 654.

(See 5 *N. S.* 655.)

FIRST District.

The debtor who suffers his creditor to have judgment after notice of the assignment of the debt cannot resist the claim of the assignee.

Oger *v.* Daunoy.   VII, N. S. 656.

The appellee may claim the reversal of the whole judgment in his answer.

The court of the first district cannot enjoin the execution of a judgment from the city courts of New Orleans.

FIRST District.

MARTIN, J., delivered the opinion of the court.

The defendant, marshal of the city court, having served out several writs of execution against Harland's property, which the plaintiff claimed as his property, the latter procured an injunction from the district court, had the defendant cited, and prayed that he might be decreed to restore the property.

The defendant prayed for a dissolution of the injunction, on the ground that the district court had no authority to interfere with the execution of the writs of the city court, nor control its officers therein; that the plaintiff ought to have sought relief in the city court.

The injunction was dissolved as to part of the property, which had been seized for rent, and sustained for the rest.

The defendant now filed an answer, averred collusion between the plaintiff and Harland, and prayed the plaintiffs in execution might be cited.

They were so, and pleaded the general issue, collusion, &c.

There was judgment that the original defendant restore the property to the plaintiff, and that the latter pay costs. From this judgment the plaintiff appealed.

The defendant denied that there was any error prejudicial to the plaintiff in the judgment appealed from, and proved that there was error to his (the defendant's) prejudice, inasmuch as the judgment was for the plaintiff, while it ought to have been for the defendant. Code of Practice, 592.

The appellant denied the right of the appellee to obtain the reversal of the judgment, under this article of the Code of Practice, alleging that it authorised appellees to procure the judgment to be set aside in those parts only in which they might be aggrieved.

The object of the legislature in this article was, to save to appellees the trouble and expense of a distinct appeal, where the case was brought up by the adverse party. It would be strange to allow the appellee a relief, without a second appeal, in case of a partial error, and deny it to him, in case the judgment was wholly erroneous.

By the Code of Practice, 617, the execution of judgments belongs to the courts by which the causes were tried in the first instance, and by the 629th article, it is for the court,'whether appellate or inferior, which rendered the judgment, to take cognisance of the manner of its execution.

The present suit is the opposition of a third party, which is defined "a demand by a third person not originally a party in the suit, for the purpose of arresting the execution of a judgment." Code of Practice, 395. Such opposition may be made, as in the present case, by a third person pretending to be the owner of the thing seized. *Ibid.* 396. But it must] be before the court that gave the judgment. *Ibid.* 397.

We however recognised an exception to these principles in the case of Lawes *et al. v.* Chinn, 4 *N. S.* 390, " to prevent an immediate injury which could not otherwise be warded off," the property being seized in a distant parish from that in which the judgment had been rendered. We thought that "*ex necessitate rei*" the injunction must have issued from the judge of the parish in which the execution was to have been carried into effect. We thought that if an execution, issued from Washita or Natchitoches, was levied in the Terre Aux Bœufs or Washington, on personal property, it would be sold, if no judge but he who gave the judgment could issue an injunction.

In the present case the judge who gave the judgment, and he who issued the execution, were in the same parish.

We therefore conclude that the injunction was improperly issued, and the district court improperly applied to, to obtain a restoration of the property seized.

But when the property of A is seized by an officer on an execution against B, the former has his action to recover damages or the value of the property from the officer, even in another court than that which issued the execution. In many cases that court can not give relief. This was determined in Vail *v.* Dumé, 7 *Martin,* 416.

[Oger *v.* Daunoy.]

But in the present case the prayer of the petition is for the restoration of the property, or its value; and the question presents itself whether, being of opinion that the restoration of the property was improperly sued for in the district court, it might have given judgment for the value, which was demanded subsidiarily; in which case it would be our duty, after reversing the judgment, to give one for the value of the property, if such value appeared on record.

The question in other words is, whether when judgment is prayed alternately, for a thing of which the court has no jurisdiction, and another of which it has—judgment can be given for the latter? We think it can. For the plaintiff, who might have made his election before suit, may still do so before trial. Besides, in the present case, there is a prayer for general relief.

As the record does not enable us to ascertain the value of the property, the case must be remanded.

It is, therefore, ordered, adjudged and decreed, that the judgment of the district court be annulled, avoided and reversed, and the case remanded for a new trial—the appellant paying costs in this court.

Morse, for the plaintiff.

Rousseau and *Moreau,* for the defendant.

Carraby *v.* Desmarre *et al.*   VII, N. S. 661.

A notarial act relating to real property must still be registered in the office of the judge of the parish in wich the property lies.

In a sale of land on the Mississippi, when no depth is stated, it becomes a question of intention what depth passes.

FIRST District.

MARTIN, J., delivered the opinion of the court.

The plaintiff sues one of the defendants as purchaser, and the other, sheriff of the parish, as vendor of a tract of land, as the property of Gravier, claimed by the plaintiff as vendee of the latter.

Desmarre insisted on his title as purchaser under an execution, and the other defendant justified under the writ.

There was judgment for them, and the plaintiff appealed.

The appellant rests his title on a notarial sale, by Gravier, execu-

33*

ted in New Orleans, long before the judgment, on which the execution issued. The land lies in the parish of Plaquemines, and the sale was never recorded there.

In the act of March 25, 1810, c. 25, sect. 7, it is provided that no notarial act concerning movable property, shall have any effect against third parties, until the same shall have been recorded in the office of the judge of the parish, in which such immovable property is situated. 3 *Mart. Dig.* 140, 7.

But the appellants' counsel urges this section has been repealed by the new Civil Code, 2415, 2417, 3318 and 3521.

The first article cited provides that sales of immovable property shall be written, by authentic or private act. Verbal sales shall be null.

The next provides that such sales, by private act, shall have effect only from the day such a sale was recorded in a notary's office, and the delivery of the thing sold took place.

The 3318th article relates to mortgages only, not to sales.

The last provides for the repeal of all acts of the legislature for which there is a special provision in the new Code.

Now, the laws anterior to the Code provided for the form and effect of sales. Those of immovable property were to be written—so they must still be under the Code. As to the effects of notarial sales, the three former ones had established a distinction; the notarial had no effect against third parties, until recorded in the office of a notary. Civil Code, 245, art. 3.

As to the effect of the notarial act, the new Code has no special provision; therefore the 3421st article does not repeal that made by the act of 1810.

As to the effect of the private sale, the new Code adds a new requisite, the actual delivery of the property, 2417. So this new special provision repeals the corresponding article of the old Code.

We therefore conclude, the district judge held correctly that the appellant could not avail himself of his notarial sale for want of a registry.

His counsel further urges that the sheriff's sale, under which the appellees protect themselves, was not recorded. Be that as it may, till the appellant produced a title, the appellees were not bound to produce any.

Lastly, the appellant's counsel contends, that a party who has no title at all can not urge the want of registry of the owner's title: and as to all the tract, except the arpent and one half immediately in front of the river, Desmarre is without any title—the sheriff having sold an arpent and one half of land on the Mississippi, without stating any depth.

In sales of land on the Mississippi, the tract is sometimes described by the extent of its front on the river, and the names of the owners of the tracts above and below. Nothing is said of the owner of the land in the rear; because generally the tract extends to another stream,

[Carraby v. Desmarre et al.]

or to an uncultivated swamp. In such a case the ordinary depth of forty arpents is presumed as that which the vendor possessed, unless the contrary appear.

The question is then one of intention as to depth, in the solution of which the court is aided by the situation of the land, and the price for which it was sold.

In the present case we do not think the district court erred, in concluding that the depth of the tract, as owned before the sale by Gravier passed.

It is, therefore, ordered, adjudged and decreed, that the judgment of the district court be affirmed with costs.

Seghers, for the plaintiff.
Denis, for the defendant.

Leblanc v. Landry. VII, N. S. 665.

If a woman marries a second time having children by the first marriage, she cannot inherit from them in case of the decease of any. The survivor or survivors are heirs. But if they and their forced heirs die before the mother, the property so inherited by them belongs to her.

FIRST District.

PORTER, J., delivered the opinion of the court.

The plaintiff has been twice married. By her first marriage she had three children. Her second marriage took place in the year 1817. In the year 1819 one of these children died, and in the year 1822 another, leaving a survivor, Artemise Le Blanc, who intermarried with the defendant in the year 1824. In the year 1825 the plaintiff passed an act by which she mortgaged to the defendant and his wife certain property to secure to them at her death the return of the inheritance of her deceased children, which she held in usufruct. There is a clause in the instrument, however, which provides that, if by law the mother had a better right to the inheritance of her children, than their sister, the mortgage should be null and void.

Since the passage of this act the wife of defendant, surviving child of the first marriage, has died, leaving an infant, who is also dead, and to whom the defendant is heir.

This action is brought to have the contract of mortgage annulled,

[Leblanc v. Landry.]

and the question to be examined is, whether the inheritance reserved to the child by a provision in our Code, of which the mother has the usufruct during life, is transmissible on the death of some of the children to the survivor, and in case of the death of the survivor and his forced heirs, whether it is inherited by the mother, or by the heirs, of the forced heirs of the child of the first marriage, who died last.

The question arises under provisions of our old Code. The 226th article, page 258, declares that, " a man or a woman who contracts a second and subsequent marriage, having children by a former one, can give to his wife, or she to her husband, only the least child's portion, and that only as an usufruct: and in no case shall the portion of which the donee is to have the usufruct, exceed the fifth part of the donor's estate.

Art. 227. " The donation mentioned in the preceding article can in no case affect any property, but the estate belonging to the man or woman who contracts a second marriage, and cannot comprise any effects which came to him or her from the deceased spouse, either by donation made before or after the marriage or otherwise or by the succession of some of the children of the preceding marriage. The effects being according to law reserved to the children of said marriage in case their father or mother marries again."

By this law the wife is forbidden to dispose of the property which she inherits from some of the children of the first marriage, these effects being reserved for the children of said marriage. On the death therefore of any one of these children, the mother inherited from them. But she could obtain nothing more than the use during her life. The right of property passed to the survivor or survivors.— The law says it is reserved to them and every other construction would be defeating the spirit as well as the letter of the statute.

It is contended, however, that the whole object, and intention of these provisions were, to secure the property to the children of the first marriage, and that when they all die before the mother she becomes owner of it in full right.

The death of the children and the consequent opening of the succession took place previous to the acts of our legislature repealing the Spanish laws. The article of our Code must therefore be construed in reference to our jurisprudence as it then existed. The provision contained in the 224th article, is not copied from the Napoleon Code, but is nearly a transcript of the 15th law of Toro, which is the 4th law of the 1st book of the *Nueva Recopilacion.*— We have repeatedly decided that the re-enactment in our old Code of the general provisions in the Spanish law did not repeal the exceptions to the provisions and that the rule would be understood and applied here with the same limitations and modifications which belong to it in Spain. In relation to this very article (227) it was declared by this court in the case of Duncan's Executors v. Hampton, that notwithstanding the prohibition contained in it against second

[Leblanc v. Landry.]

marriages, yet if the wife had been left a widow under the age of majority, the penalty there affixed did not apply to her, and she inherited in full property. Such being an exception existing in the Spanish law. 6 *N. S.* 38.

In this instance it is stated by the commentators on the laws of Spain, that the object of this provision was to secure to the children of the first marriage the property which belonged to them. That to deprive the father or mother of the right of inheriting in full property, two things were necessary: a second marriage, and children of the first or their descendants to inherit. That when all the children died before the surviving spouse, the latter became owner *pleno jure.* We see there is some difference of opinion on this subject, but the weight of authority appears to us in favor of the rule just stated, as the equity certainly is. By the contrary doctrine, the property of all the children of the first marriage would belong to the husband of one of them, in preference to their mother. See *Febrero,* p. 2, cap. 5, sect. 1, Nos. 12 and 13, and the authorities there cited.

It is therefore ordered adjudged and decreed, that the judgment of the district court be annulled, avoided and reversed; and it is further ordered, adjudged and decreed, that the mortgage given in the case by the plaintiff to the defendant, and his late wife, Artemise Le Blanc, by act before the parish judge of Iberville, on the 12th day of February, 1825, be annulled and cancelled, and that the defendant pay costs in both courts.

Moreau and *Davis,* for the plaintiff.

Williams's Executors v. Franklin *et al.* VII, N. S. 670.

When delivery does not follow sale, parol evidence is admissible to show from what causes possession was retained by the vendor.

The attorney's being entitled to a taxed fee does not disqualify him from being a witness.

A sale of movables is good against third persons, although the seller retain possession under the title of usufruct.

FIRST District.

PORTER, J., delivered the opinion of the court.

The petitioner stated that he purchased by public act from Charles A. Warfield, half of the furniture and fixings of the Planters and

Merchants' Hotel, and that the property so purchased was left in the possession of the vendor: that the sheriff of the parish of New Orleans, at the instance of one Thomas Franklin, has seized the said property, under a process from the parish court, and refuses to deliver it. He concludes by praying judgment against the defendant for the property, and in case of the failure to deliver it up for 5000 dollars, the value thereof.

The defendants pleaded several exceptions in the court of the first instance, which were overruled. One of them went to the jurisdiction of the tribunal where the suit was brought. But as that defect was not *ratione materiæ*, it might be waived, and has been waived before the court. We shall therefore proceed to decide the case on the merits.

The defendant, Franklin, pleaded first the general issue; and further that the property seized by the sheriff was the partnership property of Franklin & Warfield, found in their possession, in the Planters' Hotel, in Canal street, in this city, and that on a settlement of said partnership, and the payment of its debts, the defendant was entitled to one half the remaining balance of the partnership stock.

Morgan pleaded the general issue, and averred that he had sold the property by order of said court.

There was judgment for the plaintiff in the court of the first instance, and the defendant appealed.

There are several exceptions taken by the defendant. The first was to the testimony of the notary public who drew up the act of sale. He was introduced to prove that a counter letter, also read in evidence by the plaintiff, was given immediately after the act passed before him was executed; and to prove other circumstances which showed the transaction was *bona fide*. The objection to his evidence is, *First*, that it violates that rule of our law which forbids any thing that was said before, or at the time, or after the passing of the act, to be proved by parol evidence; and *Secondly*, that the proof established a different contract from that set forth in the petition.

Neither of these objections can be sustained by this court. The proof was not introduced to contradict the act, nor to add to its force. By the act of sale, the vendor reserved to himself the possession. The 2456th article of the Louisiana Code provides that in such cases the sale is presumed to be simulated. "And with respect to third persons, the parties must produce proof that they are acting in good faith, and establish the reality of the sale." The evidence therefore was properly offered and received to destroy the presumption of fraud created by the act of sale and there is no contradiction between the proof given of the consideration, and that expressed in the instrument passed before the notary, which would induce us to conclude the transaction was a fraudulent one. The parties may have considered the plaintiff's endorsement of the vendor's note as equivalent to money.

The same reasons justify the introduction of the curator's letter, and the protest showing the dishonor of the vendor's note and the plaintiff being compelled to take it up.

The objection to the attorney for the plaintiff being permitted to testify, is disproved by the 2261st article of our Code, which makes no exception in cases where the law gives a tax fee. Now when there is a commission on the money received, on general principles, this last objection would not be good against a factor, and we do not see why it should be a valid one in relation to an attorney. 2 Starkie, 768.

It has been contended on the merits, that there is not sufficient evidence the objects sued for are the same which have been sequestered and taken into possession by the defendants. But we think with the court below, that the evidence satisfactorily establishes the identity; and as to the objection that the court should not have received the testimony, because the objects were not specially set out in the petition, we can find no bill of exceptions taken to the proof, and if there had been, we do not think it could have availed the defendant; the one half of the furniture and fixtures in a house, was a good description in the act of sale, and the same terms were sufficiently explicit in the petition.

It is contended that the rights of the defendant, Franklin, who entered into partnership with the vendor subsequent to the act of sale, are of a higher nature on the property sold than those of the plaintiff, and that a settlement of the partnership affairs must take place before any part of the stock can be touched by the plaintiff. The soundness of this argument depends on the fact, whether the petitioner was, or was not owner of the property; and if he was, whether he sold by such a transfer, as could affect the defendant. The conveyance, there can be no doubt, transferred to the plaintiff a title to all the objects embraced by it. The deed was authentic and had a certain date against third parties. The 2243d article of the Code requires possession to follow a sale of movables, in order that it may have effect against purchasers and creditors. The defendant is certainly not a purchaser, and it may be doubted whether he is a creditor. But admitting him to be the latter, the 2456th article recognises the validity of sales of movables against third persons, when the seller retains possession under the title of usufruct, or by a precarious title. To give effect to these two provisions, we are compelled to consider the cases put in the article last cited, as exceptions to the rule contained in the 2243d.

It appears to us therefore that the plaintiff was the owner of the property, and if the defendant received into the partnership, effects which did not belong to his partner, this circumstance could not affect the right of those to whom it belonged. The owner is not obliged to have the claim settled in the *concurso* because the property did not vest in the partnership and could not be surrendered by it to the creditors.

It is, therefore, ordered; ordered adjudged and decreed, that the judgment of the district court be affirmed, with costs.

Hennen, for the plaintiff.

Nixon, for the defendant.

Herman v. Smith.   VII, N. S. 676.

When a party appeals from a judgment rendered between others, he must show it was erroneous as it respects them.

And he cannot avail himself of a technical objection which the defendant waived.

FIRST District.

PORTER, J., delivered the opinion of the court.

The appellant has brought up this case under the 571st article of the Code of Practice, and complains that he is aggrieved by the judgment rendered between the parties.

To enable him to show this, we are of opinion that he must establish the judgment rendered was erroneous between the original parties to the suit. A third person can never be aggrieved by a right judgment between others, unless there were fraud and collusion on their part. If it affects his interest in any manner he cannot complain because it is the judgment which the law requires on the legal rights of the parties.

The plaintiff in this case was the holder of a note for the second instalment of the price of real estate. It was secured by a mortgage which had the effect of a judgment: he applied for and obtained an order of seizure and sale, and without opposition on the part of the defendant, the property hypothecated was seized and sold, and the proceeds paid over.

The appellant is holder of the note due for the third instalment of the price of the same object, and he insists the order of seizure and sale was improvidently granted, because no authentic evidence was produced to show the transfer of the note to the plaintiff.

This was an objection the debtor had the right to make at any time before the sale of the property, but which not being made previous thereto, he could not make now. It was one which he might waive if he chose, and one which he has waived by his silence. The

[Herman v. Smith.]

consent cures any error in the original proceeding, and whatever will show the defendant could not avail himself of the defence, will bar the appellant.

The appellant has, however, agreed that this matter is *res judicata* between him and the appellees, because they contested his right to appeal, and the judge below decided he had a right so. to do; which judgment is unappealed from. If this be true it would be strange doctrine. It would amount in fact to this, that whenever the judge below decided that a party had a right to appeal, it followed the judgment appealed from was erroneous. Such a principle would settle all questions in this court very easily. The appellant would then in every instance succeed. The judgment of the court below in our opinion, decided nothing more than that the appellant had made out a case which enabled him to bring the cause before this court, but it left open the question when the cause came here, whether the judgment was so erroneous between the parties, that it should be reversed.

It is, therefore, ordered, adjudged and decreed, that the appeal be dismissed with costs to be paid by the appellant.

Denis, for the plaintiff.

Morphy, for the defendant.

Slidell, for the third possessor.

Xenes *v.* Taquino *et al.*   VII, N. S. 678.

Drunkenness is a vice of character, not of body, and is not redhibitory.

PARISH Court of New Orleans.

PORTER, J., delivered the opinion of the court.

This is an action of redhibition to annul the sale of a slave, and recover back part of the price paid for her, and to be exonerated from the payment of the balance due. The general issue was pleaded in the court of the first instance, and the defendant's vendor cited in warranty. The cause was submitted to a jury who found for the plaintiff. Judgment was rendered on this verdict against the defendant, and in his favor against Shiff, from whom he had purchased. From this judgment both the defendant, and the party called in warranty, have appealed.

The vice, to which the slave is charged in the petition to be subject, is habitual drunkenness. The evidence establishes satisfactorily the allegation. The only question, therefore, presented for our decision, is, whether the defect be such a one as authorises the purchaser of a slave to it, to have the sale rescinded.

The purchase was made since the enactment of the late amendments to our Code, and must be governed by them.

The 2496th article of that work defines redhibition to be, "the avoidance of a sale on account of some vice or defect in the thing sold, which renders it either absolutely useless, or its use so inconvenient and imperfect, that it must be supposed the buyer would not have purchased it, had he known of the vice."

The 2500th article divides the defects of slaves into two classes, vices of body, and vices of character.

In the 2502d article, some of the vices of body are defined, and others are stated to be contained in the 2496th article, which we have already cited.

But with regard to these of character, the next article expressly declares, that they are confined to cases where the slave has committed a capital crime, where he is convicted of theft, and where he is in the habit of running away. No reference is made, as in the article relating to their bodily defects, to the previous provision which makes any disease a cause of redhibition, which renders the services of the slave so difficult and interrupted, that it is presumed the buyer would not have purchased had he been aware of them.

And that the failure to make the reference did not proceed from inattention is manifest by the 2506th article, which succeeds that just noticed, wherein the defects in other animals are extended to the cases supposed in the 2496th article.

So that the cause turns on the inquiry, is drunkenness a vice of body, or of character? Is it mental, or physical?

We think it must be classed among the vices which our Code denominates those of character. It has of late, we believe, been made a question by physiologists whether the disposition to an immoderate use of ardent spirits, did not arise as much from physical temperament as from moral weakness. In cases of long indulgence in the habit, it is quite probable the body may require a continuance of the stimulus, and that the desire for the use of it may spring as much from physical lassitude, as from moral depravity. But on this subject the court has a safer guide than the conflicting opinions of medical men. By the ancient jurisprudence of the country, the vice of drunkenness was considered one of the mind. And the terms used in our legislation must be understood in the sense in which they were used in that jurisprudence, unless another meaning be expressly given to them by legislative authority. We conclude then that the allegation made in the petition does not furnish ground for setting aside the sale.

It has been contended, that there was fraud in the defendant concealing from the plaintiff the defect to which the slave was addicted. But unless the vice was one which furnished ground for redhibition, there was no fraud in concealing it—or, in other words, there was no obligation in the seller to communicate it to the buyer.

It is, therefore, ordered, adjudged and decreed, that the judgment of the parish court be annulled, avoided and reversed; that there be judgment for the defendant, and for the interpleader, with costs in both courts.

Carleton and *Lockett*, for the defendants.

Canon, for the plaintiff.

Ligon v. Orleans Navigation Company.
VII, N. S. 678.

COURT of Probates of New Orleans.

A copy of the registry of a vessel is not evidence in favor of the person in whose name the registry is made. For all the public purposes contemplated by the act of congress, the document is evidence, but it is not so for any other. 3 Starkie, 1153.

The subjoined papers were appended to 7 *N. S.* by Judge MAR-
TIN, and are deemed of permanent interest, sufficient to justify their
republication.

APPENDIX.

It is deemed proper to publish the following correspondence between a Committee of the
Senate and the Judges of the Supreme Court.

New Orleans, January, 1829.

GENTLEMEN:—The Committee under the enclosed resolution of
the Senate, request you to prepare for the use of the Senate a written
opinion, whether the College of Louisiana, in consequence of appro-
priations having been made by the act of March 14, 1827, to the
parishes of East and West Feliciana, for the support of their parish
schools, loses a part of the appropriation granted for its maintenance by the act of 18th February, 1825, amounting to sixteen hundred
dollars: which amount had previously, in 1824, been appropriated
to those parishes, one half thereof to each for the annual support of
parish schools.

Your attention to this request is respectfully solicited by the Committee.

ISAAC A. SMITH, *Chairman.*

To the Hon. the Judges of the Supreme Court.

New Orleans, 30*th January,* 1829.

SIR:—We have received a letter from you of the — instant, in
which, as Chairman of a Committee of the Senate, you solicit our
attention to a resolution of that body, by which the Committee are
directed " to request the Judges of the Supreme Court to prepare a
written opinion to be laid before the Senate, on the validity of the
claims of the trustees of the College of Louisiana, to be paid that part
of the appropriation granted to the said college by the act of the 18th
February, 1825, the payment of which has been refused by the Treasurer of the State, since the passage of the act of March 14, 1827."

After having given to this request, the most attentive consideration
in our power, we feel compelled to decline complying with it.

The Supreme Court of the State of Louisiana is established by the
constitution with appellate judicial power only. It can of course
exercise no other than that which is conferred on it. The request of
the Senate has suggested to us the inquiry, whether a compliance
with it would be an exercise of that power?

We have bestowed on the subject as much reflection as in our power, and we conceive it would not. There are no parties before us litigating their claims—there is no issue joined: and there is no appeal from the decree of an inferior tribunal. Did all these things combine in the present instance, the matter has not been brought before us in the mode prescribed by the acts of the legislature; and it has been again and again decided by all the judges who have filled this tribunal since its organisation, that its jurisdiction could not be exercised in any other manner than that which the law had pointed out. In addition to these objections, which to our minds appear insurmountable, another not less solid may be added. The opinions of this tribunal are its judgments, and that which we might give here, could not have such effect.

Were we to prepare and communicate an opinion, we would act on questions not growing out of a case before us: we would act out of court. We would pronounce on a contested claim, on the application of those who are not parties to it.

Should the application be considered as addressed to the judges of this tribunal in their individual capacity, and not to the court, the reasons for our declining to express an opinion are equally cogent to us, and we trust will appear fully as satisfactory to the Senate. The case on which we are called to deliver our sentiments is in relation to a claim of the College of Louisiana to a sum of money under an act of the legislature. We carefully abstain from expressing an opinion whether that institution can, or can not enforce it in a court of justice should it be well founded in law. It is sufficient for us, that we do not know whether the college may not resort to this mode of attaining what it conceives its legal rights. If it should, it is proper, on all considerations of private justice and public utility, that it should be brought before a tribunal, that had in no manner prejudged the question. The distinction of our having given the opinion in our private capacities, and not sitting as judges, would justly afford little satisfaction to the parties. The litigant to whom our conclusion was unfavorable, would know that he was before those who had already made up their minds—and he would feel that he was contending against the bias which would naturally exist in favor of preconceived notions, already made public. We hope and trust we could rise superior to any consideration of this kind, if further argument convinced us we had been in error; but we claim not exemption from the frailties of our nature, and no man, or body of men, who come before us, should unnecessarily be placed in a situation where the influence of those frailties may be arrayed against them.

In two instances, the Supreme Court of Pennsylvania have given their opinion, at the request of the executive of the state; but in both, they grew out of criminal cases before them, and were in relation to the duties which the executive might have to perform, independent of the court. 1 *Dall. Rep.* 88 and 110.

During the presidency of General Washington, the answer of the judges of the Supreme Court of the United States was requested by his cabinet to a series of questions—comprehending all the subjects of difference between the executive and the minister of France, relative to the exposition of the treaties between the two nations. Considering themselves merely as a legal tribunal for the decision of controversies brought before them in a legal form, those gentlemen deemed it improper to declare their opinions on questions not growing out of a case in court. Life of Washington, by Marshall, vol. 6, 433 and 441.

It would have been more pleasant to us, to have complied with the wishes of the Senate, but we hope we may obtain, for we are sure we will deserve, their approbation, in withholding, rather than in yielding obedience to their request.

We have the honor to be, very respectfully, your obedient servants.

F. X. MARTIN,
ALEX. PORTER, JR.

HON. J. A. SMITH, *Chairman, &c. &c.*

EASTERN DISTRICT, MAY TERM, 1829.

Depau *v.* Humphrey.   VIII, N. S. 1.

The rate of interest to be paid from the date of a note may be legally stipulated, according to the law of the place where the note is made, although it be payable in another, where the stipulation of a lesser rate is alone legal.

Interest *ex mora* is regulated by the law of the place of payment or performance, but conventional interest, *i. e.*, stipulated in the contract, is governed by the law of the place of the contract.

In a bilateral contract, where the obligations of the parties are to be performed in different places, in which different laws and usages prevail, the laws and usages of neither can offer a legitimate rule of decision for all the obligations of the contract. Each party must perform his according to the law of the place *ubi ut solveret se obligavit;* and in case he fails, he must yield to his adversary damages, equal in value to that of the thing he bound himself to deliver, at the place *ubi solutio* or *deliberatio destinatur.*

When interest is stipulated to run from the date of the contract, in a loan made in one country, but payable in another, as the object of the conventional interest is to afford to the lender a compensation for the profit he foregoes, in yielding the use of his money to the borrower, the circumstance of the place of payment differing from that in which the lender parts with his money, ought to have no influence in fixing the rate of interest.*

COURT of Probates of New Orleans.

Martin, J., delivered the opinion of the court.
The defendant, administrator of the estate of W. Kenner, deceased,

* This decree may be deemed the most masterly production of the mind of the vene

[Depau v. Humphreys.]

sued on sundry notes of the firm of W. Kenner & Co. (composed of the deceased, Clague and Oldham) given in the city of New York to the plaintiff, pleaded the statute of usury of the state of New York. On this, the plaintiff, with the defendant's consent, filed a supplemental petition, in which he prayed that, if the plea of usury was sustained, he might have judgment for the balance due him by the firm, before the notes mentioned in the original petition were given. To this supplemental petition the plea of usury was repeated.

The defendant had judgment, and the plaintiff appealed.

In this court, the appellant's pretensions have been confined to the amount claimed in the supplemental petition, and his counsel has relied on the cases of Gray v. Taylor, 1 Hen. Blackstone, 462, and Gayther v. The Bank of Georgetown, 1 Peters, 43, to show that, ad-

rable judge who pronounced it, although it does not exhibit the same glow of sentiment, nor the same classical taste in its style as the judgment in the case of Denis v. Leclerc. The conclusions of the present decree seem to be irresistible. Nevertheless, they have been impugned in a very spirited and ingenious *critique* by Mr. Justice Story, in his Conflict of Laws, chap. 8, sect. 298–307. He sifts the citations in this case, and finishes by asserting that "it may be affirmed with some confidence that the foreign jurists who have been relied on, do not establish the asserted doctrine," and that *Voët ad Pand. lib.* 22, *tit.* 1, *sect.* 6; *Ibid. lib.* 4, *tit.* 1, *sect.* 29, besides other foreign jurists, lead us to an opposite conclusion. The reader is invited to compare the two arguments: it is submitted, however, whether the statement of doctrine in the abstract is not sufficiently cogent, as far as reason is concerned; and, moreover, that the true key to the opinion of Voët on this point is found distinctly in the first sentence of that passage, section 6, *si alio in loco,* taken in connection with the third sentence of the same passage which is quoted (in English) by Mr. J. Story. " But good faith must be observed, and the place of the contract where higher interest is allowed, must not be sought for the purpose of evading the law. Why caution parties, contracting in one country with a view to payment in another, against the indulgence of bad faith in designedly availing themselves of the higher interest of the country *ubi contraxisse,* if all their craft and bad faith would be fruitless, from the certainty that, in point of law, the interest would finally depend on the law of the place *destinatæ solutionis?* Indeed, the intervening (second sentence of the passage relied on) sentence *Dummodo meminerimus* is plainly, as Judge MARTIN hints, see p. 34, a simple, reminder to the stuednt, while he imbibes this doctrine so lucidly stated, in terms which prove themselves, not to forget, meanwhile, that *proprie,* (*very accurately speaking,*) in law, *that* place wherein the business (of bargaining, that is,) was transacted, is not the *locus contractûs,* but rather that where payment was to be made under the contract. But after this good counsel, and this caution *non-obstante,* he seems to reiterate the position enunciated in the clause *si alio in loco,* for he immediately adds: But good faith must be observed, if one takes avail of the rule that interest stipulated is governed by the law of the place where " the business of bargaining was transacted;" for, if parties under cover of this admitted principle should practise a fraud on the law, (which would be done, if a citizen of New York came to New Orleans with the purpose of lending money in New Orleans, to be repaid at New York, solely to enrich himself by the difference of interest between seven and ten per cent. in contempt of the laws of New York,) then the tribunals of the place of payment ought to deny him his illconceived gains.

mitting the notes in the original petition are avoided by the statute, they present no obstacle to his recovery of the preceding debt. The appellee's counsel has not urged any authority or reason to destroy or weaken the weight of these cases.

To establish the amount due by the firm to the appellant, at the time their notes were given, his counsel has produced an account current subscribed by the firm, in the city of New York; by which they recognise themselves debtors of a balance of 14,154 dollars 93 cents, on the 31st of July, 1823, and afterwards debit themselves for 15,000 dollars, the amount of a note of Clague & Oldham, endorsed by the firm, given in New Orleans, payable in New York, bearing interest at ten per cent. from the date, that rate being the highest one of conventional interest, according to the law of Louisiana; the note being given in New Orleans. The firm debit themselves further for the sum of 500 dollars, for four months' interest then due on the note. These three items form the sum of 29,654 dollars, 98 cents.— The firm is next credited for a sum of 1313 dollars 34 cents, and a balance is struck as due from them of 28,349 dollars 59 cents, to which 459 dollars 71 cents were added as due for interest, and the final balance is stated at 28,801 dollars 30 cents due on the first of August, 1823.

On this the appellee shows that, on the ninth of the same month, the appellant received, in New York, five notes of the firm for the aggregate sum of 29,654 dollars 98 cents payable at one, two, three, four and five years; and it being the intention of the parties that he should receive interest at the rate of ten per cent. according to the law of Louisiana, but in violation of that of New York, which does not allow a higher rate than seven per cent., the notes were made payable at the latter rate, and a sixth was given, payable in three years, for the difference of three per cent. between the two rates.— The counsel, afterwards producing the statute of usury of the state of New York, which avoids all contracts, in which a higher rate of interest than seven per cent. is stipulated, has concluded that these six notes were tainted with usury, according to the laws of the place in which they were made.

The opposite counsel has not, in this court, made any attempt to controvert this proposition.

The appellee's counsel has not contested the appellant's right to the original balance of 14,594 dollars 93 cents, stated to be due on the 31st of July, 1823, but has insisted on a credit of 11,851 dollars 93 cents, the amount of two of the notes mentioned in the original petition, which were paid at maturity, reducing the balance due the appellants to 2292 dollars 66 cents.

As to Clague & Oldham's note for 15,000 dollars, it has been urged that the firm was bound as endorsers only; that the diligences, from which their liability would have resulted, were neglected; that it has been cancelled; that no obligation resulted from their debiting themselves with the amount of the note, and interest due thereon on the first of August, 1823, on the account then stated, in the city of New York, because that settlement was made to carry into effect a corrupt bargain, imposed on them by the appellant, and to which their necessities compelled them to submit, in order to obtain some delay: that the note is in itself usurious, inasmuch as it states on its face a rate of interest proscribed in the state in which payment was to be made.

We think the settlement, in which the balance due by the firm to the appellant was stated on the 1st of August, 1823, has not been proved to be tainted with usury (unles Clague & Oldham's note was so). Nothing shows that the contract for further time, according to which the notes stated in the original petition were given, eight days after, was in contemplation. At the time of this settlement, the note was not yet payable; it can not be imputed to the appellant that he neglected the diligences which charge an endorser. The firm might very fairly with their consent be charged with the amount of a note of two of its members, endorsed by the firm, and on their assuming to pay its amount as principals, and crediting the appellant with capital and interest, the surrender of the paper would not affect the liability of the firm.

So that the decision of this case must turn on the legality of the rate of interest stipulated for, on the face of the note of Clague & Oldham.

The appellant's counsel urges that the rate of interest may be stipulated, according to the law of the place in which the money is lent, and a note taken for its reimbursement, although such a note be payable elsewhere.

In support of this position, he has invoked many authorities, and principally the case of Van Reimsdich v. Kane et al., 1 *Gallison*, 375; in which Judge Story, delivering the opinion of the court, said: " This rule is well settled, that the law of the place where a contract is made to govern, as to the nature, validity and construction of such contract; and that, being valid in such a place, it is to be considered equally valid and to be enforced every where, with the exception of cases, in which the contract is immoral or unjust, or in which the enforcing of it in a state would be injurious to the rights and the interests, or the convenience of such state or its citizens. This doctrine is explicitly averred in *Huberus de Conflictu Legum*, and has become incorporated into the code of national law in all civilised countries. It would seem to follow from this doctrine, that, if a contract be void, by the law of the place where it is made, it is void every where, and that the discharge of a contract in the place where it is made shall be of equal avail in every other place. To this last proposition, there is an exception, when the contract is to be executed in a place different from that in which it is made, for the law of the place of execution will then apply."

The counsel contends that, as to the first proposition, the applicability of the law of the place where the contract is made to the nature, validity and construction of the contract, the judge speaks absolutely, and states no exception—and the exception he afterwards states is confined to the case of the discharge of the party, which is to be tested by the law of the country in which the performance was to take place.

1. The appellee's counsel has first drawn our attention to the passage of *Huberus*, referred to by Judge Story, a translation of which is to be found in 3 *Dallas*, 361.

Huberus, after stating that a contract, valid according to the law of the place where it is made is valid every where else, adds: *Verum tamen, non ita* precise *respiciendus est locus in quo contractus est initus, ut si partes alium in contrahendo locum respexerint, ille non* potius considerandus, *nam contraxisse unusquisque in eo loco intelligitur, in quo ut solveret se obligavit. ff.* 44, 7, 21.

Hence, the counsel thinks that by comparing the opinion of Judge Story with the part of *Huberus*, on which it is grounded, it follows that, as the note under consideration, was made payable in New York, its validity and construction must be governed by the laws of that place.

2. He relies next on another law of the Digest, 42, 4, 3. *Aut ubi quisque contraxerit: Contractum autem non utique in eo loco intelligitur quo negotium gestum sit, sed quo solvenda est pecunia.*

Pothier's Contrat de Change is next introduced, in which it is said that the protest of a bill of exchange is to be made according to the law of the place in which the bill is payable. *Merlin's Questions de Droit, verbo Protest*, are quoted to show the same principle, and that all the obligations, resulting from a bill of exchange, are governed by the law of the place at which it is payable.

4. The counsel then resumes the *corpus juris civilis*, to show that a question arising as to the price of wine, which the defendant had failed to deliver, it decided that if there was a place of delivery stated, the price there was to be given, otherwise that of the place in which the suit was brought. *Interrogavi, cujus loci pretium sequi oporteat, respondit si convenisset in certo loco redderetur, quanti eo loco esset, si dictum non esset, quanti ubi esset petitum. ff.* 9, 1, 3, *sect.* 4.

5. The following note of *Gregorio Lopez on Partida*, 3, 2, 32, is produced: *Quando contractus celebratur in uno loco, puta in Hispali et destinatur solutio in Cordubâ; tunc non inspicitur locus contractûs, sed locus destinatæ solutionis, ut habetur in ista lege et l. contraxisse.*

6. Voët's authority, which is next brought under consideration, appears better to support the position of the appellee's counsel than any other. *Si alio in loco, graviarum usurarum stipulatio permissa, in alio vetita sit, lex loci in quo contractus celebratur spectanda videtur, an moderatæ, an verbo modum excedentes usuræ per conventionem constitutæ sint. Dummodo meminerimus illum propie*

locum contractûs, in jure non intelligi, in quo negotium gestum est, sed in quo pecuniam ut solveret se quis obligavit. Ad Pandect. 22 *de Usuris et Fructibus.*

7. The British and American cases, cited by the appellee's counsel are Robinson *v.* Bland, 2 Burrows, 1077; 17 Johns. 519; 20 *Ibid.* 102; 2 Johns. Cas. 355; Whiston *et al. v.* Stodder *et al.,* 8 *Martin* 952; Vidal *v.* Johnson, 11 *Ibid.* 23.

The proposition, which the appellee's counsel has labored to establish, is that a contract (as to its nature, validity, effect and the manner in which it is to be performed, or the obligations of it are to be dissolved) is exclusively to be governed by the law of the country, in which the performance was to take place: *i. e.,* that there is but one *locus contract.*

The appellant's counsel urges that there are two *loci contractûs;* that in which the contract took place, and that in which the performance was intended. *Locus ubi contractus celebratus est; locus destinatæ solutionis.*

Keeping this distinction in view, let us examine the authorities, by which the first proposition is attempted to be supported.

1. Huberus says, we are not so precisely to consider the place, in which the contract was begun, that if the parties had in contracting another place in view, the latter should not more virtually *potius* be attended to. In the translation to Dallas' reports, *precise* is translated by *exclusively.* Hence the impression that our minds have received is, that the law of the place, in which the contract is entered into, may have some influence on it, even when the performance of it was to take place in another country.

This leads us to the examination of the laws *contraxisse* and *aut ubi quisque.* They are extremely short.

The first says: *Contraxisse unusquisque in eo loco intelligitur in quo ut solveret se obligavit.* Every one is understood (presumed) to have contracted, in that place where he bound himself to pay.

Godefroy, the annotator of the *corpus juris civilis,* appears to have considered this law as a mere rule of evidence; for he gives us the reason of it in the margin. *Quia ubi non apparet quod actum est, loci consuetudo attenditur.* He seems to think that, when the parties clearly express their meaning, the law is inoperative—that when the lender stipulates for a legal rate of conventional interest, and the borrower agrees to pay it, there is no necessity, in endeavoring to discover their intention, by examining what is customary at the place in which the contract is to be performed. This conclusion is strengthened by the reference he makes to another law of the digest. *Si numerus nummorum legatus sit, neque appareat quales legati sint, ante omnia ipsius patris familias consuetudo, deinde regionis in qua versatur, inquirenda est. ff.* 30, 1, 50. From this last law, Godefroy refers his readers to the laws *Interrogavi* and *item non oportet* which the appellee's counsel has cited.

II. The second law relied on, *Aut ubi quisque,* which is the.

third of the fifth title of forty-second book of the Digest, can not be understood, without considering the two preceding.

The first says: *Venire bona ibi opportet ubi quisque defendi debet id est.*   One is bound to suffer the sale of his goods, under an execution, at the place in which he is bound to defend himself, that is to say:

Law 2. *Ubi domicilium habet;* where he has his domicil.   ,

Law 3. *Aut ubi quisque contraxerit. Contractum autem non utique eo loco intelligitur, quo negotium gestum sit, sed quo solvenda est pecunia.*   Or where he contracted.   For, the contract is not understood to be where the business is done, but where the money is to be paid.

All that this law teaches us is, that at Rome the defendant was suable at his domicil, and at the place where he bound himself to pay.

III. Pothier and Merlin have often shed on matters, discussed in this court, a light which we would have sought in vain in British and American writers.   But, in the present case, a resort to the parts of their works, to which the appellee's counsel has drawn our attention, would rather embarrass, than aid our inquiry.   As protests are generally made at the place in which the bill of exchange is payable, and instruments must be in the forms prescribed by the law of the place in which they are made, it follows that the protest must generally be made according to the law of the place in which the bill is payable.   But, a bill may be drawn on London payable in Paris, or Amsterdam—the protest for non-acceptance must then be made in London, and the form of it be according to the law of England—the protest for nonpayment must be made in Paris, and consequently be regulated by the law of France.   We must dismiss those French authorities, with the observation, that, in these states, the principle, that all the obligations resulting from a bill of exchange, are governed by the laws of the place, at which it is payable, is inadmissible.   The validity, and to some purpose, the construction of the contract of the drawer, and of each endorser, must be governed by the law of the place of drawing, and endorsing; but, as each of these in effect undertakes that the drawee shall accept and pay the bill, according to its tenor, in ascertaining the obligations of the drawer and several endorsers recourse is necessarily had to the law of the place in which the bill is payable, to discover whether the holder has exercised due diligence, and what will be a fulfilment on the part of the drawee of the undertaking of the drawer and endorser, in respect to the acts to be done by him: if it appears that the undertakings of the drawer and endorser have not been fulfilled by the drawee, a resort must be had to the laws of the places of drawing and endorsing to determine what notice the holder must give, of the dishonor of the bill, and the amount of the damages to be paid by the drawer and several endorsers.   In the case of a bill drawn in New. Orleans on Philadelphia, the Supreme Court of New York,

in Hicks v. Brown, 12 Johnson, 143, said "the drawer became con-
ditionally liable for the payment, and the condition was his receiving
due notice of the dishonor of the bill, and this notice was to be given
in New Orleans; the circumstance of the bill being drawn upon a
person in another state, makes no difference.

A like decision took place in Pennsylvania, in the case of a bill
drawn in South Carolina. Hazzlehurst v. Kean, 4 Yates 19.

In Slocum v. Pomroy the Supreme Court of the United States, held
that the endorser was liable to damages, according to the law of
Virginia, having endorsed the bill in Alexandria. Chief Justice
Marshall, who delivered the opinion of the court, said: "Although
the drawer was not liable to the damages of Virginia, the endorser
is. An endorsement is not simply the transfer of the paper; but a
new and substantial contract." 6 Cranch, 221.

These decisions support the proposition of the appellee's counsel
much more strongly than the principle he invokes from Merlin;
because they show that the drawer and endorsers are bound according to the law of the place where they bound themselves respectively to pay—their undertaking is not to pay at the place where the
bill is payable, but at the place in which they contract, provided due
diligence be exercised on the dishonor of the bill: and a decision,
that they are bound according to the law of the place in which the
bill is payable, would violate the principle invoked, by the law contraxisse, under which the party is bound according to the law of the
place, ubi ut solveret se obligavit.

IV. The laws interrogavi and item non opportet, have been
stated at full length and require no observation.

V. The Partida, 3, 2, 32, to which Gregorio Lopez has annexed
the note cited by the appellee's counsel, treats of the jurisdiction of
courts, ante quien deve el demandador hacer su demanda para
responder al demandado; and Gregorio concludes that the judge of
the place, in which the defendant bound himself to pay, has jurisdiction, and not the one of the place in which the contract was made.

VI. The passage, cited from Voët, will be examined at the close of
the opinion.

We are now to attend to the British and American authorities.
The first is the case of Robinson v. Bland, 2 Burrows, 1077.

This was an action on a bill of exchange, drawn in France on
London, for money lost at a gaming table—there were other counts.
Lord Mansfield premised his opinion, by the observation that the
facts scarce left room for any question; the laws of France and England being the same. He then stated that there were three reasons,
why the plaintiff should not recover, on the bill.

The first was that the parties had a view to the law of England.
The law of the place can never be the rule, where the transaction is
entered into, with an express view to the laws of another country, as
to the rule by which it is governed. He referred to Huberus and
Voët. In every disposition in contracts, where the subject-matter

relates locally to England, the law of England must govern and be intended to govern.

Mr. Justice Denison thought that, as the plaintiff had appealed to the laws of England, his case was to be determined by them.

Mr. Justice Wilmot said the case came out to be no case at all; no point at all; no law at all.

Finally, the plaintiff recovered on a money count.

As the court was not called upon to determine, whether a contract valid at the place in which it was entered into, but otherwise at the place of payment, was void; we think that what fell from Lord Mansfield must be considered as an *obiter dictum*, on a question he was not called upon to solve.

It is true, this dictum fully supports the appellee's counsel's proposition, and comes from one of the most able judges that ever sat in a British court, and as such is entitled to much respect, but to no greater weight, than it will have after a consideration of the authorities on which it rests.

The case in 17 Johnson, 519, is a statement of the opinion of the Court of Chancery of England, which decided that a bond executed in England and made payable in Ireland, carried Irish interest where none was stipulated. Pre. Ch. 128.

This case appears to support Huberus's opinion, that the *lex loci solutionis* is to be referred to, when the parties have not expressed their intentions, *cum non apparet quid actum est*, and the distinction, that will be taken by-and-by, places the interest *ex mora* under the control of the law *contraxisse*.

In the case of Van Schaick v. Edwards, 2 Johnson's Cases, 255, a resident of Massachusetts, owning lands in New York, entered into a contract, in the former state, with an inhabitant of the latter, for the sale of the lands on a credit, and took a bond, with a rate of interest exceeding that of Massachusetts, but less than that of New York, and gave his own bond for a conveyance, on receipt of the money; the suit was on the vendor's bond, and on the question whether the bond was usurious, and whether the laws of Massachusetts were to govern, the court was divided. So, the case throws no light upon the question under consideration.

Two decisions of this court have lastly been invoked: that in Whiston *et al. v.* Stodder *et al.*, Syndics, 8 *Martin*, 95, and that in Vidat *v.* Thompson, 11 *Ibid.* 23.

In the first, we held that on a sale completed in England, where the vendor has no privilege on the thing sold, he acquires none on its being brought here; and we cited *Casaregis disc.* 179, where it is holden, that contracts are made in the country, and subject to its laws, where the final assent may have been given, viz: that of a merchant who receives and executes the order of his correspondent.

In the case of Vidal *v.* Thompson and that of Morris *v.* Eves, 11 *Martin*, we recognised principles which, if correct, must determine this case in favor of the appellant, viz:

[Depau v. Humphreys.]

1. An instrument, as to its form and the formalities, attending its execution, must be subject to the laws of the place were it is made; but

2. The law and usages of the place where the obligation, of whioh it is evidence, is to be fulfilled, must regulate the performance.

3. In Morris v. Eves, we held that a contract, made in a foreign country, is governed by its laws, in every thing which relates to the mode of construing it, the meaning to be attached to the expressions by which the parties may have engaged themselves and the nature and validity of the engagement.

If these principles be correct, there must be two *loci contractûs*, to be considered in law, in a contract which is to be performed in a different place than that in which it is entered into; *locus celebrati contractus—locus solutionis;* in many an instrument more than two places as *loci contractûs* are to be considered. The holder of a protested bill of exchange has his remedy against the acceptor; according to the laws of the place on which the bill is drawn; against the drawer according to the law of the place in which the bill was drawn; and when there are several endorsers, he may have his remedy against each of them, according to the law of the place where he endorsed. Reason points out that, in every act, the place in which it is to take place, is to be considered in ascertaining its validity and effect.

. *Locus contractûs dicitur duobus modis: primo ubi contractus, seu conventio vel obligatio perficitur; secundo, ubi solutio vel deliberatio destinatur. Pres. Everard, cons. 78.*

The distinction, as to the parts of a contract which are to be governed by the law of the place in which it was entered into, and those which are to be governed by the laws of the place in which the payment was intended, is well marked.

. In the first class, is first included whatever relates to the form and perfection of the contract, and all the ceremonies and formalities attending it.

In scriptura instrumenti, in ceremoniis et solemnitatibus, et generaliter in omnibus quæ ad formam et perfectionem contractus pertinent, spectanda est consuetudo regionis ubi fit negotium.— Debet enim servari statutum loci contractûs, quoad hæc quæ oriuntur secundum naturam ipsius contractus. Alex. cons. 37. It is incontrovertible that in this passage Alexander speaks of the *locus contractûs,* as the place *ubi fit negotium.*

Generaliter, in omnibus quæ ad formam contractus, ejusque perfectionem pertinent, spectanda est consuetudo regionis ubi fit negotiatio; quia consuetudo influit in contractus et videtur ad eos respicere et voluntatem suam eis commodare. Christineus.— Modo sic est. Quoad perfectionem contractus seu solemnitatem, adesse seu substantiam ejus requisitam, semper inspicitur statutum seu consuetudo loci celebrati contractus. Pres. Everard, cons. 78. As this writer says that the law *loci celebrati contractûs* is always attended to, we must understand him as repelling the idea, that there is any exception, as to cases in which the payment is to be made at a different place, than that in which the contract is entered into.   The *locus celebrati contractûs* is here clearly put into contradistinction with the *locus solutionis.*

In the same class, are next to be placed all matters resulting from the nature of the contract, or immediately therefrom.

Inspicimus locum contractûs, in his quæ veniunt ex natura contractus.   Burtolus ad. l. 1 ff. de usuris.

In concernentibus contractum et emergentibus tempore contractus, says *Dumoulin, spectatur locus in quo contrahitur.*

Si lis oritur ex naturu et tempore contractûs, consideratur statutum loci.   Srick. de jure in alieno territorio exercente.

Aut quæris de his quæ oriuntur secundum formam ipsius contractus,aut de his quæ oriuntur expost facto,propter negligentiam vel moram; primo casu inspicitur locus contractûs, et intelligo locus contractûs, ubi celebratur, non ubi collata est solutio.   Bartolus, ad. l. cunctos populos, Code de sum. Tr. no. 15 and 16.—Here Bartolus emphatically calls the *locus celebrati contractûs,* the *locus contractûs* in contradistinction of the *locus destinatæ solutionis.*

As to what concerns the performance of the obligation—the payment of the sum, or the delivery of the thing, which is the object of the contract, the presentation for acceptance and payment of a bill of exchange; the acceptance, days of grace, protest, weight, measures, damages arising from negligence or delay, the *locus destinatæ solutionis* is to be considered.

Sed ubi agitur de consuetudine solvendi, vel de his quæ veniunt implendi, diu ex post contractum et in alieno loco impletione destinato, tunc inspicitur locus destinatæ solutionis, Everard, cons. 78.   It is in this particular that the law *contraxisse* is particularly and exclusively applicable; because to use its expressions, every one is understood to have contracted in that place, (viz: with a view to that place,) in which he bound himself to pay.   *Contraxisse unus quisque in co loco, intelligitur, ubi ut solveret se obligavit;* there, according to the second law invoked by the appellee's counsel, he is suable, because it is the place *ubi contraxisse,* and as to him *contractum autem non utique eo loco intelligitur quo negotium gestum sit, sed quo solvenda est pecunia.*   But as to the party, with whom he who binds himself to pay money, as to the obligation of the vendor, who has stipulated for payment in a place different from that in which the sale takes place and the thing is to be delivered, the contract as to the period at which the property of the thing sold, passes to the vendee; the mode of delivery, the obligations of warranty, the manner of his being put *in mora,* the liability to the redhibitory action, or that *quanti minoris,* the law of the place, in which the vendee bound himself to pay, affords no legitimate rule of decision; for the vendor did not bind himself to perform any act there,

35*

[Depau v. Humphreys.]

that is not the place *ubi ut solveret se obligavit.* As to him, that place is the one in which he bound himself to deliver the thing sold and to warrant it: and we are to resort to the law of this last place, to ascertain whether his, the vendor's, obligations were duly performed, and to assess the damages due to the vendee, if they were not; because, as to the vendor, that place is, in the language of Everard, *locus ubi deliberatio destinatur.*

Certainly, in a bilateral or synallagmatic contract, where the obligations of the parties are to be performed in different places, in which different laws and usages prevail, the laws and usages of neither can offer a legitimate rule of decision, for all the obligations of the contract. Each party must perform his according to the law of the place, *ubi ut solveret se obligavit*—and in case he fail, he must yield to his adversary, damages equal in value to that of the thing he bound himself to deliver, at the place *ubi solutio* or *deliberatio destinatur.*

In obligations to pay money, the measure of damages is interest, according to the legal rate. The Roman law considers interest, rather as damages to be allowed for the delay of payment, than as a profit contemplated at the time of the contract. *Usuræ non propter lucrum petentium; sed propter moram solventium, infliguntur. ff.* 22, 1, 17, and 3: As such they are regulated by the law of the *locus destinatæ solutionis.*

But, in a loan of money, nothing is more common, in countries where the parties are not restrained by law to one rate of interest, to stipulate a particular one, (by their convention,) within the scope which the law allows, and this interest is called conventional by contradistinction from the legal interest *ex mora.*

In such a case, as the object of the conventional interest is to afford to the lender a compensation for the profit he foregoes, in yielding the use of his money to the borrower, it should seem, that the circumstance, of the place of payment differing from that in which the lender parts with his money, ought to have no influence, in the fixation of the rate of interest.

Accordingly we find it laid down that *usurarum modus constituendus est, in regione in qua contrahitur; et cum, redditus duodenarius, in Gallia stipulatus, in controversia incidisset, patrocinante me justicatum est in curia Flandriæ, valere pactum, nec obesse quod in Flandria, ubi redditus constitutus licet hypotecæ impositus proponeretur, usuras semisse graviores stipulari non liceat. Sed hoc intellige de usuris in stipulationem deductis, sed non de iis quæ ex mora debentur; in quibus ad locum solutionis respicere opportet. Burgundus, Tract. n.* 4, and also, *n.* 27, 28 and 29.

Quand il s'agit de decider, si des conventions faites du sujet des droits qui naissent ex natura et tempore contractûs, *sont legitimes ou non, il faut suivre la loi du lieu ou se passe le contrat. Boullinois, Ob. 46.*

Si s'agit de determiner la légitimité du taux des rentes, et que dans le lieu de la passation du contrat, le taux soit different de celui qui se paye dans le lieu du domicile du debiteur, ou dans celui du creancier; soit encore dans les lieux ou les biens hypothèques sont situes; le taux sera jugé tres légitime, s'il est conforme a la loi du lieu ou le contrat se passe. Ibid.

Let it be noticed, that although Boullinois states a case, in which no place is stipulated for, *nominatim*, he states it in such a manner as to include every place of payment which the law recognises, where none is actually mentioned; for then, he informs us, the law requires payment at the domicil of one of the parties, or on the premises. If there be no day of payment stated, the creditor may expect payment, at his domicil, otherwise he must seek it at that of the debtor, on whom a demand is to be made.

Bartolus and Boullinois consider, in the above cases, the interest paid for money in the contract of *constitution de rente*, or annuity. The rente or annuity, *redditus* cannot exceed the legal rate of interest, and they both teach that this rate must be according to the *lex loci celebrati contractûs*, in opposition to the *lex loci solutionis*.

The principle that a contract, valid in the *locus celebrati contractûs*, is void, if contrary to the law *loci solutionis*, must establish the converse of the proposition, *i. e.*, that a contract void, according to the former, is valid, if it be so according to the latter.

If this be the case, of what use is it for any legislature to pass a law for the protection of the weak and necessitous?

In some countries, the age of majority is fixed at twenty-five, in others at one-and-twenty. The minor, who cannot bind himself at home, may do so, if he engages to pay in another country.

Elsewhere, as till very lately here, contracts of suretyship are interdicted to females—they may be deprived of the protection of the laws of their country, if they be prevailed on to engage to pay in another.

A note made at Natchez, which would be null and void, as tainted with usury, according to the laws of the state of Mississippi, if payable there or at Monticello, at the distance of several hundred miles, would be perfectly valid, if made payable at Vidalia, across the river.

Courts of justice must take care that the law be not evaded. In the case of Stapleton v. Conway, 1 Vesey, 428, 3 Atkins, 727, Lord Hardwicke held that, if a contract was made in England for the mortgage of a plantation in the West Indies, and there be a covenant in the mortgage for the payment of eight per cent. interest, it would be a method to evade the statute of usury, and such a contract would be as much against the statute as any other contract.

The case of Dewar v. Span, 3 Term Reports, 425, is to the same effect. A bond was given in England, upon the purchase of an estate in the West Indies, with the reservation of interest at six per cent., and notwithstanding it was contended, in argument, that, although the bond was executed in England, it arose on a contract for the purchase of an estate in the West Indies, yet the court unanimously held the bond to be usurious, as if the attempt could succeed, it would sap the foundation of the statute of usury.

·In the same manner, if parties could free themselves from the effect of the laws of their country, by stipulating for payment elsewhere, they would sap the foundation of every law enacted. for the weak and necessitous.

The authority of the passage from Voët remains to be examined. This author says: *Si alio in loco graviarum usurarum stipulatio permissa, in alio vetita sit, lex loci ubi contractus celebratus est spectanda videtur, an moderatæ, an vero modum excedentes, usuræ per conventionem stipulatæ sint.*

" If in a place, the stipulation of higher interest be permitted, in another forbidden, the law of the place, in which the contract was celebrated, is to be resorted to, in order to ascertain whether the lesser or the greater rate of interest be stipulated by the contract."

Thus far Voët teaches what we have seen Alexander, Bartolus, Burgundus, Everard, Strickius and Boullinois teach, and the contrary of which no other commentator positively asserts, what, in our opinion, every sound principle of law dictates.

But the appellee's counsel urges that Voët unsays, in the succeeding paragraph, what he appears to have so emphatically expressed.

The words of the second paragraph are *Dummodo meminerimus illum proprie locum contractus, in jure non intelligi, in quo negotium gestum est, sed in quo pecuniam ut solveret se obligavit.*

In the argument, which the appellee's counsel draws, in this respect, he is fully supported, by what is said *arguendo* by Lord Mansfield, in Robinson *v.* Bland, and in some degree, by Judge Kent, in the same manner, in the case of Van Shaick *v.* Edwards, already cited. In endeavoring to ascertain the character of the rate of interest, stipulated in a note given in Massachusetts, Judge Kent says: " had the money, for instance, in this case, been made payable at Albany, or elsewhere in this state, (New York,) then perhaps the decision in Robinson *v.* Bland, would have applied."

If, in the second paragraph, Voët meant to introduce an exception, to the rule laid down in the first; if he meant to teach that the legality of a rate of conventional interest, arising not *ex mora* but *tempore contractûs* is exclusively to be tested by the law *loci solutionis*, even when it is different from the law *loci celebrati contractus:* then, we can not consider him as affording to us a legitimate rule of decision in the present case, because the weight of his authority is borne down by that of a crowd of the most respectable commentators of the law he cites.

Perhaps, he must be understood, in the second paragraph, to convey to the student a warning, that, by what he teaches in the first, he must not be understood to impugn the proposition, that, in a great degree, the law *loci solutionis,* influences the obligation of the party, who bound himself *ut solveret pecuniam.*

Upon the whole, we must conclude, as we did in Morris *v.* Eves and Vidal *v.* Thompson, that contracts are governed by the law of the country in which they were made, in every thing which relates to the mode of construing them, the meaning to be attached to the expressions by which the parties bound themselves, and the nature and validity of the engagement.

But that, wherever the obligation be contracted, the performance must be according to the law of the place, where it is to take place.

In other words, that in a note executed here, on a loan of money made here, the creditor may stipulate for the legal rate of conventional interest authorised by our law, although such a rate be disallowed in the place, at which payment is to be made.

Consequently, the judge of probates erred in considering Clague & Oldham's note as usurious.

It is, therefore, ordered, adjudged and decreed, that the judgment of the court of probates be annulled, avoided and reversed; and this court proceeding to give such a judgment as in their opinion ought to have been given in the lower court, it is ordered, adjudged and decreed, that the plaintiff be recognised and admitted as a creditor of W. Kenner, deceased, for the sum of seventeen thousand seven hundred and ninety-two dollars, ninety-seven cents, and the sum of four thousand seven hundred and eight dollars for interest up to this day, together with interest at ten per cent. on five thousand six hundred and ninety-seven dollars, the balance due on the note, from this date, until paid; and on the balance of the judgment, viz: twelve thousand and ninety-five dollars ninety-seven cents, at five per cent. till paid, and costs in both courts.

Livermore, for the plaintiff.

Mazureau and *Hennen,* for the defendant.

Kenner *et al. v.* Their Creditors.   VIII, N. S. 36.

If on a comparison of the day of acceptance, the day designated for payment, and the
tenor of the bill, it appears the days of grace were included with those of sight, between the day of acceptance and that designated for payment, that day is the peremptory
one of payment, and protest on it is legal.

If the acceptance be not dated, parol evidence is admissible to show on what day it was
made.*

PARISH Court of New Orleans.

MARTIN, J., delivered the opinion of the court.

The president, directors and company of the Bank of the United
States and others, complain of the judgment of the parish which
denies them, respectively, a place on the tableau of distribution,
among the creditors of the insolvents, as holders of protested bills of
the latter.

Their pretensions were opposed as those of Hicks, Lawrence &
Co., whose case was determined last week, on the grounds that the
acceptances were not according to the tenor of the bills and the protests were made too soon. 7 *N. S.* 540.

A material difference, and the only one, between these cases and
the former, is that, in this the acceptance had a date, in those, the
acceptances were without any.

But the appellants' counsel urge, that they proved, by witnesses,
in each case, the day of acceptance, and from a comparison of the
tenor of the bill, the date of the acceptance, and the day designated
for payment, it clearly appears that both the sixty days of sight,
and the three days of grace, were included in the period between

---

* While on the subject of bills of exchange, it may seem not impertinent to remind
the student, that under the unsuspected cover of " an act to repeal the act to authorise a-
special jury in certain cases, and for other purposes," approved March 27, 1823, and to
be found in 1 Moreau's Digest, 624, under the head of juries without the slightest hint
of so important an innovation in the index, (a kind of defect most faithfully imitated
from 1812, in the index to each successive volume of acts of assembly issued by the state
printer, to such a degree, that from tho index no one can surmise one half of the changes
made in the acts of that year,) there lurks the following clause: " the drawer of a note,
bill of exchange or other negotiable paper, shall never in any case whatsoever be admitted
as a witness in any civil cause or suit brought by the holder of any such note, order, bill
of exchange or other negotiable paper, against any of the endorsers of said notes, order,
bill of exchange or other negotiable paper, for the recovery of the capital and legal interest of the said notes, order, bills of exchange or other negotiable paper."

the day expressly designated as that of payment, and the conclusion is, that the latter is the peremptory day of payment, and days of grace are not to be added thereto.

They say there is no rule of law, that prohibits the drawer or acceptor, from adding the days of grace to those of sight, and including the whole between the day of acceptance and that which is designated for payment. No such rule has been shown by the counsel of the appellees, who has rested all his objections on the general principle, according to which, days of grace are allowed on all acceptances, according to the tenor of the bill. Giving this principle its full effect, it does not invalidate an acceptance, in which the days of grace have been included; because, in such cases, the days of grace, which the law adds to those of sight, are in fact added; because the day designated for payment, is the last of the days of grace, which the law would add, if the acceptance was absolute, by the mere signature of the acceptor and date under the word accepted.

It can not ever be illegal for the parties to express in their contracts the obligations, which the law would imply, if they were not expressed—where certain consequences legally result from an engagement of a particular kind, those, who enter into it, may state them at full length; consequently, when the law has provided that days of grace shall be superadded to those of sight, and the bill shall not be payable before the expiration of the days of grace, it follows that a bill at sixty days sight, being payable on the sixty-third day after the acceptance, the acceptor and holder may well agree that the former shall pay it on that day—because that is what the law would imply, had not the parties expressed it. In such a case, the days of grace, being evidently included, the acceptance is perfectly legal; the acceptor can not require that others be superadded.

We are unable to find, in such an acceptance, any ground, on which the drawers or endorsers might contend they were discharged. The holder has fully complied with the engagement he took towards them, of procuring such an acceptance, as would bind the drawee to pay the bill, according to its tenor, on the sixty-third day after presentation. The acceptance has the same force and obligation—whether made in the most common way, by the word "accepted" with a date—the words accepted to pay, at the expiration of sixty days— at the expiration of the days of sight—at the expiration of sixty-three days, or of the days of sight and those of grace.

The difficulty, if there be any, consists in ascertaining the intention of the parties.—When that is done, the legal consequence necessarily follows.

The counsel for the appellees, has, however, strenuously contended that parol evidence of the date of the acceptance was inadmissible, and they claim the benefit of a bill of exceptions, which they took to the opinion of the parish court, by which it was admitted. The authorities they rely on are, Philips on Evidence, 423, chap. 10, sect. 2; 8 Johns. 298; Norris's Peake, 119; 3 Starkie on Evidence, 995, 999; 2 *Ibid.* 579; Cowen, 750; Johns. 146; 2

Bosanquet & Puller, 509; 3 Campbell, 56; 1 Taunt. 115, 347; Chitty Com. Law, 142; 1 Chitty on Contracts, 22; 1 Mass. Rep. 27; 12 *Ibid.* 92; 8 Taunt. 98; 8 Eng. Com. Law Reps. 468.

One of the writers, cited by the appellee's counsel, Starkie, lays it down as a general principle that "evidence is admissible, that a deed was executed or a bill of exchange made at a time different from the date."

The cases, stated by Starkie, are Hall *v.* Casenave, 477, 3 Levins, 348; Giles *v.* Meeks, Addison, 384; Gress *et al. v.* Odenhemer, 4 Yates, 218; Fox's Lessee *v.* Palmer *et al.*, 2 Dallas, 214. But on examination we find that they support the position, in regard to deeds only. 3 Starkie, 46.

The same author also lays it down, that parol evidence may be received, that a party, in whose name a contract has been made for goods, was but the agent of another. *Ibid.*

In the case of Krumbhaar *v.* Ludeling, 3 *Martin*, 640, their counsel held that parol evidence was admissible, to show that the drawer of a bill, drew it as agent.

The Supreme Court of the United States has held that parol evidence was admissible, that a check (on the face of which it was doubtful whether the person, who drew it, acted in his own right or as cashier of the bank,) was drawn on account of the bank. 5 Wheaton, 286.

And in a very recent case, the Bank of the Metropolis *v.* Brent's Executors, 1 Peters, 89, the same court held that parol evidence was admissible of an agreement relative to the place, where payment of the note was to be demanded. In that case, it was contended the testimony ought not to be admitted, because it was an attempt to vary, by parol proof, a written agreement. Chief Justice Marshall, who delivered the opinion of the court, said: "this is not an attempt to vary a written agreement. The place of demand is not expressed on the face of the note, and the necessity of a demand on the person, where the parties are silent, is an inference of law, which is drawn only when they are silent. A parol agreement puts an end to this inference, and dispenses with a personal demand. The parties consent to a demand, at a stipulated place, instead of a demand on the person or maker, and this does not alter the instrument, so far as it goes, but supplies extrinsic circumstances, which the parties are at liberty to supply."

From this authority it follows, that the legal implication, resulting from an instrument, may be rebutted by parol evidence of an agreement to the contrary.

The legal meaning of an instrument may be explained by evidence of the time and place of its execution.

A contract of endorsement is, at present, ordinarily entered into by the mere signature of the party, on the back of the bill. Should the endorser be sued, the measure of damages must be sought, in the laws of the place in which he contracted; and this can only be shown by parol.

On a note, payable on a given day, the number of days of grace and the rate of interest must be sought in the law of the place, in which it is subscribed or made payable; if the place is not stated on the face of the note, parol evidence is certainly admissible.

Parol proof, not only of the place, but of the time an agreement was entered into, is sometimes important. In such a case, says Starkie (*loco citato*), " even in the case of records, which are conclusive, as far as regards their substance, averments and proofs may be received to contradict them, as to time and place."

On a bill or note, payable within a limited time after date, when there is no date, the time is to be computed, from the day it issued.—Bailey on Bills, 154.

Where an award, which directed an act to be done, within a certain number of days, had no date, the court held the time was to be computed from the day of delivery.

In both these cases, the time when the bill issued, and the award was delivered, was necessarily to be proved by parol evidence.

If it be argued that in the acceptances, under consideration, the day of payment was written, and therefore there was no necessity to resort to parol proof to ascertain it—the answer is, that a circumstance occurred from which it necessarily results, that the day designated was the peremptory day of payment, and not that from which the days of grace were to be reckoned; a circumstance which destroyed the implied right, of the acceptor to further delay, in the same manner, as the parol agreement, in the case of the Bank of the Metropolis *v.* Brent's Executors, destroyed the implied obligation of the bank making a demand from the person of the maker.

The inclusion of the days of grace and the agreement that the demand should be made at a particular place, are both circumstances, proof of which, in the language of Judge Marshall, " does not alter the instrument, so far as it goes, but supplies extrinsic circumstances which the parties are at liberty to supply."

If it be objected that, in the case first cited, the evidence was received between the parties, and in that before the Supreme Court of the United States, the endorser was presumed to be a party to the agreement, this circumstance in our opinion, cannot vary the right to introduce the parol proof, in the cases now before us. The undertaking of the holder, with the drawer and endorser, is that the former will require the drawee to bind himself to pay the bill according to its tenor; whatever is evidence against the drawee, that he had done so, will be evidence between the holder and drawer and previous endorsers, that the drawee has undergone all the obligations of an acceptor—whether the evidence when received shows such an obligation, on the part of the acceptor, as will bind the drawer and endorser, goes to the effect of the proof and not to its admissibility.

We conclude that parol evidence of the time of acceptance was properly received.

On the opposition of Hicks, Lawrence & Co. we held that, when from the comparison of the tenor of the bill, the written date of the acceptance, and the day designated for payment, it clearly appeared that the period between the day of acceptance and that designated for payment, included both the days of sight and those of grace, we would conclude that the day designated, was the peremptory day of payment, and no additional days of grace were to be claimed or allowed.

That protest on that day was timely.

The appellants, however, have urged that, according to mercantile usage, in England, the day nominally designated for payment, in an acceptance without a date, is the peremptory day.

Fairweather, cashier of the Bank of Layland & Bullers, has deposed that an acceptance, without a date, to pay on a day expressly designated, is not usual, but is occasionally resorted to. It is usual in such cases to include the days of grace, and the day designated is the third of these. He had four bills accepted in this manner; one of them was discounted by the Bank of England; three of them passed through the hands of Bankers in London. By the usage and customs of merchants in England, such a bill is payable on the day designated.

Burrell has deposed that an acceptance without a date, to pay on a day expressly designated, is not customary, but when adopted, the day designated is usually the last of those of grace, and by the usage of merchants, payment must be demanded on that day.

Frodsham deposed that in such an acceptance the day designated is usually the sixty-third, the days of grace included. This form of acceptance is used by several houses.

Ford deposed he has used the same form for several years—without any objection being made till lately; in consequence of doubts in the United States. The day designated is usually the peremptory day, and the protest is made on it.

Hooth deposed he has always accepted in this manner, for sixteen years, without any objection being ever made. His acceptances have passed through several great houses. The usage has prevailed, ever since he is in business.

Tabor deposed he has been forty years in business as a banker, and has never known any objections to be made to this form of acceptance. It is not unfrequent: a vast number of bills thus accepted, have passed through his hands.

Duncan, one of the drawees, deposed the bills are accepted according to their tenor, and law—the days of grace are included. The form of acceptance is the usual one of the drawees.

Hortsman, Wilkins, Drouet and Wilson deposed the form is used by many houses.

The same facts are substantially deposed by several other witnesses introduced by the appellants.

The appellees introduced the following witnesses.

Hall deposed there is no general usage, as to protesting a bill at sixty days sight, accepted to be paid on a day designated, without the acceptance being dated. Very few houses use that form of acceptance. He considers it as altogether irregular, and would protest the bill on the day designated, and afterwards as a matter of precaution—three days after; particularly, if the acceptor urged he should have days of grace. He would object to receive such an acceptance, for want of a date. The house of A. Haywood & Sons have refused to receive, and have sent back bills thus accepted. Since objections have been made, several houses have adopted the form of acceptance with a date.

Henderson deposed that there is no common usage, regulating the protest of a bill, accepted on a designated day, without a date. The acceptance is irregular; he would protest three days after the designated day.

Jordan deposed the acceptance without a date would be irregular, and he would be at a loss about protesting, unless he could prevail on the acceptor to add a date. This sixty-third day after presentation is the day to protest for non-payment; but by no means not without regard to the form of acceptance; because the commercial usage of England requires a date to the acceptance.

Anderson deposed he never saw such an acceptance, and would not take it, because it is liable to many objections. If he was holder of a bill, thus accepted, he would protest on the day designated. The sixty-third day is the proper day for protesting, without regard to the form of acceptance; provided the acceptance be dated; the date is essential in common usage.

Binn deposed that, presuming the day designated was the sixty-third, he would protest on that day. The proper day of protest is the sixty-third after sight, but not without regard to the form of acceptance. He considers the acceptance imperfect, without a date.

Ireland deposed the acceptance would be irregular, and contrary to commercial usage; but if the bill have been accepted sixty-three days before the day designated, the protest should be on that day. The only proper day of protest is the sixty-third after presentation; unless by a special agreement, between the drawee and holder; but such an agreement would discharge the drawer and endorsers.

Luke deposed an acceptance, without a date, is not customary; but if the day designated was really the sixty-third from the acceptance, the protest should be on that day. Common usage requires a date.

Highfield deposed that, presuming the day designated was the sixty-third from the acceptance, he would protest on it. The date is necessary.

Orford deposed the acceptance is irregular. He would think the days of grace were included, and protest, on the day designated.

The result of the testimony offered by the appellants is that, according to commercial usage, a bill at sixty days, accepted to be paid on a designated day, without a date to the acceptance, is payable on that day, without the addition of any days of grace.

The same result is given by the examination of appellee's witnesses. From the nine whom they have produced five, Hall, Henderson, Binn, Highfield and Orford depose they would protest such bill on the day designated in the acceptance, without giving any days of grace—this is to say, that day is the peremptory one, or in other words, the bill is accepted, according to its tenor.

Two of them, Ireland and Luke, deposed that, if the day designated be actually the sixty-third day from the acceptance, then it is the peremptory day—then is the bill accepted according to its tenor.

One witness only, Henderson, thinks the day designated is that, from which those of grace are to be reckoned.

Jordan expresses no opinion.

We cannot resist the impression, left on our minds by the testimony, that, according to usage in England, the bills were accepted, and the acceptors took the engagement of paying them on the day designated in the acceptance, and that protest on that day was regular.

On principles, if we were without other testimony, than that which ascertains the day of acceptance, it would be impossible to distinguish the case of the appellants from that of Hicks, Lawrence & Co. Whether the day of acceptance be written by the acceptor, at the foot of the acceptance, admitted by all parties, or ascertained by legal evidence, if it clearly appears that both the days of sight and those of grace, have been computed and included between that of acceptance, and that designated as the day of payment, the legal consequence must follow. The designated day is peremptory; days of grace cannot be claimed.

Lastly, it has been urged, with great force, that such acceptances are bad, because they leave the day, on which the bill is to be presented for payment, in uncertainty—that the holder cannot know when to protest. Therefore such a mode of acceptance must be proscribed, as leading to confusion and injury to the parties.

The objection may be considered, in relation to those who were parties to the bill, at the period of acceptance, and those who became so after. The former can only object, when they are resorted to, that the bill was dishonored; that it was not duly protested: that they were not duly notified of the dishonor. Now, if the acceptor had a right to include the days of grace, in the period between the acceptance and the day designated, the bill was duly honored. As to the uncertainty, appearing on the face of the bill, no authority has been shown to induce a belief that the drawer, or previous endorsers may claim their discharge, because the day of payment, on the face of the bill is uncertain; id certum est quod certum reddi potest. If the objection could prevail, what would become of verbal acceptances, or parol promises to accept, anterior to the drawing? In such cases, the day of presentation must be established by parol evidence, as nothing, on the face of the bill, shows when it becomes payable.

As to those, who may receive the bill after such an acceptance, with such an ambiguity on its face, and negotiate it in this state, they have no cause of complaint. No one forced them to recive such a bill, and they took it with the risk, if any, of the uncertainty of the acceptance. *Volenti non fit injuria.*

We think the parish judge erred in erasing the names of the appellants from the tableau of distribution.

It is, therefore, ordered, adjudged and decreed, that the judgment of the parish court be annulled, avoided and reversed, and it is further ordered, adjudged and decreed that the appellants be restored, on the tableau, as creditors of the insolvents for the amount of their respective bills, damages and costs resulting from the protests; the appellees paying costs in both courts.

Livermore and *Smith*, for the plaintiffs.
Mazureau and *Hennen*, for the defendants.

Kenner *et al. v.* Their Creditors.   VIII, N. S. 54.

Martin, J., delivered the opinion of the court.

A rehearing has been prayed, by the appellees, opposing creditors of the claim of the Bank of the United States, on a judgment we delivered in this case a few weeks ago, on the ground that we erred:

1. In considering the bills, holden by the bank, as duly accepted and protested.

2. In omitting to notice the objection that the bank lost its recourse against the insolvents, in consequence of sundry arrangements and transactions with the acceptors.

The arguments, in the petition, present substantially nothing, that had not been offered, on the hearing, or in the brief, with which the appellees' counsel favored us, all which, in our opinion, was victoriously answered by the counsel for the bank. On this point, therefore, no rehearing could be granted.

Before we proceed to examine the second point, it is due to the parties, in favor of whom a rehearing was solicited, to notice two of the grounds on which the application was made. The errors, into which the counsel have fallen, appear to us very great; the facts are entirely misstated, and on matters too, on which it is strange the gentlemen could have been mistaken.

In the judgment, we said, " But the appellants' counsel urge, that they proved by witnesses, in each case, the day of acceptance, and

36*

from a comparison of the tenor of the bills, the day of acceptance, and that expressly designated for payment, it clearly appears that both the days of sight and those of grace were included in the period between the day of acceptance and the one expressly designated as that of payment."

On this, the petition observes: " This argument, as far as we recollect, was never made, and could not, with any degree of propriety, have been made, at the bar, for these plain reasons:

" 1. The appellants' counsel could not say, they had proved by witnesses, the day of acceptance; they had attempted, it is true, to prove it, by witnesses; but the attempt had been resisted by us, and the court below had refused to admit the evidence offered; therefore, nobody knew what the evidence was, nor what fact could be established; therefore nothing was proved by witnesses, and therefore the appellants could not say it was.

" 2. The only question before the court was, as to the admissibility of oral evidence to prove the date. Until the decision of this preliminary question, we could not, nor could any of the parties, nor could the court say the proof was made of the date of the acceptance."

There is on the record an agreement, signed by the counsel of both parties, by which the case is submitted " on the returns to the commissions taken to Liverpool and London . . . . but the said evidence is subject to all objections, and its admissibility is expressly reserved, as well as the right to object to the admissibility of any parol evidence on the subject of these bills of exchange. On the appeal, the records may be made up of the tableau and oppositions only. The evidence, under the commissions, may be taken up in original, subject to the above exceptions."

This agreement, far from showing the evidence was rejected, in consequence of a legal exception, shows that it was admitted, subject to such exceptions.

The difference between the two modes of bringing a case before the court, is familiar to the youngest member of the bar, and their effect is quite dissimilar. In many cases, perhaps in the greatest number, parties raise the question on the admissibility of the evidence, in the lower court; and if illegal, it is rejected. This is the most regular mode; in such a case the evidence does not appear on the record, and can not be noticed by the upper court.—But this course has often the effect of retarding a final decision; for, when the opinion of the Supreme Court differs from that of the judge *a quo*, the case must be remanded to let in the proof. To avoid this, parties, who are anxious for a decision of the merits, admit the evidence, subject to all legal objections, as was done here.

It has been uniformly understood, and never till now doubted, that when the evidence comes up in this manner, this court, if it judges the evidence legal, proceeds to inquire into its effect. The consent of the parties brings the evidence before us, in the same manner, as if it had been admitted below by the judge, notwithstanding an objection to its introduction.

[Kenner *et al. v.* Their Creditors.]

The counsel of the appellants, therefore, with great propriety urged, in the argument, first, the legality of the proof, then assuming it to be admissible, contended that it established the dates of the acceptances. This court, consequently did not err in stating that, " the counsel urged that they had proved, by witnesses, in each case, the day of acceptance."

It is not the practice in this court, when a case comes before it, as this did, for the counsel first to discuss the legality of the proof, and after obtaining a favorable decision, to argue on the effect of the proof. The whole case is submitted at once, and all the points it presents are made. If the court deem the evidence illegal, it rejects it; otherwise it acts on it, and the case is decided on its merits. What is usual in all other cases, what is right in every case similarly circumstanced, was done in this, and nothing authorised the assertion that the proof of the day of acceptance was not before this tribunal; that it was not commented on, and duly and properly taken into consideration, in our judgment.

The next point, on which we deem it material to undeceive the parties, is the decision in the case of the claim of Hicks, Lawrence & Co. The counsel of the present, who were those of the then, appellees, now state the judgment of the parish court, on that claim, was not appealed from, the case was not before us, and how we could act on it, the counsel profess they do not know. Had the gentlemen, who subscribed the petition for a rehearing, bestowed a moment's consideration on their own conduct, during the hearing of the case of Hicks, Lawrence & Co. and afterwards, they would have found an easy and immediate relief from the surprise, which our pronouncing judgment on it, excited. That judgment was rendered, because the case was solemnly argued, both orally and in writing by them, and orally by the opposite counsel, as if a petition of appeal had actually been filed; the testimony, taken in relation to the very bill on which the claim was founded, had been brought up, made a part of our record, and as such, was read, commented on, and submitted to us. Not a suggestion was made, during the argument or after, that the case was not regularly before us.

By the agreement of parties, the record, on appeal, was to be made of the tableau and opposition only; the evidence was to be taken up in the original. We were, therefore disabled from detecting the informality suggested, if it exists. Whether the case was legally before us or not—whether a petition of appeal, bond, citation, &c. might not be dispensed with by consent, or the want of these or any of them, under all the circumstances of the case, cured by appearance, argument and trial on the merits—whether the judgment may be set aside or its execution resisted, on an exception—whether the conduct of the counsel requires our interference or not; it suffices that we may be resorted to for relief, to render any positive expression of our opinion improper. In the absence of the party, in whose favor that judgment was rendered, its validity can not be the subject of our inquiry.

[Kenner *et al. v.* Their Creditors.]

Had we committed an error, as is suggested, it would have been óne, into which we should have been led by implicit confidence in the character and the truth of gentlemen of high standing at the bar; a confidence, which though this court may be compelled to abandon —it will painfully and unwillingly relinquish. It could not have occurred to us, that persons, of the description just stated, would argue, both orally and in writing, the merits of a case, in which no appeal had been taken, unless under a strong obligation, subsequently to supply or waive any defect, in the manner of bringing up the case. Such was the reliance, placed by us in the ability and industry of those gentlemen, that we did not deem it necessary to inquire whether a petition of appeal was formally placed on the record, and least of all, could we have supposed, that the persons, who argued a cause, as pending before us, after they found our judgment unfavorable, would assert we had acted on a case not before us.

Upon the whole, we must consider the statement, in the petition, for a rehearing as to the impropriety of our regarding the judgment on the claim of Hicks, Lawrence & Co. to be entirely gratuitous; the authority of that decision must be the same, on the legal question, whether there was a petition of appeal or not. It is the opinion of the highest tribunal in the state, after hearing the parties, and its force and truth can not be strengthened, or weakened, by any informality in bringing the appeal before us.

II. Our opinion is, that our attention was not drawn, during the hearing, to the discharge of the insolvents, on account of an arrangement or transaction between the bank and the acceptors. The petition asserts that it was—and that we desired the counsel of the appellees to postpone any observation, on that head, till after our decision on the legality of the acceptances and protests. On this assertion, notwithstanding neither of us has any recollection on the subject, we concluded that we said so, or were misunderstood. We therefore granted the rehearing on this second point.

It has been contended that the case ought to be remanded, because the parish judge did not speak in his judgment of the objection to the claim of the bank, resulting from this real or illegal discharge.

It is obvious that this is not a sufficient cause to authorise us to refuse to act, on the whole case. The court below decides a cause, on whatever point it deems material: our duty is to revise its judgment, not the grounds on which it is rendered. Its decision on the merits, requires, nay compels us, to examine the case, on all the grounds which it presents, if that be necessary to a rightful determination of the case; for the error of the judge *a quo*, for which relief is sought at our hands, may be his failure to take into consideration; an objection, on which his judgment is silent. Under the principle contended for, there might be as many appeals, as points in a cause, if he acted on one only at a time, and decided erroneously. It has been the uniform practice of this tribunal, as it is the real intent of the statute, that the decision of the first judge on the merits, brings up the whole case. The contrary doctrine would be productive of intolerable expenses and delay.

The first piece of evidence, from which the loss of the recourse of the bank, on the insolvents, is inferred, is an agreement entered into on the 16th of November, 1825, by Brown, as agent of the bank, with the acceptors, of which he promised to procure the ratification by the bank, within a given period.

Without admitting, either that this agreement could have any effect, without the concurrence of other parties, or that, if binding on the bank, the discharge of the insolvents would follow, its counsel has contended that it is not bound, because the agreement was entered into without its authority, was never expressly or impliedly ratified, and every act of the bank, after the agreement came to its knowledge, manifested its unwillingness to be bound by it.

This throws on the appellees the burden of proving Brown's authority. The evidence of this authority, resulting from his possession of the bills, for the bank, might establish his authority to receive payment, but not that of compromising its rights.

There is no proof of any communication from Brown to the bank, nor any knowledge brought home to that institution; no implied ratification can be presumed.

No express one, is alleged.

It therefore follows that the bank is not bound by this agreement and its recourse against the insolvents is not thereby impaired.

The next piece of evidence, from which the loss of the recourse is inferred, is Brown's receipt, as attorney of the bank, for dividends of the estate of the acceptors. It is unneccessary to inquire whether the receipt had the pretended effect—for, if it had, the bank is not bound thereby, as the money was received, under a power, from which the authority of doing any act, affecting the recourse, was expressly accepted.

Finally, it has been urged, the cause should be remanded, because it must be presumed, Brown informed the bank of the agreement, he had entered into in their behalf, previous to the receipt of the power, and if the cause was again before the tribunal of the first instance, evidence could be given to that effect. This demand is addressed to the discretion of the court. The statute authorises us to remand a cause, whenever justice, in our opinion, requires it. But the necessity of such a step must be apparent. We cannot deprive a party from rights acquired in due course of law, to enable his adversary to procure proof, which, if it exist, he ought to have sought before; unless we have the strongest reasons to believe the proof exists. Now, in this case, the presumption is the other way; or rather the presumptions are equally balanced. If we presume that Brown communicated to the bank the engagement he had taken, previous to the receipt of their power of attorney, we must also presume they communicated their dissent. We have in evidence that the power contained a clause, by which they restricted him from doing any act that might impair

[Kenner *et al. v.* Their Creditors.]

their rights on the insolvents. We cannot believe that, after marking out such a course of conduct, they would soon after, have assented to a transaction, destroying those rights.

The receipt by Brown, of seven shillings in the pound, on the claim of the bank, as a dividend from the estate of the acceptors, reduces the sum they are entitled to, accordingly.

It is, therefore, ordered, adjudged and decreed, that our former judgment, so far it concerns the Bank of the United States, be amended; that the judgment of the parish court against them remain annulled, avoided and reversed, and the opposition of the appellees sustained, so far as it relates to a distribution of the claim of the bank, as now on the tableau, that a deduction of seven shillings sterling in the pound, received by its agent, be made thereon, and the claim of the bank placed on the tableau for the balance, without prejudice to the right of the appellees, on the opposition to the appellants' claim for damages, now pending in the parish court. The appellees paying the costs of the appeal, the appellees those before.

Hennen and *Mazureau,* for the plaintiffs.
Livermore and *Morse,* for the Bank of the United States.

Percy *et al. v.* Millaudon *et al.*   VIII, N. S. 68.

Directors of Banks are required to exercise ordinary care in the discharge of their duties, But if any thing occurs to awaken suspicion of the fidelity of the subordinate officers of the institution, a higher degree of diligence must be exercised.

They are responsible in their private capacity for loss arising from any illegal measure of the board of directors which they did not oppose.

They are not responsible for errors of judgment unless the error be of the grossest kind. They cannot delegate to the president and cashier the authority to discount bills or notes.

If they sell stock above the market price to the president the contract is null and void. So it is if they borrow money of the bank from the cashier, on a promise to replace it, either in cash or bank stock.

They cannot discharge themselves from the responsibility, they may have incurred as sureties of the cashier by reporting the transactions of that officer to be correct, and obtaining in this report a resolution of the board of directors, to discharge them.

FIRST District.

PORTER, J., delivered the opinion of the court.

This is an action by the plaintiffs, stockholders in the late Planters' Bank, against the defendants, who are also stockholders in the same institution, to obtain a settlement of the accounts, a liquidation of the affairs and a division of the funds belonging to the bank.

As necessary to this settlement, the plaintiffs allege, that three of the directors of the institution, viz: Laurent Millaudon, Joseph Abat and Jean Lanna, are indebted to it in a sum of 451,000 dollars for fraudulent and unfaithful conduct by them, while acting in the capacity just stated. The specifications, given in the petition of their acts, are brought under the following heads:

1. That, while acting as directors, they permitted the president and cashier of the bank, at divers times, between the 3d of August, 1817, and the 3d of November, 1819, to discount notes from the funds thereof, to a large amount, viz: 350,000 dollars without the intervention or assent of five directors, as required by the rules and regulations of the bank, by reason of which misconduct on their part, a loss was sustained, by the institution to the amount of 112,000 dollars.

2. That, after the 3d day of November, 1819, and the 1st of May, 1820, they being still directors, did aid and assist Paul Lanusse, the president, and Bailly Blanchard, the cashier, in discounting notes without the authority of the president and four directors; particularly notes of the president not endorsed, but payable to the president, directors and company of said bank, contrary to the rules and regulations thereof, and to its injury 100,000 dollars.

3. That on divers days and times, between the 1st of June, 1819, and the 1st day of July 1820, the defendants, being directors of said bank, did collusively and fraudulently cause to be transferred to the bank eight hundred shares thereof at par; although by reason of the misconduct of the defendants, the stock had become of little value, and was then currently sold in New Orleans at a great loss.

4. That on the 16th of October, 1819, the defendants were appointed a committee to examine the state of the cash of the bank, after the disappearance of the cashier, and that they fraudulently reported the cash to be correct, whereas in truth it was not so; but there was a deficiency of 49,000 dollars, which was attempted to be covered by notes or due bills of Paul Lanusse, and for which sum two notes of Paul Lanusse were afterwards fraudulently discounted, through the connivance and with the aid, of the defendants, which notes have not been paid.

5. That the defendants wilfully, improperly and fraudulently voted to discharge the sureties of the cashier, viz: Paul Lanusse and Jean Lanna, one of the defendants, and cancel the bond they had given to the bank with said cashier, while at that time he was indebted to the institution in a large sum, viz: 49,000 dollars, and also in other sums of money.

6. That they paid to the cashier and attorney of the bank 5500 dollars, fraudulently and collusively, with an intention of injuring the

stockholders; and that at divers other times, they improperly paid to other persons large sums of money, which, added to those paid to the attorney and cashier, amount to the sum of 36,000 dollars.

And 7th and lastly, That when the books of the bank were opened in 1818, and the unsubscribed stock was taken, the defendants failed to pay the amount which they subscribed or to collect that which had been subscribed for by others. That the sum so subscribed for was 126,000 dollars, no part of which was paid except the subscription of one hundred shares, and that the balance, viz: 106,000 dollars yet remain due and unpaid, for which the defendants are responsible.

Several of the stockholders, who refused to join in this petition, but who were necessarily made parties to the suit in order that a final settlement should be made between all, having an interest in the institution, have answered this petition, by declaring their ignorance of the matters therein alleged, and have required that to be done in the premises, which equity and justice may demand.

The defendants, Abat, Millaudon and Lanna, on whom fraudulent conduct is charged, and against whom such heavy responsibility is invoked, filed an answer in which they deny all the facts and allegations in the petition; more especially those which allege fraud and collusion on their part: and they further aver, that, if in all the acts complained of, any be true, they were the acts of the whole board of directors, done and made in good faith, and free from bad and corrupt intention.

On these issues, the parties went to trial in the court in the first instance. A great deal of verbal and documentary evidence was introduced. The judge was of opinion that, though a gross misapplication of the funds was established, and a consequent loss incurred by the stockholders, there was no proof adduced, which authorised him to hold the defendants responsible. That the loss was imputable to the improper conduct of the president and cashier. He gave judgment against the plaintiffs, and they appealed.

This case is one of great importance to both plaintiffs and defendants from the large amount in dispute; and of special interest to the latter, as involving charges of the most serious nature against their honesty and truth. It is also of great importance to the public, who from the number of these monied institutions and their influence on the affairs of society, as well as on those whose fortunes are embarked in them, are deeply concerned in seeing that the agents to whom their direction is intrusted should be protected while they act faithfully; but visited with the severest penalties of the law, if to the injury of the institution, they pervert the trust reposed in them, to their own emolument.

1. The first charge is the permission, given to the president and cashier to discount paper without the intervention and assent of four directors, as required by the 10th section of the act of incorporation.

Before proceeding to state the evidence, by which this charge is supported, and the effect to which in our judgment it should be entitled, it will be well to ascertain, and settle, the degree of care and diligence which the law required in the defendants, while exercising the trust of bank directors, and what responsibility such a situation imposed on them.

On this point, though there is some, we do not conceive there is much difficulty. They were the agents or mandataries of the stockholders, and as such undertook the management of its affairs, according to the rules prescribed by their charter, and by the by-laws made in pursuance thereof. By the provisions of the Civil Code, in force at the time the trust was undertaken, and at the period the breach of it was alleged to be committed, agents or attorneys in fact were made responsible not merely for infidelity in the management of the affairs intrusted to them, but also for their fault. Civil Code, p. 124, art. 17. The only correct mode of ascertaining whether there was fault in an agent, is by inquiring whether he neglected the exercise of that diligence and care, which was necessary to a successful discharge of the duty imposed on him. That diligence and care must again depend on the nature of the undertaking. There are many things which, in their management, require the utmost diligence, and scrupulous attention, and where the agent who undertakes their direction, renders himself responsible for the slightest neglect. There are others, where the duties imposed are presumed to call for nothing more than ordinary care and attention, and where the exercise of that degree of care suffices.

The directors of banks from the nature of their undertaking, fall within the class last mentioned, while in the discharge of their ordinary duties. It is not contemplated by any of the charters, which have come under our observation, and it was not by that of the Planters' Bank, that they should devote their whole time and attention to the institution to which they are appointed, and guard it from injury by constant superintendance. Other officers on whom compensation is bestowed for the employment of their time in the affairs of the bank, have the immediate management. In relation to these officers, the duties of directors are those of control, and the neglect which would render them responsible for not exercising that control properly, must depend on circumstances, and in a great measure be tested by the facts of the case. If nothing has come to their knowledge, to awaken suspicion of the fidelity of the president and cashier, ordinary attention to the affairs of the institution is sufficient. If they become acquainted with any fact calculated to put prudent men on their guard, a degree of care commensurate with the evil to be avoided is required, and a want of that care certainly makes them responsible.

It is said by a writer of great authority who treats of the doctrine of mandate, that the mandatary can not excuse himself by alleging a want of ability to discharge the trust undertaken. That it will not be sufficient for him to say he acted to the best of his ability, because he should have formed a more just estimate of his own capacity before he engaged himself. That, if he had not agreed to become the agent, the principal could have found some other person willing and capable of transacting the business correctly. This doctrine, if sound, would make the attorney in fact responsible for every error in judgment, no matter what care and attention he exercised in forming his opinion. It would make him liable to the principal in all doubtful cases, where the wisdom or legality of one or more alternatives was presented for his consideration, no matter how difficult the subject was. And if the embarrassment, in the choice of measures, grew out of a legal difficulty, it would require from him knowledge and learning, which the law only presumes in those who have made the jurisprudence of their country the study of their lives, and which knowledge often fails in them from the intrinsic difficulty of the subject, and the fallibility of human judgment. *Pothier, Traite du Mandat, no.* 48.

It is no doubt true, that if the business to be transacted, presupposes the exercise of a particular kind of knowledge, a person who would accept the office of mandatary, totally ignorant of the subject, could not excuse himself on the ground that he discharged his trust with fidelity and care. A lawyer, who would undertake to perform the duties of a physician; a physician, who would become an agent to carry on a suit in a court of justice—a bricklayer who would propose to repair a ship, or a landsman who would embark on board a vessel to navigate her, may be presented as examples to illustrate this distinction. Thus it was a provision of the Spanish law.—*Gran culpa es aquel que se trabaja de facer cosa que non sabe, o que te non convient.—Par.* 7, *tit.* 34, *ley* 5. But when the person who is appointed attorney in fact, has the qualifications necessary for the discharge of the ordinary duties of the trust imposed, we are of opinion that on the occurrence of difficulties, in the exercise of it, which offer only a choice of measures, the adoption of a course from which loss ensues can not make the agent responsible, if the error was one into which a prudent man might have fallen. The contrary doctrine seems to us, to suppose the possession, and require the exercise, of perfect wisdom in fallible beings. No man would undertake to render a service to another on such severe conditions. The reason given for the rule, namely, that if the mandatary had not accepted the office, a person capable of discharging the duty correctly, would have been found, is quite unsatisfactory. The person who would have accepted, no matter who he might be, must have shared in common with him who did, the imperfections of our nature, and consequently must be presumed just as liable to have mistaken the correct course. The test of responsibility therefore should be, not the certainty of wisdom in others, but the possession of ordinary knowledge; and by showing that the error of the agent is of so gross a kind, that a man of common sense, and ordinary attention, would not have fallen into it. The rule which fixes responsibility, because men of unerring sagacity are supposed to exist, and would have been found by the principal, appears to us essentially erroneous.

With this exposition of the duties imposed on the defendants, as directors of the bank, and the responsibility incurred by them, we proceed to the examination of the first charge contained in the petition.

The evidence on this head establishes the fact of a permission having been given, by the board of directors to the president and cashier to discount paper, which was at a longer date than sixty days, and it is also proved that two of the defendants, Abat and Lanna, were present when this power was granted on the 13th of August, 1817. But it is shown that a few days after, in consequence of a protest very properly, and judiciously made by one of the directors, De la Croix, before a notary public of this city against the legality and correctness of the proceeding, the order granting the permission was repealed. This repeal took place on the 24th of September, of the same year, and was made on the motion of one of the defendants, Millaudon. Had it been proved that an injury was sustained by the bank in consequence of this improper indulgence, accorded to its officers, we should have been of opinion that all the directors present at the deliberation of the board, who did not oppose the measure, would have been responsible to the stockholders in their individual capacities. It was an open and gross violation of the charter, which requires the president and four directors to constitute a *quorum* for discounts, and it can not be excused on the want of knowledge of its impropriety, for it was a matter on which no difficulty could exist; the language of the statute being clear, and its meaning plain. But, during the time this order was in force, it is not shown that any discounts were made by the president and cashier from which loss was sustained by the bank. It is true, we have proof that, after this time, the cashier secretly advanced the president money on his notes, but there is not a *scintilla* of evidence that the defendants had any knowledge of his doing so, or that they connived at his misconduct in this particular. We therefore conclude this charge has not been sustained.

II. The second accusation is in substance the same as the first; and is equally unsupported by proof. It alleges fraud in the defendants, by their assisting the president and cashier to discount paper, between the 3d day of November, 1819, and the 1st day of May, 1820, without the aid and intervention of four directors. Now it is established beyond all doubt, that the cashier disappeared and (as it was afterwards discovered) put a period to his existence on the 16th of October, of that year, and that Lanusse resigned his office of president on the very day on which it is alleged the connivance on the part of the defendants commenced, viz: on the 3d day of November, 1819.

III. The third specification of misconduct is the acts of the defendants, in transferring to the bank a large number of shares, to the amount of 160,000 dollars at par, when it was well known to them, and so the fact was, that the stock, at the time the transaction took place, was not of the value at which it was transferred.

This is the part of the case which has created the most difficulty in our minds, and the effect, which the evidence is entitled to, cannot be properly understood, without a full statement of all the matters connected with the transaction.

So far back as the year 1813, we find a resolution of the board of directors to purchase stock of the bank to the amount of 20,000 dollars at twenty per cent. below par. On the 10th of July, of that year, twenty-three shares were taken from a house which was unable to pay its notes. On the 13th of September, another resolution was entered into to purchase stock at not more than ten per cent. below par, so that the stock might be reduced to 200,000 dollars. By the first of April, 1815, we see the determination had been so far carried into effect, as to make the stock held by individuals amount only to 225,600 dollars. That owned by the bank on the same day was 201,800 dollars.

In the commencement of the year 1818, an attempt was made, by persons not stockholders in the bank, to take the portion of stock which up to that time had not been subscribed for. The board of directors refused them permission to do so, but afterwards opened the books and took the whole stock in their own names, for themselves and on behalf of those who were stockholders at the time. The capital being increased, we find on the 3d of April, a resolution of the board of directors was passed, two of the defendants, Lanna & Millaudon, being present, which is in the following words: "Considering the scarcity of specie, it was resolved that the president be authorised to buy shares of the bank not above par and the stock of the institution not to be less than 200,000 dollars."

Between the date of this resolution, and the first day of October, 1819, some shares were purchased, among others, forty-five from the defendant, Lanna, at par, on the 29th June, 1819; but on the 10th of October, 1819, it appears from the book of dividends that 300,000 dollars was then held by individuals, and that they were paid their dividends on this amount.

Such being the amount of stock at that time, we learn by a statement made by the cashier eight days after, and eight days before he committed suicide, that 75,000 dollars had been purchased on account of the institution within the preceding week; and that he held the defendant Lanna's notes for 25,000 dollars to represent stock to the same amount, which sum added to 75,000 dollars reduced the stock down to the amount to which it was directed to be brought by resolution of the 3d of April, namely, to 200,000 dollars.

It would greatly have aided the court, in its investigation of this matter, if the evidence afforded any clue, by which we could ascertain whose stock was purchased between these two periods of time, namely, the first and eighth of October, and at what rate it was bought. But there is an hiatus in the transfer book from the 26th of September, 1819, to the 15th of October of the same year, the time at which those transactions took place. The leaves appear to have been cut out. It would be improper in the court to indulge in any suspicion as to the cause of this mutilation of the book, or by whom it was made, for there is no evidence before us; it was in its present situation, when it came out of the possession of the defendants. The plaintiffs have offered to supply, by parol evidence, in this tribunal, the contents of that portion of the book which is wanting, by copies taken from it when it was entire, but such evidence, not having been given below, could not be received here.

We cannot, however, disguise our impressions of the extraordinary character of the transactions. The cashier, some time before he disappeared, must have been aware of the impending ruin which awaited the bank and himself. That at such a time and under such circumstances when the institution was pressed for money, and without specie to meet its engagements, he and the president, whose existence was at stake, or what is more dear to a feeling mind, whose reputation and good name depended on sustaining the credit of the bank, and preventing the disclosure of their misdeeds; that they at such a moment should pay out 100,000 dollars for bank stock is almost beyond credence. If indeed the persons whose stock was thus taken at that time, were those to whom money had been privately advanced, an explanation is given, which, though it shows highly culpable conduct on the part of the cashier and president, still enables us to account for their conduct on the ordinary principles of human action, but in any other view we have been able to take of the subject, their motives are inexplicable.

The presumption of this stock not having been transferred, in consequence of a sale duly and *bona fide* made to the president, in pursuance of the resolution of the 3d of April, 1819, is much heightened by the statement of the cashier, that there was in the vaults of the bank on the 8th of October, notes of Jean Lanna, one of the defendants, for 25,000 dollars which represented the same value in stock. These notes, we presume, were not given without value received, and the transaction only admits of two explanations; either the notes were given for money of the bank loaned by the cashier to the defendant, and the former thought proper to consider them as standing in the place of stock, or the money was obtained on a bargain for stock, by which the cash was immediately paid, and the stock was to be transferred at some future time. In either point of view, the agreement was equally reprehensible on the part of the defendant, Lanna. It was a breach of duty as flagrant as that of the president and cashier. There is no safety for monied institutions, if directors, who are appointed by the stockholders to attend to their affairs, and are placed as a check over the other officers of the bank, shall profit by the influence their station confers, to draw money out of its cof-

[Percy et al, v. Millandon et al.]

fers, in any other way but by the legal and ordinary modes, and we doubt much whether the legality of the transaction can be cured by giving any thing else in payment unless it is shown to have been as beneficial to the institution, as the money improperly obtained would have been. The disposition, which must be made of the cause at present, does not render it necessary to express a definitive opinion on this point, but our present impressions are, that any contract, or agreement, by which the director of a bank obtains money belonging to it, from any of its officers, contrary to the rules of the institution, is null and void, and that no subsequent consummation of that contract supposing it to be executory, can cure the nullity.

From whom, and on what terms, the balance of the stock found in the vault, viz, 75,000 dollars, was obtained, the evidence leaves us in the dark. The books show no regular transfer of it. A serious question therefore presents itself, whether the defendants were justified in reporting as correct, transactions of the cashier, by which this stock stood in the place of cash. It is in evidence before us, that the defendants, previous to their proceeding to an examination of the vault, were informed of the culpable transactions, which had long existed between the cashier and the president; and were also instructed that the books theretofore kept, did not exhibit the true state of the bank. This information, joined to the fact of the cashier having disappeared, was certainly sufficient to put them on their guard, and it is difficult to believe they then considered the stock worth par; under these circumstances, if they found a quantity of certificates of stock, on which the cashier had advanced money without obtaining a regular transfer of them, we do not think they acted judiciously in receiving them as cash, unless there was strong doubt of the solvency of those to whom the money had been paid. But if the stock was their own, and the title to it was not in the bank, a much higher degree of responsibility was incurred by reporting the transaction to be correct.

We are inclined, however, to think that, if the certificates so found were those of persons other than the defendants, they should not be held responsible; on the ground, that on finding the certificates there, they supposed the whole transaction correct, and that they presumed these evidences of stock had come regularly into the hands of the cashier. In the confusion and alarm necessarily attendant on the disappearance of that officer, while the doors of the bank were besieged by the multitude, who demanded payment of its notes, it would not be surprising if their inquiry was not so complete, nor their judgment so correct, as it would have been under other circumstances. But if it should turn out on a further investigation that this stock was their own, that it had not been transferred, so as to make the contract binding on the bank, or sold above the market price; and that they reported it to stand correctly in place of cash, then we should be of opinion that no statement of theirs, pronouncing the transaction regular, could at all place them in another situation than they would have stood in, had no such report been made; and that, if no regular transfer existed of the stock at the time the cashier disappeared, the defendants still owe the money, they obtained on the deposit of it.

The counsel for the plaintiffs has proposed a mode of ascertaining to whom the stock belonged, which he considered infallible. We have endeavored to avail ourselves of it; but we have been unable to come to a satisfactory conclusion, by the means indicated. An examination of the names of the persons, who held the stock on the first day of October, 1819, compared with those who were owners of it, at a subsequent time, would, if a difference existed between them, certainly raise an almost irresistible presumption, that the stock found wanting at the last period, was that which had come into the hands of the cashier in the intermediate space of time. But this fact does not establish whether the stock so wanting, came into the hands of the cashier, by a regular transfer; in consequence of a sale made to the president, or by private agreement with the cashier. We therefore think the justice of the case requires it to be remanded. The parties, being now apprised of the point which the court considers material, will be enabled to come prepared to elucidate it with all the proof in their possession, or within their reach.

As the case is one of great magnitude and embraces a variety of matter, we have thought the ends of justice would be promoted by expressing an opinion on the other heads of accusation alleged in the petition. It will narrow the grounds of contest on the next trial, and promote the discovery of truth by confining the attention of the parties in the court below, to what is really material.

IV. The fourth ground, on which responsibility is alleged is the report of the defendants when appointed to examine the officers of the bank, after the disappearance of the cashier; their reporting the cash to be correct, when there was a deficit of 14,000 dollars.

The report, made by the defendants, is found on an entry made on the book of deliberations, in the following words: " On Mr. Lanna's motion, *Resolved,* that all the transactions of this bank, as well as the vault and promissory notes, acceptances and bills receivable in the port folio, having been found correct, according to the statement of the book keeper, the late Bailly Blanchard be discharged, and his bond considered as void.

The propriety of this report, as preliminary to a motion for the discharge of the cashier and his securities, will be considered hereafter. In reference to this accusation, although it did not state the facts correctly, it does not authorise us to hold the defendants responsible. It is proved that a great deal of zeal and activity, judiciously exercised, were displayed by the defendants to secure the debt which Lanusse owed for overdrawing, that security was obtained for it, and that it was paid. It is also shown that every exertion was made to secure the balance due by him on the notes discounted. Whatever therefore may have been the motives of the committee in making the report, as the bank was not placed in a worse situation than it otherwise would have been, in relation to Lanusse, we do not think the plaintiffs can fix responsibility on the defendants, on this ground.

V. The next accusation is the note given to discharge the cashier's bond, and of all the transactions which this litigation has developed, it appears to us the most unjustifiable. It exhibits gross and culpable negligence on the part of two of the defendants, Abat and Millaudon, and on the part of the other, Lanna, who was surety, an attempt to deceive the bank to his own advantage. The defendants formed the committee which had examined the vault. They were apprised of the culpable conduct of the cashier. They had full evidence of it, furnished under his own hand, before the unfortunate man terminated his existence by a voluntary inflicted death. They knew the distress to which the institution was reduced, was owing to his, and the president's breach of duty. Yet with a perfect knowledge of all these facts, Lanna, the surety, moved the board to discharge the cashier, and consider the bond void, every thing being found correct; and the other defendants made no opposition to it. The most charitable construction of motives can find little or no apology for such conduct.

There is no doubt the defendant, Lanna, is still responsible on the bond, and whether judgment can not be given against him, on the present state of the pleadings is a question we reserve until the case be finally decided, as we do the responsibility of the defendants, Abat and Millaudon, for permitting such a determination to be taken without opposition on their part.

VI. As to the charge of voting sums to the officers of the bank, in addition to their salary, we do not see any thing which may not be reconciled to a wish to reward zeal and merit, or what they considered such, in the service of the institution.

But one of the payments, that of 1000 dollars to the attorney of the bank, stands on different grounds. The resolution granting it, is of date the 25th of March, 1820, and the following is a translation of the order, which was signed by two of the defendants, Abat and Millaudon: "*Resolved*, That in case a suit is brought by the stockholders, against the president and directors of the bank, that Mr. A. L. Duncan will be employed to defend the latter, and that 1000 dollars be allowed him for his services." When bank directors are in contest with the stockholders, and the fidelity and prudence of the agency of the former are at issue, we think each should pay their own counsel. There is just as much ground, for making the directors responsible for the attorney the stockholders would employ.

VII. The seventh accusation is completely disproved. It is shown that all the stock subscribed for has been paid.

It is, therefore, ordered, adjudged and decreed that the judgment of the district court be annulled, avoided and reversed, that the case be remanded for a new trial, and that the appellees pay the costs of this appeal.

Hennen, for the plaintiffs.

Mazureau and *Grymes,* for the defendants.

Weimprender *v.* Fleming.   VIII, N. S. 95.

FIRST District.

A party cannot proceed, at once, by the *via executiva* and *via ordinaria.* If he do, the order of seizure is to be set aside.

The plea of *non numeratâ pecuniâ* can only be met by evidence of the numeration of the money, as stated in the act, not by proof of a pre-existing debt.   •

Baudin *v.* Roliff *et al.*   VIII, N. S. 98.

In a sale under execution, if the terms be that as soon as the buyer pays, the title will pass, he must pay before he acquires it.

THIRD District.

Porter, J., delivered the opinion of the court.

This cause has been already before the court, and was remanded to have the question of alleged fraud in the conveyance to the defendants tried by a jury. The whole case has been submitted to them, and a verdict has been given for the plaintiff; from the judgment rendered in conformity therewith, the defendants appealed.

A full statement of the case will be found in the former opinion, rendered by this tribunal, a report of which is given in the first volume of the New Series of *Martin's Reports,* 165. It is sufficient for the understanding of the decision now about to be pronounced, to state:

That the suit is one for land, and that the plaintiff claims a title to the premises in dispute in virtue of a purchase, made by him from one Alston, who bought at a sale made under an execution issued at the suit of the present plaintiff, and one Conway, against a certain Oliver Pollock, their debtor. The defendants contend, that by the terms of the adjudication, as well as the general principles of law in

matters of this kind, no title ever passed to Alston, and that consequently none could be acquired by the petitioner under him.

The sale took place under the Spanish government. The adjudication is in the following words: " No bidder having appeared except
the said Don P. Lewis Alston, he is considered, as he is, the lawful
owner of said land and plantation of one thousand arpents, that did
belong to Don Oliver Pollock, as he is the last and better bidder, for
the sum of 5360 dollars, in virtue of which, I have signed this, with
the two assisting witnesses, appraisers, and their witnesses, as soon
as he pays the said sum of 5360 dollars."

Two questions are presented under this adjudication.

1. Whether any title passed to Alston, until he paid the purchase-
money? and

2. Whether it has been so paid?

We think there can be no doubt but the condition was that which
our law denominates suspensive, depending on a future event. The
purchaser is declared to be the lawful owner of the land, as soon as
he pays the money bid; he is, therefore, not the owner, until the
money be paid.

But it is contended, though the money was not actually paid, yet
this was a question entirely between the plaintiff in execution and
the purchaser, and that, if the former thought proper to release or
discharge the latter, or take any thing else in lieu of the money, the
debtor can not complain, and the title is not less vested in the buyer.
This position we consider true, provided no act between the plaintiff
and the bidder deprives the defendant of the benefit of the sale made
of his property. But to this doctrine, there are obviously the exceptions which grow out of purchases made on certain conditions and
stipulations: for, if the parties choose to make a particular agreement
on this, or on any other subject, their contract is the law which governs them, unless the agreement be void, as contravening some
principle of public policy.

The plaintiff in the present action, together with one Conway, were
the persons at whose suit the property now in dispute was sold in
execution, and purchased by Alston. Pollock, the owner of the land,
owed the petitioner a balance of a large judgment which the latter
had recovered against him several years before, and was also indebted
to Conway, who, as his surety in that suit, had paid Baudin a considerable sum of money, in discharge of the debt due by Pollock.
They joined in a petition to the Spanish tribunals for a sale of the
land; and as Conway was still surety for Pollock, it of course followed,
that whatever money could be made from the sale of the defendant's
property was to be first applied to the satisfaction of the judgment in
favor of Baudin. The balance, if any, was to be paid to Conway,
the surety.

Years elapsed after the sale without the money being paid by
Alston, the purchaser, or any steps being taken by Baudin or Conway to enforce the payment. In the year 1814, Baudin commenced

an action against the heirs of Alston, requiring them to be put in possession of the land on their paying the sum of 5360 dollars, the purchase-money, or that in default of their making said payment, the land should be sold to pay and satisfy the debt due to the petitioner. In the petition, he states the sum, yet due to him by Pollock, to be 8800 dollars, with interest and costs. To this demand the defendants appeared and answered, and, after considerable litigation, the cause terminated in April, 1817, by a judgment, which decreed that the plaintiff should recover of the defendants the sum of 5350 dollars, to be paid, however, as the judgment states, "by the defendants to the petitioner, by the sale of the right, title and interest of the said defendants to the said tract (the land purchased by their ancestor), which is hereby ordered to take place in due form of law; and it is further ordered, that if, at the sale hereby directed, the said land shall not sell for the above mentioned sum, the said defendants shall not be liable to pay to the petitioner any further sum than the proceeds of the sale to be made of the said tract of land, and that they be forever released from any further liability to the said petitioner on account of the demand made in his petition. This decree is not to affect the rights of any other party or parties, than those above named; and it is further ordered, that the costs of the suit be paid from the proceeds of the sale above ordered."

Under this judgment, an execution issued, the land mentioned in it which is that now sued for, was seized, sold, and bought by the plaintiff, for the sum of 4490.

Whether the judgment was entered up by consent, or was rendered by the court on considerations of the equity, as well as law of the case, does not appear, nor is it very material to inquire. The plaintiff by not appealing from it, and by carrying it into execution, is as much bound by it, as if it had been preceded by his assent.

The effect of it, it is contended, was to discharge the purchaser; that the plaintiff had a right to do so in any manner he chose: that the title vested in Alston, by satisfaction being made in this way as completely as it would have done by the payment of the purchase-money.

This is true: but Baudin could not discharge the defendant in execution for a larger sum than was due to him. By the original sale, Alston had purchased the premises for 5360 dollars, which money was to go, first, to the satisfaction of the balance due on the judgment to Baudin, and the remainder, if any, to be paid to Conway.

Now, if the whole amount for which the land was sold to Alston was not due to Baudin, then, he could not discharge the purchaser for the whole, and if Alston did not pay the whole amount, or was not released for the whole, no title vested in him; for, by the express terms of his purchase, he is not the owner, until he pays the entire amount, viz., 5360 dollars.

Conway was no party to the proceedings. He could not be bound by them, and a judgment by which Alston's heirs were to be discharged by the sale of the land cannot affect him. They yet owe to him the balance due between the amount coming to Baudin, and that at which their ancestor purchased, unless they have some other cause to show against the debt, than that proceeding from the judgment, rendered between Baudin and them.

The plaintiff, by his own showing only, establishes the amount due to him at that time, to be 4300 dollars. The defendants insist it does not exceed 2468 dollars. It is immaterial which we adopt, though we may remark that we have been unable to find any evidence or record that will carry the balance as high as the plaintiff states it. Either will bring us to the same result, for neither amounts to the purchase-money which Alston was to pay. It has been argued that the 4300 dollars due Baudin, with the costs of the suit, against Alston's heirs, which were directed to be paid out of the sale of the land, amounted to 4490 dollars, the price at which he purchased it. Admitting this to be true, 4490 dollars was not the price at which the land was originally sold, but 5360 dollars, and the payment of this sum, or a discharge from those entitled to receive it, was necessary to give a title to Alston, for it was on that condition he purchased.

Lastly, it has been contended that no person can set up this defence but Conway, or his heirs; that the defendants cannot, who are entire strangers to the transaction. They are in possession of the land.— The action is a petitory one. The plaintiff must show title. That which he produces shows the title of Pollock never was vested in the party in whose right he claims. He, consequently, produces nothing which could authorise the court to declare him to be the owner of the property sued for.

It is, therefore, ordered, adjudged and decreed, that the judgment of the district court be annulled, avoided and reversed; that there be judgment for the defendants as in case of nonsuit, with costs in both courts.

Moreau and *Watts*, for the plaintiff.

Preston, for the defendants.

Robinson *v.* M'Cay, Curator. VIII, N. S. 106.

The landlord's privilege is not lost, by the curator's removal of property subject thereto.

COURT of Probates, Parish of St. Tammany.

PORTER, J., delivered the opinion of the court.

The plaintiff claims 488 dollars, for house rent, and asserts that the debt is privileged, on the furniture and other movables found in the house at the decease of the tenant.

The answer contains a general denial, a plea of prescription, and averment that the debt is not privileged.

. The court below considered the debt as proved, and the plea of prescription not sustained, but it refused to allow any privilege and directed the plaintiff to be paid as a chirographary creditor. From this judgment the petitioner appealed.

. The reason given by the judge for rejecting the demand of the plaintiff to be paid as a privilege creditor, is the curator being permitted to remove the objects subject to the lien, without any assertion of claim on the part of the lessor. Louisiana Code, 2679.

We think the judge erred. The representatives of an estate can do nothing which will destroy or impair a claim existing on the deceased's person or property, at the moment of his decease. In this instance, the removal by the curator cannot have the effect of destroying the privilege, because the lessor could not exercise his privilege on the thing subject to it.

The law makes it the duty of the former to take the property into his possession, sell it, and after the sale to settle the order of privileges contradictorily with the other creditors. This power is expressly recognised by the 3223d article of the Louisiana Code. The proceeds in the hands of the curator represented the thing. The want of power in the lessor to seize, prevented the prescription from running against him.

It is, therefore, ordered, adjudged and decreed, that the judgment of the court of probates be annulled, avoided and reversed; and it is further ordered, adjudged and decreed, that the plaintiff recover from the defendant, as curator of the estate of H. H Patillo, the sum of 488 dollars; to be paid as a privilege on the movable effects of the lessee found in the house leased at the death of the lessor; and it is .further ordered, that the defendant aforesaid, pay the costs in both courts.

Bryan *v.* Turnbull *et al.*   VIII, N. S. 108.

The words of a prison bound bond need not be essentially the same, as those of the form in the act.

The sureties on it, cannot discharge themselves by surrendering the principal.

THIRD District, Judge of the Second presiding.

PORTER, J., delivered the opinion of the court.

The plaintiff brought suit against one Stewart, and obtained judgment against him. He was arrested on a writ of *capias ad satisfaciendum*, and gave the defendants as sureties to keep the prison limits. The petition charges the debtor to have violated his engagement by departing from the limits of the prison, and avers the responsibility of the defendants as a consequence of said departure.

The answer consists of a general denial, and an averment that there is no breach of the condition of the bond, because the respondents took the body of Stewart and surrendered him into the custody of the deputy sheriff, who was jailor of the parish, and that the sheriff, after his surrender, permitted Stewart to depart from the limits. The court below gave judgment against the defendants and they appealed.

Two points have been made in this court.

1. That the bond does not pursue the statute under which it was taken, and is void.

2. That the surrender of the debtor into the custody of the sheriff discharged the sureties.

I. The condition of the bond is in the following words: "Whereas on the 17th day of March last, there was issued from out of the clerk's office of the third judicial district, in the parish of West Feliciana, and state of Louisiana, a writ of *capias ad satisfaciendum*, at the suit of Mary S. Bryan against Charles Stewart, and the said Charles Stewart having surrendered his body to the sheriff, in execution of said writ. Now, therefore, if he, the said Charles Stewart will keep within the limits of the prison bounds, of said parish of West Feliciana, and state aforesaid, which bounds are prescribed and set apart by the parish judge and two justices of the peace, in conformity with the law in such cases made and provided, (it being the limit of the parish,) and not depart therefrom, without paying or satisfying the said Mary S. Bryan or her legal representatives the sum of 2682 dollars and 21 cents; ten per cent. interest on the sum of 2922 dollars and 21 cents, from the 24th of May, 1825, until the 20th of November, 1826, and like interest on 2682 dollars and 21 cents, from the last date until paid, also the sum of 22 dollars 22 cents, and 1 dollar 62½ cents for said *cupias ad satisfaciendum*, or be otherwise discharged according to law, then and in such case the obligation to be void, and of no effect, otherwise to be and remain in full force and virtue in law." The condition of the bond which the statute directs is, " That the debtor shall not break or depart from the bounds, without the leave of the court, or being released by the order of the plaintiff, at whose suit he, the debtor, is confined." The words of the bond, taken in this case, though they do not literally pursue those of the statute, are substantially the same, and do not in any respect vary the contract which would have been formed, had the very language of the act been pursued.

We have repeatedly decided that in whatever form parties chose to bind themselves, they would be bound. The law of the *Recopilacion*, under which these decisions were made, was imperative on the court, and its equity is as striking as its commands are clear. It was certainly not intended to say that every bond, which parties might sign, was valid—but that every engagement, entered into on a good and lawful consideration, was binding, no matter what form was given to the contract. The bond in this instance, had a lawful consideration, and we think the breach of the condition authorised the obligee to sue on it. The case can not in any respect be distinguished from that of Wood *et al.* v. Tick, 10 *Mart.* 196.

It has been contended that the bond was taken since the passage of the act repealing the ancient laws of the country; but a reference to the date shows it to have been given before.—Had it been entered into after, we should then have had the question presented to us, whether in the absence of any positive law, we could have adopted a better rule than that which was contained in the *Recopilacion*, but this it is unnecessary to decide.

II. The equity of permitting the sureties to discharge themselves from responsibility by surrendering the body of their principals to the sheriff, has been strongly pressed on us, and the argument is certainly not without weight. But we do not feel authorised on such a consideration, to relieve the defendants, contrary to the express terms of their obligation; having entered into an agreement by which they became responsible, unless certain events took place, it is not in the power of the court to add to, or diminish any of the grounds on which their liability was to cease. The right of bail to surrender the principal, where they are bound, for his appearance to answer the judgment of the court, is given by a provision of the Code of Practice, and no such provision is made in relation to sureties for the prison bounds.* The according of such a privilege in the one case, and the silence in regard to it on another, offer a strong reason for believ-

* This reasoning of the court it is impossible to evade; but it is amazing that the state has not (1839) after ten years, changed the condition of the bond of grace to the unfortunate.

[Bryan *v.* Turnbull *et al.*]

ing that it was the intention of the legislature to make a difference between them. We have looked through all the books within our reach, and we can not find a single case where such a right has been claimed on behalf of sureties for prison bounds, and yet the instances must have been numerous where it was their interest to surrender the debtor's body and consign him to close custody. Code of Practice, 230, 730.

It is, therefore, ordered, adjudged and decreed, that the judgment of the district court be affirmed, with costs

M'Caleb, for the plaintiff.

Watts, for the defendants.

Patin *v.* Naba.   VIII, N. S. 113.

FIRST District.

Plaintiff nonsuited, he not having proved his case.

Bailey *et al. v.* Baldwin.   VIII, N. S. 114.

PARISH Court of New Orleans.

If the party trusted be solvent at the time, his ceasing to be so does not render the party, who trusted him, liable.

The Code of Practice does not dispense with an amicable demand. See Mead *v.* Oakley, 7 *N. S.* 264, with the note of the editor.

By PORTER, J.:—The remaining question relates to the costs. The parish judge formed his opinion on the 549th and 169th articles of the Code of Practice, and concluded, that as no real tender had been made, the defendant must pay the cost, although the plaintiffs had not made an amicable demand.

[Bailey et al. v. Baldwin.]

The 169th article of the Code of Practice says, there shall no longer be any necessity for an amicable demand in writing. It is impossible not to believe it was the intention of the legislature still to require a demand should be made verbally. Had they intended to abolish it entirely, they would certainly have said, it shall no longer be necessary to make an amicable demand. The 549th article does no more than re-enact the provision, found in our laws previous to the passage of the Code of Practice. By them, the party cast was to pay the costs, and a real tender compelled the plaintiff to proceed at the risk of paying them, if he did not recover more than the sum deposited by his adversary. These laws were never understood to do away the necessity of an amicable demand, and we do not see why they should have a greater effect by being found in the Code. They could well stand together before, and they may do so now. 7 *N. S.* 264.

Rawle *v.* Skipwith *et al.* VIII, N. S. 118.

No judgment by default can be taken, until all legal objections are disposed of.

THIRD District, Judge of the Second presiding.

PORTER, J., delivered the opinion of the court.

This case has been already before the court, and was remanded for further proceedings, and on its return to that of the first instance, judgment by default was taken against the defendants, and the judgment made final. They came into court, and moved to have the judgments set aside, on different grounds alleged by them; but the judge refused to do so, conceiving, that by the 547th and 548th articles of the Code of Practice he had no power to touch the decree of the court. The defendants appealed.

When the cause was last before the court, it was presented to us on exceptions, filed to the petition. We decided that the court below had erred, in sustaining one of the exceptions, and we also examined and passed on all the others which depended on the pleadings. Those which required proof to support them, were not noticed, and one was expressly reserved, as involving an inquiry into the merits.

We, therefore, think there was an error in the court of the first

38*

instance giving judgment by default, while these exceptions were undisposed of. One of them was the allegation of the wife, that she was not responsible; because the contract, although entered into by her *in solido*, was in fact an engagement, where she was surety for her husband, and was a defence on the merits.

It is, therefore, ordered, adjudged and decreed, that the judgment of the district court be annulled, avoided and reversed; and it is further ordered and decreed, that the case be remanded to the district court, to be proceeded in according to law, the appellee paying costs of this appeal.

Fisher *et al. v.* Brig Norval *et al.*   VIII, N. S. 120.

If the master gives a receipt for goods left on the beach, they are at the risk of the ship.

FIRST District.

Porter, J., delivered the opinion of the court.

This action is brought to recover the value of thirty-five bales of cotton, which were sent by the plaintiffs to be shipped on board the brig Norval, and received by the captain. They were suffered to remain on the levee, and during the night following their delivery, were burnt and consumed. It is not shown how the fire originated.

The cotton was sent down late in the evening; but the defendants having received, and receipted for it, their responsibility must be governed by the same rules as if it had been delivered early enough to permit them to put it on board the same day.

It is proved, that the cotton was left exposed on the levee without any person to watch it, and it is proved that it is not customary in the city to put any person as a guard over cotton bales, in the situation in which they were placed.

Our Code, 2725, enacts, that carriers and watchmen may be liable for the loss or damage of things entrusted to their care, unless they can prove that such loss or damage has been occasioned by accidental and uncontrollable events.

We think the view, which the judge *a quo* took of the case is a correct one. He considered there was negligence in the defendants permitting the cotton to be exposed all night on the levee, to theft,

[Fisher *et al. v.* Brig Norval *et al.*]

fire and other accidents, without some person to take care of it. We view the transaction in the same light. It is not the care which a prudent man would take of his own property, and the defendants must show such care to excuse them from the loss which has occurred. It is not a good excuse to say, that it is not customary to place a watch over property, such as this. If any such custom has been introduced in this city, by those who have had the property of others transmitted to them for sale or transportation, the sooner they are informed, that such custom cannot control the law, and will not be recognised by courts of justice, the better.

It is, therefore, ordered, adjudged and decreed, that the judgment of the district court be affirmed, with costs.

M'Caleb, for the plaintiffs.

Eustis, for the defendants.

Mayor *et al, v.* Maighan.   VIII, N. S. 122.

PARISH Court of New Orleans.

If the matter in dispute, be under the value of 300 dollars, the Supreme Court can not act on the case.

Although the defendant alleges that this small sum is part of a larger sum that plaintiffs will continue to demand of him. See Millaudon *v.* Judge of Jefferson, 6 *N. S.* 24.

Bulloc v. Parthet.   VIII, N. S. 123.

The judgment must follow the verdict.

PARISH Court of New Orleans.

MARTIN, J., delivered the opinion of the court.

The defendant and appellant assigns as error apparent on the face of the record, a discrepancy between the judgment and the verdict, on which it purports to be grounded.

The verdict is in these words: "The jury find a verdict for 574 dollars, 96 cents in favor of the plaintiff, in cash—the said plaintiff to receive one-half of the proceeds of the outstanding debts and goods left behind by the defendant, say 751 dollars 87 cents of goods, and 946 dollars 18 cents in notes and debts, as charged in the defendant's account."

The judgment is for 574 dollars 96 cents in cash, 751 dollars 87 cents in goods and 946 dollars 18 cents in notes and debts, &c.

Now by examining the defendant's account to which the verdict expressly refers, it appears that the two last sums are the whole of the goods unsold and debts not collected, of which the jury intended the plaintiff to receive one-half only. The error is manifest and obvious.

It is, therefore, ordered, adjudged and decreed, that the judgment of the parish court be annulled, avoided and reversed; and that the plaintiff recover from the defendant the sum of five hundred and seventy-four dollars and ninety-eight cents—and that the defendant account to the plaintiff, or transfer to him one-half of the goods unsold and left behind, and one-half of the notes and debts uncollected, the plaintiff's said half being three hundred and seventy-five dollars and ninety-three cents in goods, and four hundred and seventy-three dollars and nine cents in notes and debts, the appellee paying costs in this court and the appellant, below.

Moreau and *Soule,* for the plaintiff.

Canon, for the defendant.

Bailey v. Taylor. VIII, N. S. 124.

FIRST District.

By PORTER, J.—We know of no law which authorises a surveyor of the customs to direct a forcible entry and ouster of possession of property of the United States. If the defendant held wrongfully, there were legal means of evicting him.

Jardela v. Abat. VIII, N. S. 126.

COURT of Probates of New Orleans.
Under the old Code a donation of a slave not made before a notary, and in the presence of two witnesses, was void. Civil Code, 220, art. 53.

Meilleur et al. v. Coupry. VIII, N. S. 128.

A slave under thirty years of age, cannot be presumed to have been emancipated.

COURT of Probates of New Orleans.

MARTIN, J., delivered the opinion of the court.
The heirs of Louise Rilieux, obtained a rule against Coupry, who

had obtained letters testamentary on her estate, to show cause why they should not be revoked, on a suggestion, that he was a slave, and therefore incapable of exercising the office of testamentary executor. He contended that he was a free man: the court thought otherwise. The letters were revoked, and he appealed.

His counsel urges, in this court, that the appellees have not established their heirship, and are without interest in this case. An examination of the record shows, that this point was not made below. The applicants must be considered as plaintiffs, and, as such, not bound to establish their capacity as heirs, while it was not denied. The appellant was called on to show cause; he did so, by denying he was a slave, and this was the only issue before the court.

It was admitted that he was born of a slave mother; that his mother's owner has ever resided, and still resides, in New Orleans; that he is twenty-seven or twenty-eight years of age: that he has enjoyed his freedom for fourteen years and been married as a free man.

On these facts, it is clear, he was born a slave, and must continue so, unless he was emancipated: as he is under the age of thirty years, and the lawful emancipation of a slave cannot take place before that age, the presumption of a legal emancipation which might result from his long possession of his freedom, is repelled, from the evident impossibility of his legal emancipation having taken place, and the legal impossibility of a slave becoming free, without a legal emancipation.

Prescription can no more avail him, than it would the possessor of property, evidently out of commerce.

It is, therefore, ordered, adjudged and decreed, that the judgment of the court of probates be affirmed, with costs.

Seghers, for the plaintiff.

De Armas, for the defendant.

Corkery *v.* Boyle.   VIII, N. S. 130.

PARISH Court of New Orleans.

Held, that a note given by one partner to the other, by reason of his surrendering up to him the merchandise which remained unsold, is not without consideration on the part of the payee.

Millaudon *v.* Police Jury of Jefferson. VIII, N. S. 132.

Authentic acts are full evidence against the parties and those who claim under them.

FIRST District.

MARTIN, J., delivered the opinion of the court.

The petitioner states that he is the owner of a plantation, on the right bank of the Mississippi, which is burdened with a servitude in favor of certain inhabitants of the shores of lake Barrataria, who had a right of way over his plantation, from the river to the lake; that the police jury of the parish of Jefferson pretend that he is bound to keep in repair a public road or highway over his said plantation, from its front to the depth or back line, and are incessantly harassing him with orders to keep said highway in repair, and vexatious proceedings, in consequence of said orders: he prayed and obtained an injunction, &c.

The defendants pleaded the general issue, and averred, that ever since there wus a settlement made on the shores of the lake, there has been a highway, royal or public road through the plantation of the petitioner, leading from the river to the lake, which the owner of it has ever been bound to keep in repair, &c.

The injunction was made perpetual, and the defendant appealed.

The record shows that, about the year 1779, Governor Galvez settled a few families on the shores of lake Barrataria, and he caused to be opened, at the public expense, a royal or public road or highway, taking the ground therefor, by equal proportions, from the plantations, through which it passed.

That in the act of sale of the premises in 1803, by Lartigue to Dominique Bouligny, there is a clause, by which the vendor states, that a plantation owes a public road, which it is bound to keep in repair. A similar clause is inserted in the act of sale of Dominique Bouligny to Lewis Bouligny, in 1810, as well as in the sale from Lewis Bouligny to Tricou *et al.*, from whom the petitioner bought.

Now, these authentic acts are entitled to full faith against the parties and the petitioner, who holds under the vendees, of every thing which the parties had in view, and which constitutes the object of the act. Pothier on Obligations, 701.

The object of the act was to describe the thing sold, the advantages which it had, and the burden which had been imposed on it.

Now, the parol testimony and documents establish, that Galvez laid out a public road, from the Mississippi to lake Barrataria, taking

[Millaudon v. Police Jury of Jefferson.]

the ground from the plantations along the boundaries of which it passed. After the lapse of half a century, it must be presumed that the proprietors consented to, or were indemnified for, the sacrifice: that the road was kept in repair by them and their successors is proved. In the oldest deed that is produced, executed a quarter of a century ago, the burden imposed on the land is stated; a clause recognises it in two subsequent acts of sale, to which reference is made. In one of these acts, introduced by the plaintiff, the road is traced and marked *camino real.* It is in vain that the appellant's counsel urges, that the police jury were not parties to these deeds, and therefore can not claim any right from them. We have seen that parties must be bound by their own declarations: and when the law requires these declarations to be written, it matters not into what acts they are consigned: they are not the less the declarations of the parties, who must be bound by them, and in cases like the present those who derive their rights from the parties who made these declarations, must take them affected with all the legal consequences of these declarations.

It is in evidence, that by an agreement, in 1817, subscribed by a number of proprietors, it was agreed that the road should be removed from one side of the Bayou, by which it ran, to the other; it being thought that, both those who use the road, and those who were bound to repair it, would be therefore benefitted. This circumstance does not affect the present case: the question is not as to the particular part of the petitioner's estate the road is to run through, but as to his obligation to repair it.

It is, therefore, ordered, adjudged and decreed, that the judgment of the district court, be annulled, avoided and reversed, the injunction dissolved, and that the appellee pay costs in both courts.

Seghers, for the plaintiff.

C. Derbigny, for the defendants.

EASTERN DISTRICT, JUNE TERM, 1829.

Planters' Bank of Georgia *v.* Allard.   VIII, N. S. 136.

It is now a settled rule, that a purchaser with a knowledge of an existing mortgage, cannot avail himself of the want of registry.

FIRST District.

MARTIN, J., delivered the opinion of the court.

This is an hypothecary action against the third possessor of the mortgaged premises, who resists the plaintiffs' pretensions on the ground that the premises were purchased on the production of the certificate of the recorder of mortgages, which did not mention the mortgage on which the present suit is brought; the premises lying in the parish of St. Bernard, within the county of Orleans.

The plaintiffs contended, that both the defendant and his vendor resided in the parish of St. Bernard, in the office of the parish judge of which the plaintiffs' mortgage was recorded, a circumstance with which both vendor and vendee were acquainted, that they made an attempt to obtain from the said judge a certificate which did not state said mortgage, and being unable to obtain it, they came to the city of New Orleans, where the deed of sale was executed, although the land lay in a different parish, with a view to frustrate the plaintiffs from their right of mortgage.

There was judgment against the defendant, and he appealed.

His counsel has first called our attention to a bill of exceptions to the opinion of the district judge, who admitted the testimony of the parish judge, to establish that the defendant had notice of the mortgage. The testimony was objected to, on the ground that the mortgage was not recorded in the proper office, to wit, that of the recorder of mortgages, in the city of New Orleans, and no evidence was admissible to prove notice to the defendant, but the certificate of that officer.

The appellant's counsel has contended that, the law having required that mortgagees should give legal notice to third parties of their mortgages, by causing them to be recorded in a particular office, the absence of this formality is evidence that the mortgagee is satisfied with the security which the mortgagor otherwise presents, or relies on his honesty to prevent an alienation of the mortgaged property, to the injury of the mortgagee.

2. That knowledge in the purchaser is not equivalent to notice.

3. That when the mortgagee intends to establish fraud in the purchaser, by aiding the mortgagor in committing a fraud, he ought not only to prove, but to allege the fraud, in order to enable the purchaser to disprove it.

A number of French authorities have been introduced, from which it appears, beyond contradiction, that, in the tribunals of France, knowledge in the purchaser does not prevent him from resisting the mortgagee's claim, when the legal inscription, or record of the mortgage, in the proper office, has been neglected.

But, in this country, the legislature appears to have introduced the converse of this proposition.

The old Civil Code, 464, art. 52, in order to protect the good faith of those who may be ignorant of mortgages, and to prevent fraud, required them to be recorded in the office of a recorder of the mortgages, in the city of New Orleans, for the whole territory. To permit, therefore, the bad faith of a person, who has a knowledge of the existence of a mortgage, to avail himself of the protection provided by this law, for the good faith of the ignorant, would be rather to thwart, than to promote, the views of the legislator.

In the next article, the Code speaks of mortgages not registered in the time prescribed, and authorises their registry, on an order of the judge, and directs that such mortgages shall have effect against third persons, being *bona fide; i. e.*, ignorant of the existence of the mortgage, from the date of the registry.

From a close examination of the part of the Napoleon Code, which treats of the inscription of mortgages, (3, 18, 4,) we find that no single expression is used therein which shows that the legislator had *bona fide* parties in contemplation.

Hence it is not extraordinary that the jurisprudence of our decisions has established the distinction which the legislature has pointed out.

Accordingly, in the case of Morris *v.* Trudeau, 1 *N. S.* 396, we held that a registry, made at a period in which the order of the judge was required, was sufficient notice to third parties, notwithstanding the order had not been obtained.

In Doubrere v. Grillier's Syndics, 2 *N. S.* 171, we said that when it appears from circumstances *dehors* an act, *sous seing privé*, that it was executed at the time on which it bore date, or possession of the property sold had followed it, the sale would have effect against third persons from the day of the execution of the act, notwithstanding it was not registered. See also the case of De Flechier's Syndics, v. Degruys, 5 *N. S.* 426, and Martinez v. Layton *et al.*, 4 *N. S.* 361.

These last decisions, in construction of the old Code, article 228, have not escaped the attention of the legislature, and the spirit of them has been incorporated in the 2242d article of the new Code.

We take it now to be a settled rule, that the actual knowledge of a purchaser of an existing mortgage is equivalent to the notice resulting from the registry: consequently that the absence of the record of a mortgage is no evidence of the mortgagee's intention not to rely thereon.

Pleadings in this state are confined to petition and answer. The plaintiff needs not deny the facts pleaded in avoidance of his claim, in the answer, in order to be admitted to disprove them or call on the defendant to establish them. The plaintiff may resort to the exceptions of non-age, coverture, violence, fraud, prescription, and the like, without pleading them, because he is not permitted to reply.

But the appellant's counsel has urged that fraud is not presumed, but must be proved; *ergo*, it must be alleged, and the appellee might have amended his petition for an injunction.

Non-age, coverture, violence, &c., must all be proved, yet the plaintiff to whom a release would be opposed by the answer, may avail himself of any of these exceptions without pleading it. If it were admitted, that because by an amendment, a party might bring a charge of fraud before the court, and therefore he must amend, it would follow that in every case these may be rebutted, &c., by way of amendment, whenever, by the former practice, they were necessary.

We think the court did not err in overruling the appellant's counsel's objection to the introduction of evidence to show knowledge in the purchaser before the sale of the existing mortgage.

Fagot, the judge of the parish of St. Bernard, deposed that the appellant was present at the passation of the notarial act, by which Louis N. Allard, his father and vendor, acquired the premises, that the act which contained a mention of the mortgage now sought to be enforced, was read aloud in his presence, and that the appellant went out to look for, and brought a witness, who was wanting to subscribe the act; and the witness afterwards delivered to the appellant, at his request, a copy of the said act of sale. That after the act of sale of the premises, by Louis N. Allard, to the appellant, was passed and recorded in the witness's office, the appellant brought for his signature the sketch of a certificate of the mortgage recorded in the witness's office, as affecting the premises, in which that sought to be enforced was not stated. Witness, noticing the omission, refused to sign the certificate, unless said mortgage was inserted, but the appellant said he wanted no certificate in which said mortgage was inserted; that the sketch of a certificate presented was drawn by his, the appellant's lawyer, and the object of it was to annul the mortgage sought to be enforced.

· From the above testimony, it appears to us the inferior judge did not err, in concluding that the appellant bought the premises with the perfect knowledge that they were burdened with the mortgage, against which he seeks relief in this court.

But his counsel urges that, admitting this fact, still, as it appears that the mention of the mortgage in the act of sale to his father and vendor, was accompanied by a covenant of the then vendor to relieve the vendee from the burden of the mortgage, and that in the certificate of the recorder of mortgages, stating the absence of the incumbrance, he might fairly find evidence of the performance of the · covenant of his intermediate vendor.

The district judge has thought otherwise. The appellee's counsel have invoked as an evidence of the appellant's bad faith, his attempt to induce the parish judge to violate his duty, by hiding the truth and giving a false certificate. It is true, this attempt of the appellant, though no evidence of his good faith, at the time it was made, is no absolute evidence of dishonesty at the time of the purchase. It may have had some influence on the inferior judge, and we are not ready to say it ought not to have any. Men ought to be deterred from the commission of a dishonest act, by the reflection that it will render their deviation from the path of rectitude more easily believed, in other instances.

. The magnitude of the sum for which the land was mortgaged, 20,000 dollars, and the delayed time of payment, have been presented by the appellee's counsel as violent presumptions that the appellant was not deceived by the recorder's certificate.

After a close examination of the case, we have come to the conclusion, that, as the case turns on a simple question of fact, on the solution of which it is far from clear that the district judge erred, we ought not to reverse the judgment.

It is, therefore, ordered, adjudged and decreed, that the judgment of the district court be affirmed, with costs.

Morse, for the plaintiffs.
Seghers, for the defendant.

Abat *v.* Holmes. VIII, N. S. 145.

If a party be not cited, and judgment be had against him and he imprisoned thereon, he may avail himself of the want of citation.

In a suit against partners, service on the sister of one of them, at his house, is irregular.

A party imprisoned, sued to make a surrender, may reconvene the plaintiff in damages for a wrongful imprisonment.

FIRST District.

Porter, J., delivered the opinion of the court.

The petitioner alleges, that judgment was rendered in his favor against the firm of C. C. Whitman & Co., for the sum of 1003 dollars, with interest. That this firm was composed of three partners, viz: Whitman, Howard and the defendant, who were all liable *in solido* for the debt.

That on the 3d of November, 1827, the defendant was arrested on a writ of *capius ad satisfaciendum;* that since his arrest his co-obligors have discharged part of the debt, and that there remains now due the sum of 409 dollars 16 cents, for which the defendant made no satisfaction, although he has been fourteen months imprisoned.

The petition concludes that the defendant be compelled to deliver a schedule of his property on oath, and transfer the same to his creditors, agreeably to " an act for the relief of insolvent debtors in actual custody, and for establishing prison bounds for the public jails and for other purposes," approved March, 25th, 1808.

The defendant's answer admits the imprisonment, but denies the legality of it. He denies that there is any judgment against him in favor of the plaintiff, and concludes by praying remuneration; that in consequence of the illegal, oppressive and wrongful imprisonment, he has sustained from the acts of the plaintiff, the latter be condemned to pay the sum of 1000 dollars with costs of suit.

The plaintiff filed an exception to the answer, on the ground, that, in the suit in which the writ had issued, the defendant had pleaded satisfaction of the judgment. The judge was of opinion, that no citation having been served on the defendant in the suit, in which the *capias ad satisfaciendum* had issued, the petition filed in this case should be dismissed. But he considered this was not a case in which remuneration could be asked and ordered that the defendant's prayer for damages should be overruled.

The plaintiff appealed from this decision, and the defendant has prayed, that so much of the decree as dismissed his prayer in remuneration should be amended.

39*

[Abat *. Holmes.]

The fact of the defendant not having been regularly cited in the case of the plaintiff against Whitman & Co., is clearly established. The return of the sheriff in that case was, " served a copy of petition and copy of citation in the French and English languages, on C. C. Whitman, by leaving the same with his sister, Miss Whitman, at his domicil, in Delor street, between Tchoupitoulas and Magazine streets, Dec. 29, 1826."

The Code of Practice, article 198, requires citations in suits against a partnership, to be served on one of the firm in person, or at their store or counting house, by delivery to their clerk or agent. The return here shows the service to have been made at the house of one of the partners, and does not state the citation was delivered to a clerk or agent of the firm. It was therefore contrary to law, and could not be the basis of a judgment, unless the want of it has been waived by some act of the defendants.

The first ground taken to support the waiver, is the silence of the defendant, after notice of judgment was served on him. But no such consequence can in our opinion follow the neglect to make opposition. It is not so enacted by positive law, and without such a provision, the court can see no ground for declaring the defendant abandoned his right; because he did not assert it the moment he was aware of its infringement.

It is shown the defendant has been fourteen months in confinement, under the writ of *capias ad satisfaciendum*, and it is further shown, that since he was confined, he endeavored to be restored to his liberty by application to the court, under whose authority the writ issued. This application was grounded on the fact of one of his co-debtors having been imprisoned on the same judgment, and discharged out of custody by the plaintiff in execution.

The application to be discharged out of custody, in consequence of an act of the plaintiff, did not, in our opinion, admit there was a legal cause for imprisonment. This is quite different from a man pleading *non est factum*, and payment for an obligation which, never existing, cannot have been paid. But a judgment, improperly obtained, may be discharged by some subsequent act of the party obtaining it, and such act, and the attempt by the defendant to profit by it, do not necessarily imply that the judgment was legal.

The defendant permitting himself to be arrested on the writ of *capias ad satisfaciendum* is next relied on, as evidence of his acquiescence in the legality of the judgment. If this be true, the writ had the same effect one hour, or one minute, after the defendant was arrested, as it has now. The provisions in the Code of Practice, 612 and 613, evidently apply to cases, where the party cast has stood by and suffered the money to be made by a sale of his property, as may be seen by the corresponding part of the work in French. They can have no application to the execution of the judgment by imprisonment; for then the attempt of the plaintiff to enforce the judgment, by arresting the defendant, would deprive him of all means of opposition.

[Abat v. Holmes.]

Between the seizure and sale of his goods, time is afforded to make opposition; for the execution does not obtain its object, in other words, is not executed, until the sale. So under the *capias ad satisfaciendum* the judgment is not executed, in the meaning attached to their words in the Code of Practice, until the defendant by reason of the coercion, practised on his person, pays the money.

We differ with the judge below, in regard to the plea of reconvention. We think the demand is connected with, and incidental to the claim of the petitioner, to compel him to surrender his goods. The plaintiff insists he has a sight, in consequence of the imprisonment of the defendant, to force him to make out a schedule of his goods, and abandon them to his creditors. The latter replies, that far from such a consequence following the imprisonment, he has a right to demand damages by reason of the confinement of his person being illegal. There appears to us a close connection between their demands. They both spring from the same cause.

It is, therefore, ordered, adjudged and decreed, that the judgment of the district court be annulled, avoided and reversed, and it is further ordered, adjudged and decreed, that the petition of the plaintiff be dismissed, and that this cause be remanded to try the question, arising on the defendants demand in remuneration, and it is further ordered, that the appellant pay the costs of this appeal.

Seghers, for the plaintiff.
Slidell, for the defendant.

Kennedy & Duchamp v. Develin. VIII, N. S. 150.

Every allegation, on which a prayor for judgment is grounded, may be disproved.
If a sequestration be obtained against an absent debtor, he may on his return disprove the facts sworn to.

PARISH Court of New Orleans.

PORTER, J., delivered the opinion of the court.
Under the act of assembly of the 29th of March, 1826, authorising creditors of an absconding debtor to sequestrate his property, and proceed against him as in case of a forced surrender, the plaintiffs made oath, that the defendant had absconded, and obtained an order

of sequestration against his goods and effects. The judge further directed a meeting of the creditors of the defendant, and appointed counsel to defend the rights of the absent creditor. This order is dated on the 18th of March, 1829.

Previous to the time fixed for the meeting of the creditors, the defendant returned to the state, and took a rule on the plaintiffs to show cause why the order of sequestration should not be set aside, on the ground, that the allegations in the petition, on which it issued, were untrue. This rule is dated on the 3d of April, 1829.

It came on, and was tried on the 18th of the same month. Three days after, a meeting of the creditors was had, who voted for an acceptance of the surrender of his property, and the appointment of syndics.

On the trial of the cause, the plaintiffs objected to any evidence being introduced by the defendant, on the ground, that no proof was admissible to disprove the allegations contained in the petition. The judge admitted the evidence, and a bill of exception was taken to his opinion.

The court committed no error in admitting the proof. It may be safely stated as a general rule, that all allegations in a petition, which are set forth as the ground on which a judgment is asked, are subject to be disproved by the party against whom they are made. The contrary doctrine would place every man in society at the mercy of those who thought proper to allege what was not true against him. The act of the legislature which furnishes the remedy, resorted to by the creditors in this instance, has made no exception to the principle just stated. If it had, its constitutionality might well be doubted. Acts of 1826, page 140, art. 6.

In this court it has been contended, that the case was improperly tried in the court below, on a rule to show cause, why the sequestration should not be set aside. That an answer should have been put in and the case tried in the ordinary way, after issue joined.

Admitting the position to be correct, the plaintiffs are too late in making the objection. They should have made opposition on this ground, to an inquiry on the merits, in the court of the first instance after taking the chance of, and obtaining a judgment in their favor in the tribunal below, they cannot be permitted to send the cause back and have it tried a second time. The issue, though not formally made upon the rule, was sufficiently so, in substance, to authorise a judgment on the merits.

It is alleged, that a proceeding so informal as this was, can not bind the other creditors. This again might be true, if those creditors, at the time the rule was taken and heard, had joined in the petititon. But the case was tried on the 18th, and the meeting before the notary, at which they voted for accepting the surrender, did not take place until the 21st. Until they gave their assent, the case was alone between the petitioners and the defendant.

[Kennedy & Duchamp v. Develin.]

On the merits, the opinion of the judge below was in favor of the plaintiffs, and against the defendant.

We are in the habit of paying considerable respect to the conclusion of the courts in the first instance, on questions of fact, but, in this case, the evidence has produced a totally different impression on our minds, and we yield the more readily to our conclusion; because the judge seems to have decided against the defendant, not on the fact of his having absconded, but of the plaintiffs having good cause to suppose he had.

The view, which the court below took of the case, has been much pressed on our consideration. A great deal has been said of the circumstances, under which the defendant left the city, on his voyage to New York, and that they furnished just cause for the belief entertained by the petitioners, that he had absconded. The fallacy of this reasoning, in relation to the inquiry we have now to make, appears to us obvious. All the causes of suspicion which the plaintiffs allege, may have existed at the time the writ of sequestration was taken out. But the case has to be tried by us, not only on the grounds of belief which the petitioners had at the time they sued out the writ of sequestration; but on all the facts which have been developed since the defendant's return. That return, the circumstances which occurred during his absence, the course of conduct pursued by him in New York, the fact of his having purchased goods and shipped them for this port, with many other matters which need not be stated in detail, must all be examined, as well as those in which the plaintiffs took out a writ of sequestration. The fact that we have to try is, whether the defendant was an absconding debtor at the time the proceedings commenced against him. On the proof now adduced, not a doubt exists in our minds, that he was not. The argument, used by the petitioners, might be entitled to great weight, if they were sued for damages for taking out the writ; but the belief of a fact and its existence are different things.

It is, therefore, ordered, adjudged and decreed, that the judgment of the parish court be annulled, avoided and reversed; and it is further ordered, adjudged and decreed, that the writ of sequestration granted in this case be set aside; that the cause be remanded, to be proceeded in according to law, and that the appellee pay the costs of this appeal.

M'Caleb *v.* Hart.   VIII, N. S. 155.

FIRST District.

If there be judgment against the vendee in favor of the vendor, and the party called in warranty on an appeal of both judgments, that in favor of the warrantor cannot be examined, unless he was cited.

Bushnell *v.* Brown's Heirs.   VIII, N. S. 157.

If a case be remanded the court on its return, cannot examine proceedings, anterior to the remanding.

If on remanding, the court directs a survey, and the party in whose favor it is directed, does not object to proceeding below without it, he cannot on a second appeal assign as error, that no survey took place.

THIRD District, Judge of the Fourth presiding.

Martin, J., delivered the opinion of the court.

This case was remanded from this court, at May term, 1826, 4 *N. S.* 501, with directions to the judge to grant an order of survey, and admit in evidence the records of the court against the plaintiff.

There was judgment for the defendants, the injunction was dissolved, and the plaintiff appealed.

The appellant's counsel has drawn our attention to a bill of exceptions, taken at the trial or before the judgment was reversed in May, 1826. It appears to us that we can not travel back, beyond the proceedings posterior to our last judgment.

He further says, that the order of survey, which we ordered to issue, was not granted. It was for the party for whose benefit this order was to issue, to move for it: if he did not, the presumption is, that he was satisfied that the case should proceed without it.

He complains, lastly, that the process verbal of the sale is not a title: there were no witnesses to the sale.

We have held that the process verbal of a sale by the register of wills in the city of New Orleans, is evidence of title. Habine v. Zanico, 5 *Martin*, 372.

There is no copy of the process verbal of sale coming with the record, and we can not ascertain what witnesses there were. It was the duty of the appellant, who now alleges this fact, to enable us to ascertain its existence.

It is, therefore, ordered, adjudged and decreed, that the judgment of the district court be affirmed, with costs.

Poignard v. Livermore. VIII, N. S. 158.

FIRST District.

The decision of the judge *a quo* on matters of fact respected.

Brand v. Daunoy. VIII, N. S. 159.

The vendee has a right to the land, as far as the spot called for as a boundary, though the distance given does not enable him to reach it. The ambiguity was *latent* and arose from matters within the instrument.

FIRST District.

Porter, J., delivered the opinion of the court.

The petitioner sold to the defendant a lot of ground with buildings, erected on it. The matter in dispute between the parties grows out of the sale, and relates to a passage of three feet in front on the street, with fifty in depth, adjoining the lot. The defendant insists it made a part of the property purchased by her from the plaintiff. He contends, it was not included in the conveyance.

The court of the first instance gave judgment against the petitioner, and he appealed.

In the act of sale, the property is described, as being that which the plaintiff purchase from John McDonogh, containing twenty-two feet six inches in front, with one hundred and ten in depth, bounded on one side by property belonging to Manual Andry, and on the other by a lot of the vendor.

This passage is only fifty feet in depth, and there is land enough independent of it, to supply the number of feet which the deed declares the lot to contain. So far the facts support the plaintiff's pretensions; but the description of the boundaries is inconsistent with them; for, if the three feet were retained by him, then the lot was not as the conveyance states, bounded on one side by property of Andry, and on the other by the vendor's. The limits on each side would have been land of the seller; or rather it would have been bounded on one side, to the depth of fifty feet by land of the petitioner, and on the remaining portion of one hundred and ten feet, its limit would have been the property of Andry.

With this uncertainty, in regard to the boundaries, we think the court did not err, in admitting parol evidence. The ambiguity was *latent*; and arose from matters without the instrument.

The evidence proves satisfactorily, that the passage now sued for entered into the views of the parties at the time the contract was made. We think the court below did not err, in deciding against the plaintiff.

There are two bills of exceptions taken by the plaintiff. The first relates to the permission given by the court to the appellee to prove title, when she had not pleaded it in her answer. On referring to the answer, we find it does aver the defendant to be the owner of the premises sued for. It would have been more regular, if the answer had stated under what title the defendant derived her right; but, as we can not believe the plaintiff was surprised by the production of his own deed, we see no reason for remanding the cause, more particularly as no application was made for a new trial on that ground, in the court below.

The second goes to the refusal to permit the clerk of the notary to testify, that he went to another notary's office, to examine the sale from McDonogh to Brand, and took a note of the title and boundaries, for the purpose of drawing the deed from the plaintiff to defendant. The proof was objected to, as irrelevant, and we think correctly. We are unable to perceive what effect it could have on the case.

It is, therefore, ordered, adjudged and decreed, that the judgment of the district court be affirmed, with costs.

Watts, for the plaintiff.

Pierce, for the defendant.

Donaldson v. Rouzan. VIII, N. S. 162.

SECOND District.

Held, a sheriff's deed does not pass the property of the defendant in execution, unless there be a judgment.

But if the debt has been paid, he cannot recover his property, without paying the purchaser.

Byrd v. M'Micken. VIII, N. S. 163.

A curator cannot compensate a claim of the estate, with a debt due to a firm of which he is a member.

COURT of Probates, Parish of West Feliciana.

MARTIN, J., delivered the opinion of the court.

This case was remanded from this court, in May, 1827, 5 N. S. 516. On its return, M'Micken filed an answer, averring his readiness to receive the property of the estate in the hands of Byrd, and to receive and settle his accounts, but denied Byrd's right to retain any part of the estate, for the firm of A. & W. Byrd. He urged that Byrd was chargable for the appraised value of the property of the estate, having disposed of it in an illegal manner.

Haroldson intervened, and prayed to be subrogated with his co-surety on Byrd's curator's bond, to the rights of the estate on Byrd's property.

The court decreed, that Byrd's account on file, so far as it relates to privileged debts paid by him, be allowed and passed; that the sum of 2557 dollars 11 cents, be considered as compensated with, or paid to A. & W. Byrd, and the balance, 1956 dollars 91 cents, be paid to the present curator, M'Micken, for the benefit of the creditors of the estate, with the reservation in favor of the sureties on Byrd's curator bond, and of a privilege or preference over the creditors of the firm of A. &. W. Byrd; the costs to be paid by the estate.

The court certainly erred, in allowing Byrd, the former curator, any part of the estate, or considering the same as compensated with, for the benefit of A. & W. Byrd; they must be paid with the other creditors of the estate, and the former curator must absolutely empty his hands into those of the present.

The sureties of the first curator may be subrogated to rights of his, but not to those of a firm, of which he was a member. Although a partner be appointed curator of the estate of a debtor of the firm, his acts, as a curator, are not the acts of the firm, and if he waste the estate, and his sureties suffer, their claim is against him alone, and not against the firm.

As to the demand of the present curator, that the former account for the value of the goods, at the price of the appraisement, the court of probates have not acted on it. It appears by the record, that a very large proportion of the estate was purchased by A. & W. Byrd, of the firm of whom the then curator was a partner. The case in this particular cannot be distinguished from that of Hand *et al. v.* Norris' Heirs, 11 *Martin,* 297. The sale was illegal, and as the curator received the goods, it is just he should account for them, at their appraised value.

It is, therefore, ordered, adjudged and decreed, that the judgment of the court of probates be annulled, avoided and reversed, and the case be remanded, with directions to the judge of probates to cause the former curator and appellee, Byrd, to account for the appraised value of the goods, purchased by the firm of A. & W. Byrd, and himself, and for all moneys in his hands, without allowing him to retain or compensate any part thereof, with, or for, the firm of A. & W. Byrd, and proceed therein, according to the principles here laid down; the appellee paying costs in this court.

Preston, for the plaintiff.

Livaudais *v.* Steamboat America. VIII, N. S. 166.

[When the evidence is not conclusive, the decision below is not disturbed.

FIRST District.

PORTER, J., delivered the opinion of the court.

This action is brought to recover the value of the plaintiff's slave, drowned in consequence of a pirogue, in which he was descending the river, being run against by the steamboat, and upset.

The cause was submitted twice to juries, in the court of the first instance, without a verdict being obtained. They disagreed in both instances. The case was then submitted to the judge, who decided in favor of the defendant, and the plaintiff appealed.

The evidence is contradictory and cannot be reconciled. After several perusals, our minds have been left in doubt, whether the accident was owing to the negligence of the persons in care of the boat, or not. Under these circumstances, as the burden of establishing his right to recover was thrown on the plaintiff, and, as there has been a decision in the court of the first instance in favor of the defendant, it must prevail here.

It is, therefore, ordered, adjudged and decreed, that the judgment of the court of probates be affirmed, with costs.

Maurian and *Derbigny*, for the plaintiff.

Eustis, for the defendant.

Belden *et al. v.* Rose. VIII, N, S. 167.

Evidence may be received to support a plea of tender, in which the time is not stated.
When the court is not satisfied with the verdict, the case is remanded.

FIRST District.

MARTIN, J., delivered the opinion of the court.

In this case, there is a bill of exceptions to the opinion of the court, permitting the defendant to give evidence to support a plea of tender, the period of which was not stated in the answer.

The statute does not require defendants to state the matters they urge in their defence, with all the correctness of time and place, which are required in the petition; the reason is, that the defence is more favored, than the claim. Payment may be pleaded, without saying when and where it was made, and tender is more analogous to payment, than any other defence. We think the district court did not err.

The defendant is in possession of a verdict and judgment. We have not viewed the case in the same manner as the jury, and it becomes our duty to remand the case, for a second inquiry, especially as the plaintiff made an unsuccessful attempt to set the verdict aside.

It is, therefore ordered, adjudged and decreed, that the judgment of the district court be annulled, avoided and reversed, the verdict set aside, and the case remanded for a new trial, the defendant and appellee paying costs in this court.

Maybin, for the plaintiffs.

Eustis, for the defendants.

Jayne *et al. v.* Cox. VIII, N. S. 168.

The surety on a bond, with the condition that the principal shall not depart without leave of the court may surrender him.

In the third line of 230th article of the Code of Practice, the copulative *and* has been substituted for the disjunctive *or*. In the French text, it is rightly printed *ou*.

FIRST District.

MARTIN, J., delivered the opinion of the court.

The defendant, bail of a debtor of the plaintiff, surrendered his principal, before any judgment against him, the bail. The plaintiff insisted that, as his debtor had gone out of the state, pending the suit, the bail was fixed and could not discharge himself by the surrender.

The district court gave judgment for the defendant, and the plaintiffs appealed.

The condition of the bond subscribed by the present defendant, was that the plaintiffs' debtor should not depart the state without the leave of the court, and that in case he did, the present defendant should pay, &c. Code of Practice, 219.

The 222d article provides, that a debtor, whose debt is not yet payable, on being arrested, shall give bond to appear, when the debt becomes due, &c.

The 224th article provides that an insolvent debtor, who has ceded his goods, may, in certain cases, be arrested, and obtain his liberty, by giving bond not to leave the limits of the jurisdiction of the court.

The 230th article provides, that one, who becomes surety that another shall not depart the state, or leave the jurisdiction of the court, by which the order of surety was granted, and that he will appear to answer the judgment, may be discharged from all responsibility, by surrendering to the sheriff the person of the debtor, whom he had arrested.

It is clear, that the legislature, by the 230th article, meant to provide for the discharge of sureties of ordinary defendants, sued on a debt already payable, who give bond not to depart the state; the sureties of debtors who are arrested on debts not yet payable, who give surety to appear; and the sureties of insolvent debtors, who give surety not to leave the limits of the jurisdiction of the court. By a classical or typographical error, the copulative *and*, in the third line of the 230th article, has been substituted for the disjunctive *or*, in the text. In the French version, the particle *ou* is used.

40*

[Jayne *et al. v.* Cox.]

The present defendant and appellee was, therefore, discharged from all liability, by surrendering the plaintiff's debtor.

It is, therefore, ordered, adjudged and decreed, that the judgment of the district court be affirmed, with costs.

Slidell, for the plaintiff.

Strawbridge, for the defendant.

Rochelle *et al. v.* Alvarez. VIII, N. S. 171.

PARISH Court of New Orleans.

Actions take their character from the nature of the relief sought. Code of Practice, 43, 46.

Bulloc *v.* Pailhos. VIII, N. S. 172.

PARISH Court of New Orleans.

Held, if on a verdict, there be judgment for the plaintiff, and on an appeal the court thinks it ought to have been for the defendant, the former may be indulged with a new trial, although he did not ask one below.

Donaldson *v.* Winter.   VIII, N. S. 775.

The sentence of a court of probates admitting a will is *prima facie* binding.
The copy of a sheriff's deed is no legal evidence till the absence of the original be accounted for.
A sheriff's deed must be supported by a judgment.

SECOND District.

PORTER, J., delivered the opinion of the court.

The plaintiff, as universal heir of the late Wm. Donaldson, claims from the defendant a number of lots in the town of Donaldsonville, which she alleges to be her property.

The defendant admits he is in possession of the land, mentioned in the petition; but denies that the plaintiff has any right under the will of Donaldson.

He also sets up a title under a purchase from Walker Gilbert, who bought, at a sale made by the sheriff of the parish of Ascension, under an execution or order of seizure, bearing date the   day of 1826, issued by the judge of said parish, for a duty, lately assessed on said land, of 680 dollars, for making a levee in front thereof, on the Bayou Lafourche.

And he pleads the prescription of three, five and ten years; and prays, that if he be evicted, the plaintiff may be decreed to pay him 2500 dollars, the value of improvements, put by him on the premises.

Several bills of exceptions were taken on the trial. The first was to the introduction of Donaldson's will in evidence. It was objected to on the following grounds:

1. That it should have been signed by five witnesses, not including Livingston.

2. That it was not proved according to law nor ordered to be executed.

The will concludes in these words: "which has been dictated by me to Edward Livingston, one of the witnesses thereof, written by him in my presence, and declared as my last will and testament, in the presence of the other witnesses, who have signed the same the 28th of August 1813. Signed William Donaldson. Acknowledged and declared by the said testator to be his last will and testament in our presence. Signed, George W. Dewees, Richard Relf, Benjamin Morgan, Edward Livingston, Waters Clark."

By the provisions of the old Code, in force at the time this will was opened, it is declared to suffice for the validity of a nuncupative act under private signature, that the testator in the presence of five witnesses "present the paper, on which he has written his testament, or caused it to be written out of their presence, declaring to them that, that paper incloses his last will."

It is contended the will offered here is of no effect, because it does not appear it was presented 'to all the witnesses at the same time, nor signed in presence of them, nor that the witnesses signed in presence of each other.

The proofs on which the testament was admitted to probate, consisted of the oath of three of the witnesses who declared, that it " was made at the instance and under the direction of the late William Donaldson, deceased, at New Orleans the 27th instant, is the same that the late William Donaldson caused to be written in his presence by Mr. Edward Livingston, on the 28th of August, *anno domini* 1813, and also that they recognised their signatures as well as that of the testator, given in their presence at the foot of the said last will, that the said William Donaldson told them was such, his last will and testament for the purpose therein mentioned."

This proof is literally that required by the 157th article of the Code for the admission of the will to probate. The whole proceedings by the court, which ordered the execution of it, appear to be regular, and in conformity with law. The sentence therefore is *prima facie* at least binding on all persons. Whether it is not conclusive, may be doubted, but it is unnecessary to examine that question, for, no proof was adduced on the trial to contradict the evidence, on which the probate was granted.

There are four bills of exception taken by the plaintiffs. The points of law presented by them appear to us correctly decided by the judge of the first instance: one of them, however requires a particular examination.

This bill of exceptions states, that the defendant having introduced in evidence the deed of sale of the sheriff of the parish of Ascension to Walker Gilbert, recorded in the book of records of sheriff's sales of the parish of Ascension, the plaintiff objected to its admission, &c., &c.

If the instrument offered was a copy, there was error in admitting it; the law in regard to sheriffs' deeds requires the original to be delivered up by the recording officer, and, until it is accounted for, the copy is inferior evidence. But we can not gather from the exception taken in the case, whether it was the original, which had been recorded, or a copy from the record, which was offered by the defendant. As it was the duty of the plaintiff to bring up the facts in such a manner, as to enable us to decide, whether there was error or not, he cannot have the case remanded, or the decision of the court below overruled.

The court below thought, that the sheriff's deed without a judgment did not support the defendant's right to the cause, and, in that opinion we concur.

. We are not to be understood, in giving our assent to the conclusion of the judge below, to do so, on the grounds on which its correctness has been assailed here. If the records of a court of justice be lost, we see no reason why, after their existence and loss are established, that the next best evidence, which the nature of the case is susceptible of, should not be received, and if written copies do not exist of them their contents may be established by parol testimony. But, for obvious reasons, this proof should be received with great caution, and, in the case before us, it is far from satisfactory. The keepers of the records, in which the proceedings should have been preserved, testify not only to the non-existence of any such suit among them, but they also declare, that none such is found on the docket or records which have been kept as the legal proceedings in the parish. The sheriff states in the margin, that he sold by virtue of an order to him directed without saying from what court, or judge, that order emanated. None of the witnesses prove, that a judgment or decree was regularly entered up. The parish judge came nearer it than any other, and he goes no further than to swear, "that he heard they were advertised and sold at public sale according to law—that all the formalities required by law were complied with."

In decreeing the defendant to restore possession of the premises to the plaintiff, the court directed, that previous thereto the latter should pay to the former 680 dollars, the amount made out of the sale and applied to the payment of the testator's debts, together with the sum of 2000 dollars, the value of the improvements, made by the defendant on the land.

The first part of this direction was clearly correct and requires no observation from the court. The justice and legality of the other has been impugned principally on the ground, that allowance was not made in favor of the plaintiff for the fruits made from the soil, since the institution of the suit, at which time it is asserted he appeared to be in good faith. This position we think correct; the defendant entered into possession of the premises long before the passage of the law which made good faith cease with the institution of the suit. It is a sound rule of construction never to consider laws, as applying to cases which arise previous to their passage, unless the legislature have, in express terms declared such to be their intention. If that declaration had been made in this instance, a serious question would have arisen, as to their power to do so. They have no right perhaps to add to the obligations or responsibility, which flowed from the contract at the time the defendant made it: or abridge any of the rights which it conferred. At the time the defendant made the purchase, and entered into possession; he did so *bona fide,* and as a consequence of his good faith he had a right to make the fruits his own, until his bad faith was established by the law, as it then stood. If he had a right then to contest a demand for the property, with the privilege of making the fruits his own, it would seem that a subsequent law can not change his responsibility, and say, that he shall

[Donaldson v. Winter,]

not execute that right, unless he loses the fruit. The case can not be satisfactorily distinguished from that of Brown v. Thompson, 6 N. S. 426.

· Taking the defendant's obligation to restore the fruits, by the provisions of the old Code, we think the sale from White to him, made him a possessor in good faith, and we believe he continued so until · the decision of the case in the district court.

We think the judgment below meets the equity and justice of the case, and is supported by the evidence in relation to the value of the improvements.

It is, therefore, ordered, adjudged and decreed, that the judgment of the district court be affirmed, with costs.*

M'Caleb, for the plaintiff.

Watts, for the defendant.

---

* In the above case, the court doubting the correctness of its judgment, in relation to the demand for fruits, ordered a rehearing, and it was finally decided, 1 *Lou. Rep.* 137, affirming the doctrines here advanced.

WESTERN DISTRICT, SEPT. TERM, 1829.

Meeker *v.* Muggah. VIII, N. S. 184.

FIFTH District.

An appeal made returnable at the *next* term of the Supreme Court after taken, and not filed until the *second* term thereafter, will be dismissed with costs.

Nerault's Heirs *et ux. v.* L'Enclos. VIII, N. S. 185.

The claim of the *buyer* against the *vendor* in warranty, in case of eviction, under the old Civil Code, is *defined* at page 354, art. 54, which determines the manner and amount of restitution.

Interest does not run, in case of eviction, until the warrantor is put *in mora*, by being cited in warranty, or by demanding the sum, which is the price of the thing evicted.

When the demand of the sum which is the *price* of the thing evicted, is made, *interest* is due, *only*, as in case of an ordinary debt; and interest runs from the time of the demand.

[Nerault's Heirs *et ux. v.* L'Enclos.]
FIFTH District.

This suit was brought to recover the price of a slave, evicted, with interest from the date of eviction and costs. On the 30th of June, 1813, A. L'Enclos, sold to J. B. Nerault, ancestor of the plaintiffs, a slave named Victoire, for 500 dollars. Afterwards, the wife of L'Enclos, the vendor, obtained judgment against her husband for her dotal property. . The husband was insolvent, and she restored to her tacit mortgage, and seized the slave Victoire, in the hands of the vendee, and on the 16th of January, 1816, sold her for 455 dollars. In May, 1829, the heirs of Nerault sued the tutor to the only heir of L'Enclos, and had judgment for price, interest and costs, of the slave.

Martin, J., delivered the opinion of the court.
The defendant, the appellant, complains of the judgment of the district court, because interest was allowed before the inception of the suit.
He was sued as warrantor of a slave, sold to the plaintiffs, who were evicted, and the judgment is for the consideration of the sale, with interest from the period of the eviction.
The claim of the buyer against the vendor in warranty, is defined by the old Code, (under which the sale of the slave took place,) 354, art. 54. 1. It extends to the restitution of the price. 2. The fruits received by the buyer. 3. To costs; and 4. Damages when they are suffered, besides the restitution of the price.*
The appellee has, we think, incorrectly assumed that the warrantor owes interest, in the same manner as the buyer, who withholds the price of a thing which produces fruits. The buyer knows he owes the fruits. The warrantor must be put *in morâ;* he has no means

---

* For the settlement of the doubts whether this liability of vendors for the increased value at the time of the eviction, under the old Code, has been curtailed by the new Code, see the progressive decisions in Morris *v.* Abat *et al.,* 9 *Lou. Rep.* 522, and in Bissell *et ux. v.* Erwin's Heirs, 13 *Lou. Rep.* 143, the former declaring the liability for increased value, or "profits not made," to be entirely abolished by the Louisiana Code: the latter, under a formal respect for the decision in 9 *Lou. Rep.* manifestly aiming to undermine it. The court, (1839, consisting of Martin, President, Rost and Eustis, Associate Justices,) in the case of Bissell *v.* Erwin, lay down the law thus: "The law now stands here as it did in France, before the adoption of the Code, and there the increased value of the property invariably formed part of the damages expressed on a warranty, but such increase only, as the parties could have in contemplation at the time of the contract, ought to be taken into account, and the vendor should not be made to pay the increase which results from unforeseen events, or from accidental or transient causes."

Quære, whether any possible future increase of value in real estate, sold in New Orleans since 1829, could be said to arise from transient causes and to be unforeseen or not actually guaranteed to buyers by the ardent speculators at Hewlett's or Banks's.

Quære, also, how this doctrine would apply, *e converso,* to diminished value.

[Nerault's Heirs *et al. v.* L'Enclos.]

of knowing the eviction, till the buyer apprises him of it by a demand; and that demand is of a sum of money, on which interest is due only, as in the case of an ordinary debt. In the present case, it does not appear, that any notice of the eviction was given to the appellant, till about thirteen years after it happened.

It is, therefore, ordered, adjudged and decreed, that the judgment of the district court be annulled, avoided and reversed, and that the appellee recover of the appellant the sum of five hundred dollars, with interest at five per cent. from the inception of this suit until paid, with costs of suit in the district court, and that he pay the costs in this.

Bowen, for the plaintiffs.
Curry, for the defendant.

Fux *v.* King and King *v.* Fux.   VIII, N. S. 187.

FIFTH District, Judge of the Sixth presiding.

Decided, that the Supreme Court will not rescind an order consolidating two cases, made by consent of parties, and by which one of the parties has a privileged claim compensated in judgment, by an ordinary debt, and prays for a new trial and rescission of the order.

A new trial will not be awarded on the ground that the party cast in the suit, incautiously placed his case before the court in a particular form, in which a privileged claim was compensated by an ordinary debt.

Parties must be bound by the acts of their counsel in conducting a cause, and no relief will be afforded, on the ground that a case was incautiously placed before the court for a decision and judgment.

Garahan *v.* Weeks. VIII, N. S. 191.

FIFTH District.

Decided, that a person undertaking to superintend a distillery and sugar plantation comes under an implied covenant, to possess and display the necessary skill to conduct such business.

A person exhibiting such skill in the performance of his agreement, will be enabled to recover the full amount of his wages due, in an action for work and labor done, *on a quantum meruit.*

Ducrest's Heirs *v.* Bijeau's Estate. VIII, N. S. 192.

Parol evidence is admissible under the Spanish law, to prove the alienation and acquisition of property, such as land and slaves.

A *transaction,* made before the adoption of the old Civil Code, alienating slaves, in virtue of which the heirs of the ancestor, who was the vendee, claim such slaves and their increase, must be governed by the laws of Spain.

By the Spanish law, if the money which the wife brought into marriage, whether *dotal* or *paraphernal,* was employed in the purchase of slaves, or other immovable, the property became hers if she chose.

When the purchase was made with the wife's consent, the property was hers at the dissolution of the marriage, whether her husband was insolvent or not.

If the purchase of an immovable was made with her money and without the wife's consent, she had only a subsidiary right, to be exercised in case of her husband's insolvency.

The slaves which the *second* husband of the grandmother, received in payment of a debt due the community existing between her and her *first* husband, go to the heirs of the grandmother: but the increase of the slaves belong to the community as acquests and gains.

The *produce* or *increase* of slaves and animals are considered as much the result of the care and solicitude of their possessors. as of nature, and form a part of the community of acquests and gains.

FIFTH District.

[Ducrest's Heirs s. Bijeau's Estate.]

Martha Castille married Laurent Ducrest, in 1787, and had issue
two sons—Joseph married Zelia Guidry, and had issue two sons,
Nicholas and Joseph Ducrest, who are minors—their father is now
dead. Laurent Ducrest died in 1805–6, leaving a large estate in
community, consisting of a plantation, negroes, cattle, &c. of which
an inventory was made, except the cattle. His widow Martha
Castille, married Auguste Bijeau in 1807, and had no issue. No
estimative inventory was made, or family meeting called, so that the
mother lost the tutorship of her only surviving child and son, Joseph.
Bijeau took possession of the property contained in the inventory of
the late community of the first marriage.

After the death of Laurent Ducrest, his wife Martha sold or ex-
changed a negress named Janette, to Col. Declouet, and after her
marriage with Bijeau he received from Declouet, the price of Janette
in three other slaves, viz: Honorie, Constance and Julie by paying
a small balance with the money of Martha, his wife. These three
slaves had increase, Toussant, Henry, Lerise, Sam and Henriette.
Auguste Bijeau, died in June, 1823; having sold to Joseph Ducrest,
his stepson, who was yet a minor, without a tutor or curator, at
extravagant prices, the plantation and slaves belonging to the succession of L. Ducrest.

Auguste Bijeau, died in February, 1824, leaving his affairs very
much embarrassed and his estate involved in debt. Joseph Ducrest,
the stepson, renounced his claim as testamentary heir, to Bijeau;
and Martha, the wife and mother of Joseph Ducrest by her first marriage, also renounced the community. A. Dumartrait, was appointed
curator to the vacant succession of Bijeau. Joseph, the only surviving
child by the first marriage, sued the curator for the annulment of the
sale, made to him whilst a minor by Bijeau, and for the recovery of
the slaves and other increase and all other property coming from the
succession of Laurent Ducrest. The slaves, it was admitted, were
acquired subsequent to the marriage of Martha with Bijeau; but
with the proceeds of the succession of Laurent Ducrest and the money of the said Martha.

Parol evidence was admitted to prove the transaction by which
the said slaves were acquired from Declouet.

During the pendency of this suit, Joseph Ducrest died, and it has
been revived in the name of his heirs, viz: Zelia Guidry, his wife,
in her own right, and a natural tutrix of Nicholas and Joseph Ducrest, his two children; Martha the mother of Joseph as heir to her
second son who died at the age of eleven years. The plaintiffs had
judgment for the annulment of the sale of the three slaves and their
increase. The defendant, Dumartrait as curator, &c. appealed.

PORTER, J., delivered the opinion of the court.

The contest in this case arises between the heirs of Joseph Ducrest
deceased, and the curator of the estate of Auguste Bijeau, deceased,
his stepfather. The heirs made two demands. First, that a sale

made by Bijeau to their father in his lifetime, be set aside. Secondly, that certain slaves claimed by the representative of the estate of Bijeau, as forming a part of it, be declared to be their property. The court of the first instance sanctioned both these demands by its judgment, and the defendant appealed.

The first point in the cause has not been contested before this court and the facts and the law did not authorise its being so. It is proved, that Ducrest was a minor at the time of the sale, and that it was not beneficial to him. It must of consequence be annulled.

The second has been the subject of much discussion. Previous to the death of the plaintiff's grandfather he sold a slave to one Declouet. After the second marriage of their grandmother with Bijeau slaves were received from Declouet by Bijeau in discharge of this obligation. The plaintiffs contend, that as these slaves were acquired in payment of a debt which was due to their ancestor, the property must belong to them in kind. The defendants insist they have only a right to withdraw from the succession the amount of the obligation in money.

Before entering on the merits, we must notice and dispose of a bill of exceptions. The plaintiff offered, and the court received parol evidence to show, that the slaves claimed in the petition had, as is there alleged, been obtained in payment of the note. The defendant objected to this testimony, on the ground, that by law, proof of such facts could only be made by written evidence.

In a case arising under the late Civil Code, this objection would, perhaps, be well taken; but the transaction, to establish which the proof in this case was offered, arose previous to the enactment of that work, and must be governed by the laws of Spain. It has already been decided by this court after much consideration in the case of Gonzales *et al. v.* Sanches *et al.*, 4 *N. S.* 657, that by the Spanish laws, parol evidence was admissible to establish the alienation and acquisition of immovable property. The judge, therefore, did not err in permitting the plaintiffs to introduce the testimony objected to.

On the merits, the defendant has contended, that it is only in case of the property of one of the spouses, being sold during marriage, that the object acquired with the proceeds belongs to them, or her who owned the thing sold; and in support of this position, he has relied on the authority of Pothier, who appears to support him. But this case must be determined by the laws of Spain; for they governed the country at the time the transaction took place. By them, if the money which the wife brought into marriage, whether dotal or paraphernal, was employed in the acquisition of an immovable, it became hers, whether the husband was insolvent or not at the dissolution of the marriage. But, if made without her consent, she had only what the Spanish law writers call a subsidiary right, to be exercised in case of insolvency. The circumstance of the purchase being made in the wife's name does not seem to have made, in that system, any difference. *Febrero, P. 2, lib. c. 3, sect. 1, no's 26, 27; Ibid. c. 4, sect. 1, no. 6 and 7.*

[Ducrest's Heirs v. Bijeau's Estate.]

The plaintiffs are therefore entitled to take the slaves which the husband of their grandmother received in payment of an obligation, due to the community, previously existing between her and her first husband. But have they the same right to the increase of these slaves? The law which confers the power to demand the one, refuses them the other. The increase of slaves and animals, by the early laws of Spain, belonged to the spouse who brought them into marriage. By the later statutes, however, and the modern jurisprudence of that country, the produce of these things are considered to result, as much from the care and solicitude of the possessors, as from nature; and that as such they form a part· of the gains which are to be divided between the husband and wife. *Febrero, part. 2, lib.* 1, *cap.* 4, *sect.* 1, *no.* 24; *Ibid. part. 2, lib.* 1, *cap.* 5, *sect.* 4, *no.* 44.

It is, therefore, ordered, adjudged and decreed, that the judgment of the district court be annulled, avoided and reversed; and it is further ordered, adjudged and decreed, that the sale mentioned in the petition, by which the petitioner's father, Joseph Ducrest, acquired the property, as therein stated, be annulled and made void: and it is further ordered, adjudged and decreed, that the plaintiffs do recover possession and be quieted in their title to the three slaves, acquired by Auguste Bijeau in discharge of a debt, due to the community existing between Martha Castille, one of the plaintiffs and husband, Laurent Ducrest, viz: Honorie, Julie and Constance: and that the increase of said slaves Toussant, Henry, Sam, Louise and Henriette, having become the property of the community, existing between Martha, Castille and Auguste Bijeau be equally divided between the said Martha, and the estate of the said Bijeau: and it is further ordered that the appellee pay the costs of this appeal.

Brownson and *Bowen*, for the plaintiffs.
Simon, for the defendant.

Jackson *et al. v.* Porter.   VIII, N. S. 200.

Parol evidence is admissible to prove the *nature* of a partnership, without producing the articles themselves.

Where two partners join in partnership to practise law, and in the course of business become *agents* to sell land, slaves, &c. the latter's acts or agency being agreed to by all the partners, is as much within the scope of the partnership as if a clause had been inserted, expressly authorising it.

M authorised B B, who were partners in the practice of law, as his agents to sell a tract of land for 4000 dollars: but writes to C on the subject of the land, and says he "*has a thought of asking* 6000 dollars," but does not name any price; and in the meanwhile B B sells it for 4000 dollars—the agency of B B is *not* revoked by the letter from M, the principal, to C.

Where a deed was executed by one of the partners in the name of the partnership, *parol evidence* was received to show the written assent of the other partner to the execution of the deed.

A partnership may be appointed agent or attorney to perform any act, trust or duty, within the objects of the partnership—the responsibility attaches to *all*, and the advantages resulting are enjoyed by *all* the members; although one only of the partners execute the trust in the name of the whole.

Where a partnership is appointed to perform a trust or agency foreign to its object, it is not thereby void, but the trust may be performed, if *all* the partners assent.

FIFTH District.

Thomas Martin of the state of Tennessee owned a tract of land, five arpents wide fronting on the Teche, on each side, and running back forty arpents each way, lying in the parish of St. Mary's, state of Louisiana.   Martin appointed Isaac L. and Joshua Baker, Esqrs., who were associated in practice as attorneys at law, residing in St. Mary's to sell his land for 4000 dollars; Donaldson Caffrey was commissioned as the agent of Judge Porter to buy it, which lay contiguous to a farm of the latter.   In the course of a correspondence between Caffrey and Martin, the latter wrote to Caffrey, from near Nashville, dated January 8, 1827, that he was at a loss how much to ask for the land, but had a thought of asking 6000 dollars.   The Bakers, receiving no further instructions, or advice on the subject of the land, different from that contained in their original appointment, on the 10th of February, 1827, sold the land to Judge Porter for 4000 dollars.   Isaac L. Baker executed a deed as agent of Martin in the name of the partnership (I. L. & J. Baker) which was confirmed by the written assent of Joshua Baker as one of the partners.

On the 7th of March 1827, Thomas Martin sold and conveyed the

[Jackson *et al. v.* Porter.]

same tract of land to Washington Jackson of Philadelphia, for 6000 dollars. The deed of sale and conveyance was made as well as the contract entered into at Nashville, Tennessee.

On the 24th of March, 1827, Jackson, joined by Martin and wife, filed their .petition against Judge Porter for the land in controversy, in the nature of a petitory action and jactitation of the title; petition alleging that Jackson's title was good and superior to Porter's. There was judgment for the defendant Porter in the district court. The plaintiffs appealed.

MARTIN, J., delivered the opinion of the court.

The plaintiff, Jackson, claims under a sale from the owner, a tract of land in the possession of the defendant, who purchased it from the vendor's attorney at an anterior sale.—There was judgment for the defendant and the plaintiffs appealed.

The evidence shows, that the plaintiff Martin, being owner of a strip of land between that of the defendant and that of the other plaintiff, had appointed Isaac L. and Joshua Baker, who were in partnership as attorneys at law, and for the sale of land, slaves, &c., to sell the premises, if they could obtain 4000 dollars therefor: that neither the defendant nor the plaintiff Jackson would give that price in the first instance; that the defendant employed Mr. Caffrey to endeavor to purchase the premises from the plaintiff Martin, who being written to, did not name any particular price, but said he had thought of asking 6000 dollars; and requested Caffrey to state the highest price that would be offered. In the mean while the defendant purchased the premises from the Bakers, neither he or they having any knowledge of the plaintiff Martin's answer to Caffrey: but afterwards, and before the deed was executed by the Bakers to the defendant, the answer of the plaintiff Martin was made known to the defendant, and by him immediately communicated to the Bakers.

At the trial, the plaintiffs insisted on the production of the articles of partnership of the Bakers, and opposed parol evidence of the nature of their partnership. These objections were overruled; the production of the articles was dispensed with, and parol evidence was received of the nature of the partnership.

We think the district judge did not err. Admitting that the articles would have shown, that the partnership did not extend to sales of land and slaves—if the partners afterwards agreed to an extension of its object; and as proved, actually engaged in such sales, they would be within the scope of their partnership, as much as if a clause in the articles authorised them.

But in the present case, the plaintiff Martin does not declare his intention, that the land should not be sold for 4000 dollars, but only to ask 6000 dollars: an intimation is given, that the offer of a less sum will be attended to. Under these circumstances we think the jury did not err in concluding, that the powers of the Bakers were unaffected by the knowledge they received of the contents of their principal's letter to Caffrey.

[Jackson *et al. v.* Porter.]

The deed was executed by Isaac L. Baker, who affixed to it the signature of the firm of Isaac L. & Joshua Baker as attorneys of the plaintiff Martin.

Parol evidence was received without any objection of the written assent of Joshua Baker to his partner's execution of the deed of sale.

A partnership may be appointed agent or attorney for the performance of any act or duty, which comes within the object for which the partnership is formed: and the responsibility of such trust or agency attaches to all the members, and they are entitled to all the advantages resulting therefrom; although one of them may execute the trust in the partnership name, unless it be differently provided in the partnership. Louisiana Code, 2790.

Where a partnership is appointed to perform a trust or agency foreign to the object for which such partnership is formed, the appointment is not void. It may be performed in the name of the partnership, if all the partners assent. Louisiana Code, 2791.

In the present case there is evidence, that the agency was not foreign to the object of the partnership, and of the assent of both partners. The deed was duly executed.

The land passed by the conveyance, and the subsequent sale by one of the plaintiffs to the other cannot effect the defendant's title.

We have been strongly pressed to allow damages for a frivolous appeal: but the case does not appear to justify a claim for damages.

It is, therefore, ordered, adjudged and decreed that the judgment of the district court be affirmed, with costs.

Simon and *Garland,* for the plaintiffs.
Bowen and *Brownson,* for the defendant.

Andrews *et al. v.* D. Ackerson.   VIII, N. S. 205.

A creditor who has given a complete discharge of a debt to one of the partners, and, by virtue of it, enabled that partner to deduct the amount of it on settlement with his copartners, cannot compel the latter to reimburse their parts of the sum before they shall enforce a previous mortgage which they had on the thing given in payment. Such creditor's remedy is against the partner he trusted.

Such case would not permit the application of the rule which has been often laid down by this court, viz: that a third person, who purchases, at a judicial sale, the property of minors, and whose money is applied to the payment of a debt due by them, shall have this money repaid him before the minors, for any vice in the sale, shall get back the subject for which the money was given.

[Andrews *et al. v.* D. Ackerson,]

FIFTH District.

PORTER, J., delivered the opinion of the court.

The plaintiffs, one of whom is a minor, above the age of puberty, assisted by his curator *ad litem*, stated that in 1819, their mother died, leaving them her heirs. That an inventory of her estate was made by the court of probates, and afterwards sold for 30,131 dollars 37 cents. That their father never took any measures to have himself appointed tutor or curator of either of the petitioners, who were then both under age, and disposed of the property of the community between him and their mother, without convening any family meeting, or taking any other legal step, than procuring an appraisement and inventory of the estate, as is seen by the *procès verbal* of the sale.

That the petitioners never having received any part of their said mother's estate, or any account thereof, instituted a suit in the month of February, 1828, against their father for the settlement of the affairs of the succession, and the community that had existed between their parents, and had judgment in the court of probate for 3843 dollars with interest and costs, and issued execution, which remains unsatisfied.

That they have a mortgage on the real property of their father, and the defendant; that since their mortgage attached on their father's property, a *fieri facias* issued on a judgment of the district court against their father, and several tracts of land, then belonging to their father, were sold and purchased in by defendant.

That the petitioners have given notice to the defendant of the existence of their claim against their father, of its nature and of the mortgage consequently resulting therefrom, on the premises.

The petition concludes with a prayer, that unless the defendant satisfy their said claim, interest, and costs, the premises may be sold therefor.

The defendant pleaded discussion—his plea was overruled. He next pleaded the general issue and that in 1818 and previous to the petitioners' mother's death, he sold to their father a tract of land which now constitutes part of a larger tract and owned by the defendant, and on which the petitioners seek to exercise their right of mortgage—that the petitioners' father promised to pay 3000 dollars, for the said land thus purchased from the defendant in three annual instalments, with the faculty of prolonging the time of payment during four years on payment of interest, at the rate of ten per cent., the defendant reserving to himself a mortgage till complete payment.

The defendant further pleaded that in 1819 he sold to the petitioners' father two slaves for the sum of 1600 dollars, payable also in three annual instalments, with faculty of prolonging payment four years on payment of interest at the rate of ten per cent., reserving to himself a mortgage till complete payment:—and afterwards the petitioners' father sold one of these slaves to one Rees for 800 dollars payable in three annual instalments.

The defendant admitted, that after the petitioners' mother died, an inventory, appraisement and sale of her estate took place as stated in the petition. That the said sale extended to all the property of the community and included the land purchased from the defendant, and one of the said slaves: that at the said sale the petitioners' father purchased part of the property and particularly the land on which they seek to enforce the mortgage.

That afterwards the petitioners' father, desirous to be relieved from the defendant's mortgage on the land and slaves purchased from the latter, proposed, on a release being received, to give a mortgage on the property he had purchased at the sale of the estate of the community; to which the defendant assented: and this was executed: and through the fraud of the petitioners' father, and the error or mistake of the defendant, in the release, payment of the sum due to the latter was acknowledged, though not received.

The defendant further pleaded, that the new mortgage was given for 4600 dollars, without including the interest; and payment was stipulated in two years, with. the faculty of a prolongation of the time of payment of interest at the rate of ten per cent.: but the petitioners' father absolutely neglecting to pay, the defendant instituted suit against him, in consequence of which the premises were sold and bought by the defendant.

The petitioners' father was cited in warranty, failed to answer, and judgment was taken against him by default: there was judgment for the petitioners against the defendant, and for him against the petitioners' father.

From this judgment the defendant appealed. The facts, both in the petition and answer, except the allegation of fraud in the father, and error or mistake in the defendant, as alleged in the answer, are correctly stated.

It is not contended that the district court erred in ordering a sale of the premises, but the appellant's counsel urges, that the petitioners ought to have been compelled to indemnify the defendant for the amount of the sum for which he was a creditor of the community, according to a principle often recognised by this court, viz:—that in setting aside an illegal sale in favor of a minor, he ought to be allowed whatever the vendee paid in discharge of the minor's debts. But in the present case the appellees contend, that by giving an absolute receipt for his claim, the defendant has rendered them the debtors of their father, who has had the benefit of the acknowledged payment in the same manner as if he had actually made it. The appellees, were they compelled to pay the defendant, would be twice charged with the same debt: and the appellant must impute it to his own imprudence, that he has transferred his claim to the petitioners' father, who has thereby been enabled to retain its amount from them.

This case is different from that of a third person who purchases,

[Andrews *et al.* *v.* D. Ackerson.]

at a judicial sale, the property of minors; and whose money is applied to the payment of a debt due by them. He is a stranger to the acts by which their interests are affected. It is therefore equitable—as it is the law, that the money which was applied to the payment of their debt, should be repaid by them, before they get back that thing for which the money was given. In the present instance the creditor himself entered into a transaction, by which he discharged the debt, and acknowledged the tutor had paid him. He thus furnished the latter with the means of claiming a sum from the minors, and the court of probates on settlement allowed him credit for the amount. It is therefore proper he should look to the tutor for reimbursement.

This is not a case of restitution *in integrum.* The property, belonging to the succession, and as making part of it, was sold. At the sale, the father of the minors became the purchaser, and as his property, it became liable to the mortgage which the law conferred in their favor, on the estate of their tutor. The enforcing of this mortgage does not rescind the sale, but on the contrary affirms it. The mortgage, given by the tutor to secure a debt of the community, and a sale under it, did not destroy the plaintiffs' mortgage.

The question, therefore, before us, is whether a creditor, who has given a complete discharge to one of the partners, and by virtue of it, enabled that partner to deduct the amount on settlement with his co-partners, can compel the latter to reimburse their part of the sum, before they can enforce a previous mortgage which they had on the thing given in payment; and we are of opinion he cannot. That his remedy is against the partner he trusted. The right was once extinguished by the act of the creditor as against the community, and it revives, by eviction, against him whose note was taken in place of the original debt.

It was not the property of the community which was mortgaged to secure the debt, but the property of the father, who had purchased from the community.

It is, therefore, ordered, adjudged and decreed, that the judgment of the district court be affirmed, with costs.

Garland and *Bowen*, for the plaintiffs.

Brownson, for the defendant.

Carlin *v.* Dumartrait.　VIII, N. S. 212.

FIFTH District.

Until due notice is given of the transfer of a claim, by the *transferee* to the person on whom it is given, a *creditor* of the *transferor* or assignor may legally seize it and appropriate it to his own debt.

A person employed as agent to *receive* and *pay* the debts of a succession, is *not* thereby authorised to receive legal *notice* of the assignment or transfer of a debt on the succession to a third person.

The authority to receive notice of the transfer of a debt must be *specially established,* for until notice the debtor might pay the original creditor, and while he can pay, a creditor of the first creditor might seize the debt due him.

The Court said:—This case cannot be distinguished from Bainbridge *v.* Clay, 4 *N. S. 56.*

Miles *v.* Oden *et al.*　VIII, N. S. 214.

Contracts are *governed* by the laws of the country in which they are passed: and by the comity of nations, are *enforced* according to *those laws*, by the state to which the parties have removed.

Liens, on land and slaves remaining in the hands of the owner or seller, have *no* effect against third persons, unless *they* are duly recorded.

Liens, existing on land or slaves in other states, are subject to the same rules of registering as in our own, when the parties come to this state to enforce such *liens.*

Where a creditor in Kentucky *assents* that certain property of his debtor, may be taken to Louisiana, by an agent or trustee and sold, the proceeds to be applied to the payment of his *lien* and *debt,* he cannot attack the sale of such agent as fraudulent, because by his subsequent misconduct he failed to receive the proceeds.

An agent or trustee, who is empowered to sell certain property and take a note payable to himself, may *legally sell such note to a third person,* although it be in fraud of the rights of his employers.

[Miles *v*. Oden *et al.*]

The purchaser of such note cannot be deprived of his right to it, without being repaid the money he gave for it.

It is a principle of the common law, that a *bona fide* purchaser, is not affected by *fraud in his vendor towards those from whom he obtained the property,* if he has a legal title to the thing sold.

Interest will *not* be allowed on a *note,* given for the purchase and price of slaves, when there is a contest between two adverse parties about the proceeds, until such contest is decided: because until *then,* the maker of the note is not considered *in mora.*

FIFTH District, Judge of the Seventh presiding.

Porter, J., delivered the opinion of the court.

The petitioner states, that he obtained a judgment against one Oden in the state of Kentucky, on which judgment an execution issued, that was levied on property that was afterwards replevied under the laws of Kentucky, by the said Oden, he giving his bond, with a certain O. G. Waggoner as his security. That on the 7th of June 1820, Oden executed to Waggoner a mortgage upon the articles seized, among which were certain slaves. That the debt, due to the petitioner, is yet unpaid, and that in virtue of the seizure made under the execution in Kentucky, and the assignment from Waggoner, the petitioner has a lien on the property levied on.

That one Miller, of the state of Kentucky, has fraudulently caused the said property to be transported from the state of Kentucky to defraud the mortgagee, and has sold it to one Brent.

That Miller's title, if he had any, is subordinate to his: that the proceeds of the property sold, were in fact due to Oden; Miller having lent his name to defraud the petitioner.

The petition concludes with a prayer, that Brent may be decreed to surrender up the negroes, or pay the price due for them to the plaintiff; and that an attachment may issue against Oden and Waggoner.

The attachment issued and was levied on the debt due by Brent.

Brent, who was thus made both defendant and garnishee, filed an answer in which he stated:

First: That he bought the negroes from a certain Morris L. Miller, in good faith, without any notice or knowledge of the plaintiff's claim: and if the said title should hereafter be declared fraudulent against Oden's creditors it cannot affect his rights, as he purchased in this state without knowledge of these transactions.

That the negroes purchased by him only formed a part of the property mortgaged to Waggoner, and that the plaintiffs must discuss the other portion of it in the state of Kentucky, before he can have recourse on that sold to the respondent.

That the negroes were purchased by Miller at a sale made under an execution in favor of William Fletcher, and that admitting this sale to be fraudulent, it cannot affect the respondent's title, who bought without notice.

Vol. IV.—42

That one of the slaves is affected with redhibitory defects, and the price of this slave must be deducted from the sum due.

That on the 21st of April, he received a notice from L. and M. Commagere, who state themselves the holders of the note which the respondent gave to Miller, for the slaves now claimed by the petitioner, in which notice they demand payment for the same.

Brent's answers to interrogatories, given on oath, do not state that funds of the defendants were in his hands, but acknowledges a note to have been given for the slaves mentioned in the petition, on which a deduction should be made of 400 dollars, or 450 dollars the price of one of the slaves, so affected with redhibitory diseases as not to be of any value.

On filing this answer the plaintiff prayed liberty to amend his petition, by making Miller, who sold to Brent, a party to the suit. In this amendment judgment is asked against Miller, so far as to have the sale, made by him to Brent, cancelled and set aside, and the demand is reiterated that the negroes be seized and sold to satisfy the claim of the petitioner, or that there be judgment against Oden and Waggoner for the price of the negroes sold to Brent.

The court ordered Miller and Commagere to be made parties to the suit.

At this stage of the proceedings, Raspalier intervened, and averred that he had purchased the note the defendant, Brent, had given for the slaves. That Miller's title to the property was *bona fide*. The petition of intervention concluded by demanding, that he might be decreed to be the only person entitled to receive the amount of said note with interest, and that judgment should be rendered in his favor against Brent.

Miller answered by denying any knowledge of Miles's having such a claim as that set up in the petition, and requiring him to furnish proof of it.

That Miles's mortgage is inferior to the title which the respondent acquired, because a long time previous to the date of the mortgage to Waggoner, Oden executed a deed of trust to Harrison Blanton, the said deed of trust being for the purpose of securing Robert P. Letcher and others, against damage and loss, as securities for Oden. That Letcher commenced suit, recovered judgment and issued execution against Oden. That the respondent bought the slaves at the sale made in virtue of such execution; and that he did not send them out of the state of Kentucky to defraud the petitioner.

The answer further states, that the respondent being unwilling to speculate on the misfortunes of Oden, directed the proceeds of the sale of the slaves, sent by him to Louisiana, to be paid over to Oden's creditors.

The respondent also states, that Letcher has assigned to him the mortgage under which the slaves were sold: that Waggoner, under the mortgage, in virtue of which the petitioner claims, directed the execution at the suit of Letcher to be levied on the property which the respondent purchased; and finally, that the petitioner had ratified and approved the sale.

Brent amended his answer, by stating that the title under which Miller had sold the negroes had been declared fraudulent, and pronounced null by a court of equity in Kentucky. That he believed the sale had been made with an intention to deceive him, and that he is threatened with many suits for the property.

Miller and Raspalier objected to this answer being filed, but the court received it.

The next change we find in the pleadings is that made by the plaintiff, amending the petition, and especially stating the facts attending the suit in Kentucky, which he averred, terminated by a decree annulling the sale to Miller.

The suit of Raspalier against Brent was consolidated with that in which the proceedings have been just stated, and on the consolidation being made, Brent filed another amended answer, in which, repeating all the facts already stated, he prayed that the sale might be annulled and avoided, it being fraudulent on the part of Miller.

Miller denied the allegation of Brent, and averred there was collision between him and Miles, the plaintiff, to cheat and defraud Raspalier.

Raspalier also amended the pleadings on his part, by repeating, or nearly so, the allegations of Miller.

On these pleadings the parties went to trial, and judgment was rendered in favor of the intervener. An appeal was taken to this court; the judgment was reversed, and the cause re manded, it appearing to have been tried without any answer having been put in on behalf of the defendant in attachment. 6 *N. S.* 211.

On the return of the case to the district court, the pleadings were so amended as to present the *contestatio litis* between all the parties. Another trial was had which terminated as the first, by judgment being rendered in favor of Raspalier, the interpleader.

From this judgment Miles, the plaintiff, and Brent have appealed.

The plaintiff has placed his right to recover, before this court, on two principal grounds.

1. That he had a lien on the property in Kentucky, which he has a right to enforce here.

2. That the money, due by Brent for the negroes purchased from Miller, was in fact due by Oden and Waggoner, and that as such his attachment levied on it, previous to any notification by Raspalier of his assignment, entitles him to judgment.

I. On the first ground, we are of opinion, that the lien, which the plaintiffs might have had in Kentucky, can not affect a *bona fide* purchaser in this state. The court are aware of the common principle, that contracts are governed by the laws of the country in which they are passed; and that, by the comity of nations the rights, flowing from them, are not diminished by the parties passing into other states:—*Provided,* the laws of that state afford adequate remedies to enforce the obligation. But this principle is subject to the exception, that in carrying them into effect, no injury result to the inhabitants of the country whose aid is required to enforce them. We had occasion to express our views fully on this subject in the case of Saul v His Creditors, 6 *N. S.* 599; and it is unnecessary to repeat here the reasoning on which we considered the limitation of the general principle to rest.

Our legislature have declared, that liens on land and slaves remaining in the possession of the owner, should not have effect against third persons, unless duly recorded. This rule was doubtless established to avoid the inconvenience and injury which parties, buying without notice of these liens, would sustain. Every reason, which supposes the necessity of such a regulation, as between our own citizens, applies with equal, if not greater force, to the inhabitants of another country, who come here to enforce liens given by the laws of the place, whence the property is brought.

Huberus, whose authority on this subject is justly entitled to great attention, after giving the limitation above noticed to the general rule, presents nearly this case as an example of it: and states that a mortgage, good on personal property in one country, can not be carried into effect in another state, whose laws do not recognise such hypothecations. If this be true, where mortgages of this description are not recognised as having any legal effect, we think the same rule should apply where they are only permitted against third persons, on certain conditions—such as registry, &c. This writer, indeed, gives the case of a marriage contract, binding on creditors in one country without being enregistered, as not being so if the parties remove into another, where publicity is required to be given to them by recording. His language in relation to mortgages is as follows: *Hypotheca conventionalis in re mobili dat jus prælationis etiam apud tertium possessorem jure Cæsaris et in Frisia, non apud Batavos. Proinde si quis ex ejusmodi hypotheca in Hollandia agat adversus tertium non audietur. Quia jus illi tertio in ista re mobili quæsitum per jus alieni territorii non potest auferri."* In the translation given of this passage in 3 Dallas, the sense is somewhat obscured by the omission to state in what country the mortgage would not have its effect.—*Huberus de Conflictu Legum, lib.* 1, *tit.* 3, *no.* 11; 3 *Dallas,* 375, *in notis.*

II. This point disposed of, the right of the plaintiff to recover must rest on the strength of his pretensions to attach the debt due by Brent, as belonging to his debtors, Oden and Waggoner.

Oden, who was a citizen and resident of Kentucky, was indebted to a larger amount than he was able to pay. He was pressed by some of his creditors: among others, by the plaintiff in this suit. To avoid the sacrifice of his property, he procured an execution to issue at the suit of one of them, under which several of his slaves were seized and sold, and Miller became the purchaser. It is shown clearly, that Miller's object in buying was to assist Oden and enable him to dispose of his property without too great a loss. That he had no intention of profiting by it. In pursuance of this object, the slaves purchased were sent down the river and sold to Brent, with the intention of applying the proceeds to the payment of the creditors in Kentucky. The plaintiff has attacked this act as fraudulent —insists, that by the laws of Kentuckey it was null and void; and contends, that the money due by Brent being due in reality to Oden, he had a right to attack it as the creditor of Oden.

The real character of the transaction and its legal effect, according to the laws of Kentucky, have been the subject of most elaborate discussion at the bar. We do not find it necessary to go into the question. It is shown, that after the slaves were sent down the river, and before they were sold, Miles, the present plaintiff, Letcher, ano᠁ ther creditor of Oden's, and Oden, entered into an agreement, by which, among other things, Miles consented and agreed to receive, in discharge of this debt, the proceeds of the slaves sent down the river by Miller, who, it is stated in the act, was the trustee of Oden. We are of opinion that the plaintiff, by his agreement, is precluded from saying the sale of the slaves was null and void: by consenting to take the proceeds of the sale, he sanctioned, as far as he could, the legality of the sale. It has been, indeed, contended, that by virtue of the stipulations in the instrument, Miles did not intend to waive any of his rights, in case the money was not paid to him. But the most attentive consideration of the agreement has failed to produce that conviction on our minds. It appears to us, that the reservations there made, relate to the property still remaining in Kentucky. And that there is nothing in it which would authorise us to say it was the intention of the parties, that the plaintiff should retain the right to attack the sale as fraudulent, in case he could not obtain the proceeds of it.

But there is another ground on which the plaintiff insists the attachment was properly levied. Miller, he says, was the trustee of Oden, and the debt due to him being for the benefit of the *cestui que trust*, as a creditor of the latter, he had a right to attach it. To this position the court assents; but his right to attach the equitable interest which Oden had in the funds, cannot, in our opinion, defeat a right which a third party had acquired from Miller, who had sold the negroes, and to whom the note given for them, was made payable, and in whom, consequently, the legal title was vested. This is the position in which Raspalier, the intervener is placed. He acquired *bona fide* from Miller. The note was, it is true, not negotiable, but it was a proper subject of sale; and although liable to all the equity existing between Miller, the payee, and Brent the maker, those persons who had entrusted Miller with the property, vested in him the legal title, and put him in a situation to hold himself out to the world as owner of the property, cannot deprive the purchaser of his rights without repaying to him the money which, as a consequence of the confidence reposed in the payee, he advanced. It is clear, that Oden could not do so. ·His creditors cannot have greater rights, apart from the question of fraud, which is considered as waived, by the agreement of the plaintiff to be paid out of the proceeds of sale. We are unable to distinguish between the right of the purchaser of the property and the rights of that which the vendor obtained in lieu of it, whether it was a note or any other object.

Brent, in his amended answer, has prayed a rescission of the sale, on the ground that he has not acquired a good title; but we do not see any danger to which he is exposed on this score, that would authorise us to declare the contract void. We understand it to be a clear principle of the common law, under which this transaction took place, that a *bona fide* purchaser is not affected by fraud in his vendor, who has a legal title to the property sold. 6 Cranch, 133.

The court below gave interest on the note, and in this we think it erred. There was one party claiming a lien on the slaves and a right to the proceeds, as belonging to Oden and Waggoner. The other demanded the proceeds, in virtue of an assignment from Miller. This was such a disturbance in the title as well authorised Brent to refuse paying either. Placed in so much uncertainty as to whom he was to pay, he could not be considered *in mora*.

The court decided correctly in deducting the price of the negro Charles, who had died, but the judgment must be reversed on account of the error in allowing interest.

It is, therefore, ordered, adjudged and decreed, that the judgment of the district court be annulled, avoided and reversed; and it is further ordered, adjudged and decreed, that the intervenor, C. Raspalier, do recover, against William L. Brent, the sum of two thousand three hundred and fifty dollars: and that the plaintiff, Charles Miles, pay all the costs of the proceedings, except those of appeal, which are to be paid by the intervener and appellee.

Brownson, for the plaintiff.
Simon, for the defendants.
Bowen, for the intervener Raspalier.

Gilbeaux's Heirs *v.* Cormier. VIII, N. S. 228.

FIFTH District.

Decided, that the wife may resume the administration of her paraphernal property, previously confided to her husband, whenever she chooses: and also demand restitution of what is the object or price of it.

During the pendency of a suit against the husband by the heirs of a former marriage, for a partition and restitution of the community property, the second wife may come in and interplead, and claim restitution and separation of her paraphernal property.

The tacit lien or mortgage of such wife in the estate of her husband is superior in degree or prior, to that of heirs of a former wife; and her paraphernal property, either in kind or the price, will be decreed, before the claims of the heirs are admitted. See Louisiana Code, 2368.

Dangerfield's Executrix *v.* Thruston's Heirs. VIII, N. S. 232.

Service of petition and citation on the attorney of the defendant, although made before the services of the attorney had commenced in the suit, is good, unless the party on the trial deny his authority on oath.

Such attorney may suffer judgment against his client by consent without hearing evidence in the cause, and it will be valid.

An executrix, deriving her authority from a probate court of another state, cannot exercise the character of executrix here, without first having presented the testament to a court of probates in this state.

Where a previous judgment has been obtained in one of the courts of this state by an executrix, residing in another state, and no objection or evidence to the contrary, it will be presumed she was duly qualified.

Where the copy of the record of a suit is introduced, without the judge's signature to the judgment; and another copy of *the judgment* is obtained and filed, with the signa-

[Dangerfield's Executrix *v.* Thruston's Heirs.]

ture, the record will then be taken as complete and authentic, especially where the date, amount, and number of such judgment corresponds with the other parts of the record.

In a case where there was a conditional judgment, that the defendant should have ninety days to procure evidence and establish any set-offs he might have, and no use made of the condition within the time, it is too late for the heirs in a subsequent trial to inquire into this matter.

The daughter who has received her share of her ancestor's succession, is still an incompetent witness in a suit against the other heirs of the succession.

The daughter may still be responsible to the other heirs on a final partition, if her share exceeds the disposable portion.

The district court has jurisdiction in a suit against executors *ratione materiæ*, but not *ratione personæ*.

An amendment will be admitted by filing a supplemental petition, even after issue joined, where the first petition sued only the *testamentary heirs*, and the amendment embraced *all* who had sued the instituted heirs to break the will, and prayed judgment against them, if they succeeded.

Persons suing the instituted heirs to set aside the will, thereby become liable to be sued by a creditor of the testator and made to pay the whole amount of the debt; although no part of the estate come into his hands.

FIFTH District, Judge of the Seventh presiding.

PORTER, J., delivered the opinion of the court.

This is an action to obtain from the defendants the amount of a judgment recovered against the executors of their ancestor. The petition sets out the former proceedings, and avers, that the defendants have accepted the succession, and are in possession of the property of the deceased.

The answer denies, that the plaintiff is the executrix of the person who recovered judgment against the ancestor of the defendants—puts at issue the fact of any such judgment having been rendered; and avers, that the heirs and representatives of Henry Dangerfield are indebted to the respondents in the sum of 850 dollars.

To establish the fact of the plaintiff being executrix, as she states herself to be in the petition, reference is had to a former proceeding in the court of the first district, where the judgment was rendered. It appears, that the suit was originally brought in the name of Henry Dangerfield, and judgment obtained by him in his lifetime. After his decease, a rule was taken on the defendants to show cause, why the judgment should not be revived in the name of the executrix, who is the present plaintiff. The court, after hearing the parties, made the rule absolute. It is contended, that this proceeding precludes any inquiry now into the character of the petitioner. That the matter has the authority of the thing judged.

The defendants, not contesting the principle on which the plaintiff relies, nor denying its correctness, where the proceedings have been regular, urge, that this case does not fall within its operation, because the defendants were not cited to contest the application. The rule was served on their attorney.

We have not found the decision of the point quite free from difficulty, but our minds have finally settled in the conclusion, that the service was well made, and that the proceedings which were based on it should have the same force, as if the defendants had been cited in person. It is perhaps true, as a general rule, that the authority of the attorney terminates with the judgment, and that the service made on the individual who represented the defendants in the first instance, acquires no additional force from that circumstance. But our law, from necessity, reposes great confidence in the acts of attorneys, who are admitted to practise in our courts; and it has been held, by more than one decision in this tribunal, that they would be presumed to act within the limits of their authority, unless the contrary was shown. This doctrine is, however, necessarily limited to those acts which fall within the range of the duties, which the profession have to discharge. And the question in this case is, whether the acknowledgment of service by the attorney and his appearance in consequence, and acting on behalf of the defendants, is within the limitation just stated. At first blush it would appear not, and that the agency of the attorney can only commence after the parties are cited. But in point of fact, we believe it to be no uncommon occurrence for persons who expect to be sued, to engage counsel, before the action is commenced; and that the persons, so engaged, have authority from their clients to accept service of the petition. The frequency of the practice induces us to conclude, that it arises from such authority being conferred. And when it is so usual and common, it cannot be held to be an act so out of the scope of professional duty, as to deprive the party who has acted on the faith of it, of the benefit of that presumption of correctness, which the law attaches to the acts of the sworn officers of its courts. In this very case, where an objection is taken against the irregularity of a former proceeding, because service was made on an attorney, we perceive, that an attorney has acknowledged service for all the defendants, and the whole proceedings in this action might hereafter be set aside on the same ground. The presumption of due authorisation to the counsel will, we believe, in far the greater number of instances, correspond with the truth. When an exception occurs, the party who has been represented without his consent, or contrary to his wishes, is sufficiently protected by allowing him to deny the authority of the attorney on oath; and on his doing so, requiring from his adversary proof of it.

On the same principle, we think the objection must be overruled, which contested the validity of the original judgment, on the ground of its being entered up by consent of counsel, and not after hearing the evidence.

The next question in the cause relates to the rights of the executrix, who holds her appointment under a will made and opened in the state of Mississippi, to collect a debt due to the succession in Louisiana, without first having presented the testament to a court of probate in this state, and obtaining an order for its execution. This objection we should think well founded, if such a step has not been taken by the plaintiff: but the previous judgment of the court, ordering the suit to be revived and directing execution to issue in her name, we think settles that question, and precludes any inquiry into it now. Such a judgment could not have been correctly given, without evidence before the court, of the executrix being legally authorised to collect the debts, due in this country to the succession of the original plaintiff. That evidence we must presume was furnished; at all events, no appeal having been taken from the decree of the court, it has acquired in relation to all the matters embraced by it, the authority of *res judicata.*

The plaintiff, to support the allegation in the petition, that judgment had been rendered against the executors of the defendants' ancestor, introduced a copy of the record of the suit against them. In this copy, the judgment does not appear to have been signed. To cure this defect, they then offered a copy of the judgment without the previous proceedings. In this copy the judgment appears to have the signature of the judge. It is objected, that the transcript of the proceedings does not establish any right in the petitioner, because in it the decree of the court is not final, for want of the judge's name being affixed. That the copy of the judgment which has his signature is not evidence, because it is unaccompanied with the other proceedings; and finally, that the one can not be used to eke out and support the other.

Admitting the principle, contended for, to be correct as to the necessity of producing all the proceedings in the cause, (on which we express no opinion,) we think, that in this instance, the copy of the judgment may be taken with the transcript of the record. There can be no doubt, that it is of the same suit, as that in which the copy of the whole proceedings was furnished. The language is the same, and in both, the sum which the plaintiff recovered is the same, and in both the judgment is stated to be that which was rendered in suit No. 3448. The non-insertion of the judge's signature to the decree in the transcript, we are bound to believe from the evidence before us, was a clerical error. The omission to insert it in the one instance, may be well accounted for by inadvertence. The placing it to the judgment in the other, if it were not in truth there, could not be explained in the same manner, and could have only arisen from a desire to give a false copy; which motive, it is neither legal nor charitable to presume, actuated the keeper of the record.

The judgment rendered in favor of the plaintiff's testator, against the executors of the defendants' ancestor, contained a clause, as follows: " with a stay of execution for ninety days, and with the privilege, at any time within the said ninety days, of establishing by evidence, any offsets which the defendant may have against said claim." This was on the 1st of April, 1814. No steps appear to

, have been taken by the defendants to avail themselves of the privilege, contained in the judgment. But, on the application of the present plaintiff to be made a party to the suit in 1817, the order reviving the suit and directing execution to issue in her name, contains a provision such as that just stated, and again extends to the defendants the privilege of showing, in the space of ninety days, any credits or set-offs to which they might be entitled.

Of the right thus conferred, the defendants appear to have so far profited, as to take out a commission and obtain testimony; but it does not appear, that the evidence so procured was ever laid before the court, or acted on within the limitation already stated, or indeed at any subsequent time.

The heirs contend, they may still use it in defence of this action, and their right to do so, has been a subject of much discussion at the bar. We are inclined to the opinion, that it was the duty of the original defendants to produce their proof to the court, to establish the set-offs claimed, within the ninety days, and obtain a credit on the judgment, and that their failure to do so, precludes all inquiry into these matters now. The language of the judgment is peremptory. "Ninety days are allowed, before issuing execution on this judgment, to the defendants to show and make manifest any credits or set-off which they may be entitled to." The showing, here spoken of, should have been made to the court, if the parties did not agree. The tribunal which rendered the judgment, was alone vested with the power to modify it.

But, if this objection could be got over, another, equally formidable, has been made to the introduction of the evidence. One of the depositions was returned into court, mutilated, wanting the first five pages. The other contains the testimony of the daughter of the original defendant, who, though she states herself to be without interest in the cause, having received her portion in her father's estate, may still be responsible on a final partition, if her share received should have exceeded the disposable portion.

It has been contended, that the judgment in the suit against the executors was void, from being rendered by the district court. It has been settled in the cases of Tabor v. Johnson, 3 *N. S.* 676, and Foucher v. Carraby, 6 *N. S* 548, that the courts of ordinary jurisdiction did not want power to decide causes such as this, *ratione materiæ,* but *ratione personæ.* No plea to the jurisdiction was filed here nor has any action of nullity been brought to set the judgment aside, nor appeal taken from it. We, therefore, must consider it in force. See 3 *Martin,* 676; 6 *N. S.* 548, the above cases.

This action was commenced against the testamentary heirs of the late Charles M. Thruston. In the petition, they are charged with having taken possession of his property. And judgment is prayed against them, in their individual capacity. The plaintiff, subsequent to the issue joined on this demand, filed a supplemental petition, in which she averred that several persons, some of them now residents of the state, had commenced an action against the instituted heirs to set aside the will. That the plaintiff was quite uncertain whether they would succeed in this suit or not. That, if they did, they would be responsible as well as the original defendants. She therefore prayed judgment against all, who claimed any interest in the succession.

Opposition was made to this attempt to introduce new parties, but the judge of the fifth district, presiding at the term the application was made, admitted it. And the judge of the seventh, who tried the cause, gave judgment absolutely against all the defendants.

By this judgment, the defendants, last made parties to the suit, are made responsible for the whole amount of the debt due by the succession in their individual capacity, though for aught that appears, their claim to the estate may be rejected, and no property belonging to it come into their hands. The extreme severity of this case, has induced us to examine with considerable strictness, whether it was well founded in law. An examination of the provisions in our Code has, however, satisfied us of its correctness. By the 904th article, it is provided that, "the person called to the succession, does an act, which makes him liable as heir, when, if cited before a court of justice, as heir, for a debt of the deceased, he suffer judgment to be rendered against him in that capacity, without claiming the benefit of an inventory, or renouncing the succession." Neither of these alternatives was resorted to in this instance.

It is, therefore, ordered, adjudged and decreed, that the judgment of the district court be affirmed, with costs.

Bowen, for the plaintiff.

Brownson, for the defendants.

Bell *v.* Haw *et al.* VIII, N. S. 243.

The new Civil Code (art. 3280) exempts the property and estates of all collectors of moneys, such as sheriffs, &c. from mortgage, from the time of its promulgation.

But a collector of a trade or navigation company appointed between the promulgation of the old and new Codes, would be subjected to the legal mortgage, according to the terms of his appointment, although by the new Code they ceased to exist.

The state, who is the lawgiver and a party, may constitutionally declare that all mortgages in her favor shall cease to exist, as to moneys thereafter collected.

Notice to a third party who purchases at a sale, of prior title, is sufficient to hold the property, although the title may not be regularly recorded, if such notice be given at or before the sale.

FIFTH District.

MARTIN, J., delivered the opinion of the court.

Francis Gardere, the treasurer of the State, an intervening party in the suit, complains of the judgment refusing to recognise the state's mortgage on the property of the defendant Haw, late sheriff of the parish of St. Landry, who collected the taxes due in said parish for the year 1826, without having previously given bond as the law directs and requires.

Haw was appointed sheriff a few months before the promulgation of the new Civil Code, and the law then gave the state a legal mortgage on the estates of collectors of taxes.—Civil Code, 456, art. 25. But the new Code, art. 3280, declares that there shall be no legal mortgage, but those which are recognised by that Code. The appellee's counsel has contended, that whatever may be the right of the state in regard to moneys collected before the new Code, it is clear she can claim no mortgage for the moneys thereafter collected.

The words of the old Code are " The territory, the different parishes, cities and other corporations, companies of trade or navigation, and all public establishments, have a legal mortgage on the property of their collectors, and other accountable persons, from the day when they entered into office. Civil Code, 456, art. 25.

The words of the new Code are, " No legal mortgage shall exist except in the cases determined by the present Code." Art. 3280.

Now the new Code speaks not of legal mortgages on the estate of collectors: therefore such mortgages do not exist, in cases in which the new law may constitutionally have its effects.

If a company of trade or navigation had appointed a collector between the promulgation of the two Codes, a legal mortgage would have resulted from the contracts by which the company would have entrusted, and the collector accepted, the collection of its moneys, during the continuance of the collector in office, according to the terms of his appointment; and the destruction of the legal mortgage by the legislature would not affect the obligations of the contract; and notwithstanding the law pronouncing it, the mortgage would continue to exist.

But the state may constitutionally declare, that every mortgage in her favor shall cease to exist; whether after the legislature has said so, the rights of the state in regard to moneys actually received by her servants, under the former law subsist, is a question which we shall solve, when properly called on. It suffices now that we should say, that as to moneys thereafter collected, no mortgage exists. The state is the lawgiver, and the party and she must be bound by the terms of the laws she enacts.

It has been objected, that the plaintiff's title was not duly recorded according to the provisions of the acts of 1810: Positive, indeed authentic, evidence has been produced, of due notice given to the defendants and the intervener, of the plaintiff's claim, which renders it unnecessary to inquire into the alleged irregularity of the record.

It is, therefore, ordered, adjudged and decreed, that the judgment of the district court be affirmed.

Bowen, for the plaintiff.

Garland, for the intervener.

Mayfield *v.* Cormier *et al.*   VIII, N. S. 246.

(See Mayfield *v.* Comeau, same case, in 7 *N. S.* 180.)

FIFTH District.

The purchase of property at a public sale, where all the legal formalities of the sale have not been observed, is invalid and gives no title.

Where one of the notices of the sale is directed to be put up on the church door, an omission to comply with such direction will vitiate such sale.

Evans *v.* Thomas S. Saul and Wife.   VIII, N. S. 247.

FIFTH District.

Decided, that a casual residence in another parish is not such a change of residence, as legally to transfer the domicil from the usual and permanent place of abode.

An allegation in a petition, that the defendant was a resident of

[Evans *v.* Thomas S. Saul and Wife.]

the parish where suit is instituted, but had left the state, is sufficient to ground an attachment.

But an allegation that the wife lives in another parish, will not authorise a citation to be sent there and served on the husband and wife. Such service is bad.

Where it appears that the defendant has absconded merely to avoid a criminal prosecution, and not to avoid being *cited*, the case does not warrant an attachment, but an ordinary citation left at his domicil or last place of residence is sufficient.

Where an attachment improperly issues in a suit, the ordinary proceedings will go on, but the attachment will be dismissed at the plaintiff's cost.

The word "garnishee" is inserted in the English text of 258th article, in the Code of Practice, by mistake. It should be *defendant*.

The wife has no legal domicil but that of her husband, and a citation left at his domicil, is legal service on her.

Bectel *et al. v.* Brent. VIII, N. S. 253.

FIFTH District, Judge of the Sixth presiding.

Held, that the professional services of an attorney will be determined on a *quantum meruit,* if no agreement is shown to exist.

In determining the worth of professional services of an attorney at law, on a *quantum meruit,* 500 dollars will be deemed adequate compensation for settling a claim of 3000 dollars, although two suits had been instituted.

Where the court see no ground on which an appeal is taken, to reverse the opinion of the inferior court, it will be considered as taken for delay, and as frivolous, and the judgment of the inferior court will be affirmed with costs, and ten per cent. damages on the amount of the judgment.

Marc v. Church Wardens of the Roman Catholic Church of St. Martinsville. VIII, N. S. 257.

In a case which depends on a variety of circumstances to prove its true merits, and to arrive at the justice of it, where the proof is defective and unsatisfactory, the cause will be remanded for further proceedings on the merits.

The general rule is, that he who affirms must prove, but where the affirmative involves a negative, the proof must come from the other side.

The plaintiff affirmed that the curate did not receive a salary, and it devolved on the defendants to prove that he did; for the negative, which was involved in the affirmative, could not be proved.

FIFTH District, Judge of the Sixth presiding.

PORTER, J., delivered the opinion of the court.

This action was instituted by the heirs of the late curate of the parish of St. Martin, to recover a sum of money alleged to be due to his deceased uncle, for moneys paid and advanced for the use of the church (Fabrique) during his lifetime. Annexed to the petition, is an open account by the church wardens, and signed by them. The principal defence set up in the answer is, error in the settlement. It is alleged that, according to the tariff, established by the bishop of Louisiana, in the year 1795, the curates of the parishes in the diocese had a right to receive a certain sum on each interment made by them, a portion of which was set apart for the use of the church. That the late curate acted under that tariff, and received a large sum of money to the use of the church, which he failed to pay over, or to account for in the settlement made by them, and that they were ignorant of the particular provisions contained in the tariff, until after the decease of the ancestor of the plaintiff.

This tariff has been introduced in evidence, and comes up with the record. The rights of the parties turn mainly on a correct understanding of the last clause.

It is in these words—*Ce tariff durera tant que les ministres seront salaries, mais si par quelqu' evenement leur paye est suspendue, ils peuvent demander son changement.*

We think, with the counsel for the plaintiff, that in these churches where the ministers receive no salary, the tariff was not in force. This appears to us to be its obvious meaning. It has been ingeniously argued, that the latter part of the clause, which states, "that if their salaries are suspended, they may demand an alteration of it," shows, that the suspension of the salaries does not destroy the operation of

[Marc v. Church Wardens of the Roman Catholic Church.]

the tariff, but merely gives the curates a right to demand an alteration; and that no such demand was ever made by the plaintiff's ancestor. This circumstance may perhaps be true, in those churches where the minister was once salaried, and afterwards ceased to be so. But it is a construction, which certainly does not depart from the letter of the regulations. If, however, in point of fact, the curate of St. Martin never did receive a salary, this provision cannot apply to him. For, if it never was in force in his parish, he was under no obligation to ask for a change in it.

It has been much disputed, on whom the burthen of proof was thrown, as to the existence of the salary. The general rule is, that he who affirms must prove; but where the affirmative involves a negative, as was the case here, namely, that the curate did not receive a salary, then the proof of it must come from the opposite party, for a negative can not be proved.

We think the justice of the case requires, it should be remanded.

It is, therefore, ordered, adjudged and decreed that the judgment of the district court be annulled, avoided and reversed; that the case be remanded for a new trial; and that the appellee pay the costs of the appeal.

Simon and *Brownson*, for the plaintiff.

Bowen, for the defendants.

Palfrey's Syndic *v.* François *et al.*   VIII, N. S. 260.

The question of *fraud* made by a creditor in *concurso*, against an insolvent debtor, extends no further than to deprive such debtor of the benefit of the insolvent laws.

A charge of *fraud* made against an insolvent debtor, by a creditor *in concurso* and overruled, does not form *res judicata* in a subsequent suit by the syndic of such creditor, against the debtor, on the same charge, to set aside a fraudulent sale.

In order that a judgment have the force of *the thing adjudged*, the *object* of the demand must be the same: in this case, the object in the first instance was to punish the debtor; in the *latter* case, to get back property fraudulently sold.

When the allegations in the petition, charge that the *sale* was a *sham one, without consideration*, the *admissions* and *declarations* of the parties to the act of sale, going to establish an express agreement, that the thing sold should be returned, on the vendor's repaying the price, are inadmissible evidence to prove the fraud.

Evidence, going to prove a different species of fraud from that alleged in the petition, is *inadmissible*.

43*

Evidence of the declarations of the vendor and vendee relative to the *hire* of the property alleged to have been fraudulently sold, made two years after the act of sale, is inadmissible to prove the nature of such sale.

FIFTH District.

PORTER, J., delivered the opinion of the court.

The plaintiff seeks, by this action, to set aside a conveyance, made by one Judice and wife to the defendant, François, on the ground of its having been passed to defraud their creditors. The petition alleges the fraud, and avers, that as 2000 dollars are stated to be the consideration, yet that in fact no consideration was paid; that if cash was given in presence of the notary, it was immediately returned to the vendee, and that the vendors have ever since remained in possession of the property.

Raymond François, one of the defendants, pleaded the general issue; specially denied the fraud, and averred that the sum of 2000 dollars, stated in the act of sale, was truly paid by him, and that of the money, 1414 dollars 87 cents were applied to discharge a debt due by the vendors to the firm of Raymond & Lebesque, of which he was a partner, and the balance to sundry creditors of the vendors. That he has, since the sale, hired the slaves to Judice and wife, which is the possession spoken of in the petition. He further pleaded, the prescription of one, two and three years; and, that the question of fraud could not now be raised by the syndic, as one of the creditors in the *concurso* had made such an allegation, and a decision had been given on it.

Judice and wife answered, by denying the allegations in the petition, and more especially the charge of fraud. They averred, that the sale was *bona fide*, that they had received the sum of 2000 dollars, and had employed it in paying their just debts. That the same allegation, had been made against them by one of the creditors in *concurso*, and notwithstanding the opposition on that ground, the defendant, Maximillien Judice, had, by a decree of court, been admitted to the benefit of the law of this state, for the relief of insolvent debtors, by reason of which the syndic can not now maintain another action, to set aside the conveyance in question.

The first question for examination, is that arising out of the plea which sets up the proceedings in *concurso*, or the opposition of one of the creditors as *res judicata* against the present demand, and we are clearly of opinion, that they can not have that effect. The question of fraud, which may be raised during the suit the debtor brings against his creditors, has, and by law can have, no other object than depriving the plaintiff of the right of making a cession. If found against him, it forever deprives him of the benefit of the laws passed in favor of insolvent debtors; but it leaves the conveyance in full force. That can only be set aside in a suit, in which the person to whom the conveyance was made, is a party. If found in favor of the debtor, he is admitted to the benefit of these laws; but the judgment goes no further. It only passes on the act, as incidental to the decision of the question presented. In order that a judgment should have the force of the thing adjudged, the object of the demand must be the same. That was not the case here. The object, in the former instance, was to punish the debtor; in the present, to get. back the property he conveyed without consideration. Louisiana Code, art. 2265.

The record is studded with bills of exceptions. The first is a refusal of the judge to permit the plaintiff to prove "admissions and declarations of the parties to the act of sale, attacked as fraudulent, made at the time the act was passed, going to establish the express agreement of the parties, that the slaves purporting to be sold by the said act, to Raymond François, were to be returned by him to the vendors, on their repaying to the said Raymond, the money by him actually advanced." The proof was rejected by the court, on the ground, that the allegations in the petition did not warrant the admission of such evidence.

To ascertain whether or not, this opinion was correct, particular recurrence must be had to the statements in the petition.

The petition alleges the sale to be a sham one; and charges particularly, that the consideration, expressed in the act, never had been paid, or that if any part of it was paid, the same was immediately returned to the vendee.

We are of opinion, these allegations did not authorise the introduction of the evidence. The proof offered, did not go to establish a sham sale, but one which was binding and legal, for nothing prevented the parties making such a contract: and if the creditors sought to set it aside, on the ground of inadequacy of price, they should have set forth this as the ground in their petition, and offered to repay the money advanced. On another ground it was objectionable. Admitting the sale to be fraudulent, it was a different species of fraud from that charged in the petition, and the defendants could not be presumed ready to meet it.

The next bill of exceptions was taken to the opinion of the judge, permitting a witness to prove the declarations of the vendor and vendee, in relation to the hire of the property, made out of the presence of each other, and two years after the passing of the act alleged to be fraudulent. In admitting such evidence, we think the judge erred. Parties cannot make evidence for themselves, by their own declarations. If they could, it is obvious that no sale could be ever set aside, as fraudulent.

It is, therefore, ordered, adjudged and decreed, that the judgment of the district court be annulled, avoided and reversed; and that this cause be remanded to the district court, with directions to the judge not to admit evidence of the declaration of the defendants, made subsequent to the act of sale; and it is further ordered, that the appellees pay the costs of this appeal.

Brownson, for the plaintiff.
Simon, for the defendants.

Lesassier, Curator, &c. v. Hertzel et al.
VIII, N. S. 265.

FIFTH District, Judge of the Sixth presiding.

A *surety*, who has released his principal, by a novation of the debt, is still an *incompetent* witness for the principal, to establish the novation.

Such *surety* is interested to defeat the action against the *principal;* because, if the *latter* is condemned to pay, he would have a right to call on the *surety*, who is bound by the novation, for the debt and costs incurred by his failure to discharge the obligation.

Reels v. Knight.   VIII, N. S. 266.

FIFTH District.

Held, that the *acts* of a party subsequent to a sale, may be given in evidence to show that such sale was fraudulent.

When the inquiry *is*, whether a sale was *bona fide* or not, the whole conduct of the party whose acts are assailed, *before* and *after*, as well as at the *time* the contract was made, may be inquired into.

Broussard *v.* Mallet *et al.* VIII, N. S. 269.

FIFTH District, Judge of the Sixth presiding.

Decided, that proof of minority may be made by witnesses, who have known the minor from infancy.

Although the register of baptism is higher evidence of the age of a person, than proof by witnesses, yet the existence of the former will not be presumed—it must be positively proved, that such register does exist.

Neither the births, baptisms or deaths, are so universally recorded as to enable the court to ground a legal presumption on the fact of their being so.

The obligation or contract of a minor is not *void* under the 93d article of the old Civil Code, page 76, but he cannot be required to pay more on such obligation, than the amount of one year of his revenue.

Judgment cannot be given in general terms against such minor, but only against the movables; he cannot alienate his immovable property, without authority. Emancipated minors are here spoken of only.

Execution, issuing on such judgment, shall not be levied on the immovables and slaves.

Rousseau *et al. v.* Daysson. VIII, N. S. 273.

FIFTH District.

Decided, that, in an action against a defendant for fraud, which is personal to himself, it is unnecessary to join others in the action, who were owners of the thing sold, and about which the fraud is alleged to have been committed.

In the sale of a steamboat, where the defendant represented to the purchasers, that he had bought it for them at 2500 dollars, and would sell to them at the same price, when in fact he gave but 2000 dollars,

[Rousseau *et al. v.* Daysson.]

the excess in price of 500 dollars is fraudulent, for which damages will be allowed.

But in regard to the purchaser of one-third of the boat, who was not imposed on by the misrepresentation of the price paid for it, the sale is good.

Where the jury seal up a verdict in their room, and on coming into court *vary its terms,* the latter verdict shall stand as the true one.

In a case of fraud, where the evidence is not positive, but when the jury unanimously concur in a verdict, on hearing the testimony fall from the lips of the witness, this court must be clearly satisfied the jury erred, before the verdict be disturbed.

Moore *v.* Broussard.   VIII, N. S. 277.

FIFTH District.

Held, that the 3032d article of the Louisiana Code, which provides that a prolongation of the term of payment granted to the principal debtor, without the consent of the surety, operates a discharge of the latter, applies to a case where the creditor merely suspends for a term, *his right of suing.*

The creditor, who has a surety, is not compelled to *sue* his principal debtor.

Shepherd *et al.* *v.* Carlin *et al.* VIII, N. S. 278.

FIFTH District.

This was a simple case of the application of the principle that prescription will bar a recovery of land in a petitory action, after ten years possession *animo domini* under a just title, against a resident, and twenty years against a non-resident.

WESTERN DISTRICT, OCTOBER TERM, 1829.

Mead *v.* Curry. VIII, N. S. 280.

An action does not lie against a co-partner, for any sum paid for the partnership, or funds placed in it, till after a settlement.

A suit for a specific sum, cannot be considered as one for a settlement, even when there is a prayer for general relief.

The defendant may take advantage of this, by an exception filed during the trial.

SIXTH District, Judge of the Seventh presiding.

MATHEWS, J., delivered the opinion of the court.

This is a suit brought by one partner against another, to recover from the latter the amount of funds alleged to have been advanced to him by the former, for the purpose of carrying on a trading adventure in the Spanish country, adjacent to the limits of the state of Louisiana; and also to recover one half of the gains or profits made by the traffic, which was conducted by the defendant. The petitioner states a sum, certain both in relation to the amount advanced and one-half of the profits arising from the adventure, and prays judgment for both these sums. The defendant, in answering, denies the allegations of the petition, and files an account, exhibiting a state of the transaction at its close. During the progress of the trial, in the court below, his counsel made a peremptory exception to the action, which was sustained by the judge *a quo*, and the cause dismissed. From this judgment of dismissal, the plaintiff appealed.

[Mead v. Curry.]

In support of the judgment thus rendered, the appellee relies principally on the doctrine, established by cases heretofore decided by this court, viz: that of Drumgoole *v.* The Widow and Heirs of Gardner, reported in 10 *Martin*, 433, and that of Faurie *v.* Millaudon *et al.*, found in 3 *N. S.* 476. The present action is very similar in principle, to the case first cited, and does not differ materially from the last. In both these cases, it is explicitly, stated, that one partner has no action against another, for any sum paid for the partnership, or any funds placed in it, until a final settlement takes place, &c. In the case now under consideration, a settlement, or rendition of accounts, is not demanded in the petition. The specific prayer is for a sum certain, and it is believed, that the request made, in general terms, for relief, ought not to be allowed to have the effect of changing the nature of the action; neither, in our opinion, can the petition be aided by the answer, with which an account is filed.

The defendant was certainly very tardy in filing his exception, but as it is one founded on law, it must be permitted, in conformity with the 345th article of our Code of Practice. We have looked at the law, cited from the *Curia Philipica*, 109, *no.* 7, which does not appear in a very great degree to conflict with our decisions, and if it did, must yield to the latter, as being based on commercial law, such as we conceive ought to prevail.

It is, therefore, ordered, adjudged and decreed, that the judgment of the district court be affirmed, with costs.

Scott and *Royce*, for the plaintiff.
Johnston, for the defendant.

Nuttall and Wife *v.* Kirkland.   VIII, N. S. 282.

COURT of Probates, Parish of Catahoula.

The appeal will be dismissed, if the citation be served on the attorney, and it does not appear that the appellee is absent or resides out of the state.

Dorsey *et al. v.* Kirkland *et al.*   VIII, N. S. 283.

COURT of Probates, Parish of Catahoula.
Until there be a *contestatio litis,* or judgment by default, final judgment cannot be regularly proceeded to.

Boulden *et al. v.* Hughes.   VIII, N. S. 285.

If the sum originally sued for be under 300 dollars, and a third party intervenes claiming a sum below 300 dollars, both claims cannot be cumulated to authorise an appeal, although they collectively exceed 300 dollars.

COURT of Probates, Parish of Concordia.

MARTIN, J., delivered the opinion of the court.
The petitioners state, that they are respectively creditors of the estate of Spark, who died in the parish of Concordia, leaving them a considerable estate, in land, negroes, &c., which was duly inventoried and appraised, in presence of a counsel appointed to represent the absent heirs; that he left two minor heirs, whose paternal uncle was appointed tutor, and possessed himself of the estate, sold the moveable property and removed the slaves to the parish of Washita, where he resided, and is since dead; that the defendant has caused himself to be appointed, in the court of probates of the parish of Washita, curator of Spark, and has taken the administration of the estate of the deceased.

The petition concludes, that as Spark died in the parish of Concordia, and his succession was opened, that the curator may be cited to answer, and the petitioners have, respectively, judgment for their claims, according to their rank and privileges, and other relief, according to the justice of the case.

The defendant pleaded, he was not liable out of the parish of Washita, where he resides.

The plea was sustained, and the plaintiffs appealed.

[Boulden *et al. v.* Hughes.]

Neither of their claims amounts to 300 dollars, nor do they do so collectively; but a third party, since the judgment, has intervened as a creditor of the estate, for the purpose of appealing, and has done so. His claim is also under 300 dollars, but the aggregate amount of the three exceed that sum.

It is clear, we cannot take cognisance of the case. Distinct debts, due to different persons, cannot be joined or cumulated together, to make a sum of 300 dollars, in order to give jurisdiction to this court. Preval *et al. v.* Grigg *et al.*, 5 *N. S.* 87.

But the appellants' counsel urges, that the estate of their debtor was of great value, upwards of 14,000 dollars, as appears by the inventory—and the Code of Practice, 1050, is relied on.

Before that Code, there was a doubt, whether the value of the matter in dispute (when there was a contest for curatorship or tutorship) was not the benefit the applicant could reap from the management of the estate; the Code decides, that the value is, in such a case, the amount of the whole. But the present is a case of specific debts, not of the right to curatorship.

It is further contended, that the petitioners sue for their claims, concurrently with the other creditors of the estate. This concurrency cannot avail them—for, it may lessen, but never increase the amount coming to them.

It is, therefore, ordered, adjudged and decreed, that the judgment of the court of probates be affirmed, with costs.

Ogden, for the plaintiffs.
Patterson, for the defendant.

Lewis *et al. v.* Beatty. VIII, N. S. 287.

SIXTH District, Judge of the Seventh presiding.

Parol evidence of the contents of a deed cannot be received, without proof of its loss or destruction.

The circumstance that Nugent and his wife, to whom the original had been confided, had removed to Texas and probably carried the deed with them, *decided,* to be not sufficient to authorise plaintiffs to prove its contents as a lost paper.

Lewis *v.* Blanchard.   VIII, N. S. 290.

SIXTH District.

Decided, that it is an implied condition of every contract, that the work contracted for shall be done in a sufficiently workmanlike manner, and the materials furnished shall not be spoiled.

Had the plaintiff called for the advance, he had stipulated for, before he had done any work, his claim could not have been refused, for the defendant had promised to make the advance *at any time.* But if he spoiled the defendant's timber, and the work he made was insufficient and unworkmanlike, he failed in complying with his part ·of the contract, and thereby gave the defendant a right to refuse a compliance with her part, and she was not bound to wait till the plaintiff left the work or completed it, in order to sue him for damages, or withhold the second instalment, which might not afford a sufficient remedy.

Nuttall and Wife *v.* Kirkland.   VIII, N. S. 292.

COURT of Probates, Parish of Catahoula.

Until the administrator presents his accounts, and obtains their homologation in the court of probates, or until the time expires for which he holds his appointment, any person having claim on the estate, has a right to sue him, as representing it.

Morgan *v.* Maddox *et al.*   VIII, N. S. 294.

SEVENTH District.

Held, that the defendant is bound to adduce every evidence necessary to support his plea. ·

The payee of a promissory note, is not bound to join, as plaintiff, a person not named on it, having a right to receive a part of the proceeds.

Mead *v.* Chadwick.   VIII, N. S. 296.

SIXTH District, Judge of the Seventh presiding.

Martin, J., delivered the opinion of the court.

The plaintiff moved for a new trial, on an affidavit that, being under the impression that he could give parol evidence of a deed, he had neglected to procure it, or a copy thereof; that during the trial, he discovered his error, but was taken by surprise, in having parol proof rejected; and he will be able to procure the deed, or a copy thereof, at the next term.   The new trial was refused, and he appealed.

It is clear, that no man can be relieved from the consequence of his error, on a question of law.

Hughes v. Harrison and Wife. VIII, N. S. 297.

In a suit on a promissory note, the nature of the action is not changed by an amendment, which alleges a different consideration from that originally set forth.

If, on such amendment, final judgment is proceeded to, without an answer being filed, or judgment by default taken, the judgment is erroneous.

If the defendant be interrogated as to his signature to the note, and neglects to answer, but pleads the general issue, the signature is admitted, but every other legal defence remains open.

SEVENTH District.

PORTER, J., delivered the opinion of the court.

This case has been already before the court, and was remanded. 7 N. S. 227. It was an action on a promissory note, by which the husband and wife jointly and severally promised to pay Ailes & Morris the sum of 482 dollars 16 cents, for articles furnished them for their and plantation use, as per account rendered. Judgment was rendered, in the first instance, against the wife for the whole amount, and the note, on the face, purporting to be for objects furnished for both husband and wife, that judgment was reversed, as the latter was made responsible for a debt, some part of which was the husband's.

On the cause returning to the inferior court, the plaintiff moved to amend his petition, by inserting the allegation, "that the articles of goods, wares and merchandise, in consideration of which the note, on which this suit is brought, was given, were furnished for the use and benefit of Mrs. Jemima Harrison, the wife of said Benjamin, for her family and plantation—wherefore, he prays judgment against the said Jemima and Benjamin, *in solido.*

The defendant objected to this amendment, as changing the cause of action; the court received it, and he excepted.

We are of opinion, the court did not err. The cause of the action was the note: the consideration for which it was given, the inducement: and the insertion in the amendment of a different consideration for the instrument, from that contained in the original petition, does not change the cause of the action.

The parties went to trial on this amendment, without any answer being put in. It is now objected, that the proceedings were irregular, and that the judgment must be reversed, it being rendered without the *contestatio litis*, or judgment by default.

We think the objection fatal. The answer put in to the original petition did not, and could not extend to the amendment: the case was consequently tried, without issue joined. This case cannot be distinguished from that of Freeland *v.* Lanfear, 2 *N. S.* 256.

The plaintiff, however, contends that this defect cannot be taken advantage of by the defendants, because interrogatories were annexed to the petition, calling on them to say, whether they did not execute the note on which they were sued: which interrogatories they did not reply to, but filed an answer, containing the general issue.

This point presents, for the first time, a question, as to the construction which several articles of our Code of Practice should receive.— Article 324 provides, " when the demand is founded on an obligation or an act under private signature, which is alleged to have been signed by the defendant, such defendant shall be bound, in his answer, to acknowledge expressly, or to deny his signature." In the French text, the words are *sera tenu declarer expressement dans sa response, si il reconnait ou nie sa signature.*

Art. 325 declares, that if the defendant deny his signature in his answer, it shall be proved, &c.

Art. 326. The defendant, whose signature shall have been proven, after he having denied the same, shall be barred from every other defence, and judgment shall be given against him without further proceedings.

These articles change materially the effect, of a general denial of the allegations in a petition. Heretofore, such a plea put the plaintiff on the proof of every fact necessary to maintain his action: and of course, that of the execution of the instrument on which suit was brought. The article 324 says, the defendant is bound expressly to deny or admit the execution of the instrument. If he is bound to do one or the other, and fails to do either, the conclusion is, there is no denial, because there is not such a denial as the law requires from him.

If he makes the express denial, and it is found untrue, a heavy penalty is inflicted on him—he is precluded from further defence.— Were we to hold, the defendant could escape from this penalty, by an implied denial, which would impose the same burthen of proof on the plaintiff, and create the same delay, the provision in the Code would be a dead letter. No man would deny expressly, because, by the general denial, he would get all the benefits of an express one, without incurring its risks.

In this case, there is no special denial, and from the want of it, as well as a failure to answer the interrogatories, annexed to the petition, the execution of the note was confessed. Every other legal defence is still open to the defendants.

The judgment must be reversed or rendered without issue joined.

It is, therefore, ordered, adjudged and decreed, that the judgment of the district court be annulled, avoided and reversed; that the case

[Hughes v. Harrison and Wife,]

be remanded, to be proceeded in according to law; and that the appellee pay the costs of this appeal.

Scott and *Winn*, for the plaintiff.
Flint, for the defendant.

Calvet *et al. v.* Calvet *et al.*   VIII, N. S. 301.

COURT of Probates, Parish of Rapides.
If the judge, notwithstanding there be no issue joined, and before judgment by default, give final judgment, it is error. See Freeland *v.* Danfear, 2 *N. S.* 257; and Hughes *v.* Harrison and Wife, *ante*, 522.

Scott *v.* Blanchard.   VIII, N. S. 303.

The statement of facts may be made at any time before the appeal is granted.
The record of a court of chancery, in another state, certified by the clerk, with the attestation of the chancellor that the certificate is in due form, is legal evidence.

SIXTH District.

Martin, J., delivered the opinion of the court.
In this case, the statement of facts was made after the appeal was prayed for, and the appellee cited to wait on the return day in this court.
The appellant relies on the case of M'Micken *v.* Riley *et al.*, 7 *N. S.* 393, in which we held, that the law has fixed no time within which the judge may certify.
This is certainly true; but the appellee contends, the Code of Practice requires the statement of facts to be made before the appeal.

By the 586th article, the judge is required to make a statement of facts, in the manner hereafter provided.

By the 602d article, the party intending to appeal, must require his adversary to draw, jointly with him, a statement of facts.

By the 603d article, it is provided, that if the adverse party refuse, or the parties cannot agree, the court, at the request of either, shall make such a statement.

Hence, it is urged, that the judge cannot make the statement, till the party, against whom the appeal is intended to be brought, has refused to join his adversary, or both cannot agree. This imposes on the party intending to appeal, to make the application to his adversary, before the appeal be obtained, for afterwards he is the appellant, not the party intending to appeal, and after the appeal, the case is no longer in the possession of the inferior court.

In this case, no statement of fact was made, till the return day after the citation of appeal. The judgment was rendered on the 6th day of May, 1829—the bond filed on the 14th. The day on which the appeal was granted, does not appear—but it was returned on the 5th of October, on which day the statement bears date.

In the case of a certificate, when the evidence has been taken down by the clerk in open court, or when there is documentary evidence alone, there is but little need for the exertion of the judge's memory; but when he has to relate every part of the testimony, it is meet he should be called on to do so, at a very early period after the case is tried. We do not give a forced construction to the words of the Code of Practice, when we fix as a limit, to the period within which the statement of facts is to be made, that which elapses between the judgment and the appeal.

We therefore conclude, that the statement of facts was, in the present case, made too late.

We are next to examine a bill of exceptions to the opinion of the district court, in admitting in evidence, the record of the judgment of the Superior Court of Chancery for the western district of the state of Mississippi; it is certified by the clerk, under the seal of the court, and the chancellor of that state has certified that the certificate is in due form. The act of congress (Ingersoll, 77) requires the certificate of the judge, chief justice, or presiding magistrate.

We have the certificate of the chancellor, who is the judge of the court of chancery. It is further said, the clerk, certifying the copy, had no authority to do so. The individual subscribes himself clerk of the court, and the chancellor certifies his official capacity. If he be clerk, the act of congress authorises him to certify copies of the records of his court. The judge did not err, in admitting the copy in evidence.

The suit is on a judgment of the court of Adams county, in the territory of Mississippi. That judgment was enjoined, and the injunction dissolved by the chancellor of the state of Mississippi. Admit, that the records of the court of chancery are not legal proof

[Scott v. Blanchard.]

of a judgment of the court of Adams county, yet the record of the court of chancery was the only legal evidence of the dissolution of the injunction by the chancellor; and the bill of exceptions is taken to the admissibility of the evidence, not to its effect or strength. The record was properly admitted.

It is, therefore, ordered, adjudged and decreed, that the judgment of the district court be affirmed, with costs.

Scott, for the plaintiff.
Boyce, for the defendant.

Wells *v.* Wells.   VIII, N. S. 307.

Nothing prevents a man, who has the right of possession, from taking into his hands the object which is subject to it, nor is there any necessity for his asking or obtaining the consent of a person who has no right of possession, although that person may have the possession of the thing.

But if he resort to force in so doing, he is unquestionably liable in damages.

SIXTH District, Judge of the Seventh presiding.

PORTER, J., delivered the opinion of the court.

The plaintiff states, he was in peaceable possession of five slaves, in virtue of a lease from Thomas Jefferson Wells, and that the defendant took forcible possession of them, by which the petitioner suffered damage to the amount of 2000 dollars.

The defendant avers, that the property in question was owned by his brothers, Thomas Jefferson Wells, and Madison Wells, the latter of whom was a minor, represented by his curator, S. E. Cuney, and that the curator had entrusted the defendant with the management of the minor's property, of which the defendant had possession one year before the plaintiff illegally got the slaves, and appropriated their services to his use.

That, under a contract with the brother, Jefferson Wells, the defendant had possession of that portion of the slaves which belonged to him, for one year prior to the time the plaintiff alleges he got possession thereof, and that, by contract with said Jefferson, the defendant had a right to retain them one year more. That by the illegal act of the plaintiff, interrupting defendant's possession, he has sustained 500 dollars damages, for which he prays judgment in reconvention.

The cause was submitted to a jury, who found a verdict in favor of the plaintiff for 1000 dollars, which the court below confirmed, notwithstanding an application of the defendant for a new trial. He appealed.

In this court, and we perceive, in the court below, the defendant has rested his defence on the fact of his having possession of the property previous to the time it came into the possession of the plaintiff, and that the contract, by which the latter hired it from Jefferson Wells, as alleged in the petition, was conditional, and depended on the defendant consenting to it.

The plaintiff has insisted, that his contract was simple and unclogged by any condition, and that, at all events, having possession of the slaves, the defendant could not retake them forcibly, without being responsible in damages. That if the plaintiff's possession was an illegal or tortious one, the defendant's remedy was by an action at law: he had no right to do justice to himself.

The evidence in the cause shows, that the defendant was absent from home, when the plaintiff took the slaves; that immediately after his return, he applied to the latter to give them up, and on his refusal, which was on the public road, the defendant called out to the slaves, who were at work in the field, to return to his house.

On the trial, the judge, among other things, charged, the jury, " if the jury find, that while the plaintiff was in the peaceable and honest possession of the negroes, even without a right so to possess, and the defendant, without legal authority, forcibly, or without the consent of the plaintiff, dispossessed him of the negroes, the defendant is liable. He is liable, on the ground, that he cannot, without the interposition of law, to which every citizen of the land must resort for a redress of grievances for any wrongs done him. The courts are open to the defendant for a like remedy, on the plaintiff's first possession, and he is, by parity of reasoning, entitled to damages, if it be a wrongful, tortious or violent one."

In support of this opinion, the counsel for the plaintiff has cited several authorities to show, that no man can use force or violence to redress injuries, inflicted on him, and among others, the well known law of the *Recopilacion*, which declares, that the owner of property who regains possession of it by force, forfeits all right therein.— *Neuva Recopilacion, liv.* 4, *tit.* 13, *ley* 1. And he has read from the Partidas and Pothier to establish, that it is of no moment how the force or violence is exercised, provided it deprives the possessor of the object.—*Pothier, Traite de la Possession, no.* 24. *Pa. tit.* 10, *ley* 1.

Admitting these authorities to their full extent, there exists in law, as there must do in the nature of things, a difference between a peaceable taking of possession, and that which is otherwise; and certainly all acts, by which the person entitled to possession retakes it, when lost, cannot be considered as acts of violence, although without the act, the possession would not be regained. In the present case, the judge charged the jury, "that if, while the plaintiff was in peaceable and honest possession of the negroes, even without a right so to possess, the defendant, without legal authority, forcibly, or without the consent of the plaintiff, dispossessed him of the negroes, the defendant is liable." We think the doctrine is laid down too broad in this opinion, and that, under the circumstance of the case, it had a tendency to lead the jury into error. To that part of it, which declared the defendant to be liable, if he resorted to force, no objection can be made. But that portion of it, which conveyed to the jury the idea, that the plaintiff, though he had not a right to possess, could recover damages from the defendant, for taking possession of the property, without the plaintiff's consent, although the defendant might have the right of possession, was erroneous. Nothing in our law prevents a man, who has the right of possession, from taking into his hands the object which is subject to it, nor is there any necessity for his asking or obtaining the consent of a person who has no right of possession, although that person may have the detention of the thing.

It is, therefore, ordered, adjudged and decreed, that the judgment of the district court be annulled, avoided and reversed; and it is further ordered, adjudged and decreed, that the cause be remanded to the district court, with direction to the judge not to charge the jury, " that the defendant is liable to the plaintiff, for taking possession of the slaves mentioned in the petition, without the plaintiff's consent, although the plaintiff had no right of possession therein;" and it is further ordered, that the appellee pay the costs of this appeal.

Wilson and *Bowen,* for the plaintiff.
Thomas and *Flint,* for the defendant.

Martin *v.* Ashcraft.   VIII, N. S. 313.

An appeal lies from the order of a judge, at chambers, directing the discharge of a party arrested on a *ca. sa.*

A defendant, arrested on a *ca. sa.* and discharged from imprisonment by the plaintiff, may be imprisoned again.

SIXTH District.

PORTER, J., delivered the opinion of the court.
The plaintiff was arrested, in virtue of a *capias ad satisfaciendum,*

issued under a judgment obtained against him by the defendant for 3556 dollars, and applied to the judge at chambers, under the provisions of the Code of Practice, to be discharged. After hearing the parties, the judge was of opinion, the arrest had been illegal, and directed the plaintiff to be released from confinement. The defendant appealed.

The first question is, whether an appeal lies, in the present case, to this tribunal. Two objections have been suggested. First, that it is taken from a decision on a writ of *habeas corpus;* and secondly, that the decree of the judge was not rendered in court, but at his chambers.

Neither of these objections offers sufficient ground to prevent us taking cognisance of the case.

This court has decided, it had not appellate jurisdiction, from the refusal to grant a writ of *habeas corpus,* and in a subsequent case, recognises the right of appeal from the discharge under such writ. 3 *Martin,* 42; 6 *Ibid.* 569.

These decisions are not in the least contradictory. The first was, where the writ had been resorted to in a matter growing out of the administration of penal law. The second, where it was used to obtain a discharge from imprisonment, on a writ issued in a civil action. The refusal to grant the appeal in the one case, and its accordance in the other, did not proceed from the writ, but from the case in which it was resorted to. If in a criminal prosecution, the court had not jurisdiction, because this tribunal cannot take cognisance of such matters; but, if the suit was a civil one, it had, because its jurisdiction, in cases of this kind, does not at all depend on the nature or form of the writs, or remedies which the parties may exercise, but on the fact, that the decision is final, or works an irreparable injury, and the amount in dispute is above 300 dollars.

The circumstance of the decision being given before the judge, at chambers, and not in open court, does not, in our opinion, affect the right of appeal. The case commenced by petition to the judge, the proceedings were had under the provisions of the Code of Practice, which contemplate a summary trial, and from the decision, either party had a right to appeal.

On the merits, the question is, whether a defendant, arrested on a *capias ad satisfaciendum,* and discharged out of custody by the plaintiff, can be again imprisoned, under a writ of the same description. We lately decided, in the case of Abat *v.* Whitman, that a release of this kind by the plaintiff in execution, did not discharge the debt, as it does at common law; and if it has not that effect, it does not discharge the person of the debtor. So long as the judgment debt remains unsatisfied, all the means given by the laws of the land to enforce it, are open to the creditor. The arguments addressed to this tribunal, on the hardship of the case, go rather to show the impolicy of allowing imprisonment as a means of carrying into effect judgments in civil causes, than against its exercise in the manner it was used here; and would be addressed with more propriety to a legislature, than to a court of justice, whose duty is *jus dicere,* and not *jus dare.*

It is, therefore, ordered, adjudged and decreed, that the judgment of the district court be annulled, avoided and reversed; and that the *capias,* which was stayed by the decision of said court, be proceeded on according to law, the appellee paying the cost of this appeal.

Wilson and *Briggs,* for the plaintiff.

Johnston and *Rigg,* for the defendant.

The State *v.* Wright's Administrators. VIII, N. S. 316.

Since the new Code, the state has no privilege on the estate of an insolvent sheriff, for taxes collected by him and unaccounted for.

COURT of Probates, Parish of Rapides.

MATHEWS, J., delivered the opinion of the court.

This case comes up on an appeal taken on the part of the state, as opposing creditor to the homologation of a tableau of distribution, filed by the administrators of the succession of the intestate, wherein the state was refused a privilege and preference or priority over other creditor, for an amount claimed from said succession, as being due by the deceased, on account of his defalcation to the government, in relation to money by him collected, as sheriff of the parish aforesaid, on account of taxes due to the state.

The only question presented for our consideration, relates to the preference or priority secured to the state by law, on the funds of insolvents who may be debtors to the public.

It is not contended, by the counsel for the administrators or mass of creditors, that the preference now claimed, was not accorded by our laws before the promulgation of the Louisiana Code, but that this latter law has abrogated all laws which previously existed, in relation to the right of the state, to privilege, preference, priority, or mortgage on the estates of its debtors, in cases of insolvency. We here assume as a fact not denied, that the succession of Wright is insolvent, or at least, that it is in a course of administration as such.

[The State v. Wright's Administrators.]

The cause must be decided according to the laws, as they stood at the time the sheriff made his bond, which was in 1826, after the promulgation of our new Civil Code. Previous to that event, the privilege and preference, or priority, such as the counsel for the state now contends for, was most explicitly granted by an act of the legislature, approved on the 4th of January, 1814. See acts of that year. Before this law was enacted, a legal or tacit mortgage existed on the property of public officers, and other accountable persons, in favor of the territory, and at the charge of government, accrued to the state. See Civil Code, p. 456, art. 25. As this species of mortgage is exclusively the creature of law, it can have no existence, except by express legal provisions. We are now to inquire, whether both or either of these laws, have been abrogated by the provisions of the Louisiana Code. In treating on the subject of legal mortgages, it is expressly declared, that none shall exist, except in the cases determined by that Code. See Louisiana Code, art. 3280. An enumeration of the rights and credits on which legal mortgages are founded, immediately follows this article, amongst which those of the state do not appear; and consequently, the provisions of the old Code, relating to the tacit or legal mortgage of the state, must be considered as repealed and abrogated. But, in our opinion, a legal mortgage may be considered as a thing distinct from privilege, preference and priority, although it may, in some instances, embrace them. In other words, that this species of mortgage is not necessary to support the latter rights, but they may exist without its aid.

This view of the cause, leads us to inquire into the effect, which the provisions of the new Code may have had on the rights of the state, as secured by the act of 1814. On examination, they are found to be very similar, in relation, privilege and preference, to those on the subject of legal mortgages. By the art. 3150, the property of a debtor is considered as a common pledge of all his creditors, and the proceeds of its sale must be distributed among them rateably, unless there exist among the creditors some lawful causes of preference.

The article immediately succeeding states, such causes to be privileges and mortgages. And the next declares, that privilege can be claimed, only for those debts to which it is expressly granted in this Code.

No privilege appears to be granted expressly by the Code to the state, and it seems to be excluded, by this provision, from any which might have existed previously. The repealing clause, found in art. 3521, adds to the force of the restrictive article just cited. It sweeps from our jurisprudence all laws which relate to any case, especially provided for in the Code. The case of privilege and preference is provided for by the Code, and consequently all previous laws on that subject, are repealed and abrogated. Hence, we conclude, that the act of 1814, is repealed, and hence, that the state is deprived of her legal mortgage, and of her privilege and preference on the property of her debtors, as secured by laws in force prior to the promulgation

of the new Code. As argued by the state's counsel, it can hardly
be believed, that the legislature intended, by the adoption of the Code
and the repealing clause annexed to it, to abolish the preference,
which the government had secured to itself, on the property of its
debtors. We are unable to discover the wisdom of such legislation,
which seems to us to be contrary to that of all other states and governments. *Sed ita lex*, plainly expressed, and we, as judges, are bound
to obey it.

- It is, therefore, ordered, adjudged and decreed, that the judgment
of the court of probates, be affirmed.

Wilson, for the state.

Boyce, for the defendants.

Police Jury *v.* Boissier.   VIII, N. S. 321.

A petition, claiming damages for the defendant's failure to complete a building, according to a written agreement, may be amended by a demand, under the legal warranty
resulting from the defendant's undertaking.

SIXTH District, Judge of the Seventh presiding.

Porter, J., delivered the opinion of the court.

In this case, the plaintiffs claim damages from the defendant for an
alleged failure on his part in constructing a building, in pursuance of
a written agreement, entered into between the parties. The cause
was submitted to a jury in the court below, who found a verdict in
favor of the plaintiffs, and from a judgment thereon rendered, the
defendant appealed.

The petition sets forth the written agreement, alleges a want of just
and honest compliance, on the part of the defendant, with the obligations imposed on him by the contract, and prays for remuneration
in damages, for the injury they have suffered, in consequence of his
misconduct. After the defendant had filed his answer to this petition, the plaintiffs obtained leave to put in an amendment thereto, in
which they allege, that he is liable, on an implied warranty, imposed
by law on all undertakers of buildings, that their works should be
faithfully executed. This amended petition is objected to, on the
ground that it exhibits a new cause of action, and an exception was
taken to the opinion of the judge *a quo*, by which he permitted the
amendment.

[Police Jury *v.* Boissier.]

We do not think the judge erred. The nature of the action does not appear to have been changed. It is one instituted to recover damages, in compensation of an injury, which the plaintiffs allege they have suffered, in consequence of the failure on the part of the appellant, faithfully to fulfil his obligation resulting from his contract; and whether this liability be fixed on him by special agreement, or by the warranty in such cases, created by law, makes no difference in the nature of the action.

As to the merits of the case, they seem to depend entirely on matters of fact; to these the jury have answered, and we are unable to discover any thing in the evidence, which authorises a conclusion, that their verdict is erroneous.

It is, therefore, ordered, adjudged and decreed, that the judgment of the district court be affirmed, with costs.

Rost, for the plaintiffs.
Dunn, for the defendant.

Police Jury *v.* Bullit *et al.*   VIII, N. S. 323.

The sureties on a sheriff's bond, are liable for the taxes on suits.

The power of summarily enforcing payment of a tax, cannot be exercised in regard to other taxes.

A sheriff, sued for the taxes he was bound to collect, must show he failed in doing so, after having used proper diligence.

The state is not bound to show the amount of taxes actually collected.

SIXTH District.

PORTER, J., delivered the opinion of the court.

The police jury of Natchitoches sue the sheriff and his sureties on the bond, given by him for the faithful performance of his duties, for the amount of the tax, imposed on all suits commenced in the district and parish courts.

The sheriff answers, by denying the allegation in the petition, and averring, that he has paid over all the moneys collected, to the treasurer of the parish; that not being by law authorised to enforce the payment, either against the property or person of delinquents, he could only collect as agent for the jury; that he has frequently

45*

tendered a list of the delinquents to the treasurer, to enable him to institute actions against them, which he has refused to receive. That he has paid the treasurer more than he collected, for which he prays judgment in reconvention.

The sureties deny, that they are responsible for the collection of state or parish taxes; that they are only accountable for the malfeasance of the sheriff, in the discharge of his other duties.

The court of the first instance gave final judgment in favor of the sureties, and as of nonsuit for the sheriff. The police jury appealed.

We shall first dispose of the question, as to the liability of the sureties.

The act of 1823, p. 60, sect. 3, provides, " that all persons, who shall institute a suit or suits in the said district courts, shall pay a tax of ten dollars on each and every suit; and all persons, who shall institute a suit or suits in the parish courts, above the sum of one hundred dollars, shall pay on each and every suit the sum of five dollars, to be collected by the sheriff or collector of taxes, in the same manner as is provided by law for the collection of the state and parish tax, and shall pay the same into the parish treasury, at the same time and under the same provisions as directed for the payment of the parish tax "

It has been said, that the duty, here imposed on the sheriff, cannot be considered the collection of either the state or the parish tax, for which that officer gives an annual bond, with sureties; and that for all duties, other than the collection of the taxes of the parish and state, the sureties, on the bond which the sheriff gives, on being inducted into office, are responsible.

We have given to this argument an attentive consideration, and are unable to concur with it. The law lays a tax, to be collected as other taxes. This tax is, it is true, for the benefit of the parish, but the destination of funds, to be raised by a tax, levied by state authority, does not take from the enactment its distinctive and appropriate character. Whether the money, produced, be applied to a general or special purpose, it is not less a tax: more especially, when the legislature have considered it such, so called it, and directed it to be collected as other taxes.

The defendant, Bullit, contends that, by law, no power was conferred on him to enforce the payment of this tax, and that he is not responsible, except for the amount which the persons, subject to it, voluntarily paid to him.

The act of the 20th of March, 1816, entitled " An act supplementary to the several acts relative to the revenue," by its first section conferred, on the sheriff and other collectors of the state and parish taxes, the authority to seize and sell the property of delinquents.—But this section is repealed, by the 4th section of " An act to amend the several acts relative to the revenue of this state," approved the 8th of March, 1819.

The power, therefore, to seize and sell, without due process of law, for non-payment of taxes, must be sought in some other legislative provision.

We have been unable to find any conferring it, except that of the 12th section of the act of the 27th of March, 1813, entitled " An act to lay a tax within the state of Louisiana, to determine the mode of assessing and collecting said tax, and for other purposes." By the terms of this statute, the power is limited to the tax imposed by virtue of that act.

The first section of the act, entitled " An act supplementary to the several acts relative to the revenue of this state," passed 11th of December, 1820, recognises the power in collectors to execute for taxes; for it declares they shall not do so before the first of April of that year.

The question then is, whether a power, conferred by the state on its officers, to enforce the payment of a tax, imposed by one act, extends to subsequent laws laying new taxes on other objects, and we are of opinion it does not. The right of the citizen to be heard in due course of law, before he is deprived of his property, cannot be taken away, even in favor of the state, for fiscal purposes, by implication. It must be expressly given.

We see nothing to countenance the idea, thrown out in argument, that sheriffs and collectors may not still enforce payment, in a summary manner, from delinquents of taxes on land and slaves, and the other objects made liable to taxation by the act of 1813; but no power being conferred by the act of 1823, on the sheriff, to seize and sell the property of those who do not pay the tax, imposed on suits in court, we think such power does not exist, by virtue of previous provisions, relative to taxes imposed for different purposes, and on other objects.

The court below decided, that as the plaintiffs introduced no evidence to show that Bullit, the sheriff, had collected the taxes, judgment of nonsuit should be given against them. The court erred, in considering it the duty of the plaintiffs to show the defendant had collected the money. It was the duty of the latter to establish, that he had used due diligence to perform the trust he undertook. When accounts or obligations are placed in the hands of an agent for collection, it is not merely sufficient for him, after a lapse of time, to offer to return them, without showing, that he exercised ordinary care and industry to get the money. This point was expressly decided, in the case of Collins *et al. v.* Andrews, 6 *N. S.* 195. But in that case, as the defendant might have been led into error by the opinion of the court, we·remanded the cause, to enable him to prove his diligence. We think justice requires the same course should be pursued with this.

It is, therefore, ordered, adjudged and decreed, that the judgment of the district court so far as it relates to the defendants, Burgler and Clanten, be affirmed, with costs; and so far as it relates to the defendant, Bullit, that it be reversed, and remanded to the district court for a new trial, the appellee, Bullit, paying the costs of this appeal.

Flint, for the plaintiffs.

Rost, for the defendants.

Ware *v.* Elam.   VIII, N. S. 329.

SIXTH District.

Whether a defendant, who denies his signature to a promissory note, may, by admitting it at the trial, avoid the penalty?   Code of Practice, 326.   The point not being essential to this case, was waived.

The purchaser, with a notice of an incumbrance, cannot, on account of it, resist the claim of payment.

Rachal *et al. v.* Irwin.   VIII, N. S. 331.

He who claims under an order of survey, must deduce his title from the grantee of the order.

It is not enough, that he deduces his title from a person in whose favor the commissioners granted a certificate.

SIXTH District.

PORTER, J., delivered the opinion of the court.

The plaintiffs seek to recover a tract of land, in possession of the defendant, and state in their petition, " that they claim by virtue of an order of survey, dated the 10th of February, 1799, signed by Manual Gayoso DeLemos, the governor of the province of Louisiana, and issued in favor of Diego Ramirez, under whom your petitioners hold, by a chain of regular conveyances."

The defendant sets up title under a donation from the United States. There was judgment rendered against him in the district court, and he appealed.

No conveyance was produced by the plaintiffs, from the person in whose favor the order of survey was granted. The commissioner's certificate shows, indeed, that the title was confirmed in favor of one Louis Teremazin, from whom a regular chain of conveyances was exhibited, to the plaintiffs. But this acknowledgment, on the part of the general government, that Teremazin had acquired the right of Ramirez, is not evidence against third persons. It is, as to them, *res inter alios acta.*

The plaintiffs, being thus without any title under the Spanish government, can recover only on the confirmation of the United States. It is questionable, whether he could do so under the pleadings; for he sets up title by virtue of the order of survey to Ramirez. But waiving that objection, his case is made little better. He shows a confirmation, in virtue of a survey from the Spanish authorities to which he had no right, and his settlement was not made until some years after the change of government. The case cannot, in any respect, be distingnished satisfactorily from that of Horton's Heirs *v.* Tippet. There, it is true, the party having title similar to that of the petitioners, recovered, but, as was stated by the court, it was solely on the consideration, that the plaintiffs, who sought to disturb them, had no better title. Both were declared to have no foundation, either in law or equity. 5 *N. S.* 109.

This opinion renders it unnecessary to examine into the questions raised, with regard to the mode of locating the respective titles of the parties, or the validity of the plea of prescription. The plaintiffs must recover on the strength of their title, and we are of opinion, it does not enable them to sustain the action against the defendant.

It is, therefore, ordered, adjudged and decreed, that the judgment of the district court be annulled, avoided and reversed, and that there be judgment for defendant, with costs in both courts.

Rost, for the plaintiff.

Boyce, for the defendant.

Wrinckle *v.* Wrinckle *et al.*　VIII, N. S. 333.

SIXTH District.

A wife may cumulate an action for a separation, with a prayer for an injunction to stay a sale on a *fi. fa.* against her husband.

By MATHEWS, J.,—The evidence in the cause shows pretty clearly, that the property, seized on execution, belonged to plaintiff and her children by a former husband.　The objection made to the deed, offered by her in evidence, on account of having only the mark of the vendor, need not be inquired into in the present case, as the vendee is proved to have gone into possession under it, and as the vendor recognised the act in open court, and that under the solemnity of an oath.　It is true, his testimony was opposed, on the ground of incompetency, but ·this opposition ought not to prevail, for he was called on to testify against his own interest.

Heirs of Baillio *v.* Poisset.　VIII, N. S. 336.

SIXTH District.

·The rights of the seizing creditor cannot be greater than those of the debtor.

The vendee of property on a *fi. fa.* acquires no right on property which did not belong to the debtor.

Heirs of Baillio *v.* Prudhomme *et al.*   VIII, N. S. 338.

SIXTH District.
If the demands, in two consolidated cases, exceed, together, 300 dollars, an appeal will lie.
If, after an amended petition is filed, the case is submitted to a jury, without an answer being filed, or judgment by default, the proceedings are irregular.

Haden *v.* Ware.   VIII, N. S. 340.

SIXTH District.
The vendee of slaves, mortgaged to secure the price, cannot resist payment, on the ground, that he has sold them to a third person.

Thomas *v.* Mead.   VIII, N. S. 341,

If a suit be brought to set aside a conveyance obtained by fraud, and the fraud be clearly proved, the conveyance will be set aside *between the parties*, but the rights of third persons, who are purchasers, without notice, will not be disregarded.

SIXTH District.

MARTIN, J., delivered the opinion of the court.
The plaintiff, curator of the estate of Thomas Harman, deceased,

claims two negroes, in the defendant's possession, as part of the estate. The defendant pleaded the general issue and title in himself. The plaintiff now, by leave of the court, amended his petition, alleging, that the sale to the defendant's vendor and the defendant was fraudulent, illegal and void.

There was a bill of exceptions to the opinion of the court, allowing the filing of the amended petition: so that it was properly admitted, it did not change, as is alleged, the nature of the action, and was called for by the nature of the defence.

There was a verdict and judgment for the plaintiff, and the defendant appealed.

Admitting, that the conveyance from Thomas Harman to his children was fraudulent, or made to defraud his creditors, and therefore voidable, the defendant was a *bona fide* purchaser, and cannot be affected, by a fraud committed in a transaction to which he was not a party. He purchased from a person having an apparently legal right, and paid a full consideration.

If a suit be brought, to set aside a conveyance obtained by fraud, and the fraud be clearly proved, the conveyance will be set aside, *between the parties,* but the rights of third persons, who are purchasers, without notice, will not be disregarded. Fletcher *v.* Peck, 6 Cranch, 133.

Titles which, according to every legal test are perfect, are acquired, with a confidence which is improved by the opinion, that the party is safe. If there be any concealed defect, arising from the conduct of those who had held the property, long before he acquired it, of which he had no notice, that concealed defect cannot be set up against him. *Ibid.*

And the decision of the Supreme Court of the United States, was unanimously given, that an estate, having passed into the hands of a purchaser, for a valuable consideration, without notice, his title could not be affected, by any fraud in the conveyance by which his vendee had acquired his title.

In the present case, the defendant acquired his title fairly, for a valuable consideration, without notice of any fraud in his vendor's conveyance: he, therefore, cannot be disturbed.

It is, therefore, ordered, adjudged and decreed, that the judgment of the district court be annulled, avoided and reversed: but, as the conveyance to the present defendant is urged not to be an absolute one, and the right of his vendor may, in case of fraud, be in the latter claimed by the plaintiff—it is ordered, that there be judgment for the defendant, as in case of nonsuit, with costs in both courts.

Thomas, for the plaintiff.
Flint and *Boyce,* for the defendant.

Baillio *et al, v.* Wilson. VIII, N. S. 344.

A sale made without the authority of justice, is not binding on the creditors of a succession, and they have a right to call on the person making it to pay them the value of the object sold.

Creditors are not bound by a decree of a court of probates, which they had no opportunity to oppose.

A tutor is subrogated to the rights of a creditor paid by him.

COURT of Probates, Parish of Rapides.

Porter, J., delivered the opinion of the court.

This is an appeal, taken from a decree of the court of probates, liquidating the claims against the succession of J. H. Gordon, deceased, and establishing the order in which they should be paid.

The tutrix, who administered the estate for the minor heirs, with the benefit of an inventory, has appealed, as have several of the creditors, viz. Wm. Wilson, John L. Baillio, Joseph Lattier, Francis Lattier, and Michel Lattier.

The tutrix is charged, in the account, with the amount of a carriage, belonging to the succession, sold by her at private sale. She offered, as a set-off against it, the note of the person to whom she alleges the carriage was sold. This was objected to, on the ground, that she had no right to dispose of the property of the estate at private sale, and the court below sustained the objection. We think it quite clear, the court did not err in doing so. A sale, made without the authority of justice, was not binding on the creditors of the succession, and they have a right to call on the person making it, to pay them the value of the object sold.

It was further urged, in argument, that the proceeds of the sale had, in fact, been paid to the person from whom the deceased purchased the carriage in his lifetime, and to whom he was indebted for its price at his decease. Whatever may be the facts, on this point, there is no legal evidence on the record, either of the existence of the debt, or of its payment.

She also complains, that she is debited with a note of one thousand dollars, due by Wm. Wilson to her deceased husband, although the said note was compensated by the professional services rendered by him to the estate, and that she could not collect it. The judge below allowed her 300 dollars, as the amount due the attorney, and made her responsible for the balance.

The evidence of a gentleman of the profession was taken, who made oath he was of opinion, the charge of 1000 dollars was reasonable, and that he would not have undertaken it himself for that sum, foreseeing the difficulties of the case.

According to the note of evidence, there were three suits against the succession, in which the attorney appeared and acted for the estate. We think, that 100 dollars for each of these suits, and the sum of 300 dollars for the services rendered in settling the estate, is a fair compensation, considering the amount in dispute and the labor expended.

We have next to consider the errors, alleged by Wilson, one of the appellants.

· One of the principal items in his account, consists of a debt, transferred to him by J. & S. Parkins. Of the existence of this debt,. no evidence was given on the trial, except that resulting from an account made by the administratrix, a short time after the decease of the intestate, of the claims exhibited against the estate, in which this debt of J. & S. Parkins is inserted.

This account, although probably presented to the court of probates, was not deposited there, but an order appears of that court, by which several of the creditors are directed to be paid, as privileges of the first class, and the rest of the claims, as exhibited, are to be paid proportionably, as there may be funds.

· This order, it is said, forms *res judicata* between all the creditors of the succession, and that it is now too late to dispute the amount of any account directed to be paid by it.

· To this pretension, we think the answers, given at the bar, are satisfactory and conclusive. First, that the accounts not being filed in the office of the court of probates, among the papers of the succession, none of the other creditors could know what claim was approved or what rejected; and secondly, that it appears to have been made *ex parte*, without notice or citation to persons interested. It has been argued, that we are bound to presume the creditors were regularly cited, before the judge made such a decree. But the terms of the judgment negative any such idea. It is stated to be given, at the instance of the administratrix, and no mention is made in it, that those who were interested in the estate, were present at the time the decree was rendered, that it was made after hearing the parties, or that they were notified to attend.

We therefore conclude, the inferior court did not err, in rejecting that part of the claim which the appellant Wilson complains of, and that it erred in putting the firm of J. & S. Parkins on the tableau, for the remaining portion of the debt. Wilson claims a further credit, for the sum of 100 dollars, paid a creditor an account of the estate of J. H. Gordon, and we are of opinion it should be allowed. He appears to be a privileged creditor for part of his claim, and a chirographary creditor for the balance. As the debtor had a right to impute the payment to the most onerous demand, the estate has a right to claim a deduction from the privileged debt to the amount, and the appellant is subrogated for the amount he has paid, in the place of the creditor.

The appellants, Baillio and Lettier, complain, that they were charged with 1100 dollars more than they received, and that the balance due them was erroneously diminished that much.

The tutrix opposes to this, a judgment rendered by this court, in the October term, 1826, fixing the amount due the appellants at the sum of 5840 dollars. It is contended, this decree has the force of *res judicata*, and precludes all inquiry into the claim now set up.

The appellants, not contesting the principle invoked, assert, that their debt was reduced to that amount, in consequence of credits being given to the estate from returns made by the sheriff, on several executions which had issued in their favor.—That one of these executions was credited by the sum of 1100 dollars received in a twelve months' bond, and that, subsequent to the judgment fixing the amount due the appellants, the purchaser surrendered the property back to the estate, in consequence of a defect in the title, and that the sum thus debited to them, and for which the estate had a credit, was not in fact received by them.

There is no evidence before us, that this loss occurred subsequent to the judgment liquidating the balance: it was rendered in 1826, and the property was surrendered up by the purchaser in 1824. The judge, therefore, did not err, in refusing to add to the claim of the appellants, the amount of the bond.

It is, therefore, ordered, adjudged and decreed, that the judgment of the court of probates be annulled, avoided and reversed; and it is further ordered, adjudged and decreed, that the cause be remanded to said court, with directions to amend the tableau, according to the principles established in this decree; the costs of appeal, to be paid equally by the appellants.

Thomas, for the plaintiffs.

Wilson, for the defendant.

EASTERN DISTRICT, DECEMBER TERM, 1829.

Williams *v.* Kimball.   VIII, N. S. 351.

In an attachment case, no attorney is to be appointed, by the court, to the defendant, if the citation be served on him.

The section of the Code of Practice, which treats of attachment, is extremely obscure, and the English text, which, from the relative correctness of the French, appears as a translation of it, is full of gross blunders. The title, and most of the articles of the section, seem confined to attachments in the hands of garnishees: attachments in the hands of third persons, seeming to exclude attachments of property in the hands of the party. In the 249th and 264th articles, the word *defendant* is evidently used for *plaintiff*, and in the 254th, 258th and 259th, the word *garnishee* occurs instead of *defendant*.

FIRST District.

MARTIN, J., delivered the opinion of the court.

The citation was served on the defendant in person, and three slaves were attached. Judgment was taken by default, and afterwards made final. He appealed.

His counsel assigns as error, that no attorney was appointed by the court, as is required by the Code of Practice, 260.

In ordinary cases, the defendant is made a party, by the service of the petition and citation on his person or at his domicil; in others, by such a service at his last place of residence.

If, however, the petition contains a prayer for an attachment, and the citation can not be served in any of the above manners, it may be by affixing copies of it in certain places, *Ibid.* 254, and the subsequent attachment of his property. *Ibid.* 256.

If the party, thus made a defendant to a suit, *i. e.*, without a citation on his person, at his domicil, or last place of residence, fail to appear, the court must appoint him an attorney. *Ibid.* 260. He needs this aid from the court, because the apparent impossibility of service in the ordinary way, raises a presumption, that he is abroad, and can not have timely knowledge of the action. In such a case, the proceedings are rather *in rem*, than *in personam*. *Ibid.* 265.

But when the defendant is made a party, by the service of the citation, on his person, at his domicil, or last residence, the action is essentially *in personam*, and is to be prosecuted in the ordinary way against the defendant; he has received that notice, which renders ordinary defendants liable to a judgment by default, on failure to appear and answer. He is not one of the defendants, of which the Code of Practice (258) speaks, thus made a party to a suit, *i. e.*, as provided in the 254th and 256th articles, by a citation affixed in certain places, and the subsequent attachment of his property, but has been made so by service of citation in the regular way.

Althogh the attachment has been obtained, if, after this ordinary mode of service of the citation, no property be attached, either because he has none, or has succeeded in removing his out of the sheriff's way, or even because the plaintiff has directed the sheriff to forbear levying the attachment, still, the defendant being regularly made a party, the suit is to proceed in the ordinary way, as if no attachment had been asked. There will be no need of the court appointing an attorney, to the defendant, because he has notice of the consequence of his failure to appear and answer, and may appoint an attorney, if he need one. We can not see why the actual service of the attachment should alter the case. The defendant, after having been made a party by the due service of the citation, does not cease to be so by the attachment of his property. He is not made a party, by the affixing of the citation, nor by the attachment of his property, because he was a party before the sheriff affixed the citation or attached his property. The action is an ordinary one *in personam*, and the service of the attachment is a mere incident in the suit, a conservatory act, which accompanies the demand, *Ibid.* 208, but which does not constitute it.

An attachment, like all other conservatory acts, is not, when the defendant is personally cited, a mode of bringing a suit, but a remedy or incident, which may precede, accompany, or be subsequent to the action. In the language of the Code, it may accompany a demand, or give effect to a suit, which the plaintiff has brought, or intends to bring. *Ibid.* 208 and 230.

A prayer for a writ of attachment, does not dispense with a citation of the party, any more than a prayer for the arrest of his person, the provisional service of sequestration of that in dispute, as an in-

junction.   A citation is required, on every demand in writing, (*Ibid.*
170 and 172,) and particularly in cases of attachment.   *Ibid.* 251
and 253.

We admit that, at first view, the court's naming an attorney to
defend a party present in court, appeared to us an anomaly introduced by the Code.   The section of it which treats of attachment, is
extremely obscure, and the English text, which, from the relative
correctness of the French, appears as a translation of it, is full of
gross blunders.   The title, and most of the articles of the section,
seem confined to attachments in the hands of garnishees; attachments
in the hands of third persons, seeming to exclude attachments of property in the hands of the party.   In the 249th and 264th articles,
the word *defendant* is evidently used for plaintiff, and in the 254th,
258th and 259th, the word *garnishee* occurs instead of defendant.

On a close examination of the whole section, and a comparison
of all its articles, we conclude, that the court is not bound to appoint
an attorney to a defendant, brought into court, by the regular service
of a citation on his person, at his domicil or last place of residence,
even where a prayer for an attachment precedes, accompanies, or
follows the institution of a suit, and property be thereon attached.

It is, therefore, ordered, adjudged and decreed, that the judgment
of the district court be affirmed, with costs.

Preston, for the plaintiff.
Pierce, for the defendant.

Delacroix *v.* Cenas's Heirs.   VIII, N. S. 356.

If a vendee fails to call his vendor in warranty, the latter is not liable for any costs or
damages, which result from defending the action.
The vendor called in warranty, may defend the suit, or confess judgment, as he thinks
proper.
But if the vendee supposes, he does so through collusion, he may defend the suit on his
own responsibility.

FIRST District.

PORTER. J., delivered the opinion of the court.
The plaintiff purchased, at a sale made by the ancestor of the de-

fendants, who was sheriff of the parish of Orleans, certain slaves, from which he was afterwards evicted, by a judgment of this court.

The cause of this eviction was, the misrecital in the deed of sale, of the judgments under which the seizure and sale took place.

But the money which the plaintiff had paid, for the property so purchased by him, having been applied to a discharge of a debt due by its owner, the court decreed, that he should return to the plaintiff this money with five per cent. interest from the institution of the suit; and that the plaintiff should pay the hire of the negroes, from the same time, being, in the eye of the law, a possessor in bad faith, from the period the defects of his title were made known to him.

The hire of the slaves, amounted to more than the interest which was allowed to the plaintiff; and this action is brought to recover the difference between them, together with the costs, which the plaintiff paid, in defending the suit brought against him by the original defendant, in execution. The amount is stated to be 1283 dollars, 38 cents.

The court of the first instance, refused to allow the claim, for the difference between the hire and the interest, but gave judgment against the defendant, for the costs expended by the plaintiff in defending his title. From this judgment the plaintiff has appealed, and the defendants have prayed, that it be so amended, that they may be discharged from all liability to the plaintiff.

Various questions have been raised by counsel and argued, but that which was principally relied on by the defendants, and most discussed, is in our judgment decisive of the case, and renders an examination of the others unnecessary.

It has been already noticed, that the injuries of which the plaintiff complains, arose subsequent to the commencement of the action, and were the payment by him of the hire of the negroes from the institution of the suit, and the costs incurred in defending it.

The defendants insist, they should not be made responsible for the damages proceeding from this cause, for if their ancestor had been cited in warranty, he could, and would, at once have surrendered the property, and thus have avoided the damages, which were a consequence of the obstinacy of the plaintiff, in defending the action.

To this the plaintiff replies, that the suit in revindication was pending a considerable time, before he was aware of the grounds, on which the defendants in execution asserted the nullity of the sale made to him. That a vendor has not the right, when called in warranty, to abandon his title to the property, and consent to judgment being rendered in favor of the petitioner; and finally, that by the provisions of the Civil Code, in force at the time the action was instituted, the only consequence of the plaintiff's failure to cite the defendants' ancestor in warranty, is the right reserved to them to show, that had he been called in, he could have successfully resisted the claim of those who set up title to the property he sold.

The authority of Pothier, has been principally relied on by the defendants, and it goes the whole length, of sustaining the position for which they contend. He states expressly, that although the buyer may, at any time, exercise his action against his vendor, he is deeply interested in doing so as soon as he is sued, for in default of giving notice, he has no recourse for the expenses incurred during the period which intervenes between citation and judgment. He is only responsible for the costs of the original process. A contrary doctrine, the author states, would put it in the power of the vendor, to ruin the seller, by carrying on a suit, of which he had no knowledge. *Pothier, Traité de Vente, nos.* 109 and 128.

The grounds, on which the plaintiff contests the application of this authority to his case, are next to be noticed.

And first, as to his want of knowledge that his title would be assailed, for the defect on which it was ultimately decided to be bad, and that, consequently, he could not have given notice, we think there is no strength in it. Plaintiffs, in a petitory action, do not set out in their petition, the defects in their adversary's pretensions. They state their own title. The obligation to call in warranty the vendor, does not depend on the grounds alleged for recovery by the party suing, but on the fact of the property being claimed from the vendee.

The second ground appears to us equally untenable. When a buyer, who is troubled by an action in revindication, calls on his seller to come in and defend the title of the thing sold, the management of the defence is surrendered to the latter, and as he is the person on whom the loss must ultimately fall, he has a right to conduct it in the manner which he judges most conducive to his interests. If he has sold *bona fide*, and discovers his title to be a bad one, he certainly has the right to abandon a defence, which can only increase his responsibility, and mulct him in greater damages. The opposite rule, would require him to contest a demand, which he knew was well founded, and support pretensions, on his part, which he was convinced were illegal. In a word, it would require him to do an immoral and an unjust thing. We have looked a good deal into the books, to see if any thing could be found in them, which would thus limit the rights of a vendor called in warranty, and, far from finding any thing in them, to support the position taken at the bar, they expressly sanction the contrary doctrine. *Pothier, Traité de Vente, nos.* 123 and 129; *Merlin, Repertoire,* vol. 5, *Garantie.*

If, indeed, the buyer has reason to believe, there is collusion between the party suing and his vendor, he may contest the case on his own responsibility; but unless the vendee chooses to do so on this condition, the seller may defend as he pleases, or refuse to defend, when he discovers it can not be done with the prospect of success. *Pothier, Traité de Vente, nos.* 113 and 115.

The article in the Civil Code, which declares the warranty to cease, when the buyer has let himself be cast, in a definitive judgment, without calling on his seller, if said seller prove, that he had sufficient ground or means, to have obtained a judgment in his favor, is not, in our opinion, contrary to the principle for which the defendants contend, but in consonance with it. They both rest on the same foundation, namely, that the vendor should not be made responsible for any thing, which a knowledge of the suit would have entitled him to avoid. The words of the law are satisfied, by construing it to apply (as we believe the legislature intended) to the value of the thing evicted, and all the fruits and costs anterior to the time when the vendee could have given notice. Its spirit would be essentially violated, by making the seller responsible for the consequences of a litigation, which he could have avoided. By the Spanish law, the buyer, who failed to cite his vendor in warranty, lost all recourse on him. The provision in our Code, which modified and softened the rigor of this rule, was, we presume, taken from the French jurisprudence, which, as we understand it, was that of the Roman. With that provision, stood the exception relied on here, and it may well stand with it in our law, more especially, when the limitation is in perfect harmony with the principle on which the doctrine rests. *Febrero*, p. 1, art. 7, *no* 42; *Par.* 5, *tit.* 5, *ley* 32; *Dig. liv.* 21, *tit.* 2, *law* 53.

In the case of Fleming *et ux. v.* Lockhart, the question raised here was not made, and the expressions used in the opinion, related to the general liability of the sheriff, as vendor, for the value of the thing evicted from the purchaser. 10 *Martin*, 398.

We do not think the defendants liable for any thing, except the costs of serving the original process on the plaintiff, in the suit in which he was evicted, and as the record does not afford proof of the amount, the cause must be remanded.

It is, therefore, ordered, adjudged and decreed, that the judgment of the district court be annulled, avoided and reversed; and that the cause be remanded, to be proceeded in according to law, the appellees paying the costs of this appeal.

Seghers, for the plaintiff.
Pierce and *Christy*, for the defendants.

Dufart *v.* Dufour.   VIII, N. S. 363.

FIRST District.
If partners state, in the preamble of an agreement, that they have
settled their affairs to the day of the date, no account can be claimed
by either, of any anterior transaction.

Nolte & Co. *v.* Their Creditors, on the opposition of the Tutor of the Minor Heirs of T. L. Harman. VIII, N. S. 366.

FIRST District.
A minor has a mortgage on the property of a person, who intermeddles with his estate.   Louisiana Code, 3283d article.
Held, it matters not whether the application of minors' property
for one's own benefit, be made a single act or many.   The effort to
show in this case, that the testamentary executors of T. L. Harman
had authorised, or ratified this misapplication by Nolte & Co. was
not successful.   The heirs of T. L. Harman have a legal mortgage on
the estate of the insolvents, and should be paid out of it by privilege
and preference, in pursuance of such mortgage.
· *Judgment,* that the appellants be put on the tableau for 7461 dollars 83 cents, with privilege, according to article 3283 Louisiana
Code, and the insolvents' estate is condemned to pay costs.
Grymes, for the plaintiffs.
Eustis and *Pierce,* for the defendants.

．

King v. Gayoso, for the use of Stille.   VIII, N. S. 370.

The endorser of a promissory note, with power to make such use and disposition of it, as
she thinks proper, as long as she remains bound as the payee's surety, is not bound to
admit every plea which could be opposed to the payee, such as want of consideration,
concealment or compensation.

THIRD District, Judge of the Second presiding.

Martin, J., delivered the opinion of the court.

The defendant, having obtained a writ of seizure and sale, on an
authentic act, executed by the plaintiff, the latter obtained an injunction and prayed for a jury. The prayer was opposed; the opposition sustained; and the cause tried summarily. The injunction was
dissolved, and the plaintiff appealed.

By the Code of Practice, cases on injunctions are directed to be
tried summarily, and without a jury. Art. 740 and 757.

The plaintiff and appellant, purchasers of a tract of land from
Gayoso, had given for the price a note, the payment of which was
secured by a mortgage. Gayoso endorsed the note to Stille, and by
a notarial act, made a transfer of it and of the mortgage, in order to
secure her against the consequences of a suretyship, on which she
had entered for him.

Her claim was resisted, on the ground, that she was not the absolute endorsee and actual owner of the note; but a mere pledgee, and
consequently bound to admit any defence which the maker of the note
could oppose to the payee; and that the latter, in the sale of the land,
for the payment of which the note was given, had been guilty of
such a fraud and concealment, as authorised the withholding of the
price.

The appellee's counsel has labored to show, that the allegations
of fraud and concealment are unsupported; but the case appears to
us to turn on the liability of the endorsee to admit every defence,
which might be opposed to the maker.

The note was endorsed, before maturity, and in the usual form; it
was negotiable, and the act of transfer has a clause, setting over to
the transferee all the payee's hypothecary rights, and the transfer is
stated to be made in consequence of the transferee having become
surety of the transferor, and it is added, "that the said Margaret C.
Stille, is hereby authorised, fully to make such use and disposition
of the note and mortgage, as she thinks proper, as long as she remains the surety of Gayoso, as aforesaid; and that, as soon as she is

released and discharged from said suretyship, she is to. return said note to Gayoso, or, in case she has disposed of it, in any manner whatsoever, she is to account to said Gayoso, for the full and entire value of the same."

So the endorser has a defeasible ownership in the note; for she may dispose of it, in any manner whatsoever, and is only accountable for its amount, on the contingency of her being released from the suretyship.

But the appellant's counsel urges, that she is still a mere pledgee, yet with power to dispose of the pledge; and under the Code, 3123, the destruction of the pledge, by the insolvency of the maker, would not be her loss, but that of the pledgor, who consequently remains the owner; *res perit domino,* and the pledgee can not have a better right than the pledgor, and consequently the maker can oppose, to the endorsee, every plea which he could oppose to the payee.

This argument appears inconclusive; for, even in the case of an absolute endorsement, on the destruction of the pledge, by the insolvency of the maker of the note, the loss would fall on the endorsee, and not on the endorser.

We were further referred to the same Code, 3109, where it is said that, in regard to those things in which the pledgor has a property, which may be divested, or which is subject to incumbrances, he can not transfer to the pledgee any further right in the pledge than he has himself.

This is true, under the general principle, *non dat, qui non habet. Nemo plus juris in alium transferre potest, et quam ipse habet:* but there are exceptions to it. The robber of the mail has no legal right to bank notes taken out of it, yet, by passing them in the regular course of business, he transfers to an innocent holder a right, which he has not; and the payee of a note, to whom, were he to sue, the plea of want of consideration, concealment and compensation, could be opposed, transfers to an honest endorsee, the right of resisting those pleas.

It is a general principle of commercial law, that the maker of a note. payable to order, engages to pay its amount to the innocent endorsee who took it in the usual course of business, for a valuable consideration, whatever claim the maker may have against the payee, and we are ignorant of any exception to the rule, in favor of a pledgee. Promissory notes are expressly made the subject of the contract of pledge. *Ibid.* 3123. To pledge a note, is, therefore, to make a legitimate use of it. In the usual course of business, notes and bills of exchange are used to pay debts, make purchases or raise money by discount or pledge. He, therefore, who gives a bill or note, authorises the use of it for any of those purposes and must know, by such a disposal of it, the payee will enable the endorsee to repel any clause of the maker, on the score of want of consideration, concealment, or compensation. *Volenti non fit injuria.*

In the case of Bosanquet *et al. v.* Dudmans, Starkie, 1st part,

[King v. Gayoso, for the use of Stille.]

Lord Ellenborough held, that a banker might resort to bills deposited with him by a customer, who had overdrawn, and that the right of the former, on such bills, could be extinguished by payment only.

It is, therefore, ordered, adjudged and decreed that the judgment of the district court be affirmed, with costs.

McCaleb, Rameau and *Ogden*, for the plaintiff.

Workman, for the defendant.

Dismukes *et al. v.* Musgrove. VIII, N. S. 375.

The revocation of a deed from a father to a trustee for the benefit of the son, by a suit in the court of chancery of Mississippi, cannot be pleaded here as *res judicata* against a claim of the son.

The declarations of the party who makes a *stipulation pour autrui* cannot be given in evidence.

The return of the sheriff that a witness cannot be found is not the only proof of that fact, admissible.

An appraisement of a succession in the state of Mississippi, though executed under private signature, may be given in evidence where it made part of the proceedings of the orphans' court of that state.

When the party offering a record in evidence, alleges it to be incomplete, and offers a transcript of the part omitted, the court may receive both as proof of the whole record.

The record of a suit, brought by the party who has made a conveyance for the benefit of another, may be given in evidence, to show an intention to revoke the gift.

EIGHTH District, Judge of the Third presiding.

PORTER, J., delivered the opinion of the court.

This case has been already before the court: a full statement of the pleadings and matters at issue are contained in the opinion given, on remanding the cause, and it is unnecessary to repeat them here. 7 *N. S.* 58.

A verdict has been again found for the defendant, and the plaintiffs have appealed. They rely, for a reversal of the judgment below, on alleged errors of the judge who tried the cause, in rejecting and admitting evidence.

Before examining the several bills of exception, by which the opinions of the judge *a quo* are brought before us it is necessary to dispose of the plea of *res judicata*, which the defendant offered in defence of the present action.

The suit is brought for certain slaves, which the plaintiffs claim, in virtue of a deed, of trust, as they style it, executed by their father in the year 1811; by which one Terry was created trustee, on condition of delivering the slaves and their increase to the petitioners, when they came of age and married.

The judgment relied on, as barring the claim of the petitioners, was rendered in the court of chancery of the state of Mississippi. The parties to it, were the father of the plaintiffs, complainant, and the trustee, Terry, respondent. The decree of the court annulled the deed, as having been made without consideration.

It is obvious, that a decision in this suit, between these parties, cannot have the authority of the thing judged against the plaintiffs, if any right to the property vested in them by the deed notwithstanding a subsequent change of intention on the part of the father. If, on the contrary, the father had a right to revoke the advantages, conferred on his children, and his suit in Mississippi, to annul the deed, had that effect; then its influence, on the rights of the plaintiffs, must arise from that change of will, which, whether expressed through the medium of a petition, in a suit, where the children were not parties, or evidenced by a deed of revocation, must have its effect as such, and is a defence on the merits—not one which can take the shape of an exception.

The first bill of exceptions, taken by the plaintiffs, was, to the testimony of a witness, called by the defendants to prove certain declarations of the father of the plaintiffs, in relation to the document, on which the action was instituted. The witness swore, that he had heard him say, he never knew any thing of the counter letter or obligation of Terry, until a few months before the institution of the present suit.

The plaintiffs' objection to this testimony, was on three grounds:

1. Such testimony could not be received, under the general issue, which was waived by inconsistent pleas.

2. The father was not a party to the present suit.

3. The instrument declared on, contained a stipulation *pour autrui* and could not be affected by the declaration of the maker.

The last objection may be dismissed with the observation, that it went to the effect of the proof when received, not to the legality of its introduction. And the first may be disposed of by stating, that if the declarations of the father could be received in evidence at all there was nothing in the pleadings which prevented them from being offered. The answer denies all and singular the facts in the petition, consequently it denies the existence of the instrument, on which suit was brought. The other pleas, which accompany this denial, are not, in our judgment, in any way inconsistent with it.

The second objection, we think, well taken. The father, who made the declaration, had assigned all his right in the property to Andrew.

Dismukes, under whom the defendat claimed. His declarations, therefore, could not affect the right which his children might have under an instrument previously made, to which he was a party. And the objection to his testimony, is of equal force, when his declarations are introduced to prove the non-existence of any such writing. Independent of this objection, the proof amounted to nothing more than hearsay. And though it is true, that the father could not be called as a witness, this disqualification did not authorise the proof of his declarations, for that would be to receive evidence indirectly from an incompetent witness, which could not be admitted from one that was competent.

The next exception was taken to the introduction of certain notes, which had been executed by the defendant. The plaintiffs objected: first, because the absence of the subscribing witness had not been proved by the return of the sheriff; and secondly, because the instruments offered, were executed by the party presenting them, and no one could make proof for themselves.

The return of the sheriff, that a witness cannot be found, is not the only evidence which may be given, to authorise the introduction of other proof: showing that he resides in a foreign country, or that diligent search has been made for him within the jurisdiction of the court, by witnesses who depose to these facts, will authorise evidence of his handwriting. The notes of the defendant were good evidence if they made a part of the *res gesta.* And if they did not, it was the duty of the party excepting, to place on the record all facts necessary to show the incorrectness of the opinion of the judge *a quo.* Starkie, Part 2, 342.

The plaintiffs next excepted to the introduction of the appraisement and sale of the estate of Terry, on the grounds, first, that the acts were under private signature and not proved, and the sale and inventory were not made conformably to the laws of Louisiana.

The appraisement and sale formed part of the proceedings in the orphans' court of the state of Mississippi. They were presented, under an authentication, duly made, as being a true transcript of those proceedings. There is, of course, no ground for the first objection, and as to their not being conformable to the laws of Louisiana, that might be a question, as to the effect they should have, but certainly could not prevent their introduction in proof, forming, as they did, part of a record from a sister state.

The defendant offered, in evidence, a paper, purporting to be letters of administration, granted to one David Terry, in the state of Mississippi. The plaintiffs objected to its introduction, and the defendant acquiescing in the objection, declined reading it. Upon this the plaintiffs moved the court to withdraw from the jury, a record, which had been already given in evidence, of the proceedings in relation to the succession, in which these letters had been taken out. The grounds for this motion, are alleged to be, that the defendant had shown the record not to be a complete one, and that the clerk had not certified the record to be a full, true and complete transcript. The court refused to withdraw the record, and the plaintiffs excepted.

It is not seen by us, how the court could say the record was not a complete one, by wanting a paper which was not permitted to be read in evidence. If it was on the allegation of the party offering the paper such a decision was to be made, his willingness to produce the only document necessary to make the record complete, ought to have prevented him from suffering by the omission of its not being inserted in the transcript. And the court acted correctly, in not permitting the plaintiffs, after having shut out the document necessary to the completion of the record, to take advantage of its not being complete. The necessity of producing the whole of a record is founded on the idea, that the part omitted contains something unfavorable to the party offering it, and that the construction must be gathered from the whole taken together. This rule is subject to exceptions, and none can be more proper, than that of a party, who had already given the transcript in evidence, coming forward with a document necessary to complete that which he had already presented. Starkie on Evidence, 152, 245, 246. As he apprised the opposite party of the defect, it was proper to give him the means of curing it.

The objection to the clerk's certificate, is not supported: in fact, he certifies the record to be a true copy of all the proceedings in the estate of Terry.

There are many other bills of exceptions, which it is unnecessary to examine, as the judge appears to us to have decided correctly, and no principle of law would be settled by their examination, which is not of familiar knowledge and daily application.

Among them, there are, however, two, which it may be well to notice. A question is raised by them, whether the proceedings by the father, in the state of Mississippi, to annul the conveyance to Terry could be given in evidence in this suit. It is contended, they were *res inter alios acta*, and cannot affect the children.

By the provisions of the Civil Code, in force at the time the conveyance was made to Terry, and that he gave his obligation, acknowledging to hold the property, until the plaintiffs came of age and were married, a stipulation in favor of another might be revoked at any time before acceptance. For the purpose of showing this revocation, the record of a suit, brought by the father, to annul the conveyance, which was the foundation of the promise in favor of his children, was good evidence. What the effect of the evidence would be, is another question.

It is, therefore, ordered, adjudged and decreed, that the judgment of the district court be annulled, avoided and reversed; and it is further ordered, adjudged and decreed, that this cause be remanded to the district court, with direction to the judge, not to admit the declarations of the father of the plaintiffs, that he did not know of the ex-

[Dismukes *et al. v.* Musgrove.]

:istence of the obligation on which suit is brought; and it is further ordered, that the appellee pay the costs of this appeal.

Hennen, for the plaintiffs.
Ripley, for the defendant.

Rousseau *v.* His Creditors. VIII, N. S. 384.

PARISH Court of New Orleans.

Notes given to relieve a party, who mortgages slaves for the indemnification of the payee, need not be marked *ne varietur* by a notary. Moreau's Digest, 70, sect. 4.

Here the maker was mortgagee, not mortgagor.

A mortgage is sufficiently certain, wherein money is promised with *interest*, for this, of course, means legal interest.

Kimbal *v.* Blanc *et al.* VIII, N. S. 386.

The new Code has wrought no change in the liability of steamboat owners.

By the old Code their liability was clearly not *in solido*. The art. 2796 of the Louisiana Code, declares, that an association for the purpose of carrying personal property for hire, in ships, &c., is a commercial partnership; the articles 2798 and 2823 refer to the projected Code of Commerce, as the supplement of all that part of the Louisiana Code which relates to commerce. The projected Code of Commerce, article 163, declares, that joint owners of ships, &c., are not bound *in solido*, and in case a repugnance had thus been created, it was ordered, by the articles of the Louisiana Code referred to, that the Code of Commerce should be paramount. The Code of Commerce, however, has never become law. (1839.)

To the end to reconcile the new Code, 2796, with the old law, it was now *decided*, that the provision of the Louisiana Code, is exclusively applicable to a company formed ex-

47*

pressly to conduct the business of carriers, and leaves joint owners of vessels to their former responsibility; i. e., as partners in an ordinary partnership.*

FIRST District. .

MATHEWS, J., delivered the opinion of the court.
This suit is brought by the master, against the owners of the steamboat Lady of the Lake, in which he claims from them the sum of 1567 dollars 36 cents, as a balance due to him, on account of disbursements made for the benefit of the boat and for wages.

It appears, from the record, that Blanc alone was cited in the cause, who suffered judgment by default, to be obtained against him, which his counsel afterwards made attempts to have set aside, without success, and after final judgment, took the present appeal.

Several bills of exceptions were taken to opinions of the court below, expressed in the course of the trial, on which, and on an assignment of error in law, apparent on the record, the cause now stands before this court.

The exceptions are not supported by the facts or law of the case. But we are of opinion, that there is error in law, apparent in the final judgment.

The suit is against joint owners of a steamboat, and the petition charges them as being liable in solido. The judgment is rendered against one only, for the whole amount claimed. The error, assigned, is an improper understanding and misapplication of the law, in relation to partnerships. As it existed previous to the adoption of the Louisiana Code, respecting joint owners of steamboats, we are not left in doubt, since the decision of the case of Carrol v. Waters, reported in 9 *Martin*, 500. They were liable only according to their interest in such property—not bound *in solido* in contracts concerning its management and use. The only question to be settled, in the present case, is, whether the former law has been changed or abrogated by the new Code? To prove that an alteration has been made in the law, relative to the liability of joint owners of steamboats and other vessels, we are referred to the art. 2796 of the Louisiana Code, which contains a definition of commercial partnerships, wherein it is declared, that an association, for the purpose of carrying personal property, for hire, in ships or other vessels, is a commercial partnership. The arts. 2798 and 2823 show clearly, that all the legislation contained in the Civil Code, respecting commerce, had reference to a Commercial Code, which was then made out, by the persons to whom the task of code-making had been confided, and was ready to be sub-

* It were greatly to be wished that, either by adopting this exposition, or by new legislation, the monstrous anomaly of a commercial state barbarising its practical system, by such a departure from the general maritime law, as is the daily custom of the courts of Louisiana, in holding all the part owners of ships and steamboats, liable *in solido* for debts and damages, should cease to offend our admirers abroad.

mitted to the legislature for adoption. This last code never received legislative sanction, and is therefore without the force of law; but, as the former was passed in reference to it, on matters which concern commerce, there can not be any impropriety, in looking therein for aid in interpreting the provisions of the Civil Code, on commercial subjects. In the projected Code of Commerce, by the art. 147, it is expressly stated, that a joint ownership of ships and other vessels creates a special partnership. The art. 163 declares, that in such partnership, the owners are not bound *in solido*. Now, if these rules were in force, no question could arise on the apparent contradiction betwen them and the 2796th art. of the Louisiana Code; for, in cases of repugnancy, it is expressly provided, that the Commercial Code should prevail, in matters relating to commerce. See the articles above cited, 2798 and 2823.

There is certainly something extraordinary in the reference made from the Civil Code to the Commercial Code; as, from the situation in which they were placed, we are required to look forward to a thing to be created, and which has not yet received any legal existence; but the absurdity of that course of legislation is much palliated, by the circumstance of both the Codes being at the time mere projects, and both drawn up by the same agents of the legislature. In such a state of legislation, we are unable to discover, with certainty, the will of our law-makers; it is, however, believed, that they intended to leave the laws, in relation to commerce, as they were at the time of adopting the Louisiana Code, until the Commercial Code should receive legislative sanction. Yet, if any of the provisions contained therein are contrary and wholly repugnant to the rules of the commercial system, as it existed at the time of enacting the Civil Code, they must yield to the imperative authority of the posterior law.

We are, therefore, compelled to decide, whether a just interpretation of that part of the 2796th art. of the Code, which defines that to be commercial partnership, which is formed for carrying personal property, for hire, in ships or other vessels be or be not, contrary to the law which had previously governed us in relation to joint owners of steamboats.

It is evident, that the owners of vessels may not be the carriers of goods, as contemplated by the law; they might charter them to other persons, for the purpose of being used by the latter, in any carrying trade in which they may see fit to employ them. If a ship or other vessel be hired by a partnership, formed for the purpose of carrying property, the members of such association would be bound *in solido* to those who should be injured by their negligence or that of their agents. The owners would, perhaps, be bound in the same manner, if they held themselves out to the community as partners in the carrying trade; but the bare circumstance of their being joint owners, can not produce this effect, without, in our opinion, doing violence to the will of the legislature. They passed the Civil Code, in allusion to a Code of Commerce to be made, and did not inted to alter, radically, the rules which then prevailed in matters of commerce, except by a subsequent adoption of that Code to which they alluded. In such a state of our jurisprudence, the known and established laws of the country ought not to be made to yield to subsequent enactments, unless the former are found to be wholly repugnant to the latter. If efficacy can be given to both, by any reasonable mode of construction, it should be done; and this, we think, may be effected by considering the provision of the Civil Code, as exclusively applicable to a company, formed expressly to conduct the business of carriers; leaving joint owners of vessels to their former responsibility, as partners in an ordinary partnership.

It is, therefore, ordered, adjudged and decreed, that the judgment of the district court be avoided, reversed and annulled; and it is further ordered, that the cause be remanded to said court, to be proceeded in according to law, and that the appellee pay the costs of this appeal.

Duncan, for the plaintiff.
Waggaman, for the defendants.

Dugat *v.* Babin *et al.* VIII, N. S. 391.

Separate judgments do not authorise a joint execution.
A sheriff cannot make a new levy under a writ, the return day of which has expired.
Whether the sheriff who has been enjoined from proceeding on an execution, may not, after the injunction is dissolved, proceed to sell—*Quære?*

SECOND District, Judge of the Eighth presiding.

PORTER, J., delivered the opinion of the court.
The plaintiff claimed and obtained an injunction against the execution of several writs of *fieri facias*, which had been placed in the hands of the sheriff, at the suit of the defendants. On a hearing, this injunction was made perpetual, and the defendants appealed.

There were four writs of execution, and as to two of them, the judgment of the inferior court was clearly correct. They appear to have issued jointly against the plaintiff and one Michael Bergeron, to satisfy, as the writs recite, certain judgments obtained against them. On reference to these judgments, they appear to have been rendered separately, in separate suits against Dugat and Bergeron. They consequently did not authorise a joint execution against both.

In relation to the other and remaining writs, there exists, as far as we can discover, no other objection, except that the return day had expired, when they came into the officer's hands. The facts on record show the writs to bear date the 18th of November, 1826, and to have been delivered to the sheriff the same day. In virtue of them, he levied on the property of the plaintiff the 20th of that month, and advertised the sale to take place on the 22d day of December. But on the morning of that day, proceedings were stayed by an injunction, whereupon, the sheriff returned the writs into the clerk's office, where they remained until the injunction was dissolved. On its dissolution, the defendants took the same writs out of the clerk's office, and placed them a second time in the hands of the sheriff, who levied again under them.

It has been decided by this court, that a sheriff who makes a levy, before the return day of the writ, may proceed and sell afterwards. It is attempted here to carry this doctrine still further, and sanction a new levy, made after the force and effect of the execution had expired. We can find no authority which goes so far, and there is nothing in the reason or convenience of the thing, which requires us to so extend it. The party may as well commence *de novo* under a new writ, as the old one.

The authority of the Code of Practice, art. 700, has been relied on as sanctioning the course pursued in this instance. On an examination, we find it does nothing more than declare, that so long as the injunction continues, the limitation for making a return, does not affect the writ enjoined. We are unable to say, from this enactment, that it was the intention of the legislature to confer a power on the sheriff to make a new levy, though the return day of the writ had expired. Whether he might not have proceeded to sell the property originally seized by him, this case does not require us to decide, though the authority to do even that, is doubtful, and there would be great difficulty in such a case, in ascertaining whether he should advertise it for the length of time prescribed by law for the different species of property, or only for the number of days that preceded the day fixed for sale, at the time the injunction was served. The old rule, that the writ conferred no power after its return day, except to sell where a levy had been previously made, was clear in itself, and convenient in practice. We can not, on the expression used in the Code of Practice, introduce a doctrine, from which we perceive great embarrassment and confusion must arise, though, as in most other changes and novelties, it is probable we do not see all the inconvenience to which it would lead.

It is, therefore, ordered, adjudged and decreed, that the judgment of the district court be affirmed, with costs.

Ripley and *Conrad,* for the plaintiff.

Morgan v. Peet et al.   VIII, N. S. 395.

FIRST District.

On a motion to dissolve an injunction, all the matters alleged in the petition are taken for true. A debtor in whose hands the debt due by him is attached, may enjoin an execution, issued against him by his creditor. Louisiana Code, 2145.

Garcia v. Hatchell.   VIII, N. S. 398.

THIRD District.

By MARTIN, J.—This cause presents the very intricate, and at one time very interesting question, to whom did the country between the Iberville and Perdido belong rightfully, when the title now asserted by the plaintiff was acquired?

This question, however, has very lately undergone a solemn discussion, having been acted on and solved by the Supreme Court of the United States, on a writ of error from the court of the Louisiana district, in the case of Foster et al., plaintiffs in error, v. Neilson, defendant in error.

The decision of the highest tribunal of the nation, we are bound and inclined to consider as affording to us the only legitimate rule of decision, in cases relating to the construction of treaties.

They have considered the country between the Iberville and Perdido, as part of the territory, ceded by Spain to France, and the latter to the United States. We are, therefore, bound to conclude, that the Spanish officer, who granted the premises to the plaintiff, was without authority for doing so.

Pijeau v. Beard. VIII, N. S. 401.

The third possessor is bound by the wife's judgment against the husband.

A notary cannot be allowed to give evidence of a party's declaration at the time of executing an act.

PARISH Court of New Orleans.

MARTIN, J., delivered the opinion of the court.

This was an hypothecary action, by which the plaintiff sought the sale of a slave, the property of her husband, sold by him to the defendant, on an averment, that the plaintiff's husband was indebted to her, and she had no other means of procuring payment.

The general issue was pleaded, and the defendant claimed title to the slave, under an authentic act of sale from the plaintiff's husband, who had purchased the slave from Robinson, and given, to secure payment, his note, endorsed by the defendant. That at the maturity of this note, the defendant furnished a sum of money, and a note for a less sum than the first, to take it up—and furnished since, the money to take up the second; and the two sums, thus paid by the defendant, were the consideration of the sale of the slave, by the plaintiff's husband to the defendant.

There was judgment for the plaintiff, and the defendant appealed.

To prove her claim against her husband, the plaintiff introduced a judgment, by which they were separated of goods, and she recovered a sum of money against him. But this document was excepted to by the defendant.

She then introduced her brother, who deposed, that he had seen Morel pay to the husband, the third part; the wife's portion, in a sum of money by him received from the sheriff, on account of the plaintiff's ancestor. That Morel wrote a receipt, which the plaintiff's husband signed.

To this testimony, the defendant and appellant's counsel excepted, on the ground that it was inadmissible. The judgment is *res inter alios acta*, and while there is evidence of the existence of a receipt, given by the plaintiff's husband, the paper should be produced as the best evidence of the fact of receiving the money, and of the quantum.

A third possessor, before the Code of Practice, could not be disturbed, till judgment was had against the mortgagor. This judgment the former could not attack, except on the grounds of nullity, fraud or collusion. It was against him, *prima facie* evidence.

Bernard *v.* Vignaud, 1 *N. S.* 9. We are unable to say, why the third possessor should not be equally bound by the wife's judgment against the husband.

The receipt of the husband ought to have been produced or accounted for, and parol evidence of the fact it attests, was properly excepted to.

The plaintiff next introduced an authentic act of sale for the slave, from Robinson to her husband, and the note which the latter had given, with the defendant's endorsement, with a receipt on the back for 110 dollars; and another note for 360 dollars, endorsed by the defendant, drawn by her husband.

The defendant relied on the authentic act of the plaintiff's husband to herself, and the certificate of the recorder of mortgages, that Robinson had cancelled his mortgage on the slave. These two documents bear date of the same day.

She further offered the notary, before whom the plaintiff's husband executed the act of sale for the slave to herself, (the defendant,) to prove his declaration and acknowledgment, that the sum mentioned in the act of sale, as the consideration of it was, that the defendant, as his endorsee, had furnished him with the money to take up his notes to his own vendor.

This testimony was objected to, as contradicting the averment in the act of sale, and the plaintiff's husband's declarations could not be evidence against her. We think the testimony was properly rejected, not because it was contradicting the averment in the act of sale, which was, that the vendor had received the consideration of the sale from the vendee, and to add, that it had been received for the purpose of paying a certain debt, which the vendor was liable for, but because the testimony was the declaration of a third party to the act, not part of the *res gesta*, nor sworn to.

It then follows, that by the judgment of the plaintiff, it is established, that she is credited for a larger sum than was awarded against the present defendant; that the latter is the third possessor of a slave, part owned by the husband during the contract.

The defendant has not even succeeded in showing she paid the money to the vendor, otherwise than as a consideration of the sale: it is not contended, and had she paid it to the creditor of the husband, the possession of the note by the plaintiff repels the idea that it was paid by the defendant. It is farther in evidence, that Robinson, the mortgagee, cancelled the mortgage on the very day the defendant bought: so it is evident it was not subrogated to the mortgage.

It is, therefore, ordered, adjudged and decreed, that the judgment of the parish court be affirmed, with costs.

Seghers, for the plaintiff.
De Armas, for the defendant.

EASTERN DISTRICT, JANUARY TERM, 1830.

Rawle, for the use of Russell, *v.* Skipwith and Wife.
VIII, N. S. 407.

If an amendment to an answer, presents, under another form, a defence substantially
embraced by the previous pleading, the court of the first instance need not receive it.

A continuance will not be granted on the ground of surprise, when that surprise did not
arise from the acts of the adversary, but from the application of the known rules of
law to the proceedings in the cause.

A judgment, regularly obtained in a case where the equity is doubtful, or preponderates
in favor of the plaintiff, will not be set aside to let in a legal defence, which if used in
due time, might have defeated the action.

THIRD District, Judge of the Eighth presiding.

Mathews, J.—This is the third time that this cause has been
brought before the Supreme Court. The appeal immediately preceding the present, was taken from a judgment by default, which
was allowed in the court below, in consequence of the judge believing, that no answer had been regularly put in to the merits of the
cause. The record shows, that the defendants separated in pleading
and filed various exceptions to the petition. Previous to the last
return of the cause to the district court, F. Skipwith had commenced
proceeding against his creditors, in pursuance of our insolvent laws,
and as against him the present suit was stayed, the cause is therefore
to be examined only in relation to Mrs. Skipwith.
Vol. IV.—48

[Rawle, for the use of Russell, v. Skipwith and Wife.]

The reversal of the judgment by default, was obtained on the ground, that one of the exceptions, pleaded by the wife, embraced the merits of the case, and was virtually an answer making a *contestatio litis*, which fully authorised and required the introduction of evidence, as in case of issue joined in relation to facts. The correctness of the decision in the Supreme Court, touching this point of the cause, we believe cannot be questioned, on any sound principles of reason or law: and objections to it certainly come with a bad grace from the party who received its benefit.

Without entering on a discussion of the principles laid down in our Code of Practice, relative to exceptions, whether declinatory, dilatory, or peremptory, and the whole doctrine of pleading, as therein taught, (in which the counsel for the appellant imagines he sees great confusion and want of perspicuity, and which may possibly exist,) if the third exception made by Mrs. Skipwith be opposed to the allegations of the petition, by which she is sought to be made liable for the debt now claimed from her, it will clearly appear that a contest as to facts necessarily arose. The notarial act executed by her conjointly with her husband in favor of the plaintiff, which is made a part of his petition, states especially that she binds herself *in solido* with her co-obligor, and that the debt, which they oblige themselves to pay, had been converted to the benefit of the wife. The exception amounts to a denial of these facts, by alleging others, with which they are wholly inconsistent; they cannot both be true. 1. That the debt was contracted by her husband and for his benefit. 2. That in truth she bound herself as surety, which according to law could not be validly done. The cause was tried in the court below, without the introduction of any evidence in support of the defence contained in the exception above stated; and judgment was rendered. subjecting property which had been mortgaged to the defendants, and the mortgage by them transferred to the plaintiff, to be sold to satisfy his claim; from which Mrs. Skipwith appealed.

I find in the record four bills of exceptions taken to the opinions of the judge *a quo* pronounced on matters which occurred in the course of the trial of the cause. The first was on a motion made by the defendant's counsel to have the cause dismissed on the grounds stated in the third exception contained in the original answer of the appellant. In my opinion, the judge did not err in refusing to dismiss the petition on those grounds. He was correct in considering that exception as embracing a plea to the merits; it formed, according to the arguments above stated, *a contestatio litis*, on the decision of which principally depended the defendant's liability or exoneration from the debt claimed. The second bill was produced by the refusal of the judge to permit a peremptory exception to be filed, when the cause was called up for trial. Notwithstanding the counsel chose to denominate it as one arising from law, I am of opinion with the district judge, that it rather relates to form, and was offered too late. See Code of Practice, p. 122, art. 343, 344 and 345. The third has relation to an answer which the defendant offered to file. Part of it was received, and part rejected, as " changing the issue between the parties, and might operate a continuance, on the ground of surprise." The part rejected was an allegation that the appellant was separated in property from her husband by a marriage contract made in France, consequently not bound for his debts; and that the land and negroes, which the contract shows to have been sold to Josias Gray (as stated in the petition) by her and her husband jointly, and on which the mortgage was stipulated in their favor by the vendor, and afterwards in part transferred to the plaintiff, were her separate property, &c.

Taking, as I have done throughout, in this cause, the exceptions first filed on the part of Mrs. Skipwith, as embracing a plea to the merits, and holding the place of an answer, the pleading offered to be filed in the last instance before the district court must be viewed in the light of an amendment or amended answer. According to the Code of Practice amendments may be made to both petitions and answers, after issue joined, if permission be obtained from the court; the granting of such permission is restrained absolutely, only in cases where the amendments would change the substance of the demand, or that of the defence. Code of Practice, arts. 419, 420. The effects of amendments allowable, is regulated by art. 421.

When leave to amend is asked, the first inquiry to be made by the court from which it may be requested, is whether the amendment proposed will have the effect of substantially altering the claim, as set forth in the original petition, or the defence contained in the answer, according as the application may be made by either plaintiff or defendant; for if this effect would necessarily be produced, the law positively prohibits these amendments, leaving no discretion to the courts.

The amendment to the answer proposed in the present case, seems to have been rejected by the judge a quo, under a belief that it changed the issue between the parties, and might operate a continuance of the cause (which was then on trial) on the ground of surprise. It is not readily perceived in what manner this amendment could change the issue already made by some of the allegations of the petition, and the third exception filed by the defendant. The payment of the debt is claimed from her, as being bound in solido with her husband, and as having been contracted for her benefit. She denies the truth of these facts, by alleging that, although the contract was made in the form of an obligation in solido, and in the preamble contains an acknowledgment that the debt secured by it had been beneficial to her, yet in truth she only became surety to her husband for the payment of a debt entirely his own, and from which she derived no benefit. In consequence of his insolvent situation (as above stated) proceedings in the suit on the last trial were carried on against her alone; and it is her property only that could be made liable to seizure under the judgment, either as an interest in the com-

[Rawle, for the use of Russell, v. Skipwith and Wife.]

munity of goods (if any exist) between her and her husband, or such as she holds separately. Consequently, any additional allegation in the answer, that she is separated in property from her husband, could not materially change the issue between the parties; or in the language of the Code of Practice, alter the substance of her defence. It was therefore within the discretion of the court below, to have permitted or rejected the amendment proposed.

Whether this discretion was properly exercised by that tribunal, is believed to be a legal subject of inquiry by this court. As the additional plea offered was not, in my opinion, very material to the issue already joined, and could not in any degree affect the interest of the defendant in the present action, and as it was proposed when the cause was on trial, and might have produced unnecessary delay, I think that the district court did not err in refusing it.

The investigation of the last bill of exception, that which was taken to the opinion of the judge, in refusing a continuance of the cause, on the affidavits of the defendant and her counsel, necessarily leads to an examination of the merits.

The judgment rendered by the district court in relation to facts, is based entirely on the notarial act executed by the defendant and F. Skipwith with her husband, in favor of the plaintiff and her acknowledgments and renunciations therein contained. She renounced the benefit of the laws which would have released her from the obligation of a contract *in solido*, without proof that it turned to her advantage, and acknowledged that the debt, for which she then bound herself had been converted to her own benefit. If the contract contained nothing, in any manner repugnant to these declarations, the act would be conclusive as to all facts necessary to create a legal obligation on the part of the wife. She bound herself *in solido* with her husband and the debt was created for her own benefit. But in the answer or third exception of the pleadings, it is stated that she was merely surety for a debt of her husband, from which she never derived any advantage. That these allegations are true, notwithstanding the acknowledgment of the defendant to the existence of facts directly contrary, in the first part of the notarial act, a strong presumption is raised, by a statement made in the last clause of the instrument, which shows that the obligation was entered into to secure the payment of six notes which had been executed by F. Skipwith alone to the plaintiff in 1818, amounting altogether to the sum now claimed from the defendant. A wife who has made up her mind to become surety for her husband, will readily accede to all the forms of law required to give validity to her obligation, although there may not be a single word of truth in any of her acknowledgments. The law is settled and clear, that at the time this contract was made, a wife could in no case bind herself as security for her husband. See 4 *N. S.* 230, where all the cases previously decided in relation to the present subject are collated.

The evidence of the cause, as exhibited on the record, does perhaps preponderate in favor of the plaintiff's claim: but as doubts may fairly be entertained of its legality under the existing circumstances of the case, I am of opinion that it might have been in aid of justice to have continued the cause on the showing of the defendant in the court below. It cannot be considered as having arisen from very gross neglect, that the defendant was not prepared with all her testimony on the last trial; when we take into view the manner in which the suit has been bandied about from one court to the other, on the petition and what the counsel for the appellant considered as exceptions, which in his opinion ought to have been disposed of, before an answer to the merits could regularly be required. If in this he was in error, the effects of it should not be too rigorously visited on his client. I have been always opposed to a course in judicial proceedings which may have a tendency to affect the legal rights of suitors, by too strict an adherence to forms of practice.

It must ever be painful to a judge to witness a probability of injustice to a client, by the mistakes of his counsel; and when a remedy can be applied by a little delay, without doing great violence to general rules of procedure in suits it ought to be granted. In the present case it may be presumed that the defence was conducted principally by suggestions from the husband, and that it did not seriously occupy the attention of his wife, until since his failure. This circumstance, in addition to the inaptitude of women to manage affairs, relative to property, and particularly such as concern law suits, ought to excuse the appellant for neglect in communicating to her counsel her means of defence, at a more early period.

PORTER, J.—I fully concur in the opinion which the presiding judge of the court has prepared in this case, except that part of it which considers the decision of the inferior court erroneous, in not continuing the cause.

I do not think there was any legal ground presented for delaying the trial, and I do not believe the justice of the case requires our interference.

The cause was commenced on the 22d of May, 1827, and the trial was had in June, 1829. It appears to have been delayed during this time, by the various proceedings had on the matters set up in defence by the pleadings of the defendants.

When filed, they were stated to be exceptions to the plaintiff's petition, and on examination, they were found to contain not only exceptions, but an answer on the merits. The district court sustained the exceptions, and the plaintiff was compelled to appeal. In this tribunal, the decision was reversed, and the cause remanded. On its return to the district court, no further answer was put in. The plaintiff, misled, I presume, by the defendant's having stated his defence to consist of exceptions, took a judgment by default, and the court made it final. From this judgment, the defendant, in turn, appealed, and it was reversed—this court expressly declaring, that the original answer contained not only exceptions, but a defence on the merits.

After the defendant was thus relieved from the effects of a final judgment, and relieved, too, on the express ground that she had pleaded to the merits; as soon as the cause was called for trial in the court below, she moved for a continuance, on the ground, that she had never conceived her cause at issue; and her counsel made an affidavit that he had also been of that opinion.

In addition to this affidavit, we have that of the defendant, who swears, that she had been informed by her husband, and verily believes it to be true, that he had been sued for the debt due Russell, in 1809, in Philadelphia, and that a copy of the record of said suit would show, that the said debt was originally due by her husband; that, deponent not being aware of the importance of such information never communicated the same to her counsel, until it was too late to procure the said record for the present term of the court.

If, on such facts, a party can claim a continuance, and the cause is to be remanded from this tribunal, to be tried again, because it was refused, I do not see well in what kind of a case it can hereafter be denied, where ignorance or surprise is laid as the ground. The well established rule is, that new trials should never be granted, for the discovery or want of evidence, which the party might, by due diligence, have procured; or for surprise, which was not caused by some art of the adversary, but from the application of the known rules of proceeding, to the cause. This rule, like all the others on this subject, is, for obvious reasons, one of great utility, and should never be deviated from, unless in cases whch plainly show, that the want of diligence, or surprise, was attributable to causes which satisfactorily take the case out of the reasons on which the rule is founded. In this instance, nothing of that kind has been shown. The defendant's want of diligence is excused by no one circumstance, but an allegation that she did not know the information was of any importance, and, therefore, did not communicate it to her counsel. Two years before, she apprised those intrusted with her defence, that she was only surety for her husband, and pleaded expressly in her answer, that she was not responsible for his debts.

The surprise alleged on the ground, that the defendant was not aware there was a plea to the merits, although she had pleaded the engagement never had any legal force against her, being signed as surety, does not require a particular examination. It is most clear, it was a defence on the merits, and it is equally clear, the defendant can claim no advantage from such a mistake.

The law presumes a certain degree of legal knowledge in all parties litigant in courts; or supposes the means of obtaining it through a certain class of persons, whose lives are devoted to the acquisition of that knowledge, and whose profession and duty it is, to afford their aid to all who may honestly demand it. Without this presumption, and the rules predicated on its existence, no cause could be terminated. Parties would come before us again and again, with pleas of ignorance, inattention, misapprehension and mistakes. In some instances, they would be well founded. In others, they would be used by the crafty and unprincipled, as an engine of delay, and as a means of trying a cause a second or third time, or oftener, if the decision was unfavorable.

If the rule, to an observance of which I attach so much importance, should be ever deviated from, it ought only to be in cases where there is a strong probability injustice has been done. Not merely injustice, by depriving a party of a strictly legal defence, but one in which equity too enters for its share. That this view is correct, I think is manifest, from the reflection, that no defence which was purely legal, could give a stronger right to the defendant to have the judgment set aside, than her inattention to, or violation of, the rules of proceeding conferred on the plaintiff to have that judgment maintained. In the instance before us, that equity has not been shown to my satisfaction. It was strongly pressed in argument, that the obligation by which the wife acknowledged the debt had turned to her benefit, proved the contrary, because it showed that debt to have been originally contracted by the husband. But the debt may have been so contracted, and yet the wife have derived great benefit from it. The contract of marriage comes up with the record, and is placed before us. By it, we see that neither party had any property at the time of its celebration, except their wearing apparel. It is not shown the wife carried on a separate commerce, nor that she has received property by succession, or otherwise. The husband is now insolvent. The wife owns either a plantation and slaves, sold to Gray for 45,000 dollars, or the debt due for them. How this property was acquired, the evidence affords no information, except the declaration in the contract with the plaintiff, by which the wife acknowledges the debt due to him had turned to her benefit. If this declaration be true, the presumption is, that the money, or the value received from Russell, was applied to the acquisition of property for her. It is possible this view may be erroneous; but when a party seeks to set aside a judgment which has been regularly obtained on a clear legal right, she ought to show more than that she would have had a legal defence. Equity, on a consideration of the whole case, should also appear to be in her favor.

I conclude that, as the law is clearly with the plaintiff, and the equity, to say the least of it, doubtful, the judgment of the inferior court should be confirmed, except in relation to the interest. The obligation which the wife contracted for her husband, was novated by the acceptance of an assignment of a debt due by Gray, and the judgment of the inferior court enforces this assignment on the property mortgaged by Gray, which has since come into the hands of the husband of the appellant. It also gives interest on the sum due to Russell at the time of the acceptance of Gray's debt, in lieu of the notes then held by the former. I can discover nothing in the transfer of the debt which authorises this. It is for the sum of 11,500 dollars, to be paid at certain periods, and is silent in respect to any interest.

I, therefore, think the judgment of the district court should be reversed, so far as it gives interest, and that it be confirmed for the principal.

MARTIN, J.—I concur with the opinion of the presiding judge in every part of it, except that which relates to the remanding of the cause, on the ground, that the district court erred in denying a continuance to the defendants. In this part of the case, I concur with the junior judge of this court, for the reasons he has given.

It is, therefore, ordered, adjudged and decreed that the judgment of the district court be annulled, avoided and reversed; and it is further ordered, adjudged and decreed, that the assignment by the defendant, L. V. Skipwith, to plaintiff, of a portion of the mortgage of Josias Gray to herself and husband, on the 8th day of September, 1821, be considered good and valid to the amount of eleven thousand five hundred dollars; and it is further ordered and decreed, that the plaintiff be at liberty to exercise against the lands and slaves mentioned in said act of mortgage from Josias Gray, to defendant, all rights of actions which she, the said Louisa V. Skipwith, could or might of right exercise, had the assignment mentioned in this decree of that part of said mortgage never have been made; the defendant paying costs in the court of the first instance; the plaintiff that of appeals.

Morgan, for the plaintiff.
Watts, for the defendant.

Buhol, Wife of Bouguignon, *v.* Boudousquie & Destrehan, VIII, N. S. 425.

When the statute directs a jury to be drawn within thirty days after the passage of the act, and it is done afterwards, the jury is not legally empannelled.

The legislature has the power to declare that laws shall have effect from and after their passage.

FIRST District.

[Buhol, Wife of Bouguignon, *v.* Boudousquie & Destreban.]

PORTER, J., delivered the opinion of the court.

This case has been frequently before the court. The proceedings which have given rise to this appeal, have grown out of our judgment, declaring the plaintiff to be the proprietor of the premises in dispute, and remanding the cause for inquiry into the damage she had sustained by the illegal possession of the defendant. See 6 *N. S.* 653 and 697; 7 *Ibid.* 156.

That inquiry has resulted in a verdict of a jury who assessed her damages at 1320 dollars. From the judgment confirming this verdict, the party cited in warranty has appealed, after having made an unsuccessful attempt to obtain a new trial in the court of the first instance.

He alleges two errors were committed by the judge *a quo.*

First, in refusing to sustain his challenge to the array of the jury.

Secondly, in charging the jury incorrectly after the evidence was gone through.

The challenge to the array was founded on an alleged non-compliance by the sheriff with the provisions of an act of the legislature passed the 7th of February 1829, which among other things set forth in the title, is declared to have for its object, "to reform the mode of designating and summoning jurors of the several courts within the first district."

The third section of the act directs, "that within thirty days of the passing of the act, and annually thereafter, on or before the first Monday of December of each succeeding year, it shall be the duty of the sheriff of the parish and city of New Orleans, to make, or cause to be made, in writing, and keep a register," &c., &c.

The fourth section provides for the judges selecting from this list within thirty days after the passage of the act, and annually thereafter, on the Saturday next after the first Monday of December of each succeeding year, the names of persons to serve as jurors," &c., &c.

And the 13th section declares, that all previous enactments, inconsistent with that act, are repealed.

This act, as already stated, was not published or promulgated, until the 6th of March, 1829; and the list of names directed by the sections already quoted, was not made until the 13th and 14th of the same month. The defendant contends that this failure, to comply with the directions of the statute, vitiates the panel.

It has been urged on the court, that the words thirty days from the passage of the act, which in French are rendered, *trente jours apres l'adoption de cet acte,* mean thirty days after its promulgation. But whether we take the technical sense, uniformly, and we believe we might say universally given to these terms, when used in relation to law, or consult the sense of the words as given by philologists, we are led to the directly opposite result. *Pass,* as stated by Johnson, when applied to law, is synonymous with enact. The legal meaning of the word in that country from which our language comes, has not been disputed. Our legislature, in numerous instances, have used it in contra-distinction to promulgation, of which an example may be given from the very title to the act we are now construing; one of its objects is declared to be the repeal of a law, passed the 1st of April, 1826, which law, on reference to it, appears to have received the governor's signature on that day. And the common understanding attached to the words *pass an act*, is, we believe, entirely opposed to that contended for by the appellee. There is still, however, a higher authority on this subject, and that is the constitution of the state. The 20th section of the third article, clearly contemplates the passing of a law, to be distinct from its promulgation; for it provides, "that every bill which shall have passed both houses, shall be presented to the governor;" if not approved by him, it is to be sent back: and when reconsidered, if two-thirds of all the members elected to the house in which it originated, "shall agree to pass the bill," it shall be sent to the other house; and if sanctioned by an equal number there, it shall be a law. A perusal of this article, we think, can leave no doubt on the mind, that by the constitution, a bill is passed into a law, the moment it receives the sanction of those branches of the government, to whom the power of legislation is granted. We conclude, therefore, not only that a law may be passed before it is promulgated, but that it necessarily must be; and that to adopt the opposite construction, would be to deprive the legislature and mankind (if our opinions could have that effect) of the use of the most clear and apposite terms in the language, to express the idea of enactment, in opposition to publication, or promulgation.

The expressions, therefore, in the statute, *thirty days from the passage of the act* we think, clearly means, thirty days after its receiving the sanction of the governor. The next question is, whether it is our duty to carry it into effect.

The inconvenience of the construction contended for by the appellant, and the absurd consequences that would result from an obedience to the literal terms of the law, have been forcibly presented to us in argument, and the objection is certainly entitled to much consideration. When the terms of part of a law, taken in their literal sense, lead to absurd and inconvenient results, or violate any great principle of natural or social rights, courts of justice, in all countries, have been in the habit of seeking for the intention of the legislature in the scope and object of the whole enactment; and if from a view of the whole law, or from other laws in *pari materia*, the evident intention is different from the literal import of the terms employed in a particular part of the law, that intention is held to control, because it is really the will of the legislature. But a slight consideration will satisfy all, that this power is to be exercised with great caution. The very ground on which courts assume the right, proves indeed the necessity of doing so. Bound, as judges are, to carry into effect the will of the legislature on all subjects, where its commands do not violate the provisions of the constitution, they never can refrain from, or refuse enforcing a law, unless where they are clearly and satisfactorily convinced, that the literal terms of the act convey a different idea from that which was contemplated; and that in adopting a different construction, they have sought for, and found the true intention and will of the law maker.

We have given to this case a great deal of attention: and we have repeatedly asked ourselves: Was it the intention of the legislature, the register should be made thirty days after the passage of the act, or thirty days after its promulgation?   We have been unable to give any other answer, but that it was contemplated by them to be made thirty days after the passage of the law. Such is the literal meaning of the language, expressed by terms which they are in the habit of repeatedly using, and always to express the same idea. Then there is nothing extraordinary in the enactment, nor any thing that could have led to unjust or inconsistent consequences, had it been promulgated in proper time by the officers charged with that duty. By a previous act of the legislature in force when this statute was passed, all laws were to be sent to the public printer in seven days from their passage, and by him was to be printed immediately. Had this been done, as we presume it was contemplated it would have been done, no inconvenience could have been produced. Knowledge of the regulation would have come to those who were to act under it, in full time to have enabled them to obey it. Moreau's Digest, 267.

We have been asked: Can it be believed the legislature contemplated there should be no jury for the first judicial district, for the space of one year? To this question our answer must be that of every one who looks to the object of the law: certainly not. And had the enactment necessarily produced such an effect, then it would have fallen within the rule already-noticed, by which the will of the legislature must be sought in something else than the literal import of a particular clause. But no such consequences followed, or ought to have followed the provision introduced in the statute. It is from a circumstance arising, after its passage, not from the meaning of the terms used, the inconvenience has proceeded. For us, then to say, that matters arising subsequent to the passage of the law, in relation to its promulgation, will authorise a deviation from the plain and unambiguous commands of the legislature, would be going farther, we believe, than any tribunal has yet gone, and certainly farther than we are prepared to go.

There is still another consideration which has entered into the judgment we are about to pronounce. The legislature have the power to declare, that laws shall have effect from and after their passage.—They have already done so, they may do so again. This mode of legislation is certainly not a convenient one to the citizen, and we presume will not be frequently resorted to. But times may come, and circumstances arise, when the public interest will imperatively require such a provision. When it does, and a law of this description is passed, every argument urged in this instance against giving effect

[Bubol, Wife of Bouguignon, v. Boudousquie & Destrehan.]

to the legislative will, will apply to any subsequent enactment which is declared to be in force from and after its passage. Clearer terms could not be used in any subsequent law, and there would be few with such a clause that would not produce as much inconvenience, and lead to as absurd consequences as that before us.

It occurred to us, as worthy of consideration, whether the time in which the sheriff was to make the register, was not merely directory and whether it was not good if done in any month in the year. But the legislature, by fixing a precise period, must have considered it material, and if the time of making it could be enlarged for months, it might be for years, and thus the whole of the legislation become a dead letter. In conformity with this principle, the case of Flower v. Livingston was decided. 12 *Martin*, 681.

On the whole, we conclude that, as the cause was not tried in the court of the first instance, by a jury legally summoned, the case must be remanded.

It is, therefore, ordered, adjudged and decreed, that the judgment of the district court be annulled, avoided and reversed; and that the cause be remanded for a new trial, the appellee paying the costs of this appeal.

Conrad, for the apellant.
Hennen, for the appellee.

Bauduc *v.* Domingon *et al.*　VIII, N. S. 434.

PARISH Court of New Orleans.
Held, a defendant may be cited, though the petition contain no prayer to that effect.
Held, a supplemental petition, asking more than the original, does not alter the substance of the demand.

By PORTER, J.—The substance of the original petition was not changed by the amendment. One of the tests for ascertaining this, is to inquire, whether the matters contained in the two petitions, might not have been cumulated in one, and of this there can be no doubt. The 151st article of the Code of Practice provides that, if the plaintiff has several causes of action, tending to the same conclusion, not contrary to, nor exclusive of, each other, he may cumulate and bring them in the same suit. Now, in the instance before us,

[Bauduc *v.* Dormingon *et al.*]

the plaintiff might well have brought these demands in the same petition: for the matter set forth in the supplemental, grows out of that in the original, is cumulated with it, and has for its object the giving of greater efficacy to the judgment originally asked for. There may be, it is true, cases joined in one action, which could not, perhaps, be presented in the shape of amendment, but we are satisfied this is not one of them. It is true, the supplemental petition asks for more than the original; if it did not make some change, there would be no necessity for it; but it does not alter the substance of the demand.— That, at first, was for judgment against the defendant for moneys due; now, it is for conservatory measures to give efficacy and effect to the judgment. This changes the mode of relief, but in no means alters the substance of the demand, which was, to have a judgment against the defendant that might restore to the plaintiff what was due to him, for the causes set out in the petition. The amendment only indicates to the court the measures necessary to accomplish this end.

Another objection was made in argument, namely: the want of allegation, in the supplemental petition, that the defendant was insolvent. But this ground was not pleaded below, and when a cause comes up here on exceptions, we cannot notice any others but those which were placed in writing before the court of the first instance, as the law directs.

Love *v.* Dickson.   VIII, N. S. 440.

EIGHTH District.

No proceedings can be had in the inferior court, while the case is pending before the appellate court; even after judgment above, till the expiration of three judicial days.

Franklin *v.* Warfield's Syndic.   VIII, N. S. 441.

Personal property cannot be mortgaged.

FIRST District.

Mathews, J., delivered the opinion of the court.

This action was commenced originally in the parish court; and after the failure and cession of goods by the defendant Warfield, was transferred to the district court, wherein proceedings had been instituted by the insolvent.

The object of the suit in the first instance, was to dissolve a partnership which existed between the plaintiff and defendant, in relation to their business as inn-keepers, and to obtain a settlement of their accounts, &c.

In the progress of the cause since it has been cumulated with the *concurso,* M'Call intervened, and claims one half of the furniture of the house which was occupied by the partners, as having been sold to him by Warfield, previous to his partnership. He obtained a decree in his favor, from which the plaintiff appealed.

The only question which the case at present presents, relates to the claim of the intervening party.

His rights depend on an interpretation of two notarial acts, in virtue of which he pretends title to the property in dispute.

The first of these bears date on the 14th of March, 1828, and the second on the 24th of June, of the same year. The last act purports to be explanatory of that which preceded it; but as it was made at a time when the insolvent could not legally and validly make any alteration in the state of his property to the prejudice of the mass of his creditors, it may be dismissed without comment. The act of the 14th of March, was passed by the parties, to secure M'Call against any loss which might occur to him in consequence of his endorsement on Warfield's note of 2500 dollars; and no doubt they intended to make it effectual for that purpose. But we believe that it was executed in such a manner and form as to frustrate their intentions. It is an hypothecation of personal property, which is not tolerated by law. The expression, *assign over,* found in the act conjoined to the terms " mortgage, affect, and especially hypothecate," does not alter its nature. It is not usual, in contracts of sale, to introduce an expression like this, unless in transfers of debts. Coupled as it is with the words " mortgage, affect, and especially hypothecate," such meaning should be given to it as will correspond with them. The

[Franklin v. Warfield's Syndic.]

property is assigned over by hypothecation. If the act had relation to immovable effects, no doubt would be entertained in relation to its character; it could be considered as nothing more than a mortgage. A pledge it can not be, for it is of the essence of such contracts, that the property should be delivered to the pledgee. Being neither a sale nor pledge, the intervening party has, in our opinion, acquired no right to the furniture intended to be affected by his contract with the insolvent.

It is, therefore, ordered, that so much of the judgment of the district court as decreed the half of the proceeds arising from the sale of the furniture and goods which were sequestered by the sheriff, to be paid to M'Call, the intervening party, be annulled, avoided and reversed; hereby affirming that part of the judgment which settles the sum due by Warfield to the plaintiff. And it is further ordered, &c., that the case be sent back to the court below, for the purpose of directing distribution of the insolvent's estate, according to law; the appellee to pay the costs of this appeal.

Nixon, for the appellant.

Hennen and *M'Caleb*, for the appellee.

Michoud, Syndic of the Creditors of Dalon, *v.* Lacroix. VIII, N. S. 445.

If A purchases slaves for B, who refuses to recognise A's agency, no title passes to B.

Parol proof of simulation in written contracts is not admissible in cases where the party whose interest it may be to prove it might have taken a counter-title.

FIRST District.

MATHEWS, J., delivered the opinion of the court.

In this case the syndic sues to recover from the defendant, certain slaves described in his petition, and their hire for the time during which they have been in possession of the latter.

It is alleged that the insolvent is the owner of said slaves, as having been paid for with his money and notes, and that he was in possession of them until they were taken from him by a writ of attachment obtained by the defendant, against property of one Louis Menard, wherein they were seized, &c.

The answer contains several exceptions to the action, a general denial, and sets up title in the present possessor. The court below gave judgment of nonsuit on a trial of the merits, from which the plaintiff appealed.

The evidence of the case shows, that the slaves now in dispute, together with a tract of land, were purchased from François Lambert, for Louis Menard, by an assumed agency on the part of François Menard, his brother; the whole property was paid for by promissory notes of divers persons, endorsed by François Menard, as agent for his brother Louis, amongst which, one for 925 dollars, made by Dalon, came by regular transfer into the possession of the present defendant. It was protested for non-payment, and suit was commenced by attachment against Louis Menard, and the slaves now in dispute, were seized as his property. In that suit Dalon intervened, claiming the slaves as belonging to him, and prayed a trial by jury, which the district court refused, and proceeded to give judgment in favor of the plaintiff, for the sum claimed. Dalon appealed; the judgment was reversed in the Supreme Court, and the cause sent back to be tried de novo. The appeal was not taken in such a manner as to stay execution, and the sheriff proceeded to sell the property attached on a fieri facias. At the sale the plaintiff in execution became the purchaser, and obtained a sheriff's deed. After the cause went from the supreme to the district court, it was discovered that Louis Menard, had refused to sanction the purchase made by his brother François, consequently acquired no title to the property bought, and the attachment suit was dismissed. Another appeal was taken, and the judgment of the district court was affirmed. Nothing definitive in relation to Dalon's claim, was determined in this suit, and he having become insolvent, the syndic of his estate renews it in the present action.

Whether the defendant, under all the circumstances of the case, is entitled to the protection accorded by law to innocent purchasers, we need not inquire: he has been so long in possession of the slaves, that he can only be disturbed by a person showing a better title than that under which he claims. The present is, in truth, a petitory action, and the plaintiff can recover only by showing title in the insolvent. The property was transferred by Lambert, to Louis Menard, who refused to accept it, by disavowing the purchase made by his brother and therefore never had any title to it. The claim of the title in favor of Dalon, as alleged in the petition, is founded on a possession which he had previous to the seizure under Lacroix's attachment, and the circumstance of the price having been paid out of his funds. The loan of money to pay the price of property bought, can not of itself give title to the lender in any case: and according to our law, all sales of immovable property or slaves, must be made by authentic act, or under private signature. Louisiana Code, art. 2415. Title to this species of property can not be passed by parol. It is therefore clear, that although the allegations of the

[Michoud, Syndic of the Creditors of Dalon, v. Lacroix.]

petition should be taken as true, the plaintiff has shown no legal title in the insolvent, to the property claimed: but it does not appear that the price was paid by Dalon, at least so far as it has relation to the sum of 925 dollars, for which Lacroix recovered a judgment as above stated. In the course of the trial of the cause in the court below, witnesses were offered on the part of the plaintiff, to prove that the act of sale to Menard, was simulated, and was really intended to convey the property in these slaves to Dalon. Testimonial proof of this nature was rejected by the judge, and a bill of exceptions taken, &c. We are of opinion that the court did not err in rejecting the testimony.

1. Because simulation or fraud is not alleged in the petition.

2. Because parol proof of simulation in written contracts, is not admissible in cases where the party, whose interest it may be to prove it, might have taken a counter-title.

Now, if at the time when the purchase was made by Menard from Lambert, it was intended to give title to Dalon, in the slaves which were bought, although by the act of sale they were conveyed to Menard, Dalon, who it is alleged paid the price, must be presumed to have known this fact, and could have requested a counter-title. 1 *N. S.* 451; 4 *Ibid.* 123.

It is, therefore, ordered, adjudged and decreed, that the judgment of the district court be affirmed, with costs.

Seghers, for the plaintiff.
Denis, for the defendant.

Flower *et al. v.* Swift. VIII, N. S. 449.

Witnesses cannot be examined after the day stated in the notice for their examination.

EIGHTH District, Judge of the Seventh presiding.

MARTIN, J., delivered the opinion of the court.

The defendant, who is executor of M'Elroy, took from a debtor of his testator, a note payable to the estate, or order, and endorsed it to the plaintiff, adding to his name on the endorsement, the words *executor of M'Elroy.* The note was duly protested, due notice was

49*

given him; he resisted the claim, but judgment was given against him, as endorser of the note, and he appealed.

His counsel has drawn our attention to two bills of exceptions. The first is, to the opinion of the court below, who sustained the plaintiff's opposition to the reading of testimony, taken after the day from which the commission was made returnable.

The party against whom testimony is intended to be used, is informed by the notice of the day on which the commission is made returnable, that it is not to be taken after that day. He may therefore rightly conclude, that his adversary declines examining witnesses, not brought before the commissioners at such a period. He has a right to be present at the examination and when, through the negligence of his adversary, he is deprived of that right, he may oppose the reading of the testimony so tardily taken.

The other bill was taken to the rejection of the testimony, taken down in writing in the court of probates, in a suit erroneously brought there between the same parties, as the court was without jurisdiction.

We think the testimony was properly rejected. Proceedings before a court, or judges, who have no jurisdiction of the matter, *ratione materiæ*, are absolutely *coram non judice*. An oath taken in such a case, is in law a nullity; it cannot prejudice any one. We have been referred to Moreau's Digest, Crimes, art. 365, 16 and 17, but cannot adopt the construction for which the appellant's counsel contends, and in which he invokes the authority of Kerr's exposition, and under which he argues, that a court or magistrate, having authority to administer oaths, in certain cases, perjury may be committed in an oath taken before it or him, in a case in which he is without authority or jurisdiction.

On the merits, the appellant's counsel has urged, that the paper sued on, is not a promissory note, but the mere acknowledgment of a debt due the estate; that the transfer of it entitles the appellee to recover what is due to the estate by the maker of the note: the appellant having endorsed the note in his capacity of executor, is not personally liable.

We are of opinion the district judge did not err, in considering the endorsement as a new contract, the drawing of a bill of exchange. Such a contract is not in the scope of an executor's authority; *i e.*, he cannot thereby bind the estate to pay damages or even to refund the amount of the note; for if he could, he could ruin the estate, by making it liable to pay the amount of notes of its insolvent debtors. As the executor cannot bind the estate by endorsement, it follows, that the liability resulting from those he makes, is personal.

It is, therefore, ordered, adjudged and decreed, that the judgment of the district court be affirmed, with costs.

Hennen, for the plaintiffs.
Workman, for the defendant.

Sanchez *v.* French Evangelical Church Society. VIII, N. S. 452.

FIRST District.
Decided, if what ought to be pleaded in bar, be pleaded as an exception, it is not error to refuse to dismiss the suit on it.
Also, if the allegation of the purchase of a litigious right be not made in the court below, as considered by court or jury, it cannot be inquired of in the court above.

· Caldwell *v.* Benedict. VIII, N. S. 454.

FIRST District.
This was a question of fact.
Held, that fraud is not to be inferred from slight presumptions.

Cormier *v*. Leblanc.   VIII, N. S. 457.

The corroborating circumstance which the Code requires, in addition to the testimony
of one witness, cannot be drawn from his testimony.

FIRST District.

Martin, J., delivered the opinion of the court.

The defendant and appellant claims the reversal of the judgment, which is for 600 dollars, claimed from him as a surety for a third person, or on a promise of his, the defendant, to pay the note of that third person. His counsel shows, that there is not on the record any evidence of the contract on which the plaintiff sues, except that which results from the testimony of one witness, unattended with any corroborating circumstance. He has relied on the Civil Code, 2257.

The appellee's counsel has built all his hopes of success, on an allegation, that the claim of the plaintiff rests on a promissory note, which is evidence of a commercial contract and the presence of a very corroborating circumstance.

Bijotat, a debtor of the plaintiff, being about to depart from the state, the latter conceived himself entitled to demand from him security for the payment of a note not yet payable, and as stated in the petition, the defendant promised to pay the note. Now, the suretyship which may be required in such a case, is not necessarily a commercial transaction; and we think the first ground of defence fails.

The second ground is, that a corroborating circumstance is presented by the testimony, *i. e.*, that the defendant made a partial payment on the note, by inserting on the back of it a receipt therefor.

The Code requires for proof of a contract for the payment of a greater sum than 500 dollars, the testimony of one credible witness, and other corroborating circumstances.* Now the circumstance relied on, is found in the testimony of the single witness. This we think does not suffice; the corrobarating circumstances the Code requires, are not those stated by the single witness in his testimony; but these that appear *aliunde*.

It is true, the partial payment is stated by the defendant in his answer, but he states it to have been made by him as the agent of the maker of the note out of moneys of the latter in his hands, and not in discharge of any obligation of his, the defendant.

* Under the actual adjudications and practice the proof by one witness with the *corroborating circumstance* of a provisional judgment by default, remaining not set aside, is sufficient to make the judgment by default final.

[Cormier *v.* Leblanc *et al.*]

We think the district court erred.

It is, therefore, ordered, adjudged and decreed, that the judgment be annulled, avoided and reversed; and that there be judgment as in case of nonsuit, with costs in both courts.

Seghers, for the plaintiff.

Moreau and *Soule,* for the defendant.

Beard *v.* Pijeaux.   VIII, N. S. 459.

Judgment obtained by the wife against the husband, is evidence of the debt in an hypothecary action.

But where the answer charges the judgment to have been obtained through fraud and collusion, the wife must give evidence to prove it was *bona fide.*

PARISH Court of New Orleans.

PORTER, J., delivered the opinion of the court.

The plaintiff seeks, by this action, to enforce an hypothecary right arising out of claims against her husband, in a slave once owned, and sold by his heirs to the defendant.

The general issue is pleaded, and title set up to the slave, on the ground that the defendant paid the vendor of the husband, the price which the latter had contracted to give for the property when he acquired it. There is a further allegation, that the judgment which the plaintiff had obtained against her husband, was obtained by fraud and collusion.

There was judgment for the plaintiff, and the defendant appealed.

The defendant excepted to the opinion of the judge, permitting the plaintiff to offer as evidence of the debt due by the husband, the judgment which the wife had obtained against him, in a suit wherein a separation of property had been decreed, and the amount of her estate received by him, liquidated. In this opinion, however, we can perceive no error. The law makes the judgment against the debtor, evidence on which the hypothecary action may be instituted, and makes no distinction between that rendered where the wife is creditor, and any other person.

The plaintiff then introduced her brother, who deposed that he had seen Morel pay to the husband, the wife's part, in a sum of money by him received from the sheriff, on account of the plaintiff's ances-

tor. That Morel wrote a receipt, which the plaintiff's husband
signed. To this testimony the defendant excepted, and we think the
court erred in admitting it. The receipt of the husband was higher
evidence, and it should have been produced, or the want of it accounted for, before inferior testimony was admitted.

The first question for our consideration on the merits, is the effect
which ought to be given to the judgment rendered between the wife
and husband. The answer avers it was obtained through fraud and
collusion.

No evidence of the fraud and collusion was given by the defendant. She insists, however, on not being compelled to furnish it, and
contends that the moment the validity of the judgment is put at issue,
by a plea, such as that presented in this case, the plaintiff is bound
to offer proof of the truth of the facts on which it purports to be
based. The general rule of evidence, founded on the familiar maxim
ei incumbit probatio qui dicit, non qui negat, is opposed to this
position. And at first blush, no good reason is perceived, why the
allegation of fraud should form an exception, more especially where
applied to the judgment of a court. But when the subject is looked
at a little more closely, it will be seen that the charge of collusion
involves a negative, and must be governed by the rules relating to
allegations of this description. The plea is in these words. " This
defendant expressly denies that the said Lecesne ever received any
money belonging to his wife, and she maintains that the judgment
rendered in favor of the latter, was obtained by fraud and collusion."
The whole of this sentence taken together, clearly presents the idea
of the fraud and collusion, consisting in confessing judgment, or in
permitting it to be rendered for a sum due to the wife, which in fact
never had been received by the husband. Such a plea contains a
negative, and the burthen of proof must be on the party who denies
the judgment was collusively rendered, because the assertion of his
adversary is not susceptible of proof. Take the case either of no
money received, or a less sum than the parties confessed had been
paid. Place the burthen of proof on the person denying it, and we
would have as a consequence, that though the fraud might exist, it
never could be established, for it would be impossible for the party
against whom the judgment was offered, to prove the money had not
been paid.

This doctrine receives additional force in this case, from the jea-
lousy with which our law views all acknowledgments from the husband to the wife, admitting the receipt of money. It is expressly
declared, that they do not make evidence against persons not parties
to them, unless supported by other circumstances. The judgment
rendered between them, should not have more force than the confession of the husband in a public act, because that confession would
authorise the court to render judgment against him at the suit of the
wife.

There being no other evidence of money received by the husband

[Beard v. Pijeaux.]

of the plaintiff, than that offered by the judgment obtained against him, we think the judge erred in sustaining the action.

It is, therefore, ordered, adjudged and decreed, that the judgment of the parish court be annulled, avoided and reversed, and that there be judgment against the plaintiff as in case of nonsuit, with costs in both courts.

Seghers, for the plaintiff.
De Armas, for the defendant.

Reynolds *et al. v.* Kirkman *et al.* VIII, N. S. 464.

PARISH Court of New Orleans.

Held, a factor, who employs an agent to sell goods without the authority of his principal, is responsible for the agent.

Cuebas *v.* Venas. VIII, N. S. 465.

PARISH Court of New Orleans.

A judgment derives its force and effect from what is decreed by the court, not from what is admitted by the parties. A judgment, confessed by an attorney, in presence of his client, has no preference over one confessed out of the client's presence.

A judgment cannot be given with preference, without a prayer for a writ of seizure and judgment by privilege.

Sainet *v.* Sainet.   VIII, N. S. 468.

COURT of Probates of New Orleans.
Decided, that if an attorney claims 500 dollars, as attorney of absent heirs, and 75 dollars for services to the deceased, on evidence, that the former services are well paid for by 250 dollars, the court cannot allow 500 dollars, for the total of his two claims, that is, 250 dollars as attorney of absent heirs, and 250 dollars for services to the testator, whereas he had only demanded 75 dollars for the latter.

Adams *v.* Duprey.   VIII, N. S. 470.

FOURTH District.
Under the act of 1817, a sheriff who sold property, subject to a mortgage, could not collect from the purchaser, the amount of the mortgage.   But see Code of Practice.

Hepp *v.* Parker.   VIII, N. S. 473.

Parol evidence may be given, that [one of the parties to an act, perused it several days before he affixed his signature.
Knowledge in a purchaser, that a slave is diseased, will not defeat his action of redhibition: it must be shown, he knew the disease was incurable, or that, without knowing that, he bought the chance of the slave's recovery.
Parol evidence cannot be given to contradict the date of an authentic act.

PARISH Court of New Orleans.

PORTER, J., delivered the opinion of the court.

This is a redhibitory action, in which there was judgment in the court of the first instance, in favor of the plaintiff. The defendant appealed.

The cause was submitted to a jury, and, on the trial, the appellant took two bills of exceptions. One of them was to the opinion of the court, preventing a witness answering the following question: "How many days before the plaintiff signed the bill of sale, was it, that he came and perused the bill of sale, as written in the records of G. R. Stringer, Esq., notary public?" We think the judge erred. The answer to the question could not, in any respect, contradict the act, not even its date; for, *non constat* whether the date was affixed when the instrument was drawn out, or at the time it became a public act by the signatures of the parties.

The object declared in the bill of exceptions, of putting this question, was to show that the plaintiff had the slave in possession, and was acquainted with him, before he signed the sale. The appellee urges, that if this were the object, it could not have in any respect weakened his case, or strengthened his adversary's, supposing the witness to have answered as the party calling expected. Because, whether the plaintiff knew of the fact or not, at the time of the purchase, he is still protected under the warranty.

To this objection it has been answered, that the disease of which the slave died, was not one of those which the law classes as an absolute vice of body; that consequently the action can only be maintained under the 2496th article of the Code, which confers it on the buyer, when the thing bought is either absolutely useless, or its use so inconvenient and imperfect, that it must be supposed the buyer would not have purchased it, had he known of the vice: and that, if the answer to the interrogatory would have induced the belief of the purchaser having a knowledge of the disease at the time he bought, then it was material it should be answered, because the presumption of ignorance, on which the law gives an action, would be destroyed.

This argument has also been supported, by reference to the 2497th article of the Code, which declares, that apparent objects, such as the buyer might have discerned by simple inspection, are not among the number of redhibitory vices.

Knowledge, that a slave was diseased at the time of the sale, and a knowledge that he was afflicted with an incurable disease, are two distinct things, and their effects on the right of the parties, quite dissimilar. It is almost incredible, that any person, in his senses, would buy property of this kind, and give a full price for it, unless he conceived he was protected by the warranty, and even then it is difficult to conceive any object in such a contract. If indeed, as was said in the case of St. Rome v. Poré it appeared clearly, that the purchaser knew the nature and extent of the disease, and consented to purchase under all risks, the action of redhibition could not, perhaps, be maintained. But when the evidence is in the least degree equivocal, the presumption would be, that where a full price was given, the purchaser conceived the disease was other than incurable; one that would yield to medicine. It is established in the present instance, that the slave died of an abscess in his lungs. When the physician was first called in, which was seven or eight days after the date of the bill of sale, the negro was found to be afflicted with a cough, and difficulty of breathing. This cough existed at the time the contract was made, for it is in evidence, that the defendant, when questioned in relation to it by the plaintiff, said, it was the remains of dysentery. Now, supposing the witness had established the fact of the plaintiff's having the slave in his possession some time before he signed the note, we do not see how it could have aided his defence. The presumption flowing from it, would only have confirmed a fact proved by other testimony, and in relation to which, there does not appear to have been any dispute, namely, that the plaintiff knew at the time he purchased the slave, he was afflicted with a cough. We are clear this knowledge did not defeat his recourse in warranty, for there must not only be knowledge of a disease, but knowledge of one that is incurable and of such a nature as to render the slave useless, or his use so inconvenient and imperfect, that the buyer bought the hope or chance he might recover. 10 *Martin*, 820.

Although, therefore, the judge might very properly have admitted the evidence, we do not see any possible influence it could have had in the cause which would authorise us to remand it for a new trial.

On the other bill of exceptions, we think the judge did not err. The evidence offered was to contradict the date of an authentic act. The date made a part of the instrument. And by the positive provisions of our law in relation to public acts, they make full proof against the parties signing them, their heirs and assigns, unless declared and proved a forgery. Louisiana Code, 2233.

It is, therefore, ordered, adjudged and decreed, that the judgment of the parish court be affirmed, with costs.

Carleton and *Lockett*, for the plaintiff.

Preston, for the defendant.

Landreaux *et al. v.* Campbell.   VIII, N. S. 478.

. FIRST District.

Held, that when the redhibitory malady did not manifest itself within three days after the sale, evidence must be given of its previous existence.

This was a case of counter-balancing evidence, in which the court below decided for the plaintiff, but this court *è contra.*

Garretson *et al. v.* Zacharie.   VIII, N. S. 481.

The surety, on an attachment bond, is not liable, when the principal had a cause of action, but fails to recover, on account of some irregularity in the proceedings, posterior to the bond.

PARISH Court of New Orleans.

PORTER, J.—The defendant is sued on a bond, in which he was surety of Cochrane, in a suit of the latter against one Smith, who, with the present plaintiffs, were joint owners of the steamboat Leopard. The bond was given, on obtaining an order of seizure. Pending the proceedings, the boat was sold, and there being ultimately judgment for the present plaintiffs in that suit, they brought this action, in which, after setting out these facts, they aver they have suffered damage to the amount of 3854 dollars.

The defendant pleads the general issue.

The parish judge gave judgment in favor of the plaintiffs for 600 dollars, being the one half of the price for which the boat was sold. The defendant appealed, and the appellees have complained of the judgment, as not allowing a sufficient sum in damages.

Various grounds of defence have been set up in this court. Those which require a particular notice, are as follow:

First, that the seizure was not wrongfully made, because the co-defendant in the suit of attachment, sued the plaintiff in that case, and judgment was obtained against him.

This circumstance, in my opinion, did not authorise the seizure of the plaintiffs' share in the boat, nor the suit against them; and for that seizure and failure to legalise it by a judgment, the principal and surety on the bond are responsible.

Secondly, that the boat was sold *pendente lite*, on the demand of one of the defendants.

It cannot affect the rights of the plaintiffs, who, though sued, were never legally before the court below, at whose instance the boat was sold. It is enough, that she was disposed of, in an action to which they were not a party. The sale was a consequence of the seizure, illegally made, as it respects the plaintiffs.

The third objection is, that at the time the seizure was made, the plaintiffs really owed the plaintiff, in sequestration. This objection will be noticed, after the others are disposed of.

The fourth ground is, that there is no evidence of damage. The record shows the plaintiffs' interest in one half of the boat has been sold. They, of course, have lost the value of that half, and the evidence proves it to be 600 dollars.

The fifth objection is, that the bond was not required by law, and that the defendant is only responsible for the one half. But this ground is quite untenable, for the law required a bond before the boat could be seized or sequestered, and a judicial surety cannot plead discussion.

Lastly, it has been urged, that divers creditors of the boat intervened in the suit., proved their claims against the boat, and had their claims allowed, and paid out of the proceeds of the sale. That, consequently, the plaintiffs have sustained damages, unless the amount of their debts are satisfied. But we have no evidence before us, of the existence, or amount of these debts, except that which the record in the suit of sequestration presents, and as the present plaintiffs were not parties to it, not being legally cited, none of the testimony, there taken, can make evidence against them.

The condition of the bond was in the following words: " Whereas the above bounden Richard Cochrane, has this day sued out a writ of seizure, from the honorable the parish court of New Orleans, against the steamboat Leopard, the property of the said Garreston, Bowan, Warster and L. Smith: Now, therefore, the condition of this obligation is such, that if the said Richard Cochrane shall prosecute his said writ of seizure with success, and shall pay all such damage as the said Garretson, Bowan, Warster and Smith shall suffer, in case it shall appear, that the said writ of seizure was wrongfully sued, then the above obligation to be void, else to remain in full force and virtue."

It is very clear, that if the obligor, either prosecuted the writ with effect, or paid the damages that ensued from his wrongfully suing it out, the bond was discharged. The counsel for the appellee has

[Garretson *et al. v.* Zacharie.]

argued the case, as if the failure to prosecute with success, was conclusive evidence the sequestration was wrongfully sued out. This, I think, is not correct. There may be cases, where a sequestration or attachment was most rightfully sued out, and yet, from circumstances attending the progress of the suit, after it was commenced, judgment of nonsuit would be given against the plaintiff. In such a case, when sued on the bond, he ought not to be concluded by the judgment, and it would be open to him to show all the grounds, on which he resorted to this mode of enforcing his rights. But, granting to the appellant, in the present case, the full benefit of this doctrine, he has offered no proof, that the writ of sequestration was rightfully levied on the property of the plaintiffs. The judgment, rendered against him in the first suit, is *prima facie* evidence it was wrongfully sued out. The presumption, created by that judgment, has been destroyed by any legal evidence. There is no legal proof, the plaintiffs owed him one cent, at the time the writ was sued out. The testimony, taken in a case where they were not cited, can not be used against them. The circumstance of the action being brought by the captain of a steamboat, in the employment of the plaintiffs, affords no presumption of the existence of a debt, when the owners lived in another country, and the officer was running her in this state, on their account. He had the means of paying himself, from the proceeds of her freight.

The impression on my mind is, that the suit of the captain, in the first instance, was a harsh one, and that he and his sureties ought to bear all the consequences of his not succeeding in it. He was captain of the boat, entrusted by the owners, living in another country, with the care and management of her, bound by his contract, to run her to the best advantage for their interests, and return her to them at the place where he received, unless otherwise directed. Instead of doing this, he profits by the confidence which placed the property in his hands, to seize the vessel, for a debt due to himself, and sell her. At the first sale, she brought upwards of 3000 dollars. The purchaser not being able to comply with the contract, she was put up at auction a second time, at three days' notice, and then the party sequestrating buys her in for 1200 dollars. Our attachment law has conferred a great privilege on strangers, by permitting them to attach the property of their debtors, living abroad, when found in this state, and it is exacting no harsh measure from them, to require these laws to be strictly fulfilled. If any case can be less favorable than another, it is that of a captain of a ship or boat, attaching, in a foreign port, the property which he was to take care of, while in his possession, and return to the owners. If any thing was due, it does not appear, that he ever made a demand of it, before seizing the vessel. I think the strict law of the case, and its equity too, in favor of the plaintiffs, and that the judgment of the court below should be affirmed, with costs.

MARTIN, J.—The defendant, sued as surety on a bond, for obtaining a writ of seizure of a steamboat, pleaded the general issue; there was judgment against him, and he appealed.

The bond was given, in the case of Cochrane *v.* Smith *et al.,* 2 *N. S.* 552.

Cochrane was master of a boat, one-half of which was the property of Smith, and the other of the present plaintiffs; he obtained a writ of seizure (on the bond now sued on) against all the owners. Smith was served with a citation, but the others, being absent, were not. The boat was seized, and Cochrane procured an attorney to be appointed for the latter. Afterwards, on the motion of Smith, and without any opposition from the attorney appointed to the other defendants, or Cochrane, the sale of the boat was ordered, and she was accordingly sold. The attorney had obtained sixty days, to correspond with the absent defendants, but afterwards, and before the expiration of that delay, he pleaded the general issue. Smith made default, and judgment was finally given against all the defendants. The attorney obtained an appeal, and on showing, that the absent defendants, whom he had been appointed to represent, had never been cited, and urging that they were not bound by his plea, as they were not afforded the opportunity of appointing an attorney, procured the reversal of the judgment, and brought suit on the bond against the present defendant, the surety of Cochrane.

The condition of this instrument is, that if the writ of seizure be prosecuted with success, and the plaintiff pay all such damages as the defendants may sustain, in case it shall appear the writ of seizure was wrongfully sued out, &c.

I am of opinion, that although the copulative *and* is used in the bond, the disjunctive *or* was intended by the parties; for, if the writ of seizure was successfully prosecuted, there could be no obligation to pay damages; and if the damages were paid, no claim could exist, for the want of a successful prosecution of the writ; and that the damages, for which the surety is bound, are those resulting from the writ being wrongfully sued out.

Indeed, it is proper, that the surety for a writ of seizure should be protected, if it be true, that the principal has a right to the writ, for he is to pay such damages only, as result from its being wrongfully sued out.

In the present case, the plaintiffs admit they were owners of one-half of the boat, and Smith of the other—that Cochrane was, with their consent, master of her. This latter circumstance establishes, that Cochrane had some claim on them, for his wages, and had a privilege on that part of the boat. He established his claim, with so very minute a diminution, contradictorily with Smith, as to show, the writ of seizure was sued out and prosecuted with success.

As to the other defendants, the present plaintiffs; the writ, owing to a technical objection, as to matter posterior to the issue of the writ, the judgment of the inferior court, against the latter, was reversed—

[Garretson *et al. v.* Zacharie.]

so that the appellant, to be relieved, must show, the writ was not *wrongfully* sued out. So, it is in evidence, that Cochrane was a creditor of all the defendants, as owners of the boat, and as such, might obtain a writ of seizure rightfully. It is said, the amount due by the plaintiffs is not established, to a definite amount. We are not ready to.say, that the surety, on a writ of seizure, is liable to damages, if his principal fail in establishing every item of his claim. It certainly suffices, that he had a real claim, and if the adverse party complain, that it was grossly exaggerated, for the purpose of injuring him, he must give some evidence of this.

MATHEWS, J.—The difference of opinion, expressed by the judges, who have preceded me in this case, makes it necessary for me to express mine also. They seem to concur in every thing, except as to the evidence required, to show the existence of the debt, from the plaintiffs to Cochrane, on which the seizure and sequestration of the steamboat was obtained. If the former, as part owners of the boat, were indebted to the latter, as master, at the time of suing out the writ of seizure, it seems to be agreed, that the writ was not wrongfully obtained, and consequently, the bond, given to secure the defendant in that action, never became obligatory on the surety.

I concur in opinion with Judge Martin, that, as the evidence of the case shows, the plaintiff, in the writ of seizure, to have been master of the boat, at the time he proceeded against the present plaintiffs, who were part owners, and that it had been under his management some time previous, we are bound to presume, that he had earned wages, which were then due. I do not believe, that this presumption is in any manner disproved, by the eventual success with which the action, on the writ of seizure, was defended; when we recollect, that it was finally dismissed, on account of irregularities in forms of proceeding.

It is, therefore, ordered, adjudged and decreed, that the judgment of the parish court be annulled, avoided and reversed; and that there be judgment for the defendant, with costs in both courts.

Pierce, for the plaintiffs.
M'Caleb, for the defendant.

Nichols *v.* Hanse *et al.* VIII, N. S. 492.

FIRST District.

If a party agrees to go to New York, and report himself as ready to commence work in the capacity of an engineer, for building one or more steam engines, and to attend to the casting, erecting and putting up said engines, in complete operation, his claim for compensation, is not that of an overseer, but that of a workman, which is prescribed by the lapse of one year. Louisiana Code, art. 3499.

And an agreement, that he will guided by the defendants, does not affect their claim for damages, if the work be not performed in a skilful and workmanlike manner.

Barkley *v.* Bills. VIII, N. S. 496.

PARISH Court of New Orleans.

Decided, that it is allowed to give a witness's declarations in evidence in order to discredit him.

Hebert *v.* Esnard. VIII, N. S. 498.

FOURTH District, Judge of the Second presiding.

Decided, that if justice appears to have been done by the verdict, and no attempt was made below, to set it aside, the Supreme Court will maintain the judgment given thereon, although the evidence might have sustained a different verdict.

Gardiner *v.* Mariners' Church Society. VIII,
N. S. 500.

FIRST District.
Appeal considered to be taken for delay; judgment confirmed with
ten per cent. damages.

Savenet *et al. v.* Le Breton *et al.* VIII, N. S. 501.

A wife may introduce her husband's acknowledgment, in an act to which she was not a
party, to show that he received part of her property.
If a notarial act be subscribed by one witness only, it is valid as a *sous seing privé* only.

PARISH Court of New Orleans.

MARTIN, J., delivered the opinion of the court.
The plaintiff claims a lot of ground, part of her paraphernal estate,
received by her husband from the person who had in his hands her
father's estate.
She introduced as evidence of her title, a notarial act, by which her
husband acknowledged he had received the lot as part of the plaintiff's paraphernal estate.
The admission of the document was objected to on two grounds.
1. Because she was not a party to the act.
2. Because it was not attested by two witnesses, one only having
subscribed it.
The act was received in evidence, and the defendant's counsel
took a bill of exceptions.
I. We think the first objection was properly overruled—the document was introduced to show against the husband's vendee, that
the husband had received the lot, part of the plaintiff's paraphernal
estate.
II. An authentic act is that which is received by a notary assisted

by two witnesses. He and they must subscribe it; if the act wants
the signature of the notary or of either of the witnesses, it is a private
act only, and proof of its execution does not result from its inspection.

The court erred in receiving the document as an authentic act.—
Proof of its due execution ought to have been required before it was
admitted in evidence.

It is, therefore, ordered, adjudged and decreed, that the judgment
of the parish court be annulled, avoided and reversed, and the case
remanded with directions to the parish judge not to receive the act;
objected to in evidence, as an authentic act—the plaintiff and appellee paying costs in this court.

Palfrey *v.* Kerr *et al.*   VIII, N. S. 503.

The party who claims from the owners of a steamboat, for a slave carried away in her,
must show, that they could have prevented it.

FIRST District.

MARTIN, J., delivered the opinion of the court.

The defendants, owners of a steamboat, resisted the plaintiff's
claim for damages, resulting from the master having hired, as a hand
a slave of the plaintiff, and carried him out of the state, by pleading
the insufficiency of the petition and the general issue. There was a
verdict against them, on the latter plea; but the court gave judgment
for them on the first, being of opinion, that " the law of the case is
against the plaintiff, that the act of the master was an illicit one, not
within the scope of his agency, and consequently, the defendants,
the owners, were not responsible." From this decision, the plaintiff
appealed.

We have two statutes, that have some bearing on this case. 1
Moreau's Digest, 119 and 121. The first provides, that he who
hires a slave, without the owner's consent, shall pay a daily compensation, and all damages; and in case of inability to pay, be imprisoned.
The second superadds a fine. Hence, the act is constituted a legal
misdemeanor, for which the offender is liable in damages *civiliter*,
and condemned to pay a fine to the state. The district court, there-

fore, did not err, in concluding that, in the present case, "the act of the master was an illicit one."

But the appellee's counsel urges, that, according to the former and present Code of this state, (322 art. 21 and 2299,) principals are accountable for damages, resulting from the conduct of their agents, when they might have prevented the act which caused the damage, and have not done it; and, in the present case, the possibility of the defendants to prevent the act complained of, is neither proved nor alleged.

The appellant's counsel has contended, that his client's claim arises under the merchant or maritime law, not under the new Civil Code, which professes not to extend to commercial matters, which were left to be regulated by a Code of Commerce, the benefits of which we do not as yet enjoy; that the new Code has recognised partnerships, in boats for the carriage of merchandise, as commercial ones. 2796, 2698. So that we are to be governed, in commercial matters, by the merchant law, as contradistinguished from the municipal law, embodied in what is called the Louisiana or Civil Code.

We are of opinion, that the parts of the new and former Code, which ascertains the liability of principals for the acts of their agents, is not at all controlled by the commercial law, and that the plaintiff cannot recover, because he has not shown, that the defendant could have prevented the acts, from which the damages they claim, are said to have resulted.

It is, therefore, ordered, adjudged and decreed, that the judgment of the district court be affirmed, with costs.

Slidell, for the plaintiff.
Duncan, for the defendants.

Mathews v. Heirs of Delaronde. VIII, N. S. 505.

FIRST District.
Decided, that after defendants have joined in their answer, they cannot be permitted to sever in their defence.

Bourg *v.* Bringier.   VIII, N. S. 507.

COURT of Probates, Parish of St. James.

The endorser, who has not been duly notified of protest, is a competent witness on the part of the maker, to prove payment.

A note, endorsed in blank, authorises payment to the holder.—Chitty on Bills, (1821,) p. 532; Starkie, p. 4301.

Monroe *v.* M'Micken.   VIII, N. S. 510.

THIRD District.

Decided, that an execution will not be enjoined, for matter which might have been pleaded to the action.

An answer, put in the papers of a cause, without being handed to the clerk and by him endorsed and filed, is not a part of the record.

By PORTER, J.—After the jury was sworn, the plaintiff moved for a continuance, from having discovered that no answer was filed, nor judgment of default taken, to form the *contestatio litis.* The court refused to continue the cause on this ground, and the plaintiff excepted.

It appears the answer was not endorsed by the clerk, as filed, but the evidence no doubt satisfied the judge below, that it had been placed among the papers of the cause, several days before. We think the weight of the evidence is in favor of that conclusion. Admitting there is no doubt of the fact, the difficulty still remains. The 463d article of the Code of Practice provides, that as soon as the answer has been filed in a suit, the clerk shall set down the cause on the docket of the court, in order that it be called in its turn, and a day fixed for its trial.

From this provision, we think it follows, the cause was irregularly set down for trial, before the answer was filed. The only doubt then, which can remain in this case, is, whether the plaintiff took advantage of the objection in proper time. The bill of exceptions, at its commencement, states, that after swearing the jury, the plaintiff moved for a continuance, on this ground. But from the language used in another part of the bill, it would seem doubtful whether the jury was not sworn, without allowing the plaintiff sufficient time to examine the answer, and see if the case was at issue. The statement is as follows: "After the overruling of the motion to continue on affidavit, at this moment the court 'ordered a jury to be sworn. Gen. Ripley, attorney for plaintiff, objected, because he had not yet examined the answer; the papers were handed to him by the clerk, and while he was reading the paper marked A, defendant's counsel moved to amend the same, by striking out the word *court* and inserting the word *curator*, which was opposed by plaintiff's counsel, the same not being endorsed, as filed by the clerk; after taking the testimony of E. Cowley and James Turner, the court ordered the same to be filed."

The plaintiff was not bound to notice the answer until filed. It was not one in the cause, until handed to the clerk, and endorsed by him, consequently no argument can be drawn, upon the implied notice which the law raises as to the knowledge of the parties to a suit, of the pleadings in it. The plaintiff then as soon as the paper was presented to him, had a right to take advantage of the defect, and the swearing of the jury did not waive it. If our construction be correct, as we think it is, that until the answer is filed, it is not a part of the record, it follows, the jury were sworn before issue was joined, and the cause must be remanded.

We are always reluctant to yield to these technical objections, but we apprehend great confusion would result, if any other principle was adopted in relation to such matters. If papers can be considered as belonging to a cause. and the pleadings be made up by a party putting them in the bundle without the endorsement of the clerk, there will be constant dispute as to the time they are placed there, and that which the law contemplates to appear by record, will have to be proved, as in this instance, by parol evidence. We think the safety of suitors will be promoted, and we are sure much confusion will be avoided, by adhering strictly to the rule of considering them as private, until regularly filed.

It is, therefore, ordered, adjudged and decreed, that the judgment of the district court be avoided, reversed and annulled, and that the cause be remanded to be proceeded in according to law, the appellee paying costs of appeal.

EASTERN DISTRICT, FEBRUARY TERM, 1830.

Harty *et al. v.* Harty *et al.*   VIII, N. S. 518.

A decree of a court of probates may be annulled by it.
A parent may demand the adjudication of any property, held in common with his children.

COURT of Probates of New Orleans.

MATHEWS, J., delivered the opinion of the court.
This suit is brought by the heirs of Simon Harty for the purpose of obtaining a decree to annul a judgment of adjudication of certain property, (described in the petition,) which was made to their mother as being common between her and them at the decease of their father and to have said property partitioned off. Sinnott was made a defendant, and damages are claimed against him and Mrs. Harty *in solido* on account of alleged misconduct by them in their respective capacities of curatrix and tutrix, and under tutor and curator *ad lites.* They separated in their answers—the widow pleaded general denial—and Sinnott to the jurisdiction of the court. The plea of the latter was sustained, and the suit as to him was dismissed. He afterwards prayed leave to intervene, alleging that his interest might be affected by the final decision of the cause, and that he believed it was proceeding collusively between the plaintiffs and their mother. He obtained the privilege of intervening, and after judgment in favor of the plaintiffs, took this appeal.

The objections to the correctness of the judgment rendered by the court below, may be reduced to two: 1. Want of jurisdiction in that court *ratione materiæ*. 2. Complete legality in all the proceedings by which the property now in dispute was adjudicated to the defendant Mrs. Harty.

To prove that the probate court is without jurisdiction in actions brought to rescind and annul judgments, we are referred to the provisions of the Code of Practice on this subject. The art. 924, of the 3d title, enumerates the cases in which courts of probate have exclusive power: and the following art. limits that jurisdiction to these cases, or those mentioned in the remaining part of this title. It is believed that authority to take cognisance of suits in which the nullity or rescission of judgments is demanded, is not expressly given in any part of the title of the Code of Practice which treats exclusively of probate courts and of their jurisdiction. It is confined to cases relating to successions, whether administered by testamentary executors, tutors or curators, and the estates of persons intestate, &c.

The adjudication of which the plaintiffs complain in the present suit, was clearly within the province of the court of probates; and the question now is, whether its power extends to the revision of that judgment by means of an action to annul or rescind it? Although the Code of Practice makes a distinction between the nullity and rescission of judgments, and establishes rules somewhat different in relation to each; yet they are so identical in their effects, that they may properly be considered together in a legal discussion. According to the art. 608. the nullity of a judgment may be demanded from the same, &c. By the art. 616, the action for rescinding a judgment must be pursued by presenting a petition to the court by which such judgment was rendered. The art. immediately preceding allows to minors four years after they have arrived to the age of majority to bring this kind of action. The present suit was commenced within the time prescribed by law, and in our opinion before the proper tribunal. The court below had jurisdiction of the case in its origin, as relating to a succession, and this jurisdiction is extended by the art. 616 above cited, to a revision of its former judgment.

In investigating the second ground of opposition to the judgment from which the present appeal is taken, we must first look into the right of the defendant, Mrs. Harty, to cause the property of her husband's estate to be adjudicated to her as being held in common between her and his heirs: and secondly, the legality of the proceedings by which the adjudication was effected, must be examined. The right of a surviving parent, (either father or mother,) to cause property held in common with his or her minor children, to be adjudicated to the former, depends mainly on a proper construction of the act of the legislature, passed in 1809, relative to minors. By the 2d section of that act it is declared that, " When the legitimate father or mother of a minor has an estate in common with said minor, said father or mother may cause either the whole or part of said estate to

be adjudicated to him or her, by the judge, according to the estimated
value of the inventory, provided this estimation has been made by
appraisers duly sworn; and provided, likewise, said adjudication be
deemed convenient to the interest of the minor, by the assembly of
the family; and provided moreover the same has been assented to by
the under tutor."

The adjudication which the plaintiffs require to be annulled, was
made of property which belonged to their father exclusively, and
formed no part of the community of acquets and gains at the time of
his decease. He, however, willed a certain portion of it (by a testament made in due form,) to his wife, and she subsequently inherited
another part by the death of some of her children, previous to the
adjudication which is now attacked. From these facts a question is
raised, whether she held the property which was adjudicated as an
estate, in common with her children who were then minors, according to the intent and meaning of the act. The counsel for the appellees contend that the privilege granted by this law to a surviving
father or mother, must be restricted to the community of acquets and
gains; and cannot legally be extended to property common to the
parent and children, under any other title. Whatever may have been
the intention of the legislature, it is clear that the act itself makes no
distinction with regard to right or title by which an estate may be
thus held in common. If the provisions of the law be wise in relation to a community of gains made by partners in the marriage state,
it is difficult to perceive their want of wisdom, with respect to any
other community of property similarly situated. We therefore conclude that the adjudication to Mrs. Harty was made of part of an
estate, subjected by law to that mode of transfer. It now remains to
ascertain whether this transfer or alienation was made in pursuance
of the requisite formalities. These are prescribed by the provisos of
the act above cited. 1. The property to be estimated by appraisers
duly sworn. 2. The adjudication must be declared convenient to
the interest of the minors, by a family meeting. 3. It must be
assented to by the under tutor.

The plaintiffs contend that none of these formalities have been
legally fulfilled. Their father made a will and appointed executors,
whom he authorised to make an inventory of his estate, without the
intervention of justice: in pursuance of this authority they proceeded
to have the property inventoried and appraised, without being assisted by the parish judge or a notary, duly authorised; but the appraisers verified their estimation by an oath, subsequent to the completion
of the inventory, and these proceedings were approved and registered
by order of the court of probates. We are therefore of opinion that
the estate of the testator was legally inventoried and appraised by
appraisers duly sworn, and that consequently, the first formality required by law, to give validity to the adjudication, has been complied
with. A family meeting took place (in pursuance of an order from
the court of probates to that effect) in presence of a justice of the

peace, who made a process verbal of their deliberations and final declaration, that the proposed adjudication would be convenient to the interest of the minors, which received the approbation of a curator *ad litem*, of those who were above the age of puberty, and under tutor of one who was under that age.

In these respects the proceedings seem to have been correct; but the members of the assembly were not sworn.

It is true that neither the Civil Code nor the act of 1809 requires this solemnity; but it is ordered by an act of the legislature, passed in 1811. See 3 *Martin's Digest*, p. 182. This law declares that the property of minors shall be kept unsold, unless the tutor, with the consent of the under guardian, and of at least five of the nearest relations of the minor, or of an equal number of friends, if there be no relations, duly sworn to declare the truth, the whole truth and nothing but the truth, that it is for the interest of the minor that said property or part thereof be sold. Since this act has been in force, it is clear that the decisions of family meetings, in relation to the sale of the property of minors, must be made under the solemnity of an oath, so far as they respect ordinary sales, and that without it such sales might be avoided by the minors, if their rescission should be demanded within the time prescribed by law.

It may, however, be questioned, whether the same formality is required, to give validity to the special and extraordinary mode of alienation and transfer of property held in common between minors and their surviving father or mother by an adjudication, according to the estimated value in the inventory.

This is a privilege granted to the parent, in derogation to general rules, established for the protection of those, who, from want of age and experience, are supposed to be incapable of guarding their own interest; and ought to be restricted within the precise limits of the provisions under which it is awarded. The alienation allowed by it, has all the principal features of a sale; parties, property and power. The incapacity of the minor to consent, is supplied by that of his relations or friends, and his under tutor. The law of 1811 requires that the consent on the part of the relations or friends should be given under the sanction of an oath; under the rule of interpretation, that special provisions of law are not abrogated by those which are general.

We are of opinion that this rule is not applicable to the present case. The last law requires the property of minors to be kept unsold if a sale be not authorised by a family meeting acting under oath; and we have already seen that an adjudication made to a surviving father or mother, is a sale. The oath prescribed is an additional formality, and if not attended to in the deliberations of assemblies of relations or friends, relative to the sales of the property of minors, such decisions must be considered as null and without effect.

The record affords no evidence that the friends of the plaintiffs who met to consider of the propriety and convenience to the interest

51*

of the latter, (then minors,) that their property should be adjudicated
to their mother, were sworn as required by law: and it is believed
that the presumption (which is sometimes applied to the proceedings
of public officers) of every thing having been rightly done, does not
supply the want of this evidence, as such assemblies should rather
be considered to be acting in a private capacity. The neglect to
comply with this formality, is fatal to the adjudication.

In relation to the objections made to the claim of Arthemise Harty
one of the plaintiffs, as having by her acts, since she became of age,
ratified the adjudication, we are of opinion that they will be more
properly taken into consideration in the proceedings to be had in the
partition decreed by the court below.

It is, therefore, ordered, adjudged and decreed, that the judgment
of the court of probates be affirmed, with costs, reserving to the appellant any rights or claims which he may have, on that portion of
the property to be partitioned, which may fall to the share of Arthemise Harty, should it be made appear that she has ratified the adjudication to her mother.

Avart *v.* His Creditors.   VIII, N. S. 528.

A suit to set aside a mortgage injurious to creditors is prescribed by the same limitation
of time as suit to avoid any other contract.

FIRST District.

MATHEWS, J., delivered the opinion of the court.

This case comes up on an opposition made by a creditor of the
insolvent to the homologation of a tableau of distribution filed by the
syndics of his estate. The cause was formerly before this court, on
an appeal from a judgment, by which the opposition of the complainant was dismissed. See 6 *N. S.* 652. The judgment of the district
court was then reversed, and the cause remanded to be proceeded in
according to law. The opposing creditor, on the last trial in the
court below, having obtained judgment in his favor, Delasize, another
creditor and syndic of the insolvent's estate, whose interest was materially affected by said judgment, appealed.

The opposition is made to a privilege or preference, claimed by the appellant, on the funds of the bankrupt, in consequence of a mortgage, executed on the 24th of April, 1823. The cession of his property was made, on the 4th of June of the same year, and the principal ground on which the claim of privilege is opposed, is assumed under the provisions of 1817, relative to the voluntary surrender of property, &c., which reprobates all unjust preferences granted by an insolvent, to one or more of his creditors, over the others, and annuls all acts and deeds executed by him, (with the intent of giving such preference) within the three months next preceding his failure, &c. According to this law, it is contended on the part of the appellant, that the act of mortgage, although executed within the time prohibited, can not be declared null, without previously convicting the insolvent of having thereby intended to give an unjust preference. This appears to have been the main defence against the pretensions of the appellee in the court below: but since the appeal is a peremptory exception founded on prescription, as established by art. 1982, of the Louisiana Code, has been pleaded, which we believe to be decisive of the cause. This article is found in the article 4, chap. 3, sect. 7, of the Code on the subject of conventional obligations. The section treats of contracts which may be avoided by persons not parties to them; and the first paragraph relates to "the action of creditors in avoidance of contracts and its incidents." The second designates what contracts shall be avoided by this action; and the article cited, limits the time within which it may be commenced with effect; it is expressed in the following terms: "No contract for securing a just debt, shall be set aside under this section, although the debtor were insolvent to the knowledge of the creditor with whom he contracted, and although the other creditors are injured thereby, if such contract were made more than one year before bringing the suit to avoid it; and if it contain no other cause of nullity, than the preference given to one creditor over another."

It is evident, according to this provision, that after the lapse of one year, a suit to avoid a contract, such as described in the act, would be barred. The application to the court below, in the present instance, to annul the contract of mortgage (by which the appellant obtained the preference complained of) on account of injury to the other creditors of the insolvent, is not made directly in the form of an action, to have the contract set aside. But in our opinion, it is virtually the same thing. In *concurso*, a mixed proceeding takes place between the insolvent and his creditors, and the latter as opposed to each other. In the event of a contest between the mass of creditors and any one of them, by which the apparent rights of the individual are assailed, the first would hold the place of plaintiffs; the same would be the situation of any one of the creditors who should claim the interference of the court to set aside any instrument on the ground of unjust preference, or legal fraud, executed in favor of another. Viewed as a plaintiff, he would be subject to all constructions and disabilities, which appertain to a person who com-

[Avart v. His Creditors.]

mences an original action; consequently the same prescription is
alike applicable to such a demand made either collaterally or directly.
In the present case, we have been unable to discover any thing which
can shelter the appellee from the operation of the prescription invoked
against him. He received a dividend of the insolvent's estate, as a
chirographic creditor, in pursuance of a tableau of distribution, filed
on the 20th of December, 1825. On the 2d of January, 1826, that
tableau was amended, at the suggestion of his counsel, so as to place
him thereon, as a creditor to a larger amount than had hitherto
appeared in his favor; the present opposition was not filed until the
28th of April, 1827.

In the judgment heretofore rendered in this court, the present plea
of prescription was not taken into consideration; it was not pleaded.

It is, therefore, ordered, adjudged and decreed, that the judgment
of the district court be avoided, reversed and annulled; and it is further ordered, that the opposition of the opposing creditor and appellee be dismissed, at his costs in both courts.

De Armas, for the plaintiff.
Seghers, for the defendants.

Clamagaran v. Sacerdotte.   VIII, N. S. 533.

A debtor who makes a *concordat* with his creditors, must pay the expenses of collecting
the debts assigned to the trustees.
He is not responsible for fees paid gratuitously to counsel.
Evidence may be given to show that money was paid previous to the day on which the
receipt is executed.

FIRST District.

PORTER, J., delivered the opinion of the court.
The defendant, some years since, was in embarrassed circumstances,
and being unable to discharge his debts, made an arrangement with
his creditors, by which, time was accorded him to pay them. The
conditions of this indulgence, among other things, were, that he
should place, in the hands of persons designated by the creditors,
notes due to him for the sale of landed estate, and that these agents
should have the power to collect the rents of certain houses belong-

ing to the defendant. He was also to pay into their hands, a sum of money, sufficient, with the notes and rents already stated, to discharge the principal of the debts due by him; the interest being abandoned. Out of these moneys the agents were to pay the creditors, according to the rank which their respective demands entitled them to hold on their debtor's estate. The plaintiff, together with one Macarty, was designated by the creditors in the act. They are called syndics, throughout the whole of it, and are authorised to raise mortgages on his estate, which he was about to sell, and receive a mortgage from him, on the property which he was partly to receive in exchange for it. Macarty, soon after the execution of the act, died, and the plaintiff was empowered by the creditors, to act alone. He did so, and brought this action, as well in his own name as in that of the other creditors, to compel the defendant to pay the balance due by him, after crediting him with the amount received on the notes, and on the rents of the houses.

The defendant, in his answer, denies that the other creditors had authorised the plaintiff to sue him; and averred that he was indebted to the respondent, for which he prayed judgment in reconvention. The names of these creditors were subsequently struck from the record, on application of the petitioner, and the cause continued between him and the defendant.

There have been three trials in the court below, and as many verdicts in favor of the plaintiff. In the first, the jury found for the plaintiff the sum of 230 dollars 77 cents, but the court below granted a new trial. In the second, the verdict was for 1560 dollars 21 cents. On appeal, the judgment rendered in conformity therewith, was reversed, and the cause remanded. It now returns to us with a verdict, and judgment thereon, for 404 dollars.

The points in dispute between the parties, are three. The first is in relation to the commission claimed by the plaintiff, for transacting the business of the defendant. The second, is in respect to a fee paid to the counsel, by the petitioner, for advice, &c. The third, relates to a credit of 500 dollars, to which the defendant says he is entitled, and which he insists the plaintiff has not allowed him.

I. The character in which the plaintiff acted, and his right to fees, for collecting rents, raising mortgages, and paying over the moneys received by him, has been the subject of vehement contestation at the bar. His counsel has placed his claim to remuneration, on the ground of his being called syndic, in the act of concordat, and insists that the appellation thus bestowed on him, conferred a right to all the compensation which the law grants to agents of this kind, when the debtor makes a *cessio bonorum;* but to this position we can not accede. The statute only gives commissions to syndics who are appointed under the act by which the rate of these commissions are established. Agents appointed in any other case, or in any other mode, may have a claim to compensation from their principal, for services rendered, but they can not demand it under the provisions

[Clamageran v. Sacerdotte.]

of the act in relation to insolvent debtors, because they are not acting
in the cases provided for by the statute.

Equally unsupported do we consider the argument of the defendant, that the concordat amounted to a *dation en paiement*. We
have examined with attention, the act, and we are satisfied no such
deduction can be made from it. In no part of the instrument do the
creditors declare that their claims are discharged, nor is there any
thing found in it to induce us to conclude they received the promise of the defendant, to pay them in the manner therein stated, as
payment of their credits. On the contrary, the opposite conclusion
may be fairly drawn from it. The whole contract is executory.
The defendant promises to put the syndics in possession of the notes
to be given in the sale of his property to Andry; he engages that the
rents which they are authorised to collect from his tenants, will
amount to 1000 dollars a year; and that if they do not, he will annually make good the defect. At the expiration of three years, he
promises to pay the sum of 3400 dollars, to complete the amount due
to his creditors.

After these stipulations, and some others not necessary to be set
out, the creditors declare that *" au moyen du present concordat et
son execution;"* "in consequence of the present concordat, and its
execution, the mass of the creditors abandon to Sacerdotte, all interest
due them up to that day, on their respective credits, and the said creditors grant him a delay of three years, to pay the whole amount of
the capital, and do also release and abandon to him, all the interest
which might accrue to them until the end of three years."

The final release of the debtor is thus made to depend expressly
on the execution of the concordat. If, then, the notes arising from
the sale of the property, had not been delivered up to the syndics; if
the rents had not annually amounted to 1000 dollars, or the defendant had not supplied the balance that might be wanting; and finally,
if the 3400 dollars had not been paid, as promised by him, we think
it quite clear, the original claims of the creditors, which were suspended by the concordat, would have revived in full force. And
hence we conclude that this part of the defence furnishes no ground
for saying the defendant had no interest in the collection of the debts
placed in the hands of the agent, and was not responsible for the expenses attending it.

Each party has insisted the plaintiff was the agent of the other.
In this, as in many other instances, truth lies between the litigants.
He was the agent of both, for both had an interest in seeing the
moneys collected, and the claims liquidated. The plaintiff was the
agent of the creditors, in receiving the money from the defendant,
and in paying it over to them. He was the agent of the defendant
in collecting money from others. As the latter was compelled to
make good the deficit which might exist, he had a right to call on
the former for an account, and could have forced him to have furnished it. We are unable to distinguish this case from several others

[Clamageran v. Sacerdotte.]

decided in this court, where attorneys, charged with the collection of debts, have received from the debtor, obligations to put in suit, out of the funds proceeding from which, they were to discharge the claims first placed in their hands. In such cases, we have uniformly considered that the expenses of collection, should be borne by the party who placed the obligations in the hand of the agent, to discharge his debt. The legal correctness, and the equity too, of such a rule, where there exists no express stipulation to the contrary, we think can not be doubted. See Johnson *v.* Stirling, 3 *N. S.* 483; Benson *v.* Skipp, 5 *Ibid.* 154; O'Connor *v.* Bernard, 6 *Ibid.* 572.

To the services, therefore, rendered to the defendant, in making the collections, we think the plaintiff has a right to claim compensation from him, and we see nothing in the record which enables us to say the jury placed too high an estimate on them.

II. The next matter in dispute, is the fee of 500 dollars paid to an attorney. In the account of the plaintiff, this charge is made as follows: " Paid to P. A. Cuvillier, for his fees, as well for his services rendered to the insolvent, in the cession of his property, as for those rendered to the syndics posterior to the failure."

There never was any cession made by the defendant of his effects. A respite was, it is true, obtained previous to the concordat, under which the plaintiff acted, and if it were for the services rendered by the attorney, in procuring that respite, we think the payment was erroneously made. The defendant had a right to settle his own account with the attorney for these services. The appellee could not legally do so, unless it was for the benefit of the appellant, or at his request, neither of which is shown here. Then as to the services rendered since the concordat, we think that if the plaintiff, as agent of the defendant, has expended money in discharging the duty devolved on him, it is right, and law, the latter should reimburse him. But this money must not have been gratuitously, but necessarily expended, and the necessity can not be presumed, it must be proved, to enable the agent to recover. That has not been done in this instance. There is no proof that any difficulty occurred in collecting the debts; that any of the debtors were in default; any suits brought; any compromises made; any thing on which legal advice could be required. The attorney, indeed swears, he had fifty consultations with the plaintiff; on what subjects we are not informed, and these conversations the defendant should not pay for, unless they were necessary for the execution of the business entrusted to the plaintiff.

III. Before entering on the merits of the last subject of contestation, which relates to a credit claimed by the defendant, for 500 dollars, it is necessary to dispose of a bill of exceptions, taken to the testimony of a witness, on the part of the plaintiff, who proved, that the money, for which he had given a receipt, had been credited to the defendant, previous to its date. His testimony was objected to, as proving against, and beyond the contents of the written document.

We are of opinion the court did not err. The receipt is in these words: *J'ai recu de M. Sacerdotte, la somme de cinq cent piastres sur ce qu'il me doit. Nouvelle Orleans*, 18 *Mai*, 1824. P. H. Clamageran. The act is a private, not a public one. The prohibition in our Code, against the reception of evidence, against or beyond what is contained in written instruments, applies particularly to those which relate to real estate. Those in relation to personal property are governed by the general rules of evidence. In that system of jurisprudence, from which we have derived our principles in relation to proof, receipts are considered as exceptions to the general rule, and parol evidence may be given to explain, or even to contradict them. Without adopting that exception to its whole extent, we can find sufficient reason for admitting the parol evidence in this instance. Proof, that the money had been paid at a previous time, did not contradict the time of the receipt, for it does not say the money was paid on that day. It only affords a presumption of it. Starkie on Evidence, p. 4, 1044; 1 *N. S.* 145; 2 *Ibid.* 378; 5 *Ibid.* 68; 9 *Ibid.* 310; 8 *Ibid.* 389.

On the merits of this point, we concur with the jury. We think they did not err in concluding the money had been paid, previous to the date of the receipt, and crediting in account, at the time it was paid.

Much has been said by the counsel on both sides, of the influence which the verdict of the jury should have on our deliberations. We thought the jurisprudence of the court so firmly established in this matter, and so well understood, that it scarcely afforded room for aberration at this day. The verdict of a jury has great weight in all cases, when questions of fraud, or damages, are involved. It turns the scale, when the evidence is conflicting on matters of fact, and the truth doubtful; but it has no influence, nor should it have any, where the facts being established, the rights of the parties depend on the law arising out of them. In such cases, the conclusions of the court can be more safely relied on, than those of the country. Such is the instance before us. The jury have erred, in allowing the plaintiff credit for a sum of money paid by an agent, without any evidence that this money was necessarily expended for the benefit of the principal.

This sum of 500 dollars deducted, the moneys paid by the plaintiff, on account of the defendant, and his own claim, amounted to 4091 dollars 74 cents. He has received 13,804 dollars, and is consequently entitled to judgment for the balance, 205 dollars 74 cents, deducting 171 dollars 74 cents the balance on another account.

It is, therefore, ordered, adjudged and decreed, that the judgment of the district court be annulled, avoided and reversed; and it is further ordered, adjudged and decreed, that the plaintiff do receive of the defendant, the sum of thirty-three dollars, with costs in the court below, except those occasioned by making other parties plaintiffs: these, with the costs of the appeal, to be paid by the defendant.

Canon, for the plaintiff.
Seghers, for the defendant.

Gasquet *et al. v.* Johnston. VIII, N. S. 544.

A confession of judgment which will preclude the necessity of filing an answer, or forming the *contestatio litis*, can only be made by the defendant or one specially authorised to that effect.

FIRST District.

PORTER, J., delivered the opinion of the court.

The defendant in this case, took a rule on the plaintiffs to show cause why the judgment rendered against him should not be set aside, on the ground of certain irregularities practised in obtaining it. The court below after hearing testimony, ordered the rule to be discharged.

The petition of appeal is " from a certain judgment rendered against him," the defendant. It has been contended that this appeal only brought legality and correctness of the judge's decision in relation to the rule before us; that the merit of the original judgment could not be inquired into.

We think otherwise. The rule to show cause why the judgment should not be set aside, and the order of the court discharging it, can not be distinguished, for the purpose for which we are now considering them, from the ordinary motion made for a new trial. An appeal from the judgment rendered in the latter case, has never been supposed an appeal solely from the decision, or an attempt to abstain a revision of it. The terms used in the petition of appeal, we think, apply more pertinently to the judgment rendered, than to an order to discharge a rule to show cause.

The case commenced by attachment, and an attorney was appointed to defend the absent debtor. The agent left the city during the summer months; pending his absence, a paper was forwarded by the defendant to another person, containing the following declaration: " I confess judgment on the following attachments." The first enumerated is that which was levied by the plaintiff in this suit.

The instrument concludes with an authorisation to the sheriff of New Orleans, to proceed forthwith to sell any goods in his possession to satisfy the attachments, and pay the amount over to the creditors or their agents.

On the same sheet of paper was a power of attorney to the counsel who had been appointed by the county, authorising him to sell or cause to be sold, the goods belonging to the principal, in the hands of the sheriff—to confess judgment, on said attachments if necessary, and to do all other acts necessary to carry the power into effect.

[Gasquet *et al. v.* Johnston.]

This paper came to the individual to whom it was directed, during a sickness which terminated by his death. After his decease, the person who was authorised to open his letters, on discovering the nature of the instrument, gave information of its contents to the plaintiffs, and by their advice, and that of their attorney, he deposited it in court.

Shortly after it was placed there, the plaintiffs had judgment entered up on the demand in the petition, on the ground of the confession contained in the document already referred to. The instrument purported to be executed before a notary, in Nashville, Tennessee, but owing to its not being signed by witnesses, it had not the force of an authenticated act: and testimony was called and heard, to establish the verity of the defendant's signature.

The use which the plaintiffs made of the confession or acknowledgment thus obtained, has been objected as irregular and unauthorised, and as giving them a preference in obtaining judgment, contrary to the intention of the debtor, who desired that all his creditors should share alike in the goods attached.

We think from the whole tenor of the act that such was the defendant's intention, and we are of opinion the judgment was irregularly obtained. A technical confession of judgment which will preclude the necessity of filing an answer, or forming the *contestatio litis* can only be made by the defendant, or some one authorised by him to that effect. The document in the plaintiffs' hands, can be considered in no other light, than evidence of the debt claimed; and as such, it could only be used by them on the trial of the cause contradictorily with the defendant.

It is, therefore, ordered, adjudged and decreed, that the judgment of the district court he annulled, avoided and reversed; and it is further ordered and decreed, that this cause be remanded, to be proceeded in according to law, the appellee paying the costs of the appeal.

Tourné *et al. v.* Lee *et al.*   VIII, N. S. 548.

Trespassers cannot call in warranty those under whose authority they acted.

The corporation of New-Orleans have the right to consider an act in violation of their ordinances relative to the port of New Orleans, as a nuisance, and have the power to abate it.

PARISH Court of New Orleans.

PORTER, J., delivered the opinion of the court.

The defendants, acting under the order of the mayor of the city of New Orleans, cut loose, and turned adrift, a raft of wood, belonging to the plaintiffs, which they had moored in the port opposite Faubourg St. Mary, and suffered to remain there for a longer period of time, than the city ordinance permitted.

The defendants pleaded, that they were acting as officers of the corporation, under orders from the head of it. They prayed that the mayor, alderman and inhabitants of the city, might be cited in warranty, and they discharged. The court correctly refused this demand. Trespassers, or those accused of trespassing on the rights of others, cannot relieve themselves from responsibility, by pleading, in defence, the authority of third persons.

The jury found a verdict for the defendants, and the plaintiffs appealed, after having fruitlessly attempted to have the verdict set aside, and a new trial granted in the court below.

The cause presents two questions. First, of fact: whether the raft was moored opposite the levee, in a place forbidden by the city regulations, and had remained there a sufficient length of time, to be obnoxious to their penalties: and secondly, of law, whether the ordinance was constitutional. The first we consider correctly settled, by the verdict of the jury, and shall proceed to examine the second.

We have no doubt the ordinance of the city council was constitutional in its prohibtion, and the remedy it accorded for a violation of it. It is essential to the good police of the city, and the general convenience, that the corporation should be vested with the .power to prescribe what portion of the port is appropriated to particular craft, and for what length of time, and on what conditions they can remain in the place assigned them. This, indeed, the appellants have not much contested, but it has been strenuously contended, that the remedy was a violation of the fundamental law of the state, because it deprived the citizen of his property, without a judgment of the court, pronounced after hearing him, or giving him an opportunity to be heard. As the corporation had the power of making regulations as

[Tourne *et al. v. Lee et al.*]

to the place where rafts of wood should land, and how long they
might remain, they had, in our judgment, the right to consider a violation of their ordinance on these matters, as a nuisance, and to treat
it accordingly.   Counsel has read from 3d Blackstone to show that
the act of the defendants does not fall within the definition of a nuisance.   The nuisances treated of in the passage cited, are those which
are private.   The offence of the plaintiffs falls within the class of
public ones.   The same author specifies, as one of the latter kind,
" annoyances in public rivers, rendering the same inconvenient."
But it was said, the evidence showed that no inconvenience resulted
from this raft, at the time it was moved; owing to the state of the
waters, the batture, and other causes.   This may be so, and the plaintiffs' case not be made stronger, because the court were bound to conclude, that in general, it is inconvenient to the public, and a nuisance, that rafts of wood should remain longer than 48 hours, where
this was placed.   The city council, in whom the right of legislation
is vested, have said so by their ordinance, and as they have made no
exception, we can make none.   If, in the greater number of instances,
the public convenience is opposed to mooring rafts where the defendants placed theirs, the corporation had a right to consider all such, and
place all under the same penalties.   They may have wisely considered,
that the introduction of any exception into the ordinance, would
have defeated its object, and that the inconvenience of settling
whether particular cases came within the exception, would be a
greater inconvenience to the public, (of which the plaintiffs form a
part) than a prohibition which embraced all cases.   Considering,
therefore, the act of the defendants, permitting the raft of wood to
lie longer in a place than the regulations of the city authorised, as
producing a nuisance which was public in its nature, any person,
and more especially the city authorities, had a right to abate it:
because, in the language of the great judge and constitutional lawyer
already quoted, " injuries of this kind, which obstruct or annoy such
things as are of daily convenience and use, require an immediate
remedy; and cannot wait for the slow progress of the ordinary forms
of justice."   3 Blackstone's Comm. 5, 216; 4 *Ibid.* 167.

It is, therefore, ordered, adjudged and decreed, that the judgment
of the parish court be affirmed, with costs.

Canon, for the plaintiffs.

Moreau and *Armar*, for the defendants.

Winter v. Corporation of Donaldsonville.
VIII, N. S. 553.

SECOND District.

Decided, that the act of 1823 professedly changed the limits of Donaldson, as fixed by the act of 1813, and Winter's land was excluded by the last legislation.

Flower v. O'Connor.   VIII, N. S. 555.

THIRD District, Judge of the Second presiding.

Held, that to repel the plea of *coverture*, the wife's petition to be admitted as heir, accompanied by the husband's authorisation, is admissible evidence.

The property of the succession, when received by the wife, is paraphernal, which she may administer herself, nor ask her husband's approbation.

By MARTIN, J.—We cannot agree with the appellee's counsel, that the 983d article of the new Code refers to the acts mentioned in the third paragraph of the preceding article, as evidence of a tacit acceptance of a succession. The collection of the actual debts of a succession, the sale of the goods, the payment of the passive debts are all facts, or acts, which may be given in evidence, to charge a party as heir, and show that he tacitly accepted the succession.

The 983d article refers to instruments in written acts, which are stated, in the second paragraph of the preceding article, as evidence of an express acceptance.

Russell *et al. v.* Hall.   VIII, N. S. 558.

FOURTH District, Judge of the Second presiding.
The principle that want of consideration may be proved between
the maker and payee of a note fully recognised.

Walker *v.* Vanwinkle *et al.*   VIII, N. S. 560.

It is always in time for the defendant to move for the dissolution of an injunction, for
matters appearing on the face of the petition.
It may be done after an answer put in.
The assignee of leased premises, may remove the lessee by summary process.
No matter what may be the value of the improvements placed on the premises, the jus-
tice of the peace has jurisdiction under the act of 1819.

FOURTH District, Judge of the Second presiding.

PORTER, J., delivered the opinion of the court.
The plaintiff states that he leased from one Stewart, four acres of
land on the Mississippi river, for an indefinite period of time, and
that confiding in his lessors remaining proprietors of the premises, he
put valuable improvements on them to the value of 700 dollars.—
That at the time of the lease the property was mortgaged, and has
been since sold by the mortgagee.   That the purchaser, at the public
sale made in virtue of an execution issued on the act of mortgage,
has procured an order from a justice of the peace to dispossess the
petitioner, and that he fears the sheriff will carry it into execution.—
The petition avers, that the purchaser must pay the value of the improvements before he can evict the possessor; and concludes by a
prayer for an injunction.
The defendant, Montgomery, who had bought the premises, answered, by praying that the injunction be dissolved, as granted in a

case where no such process is allowed by law, and by a court not having jurisdiction.

On the merits he denied all the allegations in the petition, except some facts not necessary to set forth; and concluded by a demand in reconvention.

After issue thus joined, the defendant moved to dissolve the injunction, on the matters appearing on the face of it. The court, notwithstanding the opposition of the plaintiff, went into the inquiry, and the correctness of this proceeding, is the first question for our decision.

We think the court did not err. It is always in time for a motion to dissolve an injunction, on the facts alleged in the petition. The defendant's denial in the answer of the truth of the plaintiff's statements, did not preclude him from subsequently admitting them to be true. Nor is there any force in the objection, that the cause having been submitted to a jury by the pleadings, the injunction could not be dissolved until they passed on it. The only object of an investigation before them, viz., the ascertaining of the truth of the facts at issue, ceased by an admission, on the part of the defendant, of the truth of the plaintiff's allegations.

The court, after hearing the parties, dissolved the injunction, and the plaintiff appealed.

In this court he has principally relied on two grounds.

1. That the remedy given by the act of assembly, is limited to the immediate lessee, and does not extend to those who acquire from him.

2. That the plaintiff's demand for improvements, placed the case out of the jurisdiction of a justice of the peace.

The counsel for the appellant has presented this case to our consideration, on the act of assembly passed the 3d of March, 1819, and has argued on the particular phraseology of the statute, that it was the intention of the legislature to confine the privilege of removing the lessee by summary process to the immediate lessor—and that it did not extend to his assignees. There has, however, been later legislation on the subject than the act cited in argument, and upon a proper construction of it, depends the rights of the parties. By the 2683d article of the Louisiana Code, it is provided, "When the lessor has given notice to the lessee, in the manner described by law, to quit the property, and the lessee persists in remaining on it, the lessor may have him summoned before a justice of the peace, and condemned to depart; and if, three days after notice of the judgment, he has not obeyed, the justice of the peace may order that he shall be expelled, and that the property shall be cleared by the constable, at his expense."

We are of opinion that the lessor, and the representatives and assigns of the lessor, may exercise the remedies given by this enactment. According to the 2704th art. of the Code, the purchaser of the thing leased, takes the property subject to the lease, and bound by the contract of the orignal lessor. Being thus subject to all his obligations, it clearly follows, that the lessee is entitled to every remedy given to enforce the rights growing out of these obligations.

The second point in the cause, we think, is clearly with the appellee. The value of the improvements, placed by the lessee on the land, does not take away jurisdiction from the justice of the peace, no more than the land itself being of greater value than the sums of which these officers can take cognisance in ordinary actions, would. The object which the legislation on this subject had in view, would be completely defeated if it did. The law intended to give a speedy and efficacious means of putting the lessor in possession, and leaves the other questions growing out of the contract, to be settled in due course of law, after possession is obtained. It is very questionable whether under the 2697th art. of the Louisiana Code, the lessee can compel the lessor to pay for his improvements, unless, in the words of the law, they were made " with lime and cement;" as to all other ameliorations, his right perhaps extends no farther than removing them from the premises. But as the decision of this point is not necessary in the present case, we refrain from expressing an opinion on it.

It is, therefore, ordered, adjudged and decreed, that the judgment of the district court be affirmed, with costs.

Walden v. Grant et al.   VIII, N. S. 565.

Enregistering an act under private signature in a notary's office, does not give it the force of an authentic act.

Recording a mortgage in the name of an assignee is not proof against third persons of the assignment.

An attorney at law cannot alienate a judgment obtained by his client, without special authority.

FIRST District.

PORTER, J., delivered the opinion of the court.

The petition states the plaintiff to be assignee of the judgments, against Edward Livingston, on which, notwithstanding a sum of money has been made by the sheriff of the parish of Orleans, on two writs of *fieri facias*, a balance is still due, and unpaid.

[Walden *v.* Grant *et al.*]

It further states, that these judgments were duly received in the office of the recorder of mortgages: by reason whereof, they created a mortgage on all the real estate of the defendant, from the day they were respectively recorded. That at the date of enregistering, Livingston had a right, interest and title, in, and to, three lots of ground on the batture in front of the fauxbourg St. Mary, which lots have come into possession of the defendants, Grant and Alden. That more than ten days previous to the institution of this suit, they had notice in writing, that payment had been in vain demanded of Livingston, for the balance due by him on the judgments, and that the property before mentioned, would be seized and sold, unless paid by them in ten days.

It concludes, by an averment of the money yet due by Livingston, not being paid either by him or the defendants, and a prayer, that the lots be seized and sold, to satisfy the claim of the petitioner.

To the petition, an exception was filed, alleging an informality, for which it should be dismissed; the want of a declaration on oath, by the plaintiff, of the existence of the debt, and demand of payment. The court of the first instance overruled the exception, and an answer on the merits was put in. In this answer, all the allegations in the petition, were put at issue, except certain sacts, which it is not deemed material to specially notice. There was judgment for the plaintiff, and the defendant appealed, after an unsuccessful attempt to obtain a new trial.

In this court, the appellants have filed several points, on which they allege, the judgment below should be reversed. In argument, they have principally relied on the two following:

1. The court below erred, in overruling an exception of the defendants, that the affidavit required by the 70th article of the Code of Practice, was not made by the plaintiff.

2. There is no proof in the record, that the plaintiff was the assignee of the judgments against Livingston.

We deem it unnecessary to state, what conclusion we should come to on the first ground, being of opinion, that the second is decisive of the plaintiff's pretensions in this suit.

The first evidence on which the plaintiff relies, to establish this assignment, is an act passed by a notary public of this city, in which it is stated, that the petitioner personally appeared before him, and presented three certain instruments, in writing, purporting to be three transfers of judgment, in his favor, which the appearer required him (the notary) to transcribe into his current register of notarial acts, there to remain as on record, and serve as occasion may require, whereupon, &c., &c.

After reciting these instruments, which appear to be all *sous seing privé*, the act concludes as follows: " Thus done and recorded, in the city of New Orleans, in the presence of Felix Brunel and William M'Cauley, witnesses, who hereunto subscribe their names, with me, the said notary."

By an agreement on record, this evidence was received, subject to all legal exceptions, and the exception now made to it, is, that this is not the authentic act, which establishes against third persons, the execution of the instruments under private signature, recited in it.

We think the objection well taken. The act proves, that the notary committed the writings *sous seing privé* to record. But his doing so does not give authenticity to the instruments. Those on which the law invests him with power to confer that privilege, are acts passed before himself, as private instruments legally acknowledged before him, and subscribed by the parties, in presence of two witnesses. Neither of these indispensable requisites is found in the act under consideration. The makers of the private writings did not appear before the notary. The party in whose favor they were made, alone presented himself, and had them enregistered. Were we to hold, that such recording gave to the instruments received by the notary, the force and effect of a public act, and dispensed with the necessity of proving them, in the ordinary mode, we would be enabling litigants, by their own acts, to make proof for themselves. Marie Louise v. Cauchoix, 11 *Martin*, 243; Seymour v. Cooley, 3 *N. S.* 396.

The next proof on which the plaintiff rests, is the certificate of the recorder of mortgages.

By this certificate, the judgments appear to be enregistered in the name of the plaintiff, and this, it is contended, is *prima facie* evidence, they were assigned to him.

On looking into the certificate, it is seen, that the register admitted the judgments to record, on the act passed before the notary, which we have just examined, and considered not to furnish, *per se*, legal proof of the fact for which it was produced. It is therefore necessary to inquire, whether its force and authenticity be increased by the recorder of mortgages having acted on it as evidence, which satisfied him the assignment had been made. The different provisions of our law, in relation to this officer and his duties, have been attentively considered, and nothing has been found in them to justify such a conclusion. Indeed, nothing short of express and positive legislation, would authorise the court so far to depart from general principles, as to consider the act of the recorder, evidence against the possessor. So far as the mere fact of enregistering is in question, it is indeed proof, because it is the highest evidence of that fact. But although it proves a mortgage was recorded, it does not establish the proof of the facts on which that recording was made, for from fraud in the parties or error in the recorder, the one may exist without the other. The act of mortgage and the assignment, in the instance before us, must have existed prior to their being recorded, and the certificate of the register, therefore, is only secondary evidence of them. To receive it in place of the higher proof, which the law presumes in the possession of the creditor, would be a violation of the rule, that the best evidence of which the case is susceptible, must be produced.

[Walden v. Grant et al.]

But although the act of the recorder of mortgages is not evidence against the third possessor, it may, under certain circumstances, be evidence for him. As when the mortgage is enregistered for a less sum than its real amount, or where it is cancelled in part, or for the whole, because it is the enregistering alone which gives it effect against third persons. It was on this principle, the case of Le Farge v. Morgan et al. was decided, which was so much pressed on us in argument. 11 *Martin*, 526.

It was next contended, that the records of the judgments furnished evidence of an assignment, in a motion made by the plaintiff's counsel, recognising Walden as assignee. But to make this a legal transfer of the assignee's interest, it should have been shown that the attorney had authority to alienate his client's interest in the debt, and nothing of that kind has been proved.

Lastly, it was urged, that possession of the mortgage was evidence of right to it, and this position we consider less tenable than any we have been examining. Possession of a written title, is in no ways proof of ownership, unless it be an obligation payable to bearer. Even in the case of a bill of exchange, or promissory note, endorsed in blank, proof of the hand writing of the payee, is indispensable to recovery.

Being thus of opinion, that the plaintiff has not established the assignment, under which he claims title to the judgments set out in his petition, the judgment of the court below must be reversed, and ours be for the defendants, as in case of nonsuit.

It is, therefore, ordered, adjudged and decreed that the judgment of the district court be annulled, avoided and reversed; and that there be judgment for the defendants as in case of nonsuit, with costs in both courts.

Hoffman, for the plaintiff.
Maybin, for the defendants.

Cambre *et al. v.* Kohn *et al.* VIII, N. S. 572.

In a sale of a certain and limited part, taken from a whole tract, leaving another part between the premises sold and the river; the words *from to the river*, are merely descriptive of the position of the land sold, and no land passes beyond the expressed limits.

FIRST District.

MATHEWS, J., delivered the opinion of the court.

This case was formerly before the Supreme Court, on an appeal taken from a judgment rendered by the district court, in relation to exceptions which were pleaded to the action. It was remanded, and trial has since taken place on the merits.

The plaintiffs claim, as heirs of Veronique Cambre, who was the wife of Andrew Velliamil, the purchaser of a certain lot of ground, in the fauxbourg St. Mary, from Claude F. Girod, who derived his title from Bertrand Gravier. One half of this property is claimed in right of their ancestor, as having been acquired during her marriage with Velliamil, and the defendants are sued as possessors without title.

The object of the suit is to recover from them, certain portions of the batture, in front of the fauxbourg, of which they have had possession for some years. Their answers contain a general denial, and allege title, &c. The cause was submitted to a jury, who found a verdict in their favor, and from a judgment rendered in conformity thereto, the plaintiffs appealed.

In investigating this case, we consider, as wholly unnecessary, any disquisition on the doctrine of alluvion, in relation to the rights of riparious proprietors of land on navigable rivers, or other water courses in this state, viewing them to be settled by many decisions of its competent judiciary.

We will, therefore, come directly to the consideration of the title of the plaintiffs, as supported by the written documents and testimony adduced in the cause. The main foundation of their claim to the premises in dispute, is founded on an act of sale, made by Bertrand Gravier, to Claude F. Girod, executed on the 22d of March, 1794, of a certain parcel of land described in said act. The latter person having transferred to Velliamil, all his rights and claims on the batture, in front of a lot, of which the tract or parcel of land purchased from B. Gravier, made a part, in the act of sale passed between them, on the 23d of April, 1807. The expressions principally relied on in the deed from Gravier to Girod, are, that the piece or patch of land *(pano de terra)* sold, was situated without the walls of the city, and fronted to the river *(frente al rio)*, and that it passed to the purchaser by express terms *"con todas sus entradas y salidas usos, costumtres derechos,"* &c. From these expressions, the counsel for the appellants contend, that the vendor became the owner and possessor of a rural estate, limited in front by the river, and consequently acquired a right to any alluvion which was then attached to it, or might thereafter accrue. The sale purports to be of a piece of land, composed of 52½ feet front to the river Mississippi, and 160 in depth, bounded on one side by the land of Nicholas Gravier, and on the other, by land of the vendor, making a superficies of 8290 square feet. The testimony of the case shows, that at the time of this sale, a considerable extent of alluvion, or batture, was then formed and attached to the lot of ground sold, indeed to an extent greater than the land embraced by lines corresponding with the limitations of the deed, which fixed the quantity to the amount as stated (8290 square feet.) The proof of this fact renders useless any inquiry into the privilege of the vendor, to acquire, by right of accession, alluvion which might have attached itself to his lot, after he became the proprietor, under the sale from B. Gravier. That the purchaser took possession of the parcel of land really intended to be sold, cannot be denied, and it is clear, from the evidence, that it was a small portion of a large tract, then held by the seller, and whether, at that period, the whole front of the tract was established as a faux-bourg to the city of New Orleans, need not be inquired into, believ-ing, as we do, that even considering the property sold, as a rural estate, the expression in the act of sale, did not convey to the vendor, any right to the alluvion there formed and attached to the lot which he bought. It is contended, that it passed as an accessory. In the sense in which we now use this word, it means that which accedes to some principal thing, and the idea which it generally conveys, is of something less than the principal. It may happen, however, that the accessory is more valuable than the principal thing, as in the example adduced by the counsel for the appellants, of a costly house placed on a small lot of ground; and the sale of the lot, without any restrictive expressions, would convey the house to the purchaser. But to effect a transfer of any thing more than is expressly stipulated in a deed, it must be clearly shown by the buyer, that what he claims in addition to the property actually sold, is an accessory, and depen-dent on the principal.

It is true, that riparious owners of land acquire alluvions by the right of accession as established by law; but so soon as they are com-pletely formed and attached to the original soil, they are considered as making a part of the estate to which they are joined. This doc-trine, so fully in accordance with common sense, is established by some of the authorities cited in this case. In the original *Encyp. verbo,* under the word alluvion, after stating it to be a mode of ac-quiring property according to the provisions of the Roman law; it is

further declared, that the portion thus added, is not considered as
new land, it is a part of the old, which acquires the same qualities,
and which belongs to the same owner, in the same manner as the
increase by the growth of a tree makes part of the tree, &c. This
right of acquisition by alluvion, is founded on the general rule of
justice and equity, which accords the profit and advantage of a thing,
to him who is exposed to damage and loss. The same doctrine is
found in Ferriere's Com. on the Custom of Paris, nos. 37 and 38 of
art. 326, *lit.* 25. After pointing out the manner in which an augmentation is made to an inheritance, by alluvion, it is said "cette
augmentation est tellement unie a l'heritage qu'elle prend ses quali-
tes, et par consequent devient propre, comme l'heritage auquel elle
a ete unie, selon Dumoulins sur l'art 1 de cette costume. Glos. 5,
nos. 115 and 116, ou il dit, *incrementum alluvionis nobis acquiri-
tur eo jure, quo, ager augmentatus primum ad nos pertinibet,
nec istud incrementum consetur novus ager; sed pars primi.* We
have assumed as proved (a fact well established by the testimony of
the cause) that at the time of the sale of the parcel of land to Girod,
under whom the plaintiffs claim title to the batture in front of the
land sold, an alluvion had been formed, and attached thereto, whereas
the lot sold was the property of B. Gravier, the original vendor, and
made a part of his plantation, which was of an extent much greater
than the land sold. Now, according to the authorities above cited,
and according to the decision of the Superior Court of the late territory of New Orleans, in the case of J. Gravier *v.* The Corporation,
this alluvion must be considered as having formed an integral part of
the plantation of B. Gravier, at the time he sold out the lots separately on its front, and did not pass to any purchaser of a restricted
part of the whole plantation, unless it were embraced within the
limits of the part thus sold. The titles adduced by the appellants,
show, that B. Gravier conveyed by act of sale, to Girod, a parallelo-
gram of land, of 160 feet by 51½, of which the vendor took full and
entire possession, and by this course of proceeding, all the obligations on the part of the vendor, arising from his contract of sale, were
satisfied and discharged, unless the expressions in the act can be
legally interpreted, in such a manner as to give to the purchaser an
additional quantity of land greater in extent than that conveyed by
express limitation to a certain number of square feet. The first of
these expressions, is *frente al rio,* and it is contended, that such a
clause in the sale of lands, which are bounded by the river, gives to
purchasers all contained within lateral lines up to that boundary.
The truth of this doctrine can not be denied, as it relates to a sale
and transfer of the whole of a plantation, held by a riparian owner:
and is true, according to the judgment of this court, in the case of
Morgan *v.* Livingston, so far as to give to the buyer of a part of the
front of a plantation, the privilege of acquiring, by right of alluvion,
when it appears that the river was the real boundary at the time of
sale, and that nothing intervened, worthy of being considered a fit

[Cambre *et al. v.* Kohn *et al.*]

subject for exclusive ownership. But we are of opinion, that it is not applicable to a sale made of a certain limited part, taken from a whole tract of land, when at the time of sale the vendor held in full property another part between that sold and the river. In this last case, the words front to the river, must be taken as merely descriptive of the situation of the property sold at the time of sale, and ought not to be construed in such a manner as to extend the grant of the seller beyond the express limits contained in the act of sale, in relation to quantity.

We do not believe that the pretensions of the plaintiffs can be supported by the formal part of the act, which grants to the vendor every thing appertaining to the lot sold. For it has already been shown, that the alluvion did not appertain to it as an accessary, but made a part of the whole plantation from which it was separated in the sale to Girod.

The conclusion to which we have come, in this cause, is entirely conformable to the principles established by the decisions in the cases of Livingston *v.* Herman, Cochran & Ray *v.* Story & Fort, and J. Gravier *v.* The Corporation of New Orleans, decided under the territorial government. And we are of opinion, that the most rigid interpretation of the act of sale now under consideration against the vendor, would not give the alluvion in question to the vendee, or those claiming under him.

It is, therefore, ordered, adjudged and decreed, that the judgment of the district court be affirmed, with costs.

Moreau and *Soulé,* for the plaintiffs.
Livermore, for the defendants.

Questi *v.* Rills.   VIII, N. S. 581.

FOURTH District.

Decided, that the office of administrator is created by the Louisiana Code; see article 1042 for his powers. Article 1009 lays down the duty of taking an oath before entering into function. The present administrator had omitted this: hence, he may well be opposed with this, when he attempts seizure and sale on mortgaged property. He is without legal authority to do any such acts.

State *v.* Probate Judge of Iberville. VIII, N. S. 585.

DECIDED, that a will made in one state, and admitted to probate in another, may be ordered for execution in this state, on producing the record of its having been admitted to probate by any court of competent jurisdiction. Louisiana Code, article 1682.

The meaning of the terms, " the place where it was received," in that article, adjudged to be that, if the will was proved and received before any court of competent jurisdiction in another country, the judge here should have admitted it to probate in this state. We admit to probate wills made out of the state, which had been received elsewhere, but we require proof of their execution where this sanction has not been bestowed on them.

Morgan's Syndics *v.* Fiveash. VIII, N. S. 588.

SECOND District.

Decided, that a planter who permits his slaves to earn money for themselves, by cordelling ships, has no action in case one of them be drowned accidentally in doing so.

Flower *v.* O'Connor.   VIII, N. S. 592.

THIRD District, Judge of the Second presiding.

An affidavit for a continuance need not state that the testimony wanted could not have been discovered by proper diligence before the trial.

The words of the Code of Practice, art. 561, may be literally pursued without it.

Poirot *v.* Vesser.   Vesser *v.* Poirot.   VIII, N. S. 595.

PARISH Court of New Orleans.

Held, that a vacant estate cannot be sued except in a court of probates.

Kirkland *v.* His Creditors.   VIII, N. S. 597.

If the appellant is prevented by circumstances beyond his control, from obtaining and filing the transcript, he may be released although the clerk's certificate has been delivered to the appellee.

THIRD District.

MARTIN, J., delivered the opinion of the court.

The transcript not having been filed by the appellee in proper

53*

time, obtained the clerk's certificate, and afterwards, the appellant's counsel read an affidavit, to show that there had been no neglect, and prayed leave to file the transcript.

The appellee's counsel has had the candor to admit the sufficiency of the affidavit, if the application is not too tardy.

He has urged, that the judgment of the inferior court is now irrevocable. Code of Practice, 589. That the appeal has been abandoned, and can not be renewed. *Ibid.* 594; *French Code de Procedure Civille,* 489; *Traité des Obligations,* 864.

The right of the appellee to take out the clerk's certificate, is only given in the case of the appellant's neglect to file the transcript. *Ibid.* 588. Although the defence of the transcript is *prima facie* evidence of that neglect, and authorises the delivery of the certificate.

But accidents, beyond the appellant's control, may prevent the appellant from bringing up the record in due time. The clerk of the inferior court may die, be disabled by sickness, or a great pressure of business, from making out the transcript, or he may neglect, or wilfully omit. Other events may cause a delay. In such a case, the transcript will be received; and no objection allowed, if the appellee has taken no steps, and the delay is accounted for.

Evidence that there has been no neglect, establishes that the certificate was improvidently applied for; and the court, on being satisfied of this, must release the appellant by avoiding the certificate and refusing the execution that issued on it. To do so, the court requires no legislative permission.

The legislature, however, has made one, to enable the appellant, who has not the transcript ready to be filed, to obtain a delay for that purpose, and even the recall of the clerk's certificate, if one has issued at the time he applies for relief, and even to enjoin the execution of the judgment.

The Code of Practice, 883, authorises the court to grant the appellants an injunction to suspend the execution of the judgment appealed from, if, at the time of his petition for delay, the appellee has already acquired from the clerk the necessary certificate for the purpose of such execution.

Surely the legislature has not made this provision for the sole case of a certificate illegally issued before the period at which it might be legally applied for.

It is true the party seeking relief in this case, must do it within the period fixed by law, if possible; but if he be prevented from doing so by accidents, over which he had no control, we believe, that on showing it, he may he listened to in proper time, as soon as it is within his power.

The transcript must therefore be admitted to be filed.

Ripley, for the appellant.

Morgan *v.* His Creditors.   VIII, N. S. 599.

Partnership creditors have both by the Civil Code and the Louisiana Code, the right to be paid out of the partnership effects by preference to the private, or separate creditors. But the Louisiana Code, unlike the Civil Code, contains no provision for the converse proposition, viz: that private creditors have a right to be paid out of the individual property of a partner by preference to the partnership creditors of the firm to which he belongs. This counter-proposition cannot be deduced as a corollary from article 2894, because article 3152 rejects every privilege not *expressly* recognised by that Code.

MARTIN, J., delivered the opinion of the court.

Morgan, an appealing creditor, claims payment and distribution of the separate estate of the insolvent, before the creditors of the firm of Morgan, Dorsey & Co., of which the insolvent was a member.

He claims two distinct debts.

1. The first of 72,613 dollars 17 cents, is the amount of the five bonds executed by the insolvent in Philadelphia, on the 13th of September, 1824, bearing interest at the rate of six per cent. from the 1st of January following.

2. The second of 25,000 dollars, is the amount of a promissory note of the insolvent, subscribed in Philadelphia, in the month of October, 1825; and duly protested in the month of December following; bearing interest according to the law of Pennsylvania, at the rate of six per cent. per annum, from the date of the protest.

The appellant's claim, as to the first debt, was sustained; but the district court denied him any preference on the separate estate, over the creditors of the firm, in regard to the second debt.

The syndics and appellees, claim the reversal of the judgment *in toto.*

I. As to the first debt, they insist that the obligation of a contract, settles the right of the parties; the estate of the debtor represents his person, and is pledged for the performance of his obligations. Civil Code, 2089, 3152.

If the appellant claims a privilege in preference, he must produce a law which authorises it.

II. As to the second: The note was an accommodation paper, taken up and holden by C. Price & Morgan; of which firm the appellant is a member. They were not creditors for the whole amount, but only for the sum actually paid by them as endorsers for the insolvent.

The counsel for the appellant has replied, that the articles of the new Code relied on by the appellees, have no particular bearing on the first debt. The 298th article introducing no new principle; the 3152d article being inapplicable; because the debt under consideration was contracted before the adoption of the new Code.

The appellant's counsel does not deny that the creditor of an obligation *in solido*, may apply to any one of the debtors he pleases, without the debtor having the right to plead the benefit of division in the 2089th article; but he contends that partnership debts must be paid out of the partnership estate; and the private or separate debts, out of the private or separate estate; and that the partnership creditors who are unable to obtain payment out of the partnership estate, cannot resort to the separate or private estate, till its particular creditors are satisfied.

This principle, first acknowledged by the Roman law, was adopted by the jurisprudence of Spain, and makes a part of that of England and that of the United States.

"Si plures habuit servus creditores sed quosdam in mercibus certis, an omnes in iisdem confundendi erint et omnes in tributum vocandi; ut putes sagariam et linteariam et sep*a*ratos habuit creditores? Puto eos separatim in tributum vocari, unusquisque eorum merci magis quam ipsi credidit." *Ff. de Tribut. act. l. et si plures.*

"Sed si duas tabernas ejusdem negotiationis exercuit, et ego fui tabernæ, *v. g.* quod ad Boxinum habuit raciocinator, alius ejus quam trans Tiberim, equissimum puto separatim tributionem faciendam; ne ex alterius re mercive alii indemnes fiant, alii damnum sentiant." *Ibid. b. 5.*

"Teniendo el deudor varias negotiationes y por ellas acreedores personales, los de una notienen accion a pedir contra los bienes de la otra, hasta, que los de esta sean satisfechos, y solo pueden pretender su credito del sobrante; porque cada uno se considera mas acreedor en aquella que en la persona del deudor." *7 Febrero, ad. 2, 3, 3, D. 2.*

"Et quando sunt diversæ negotiationes non veniunt omnes creditores, communiter ad omnia: Sed quislibet in suam negotiationem. Quod non est in aliis creditoribus qui non contraxerunt ratione negotiationis: nam illi possunt ire ad quæcumque bona; et declarat hæc Paul. de Cart. in dicta, sect. Si plures, et tene ista menti." *Gregorio Lopez, Partida, 6, 14, 11.*

Merlinus teaches that the conclusion is the same, whether the negotiations be of different kinds of merchandise; 2. or of the same kind; 3. where the negotiations of the same, or of different kinds of merchandise are carried on in different parts of the same town; or 4. in different towns or provinces. *De Pignoribus*, 557, 4, 1; *Quest.* 13, 1; *Casaregis*, 140; *Dist.* 39, *n.* 18, 20; *Voel, ad Pandect*, 14, 4, 26, 7 and 8.

"Si un deudor tiene dos or mas negotiationes los acreedores de una de estas han de ocurir a cobrar de los bienes de ella, sin poder hacerlode los de la otra; sino en lo que sobrare, pagados los acreedores de ella; porque cada acreedor se creye mas en la negociacion en que lo fue, para serlo, que en la persona del deudor, lo qual no es en los demas acreedores, que non contraxeron por ocasion, de negociacion; los quales pueden ocurir a cobrar qualesquieras bienes del deudor.— Y lo mismo teniendo una sola negociacion aunque ocurran los acreedores de ella; u otros qualesquiera, porque no se creyeron mas en ella, que en la persona del deudor." *Cur. Phil. Prelacion, n.* 59 and 60, 2; *Curia Phillipica, Ill.* 395, n. 58, 59.

" Quando quis habet plures negotiationes, quilibet creditor debitum suum de illa negotiatione, cui credit, petat; nam videtur illi negotiationi credidisse et sic quasi separationis bene beneficium hic habetur." 2 *Bruneman,* 768.

The Civil Code, 1808, has made no alteration in this part of the Spanish law.

In the United States and in England, it is true, where there is no insolvency, the separate creditor of a partner may levy his execution against the estate of his debtor, on any part of the partnership estate; but in case of bankruptcy, the partnership estate is first applied to partnership debts. Com. 368 and 405; Hovenden's Supplement to Vesey, in 1 Vesey 236; Hankey *v.* Garrett, no. 3 and 4, Hammond's Equity Digest, 150, 158; 2 Day's Com. 161—3; 3 Vesey, 341; Chitty's Com. Law, 254; Desse's *v.* Plantin's Syndics, 6 *Martin,* 699.

From the above authorities, we conceive the district judge did not err, in supporting the appellant's claim on the first debt.

II. On the second, the inquiry is, whether the new Code, which was promulgated a few months before the note on which the claim rests was executed, has altered the old law.

The new Code expressly recognises the right of partnership creditors, to be paid out of the partnership estate, by preference to the private or separate creditors; art. 2794; but it also provides, that a privilege can be claimed only for those debts to which it is expressly granted by the Code, art. 3152.

Perhaps we might deduce, as a corollary from the principle recognised in the 2794th article, that, as partnership creditors exclude separate ones from the partnership estate, the latter must exclude the former from the separate; but this would be a distinction by implication; and the 3152d article rejects every privilege not expressly recognised by the Code.

It is true, at the time the new Code was adopted, the legislature contemplated the formation of a Code of Commerce; they frequently refer to it in the Civil Code, and expressly declare that its provisions will be paramount to those in the Civil. How far the commercial law of the country, as existing at the period of the adoption of the Civil Code, is to control the provisions of the latter till the enactment of the contemplated Code of Commerce, need not be inquired into in this case. Had the new Code been absolutely silent on the distribution of the property of persons engaged in commercial partnerships, in case of insolvency, we might conclude they have left the matter to be regulated by the pre-existing provisions. But they have acted on the subject; they have given a privilege to creditors of a partnership, on the partnership estate; have, by a general clause, abolished the privilege of separate creditors of a partner, on his separate estate. It is our duty to conclude, that the legislature has acted on the whole subject, in the Civil Code, and left nothing in this particular, to be regulated by the commercial law.*

It is, therefore, ordered, adjudged and decreed, that the judgment of the district court be affirmed, with costs.

Hennen, for the plaintiff.

Eustis, for the defendants.

---

* After this explicit decision that the most reasonable and beneficent principle in question was utterly abolished by the Louisiana Code, it will be seen with surprise that the organ of the court in this case should, in the case of *Hagan et al. v. Scott,* 10 *Lou. Rep.* 249, (a case arising in the year 1832, and so, entirely under the dominion of that Code,) decree the contrary of this decision, and refer to this decision as the basis of its conclusions: "These last debts were separate ones of W. P. Scott, and his separate creditors had a right to be paid out of his separate property, paramount to the claims of any partnership in which he had been concerned, 8 *N. S.* 599." Which is law, between these two antinomies?

EASTERN DISTRICT, MARCH TERM, 1830.

Daquin *et al. v.* Coiron *et al.*   VIII, N. S. 608.

Under the provision of the old Code, the possessor was not necessarily in bad faith from the time suit was commenced: but he owed fruits from the judicial demand.

The party cited in warranty has a right to receive the money which the plaintiff is directed to pay before he can recover possession, in case it is shown the defendant had not paid the purchase-money.

When the plaintiff recovers but is directed to pay a sum of money before he can enter on the premises, a certain time will be fixed for the payment thereof, and in default of his doing so, execution may issue against him.

When the interest is a legal consequence of the debt, a demand for the principal, is a demand for the principal and interest.

FIRST District.

Porter, J., delivered the opinion of the court.

This is an action in which heirs have sued, to obtain restitution of property descending to them from their ancestors, which was sold contrary to law. The legality of the alienation was examined when the case was last before us, and the plaintiffs' pretensions were declared to be well founded. The cause was remanded for inquiry into the value of the improvements, and the fruits: See 6 *N. S.* 674.

It now returns to us with a mass of evidence taken on these points, and a judgment of the court so unpalatable to the petitioners, and to the defendants, that they have both appealed from it.

The property, from the time it was first sold, passed through various hands, before it came into possession of the defendant Coiron. The respective vendors cited each other in warranty, in the order in which the sales had been made, but in the court below, as here, the case has been contested by the party, (Millaudon,) who sold to the person now in possession; and in the conflicting interests which have grown out of the respective situations of the parties, the warrantor is found opposing the plaintiffs' claim against the defendants, and contesting the defendants' demand to be paid for ameliorations.

By law, the owner who evicts a *bona fide* possessor, has the choice, either to pay him the value of the materials and workmanship employed in putting improvements on the property, or to reimburse him the enhanced value which they confer on it. That privilege was exercised in this instance by the plaintiffs, and they chose the latter alternative.

The court below considered that the property had been increased in value, in the sum of 24,750 dollars, from which it deducted the fruits made since the decision in this tribunal, annulling the defendants' title.—These fruits the judge estimated at 5136 dollars. To the balance remaining after deducting the latter from the former amount, he added 19,583 dollars, which had been paid by the original purchaser, in discharge of a debt due by the ancestor of the petitioners, and directed these sums to be paid by them before they took possession.

The court further considered, that as the mortgage existing on the plantation had been discharged by the warrantor, and not by the defendant in possession, the plaintiffs must pay its amount to the former, with interest at five per cent. from the date of the judgment in this court, in relation to the title; but that the enhanced value should be paid to the latter. In default of these payments being made within two months, the judgment authorised execution to be issued against the plaintiffs. The costs were directed to be paid equally by the petitioners and the defendant.

The claims of the plaintiffs, and defendant, who are both appellants, as against Millaudon, who is cited in warranty, require a distinct and separate consideration. We shall first take up those of the petitioners.

They complain of the judgment below, on the following grounds.

1. The mode of ascertaining the enhanced value of the land in litigation, adopted by the judge *a quo*, is correct and equitable, but the judge's calculations are erroneous, and the estimate of the improvements on the premises, far from being underrated, is beyond the real amount of the said enhanced value.

2. The plaintiffs are allowed a share in the revenue, or crops of the plantation, only from the date of the judgment declaring the

[Daquin *et al. v. Coiron et al.*]

defendants' title null, when by law they are entitled to fruits from the institution of this suit. Civil Code, 103, art. 7; 481, art. 30.

3. Admitting that the plaintiffs can claim fruits from the date of the judgment only, viz. from the 31st of December, 1827, they are entitled to a share in the crop of 1827, or such part thereof as was gathered after the 31st of December, 1827. And moreover, there should be a clause in the judgment, reserving to the plaintiffs the right of claiming by a further action their share in the crop made on the plantation, from and after the date of the latter judgment, namely, in the crop of 1829, until they take possession of the premises.

4. No interest is to be allowed to the defendants, because they claimed none in their answer, and because the sum to be paid to them was not liquidated. And if any interest be allowed, it must be only from the date of the latter judgment, viz., from the 6th of July, 1829, and not from the date of the former judgment, of 31st of December, 1827, when the amount to be paid to the plaintiffs was unliquidated. Code of Practice, 553.

5. No execution, as contemplated by the judge *a quo*, can issue against the plaintiffs, unless they take possession of the premises; at all events, too brief a delay was allowed to the plaintiffs.

6. Costs ought not to be divided, but must be borne by the defendant.

I. The judge of the first instance, finding it impossible to reconcile the testimony of the witnesses introduced by the plaintiffs and warrantor, respectively, and believing them all equally entitled to credit, added together the whole amount of their estimations of the value of the land in 1812, and the present time; and dividing the sum obtained from the addition, by the number sworn, adopted the product as the real value of the property, at the two epochs just mentioned. His decision is complained of by both parties. The appellants think he adopted the true mode of reaching the truth, but contend he erred in his calculations. The appellee denies the correctness of the course pursued by him, and insists that proof should be weighed, not counted. Of the truth of the last observation, there can be no doubt, but the difficulty in this case is, to obtain any satisfactory result from weighing it. We have balanced it repeatedly, and are free to confess we find it impossible. A number of the witnesses on each side, appear equally respectable; their means of information about the same; their integrity unimpeached; yet their conclusions are utterly variant and contradictory. Without, therefore, adopting the mode resorted to by the judge, to arrive at the result obtained by him, we are of opinion that we could make no decision in the case which, if it did not almost entirely disregard the evidence on one side or other, would be freer from objection, than that which the judge *a quo* has come to. Admitting his calculations to be erroneous, (and they are not materially so,) the conclusion appears to us a fair medium of the opposite and conflicting proof exhibited. If there be a preponderance in the proof on either side, it is in favor of the warrantor, and the difference between the amount allowed by the judgment, and that which would be obtained by a calculation, allowing the same weight to the testimony of all the witnesses, is not so great as to authorise us to make any change in the decision of the court below.

II. The second ground contests the correctness of the judgment, in relation to the time from which the defendant was condemned to account for the fruits. If the judge of the first instance has erred in this respect, it is an error into which he has fallen with this court, as the point in question was decided in the case of Donaldson *et al. v. Dorsey's* Syndics, 7. *N. S.* 376. A single decision, however, on any question, can not be considered as settling the jurisprudence in relation to it, and we have examined the subject again, as if it were presented to us for the first time.

The argument at the bar extended not only to the doctrine respecting fruits, but to that in regard to improvements which might be placed on the soil by a possessor, who was evicted in virtue of a superior title.

In the case of Packwood *v.* Richardson, 1 *N. S.* 405, we decided, that a possessor in good faith, did not necessarily cease to be so, by the commencement of a suit for the property possessed. We came to that conclusion on the provision of the old Civil Code, which declares, that a person who had entered upon property with a just title, and who is a *bona fide* possessor, ceases to be one, from the moment the defects are made known to him in the title under which he holds. We thought, that knowledge of an adverse title, was not in every instance, knowledge that it was a better one, and that until such knowledge was communicated to the possessor, the defects of his own title were not known to him; and we supposed ourselves fortified in this construction, by a reference to commentators on the Napoleon Code, the provisions of which on this subject, are *verbatim* ours.

The authorities cited by the court in that case, we still think sustain the ground assumed by us. It is true a passage from another part of Toullier's works seems to countenance a contrary doctrine, and decisions have been made in some of the tribunals of France, giving a different construction to the law, from that which this court considered the true one. We leave to others the task of reconciling the opinions which may exist in that country. It is possible we may have misunderstood those cited when the subject first came under our consideration. But if we did, it does not follow we have erred in the construction given to our law. Such a consequence could only result from these decisions and opinions being of binding authority in this state. As they are not, the correctness of our opinion must be tested by reason and common sense, which ought to have, and we trust do possess, more authority within these walls, than the doctrine of any jurist, ancient or modern. Great respect is due to the opinions of enlightened men and learned tribunals of any country.

[Daquin et al. v. Coiron et al.]

In cases where the understanding of the court is in suspense, or doubt, they may well give it a direction; but when the judges who compose this tribunal, have a clear and perfect conviction of their own, on a legal question, they would fail in their duty to express that conviction, although others may consider it wrong, because it is opposed to great names, and foreign opinions. 1 *N. S.* 409; *Toullier's Droit Civil Francais, vol.* 3, *no.* 76; *vol.* 4, 332, *no.* 313; *Pothier's Traité de Propriété, no.* 342 *(ed.* 1807*) in notis; Jurisprudence du Code Civil, vol.* 3, *p.* 64; *Denever's Journal de la Cour de Cassation, vol.* 11, *p.* 207.

The article of our Code already referred to, declares the good faith of him who has entered into possession under a just title, to cease, so soon as the defects in his title are made known to him. The first question which this law presents, is, what is meant by the expression, *made known to him.* Taken literally, they may mean either certain knowledge of the defects, or mere notice, that others consider them to exist. Construed in relation to the subject matter, they must be understood in the former sense. For, as good faith consists in the belief of a just title, a possession *animo domini,* bad faith can only arise on the destruction of that belief. The next question is, whether the commencement of a suit always makes these defects known; whether it produces a conviction in the mind of the possessor, that his title is bad, and his adversary's good? The law has not said it shall, therefore there is no technical bad faith created by the action being commenced. In point of fact, such conviction is not produced on the mind of the possessor, in all cases. In the greater number, we believe he honestly thinks he has a better title than the party to whom he is opposed, up to the very moment when judgment is pronounced by the tribunal, which decides in the last resort. This belief of ours, we imagine, will be shared by all those who have had any experience of the motives which operate on men's minds in defence of their rights, real or imaginary. Independent of the delusions of self-love, there are cases where the coolest and most unbiassed mind might fall into error. Facts may be essential to a correct understanding of the case, which are never known until the testimony is heard on the trial, and never can be known before it. The law may be so unsettled and uncertain, that the counsel who advise, may well draw different conclusions from the judges who decide. So that under the interpretation contended for, cases might occur, where the party who entered into possession *bona fide,* would be advised by his counsel, he had the better title; where the court which tried it in the first instance thought so; where even this court might think so; and on an application for a rehearing, change its opinion; and yet during all this time, while this general delusion prevails as to the validity of his pretensions, the possessor is to be considered in bad faith, because he did not know the law better than his counsel who advised—the judge who tried his cause in the inferior court, and because he shared, for a time, with the tribunal, in the last resort, a conviction, that he had a better title than his adversary.

A conclusion which is so contrary to reason and an acquaintance with the affairs of men, never could have been adopted in any country, if a positive rule had not existed in it, that good faith should cease with the commencement of a suit. The minds of men who live long under regulations of almost any kind, naturally come to consider them founded in reason and truth, and the bias, which habits of thought thus produce, insensibly extends itself to the examination of every question arising out of a change in these rules.— With the destruction of the rule, however, we think all argument derived from it should cease.

We still, therefore, remain satisfied, that, according to the provisions of the old Code, bad faith was made to depend on an investigation of all the circumstances of each case, and not on the particular period the possessor received notice his title was contested. And in the three several cases in which we applied this doctrine to the right of the defendant, to be paid for improvements, we do not believe any error was committed. 1 *N. S.* 409; 7 *Ibid.* 376. 650.

But in relation to the right of enjoying fruits, the legislature has thought proper to make a special provision. By the 30th article of the old Code, p. 480, it is provided, that all which are reaped after demand, shall be restored to the party recovering possession.

There is perhaps a sound reason for this distinction. In the case of improvements placed on the soil, the owner is enriched by the money expended by the possessor; the property is increased in value. But where fruits are reaped, he is benefitted. In the case of eviction, then he presents himself in first hypothesis, *damno evitando*—in the latter, *lucro captando.* The equity arising from these different positions, is by no means the same. The 39th and 41st laws of the title of the 3d Partidas, seem to recognise a rule of the same kind. By them, the defendant was to pay the fruits gathered, after issue joined. But no limitation is affixed in respect to his right to be paid for improvements.

We conclude, therefore, that the plaintiffs are entitled to claim the fruits from the institution of the suit.

III. The third point will be noticed, when we proceed to examine the facts of the case, and apply the law to them. The fourth relates to the interest allowed by the judgment.

It is objected, that it was not claimed in the answer, and that it was allowed on a sum not liquidated.

The 553d article of the Code of Practice declares that interest shall not be allowed by the judgment, unless the same has been expressly claimed, and then only in cases in which the law permits such interest to be stipulated.

We do not understand this provision to apply to cases, where the interest is a legal consequence of the obligation, on which suit is brought. It was made, as the last clause of the article shows, for those cases where the payment of interest was stipulated, and where interest could not be given without that stipulation. In such cases, where the petition, or claim in reconvention, as the case may be, only asks for an execution of part of the contract, the judgment cannot go beyond the demand in the pleadings.

But where the interest due, is a legal consequence of the debt, without any stipulation, a demand for the principal, is a demand of both principal and interest; the one necessarily follows the other.—The amount claimed here was sufficiently liquidated, and we do not see, that in this part of the judgment, any error was committed.

The property which the plaintiffs had recovered, was sold to pay a debt of their ancestors; and the judgment of the inferior court directed that money to be repaid, before they took possession of the premises, together with the increased value of the plantation. In default of these payments being made in two months, the decree authorised execution to issue against the plaintiffs.

They complain of this, and admitting the correctness of the principle, they contend that the time allowed for them to make payment was too short; that a greater delay should have been granted.

The question presented to the court by this objection, is quite novel. The plaintiffs, who have sued for the premises, and who have obtained judgment for them, certainly can not expect that the defendant should remain their tenant at will, for years, liable to be evicted at any moment they choose. If he is deprived of the land, and its free enjoyment, by a judgment which they have provoked, he has as much right to receive the money decreed to him in consequence of that judgment, as they have to get possession of the plantation. His demand in the answer, was one in reconvention; it is the very instance put in the Code of Practice to illustrate this species of action, article 375. We think the principle on which the judge decided correct; but the judgment requires some modification. The plaintiffs have no right to the premises, until they make a tender of the money. The defendant, or warrantor, has no right to the money until the property is tendered to the plaintiffs.

According to the estimation of the court of the first instance, which we adopt, the increased value of the property is 24,750 dollars. From this must be deducted the fruits reaped since the inception of the suit. It was commenced in December, 1826, and there are the crops of two years accounted for. The judge below considered, that as the plaintiffs had furnished the land and buildings, with some slaves; and the defendant, slaves, animals and plantation utensils, and superintended the whole, that each should take one-half of the net product. We think the judge did not err by so deciding; it appears equitable, and is supported by the evidence given on the trial. The crops of the two years already stated, amount to 24,342 dollars 46 cents, to the half of which, 12,171 dollars 23 cents, the plaintiffs are entitled. This deducted from 24,750 dollars, leaves 12,578 dollars 77 cents, which they must pay before they can take possession of the premises.

They must also pay the sum arising out of the original sale of the plantation, which was appropriated to the discharge of their ancestors' debts. The amount is contested. The warrantor, Millaudon, insists it is 23,500 dollars. The plaintiffs say it is only 19,583. This difference arises from a payment made by Dufau, who was surety for the ancestors of the plaintiffs, in the contract with Evans. Dufau, who was examined, states that he paid this amount out of his own funds, and that Daquin afterwards repaid him a certain sum: he could not recollect how much. It is clear, therefore, the whole sum of 23,550 dollars is not due. Nor do we think any part of this payment can be claimed by the defendants. The money was paid by Dufau, as surety of the Daquins, before the land was decreed to him, in consequence of his purchase in the name of Massicot. It is only those who have purchased in consequence of a sale made to discharge the ancestor's debts, that can demand repayment from the minors. Now the sale made on the demand of Evans, was not for 23,500 dollars, but for the sum allowed by the judge. That sum the plaintiffs must repay, with interest at five per cent. from the commencement of the suit.

By the judgment of the court of the first instance, this sum was directed to be paid to Millaudon, who was cited in warranty, and the balance due for the improvements was decreed to the defendant, Coiron. The latter has appealed, and has contended that the whole amount is due to him; that if Millaudon should be considered as representing the previous purchasers, he represents all the rights which Millaudon had.

As a general rule this is perhaps correct. *Prima facie,* the money should be paid to the possessor. But if he abandons the defence as he did here, throws it on his warrantor, and asks for judgment against him for all damages which arise out of the eviction; it is open to the warrantor to show, that the party in possession is indebted to him, in a larger amount than that for which the judgment is demanded. The plaintiff's right to receive the money, which the original purchaser paid in discharge of the plaintiff's ancestor's debts, depends not only on having bought the property, but having paid for it. He has no right to the reimbursed money, which he has not expended.

The case was argued before us, as between the defendant and his warrantor. But no judgment was given in the court below on the issue formed between them; and when this cause was last before us, we gave as one reason why he could not render a final judgment, that the rights of the vendors, cited respectively in warranty, had not been passed on. It is clear we can not decide a case between parties in this tribunal, on whose conflicting claims no judgment has been rendered in the inferior court. We must either affirm or reverse, and we could do neither here.

The greatest difficulty we feel in remanding the cause, is created by the situation in which the plaintiffs are placed. They should not be deprived of the possession of their property, during the period the

[Daquin,*et al. v.* Coiron *et al.*]

defendant and his warranty are settling their pretensions to the money which the petitioners are compelled to pay one or the other. We think the interests of all will be best preserved by permitting the plaintiffs to obtain possession, on depositing the money in court; and in case they do not do so, to reserve to the defendant and his warrantor, the right to enforce payment, so soon as it is decided which of them is entitled to the money.

· It is, therefore, ordered, adjudged and decreed, that the judgment of the district court, be annulled, avoided and reversed, and it is further ordered, adjudged and decreed, that the plaintiffs do recover of the defendants, the property claimed in the petition; but that before entering on, or taking out a writ of possession for the same, they deposit in the hands of the clerk of the district court, the sum of thirty-two thousand one hundred and sixty-one dollars seventy-seven cents, with interest at five per cent. on the sum of nineteen thousand five hundred and eighty-three dollars, from the 13th of December, 1826. Reserving, however, to the defendant, I. Coiron, andt he warrantor Laurent Millaudon, the right to enforce payment of the same, on a final decision of the cause, in case the plaintiffs previous thereto, do not pay the said sum into court.

· And it is further ordered, adjudged and decreed, that this case, so far as it respects the rights of the vendor, cited in warranty, be remanded for further proceedings, and that the appellee pay the costs of this appeal.

Quemper, for the plaintiffs.
Denis and *Mazureau*, for the defendants.

The Louisiana Insurance Company *v.* Morgan, Sheriff of Orleans, and Gardere, Treasurer of the State. VIII, N. S. 629.

A tax levied on the stock in trade of an insurance company, extends to capital secured as well as paid in.

The oath of the president and directors is not conclusive as to the amount of stock.

FOURTH District.

Porter, J., delivered the opinion of the court.

By an act of the legislature approved the 27th of March, 1813, an annual tax of twenty-five cents, is imposed on every 100 dollars of the stock in trade of banks, insurance, and other incorporated companies.

The stock of the company who are plaintiffs in this suit, is divided into 300 shares, of 1000 dollars each, one-tenth of which has been paid in, and securities taken for the remaining nine-tenths, pursuant to the first section of the act of incorporation.

The treasurer of the state, acting under the advice of the attorney-general, conceived that the company should pay this tax, not only on the sum which the stockholders had paid in, but on that which they had furnished security to pay, and the company refusing to acquiesce in this construction of the law, he issued a writ of seizure, to compel them.—This writ they enjoined, and the proceedings which followed, form the case now presented for our decision.

The judge below, after hearing the testimony, and the arguments offered on it, made the injunction perpetual. The state appealed.

From the facts established on the trial, it appears, that up to the present time, the treasurer has been accustomed to demand nothing more, than the sum due to the state on the amount of the capital stock paid in. But the attorney-general urges it was through error, this construction was given to the act, imposing a tax on the stock of the company, and insists the state has not only a right to claim the tax for the past year, according to the interpretation which she now puts on the law, but also the arrearages which would be due on the former payments, if that interpretation be correct. The order of seizure, enjoined, issued for both.

It was admitted, that the president of the company declared, to the state treasurer, that the capital stock of said company, was all subscribed, that one-tenth of it was paid in cash, and the remaining nine-tenths of it secured.

The first objection made to the present claim, on behalf of the state, is derived from the 36th section of the act of the legislature, imposing the tax. It provides, " That the treasurer of the state shall be, and is hereby authorised, to demand from the president and directors of banks, insurance, or other incorporated commercial companies, by writing, and under oath, a declaration of the amount of their stock in trade; and from these declarations, he, the said treasurer, shall establish the amount of the tax, due by each of the said incorporated banks, insurance, or other commercial companies; and the said president and directors of such companies, shall be bound to pay the said tax, quarterly, into the hands of the state treasurer," &c., &c.

That the state might, in levying a tax, think proper to consider, and so enact, that the oath of the party interested in diminishing it, should be conclusive as to the amount due, cannot be called in question. But a clear and unequivocal declaration of their intention would be necessary, to justify such a conclusion. The very existence of legislation, and the necessity for laws of any kind, rest on a presumption of feelings in our nature, and motives of action governing men, totally opposed to such a construction. We do not recollect a single instance, in any statute, by which duties were imposed, or obligations created that the right of furnishing evidence, which would be conclusive as to their being correctly discharged, is conferred on the party burthened by them. It would be well, if this could be safely done. But in all these cases, law makers presume, that there may be fraud; that with the purest intentions, there may be error; and that the delusions of self-love, render it as unsafe to trust men with power over the proof, as it would be to permit them to sit in judgment, and decide their own case.

Our legislature was not so imprudent, as the argument addressed to us on this subject supposes. By the latter part of the section relied on, it is provided, "that in case of negligence or refusal of the president and directors of the above mentioned companies, to make a fair declaration of the stock in trade, in the manner prescribed by this act, they shall be liable to pay a double tax," &c.

We have seen, that it is not from negligence or refusal to make any return, but from negligence or refusal to make a fair one, that the penalty is incurred. That the legislature intended this penalty to follow an unfair return, as well as making none at all, is evident, from their annexing a condition to it; for whether it was fair, or not, could only be ascertained after it was examined. It is equally clear, they did not understand the declaration was to be taken as conclusive, for if they had so contemplated, the requiring it to be a fair one, was vain and nugatory. Why impose a penalty for an unfair return, if every return was to be taken as fair? Why require the declaration of the president and directors to be made in a particular manner, if that declaration, no matter how contrary to the manner prescribed, was to be evidence, and conclusive evidence too, of its being given in the mode required by the statute?

We have been unable to find any satisfactory answers to these questions; and even if we had found them, the present case would not authorise the application of the doctrine on which the appellees rely. The statement of facts contains an admission, "that the president of the Louisiana Insurance Company declared, to the state treasurer, that the capital stock of said company was all subscribed, that one-tenth of it was paid in cash, and the remaining nine-tenths secured." This declaration does not confine the stock in trade, to the amount paid in. It states the facts, in relation to the mode the stock is held, and leaves the inference to be drawn, whether all, or part of it, is to be considered as the stock on which the company is trading. This statement, if it be different from the terms used in the treasurer's receipt, as making a part of the admissions of the parties, on record, controls it.

This objection disposed of, we are required to examine the case on what may be properly called its merits.

The clause in the act of our legislature, on which this contest has arisen, is in the following words:

"Stocks of all banks, insurance, and other incorporated commercial companies, established, or to be established in this state, by any authority whatever, shall, after the passage of this act, be liable to an annual tax of twenty-five cents, on every 100 dollars of their stock in trade, to be collected as prescribed by this act.

The decision of the case, therefore, turns on the correct interpretation to be given to these expressions in the law, *stock in trade*. It would appear to lie in a narrow compass, and yet the discussion has extended far and wide, in search of the meaning of these terms.

. The intention of the legislature is to be collected from the whole context of the act, in which the passage already cited is found; from that of the act incorporating the company; from the literal meaning of the language; and from the meaning which should be attached to that language, when used in relation to the subject matter.

We shall first consider it under the means which the acts themselves afford, for obtaining a correct knowledge of the meaning of the law maker.

The act incorporating the company which are plaintiffs in this suit, by its first section, among other things, provides, "that the capital stock of the said corporation shall not exceed the sum of 300,000 dollars divided into 300 shares of 1000 dollars each; to be paid, one-tenth part at the time of subscribing, either in money, or in bank notes of any of the banks established in New Orleans; the remaining nine-tenths, by such instalments as the directors, hereinafter mentioned, shall appoint. Provided, however, That the first board of directors to be chosen, as hereinafter directed, shall within one month after their appointment, take good and satisfactory security, to consist either in bank, or other stock, or mortgages on real estates, for the payment of the remaining nine-tenths, whenever it shall be deemed expedient to call for the same; and in case of losses accruing to the said company, the stockholders shall in no case be liable, or in any way answerable, for more than the amount of their respective shares."

The 14th section declares that "no insurance shall be made by the said corporation, until the several securities to be taken for the nine-tenths of the said capital stock, shall have been received by the directors of said company.

Under these provisions, the company say, their only stock in trade is the one-tenth paid in; and yet the act of incorporation says, they shall make no insurance, that is, they shall not trade at all, until the one-tenth is paid, and the remaining nine-tenths secured. If then the capital paid in is alone the stock in trade, we are forced to conclude that it was the intention of the legislature, the company should not do business on their stock in trade, but that they might do it on that, which, according to the argument now used, is not a part of their stock in trade.

A construction which at once carries us to such strange consequences, certainly requires no particular refutation from the court. Unless the company has violated its charter, the position it now assumes must be untrue. It is prohibited from making any insurance on the one-tenth of the stock paid in. It then follows, that it must have either not complied with the conditions on which it was incorporated or that it has done business on the capital paid in, and something else. If there were any thing more than the 30,000 dollars the declaration of the directors and president have been made in error since the first payment of the tax. We are left in no doubt, as to what formed the addition to the money paid in, and on which the appellees have been doing business. It was the securities obtained for the payment of the nine-tenths of the stock, for without them, the company were prohibited from making any insurance, whatever.

Supposing us without this strong and unequivocal expression of the understanding of the legislature, and that we were compelled to decide the case alone on the meaning of the words used, would there be any more difficulty? We think not. The terms, *stock in trade*, mean the capital on which the company transacts its business—that which it uses to accomplish the purpose for which it was formed. The attempt to restrain the capital to the amount of cash paid in by the partners, is to us of the first impression. We are unable to see why it should be so limited. Stock may consist of other things, on which, either an individual or a company, may trade as surely, and perhaps as successfully, as on money. In the case of an ordinary partnership, where all the members of the firm, but one, had contributed a certain sum, for the formation of a common stock, and that one gave his obligation to pay his share when called on, could it be doubted, that the debt thus due by the individual partner, would make a part of the stock in trade of the company? We should suppose not. Louisiana Code, 2779. The case before us is stronger. This association was formed alone for the purpose of effecting insurance. Its business, unlike that of a bank, was not to lend out money. Its transactions produce only a responsibility depending on contingencies. It may trade for a long time without disbursing a dollar, except for ordinary expenses. All that it requires to enable it to do business, is to inspire the public with confidence in its integrity and capacity to meet any losses for which it may become liable. Under such circumstances, where the security furnished by the stockholders, to pay whenever the necessities of the corporation may require it, enables that corporation to insure with the same freedom, and to the same extent, as if the cash was in their vaults; there is not a shadow of reason, for distinguishing between that part of the stock which is secured, and that which is paid in. Both are the stock in trade, because both are the stock on which the company does trade: both serve the same purposes: both contribute to the production of profits. It is not pretended the company has restrained its operations to the amount paid in. It has not been shown that the securities it has obtained from the stockholders, do not enable it to make insurances to the whole amount secured. In the absence of any proof, we are bound to presume from the nature of the business, that the unpaid part of the stock, enables the company to do so, and it can not be doubted that its operations are conducted in reference to them. When to these considerations, we add those drawn from the act of incorporation, we feel compelled to state, that we think the claim set up by the appellees, to be wholly without foundation.

It is the strong conviction of the error into which the company, and the former officers of the state have fallen, that prevents us from giving that weight to the interpretation so long put on the act, which the judge of the first instance considered it his duty to do.—The state is not bound by the error of one of its officers. It is not placed beyond the protection of its own law, that where there has been a mistake, there exists a remedy to rectify it. Much stress has been laid on the accounts of the treasurer being annually submitted to the examination of a committee of the legislature; the report of that committee to both houses; and their acquiescence in the construction given to the law by the treasurer, from no steps having been taken to correct his error. This argument is entitled to some weight, but not to all that which was given to it. We can not shut our eyes as to the manner these things are done. The committee who examine the accounts of the treasurer do not report the details of them to the legislature. So that it is only the presumption of their acquiescence, and not that of both branches of the legislature, which can be invoked. It is only theirs, too, without its being shown their attention was ever drawn to the matter under consideration. It rarely happens, we apprehend, that the gentlemen charged with that duty, take the statute book in hand, to see whether the collecting officers have properly interpreted the laws imposing taxes. Special circumstances may make them do so in some cases. Generally, we believe their principal attention is directed to see that all the money received, is accounted for. A point which has passed *sub silentio* in courts of justice, is justly entitled to little consideration, in establishing a legal principle. The silence of a committee of the legislature, is not worthy of much more, when invoked as a guide for a judicial decision. It might make some weight in the balance of a doubtful case. It can effect but little, the scales of a clear one.

It has been contended, that the terms used in the French text of the law, namely, *chaque cent piastres effectives*, are different from those used in the English, *every hundred dollars of their stock, used in trade*, or at least show the propriety of restricting them to the capital paid in. The literal translation of the French words just quoted, would be, *every one hundred dollars that are effective*. We believe, that every 100 dollars of the capital, secured, as directed by the charter, are as effective in the hands of the president and directors, as the same sum paid in, and we do not, therefore, see, how the appellee's case is strengthened by the argument drawn from this source.

A great deal has been said on the term *stock*, used in the first part of the section imposing this tax; and those of *stock in trade*, employed in the latter part of the section, to designate, on what portion of that stock the tax should be levied. They meant, it is said, something different, and they can only mean that for which the appellees contend; because there can be no stock until it is subscribed for, and after it is subscribed, it admits of no other division, than that of capital paid in, and capital secured.

We see no difficulty in this; it is true there can be no stock until it is subscribed; but after subscribed for, it may not be in trade. It may be swallowed up by losses, and though in the charter of incorporation, the directors are prohibited, on such an event, to make any dividend until the stock is restored, yet, until that is done, the company are trading on less than the stock subscribed for. The provision of the law, making the tax depend on the capital used, not on that subscribed, was wise and equitable. And as the amount must fluctuate, the oath of the president and directors was required to ascertain it.

The plea of prescription is disposed of, by the law of the 29th title of the 3d Partidas, which was in force to the year 1828.

It is, therefore, ordered, adjudged and decreed, that the judgment of the parish court be annulled, avoided and reversed; that the injunction granted in the case be dissolved, and that the appellees pay costs in both courts.

Maybin, for the plaintiffs.
Morphy, Attorney-General, for the defendants.

Boatner v. Ventress. VIII, N. S. 644.

The decision of the board of commissioners under the authority of the United States, in regard to donation claims in Florida, is final, and cannot be re-examined in a court of justice.

The recitals in a title emanating from government are evidence against the possessor without title.

That a patent is not necessary in all cases to confer a legal title to soil, of which the government is the proprietor, cannot be doubted.

In many of the States, no action of ejectment can be maintained by a donee without a patent, but in Louisiana an equitable title may be enforced in a court of law.*

THIRD District, Judge of the Eighth presiding.

PORTER, J., delivered the opinion of the court.

This is a petitory action. The petitioner states, that he is owner legally and equitably, of 586$\frac{84}{100}$ acres of land, situate in the parish of Feliciana, under the laws of the United States, by virtue of a settlement originally made by John Cooper. That his claim has been contested by Edwin O'Neale, and the heirs of Lovill Ventress, before the register of the land office and receiver of public moneys of the United States, at St. Helena court house, who have passed upon the merits of their pretensions, and decided the land to be the property of the petitioner. That in virtue of their decree, the land has been surveyed, and every thing has been done preparatory to the issuing of a patent by the government of the United States. The petition concludes, by stating, that one Glover had entered on the premises, and held the possession of them, which he refuses to deliver up.

Glover disclaimed all title to the property, and averred, that he held under the heirs of Ventress. He prayed that he might be discharged. This prayer was granted, on the heirs of Ventress appearing and pleading to the action.

* This case was very advantageously used by the committee on elections of the House of Representatives of Louisiana, in its ingenious report on the contested election of the Parish of Jefferson, in 1838, I. T. Preston, Esq., sitting member. Quære, how complete must a purchaser's or donee's title to United States land be, before he is admissible to the polls as a voter? Is the receiver's receipt of the price sufficient evidence of title for a citizen who claims to vote under the eighth section of the second article of the constitution? The house ultimately rejected the votes of such persons, but for a combination of reasons, whereof the chief was the want of any bona fide intention to purchase land.

[Bonner v. Ventress.]

In their answer, they state, that they are entitled by law, to the estate of their late father, who was justly entitled to the premises, under the several acts of congress in relation to lands in that section of country, where the *locus in quo* is situated;—that he held it under an actual settlement, occupancy and improvement, made by John James Simmonds, about twenty years ago; and that in the month of July, 1820, a certificate, on the claim of Simmonds, was issued by the register and receiver of the land office, to one Pulaski Cage, who has transmitted the same to the respondents.

They further pleaded prescription, and in case of eviction, claimed the value of their improvements.

The cause was twice tried in the inferior court, and in both instances there was a verdict for the defendant. On the first trial, the judge charged the jury in favor of the defendant, on the plea of prescription, and afterwards set the verdict aside, on a motion for a new trial, being convinced he had erroneously expounded the law on that point.—On the second trial, the court instructed the jury, that the plaintiff could not recover, because he had failed to prove an assignment to him, of the right of the settler, under whose improvement and occupancy the certificate and order issued.

This case was argued last year, but the bench not being at that time full, owing to the indisposition of the presiding justice, and the judges who heard it not being able to come to a conclusion satisfactorily to themselves, it has been again very fully discussed. As the decision of the points involved in the cause is of importance to a considerable portion of the citizens of the state, we have bestowed on it a great deal of our attention.

From the statement already made of the allegations in the petition it is seen, that the plaintiff mainly relies on the decision of the commissioners of the United States in his favor. The evidence introduced in the cause, shows such a decision to have been made, and the first and by far the most important inquiry devolving on us, is the effect which should be given to it.

For a proper understanding of this point, reference must be had to the several acts of congress, for the adjustment and settlement of land claims in Florida.

Both parties claim by donation from the United States, and the first provision we meet with in respect to those who acquired property in this manner from the general government in that section of country is found in the eighth section of an act of congress, passed the 25th of April 1812, by which it is enacted, "That the said commissioners be, and they are hereby authorised and required to collect and report to congress at their next session, a list of all the actual settlers on land in said district, respectively, who have no claim to land derived from the French, British or Spanish governments, at the time at which such settlements were made." Land Laws, page 606.

Whether the report was made within the time prescribed by the act, the evidence in the case does not inform us. The next legislation we find on the subject, is an act entitled, " An act for adjusting the claims to land, and establishing land offices in the districts east of the island of New Orleans," passed the 3d of May, 1829. By the 8th section of which it is provided, " That every person, or his or her legal representative, whose name is comprised on the lists, or register of claims, reported by the said commissioners, and the persons embraced in the list of actual settlers, or their legal representatives, not having any written evidence of claim reported as aforesaid, shall where it appears by the said report, or by the said lists, that the land claimed or settled on, had been actually inhabited or cultivated by such person or persons in whose right he claims; on or before the 15th day of April, 1813, be entitled to a grant for the land so claimed, or settled on as a donation."

The 12th section of this act provides for the issuing a certificate by the register and receiver, for all claims confirmed by it, and declares, that if, on presentation to the general land office, of such certificate, the commissioner thereof shall be of opinion, that it " has been fairly obtained, according to the true intent and meaning of this act, then, and in that case, a patent shall be granted in like manner as for other lands of the United States." Land Laws, 75, p. 759.

In the year 1822, the legislature of the United States again acted in relation to these lands, and in the 4th section of an act passed by them on the 8th of May, of that year, after having made provision for the manner in which they should be surveyed, it is declared, " that in relation to all such claims which may conflict, or in any manner interfere, the said registers and receivers of the public moneys of the respective districts, shall have power to decide between the parties, and shall in their decision, be governed by such conditional lines or boundaries, as may have been agreed on between the parties either verbally or in writing, at any time prior to the passage of this act." *   *   *   *   *   *   *

" Provided, however, That, should it be made appear, to the satisfaction of the register and receiver of public moneys, of the respective districts in any such case, that the subsequent settler had obtruded on the claim of the former, and had made his establishment after having been forbid so to do, the said register and receiver of public moneys, shall have power to decide between the parties, according to the circumstances of the case and the principles of justice. Land Laws of the United States, 824.

In virtue of the authority thus conferred, the register and receiver decided, that Simmonds, under whom the defendants claim, having made and sold another improvement, before he settled on the *locus in quo*, and having been forbid to do so by Cooper, under whom the plaintiff sets up title, neither the heirs of Ventress, nor any other person claiming from Simmonds, had a just or equitable title to the land in question.

The defendants resist the force and effect which the plaintiff seeks to give to this decision. They contend, that by virtue of the provisions of the act of 1819, the quantity of land therein mentioned, was given to them, and that a legal title is vested in them to the premises, of which they cannot be deprived, except by a judgment of a court of justice, and the law of the land.

The solution of the question on which the cause turns, depends on the correctness of this position. If a legal title was vested in the claimants, under the acts of Congress already cited, at any time previous to the decree of the commissioners, it is very clear, that a decision by officers of the government cannot have the force of *res judicata*, nor deprive them of any right which they may have had previous to such decision.

In the case of M'Clung *v.* Silliman, the Supreme Court of the United States said, that whatever doubts may have, from time to time, been suggested, as to the supremacy of the United States in its legislative, judicial or executive power, no one has ever contested its supreme right to dispose of its own property in its own way. Without this authority, no one could rightfully entertain any other opinion. The parties to this suit, and others, who have received donations from the government, must, therefore, be content to take them with all the conditions it has thought proper to annex to its gift. 6 Wheaton, 605.

On a question of this kind, great respect is due to the opinions of those from whom the title emanates: originating, as did these opinions, in a desire to benefit the *bona fide* settler, we are bound to presume that the same liberal motives which operated in the commencement of their legislation on this subject, governed them to the end: more especially as nothing has been taken back, which was given; and the object of their later enactments, was only to carry into effect, the principle which it is presumed governed them throughout. Now, the act of 1822, is the legislative construction, by those best acquainted with their own motives, of that of 1819. It is manifest, congress did not understand that a legal title was vested in the settler, by the provisions of this statute. For if they thought so, they would have left the grantees to their rights at law, well knowing they could not be deprived of them, by an extraordinary tribunal, vested with powers such as those conferred on the register and receiver.

That a patent is not necessary in all cases, to confer a legal title to soil, of which the government is the proprietor, cannot be doubted. An act of congress may divest the United States, at once, of all property in a portion of the public lands, and transfer it to an individual. But it is perfectly clear the government may legislate in such a manner, as to make the issuing of the patent necessary, to effectuate this object, and we believe their ordinary legislation in respect to the public domain, which is given away, contemplates the retention of entire power over the object given, until that is done.

Indeed, when there is no expression in the statute conveying a different idea, we should think, that the obligation imposed on the donee, to apply for, and obtain, a patent, is strong evidence that his title is not to be considered complete, until it is obtained. In many, perhaps the greater number, of our sister states, no action of ejectment can be maintained without it. In this, and some others, an equitable title may be enforced in a court of law. But in relation to the Florida lands, we think there is strong evidence, beyond the obligation imposed on the settlers to apply for a patent, that the government retained complete power over the soil until the patent issued.

The provision contained in the act of 1819 is that on which the defendants principally rely. The 3d section declares, that the persons who appear, by the commissioners' report, to have actually settled and cultivated the land claimed by them, on or before the 5th of April, 1813, shall be entitled to the land so claimed and settled as a donation.

The particular language here used, cannot escape the attention of those who are called on to interpret it. The act does not say, that such settlers are confirmed in their right and title to the land: it declares they shall be entitled to a grant for it. It does not divest the United States of the soil, but furnishes a claim to ask them to do so.

In the case of Foster & Elam v. Neilson, which decided the right to so large a portion of the lands of that section of our state, in which, those involved in the present controversies are situated, the Supreme Court of the United States, in construing the terms of the treaty between our government and Spain, said, there was an important difference between the expressions therein contained—*all grants of land shall be ratified and confirmed*, and the words, *are hereby ratified and confirmed*. That the latter acted directly on the subject-matter, the former only contained an engagement, congress would ratify and confirm them; and that until it did so, the court could not consider them as confirmed. 2 Peters, 315.

If we now turn our attention to the language used in the 12th section of the act of 1819, it will be seen, that the case before the court is much stronger:—that the construction we have given to the words, shall be entitled to a grant, far from being refined, is in exact consonance with the sense in which the legislature used them, and that such construction is, in fact, the only one, by which all parts of the law can be carried into effect.

It provides for the issuing a certificate, and declares, that on the presentation of it to the general land office, if the commissioner thereof shall be of opinion that it has been fairly obtained, according to the true intent and meaning of the act, a patent shall issue. If the third section conferred a title to the land, and put an end to all power in the government over it, that just cited was useless, and can have no effect. The commissioner had no power to judge of its fairness or unfairness. We think this provision shows conclusively, that congress retained power over these donations, up to the time the patent issued, and that until it did issue, no title vested in the donee.

Under this view of the subject, we are of opinion we cannot interfere with the decision of the register and receiver. The government of the United States has deemed it proper to intrust them with the power of deciding, in case of a conflict between donees, which of them should enjoy its bounty; and as they had no title but that which flowed from the liberality of the donor, they must take with such conditions as he has thought proper to affix to his donation.

The only other question in the case, of importance, is in relation to the want of proof of the right of Cooper, who was the original settler, being transferred to the plaintiff. There is no evidence of it, except the recital in the certificate of confirmation. The judge below, was of opinion it was not sufficient. This is the first time such a point has been presented for our decision. The general rule certainly is, that the assignee must prove the right of the assignor is vested in him: and that recitals in a deed are not evidence against third parties. In the case of Penrose v. Griffith, the Supreme Court of Pennsylvania was divided on a similar question. A majority of the court held, that recitals in the patent bound all who claimed subsequently from the state, but not those who had a title before the patent issued. One of the judges thought it was *prima facie* evidence against both. In a subsequent case, the same tribunal determined, that where the defendant showed no title, the recitals in the patent were evidence against him. Such was this case; after the decision of the register and receiver, the defendants had no title to the premises, and as we think the rule well founded in principle, we are of opinion the court below erred in its charge to the jury. 4 Binney, 231; 2 Serg. & Rawle, 455.

Having come to the conclusion just expressed, it is unnecessary to examine the other questions raised by the several bills of exceptions, for, supposing them all decided in favor of the defendants, the plaintiff must recover. The cause, however, will have to be remanded, to inquire into the value of the improvements placed on the land, while the appellees were in good faith.

It is, therefore, ordered, adjudged and decreed, that the judgment of the district court be annulled, avoided and reversed; and it is further ordered, adjudged and decreed, that the case be remanded, to ascertain the value of improvements made by the defendants while in good faith, and that the appellee pay the costs of this appeal.

Preston, for the plaintiff.

Morgan, for the defendants.

Gayosos *v.* Executors of Baldwin. VIII, N. S. 658.

The want of a survey does not exclude parol proof of boundaries.

THIRD District.

Porter, J., delivered the opinion of the court.

By the pleadings in this action, which is a petitory one, the plaintiffs are put on the proof of their title to the premises sued for. To establish it, they produced a concession from the Spanish government and offered parol evidence of the boundaries. This evidence was objected to, and the court declared its opinion to be, that the plaintiffs having never had a survey made of the land claimed by the succession of C. Baldwin, deceased, which is the land in contest, could not prove by parol, the metes and bounds.

We are of opinion the court erred. It appears from the evidence on record, that the land claimed by the petitioners, had been surveyed under the authority of the Spanish government, and a plat of this survey is produced. The land embraced by the limits there given, may be shown by parol evidence. Frequently it can be proved in no other way; the plat of survey being nothing more than a representation of that which is essentially matter *en pais.* On the trial of land cases, it is usually the practice for courts of justice, on application of either party, to order a survey, with directions to the surveyor to run such lines as may be required by the litigants. This is done as a matter of convenience, to enable the court and jury to apply with more facility and correctness, the other proof which may be offered of the *locus in quo.* But this survey makes no proof in itself of the truth of the lines traced on the plat returned into court. It is not evidence *per se,* but the means used to apply evidence. The want of it, therefore, does not prevent the introduction of parol proof, though its absence may render the application of that proof more difficult. If the plaintiff's title calls for natural boundaries, or other limits which exist in fact, and the defendant's claim or concession does the same; there is often no other means of showing where these boundaries are, but by parol evidence. The lines traced by the surveyor on paper, might give a picture of them, but could not establish their existence. If, from the nature of the case, it was impossible for the court to ascertain the extent of the interference of the titles without a survey, the judge had the power to continue the cause, and order one, or after having heard the testimony, nonsuit the plaintiff, for not making his case sufficiently clear. But the bill of exceptions presents for our opinion the naked question, whether the want of a survey, giving a representation of the lines of the land claimed, excludes parol proof of the boundaries? and that question we feel compelled to answer in the negative.   See the case of Milligan's Heirs v. Hargrove, 6 *N. S.* 344, where the effect of surveys made under an order of court was fully gone into.,

It is, therefore, ordered, adjudged and decreed that the judgment of the district court be annulled, avoided and reversed, and it is further ordered, adjudged and decreed, that the case be remanded to the district court, with directions to the judge not to reject parol proof on behalf of the plaintiffs, to show the boundaries of the land in dispute, because a survey had not been made by them of it.   And it is further ordered and decreed, that the appellees pay the costs of this appeal.

Smith and *Conrad*, for the appellants.
Hennen, for the appellees.

Lacy v. Buhler.   VIII, N. S. 661.

The sheriff cannot surrender property, seized on a *fi. fa.* to a claimant, who obtains an injunction to stay the sale.

THIRD District, Judge of the Eighth presiding.

MARTIN, J., delivered the opinion of the court.

This is a suit against the sheriff of East Baton Rouge, in which, damages are claimed from him, on account of negligence and misconduct in his official capacity, in relation to the execution of a judgment which the plaintiff had obtained against Andrew Miller.

The answer is a genereal denial, and judgment being rendered in favor of the plaintiff, the defendant appealed.

The important facts of the case, as shown by the evidence, are as follows: the present plaintiff obtained a judgment against one Milton, on which a *fieri facias* issued, and was levied by the defendant, acting as sheriff, on a mare, and a certain quantity of cotton in the seed, which were afterwards claimed by R. Frickling, and the sale of the property was arrested by an injunction which the claimant had obtained against the sheriff, as appears by the return of the *fieri*

[Lacy *v.* Buhler.]

facias. This injunction was subsequently dissolved, and another writ of execution issued, on which a small portion of the plaintiff's judgment was satisfied, independent of costs, by the seizure and sale of other property, than that which had been seized under the former execution.

The question of law, arising out of these facts, is, whether the sheriff is justifiable in the surrender of the property which had been seized in virtue of the first suit, to the claimant, in consequence of the injunction by which the sale had been delayed?

Its solution depends principally on the provisions of our Code of Practice, relative " to the opposition of third persons." The art. 395, defines it to be a demand brought by a third person, not originally a party in the suit, for the purpose of arresting the execution of an order of seizure or judgment, rendered in that suit, or to regulate their effects in what relates to him.

If the opposition has for its object, to set aside the order of seizure as having been effected on property not belonging to the party against whom the order was directed, but owned, on the contrary, by the third person making the opposition, it must be done by means of a petition and citation, served on the party making the seizure, as in ordinary suits; but such opposition shall be considered as a separate demand, distinct from the suit in which the order was granted. Art. 398.

They court may, nevertheless, at the request of the opponent, enjoin the sheriff not to proceed to the sale of the property thus claimed, provided such opponent give security to the plaintiff for such an amount as the court shall determine, to be responsible for all damages which said plaintiff may sustain, should the opposition be wrongfully made. Art. 399.

When a sheriff is in possession of property by virtue of a seizure, under writ of execution, he must be considered as a rightful possessor holding for the benefit of the plaintiff in the writ, until it be clearly shown, that the property seized belongs to some third person, and not to the defendant, from whom it may have been taken. An injunction to arrest the sale, would not, therefore, destroy the right of possession acquired under the seizure: and the officer, holding as agent for the plaintiff, cannot surrender property thus held, to a claimant, without making himself responsible in damages for any injury which the plaintiff sustains, in consequence of such unauthorised and illegal surrender. And that which took place in the present case, appears to us to have been entirely gratuitous on the part of the sheriff.

It is, therefore, ordered, adjudged and decreed, that the judgment of the district court be affirmed, with costs.

Lawrence and *Eustis,* for the plaintiff.
Watts, for the defendant.

Brooks v. Pool. VIII, N. S. 665.

THIRD District, Judge of the Eighth presiding.
A minor cannot sue his tutor, for the delivery of his estate, till after settlement, in the court of probates.
That court would have power to order a transfer of the property from the tutor to the curator *ad bona.*

Martinez v. Perez *et al.* VIII, N. S. 668.

The agent, who carries on a suit, has no lien or preference on the amount of the judgment, in the hands of the defendant, attached by a creditor of the principal.

FIRST District.

MATHEWS, J., delivered the opinion of the court.
This suit is commenced by attachment, and Miranda, a debtor of the defendants, is made garnishee: Currell, Kilshaw & Co. intervened and claim a privilege on the debt attached, for money by them expended in the prosecution of a suit, instituted by the defendants against the garnishee, in which a judgment was obtained against him, for the sum of 7373 dollars 43 cents. Judgment was rendered by the court below, in favor of the plaintiffs, against the original defendants, and the petition of intervention dismissed; from this decree of dismissal the intervening party appealed.
They base the privilege or preference claimed, principally on the arts. of the Louisiana Code, which treat of the rights acquired by possessors of property belonging to others, where the possessor has incurred expenses for its preservation. Against the owner, the species of right acquired, is in the nature of that of pledge, by virtue of which he may retain the thing, until the expenses which he has incurred are repaid. He possesses this unqualified right of pledge, even against the creditors of the owner, if they seek to have the thing sold, &c.—

[Martinez v. Perez et al.]

Finally, he who has incurred these expenses, has a privilege against the creditors, which gives him a preference over them, on the price of the thing sold, &c. Louisiana Code, 391, 392, 393.

These provisions of our law evidently relate to the possession of corporeal things. There can be no positive possession of incorporeal rights; it is only *quasi;* it is nothing more than the use of such rights. They are not susceptible, properly, of a real possession, and perhaps no qualified or limited right on the incorporeal thing could be created by this *quasi* possession.

An agent or attorney appointed to collect debts, who expends money in prosecuting the claims of the creditor to judgments, would have no lien on such judgments, to give him a preference over other creditors of his employer. An attorney at law might retain the title papers of his client, until the latter should pay to him the fees stipulated between the parties; so a person who is in possession of any papers, intrusted to him to have them recorded, might lawfully hold them until the fees for recording, by him advanced, should be refunded. But such privileges result from the possession of things corporeal.

In the present case, it is believed, that Currell, Kilshaw & Co. could not have prevented the debtor of their principal, from paying to them the amount recovered against him, free from any lien or privilege of the agents, on the money thus paid. The evidences of the debt on which judgment was obtained, were merged in that judgment, as being an evidence of higher dignity; and of this last, they never have been in possession. We are of opinion, that the decision of the court below, in relation to the petition of intervention, is correct.

It is, therefore, ordered, adjudged and decreed, that the judgment of the district court be affirmed, with costs.

Strawbridge, for the appellee.
Eustis and *Duncan,* for the appellants.

Perillat v. Puech. VIII, N. S. 671.

PARISH Court of New Orleans.

The part of a witness's testimony, relating what he heard others say, must be rejected.

Williamson *et al.* *v.* Spencer and Wife. VIII, N. S. 673.

COURT of Probates, Parish of East Feliciana.
The citation of appeal herein being served after the return day, the appeal was for that reason dismissed.

Rivas *v.* Gill. VIII, N. S. 674.

A suit, by a creditor to avoid a sale in fraud of his rights by his debtor, is prescribed by one year.

THIRD District, Judge of the Eighth presiding.

MATHEWS, J., delivered the opinion of the court.
This suit is brought to avoid a contract, by which certain property was sold and transferred from Joseph Gill and his wife, to the defendant.

The plaintiff alleges himself to be a creditor by judgment, of the vendors, and that the sale is feigned, simulated and fraudulent, &c. The defendant pleaded the general issue and prescription to the action. The cause was submitted to a jury who found a verdict for the plaintiff, and judgment being rendered thereon, the defendant appealed.

The species of action resorted to in the present instance, is that which is ordained by the Louisiana Code, for the avoidance of contracts by persons not parties to them: see p. 640, sect. 7. The art. 1965 declares, that "the law gives to every creditor, where there is no cession of goods, as well as to the representatives of all the creditors, where there is any such cession, or other proceeding, by which they are collectively represented, an action to annul any contract made in fraud of their rights." As simulated acts of sale, by which a debtor intends to place his property out of the reach of his creditors,

[Rivas v. Gill.]

is clearly a contract made in fraud of their rights; and on the establishment of facts, showing the simulation and fraud, ought to be declared null and void; provided the suit to set it aside, be brought within the time prescribed by law. The action given by this section, is limited to one year; if brought by a creditor individually, to be counted from the time he has obtained judgment against the debtor; if brought by syndics, or other representatives of the creditors, collectively, to be counted from the day of their appointment. See art. 1989.

The sale, sought to be avoided by the present suit, was made under private signature; but the act was afterward regularly recorded in the office of a notary public, and the property conveyed by it, had been previously delivered to the vendee, and all these proceedings more than one year before the plaintiff had obtained judgment against the vendors, and before the institution of this action, which was therefore fraud by the express provisions of the law, which gave it to the individual creditor. By invoking the aid of the court, to avoid the contract, which stands in his way in the execution of his judgment, the creditor seems to us to have subjected himself to all the disabilities and restrictions created by the law which gave him the right of action.

It is, therefore, ordered, &c., that the judgment of the district court be avoided reversed and annulled; and that judgment be now entered for the defendant with costs in both courts.

Watts, for the appellant.
Conrad, for the appellee.

Russell *et al. v.* Wolff *et al.*   VIII, N. S. 676.

PARISH Court of New Orleans.
If there be two defendants, and one of them makes a cession of his goods—the suit, as to him will be transferred to the court before whom the *concurso* is pending, and retained as to the other defendant.

Martinstein *et al. v.* Wolff. VIII, N. S. 679.

PARISH Court of New Orleans.

On the failure of a debtor *in solido,* the co-debtor may be proceeded against, without waiting for the issue of the proceedings in the *concurso.*

Louisiana State Insurance Company *v.* Morgan *et al.* VIII, N. S. 680.

A legislative exposition can only result from proceedings of both houses, approved by the executive, or persisted in according to the constitution, without their approbation. The act of 1813, imposing a tax on stock does not require the president and directors of stock companies *all* to swear to their declarations: the affidavit of either or one suffices.

FIRST District.

MARTIN, J., delivered the opinion of the court.

There is hardly any difference between the present case and that between the Louisiana Insurance Company and the present defendants, determined a few days ago.

An injunction was obtained against the treasurer of the state and the sheriff of the parish, to stay proceeding on a treasury execution, for arrearages of taxes. During several years, the preceding treasurer having construed the act of assembly of 1813, as imposing the tax on stock actually paid in, and not on that which was subscribed and payment secured by mortgages, deposit of stock, or other means.

The same argument was used, as at the hearing of the former case, and that through which a legislative exposition of the act under consideration was endeavored to be impressed on us, has been peculiarly urged.

The silence of a committee of the legislature, in a report concurred with by the houses, in regard to a tax, the collection of which has been omitted or but partially enforced, cannot be considered a legislative exposition, sanctioning the omission or partial collection.

A legislative exposition can only result from proceedings of both houses, approved by the executive, or persisted in, according to the constitution, without their approbation.

In this case, however, the argument had much less force than in the preceding case, as the amount of the tax collected from these plaintiffs, was not even communicated to the legislature.

But a technical objection has been raised here, to which nothing in the pleadings gives rise, and which does not appear to have been acted on below.

It is that the declaration, which is to be the basis of the treasurer's assessment of the tax, was demanded and received by that officer from the president, and not from the president and directors.

The dissolution of an injunction is asked, or its being made perpetual resisted, on disproving the allegations on which it was obtained; the party enjoined cannot be prepared to adduce any evidence to disprove facts, to which his attention is not directed by the pleadings.

The act requires the declaration to be demanded from the president and directors, and to be given by them under oath, not under their oaths. It is not required they should all swear. When a corporation wants one of those writs, which cannot be obtained without an affidavit, one of their officers or clerks makes it. If two plaintiffs want such a writ, the affidavit of either suffices. We are not ready to say, that the board could not have satisfied the obligation imposed on them, by the act, if they had directed the cashier, the officer of the institution best acquainted with the fact, to state on his oath, the amount of stock subscribed, distinguishing the part actually paid in, from that the payment of which was secured by mortgages or otherwise; but we are clear, that the president and directors were not all necessarily to swear; the affidavit of either would suffice; the words of the law are, under oath, not under their oaths. Did it therefore appear, that the president made the declaration or affidavit, by order of the board, the treasurer might have received it, as a legitimate basis of his assessment, even if he had demanded it from the president alone.

But it appears, from the plaintiffs' own showing, that the president made a correct declaration; and they have annexed to their petition, a statement of the part of the stock paid in; which, as it is one-tenth of that subscribed, the other nine-tenths being to be secured, gives the total of *stock in trade*, as stated by the president. So that, if the injunction was sustained on the technical objection, justice would require us to save the right of the state to another execution. As we do not dissolve injunctions, which must necessarily be immediately issued *de novo*, we cannot perpetually enjoin a remedy, which every circumstance in the case demands, that the party should be immediately permitted to resort to.

[Louisiana Insurance Company *v.* Morgan *et al.*]

The plaintiffs' argument has been considered on the merits, to show that the words *stock in trade*, used by the legislature, do not cover that part of the stock, the payment of which is secured; they have not pretended that there is the least inaccuracy in the president's declaration.

As this technical objection was not presented by the pleadings to the state officers, they cannot be permitted to offer evidence on it in this court, nor could it be expected from them they should produce it below; and as it does, by no means, reach the merits of the case, we think it our duty to disregard it.

It is, therefore, ordered, adjudged and decreed, that the judgment of the district court be annulled, avoided and reversed; the injunction dissolved, and that the appellees pay costs in both courts.

Eustis, for the plaintiffs.
Morphy, for the defendants.

Caldwell *v.* Cline. VIII, N. S. 684.

Whether the circumstance of a party having an action for damages, prevents his obtaining an injunction?

FIRST District.

MARTIN, J., delivered the opinion of the court.
The plaintiff, manager of a theatre in the city of New Orleans, applied to the court of the parish and city, for an injunction, to prevent the defendant, a rope dancer, whom he had engaged in New York, performing in another theatre. The judge below refused the injunction, and the plaintiff obtained from this court, a rule on the inferior judge, calling on him to show cause, why he did not grant the injunction.

The judge showed cause that,

1. The plaintiff, on a breach of the contract by the defendant, had his remedy in damages.

2. If the judge had power to prevent the defendant from performing, he must have that of compelling him to perform; and he was ignorant of the means by which the latter power could be enforced.

3. The contract of the parties had no restrictive clause.

The contract, which is annexed to the petition, shows, that in Sep-

56*

[Caldwell v. Cline.]

tember, 1829, in the city of New York, the defendant agreed with
the plaintiff, to play on the plaintiff's theatre, in New Orleans, two
engagements, of six nights each, commencing on the 10th of February, 1830, with an allowance of ten days for detention.

The plaintiff agreed the defendant should have the surplus of each
night's receipts, after a deduction of 250 dollars, and further, one
clear half of the seventh and fourteenth nights' receipts, as a benefit.

The plaintiff made oath, that the defendant, according to his engagement, performed during five nights, on the plaintiff's theatre,
and refused to perform any more, and entered into an engagement to
perform in another theatre than the plaintiff's.

We are not ready to say with the parish judge, that as the plaintiff had a claim for damages, on the breach of the contract, he could
not, if a proper case had been made, have been entitled to an injunction.

It is unnecessary to examine whether the court's power to enjoin,
depends on that of compelling a specific performance, nor by what
means the latter power could be exercised.

But we agree with him, that there is nothing alleged here or
proved, that the defendant should not perform on any other theatre
than the plaintiff's, till he had complied with his engagement with
the latter.

It is therefore ordered, that the rule obtained on the parish judge,
be discharged, and that the plaintiff pay costs.

Morris *et al. v.* Thames.   VIII, N. S. 687.

Title cannot be claimed to the property of an intestate, in this state, under a sale by an
administrator appointed in Georgia.

EIGHTH District, Judge of the Second presiding.

Martin, J., delivered the opinion of the court.

The petition charges that the defendant wrongfully took possession
of a slave, the property of the plaintiffs, whom she removed out of
the state. The claim is for the return of the slave, or his value and
damages.

The defendant pleaded, as a peremptory exception, the want of

[Caldwell *v.* Cline.]

the averment of a demand, while the slave was in her possession, and the general issue.

The plaintiff had judgment for 450 dollars and costs, and the defendant appealed.

The points made by her counsel in this court, are, that,

1. Her peremptory exception was improperly disallowed.

2. There is no proof of the death of the person, under whom the plaintiffs claim as heirs.

3. There is no proof of title in them.

4. The title of the plaintiffs is good and valid.

The case has been submitted to us on these points, without an argument.

I. We have been unable to discover any weight in the peremptory exception. The possession of the defendant, and her removal of the slave out of the state, are alleged.—A demand is averred; but whether it was made previous to, or after the removal, does not appear, nor do we think it material. If one takes my slave, and sends him out of the state, there can not be any good reason shown why I should not, after a request that the slave be sent for and returned, have an action for his return, or the value.

II. III. There is proof of the death of Jared Morris, the plaintiffs' father, and that they are his children.

IV. The defendant's claim, under an administrator of Jared Morris' estate, appointed by a court of the state of Georgia, can not entitle her to part of the estate in this.

It is, therefore, ordered, adjudged and decreed, that the judgment of the district court be affirmed, with costs.

Hennen, for the appellant.

Shaw *et al. v.* Canter.   VIII, N. S. 689.

PARISH Court of New Orleans.

The Supreme Court pays less deference to the decision of the judge *a quo,* in a question of fact, where the principal part of the testimony is taken on a commission, than where he personally heard the witnesses.

Dicks *et al. v.* Chew *et al.*   VIII, N. S. 690.

THIRD District, Judge of the Second presiding.
No appeal lies from the order of the inferior court, discharging a jury, who cannot agree, and continuing the cause.

Pilié *v.* Patin, Wife of Delâge, and her Husband.
VIII, N. S. 692.

The wife cannot be surety for the husband. And, where she binds herself as principal, she may show the contract was one of suretyship, although she did not take a counter-letter.

FIRST District.

PORTER, J., delivered the opinion of the court.
The plaintiff, endorsee of a promissory note secured by a mortgage, prayed for, and obtained, an order of seizure against the property of the wife. This seizure the latter enjoined, alleging, that the obligation she had signed, was given for a debt of her husband, which had not turned to her benefit.
The court below, after hearing testimony, made the injunction perpetual, and the plaintiff appealed.
By the act of mortgage, the defendant states, that she owes to Francois La Brouche Dusin, 1217 dollars, for so much that he lent her to repay her sister, Gertrude Patin, wife of Pierre Abadie, the two instalments, which the latter had advanced to her, on a contract for the hire of ten negroes for three years, and to insure the payment of this sum, for which she had given her two notes for 608 dollars 50 cents each, she mortgaged certain slaves, &c.
The court, notwithstanding the objection of the plaintiff, permitted the defendant to prove by parol testimony, a consideration for the act of mortgage, different from that expressed in it. The legality of this decision is brought before us, by a bill of exceptions.

We are of opinion the judge did not err. The plaintiff has relied on the often cited articles of our Code, which forbid the introduction of evidence, against, or beyond, what is contained in 'public acts.— These articles have never been understood to apply to cases, where the contract was never entered into, in contravention of other provisions of the law. When certain persons, such as minors, or married women, are incapacitated from contracting engagements of a particular kind, any stipulations obtained from them, contrary thereto, are *in fraudem legis*, and if it were not open to them to show the real nature of the transaction, the laws made for their protection, would have no effect. It is not a good answer, to say, that persons so incapacitated, should take a counter-letter, for, to admit this argument, would be to make them the victims of the weakness which induced the law to throw its shield over them. If they had knowledge enough to guard themselves in this way, they would not require any other protection. In the case of the Louisiana State Bank *v.* Rowell we said, "When the law incapacitates persons from making contracts of a particular kind, its provisions cannot be evaded by giving to these contracts a different form from that forbidden by law, when in substance the contract is that prohibited. To sanction such agreements, would be permitting that to be done indirectly, which the law will not permit to be done directly." 7 *N. S.* 341; 5 *N. S.* 54.

The evidence shows, we think, satisfactorily, the following facts: The defendant had bound herself jointly with her husband, for a debt, which he had contracted to the plaintiff. Suit was brought against them, in which, the plaintiff recovered judgment against the husband, and failed in his action against the wife. At, or about, the same time, one Poydras, recovered judgment against the defendant, with which judgment she was dissatisfied, and desired to appeal.— Being embarrassed to obtain security for the prosecution of the appeal, the plaintiff offered to become her surety, on the condition of her securing the former debt, in the manner it was done in the act on which this suit was instituted.

On these facts, we have no doubt the contract of the appellee was not binding on her, and it is therefore ordered, adjudged and decreed that the judgment of the district court be affirmed with costs.

Cannon, for the plaintiff.

Eustis, for the defendants.

Heirs of Farrar v. Warfield and Wife.   VIII, N. S. 695.

A surveyor cannot give his opinions in evidence, as to the proper location of a grant.
He must state the facts.
Papers in a foreign language need not be translated by the sworn interpreter of the court.
Doctrine in Gayle v. Gray, 6 N. S. 693, recognised.

THIRD District.

Porter, J., delivered the opinion of the court.
This is a petitory action.   One of the principal points in issue, is
the location of the grant under which the plaintiffs claim the premises.   The jury found a verdict for the defendants, and the plaintiffs
appealed.
They require the cause to be remanded for a new trial, on alleged
errors of the judge, in admitting and rejecting testimony.
The surveyor, who had been appointed by the court, to make a
survey of the premises in dispute, was asked by the plaintiffs the
following question: " Have you any doubt in your mind, that from
the antiquity of the appearance of the improvements on the land,
near and adjoining the bluffs, as described in your survey; from the
locality of the ground; from the correspondence marked on the diagram in the patent, and in your own survey, particularly as to the
meanders of Thompson's creek, and the actual position of the bluff,
as you found them, that the land you surveyed, is the same marked
on said diagram."   The court would not permit the witness to answer this question, and acted correctly in doing so.   Whether the
facts stated in the interrogatory, left any doubt on the mind, was a
question to be decided by the jury, and not by the witness.   The
plaintiffs say, that as a professional man they had a right to his opinion.   The cases in which testimony of this kind is received are those
where the solution of the question requires a degree of skill and
judgment, which is usually confined to a few individuals, exercising
a particular art or profession, and where the jury are supposed incapable of drawing a correct inference from the facts.   The location of
of a patent, does not, in our opinion, present a question of science,
which calls for opinion from the witnesses, instead of facts.   We do
not recollect a single case, where such a question has been put to
surveyors, and this, in itself, is an argument of considerable weight
against its legality, as the instances must have been numerous where
there was a motive for putting it.   Starkie on Evidence, p. 1. 74.
The plaintiffs also objected to the introduction of certain documents

in the French and Spanish languages, on the ground, "that there was no interpreter to the court, by which the contents of said papers could be known, either to the jury, or the counsel for the plaintiff." If the law made it compulsory on the judge, to appoint an interpreter to the court, then, perhaps this objection would have been legal. But the statute leaves it discretionary with the tribunals of the state, to do so, and in the absence of such an officer, any person, who is qualified by his knowledge, may discharge the duty. Moreau's Digest, 1, 296.

Another objection was taken to the introduction of the defendants' title, on the ground that it was a patent issued at a time when the Spanish government had no authority to grant lands in West Florida. This objection is disposed of by the decision of the case of Gayle v. Gray, 6 N. S. 693, with which we see no reason to be dissatisfied.

On the merits, the evidence does not present a case, which authorises us to interfere with the verdict of the jury, and it is, therefore, ordered, adjudged and decreed, that the judgment of the district court be affirmed, with costs.

Roman v. Hennen et al. VIII, N. S. 698.

FIRST District.

Held, that one creditor cannot bring a suit, after the insolvency to set aside a conveyance made by a debtor. Suits for property belonging to the insolvent and alleged to make a part of his estate surrendered, must be brought by the representatives of those to whom the surrender was made; that is, by the syndics.

Merry *v.* Chexnaider.   VIII, N. S. 699.

FIRST District.

By Porter, J.—The plaintiff sues, in this action, to recover his freedom, and from the evidence on record, is clearly entitled to it.— He was born in the northwestern territory, since the enactment of congress, in 1787, of the ordinance for the government of that country, according to the sixth article of which, there could be therein, neither slavery or involuntary servitude. This ordinance fixed forever the character of the population in the region over which it extended, and takes away all foundation from the claim set up in this instance, by the defendant. The act of cession by Virginia, did not deprive congress of the power to make such a regulation.

Lloyd *v.* Graham *et al.*   VIII, N. S. 700.

A married woman, who, jointly with her husband, purchases property from her father, cannot contradict the act of sale, and prove by parol evidence, that the donation of it was contemplated.

COURT of Probates, Parish of East Feliciana.

Porter, J., delivered the opinion of the court.
· The plaintiff, by this action, seeks to have a partition made of property, which she alleges she inherited from her deceased father, and now holds in common with her mother, and the other heirs of her father.
The mother claims the property in her own right, and denies the right of the plaintiff to have a division made of it.   The court of the first instance decided in her favor, and the plaintiff appealed.
In support of the allegation in the petition, of the property being common, the plaintiff introduced an instrument *sous seing privé*, by

which it appears, the land in question had been sold by the father of defendant, to her and her husband, for the sum of 1550 dollars.

Testimony was offered to show, that this sale was, in fact, a donation; that the deed was simulated. It was objected to, and we think the court erred in receiving it. This contract, on the face of it, was not such a one as the law prohibited the defendant from entering into, nor does the allegation on which she seeks to avoid it, show it to have been one of those, where she was incapacitated from binding herself. She is, therefore, within the operation of that principle of our jurisprudence, which forbids parol proof being received against the contents of a written instrument. 1 *N. S.* 451; *Ibid.* 454.

The counter-letter, which, it was contended, proves the allegation in the answer, we think strengthens the case of the plaintiff. The estimation given to the property received, taken with the sale, proves that it was the intention of the parties, the land and slaves should enter into the community, and the husband be responsible for their value.

It is, therefore, ordered, adjudged and decreed, that the judgment of the probate court be annulled, avoided and reversed; and it is further ordered, adjudged and decreed, that the case be remanded to the said court, with directions to the judge, to proceed, and make the partition claimed in the petition; and it is further ordered, that the appellee pay the costs of this appeal.

Ripley, for the appellants.

Hyde v. Wolff. VIII, N. S. 702.

PARISH Court of New Orleans.
Same point as in Martinstein *et al.* v. Wolff, *ante*, 663.

House *v.* Croft.　VIII, N. S. 704.

Minority must be pleaded; the plaintiff is not obliged to prove the defendant to be a major.

A prayer for judgment, is a sufficient allegation that the money alleged in the petition to be due, is unpaid.

When suit is brought on a judgment of a sister state, it is not necessary to allege that the court which rendered judgment is a court of competent jurisdiction.

Payment of a debt cannot be pleaded in reconvention.

The faith and credit due to judgments of the courts of other states of the Union, extends as well to their competency, as to the correctness of the matters decided by them.

THIRD District, Judge of the Fourth presiding.

PORTER, J., delivered the opinion of the court.

The plaintiff alleges, the defendant was appointed his guardian, in South Carolina, and gave bond for the faithful discharge of the duties of his office; that he failed to perform them; that the petitioner was compelled to sue him in a court of equity, in that state, and that judgment was rendered against him for 3158 dollars 31 cents, which has been demanded from him, and for which, this suit is brought.

The defendant filed exceptions to the petition.

1. That the plaintiff had not alleged he was of lawful age and capable to sue in his own name.

2. That he had not given the date of the decree of the court of chancery, and had not alleged it was a court of competent jurisdiction, nor that the money was still due.

The district court overruled these exceptions, and the correctness of its doing so, is the first question for our consideration.

We think the court did not err. The plaintiff, if he was of age, was not required to allege it. If he was not, the defendant should have set the matter up as a defence, and proved it. There was nothing in the circumstance of the petitioner having been a minor, to take this case out of the general rule, as every man of full age, was so, at some period of his life.

The decree of the court of chancery was annexed to, and made a part of the petition, consequently, its date made a part of the petition. This demand for judgment against the defendant, is a sufficient allegation, that the money, alleged in the petition to be due, is unpaid.

It was not necessary to allege that the court which rendered judgment against the defendant, in South Carolina, was a court of competent jurisdiction. Its competency is presumed, until the contrary is shown. And the pleadings are sufficiently certain, when they conform to the presumptions of law.

[House v. Croft.]

The defendant answered to the merits, and pleaded, first, the general issue: secondly, the nullity of the judgment, as being rendered without citation. He also set up a demand in reconvention: 157 dollars of which, he alleges, was advanced to the plaintiff, in the defendant's capacity as guardian, and another sum of 1579 dollars 15 cents, he averred was paid to the petitioner, but on what account, is not stated.

A motion was made to strike the plea of reconvention from the answer, because the things therein demanded, are not connected with, or incidental to, the claim in the petition.

The court sustained this motion, but at the same time declared the defendant was at liberty to file any plea, which might go to extinguish the plaintiff's demand, in whole, or in part. The defendant excepted.

One of the matters set forth in the answer, not being shown to have any connection with the demand in the petition, could not be pleaded in reconvention. The other, which averred payment of a portion of the claim sued on, should have been pleaded as such, and could not be presented in the shape of a separate demand, for payment necessarily extinguishes the obligation on which the payment is made. We are at a loss to conceive why the defendant refused to plead these matters, as payment, although offered permission by the court to do so. If his object was to escape from the acknowledgment of a debt once existing, which an allegation of payment of it would have produced, we are furnished with an additional reason for not permitting it to be offered in reconvention, for he should not have the advantage of showing he paid part of the debt, without taking the consequences that would have followed pleading it regularly.

The court below decided correctly, in presuming the competency of the court which gave judgment. Under the constitution of the United States, full faith and credit is due to the decrees of the courts of our sister states; and that faith and credit extends, as well to the jurisdiction of the court, as to the fact that judgment was rendered.

There was no error in giving interest from judicial demand, and it is, therefore, ordered, adjudged and decreed, that the judgment of the district court be affirmed, with costs.

Turner, for the defendant.

Woodruff *v.* Wederstandt *et al.*　VIII, N. S. 708.

Whether a sale of land on a mortgage executed by the vendor, is an eviction of the
vendee, which will authorise him to resist payment? *Quære.*
If the vendor, after the sale, does any act to impair the title, or possession, of his vendee,
he cannot recover until he replaces the buyer in the same situation he was in at the
time of the purchase.

THIRD District, Judge of the Fourth presiding.

Porter, J., delivered the opinion of the court.
The plaintiff brings this action, on a note made to him by the
defendants, in consideration of a tract of land sold to them.　In the
act of sale, it is stipulated, " that no delay is to be made in the payment of the purchase-money, unless, or until, an actual eviction takes
place."
The plaintiff, it appears, had bought the property at a sheriff's sale,
at twelve months' credit, and at the the time of selling, the purchase
money was still due by him.　Failing to pay at the expiration of the
credit, execution issued against him, on the twelve months' bond,
and the premises, which the defendants had purchased, were seized
and sold, to one Charles M'Micken.　The purchaser took no step to
evict the defendants, but some time after the sale by the sheriff, they
removed from the land.
The case was submitted to a jury, in the court of the first instance,
who found a verdict for the defendants, and the plaintiff appealed.
On the trial, he requested the court to charge the jury,
1.　That a sale of lands, under an execution, which are, at the time
the levy is made, in the possession of a third party, by title under an
authentic act, does not operate as an actual eviction.
2.　That the purchaser of property cannot resist the payment of
the purchase-money until, and unless, suit has been actually brought
against him.
3.　That as no demand was made before the levy, the defendant in
execution, could have successfully resisted the sale of the property, if
notice of the levy had been given to him, and that the defendant was
bound to give such notice.
The court refused to charge the jury affirmatively on these propositions, and the plaintiff excepted.
We do not find any proof on record, that the defendants had notice
of the execution and the seizure, and if we are to presume it, we may
rightfully presume the defendants supposed the plaintiff had knowledge a writ of execution was issued against him, for a debt which

he owed, which he had not paid, and which it was his duty to pay. Another part of the defence is, that no actual eviction took place. This is supported by evidence, which shows, the sheriff did not actually seize and take into his possession, the property, for if he had, there would have been an actual eviction. · If he did not, we are unable to see how we can presume greater knowledge of the proceedings in the defendants, than the debtor; the latter was certainly more privy to the pursuit of his creditor, than the former could have been.

The case turns on the effect to be given to the terms, *actual eviction.* The plaintiff contends, that nothing less than a forced eviction under the authority of justice, can authorise the defendants to retain the purchase-money in their hands. After the property was sold, under the authority of justice, and the right of the purchaser to evict was absolute, we are not prepared to say, it was necessary for the vendees to remain tenants at will of the buyer. If the case called on us to decide it on that point, we are strongly inclined to think, they were authorised to consider such a change in their situation, as an actual eviction, and abandon the premises. But the facts of the case present other grounds, on which, we have no doubt the decision of the jury and the court below, was correct.

If the defendants had been disturbed by the exercise of a right in a third party, independent of any fault in the plaintiff, he would have been protected under the clause in the contract, by which he was responsible only, in case of actual eviction. But when the disturbance is the consequence of the vendor's conduct after the sale; by his failure to comply with his engagement to another, he has weakened the title, and impaired the possession of his vendees, and he cannot recover the purchase-money, until he has replaced them in the same situation they were, when the disturbance took place. It would be a grievous hardship, to compel the purchaser to pay for property which, since he bought has been sold to pay the debts of his vendor. It would be permitting a party to do, what it is an elementary principle no one shall do; that is, profit by his own wrong.

It is, therefore, ordered, adjudged and decreed, that the judgment of the district court be affirmed, with costs.

Pierce, for the plaintiff.

TABLE OF CONTENTS

INDEX.

INDEX

TO

THE WHOLE WORK.

ABSENTEE.

1. The law gives a mortgage on the estates of those who intermeddle in the administration of absent persons' property. *Quære*, whether the absent persons alluded to are not those declared absent? Ward *v.* Brandt *et al.*, Syndics, ii, 212.

2. When a person owning property in this state, does not appear at the place of his residence for five years, and has not been heard of, his presumptive heirs may cause themselves to be put in possession of the estate which belonged to him, and they enjoy a portion of the revenue. Their right yields to the testamentary heir, and both to the claim of the husband and wife, who wish to continue the partnership. Westover *et al. v.* Aimé and Wife, ii, 220.

3. The right of the presumptive heir, to receive the revenues of his ancestor, who has disappeared, is a personal interest, and does not partake of the realty. *Ibid.*

4. The Civil Code points out the cases in which attorneys may be appointed to represent absentees. Holliday *v.* M'Culloch *et al.*, iii, 53.

5. Persons, out of this state, can only be made amenable to our tribunals by having *their* property attached. A writ of attachment duly executed, stands in the place of a citation. The credits, goods, and effects of the defendants, represent his person. If they be not levied on, he is not legally before the tribunal, any more than in an ordinary case where the citation is not *served*. Schlatter *et al. v.* Broaddus *et al.*, iii, 95.

6. The party is not precluded by the acts of the attorney appointed to defend him in his absence. Fisk *v.* Fisk, iii, 434.

7. A curator may be appointed to an absentee in the service of the public. Ramsay *v.* Livingston, iii, 725.

ACCOUNT.

1. By accepting a general account of an agency including the commissions of the agents, and in which are expressed what accounts have been, and what remain to be collected, the principal discharged the agents; their agency was at an end, and they were no longer accountable for payment of any item said to have been left uncollected through their negligence. Rion *v.* Gilly *et al.*, i, 492.

2. The omission to charge an item in an account that is shown to be justly due, does not prevent a subsequent demand for it. Pavie *v.* Noyrel, iii, 461.

3. If a party is bound to furnish an account, his adversary may use that part which is against him, without being compelled to admit the items in it that are in his favor. Smith *v* Harrathy, iii, 559.

ACT AUTHENTIC.

1. The laws of Spain did not require all that strictness in the execution of acts in distant colonies which was required in the cities of Europe. Commandants might receive acts whatever the value of the property. Pizerot *et al. v.* Meuillon, i, 99.

2. The process verbal of the sale of property by the register of wills who sold it, is evidence of the sale, and no act under the signature of the parties is necessary to perfect it. Zanico *v.* Habine, i, 384.

3. The witness to a notarial act may, in certain cases, impeach it. Langlish *v.* Schons *et al.*, i. 390; Marie *v.* Avart's Heirs, i, 677.

4. A party who is named in a notarial act, but whose signature is not thereto, is not bound thereby. Lombard *v.* Guillet and Wife, ii, 224.

7. An amendment can only take place on account of some error of the court in rendering the judgment. Lynch v. Postlethwaite, i, 564.

8. Amendments may be allowed at any stage of the pleadings, but if it appear that the cause has been as fully tried on its merits, as it would have been with the amendment, the Supreme Court will not remand the cause. Johnston's Executor v. Wall et al., ii, 539; Debays et al. v. Mollere, ii, 763.

9. In the first district, an application for leave to amend, is too late on the day the causes are set down for trial. Chalmers et al. v. Stow, iii, 94.

10. A defendant cannot amend his answer, so as to change the substance of the issue joined. Abat v. Bayon, iii, 374.

11. The petition may be amended by praying for the restitution of the property, instead of its value. Castille v. Dumartrait, iii, 455.

12. The plaintiff may be allowed to amend his pleadings, by alleging the nullity of the judgment under which the defendant claims. There is no incompatibility in uniting a prayer for nullity, with one for the recovery of the property. Murdock v. Browder, iii, 706.

13. In an action for damages for killing the plaintiff's slave, he may be permitted to strike out a charge of neglect in the defendant, in the management of his own farm. Perrie v. Williams, iii, 713.

14. An opposition filed to a tableau of distribution cannot be amended without leave. Kirkland v. His Creditors, iv, 336.

15. In a suit on a promissory note, the nature of the action is not changed by an amendment which alleges a different consideration from that set forth. Hughes v. Harrison and Wife, iv, 522.

16. A petition claiming damages for the defendant's failure to complete a building, according to a written agreement, may be amended by a demand, under a legal warranty, resulting from the defendant's undertaking. Police Jury v. Boissier, iv, 532.

17. If an amendment to an answer presents, under another form, a defence substantially embraced by the previous pleading, the court of the first instance need not receive it. Rawle, for the use of Russell, v. Skipwith and Wife, iv, 565.

18. An amendment will be admitted by filing a supplemental petition, even after issue joined, where the first petition sued only the *testamentary heirs*, and the amendment embraced *all* who had sued the instituted heirs to break the will, and prayed judgment against them, if they succeeded. Dangerfield's Executors v. Thurston's Heirs, iv, 499.

19. A supplemental petition, asking more than the original, does not alter the substance of the demand. *Ibid.*

ANNUITY AND RENTE FONCIERE.

A suit on a contract of sale, accompanied by a contract of annuity. Mayor, &c. v. Duplessis, i. 374.

APPEAL.

A. *From what judgments Appeal will lie.*
B. *From what judgments Appeal will not lie.*
C. *Of Petition and Citation of Appeal; and Sheriff's return.*
D. *When returnable.*
E. *When to be filed.*
F. *Of Appeal Bond.*
G. *Of the Answer on Appeal Bond, and Motion to dismiss.*
H. *Of Appeal by third persons.*
I. *Of the different manners of bringing up Appeals, and of informalities in so doing*
K. *Of Errors apparent on the face of the Record.*
L. *Of Certiorari, and other relief granted to Appellants.*
M. *Of the effect of Appeal.*
N. *Of damages on Appeal.*
O. *Of practice on Appeal relative to Facts.*
P. *Of the voluntary Execution of Judgment as affecting Appeal.*
Q. *Of Appeal generally.*

A. *From what judgments Appeal will lie.*

1. An appeal lies from a judgment of nonsuit. Lefevre v. Broussard, i, 51.

2. An order maintaining an injunction, may be the subject of an appeal. Riley v. Lynd, i, 115.

judgment, and does not work a grievance irreparable, therefore cannot be appealed from; Fortin v. Randolph, ii, 191.

9. An appeal from the grant of a new trial (before final judgment) is premature. Dresser v. Cox, ii, 365; Belanger v. Gravier, ii. 408.

10. No appeal lies from the continuance of a cause, there being no final judgment yet. Compton et al. v. Patterson, ii, 556.

11. No appeal lies on a *quo warranto* to a justice of the peace, to ascertain whether he has jurisdiction of a cause. State of Louisiana v. Knight, ii, 571.

12. An order for the syndic to produce his book is but a preparatory step towards a final judgment, and any appeal from it is premature. Bargebur et al. v. Their Creditors, ii, 722.

13. No appeal lies from an order to transfer a cause. What is grievance irreparable? Todd et al. v. Andrews, iii, 10.

14. No appeal lies from a judgment given against a sheriff, on account of his having taken insufficient bail when less than 300 dollars is claimed from him, although more was demanded from the defendant in the original suit. Richards et al. v. Morgan, iii, 239.

15. No appeal from a decision refusing to sustain exceptions to the petition: such judgment not being final. Spencer v. Lambert, iii. 323; Ponsony v. Debaillon et al., iv, 211.

16. No appeal can be taken from an order of the judge homologating the inventory, made by the executor. No relief can be had until after final judgment. Rieffel et al. v. Boissiere, iii, 322.

17. If there be a reconvention, and the sum so demanded added to that claimed by the plaintiffs, makes an aggregate of more than 300 dollars, this circumstance will not authorize an appeal. Jewell v. Andrews, iii, 661.

18. No appeal lies from an order directing plaintiff to answer interrogatories. The delay that the plaintiff feared, and alleges for injury, is only increased by the appeal. If the answer be wrongly exacted, that may be made appear after it is put in, as well as, here on appeal. M'Donough v. Rogers, iii, 813.

19. A decree of partition cannot be appealed from. The partition must be made and, homologated, to authorise an appeal. Stokes v. Stokes, iii, 867.

20. No appeal lies from the refusal of a court of this state to transfer a suit to the, federal court. Higgins v. M'Micken, iv, 126.

21. No appeal lies from an order directing a purchaser to bring into court the price of the premises, to await the decision of the court on the claim of a mortgage. Kenner v. Young, iv, 152; Delancy v. Grymes et al., iv, 315.

22. No appeal lies from a judgment overruling a plea in the jurisdiction, and an exception to the right of the plaintiff to sue the defendant, without making his other partners parties. Howard v. Cox, iv, 169.

23. No appeal lies from the order of the inferior court, discharging a jury, who cannot agree, and continuing the cause. Dicks et al. v. Chew et al., iv, 668.

C. Of Petition and Citation of Appeal and Sheriff's Return.

1. An alias citation allowed, the first having been irregularly served. Lafon v. Riviere, i, 410.

2. If the appellee accept service of the appeal, after the return day is expired, he waives his right to have it dismissed. Veches v. Grayson, ii. 415.

3. Where appellant obtained the judge's order for an appeal within the two years: *Held*, immaterial that he did not cause citation of appeal to be served until afterwards. Baldwin v. Martin et al., ii, 552.

4. Admission of service of citation of appeal cannot have a greater effect than service, would. Leglise v. His Creditors, iii, 283.

5. The appellant may bring up either the original petition of appeal, or a copy. Louisiana Bank v. Morgan, Dorsey & Co., iii, 318.

6. Service of citation of appeal on the attorney of the appellee, is not sufficient, unless it is shown the latter was absent from the state. M'Micken v. Smith and Wife, iii, 605;

7. Nothing will cure want of citation but appearance and pleading to the merits. *Ibid.*

8. It is not a good service of a citation of appeal, that it may be made on a curator *ad hoc* when the party dies *pendente lite*. His heir should be cited. *Ibid.*

9. A citation of appeal is improperly served on the attorney on record, when the appellee resides in the state. Phelps et al. v. Overton, iii, 852; Nuttall and Wife v. Kirkland, iv, 517.

10. When the appellee is absent, and has two attorneys on record, the citation may be served on either. M'Micken v. Riley et al. Administrators, iv, 288.

4. An appeal can not be granted to a party who is without pecuniary interest. La-
fitte v. Duncan, iii, 415.

5. When a third person appeals, and his right to do so is denied in the Supreme Court,
the case must be remanded, in order that the issue be tried in a court of original jurisdiction.
Hermann v. Smith, iii, 791; Oakley v. Phillips, iii, 851; Ibid. iv, 254.

6. The third possessor may appeal from a judgment against the mortgager. Planters'
Bank of Georgia v. Proctor, iv, 48.

7. When there has been an appeal and judgment in the appellate court, third parties
can not have the case again examined on appeal. Lacroix v. Menard et al., iv, 268.

8. When a party appeals from a judgment rendered between others, he must show it
was erroneous as it respects them. Hermann v. Smith, iv, 396.

9. And he can not avail himself of a technical objection which the defendant waived.
Ibid.

I *Of the different Manners of bringing up Appeals, and of Informalities in so doing.*

1. Statement of facts may be made at any time before the judgment is actually signed;
if made subsequently, it must be by consent of parties. Syndic of Hellis v. Asselvo, i, 108.

2. On the appellant's failure to do so, the record can not be brought up by the appellee.
Carson v. Wallace, i, 362.

3. A certificate of the judge that the record contains all the evidence adduced on the
trial, under the act of 1817, is good, though made one year after judgment. Franklin v.
Kemble's Executor, i, 438.

4. It is not necessary that the judge certify that all the testimony in the cause accompanies the record, when the evidence was reduced to writing. Barnwell v. Kumbel, i,
533.

5. A statement of facts, without a date, made *as well as is recollected,* and stating that
other facts were proved which the judge considered immaterial, is not good. Ship et al.
v. Cuny et al., i, 702.

6. Formal imperfections do not prevent the Supreme Court from proceeding to judgment. Dussuau et al. v. Rilieux, i, 731.

7. When the parol evidence is not reduced to writing in open court, the appellant has
no right to bring it before the Supreme Court, otherwise than by a statement of facts
agreed on, or by the judge. Wiltz v. Dufau et al., ii, 59.

8. If a defendant do not, at the trial, move to dismiss the suit for want of an answer
to his interrogatory, he cannot assign it as error on appeal. Gitzander v. Macarty, ii, 73.

9. The clerk's certificate that he has given a true transcript of the record, insufficient.
This certificate may be true, and yet the record not contain all the matters on which the
cause was tried. Moulon v. Brandt et al., ii, 144; Burch v. Chew, ii, 597.

10. The judge a quo cannot, after the record comes up, certify facts which must, if
received, make part of the statement; nor has he any authority to certify what transpired
in his court during the trial, such as the admission of parties that certain evidence given
should not be reduced to writing: any such admission should have been part of the record.
Mitchell v. Jewell, ii, 141.

11. If, nearly a year after the trial of a cause, the judge certify that the record contains all the facts upon which the trial was had, *as well as he can now say,* the certificate
will not enable the Supreme Court to examine the case. Girod v. Perroneau's Heirs,
ii, 162.

12. When the cause is tried or written documents alone, the judge may certify at any
time as long as his memory permits him. Ibid. 184.

13. The Supreme Court cannot take as evidence what the court a quo states in the
judgment. Lombard v. Guillet and Wife, ii, 224.

14. What is related in the opinion of the judge a quo cannot be noticed as evidence of
the facts. Blossman v. His Creditors, ii, 278.

15. The record not containing the petition of appeal, the counsel who argued on behalf
of defendant, urged that this court could only dismiss the parties from before them. The
certificate of the clerk that there was a petition which was taken out by the appellant is
not sufficient to establish the fact of an appeal, but as the manuscript filed contains an
appeal bond, the defendant, by signing that, has furnished sufficient proof that he appealed.
Mulanphy v. Murray, ii, 338.

16. The party excepting must put on the record so much of the testimony as is need-
ful to a full understanding of his bill of exceptions. Butler v. De Hart, ii, 429.

17. The statement of the judge is presumed to be made in consequence of the parties
having disagreed. Gayoso de Lemos v. Garcia, ii, 469.

18. A certificate that the record contains all the material testimony is sufficient. Ibid.

19. If it appear all the evidence was not taken down by the clerk, the court will remand the cause, although the knowledge of the defect reaches it irregularly. Davis *s.* Dancy *et al.*, ii, 552.

20. The judge's certificate cannot control or eke out the facts appearing on the record. Wood *et al. v.* Lewis, ii, 555.

21. Where special facts were submitted to the jury by each party, the case was not one in which, under the 18th sect. of the act of 1817, c. 32, the taking down the evidence in open court may dispense with a statement of facts, as required by the act of 1813. Hermann *v.* Livingston, 9 *Martin,* 674. As, therefore, the clerk was not bound to take it down, or any part of it, this court cannot conclude that he took down the whole, and cannot act on it. Wall *v.* Hampton *et al.*, ii, 684.

22. If a case be submitted on special facts, the evidence cannot be legally brought before the Supreme Court. Syndics of Weimprender *v.* Trepagnier, ii, 740.

23. A judge cannot certify, after judgment, that the record contains all the matters on which the case was decided, unless it appears it was tried on written documents. Conway *et al. v.* Chinn, iii, 366.

24. The judge of probates may certify the record at any time after judgment. Roman Catholic Church *v.* Miller, iii, 465.

25. Where the motion for a new trial is not shown by the record to have been made before the judgment was signed, the cause will not be remanded, because that motion does not appear to have been acted on. Reynolds *v.* Thomas, iii, 487.

26. A certificate of the clerk that the record contains a true and complete transcript of all the proceedings had, and of all the documents on file in the suit, does not enable the court to examine the case on its merits. Ditto *v.* Barton, iii, 775.

27. A mistake in writing the sum for which the judgment appealed from was rendered, is fatal. Martin *v.* Rutherford *et al.*, iii, 840.

28. When the judge certifies, the presumption is that the counsel did not agree on the statement. M'Micken *v.* Riley *et al.*, Administrators, iv, 288.

29. The law has not fixed the period during which the judge may certify. *Ibid.*

30. The statement of facts may be made at any time before the appeal is granted. Scott *v.* Blanchard, iv, 524.

K. *Of Errors Apparent on the Face of the Record.*

1. Errors in law, apparent on the record, may be assigned, although there be neither statement of facts, special verdict, or bill of exceptions. Denis *v.* Cordeviolle, i, 316.

2. Want of evidence to support a judgment, cannot be assigned as error, apparent on the record. Mollon *et al. v.* Thompson *et al.*, i. 726.

3. Nothing can be assigned as error appearing on the face of the record, but matter of law, which (without the adversary's consent) could not have been cured by other proceedings in the cause. Daunoy *v.* Clyma *et al.*, ii, 238; Butler *v.* Despalir *et al.*, ii, 315; Fitz *v.* Cauchoux, ii, 658; Caldwell *v.* Townsend *et al.*, iv, 94.

4. Evidence introduced by a party on the trial of a cause, cannot be assigned as error on the face of the record, by himself. Albert *v.* Davis, ii, 316.

5. The appellant cannot assign any thing for error apparent on the record which might have been cured by legal evidence. The presumption is, that evidence was introduced. Hill *v.* Tuxxine, ii, 557.

6. A minor above the age of puberty must be assisted in his suit by a curator, and if he be not, the circumstance may be assigned as error, apparent on the face of the record, on the appeal. Gassiot *v.* Gicquel, ii, 642.

7. A mistake in the report of referees cannot be assigned as error. The errors which may be assigned as apparent are those into which the court itself falls, not those of referees, which are always cured by the submission of the party without objection. Baudin *v.* Dubourg & Baron, iii, 368.

8. The appellant cannot assign as an error, that the judgment was signed too soon. Weathersby *v.* Hughes, iv, 222.

L. *Of Certiorari and other Relief granted to Appellant.*

1. Writ of *certiorari* obtained. Mitchell *v.* Jewell, i, 712.

2. If the parties agree that a statement of facts be made by the judge, and he decline doing so, having forgotten the facts and lost his notes, the appellant will be relieved. Porter *v.* Dugat, i, 703.

3. The Supreme Court may relieve on the refusal of a new trial; but a very clear case must be made to induce it to do so. Sanchez and Wife *v.* Gonzales, ii, 177.

4. Where a *certiorari* has been granted to obtain the judge's certificate, due diligence

must be used to have it returned, or the appeal will be dismissed. Prudhomme v. Murphy, iii, 460.

5. If the sheriff actually swore to his return of a citation of appeal, and the clerk omitted to add the *jurat*, the appellant has a right to have the omission supplied. Breaux v. Gireaud, iii, 637.

6. If the cause be tried without evidence, and out of the regular time of the court, the party cannot be relieved by a *certiorari*, but is driven to his appeal. Stewart v. Barrow, iii, 881.

7. If the appellant is prevented by circumstances beyond his control, from obtaining and filing the transcript, he may be released, although the clerk's certificate has been delivered to the appellee. Kirkland v. His Creditors, iv, 629.

See MANDAMUS.

M. *Of the Effect of Appeal.*

1. When the appeal does not stay execution, the reversal of a judgment in the appellate court does not avoid the sale made under an execution issuing from the inferior court in virtue of the judgment. Baillio *et al.* v. Wilson, iii, 514.

2. But if the judgment of the inferior court was for the delivery of a specific thing, and this object was delivered in consequence of the party not being able to give security on the appeal, the reversal of the judgment would enable the appellant to get back the property detained in satisfaction of it. *Ibid.*

3. An appeal suspends all proceedings before the judge *a quo.* Williams v. Chew, iv, 18; Love v. Dickson, iv, 577.

4. Whether appeals or writs of error, by the United States as appellant, do not in every case suspend executions? *Quære. Ibid.*

5. Pending an appeal from the homologation of a tableau of distribution, none of the creditors can compel payment of the sum for which they are placed on the tableau. Dreux v. His Creditors, iv, 35.

6. An appeal from a judgment of partition, where the property is in the actual possession of the appellee, is suspensive, although security was only given for costs. Millaudon v. Percy's Syndic, iv, 271.

N. *Of Damages on Appeal.*

1. If the record does not show the facts of the case, and that the appeal was taken for delay only, damages can not be given. Stringer v. Duncan *et al.*, i, 570.

2. If the appellant fails to bring up his case according to law, the appellee may have the judgment affirmed, with damages for delay. Yeiser v. Smith, ii, 313; Henson *et al.* v. Ogden *et al.*, ii 330.

3. When evidence is contradictory, damages will not be given on an appeal for frivolity. Troppe *et al.* v. Bayon, iii, 414.

4. In a hard case, the court will not mulct a defendant in damages. What is to be called *a hard case?* White v. Cumming, iii, 507.

O. *Of Practice on Appeal relative to Facts.*

1. Where the court has the entire evidence, they will not remand the case, although they think the inferior court erred in refusing to charge the jury as prayed. Abat v. Doliole, i, 252.

2. A general verdict is not conclusive in this court as to the matter of fact: we must pronounce on it after the consideration of the statement of facts: if there is no statement, &c., the case will be remanded. Chetodeau's Heirs v. Dominguez, i, 593.

3. The decision of the inferior court on a question of fact will prevail in the Supreme Court, if not clearly erroneous. Rachel v. St. Amand, i, 643; Evans v. Richardson, ii, 278; Vialet v. Lalande, iv, 47.

4. If it be doubted which of the parties introduced a document below, the Supreme Court will presume it introduced by him whose interest it was to do so. Sassman v. Aimé and Wife, i, 721.

5. Where fraud is put at issue, and the Supreme Court think that the weight of evidence is against the verdict, they will remand the cause for a new trial. The court has the power to decide differently from the jury, but it is one which, in cases of that description, is to be exercised with great caution. Bradford v. Wilson, ii, 171.

6. The conclusion of the district court in a matter of fact allowed to prevail, if appellant do not show error in it. Elishe v. Voorhees, ii, 337; Boissier's Syndics v. Belair *et al.*, iii, 12.

18. Inconsistency in pleas, not objected to below, cannot be complained of on the appeal. Ray *et al. v.* Cannon *et al*, ii, 580.

19. It suffices that the judgment states "that upon evidence of the nature and value of the plaintiff's claim, &c." Shuff *v.* Palfrey, ii, 590.

20. If a party establishes his right to a property under a different title, than that which he set up, and judgment be rendered thereon in his favor, this court will not disturb the judgment by which substantial justice has been done. Wyer *v.* Winchester, ii, 597.

21. When the law of the country in which the parties contracted is not set forth, the court must take that of the state as their rule. Campbell *v.* Henderson, iii, 46.

22. When the cause was tried by a jury below, and the judgment is reversed, it is sent back, although there be sufficient evidence to act on. *Ibid.*

23. A decision on any point connected with the merits, authorises an examination of the whole case in the Supreme Court. Miller *et al v.* Mercier *et al,* iii, 75.

24. If a paper be evidence of one fact, and not of another, it will be presumed to have been read, to prove that which could be legally established by it. Fougard *v.* Tourregand, iii, 130.

25. If the point really at issue was not contested in the court below, and the evidence is not satisfactory, the Supreme Court will remand the cause. Bailly *v.* Robles *et al.*, iii, 322.

26. Where the appellant, without any fault of his, is unable to bring up the case, so that the merits can be examined, the cause will be remanded for a new trial. See Porter *v.* Dugat, 9 *Martin*, 92. William Watson & Co. *v.* Clare, Curator, iii, 465.

27. When the record enables the court to act on the merits, their attention may be drawn, without a formal assignment, to any error in the proceedings, after ten days have expired from the filing of the record. The State *v.* The Bank of Louisiana, iii, 563.

28. When one of the judges of the Supreme Court is unable to sit in a cause and the other two differ in opinion, no judgment can be rendered, nor is that of the court below affirmed by the failure to reverse. Bowman *v.* Flower, iii, 596.

29. A party who is neither appellant nor appellee, can not have a judgment amended in his favor. Bernardine *v.* L'Espinasse, iii, 761.

30. The inferior court must carry into effect the decree of the Supreme Court, as the former understands it. Holstein *v.* Henderson, iii, 835.

31. But the latter may interfere of its decree be misunderstood. *Ibid.*

32. If the defendant, who has obtained a new trial, waives it, and consents that judgment should be signed on the first verdict, and that the record should consist of the evidence given on the first trial, he is not thereby precluded from his appeal. Ford *v.* Miles, iii, 879.

33. When there is neither statement of facts, bill of exceptions, &c., the judgment is never disturbed, if any duly admitted evidence would support it. Mitchell *et al. v.* White *et al.*, iii, 894.

34. A case will not be remanded because irrelevant testimony was received. Thompson *v.* Chaveau *et al.*. iv, 15.

35. A defendant who did not appeal can not be heard. Plauche *et al. v.* Gravier *et al.*, iv, 15.

36. Where, from the time and manner of trying a suit, a party has had no opportunity of being heard, the cause will be remanded. Barrow *v.* Steward, iv, 93.

37. The appellant cannot be relieved, unless there is a judgment which the Supreme Court may reverse. Pradere *v.* Bertholet, iv, 183.

38. If the appellant fail to bring up the record, the appellee may do so, and claim an affirmance of the judgment and damages. Mead *v.* Tippet, iv, 226.

39. If justice appears to have been done by the verdict, and no attempt was made below to set it aside, the Supreme Court will maintain the judgment given thereon, although the evidence might have sustained a different verdict. Hebert *v.* Esnard, iv, 596.

APPRENTICE.

A master may punish his apprentice. Mitchell *v.* Armitage, ii, 67,

ARBITRATOR.

1. The sentence of arbitrators is a judgment in itself, over which the court has no control except to place it on record and order its execution: and whether it be, or not, a judicial proceeding, to be homologated it must be written in that language in which is written the constitution of the United States. Ditman *v.* Hotz, i, 717.

2. As arbitrators are not required to keep a written account in detail of all their pro-

ceedings, parol evidence may be admitted to show when they met. All the arbitrators must be present at the award, but if a majority concur it suffices for them to sign. Porter v. Dugat, ii, 309.

3. If the submission be to an award under the hands and seals of the arbitrators, the seals are essential, and if the contract arise in another country, it is for this court *jus dicere* not *jus dare*, how much soever it might condemn such technicality. Bell v. James, iii, 720.

ARREST.

1. Arrest before debt is payable not permitted. Whetton v. Townsend, i, 20.

2. On failure of plaintiff to make the advance for the maintenance of his debtor in jail, the latter can not be discharged *ex parte*, without notice to plaintiff. Dodge's Case, i, 507.

3. A debtor within the prison bounds, may avail himself of the act of 1808, in favor of debtors in actual custody. Brainard v. Francis, ii, 624.

See also ATTACHMENT and BAIL.

ASSIGNMENT.

1. No particular form and specific instrument is requisite in the assignment or transfer of debts. It may as well be done by an order on a debtor to pay a third person, as by giving up the evidence of the debt. Gray v. Trafton *et al.*, ii, 392.

2. The service on the debtor of a copy of the assignment, is not essentially requisite, to vest the debt in the assignee. Notice to the former suffices. Touro v. Cushing, ii, 504.

3. If debts be assigned as collateral security, by public act, the assignee is not obliged to use the same diligence as the endorsee of negotiable paper. Johnson *et al.* v. Sterling, iii, 137.

4. An agreement that the expenses of collection shall be borne by the assignor, does not authorise the assignee to charge a fee for his own trouble. *Ibid.*

5. Notice received by garnishee previous to attachment of an assignment made in New York, of the property in his hands, invalidates the attachment. Chartres v. Cairnes *et al.*, iii, 208.

6. The creditors of the assignor may seize the debt assigned, as long as the assignee has not given notice of the assignment to the debtor. Bainbridge v. Clay, iii, 226.

7. The transfer of a debt vests only an inchoate right in the assignee, and until notice to the debtor, any creditor of the assignor may pursue it. Carlin v. Dumartrait *et al.*, iii, 445.

8. The recording of a transfer of a debt in the office of a parish judge, does not operate as a notice to third persons. Thomas v. Callihan's Heirs, iii, 498.

9. The surety is affected by notice of assignment given to the principal. Reeves *et al.* v. Barton *et al.*, iii, 841.

10. If the transferee neglects to give notice of the transfer to the debtor, payment compulsorily made by the latter to the transferor, destroys the transferee's right against the debtor. Styles v. M'Neil's Heirs, iii, 847.

11. The debtor who suffers his creditor to have judgment after notice of the assignment of the debt can not resist the claim of the assignee. Ramsay v. Littlejohn, iv, 387.

ASSUMPTION.

The assumption of the debt of another must be strictly proved. Old *et al.* v. Fee, i, 611.

ATTACHMENT.

A. *When Attachment will lie, and of Affidavit to obtain it.*
B. *Of the conflict between Attaching Creditors and persons claiming under debtor.*
C. *Of Garnishees; their rights, duties, and liabilities.*
D. *Of the motion to dissolve Attachment.*
E. *Different decisions on the law relative to Attachments.*

A. *When Attachment will lie, and of Affidavit to obtain it.*

1. A shipper suing the master and owners of a vessel for goods lost through their neglect, may attach their property. Hunt v. Norris, i, 282.

2. A ship sold in Philadelphia, while she is in the port of New Orleans, may be attached

by a citizen of Louisiana, for a debt of the vendor, before the vendee takes possession. Price v. Morgan, i, 607.

3. An affidavit to procure an attachment may be sworn to before a deputy clerk. Kirkman v. Weyer, ii, 85.

4. The affidavit necessary to hold the defendant to bail, may be annexed to a supplemental as well as to an original petition. Vidal v. Thompson, i, 168.

5. Attachment is not given by our law to compel the delivery of a specific thing. Hanna's Syndics v. Loring, i, 191.

6. Swearing, that the defendant owes the affiant as he believes, is not that declaration which the law requires. It should be positive, when the creditor makes the oath. Penrice v. Crothwaite et al., ii, 233.

7. A party may attach the amount of a judgment recovered against himself. Grayson v. Veeche, ii, 386.

8. The oath to obtain attachment, when made by the agent, need only be to the best of his knowledge. Bridger v. Williams, ii, 410.

9. If the property of the estate of a person who has died abroad comes into this state it cannot be attached: it must be represented by a curator. John Brown et al. v. Richardsons, ii, 434.

10. An attachment will not lie against a non-resident executor. Deboys et al. v. Yerby, Executor, ii, 491.

11. An attachment lies against a non-resident, although he be in the state at the time it is sued out. Bryans et al. v. Dunseth et al., ii, 497.

12. One who has obtained a respite, and meditates a removal, may be arrested, and his goods seized. S. J. Picquet et al. v. W. Golis, ii, 510.

13. When he is brought before the judge, his person and goods may be secured, notwithstanding a defect in the process on which he was arrested. Ibid.

14. An attachment lies for damages claimed. The affidavit is then sufficient, when it is so clear, positive, and certain, that it will support an indictment for perjury, if the facts be untrue. Therefore, an affirmation that the facts as "set forth in the petition" are true, is sufficient. Cross v. Richardson, ii, 671.

15. A bail bond given by a person held to bail on an affidavit, wherein Antoine Turcas makes oath that the sum mentioned in the petition is really due to him the said François Turcas by the said John Rogers. The affidavit was otherwise sufficient. The Supreme Court held, that this bond could not be avoided on the ground of the irregularity of the affidavit. See Etzberger v. Menard, 11 Martin, 434. Turcas v. Rogers, ii, 770.

16. Partnership property may be attached in a suit against one of the members of the firm. Cucullu v. Manzenul et al., iii, 265.

17. An affidavit made before the mayor of Cincinnati does not authorise an attachment to issue on it in Louisiana. Tallant v. Thompson & Musselman, iii, 373.

18. If the consignor direct his goods to be sold for the payment of one of his creditors, and the consignee promises the latter to do so, the goods are not liable to be attached for another debt of the consignor. Armor v. Cockburn et al., iii, 432.

19. When attachment will lie on a debt not yet due. McClintock et al. v. Cairnes, iii, 615.

20. Although a party be a resident, an agent may swear for him if he be absent. Morgan's Syndics v. Fiveash, iv, 296.

21. In an affidavit to hold to bail the agent need not state he swears from his personal and direct knowledge. Ibid.

22. Affidavit of debt, by a person who has no knowledge of it but what he derives from plaintiff, bad. Baker v. Hunt et al., i, 21.

B. *Of the conflict between Attaching Creditors and persons claiming under debtor.*

1. The creditors of the vendor may attach the thing sold, if it be not delivered. Norris v. Mumford, i, 208; Peabody et al. v. Carrol, i, 727.

2. Property attached cannot be mortgaged after the beginning of the suit, so as to defeat the attaching creditor's lien. Harvey v. Grymes et al., i, 646.

3. Credits assigned are liable to attachment before notice to the debtors. Randal v. Moore et al., i, 755.

4. Goods shipped cannot be attached after the bill of lading has come into the hands of the consignee. M'Neil et al. v. Glass et al., ii, 452.

5. Creditors can no longer attach the property of the debtor, when he has lost all control over it, and cannot change its destination. Babcock v. Malbie, iv, 185.

C. *Of Garnishees—their Rights, Duties and Liabilities.*

1. An attachment in the hands of a garnishee is sufficient to place the property in the custody of the law, and the sheriff has no right, after service of such an attachment, to take the property from the garnishee without a further order of the court. Scolefield *et al. v.* Bradlee, i, 699.

2. Testimony cannot be received to contradict the answer of garnishees to interrogatories, without giving them notice that the answer would be disproved by testimony. Allyn *v.* Wright, i, 726.

3. A garnishee who, by not answering, admits that he has funds of defendant sufficient to cover the plaintiff's demand, is entitled to retain so much from defendant, until the latter releases him from liability by giving bond to the sheriff. Lecesne *v.* Cottin, ii, 174.

4. A garnishee, as such, has no right to plead for the defendant. All he has to do in court is to tell the truth. Hanna's Syndics *v.* Lauring *et al.,* ii, 132.

5. The money in the garnishee's hands cannot be taken from him before final judgment against the defendant in attachment. Caldwell *v.* Townsend, iii, 554.

6. Judgment against a garnishee does not prevent his creditor from showing that a larger sum is due. Robeson *et al.,* Syndics, *v.* Carpenter, iv, 141.

7. When the plaintiff in attachment releases the garnishee against whom he has judgment, the claim of the defendant in attachment is revived. But the latter cannot issue execution till the satisfaction be entered on the judgment of the plaintiff in attachment. *Ibid.*

D. *Of the Motion to Dissolve Attachment.*

1. On motion to quash attachment, the merits of the case cannot be inquired into. Smith *et al. v.* Elliott *et al.,* i, 132.

2. A motion to dissolve an attachment is in the nature of a plea in abatement. It ought, therefore, to be made in *limine litis,* and cannot be attended to after the trial of the cause has begun. Watson *et al. v.* M'Allister, i, 572.

E. *Different Decisions on the Law relative to Attachments.*

1. Attachment gives no lien in case of failure of defendant. Marr *v.* Lartigue, i, 47; Hanna *v.* His Creditors, ii, 279.

2. If A buys goods for B, giving his own note, and draws on B, who pays the draft, the goods cannot, on the failure of A, be arrested in the hands of another agent of B, for the debt of A. Emmerson *v.* Gray & Taylor, i, 198.

3. Creditors of the vendor may attach the thing sold, if it be not delivered. An order to deliver is not delivery. Norris *v.* Mumford, i, 208.

4. If a debtor in another state executes an assignment of all his estate to trustees, for the benefit of all his creditors, any part of it found in Louisiana may be attached before the trustees obtain the possession of it. Rainacy *v.* Stevenson, i, 338.

5. Where the share of a part owner of a boat is attached, and the others obtain delivery on their bond, their liability does not exceed the interest of the defendant at the time of attachment. Nancarrow *v.* Young *et al.,* i, 522.

6. If two persons jointly ship a cargo, and the consignee sell it, and credit each for his share, this share is subject to attachment of the owner's private creditors, the joint ownership being at an end. Tappan *et al. v.* Brierly, i, 586.

7. A vessel of the United States cannot be seized to compel payment of toll. Orleans Navigation Company *v.* Schooner Amelia, i, 601.

8. Whether or no, forced heirs, absent from the state, are seised of an inheritance in such a manner as to subject it to be attached by their creditors, before acceptance? Astor *v.* Winter, i, 630.

9. If the petition concludes with a prayer for the attachment of a specific debt, the sheriff cannot attach any thing else. *Ibid.*

10. The property of a debtor does not become the common stock of his creditors, except in case of insolvency. Scolefield *et al. v.* Bradlee, i, 699.

11. Property attached cannot be mortgaged after the beginning of the suit, so as to defeat the attaching creditor's lien. Harvey *v.* Grymes, i, 646.

12. Although an attachment be set aside as irregular, yet if, mean while, the defendant has been cited, plaintiff may take judgment by default. Sompeyrac *v.* Estrada, i, 692.

13. Credits assigned are liable to attachment for the debts of the transferer, before notice to the debtors. Randal *v.* Moore *et al.,* i, 754.

14. By the practice at this time, an execution operated as a lien on all the movable property of the defendant, from the day it came into the sheriff's hands. Duffy *v.* Townsend *et al.,* ii, 26.

15. The sheriff's return on an attachment is not open for amendment during the pendency of a suit on the attachment bond. The latter is not a continuation of the former case. Hatton v. Stillwell, ii, 76.

16. Third parties, claimants of goods attached, having a privilege on the property attached, at the time of levying of the attachment, to an amount exceeding its value, bonded the same, with condition to abide the order of the court—and subsequently bought of defendant other property of the same kind, for which they paid him, after reimbursing themselves for their balance formerly due above the value of the property attached: *Held*, they did not by this destroy their lien on the property attached and bonded. Canfield v. M'Laughlin, ii, 69.

17. In attachments, the priority does not apply to the first judgment, for the lien commences with the seizure. Carrol v. M'Donogh, ii, 137.

18. Where garnishee, in his answers, sets up the pendency of a prior attachment in another state, time will be given to await the decision of that attachment, before judgment is entered up here. *Ibid.*

19. If the attachment was wrongfully sued out, the proper remedy is an action on the bond. Lloyd v. Patterson *et al.*, ii, 477.

20. If property be transferred and delivered to one as security for the reimbursement of disbursements made on account of the owner, it may be attached by a creditor, but the attaching creditor will be postponed to this third person for the amount of the disbursements so made by him. Skillman v. Bethany *et al.*, ii, 611.

21. A creditor may use all legal means against any of the debtors *in solido:* hence, if he issue an attachment against the goods of one of them, who is permanently removing out of the state, this is not illegal, although the co-debtors be solvent and resident. Maxwell *et al.* v. Gunn, ii, 620.

22. The defendants may offer evidence to show that no property belonging to them was attached. It is not for the owner alone to plead this. Schlater v. Broaddus, iii, 95.

23. If A recover money for the use of B, it cannot be attached as the funds of A. Davis *et al.* v. Taylor,.iii, 252.

24. If a defendant, who is about to absent himself, be arrested on an affidavit that he does not leave property to satisfy the demand, he may be discharged on showing he does leave enough to pay that sued on, though it may be doubtful whether he is able to pay all his debts. Carraby v. Davis, iii, 792.

25. Plaintiff cannot arrest the person of his debtor, and attach his property, unless both remedies are necessary to insure the execution of the judgment. John K. Ferguson v. Wm. L. Foster, iv, 339.

26. A rule to show cause why an order of arrest should not be set aside, does not put the truth of the allegations contained in the affidavit at issue. *Ibid.*

27. In an attachment case, no attorney is to be appointed, by the court, to the defendant, if the citation be served on him. Williams v. Kimball, iv, 544.

28. The section of the Code of Practice, which treats of attachment, is extremely obscure, and the English text, which, from the relative correctness of the French, appears as a translation of it, is full of gross blunders. The title, and most of the articles of the section, seem confined to attachments in the hands of garnishees: attachments in the hands of third persons, seeming to exclude attachments of property in the hands of the party. In the 249th and 264th articles, the word *defendant* is evidently used for *plaintiff*, and in the 254th, 258th and 259th, the word *garnishee* occurs instead of *defendant*. *Ibid.*

29. An allegation in a petition, that the defendant was a resident of the parish where suit is instituted, but had left the state, is sufficient to ground an attachment. But an allegation that the wife lives in another parish, will not authorise a citation to be sent there and served on the husband and wife. Such service is bad. Evans v. Saul and Wife, iv, 506.

30. Where it appears that the defendant has absconded merely to avoid a criminal prosecution, and not to avoid being *cited*, the case does not warrant an attachment, but an ordinary citation, left at his domicil or last place of residence, is sufficient. *Ibid.*

31. Where an attachment improperly issues in a suit, the ordinary proceedings will go on, but the attachment will be dismissed at the plaintiff's cost. *Ibid.*

32. The word "garnishee" is inserted in the English text of 258th article, in the Code of Practice, by mistake. It should be *defendant*. *Ibid.*

ATTORNEY AT LAW.

1. In this state an attorney and counsellor may sue for the reward of his services, according to their real value; that this real value is not to be fixed by any previous contract, but may be by allowance of the suitor after services performed; but that it cannot,

ATTORNEY GENERAL.

is concerned, results from his office, and is expressly given by statute. The State v. Bank of Louisiana, iii, 563.

ATTORNEY FOR ABSENT CREDITORS.

The fees of counsel appointed to represent absent creditors, are in no case to be paid by the mass. M'Coy v. His Creditors, iii, 229.
See also INSOLVENT.

ATTORNEY FOR ABSENT DEBTORS.

1. The fees of counsel appointed to defend an absent debtor, must be fixed by the court. Ellery v. Gouverneur et al., i, 482.

2. Seven months are not too long a period for the counsel of an absent debtor residing in France to obtain information as to the nature of his defence. Lecesne v. Cottin, ii, 1.

3. Attorney for absent debtors may be heard in court, although no property is attached. Hicks v. Duncan et al., iii, 306.

4. Whether an attorney for absent debtors can confess judgment. Quære? Caldwell v. Townsend, iii, 554.

ATTORNEY FOR ABSENT HEIRS.

1. The attorney of absent heirs, appointed by the court of probates, may sue the curator of the estate for a balance due by him, without suing him and his sureties on the bond. Denis v. Cordeviella, i, 316.

2. In such an action the balance is not to be paid to the attorney of absent heirs, but deposited in the state treasury. Ibid.

3. The attorney appointed by a court of probates to represent absent heirs, cannot do so in another court under that authority. Harrod et al. v. Norris's Heirs, ii, 58.

4. The alleged attorney of absent heirs is bound to show his authority, and establish the quality of his clients. Sibley v. Slocum, ii, 567.

5. The counsel for the absent heirs needs not any specific authority to institute a suit, under the 1207th article of the Louisiana Code. Rawle v. Fennessey, iii, 441.

AUCTIONEER.

1. A bond given by an auctioneer, instead of a recognizance, is valid. Clairborne v. Debon et al., i. 172.

2. Under the act of the legislative council, auctioneers can claim commissions only on sales; for services rendered in disposing of property for a term of years, they may claim such sum as may be due them on a quantum meruerunt. Dutillet et al. v. Chardon, i. 301.

3. If one gives goods to another to sell, and that other procure an auctioneer to sell them, the auctioneer is accountable to that other only. Hewes v. Lauve, ii, 59.

AVERAGE.

1. The expenses occasioned by the detention of vessels in consequence of embargo, or orders of a sovereign power, are not to be brought into general average. Harrod et al. v. Lewis et al., i, 129.

2. Goods taken out of a vessel to lighten her and put on the beach, in case of damage, furnish cause for a claim of general average. Hennen v. Monro, iii, 350.

3. Lenders on bottomry and respondentia, are liable to contribution on general average. Chandler et al. v. Garnier, iv, 76.

4. Losses, casual and inevitable, are not a subject of general average. Shiff v. Louisiana State Insurance Company, iv, 90.

BAIL.

1. Bail not demandable on penal statutes, by the practice. Saul v. Allier, i, 4.

2. A stay of proceedings, without a discharge granted by the creditors, does not release bail. Henderson v. Lynd, Bail of Brown, i, 44.

3. Time given to the bail, on proof of collusion between plaintiff and a creditor of the principal in another state. Berret v. Bail of Lewis, i, 21.

4. The proceedings by motion against bail, is in its nature an original action, and he is entitled to a trial by jury. Labarre v. Fry's Bail, i, 746.

5. Although the proceedings on a bail bond partake of the nature of a new action, the form need not be the same: and the notice of motion in court required by law may be signed by an attorney. Hall v. Farrow's Bail, i, 749.

14. The profits made by the Louisiana Bank on the sale of the state bonds, are to be divided like any other profits made by it in ordinary transactions. *Ibid.*

15. The object for establishing a bank with corporate powers, is not merely the division of profits among its members. *Ibid.*

16. The directors of the Bank of Louisiana, in selling the bonds of the state, had a right to pledge the faith of the institution that the profits arising from the sale should not be divided until payment was made by the state of her bonds to that amount, and the contract is binding on the state. *Ibid.*

17. Directors of banks are required to exercise ordinary care in the discharge of their duties. Percy *et al.* v. Millaudon *et al.*, iv, 430.

18. But if any thing occurs to awaken suspicion of the fidelity of the subordinate officers of the institution, a higher degree of diligence must be exercised. *Ibid.*

19. They are responsible in their private capacity for loss arising from any illegal measure of the board of directors which they did not oppose. *Ibid.*

20. They are not responsible for errors of judgment unless the error be of the grossest kind. *Ibid.*

21. They cannot delegate to the president and cashier the authority to discount bills or notes. *Ibid.*

22. If they sell stock above the market price to the president, the contract is null and void. *Ibid.*

23. So it is if they borrow money of the bank from the cashier, on a promise to replace it, either in cash or bank stock. *Ibid.*

24. They cannot discharge themselves from the responsibility they may have incurred as sureties of the cashier by reporting the transactions of that officer to be correct, and obtaining in this report a resolution of the board of directors to discharge them. *Ibid.*

BANK NOTE.

1. If a bank note without any signature were fairly to go into circulation, would not the bank be bound? *Quære?* Miner *v.* Bank of Louisiana, i, 3.

2. It would if the signatures were torn from a genuine note. *Ibid.*

3. Possession is *prima facie* evidence of property, in a bank note. Louisiana Bank *v.* Bank United States, i, 752.

4. A note neither proved to have the signature of the president or cashier, nor acknowledged by them, cannot be laid before experts as a ground of comparison. Evidence was properly rejected of the defendant's agents having paid notes which the witness offered, and considered as perfectly similar to the one sued on. Evidence of the engraving was proper to go to the jury, though not conclusive. Conrad *v.* Louisiana Bank, ii, 151.

BARRATRY.

1. The presence of the owner is not conclusive evidence of his assent to any act which is alleged to constitute barratry. Millaudon *v.* New Orleans Insurance Company, ii, 241.

2. When proof is once given of any act which amounts to barratry, the *onus* of establishing every fact that goes to excuse it, is thrown on the insurer. *Ibid.*

3. Barratry cannot be committed by a master who has the equitable title in the vessel. Barry v. Louisiana Insurance Company, ii, 257, 354.

An act of barratry once proved, the *onus* of establishing every fact that goes to excuse it is thrown on the insurer. *Ibid.*, 400.

See INSURANCE.

BATTURE.

1. The words "front to the river" *prima facie* designate a riparious estate. Morgan *v.* Livingston *et al.*, i, 451.

2. The vendee of a riparious estate acquires a qualified property in the bank of a river, and consequently the batture which may thereafter arise. *Ibid.*

3. Nor does an intervening highway prevent this, when the owner is bound to repair it, and the soil of it is at his risk. *Ibid.*

4. The words *frente a la levee* do not signify a boundary on the river. The purchaser of a riparious estate, under these expressions, does not acquire land on the river, when it is proved that there was property susceptible of private ownership beyond the levee. Livingston *v.* Herman, ii, 40.

5. By the formation of the batture of the faubourg St. Mary, the place it occupied ceased to be a part of the port. After the change, it became the property of the city. Packwood *v.* Walden, iv, 159.

6. The principle established in the case of Livingston *v.* Herman—that a sale of so

many feet, *front to the river Mississippi, conformably to a plan,* which plan exhibits the front line of the lot in question, not extending to the river, but passing within the levee, does not pass the alluvion, provided any alluvion of sufficient height and magnitude was formed at the time said sale took place, but *that* the said alluvion remained the property of the vendor—*re-affirmed* very emphatically by the court. Cochran *et al. v.* Fort *et al.,* iv, 375.

7. The court decide that the weight of evidence is clearly in favour of the affirmative of the proposition of fact, that there did exist alluvion, opposite the lot now in question, of sufficient height and magnitude to be susceptible of ownership. Out of sixteen witnesses, nine depose to its existence from 1793 to 1803. *Ibid.*

8. It seems that, in the last mentioned year, it was only covered at high water to the depth of five feet. There is no positive evidence at what height batture may be reclaimed from the river and applied to private use. *Ibid.*

9. But supposing, contrary to the conclusion of the court, that no batture susceptible of ownership existed in February, 1803, the plaintiff's case would still labor under a difficulty from a new quarter. *Ibid.*

10. The fauxbourg was incorporated two years after. To enable them, therefore, to recover in this action, they must show a batture created between the day of their purchase and the date of the act of incorporation, which was susceptible of ownership; for if the alluvion was formed afterwards, it became the property of the city, and not of the front proprietors. *Ibid.*

BILL OF EXCEPTIONS.

1. An erroneous opinion voluntarily given to the jury by the judge, may be excepted to. Rochelle & Shiff *v.* Musson, i, 98.

2. No exception can be taken to a judge's charge after verdict. Vaughan *v.* Vaughan, i. 110.

3. If counsel take an exception and offer to draw a bill, but the judge insists on doing it himself and neglects it, the Supreme Court will order it to be drawn and sent up. Broussart *v.* Truban's Heirs, i, 204.

4. No bill of exceptions lies to a final judgment. Fagot *v.* David, i, 207; Moore *v.* Maxwell *et al.,* ii, 262; Goodwin *v.* Heirs of Chesneau, iii, 110.

5. No notice should be taken of a bill of exceptions to the competency of a witness, when the same fact was proved by an unexceptionable witness. Johnson *v.* Duncan *et al.,* Syndics, i, 352.

6. Where the whole evidence comes up with the record, it is useless to consider a bill of exceptions to the opinion of the court in refusing to receive a conditional verdict presented by the jury. Duncan *et al.,* Syndics, *v.* Martin *et al.,* i, 361.

7. This court is bound to notice the refusal to grant a new trial in the district court, without having its attention drawn to it by a bill of exceptions. Muse *v.* Curtis *et al.,* i, 692.

8. A party dissatisfied with the opinion of a court stating his objection at the time, may draw up his bill of exceptions at any time during the trial. Livingston *v.* Herman, i, 717.

9. The party who excepts, is bound that the bill contain sufficient matter to enable the Supreme Court to test the opinion of the judge *a quo.* Villeré *v.* Armstrong *et al.,* iii, 212.

BILL OF EXCHANGE.

A. *Of the Demand of Acceptance and Payment.*
B. *Of the Notice and Waiver of Notice.*
C. *Of the Consideration.*
D. *Accommodation Paper.*
E. *Causes which Discharge Liability.*
F. *Evidence on Bills and Notes.*
G. *Of Bills and Notes in General.*

A. *Of the Demand of Acceptance and Payment.*

1. Whether due diligence had been used? Durnford *v.* Johnson, i, 56; Lanusse *v.* Massicot, i, 121.

2. A bill from the quarter-master-general on the secretary of the United States, need not be protested for non-acceptance. Baker *v.* Montgomery *et al.,* i, 224.

3. Holders may demand immediate payment of a bill protested for non-acceptance, without waiting for day of payment and finally protesting. Morgan *v.* Towles, i, 695.

15. A certificate of protest is bad if it states that notice was put into the "post office," without saying into *what* post office. Laporte *v.* Landry, iii, 250.

16. The waiver of notice must be express, and can not be inferred. *Ibid.*

17. The certificate of the notary that he notified the endorser by express, although read without opposition, does not establish a legal notice. Duraldo's Heirs *v.* Guidry, iii, 455.

18. In an action against an agent for endorsing a note without authority, proof must be given of notice of protest to him or to the principal. Clay *v.* Oakley, iii, 480.

19. Depositing the notice in a post office is not sufficient if the endorser lives in the place where the post office is situate. And if he lives out of the place, the notice is bad if directed to him as living in it. *Ibid.*

20. A post-office is not the proper place to deposit a notice when the endorser lives in the same town or adjoining it. M'Crummen *v.* M'Crummen *et al.,* iii, 489.

21. The post-office is not a place of deposit for notices of protest, but the mail may be used as a means of their conveyance. Laporte *v.* Landry, iii, 576.

22. The offer of an endorser to endorse a note for the same sum, is not a waiver of notice. *Ibid.*

23. The declaration of a notary that he gave notice of the protest of a note, must be recorded under his signature and that of two witnesses. Allain *v.* Whitaker *et al.,* iii, 637.

24. Whether it ought not to state in what post-office the notice was put. *Ibid.*

25. The notary should state in what post-office he put the notice. Pritchard *v.* Hamilton, iv, 14.

26. Where the endorser lives within three miles of the post-office, notice put there is not sufficient. Louisiana State Bank *v.* Rowel *et al.,* iv. 37.

27. Since the act of assembly of 1823, the post-office is, in certain cases, a proper place of deposit for notices to endorsers. Before that time, *alias.* Pritchard *v.* Scott, iv, 328.

C. *Of the Consideration.*

1. The maker of a note can not, against a fair endorsee, avail himself of an equity which would have destroyed the claim of the original payee. Hubbard *et al. v.* Fulton's Heirs, i, 700.

2. There is no difference between a *want* and a *failure* of consideration. Each may be set up as a defence, not only against the original payee, but also against an endorsee who took the note with the knowledge of an equitable circumstance entitling the maker to avail himself of the defence. Leblanc *v.* Sanglair *et al.,* ii, 334.

3. The acceptor of a bill of exchange has no right to go into the consideration between the drawer and drawee. Debuys & Longer *v.* Johnson, iii, 300.

4. A note given by one partner to the other, by reason of his surrendering up to him the merchandise which remained unsold, is not without consideration to the payee. Corkery *v.* Boyle, iv, 454.

See BILLS IN GENERAL.

D. *Accommodation Paper.*

1. Notes avowedly made to a merchant for the sole purpose of obtaining his endorsement, and by this means his responsibility, are as strictly mercantile paper as a bill of exchange. Harrod *et al. v.* Lafarge, ii, 277.

2. The endorser of an accommodation note is merely a surety, and can recover no more than he has paid. Nolte *et al. v.* Their Creditors, iv, 135.

3. A party who endorses a bill for the accommodation of the drawer, is not entitled to receive damages from the latter beyond what he has actually paid. Dorsey *et al. v.* Their Creditors, iv, 331.

E. *Causes which Discharge Liability.*

1. The endorser is discharged if the holder neglects the proper means of discovering the maker's residence and makes no demand. Hennen *v.* Johnston *et al.,* i, 571.

2. It cannot be opposed to the endorsee that the note was given to the original payee in discharge of a debt, which it appears he had no right to demand or receive. Hubbard *et al. v.* Fulton's Heirs, i, 557.

3. If an endorser, ignorant that no demand was made of the maker, promises to pay, he will be relieved. Hennen *v.* Desbois *et al.,* i. 625.

4. The maker of a note can not, against a fair endorsee, avail himself of an equity which would have destroyed the claim of the original payee. Hubbard *et al. v.* Fulton's Heirs, i, 700; Thompson *v.* Gibson, ii, 420.

21. A witness swearing that he had no recollection of giving the notice of a except from the memorandum on the back of it, but that he had no doubt he had it, or he would not have made such a memorandum, is legal proof that the notice given. Ballard v. Wilson, iii, 505.

22. Notes taken up with the endorser's name in them are *prima facie* evidence of ment by the maker. Miller v. Reynolds *et al.*, iii, 702.

23. The certificate of the notary who protested the note, is admissible in ev although it does not establish every fact necessary to prove plaintiff's claim. Dicks v. Chew *et al.*, iii, 888.

24. Repossession of a note once specially transferred by the endorser, is not evi of title, but it is if the transfer was in blank. Sprigg v. Cuny's Heirs, iv, 230.

25. If the acceptance be not dated, parol evidence is admissible to show on what day was made. Kenner *et al.* v. Their Creditors, iv, 418.

H. Of Bills and Notes in general.

1. Although defendant added "Parish Judge" to his name he is personally sua Pailletté *et al.* v. Carr, i, 152.

2. A blank endorsement may be stricken out at the trial. Baker v. Montgomery *et* i, 224.

3. The endorser of a note can not claim its amount, if it be not re-indorsed to unless he has paid it to one of the subsequent indorsees. Arnold v. Bureau, i, 563.

4. A note payable " on the first of May next *fixed*" is payable on that day, and no of grace are allowed on it. Durnford v. Patterson *et al*, i, 587.

5. The payee's writing on the back of a note " I guarantee the payment of this n does not render the transferee an endorsee. Canfield *et al.* v. Vaughan *et al.*, i, 684.

6. *Quære*, whether a note is said to be due on the day its term expires, or on the day of grace, with reference to its becoming burthened, in case of transfer, with equities existing on that day in the hands of the maker. *Ibid.*

7. The endorser of a note not negotiable is not suable until the insolvency of the ma Rappey v Dromgoole *et al.*, i, 689.

8. It may lawfully be stipulated that in case a note be not paid at maturity it bear interest *ten per cent.* from its date: whether this stipulation be regarded as a per or simply as an agreement to pay interest on the condition expressed, there is no why the promissor should not be bound by it. Lauderdale v. Gardner, i, 690.

9. A blank endorsement gives a right of action to the holder of a note. Abat v. Ri ii, 4.

10. A wife is not bound by a note, on which the name of her husband is written abo hers, where his signature is denied and not proved. Lombard v. Guillet and Wife, 224.

11. The wife is not bound by a note executed jointly with her husband. *Ibid.*

12. A note, the payment of which is secured by special mortgage, may be sued on the ordinary way. Croghan v. Conrad, ii, 237.

13. The endorsement and negotiability of a note is not restrained by its being phrased *ne varietur* by a notary. Fusilier v. Bonin *et al.*, ii, 308.

14. A person to whom a negotiable note is offered, is fairly obliged to inquire into validity in the single case of *circumstances reasonably creating suspicion*. If one transf a note purporting to be *value received in a horse*, that does not place the endorsee in different situation from that of endorsee of a note *for value received;* this creates reasonable suspicion. *Ibid.*

15. A note payable in sugar is not negotiable. Pepper v. Peytavin, ii, 383.

16. A promissory note is not invalid because the sum is stated in figures. Nugent Roland, ii, 381.

17. If a note be marked *ne varietur*, it would not oblige the endorsee receiving it, go to the notary's office to examine into the original consideration of it, nor does it any suspicion on the note. See 12 *Martin*, 237. Canfield v. Gibson, ii, 418.

18. If a partner, after his copartner's death, endorse a note due to the partnersh though it do not validly transfer the title to the said note, at least transfers all the ri of him who endorsed it, and leaves no property in it of his, for attachment. Jones *et* v. Thorn, ii, 709.

19. The law of March 14th, 1823, providing that unless the sum of money specified a note, bill, &c., to be due or payable, be expressed in *words at full length* when made drawn in or out of this state, except that when made out of the state, it be shown to made according to the laws and usages of such state, it shall not be obligatory, or ad sible as evidence of a debt—was introductory of a principle entirely new to the law mer

chant; Nugent *v.* Roland, 12 *Martin*, 659; Debuys & Longer *v.* Mollere, 2 *Martin*, *N. S.* 625. It only governs notes, &c., made after its passage. White *et al. v. Brown et al.*, iii, 9.

20. That if a bill of exchange be given in payment of a precedent debt, the drawer is responsible if it return dishonored. Turner *v.* Hickey, iii, 82.

21. A note endorsed by one partner, does not render the endorsee responsible to the firm for laches. Collins *el al. v.* M'Crummen *et al.*, iii, 50.

22. If the note alleged to have been lost, is admitted to have been executed, and it was proved it was protested and afterwards returned to the plaintiff, so that an endorsee would acquire it subject to all the equity, that might be opposed to the plaintiff, he will not be compelled to give surety. Brent *v.* Erwin, iii, 92.

23. If the note be regularly endorsed, the defendant cannot put the plaintiff on the proof of his right to it; unless there is an allegation that the plaintiff did not come to it *bona fide.* Banks *v.* Eastin, iii, 90.

24. An endorsement in blank, makes the note payable to bearer. *Ibid.*

25. The place of payment is accidental to the contract, not of the essence of it. Mullen *v.* Croghan, iii, 116.

26. What is full value *in money* for a note, is a question of law. Flood *et al. v.* Shaumburgh, iii, 180.

27. The endorsee of a note, after its maturity, must allow any equitable defence to the maker. Turcas *v.* Rogers, iii, 204.

28. If a note sued upon, as lost, is admitted by the defendant to have existed and not pretended to have been paid, presumptive evidence of its loss will suffice. Lewis *v.* Peytavin, iii, 209.

29. But the plaintiff will be made to give security for the defendant's indemnification *Ibid.*

30. The obligation resulting from an endorsement, is a legal consequence, and if it render the endorser necessarily liable to pay, the law must determine in what capacity, and to whom. Shelmerdine *v.* Duffy, iii, 219.

31. A note made in another state is governed by the laws of that state, although endorsed to a citizen of this. Ory *v.* Winter, iii, 296.

32. The right of a defendant in a note may be sold in execution. Brown *v.* Anderson iii, 339.

33. The attorney in fact to whom the plaintiff had endorsed a note for collection, may be permitted to strike out the endorsement at the trial. Perry *v.* Gerbeau and Wife. iii, 442.

34. A wife is not bound by a note executed jointly and severally with her husband, on a contract which did not turn to her advantage. *Ibid.*

35. Whether the endorsee take up a note by payment or by novation, his recourse against the endorser is the same. Bullard *v.* Wilson, iii, 505.

36. The endorsee need not give notice to the maker of the transfer of the note on which suit is brought. Dicks *et al. v.* Burton, iii, 698.

37. If a transfer be written on the back of the note, but not signed, and the note remains in the payee's hands, the transfer must be considered as inchoate. Ramsay *v.* Livingston, iii, 725.

38. If the plaintiff has parted with his interest in the bill and gives no other evidence of title but that resulting from possession, he will be nonsuited. Dicks *et al. v.* Cash *et al.*, iii, 738.

39. When the endorser of a note is present, and is a party to an instrument, by reason of which the note was given which he endorses, he cannot claim the protection of the *lex mercatoria.* Martel *et al. v.* Tureaud's Succession, iii, 771.

40. When a man gives two endorsers, the first is liable to the second and subsequent endorsers. Stone *et al. v.* Vincent, iv, 41.

41. When the consideration of a note to bearer, and the right of the holder are put at issue he must show he came by it *bona fide.* Bowen *v.* Vial, iv, 61.

42. The names of the endorsers make no part of the bill unless they are necessary to trace a title to it in the plaintiff. Those which are subsequent to plaintiff need not be set out. Abat *v.* Tournillon, iv, 98.

43. The holder of a negotiable note, by blank endorsement, may maintain suit on it, without filling up the same to himself. Sprigg *v.* Cuny's Heirs, iv, 230; Gabaroche *v.* Herbert *et al.*, iv, 341.

44. An endorsee of a bill of exchange, who has no interest in the bill, but endorses it to facilitate its discount, is not always to be considered merely as a surety. Weir *et al. v.* Cox, iv, 277.

45. As between the drawer and the payees who had agreed to endorse for his accommodation, the contract of suretyship was formed; as has already been decided in this court in the case of Nolte *et al. v.* Their Creditors. So also the payees and endorsers became sureties to all persons who might take the bill in the due course of trade. But the engagement of the acceptor was absolute to pay to *them*, and there is nothing in the terms of the obligation, nor we believe in the understanding of the parties, at the time they endorsed it, which creates the slightest presumption they intended to become sureties to the acceptor, or that he honored the draft on their responsibility; or that they were to be bound not only to the persons to whom the bill was to be paid, but also to the person who promised to pay it. *Ibid*

46. The endorser of a promissory note, with power to make such use and disposition of it, as she thinks proper, as long as she remains bound as the payee's surety, is not bound to admit every plea which could be opposed to the payee, such as want of consideration, concealment or compensation. King *v.* Gayoso for the use of Stille, iv, 551.

BOND.

1. The performance of either of the conditions of the bond discharges the obligor. Reagan *v.* Kitcher *et al.*, i, 142.

2. Although the proceedings on a bail bond partake of the nature of a new action, the form need not be the same: and the motion in court required by law may be signed by an attorney. Hall *v.* Farrow's Bail, i, 749.

3. The sealing, or formal delivery of a bond or obligation is not required by any law of this state. Labarre *v.* Durnford, ii, 89.

4. The plaintiff may sue the surety on a prison-bound bond without the principal and before judgment against the latter. A bond need not pursue the statute literally. Signature of an officer to a bond he is bound by law to take, proves itself. Wood *et al. v.* Fitz, ii, 90.

5. A bail bond taken under the act of 1808, c. 16, does not need to be assigned by the sheriff; but one taken under the act of 1805 requires assignment. Sompeyrac *v.* Cable, ii, 108.

6. The surety to a bail bond binds himself as principal, jointly and severally with the person arrested, and cannot avail himself of exceptions which the law grants to sureties alone. Etzberger *v.* Menard, ii, 218.

7. Penalty of a bond claimed. Hunter's Syndics *v.* Hunter *et al.*, ii, 271.

8. A bond given on the suing out of an injunction cannot be cancelled on motion of the obligor. Leake *v.* Breedlove *et al.*, ii, 451.

9. No action lies on an injunction bond, where the injunction is dissolved by consent of parties. Breedlove *et al. v.* Johnston, ii, 729.

10. Defendants who have subscribed a bond as executors may not sign it as sureties also, in their private capacity. Lafon *v.* Testamentary Ex. of Lafon, ii, 744.

11. An injunction bond executed before an order of court has been made, is as binding as if executed after. Collins *v.* Welsh, iii, 27.

12. A twelve-months bond is not void if taken for more than the property sold for. Aubert *v.* Buhler, iii, 138.

13. The surety of a twelve-months bond can not be released on the ground that the sheriff neglected to file the bond with the execution. Evans *v.* Nash, iii, 193.

14. If property attached, be released on bond, they who give the bond cannot afterwards plead that the sheriff had no right in the goods. Morgan *v.* Furst *et al.*, iii, 249.

15. In whatever way a man appears to bind himself he is bound. *Ibid.*

16. The law has not left the party a judge of the amount of the bond, even on a devolutive appeal, but it requires him to give bond and surety "to such an amount as the court may determine, as sufficient to secure the payment of the costs." Code of Prac. (ice, 578. Glaze *v.* Russell, iii, 523.

17. The surety on a twelve-months bond cannot be discharged from responsibility on the ground that the law is unconstitutional, in virtue of which the bond was given. Bradford *v.* Skillman, iii, 773.

18. Surety on a sequestration bond, has no right to the discussion of his principal's property. Penniman *v.* Barrymore, iv, 32.

19. A bond dated the 9th may be shown to have been delivered the 10th. *Ibid.*

20. The words *fourteen hundred and ten* may be understood to be *fourteen hundred and ten dollars. Ibid.*

21. A bond given in a court of the United States, on taking out a writ of error, may be put in suit in a state court. Saunders *v.* Taylor, iv, 42.

22. The surety on a bond, with the condition that the principal shall not depart without leave of the court may surrender him. Jayne *et al. v.* Cox, iv, 473. See also, ATTACHMENT, BAIL, and SURETY.

CARRIER.

1. The liablity of a carrier does not begin till the goods are delivered to him. Williams *v.* Peytavin, i, 251.

2. In case of loss, carriers are bound to disprove negligence. Hunt *v.* Morris *et al.,* i, 525.

3. In this case the defendant, master of a boat, negligently suffered a box of drugs, entrusted to him to be landed on the way, and had it not ready to be delivered on the arrival of the boat at the place of delivery. The plaintiff had a right to procure other drugs, and bring his action *instanter:* he was not bound to wait. Frisby *v.* Sheridan, iii, 80.

4. If a carrier converts goods to his own use by failing to deliver them according to his contract, the measure of damages is the full value of the property, and not the diminished value of the goods by the change of voyage. Boyle *v.* Dickenson *et al.,* iii, 673. See also SHIPPING.

CHECK.

A power to fill up a blank check is personal, and will not descend to one's representatives. Musson *v.* Bank United States, i, 530.

CITATION.

1. A citation need not be headed state of Louisiana. Bludworth *v.* Sompeyrac, i, 205.

2. A plaintiff may obtain a citation of defendant without praying for it in his petition. Sompeyrac *v.* Estrada, i, 692.

3. Although an attachment be set aside as irregular, yet if meanwhile the defendant has been cited, plaintiff may take judgment by default. *Ibid.*

4. Appearance cures want of citation. Dyson *et al v.* Brandt *et al.,* ii, 10.

5. The want of citation in the mode prescribed by law, is a fatal objection to a proceeding by attachment. Stockton *et al v.* Hasluck *et al.,* ii, 129; Cochran *v.* Smith *et al.,* ii, 738.

6. According to a provision of the *Partida,* 3, *tit.* 7, *ley.* 1, *in princ.* citation is the root and foundation of every suit. Weimprender's Syndics *v.* Weimprender *et al.,* ii, 167.

7. Neither the petition nor the citation need be in the French language. Fleming *v.* Conrad, ii, 201.

8. But copies must be served in the English and French. *Ibid.*

9. If the sheriff's return show that the petition and citation were served on the defendant, it will be presumed they were served as the law requires. *Ibid.*

10. If the sheriff, in copying a citation, insert words not in the original, it will not be void on that account. Herman *v.* Sprigg, iii, 58.

11. The return of a citation can not be explained by parol, even by the sheriff or deputy. Killman *v.* Jones, iii, 199.

12. Although this court has decided in the case of Bludworth *v.* Sompeyrac, 3 *Martin,* 719, that by the practice of the courts under the territorial government, the style of the state was not necessary to a citation in a civil suit, yet, as the form of citation in appeals is now established by law, and as, according to the constitution, all process must issue in the name of the state, a citation not having this caption will be treated as imperfect, and the appeal dismissed. Martin *v.* Martin, iii, 468.

13. If a party be not cited, and judgment be had against him and he imprisoned thereon, he may avail himself of the want of citation. Abat *v.* Holmes, iv, 461.

14. In a suit against partners, service on the sister of one of them, at his house, is irregular. *Ibid.*

CITIZENSHIP.

1. The inhabitants of the Territory of Orleans became citizens of Louisiana and of the United States by the admission of the country as one of the United States. Desbois's Case, i, 57.

2. The sale of a citizen's right, though in the Spanish law, null, and of no effect, *has effect* of a certain sort by the Civil Code. See *Partida* 3, *tit.* 7, *l.* 13; Civil Code, 368. 131. Simmons *v.* Parker, iii, 272.

CIVIL CODE.

1. Such parts only, of the civil laws which were in force in this country when the Civil

Code was adopted, are repealed, as are either contrary to or incompatitble with the provisions fo the Code. Cottin *v.* Cottin, i, 432.

2. The re-enacting in the Civil Code the general provisions in the ancient laws of the country, does not repeal the exceptions with which the general rule was limited. Miller *et al. v.* Mercier *et al.,* iii, 78.

3. The new Code can not affect any contract anterior to its promulgation. Duncan's Executor *v.* Hampton, iii, 732.

4. The omission to print, in the new Code, articles contained in the old, does not repeal them. Flower *et al. v.* Griffith, iii, 758.

5. The twenty-first title of the third book of the old Code, is yet in force. *Ibid.*

6. The Code of 1808 received legislative sanction from the territorial assembly; the amendments to that Code were adopted by the legislature of the state, and if the book, printed in 1825 as the Code of Louisiana, contains the old Code and amendments faithfully transcribed, then all the provisions in it are binding, and have the force of law; but if it contains any thing more, what has been added *has not.* If any thing has been omitted, that omission does not prevent the law which had been already promulgated in the old Code, from being still in force. *Ibid.*

7. In sales made before the promulgation of the new Code, the rights of the parties are to be regulated by the provisions of the former Code. Brown *v.* Thompson, iii, 901.

8. Observe, it is by the Louisiana Code that the innovation was introduced, that danger of eviction without *actual* disturbance *does authorise* the vendee to retain the price, unless the vendor will give him security. *Ibid.*

CLERKS OF COURT.

1. The Supreme Court will not issue a mandamus to restore the clerk of a district court to his office. State *v.* Dunlap *et al.,* i, 364.

2. Clerks of courts have had deputies ever since the establishment of the American government in this country; and the act of 1817 appears to have recognised such deputies: an affidavit to procure an attachment may be sworn to before a deputy clerk. Kirkman *v.* Wyer, ii, 85.

3. A clerk cannot certify to the contents of a paper in his possession; he must give a transcript of it. Smoot *et al. v.* Russell, ii, 532.

4. "Frequent intemperance" and "habitual indolence" charged against a clerk, are too general, and evidence cannot be received in support of them. A clerk will not be removed for having acted incautiously, if his acts have occasioned injury to no one. State of Louisiana *v.* Winthrop, Clerk of East Baton Rouge, ii, 733.

5. Procuring the means of producing an abortion is a breach of good behavior, for which a clerk may be removed from office. The State *v.* Bell, ii, 780.

COLLATION.

1. When a father has sold a thing to his son at a very low price, the advantage thus conferred is subject to collation: but the price obtained for land two years and a-half after, is a fact entirely equivocal as to this point. Boissier *et al. v.* Vienne *et al.,* ii, 336.

2. Grandchildren coming to the partition of their grandfather's estate, with uncles and aunts, are not obliged to collate an onerous obligation due by their father. Destrehan *v.* Destrehan's Executors, iii, 391.

3. A donation of community property, by the husband to one of the children, must be collated one half to the father's estate and one half to the mother's. Baillio *v.* Baillio, iii, 519.

4. A child must collate the value of the hire of slaves lent to him by his father, to enable him to procure others. Hamilton *v.* Hamilton *et al.,* iii, 783.

5. But not that of one sent to attend the child as a domestic. *Ibid.*

COMMITMENT.

A mittimus in French is bad since the constitution, which requires all judicial proceedings to be in the language in which the constitution and laws of the United States are written. W. F. Macarty's Case, i, 71.

COMPENSATION.

1. In a suit on an unsettled account-current, compensation need not be pleaded. Fram *v.* Allen, i, 134.

2. A private debt can not be set off against a partnership debt. Thomas *et al. v.* Elkins, i, 260.

3. A debt is liquidated so as to be susceptible of being set off when it appears something, and how much, is due. Carter *et al. v.* Morse, i. 647.

4. Private debts cannot be set off against partnership demands—hence, where A was a partner of a commercial firm in Kentucky, and of one in New Orleans: *Held,* that in case of insolvency of the latter, the house in Kentucky might prove its debt, although one of its partners was responsible to the creditors of that which had failed. Ward *v.* Brandt *et al.,* ii, 212.

5. Plaintiffs claim the rent of a tract of land rented by their ancestor to defendant: a note of R. Martin, one of the plaintiffs, is offered in compensation: *Held,* R. Martin is a claimant in *his own right,* although he claims as heir; that is, the sum, if any, will be his own absolute property, although his claim results from a debt originally created by his ancestor; and any debt due by him may be set off. In the same manner that a plaintiff who sues as assignee or endorsee, though he claims what was once due to his assignor or endorser, is bound to suffer the compensation of what he owes, or of contracts entered with him. Martin's Heirs *v.* Overton, ii, 552.

6. The word *set-off* is synonymous with *compensation.* Pierce *v.* Millar, iii, 99.

7. Compensation must be specially pleaded. Robinson *et al. v.* Williams, iii, 192.

8. Partnership debts cannot be compensated by a demand against an individual member of the firm. Finley *v.* Breedlove *et al.,* iii, 244.

9. If a tutor take a note in his own name for moneys due the minor, a debt due by the tutor, in his own right, may be offered as a defence to it. Ory *v.* Winter, iii, 296.

10. Compensation may be pleaded in case of insolvency, when the credit accrues before bankruptcy, and is unattended with suspicious circumstances. Buard *v.* Buard's Heirs, iii, 478.

11. Syndics are not to admit the compensation of a debt of the insolvent transferred since the failure. Kenner's Syndics *v.* Sims, iii, 748.

12. A debt offered as compensation must be as liquidated as the plaintiff's. Lacoste *v.* Bordere *et al.,* iv, 338.

CONFLICT OF LAWS.

A. *Of Different Dates.*
B. *Of Different Places.*

A. *Conflict of Laws of Different Dates.*

1. Subsequent statutes do not repeal previous ones by containing different provisions. They must be contrary. Saul *v.* His Creditors, iii, 663.

2. Where the personal statute of the domicil is in opposition to a real statute of situation, the real statute will prevail. *Ibid.*

3. One born in Louisiana, in 1802, when the law made twenty-five the age of majority, and remaining in Louisiana until 1808, when the Civil Code established twenty-one as the period of majority, but subsequently removing to and residing in Spain, where twenty-five is the age, will be regarded as a major, if he or she come back to Louisiana "when above twenty-one, but under twenty-five." Barrera *v.* Alpuente, iii, 748.

4. For the rules of construction applicable to repealing statutes, see the repeated declarations of the court in 1 *N. S.* 158; *Ibid.,* 73; 3 *N. S.* 190, 236. Peet *et al. v.* Morgan, iv, 68.

See SPANISH LAWS.

B. *Conflict of Laws of Different Places.*

1. In a conflict of foreign laws with our own, the vendor's privilege is to be distinguished as belonging to the contract itself, and not to the remedy for enforcing its execution: and if a sale be made in England, and the goods be brought into Louisiana, no vendor's privilege will spring up in Louisiana to the English vendor, there being no privilege by the laws of England. Whiston *et al. v.* Stodder *et al.,* Syndics, i, 621.

2. If a slave be claimed by prescription, the question is to be examined according to the laws of the country in which he was thus acquired. Broh *v.* Jenkins, ii, 20.

3. Contracts made in a foreign country are governed by the laws of that country, in expounding them. Morris *v.* Eves, ii, 267.

4. But the remedies by which they are enforced, must pursue the forms, and be controlled by the regulations of the country where the suit is brought. *Ibid.*

5. The maxim *actor sequitur forum rei* is a part of the public law, or law of nations. *Ibid.*

6. The law *loci contractus* governs the contract as to its nature and validity; that *loci fori* governs the remedy. Hence, if the contract be made in a country governed by the

common law, where it seems a *failure* of consideration might not be pleaded to a suit for the purchase money, but the buyer must resort to his action of warranty for a deduction, still the purchaser might have pleaded that failure of consideration. *Evans et al. v. Gray et al.*, ii, 349.

7. In Louisiana a creditor may attach the property of his debtor before it is transferred by sale and *delivery;* and that too although a different rule prevail in the country of the domicil of the debtor. *Olivier v. Townes*, ii, 606.

8. When one government permits the municipal laws of another to be carried into effect in her jurisdiction, she does it on a principle of comity; she must take care that no injury is inflicted on her own citizens thereby. *Ibid.*

9. What the law protects, it has a right to regulate. *Ibid.*

10. The liability of partners on a contract made in this state, is governed by our laws, not of that where the partnership was entered into. *Baldwin v. Gray*, iii, 269.

11. A note made in another state is governed by the laws of that state, although endorsed to a citizen of this. *Ory v. Winter*, iii, 296.

12. A conveyance made by a citizen of this state, in New York, though valid by the laws of that state, is void here, if made in *tiempo inhabil.* *Thorn & Co v. Morgan et al.*, iii, 302.

13. Partners in steamboats, residing in Louisiana, are bound in *solido* for necessaries furnished the boat, in a country where the law creates that obligation. *Ferguson v. W. & D. Flower*, iii, 305.

14. If the party claims under the laws of another state, and fails to prove them, the case will be decided by those of our own. *Bray v. Cumming*, iii, 528.

15. Contracts are governed by the laws of the country where they are made, but they cannot be enforced to the injury of a state whose aid is required to carry them into effect. *Saul v. His Creditors*, iii, 663.

16. Nor where they are in opposition to the positive laws of that state. *Ibid.*

17. In the conflict of laws, where it is doubtful which should prevail, the court that decides should prefer the law of its own country to that of the stranger. *Ibid.*

18 Personal statutes of the country where a contract is sought to be enforced, may sometimes control the personal statutes of the country where the contract was made. *Ibid.*

19. When the record does not show the law that regulates contracts entered into abroad, the court tests them by the laws of this state. *Coleman et al. v. Breaud*, iii, 811.

20. The contract of insurance is to be construed with reference to the laws of the country where made. *Shiff v. Louisiana Insurance Company*, iv, 90.

21. The *lex fori* regulates the plea of prescription. *Union Cotton Manufactory v. Lobdell*, iv. 171.

22. The rate of interest to be paid from the date of a note may be legally stipulated, according to the law of the place where the note is made, although it be payable in another, where the stipulation of a lesser rate is alone legal. *Depau v. Humphrey*, iv, 493.

23. Interest *ex mora* is regulated by the law of the place of payment or performance, but conventional interest, i. e., stipulated in the contract, is governed by the law of the place of the contract. *Ibid.*

24. In a bilateral contract, where the obligations of the parties are to be performed in different places, in which different laws and usages prevail, the laws and usages of neither can offer a legitimate rule of decision for all the obligations of a contract. Each party must perform his according to the law of the place *ubi ut solveret se obligavit;* and in case he fails, he must yield to his adversary damages, equal in value to that of the thing he bound himself to deliver, at the place *ubi solutio* or *deliberatio destinatur. Ibid.*

25. When interest is stipulated to run from the date of the contract, in a loan made in one country, but payable in another, as the object of the conventional interest is to afford to the lender a compensation for the profit he foregoes, in yielding the use of his money to the borrower, the circumstance of the place of payment differing from that in which the lender parts with his money, ought to have no influence in fixing the rate of interest. *Ibid.*

See HUSBAND and WIFE.

CONSIDERATION.

1. A promise, in consideration of the governor being prevailed on by the promise to appoint the promisor to an office, is not binding. *Faurie v. Morin's Syndics et al.*, i, 214.

2. The past use of money is a good consideration to support a promise to pay interest. *Garland v. Lockett*, iii, 448.

3. The use of the money forms a good *consideration* for such promise. This contract is called in our law *constitutæ pecuniæ*. *Ibid.*

4. A debt due by another, is a sufficient consideration to support the promise of a third party to pay it. Flood *v.* Thomas, iii, 658.

5. The promise of a father to pay part of the debt of his insolvent son, to a creditor, (who alleges fraud in the insolvent, and threatens a prosecution, and promises to procure a dischare from the creditors, on being secured) is without a good consideration and void. Perry *v.* Frilot, iii, 816.

'See CONTRACTS and same title under BILLS.

CONSTITUTION.

1. A law which provides means for the recovery of debts contracted before its passage is not contrary to the constitution. Police Jury *v.* M'Donough, i, 537.

2. The constitution of Louisiana began to be binding on the people, and all the parts of the government, legislative, executive and judicial, were to be administered according to its provisions, as soon as the state was admitted into the Union, and thenceforth judicial proceedings were to be preserved in the language in which the constitution of the United States is written. Bouthemy *et al. v.* Dreux *et al.*, ii, 52.

3. The law in force in this country, at the change of government, on the subject of *cessio bonorum*, is not unconstitutional. Blanque's Syndics *v.* Beale's Executors, ii, 505.

4. The act of 1813, in that part which requires the registry of marriage contracts theretofore passed, to be recorded within a year from the passage of the act, &c., &c., is not unconstitutional as regards the constitution of the United States. Dutillet *v.* Dutillet's Syndics, iii, 131.

5. A law imposing a tax on a particular parish, the object of which is the payment of a debt due by the state, is not unconstitutional. Le Breton *v.* Morgan, iii, 253.

6. The judiciary possess the power to declare laws, contrary to the constitution, void. *Ibid.*

7. The state constitution extended over East Baton Rouge from the date of the promulgation of the act accepting the territory ceded by the United States. Legendre *v.* M'Donough, iv, 39.

CONTEMPT OF COURT.

1. A disturbance of a parish judge while acting as sheriff or auctioneer is not a contempt of his judicial authority. Detournion *v.* Dormenon, i, 15.

2. An attorney suspended from his practice for using indecorous language to the court. Michel de Armas's Case, ii, 78.

CONTINUANCE.

1. Continuance will be granted though the other party offer to admit that the witness would swear to a certain fact. Larrat *v.* Carlier, i, 17.

2. The court re-affirmed the position in Locesne *v.* Cottin, 9 *Martin*, 545, that whenever the propriety of granting a continuance to a defendant was doubtful, the duty of the court was to accord it; because if there was error on that side it produced but delay, if on the other, irreparable injury might ensue. Lee *v.* Andrews *et al.*, ii, 146.

3. It is too late to pray for a continuance after the trial has begun and evidence is heard. Rousseau *v.* Henderson *et al.*, ii, 373.

4. A continuance should never be granted on an allegation of a want of testimony, unless its materiality is shown, diligence to procure it, and the expectation that it will be had. Lafon's Executrix *v.* Gravier *et al.*, ii, 448.

5. Every affidavit for a continuance, should contain a declaration that the evidence is material, that due diligence has been used to procure it, that there is an expectation it will be had, and that the application is not made for delay. Allard *et al. v.* Lobau, iii, 90.

6. When the counsel who had the principal charge of the cause, and on whom plaintiff placed his greatest reliance, was unable to attend from illness, this was a good reason for postponing the trial. The contrary doctrine would lead to the most intolerable hardships. Patin *v.* Poydras's Executors, iii, 691.

7. An affidavit asserting a belief that a witness is material, will not authorise a continuance. Gilman *v.* Horseley, iii, 701.

8. During the pending of the cause in the admiralty court, the suit between the insured and the insurer may be continued for a reasonable time. Leno *v.* Louisiana Insurance Company, iii, 746.

9. Sickness of leading counsel is good ground for a continuance. Baillio *et al. v.* Maria C. and Wm. Wilson, iii, 861.

10. Where plaintiff swears positively that an absent witness will prove *all the facts alleged* in his petition, the court will hardly declare that his facts are irrelevant, and so refuse a continuance. Winter *v.* Donaldsonville, iv, 48.

11. The absence of an attorney in the service of the state, and having his client's papers too in possession, is a good reason for a continuance. Patin *v.* Poydras, iv, 364.

12. A continuance will not be granted on the ground of surprise, when that surprise did not arise from the act of the adversary, but from the application of the known rules of law to the proceedings in the cause. Rawle, for the use of Russell, *v.* Skipwith and Wife, iv, 565.

13. An affidavit for a continuance need not state that the testimony wanted could not have been discovered by proper diligence before the trial. The words of the Code of Practice, art. 561, may be literally pursued without it. Flower *v.* O'Connor, iv, 629.

CONTRACTS.

A. *Of Consent necessary to form Contracts.*
B. *Of Parties to Contracts and Stipulations pour autrui.*
C. *Of Different Kinds of Contracts.*
D. *Of Causes and Effects of Nullity in Contracts.*
E. *Of Synallagmatic or Commutative Contracts.*
F. *Of putting in Default of Damages and Penalties.*
G. *Of Avoidance.*
H. *Of Extinction.*
I. *Of Contracts generally.*

A. *Of Consent necessary to form Contracts.*

1. If the agent evidently meant one voyage, and the principal understood another, no contract of mandate can be said to have taken place between them. Terril *et al. v.* Flower *et al.,* i, 512.

2. A party who is named in a notarial act, but whose signature is not thereto, is not bound thereby. Lombard *v.* Guillet and Wife, ii, 224.

3. If one of the parties to a contract refuse to sign, it is not binding on others who have already affixed their signatures. Wells *v.* Dill, ii, 554.

4. If A propose to B to take charge of his plantation as an overseer, for a certain allowance, B's going on and taking charge of it, is evidence of his assent to the terms.— Seal *v.* Erwin *et al.,* ii, 650.

B. *Of Parties to Contracts and Stipulations pour autrui.*

1. If A has promised B to do a certain thing, and fails to do it, C cannot maintain an action for the breach of this promise, because a knowledge of this promise was the leading motive that induced him to contract with B. Gales's Heirs *v.* Penny, i, 718.

2. He who has stipulated in favor of another may revoke the stipulation any time before acceptance. Gravier *v.* Gravier's Heirs, iii, 65.

3. The party in whose favor a stipulation is made by another, may bring an action to enforce it. Flower *v.* Lane *et al.,* iii, 786.

4. If, in a contract, certain advantages be stipulated in favor of a third person, in consideration of services to be by him performed, the parties may alter their minds, provided the third person be not injured in regard to services prior to the change. Thompson *v.* Linton *et al.,* iv, 66.

C. *Of Different Kinds of Contracts.*

1. If one give a quantity of pork and some money for the note of a third party, this is an *exchange,* wherein each party is vendor and vendee. Shuff *v.* Cross, ii, 286.

2. The obligor who gives his signature in blank, is bound by the obligation which may be written above it. Breedlove *et al. v.* Johnston, ii, 729.

3. An agreement by which A *sells* cotton to B, on condition that the latter shall take it to another place, sell it, and pay over the proceeds to the creditors of the vendor, is not a contract of sale. Bynum *v.* Armstrong, iii, 490.

D. *Causes and Effects of Nullity in Contracts.*

1. If the vendor points out a vacant lot for sale, telling the vendee it has two hundred feet in front, and it turns out that space shown consists in the lot, and a space of thirty feet in front belonging to another, the error of the vendee, who believes that the two hundred feet include the thirty, does not vitiate the contract. Wikoff *v.* Townsend *et al.,* i, 585.

2. A contract to rent a house for a purpose forbidden by a city ordinance is illegal, and cannot be enforced in a court of justice. Milne *v.* Davidson, iii, 597.

3. An instrument is not void because it wants a date. Barfield *v.* Hewlett, iii, 752. See SALE, D.

E. Of Synallagmatic or Commutative Contracts.

1. In contracts which are reciprocally beneficial to both parties, the same care is exacted of the bailee which every prudent man takes of his own goods. Nichols *v.* Roland, ii, 171.

2. In synallagmatic agreements, the dissolving condition is always understood. Turner *v.* Collins, ii, 755.

3. But it must be sued for at law, and delay may be allowed the defendant according to circumstances, and after he is *en demeure*. *Ibid.*

4. In an alternative obligation, the choice is with the party promising. Galloway *v.* Legan, iii, 263.

5. A synallagmatic agreement, neither made double nor executed, is null. Herriot *et al. v.* Broussard, iii, 290.

6. A synallagmatic contract, though not made double, is good as a commencement of proof in writing. Strong *v.* Morgan, iii, 483.

F. Of putting in Default of Damages and Penalties.

1. The whole penalty only recoverable on showing the absolute failure to perform the contract. M'Nair *v.* Thompson, i, 413.

2. If a hired horse be driven further than was agreed upon, and in consequence thereof the horse die, the owner may recover his value, and interest may be allowed on the score of damages for the detention. Guillot *v.* Armitage, i, 609.

3. If one bind himself to deliver sugar on a day fixed, and fail, he is liable to damages in money. Pepper *v.* Peytavin, ii, 383.

4. If books which were delivered to be bound are not returned, the binder owes damages for his non-compliance, and if absent, an attachment may issue to seize his goods. Turner *v.* Collins, ii, 487.

5. The penalty cannot be superadded to the damages, for these are the compensation for the damages which the creditor sustains. Churchwardens *et al. v.* Peytavin, ii, 493.

6. The penalty is forfeited only when the debtor is *in mora*. Under a prayer for a general relief, the rent of the premises may be allowed. *Ibid.*

7. Damages cannot be claimed, on a contract to deliver slaves, till the party is *in delay*, although the day of delivery be fixed by the contract. Erwin *v* Fenwick, iii, 820.

8. The putting the debtor *in delay* is a condition precedent to recovery, and need not be pleaded in defence. *Ibid.*

9. The creditor can put the debtor *in mora*, in no other manner than by a suit, writing, notarial protest, or a demand proved by the testimony of two witnesses. Hagan *et al. v.* Clark, iv, 53.

10. The obligor in a penal obligation, must be put in delay, in one of the modes prescribed by the Code, before the penalty can be exacted. Llorent *v.* Gaitrie, iv, 88.

11. When the creditor has, by his own failure, prevented the debtor from complying with his engagement, the penalty is not recoverable. Landry *et al. v.* Peytavin, iv, 196.

G. Of Avoidance.

1. Licitation, like any other contract, may be avoided by the parties thereto. Haynes *v.* Cuny, i, 700.

2. An heir cannot set aside his ancestor's deed, on the ground that it was made in fraud of his creditors. Terrel's Heirs *v.* Cropper, i, 733.

3. To set aside an alienation, fraud in the alienor, knowledge in the alienee, and injury to a third party must be shown. Kenney *v.* Dow, ii, 133.

4. Threats of legal process is not such a violence as will avoid an agreement. Bradford's Heirs *v.* Brown, ii, 181.

5. Actions to set aside contracts as fraudulent, must be brought within one year from the time the fraud was discovered. Syndics of Weimprender *v.* Weimprender, ii, 751.

6. But where the debtor is insolvent, the action need not be commenced until a settlement of the estate. *Ibid.*

7. A contract, by which a tutor agrees to pay interest on a claim due by the minor, on being allowed a longer term of credit, is not void, but voidable. And if the minor is not injured by it, the contract will not be set aside. Collins *et al. v.* Andrews, iii, 803.

See SALE, B.

H. *Of Extinction.*

1. An obligation to deliver on a certain day a quantity of cotton, in lieu of a sum of money due at the date of the contract, is not discharged by the payment of that sum. Williams *v.* Gilbert, vi, 553.

2. If a man and woman contract to carry on business together, their subsequent cohabitation does not lessen her rights. Viens *v.* Brickle, i, 611.

3. The act of extinguishing a debt dispenses with a previous declaration of the intention of extinguishing it. Baldwin *v.* Williams, ii, 564.

4. A promise to deliver cotton in payment of a debt, which the obligee *is to sell*, is not discharged by the death of the latter. Ferguson *et al. v.* Thomas *et al.*, iii, 24.

5. A receipt to a debtor *for his part*, extinguishes the obligation *in solido.* Baldwin *v.* Gray, iii, 269.

6. An engagement to furnish security that the affairs of a partnership will be liquidated, is not complied with by giving bond to pay the debts of it. Abat *v.* Bayon, iii, 374.

See PAYMENT, and other modes of extinguishing contracts.

I. *Of Contracts Generally.*

1. Where it has been agreed that the contract should be reduced to writing, until it is actually written and signed by all the parties, either of them may recede. Villere *et al. v.* Brognier, i, 131; Casson and Wife *v.* Fulton's Executors, i, 439; Miltenberger *v.* Canon, ii, 76; Des Boulets *v.* Gravier, ii, 502.

2. If a negro be staked on a race to be run, and a second race is run in lieu of the first, the negro is no longer in stake. Vernot *v.* Yocum, i, 140.

3. A promise in consideration of the governor being prevailed on by the promise to appoint the promissor to an office, is not binding. Forie *v.* Morin's Syndics *et al.*, i, 214.

4. A joiner who was bound to execute " all the joiner's work necessary to" the New Orleans' Theatre, must likewise execute such things as seem merely ornamental, for in such case ornaments are necessary. Sauzenau *v.* Delacroix *et al.*, i, 387.

5. Writing is not of the essence of a convention to pay a particular rate of interest. Delacroix *v.* Prevost's Executor, i, 482.

6. The nature, validity, and construction of a contract is determined according to the *lex loci*, the remedy according to *lex fori.* Lynch *v.* Postlethwaite, i, 540; Morris *v.* Eves, ii, 267.

7. The vendee of real property which is liable in his hands to an action of mortgage, is personally liable on his promise to pay the price. Durnford *v.* Jackson *et al.*, i. 615.

8. In cases of contracts made between persons who are absent from each other, by means of letters or authorised agents, the contracts are considered *made* in *that* country and subject to its laws, where the final assent may have been given, which is that of a merchant who receives and executes the order of his correspondent. Whitson *et al. v.* Stodder *et al.*, Syndics, i, 621.

9. A contract, by which one party gives a quantity of cattle and all the land he has, in consideration of the promise of the other that he will support him, is valid. Vick *v.* Deshautel, i, 699.

10. On a stipulation between defendant and plaintiff that the latter should keep the former's keel boat at two dollars a-day, and that in case she was lost, or defendant thought proper to keep her, he should pay 200 dollars for her, besides two dollars a-day, until the purchase money was paid: *Held*, that this contract was in the light of a sale, 200 dollars the purchase-money, and plaintiff might recover this, but not the two dollars per day in addition, which would be usurious interest. Boniol *et al. v.* Henaire *et al.*, ii, 107.

11. One who, on his father's death, takes home a destitute brother and employs him on a farm, is not necessarily bound to pay him wages, but circumstances may entitle the latter to them. Smith *v.* Smith, ii, 111.

12. Wherever the obligation be contracted, the performance must be according to the laws of the place where it is to take place. Vidal *v.* Thompson, ii, 168.

13. Accidental or overpowering force does not excuse the performance of an aleatory contract. Henderson *v.* Stone, ii, 567.

14. The place of payment is accidental to the contract, not the essence of it. Mellon *v.* Croghan, iii, 116.

15. If a contract be not obligatory when entered into, a change in the law cannot make it so. White *et al. v.* Noland, iii, 186.

16. No person has such an interest in the renewal of a license to keep a gambling-house as may be the object of a contract. Sacerdotte *v.* Matossy, iii, 214.

17. A farmer who takes in cattle to pasture for hire, must keep his ground under a good

9. In a suit by one partner against another for a dissolution and settlement, to which the defendant consents, the referees may adjudge that the expenses and costs should be paid out of the common stock. Philpot v. Patterson, ii, 538.

COURTS.

1. The decisions of the Supreme Court are evidence of what the law is. Breedlove et al. v. Turner, i, 735.

2. The Supreme Court is bound to solve doubtful questions of law and cannot refer them to the legislature. *Ibid.*

3. The courts of this state are not limited to the determination of questions of law:— they may try issues of fact. Desdunes v. Miller, ii, 592.

4. It is not too late to pray for the transfer of a suit to the court of the United States under the 12th section of the judiciary act of congress after setting aside a judgment by default. The court was divided on this point. Duncan v. Hampton, ii, 287.

5. An application to remove a cause must be simultaneous with the appearance. Johnson's Ex. v. Wall et al., ii, 539.

6. On the death of the defendant, and the appointment of a curator to his estate, the plaintiff may demand the removal of the case to the court of probates. Prentice et al. v. Waters, iii, 150.

7. On an application to remove a cause to the United States Court, evidence must be given that the defendant is a citizen of another state. Louisiana State Bank v. Morgan, Dorsey & Co., iii, 318.

8. A petition to remove a case to a court of the United States, need not be filed personally. Fisk v. Fisk, iii, 434.

See APPEAL, and JURISDICTION.

DAMAGES.

1. If an editor abandon a newspaper, because contrary to an agreement the insertion of an article be insisted on, he will not be entitled to damages. Mortmain v. Lefaux, i, 520.

2. Damages not given for the value of a slave killed by defendant in an attempt to arrest him. Allain v. Young, i, 719.

3. Although damages are not incurred beyond the costs, for bringing an action, in which one fails, yet he who resorts to extraordinary remedies, as an injunction, &c., must compensate his adversary in case of failure. Jackson v. Larche, ii, 194.

4. Damages may be given in such a case, beyond the penalty of the bond. *Ibid.*

5. A defendant who appears not to have been ignorant of his want of title may be decreed to pay the wages of the slave recovered of him, even before the demand. Mulhollan v. Johnson, ii, 551.

6. If the defendant deceitfully obtain possession of a slave of the plaintiff, and afterwards has an execution levied on him, and purchases him, the only measure of damages is the hire till the seizure. Williams v Raby, iii, 206.

7. Damages on the warranty of goods sold, is not confined to the price of them. Findley v. Breedlove, Bradford and Robinson, iii, 244.

See CONTRACTS, F.

DATION EN PAYEMENT.

1. In a *dation en payement* delivery only can transfer property. Durnford v. Syndics of Broouks, i, 112.

2. A *dation en payement* does not require the forms prescribed by law for donations pure and simple. This subject was fully gone into in the case of M'Guire v. Amelung, 12 *Martin*, 649. M'Neely v. M'Neely, ii, 570.

See PAYMENT.

DEATH.

1. An absentee is reputed living until his death be proved, or until one hundred years have elapsed since his birth. Hayes v. Berwick, i, 51; Sassman v. Aimé and Wife, i, 721.

2. While the cause was before the Supreme Court the defendant died: this being suggested on the record, his representative Arnauld Lartigue was made a defendant in his stead. Olinde v. Gougis, i, 227.

3. Parol evidence may be received of the death of a person where it does not appear any record was made of it. Dufour v. Delacroix, ii, 266.

4. When the party dies *pendente lite*, his heir should be cited. M'Micken v. Smith and Wife, iii, 605.

5. The certificate of a jailor, of the death of a prisoner is not legal evidence; is not the best the nature of the case admits, not even so good as the jailor's oath. Gill v. Phillips *et al.*, iii, 847.

6. When a defendant dies a judgment rendered against him must be declared executory against his representatives. Lagendre v. M'Donough, iv, 39.

DELIVERY.

1. Under certain circumstances defendant was adjudged to have given plaintiff tradition by consenting that he should take possession. Cuvillier v. M'Donough, i. 506.

2. The deed in this case is of itself evidence of the vendor's consent that the vendee should take possession when the thing sold is not, at the time, in that of a third party, and this consent is itself a legal delivery. Fortin v. Blount, ii, 429.

See SALE.

DEMAND.

1. The party from whom land is recovered, ought to be charged for the use, and occupation from the day of legal demand. Walsh v. Collins, ii, 239.

2. A possessor in good faith, does not owe fruits till after a judicial demand. Dufour v. Camfranc, ii, 243.

3. In an action against husband and wife, on a debt of hers before marriage. Amicable demand need not be made on the husband. Flogny v. Hatch, ii, 285.

4. A suit to be put on the tableau according to rank and privilege, is not a suit for the *payment* of any sum of money, on which the act of 1813, 2 *Martin's Digest*, 196, requires an amicable demand. Marigny v. Johnston's Syndics, iii, 160.

5. The defendant cannot resist the plaintiff's claim, for his, the plaintiff's, negro, and the hire, on the ground that there was do demand. Stafford v. Stafford, iii, 483.

See CONTRACTS.

DEPOSIT.

1. The depository must return the thing deposited only to him who deposited it, or in whose name the deposit was made, or who was pointed out to receive it. No other person can claim the thing till he has obtained a cession of the depositor's right, or has established his claim in a suit to which the latter was a party. Jenkinson v. Cope's Executors, i, 563.

2. An attorney who collects and retains money in his hands is not the depository of his client. Durnford v. Seghers's Syndics, ii, 6.

3. And in case of his insolvency no privilege exists in favor of the latter. *Ibid.*

4. The party who takes a deposition, must see that the commission be duly executed and returned, and to this end must see that the questions of his opponent be answered. Baker v. Voorhies, iii, 853.

5. The privilege on contracts of deposit entered into before the promulgation of the Louisiana Code, is not affected by its provisions. Sabatier *et al.* v. Their Creditors, iv, 70.

DEPOSITIONS.

1. Where the commission to take depositions is addressed to a particular person, his authority to administer an oath need not be proved. Dunn v. Blunt, i, 319.

2. Notice of the taking of depositions out of the state is to be given as in case of depositions taken within. Doane v. Farrow, i, 719.

3. But, it is not necessary that the giving notice should appear by the return of the commissioner; it may be proved by affidavit. *Ibid.*

4. The day should be mentioned in the notice. *Ibid.*

5. Notice must be served on the parties if they are in the state; if they are absent, or cannot be found after reasonable diligence, it may be served on the attorney. *Ibid.*

6. The deposition of a witness must be reduced to writing by him, by the justice, or an indifferent person. It is inadmissible in the handwriting of the party or his counsel. Key's Curator v. O'Daniel, ii, 118.

7. Proof of the official capacity of the *person* who executes a commission out of the state, cannot be dispensed with, although he subscribes himself a magistrate or justice. M'Micken v. Stewart, ii, 133.

8. Directing a commission to one by name makes him an officer of the court *ad hoc*,

and dispenses with any proof of his qualification to discharge the duty imposed on him. His certificate is full proof of what it states. Robertson v. Lucas, ii, 430.

9. The certificate of a commissioner, that a deposition was taken in his presence, is evidence that every thing which appears on the face of it was done in his presence. Bowman v. Flower, ii, 659.

10. Affidavits made before a notary in New York, are not sufficiently authenticated by the seal of the notary. Hicks v. Duncan et al., iii, 306.

11. Depositions in another state, taken under a rule of court of this, must pursue the rules prescribed by our law. Commandeur v. Russell, iii, 616.

12. Notice to take depositions may be left at the domicil and this suffices as if served personally. Cohen v. Havard, iii, 513.

13. The party who takes a deposition, must see that the commission be duly executed and returned, and to this end must see that the questions of his opponent be answered. Baker v. Voorhies, iii, 853.

DOMICIL.

A defendant who removes into Rapides, buys a house and lives there for three months, without having left any property in Natchitoches the parish he removed from, cannot plead that he is unable only in Natchitoches, from not having acquired a domicil in Rapides; either his residence is in Rapides, and then he is rightly sued, or nowhere, and thus he may be sued anywhere. Rippey v. Dromgoole et al., i, 689.

2. Declarations operating a change of domicil must be made both in the parish the party removes from, and that to which he removes. Civil Code, 19, art. 1 and 2. Hyde et al. v. Henry, iii, 225.

3. The last residence of a person who has removed out of the state, is the house in which he lived, not that occupied after his departure by the family with whom he lived. Zacharie v. Richards, iv, 20.

4. A casual residence in another parish is not such a change of residence, as legally to transfer the domicil from the usual and permanent place of abode. Evans v. Thomas S. Saul and Wife, iv, 506.

DONATION AND TESTAMENT.

A. *Donation inter Vivos.*
B. *Donation Mortis Causa.*
C. *Forced Heirs and Disposable Portion.*

A. *Donation inter Vivos.*

1. By the Spanish laws, a donation to an infant of slaves delivered to the donee's father is irrevocable, notwithstanding there was no formal acceptance. Pierce v. Grays et al., i, 381.

2. A deed of sale not valid as such may be good as a donation;—a donation is valid though the donor die without delivering the deed or the property, if he do not make any other disposition of the property. Holmes et al. v. Patterson, i, 441.

3. A donation of slaves without estimation, is void, though accompanied by delivery; for delivery cures want of estimation of property given only in case of movables. Williams et al. v. Horton, Curator, iii, 357.

4. If land be given, on condition that the public buildings be erected thereon, it reverts to the donor, on the seat of justice of the parish being moved to another spot. Police Jury of the Parish of Lafayette v. Reeves, iii, 817.

5. But the police jury may remove the buildings they erected thereon. *Ibid.*

6. Every act in which the word donation is used, is not necessarily a donation. Delahoussaie v. Judice, iii, 829.

7. Donations *inter vivos* cannot be made in the form of onerous contracts. Heirs of Cole et al. v. Cole's Ex., iv, 298.

8. Under the old Code a donation of a slave not made before a notary, and in the presence of two witnesses, was void. Jardela v. Abat, iv, 453.

B. *Donations Mortis Causa.*

1. The notary must write the will with his own hand. Knight v. Smith, i, 101.

2. Notwithstanding a will be null and void as a mystic will, which the testator intended to make it, it will be valid as an olographic will, if it possess all requisite formalities Brouten et al. v. Vassant, i, 352.

3. If husband and wife by their marriage contract, give to the survivor the property of the party first dying, provided there be no child born, the donation is revoked by the birth of a child, and not revived by its death. *Frideau v. Frideau*, i, 687.

4. A will clothed with all the requisites of the law can only be avoided by attacking its genuineness. *Haynes v. Cuny*, i, 700.

5. After the court of probates has ordered the execution of a will, any person interested in setting aside the will may be heard against it in the district courts. *Bouthemy et al. v. Dreux et al.*, ii, 52.

6. In the country, it is sufficient for the validity of nuncupative wills under private signature, if they are passed in presence of three witnesses residing in the place where the testament is received, or of four residing out of it. Civil Code, 228—98: *Held*, that such a will, executed in the country in presence of five witnesses, most of whom were nonresidents of the place, three of whom swear that they were present at the making of the will, and do not think it was possible to procure more witnesses, is valid. *Fleckner v. Nelder*, ii, 361.

7. But it must appear that more than three *can not* be procured. *Fruge et al. v. Lacasse*, ii, 529.

8. One witness may prove a will. *Bouthemy v. Dreux et al.*, ii, 374.

9. Witnesses to a will may contradict enunciations in it. *Ibid.*

10. The names of the witnesses to a nuncupative will under private signature need not be inserted in the body of the will. *Ibid.*

11. Facts which depend on proof should be alleged, so that the adverse party may disprove them in the inferior court. *Ibid.*

12. Presentation of the will to witnesses need not be *manual*. *Ibid.*

13. An olographic will is not marred by the attestation of subscribing witnesses. *Heirs of Andrews v. Executors of Andrews*, ii, 395.

14. If the proof of a will's being read over to the testator in the presence of witnesses is furnished by the testament itself, it matters not in what words it is conveyed. *Seghers, Attorney for absent Heirs, v. Antheman, Executor*, ii, 402.

15. Where a will is witnessed at intervals of time, and there are alterations made in the testament between the first and last attestation, it is void. *Crane et al. v. Marshall*, ii, 550.

16. If a will be not void, but voidable, no one but the heir at law can take advantage of the defect. *Bonne et al. v. Powers*, iii, 127.

17. The validity of a will, which has not been presented to the judge of probates, will not be inquired into in the district court. *Bradford's Curator v. Beauchamp*, iii, 134.

18. Till such a will has been so presented, it cannot authorise prescription. *Ibid.*

19. A devise to the mother for life, remainder to the children, in equal parts, to be held for the survivors, down to the last, in the event of death before marriage or without issue, is a substitution which the law reprobates. *Farrer et al. v. M'Cutcheon et al.*, iii, 293.

20. General expressions in a will are to be restrained by what precedes and follows them. So a bequest of "1000 dollars, my movable estate, plate and jewels" will not entitle the legatee to *all* the movable or personal estate. *Lartigue et al. v. Duhamel's Executor*, iii, 430.

21. The process verbal of the probate of a will is void, if it does not state, "that the will was read in an audible and distinct voice to the witnesses and bystanders. See Code of Practice, art. 942. *Johnson v. Kirkland*, iii, 500.

22. A donation of community property, by the husband to one of the children, must be collated one half to the father's estate and one half to the mother's. *Baillio v. Baillio*, iii, 519.

23. A bequest to a master of a slave, of a sum of money in payment of the slave, is not a *fidei commissum*, and therefore prohibited by law. *Mathurin v. Livaudais*, iii, 551.

24. A trifling variance between the expressions used by the testator and the words written by the notary, is not fatal. *Hamilton v. Hamilton et al.*, iii, 783.

25. The clause declaratory of the testator's sanity, is a mere formula. *Ibid.*

26. The notary may ask of the testator in what manner he wishes to dispose of his property. *Ibid.*

27. It is a fatal objection to a will offered as an authentic nuncupative one, that no mention is made of its having been written by the notary. *Masse's Heirs v. Pierre et al.*, iii, 834.

28. On the allowance of the various objections, the court will not reserve to the party offering it the faculty of presenting it as a nuncupative will by private act. *Ibid.*

29. A grant of letters testamentary, is an order that the will be executed. Swift v. Williams *et al.*, iii, 891.

30. In cases of doubt whether a will presents a substitution or not, it should be maintained. Heirs of Cole *et al.* v. Cole's Executors, iv, 298.

31. A will made in one state, and admitted to probate in another, may be ordered for execution in this state, on producing the record of its having been admitted to probate by any court of competent jurisdiction. State v. Probate Judge of Iberville, iv, 628.

C. *Forced Heirs and Disposable Portion.*

1. If a father bequeath the whole of his property to his natural children the legacy must be reduced to the amount limited by law. Sennet v. Sennet's Legatees, i, 142.

2. The new Code recognises the father and mother only as forced heirs in the ascending line: this repealed the provisions of the old Code which recognised as such all ascendants. Johnston v. Kirkland *et al.*, iii, 864.

3. When the deceased leaves a father or mother, he or she is forced heir for the one-fourth of the estate. And the child may dispose of three fourths by last will and testament. Heirs of Cole *et al.* v. Cole's Executor, iv, 298.

See LEGACY and SUCCESSION.

DONALDSONVILLE.

1. The act of 1823 professedly changed the limits of Donaldson, as fixed by the act of 1813, and Winter's land was excluded by the last legislation. Winter v. Corporation of Donaldsonville, iv, 617.

EMANCIPATION.

1. Parol evidence of an agreement for the freedom of a slave is inadmissible. Victoire v. Dussau, i, 240.

2. The *Code Noir* of Louis XV, requiring written acts of emancipation, was for a short time only in force in Louisiana. Beard v. Poydras, i, 256.

3. A deed of emancipation of a slave under the age of thirty, is void. Trudeau's Executor v. Robinette, i, 592.

4. A master who has agreed to free his slave for a fixed price, can not be compelled to free him after he has received a partial payment only. Cuffy v. Castillon, i, 407.

5. Under Spanish laws freedom may be obtained by prescription. Metayer v. Moret, i, 415. And the time necessary may be spent partly in Havanna, and partly in Louisiana, Metayer v. Metayer, i, 450.

6. The marriage of a slave has its civil effects on his emancipation. Girod v. Lewis, i, 505.

7. An act of emancipation passed by a person who at the time held and possessed the negro as a slave is *prima facie* evidence that it was done by the owner. Simmins v. Parker, iii, 272.

8. A slave under thirty years of age, cannot be presumed to have been emancipated.— Meilleur *et al.* v. Coupry, iv, 453.

ERASURES AND INTERLINEATIONS.

1. The interlineation in a deed of the words " in front" is not material when the number of arpens may be correctly ascertained. Barrabine *et al.* v. Bradshears, i, 356.

ERROR.

A party who had agreed to pay damages for a trespass on the plaintiff's land, cannot allege his error as to the title of the plaintiff without proving it. Labolais v. Bernard, iii, 810.

EVIDENCE.

A. *Of Witnesses.*
    1. *Competency.*
    2. *Of the rights and duties of witnesses, and mode of examination.*
B. *Of Evidence as admissible under the allegata or Pleadings.*
C. *Of the Burden of Proof.*

D. *Of Parol Evidence.*
    1. *As affecting written evidence.*
    2. *As affecting immovable property.*
    3. *Of the admissibility of parol evidence generally.*
E. *Of the Confessions and Declarations of the parties and of third persons.*
F. *Of Books of Account and of Vouchers.*
G. *Of Evidence and Proceedings in a different Suit, or on a former Trial.*
H. *Of Authentication of Records and Documents from other States and Countries, and of printed Statutes.*
I. *Of Admissibility and Effect of Judgments, Decrees, and Judicial Proceedings.*
K. *Of Certificates of Judges, Clerks, Sheriffs, and other Officers of State.*
L. *Of Plans and Surveys.*
M. *Of the proof of Signatures and Execution of Written Documents not Authentic.*
N. *Of Copies.*
O. *Of Loss of Writings, and of Parol Proof of the Contents of Written Documents.*
P. *Of Evidence generally.*

A. *Of Witnesses.*—1. *Of their Competency.*

1. He who bespeaks work for another is a good witness. Trouard *v.* Beauregard, i. 10.

2. In an indictment for forgery, the person whose handwriting was forged is a competent witness. Territory *v.* Barreau, i, 26.

3. The rule of the Civil Code relative to the competency of witnesses was not intended to affect the right of suitors to require the testimony of persons against their own interest. When a person is offered as a witness, and sworn on his *voir dire*, the examination ought to be suffered to ascertain in favor of *which* party is his interest. To discover the interest of a witness, it is immaterial whether it is done on an oath administered in chief or on his *voir dire.* Rochelle & Shiff *v.* Musson, i, 98.

4. Attorney in fact is an admissible evidence. Duplantier *v.* Randolph, i, 108.

5. The counsel of a party is not an incompetent witness for him. Menendez *v.* Syndics of Larionda, i, 121.

6. Defendant's co-trespasser may be a witness for him. Harang *v.* Dauphin, i, 209; Curtis *v.* Graham, ii, 312.

7. An attorney at law, whose fee is nearly the same whether he gain or lose the suit, is a good witness. Caune *v.* Sagory, i, 221.

8. An agent under certain circumstances may testify. Peytavin *v.* Hopkins, i, 479; Butler *v.* De Hart, ii, 429; Robertson *v.* Nott, ii, 614.

9. Ceding debtors can not be used as witnesses by their syndics, unless they renounce their right to the surplus of their estates. Clay's Syndics *v.* Kirkland, i, 268.

10. A creditor of a person, for whose debt defendant is sued, is not an incompetent witness for plaintiff, particularly when the absolute insolvency of his debtor does not appear. Hewes *v.* Lauve, i, 495.

11. A stockholder can not be a witness for the corporation. Lynch *v.* Postlethwaite, i, 540.

12. *Quære*, whether the payee of a lost note be a legal witness to prove it? Latapie *v.* Gravier, i, 640.

13. A party cannot make himself a legal witness by depositing a sum of money sufficient for the payment of the costs to which he may be liable. Meeker's Assignee *v.* Williamson *et al.*, Syndics, i, 643.

14. A father-in-law is an incompetent witness: *reversed on rehearing.* Bernard *et al. v.* Vignaud, i, 650.

15. A clerk may be a witness for his employer. Finlay *et al. v.* Kirkland, ii, 3.

16. The oath of an agent whose knowledge is derivative from his principal, is not legal evidence of the debt. Planters' Bank *et al. v.* Lanusse, ii, 146.

17. The maker of a deed is a good, and the best, witness to prove its execution. Robertson *v.* Lucas, ii, 430.

18. The court may order a change of surety, so as to enable the actual surety to testify. Butler *v.* De Hart, ii, 429.

19. A vendor who has obtained from his vendee a release of his obligation to guarantee the title of the latter, is a competent witness in an action against a third party. Vannorght *v.* Foreman *et al.*, ii, 480.

20. One who may directly be a winner or loser by the event of the suit, *cannot testify.* Pratt *v.* Flowers, ii, 674.

21. An agent is a good witness. *Ibid.*

61*

22. A district judge cannot be examined as a witness on the trial of a suit where he sits as judge. Ross *et al. v.* Buhler *et al.,* ii, 665.

23. An insolvent cannot testify, in an action between a creditor and the syndics. Seghers v. Moulon's Syndics, ii, 756.

24. When the witness has an interest in the question to be determined, and none in the event of the suit, the objection goes to his credibility, not to his competency. Broussard *v.* Duhamel, iii, 6.

25. An attorney on record cannot become a competent witness by striking his name off the docket, and renouncing his fee. English *v.* Latham, iii, 28.

26. A witness who acknowledges he is responsible for costs, but has means secured to pay them, is not incompetent. Collins *et al. v.* M'Crummen *et al.,* iii, 50.

27. A witness, whose interest it is to defeat the claim, is a good one for the plaintiff. *Also,* a witness may be excluded as to the items of an account in which he is interested, yet he must be heard on the others. M'Micken *v.* Fair, iii, 264.

28. A partner who has sold to his co-partners any debts that may be due to the firm, and who receives a release from the partnership, is a competent witness. Meriam *et al. v.* Worsham *et al.,* iii, 271.

29. The mate is a good witness for the captain, in a suit against him for negligence. Jordan *v.* White, iii, 315.

30. In a suit against the part owner of a steamboat, another owner is a good witness for the defendant. *Ibid.*

31. An interest in the event of the suit, alone renders a witness incompetent. Marburg *v.* Canfield, iii, 383.

32. A churchwarden is an admissible witness in behalf of the corporation of a church. Marc *v.* Church of St. Martins, iii, 438.

33. The party who calls a witness, and examines him in chief, can not afterwards object to his competency. Buard *v.* Buard's Heirs, iii, 478.

34. An attorney may be called on by his client's adversary to testify in the cause in which he is employed. Cox *v.* Williams, iii, 481.

35. A payee and endorser of a note is a good witness to prove that he acted as agent for another in taking the note payable to himself. *Ibid.*

36. An agent is a competent witness, in all matters connected with his agency, without a release. Martial *v.* Cotterel, iii, 538.

37. A witness whose interest is equal, is competent. *Ibid.*

38. And his being liable for costs, will not render him incompetent, if he is at the same time agent. *Ibid.*

39. In an action against one executor of an estate, a co-executor may be called as a witness by the plaintiff. Taylor *v.* Hollander, iii, 548.

40. So if he has been discharged from his office he is a good witness. *Ibid.*

41. The teller of a bank who has overpaid a check, is a good witness without release. O'Brien *v.* Louisiana State Bank, iii, 554.

42. And so universally of agents in the ordinary course of their employment. United States Bank *v.* Johnson, iii, 555.

43. An attorney is a good witness when he is not called on to disclose facts that came to his knowledge when consulted in his professional capacity. Reeves *et al. v.* Burton *et al.,* iii, 841.

44. In testing the competency of a witness, the main question is, whether the judgment to be rendered may be given in evidence in a future suit against him. *Ibid.*

45. A witness who testifies against his interest, is a good witness. Levergue *v* Anderson, iii, 846.

46. A witness is not to be rejected because he is a creditor of the estate of the defendant's ancestor. Thompson *v.* Chaveau *et al.,* iv, 15.

47. Nor because having a mortgage on a tract of land purchased by the plaintiff, he received from the latter part of the price, in payment of his debt, and released his right on the mortgage. *Ibid.*

48. When the witness who declares a fact which will render him incompetent, states at the same time facts to restore his competency, his evidence cannot be rejected. M'Micken *v.* Fair, iv, 39.

49. The curator of an estate is not a good witness where the legality of his conduct is at issue. Barbineau's Heirs *v.* Castille *et al.,* iv, 204.

50. An agent is a competent witness without a release. A surety on a bond given to release property from sequestration, is not a competent witness. See United States Bank *v.* Johnson, 5 *N. S.* 210. Lane *et al. v.* De Peyster, iv, 279.

51. The daughter who has received her share of her ancestor's succession, is still an

incompetent witness in a suit against the other heirs of the succession. The daughter may still be responsible to the other heirs on a final partition, if her share exceeds the disposable portion. Dangerfield's Executor *v.* Thurston's Heirs, iv, 499.

52. A *surety*, who has released his principal, by a novation of the debt, is still an *incompetent* witness for the principal, to establish the novation. Such *surety* is interested to defeat the action against the *principal;* because, if the *latter* is condemned to pay, he would have a right to call on the *surety*, who is bound by the novation, for the debt and costs incurred by his failure to discharge the obligation. Lesassier, Curator, &c. *v.* Hertzel *et al.*, iv, 612.

2. Of the Rights and Duties of Witnesses, and of the Mode of Examination.

1. It is in the discretion of the judge to permit a witness who had been attached, to be examined after the parties had closed their evidence. Richardson *v.* Debuys & Longer, iii, 250.

2. A witness is not protected from answering a question, on the ground that he may thereby make himself liable to a civil suit. In questions of this kind Spanish laws can afford no assistance. Planters' Bank *v.* George, i, 523.

3. The criminality of a witness can not be otherwise proved than by record of his conviction. Castellano *v.* Paillon, ii, 710.

4. An attachment may issue to compel the attendance of a witness without an affidavit of his materiality, where the issuing it will not delay the trial of the cause. Southward *et al. v.* Bowie, iii, 486.

5. A witness is not to be entirely believed if it be shown that the facts related took place on a different day from that which he stated. Flood *v.* Thomas, iii, 658.

B. Of Evidence as admissible under the Pleadings.

1. Where there is a written contract the plaintiff will be allowed to resort to it, although he has presented an account claiming less than was stipulated. Brand *v.* Livaudais *et al.*, i, 482.

2. Although the party introduces a will emancipating her, she may give parol evidence of her being born free. Beard *v.* Poydras, i, 256.

3. An heir seeking to establish his claim, and repelled by a charge of fraud, may prove what was allotted to some of his co-heirs some years before the suit was brought, while he was an infant, to show the fairness of his present claim. Trepagnier's Heirs *v.* Durnford, i, 400.

4. Although in cases in which the obligation of the defendant to remunerate is founded on negligence or fraud, it is incumbent on the plaintiff to set forth the charge in his petition, yet if it be evident that counsel for defendant, had perfect knowledge of the charges which they were called on to contest, their exception to the admissibility of evidence will not be sustained. Ralston *v.* Barclay *et al.*, i, 519.

5. If the petition charges that there is an error in a release, being a reference to a mortgage by a wrong date—it must be read, if proved, and the party left to establish the mistake by legal evidence. Hipkins *v.* Salkeld, i, 597.

6. In an action for separation from bed and board, when adultery is at issue, a witness cannot be asked the general character of the defendant for chastity. A. Trudeau *v.* J. Le Bean Trudeau, ii, 414.

7. Evidence that a curator was appointed in 1813, will be admitted under an allegation that the appointment was made in 1815. Pigeau *et al. v.* Commeau, iii, 268.

8. Evidence may be given that a partner endorsed the note for the firm, although it be not averred that the partnership was a commercial one, nor that the partner had authority to administer its affairs. Hodge *v.* Eastin, iii, 453.

See same title under PRACTICE.

C. Of the Burthen of Proof.

1. Where one party charges the other with culpable neglect, the person who claims the damage, is bound to prove it, though it may involve a negative. Hicks and Wife *v.* Martin, i, 697.

2. Where a defendant, in the course of the transaction on which the action is founded, has acted with the plaintiff as possessing a certain character, and acknowledged the title by virtue of which he sues, this is *prima facie* evidence that he is entitled to sue; and if he is not, the burthen of proof is then thrown on the defendant. Prevosty *v.* Nichols, ii, 167.

3. In an action for property delivered to bailee, and not returned, the burthen of proof

as to the facts which excuse the failure to restore it, lies on the bailee. Nichols *v.* Roland, ii, 17.

4. The burthen of proof lies on him against whom prescription is pleaded to a right of passage: he must give evidence of such acts as take his case out of prescription. Powers *v.* Foucher, ii, 282.

5. The burthen of proof lies on the party who has to support his case, by the proof of a fact of which he is supposed cognisant. Denis *v.* Veazy, ii, 282.

6. An act of barratry once proved, the onus of establishing every fact that goes to excuse it is thrown on the insurer. Barry *v.* Louisiana Insurance Company, ii, 400.

7. When the maker of a note is sued, and relies on payment before endorsement, or any other legal defence, the burthen of proof of the time of endorsement rests on him. Canfield *v.* Gibson, ii, 418.

8. Where the issue is on the life or death of a person once existing, the burthen of proof lies on the party asserting the death. M. & T. Gayoso de Lemos *v.* Garcia, ii, 469.

9. Dilatory exceptions must be proved by the party making them, unless the affirmation on which they rest, involves a negative. *Ibid.*

10. In a suit for settlement of a partnership, the partner who alleges losses must prove them. Profits are always presumed. Marquez *v.* Vioso, ii, 515.

11. It is the duty of an agent to prove those facts which will discharge him from responsibility in not collecting debts put into his hands for collection. Collins *et al. v.* Andrews, iii, 803.

12. The plaintiff affirmed that the curate *did not* receive a salary, and it devolved on the defendants to prove that he *did;* for the negative which was involved in the affirmative could not be proved. Marc *v.* Churchwardens &c., iv, 508.

13. Where the answer charges the judgment against the husband to have been obtained through fraud and collusion, the wife must give evidence to prove it was *bona fide.* Beard . Pigeaux, iv, 585.

14. The party who claims from the owners of a steamer, for a slave carried away in her must show that they could have prevented it. Palfrey *v.* Kerr *et al.,* iv, 598.

D. *Of Parol Evidence.*

1. *As Affecting Written Evidence.*

1. Evidence of a promise to pay interest shall not be admitted if no mention is made of it in the note. Toussaint *v.* Delogny, i, 45.

2. The witness to a notarial act may in certain cases impeach it. Langlish *v.* Schons *et al.,* i, 390.

3. Although the vendor avails himself of the exception *non numeratæ pecuniæ,* the vendee may not gainsay any other thing averred in the act; particularly he shall not be admitted to prove by parol evidence, that the consideration was a lesser one than that acknowledged in the deed. Berthole *v.* Mace, i, 415.

4. It is not enough to prove that a paper, purporting to be an act of sale under private signature was seen in the hands of the adverse party, but proof must be given of its genuineness. Bradley's Heirs *v.* Calvit, i, 436.

5. When an act is attacked as fraudulent or false, parol evidence must, of necessity, be admitted, not indeed to alter or modify the contents, but to support the truth of the act and the good faith of the parties. Fouque's Syndics *v.* Vignaud, i, 493.

6. To come at a knowledge of the facts from which the verity of the contract, and the good faith of the parties to the act may be ascertained, oral evidence must be heard. The heir may show that a sale made by his ancestor is feigned. *Quære*—Whether oral evidence alone, unaided by any written testimony be sufficient for this. Croizet's Heirs *v.* Gaudet, i, 498.

7. Parol evidence cannot be received of the irregularity of the proceedings of a family meeting before a parish judge, except only where the record is attacked as false. Tregre *v.* Tregre, i, 523.

8. It is agreed, that on suggestion of fraud, testimonial proof may be received against an instrument: but this can only be regularly done, in cases in which one of the parties to a suit may be subject to injury, by such fraud, in rights and claims which existed at the time of its perpetration. Sides *v.* M'Cullough, i, 605.

9. A public act may be impeached by the subscribing witnesses. Marie *v.* Avart's Heirs, i, 677.

10. Parol evidence offered against the contents of a bill of lading rejected. Center *v.* Torsey, i, 633.

11. If a slave be delivered on trial, parol evidence may be received to show under what circumstances. Nichols v. Roland, ii, 171.

12. The prohibition of receiving parol evidence against or beyond the contents of a written instrument, only extends to the parties—third persons are not affected thereby. Barry v. Louisiana Insurance Company, ii, 257.

13. To a bill of sale which stated that the *purchasers* (of whom they are two) gave *his* note for 1500 dollars, they may show that each gave a note for 750 dollars. The pronoun *his* implies the fact that *each* gave a note, which must have been for 750 dollars: to pay 1500 dollars in *his* note of hand is not inconsistent with two notes of 750 dollars being given. Lafariere v. Sanglair *et al.*, ii, 234.

14. Evidence that what an act shows to have been a sale was a *dation en paiement* is evidence against what is contained in the act, and must not be received. Skillman and Wife v. Lacey *et al.*, ii, 334.

15. Parol evidence cannot be received to prove that a note which is expressed to be paid in dollars, was to be discharged in bank notes of the bank of Kentucky. Veeche v. Grayson, ii, 415.

16. Ambiguity arising from matter *dehors* the instrument may be explained by parol testimony. Lafon's Ex. v. Gravier *et al.*, ii, 448.

17. A party to a sale cannot prove its simulation by *parole*. Delery v. Bunle's Under Tutor, ii, 515. Brocard v. Camp's Curator, ii, 517. Copell v. Dalton, iii, 249.

18. A wife claiming as legatee of her husband, cannot show the simulation of a sale by parol evidence. Otherwise, when she claims in her own right. Guidry v. Grivot, ii, 577.

19. Plaintiff may prove payment of a written order in favor of defendant without producing it, if the existence of the order be admitted. Spraggins v. White, iii, 190.

20. Parol evidence cannot be received from a purchaser at sheriff's sale, to show the property was worth less than the conveyance expresses he was to give for it. Balfour v. Chew, iii, 257.

21. Oral evidence cannot be given of the contents of a paper in the hands of an adversary, without notice to him to produce it on the trial. Erwin v. Porter, iii, 793.

22. A party to a public act, who has not a counter-letter, cannot be permitted to prove that it was feigned and simulated. Rawle v. Fennessey, iii, 810.

23. Parol evidence cannot be admitted to contract written. Walsh v. Texada's Syndic, iv, 221.

24. Parol evidence is inadmissible to show that a payment was made, *in a note*, when the receipt expresses generally that the debt had been paid. Chew v. Chinn, iv, 342.

25. Parol evidence may be given, that one of the parties to an act read it several days before he affixed his signature. Hepp v. Parker, iv, 588.

26. Parol evidence cannot be given to contradict the date of an authentic act. *Ibid.*

27. Evidence may be given to show that money was paid previous to the day on which the receipt is executed. Clamageran v. Sacerdotte, iv, 608.

28. Where a wife binds herself as principal, she may show the contract was one of suretyship, although she did not take a counter-letter. Pilié v. Patin and Her Husband, iv, 668. Louisiana State Bank v. Rowell, iv, 266.

29. A married woman, who, jointly with her husband, purchases property from her father, cannot contradict the act of sale, and prove by parol evidence, that the donation of it was contemplated. Lloyd v. Graham *et al.*, iv, 672.

30. A commencement of proof in writing, is presented by every instrument which requires parol evidence to establish its reality. And, therefore, where the contract is for land, if the agreement has been reduced to writing, proof of its being signed by the parties, may be given by parol, though it was not made double. Pignatel v. Drouet, iv, 129.

31. Parol evidence may be received to show that the contract sued on is not what it appears to be, but a cover to an usurious transaction. Perillat v. Pueche, iv, 129.

32. A notary cannot be allowed to give evidence of a party's declaration at the time of executing an act. Pijeau v. Beard, iv, 563.

D. *Of Parol Evidence as Affecting Immovable Property.*

1. Parol evidence of the sale of land cannot be admitted, though the vendee be in possession. Grafton v. Fletcher, i, 152.

2. It appearing that the wife brought land to her husband, the judgment will not be reversed because parol evidence was received to show that it was brought *in marriage.* Robillard v. Robillard, i, 299.

3. Parol evidence is not admissible to prove that a grant to L. L. was intended and

understood at the time to be in lieu of, and to operate an extinguishment of the grant to
F. L., under whom defendant claims. Chabot *et al. v.* Blanc, i, 377.

4. Where a sale has been made in a country where it might lawfully have been made
verbal, parol evidence may not be received of the sale without proof of the loss of the
writing. Toustin *v.* Lucile, i, 422.

5. Oral evidence to prove that the vendee of land did possess in his own name, speak of
it as his own property and even offer to sell it, is legal and pertinent, where vendee pretends that he purchased for account of plaintiff and offers to reconvey to him, on being
sued for the price. Peytavin *v.* Hopkins, i, 397.

6. To come at a knowledge of the facts from which the verity of the contract and the
good faith of the parties to the act may be ascertained, oral evidence must be heard. The
heir may show that a sale made by his ancestor is feigned. *Quære.*—Whether oral evidence alone, unaided by any written testimony, be sufficient for this. Croizet's Heirs *v.*
Gaudet, i, 498.

7. In giving judgment the court said: "It is agreed, that on suggestion of fraud, testimonial proof may be received against an instrument: but this can only be regularly done,
in cases in which one of the parties to a suit may be subject to injury, by such fraud, in
rights and claims which existed at the time of its perpetration." Sides *v.* M'Cullough, i,
603.

8. Parol evidence of ownership, unless to establish that the plaintiff had acquired the
slave by inheritance, bad; but as to possession, good. M'Guire *v.* Amelung *et al.*, ii, 378.

9. The rule, that the objection to illegal testimony was not waived by a failure to
except to it at the trial, (3 *Martin*, 252, 353,) repudiated, and that in 5 *Martin*, 442, re-
affirmed. Babineau *v.* Cormier, ii, 518.

10. Payment of the price of real estate may be proved by parol, but such proof of that
fact will not establish there was a sale. L. & F. Frique *v.* Hopkins *et al.*, iii, 273.

11. A verbal power of attorney if given in a state where slaves pass by parol, is legal
proof of the authority under which a written sale was made in this state. Thatcher *v.*
Walden, iii, 633.

12. When fraud is not in issue, evidence cannot be given of the consent to a sale of
slaves. Gill *v* Phillips *et al.*, iii, 847.

13. Parol evidence may be received of the disclosure to vendee, by the vendor, of a
redhibitory vice in a slave, before the sale. Dunbar *v.* Skillman, iii, 51.

14. When delivery does not follow sale, parol evidence is admissible to show from
what causes possession was retained by the vendor. Wiliams's Executors *v.* Franklin
et al., iv, 393.

15. The want of a survey does not exclude parol proof of boundaries. Gayoaos *v.*
Executors of Baldwin, iv, 656.

3. Of the Admissibility of Parol Evidence Generally.

1. A marriage celebrated in North Carolina may be proved by parol evidence. White
et al. v. Holstein *et al.*, i, 274.

2. If there be no suggestion of fraud or simulation, parol evidence can not be admitted
to prove that a deed was intended as a collateral security. Spicer *et al. v.* Lewis *et al.*,
i, 547.

3. Parol evidence will be received to show that a proxy purchased land for his principal, although the purchaser took the deed in his own name. Hall *v.* Sprigg, i, 557.

4. Parol evidence may be received of the death of a person where it does not appear
any record was made of it. Dufour *v.* Delacroix, ii, 266.

5. Parol evidence of ownership, unless to establish that the plaintiff had acquired the
slave by inheritance, bad; but as to possession, good. M'Guire *v.* Amelung *et al.*, ii,
378.

6. Parol evidence may be received to establish services rendered by an attorney before
a justice of the peace. Veeche *v.* Grayson, ii, 415.

7. To receive parol evidence of the authority given by the directors of the Louisiana
Bank to the president to sign the *concordat* of the defendant and his creditors, when it is
shown that no entry was made of his authority in the books of the bank, was not error
in the district judge. Wolf *v.* Bureau, ii, 492.

8. Oral proof may be introduced to establish the identity of a person who sues as the
heir instituted in a testament. Lafon's Executor *v.* Gravier *et al.*, ii, 448.

9. Parol evidence that the sale in question was not intended to be an absolute one, as
the deed expresses, ought not to have been admitted, in a case where, although the petition contains a charge of error or fraud, yet neither error nor fraud were put in issue to

the jury, and the allegation of them must be considered as abandoned before the jury. Wall v. Hampton et al., ii, 684.

10. The lading of goods may be proved by parol, if it does not appear there was a bill of lading. Giraudel v. Mendiburne, iii, 146.

11. Latent ambiguity may be explained by parol evidence. Pegeau v. Cómmeau, iii, 268.

12. If, after the work is commenced, the contract for which was reduced to writing, a subsequent agreement is entered into by parol, it may be proved by oral testimony. Commandeur v. Russel, iii, 116.

13. A verbal power of attorney, if given in a state where slaves pass by parol, is legal proof of the authority under which a written sale was made in this state. Thatcher v. Walden, iii, 633.

14. Parol evidence can not be received of a promise to pay conventional interest. Kenner's Syndics v. Sims, iii, 748.

E. Of the Confessions and Declarations of the Parties and of Third Persons.

1. Conversation of a party, while a compromise is in view, admitted to prove a fact, Delogny v. Rentoul, i, 55.

2. A man's own allegations on the record are the highest evidence against him: the effect of them cannot be destroyed or weakened by any contradictory evidence. Delacroix v. Prevost's Executors, i, 482.

3. The admission of a party, that he is one of the partners of a firm, may be received in evidence, although it appear that written articles of the partnership exist which have not been called for: alias in a contest between partners. Drane v. Farrow, i, 75.

4. Declarations of the father of the child, are good evidence of it, if made before the cause of action arose. David v. Sittig, ii, 418.

5. Declarations of the vendor, out of the presence of the vendee, may be given in evidence against the latter. Guidry v. Grivot, ii, 577.

6. But they are no evidence of fraud in the latter. Ibid.

7. The acknowledgments of the vendor in the deed of sale, are evidence against a subsequent vendee. Martin v. Curtis et al., iii, 33.

8. The acts of a party are good evidence when they make a part of the res gesta. Bedford, Breedlove & Robeson v. Jacobs, iii, 379; Ponsony v. Debaillon et al., iii, 624.

9. Between creditors, the acknowledgment of their solvent debtor is prima facie evidence of the debt. Armor v. Cockburn et al., iii, 432.

10. Where the title of slaves, alleged to be given by the father to the son-in-law, in consideration of marriage, is at issue, declarations of the wife are not good evidence, Bray v. Cumming, iii, 528.

11. If a suit be brought to recover slaves which are named in the petition of the plaintiff, and the defendant admits that he is in possession of slaves as designated in the petition, it is prima facie evidence the slaves sued for, and possessed, are the same. Johnson v. Field, iii, 690.

12. A party cannot give his own conversation in evidence. Pierre v. Williams, iii, 713.

13. Any legal evidence may be offered in support of the confession of an insolvent, that he owes one of the creditors in the concurso. Sabatier et al. v. Their Creditors, iv, 70.

14. Evidence of the declarations of the vendor and vendee relative to the hire of the property alleged to have been fraudulently sold, made two years after the act of sale, is inadmissible to prove the nature of such sale. Palfrey's Syndic v. François et al., iv, 509.

15. The declarations of the party who makes a stipulation pour autrui can not be given in evidence. Dismukes et al. v. Musgrove, iv, 553.

16. The letters of third persons are not evidence. Chain v. Kelso, iv, 236.

F. Of Books of Account and of Vouchers.

1. In a contest as to the legitimacy of claims amongst creditors, the confession of the insolvent, or the books of insolvent which had been withholden from the syndics, make no proof except as to his liability to pay. Menendez v. Syndics of Larionda, i, 121.

2. Either party has a right to have the other's books of account brought into court with due notice. Godel v. M'Lanahan, ii, 703.

3. Books of account are not in themselves evidence in favor of those who keep them. Syndics of Johnson v. Breedlove et al., ii, 728.

4. Vouchers filed by an executor in support of his account are *prima facie* evidence of its correctness. Casanovichi *et al. v.* Debon *et al.,* ii, 754.

5. Insolvents' books not admissible in an action between creditors. Canfield & Dixon *v.* Maher *et al.,* iii, 264.

6. Partnership books are good evidence between partners. Jordan *v.* White, iii, 315.

7. Merchants' books are not in themselves evidence against merchants. Herring *v.* Levy, iii, 330.

8. Merchants' books are evidence, on proof of the clerk's handwriting and his death; but extracts from them are not. *Ibid.*

9. If a party *is bound to furnish an account,* his adversary may use that part of it which is against him, without being compelled to admit the items in it that are in his favor. Smith *v.* Harrathy, iii, 559.

10. An account referred to in a deed of partition, is evidence against the heirs. Gill *v.* Phillips *et al.,* iii, 847.

11. The handwriting of a clerk who is dead, in entries in his employers' books, may be proved. Hunter *v.* Smith, iii, 868.

12. A bankrupt's books are evidence of fraud as against himself. Marmiche *v.* Commagere *et al.,* iv, 103.

G. *Of Evidence and Proceedings on a Different Suit or on a Former Trial.*

1. The record of a former suit between the parties is evidence, although it was dismissed. Bore's Executor *v.* Quierry's Executor, i, 284.

2. The record of a suit in which there was judgment against his principal, is not sufficient to settle the question of damages between surety and plaintiff. Lartigue *v.* Baldwin, i, 356.

3. A deposition taken in a suit against one of two defendants, cannot be read in a suit against both. Hatton *v.* Stillwell, ii, 76.

4. A judgment in a suit by attachment is evidence of the debt in another suit brought in the same state. Gray *v.* Trafton, ii, 189.

5. If a case be remanded, with the view of correcting a partial error, the district judge acts correctly, in assuming a former report of referees not excepted to, as the state of the accounts between the parties, and in ordering a partial reference only, with a view to comply with this decision of the Supreme Court. Parquin *v.* Finch *et al.,* iii, 11.

6. A party who has taken no step to bring in a witness, cannot use his testimony taken down by the clerk in another case. Hunter *v.* Smith, iii, 868.

7. The defendant may offer in evidence his own answers to interrogatories propounded to him by the plaintiff in a former suit. *Ibid.* 497.

8. Where a witness is dead, ill, or cannot be brought into court, his evidence taken down on a former trial in the cause may be read in evidence. Miller *v.* Russell, iv, 266; Hennen *v.* Monro, iii, 350.

9. Testimony taken under the act for perpetuating it, if it be reduced to writing by the attorney of the party applying for it, will be rejected. Mayer *v.* Gillard's Heirs, iv, 254.

10. To repel the plea of coverture, the wife's petition to be admitted as heir, accompanied by the husband's authorization, is admissible. Flower *v.* O'Connor, iv, 617.

H. *Of Authentication of Records and Documents from other Countries, and of Printed Statutes.*

1. The signature and official capacity of a notary in a foreign country may be proved by a witness who knows him to be a notary *de facto.* Las Caygas *v.* Larionda's Syndics, i, 245.

2. Answers to interrogatories received by the mayor of New York, and accompanied by the certificate of the governor and the seal of the state, are sufficiently authenticated. Woolsey *v.* Paulding, i, 727.

3. A Spanish notarial instrument, attested by three notaries of the district and the constitutional *alcalde,* with a certificate of the American consul, received in evidence, on proof of the handwriting of the notaries. Ferrers *v.* Bosel, ii, 67.

4. The capacity and signature of a justice of the peace in another state to the *jurat* of an answer to interrogatories is not to be certified as the record of a court under the act of congress. Gitzander *v.* Macarty, ii, 73.

5. A certificate of a record of judical proceedings in another state, ought to contain intrinsic evidence of the official capacity of the person who certifies. Kirkland *v.* Smith, ii, 724.

INDEX. 733

6. Affidavits made before a notary in New York, are not sufficiently authenticated by his seal. Hicks *v.* Duncan *et al*, iii. 306.

7. Whether the printed statutes of another state are evidence: *Quære.* Wakeman *v.* Marquand *et. al.*, iii, 535.

8. But they are when the copy introduced has been sent by the executive of the state where they were passed to the governor of this. *Ibid.*

9. The common law of a sister state may be proved by parol. *Ibid.*

10. The copy of the probate of a will is the copy of a judicial proceeding, which must be certified under the act of congress of 1790. Balfour *v.* Chew, iii, 639.

11. Foreign records must be proved according to the act of congress. Johnson *v.* Rannels, iv, 86.

12. A will need not be probated in this state, when used merely as evidence of title. *Ibid.*

13. The record of a court of chancery, in another state, certified by the clerk, with the attestation of the chancellor that the certificate is in due form, is legal evidence. Scott *v.* Blanchard, iv, 524.

I. *Of the Admissibility and Effect of Judgments, &c.*

1. The sentence of a foreign court of admiralty is conclusive as to the national character of the ship. Blanque *v.* Peytavin *et al.*, i, 271.

2. The record of a former suit between the parties is evidence, although it was dismissed. Bore's Executor *v.* Quierry's Executors, i, 284.

3. A judgment in favor of an Indian woman of the Natchez tribe, to which none of the present parties was a party, not admissible in evidence. Ulzerre *et al. v.* Poeyfarré, i, 626.

4. The record of the conviction of a slave cannot be offered in evidence against the owner in a civil action against him for the damage resulting from the criminal act of the slave. Steel *v.* Caseaux, i, 641.

5. The judgment obtained by a minor against his tutor is evidence of his claim on the tutor's property sold to a third person. Bernard *et al. v.* Vignaud, i, 650.

6. The record of a suit is legal evidence, although proceedings were not continued till a judgment was had. Barlow *v.* Dupuy, ii, 512.

7. The record of a suit against a debtor, in which judgment was rendered for an intervening creditor, is sufficient proof of the said creditor's claim. Hodge *v.* Morgan, ii, 592.

8. The mention in the judgment of a court before whom a debtor is discharged, that he took the oath required by law, is evidence of the fact. Brainard *v.* Francis, ii, 624.

9. The record of a slave's conviction of theft, cannot be read in a suit between other parties. Lewis v. Peytavin, iii, 209.

10. The parish judge who received the sheriff's bond is a good witness to prove its contents in case of loss. Villere *v.* Armstrong *et al.*, iii, 212.

11. A record is the best evidence of what was done in a cause, and it cannot be contradicted by parol. Williams *v.* Hooper, iii, 264.

12. A power of attorney, executed before a justice of the peace in another state, is not a record or a judicial proceeding, under act of congress. Parham *v.* Murphy, iii, 319.

13. The sentence of a foreign court of admiralty is conclusive on the matters on which it decides. Cucullu *v.* Louisiana Insurance Company, iii, 620.

14. But in an action between the insurer and insured, the court may examine whether the tribunal which condemned was rightfully constituted by the law of nations. *Ibid.*

15. But the regularity of its proceedings cannot be inquired into. *Ibid.*

16. When the judgment of a criminal court is the foundation of a civil suit, it may be given in evidence thereon. Parish of Orleans *v.* Morgan, iii, 721.

17. A sentence rendered in the court of admiralty, which is appealed from, does not prove a falsification of the warranties contained in the policy. Zino *v.* Louisiana Ins. Company, iii, 746.

18. A party may use as evidence any document filed in the case. Hunter *v.* Smith, iii, 868.

19. The order of a court of probates for appointing a curator is evidence of that appointment, between persons not parties thereto. Thompson *v.* Caveau *et al.*, iv, 15.

20. When the party offering a record in evidence, alleges it to be incomplete, and offers a transcript of the part omitted, the court may receive both as proof of the whole record. Desmukes *et al. v.* Musgrove, iv, 553.

VOL. IV.—62

EXCHANGE.

EXECUTION.

cution, and may not insist on selling the personal property of defendant first. Miller v. Morgan, iii. 757.

32. A plaintiff in execution cannot seize property of the defendant in the hands of third persons, on the ground that the sale to them is fraudulent. *Ibid.*

33. But when the conveyance is *sous seing privé*, he may if the sale was *antedated. Ibid.* Peet *et al. v.* Morgan, iii, 780.

34. Property fraudulently sold by defendant can not be sold under execution against him until the sale be set aside. Yocum *v.* Bullit *et al.,* iii, 858.

35. A defendant, arrested on a *ca. sa.* and discharged from imprisonment by the plaintiff, may be imprisoned again. Martin *v.* Ashcraft, iv, 528.

36. Execution may issue on a judgment, which does not settle every claim of the parties: as for example, when there is a decree that plaintiff be put into possession of the land, but the cause to be remanded for inquiring into damages. Bourguignon *v.* Boudousquic, iv, 193.

37. Plaintiff who takes a twelvemonths' bond and sues on it, is not estopped from denying that he took it in discharge of his debt. Williams *v.* Brent, iv, 211.

38. The return of the sheriff that a debt is satisfied, does not conclude the creditor. *Ibid.*

39. There is no difference in the effect of a sale made to a stranger and that made to the defendant in execution. *Ibid.*

40. A twelvemonths' bond is not a payment of the debt on which execution issued. *Ibid.*

41. Nor does it operate a novation. *Ibid.*

42. An execution from the city court to seize goods and chattels does not authorise the marshal to seize and sell real estate. Thompson *v.* Chauveau, iv, 261.

43. The rights of the seizing creditor cannot be greater than those of the debtor. The vendee of property on a *fi. fa.* acquires no right on property which did not belong to the debtor. Heirs of Baillio *v.* Poissot, iv, 538.

44. When a property is sold by the sheriff, subject to a mortgage, and not subject to the *payment* of the mortgage, the purchaser is not responsible for the lien. Mounot *v.* Williamson, iv, 282.

45. And if the property sold does not amount to the mortgage, there is no sale. *Ibid.*

46. It is sufficient notice of such mortgage, that it is mentioned in the act of sale. *Ibid.*

47. Separate judgments do not authorise a joint execution. Dugat *v.* Babin *et al.,* iv, 560.

48. A sheriff cannot make a new levy under a writ, the return day of which has expired. *Ibid.*

49. Whether the sheriff who has been enjoined from proceeding on an execution, may not, after the injunction is dissolved, proceed to sell—*Quære? Ibid.*

50. Under the act of 1817, a sheriff who sold property, subject to a mortgage, could not collect from the purchaser the amount of the mortgage. But see Code of Practice, Adams *v.* Duprey, iv, 588.

51. A *fi. fa.* may be levied on a sum of money directed by the legislature to be paid the defendant. Flower *et al. v.* Livingston, ii, 758.

52. The defendant cannot oppose to the plaintiff in the *fi. fa.* that this money is in the constructive possession of a third party. *Ibid.*

EXECUTORY PROCESS.

1. The vendor of real estate must produce an authentic act of sale to entitle him to a writ of seizure. Day *v.* Fristoe, i, 556.

2. Where the plaintiff obtained an order of seizure of a slave, on exhibition of a deed of mortgage executed by the vendee, and it appeared by the opposition of a third person that the slave was not in possession of the vendee, the court ought to have given judgment for the amount of the note taken at the time of sale, and let the plaintiff have his remedy afterwards against the third possessor, in the manner pointed out by law. Knight *v.* Hall, i, 576.

3. The vendor cannot have an order of seizure after the failure of the vendee, but must be paid by the syndics. Chiapella *v.* Lanusse's Syndics, ii, 121.

4. A note, the payment of which is secured by special mortgage, may be sued on in the ordinary way. Croghan *v.* Conrad, ii, 237.

5. An acknowledgment of the debt and mortgage in a public act, amounts to a confession of judgment. Tilghman *v.* Dias, ii, 387.

6. On an authentic act, written in the French language, an order of seizure and sale may issue. *Ibid.*

7. An assignee by an act *sous seing privé* cannot obtain an order of seizure and sale. Gilly v. Lee, ii, 446.

8. The endorsee of a note, secured by a mortgage, may, after he has paid it, have an order of seizure and sale; but he must prove the facts that entitle him to do so, by evidence of as high a nature as the deed of mortgage. Nichol v. De Ende, iii, 94.

9. If the proceedings have been changed from the *juicio executivo* to the *juicio ordinario*, judgment may be given generally against the defendant. Clay v. Oldham, iii, 87.

10. Plaintiff cannot proceed at the same time with an order of seizure and a suit in the ordinary way. If they be both resorted to, the *via executiva* merges in the *via ordinaria*. Shipwith et al. v. Gray, iii, 180; Weimprender v. Fleming, iv, 441.

11. An assignment *sous seing privé* does not authorise the assignee to take out an order of seizure and sale. Gray v. Baldwin, iii, 271.

12. The surety who pays for the principal, is not entitled to take out execution in the name of the creditor. See 1 N. S. 237. *Ibid.*

13. The copy of a copy of an act of mortgage does not authorise a suit of seizure. Even when this copy makes a part of the record of a suit against the mortgagor, in which the third possessor intervened, if he did so to be relieved from a sequestration. Poydras v. Hiriart, iii, 891.

14. A clause in an act, authorising any attorney to confess judgment, does not authorise the issue of a writ of seizure and sale, but is irreconcilable with the idea of an execution on the act without a previous confession of judgment in court. Oldham v. Polk, iv, 19.

15. The mere endorser of a note secured by mortgage, cannot obtain an order of seizure and sale out of court. Planters' Bank of Georgia v. Proctor, iv, 48.

16. The right of the assignee must be established by matter of record, before he claim a writ of seizure and sale. Crane v. Baillio, iv, 239.

17. The notice in the 735th and 736th articles of the Code of Practice, is that which the sheriff is to give to the defendant, before seizure. Rowlett v. Shepherd, iv, 336.

18. The act of 1828 has repealed those parts of the former laws which required an assignee to prove the consideration of the assignment before he obtained a writ of seizure. *Ibid.*

19. The demand which must precede the seizure, is the only notice required before payment be enforced by a writ of seizure, by an assignee. *Ibid.*

20. That part of the old Code which required the plaintiff's oath before a writ of seizure issued, is repealed. *Ibid.*

21. An order of seizure and sale cannot issue on property in the hands of a third person, unless on the production of an act of mortgage duly recorded. Sinnott v. Michel, iv, 360.

22. On a rule to shew cause why an order suspending an order of seizure and sale should not be set aside, the merits of the case cannot be inquired into: irregularity in the granting the order alone is proper to be inquired into. Abat v. Poyfarré, i, 650.

EXPERTS.

1. The report of experts can not become a judgment until the court is satisfied of its correctness. Mericult v. Austin, i, 130.

2. The task of experts appointed to judge of signatures, is confined to comparison. Lecarpentier v. Delery's Executor, i, 269.

3. A report of referees in one case cannot be used in another, unless it was made the judgment of the court, and a report confirmed in part is of no force as to the rest. Lefevre v. Bariteau, i, 580.

4. Experts cannot be appointed to examine property, in order to ascertain its value—nor to their report legal evidence. Millaudon v New Orleans Water Company, ii, 192.

5. Expert appointed by the court of probates to value a certain building, not allowed two and a-half per cent. on the amount of property. Lennatt v. Pierce et al., ii, 431.

6. If the report be sworn to after it was written, it is not therefore to be rejected. Nott v. Daunoy, ii, 576.

7. The report of the experts on the expediency of selling, is not conclusive. Millaudon v. Fercy et al., iii, 654.

8. If the two experts disagree on the genuineness of a signature submitted to them, a third cannot be appointed: unanimity is required. Barfield v. Hewlett, iii, 758.

9. Experts cannot proceed with one piece of comparison only. *Ibid.*

FAMILY MEETING.

1. At a family meeting the under tutor should be present.
2. Co-heirs of a minor, under the pre-existing law, might be members of a family meeting. Raguet's Heirs *v.* Barron, iv, 103.

FATHER AND CHILD.

1. Alimony granted to children because their father constrained them to associate with his concubine. Heno *et al. v.* Heno, ii, 38.
2. A father who is not indebted, may purchase property for his child, and in its name, and subsequent creditors cannot attack the act as fraudulent. Henry *v.* Hyde *et al.*, iii, 689.
3. A mother has no right to purchase property for her minor child. Sarapure *v.* Debuys, iii, 727.
4. A sale from a father to a minor child, paid for by the child's notes, the property remaining in the father's possession, will be presumed simulated, and the notes null, as regards drawer and his heirs. Beal *v.* Delancy *et al.*, iv, 95.
5. The condition of a child born during marriage, cannot be affected by the declaration of one or both spouses. Tate *v.* Penne, iv, 349.
6. The law presumes the husband the father of the child born during marriage. *Ibid.*
7. A parent may demand the adjudication of any property held in common with his children. Harty *et al. v.* Harty *et al.*, iv, 602.
See NATURAL CHILD.

FERRIES.

1. The police-jury of the parish and the city council have both the right of establishing a ferry before the city. Police Jury *et al. v.* Mayor *et al.*, i, 203.
2. It is no violation of an exclusive right to keep a ferry, to cross persons without demanding toll. Chapello *v.* Wells *et al.*, iii, 341.
3. The Opelousas Steamboat Company can not prevent other steamboats than their own from landing passengers at one of the *termini* of their ferry, if they have not been taken at the others, or on the route between the two. State *et al. v.* Wilson, iii, 798.

FOREIGN LAWS.

1. Laws of other states, or of foreign countries must be proved. Boggs *v.* Reed, i, 438.
2. When the law of the country in which the parties contracted is not set forth, the court must take that of the state as their rule. Campbell *v.* Henderson, iii, 46.
3. If the party claims under the laws of another state, and fails to prove them, the case will be decided by those of our own. Bray *v.* Cumming, iii, 528.
4. Whether the printed statutes of another state, are evidence: *Quære.* Wakeman *v.* Marquand *et al.*, iii, 535.
5. But they are, when the copy introduced has been sent by the executive of the state where they were passed to the governor of this. *Ibid.*
6. The common law of a sister state, may be proved by parol. *Ibid.*
7. Whether, on a change from one form of government to another, the authorities and laws of the previous one exist until the new government goes into operation.— *Quære.* Cucullu *v.* Louisiana Insurance Company, iii, 620.

FRAUD.

1. He who alleges ill faith is bound to the strictest proof. Fort and Wife *v.* Metayer, ii, 117.
2. The acts of the vendor, after the sale, are against the vendee evidence of fraud in the vendor: so are his declarations as part of the *res gesta;* but neither is evidence of fraud in the vendee. Martin *v.* Reoves *et al.*, iii, 90.
3. A conveyance alleged to be fraudulent, cannot be tried by seizing the property as belonging to the vendor and setting up the fraud as a defence. An action must be brought to annul the conveyance. Barbarin *v.* Saucier, iii, 577.
4. The issue *fraud vel non* is peculiarly of the cognisance of the jury. Abat *v.* Segura, iii, 824.
5. Fraud is not to be inferred from slight presumptions. Caldwell *v.* Benedict, iv, 583.
See INSOLVENCY and SALE.

HABEAS CORPUS.

Habeas Corpus seems not the rightful proceeding when petitioner is in prison bounds. Dodge's case, i, 507.

HUSBAND AND WIFE.

A. *Of Marriage Contracts.*
B. *Of Dowry and Paraphernalia.*
C. *Of the Community.*
D. *Of the Wife's Mortgage and Privilege.*
E. *Of the Contracts of the Wife.*
F. *Of the Law of Husband and Wife generally.*

A. *Of Marriage Contracts.*

1. A contract of marriage entered into here, cannot provide that the rights of the parties shall be according to the custom of Paris. Boucier *v.* Lanusse, i, 174.

2. Marriage contract not recorded in pursuance of the act of 1813, has no effect against third parties. De Armas and Wife *v.* Hampton, ii, 236.

3. An estimation of property in a marriage contract previous to the passage of the Civil Code operated a sale. Frere *et al. v.* Frere *et al.,* ii, 521.

4. A clause in a marriage contract, by which the whole of the acquests and gains is to go to the survivor in case there are no children, is not illegal. Parquin *et al. v.* Finch, ii, 521.

5. The act of 1813, in that part which requires the registry of marriage contracts theretofore passed, to be recorded within a year from the passage of the act, &c. &c., is not unconstitutional as regards the constitution of the United States. Dutillet *v.* Dutillet's Syndics, iii, 131.

B. *Of Dowry and Paraphernalia.*

1. A sale of land, by a husband to his wife, to replace the value of real estate, part of her paraphernal property, by him sold, is valid. Provost *v.* Provost and Hennen, i. 279.

2. A woman having married without constitution of dowry, and her husband having received and sold slaves bequeathed her before marriage, and also received from the executors of her father a sum of money, *decided,* that this property of the wife's was paraphernal. Hannie *v.* Browder, i, 450.

3. There being no *dot,* all the wife's property is paraphernal. The child issued from a paraphernal slave is itself paraphernal. A widow has no right to interest on the proceeds of her paraphernal property in the hands of her husband's representatives. Frederic *v.* Frederick, ii, 90.

4. When the dowry is to be paid *en deniers un fois payée,* a sum of money once paid, interest is only due from the judicial demand. Chamerd *v.* Sibley, ii, 110.

5. *Quære.* Has the vendee of dotal property, sold him by the husband, while he remains in undisturbed possession, a right to claim a rescission of the sale and restitution of the price, on the ground of the nullity *absolute,* or *relative* of the contract? Bonin *et al. v.* Eyssaline, 302.

6. A husband who sells the dotal property of his wife, and afterwards acquires an absolute right to it may avail himself of such posterior right in opposition to the vendee's claim for a rescission of the contract of sale, *provided* the complete title has been obtained previous to institution of suit for rescission. *Ibid.*

7. A question of marital rights decided according to Spanish law. Is the husband's estate responsible for the value of the paraphernal property of his wife alienated by their joint act? Degruy *v.* St. Pé's Creditors, iii, 335.

8. The wife has no claim on her husband's estate for improvements made on her property during marriage. They belonged to, and made a part of the community of acquests and gains. *Ibid.*

9. The wife most, against creditors, produce other proof of the payment of the *dot,* than the husband's confession in the marriage contract. Buisson *v.* Thompson, iv, 345.

10. The wife may resume the administration of her paraphernal property, previously confided to her husband, whenever she chooses: and also demand restitution of what is the object or price of it. Gilbeaux's Heirs *v.* Cormier, iv, 499.

11. The property of the succession, when received by the wife, is paraphernal, which she may administer herself, nor ask her husband's approbation. Flower *v.* O'Connor, iv.

C. *Of the Community.*

1. When a marriage was contracted in Hispaniola, and the contract of marriage stipulated that there should be a community of acquets and gains, whithersoever the parties might remove, and the parties remove to Charleston, where the wife died leaving children

6. When this is done, the creditor need not prove that the engagement turned to her advantage. *Ibid.*

7. She cannot bind herself as surety for her husband. *Ibid.*

8. Nor even by binding herself *in solido* with him. *Ibid.*

9. The wife is not bound by a note executed jointly with her husband, even in the hands of an endorsee: and when it was given for property, bought by the husband during the marriage. Sprigg *v.* Boissier and Wife, iii, 451.

10. The circumstance of the wife having had a separate advantage in a contract, joint and several of husband and wife, being of the essence of her obligation, must be proved by some other evidence than proof that she touched the money. Brandegee *v.* Kerr and Wife, iv, 156.

11. The wife cannot be surety for the husband. And, where she binds herself as principal she may show the contract was one of suretyship, although she did not take a counter-letter. Pilié *v.* Patin, Wife of Delâge, and Her Husband, iv, 618.

F. *Of the Law of Husband and Wife Generally.*

1. A couple domiciliated in Louisiana eloping to and marrying in Natchez, under circumstances which prove they had Louisiana in contemplation for their residence at the time of marriage, have their conjugal rights regulated by the laws of Louisiana. Le Breton *v.* Nouchet, i, 93.

2. If the wife behaves outrageously to her husband, a separation from bed and board will not be granted to her on account of his ill treatment of her. Durand *v.* Her Husband, i. 235.

3. When a couple remove from the country in which they were married, their respective rights to the property which they acquire in the country to which they migrate, are to be regulated by its laws. Gale *v.* Davis's Heirs, i, 312.

4. A wife who bound herself with her husband, and who expressly renounced the benefit of the laws in her favor, cannot demand proof that the debt was created for her advantage. Chapillon and Wife *v.* St. Maxent's Heirs, i, 351.

5. The Spanish law did not require, as the Civil Code of 1808 does, any express declaration, that the property appraised and delivered to the husband is intended to be thus conveyed to him. Jourdan *et al. v.* Williams *et al.*, i, 522.

6. Where defendant's intestate married the plaintiff, although the former had a wife then living, she was not to be regarded in the light of a partner and entitled to nothing because there was no profit; but her marriage contract being illegal and void, she has a right to be indemnified against the consequences of his deceit, and will be allowed for her services in his house, the use of her furniture, hire of her negroes, moneys of hers received by him, and debts of his paid by her since his death. Fox *v.* Dawson's Curator, ii, 690.

7. The allowance to widows for mourning dresses should be made them without distinction between richer than their husbands and others. Frederic *v.* Frederick, ii, 90.

8. Property acquired by wife, for a valuable consideration, during marriage, may be sold by husband and wife. De Armas and Wife *v.* Hampton, ii, 236.

9. There is nothing in the law which makes provision for the support of the wife, during a suit for separation, of bed and board, conditional on her success. It is only required that she shall prove that she constantly resided in the residence assigned her, and in this case the fact of a short visit by her made to Baton Rouge, does not take away her right. Le Beau *v.* Trudeau, ii, 409.

10. In an action for separation of bed and board, where adultery is at issue, a witness cannot be asked the general character of the defendant for chastity: the wife did not forfeit her matrimonial right by the reputation of being an adultress, but by proof of the fact that she was one. The jury would not be authorised to infer it from bad character. Neither can the rights of these suitors depend on a witness's opinion of what is modest conduct. The facts must be told and the jury judge. Alexis Trudeau *v.* Julie Le Beau Trudeau, ii, 414.

11. A notarial act showing that the wife, authorised by the husband, and in his presence, acknowledged that she received a sum of money, and discharged her father's executors, while nothing shows that the money came to the husband's hands, does not suffice to charge him with that sum on a separation of bed and board. Faussier *v.* Faussier *et al.*, ii, 479.

12. Publication of a separation of property between the husband and wife is expressly required by law; but the pain of nullity is not denounced against a neglect of such publication.. It is not a prohibitive regulation, which might in some instances imply nullity. The court is therefore of opinion that a judgment of separation, unattended by publica-

tion is not *ipso facto* void; it can only be decreed null on showing fraud or injury to third parties resulting from such laches. Turnbull *v.* Davis *et al.,* ii, 546.

13. The matrimonial rights of the wife who marries with the intention of instant removal into another state, must be governed by the laws of her intended domicil. Ford's Curator *v.* Ford, ii, 744.

14. The want of recording a marriage contract, cannot be objected by the representative of the husband. *Ibid.*

15. A widow left in necessitous circumstances, when her husband died rich, is entitled to the marital portion, although she was married and resided out of Louisiana, and her husband died out of this state. Abercrombie *v.* Caffray *et al.,* iii, 1.

16. A woman who was deceived by a man, who represented himself as single, and her children born while the deception lasted, are entitled to all the rights of a legitimate wife and children. Clendenning *v.* Clendenning *et al.,* iii, 120.

17. Husband joining with the wife in a suit, is sufficient evidence of his authorising her to bring the action. Lawes *et al. v.* Chinn, iii, 332.

18. The wife is bound to follow her husband wherever he determines to go. Chretien *v.* Her Husband, iii, 453.

19. When a note is payable to the wife, the husband cannot transfer her right, nor bring nor defend a suit respecting it without her. Sterling *v.* Johnson and Wife, iii, 578.

20. Married women cannot under any circumstances become sureties for their husbands. M'Micken *v.* Smith and Wife, iii, 605.

21. The exception in the *Partidas* in favor of women who become widows before they are of age, in regard to estates inherited from their children, is unrepealed by any act of the legislature of the state or late territory. Duncan's Executors *v.* Hampton, iii, 732.

22. In the case of Saul *v.* His Creditors, the statute which regulates the rights of husband and wife, was decided to be *real,* not *personal,* and hence, property found in this state at the dissolution of the marriage was declared to be subject to distribution according to the laws of Louisiana, without regard to the fact that the marriage had been contracted, and that either or both spouses had always resided elsewhere. Cole's Widow *v.* His Executors, iv, 146.

23. The law of the *Fuero Real,* viz: "every thing which the husband and wife acquire while together, shall be equally divided between them," is not repealed by the 2370th article of the Louisiana Code; which declares, that "a marriage contracted out of the state, between persons who afterwards come to live here, is also subjected to the community of acquests and gains with respect to such property as is acquired after their arrival;" but the latter is a positive statutory provision covering only part of the ground of the original principle. *Ibid.*

24. Nor does the 3521st article of the Louisiana Code repeal that provision of the *Fuero Real,* for it only forbids the invoking of the former laws of Louisiana, where their objects are specially provided for by actual legislation. Now, the case of one of the married couple moving into this state, is not specially provided for: the former law, therefore, in relation to it, is not repealed by this general provision. *Ibid.*

25. The law presumes the husband the father of the children born during marriage. Tate *v.* Penne, iv, 349.

26. In case of voluntary separation access is always presumed unless cohabitation has been physically impossible. *Ibid.*

27. The condition of a child born during marriage cannot be affected by the declaration of one or both the spouses. *Ibid.*

28. The wife has no legal domicil but that of her husband, and a citation left at his domicil, is legal service on her. Evans *v.* Saul and Wife, iv, 247.

INDIANS.

1. Under the French government in Louisiana, some Indians were held in slavery, and the establishment of the Spanish government did not restore such to freedom. Seville *v.* Chretien, i, 367.

2. The issue of an Indian woman is free. Ulzere *et al. v.* Poeyfarré, ii, 727.

3. Under the former government of Louisiana, a sale by Indians, of land assigned to them, did not incapacitate them from acquiring a right to soil in land to which they removed. Spencer's Heirs *v.* Grimball, iii, 870.

4. If a sale by the Indians was followed by payment of the price, and delivery of the property, no person can take advantage of an informality in the mode of making it, but the Indians. The nullity is relative. Absolute and relative nullities discussed. *Ibid.*
See LANDS.

INDICTMENT.

The caption not a part of the indictment. *Vi et armis* not necessary in an indictment for murder. Territory *v.* McFarlane, i, 27.

INJUNCTION.

1. Defendant in injunction not bound to answer on oath, and cannot take advantage of his voluntary affidavit. Orleans N. Co. *v.* The Mayor, &c. of New Orleans, i, 4.

2. An injunction not to molest, does not prevent a suit to ascertain a right. Mayor *v.* Magnon, i, 207.

3. If a sheriff levies an execution on the property of a third person, [the sale may be enjoined by the judge of the district in which the seizure was made, although the execution issue from another district. Davenport *v.* Turnbull's Heirs, i, 616.

4. Whether the plaintiff may be perpetually enjoined from claiming the premises? Certainly not, when it was not prayed for in the answer. Porter *v.* Dugat, i, 703.

5. When an act of assembly directs that the judgment of a justice of the peace shall be executed, notwithstanding an appeal, it cannot be suspended by an injunction. The State *v.* Judge Pitot, ii, 232.

6. An injunction cannot be granted unless bond and security are given. Lafon's Ex'rs. *v.* Gravier *et al.,* ii, 448.

7. A party cannot on a partial set-off enjoin the whole execution. Nor ought a court to enjoin the execution of its own judgment, because the defendant therein has acquired rights or claims against the plaintiff. Palfrey *v.* Shuff, ii, 591.

8. An injunction improperly taken against one partner, where his partners shared the injury resulting from the obstacle, authorises an action for damages at the suit of the firm. Mitchell *et al. v.* Gervais, ii, 743.

9. An injunction will not be dissolved although originally improperly granted, if it appear that a subsequent event will require it to issue, if dissolved. Exnicios *v.* Weiss, iii, 136.

10. If the party who, on a *fi. fa.* points out property as belonging to the defendant, and becomes the last bidder, he cannot have an injunction, on the ground that the property belonged to another, and so he acquired no title. Dubreuil *v.* Soulié, iii, 240.

11. The sheriff's vendee cannot have an injunction because his deed is not in the form prescribed by law. *Ibid.*

12. The merits of an action to which an injunction is accessory, cannot be examined on a motion to dissolve the injunction, any more than a debt can be disproved on a motion to set aside an attachment. Dupau *v.* Richardson, iii, 265.

13. An injunction which has been granted unadvisedly, will not be dissolved if it appear from the evidence that it must be issued again. Bushnell *v.* Brown's Heirs, iii, 370.

14. The execution of a judgment cannot be enjoined, until a claim of the defendant sounding in damages be examined. Havard *v.* Stone, iii, 475.

15. A party may always have an injunction when the act would give rise to a claim in damages. Carraby *et al. v.* Morgan, iii, 635.

16. If the defendant plead that the injunction was improperly issued by a judge of another district, when that of the district was absent, he cannot give, in evidence, that the plaintiff is without title, as the slave was brought into the state contrary to law; for, inasmuch as possession enables plaintiff to maintain the injunction, a forfeiture for breach of positive law, cannot be set up and examined collaterally in such a case as this. Wells *v.* Hunter, iii, 852.

17. On motion to dissolve an injunction, all the matters alleged in the petition are taken for true. A debtor in whose hands the debt due by him is attached, may enjoin an execution, issued against him by his creditor. Louisiana Code, 2145. Morgan *v.* Peet *et al.,* iii, 562.

18. An execution will not be enjoined, for matter which might have been pleaded to the action. Monroe *v.* M'Micken, iii, 600.

19. It is always in time for the defendant to move for the dissolution of an injunction, for matters appearing on the face of the petition. It may be done after an answer put in. Walker *v.* Vanwinkle *et al.,* iv, 618.

20. Whether the circumstance of a party having an action for damages, prevents his obtaining an injunction? Caldwell *v.* Cline, iv, 685.

INSANITY.

1. The acts of an insane or imbecile man, anterior to the petition for interdiction, will

not be annulled, except it be proved that the person with whom he contracted could not have been deceived as to the state of his mind. Louisiana Bank v. Dubreuil, i, 394.

2. The heir may avail himself of the testator's insanity, although his interdiction was not provoked. Marie v. Avart's Heirs, i, 677.

3. Proof cannot be received of the insanity of a vendor, whose interdiction was not provoked. Daunoy v. Clyma et al., ii, 238.

4. Ex parte evidence affords no legal proof of insanity. Stafford v. Stafford, ii, 542.

IN SOLIDO.

1. The members of an unincorporated company are bound in solido for its debts. Lynch v. Portlethwaite, ii, 540.

2. In cases of solidary obligations, the creditor may sue either of his debtors alone. Ibid.

3. Solidarity is never presumed. Slocum v. Sibley, i, 440; Dean v. Smith et al., ii, 317.

4. A receipt to a debtor for his part extinguishes the obligation in solido. Baldwin v. Gray, iii, 269.

5. Bail are not responsible in solido, unless in case of insolvency of one of them, or unless when sued they fail to claim the benefit of division. U. S. et al. v. Hawkins's Heirs, iii, 308.

INSOLVENCY.

A. Of the Forced Surrender.
B. Of the Cession.
C. Of the Meeting of Creditors, and the Homologation of their proceedings, and of opposition thereto.
D. Of the Syndics.
    1. Of their appointment.
    2. Of their duties and responsibilities.
E. Of the stay of Proceedings, and the effects thereof.
F. Of the omission of a creditor's name on the Bilan, and the effects thereof.
G. Of the Sale of Property.
H. Of the Tableau and its Homologation, and of opposition thereto; and herein of the rank of creditors, of the proof of their claims and their payment.
I. Of the Charge of Fraud.
K. Of the Contracts of Insolvent, which are fraudulent and invalid as to creditors.
L. Of Respite.
M. Of Insolvency generally. See Costs.

A. Of the Forced Surrender.

1. Insolvent cannot withhold part of his goods, on the ground that he has delivered enough to pay his debts. Duncan & Jackson's Synd. v. Duncan, i, 115.

2. The insolvent cannot complain of irregularity in the proceedings after the forced surrender is ordered; it is a question in which the creditors are alone concerned. Dyson et al. v. Brandt et al., ii, 10.

3. Where two suits to compel a "forced surrender" are carried on by different creditors at the same time, the order of a stay of proceedings made on the second application, does not estop the defendant to contest the legality of the first. Ward v. Brandt et al., ii, 31.

4. A "forced surrender" is that which is ordered at the instance of the creditors of an insolvent; whenever the application for relief comes from the debtor it is the "voluntary." Ibid.

5. This "forced surrender" may be ordered in all cases where the insolvent, being a merchant or trader, is in failing circumstances. Ibid.

6. But the oath of the creditor alone, is not sufficient to obtain an order, to sequestrate the property of the insolvent, and call a meeting of his creditors. Wikoff et al. v. Duncan's Heirs, ii, 114.

7. The act of 1817, relative to voluntary surrenders, does not govern those which are forced. Planters' Bank et al. v. Lanusse et al., ii, 146.

8. A forced surrender cannot be ordered unless the party alleged to be a bankrupt is made defendant, and cited as in ordinary civil actions; it is not sufficient that he has knowledge that a suit is pending against him. Weimprender's Syndics v. Weimprender et al., ii, 157; Guirot v. Her Creditors, ii, 380.

9. In case of a forced surrender one of the creditors cannot carry on legal proceedings

in a distinct suit against insolvent for the recovery of his debt. Mayhew v. M'Gee, i" 383.

10. A forced surrender cannot be ordered of the estate of a deceased person; it must administered under the authority of the court of probates. Dupuy et al. v. Greffin's Executor, ii, 432.

B. Of the Cession.

1. Insolvent cannot withhold part of his goods on the ground, that he has delivered enough to pay his debts. Duncan and Jackson's Syndics v. Duncan, i, 115.

2. After a cession, the debtor who does not obtain a release, is not suable till the property ceded be liquidated. Fitzgerald v. Phillips, i, 246.

3. A ceding debtor who has not obtained his discharge, is liable to a simple contra debtor, when it is clear that the privileged debts absorb all the ceded property, althou the estate be yet unliquidated. Fitzgerald v. Phillips, i, 286.

4. If the cession be refused on allegation of fraud, and the sheriff be appointed syndi the debtors cannot be ordered to assign their property to the sheriff as trustee. W. & 1 Crommelin v. Their Creditors, i, 340.

5. The law in force in this country, at the change of government, on the subject cessio bonorum, is not unconstitutional. Blanque's Syndic v. Beale's Executors, ii, 505.

6. The act of 1817 has not repealed the former laws relative to the voluntary surrende It introduces a cumulative remedy, from which certain insolvents are excluded. Kelse v. His Creditors, ii, 585.

7. The loss of credit is a good cause for a debtor to obtain relief by a cession of h 'goods. Section of act of 1817, relative to production of books of insolvent, commented on. Richards v. His Creditors, iii, 550.

C. Of the Meeting of Creditors and the Homologation of their Proceedings.

1. If one of a firm, not shown to be a creditor in his private name, sign a concordat, the firm is concluded by the signature. Arnold v. Bureau, ii, 180.

2. The wife of the insolvent may vote though she has not renounced. Planters' Bank et al. v. Lanusse et al., ii, 293.

3. It is not enough that creditors, making opposition to the homologation of the p eedings of creditors in an appointment of syndics, should charge that the election was illegal "because the persons who voted were not creditors of insolvent to the amount by them stated, nor had any claim on his estate;" the statute requires that an opposing creditor should within ten days lay before the court his written deposition stating especially the several facts of nullity, or of fraud. Bierra v. His Creditors, ii, 590.

4. The ten days allowed by law for filing an opposition to the appointment of syndics to an insolvent's estate, commence running from the day on which the proceedings, had before the notary for that purpose, were closed. Dreux v. His Creditors, ii, 594.

5. To the formation of a concurso three creditors are necessary, but it is not necessa they should be present at the meeting. Turcas et al. v. L'Eglise, iii, 356; Mayfield Comeau, iv, 202.

6. After the process-verbal of the meeting of the creditors of an insolvent is closed, notary cannot, on a subsequent day, receive the votes of creditors who did not met Broussard v. His Creditors, iii, 458.

7. An imprisoned debtor who applies for the benefit of a cessio bonorum, cannot ha' his creditors called before a notary: but into open court, or before the judge. See act assembly. 2 Martin's Digest, 142. Stewart v. His Creditors, iv, 368.

8. General rules which govern a concurso. Saul v. His Creditors, iv, 302.

D. Of the Syndics.

1. Of their Appointment.

1. A majority in amount is necessary for the appointment of a syndic. Enet v. His Creditors, i, 251.

2. Unless all the creditors agree, the syndic must be chosen from their own number. Clamageran v. Degruy, ii, 626.

3. Mortgage creditors are entitled to vote for syndics. Enet v. His Creditors, ii, 268, 298.

4. An insolvent cannot contest the legality of the choice which his creditors make of syndics. Seghers v. His Creditors, i, 622.

5. The appointment of syndics made in the French language, in the proceedings be-

fore the notary, is unconstitutional, and not cured by the homologation of the proceedings. Viale's Syndics v. Gardenier *et al.*, i, 731.

6. Syndics must be appointed by the majority of creditors in amount, and if the claim of creditors offering to vote is disputed, it must be proved, as in ordinary cases, by legal evidence. Planters' Bank *et al.* v. Lanusse *et al.*, ii, 148.

7. Claims of creditors may properly be investigated before voting for syndics. The notary must record the proof each party presents, and return it to court, where it can be acted on. *Ibid.* 146.

8. In cases of this kind all the creditors are at once plaintiffs and defendants. Trial by jury may be demanded for the ascertainment of the facts at issue. *Ibid.*

9. An endorser who has not paid his endorsee has no right to vote. *Ibid.*

10. The creditors of an insolvent have a right to change the syndics, who are but their mandatories, in case they make a cession of their goods. Seghers v. His Creditors, ii, 517.

11. A judgment reversing that by which a syndic was appointed, does not avoid acts done by him in the meanwhile. Saulet v. Dreux's Syndics, iii, 179.

12. The insolvent may be appointed syndic. Turcas *et al.* v. L'Eglise, iii, 356.

2. *Of their Duties and Responsibilities.*

1. There is nothing in the laws which authorises the syndics of an insolvent debtor to throw their own goods into the mass of his estate, sell them on credit, take to themselves all the benefits of the good debts and make the estate responsible for the bad. Syndics of Williamson v. Syndics of Phillips, iii, 205.

2. Syndics become responsible by their own misconduct only. Seghers v. Visinier *et al.*, i, 211.

3. The functions of syndics cease as soon as their accounts are rendered and approved. Fitzgerald v. Phillips, i, 177.

4. Syndics cannot act without the confirmation of a competent tribunal. Dukelus's Syndics v. Dumountel *et al.*, i, 273.

5. Syndics, before the act of 1817, had the power to release the mortgages on insolvent's property. Williamson *et al.* v. Their Creditors, i, 423.

6. Syndics cannot take possession of an estate on the ground that the possessor obtained it from their insolvent by a fraudulent sale. St. Avid *et al.* v. Weimprender's Syndics, ii, 39.

7. A syndic cannot sue his co-syndic for funds of the estate, in the hands of the latter. Preval v. Moulon, ii, 230.

8. After insolvency, the syndics may sue for any property, the alienation of which was null and void as to creditors. Martinez v. Layton & Co., iii, 324.

9. But when the object of the action is to enforce a lien, which one of the creditors may have on immovables alienated before failure, they cannot. *Ibid.*

10. When damages are claimed from syndics for malfeasance, suit ought to be brought against them in their individual capacity. Pimpinella v. Lanusse's Syndics, iii, 774.

11. Syndics have no control over the suits which the individual creditors may raise with each other in the concurso. Saul v. His Creditors, iv, 302.

E. *Of the Stay of Proceedings, and the Effects thereof.*

1. The order on a *cessio bonorum* stops all proceedings as well against the person, as the general estate, or those *in rem.* Elmes v. Estevan, i, 21.

2. If, pending suit, a stay of proceedings be ordered and suit proceed, no new trial will be granted, it appearing that defendant had gone to trial, and that the proceedings against creditors had not been continued. Livaudais v. Henry, i, 52.

3. If a debtor does not make a cession of his goods at the meeting of his creditors, the order for staying proceedings may be rescinded. Deglane v. His Creditors, i, 323.

4. The stay of proceedings does not prevent the record of a mortgage. Torrey *et al.*, Syndics, v. Shamburgh, ii, 60.

5. The stay of proceedings granted to an insolvent does not prevent the seizure of the goods of a third person found on the premises leased. Ritchie *et al.*, Syndics, v. White *et al.*, ii, 186.

6. The order for staying all proceedings against the person and property, ordinarily, granted at the beginning of proceedings to procure a respite, ceases with the granting of it. Abat v. Michel, ii, 447.

7. The District Court cannot proceed in a suit against a debtor who has obtained a stay of proceedings from the Parish Court of New Orleans. Hunimin v. Jones, ii, 630.

ledgment of it, will not establish it against his creditors. But otherwise, if *adminiculada* (supported) by circumstances. The Planters' Bank *et al. v.* Lanusse *et al.,* ii, 293.

8. The judgment of homologation is incomplete until signed by the judge. Abat *v.* Michel, ii, 447.

9. If a bill is accepted on the promise that a mortgage will be given to secure the acceptor, and it be subsequently given, if the mortgagor fail, the date of the promise will be considered in inquiring whether it should be set aside. Wyer's Syndics *v.* Sweet *et al.,* ii, 750.

10. A suit to be put on the tableau according to rank and privilege, is not a suit for the *payment* of any sum of money, on which the act of 1813, 2 *Martin's Digest,* 196, requires an amicable demand. Marigny *v.* Johnston's Syndics, iii, 160.

11. The endorser of an insolvent, who is also a debtor of his, has only a right to be placed on the bilan for the balance. Moulon *v.* His Creditors, iii, 216.

12. Creditors who sign a concordat, do not waive the right of contesting, thereafter, the claims of each other, on the syndic filing a tableau of distribution. See 10 *Martin,* 690. Garidel *v.* Fogliardi, iii, 343.

13. The tableau of distribution cannot be homologated till the creditors are cited, and this should appear on the record. Barbegur *et al. v.* Their Creditors, iii, 414.

14. If a creditor claim to be paid by the preference on the insolvent's bank stock, pledged to him, his claim must be settled contradictorily, with all the other creditors, after the tableau is made. Astor *v.* Syndics of Saul *et al.,* iii, 417.

15. A mortgage creditor does not lose his rank, because the register overlooked his mortgage. Dreux *v.* His Creditors, iii, 417.

16. If the mortgagor's wife renounces her right, she will be postponed to the mortgagee. *Ibid.*

17. If the law, which prescribes the mode of citing an insolvent's creditor, when the syndics present the tableau, be repealed, and the proceedings are continued on to final judgment, without any objection below or in this court, the error is waived. Ludeling's Syndics *v.* Poydras's Executors, iii, 419.

18. Creditors are cited to oppose the tableau, by publications, but to bring them into court in the first instance, personal notice is necessary as to those who reside in the parish. In New Orleans, publication in the papers, or a notice stuck up may be resorted to. *Ibid.*

19. Judgment of homologation regularly obtained, has the authority of the thing judged against all the creditors who were placed on the bilan. Louisiana Insurance Company *v.* Campbell, iii, 777.

20. Pending an appeal from the homologation of a tableau of distribution, none of the creditors can compel payment of the sum for which they are placed on the tableau. Dreux *v.* His Creditors, iv, 35.

21. When a creditor lays claim to a better place on the tableau, it may be opposed by any other thereafter, who deems it expedient and he cannot be said to be *in mora,* where he received notice of this claim. He who pays the note of another, cannot avail himself of the mortgage the latter had given for the benefit of his endorser, unless the mortgage be assigned him. Kirkland *v.* His Creditors, iv, 181.

22. A party who has no share in the money to be distributed cannot oppose the homologation of the tableau of distribution. Gravier *v.* Lafon *et al.,* iv, 371.

23. If a cause be remanded, with directions to amend the tableau according to the principle, laid down by the Supreme Court, the district court has no authority to touch the tableau in other parts. Nolte *et al. v.* Their Creditors, iv, 381.

24. Creditors may oppose the tableau of distribution at any time previous to the signing of the judgment of homologation. Avart *v.* His Creditors, iv, 100.

I. *Of the Charge of Fraud.*

1. Fraud is to be presumed in all the acts of a bankrupt whereby he undertakes to divest himself of his property to the prejudice of his creditors. Misotiere's Syndics *v.* Coignard, i, 171.

2. Fraud is presumed in all cases of bankruptcy. Menendez *v.* Larionda's Syndics, i, 202; Brandt *et al.,* Syndics, *v.* Shaumburgh, ii, 671.

3. When creditors refuse to accept the cession, and allege fraud, insolvent can not dismiss his petition. Clague *et al. v.* Lewis *et al.,* i, 317.

4. The fact of a defendant in insolvent circumstances having waived apparently good grounds of defence, does not necessarily import bad faith in him. Meeker's Assignees *v.* Williamson *et al.,* Syndics, i, 643.

M. *Of Insolvency Generally.*

1. Bail discharged, in case of defendant who contracted a debt prior to insolvency, and subsequently assumed to pay it. Packwood *v.* Foelckell, i, 7.

2. The services of the counsel employed by insolvent to make his cession of goods, are in reality services done to the creditors themselves; they do not form a privileged claim against insolvent, but against the funds in syndic's hands, belonging to the mass of creditors, and it is for the court to fix the *quantum* of remuneration. Morel *v.* Misotière's Syndics, i, 132.

3. The period of insolvency, or want of means in the debtor to pay all his debts, if evinced by a subsequent failure, is certainly the most rational period after which he should not be allowed to make any change in the state of his affairs, to the benefit of part of his creditors and injury of others. To fix this period with precision is difficult, on which account every case must rest on proofs and circumstances of its own. Brown *v.* Kenner *et al.*, i, 123.

4. A law of the Partidas was cited to show that a prescription of one year bars creditors from annulling sales made by debtors in fraud of their rights. *Held*, not applicable to the right of the mass of the creditors to oppose the fraudulent pretensions of other creditors who are making claims injurious to all. *Ibid.*

5. Foreign proceedings in bankruptcy, no protection against debts contracted here. Mitchell *v.* M'Millan, i, 196.

6. If a part of the property ceded be lost by the misconduct of the syndics, the debtor is entitled to a proportionate allowance from each creditor. Fitzgerald *v.* Phillips, i, 286.

7. The bare circumstance of his surrendering no property, is not sufficient to deprive an insolvent in actual custody of the benefit of the act of 1808, c. 16, when no fraudulent conduct was proved against him. Miles *v.* His Creditors, i, 494.

8. On failure of a debtor, his note, though not yet payable, may be put in suit. Fisk *v.* Chandler, i, 539.

9. The discharge of a member of a commercial partnership, under an insolvent law, does not release the other. Russel *v.* Rogers *et al.*, ii, 27.

10. The act of 1817, (relating to insolvents,) does not deprive persons who have not a year's residence of any right which previous acts gave them. Shreeve *v.* His Creditors, ii, 169.

11. Debts, other than those arising from consignment, may be proved on insolvency against a commission house in this city. Ward *v.* Brandt *et al.*, Syndics, ii, 212.

12. A discharge in a sister state, which liberates the person of the debtor, but leaves the contract in force, does not protect him from imprisonment here. Morris *v.* Eves, ii, 267.

13. In a *concurso* all the creditors are at once plaintiffs and defendants, nor is there any difference between the syndics and those who nominate them. Walton *v.* Watson *et al.*, ii, 479.

14. Several creditors, standing in the same predicament, and seeking the same relief, may join in one application. S. J. Pecquet *et al. v.* W. Golis, ii, 510.

15. Syndics have no right to take the whole proceeds of a vessel of which their insolvent was part owner only. Nor can those who have a right of action against the part owner be compelled to await the settlement of the insolvent's estate before they obtain the benefit of the proceedings against their debtor, who had not failed. Canex *et al. v.* Schooner James M'Kinley, ii, 667.

16. An insolvent cannot employ counsel after his failure, at the charge of his estate. Seghers *v.* Moulon's Syndics, ii, 756.

17. An acknowledgment of one of the syndics, that the person so employed was counsel, is not evidence that they agreed to compensate him for his services. *Ibid.*

18. A man's solvency cannot be better tested than by the return of an execution against him, on which no property can be found. Taylor *v.* Curtis, iii, 40.

19. The legal mode of showing the insolvency of an estate is by a settlement in the court of probates. Semple *v.* Fletcher, iii, 102.

20. If a person, who advances the price of a slave, take the bill of sale in his own name for his security, he cannot be disturbed by the creditors for the person for whom the purchase was made till he be reimbursed. Villars *v.* Morgan, iii, 153.

21. When a negotiable note is the evidence of the debt, it is the duty of the insolvent to find out the endorsee; putting the debt in the schedule in the name of the payee is not sufficient. Clark *v.* Wright, iii, 474.

22. An insolvent debtor does not acquire a discharge of his debts when the creditors fail to appear; or having made a change of parish, withdraw it. Dufau *v.* Massicot's Heirs, iii, 800.

23. The creditor of an insolvent who is put on the *bilan*, cannot object to the regularity

parts of the vessel cannot be used as before the accident, without repairs equal to half the value the insured may abandon. *Ibid.*

6. But if repairing the injury which has arisen from one of the perils insured against, will replace her in the same situation she was before, no matter how unsound, the insured cannot abandon. *Ibid.*

7. Abandonment transfers the property to the insurers without any acceptance on their part. Mellon *v.* Bucks *et al.*, iii, 580.

8. And after abandonment the insured cannot maintain an action against the owners, and master of the vessel for not having delivered the property. *Ibid.*

9. Nor can he maintain it on the ground that he is a *negotiorum gestor* of the insurers, when one of the objects of the suit is to take funds out of their hands which they have a right to hold in consequence of the abandonment. *Ibid.*

10. In case of a total loss, the assured must abandon within a reasonable time. Mellon *v.* Louisiana State Insurance Company, iii, 659.

11. And whether the abandonment was made within a reasonable time, is a proper question to be submitted to the jury. *Ibid.*

12. A demand of payment for a total loss amounts to abandonment. Cassedy *v.* Louisiana State Insurance Company, iii, 899.

13. An abandonment rightfully made, reverts back to the time of the loss. Clamageran *v.* Banks *et al.*, iv, 55.

D. *Of Insurance generally.*

1. The question as to sea-worthiness is one of fact for the jury. Trimble's Syndics *v.* N. O. Insurance Company, i, 138; Cole *v.* Louisiana Insurance Company, ii, 630.

2. A joint owner who had exclusive management, rendered liable for not having insured the entire vessel. Ralston *v.* Barclay *et al.*, i, 519.

3. Insurance may be had on freight to be carried. Cole *v.* Louisiana Insurance Company, ii, 630.

4. The insured will recover on a valued policy, although the invoice cost of the goods be below the sum insured. Akin *et al. v.* Mississippi Marine and Fire Insurance Company, iii, 428.

5. If a voyage be insured to *Key West* and the *Havana*, and the ship unnecessarily proceed to the last place first, this is a deviation. *Ibid.*

6. But if she did so through bad weather, and the voyage to *Key West* fail, a recovery, will be had for a total loss. *Ibid.*

7. In a policy of insurance the written controls the printed part. Brooke, Allen & Co.. *v.* Louisiana State Insurance Company, iii, 420.

8. Discussion of the principle, *that a total loss of any part, is a total loss* within the meaning of the policy. *Ibid.*

9. The insured is not obliged to communicate a fact respecting the situation of the port of destination, in relation to pilotage, for example, the knowledge of which was, equally within the reach of the insurer. Nelson *v.* Louisiana Insurance Company, iii, 545.

10. Whether an article be perishable in its nature, or not, is to be ascertained by the usage and custom of the port where the goods are shipped. *Ibid.*

11. The particular enumeration of perishable articles in an ordinary policy does not prevent the insured from showing, under the general clause, that other articles are perishable. *Ibid.*

12. When it becomes necessary to place goods in launches to transport them from the ship to the port of destination, they are at the insurer's risk until landed. Oscar *v.* Louisiana State Insurance Company, iii, 587.

13. The law of insurance is the same in this state as in the other states of the Union. Brooke *et al. v.* Louisiana State Insurance Company, iii, 645.

14. Insurers are responsible until the vessel is moored in good safety at the port of discharge. Zacharie *v.* The Orleans Insurance Company, iii, 690.

15. A sentence rendered in a court of admiralty which is appealed from, does not prove a falsification of the warranties contained in the policy. Zino *v.* The Louisiana Insurance Company, iii, 746.

16. During the pendency of the cause in the admiralty court, the suit between the insurer and insured may be continued for a reasonable time. The appeal meanwhile prevents that judgment from having the force of *res judicata.* *Ibid.*

17. The contract of insurance is to be construed with reference to the laws of the country where it was made. Shiff *v.* Louisiana State Insurance Company, iv, 90.

18. Nothing but necessity justifies a deviation. The necessity is not to be tested by

the event, but by all the circumstances attending the case. Byrne v. Louisiana State Insurance Company, iv, 179.

See BARRATRY.

INTEREST.

1. Interest cannot be sued for in a distinct action. Faurie v. Pitot et al., Syndics, i, 46.

2. Legal interest is fixed at 5 per cent., and is by law recoverable, in all cases of money due, from the date of the judicial demand; it is also recoverable when no demand has been made, in cases where the debt is owing for things which, from their nature, may be supposed to produce revenue or fruits. Domat, book 3, tit. 5, sect. 1, art. 4, lays down that the purchaser of a farm owes interest on the price which has not been paid, agreeably to the terms of sale, although no demand has been made, and even should he receive less revenue from the land than the interest of the price. Syndics of Segur v. Brown, i, 98.

3. Purchaser in possession of the land is bound to pay interest on every instalment of the price due. Duplantier v. Pigman, i, 116.

4. Interest not allowed on running accounts, except where an understanding to that effect is shown. Merieult v. Austin, iii, 318.

5. The court cannot allow interest on the sum awarded in the verdict, which was before unliquidated. Morgan v. Bell, i, 302; Parker v. Walden, iv, 127.

6. Interest cannot be allowed on an unliquidated claim for any period anterior to the suit. Foster et al. v. Dupré, i, 333.

7. Interest should not be allowed on a demand liquidated by the verdict only. Pierce v. Flower et al., i, 387; Andry et al. v. Foy, i, 525.

8. Where interest has been paid by debtor above the legal rate, he is entitled to a credit on the debt for the amount thus paid. Durnford v. Bariteau, i, 410.

9. Writing is not of the essence of a convention to pay a particular rate of interest. Delacroix v. Prevost's Ex'rs, i, 482.

10. If the vendor covenant to clear the estate of an incumbrance, until he does it, and the vendee has knowledge of it, interest will not run. Bouthemy's Ex. v. Ducournau, i, 521.

11. Interest cannot be claimed, under the custom of merchants, when the goods do not appear to have been bought for the purpose of trade and the vendee is not a merchant. Davis v. Turnbull et al., i, 551.

12. A promise to pay interest for the renewal of a note means no more than bank interest: it cannot be presumed to mean usurious interest. Boismarre v. Jourdan, ii, 464.

13, If interest be promised on a privileged debt, the interest is not therefore privileged. Roman v. Degruy et al., ii, 613.

14. An agreement to pay ten per cent. on the purchase-money for three years, which is afterwards extended to the fourth year, does not entitle the creditor to interest at this rate, on further indulgence. Hepp et al. v. Ducros et al., iii, 55.

15. The buyer owes interest on the price of slaves from the time the debt becomes due. Ibid.

16. The liquidation and judgment of the Spanish tribunal in 1797, made with consent of those interested, conclusive. Slaves are not considered as producing revenue per se, though they do so by being hired out or employed in agriculture, &c.; land alone strictly and literally can be said to bear fruits, so that interest may be claimed on debts contracted on account of it. St. Maxent's Syndics v. Sigur, i, 132.

17. Interest on a twelve-months' bond is to be paid at the rate of ten per cent. if by the judgment the debtor was to be charged at that rate till payment. See Acts of 1817, p. 134. Rees v. Dejean, iii, 456.

18. Property subject to mortgage for principal and interest of the price of a a tract of land, is not subject to a demand for interest on interest growing out of a subsequent agreement of the parties. Overton v. Archinard, iii, 511.

19. When the case is tried by a jury, the court cannot give interest on the sum found by the verdict. Bedford et al. v. Jacobs, iii, 614; Commandeur v. Russel, iii, 616.

20. But if the verdict is for a certain sum with interest, the court may decide the rate. Overton v. Gervais, iii, 619.

21. Interest cannot be allowed on a contract made in Ireland on evidence, that it is customary, without showing that it is authorised by law. Glascow v. Stevenson, iv, 62.

22. The jury are not bound to say a debt is paid because a witness swears he thinks it is. Interest must now be allowed on a protested note from the day of protest. O'Conner v. Bernard, iv, 64.

23. Conventional interest is chargeable only when supported by an agreement in writing. Ory v. Winter, iv, 79.

24. If interest be demanded in the petition, and the judgment be silent on it, a subsequent demand can not be made for interest. Saul v. His Creditors, iv, 302.

25. A mortgage is sufficiently certain wherein money is promised with *interest*, for this, of course, means legal interest. Rousseau v. His Creditors, iv, 557.

26. When the interest is a legal consequence of the debt, a demand for the principal is a demand for the principal and interest. Daquin et al. v. Coiron et al., iv, 635.

27. If the jury give more than legal interest, the plaintiff may release the overplus and have judgment. Dicks et al. v. Cash et al., iv, 275.

28. *Interest* will *not* be allowed on a *note* given for the purchase and price of slaves, when there is a contest between two adverse parties about the proceeds, until such contest is decided: because until *then* the maker of the note is not considered *in mora*. Miles v. Oden et al., iv, 492.

INTERPRETER.

Papers in a foreign language need not be translated by the sworn interpreter of the court. Heirs of Farrar v. Warfield and Wife, iv, 670.

INTERROGATORIES ON FACTS AND ARTICLES.

1. The answer of a partner to interrogatories suffices, if not excepted to. Martineau et al. v. Carr et al., i, 153.

2. Where the answer of one party to interrogatories has been excepted to, the answer can not be withdrawn, and may be used against respondent by the other party. Poston v. Adams, i, 365.

3. The defendant may avail himself of his own answer to an interrogatory put to him by the plaintiff, though plaintiff decline to use it himself. Berthole v. Mace, i, 417.

4. Executors interrogated as to the genuineness of testator's signature to the note sued on answering they believe it genuine, but believe it to have been paid by him, do not by this answer prove payment. Franklin v. Kemble's Executor, i, 438.

5. Answers to interrogatories received by the Mayor of New York, and accompanied by the certificate of the governor and the seal of the state, are sufficiently authenticated. Woolsey v. Paulding, i, 727.

6. Answers to interrogatories must be taken together; they cannot be divided. Bradford's Heirs v. Brown, ii, 181; Rogers v. Parmetti, ii, 492; Hunter v. Smith, iii, 35.

7. The article of the Civil Code, 316, art. 261, providing that, if either party refuses or neglects to answer interrogatories on facts and articles, the fact on which he refuses to answer shall be taken for confessed, and the judge shall proceed, in consequence of that proof, to render judgment: *Decided*, to be *cumulative* of that provision in the act of the legislative council, (2 *Martin's Digest*, 160, n. 9,) that on failure of plaintiff to answer defendant's interrogatories "his suit shall be dismissed at his costs on the motion of the defendant," and does not repeal the last mentioned. Patterson v. Lafarge, ii, 431.

8. When a party answers evasively an interrogatory propounded to him, this raises a violent presumption that a direct answer would have been against his interest. Baron v. Sterling, ii, 503.

9. Nothing requires the defendant's answer to the plaintiff's interrogatories to be inserted in the answer to the petition. Seal v. Erwin et al., ii, 650.

10. Where plaintiff files interrogatories to be answered by a witness, whose deposition is to be taken, and the adverse party filed his cross interrogatories under them, this is a waiver, *perhaps*, of the objection that some of plaintiff's are leading questions. Sowers v. Flower et al., ii, 759.

11. Interrogatories propounded to a party in a suit cannot be answered by his agent. Buford v. Valentine, iii, 21.

12. If the answers to interrogatories are evasive, the cause will be remanded. Bird v. Bowie, iii, 36.

13. If part of plaintiff's answer to interrogatories be stricken out, the defendant is not entitled to further time to except to what remains. Clay v. Oldham, iii, 87.

14. If a party be called on by an interrogatory to state whether he have a paper in his possession, and he answer in the affirmative, it is sufficient if he produce it on the trial, and the opposite party is not entitled to a continuance to examine it. *Ibid.*

15. A party interrogated on facts and articles cannot, by his answer, make the copy of an instrument evidence, without accounting for the loss of the original. Lafarge v. Ripley, iii, 304.

16. Nor make conversation between himself and a third party, in the absence of his adversary, evidence against the latter. *Ibid.*

17. The defendant me . offer in evidence his own answers to interrogatories propounded to him by the plaintiff in a former suit. Hunter *v.* Smith, iii, 497.

18. A party interrogated on facts and articles, is not compelled to answer categorically, if he swears that his memory will not permit him to do so. Lewis *v.* Decoux, iii, 694.

19. Although the party against whom a witness is examined on interrogatories may not be entitled to cross examine—if his opponent consents to his doing so, and gives him notice of time and place, the latter may not deceive him, by taking the deposition elsewhere, and on another day. Gill *v.* Jett, iii, 839.

20. If the testimony leave it doubtful whether notice to file cross interrogatories was given, the deposition ought to be rejected. Gill *v.* Phillips *et al.,* iii, 847.

21. A plaintiff, from whom the fact of the delivery of a bill is drawn by an interrogatory, may prove its loss by the answers admitting the delivery. Glasgow *v.* Stevenson, iv, 62.

22. A party interrogated whether he did not agree to erect a saw-mill for defendant, may well answer that he agreed to put up one in partnership with him, but that he, the defendant, failed to comply with his part of the contract, whereupon they had rescinded the contract. Nichols *v.* Pierce, iv, 123.

23. It is not necessary for a defendant to swear that the answer of the plaintiff to his interrogatories is *material,* if he swear they will assist him in his defence. Fisk *v.* Bynum, iv, 238.

24. The answer of the plaintiff to interrogatories may be taken under a general commission to examine all witnesses. Gabaroche *v.* Herbert *et al.,* iv, 341.

25. An answer to interrogatories must be categorical, but it is immaterial in what words the answer is made, provided an affirmance or denial result. *Ibid.*

INTERVENTION.

1. The intervening party who claims the property seized under an attachment, has no right to take advantage of any irregularity in the proceedings between the plaintiff and defendant; he is only permitted to show that the property attached is verily his. Lee *et al. v.* Bradlee, i, 613.

2. In an ordinary partnership, dissolved by the death of one of the partners, the heirs of the deceased partner have a right to participate with the survivors in the liquidation. Norris's Heirs *v.* Ogden's Executor, ii, 226.

3. Therefore, if a suit is commenced by one of the partners to recover a debt due the partnership, the other partners have a right to intervene; *aliter* if they have a joint interest with the defendant. *Ibid.*

4. An intervening party may demand to have his case tried by a jury. 9 *Martin,* 381. Lacroix *v.* Menard, iii, 96.

5. He who interpleads, cannot change the nature of the action in which he intervenes. Carraoy *et al. v.* Morgan, iii, 635.

6. A creditor has no right to interfere in a suit between his debtor and a third party. Brown & Sons *v.* Saul *et al.,* iii, 343.

7. The opening of the argument in a case belongs to him who is emphatically the plaintiff; i. e., to him who instituted the suit. This right does not belong to the intervenor, notwithstanding art. 392 of Code of Practice. Murmiche *v.* Commagere *et al.,* iv, 108.

8. A party who wishes to interplead, must show that the decision of the case is to affect his rights. Pierre *et al. v.* Massey *et al.,* iv, 208.

9. It is not enough that he shows that he has claims to enforce against either of the parties. *Ibid.*

10. An intervenor can not retard the cause in which he interpleads. Walker *v.* Dunbar *et al.,* iv, 361.

INVENTORY.

1. The presence of the under tutor of an inventory is necessary. Frere *et al. v.* Frere *et al.,* ii, 521.

2. There is no law requiring that in an inventory of minor's property, a distinction should be made between what was inherited from his father, and what from his mother. Agnisse *et al. v.* Gucdron *et al.,* ii, 599.

3. An inventory is to precede the partition of every estate. Millaudon *v.* Peroy *et al.,* iii, 654.

4. But it may be made after the partition is ordered. *Ibid.*

JUDGE.

1. A parish judge has no authority to receive the acknowledgment of a deed. Marie Louise v. Cauchoix, ii, 186; Seymour v. Cooley, iii, 107.

2. A parish judge charged with the settlement of an estate, can not give professional aid therein, nor receive a fee as an attorney at law. Duverney v. Vinot, ii, 267.

JUDGMENT.

1. A judgment which does not contain any of the reasons which influenced the court rendering it, is unconstitutional and void. Gray et al. v. Laverty et al., i, 273; Millon v. Delisle, ii, 649.

2. It is now settled that they are not so; and that the nullity must be pronounced on an appeal, or by judgment in the court which rendered the judgment. Legendre v. M'Donough, iv, 39.

3. A judgment of dismissal ought to contain the reasons on which it is grounded. Sierra v. Slort, i, 297.

4. When the judge gives no reasons, the court will annul the judgment upon the appellee's objecting, but will give such judgment as the case requires. T. & D. Urquhart's Executor v. Taylor, i, 360.

5. A judgment is valid if the reasons of giving it appear on reference to the petition. Doubrere v. Papin, i, 409.

6. The want of reasons in a judgment by default held an error. Montserrat v. Godet, i, 412.

7. In awarding the restitution of a note which the plaintiffs are liable to pay if not returned, the court had a right further to provide, that in defect of such restitution, the amount of the note should be paid; although the petition prayed only the restitution of the note and general relief. Dubourg et al. v. Anderson, i, 560.

8. Three judicial days must elapse before judgment taken by default becomes final. Gorham v. De Armas, i, 571.

9. The court need not give any reason, in a judgment taken by default on a liquidated claim. Dehart v. Berthoud et al., i, 580.

10. A judgment of this court set aside by consent of parties and cause remanded. De Armas and Wife v. Hampton, i, 649.

11. A judgment may be so far final, as to be appealable from without being final, as to the point in issue. Clay v. His Creditors, ii, 17.

12. The validity of a sentence, rendered by a court of competent jurisdiction, cannot be inquired into collaterally. Dufour v. Camfranc, ii, 243.

13. The recording, not the docketing the judgment, creates the lien. Hanna v. His Creditors, ii, 279.

14. A judge may well sign a judgment after the three days. Thompson v. Chretien et al., ii, 309.

15. A district court cannot, by a new decree, change its former judgment after the expiration of the term in which it was rendered, unless on a new trial granted. Baillio v. Wilson, Tutrix, &c., ii, 322.

16. The circumstance of a judgment being rendered on a petition written in French, does not make it void. Whether voidable? Bouthemy v. Dreux et al., ii, 374.

17. It is not in the power of an inferior court to deprive a party, in whose favor it has rendered judgment, of the benefit which results from it, on the allegation of any fact that might have been objected to him, and prevented his obtaining judgment. Lafon's Executors v. Dessessart, ii, 401.

18. Judgment cannot be given for defendant for a balance which may be found due him, unless specially claimed in his answer. Coulory's Heirs v. Dufau, ii, 409.

19. A judgment of dismissal is nothing more than one of nonsuit, and does not form rem judicatam on any of the matters at issue. Baudin v. Rolliff, Robertson et al., Interpleaders, ii, 423.

20. The judgment of homologation is incomplete until signed by the judge. Abat v. Michel, ii, 447.

21. Judgment cannot exceed the amount claimed in the petition. Barckley v. Evans'b Executors, ii, 650.

22. Where the fact is doubtful, judgment will be given against him holding the affirmative. Walton et al. v. Grant et al., ii, 721.

23. A judgment is valid, although the sum adjudged be not stated therein, when the sum appears on record. Melançon's Heirs v Duhamel, iii, 4.

24. A judge need not in all cases refer to the law which he decides. Henderson for the use of Hunter v. Bowles, iii, 46.

25. If the proceedings have been changed from the *juicio executivo* to the *juicio ordinario*, judgment may be given generally against the defendant. Clay *v.* Oldham, iii, 87.

26. The plaintiff may, by the introduction of evidence by the defendant, obtain judgment, on a different ground from that prayed for in the petition. Labarre *v.* Lambert, iii, 91.

27. The absence of the reasons on which a judgment is grounded, is only a relative nullity. Whitehurst *v.* Hickey *et al.*, iii, 169.

28. A judgment against two, without stating the parties are condemned *in solido*, makes each responsible for his *virile* share. United States *et al. v.* Hawkins' Heirs, iii, 308.

29. Judgments are presumed to follow the obligation they enforce. But when the prayer in the petition does not follow the obligation, this presumption does not exist. *Ibid.*

30. A judgment given on erroneous evidence, is valid until reversed. Clark's Heirs *v.* Barham's Heirs, iii, 337.

31. When the defendant is sued as *attorney in fact*, and the judgment is general, the judgment does not affect the defendant in his own right. Baudin *v.* Dubourg & Barron, iii, 368.

32. Judgment is not final until signed by the judge. Sprigg *v.* Wells, iii, 467.

33. When judgment is given against a defendant in a representative capacity, but this fact is not mentioned in it, recording the judgment will not give a lien on the property of the principal. Douglas *et al. v.* Curtis, iii, 469.

34. If a judge signs a judgment before the proper time, the party may still move for a new trial, in the same manner as if the judgment was unsigned. Gardere *et al. v.* Murray, iii, 526.

35. If the party, instead of doing this, appeals, he is precluded from urging that the judgment was not final. *Ibid.*

36. After a cause is argued, no motion can be made to hasten judgment until the time given by law for rendering it has elapsed. Dicks *et al. v.* Barton, iii, 698.

37. After a motion for a new trial is overruled, the court may proceed at once to give final judgment. *Ibid.*

38. When a criminal court, without exceeding its authority, directs the payment of a fine, it cannot be decreed to another person while the judgment remains in force. Parish of Orleans *v.* Morgan, iii, 721.

39. A judgment under the third section of the act of March 27th, 1823, ought, perhaps *must* direct, that the fine should be paid to the hospital as the act directs. *Ibid.*

40. When a defendant dies, a judgment rendered against him must be declared executory against his heirs or representatives, because property which has ceased to be his cannot be affected by a judgment to which the new owners are not made parties; but on the death of the plaintiff, nothing prevents his heir or representative from taking out execution. Legendre *v.* M'Donough, iv, 39.

41. Where a previous judgment has been obtained in one of the courts of this state by an executrix, residing in another state, and no objection or evidence to the contrary, it will be presumed she was duly qualified. Dangerfield's Executor *v.* Thurston's Heirs, iv, 199.

42. Judgment cannot be given in general terms against a minor, but only against the movables; he cannot alienate his immovable property without authority. Emancipated minors are here spoken of only. Execution, issuing on such judgment, shall not be levied on the immovables and slaves. Broussard *v.* Mallet, *et al.*, iv, 513.

43. Judgment obtained by the wife against the husband, is evidence of the debt in an hypothecary action. But where the answer charges the judgment to have been obtained through fraud and collusion, the wife must give evidence to prove it was *bona fide*. Beard *v.* Pijeaux, iv, 585.

44. A judgment derives its force and effect from what is decreed by the court, not from what is admitted by the parties. A judgment, confessed by an attorney, in presence of his client, has no preference over one confessed out of the client's presence. Cuebas *v.* Venas, iv, 587.

45. A judgment cannot be given with preference, without a prayer for a writ of seizure and judgment by privilege. *Ibid.*

46. A confession of judgment which will preclude the necessity of filing an answer, or forming the *contestatio litis*, can only be made by the defendant or one specially authorised to that effect. Gasquet *et al. v.* Johnson, iv, 613.

JUDGMENT BY DEFAULT.

1. When judgment is taken by default, the verdict cannot be for the defendant, although no damage be proved. Allen *v.* Lioteau, ii, 1.

2. A judgment by default may be made final, even when the object of the suit is the recovery of land. Conrad v. Fleming, ii, 201.

3. The appearance made by the defendant's attorney for the sole purpose of having a judgment by default set aside, is not such an appearance as to destroy his client's right to have the cause removed to a court of the United States. Duncan v. Hampton, ii, 287.

4. The want of an answer does not authorise the confirmation of the judgment by default without evidence, except where the demand is liquidated. Mine v. Labo et al., ii, 604.

JUDICIAL PROCEEDINGS.

1. The proceedings of a parish judge, presiding as such at the partition of an estate, and decreeing the adjudication of it according to law, are *judicial* proceedings, and if not written in the English language, are void. Tregre v. Tregre, i, 523.

2. The proceedings of the meeting of the creditors of an insolvent, are judicial proceedings. They are ordered by the court, and constitute a part of the proceedings of the suit, instituted by the debtor against his creditors, and are the basis on which rests the judgment which terminates it. Durnford v. Segher's Syndics, i, 576; Viale's Syndics v. Gardenier et al., i, 731.

3. The constitution of Louisiana began to be binding on the people, and all the parts of the government, legislative, executive, and judicial, were to be administered according to its provisions, as soon as the state was admitted into the Union, and thenceforth judicial proceedings were to be preserved in the language in which the constitution of the United States is written. Bouthemy et al. v. Dreux et al., ii, 52.

4. The *procès verbal* of the sale of a minor's real estate by the parish judge is valid, though it be reduced to writing in French, as the sale might have been made by any auctioneer not judicial. Melançon's Heirs v. Duhamel, ii, 96.

5. Every thing in judicial proceedings is to be presumed rightly done. Trepagnier's Heirs v. Butler et al., ii, 363.

6. A power of attorney, executed before a justice of the peace in another state, is not a record or a judicial proceeding, under the act of congress. Parham v. Murphee, iii, 319.

7. The copy of the probate of a will is the copy of a judicial proceeding, which must be certified under the act of congress of 1790. Balfour v. Chew, iii, 639.

JURISDICTION.

A. *Of the Jurisdiction of the Supreme Court.*
B. *Of the Jurisdiction of the Court of Probates, as distinguished from that of Courts of ordinary jurisdiction.*
C. *Of Jurisdiction generally.*

A. *Of the Jurisdiction of the Supreme Court.*

1. No criminal appellant jurisdiction given to this court. Laverty v. Duplessis, i, 84.

2. This court cannot exercise a general superintending jurisdiction over the inferior courts. Ibid. The State v. Judge Esnault, ii, 360.

3. This court, as an appellant court, has the right to issue a mandate. Agnes v. Judice, i, 105.

4. The sum claimed, not that recovered ascertains the jurisdiction of the court. Harang v. Dauphin, i, 209.

5. In an action for freight, the defendant having pleaded that the contract was made in Kentucky, the court waived the validity of this plea, in deciding that the defendant impliedly contracted to pay the freight by taking the merchandise, and so his obligation originated at New Orleans. Smith v. Flowers et al., i, 449.

6. When the inferior court refuses to examine the case on the merits, the Supreme Court cannot decide on them. Martin v. Heirs of Martin et al., iii, 19.

7. The constitution does not authorise the court to take cognizance of any case where the object in dispute is below 300 dollars. Whether the legislature can confer the power? —Quære. M'Rea v. Bushnell, iii, 364.

8. An appellate court cannot give a judgment which the court a quo could not. Reels v. Knight, iii, 440; Pritchard v. Hamilton, iv, 14.

9. The Supreme Court cannot give relief against the imposition of a fine of forty dollars. Millaudon v. The Judge of the Parish of Jefferson, iii, 730.

10. The Supreme Court cannot take cognizance of a case referred to it by a district court, without an appeal having been prayed for and granted; the case having stood several years in the court a quo, and the district judge, doubting his jurisdiction over it, and thereupon referring it to this court. Hughes v. Hook's Heirs, iii, 858.

11. If the matter in dispute be under the value of 300 dollars, the Supreme Court cannot act on the case. Although the defendant alleges that this small sum is part of a larger sum that plaintiffs will continue to demand of him. Mayor *et al. v.* Maighan, iv, 451.

12. If the sum originally sued for be under 300 dollars, and a third party intervenes claiming a sum below 300 dollars, both claims cannot be cumulated to authorise an appeal, although they collectively exceed 300 dollars. Boulden *et al. v.* Hughes, iv, 518.

13. The legislative construction of the constitution as to jurisdiction of this court, in article 876, Code of Practice, is to be respected. Carraby *v.* Carraby, iv, 318.

14. If the demands, in two consolidated cases, exceed, together, 300 dollars, an appeal will lie. Heirs of Baillio *v.* Prudhomme *et al.*, iv, 539.

B. *Of the Jurisdiction of the Court of Probates.*

1. The jurisdiction of a court of probates extends over the acts of persons appointed under its authority; but not over claims against the estates which they administer. Abat *et al. v.* Songy's Estate, i, 561.

2. Before the act of 1890 the court of probates had power to decree the exhibiting and filing of an executor's account, and a *distringas* was the proper writ of execution. Casanovichi *et al. v.* Debon *et al.*, ii, 56.

3. The court of probates has exclusive jurisdiction of all claims against a vacant estate. Vignaud *v.* Tonnacourt, ii, 305; Poirot *v.* Vesser, iv, 629.

4. The court of probates has but a limited jurisdiction. If it issue a *fieri facias*, and the title of the debtor to the property seized be contested, it cannot try the right of the party claiming it. Menard *v.* Rust *et al.*, ii, 62.

5. The court of probates has not jurisdiction of a demand against a surviving partner for a partnership debt. Turner *v.* Collins, ii, 487.

6. An action against a curatrix can only be brought in the court of probates. Sanders *v.* Highland's Curatrix, ii, 649.

7. If property forming part of a succession be irregularly sold, and an action of warranty be grounded thereon, the action does not appertain to the court of probates. Montamat and Wife *v.* Debon, ii, 688.

8. When an executor has become insolvent, the court of probates retains jurisdiction of action against him for property in his hands belonging to the estate. *Aliter* where judgment is demanded for a sum of money. Taylor *v.* Hollander, iii, 382.

9. The court of probates has jurisdiction in all cases that relate to putting into provisional possession the heirs of the absentee, but it cannot try the question of title. Donaldson *et al. v.* Dorsey *et al.*, iii, 373.

10. If in a suit for partition, the defendant set up a title in himself which is alleged by the plaintiff to be simulated, the court of probates has no jurisdiction of the case. Reels *v.* Knight, iii, 440.

11. The court of probates is not without a jurisdiction *rations materia* in a case in which some of the defendants are minors and some majors. Skillman and Wife *v.* Lacy, iii, 450.

12. The court of probates has jurisdiction of applications for the interdiction of insane persons. Stafford *v.* Stafford, iii, 479.

13. The court of probates may decide on the validity of a sale of land, when the question arises collaterally in the examination of other matters of which it has jurisdiction. Baillio *et al. v.* Wilson *et al.*, iii, 514.

14. An executor is not suable in the court of probates, on his endorsement of a note payable to the estate. Flower *et al. v.* Swift, iii, 645.

15. The court of probates has power to decide on sales of the immovable property of a succession. Gill *v.* Phillips *et al.*, iii, 847.

16. That the court of probates has no power to decide directly, on the validity of sales of real estate, or to try titles thereto, is a position to which this court readily accedes. But that court possesses all powers necessary to carry its jurisdiction into effect, and when in the exercise of that jurisdiction, questions arise collaterally, it must, of necessity, decide them, for if it could not, no other court could. It is immaterial, whether these questions arise out of the sale of land, slaves, or in any other manner, if the examination of them is necessary to the decision of the issue joined. *Ibid.*

17. The court of probates has alone jurisdiction of a suit against a curator to compel him to account. Balsineur *v.* Bills, iv, 170.

18. The law disqualifying judges of probates from sitting in cases where they were witnesses, was repealed by the act of 1828, p. 152, sect. 6. *Ibid.*

19. A decree of a court of probates may be annulled by it. Harty *et al. v.* Harty *et al.*, iv, 602.

The court of probates has not jurisdiction of a case where the heirs of a succession claim property from those who hold under a title adverse to them and their ancestor. Harris's Tutor *v.* M'Kee *et al.*, iii, 365.

C. *Of Jurisdiction generally.*

1. If a sheriff wrongfully execute the process of a court, he may be sued therefor in another court. Clarke's Ex'rs *v.* Morgan, i, 223.

2. Where a court has no jurisdiction over the *subject* of the suit, no admission of the parties can give it. Abat *et al.* Songy's Estate, i, 561.

3. The marshal of the United States is suable in a state court for a trespass, committed under color of an authority, under a process issued out of a court of the United States. Dunn and Wife *v.* Vail, i, 577.

4. On a notice that an order will be moved for to put in force a treasury execution, the district court had no right to pronounce a judgment for the sum with interest and costs, but only that the execution be put in force. The State *v.* Montegut *et al.*, i, 583.

5. The jurisdiction of the court of the parish and city of New Orleans does not extend to contracts or torts originating out of the parish. Breedlove *et al. v.* Fletcher, i, 593.

6. Where plaintiff's testator was drowned in the parish of St. Martin, and the defendant took a large sum of money from the body, which he brought to New Orleans and deposited in a bank in his own name, and refused to pay the same when requested by the executor: *Held,* that the plaintiff might either have against him an action similar to that of money had and received, in St. Martins, or one for tortious conversion in the parish court of New Orleans, the refusal to pay the money being a conversion in New Orleans. Cost *v.* Jennings, i, 629.

7. After the court of probates has ordered the execution of a will, any person interested in setting it aside, may be heard against it in the district court. Bouthemy *v.* Dreux *et al.*, iii, 374.

8. An attorney appointed by the court, cannot give jurisdiction by pleading informally. Debays *et al. v.* Yerby's Ex'rs, ii, 491.

9. The district court has jurisdiction of a suit where the heirs at law claim the whole estate from a person they allege has no title to it. Crane *et al. v.* Marshall, ii, 550.

10. A court may at any stage of the case dismiss it, if it appear it has no jurisdiction. Lafon's Ex'rs *v.* Lafon, ii, 573.

11. The district court does not lose jurisdiction of a cause before it, when the defendant leaves no property within the reach of the court of probates. Lecesne *v.* Cottin, ii, 713.

12. Sureties on curator's bonds may be sued in the district court, and if they plead discussion, the creditor may go into the court of probates to do it. Beneficiary heirs may also be sued in the district court, when a breach of duty is alleged which renders them personally responsible. Martin *v.* Heirs of Martin *et al.*, iii, 19.

13. A husband can only sue the heirs of his wife, in the district court, in order to establish contradictorily with them the amount of the debts of the community. Broussard *v.* Bernard *et al.*, iii, 14.

14. Courts in this state cannot enlarge their jurisdiction by fiction. Shiff *et al. v.* Wilson, iii, 28.

15. A curator, or beneficiary heir, ordered by the court of probates to pay a debt, may be sued in the district court. Waters *v.* Wilson *et al.*, iii, 42.

16. The district court is not ousted of jurisdiction, because a corporation has the right of enforcing its regulations. Trustees of Natchitoches *v.* Coe, iii, 44.

17. Heirs may sue the widow in the district court for a partition of the common estate. The Civil Code, 176, art. 133, in giving jurisdiction to the court of probates does not give it exclusively. Heirs of Gague *v.* Gague *et al.*, iii, 51.

18. Heirs who accept purely and simply, may be sued in any court. Ingrem *et al. v.* Ingrem *et al.*, iii, 100.

19. The widow who accepts the community, may be sued in the district court. Flood *et al. v.* Shamburgh, iii, 180.

20. The district court is not wholly deprived of jurisdiction, *ratione materiæ*, in suits for the recovery of debts against a succession. Tabor *v.* Johnson *et al.*, iii, 194; Foucher *v.* Carraby *et al.*, iv, 54.

21. An inhabitant of the city of New Orleans, cannot be sued in the court of probates of East Baton Rouge, on the ground that he was executor to a deceased person, whose

JUSTICE OF PEACE.

lord's, he took cognisance of a suit between landlord and tenant, brought before him as a justice. Dressen v. Cox, ii, 766.

4. A justice of the peace derives no protection from his official capacity, when he does not act within his jurisdiction. Bore v. Bush et al., iii, 720.

5. The assignee of leased premises may remove the lessee by summary process. No matter what may be the value of the improvements placed on the premises, the justice of the peace has jurisdiction under the act of 1819. Walker v. Van Winkle et al., iv, 618.

LAND.

1. In the Spanish colonies, the manner of locating the lands assigned to the Indians was not by fixing their boundaries by actual survey. They obtained permission to settle on a certain spot, and around that spot they were entitled to possess an extent of one league. Reboul v. Nero, i, 407.

2. A confirmation of title by the commissioners of the land office of the United States can not avail against a complete title under the crown of Spain. White v. Wells's Executors, i, 431.

3. The laws of the Indies require the property of Indians to be sold at auction; but if a private sale be made by them, held, that the Indians themselves, or some one claiming under them, must take advantage of this illegality, and until then the purchasers hold in their right, and cannot be disturbed. Martin v. Johnson et al., i 433.

4. Where plaintiff had obained from the Spanish governor an order of survey and a conditional grant, which he afterward surrendered into the hands of the commandant: Held, that he had abandoned his inchoate right. Boissier v. Metayer, i, 439.

5. Though plaintiffs do not show a title derived from the sovereign of the country, yet possession under written deeds will enable them to be maintained in it, when the defendants have no title. Davenport v. Turnbull's Heirs, i, 616.

6. When both parties have obtained, from the commissioners of the land office, a relinquishment of the rights of the United States on the land, their previous titles should be weighed independently of these relinquishments. Hooter v. Tippet, i, 679.

7. The purchaser from a claimant who has obtained the commissioner's certificate, shall not be disturbed by another claimant alleging that he has bought from a person having a right of pre-emption. Tippet et al. v. Everston, i, 691.

8. The commissioner's certificate will not avail against title or possession in another. Carmichael v. Brisler, i, 694.

9. When the defendant pleads the general issue, and does not set up a title, the plaintiff is not relieved from the necessity of proving a legal title in himself, by showing that the defendant has a defective one, emanating from the same source as his own. Sassmann v. St. Aimé and Wife, i, 721.

10. A person who slanders the title of another to real estate, may be compelled to bring suit, to prove the truth of what he has said. Livingston v. Herman, ii, 40.

11. It is not necessary, to enable the court to decide on the title for land, that there should be a prayer in the petition to be put in possession. Ibid.

12. A case depending on boundary lines. Meaux's Heirs v. Breaux, ii, 40.

13. The party from whom land is recovered, ought to be charged for the use and occupation, from the day of the legal demand. Walsh v. Collins, ii, 239.

14. A just title is that which is of a nature to transfer the property. So that, if it be not transferred, it is owing to a want of right in the grantor. Dufour v. Camfranc, ii, 243.

15. A purchaser at a sheriff's sale, by a defective title, owes fruits from the judicial demand. Ibid.

16. Where property is put up at sale and bid for as such, but afterwards and before adjudication is described as having a known quantity, and purchased by a particular designation of its limits, it will require the strongest proofs to justify the court in rejecting the positive description given in the act by which plaintiff acquired, and declaring the overplus of land to have been sold in the sale of the designated portion. Macarty v. Foucher, ii, 273.

17. Disputes about the limits of adjoining tracts of land. Martin v. Trumbull, ii, 332.

18. Case in which are laid down principles for guidance in uncertainty respecting the location of land. Holstein v. Henderson, ii, 317.

19. Whether the vendee can recover land which the vendor before the sale has sworn to belong to the person in possession. Davis's Heirs v. Prevost's Heirs, ii, 345.

20. Lands granted by the king of Spain did not enter into the community of acquests and gains. Gayoso de Lemos v. Garcia, ii, 469.

11. A landlord allowed an order of seizure in the first instance upon an authentic act of lease. Sterrett *v.* Smith, ii, 706.

12. If, on a lease for years, the tenants abandon the premises, the landlord may demand the rent for the whole term. Christy *v.* Casanave, ii, 707.

13. The legal lien of the landlord is of a higher nature than the claim of the United States on custom house bonds. Jackson *v.* Oddie, ii, 538.

14. The lessor may expel the lessee, if he do not pay the rent, and may demand bail of him though he exercises his right in part on the furniture. Dressen *v.* Cox, ii, 766.

15. The landlord has a privilege on the tools of a tradesman found on the premises, for the payment of rent. Parker *v.* Starkweather, iv, 264.

16. Landlord's privilege is not lost by the curator's removal of the property subject thereto. Robinson *v.* M'Coy, Curator, iv, 445.

17. The assignee of leased premises may remove the lessee by summary process. Walker *v.* Van Winkle *et al.,* iv, 618.

LEGACY.

1. Before a legatee can be compelled to suffer a deduction from his legacy, in order to pay a debt of the succession, the debt must have been established contradictorily with the heirs or executors. White *v.* Hepp *et al.,* vi, 704.

2. A legacy is not subject to attachment without its being first shown that the succession is insolvent. *Ibid.*

3. The legacy of a debt includes that of the interest due thereon. Hepp *et al. v.* Lafonta's Ex'rs, ii, 705.

4. Accretion takes place among the legatees in case of the legacy being made to several conjointly, though the testator should, by a subsequent member of the sentence in which this bequest is made, assign a part to each legatee. Parkinson *et al. v.* M'Donough *et al.,* iii, 287.

5. If a specific legacy is made of a note, and afterwards, but before the death of the testator, a payment is made on it, the legatee cannot claim that the amount of the note should be paid by the executors. Hepp *et al. v.* Lafonta's Ex'rs, iii, 342.

6. A legacy of so much money in a drawer, is only good for the sum found there at the decease of the testator. Roman Catholic Church *v.* Miller, iii, 465.

7. Where the right of a legatee is disputed, he may bring suit to have the claim recognised, though judgment cannot be given for any specific amount, until the curator renders his account. And a jury may be called to try the facts on which the legatee's claim is disputed. Wooter *v.* Turner, iv, 8.

8. A sale by a legatee, who holds under a will giving the whole of the estate, while there exists a *forced heir,* is not void, but voidable. Toten *v.* Case, iv, 235.

LETTER.

A letter is an object of property, which still continues to a certain degree in the writer after it is received by his correspondent; and may not be published without his consent. Denis *v.* Leclerc, i, 30.

LICITATION.

Licitation is a mode of dividing estates held in common, and may be avoided, like any other contract, by the parties thereby. Haynes *v.* Cuny, i, 700.

LITIGIOUS RIGHTS.

A purchase of land, for the recovery of which no suit is commenced, is not the purchase of a *litigious right.* Prevost's Heirs *v.* Johnson *et al.,* i, 704.

LOUISIANA.

1. The state of Louisiana is suable by one of her own citizens. State *v.* Montegut *et al.,* i, 583.

2. Louisiana is a member of the Union, on a footing with the original states, and is not bound by any condition subsequent, annexed to her admission. The State *v.* New Orleans Navigation Company, ii, 203.

MANDAMUS.

1. The Supreme Court has a right to issue a mandamus. Agnes *v.* Judice, i, 105.

2. On the dismissal of an appeal, no mandate can issue to the inferior court to execute judgment. Louisiana Bank *v.* Hampton, i, 250.

MANDATE.

A. *Of the Constitution of the Agency and the Extent of the Agent's Powers.*
B. *Of the Agent's Rights, Duties, and Responsibility, as regards his Principal.*
C. *Of the Agent's Responsibility to those with whom he Contracts.*
D. *Of the Principal's Responsibility for the Acts of his Agent.*
E. *Of Mandate Generally.*

A. *Of the Constitution of the Agency, &c.*

thereby authorised to receive legal *notice* of the assignment or transfer of a debt on the succession to a third person. The authority to receive notice of the transfer of a debt must be *specially established*, for until notice the debtor might pay the original creditor, and while he can pay, a creditor of the first creditor might seize the debt due him. Carlin *v.* Dumartrait, iv, 492.

See MANDATE GENERALLY.

B. *Of the Agent's Duty.*

1. Agent disobeying orders liable for the injury sustained, not for the whole value of the object. Nelson *et al. v.* Morgan, i, 69.

2. If A buys land for B he cannot rescind the sale without B's consent. Kemper *v.* Smith, i, 186.

3. By accepting a general account of an agency, including the commissions of the agent, and in which are stated what the accounts have been, and what remain to be collected, the principal discharged the agent. Rion *v.* Gilly *et al.*, i, 492.

4. Where the consignee in his letter of instructions makes no *positive* restrictions as to price, a draft for the proceeds justifies a sale, although the state of the market might demand a further delay. Briggs *et al. v.* Ripley *et al.*, i, 540.

5. If a proxy purchases land for the principal, and pays for it with money belonging to his principal, he will be compelled to convey it. Parol evidence will be received to show that it was so bought, although the purchaser took the deed in his own name. Hall *v.* Sprigg, i, 557.

6. The liability of a factor who sells goods on credit, depends much on the prevailing custom. Reano *v.* Mager, ii, 260.

7. Where an agent, without authority to sell otherwise than for cash, sold upon credit, if the principal sue both agent and his vendee for the value of the goods, and demand the interest which had been stipulated as the consideration of the extension of the period of the credit: *Held,* that he thereby approves and ratifies the act of his agent. Surgat *v.* Potter *et al.*, ii, 325.

8. He who undertakes, though gratuitously, the business of another, is bound to indemnify the latter from the consequence of his neglect of the business undertaken. Montillot *v.* Bank United States, ii, 465.

9. But if the employer does not avail himself of the advantage this inattention gives him, and he approve of a contract evidently made for his best advantage, though not strictly according to order, he cannot be allowed to recall his approval. Breedlove *et al. v.* Wamack, ii, 635.

10. A factor who sells at sixty days, cannot excuse his neglect to demand payment at the expiration of that time, by showing that it was his practice not to call for a note until the amount sold was sufficient to render it necessary, and then take it at sixty days. A factor, purchasing goods for his principal, which he promises to ship him, cannot afterwards cancel or renounce the sale. Gilly *et al. v.* Logan, ii, 638.

11. If a factor, who had given credit on a sale of lumber, gives a new credit at the expiration of the first, by receiving a note payable to himself, (and for more than the price of the lumber due plaintiff,) he thereby makes the debt his own. Hosmer *v.* Beebe, ii, 685.

12. The right of factors to sell on credit and in what manner: principal ought to receive due information of the manner of sale, &c. Fisk *et al. v.* Offit *et al.*, iii, 160.

13. If goods are sent to commission merchants, and they hand them over to a third person for sale without the order of the principal, they are responsible. Mark *v.* Bowers, iii, 241.

14. A factor who extends the time of credit, though he did it not in bad faith, makes himself personally liable for the debt. Richardson *et al. v.* Weston, iii, 286.

15. An agent who sells goods on credit, is not responsible to the principal until the price is received, unless the sale was made improperly. A. & W. Bird's Syndic *v.* Dix's Estate, iii, 290.

16. If an agent, who is to be paid on condition that he succeeds in the business entrusted to him, be dismissed without cause, he can claim a sum equal to the trouble he has been put to. Lanusse's Syndics *v.* Pimpienella, iii, 346.

17. An agent who surrenders a note belonging to his principal, and takes one payable, at a distant day, to himself, and delays bringing suit at maturity, is chargeable with its amount. Littlejohn *v.* Ramsay, iii, 425.

18. He who remits a bill, his own property, must abide the consequences. If Titius directs Caius to remit the balance of his account, and this be done by Antonio's bill payable to Caius, *supra protest*, and Antonio fail, by whom will the loss be borne? If Caius,

in taking the bill, did not act as Titius' agent, as if he possessed the bill, or acquired it before he received the order—or if, having taken it after the order, it appears be acquired it for himself, as e. g. if he remitted it a different rate of exchange, by which he gained something, the sale of the bill is at his risk; for he is considered as a drawer. Cass regis, 62, 63, p. 49, 50. Akin et al. v. Bedford et al., iii, 635.

19. It is the duty of an agent to prove those facts which will discharge him from responsibility in not collecting debts put into his hands for collection. Collins et al. v. Andrews, iii, 803.

20. Agents with general powers are not bound to exercise more than ordinary diligence, and such as is customary in similar undertakings. Millaudon v. M'Micken, iv, 143.

21. The principal must relieve the agent from any responsibility properly incurred. Flower et al. v. Jones & Gilmore, iv, 187.

22. The agent can maintain a suit against the principal not merely for repayment, but for indemnity, and the latter can only be released by producing an act by which the creditor accepts him in the place of the agent, or by paying the debt. Ibid.

23. A merchant who has funds of another in his hands, and is compelled by political events to send them away, must as much as possible retain a control over them, and as soon as the cause which induced him to part with them ceases, must dispose of them according to orders. Perez et al. v. Miranda, iv, 329.

24. If the party trusted be solvent at the time, his ceasing to be so does not render the party who trusted him liable. Bailey et al. v. Baldwin, iv, 448.

25. A factor, who employs an agent to sell goods without the authority of his principal, is responsible for the agent. Reynolds et al. v. Kirkman et al., iv, 587.

C. Of the Agent's Responsibility to those with whom he contracts.

Quoad the importation and entry of goods at the custom house, the consignee is considered as owner, and the real owner contracts no debt with the United States when the consignee makes the entry and gives bond for duties. Hewes et al. v. Pierce, ii, 482.

D. Of the Principal's Responsibility.

1. A factor contracting to import goods for another can only bind that other to the extent of the authority given, which, if not exactly attended to, must free him from every obligation arising out of the agreement. Nor ought it to be prejudicial to the person for whom the goods were imported, that he had them in possession for the purpose of entering them at the custom-house and securing the duties, for this act was beneficial to all interested in the property. Ralston v. Palmer, i, 332.

2. When the agent exceeds his authority, the principal may set the contract aside, but he cannot enforce it, according to his instructions to the agent. Findley v. Breedlove, Bradford & Robinson, iii, 244.

3. An agent who acts without authority (as in this case, under a void power, so become by the dissolution of the mandant firm, void at least in relation to those persons who were acquainted with that event) does not bind his principal even though the act was done with intent to benefit him. Ure et al. v. Currell, iii, 372.

4. If A requests B to purchase bills, and B procures them on his own credit from C, and delivers them to A, who credits him therewith: on the failure of B, C will have no action against A, if there be no fraud or collusion on his part. Amory et al. v. Grieve's Syndics, i, 307.

5. Where nothing shows that defendant authorised or even ratified the use of his name in the contract, on which action is brought, although his brother se fit forte, i. e., covenanted that he had authority, and would procure a ratification of the defendant for his acts, the defendant is not bound. Lacroix v. Menard, iii, 763.

6. When goods are sold to an agent for an unknown principal, the latter is suable when discovered, although no injury was made by the vendor; unless the latter let the day of payment go by without demand on the principal, who afterwards pays the agent. Williams et al. v. Winchester, iv, 139.

7. The party who claims from the owners of a steamboat, for a slave carried away in her, must show, that they could have prevented it. Pulfrey v. Kerr et al., iv, 598.

E. Of Mandate Generally.

1. An authority to sell a slave must be in writing. Stockdale v. Escaut, i, 288.

2. A merchant who has made advances to a planter on his crop, (but which crop was withheld,) cannot charge commission on the amount of the crop as if sold by him. Harrod et al. v. Constant, i, 417.

3. An attorney in fact appointed to receive an instrument of mortgage, is not responsible for not giving notice of it, unless he was specially directed so to do. Hodge's Heirs v. Durnford, ii, 410.

4. He who enters on an office without proper authority, subjects himself to all the responsibilities of the situation he usurps, and cannot claim the benefits of it. Abat v. Bayon, iii, 374.

5. A verbal power of attorney if given in a state where slaves pass by parol, is legal proof of the authority under which a written sale was made in this state. Thatcher v. Walden, iii, 633.

6. Where possession has followed a sale by an agent, for twenty years, his authority may be presumed. Buhols, Wife of Bourguignon v. Boudousquie, iii, 787.

7. Where the mandate gives a power to sell, the opinion expressed by the principal, that the property should bring a certain sum, will not invalidate a sale by the agent for less. Executor of Sprigg v. Herman, iv, 38.

8. If A purchases slaves for B, who refuses to recognise A's agency, no title passes to B. Michaud, Syndic of the Creditors of Dalon, v. Lacroix, iv, 579.

MARTIAL LAW.

Martial law, what? An act suspending legal proceedings during an actual invasion is not a law impairing the obligation of contracts. Johnson v. Duncan et al., Syndics, i, 157.

MINOR.

A. Of Tutors and Curators of Minors.
B. Of the Contracts of Minors.
C. Of Suits by and against Minors.
D. Of the Sale, &c. of Minors' Property.
E. Of Minors' Mortgage.
F. Of Minors generally.

A. Of Tutors and Curators of Minors.

1. A tutor by nature moving out of the state, retains the tutorship. Delacroix v. Boisblanc, i, 329.

2. A father, being natural tutor, has no need of the interference of courts of justice to assume the rights and privileges which belong to the office. Montegut et al. v. Trouart et al., i, 571.

3. A tutor's liability is not prevented by his neglecting to take the oath, give security, &c. Bernard et al. v. Vignaud, i, 650.

4. Tutors are not bound to pay compound interest. The provision of law that requires that the tutor render his account, before the judge, is introduced for the exclusive advantage of the minor, and none other can have any interest in it. Jarreau v. Ludeling, ii, 290.

5. On an application to dismiss a tutor, evidence may be given of his incorrect conduct in transactions with other persons, when they have been specifically stated in the complaint. He cannot be allowed to show that the petitioner (who does not solicit the tutorship) lives with a woman of color. On a charge of bad morals in the tutor, and of such neglect as endangers the minor's property, evidence cannot be given of the neglect of their education. Ozanne v. Delille, iii, 445.

6. It is not a good ground for the removal of the natural tutor, that he failed to make an inventory in ten days after his appointment. Ibid.

7. Neither is his insolvency before his appointment, a cause of removal. Ibid.

8. Tutors, other than those by nature, are deprived of the tutorship, ipso facto, by removing out of the state. And if they take with them the minor, his domicil remains that of his origin. Robins v. Weeks, iii, 584.

9. The mother who loses her tutorship by marriage, and is afterwards reappointed, holds the office under the law, and not by natural right. Ibid.

10. The liability of a tutor is not affected by his neglect to give bond and security; this would be taking advantage of his own wrong. Butler v. Her Creditors, iii, 686.

11. A mother has no right to purchase property for her minor child. Sarapare v. Deboys, iii, 727.

12. Tutor rendering account, should be allowed a reasonable time to answer objections to his account. Baillio et al. v. Wilson, iii, 861.

13. The grandfather has a right to the tutorship, after the father and mother, without

65*

being recommended by a family meeting, who are, however, to pass on the sureties he offers. Commaux v. Barbin, iv, 13.

14. At such a meeting the under tutor should be present. *Ibid.*

15. There is no tutorship until the death of the father or mother. Acosta v. Robin, iv, 285.

B. *Of the Contracts of Minors.*

1. A minor above the age of puberty may contract, if the engagement be advantageous to him. Southworth et al. v. Bowie, ii, 537.

2. A minor, not emancipated, is incapable of binding himself by a contract, Civil Code, 264, art. 14, unless it be proved that the contract turned to his benefit. Guirot v. Guirot's Syndics, iii, 109.

3. Minors in trade are not bound by contracts in trade, unless they be emancipated. Babcock v. Penniman, iii, 695.

4. Marriage in the state of Mississippi does not produce emancipation, nor make a promise binding, though the promise should be of this state. *Ibid.*

5. A minor can neither alienate nor purchase property, without the authority of justice. *Ibid.*

6. But on his coming of age, he may ratify an acquisition or alienation of property made for him during his minority. *Ibid.;* Sarapore v. Debuys, iii, 727.

7. The obligation or contract of a minor is not *void* under the 93d article of the old Civil Code, page 76, but he cannot be required to pay more on such obligation than the amount of one year of his revenue. Broussard v. Mallet et al., iv, 612.

8. Judgment cannot be given in general terms against such minor, but only against the movables; he cannot alienate his immovable property, without authority. Emancipated minors are here spoken of only. *Ibid.*

C. *Of Suits by and against Minors.*

1. A minor above the age of puberty must be assisted in his suit by a curator. Gassiot v. Gicquel, ii, 643.

2. A minor is not properly represented in court by a curator *ad litem.* Heno v. Heno et al., ii, 38.

3. When a minor is absent from the state, service of citation in an action of partition may be made on his curator. Martin v. Martin's Heirs et al., iii, 492.

4. And if duly represented in that action, the judgment is conclusive against him until set aside. *Ibid.*

D. *Of the Sale of Minors' Property.*

1. If a tutor sell the real estate of his ward, the purchaser will be quieted by a possession of four years after the ward comes of age. O'Connor et al. v. Barre, i, 144.

2. If a mother lose the tutelage of her children by a second marriage, she cannot alienate their property. *Ibid.*

3. The sale of a minor's property must be made at the place where the family meeting have decided it is most advantageous it should be sold. In the case of Julia Pierce, ii, 2.

4. The proceedings of the court of probates of a parish, in which neither the minor, his tutor or under tutor reside, for the sale of his property, are void. Leonard's Tutor v. Mandeville, i, 8.

5. The process-verbal of the sale of a minor's real estate by the parish judge is valid, although it be reduced to writing in the French language, inasmuch as the sale might legally have been made by any other auctioneer not judicial. Melançon's Heirs v. Duhamel, ii, 96.

6. The formalities which the law prescribes for the sale of a minor's estate are introduced for his exclusive advantage, and a vendee cannot allege the want of any of them—so that such vendee cannot resist the payment of the purchase-money on the ground that the inventory and other proceedings prior to the sale are in the French language. *Ibid.*

7. The tutor cannot make a compromise respecting the immovable property of the minor without a judicial decree which sanctions it. Chesneau's Heirs v. Sadler, ii, 126.

8. A contract for the property of persons under age, is absolutely null, if entered into without the formalities which the law prescribes. Nor is it necessary, when they sue for the property, to show that they were injured by the transaction. If the minor, however, approves expressly or tacitly of the alienation, after coming of age, he cannot afterwards sue for the property. *Ibid.*

9. The prescription of four years against minors, runs only against them for those acts

where the forms of law have been pursued in the alienation of their property. **M. & F. Gayoso de Lemos v. Garcia**, ii, 469.

10. If the sale of minors' property is sought to be rescinded on account of lesion by the remedy of *restitutio in integrum*, the circumstance that the property was, some time after judicial sale, sold for a much higher price, does not prove the lesion conclusively, when the price at the judicial sale was equal to the amount of appraisement. **Agarace et al. v. Guedron et al.**, ii, 599.

11. The minor may consider an illegal sale of his property by the guardian as a conversion to the latter's use, and demand the price with interest. **Chesneau v. Girod**, ii, 757.

12. Minors are not bound by a sale of their property made under judicial proceedings to which they were not parties. **Donaldson et al. v. Dorsey's Syndics**, iii, 696.

E. *Of Minors' Mortgage.*

1. The minor has a tacit mortgage on the estate of his tutor: he has no privilege. **Welman v. Welman et al., Syndics**, i, 416.

2. Under the laws previous to the promulgation of the Civil Code, the tacit mortgage on the property of tutors and curators in favor of minors, began to operate with the tutorship, which takes place in various ways, either by the appointment of the judge, by will, or by nature. **Montegut et al. v. Trouart et al.**, i, 571.

3. Common property adjudicated to the surviving husband or wife, cannot be relieved from the mortgage the law lays it under, by the substitution of another mortgage on other property. **Musson v. Olivier**, iv, 167.

4. A minor has a mortgage on the property of a person who intermeddles with his estate. Louisiana Code, 3283 article. It matters not whether the application of minors' property for one's own benefit, be made a single act or many. **Nolte & Co. v. Their Creditors et al.**, iv, 550.

F. *Of Minors Generally.*

1. A professor cannot avail himself of prescription against a minor. **Calvit v. Innis**, ii, 99.

2. Proof of minority may be made by witnesses who have known the minor from infancy. **Broussard v. Mallet et al.**, iv, 513.

3. Although the register of baptism is higher evidence of the age of a person than proof by witnesses, yet the existence of the former will not be presumed—it must be positively proved that such register does exist. Neither the births, baptisms, or deaths, are so universally recorded as to enable the court to ground a legal presumption on the fact of their being so. *Ibid.*

4. Minority must be pleaded; the plaintiff is not obliged to prove the defendant to be a major. **House v. Croft**, iv, 674.

MORTGAGE.

A. *Conventional.*
B. *Tacit and Legal.*
    1. *Of Wife's Mortgage and Privilege.*
    2. *Of Mortgage in Favor of Minors.*
    3. *Of Tacit and Legal Mortgage Generally.*
C. *Of the Registry of Mortgages and Privileges.*
D. *Of Third Possessors—their Rights, and Actions against them.*
E. *Of the Extinction of Mortgages.*
F. *Of Mortgage Generally.*

A. *Conventional' Mortgage.*

A special mortgage, although taken at the time that the mortgagor had no title to the mortgage-subject, attached to it the instant he became owner, and the mortgagee has a preference over a subsequent vendee. A general mortgage operates on all the property of the mortgagor, as well that which he owns at the time of passing the act as that which he subsequently gets a title to. There is the same reason why a special mortgage on a particular object should attach to that object, when subsequently acquired by the mortgagor. **Deshautel v. Parkins, use of Campbell, Rich & Co.**, ii, 542.

9. If a bill is accepted on the promise that a mortgage will be given to secure the acceptor, and it be subsequently given, if the mortgagor fail, the date of the promise will be considered in inquiring whether it should be set aside. Wyer's Syndics v. Sweet et al., ii, 750.

10. Property specially mortgaged cannot be sold at the suit of a third party, unless it bring more than the amount for which it is mortgaged. Du Armas v. Morgan, iii, 175.

11. Selling the land as subject to a mortgage, does not make the purchaser personally liable. Balfour v. Chew, iii, 257.

12. The court of probates is not without a jurisdiction ratione materiæ in a case in which some of the defendants are minors and some majors. The issue of a mortgaged female slave, born after a sale by the mortgagor, are in the hands of the vendee unaffected by the mortgage. Skillman and Wife v. Lacy, iii, 450.

13. When a creditor lays claim to a better place on the tableau, it may be opposed by any other thereafter who deems it expedient, and he cannot be said to be in mora, where he received notice of this claim. He who pays the note of another, cannot avail himself of the mortgage the latter had given for the benefit of his endorser, unless the mortgage be assigned him. Kirkland v. His Creditors, iv, 181.

14. The wife by renouncing her mortgage on property sold by her husband, does not abandon her right on that previously alienated by him. Dreux v. His Creditors, iv, 35.

15. Personal property cannot be mortgaged. Franklin v. Warfield's Syndic, iv, 578.

16. Notes given to relieve a party, who mortgages slaves for the indemnification of the payee, need not be marked ne varietur by a notary. Rousseau v. His Creditors, iv, 537.

NATURAL CHILDREN.

1. He who claims the estate of a natural child, must prove that he has acknowledged him by a formal act, according to law. Pigeau v. Duvernay, i, 244.

2. The natural father cannot compel the mother of a natural child to give up to him the possession of such child. There is no tutorship until the death of the father or mother. Acosta v. Robin, iv, 285.

NEW ORLEANS.

1. Although corporations, the charters of which are silent as to the right of laying taxes, must have that right as incident to their incorporation, yet where the power of raising money is expressly granted, it may be limited, either positively, by exclusion of certain articles from taxation, or negatively by specification, which excludes from it objects not specified. Blanc et al. v. The Mayor, &c. of New Orleans, i, 13.

2. Quere. Whether the city council may lawfully withhold a license for one of the three objects, keeping tavern, billiard-tables, and retailing liquors, in order to compel the applicant to take one for the other two also? Ramozay et al. v. The Mayor, &c. of New Orleans, i, 28.

3. The front squares on Levee street in New Orleans having been extended, by encroachment in 1776, have still their original back line. Riviere v. Spencer, i, 46.

4. Master and Wardens of New Orleans not exclusively empowered to collect pilot's fees. Allen v. Guenon et al., i, 100.

5. The city council cannot levy taxes on other than real and personal property within the limits of the city. Rabassa et al. v. Mayor, &c. of New Orleans, i, 111.

6. The land near New Orleans granted by the King of Spain, as part of the royal demesne and commons, on a breach of the condition, is to be considered as part of the commons of the city. Mayor, &c. v. Bermudez, i, 127.

7. The city derives no title from congress to land not part of the commons. Mayor, &c. v. Casteros, i, 194.

8. Mayor, &c. may sue for the removal of a nuisance. Mayor v. Magnon, i, 207.

9. The authority of the corporation of New Orleans, to prevent or abate nuisances, is of a very extensive nature, and a strong case of abuse must be shown to induce the court to interfere with its exercise. Milne v. Davidson, iii, 597.

10. If the corporation of New Orleans neglect enforcing their ordinances, the farmers of their duties may claim a diminution in the price of adjudication. Mayor et al. v. Peyroux, iii, 788.

11. The city council are, by law, judges of the election of their members. No mandamus lies to compel them to admit a member whom they do not think duly elected. And the sheriff who executes a writ of distringas, to compel obedience to a mandamus in such a case, is a trespasser. Mayor et al. v. Morgan, iv, 131.

NEW TRIAL.

1. Name of witness and nature of evidence must be stated in order to obtain new trial. André v. Bienvenu, i, 17.

2. The misbehaviour of the counsel or of the jury must be taken advantage of by a motion for a new trial. Morgan v. Bell, i, 302.

3. This court is bound to notice the refusal to grant a new trial in the district court, without having its attention drawn to it by a bill of exceptions. Muse v. Curtis et al., i, 692.

4. A party has a right to have spread on the records the reasons which he alleges as ground for a new trial. Livingston v. Hermann, i, 717.

5. New trial will not be granted on the ground of the late discovery of evidence to be obtained from the conscience of the opposite party. Muirhead v. M'Micken, ii, 75.

6. A party who has not pleaded a release, cannot have a new trial on his affidavit that he has discovered, since the trial, the means of proving it. Smith v. Crawford, ii, 75.

7. A new trial will not be granted on the ground that it does not appear on what the jury based its verdict. Harrod et al. v. Lafarge, ii, 277.

8. The absence of one of the attorneys in a cause is not a ground for a new trial, when the other declared himself ready to proceed when the cause was called. Flower v. M'Micken, ii, 618.

9. Motions for new trials are always addressed to the legal discretion of the court. Roberts v. Rodes, iii, 32.

10. A new trial refused, because the party applying for it had not used due diligence to procure the missing evidence. Stafford v. Callihan, iii, 38.

11. The court, not the party, must judge whether due diligence was used to procure testimony. Loccard v. Bullitt, iii, 51.

12. A new trial may be moved for, three days after judgment is pronounced, though the cause has been tried by a jury. Bedford, Breedlove & Robeson v. Jacobs, iii, 379.

13. New trial may be prayed for, after three days, if judgment be not signed. Smith v. Harrathy, iii, 559.

14. An affidavit to obtain a new trial, on the ground that part of a letter, on a different sheet, was not read, should state the contents of that part. Sorbé v. Salavignac, iv, 179.

15. If a paper, rejected when offered as evidence, be accidentally put with the rest, and taken out with the jury, this circumstance will not necessarily require a new trial. Flower et al. v. Jones & Gilmore, iv, 187.

NONSUIT.

1. The court may, in its discretion, when the plaintiff's claim is not established, give judgment as in case of a nonsuit. Abat v. Rion, i, 598.

2. In a petitory action for a slave, the answer being the general denial, and the evidence not establishing any title in plaintiff, the judgment of the court below should be one of nonsuit, not judgment in favor of defendant. Harper v. Destrehan, ii, 279.

3. When plaintiff fails to make out his case, there will be judgment of nonsuit. Hervy et al. v. Russell, iii, 21.

4. Plaintiff can not take a nonsuit after a general verdict. Applegate et al. v. Morgan et al., iii, 691; Pritchard v. Hamilton, iv, 14.

5. The plaintiff has a right to put his case to the jury, and cannot be nonsuited by the court contrary to his will. Bore v. Bush et al., iv, 720; Kernion v. Guenon, iv, 197.

NOTICE.

1. The ten days in which a party may appeal do not run till notice of judgment has been served on him: and this notice can not be given till after the judgment is signed. Turpin v. His Creditors, ii, 16.

2. Notice to take depositions may be left at the domicil, and this suffices as if served personally. Cohen v. Havard, iii, 513.

See BILLS OF EXCHANGE and ASSIGNMENT.

NOVATION.

1. Where a note was originally taken for the price by vendor's agent, and afterwards a fresh note, with a prolongation of credit, for the payment of that price, was taken by the vendor in person, this does not amount to a novation. Hobson et al. v. Davidson's Syndic, i, 648.

9. It is a fiction of law to prevent lesion, that all acts which put an end to the community of property are to be regarded as *partitions*. *Ibid*.

10. A contract by which the step-father renounces all right to his wife's estate on receiving specific property, is not a partition. *Ibid.*; Goodwin *v.* Heirs of Chesneau, iii, 110.

11. Grandchildren coming to the partition of their grandfather's estate, with uncles and aunts, are not obliged to collate an onerous obligation due by their father. Destrehan *v.* Destrehan's Executors, iii, 391.

12. An inventory is to precede the partition of every estate. But it may be made after the partition is ordered. Millaudon *v.* Percy *et al.*, iii, 654.

13. Under the old Code, the heirs in partition had a tacit mortgage, for the execution of all the engagements therein contained. Civil Code, 200, art. 246. By the new Code a special mortgage is required in such case. Walsh *v.* M'Nutt's Syndics, iv, 253.

PARTNERSHIP.

A. *Of the Constitution and Nature of Partnership, and its Several Kinds.*
B. *Of the Rights and Liabilities of the Partners as regards each other.*
C. *Of the Liabilities of Partners as regards Third Persons.*
D. *Of the Dissolution of Partnership, and its Consequences.*
E. *Of Partnership generally.*

A. *Of the Constitution and Nature of Partnership, and its Several Kinds.*

1. A partnership, "to do commission business as factors, in the city of New Orleans," is not a particular partnership. Ward *v.* Brandt *et al.*, Syndics, ii, 212.

2. It is not necessary that the style of such partnership should contain the name of each partner. *Ibid.*

3. A partnership to carry on business as ironmongers, is not a special or corporate partnership. Norris's Heirs *v.* Ogden's Executors, ii, 226.

4. Although there are but two members of a firm, it does not follow that their interest is equal. Allen *v.* Brown *et al.*, ii, 477.

5. The name of one of the partners may be the *nom social* of the firm, and the other partners are bound by contracts entered into by him, whose name is used, in his individual name in such case. Phillips *v.* Paxton *et al.*, iii, 15.

6. The partner of my partner is not my partner. Hazard *v.* Boyd, iii, 319.

7. Partners for the buying and selling negroes are not commercial partners. Castleman *v.* Stone, iii, 542.

8. If it be admitted that two persons have taken a third in business, and it appears they made him an advance of several thousand dollars, the interest of which is to be regulated by the profit: then they supply him with goods, pay for others shipped to him, supply him with money, and pay his drafts, a partnership will be inferred. Dennistoun *et al. v.* Debuys *et al.*, iii, 739.

B. *Of the Rights and Liabilities of the Partners, as regards each other.*

1. In particular partnerships one partner can not bind the other without authority, nor are they then bound *in solido*. C. Slocum *v.* Sibley, i, 440.

2. Where, in a commercial partnership, it was provided that real estate should be purchased for the purpose of convenience in carrying on the sale of goods and merchandise, and one partner bought twenty thousand arpens of land on account of the partnership: *Held*, that the purchase did not bind the other partners, as being entirely out of the course of trade. Brooks's Syndics *v.* Hamilton, ii, 98.

3. A partner has no action against another for any sum paid for a partnership, or any funds placed in it, until a final settlement takes place, and then only for the balance which appears due him. Dromgoole *v.* Gardner's Widow and Heirs, ii, 117.

4. Partners are joint owners of the property belonging to the partnership, and have each an equal right to take it into possession. Johnson *et al. v.* Brandt *et al.*, ii, 140.

5. One partner may accept title to real property for the benefit of the whole firm, but cannot alienate to their prejudice, without express consent on their part. Richardson *v.* Packwood, ii, 457.

6. In a joint speculation the party who acts ought to take the necessary steps to secure the price, or to give warning to his partner of the dangerous situation of the debt; by his neglect he may subject himself to the whole loss. Barron *et al. v.* Blanchard, ii, 772.

7. An authority to a partner to settle the affairs of a partnership, does not authorise him to endorse notes belonging to it. Poignaud v. Livermore, iii, 561.

8. A partner has no action against his copartner for any sum paid by the former for the partnership, until a final settlement takes place. Wood v. Steamboat Fort Adams and Owners, iii, 754.

9. Even when the claim has been settled and acknowledged. Case of Dromgoole v. Gardner's Widow and Heirs, 10 Martin, 433, re-affirmed. Ibid.

10. Joint owners must contribute rateably to useful expenses incurred on the property by a joint owner having the management of it, when no opposition on their part has been made to such expenses. Percy v. Millaudon, iv, 84

11. An action does not lie against a co-partner for any sum paid for the partnership, or funds placed in it, till after a settlement. Mead v. Curry, iv, 516.

12. A suit for a specific sum cannot be considered as one for a settlement, even when there is a prayer for general relief. The defendant may take advantage of this, by an exception filed during the trial. Ibid.

C. *Of the Rights and Liabilities of Partners, as regards Third Persons.*

1. The creditors of a partner have no claim on the partnership, much less on the co-partners. Desse's Syndics v. Plantin's Syndics, i, 528.

2. Members of an unincorporated company are bound *in solido*. Lynch v. Postlethwaite, i, 540.

3. The part owners of a steamboat are not liable *in solido* to the freighters. Carrol v. Waters, ii, 13.

4. The discharge of a member of a commercial partnership under an insolvent law, does not release the other. Russel v. Rogers *et al.*, ii, 27.

5. In case of insolvency of the partnership, if two of the partners owe the firm, their debt passes with others to the creditors, and the other partners, who are solvent, have no right to be paid out of the debts until all claims on the partnership are discharged. Ward v. Brandt *et al.*, ii, 212.

6. A mortgage executed by two of the partners, after the acting partner had prayed for a respite, which was accorded, gives no preference to the mortgagee. Ibid.

7. The partners in an ordinary commercial partnership, are bound *in solido*, and cannot prove or be paid their respective claims until the partnership debts due to other creditors are paid. Ibid.

8. If judgment has been given against one of the co-partners in a sister state, and the plaintiff sues another in this, he can not recover but on terms. Bryans *et al.* v. Dunseth *et al.*, ii, 497.

9. If a partner, after his co-partner's death, endorse a note due to the partnership, though it do not validly transfer the title to the said note, at least transfers all the right of him who endorsed it, and leaves no property in it of his for attachment. Jones *et al.* v. Thorn, ii, 709.

10. An injunction improperly taken against one partner, where his partners shared the injury resulting from the obstacle, authorises an action for damages at the suit of the firm. Mitchell *et al.* v. Gervais, ii, 743.

11. The name of one of the partners may be the *nom social* of the firm, and the other partners are bound by contracts entered into by him, whose name is used, in his individual name in such case. Phillips v. Paxton *et al.*, ii, 15.

12. Whosoever holds himself out to the world as partner in a commercial firm, cannot be permitted to escape from the responsibility he has incurred by that declaration, though he be not in fact a partner. Richardson v. Debuys & Longer, iii, 250.

D. *Of the Dissolution of Partnership, and its Consequences.*

1. All the parties to a dissolved firm may join in the same suit for claiming property which is in common between them. Terrill *et al.* v. Flower *et al.*, i, 512.

2. If, after the dissolution of the partnership, one of the partners endorse a note due them, the endorsee is not bound so strictly to give notice, in case of non-payment, as if the note were regularly endorsed. Walker *et al.* v. M'Micken, i, 715.

3. In an ordinary partnership, dissolved by the death of one of the partners, the heirs of the deceased partner have a right to participate with the survivors in the liquidation. Norris's Heirs v. Ogden's Executor, ii, 226.

4. Therefore, if a suit is commenced by one of the partners to recover a debt due the partnership, the other partners have a right to intervene; *aliter*, if they have a joint interest with the defendant. Ibid.

5. A partner cannot alienate real estate belonging to the firm, though it would be perhaps correct to say, that he may legally sell the right of warranty against the vendor from whom the firm purchased, *in case the partnership* was in existence at the time of the sale. *Aliter*, if the firm was dissolved at the time of the conveyance made from the surviving partner to the defendant. Simmins *v.* Parker, ii, 272.

6. Proof of the dissolution of a partnership need not be in writing. Poignaud *v.* Livermore, iii, 561.

E. Of Partnership Generally.

1. If two persons jointly ship a cargo and the consignee sell it, and credit each for his share, this share is subject to the attachment of the owner's private creditors, the joint ownership being at an end. Tappan *et al. v.* Brierly, i, 586.

2. If one of a firm, not shown to be a creditor in his private name, sign a *concordat*, the firm is concluded by the signature. Arnold *v.* Bureau, ii, 180.

3. Private debts cannot be set off against partnership demands—hence where A was a partner of a commercial firm in Kentucky, and of one in New Orleans: *Held*, that in case of insolvency of the latter, the house in Kentucky might prove its debt, although one of its partners was responsible to the creditors of that which had failed. Ward *v.* Brandt *et al.*, Syndics, ii, 212.

4. Although there are but two members of a firm, it does not follow that their interest is equal. Allen *v.* Brown *et al.*, ii, 477.

5. Whosoever holds himself out to the world as partner in a commercial firm cannot be permitted to escape from the responsibility he has incurred by that declaration, though he be not in fact a partner. Richardson *v.* Debuys & Longer, iii, 250.

6. A partner cannot alienate real estate belonging to the firm, though it would be perhaps correct to say, that he may legally sell the right of warranty against the vendor from whom the firm purchased, *in case the partnership* was in existence at the time of the sale. *Aliter*, if the firm was dissolved at the time of the conveyance made from the surviving partner to the defendant. Simmins *v.* Parker, iii, 272.

7. An authority to a partner to settle the affairs of the partnership, does not authorise him to endorse notes belonging to it. Poignaud *v.* Livermore, iii, 561.

8. A person who is a partner of the defendant, in a particular adventure, for which he has advanced the funds, will have a preference, on the object of such adventure, over attaching creditors of defendant. Purdy *et al. v.* Hood *et al.*, iii, 686.

9. If it be admitted that two persons have taken a third in business, and it appears they made him an advance of several thousand dollars, the interest of which is to be regulated by the profit: then they supply him with goods, pay for others shipped to him, supply him with money, and pay his drafts, a partnership will be inferred. Dennistoun *et al. v.* Debuys *et al.*, iii, 739.

10. In a suit to ascertain the share of one partner, all must be made parties. Dufau *v.* Massicot's Heirs, iii, 800.

11. After the death of a partner, the affairs of a firm may be carried on in the social name, for the benefit of the survivor and the heir of the deceased. Ganiott *v* Havard, iii, 844.

12. The vendee of a partnership stock and credits, cannot sue one of the partners (vendors) for charges against that partner on the books of the partnership. Leeds *v.* Holmes, iv, 102.

13. Partnership creditors have both by the Civil Code and the Louisiana Code, the right to be paid out of the partnership effects by preference to the private, or separate creditors. But the Louisiana Code, unlike the Civil Code, contains no provision for the converse proposition, viz: that private creditors have a right to be paid out of the individual property of a partner by preference to the partnership creditors of the firm to which he belongs. This counter-proposition cannot be deduced as a corollary from article 2894, because article 3152 rejects every privilege not *expressly* recognised by that Code. Morgan *v.* His Creditors, iv, 631.

PAYMENT.

1. Although the salary of the mayor may not be reduced, his receipt for a less sum for his salary will bind him. Girod *v.* Mayor, &c., i, 324.

2. If there be a standing account between two, and one produces his own checks out of bank, payable to and with the receipt of the other on them, he will be entitled to credit for these, unless it be shown that the checks were given for some other distinct claim. Joublanc's Executors *v.* Delacroix, i, 403.

3. The payment of property, part of a succession, to a person declared heir to it; by the

judgment of a court of competent jurisdiction, unappealed from, is valid even after the judgment is reversed. Phillips v. Johnson *et al.*, i, 549.

4. The payment of *personal* property belonging to the succession to a person recognised as heir to the *real* only, is invalid. Phillips v Carson, i, 552.

5. If payment be made of a debt to the succession to a person declared heir to it, pending the appeal of the judgment which declared him so, and on the affirmance of the judgment a devolutive appeal is taken from the affirming judgment, the payment will be valid notwithstanding the payee is at last decreed not to be the heir. Phillips v. Curtis, i, 555.

6. A note, payable in merchandise, cannot be offered in payment of a cash debt. Canfield *et al. v.* Notrobe, i, 565.

7. Payment of a note to a person who has not at the time the possession of the note, or any authority to receive its amount, cannot avail the debtor, although the other afterwards receive the note from its holder with authority to collect it. Welsh v. Brown, ii, 104.

8. A promise to deliver " a sound and likely negro boy, aged, &c., which *is* valued at 1200 dollars," is discharged by the delivery of a sound and likely negro boy, aged, &c.; the words *is valued*, mean is to *be received.* Cavenagh v. Crummin, ii, 316.

The act of 1821, relative to tenders of payment, relates exclusively to cases where suits are actually commenced, and operates principally on cost, or *fraix de justice:* it did not repeal the provisions of the Civil Code, 292. *Ibid.*

9. Giving a slave, in payment of one's services as housekeeper, is not a donation pure and simple, and need not be by public act. M'Guire v. Amelung *et al.*, ii, 378.

10. The true mode of applying a partial payment. Interest is to be calculated from the maturity of the note, till the day of a partial payment, and added to the principal: the partial payment is then to be deducted from the aggregate. Hynson *et al. v.* Maddens *et al.*, ii, 547.

11. A payment when not applied by the payor, must be imputed to the debt he had the greatest interest to discharge. Wickner v. Croghan, iii, 235.

12. *Quære*, if goods were consigned to M'Coy & Scallan, and were sold at auction by a firm of auctioneers called M'Coy & Co., whereof M'Coy was also a partner, and payment made by the purchaser at auction to M'Coy, is this payment to M'Coy acting in a separate capacity, a payment to the house of which he is a member, the consignees of these goods? Dennison and Connaire v. Nicholson, iii, 304.

13. An obligation to A, which B the obligor promises to settle with C, is not discharged by showing, in a suit by A against B, that C is indebted to the latter. Fluker v. Turner, iii, 389.

14. The imputation of a payment is by law made to the most onerous debt, as to a mortgage, when there are other ordinary debts. Pattin Abadie v. Poydras, iii, 730.

15. In making the imputation of payment, it is not the debt first contracted, but that first due, which is considered to be the most ancient. Lanusse v. Lana, iii, 765.

16. If the transferee neglects to give notice of the transfer to the debtor, payment compulsorily made by the latter to the transferor, destroys the transferee's right against the debtor. Styles v. M'Neil's Heirs, iii, 847.

17. The delay of a demand during seven years, and the circumstance of the plaintiff having, since the debt accrued, made a cession of his goods, without including the debt in the schedule, are not evidence of payment. Tremoulet v. Cenas's Heirs, iv, 51.

18. The receipt of a draft *in payment*, extinguishes vendor's privilege on thing sold. Abat *et al. v.* Nolte *et al.*, Syndics, iv, 94.

19. Plaintiff who takes a twelvemonths' bond and sues on it, is not estopped from denying that he took it in discharge of his debt—giving the bond is not payment. Williams v. Brent, iv, 211.

20. A payment made under the provisions of the old Code, to the holder of the obligation, is valid, although the possessor be afterwards evicted of it. Dean v. Carnahan, iv, 233.

21. Anything may be accepted in payment. Rison v. Young and Turnbull, iv, 246.

22. Giving credit on account is evidence of the thing given being accepted in payment. *Ibid.*

23. By MATHEWS, J.—Proof which shows that credit has been given on account with the original debtor, in consideration of a delegation made by him to his creditor, is evidence that the latter accepted the debt thus delegated in payment. Cox v. Williams, iv, 249.

By MARTIN, J.—There cannot be better evidence of the partial or entire payment of a debt than the express acknowledgment of the creditor evidenced by his giving credit to his debtor. *Ibid.*

By PORTER, J., dissenting.—I cannot assent to the proposition contained in the opinion just delivered by the presiding judge of the court, "proof which," &c. In my mind—if the act of the creditor can be explained in any other way but that of discharging the debtor, the provisions of our Code prohibit such a construction being put on his act. Cases of Barron *v.* How, 2 *N. S.* 144, and Gordon *et al. v.* M'Carty, 9 *Martin*, 288, reviewed. *Ibid.*

24. A party is not obliged to accept several drafts for one debt. Russell *et al. v.* Ferguson, iv, 332.

PENALTY.

1. The penalty cannot be superadded to the damages. Churchwardens *et al. v.* Peytavin, ii, 493.

2. The penalty is forfeited only when the debtor is *in mora. Ibid.*

3. The penalty cannot exceed double the amount of the injury. English *v.* Latham, iii, 28.

See CONTRACTS.

PERJURY.

No action will lie for a charge of perjury made in the course of judicial proceedings. Wamack *v.* Kemp, iv, 25.

PILOTS.

Master and Wardens of New Orleans not exclusively empowered to collect pilot's fees. Allen *v.* Guenon *et al.*, i, 100.

PLEDGE.

1. A contract of pledge is a contract *in rem*, in which the *delivery* of the thing is not a consequence of the contract, but is of the very essence of it. Lee *et al. v.* Bradlee, i, 613.

2. A pledge does not amount to an alienation. Clay *v.* His Creditors, ii, 17.

3. A contract of pledge, in the form of one of sale, will not protect the property of the pledgor, in the hands of the pledgee, from the creditors. Williams *et al. v.* Schooner St. Stephens, ii, 500.

4. The contract of pledge of incorporeal things will not give a preference unless evidenced by an authentic act, or one *sous seing privé*, duly recorded, at a time not suspicious. And this contract *sous seing privé*, though made long before insolvency, cannot be recorded, at the time when the debtor would be incapable of giving a preference by any act of his. Saul *v.* His Creditors, iii, 663.

POLICE JURY.

1. A court cannot compel the police jury to comply with the directions of an act of legislature, in levying a tax. Claiborne *v.* Police Jury, i, 536.

2. For certain rights of police juries. See Police Jury *v.* M'Donough, i, 537.

3. The police jury of New Orleans may order repairs on levees at any season of the year. Notice to the proprietor must be in the English language, if it be his mother tongue. Police Jury *v.* Hampton, iii, 588.

4. If the forms of the law, in giving notice, are not strictly complied with, no action can be maintained against the owner for a breach of the police regulations, but the jury may recover the value of the repairs put on his plantation if they were useful and necessary to him. *Ibid.*

POSSESSION.

1. When an usurper enters on land he acquires possession inch by inch, of the part which he occupies. Prevost's Heirs *v.* Johnson *et al.*, i, 704.

2. The possession of one who shows no title, when the extent of it is not shown to have reached within a mile of the *locus in quo* cannot be considered a possession of it. *Ibid.*

3. Feeding cattle and hogs, cutting wood, building pens, are not necessarily acts of possession of the land—as clearing land, cultivating it, building houses, &c. *Ibid.*

4. Digging a canal and felling trees are not such acts of possession as may be the basis of the prescription of thirty years. Macarty *v.* Foucher, ii, 273.

5. If a person possesses under a title which proves on investigation to be deficient, and

may reasonably have believed it was perfect, and valid, he ought not to be considered as a knavish possessor. Richardson v. Packwood, ii, 457.

6. A possessor is not necessarily in bad faith from the time an action is commenced against him. Packwood v. Richardson, ii, 494.

7. Possession of a note is *prima facie* evidence of title to it, but not evidence the possessor is acting for a third party. Parham v. Murphee, iii, 319.

8. When property is held by husband and wife, to which one of them has a title, possession follows the title. Clark's Heirs v. Barham's Heirs, iii, 337.

9. In a suit for land where the pretensions of parties are equal in law and equity, he who is in possession will prevail. Hooter's Heirs v Tippet, iii, 469.

10. The possession acquired by actual occupation, though not maintained during the whole period required for prescription, cannot be interrupted by possession merely civil. Where both claimants have obtained a relinquishment from the United States, he who had the best title from the Spanish government will prevail. Sterling and Wife v. Drew et al., iii, 509.

11. The possessor without a just title, owes the fruits from the beginning of his possession. Donaldson et al. v. Hull, iv, 173.

12. A possessor in good faith is only responsible for the fruits from judicial demand. Balfour v. Chinn, iv, 273.

13. The district court was not without jurisdiction *ratione materiæ* in suits against an estate administered by an executor. And a possessor under a sale made in virtue of a judgment of that court, is not *mala fide*. Donaldson et al. v. Dorsey's Syndic, iv, 280.

14. We know of no law which authorises a surveyor of the customs to direct a forcible entry and ouster of possession of property of the United States. If the defendant held wrongfully, there were legal means of evicting him. Bailey v. Taylor, iv, 453.

15. Nothing prevents a man, who has the right of possession, from taking into his hands the object which is subject to it, nor is there any necessity for his asking or obtaining the consent of a person who has no right of possession, although that person may have the possession of the thing. But if he resort to force in so doing, he is unquestionably liable in damages. Wells v. Wells, iv, 526.

16. Under the provision of the old Code, the possessor was not necessarily in bad faith from the time suit was commenced: but he owed fruits from the judicial demand. Daquin et al. v. Coiron et al., iv, 635.

PRACTICE.

A. *Of the Parties who may Sue and be Sued.*
B. *Of the Petition, its Requisites and the Service thereof.*
C. *Of the Answer; Exceptions and Pleadings generally.*
D. *Of the Evidence as admissible under the Pleadings or not.*
E. *Of the Contestatio Litis.*
F. *Of Possessory and Petitory Actions, and their Rules.*
G. *Of the Hypothecary Action, and its Rules.*
H. *Of Suits against several Defendants.*
I. *Of Consistent and Inconsistent Demands, and Cumulations.*
K. *Of Practice generally.*

A. *Of the Parties who may Sue and be Sued.*

1. Suit may be brought by two executors, one of whom only has qualified. Clark's Ex'rs v. Farrar, i, 118.

2. If a sheriff dies before receiving the amount of a sale on a *fi. fa.* his representatives cannot enforce the payment. Pavie's Heirs v. Cenas, i, 136.

3. The majority of the administrators of a public school may sue in their own names. Paillette et al. v. Carr, i, 152.

4. A consignee may sue for injury done to the goods. Morgan v. Bell, i, 302.

5. Attorney for absent heirs may sue the curator of an estate for a balance due by him without suing him and his sureties on the bond. Denis v. Cordeviella, i, 316.

6. The holder of a negotiable note endorsed in blank may sue thereon. Allard v. Ganushaw, i, 316.

7. One may have a direct action on a stipulation in his favor in a deed to which he was not a party. Mayor, &c. v. Bailey, i, 375.

8. An agent who stipulated in his own name, and sues for the use of his principal, transfers his right of action, and thus enables the principal to appear in the case as the real plaintiff. M'Nair v. Thompson, i, 413.

4. Bail may be prayed for in the petition. Labarre v. Durnford, ii, 89.

5. Neither the petition nor the citation need be in the French language. Fleming a. Conrad, ii, 201.

6. But copies must be served in the English and French. *Ibid.*

7. If the sheriff's return show that the petition and citation were served on the defendant, it will be presumed they were served as the law requires. *Ibid.*

8. When a defendant cannot be found, service of petition must be made at the usual place of abode of the defendant, which does not mean *last* place of residence. According to the first expression, the person alluded to would be considered as being no longer a resident in the same place; while the second implies only a temporary absence. Baldwin v. Martin *et al.*, ii, 532.

9. A party who, in setting forth his claim, omits the necessary circumstances of dates, places, &c., and sues in the common law mode, for money had and received, money lent, money laid out and expended, &c., can claim no such latitude as is taken in common law courts. Stroud v. Beardslee, ii, 604.

10. The plaintiff need not support his petition by his oath. Bingey v. Cox, ii, 713. The case of a justice sued for malfeasance in office, forms no exception to this rule. *Ibid.*

11. In the description of a note in the pleading, an error in the fractional part is fatal. Pilié v. Mollere, ii, 772.—*Contra*, 16 *Infra*. See BILLS H.

12. The return of the sheriff that he served petition and citation, is sufficient to show that he served it in both languages. Cox v. Wells *et al.*, iii, 48.

13. The goods sold need not be described in the petition when the defendant has assumed payment of the amount. Collins *et al.* v. M'Crummen *et al.*, iii, 50.

14. The sheriff may, at any time, be allowed to perfect his return, by signing it. Nichol v. De Ende, iii, 94.

15. A petition against the drawer of a bill, which does not set out demand and notice, does not set forth any cause of action, and if judgment be given on it, it will be arrested. Barbarin v. Descahaut's Heirs, iii, 186.

16. If the fractions of a dollar be expressed in figures, the note is not therefore void, but the fractions will be rejected. Pilié v. Mollere, iii, 221.

17. The defendant on whom citation has been irregularly made, waives the objection resulting therefrom, if he goes to trial without relying on it. Debuys and Longer v. Johnson, iii, 300.

18. Plaintiff describing himself as " of the kingdom of France," gives himself a sufficient domicil. Perry v. Belieyre, iii, 456.

19. When a note is annexed to *and made a part of the petition*, there can be no variance between the *allegata et probata*. Ditto v. Barton, iii, 775.

20. When suit is brought on an attachment bond, it is the duty of the obligee to allege and prove the damage he has sustained by a breach of the condition. Ponsony v. Debaillon *et al.*, iii, 824.

21. If there be a variance between the date of the deed annexed to the petition, and that stated in it, the former corrects the latter. Code of Practice, art. 690, 694. Hughes v. Harrison, iv, 219.

22. There cannot be a variance between the instrument sued on and that given in evidence, when it is made part of the petition. Deblieux v. Case, iv, 234.

23. It is not necessary after stating the residence of the defendant to be in *such a county*, to add the words state of Louisiana. Adams v. Lewis, iv, 291.

24. If a writ of seizure and sale be set aside, the plaintiff may amend his petition, without giving the debtor notice of the motion to amend or serving him with a copy of the amendment. Ursuline Nuns v. Depassau, iv, 383.

25. Service of petition and citation on the attorney of the defendant, although made before the services of the attorney had commenced in the suit, is good, unless the party on the trial deny his authority on oath. Dangerfield's Executrix v. Thruston's Heirs, iv, 499.

26. A defendant may be cited, though the petition contain no prayer to that effect. Banduc v. Domington *et al.*, iv, 576.

27. A prayer for judgment, is a sufficient allegation that the money alleged in the petition to be due, is unpaid. House v. Croft, iv, 674.

28. When suit is brought on a judgment of a sister state, it is not necessary to allege that the court which rendered judgment is a court of competent jurisdiction. *Ibid.*

C. Of the Answer, Exceptions, and Pleadings generally.

1. A general denial is sufficient to require of plaintiffs full power and authority to

proceed in the suit as syndics or administrators legally empowered. Dukelus's Syndic v. Dumountel *et al.*, i, 273.

2. If a rule to show cause is neither enlarged nor made absolute on the day given, it cannot afterwards be discharged or made absolute without notice to the other party. D'Auterive v. Neto, i, 570.

3. A different contract ought to be pleaded specially, and under the general issue, cannot be shown in avoidance of the contract sued on. Center v. Torrey, i, 633.

4. As the pleadings in our practice consist only of the petition and answer, and no such thing is known to us as a plea *puis darrein continuance*, all that can be reasonably required is, that the party be not taken by surprise, but be allowed time to make his defence in case of any new occurrence in the suit. Dufour v. Camfrancq, i, 636.

5. When answer sets forth some new fact, in avoidance of the claim, the replication, under the practice, was held to admit it if not specially denied. Lewis v. Peytavin, ii, 67.

6. An exception to the right to sue of an administrator appointed by the authority of another state should be pleaded *in limine*. M'Grew v. Browder, ii, 579.

7. The pendency of a suit in another state, cannot be pleaded in abatement of an action brought in this. Stone *et al.* v. Vincent, iv, 41.

8. An answer praying for damages cannot be filed the day the cause is set for argument. Mead v. Oakley, iv, 236.

9. In a suit on an unsettled account, compensation need not be pleaded. Fram v. Allen, i, 134.

10. If defendant pleads the general issue, he cannot show that the plaintiff agreed to receive payment in Bordeaux, and made no demand there. Doubrere v. Papin, i, 237.

11. After the jury is sworn, it is too late to move that the suit be dismissed, because the plaintiff did not answer the defendant's interrogatories. Woolsey v. Paulding, i. 727.

12. Appearance of an insolvent debtor to the proceedings had against him by his creditors, and contesting their validity, cure want of citation. In order that a suit pending be pleaded in bar, it must be shown that it was between the same parties as well as for the same thing. Dyson *et al.* v. Brandt *et al.*, ii, 10.

13. Pleas which tend to prevent an examination of the case on its merits, cannot be aided by inference. Clay v. His Creditors, ii, 17.

14. The facts submitted to a jury need not specially be set out in the petition and answer; it is sufficient if they grow out of the pleadings. Livingston v. Hermann, ii, 40.

15. Case for the rescission of the sale of a slave; defendant pleaded the general denial only—the judge *à quo* charged the jury to disregard plaintiff's evidence, inasmuch as he had not brought suit within six months after the discovery of the disease, whereupon the jury found for defendant. This was error: if prescription be relied on, it must be pleaded, and the court cannot *ex officio* supply it. Case remanded for a new trial, with instructions not to give such charge. Dunbar v. Nichols, ii, 89.

16. If the plea of the general issue be followed by an averment that the defendant has a better title than the plaintiff, this does not impair the force of the plea of the general issue, so as to admit the *locus in quo*. Murray v. Boissier, ii, 99.

17. Evidence of the nonage of defendant cannot be gone into on a motion to discharge him from bail. David v. Sittig, ii, 137.

18. If a party mis-state his right in the petition, but offers evidence which clearly establishes it, and the opposite party does not object to the evidence, the error is cured. Bryan and Wife v. Moore's Heirs, ii, 168.

19. The defendant cannot plead in bar that the plaintiff brought a suit for the same cause of action, which he dismissed. Jackson v. Larche, ii, 194.

20. Nor that other persons have sued him for the same trespass, and that these suits must be cumulated. *Ibid.*

21. A defendant praying for the removal of a suit to the court of the United States, on the ground that he is a citizen of another state, must show that the plaintiff is a citizen of this state. It is not enough that the plaintiff in his petition avers himself a resident of this state. Beebe v. Armstrong, ii, 220.

22. Pleadings should not be argumentative or loaded with extraneous matter. Norris's Heirs v. Ogden's Executors, ii, 236.

23. The defendant cannot amend by withdrawing an answer which contained an admission, and pleading the general issue. Vavasseur v. Bayon, ii, 261.

24. Inconsistent pleas cannot be received. *Ibid.*

25. Where there was no proof of the quality of the justice before whom the plaintiff's answer to defendant's interrogatories was sworn to, defendant cannot move to dismiss the

suit, after going to trial on the merits. Dean *for the use of* Vineyard *v.* Smith *et al.*, ii, 317.

26. If a defendant does not plead *in limine*, he admits that his residence and that of the plaintiff are rightly set forth. Crouse *v.* Duffield, ii, 366.

27. A mistake in a name by omission of a letter, cannot be taken advantage of on the general issue: it must be specially pleaded *in limine*. Boyer and Wife *v.* Aubert *et al.*, ii, 380.

28. The defendant cannot offer pleas that contradict each other. Dean *v.* Jackson, ii, 413.

29. Allegations contained in a petition cannot be taken as true when the general issue is pleaded. Gravier *v.* Brandt *et al.*, ii, 423.

30. After a cause has been at issue nine years, it is too late for defendant to plead in abatement that her office of executrix had long since been discharged. Lafon's Executors *v.* M. Riviere, Executor of Riviere, ii, 414.

31. When the defect of the thing sold is established, there is no need of an allegation of fraud or warranty. Brown *et al. v.* Duplantier, ii, 465.

32. If the general issue and satisfaction be pleaded, the former will be considered as waived. Bryans *et al. v.* Dunseth *et al.*, ii, 497.

33. An application to remove a cause to the court of the United States, must be simultaneous with the appearance. Johnson's Executors *v.* Wall *et al.*, ii, 530.

34. Attachment may be prayed for in a supplemental petition. Eshom *v.* Lamb *et al.*, ii, 642.

35. The defendant is entitled to oyer of the instrument sued on, even when he has not answered within the ten days, provided no judgments by default have been yet taken. Maxwell *v.* Walker *et al.*, ii, 639.

36. If the vendee promise to pay the price to the vendor of his own vendor, he cannot delay the suit of the first vendor till he obtain judgment against his immediate or second vendor, or an alleged deficiency in the quantity of the land sold to him. Desblieux *v.* Darbonneaux, ii, 639.

37. A plaintiff who sues as guardian, need not prove his authority on the general issue. Harper *v.* Destrahan, iii, 686.

38. Inconsistent pleas can not be received. Ferguson *et al. v.* Thomas *et al.*, iii, 24; Nuba *v.* Carlin, iii, 100.

39. The pleas of usury, fraud, and want of consideration, do not waive the general issue. Durnford *v.* Ayme, iii, 84.

40. Where the rules of court do not require a replication, all means of defence are left open to the plaintiff. Flood *et al. v.* Shamburgh, iii, 180.

41. Failure of plaintiff to comply with a condition precedent, may be taken advantage of on the general issue. Abert *v.* Bayon, iii, 188.

42. The plaintiff need not file any replication. Fraud may be shown by him without having alleged it in his replication. If there be a replication, it may be read to the jury to place before them a charge which might be made *ore tenus*. Defendant cannot be admitted to demur to the evidence, unless he admits the facts which may be presumed from the evidence by the jury, as well as the direct facts. Skillman *v.* Jones, iii, 199.

43. Dilatory and declinatory pleas should precede answering on the merits; but when there is a total want of right disclosed by the petition, it may be taken advantage of at any stage of the proceeding. Brown & Sons *v.* Saul *et al.*, iii, 343.

44. The action cannot be defeated on the ground that there are other owners, unless the plea discloses who they are. Hennen *v.* Monro, iii, 350.

45. The plaintiff is not bound to exhibit any proof of his allegations which are not denied. Akin *et al v.* Bedford *et al.*, iii, 413.

46. Pleas of payment and want of consideration are not inconsistent. A man may pay a note, and not discover until after the payment is made that the consideration on which he gave it was wanting. Miles *v.* Miller, iii, 367.

47. No change can be made in the pleadings, without leave of the court or consent of the opposite party. Rost *v.* St. Francis's Church, iii, 503.

48. A clause in a contract, that differences arising under it shall be settled by arbitrators, cannot be urged at the trial, if not pleaded. Buquoi *v.* Hampton, iii, 723.

49. The plea of general issue is waived by that of payment. Judice's Heirs *v.* Brent, iii, 820; M'Micken *v.* Brent, iii, 829.

50. On the plea of the general issue, the defendant may avail himself of the defence, that the parties were partners. Noble *v.* Martin *et al.*, iv, 244.

51. A plea, that the time when the debt sued on became due, was subsequent to the

that a deed was dated at another day than that which it purports.   Executors of Sprigg
v. Herman, iv, 38.

19. When the principal appears in court to support the act of the agent, whatever is
evidence against the latter, is evidence against the former.   Thompson v. Chaveau, iv,
261.

20. Every allegation, on which a prayer for judgment is grounded, may be disproved.
Kennedy & Duchamp v. Develin, iv, 463.

21. When the allegations in the petition, charge that the *sale* was a *sham one, without
consideration,* the *admissions* and *declarations* of the parties to the act of sale, going to
establish an express agreement, that the thing sold should be returned, on the vendor's
repaying the price, are inadmissible evidence to prove the fraud.   Palfrey's Syndic v.
François *et al.,* iv, 589.

22. Evidence going to prove a different species of fraud from that alleged in the petition, is *inadmissible. Ibid.*

23. The *acts* of a party subsequent to a sale, may be given in evidence to show that
such sale was fraudulent.   Reels v. Knight, iv, 512.

24. When the inquiry *is,* whether a sale was *bona fide* or not, the whole conduct of the
party whose acts are assailed, *before* and *after,* as well as at the *time* the contract was
made, may be inquired into.   *Ibid.*
See EVIDENCE.

E.   *Of the Contestatio Litis.*

1. If the plaintiff proceed to final judgment without the defendant having answered,
and without having taken judgment by default, the final judgment will be set aside, as
the *contestatio litis* was not formed by the pleadings.   Miles v. Oden *et al.,* iii, 813; Dorsey *et al. v.* Kirkland *et al.,* iv, 518.

2. No examination of the merits of a case can take place until issue be joined.   The
contestatio litis in the language of the Code of Practice is the foundation of the suit.
The Spanish law considered it the *raiz piedra angular, y fundamento del juicio,* and that
no judgment was valid in which it was omitted.   Beatty v. Wright's Estate, iv, 245;
Calvet *et al. v.* Calvet *et al.,* iv, 524.

F.   *Of Possessory and Petitory Actions.*

1. An overseer on a plantation who has contracted for a share in the profits, in return
for his labor, on being turned off is not entitled to the possessory action.   Castanedo v.
Toll, i, 504.

2. It is not necessary to enable the court to decide on the title for the land, that there
should be a prayer in the petition to be put in possession.   Livingston v. Herman, ii, 40.

3. When the defendant pleads the general issue and does not set up a title, the plaintiff
is not relieved from the necessity of proving a legal title in himself by showing, that the
defendant has a defective one, emanating from the same source as his own.   Sassman v.
St. Aimé and Wife, i, 721.

4. By our law after the lessee has disclaimed title, and called in his lessors, nothing
can be tried between him and the plaintiff but the possessory right.   Bayoujon's Heirs v.
Criswell, iii, 521.

5. The defendant cannot plead title in himself to a possessory action.   Gayoso v.
Wikoff, iv, 326.
See SALE, G. H.

G.   *Of the Hypothecary Action.*

1. " In real actions, where there are two or more persons concerned and residing in
several districts, in matter of partition, mortgage or revindication of property, the judge
of the place where the property is situated shall have cognisance of the case."   Davenport's Heirs v. Fortier *et al.,* ii, 685

2. Plaintiff in an hypothecary action need not allege ownership in defendant; allegation of possession suffices.   Walker v. Dunbar, iv, 89.

3. The third possessor is bound by the wife's judgment against the husband.   Pijeau
v. Beard, iv, 563.
See EXECUTORY PROCESS and MORTGAGE, D.

H.   *Of Suits against Several Defendants.*

1. If there are several defendants, and they plead separately, they may have the cause
tried separately, but if they go to trial jointly, and suffer a verdict to be given against
them, they cannot afterwards object to it as error.   Seré v. Armitage *et al.,* i, 750.

2. When distinct claims against distinct defendants, are presented together to a jury,

and they find generally, the verdict will be set aside. Thompson *v.* Linton *et al.*, iii, 533.

3. After defendants have joined in their answer, they cannot be permitted to sever in their defence. Mathews *v.* Heirs of Delaronde, iv, 598.

I. *Of Consistent and Inconsistent Demands and Cumulation.*

1. Where two suits to compel a "forced surrender" are carried on by different creditors at the same time, the order of a stay of proceedings made on the second application, does not estop the defendant to contest the legality of the first. Ward *v.* Brandt *et al.*, ii, 31.

2. It is not sufficient, that the facts necessary to be stated in the petition to create responsibility as heir, establish liability as maker of a promissory note, to authorise the conclusion that defendant was sued in both characters; but if defendant, sued in one character, suffers inquiry to prove him responsible in another, judgment will be given in pursuance of the proof. John Brown *et al. v.* Richardsons, ii, 434.

3. Several creditors standing in the same predicament, and seeking the same relief, may join in one application. Pecquet *et al. v.* Golis, ii, 510.

4. One suit may be brought on two different causes of action, if they be not inconsistent. Cross *v.* Richardson, ii, 671.

5. If an executor, who has become insolvent, is sued in the court of probates for notes and obligations belonging to the estate, and it appears he has transferred them, the cause must be cumulated with the proceedings in the *concurso.* Taylor *v.* Hollander, iii, 548.

6. The cumulation of actions is the forming together several demands against the *same* defendant; the bringing two demands together against *two* distinct defendants is no where forbidden. Lafonta *v.* Poultz, iii, 887.

7. If the plaintiff bring inconsistent demands in different actions, he may renounce all benefit to be derived from the first, in the court where the second is pending, and proceed with the last instituted. Adams *v.* Lewis, iv, 291.

8. A wife may cumulate an action for a separation, with a prayer for an injunction to stay a sale on a *fi. fa.* against her husband. Wrinckle *v.* Wrinckle *et al.*, iv, 538.

K. *Of Practice Generally.*

1. If petition be amended by inserting the plaintiff's residence, no time to answer will be granted. Sinnet *v.* Mulhollan *et al.*, i, 139.

2. On a rule to show cause, in favor of a police jury, for expenses incurred in repairing the levee, if the defendant denies every thing charged, the judge cannot proceed to judgment without a trial. Syndics, &c., *v.* Mayhew, i, 235.

3. If there be a prayer for general relief damages may be given beyond a specific sum prayed, if the petition shows that they are due. Morgan *v.* M'Gowan, i, 245.

4. If either party dies after the *contestatio litis*, his attorney shall prosecute it to judgment. Rochon *v.* Montreuil, i. 277.

5. The misbehaviour of counsel or of the jury, must be taken advantage of by a motion for a new trial. Morgan *v.* Bell, i, 302.

6. Plaintiff may be allowed to discontinue even after entering on the trial; and a discontinuance leaves to the party the right of supporting a new suit for the same cause of action. Petit *v.* Gillet, i, 337.

7. Contracts which are founded on smuggling transactions, wherein both parties were concerned, are plainly such as will not be enforced by a court of justice. But the defendant cannot take advantage of the illegality of the contract, without having alleged it in his answer. Harvey *v.* Fitzgerald, i, 501.

8. Inferior courts may grant leave to discontinue, as well before as during trial. Hunt *v.* Morris *et al.*, i, 525.

9. The court may, in its discretion, when plaintiff's claim is not established, give judgment as in case of a nonsuit. Abat *v.* Rion, i, 598.

10. On a rule to show cause why an order suspending an order of seizure and sale should not be set aside, the merits of the case cannot be inquired into: irregularity in the granting the order alone is proper to be inquired into. Abat *v.* Poyefarré, i, 650.

11. When a case is remanded to be proceeded on, after a reversal of the judgment, the district court may act on the verdict theretofore rendered. Muse *v.* Curtis, i, 698.

12. If a plea of prescription be received at the trial, the party pleading it must be permitted to submit the fact of his possession to the jury. Porter *v.* Dugut, i, 703.

13. A party has a right to have spread on the records the reasons which he alleges as ground for a new trial. Livingston *v.* Herman, i, 717.

14. If A has promised B to do a certain thing and fails to do it, C can not maintain

an action for the breach of this promise, because a knowledge of this promise was the leading motive that induced him to contract with B. Gales's Heirs v. Penny, i, 718.

15. When defendant pleads the general issue, and does not set up a title, the plaintiff is not relieved from the necessity of proving a legal title in himself by showing that defendant has a defective one emanating from the same source as his own. Sassman v. St. Aimé and Wife, i, 721.

16. If it be doubted which of the parties introduced a document below, the Supreme Court will presume it introduced by him whose interest it was to do so. *Ibid.*

17. If the defendant sued on an appeal bond, in the court in which it was given, crave oyer, and, the copy being tendered to his counsel and refused, the bond is spread on the record, this will suffice. Dussuau *et al. v.* Rilieux, i, 731.

18. The proceeding by motion against bail is in its nature an original action, and he is entitled to a trial by jury. Labarre v. Fay's Bail, i, 746.

19. A party can not complain of the withdrawing of a paper which has been received in evidence, if he accompanies his objection by the declaration that he does not intend to make use of it. Livingston v. Herman, ii, 40.

20. The sheriff's return is not open for amendment during the pendency of a suit on the attachment bond. The latter is not a continuation of the former case. Hatton v. Stillwell, ii, 76.

21. Where an endorser was sued on the protest for non-acceptance, in order to compel him to give security, and afterwards on the protest for non-payment, and there was judgment in the latter suit: *Held,* that the endorser could not be condemned to pay even costs on the first case, after payment of the judgment in the second. The court cited Pilot v. Faurie, 2 Martin, 83, 383. Bolton *et al. v.* Harrod *et al.,* i, 77.

22. A party who, without opposition, suffers evidence to go to the jury, on a fact not put in issue, is bound by their decision on it. M'Micken v. Brown, iii, 756.

23. It is no defence to an action on that part of the *Black Code* which forbids the sale of spirits to slaves, &c., that the defendant did not know the negro to be a slave. Delery v. Mornet, ii, 164.

24. If a claim be made in one capacity, and proved to be due in another, the court will give judgment on the merits, if the adverse party makes no objection. Floguy v. Adams, ii, 234.

25. The party from whom land is recovered, ought to be charged for the use and occupation, from the day of the legal demand. Walsh v. Collins, ii, 239.

26. The petition and answer not making up any conflict, there should be verdict for defendant. Guilbert v. De Verbois, ii, 395.

27. If judgment has been given against one of the co-partners in a sister state, and the plaintiff sues another partner in this, he cannot recover but on terms. Bryant *et al.* v. Dunseth *et al.,* ii, 497.

28. The defendant cannot attack the title under which he claims. Crane *et al.* v. Marshall, ii, 550.

29. Where a party submits certain points, as *involving questions of law,* to be decided by the court, the facts involved in those points are to be taken for granted.

If parties on going to trial agree on certain facts, and proceed to investigate those on which they differ before the jury, the duty of the court is, after a verdict has established the contested facts, to take them together with those agreed on, and pronounce their judgment on the whole case. Golis v. His Creditors, ii, 612.

30. If a suit be brought on a bill of exchange, and defendant plead that this same bill as between the same parties is the subject of a judgment in New York: *Held,* that this judgment must be taken to have merged the right of action on the bill in itself and destroyed it: hence no replication on part of plaintiff here, on the merits of the original case, will be heard. Mackee *et al. v.* Cairnes *et al.,* ii, 754.

31. No action can be maintained on a corrupt bargain. Mulhollan v. Voorhies, iii. 18.

32. A denial that the plaintiff performed one part of his contract is not an admission that he performed the rest, if this denial follows the general issue. Cornell and Wife v. Hope Insurance Company, iii, 73.

33. The neglect of one party to prove what is essential to his recovery, is not cured by the evidence of the other leaving the fact doubtful. *Ibid.*

34. The allegata and probata must agree. White *et al. v.* Noland, iii, 186.

35. A suit dismissed, is the same as if it had never been instituted. Garderre v. Fescher *et al.,* iii, 319.

36. A petition to remove a case to the court of the United States need not be filed personally. Fisk v. Fisk, iii, 434.

19. A suit, by a creditor to avoid a sale in fraud of his rights by his debtor, is prescribed by one year. Rivas v. Gill, iv, 661.

C. Of the time when Prescription begins to Run and of the Causes which Interrupt or Repel it.

1. In order that the prescription which does not run against minors may also be suspended in favor of the co-interested who are of age, their claim must be indivisible. O'Connor et al. v. Barre, i, 144.

2. The renewing of a note interrupts prescription. Turpin v. Creditors, ii, 25.

3. In a redhibitory action brought to rescind a contract of sale of certain slaves, and alleging fraud against the seller, to which defendant pleaded prescription and the general issue, the lapse of one year from the date of the sale does not form a bar to the action as established by the Civil Code, 358, art. 75, where the plaintiff proves the absence of the defendant from the state, for about eight months of the full year, which commenced with the sale and expired about a month before suit. Contra non valentem agere non currit praescriptio, is recognised by the Spanish law. Morgan v. Robinson, ii, 284.

4. The prescription of four years against minors, runs only against them for those acts, where the forms of law have been pursued in the alienation of their property. Gayoso de Lemos v. Garcia, ii, 469.

5. Prescription in redhibitory actions runs from the time the defects in the slave are known to the purchaser. Reynaud & Sucko v. Guillotte & Boisfontaine, ii, 441.

6. Debt due on a condition, prescription does not begin to run until the condition is accomplished. Lechangeur v. Gravier's Heirs, ii, 737.

7. Prescription is interrupted by an action wherein plaintiff was nonsuited. Chretien v. Theard, ii, 747.

8. Prescription is not interrupted by filing the petition, but by its service. Bonnet et al. v. Ramsay, iii, 776.

9. The right of pre-emption accorded by the act of congress of 1814, is not such a title as enables the settler to plead prescription before the time he purchases. Mulligan's Heirs v. Margrove, iii, 861.

D. Of Prescription Generally.

1. Settlers coming within the purview of the act of congress of the 2d of March, 1805, may prescribe from the day that they were embraced by the dispositions of that law. King et al. v. Martin, i, 358.

2. Prescription is presumed to be waived when not pleaded. Brown et al. v. Duplantier, ii, 465.

3. Prescription does not run against him who can not sue. Hernandez et al. v. Montgomery, ii, 697.

4. Purchasers under the same title, without partition, cannot prescribe against each other by the lapse of ten years. Broussard v. Duhamel, iii, 6.

5. Prescription does not run against the wife in favor of the purchasers of her property, although separated. Prudhomme v. Dawson et al., iii, 48.

6. Possession cannot be pleaded against the public, unless it is immemorial. Allard et al. v. Lobau, iii, 90.

7. Acts of limitation do not apply to matters which are presented as exceptions. Bushnell v. Brown's Heirs, iii, 370.

8. The lex fori regulates the plea of prescription. Union Cotton Manufactory v. Lobdell, iv, 171.

9. Prescription does not run against one who cannot sell. Ayraud v. Babin's Heirs, iv, 321.

PRIORITY OF THE UNITED STATES.

1. The United States have no lien for debts due them. They have only a right to priority of payment out of funds in the hands of the representative of the insolvent. Jackson v. Oddie, ii, 538.

2. The United States have not a preference in an insolvent estate above the mortgage creditor. United States et al. v. Hawkins's Heirs, iii, 308.

3. According to the technical rules of the law of Louisiana, the mortgagee has a right to the property of the mortgaged; and there is no difference between his claims when opposed to the United States, and those of a mortgagee at common law. Ibid.

4. The United States have no privileged claim on the property of a firm of which their debtor is a member, till the debts of the firm be paid. The United States v. Baulos's Executor, iii, 662.

PRISON BOUNDS BOND.

1. The words of a prison bound bond need not be essentially the same as those of the form in the act. Bryan v. Turnbull et al., iv, 446.
2. The sureties on it cannot discharge themselves by surrendering the principal. *Ibid.*

PRIVILEGE.

A. *The Wife's.*—See MORTGAGE, B. 1.
B. *Of the Registry of Privileges.*—See MORTGAGE, C.

C. *Of Privilege Generally.*

1. An attorney's privilege for fees on the estate of an insolvent, extend to tax fees only. Morse v. Syndics of Williamson & Patten, v, 124.
2. Vendor's privilege will be postponed until law charges are paid. Delor v. Montegut's Syndics, i, 402.
3. Taxed costs of every kind are privileged. Turpin v. His Creditors, i, 539.
4. Factors have a lien for all sums advanced by them. Rogers et al. v. Torrey, i, 619; 2 Patterson v. M'Gahey, i, 668; 2 Kirkman v. Hamilton et al., i, 728; Canfield v. M'Laughlin, i, 730.
5. If cotton be sold, payable in two days, and the vendee instantly procures advances thereon, delivering it to the lender who ships it in his own name, the vendor can not claim it without refunding the sum advanced and charges. *Ibid.*
6. Both by the Civil Code and the Spanish Commercial law, vendors of movable goods, unpaid for, retain a privilege on them so long as they remain in the possession of the buyer. Hobson et al. v. Davidson's Syndic, i, 648.
7. If the lessee gives his notes for rent, and afterwards fails, the landlord has a privilege on the goods in the house. Paulding v. Ketty et al., Syndics, i, 713.
8. In case of the insolvency of an attorney at law, no privilege exists in favor of the client for money in his hands. Durnford v. Segher's Syndic, ii, 6.
9. In case of insolvency, the vendor has a privilege on the proceeds of the movable sold by him, which is in the debtor's possession at the time of failure, and has been disposed of by the syndics. Millaudon v. New Orleans Water Company, ii, 192.
10. Persons sending property to be sold on commission, have not a privilege for the debt which arises from the goods being sold, in case the proceeds cannot be traced and identified, in the insolvent's hands. *Ibid.*
11. The law gives a mortgage on the estates of those who intermeddle in the administration of absent persons' property, not on those who administer it under authority from the proprietor. *Quære*—whether the absent persons, alluded to, are not those who are *declared absent.* Ward v. Brandt et al., Syndics, ii, 212.
12. The foreman of a tailor has not a privilege for his salary. *Gens de service* are *domestics.* Lauran et al. v. Hotz, ii, 417.
13. An agent has a lien on goods placed in his hands for sale, which is not lost by depositing them in the hands of a third person with notice of his claim. Ganseford v. Dutillet et al., ii, 456.
14. If notes are placed in a man's hands for collection and to secure him for advances made and to be made, he may resist a demand of them till he be indemnified. King's Curator v. Osborne et al., ii, 651.
15. A teacher in the insolvent's school is not among the *gens de service*, and hence has no privilege for his wages. Labat v. Labat's Syndics, ii, 771.
16. A person who is a partner of the defendant, in a particular adventure, for which he has advanced the funds, will have a preference, on the object of such adventure, over attaching creditors of defendant. Purdy et al. v. Hood et al., iii, 686.
17. Privilege of material-men and workmen. See *Undertakers.*
Overseers have not the privilege of *domestics.* M'Nult v. Boyce's Syndic, iii, 851.
18. He who has a superior privilege, cannot prevent a sale, but must exercise his privilege on the proceeds. Casson v. Louisiana State Bank, iv, 241.
19. A contractor employed to improve a lot of ground acquires a privilege for the value of the amelioration. See Louisiana Code, art. 3216; Parker v. Walden, 6 N. S. 713. M'Nair v. Richardson et al., iv, 138.
20. A judicial sale to enforce the payment of the first instalment is necessary to protect the vendee against the vendor's privilege for subsequent ones. Ayraud v. Babin's Heirs, iv, 321.
21. A resale and delivery by a purchaser destroys the privilege of his vendor on the property so resold. Willard v. Parker, iv, 326.

PROMULGATION.

1. Acts of legislature are not in force until after promulgation. St. Avid v. Weimprender, i, 334.

2. The publication of the State Gazette is not a promulgation of the acts of the legislature, pursuant to the provisions of the Louisiana Code, arts. 4, 5, 6, 7. Jewett v. Davis, iii, 608.

3. Three days after the laws are sent to the clerk of the parish in which the seat of government is held, they are to be considered in force there, and thence in the other parishes at the interval of one day for every four leagues, according to the sixth article of the new Code. *Ibid.*

4. The Louisiana Code obtained the force of law in the city of New Orleans on the 20th of May, 1825; it was most probably received in the parish of West Feliciana before the month of November of that year. Fisk v. Browder *et al.,* iv, 118.

PROVISIONAL SEIZURE.

A privilege creditor has a right to a provisional seizure. The seizure accorded by articles 284 and 285, Code of Practice, is not limited to cases in which the pledge was in possession of the creditor. Adams v. Lewis, iv, 193.

PUBLIC THINGS.

1. Public places cannot be appropriated to private use; and if the Spanish government had given away such places, such grants might be declared void. Mayor, &c. v. Metzinger, i, 125.

2. Any inhabitant has the right to forbid the erection of houses, or other edifices on public places. Mayor, &c. of New Orleans v. Gravier, ii, 253.

3. And in a suit already commenced by the corporation of a city, he may intervene and urge his private right to strengthen that set up by the public. *Ibid.*

See ROADS AND LEVEES.

RAPIDES.

Ray's ferry recognised as the limit of the Spanish post of Rapides. Baldwin v. Stafford *et al.,* ii, 113.

RATIFICATION.

1. When one has acted without previous authority for another, the ratification of his acts, when not express, is a mere legal presumption arising from some act of the principal relating to the business: his refusal to ratify destroys the presumption. Mayor, &c. v. Hunter, ii, 273.

2. The receipt by the owner of the price of the slave sold by an agent is a ratification of the sale. Adams v. Gainard, iv, 227.

3. The ratification of a void contract, cannot affect the interest of third parties. Burroughs v. Jayne *et al.,* iv, 280.

RECONVENTION.

1. Damages for an injury cannot be claimed in reconvention, one year after its infliction. Ritchie v. Wilson, iii, 167.

2. The nature of the plea of reconvention. The plaintiff against whom a plea of reconvention is filed cannot discontinue. Lanusse's Syndics v. Pimpionella, iii, 346.

3. Reconvention may be pleaded in a supplemental petition, when the defendant has set up a reconventional demand, superior in amount to the sum claimed in the petition, and this does not conflict with the ancient law of this country, that *reconvention is not permitted.* Parker v. Starkweather, iv, 81.

4. Damages claimed, as growing out of proceedings originating in the same demand may be the object of reconvention, as in this case, damages suffered by the owners, through an attachment issued by the overseer of his plantation for the same cause of action as the present suit. Boyd v. Warfield, iv, 109.

5. He who reconvenes is considered as a plaintiff, and a finding in his favor, without limitation, must be viewed as embracing his whole claim. Orleans Navigation Company v. Bingay, iv, 116.

6. An unliquidated demand cannot be pleaded in compensation, but may in reconvention. This was decided in Agaisse *et al.* v. Guedron *et al.,* 2 N. S. 73. By Code of Practice, art. 374–377, demands in reconvention are required to be connected with the original demand. Montgomery v. Russell, iv, 246.

7. If there be a demand in reconvention, plaintiff cannot dismiss the suit, so as to prevent the defendant having judgment against him, but he may waive benefit to be derived from it. Adams v. Lewis, iv, 291.

8. Reconvention must be, on matter necessarily connected with his claim. Code of Practice, 375. Lacosta v. Bordore et al., iv, 338.

9. A party imprisoned, sued to make a surrender, may reconvene the plaintiff in damages for wrongful imprisonment. Abat v. Holmes, iv, 461.

10. Payment of a debt cannot be pleaded in reconvention. House v. Croft, iv, 674.

RECORDER OF MORTGAGES.

1. The certificate of the register of mortgages is *prima facie* evidence of the truth of the facts therein alleged; which must be proved false, not made doubtful, by one opposing its effect. Lafarge v. Morgan et al., ii, 229.

2. The recorder of mortgages is bound to record, on the order of the judge, proceedings by *scire facias* to revive a judgment in a court of the United States in another district, and to state such a record on his certificate. Walden v. Duralde, iv, 316.

REFEREES.

1. The report of referees can not become a judgment until the court is satisfied of its correctness. Merieult v. Austin, i, 130.

2. A report of referees in one case, cannot be used in another, unless it was made the judgment of the court, and a report confirmed in part is of no force as to the rest. Lefevre v. Bariteau, i, 580.

3. Attendance before referees waives want of notice, and a consent to refer a cause and to receive a report of referees, waives the trial by jury. Hatch v. Watkins, ii, 421.

4. A reference which appears to have been made without consent of parties, will be presumed referred under the act for the reference of long and intricate accounts. Syndics of Brooke v. Hamilton, ii, 566.

5. Courts have the power *ex officio* to send causes before referees, under the acts of the Legislative Council, 1804, 6; 1805, 256; Caulker v. Banks, 3 *N. S.* 532. Spraggins v. White's Executors, iii, 304.

6. If opposition to the report of referees be made *ore tenus*, and no objection taken to that mode, that suffices. Zoit v. Millaudon, iii, 359.

See Experts.

REGISTRY.

 • A. *Of Mortgages and Privileges.* See Mortgage, C.
   B. *Of Conveyances and other Deeds.*

1. A building contract must be registered, according to the provision of the act of 1813. Jenkins v. Nelson's Syndics, ii, 218.

2. A sale of a slave made in another state, need not be recorded here. Smoot et al. v. Baldwin, ii, 535.

3· The want of recording a marriage contract can not be objected by the representatives of the husband. Ford's Curator v. Ford, ii, 744.

4. The recording of a transfer of a debt in the office of the parish judge, does not operate as a notice to third persons. Thomas v. Callahan's Heirs, iii, 498.

5. A builder who does not record his contract, is not entitled to any privilege.
Even if he obtains judgment against the debtor, but the judgment be pronounced two days after the cession, and remain unrecorded, yet is his situation not bettered. Oddie v. His Creditors, iv, 23.

6. When the contract states a privilege existing on the thing sold, and the vendee discharges the vendor from the consequences, he cannot resist the privilege on the ground that the act from which it results was not duly registered. Parker v. Walden, iv, 127.

7. A notarial act relating to real property must still be registered in the office of the judge of the parish in which the property lies. Carraby v. Desmarre et al., iv, 389.

RES JUDICATA.

1. By the practice of the late Superior Court, (in which appeal cases were tried as original,) a judgment of nonsuit obtained by appellant against appellee who was plaintiff below, does not amount to a desertion of the appeal by appellant: nor give the original judgment the force of *res judicata*. Seville v. Chretien, i. 367.

2. To support the plea of *res judicata*, the demand must be founded on the same cause of action. Hawkins v. Gravier et al., ii, 51.

3. The decree which a tribunal of competent jurisdiction renders directly on the point

reviewed, is, as a plea, a bar, or evidence, conclusive between the same parties, or those claiming under them, for the same thing. Dufour *v* Camfranc, ii, 243.

4. A judgment in a sister state between the same parties, for the same thing, sustains the plea of *res judicata*. 7 Cranch, 481; 3 Wheaton, 234; Mackee *et al. v.* Carnes *et al.*, ii, 754; Gilman *v.* Horsley, iii, 701.

5. A judgment against a person who sues to abate a nuisance, does not form *res judicata* against another who brings a similar action. Allard *et al. v.* Lobau, iii, 90.

6. A judgment of eviction cannot be pleaded as *res judicata* against a claim of the vendee for damages. Goodwin *v.* Heirs of Chesneau, iii, 109.

7, When a judgment dissolving an injunction is given on a plea to the merits, it forms *res judicata* on the matters at issue. Wells *v.* Hunter, iii, 472.

8. A judgment does not give to the plaintiff the plea of *res judicata*, as to a claim of the defendant against the plaintiff, existing before the judgment, when the claim was not pleaded in compensation. De Lahoussaie *v.* Judice, iii, 829.

9. A judgment against the assignee of part of a debt on the ground that he acquired no interest by the assignment, forms no *res judicata* against the original creditor. Ganiott *v.* Havard, iii, 844.

10. A judgment of nonsuit forms no *res judicata*. Thomas *v*, Callihan's Heirs, iii, 860.

11. Judgment on a suit for the price of a vessel, forms no *res judicata* as to a suit for damages occasioned by illegal detention. Desboulets *v.* Gravier, iv, 140.

12. A judgment of nonsuit cannot be pleaded as *res judicata*, even after payment of costs. Dicks *et al. v.* Cash *et al.*, iv, 275.

13, In order that a judgment have the force of *the thing adjudged*, the *object of the* demand must be the same: in this case, the object in the first instance was to punish the debtor; in the *latter* case, to get back property fraudulently sold. Palfrey's Syndics *v.* Francois *et al.*, iv, 509.

14. The authority of the thing judged does not depend on the points raised in argument, but on the matters put in issue by the pleadings. Saul *v.* His Creditors, iv, 302.

15. When the syndics are suffered to litigate the claim of a creditor without any interference or opposition of the other creditors, the judgment rendered has the force of *res judicata* against all the parties to the *concurso*. *Ibid.*

16. Whether a judgment rendered between two of the creditors would have that effect, *quære*. Interest does not run on a judgment. *Ibid.*

17. When a judgment is set up as the basis of a demand, the party to whom it is opposed, may avail himself of any limitation in his favor without pleading it. *Ibid.*

18. The revocation of a deed from a father to a trustee for the benefit of the son, by a suit in the court of chancery of Mississippi, cannot be pleaded here as *res judicata* against a claim of the son. Dismukes *et al. v.* Musgrove, iv, 553.

ROADS AND LEVEES. ·

1. The soil of highway is public property, and cannot be recovered in an action between individuals. Renthorp *et al. v.* Bourg *et Ux.*, i, 227.

2. Individuals summoned to work on the levee, if a delinquent planter, have to be paid out of the parish treasury, and have no action against him. Fortier *v.* M'Donough, i, 330.

3. An individual who complains of an obstruction to a highway, can maintain an action for it in the District Court. Allard *et al. v.* Lobau, ii, 668.

4. The right conferred on the Navigation Company, to make a road along the banks of the bayou St. Jean, is not a surrender of the sovereignty of the public. Allard *et al. v.* Lobau, iii, 90.

5. A squatter on public lands has no right to object to a road being run through his possessions. *Ibid.*

6. The right of the public to make roads, is not limited to the banks of navigable streams. *Ibid.*

SALE.

A. *Of the Requisites of the Contract of Sale, and Forms necessary in the Sale of Immovables.*

B. *Of the Causes of Nullity and Rescission.*

C. *Of the Delivery, and consequences of Non-delivery of the thing sold.*

D. *Of the Causes which authorise Vendee to refuse to take the property, or pay the price.*

E. *What constitutes Eviction.*

F. *Of the Consequences of Eviction as between Vender and Vendee.*

A. *Of the Requisites of the Contract of Sale, and Forms necessary in the Sale of Immovables.*

1. A verbal promise to pay to the vendor the difference between the price at which a tract of land is purchased, and that at which it may be sold, cannot support an action. Hart v. Clarke's Executors, i, 422.

2. A parish judge may record his own bill of sale. Tessier v. Hall, i, 577.

3. The sale is not completed until the notarial act intended for it be signed by the parties. Villere et al. v. Brognier, iii, 326; Miltenberger v. Canon, ii, 76.

4. A contract for the sale of a slave must be reduced to writing. Nicholls v. Roland, ii, 171.

5. The assent of the vendee to an act of sale, may be proved by matter *aliunde.* Bradford's Heirs v. Brown, ii, 181.

6. A want of title in the vendor does not make void a conveyance of property if he afterwards acquire the right of the true owner. M'Guire v. Amelung et al., ii, 378.

7. A sale made in another state of the Union for a slave, need not be recorded here. Smoot et al. v. Baldwin, ii, 535.

8. Delivery of slaves takes place by the delivery of a title which states that the slave sold has been delivered. *Ibid.*

9. A receipt acknowledging *payment* for a lot, is evidence of a sale. Richards v. Nolan et al., iii, 96.

10. Defendants claimed title, under a memorandum running, " I do sell," &c., signed by plaintiff, not signed by defendant. This was a sale *sous seing privé* of the premises; there is price, thing and consent; vendee's consent may be given afterwards and be proved *aliunde.* Crocker v. Nuley et al., iii, 167.

11. An endorsement of a title which remains in the possession of the endorser does not transfer the property to the endorsee. Herriot et al. v. Broussard, iii, 290.

12. The purchaser of real estate by public act, cannot be affected by a previous alienation *sous seing privé,* which was not accepted by the person in whose favor it was made. Wells's Heirs v. Baldwin, iii, 484.

13. An act *sous seing privé,* not followed by actual delivery, has no effect against third persons. De Flechier's Syndics v. Degruys, iii, 603.

14. Land sold *sous seing privé* where the sale is not followed by actual delivery may be attached by a creditor of the vendors. See 5 *N. S.* 423.
That constructive possession which the law presumes to follow the deed, will not protect the buyer against his neglect to register the act. M'Micken v. Sims, iv, 360.

15. Notice to a third party who purchases at a sale, of prior title, is sufficient to hold the property, although the title may not be regularly recorded, if such notice be given at or before the sale. Bell v. Haw et al., iv, 504.

B. *Of the Causes of Nullity and Rescission.*

1. The commission of a capital crime by a slave, immediately after the sale, is not ground sufficient for the rescission of the sale. Zanico v. Habine, i, 384.

2. The sale of a slave rescinded, because the slave's services were so inconvenient, difficult and interrupted, that it was presumed the buyer would not have bought her at all, if he had been acquainted with the defect. Blondeau v. Gales, i, 640.

3. The vendor may not avail himself of the exception *de non numerata pecunia* after thirty days; the opinion of *Gregorio Lopez* preferred in this case to that of *Febrero.* Lepretre et al. v. Sibley, ii, 101.

4. An act cannot be attacked as fraudulent after the vendor has paid all his debts. Copelly v. Deverges, ii, 262.

5. The vendee of an estate can not be disturbed on the score of lesion, in the sale by which his vendor acquired it; the sale is not, therefore, void; and if the first vendor wishes to avail himself of the benefit of the law, he must bring suit to have the act set aside. Bradford's Heirs v. Brown, ii, 181.

6. The exception *de non numerata pecunia* may be made in case of an authentic act.

9. The mere execution of a notarial sale does not dispense with a delivery. Copelly v. Deverges, ii, 262.

10. To avail himself of a feigned delivery against a posterior, real one, the party must bring himself strictly within the law that sanctions his claim. *Ibid.*

11. No delivery is necessary where the thing sold is already in the vendee's possession, though in *autre droit*. Peet *et al. v.* Morgan, iv, 68.

12. The deed in this case is of itself evidence of the vendor's consent that the vendee should take possession, when the thing sold is not, at the time, in that of a third party, and this consent itself is a legal delivery. Civil Code, 350, art. 30, 29. Fortin *v.* Blount, ii, 429.

13. Land sold *sous seing privé* where the sale is not followed by actual delivery, may be attached by a creditor of the vendors. See 5 *N. S.* 423. M'Micken *v.* Sims, iv, 360.

14. When delivery does not follow sale, parol evidence is admissible to show from what causes possession was retained by the vendor. Williams's Executors *v.* Franklin *et al.*, iv, 393.

15. A sale of movables is good against third persons, although the seller retain possession under the title of usufruct. *Ibid.*

See DELIVERY.

D. *Of the Causes which Authorise the Vendee to refuse to pay the Price, or to take the Property.*

1. Purchaser in danger of eviction may withhold payment unless his vendor offer him security against the danger. Duplantier *v.* Pigman, i, 116; Brown *v.* Thompson, iii, 901.

2. If one purchases a crop of sugar after viewing it, he cannot claim any abatement on account of its inferior quality. Decuir *v.* Packwood, i, 373.

3. Although the register of mortgages certifies that the land is free of mortgage, yet the purchaser will not be compelled to pay the price, if it appear that the order of court by which a mortgage was ordered to be cancelled, was obtained in the absence of the mortgagee. Dreux, Executor, &c. *v.* Ducourneau, i, 426.

4. The vendee cannot refuse payment of the price, nor can he require security, till suit be actually brought to evict him. Fulton's Heirs *v.* Griswold, i, 548.

5. Defendant who had given two notes not negotiable, for certain slaves, bought at the sale of intestate's property, justified in the refusal to pay without security against eviction. Smith *v.* Roberts *et al.*, ii, 340.

6. The purchaser of a tract of land of 1400 arpents, cannot refuse payment on the ground that the United States have only confirmed the title to 640. Guidry *v.* Green, ii, 525.

7. A vendee cannot resist payment on the ground that there are other persons who have titles to the land sold him, there being no suit brought, no certainty that these persons will ever disturb him, nor any means of trying whether their titles are better than his. Winkle *v.* Tyler, iii, 36.

8. If the vendor, after the sale, promises to send the thing on board of a vessel, and through the neglect of the person he employs, it be lost, the vendee may refuse the payment of the price. Lincoln *et al. v.* Vioso, iii, 96.

9. If one buy a judgment debt, he cannot be forced to pay the price if the claim was only in suit at the time of sale. Henderson *v.* Griffin, iii, 109.

10. A vendee who is not evicted cannot resist payment of the purchase-money. Garderre *v.* Foucher *et al.*, iii, 319.

11. The purchaser of three lots, who is disturbed in the possession of one of them, cannot suspend the payment of the price of the other two. Pierce *v.* Morgan, iv, 44.

12. A buyer, while in the peaceable and undisturbed possession of the thing sold, cannot, by law, withhold the price, simply on a plea of want of title in the vendor. The negation of right in a buyer, who purchased under the old Code, to suspend payment of the price when he dreads eviction, is not modified, as relates to such buyer by the provisions of the Louisiana Code. Brown *et al. v.* Reves *et al.*, iv, 223.

13. Under a promise to save the vendee harmless from a mortgage, judgment against the principal debtor will not enable the purchaser to resist the payment of the price. Murray *v.* Bacon, iv, 238.

14. Whether a sale of land on a mortgage executed by the vendor, is an eviction of the vendee, which will authorise him to *resist* payment? *Quære.* Woodruff *v.* Wederstardt *et al.*, iv, 676.

15. If the vendor, after the sale, does any act to impair the title, or possession of his

I. Of Redhibition and the Action Quanti Minoris.

claim for a rescission of the contract of sale, *provided* the complete title has been obtained previous to institution of suit for rescission. *Ibid.*

8. The ignorance of the defect, in the vendor, does not protect against the action of *quanti minoris*, though it does against the redhibitory action. Moore's Assignee *v.* King *et al.*, ii, 310.

9. An action to rescind a contract on the ground of fraud, must be brought in two years. Mitchell *v.* Jewell, ii, 407.

10. Where vendor of a slave stipulated that he should not be liable for the vice of running away, while the slave was in fact, to his knowledge, addicted to that vice, a circumstance which was not communicated to the vendee, vendor remains liable. The redhibitory defect must have been excluded *bona fide.* Macarty *v.* Bagnieres, i, 18.

11. The purchaser cannot claim a diminution of the price for a deficiency of measure, unless the real quantity falls short of that expressed in the contract by one-twentieth part. And if he could demand it for a larger difference, it must be done within one year from date of deed. Fortin *v.* Blount, ii, 429.

12. An action *quanti minoris* lies for a vendee who has sold the thing. Prescription is presumed to be waived, when not pleaded. Brown *et al. v.* Duplantier, ii, 465.

13. It is no defence to an action *quanti minoris*, that the vendee sold the thing advantageously. *Ibid.*

14. Redhibitory defects in a slave may be pleaded after twelve months in defence of an action brought for the price. Thompson *v.* W. & H. Milburn, ii, 522.

15. Any disease of which a slave is afflicted at the time of sale, which has progressed so far as to be incurable, may be pleaded as a redhibitory vice. *Ibid.*

16. If the slave die, the burthen of proof that the disease was curable, is cast on the seller. *Ibid.*

17. The vendee may recover against his warrantor, without returning the slave, if he be a runaway. Castellano *v.* Peillon, iii, 710.

18. The purchaser at a sale by order of the court of probates is not entitled to the action of redhibition. Pintard *et al. v.* Deyris, iii, 12.

19. A case depending on the rescission of an exchange. Roberts *v.* Rodes, iii, 32.

20. Action of redhibition does not take place in sales made by authority of justice. Abat *v.* Casteres, iii, 70.

21. The action of *quanti minoris* must be brought within one year. Millaudon *v.* Soubercase, iii, 88.

22. Although the time to bring the action of a rescission *a quanti minoris*, be elapsed, the vendee may successfully oppose the vendor's suit. Davenport's Heirs *v.* Fortier *et al.*, iii, 202.

23. Although the action of *quanti minoris* does not lie on a judicial sale, on account of a vice or defect in the thing sold, the vendee may avail himself of a want of quantity. *Ibid.*

24. The vendee is estopped from asserting that the slave's habit of running away was disclosed to him as a qualified vice, whilst the deed contains an averment that it was stated as an absolute vice. Bayon *v.* Towles, iii, 436.

25. The 2522d article of the Louisiana Code places the causes which justify a reduction of price (the action *quanti minoris*) on the same ground as those of redhibition; and concluded that, as in the latter action, the contract could not be set aside unless the slave was afflicted with some vice or defect which rendered him absolutely useless, or his use so inconvenient and imperfect that it must be supposed the buyer would not have purchased him had he known of his imperfections; the plaintiff could not demand any reduction for a defect which did not fall within either of the causes that furnish ground for redhibition. Millar *v.* Coffman, iv, 352.

26. The causes for which a reduction in the price of a slave can be claimed are the same as those for which the rescission of the sale may be demanded. Lawrence *v.* M'Farlane, iv, 353.

27. Inquisition, whether a chronic rheumatism, under certain circumstances be a redhibitory vice? *Ibid.*

28. In a redhibitory action, the plaintiff may prove that the slave ran away after he was purchased, as showing the continuance of the habit of running away. Pilié *v.* Lallande *et al.*, 384.

29. Drunkenness is a vice of character, not of body, and is not redhibitory. Xenes *v.* Taquino *et al.*, iv, 397.

30. Parol evidence may be given, that one of the parties to an act, perused it several days before he affixed his signature. Hepp *v.* Parker, iv, 588.

31. Knowledge in a purchaser, that a slave is diseased, will not defeat his action of

redhibition: it must be shown, he knew the disease was incurable, or that, without knowing that, he bought the chance of the slave's recovery. *Ibid.*

32. When the redhibitory malady did not manifest itself within three days after the sale, evidence must be given of its previous existence. Landreaux *et al. v.* Campbell, iv, 591.

K. *Of Judicial and Forced Sales and of their Rules.*

1. In sales of real property by the sheriff on credit, a deed of mortgage signed by the vendee is not necessary. Clark's Executor *v.* Morgan, i, 244.

2. A constable selling land under a justice's execution must advertise it in the same manner as the sheriff under an execution from the parish court. Reeves *v.* Kershaw, i, 281.

3. When a sale under execution does not take place on the day appointed, it must be advertised anew. Crocker *v.* Watkins, i, 284.

4. The neglect of the tax collector to advertise the sale in a newspaper does not affect it. If plaintiffs wish to claim the right of redemption, they must comply with the requisites of the 18th section of the act of 1813, c. 13. Smeltzer and Wife *v.* Bouth, i, 443.

5. A bid at a sheriff's sale must be followed by a tender of the money; otherwise it may be disregarded. Landed property sold at sheriff's sale does not pass by the return; there must be a conveyance. Durnford *v.* Degruys *et al.*, Syndics, i, 635.

6. A forced alienation results from a sale made at the time, and in the manner prescribed by law, in virtue of an execution issuing on a judgment already rendered by a court of competent jurisdiction. If a sale is made where these requisites are wanting, the purchaser does not acquire the "right, title, and interest" which the debtor had in the thing sold. Dufour *v.* Camfranc, ii, 243.

7. Laws which deprive men of their property, without their consent, should be strictly pursued. *Ibid.*

8. When an alienation of property is not expressed in the instrument, it must clearly result from the act. *Ibid.*

9. If proceeds arising from property irregularly sold at sheriff's sale, have been applied to the payment of the owner's debts, he cannot recover the property until he repays the purchaser the amount. *Ibid.*

10. Immovable property, at a sheriff's sale, does not pass by the adjudication: his deed is essential. *Ibid.*

11. Parol evidence cannot establish the sale. Dufour *v.* Camfranc, 243.

12. In the case of a sale by the parish judge of various articles, the whole sale is one entire act which receives its perfection by the signature of the judge at the close of the sitting: and neither purchaser is prior or posterior to the others. Jackson *et al. v.* Williams, ii, 319.

13. Action of redhibition does not take place in sales made by authority of justice. Abat *v.* Casteres, iii, 71.

14. The purchaser at sheriff's sale cannot refuse payment on the ground that he has bought without title; he must be *evicted.* Stille *v.* Brownson, iii, 449; Foster *v.* Murphy, iii, 457.

15. The power to imprison a purchaser at sheriff's sale, until he comply with the contract, is not unconstitutional. Abat *v.* Carteres, iii, 71.

16. Purchasers at sheriffs' sales cannot be affected by irregularities which occur after the sale. If a levy be made before the return day, a sale may be made after. Aubert *v.* Buhler *et al.*, iii, 138.

17. A debtor, the claim on whom has been seized and sold, may retain against the purchaser whatever he might retain against his creditor before the sale. Flower *et al. v.* Arnaud, iii, 232.

18. Unless property sold by a sheriff brings more than the amount of the previous mortgages there is no sale. Balfour *v.* Chew, iii, 257.

19. A bid at a sheriff's sale, is a bid for the absolute value, and when it is incumbered, is not a bid over and above the incumbrances. *Ibid.*

20. But this bid may be made for the entire value, with the obligation to pay the mortgage; or for the value above the mortgage, subject to the prior incumbrance. *Ibid.*

21. Selling the land as subject to a mortgage, does not make the purchaser personally liable. *Ibid.*

22. Purchasers at sheriff's sales are not responsible for irregularities antecedent to issuing the order of sale. Livingston *v.* Waldron, iii, 353.

25. A sale by the sheriff of New Orleans, for taxes, is legal, if it pursue the same formalities which are directed for the sale of lands in other parts of the state. *Ibid.*

24. When a debt is due at several instalments, and the transferee of the second causes the property to be seized and sold, the purchaser at the sale cannot be disturbed by an option at the suit of a creditor to whom the first instalment was assigned. How the proceeds of the sale should be divided.—*Quære.* Parkins *et al. v.* Campbell *et al.*, iii, 485.

25. In order to support a sheriff's deed made for properly sold under execution, the party relying on such deed is bound to show judgment and execution. Nancarrow *v.* Weathersbee, iii, 866.

26. A mortgaged square may be sold in separate lots. Plauche *et al. v.* Gravier *et al.*, iv, 75.

27. Privileges on property seized do not form a good ground for suspending the sale. Herbert's Heirs *v.* Babin *et al.*, iv, 83.

28. He who claims under a sale on a *fi. fa.* is bound to produce the judgment and writ, but no other part of the record of the suit; and the certificate of the record from below, should simply be, that the copy is a true one. Thompson *v.* Chaveau, iv, 15.

29. It is an essential pre-requisite of sales under execution, that public notice should be given of the time and place at which they are to be made. A purchaser under a forced sale does not acquire a good title when the formalities of law have not been pursued. Mayfield *v.* Comeau, iv, 202.

30. There is no difference in the effect of a sale made to a stranger, and that made to the defendant in execution. Williams *v.* Brent iv, 211.

31. In a sale on a *fi. fa.* the property passes by the adjudication. Hughes *v.* Harrison, iv, 219.

32. A possessor under a sale made in virtue of a judgment of the district court in a suit against an estate administered by an executor, is not *mala fide.* Donaldson *et al. v.* Dorsey's Syndics, iv, 281.

33. In a sale under execution, if the terms be that as soon as the buyer pays, the title will pass, he must pay before he acquires it. Baudin *v.* Roliff *et al,* iv, 441.

34. A sheriff's deed does not pass the property of the defendant in execution, unless there be a judgment. But if the debt has been paid, he cannot recover his property, without paying the purchaser. Donaldson *v.* Rouzan, iv, 469.

35. The purchase of property at a public sale, where all the legal formalities of the sale have not been observed, is invalid and gives no title. Where one of the notices of the sale is directed to be put up on the church door, an omission to comply with such direction will vitiate such sale. Mayfield *v.* Cormier *et al.,* iv, 506.

36. The copy of a sheriff's deed is no legal evidence till the absence of the original be accounted for. Donaldson *v.* Winter, iv, 475.

37. A sheriff's deed must be supported by a judgment. *Ibid.*

See EXECUTION AND SALE, D.

L. *Of Sales at Auction.*

1. The process verbal of the sale of property by the register of wills who sold it, is evidence of the sale and no act under the signatures of the parties is necessary to perfect it. Zanico *v.* Habine, i, 384.

2. A bidder may refuse to take land struck to him, on the discovery of an incumbrance, and the auctioneer's proclamation before the bids began, is no evidence of the bidder's knowledge of the incumbrance. Porter *et al. v.* Liddle, i, 538.

3. A case in which plaintiff seeks to rescind a sale of land of his under execution, on the ground of illegal conduct of the sheriff. Brasbears *v.* Barbarino *et al.,* i, 681.

4. Where property is put up at sale and bid for as such, but afterwards and before adjudication is described as having a known quantity, and purchased by a particular designation of its limits, it will require the strongest proofs to justify the court in rejecting the positive description given in the act by which plaintiff acquired, and declaring the overplus of land to have been sold in the sale of the designated portion. Macarty *v.* Foucher, ii, 273.

5. He who bids at an auction for, and in the name of another, has not the right of availing himself of the bid, in case that other disowns his authority, without the assent of the owners who were the vendors. Daquin *et al. v.* Coiron *et al.,* iv, 110.

M. *Of Sales per Aversionem.*

1. When property is sold by certain bounds, and *per aversionem,* if there be a surplus over the quantity mentioned, it passes to the vendee. Innis *v.* M'Crummin, ii, 337.

2. When, in the sale of a tract of land there is error as to the quantity contained within certain limits, but none as to the limits, the vendor cannot claim any land lying within

these limits. The doctrine of sale *per aversionem* explained. Cuney *v.* Archinard, iii, 523.

3. The vendee has a right to the land, as far as the spot called for as boundary, though the distance given does not enable him to reach it. The ambiguity was *latent* and arose from matters within the instrument. Brand *v.* Daunoy, iv. 467.

N. *Of Sales Generally.*

1. If a third person unauthorised, accept a sale for vendee, his subsequent ratification will have a retroactive effect. Fleckner *v.* Grieve's Syndics *et al.*, i, 319.

2. If the vendee refuses to take away the goods, the vendor may, after proper notice, sell them for account of the vendee. Gilly *et al. v.* Henry, i, 648; Zoit *v.* Millaudon, iv, 470.

3. The vendee is bound by the contract of lease made by his vendor. Clague *v.* Townsend *et al.*, ii, 454.

4. Purchaser is not necessarily in bad faith from the inception of suit. Prudhomme *v.* Dawson *et al.*, iii, 48.

5. It is not necessary to the completion of the contract between vendor and vendee, that the article sold should be weighed in presence of the latter. Hill *v.* Morgan, iii, 360.

6. Payment is not a suspensive condition of a cash sale. *Ibid.*

7. The right of the vendor to claim back the thing sold within eight days, can only be exercised when it is in possession of the vendee. *Ibid.*

8. If the farmer of the city revenue has notice, at the time of adjudication, that an ordinance then in its passage in the city council, if passed into a law, is to form a part of the conditions of the contract, he cannot resist its effect, on the ground that it was not a law at the time that he contracted. Griffon *v.* Mayor *et al.*, iii, 541.

9. Selling flour by the barrel, or bacon by the single ham, on the levee, is selling by retail. *Ibid.*

SEQUESTRATION.

1. The oath of the creditor alone, is not sufficient to obtain an order to sequestrate the property of the insolvent. Ward *v.* Brandt *et al.*, ii, 31.

2. A writ of sequestration is not the proper mode to compel the appearance of an absent debtor, and obtain a judgment for a debt. Stockton *et al. v.* Hasluck *et al.*, ii, 129.

3. Conventional sequestrators, acting for both parties and without compensation, are liable to the same obligations as are created by the real contract of deposit. Lafarge *v.* Morgan *et al.*, ii, 228.

4. The sequestrators are not liable for damages for withholding them in a crisis wherein one of the depositors alleged that the incumbrances were raised, the other denied that fact and forbade their surrender. *Ibid.*

5. In case of sequestered property the legal effect of a judgment of nonsuit is the same as that of a voluntary discontinuance: it leaves the parties in the situation they were in before suit, and the sheriff should restore the property to the hands from which it was taken. In this case the plaintiffs were the factors in whose hands tobacco was seized: their agency was not destroyed by bringing the suit; hence they are again entitled to the possession of the tobacco after nonsuit, unless their power is positively revoked. Hasluck *et al. v.* Morgan, ii, 577.

6. A writ of sequestration can not issue on an affidavit that the defendant intends to remove his property out of the parish. Debaillon *v.* Ponsony, iii, 449.

7. The provisions of the Code of Practice which require the judge to fix the amount of the bonds to be taken on a writ of sequestration, and the sheriff to return it into court are directory only. They do not authorise a recourse on the sheriff for a neglect, from which the plaintiffs receive no injury. Vawter *v.* Morgan. iii, 738.

8. If a sequestration be obtained against an absent debtor, he may on his return disprove the facts sworn to. Kennedy & Duchamp *v.* Develin, iv, 463.

SERVANT.

1. A cook, hired for eighteen months, may be dismissed at any time. Bethmont *v.* Davis, ii, 173.

2. If the master was bound to pay his passage back to France, at the end of his services, his representatives may recover the value of such a passage, though the cook died during the pendency of a suit brought on the master's refusal to pay the passage money. *Ibid.*

SERVITUDE.

1. Whether a right of servitude claimed by defendants, might have passed without a grant? Orleans Navigation Company v. Mayor, &c., i, 66.

2. A case of the loss of servitude by non-usage. Denis v. Veazy, ii, 284.

3. The existence of a servitude must be established by proof positive, or otherwise irresistible. Randolph v. Daunoy, iv, 198.

SHERIFF.

1. Sheriff seizing property on which a third person has a lien, is not liable to a suit sounding in damages. Kenner et al. v. Morgan, i, 109.

2. If a sheriff dies before receiving the amount of a sale, on a fi. fa., his representatives cannot enforce payment. Pavie's Heirs v. Cenas, i, 136.

3. If a sheriff wrongfully execute the process of court, he may be sued therefor in another court. Clarke's Ex'rs v. Morgan, i, 220.

4. If sheriff, in selling a runaway slave, omit the formalities of law by which the slave is recovered from his vendee, he is liable in damages; nor need sheriff have notice of the former suit to recover the slave, but he acquires, from such want of notice, the faculty of showing any thing in the present action which might have prevented the recovery in the former. Fleming and Wife v. Lockhart, ii, 103.

5. It is not a good defence against the claims of a sheriff for fees of office, that he has not resided within the state during the time the services were rendered. Morgan v. Mitchell, iii, 166.

6. In an action against a sheriff for not returning process, if a writ of sequestration issued, the presumption is that citation did also. The measure of damages is, the amount claimed in the previous suit. Dupuy v. Barlow, iii, 284.

7. A sheriff who neglects to arrest a defendant, at the suit of a creditor who is not placed on the bilan, is responsible in damages—but they will be only nominal. Clark v. Wright, iii, 474.

8. Sheriffs cannot demand the fees given by law for keeping slaves, unless they are detained in actual custody. Wright v. Harman et al., iii, 522.

9. But they may recover on a *quantum meruit* for the moneys actually expended by them. *Ibid.*

10. A sheriff who seizes property not subject to execution, is liable to an action for damages. Carraby et al. v. Morgan, iii, 635.

11. An action lies against a sheriff, who seizes goods other than those of the defendant in execution. Peet et al. v. Morgan, iii, 780.

12. A plaintiff does not lose his claim on a sheriff who has taken a twelvemonths' bond without proper surety by receiving the bond and attempting to procure the money. Semple et al. v. Buhler, iv, 21.

13. Nor by failing to oppose the rightful claim of a third party. *Ibid.*

14. A sheriff who has received money on an execution, cannot invoke the prescription of five years. Tremoulet v. Cenas's Heirs, iv, 51.

15. A legislative declaration, Code of Practice, art. 400, that if the intervening party does not give security, and the sheriff proceeds to sell, the latter shall be responsible for damages, does not repeal all other parts of the law under which he was responsible before. Peet et al. v. Morgan, iv, 68.

16. Whether two sheriffs may be sued together for illegal returns, on different writs in the same suit? Fisk v. Browder et al., iv, 118.

17. The action for an illegal return, is prescribed by one year. *Ibid.*

18. The return of the sheriff that a debt is satisfied, does not conclude the creditor. Williams v. Brent, iv, 211.

19. The sureties on a sheriff's bond, are liable for the taxes on suits. Police Jury v. Bullit et al., iv, 533.

20. The power of summarily enforcing payment of a tax, cannot be exercised in regard to other taxes. *Ibid.*

21. A sheriff, sued for the taxes he was bound to collect, must show he failed in doing so, after having used proper diligence. *Ibid.*

22. The sheriff cannot surrender property, seized on a fi. fa. to a claimant, who obtains an injunction to stay the sale. Lacy v. Buhler, iv, 657.

23. Since the new Code, the state has no privilege on the estate of an insolvent sheriff, for taxes collected by him, and unaccounted for. The State v. Wright's Administrators, iv, 530.

SHIPPING.

1. If the consignor prevent the master from fulfilling his engagement, full freight may be claimed of him. Blake et al. v. Morgan, i, 133.

2. The master of a vessel cannot claim wages when she is lost by his fault. Latham v. West, i, 416.

3. The consignee who receives the goods thereby, contracts to pay the freight. Smith v. Flowers et al., i, 449.

4. If the freighter refuses to receive goods on the ground that they are damaged, and the master says, "they may be received, and the matter will be afterwards settled," the freighter may stop the freight till an allowance be made for the damage. Bernadon v. Nolte et al., i, 563.

5. The quantum of salvage is a matter to be left to the sound discretion of the original court. Chaveau v. Walden, ii, 76.

6. The court re-affirmed the decision in Urquhart v. Robinson, 1 Martin, 236, that the invoice accompanying the bill of lading is not legal evidence per se of the value of the goods. Watson v. Yates et al., ii, 146.

7. The master of a packet between Pensacola and New Orleans, not drawing more than five feet, is not bound to take a pilot. Ibid.

8. The master who fails to deliver the goods, is accountable for the value: the fundamental rule for appreciating the loss in such case is given by the price as estimated in the invoice. Ames et al. v. Reed, ii, 236.

9. The owner of a vessel is responsible for the damage done by her, although a pilot be on board. Williamson v. Price & Morgan, iii, 333.

10. The shipper of goods is not responsible for the cost of defending the ship and other property on board, which is seized and prosecuted for illegal trade. Duncan's Executors v. Poydras's Ex'rs, iii, 632.

11. A shipper, suing the master and owners of a vessel for goods lost through their neglect, may attach their property, Hunt v. Norris, i, 282.

12. If the master gives a receipt for goods left on the beach, they are at the risk of the ship. Fisher et al. v. Brig Norval et al., iv, 450.

13. The new Code has wrought no change in the liability of steamboat owners. By the old Code their liability was clearly not in solido. The art. 2796 of the Louisiana Code, declares, that an association for the purpose of carrying personal property for hire, in ships, &c., is a commercial partnership; the articles 2798 and 2823 refer to the projected Code of Commerce, as the supplement of all that part of the Louisiana Code which relates to commerce. The projected Code of Commerce, article 163, declares, that joint owners of ships, &c., are not bound in solido, and in case a repugnance had thus been created, it was ordered, by the articles of the Louisiana Code referred to, that the Code of Commerce should be paramount. The Code of Commerce, however, has never become law. (1839.)

To the end to reconcile the New Code, 2796, with the old law, it was now decided, that the provision of the Louisiana Code is exclusively applicable to a company formed expressly to conduct the business of carriers, and leaves joint owners of vessels to their former responsibility; i. e., as partners in an ordinary partnership. Kimbal v. Blane et al., iv, 557.

See Carrier.

SIMULATION.

1. The apparent vendee in a simulated sale will be condemned to make restitution. Greffin's Ex'r v. Lopez, i, 349.

2. A case of simulated sale. Kemble v. Kemble et al., ii, 566.

3. A case of simulated donation inter vivos. Montamat and Wife v. Debon, iii, 256.

SLANDER.

1. A charge of robbing the plaintiff of his tobacco, in an action of slander, is not supported by evidence of his dishonestly obtaining the tobacco. Freeland v. Lanfear, ii, 655.

2. Under the act of 1817, which limited process of attachment to cases of damages ascertained and specific, an action of slander could not begin with an attachment. See Cross v. Richardson, 2 N. S. 323. Banne v. Thomassin, iv, 60.

3. No action will lie for a charge of perjury made in the course of judicial proceedings. Wamack v. Kemp, iv, 25.

SLAVES.

1. Persons of color presumed free; negroes otherwise. Adele v. Beauregard, i, 20.

2. A negro will be presumed free, though purchased as a slave, if the purchase was made in a country in which slavery is not tolerated, unless it be shown that he was before in one, in which it is. Forsyth *et al. v.* Nash, i, 262.

3. An authority to sell a slave must be written. Stockdale *v.* Escaut, i, 288.

4. If a slave be described in the bill of sale as a *bon domestique, cocher et briquetier*, and he be proved to be a good servant, and a coachman and brickmaker, this will suffice. Duncan *v.* Cavallo's Ex'r, i, 291.

5. When the person who claims the defendant as a slave, has proved her slavery, she can not contest his title. Trudeau's Ex'r *v.* Robinette, i, 292.

6. By the Spanish laws a slave can obtain his freedom by prescription, whether this provision is not repealed by our Code. Metayer *v.* Noret, i, 415.

7. Prescription is never pleadable to a claim of freedom. Delphine *v.* Deveze, ii, 769.

8. In an action for an injury done to plaintiff's slave in putting out his only eye, so as to render him wholly useless, defendant was adjudged to pay the expenses which had been incurred for the attendance on the slave and the full value of the slave, and to receive him as his own property. Jourdan *v.* Patton, i, 423.

9. Under the laws of the United States existing in 1819, slaves introduced into the country in contravention of law, acquire no personal rights; they are mere passive beings, who are disposed of according to the will of the several legislatures. Gomez *v* Bonneval, i, 521.

10. A slave may sue another than her master for her freedom. Marie *v.* Avart, i, 534.

11. Suit brought by a negro to recover his freedom: not having fulfilled the conditions of his emancipation, the deed was revoked. Julian *v.* Langlish, i, 717.

12. No defence to an action on that part of the *Black Code* which forbids the sale of spirits to slaves, &c., that the defendant did not know the negro to be a slave. Delery *v.* Mornet, i, 164.

13. A contract for the sale of a slave must be reduced to writing. Nicholls *v.* Roland, ii, 171.

14. If the owner of a slave remove her from Kentucky to Ohio, *animo morandi*, she becomes free, *ipso facto*. Lunsford *v.* Coquillon, ii, 689.

15. If slaves be committed as felons and runaways, an acquittal of them as felons, does not authorise a discharge of them as runaways.

It is not a good defence that the slaves were not kept in close custody. Morgan *v.* Mitchell, iii, 166.

16. If a sheriff fail to advertise runaway slaves, he cannot recover his legal fees, but he may recover the value of his services, if the owner knew of their confinement and refused to take them out. *Ibid.*

17. Where a slave is directed by the will of the master to be set free, the purchaser of him before the time arrives, has a right to the slave's labor wherever he chooses to have it performed: *Quære*, whether he may carry him out of this state? Perhaps, the slave may be allowed the aid of the magistrate, in case of an evident attempt to transport him out of the jurisdiction of the state, in order to frustrate his hope of emancipation, under the will and sale. by compelling the purchaser to give security for the forthcoming of the slave, in due time, or otherwise. Moosa *v*, Allain, iii. 243.

18. The issue of a mortgaged female slave, born after a sale by the mortgagor, are in the hands of the vendee unaffected by the mortgage. Skillman and Wife *v.* Lacey, iii, 450.

19. Free persons of color are entitled to a trial by jury, and can not be tried for offences by a justice of the peace. See 1 *Martin's Digest*, 688, 100, 648, 46. Bore *v.* Bush *et al.,* iii, 720.

20. The article in the constitution of the United States relative to fugitive slaves, does not apply to a case where a right of property is claimed in them by a citizen of the state where he is found. Volant *v.* Lambert, iv, 57.

21. Whether the vendor of a slave in this state, warrants a good title according to the laws of another state into which the slave is removed? *Quære. Ibid.*

22. Warranty of title in a slave is not limited to title with possession, but extends to cases where possession is lost, and the vendee is compelled to bring suit for him. *Ibid.*

23. A planter who occasionally permits his slaves to earn money by cordelling, cannot complain of those who hire them for that purpose. Morgan's Syndics *v.* Fiveash, iv, 296.

24. The presumption of slavery arising from color is confined to blacks. Pile *v.* Lalande, iv, 384.

25. A planter who permits his slaves to earn money for themselves, by cordelling ships, has no action in case one of them be drowned accidentally in doing so. Morgan's Syndics *v.* Fiveash, iv, 628.

56. The plaintiff sues in this action, to recover his freedom, and from the evidence on record, is clearly entitled to it —He was born in the northwestern territory, since the enactment of congress, in 1787, of the ordinance for the government of that country, according to the sixth article of which, there could be therein neither slavery nor involuntary servitude. This ordinance fixed for ever the character of the population in the region over which it extended, and takes away all foundation from the claim set up in this instance, by the defendant. The act of cession by Virginia, did not deprive congress of the power to make such a regulation. Merry v. Chexnaider, iv, 672.

See Emancipation and Statu Liber.

SPANISH LAWS.

1. The law of the *Recopilacion*, which requires, as a legal presumption of a child's capacity to live, that it should live twenty-four hours, is still in force. Cottin v. Cottin, i, 344.

2. By the laws of Spain, a slave can acquire his freedom by a possession of ten years in the presence of his master, or of twenty years in his absence. Whether this provision has been repealed by our Code? Metayer v. Noyer, i, 415.

3. The Spanish insolvent laws in force before the adoption of the constitution of the United States by the people of Louisiana, are not affected by that instrument. Ray et al. v. Cannon et al., ii, 580.

4. Under the Spanish law, valuation in the contract of marriage did not transfer property to the husband. Prudhomme v. Dawson et al., iii, 48.

5. The forfeiture of the right to recover, on account of having seized and taken property from the defendant, to satisfy the amount claimed by suit, a principle of Spanish law, (*N. Recopilacion, b. 4, tit. 13, l. 1, and b. 5, tit. 17, l. 10, of same work,*) only takes place in consequence of a taking with force, as it was the intent of the law maker to prevent breaches of the peace. Ware v. Innis, iii, 38.

6. The Spanish law did not require that all the formalities necessary to give effect to a will should appear on the face of it. Bonne et al. v. Powers, iii, 127.

7. Lands granted by the king of Spain to the husband alone, did not make a part of the community of acquests and gains. But the improvements made on them do. L. & F. Frique v. Hopkins et al., iii, 273.

8. A question of marital rights decided according to Spanish laws. Degruy v. St. Pé's Creditors, iii, 335.

9. By the Spanish law opposition to a tableau of distribution in a case of bankruptcy must be made in writing. Ludeling v. His Creditors, iii, 408.

10. The nature of the Spanish action *juicio de concurso* considered. *Ibid.*

11. An ordinance of a Spanish governor, in 1770, of which neither the original nor a copy can be had, requiring all sales of land to be made before a notary, when no authority in the governor is shown to change the general law of the land, and when the Superior Court of the late territory refused to recognise it, will not now be regarded. Gonzales et al., v. Sanchez and Wife, iii, 426.

12. Land given by the Spanish government to the husband, did not enter into the community. Heirs of Rouquier v. Executors of Rouquier, iii, 464.

13. The jurisprudence of Spain makes a part of the law of Louisiana. Saul v. His Creditors, iii, 663.

14. The exception in the *Partidas* in favor of women who become widows before they are of age, in regard to the estates inherited from their children, is unrepealed by any act of the legislature of the state or late territory. Duncan's Executors v. Hampton, iii, 732.

15. Parol evidence is admissible under the Spanish law, to prove the alienation and acquisition of property, such as land and slaves. Ducrest's Heirs v. Bijeau's Estate, iv, 482.

16. A *transaction*, made before the adoption of the old Civil Code, alienating slaves, in virtue of which the heirs of the ancestor, who was the vendee, claim such slaves and their increase, must be governed by the laws of Spain. *Ibid.*

17. By the Spanish law, if the money which the wife brought into marriage, whether *dotal* or *paraphernal*, was employed in the purchase of slaves, or other immovable, the property became hers if she chose. *Ibid.*

18. When the purchase was made with the wife's consent, the property was hers at the dissolution of the marriage, whether her husband was insolvent or not. *Ibid.*

19. If the purchase of an immovable was made with her money and without the wife's consent, she had only a subsidiary right, to be exercised in case of her husband's insolvency. *Ibid.*

STATUTE.

1. Laws in this territory being passed in French and English form two originals which must be construed together. Hudson v. Grieve. i, 16, 56.

2. The two originals, English and French, of an act of the legislature cannot be considered otherwise than as parts of a whole, and not as distinct expressions of its will. In a criminal statute the mode of construction most favorable to the defendant will control. State v. Dupuy, ii, 177.

3. Acts of legislature are not in force immediately after they receive the governor's signature, but after promulgation. St. Avid v. Weimprender, i, 334.

4. When the English and French part of a statute differ, if the expressions in the former be clear and unambiguous, the latter is to be disregarded. But, if they leave the meaning of the legislature uncertain, the latter part may be referred to, in order to clear the doubt. Breedlove et al. v. Turner, i, 735.

5. An affirmative statute containing provisions different from, but not contrary to, a former statute, does not repeal it. Seghers, Att. for Abs. Heirs, v. Antheman, Ex. of C. André, f. w. c. ii, 402.

6. An act of legislature cannot affect instruments executed before its passage. Durnford v. Ayme, iii, 84.

7. Subsequent laws do not operate a repeal by containing provisions *different* from former ones; they must be contrary to them. Herman v, Sprigg, iii, 58.

8. Whether the distinction of *public* and *private* acts of the legislature, be known in this state? If it be, the act incorporating the state bank is a public one. Louisiana State Bank v. Flood, iii, 96.

9. Powers confirmed by the terms it *shall be lawful*, need not *necessarily* be exercised. Acts of Legislative Council, 1804, p. 6; 1805, p, 256. Caulker v. Banks, iii, 155.

10. A law imposing a tax on a particular parish, the object of which is the payment of a debt due by the state, is not unconstitutional. Le Breton v. Morgan, iii, 253.

11. The judiciary possess the power to declare laws, contrary to the constitution, void. *Ibid.*

12. The rules in relation to real and personal statutes, apply also to unwritten laws or customs. Saul v. His Creditors, iii, 663.

13. Laws are never presumed to have a retrospective operation. Miller v. Reynolds et al., iii, 702.

14. The legislature cannot delegate the power of making laws. Flower et al. v. Griffith, iii, 758.

15. All laws except those in relation to remedies, are presumed to be made for cases which are subsequent to them. Dean v. Carnahan, iv, 233.

16. An act of the legislature, the execution of which is suspended by one of its clauses, or by a delay of its promulgation may in the meanwhile be modified or repealed by a posterior act. Gosselin et al. v. Gosselin, iv, 320.

17. A legislative exposition can only result from proceedings of both houses, approved by the executive, or persisted in according to the constitution, without their approbation. Louisiana State Insurance Company v. Morgan et al., iv, 663.

18. When the meaning of the words of an act presents no ambiguity, there is no room for interpretation, on the allegation of hardship. Waters v. Backus, i. 610.

19. The legislature has the power to declare that laws shall have effect from and after their passage. Buhol v. Bundousquie et al., iv, 575.

20. The state, who is the lawgiver and a party, may constitutionally declare that all mortgages in her favor shall cease to exist, as to moneys thereafter collected. Bell v. Haw et al., iv, 504.

STATU LIBER.

1. A female slave whose deed of emancipation ran thus: "I emancipate and liberate from all subjection, captivity and servitude the said negro, Catin, my slave, with the qualification and condition that she shall hold and enjoy freedom immediately after my death," is a *statu liber* during the grantor's lifetime, and children born from her, while in such state, are not entitled to freedom. Catin v. D'Orgenoy's Heirs, i, 634.

3. A *statu liber* has no action for relief for ill treatment. Dorothée v. Cequillon et al., iv, 276.

STOLEN PROPERTY.

1. The *bona fide* vendee of a stolen negro, is not entitled to demand the price from the lawful owner. Harper v. Destrahan, ii, 686.

2. Purchasing a horse that has been stolen, in market overt, does not give a right to him unless there be three years possession following the sale. Davis v. Hampton, iii, 300.

SUBROGATION.

1. A surety who pays the debt is subrogated, *ipso facto*, to the rights of the creditor. Civil Code, 290, art. 151. Curtis v. Kitchen, i, 687.

2. The endorser of a note (given for the purchase of a slave, by the maker) is by the payment, subrogated to the vendor's rights, and may demand the rescission of the sale. Torregano v. Segura's Syndics, ii, 628.

3. Subrogation does not take place in favor of all who pay a debt, but only of him who being bound for it, discharges it. Nolte & Co. v. Their Creditors, iv, 368.

4. A tutor is subrogated to the rights of the creditor paid by him. Baillio v. Wilson, iv, 541.

SUBSTITUTION,

1. A devise to the mother for life, remainder to the children, in equal parts, to be held for the survivors, down to the last, in the event of death before marriage or without issue, is a substitution, which the law reprobates. Farrar et al. v. M'Cutcheon et al., iii, 223.

2. A debtor cannot be compelled to pay several transferees to whom the creditor may have assigned separate portions of the debt. King et al. v. Havart, iii, 504.

3. A bequest to a master of a slave, of a sum of money in payment of the slave, is not a *fidei commissum*, and therefore prohibited by law. Mathurin v. Livaudais, iii, 551.

SUCCESSION.

A. *Of the Place of Opening the Succession.*
B. *Of the Appointment of Curators and Administrators.*
C. *Duties, Powers, Rights and Responsibilities of Curators, Executors and Administrators.*
D. *Of the Sale of Property belonging to Succession.*
E. *Of the Payment of Debts and the Legacies, and of Rendition of Account.*
F. *Of the Liabilities of Heirs.*
G. *Of Succession Generally.*

A. *Of the Place of Opening the Succession.*

If a parish be divided into two, proceedings on the *mortuaria* are to be commenced in the new parish, if the domicil of the deceased makes part of it, although he died before the division. Harang v. Harang et al., iv, 151.

B. *Of the Appointment of Curators and Administrators.*

1. Although, perhaps, the circumstance of a person not being domiciliated in the state, would not exclude him from the office of curator *ab intestato*, claiming as a relation or creditor against strangers or persons wholly uninterested in the succession, yet where two parties are contending for a preference, whose pretensions are in other respects nearly equal, it would be nothing more than an exercise of sound discretion in the judge to prefer the citizen of the state who possesses property, which is tacitly mortgaged for the faithful performance of his duties as curator, to strangers not possessing this additional qualification. Rush v. Randolph, i, 260.

2. If one who was a creditor at the time of his application for the curatorship cease to be a creditor before appointment, he thereby destroys his claim to the curatorship. *Ibid*. 344.

3. If the testator dispose of property to his natural children, which the law requires should go to his legitimate brothers and sisters, and name an executor, the proper course is for the court of probates not to appoint a curator to the absent brothers and sisters until partition, but meanwhile to appoint a defensor to protect their rights in making the same. Johnson v. Davidson, i, 495.

4. Although while all the co-heirs were present, and the minor ones represented by their tutrix, there could not legally be a curator *ad bona*, yet the eldest son of the deceased, who had taken on himself the management of the estate, with the consent of his co-heirs of age, and among them of Mrs. Ware, plaintiff, under the appellation of curator *ad bona* of the estate, is answerable as their agent. Ware and Wife v. Welsh's Heirs, ii, 116.

5. An heir, who has accepted, with the benefit of an inventory, is entitled to the pos-

session and administration of the estate. If there be other heirs, their rights will be noticed when they appear. Dufour v. Camfranc, ii, 243.

6. An executor cannot, because he has been unable to liquidate the estate within a year, refuse to give it up to the heir after the expiration of that time. He may retain it for a longer time if he is so authorised by the will, but cannot refuse to render an account at the end of the year. Lafon's Executor v. Gravier et al., ii, 448.

7. The amount expressed in the bond of a curator is *prima facie* that which is due the heirs. Eggleston v. Colfax et al., iii, 363.

8. If letters of curatorship be granted without legal citation, as demanded by the Code of Practice, they will be annulled at the suit of any person interested. Elkins v. Canfield, iii, 636.

C. *Duties, Rights, and Responsibilities of Curators, Executors, and Administrators.*

1. An executor who has taken a note from a debtor of his testator, may, after a year, sue either in his own name or as executor. T. & D. Urquhart, Executors, v. Taylor, i, 360.

2. If the appointment of a curator be revoked on appeal, and he delays the delivery of the estate until the heirs come, the commissions belonging to the curator for administering the estate, rightfully belong to the curator appointed by the court of appeal. Preval v. Debuys et al., i, 395.

3. One whose slave has been sold as part of another's succession, has a claim against the curator for the price, and is not to be classed with the creditors of the succession. Donaldson v. Rust, i, 479.

4. The per centage allowed to the special administrator does not extend to any goods which may be found blended with those of the estate. Labatut v. Rogers, i, 481.

5. Upon judgment against an executor for a debt of his testator, he is at once liable to execution against his own property, but he may obtain immediate relief by offering to render his account, showing that he has legally and fully administered. Querry's Executor v. Faussier's Executor, i, 516.

6. An executor, suing for money had and received to his use as such, needs not style himself as executor, and if he do, the defendant cannot contest his capacity. Hunter v. Postlethwaite, ii, 125.

7. If an executor suffer three years to elapse without taking any steps for the recovery of a debt, and afterwards gives further credit, incorporating this debt with one of his own, into a mortgage in his own name, he becomes liable to the estate. Norwood's Executors v. Duncan et al., ii, 153.

8. When money is given by an executor, on a quite uncertain event, he should show that the interests of the succession required it, or at least make out a strong case, to induce a belief they did. Forrer v. Boffil, ii, 185.

9. An executor to whom power is given to act beyond the year, and settle the estate, may act as long as it is necessary to accomplish the object. M. & F. Gayoso v. Garcia, ii, 469.

10. An executor cannot sell property of his testator by private sale, although authorised to act, extrajudicially. Minor's property cannot be alienated in any other mode but that prescribed by law. *Ibid.*

11. Executors, who reside abroad, cannot compel legatees of property in the state, to sue them elsewhere. Hepp et al. v. Lafonta's Executors, ii, 705.

12. An executor may be sued before he is ready to pay, on a debt of the succession which he refuses to acknowledge: the justice of the debt may be as well ascertained before, as after the representative of the estate has funds to meet it. Herman v. Flood et al., ii, 771.

13. The judgment against the executor, however, in such case should not be absolute so as to authorise an instant execution against him: it should order that the debt be paid by the executors in the due course of administration. *Ibid.*

14. A curator is according to law *functus officio* after the expiration of a year. Civil Code, 180. He must then render an account of what he has done, but cannot be compelled to do more under an expired authority. The court of probates has no jurisdiction of a subsequent suit against him. Johnson v. Brown, iii, 174.

15. When the will does not give seisin to the executors, they are all entitled to commission only on the sum which came into their hands to pay debts and legacies. Baillio v. Baillio, iii, 519.

16. The expiration of the office of a curator does not prevent the execution of a writ issued in his name while he legally represented the estate. Roberts v. Kinchen et al., iii, 602.

17. An executor may novate a debt of the estate. Turnbull *et al. v.* Freret, iii, 717.

18. Whether an executor can do any act to defeat the duties imposed on him by the will—*Quære?* Bernardine *v.* L'Espinasse, iii, 761.

19. An administrator does not become personally liable, on his letter announcing the sale of the property of the estate, and that the debt would be paid as soon as the money was collected, even on proof of such collection. Talmadge *et al. v.* Patterson, iv, 78.

20. A curator cannot be allowed credit for higher than legal fees paid by him to the parish judge. The fees of the parish judge are fixed by law; of this law no one can plead ignorance; if the curator paid higher fees he did so in his own wrong, and it is no justification that they were demanded of him. Arsenaux *v.* Michel, iv, 119.

21. He must suffer by the neglect of a person whom he entrusts with the collection of a note of the estate. *Ibid.*

22. Sureties of a curator are not responsible for debts of the estate of which the curator could not enforce payment. Cox *v.* Williams, iv, 294.

23. A co-executor may appear in a suit when a person prays to be admitted as heir, and the admissions of his co-executor, and the attorney for the absent heirs, will not prevent him insisting on strict and legal proof. Babin *v.* D'Astugue, iv, 372.

24. Though the time for which executors were appointed have expired, they may contest the right of a party claiming the estate as heir. *Ibid.*

25. A curator cannot compensate a claim of the estate, with a debt due to a firm of which he is a member. Byrd *v.* M'Micken, iv, 469.

26. An executrix, deriving her authority from a probate court of another state, cannot exercise the character of executrix here, without first having presented the testament to a court of probates in this state. Dangerfield's Executrix *v.* Thurston's Heirs, iv, 499.

27. Until the administrator presents his accounts, and obtains their homologation in the court of probates, or until the time expires for which he holds his appointment, any person having claim on the estate has a right to sue him as representing it. Nuttall and Wife *v.* Kirkland, iv, 520.

28. Title cannot be claimed to the property of an intestate, in this state, under a sale by an administrator appointed in Georgia. Morris *et al. v.* Thames, iv, 666.

D. *Of the Sale of Property belonging to Succession.*

1. If one of the partners be executor, the partnership cannot buy property at the sale of the testator's estate. Harrod *et al. v.* Norris's Heirs, ii, 200.

2. Any irregularity in the sale must be complained of before the homologation of the curator's account. Lafon's Executors *v.* Phillips *et al.*, ii, 644.

3. The purchaser of the land of an estate, under the directions of a Court of Probates, acquires it free from incumbrance. De Ende *v.* Moore, ii, 675.

4. Purchasers of land at probate sale, cannot call on the succession for the value of improvements put on it by third persons, if it were sold such as it belonged to the succession. Rutherford's Representatives *v.* Martin's Heirs, iii, 22.

5. If a probate sale be made to satisfy a mortgage, and the mortgagee become the purchaser, he will be allowed to retain the price. Bacon *v.* M'Nutt *et al.*, iii, 39.

6. Sales of deceased persons' estates are made with reference to the inventory and appraisement. Hamilton *v.* Hamilton *et al.*, iii, 783.

7. A purchaser of the property of a succession cannot offer in compensation a note of the testator. Green *v.* Davis *et al.*, iv, 225.

8. If a creditor's claim depends on a condition precedent, he has no right to interfere with the proceedings of the other creditors in relation to the sale of the estate. Beatty *v.* Wright's Estate, iv, 245.

9. A sale made without the authority of justice, is not binding on the creditors of a succession, and they have a right to call on the person making it to pay them the value of the object sold. Baillio *et al. v.* Wilson, iv, 541.

10. Creditors are not bound by a decree of a court of probates, which they had no opportunity to oppose. *Ibid.*

E. *Of the Payment of Debts and the Legacies, and of Rendition of Accounts.*

1. After a decree awarding a balance in favor of the widow and heirs, and ordering the executors to pay it to them, and also to deliver up all the items of uncollected debts, the executors have no right to bring the widow and heirs into court to hear new accounts, and debate new charges. Robin's Widow *et al. v.* His Ex'rs, i, 411.

2. One whose slave has been sold as part of the succession, is not to be classed with the creditors of the succession, but has a claim against the curator for the price. Donaldson *v.* Rust, i, 479.

. 3. Opposition being made to the payment of plaintiff's debt, is enough to require a classification of creditors before payment by the beneficiary heirs. Cox v. Martin's Heirs, ii, 323.

4. Vouchers filed by an executor in support of his account, are *prima facie* evidence of its correctness. Casanovichi *et al.* v. Debon *et al.*, ii, 754.

5. Creditors of an estate accepted with the benefit of inventory, must go into the court of probates, and be there paid according to the rank and order of their privilege. The circumstance of the creditor having a mortgage does not take him out of the general rule. Wilson v. Baillio *et al.*, iii, 23.

6. Executors cannot safely pay a mortgage creditor until his claims be settled contradictorily with the other creditors. Kenner *et al.* v. Duncan's Ex'rs, iii, 164.

7. If the representative of an estate fail to settle it, the regular course is to compel them to file a tableau of distribution. And if they fail to comply with an order to that effect, they will render themselves liable in their private capacity. *Ibid.*

8. The executor cannot pay any debt, without the order of the court, especially one against which the plea of prescription lies. Lafon's Heirs v. His Ex'rs, iii, 206.

9. Where the right of a legatee is disputed, he may bring suit to have the claim recognised, though judgment cannot be given for any specific amount, until the curator renders his account. And a jury may be called to try the facts on which the legatee's claim is disputed. Wooter v. Turner, iv, 8.

10. When the court of probates orders a syndic to account with a creditor according to his rank, the rights of the parties in relation to particular demands which may form a portion of that account, cannot be inquired into until it is rendered. Percy's Syndic v. Percy *et al.*, iv, 269.

F. *Of the Liabilities of Heirs.*

1. Children are not heirs till they accept. L. & M. Cresse v. Marigny, i, 216.

2. The heir cannot be sued till he accepts. Johnson v. Boon's Heirs, i, 261.

3. He who takes the quality of heir in acts, accepts the succession simply. Bingey v. Cox, ii, 713.

4. The heirs are bound only to the amount of what the estate was worth at the death of the ancestor. Changeur v. Gravier's Heirs, iii, 230.

5. If a debtor on receiving a release, bind himself to pay the debt if he becomes able, his heirs will be bound to apply his estate to the discharge of the debt. *Ibid.*

6. Persons suing the instituted heirs to set aside the will, thereby become liable to be sued by a creditor of the testator and made to pay the whole amount of the debt; although no part of the estate come into his hands. Dangerfield's Ex'rs v. Thurston's Heirs, iv, 499.

G. *Of Succession Generally.*

1. The office of special administrator is legal, and has not been abolished. Rogers v. Beiller, i, 192.

2. Judgment cannot be rendered against an estate till it be represented by an heir, or curator, Johnson v. Boon's Heirs, i, 261.

3. The estate of a deceased in the hands of his widow and heirs, is bound by a judgment obtained against his administrator. Randal's Widow and Heirs v. Baldwin *et al.*, i, 270.

4. The attorney for absent heirs may sue the curator of the estate for a balance due by him, without suing him and his sureties on the bond. In such an action the balance is to be deposited in the state treasury. Denis v. Cordeviella, i, 316.

5. The payment of property, part of a succession, to a person declared heir to it, by the judgment of a court of competent jurisdiction, unappealed from, is valid even after the judgment is reversed. Phillips v. Johnson *et al.*, i, 549.

6. If payment be made of a debt of the succession to a person declared heir to it, pending the appeal of the judgment which declared him so, and on the affirmance of the judgment a devolutive appeal is taken from the affirming judgment, the payment will be valid notwithstanding the payee is at last decreed not to be the heir. Phillips v. Curtis, i, 555.

7. The payment of *personal* property belonging to the succession, to a person recognised as heir to the *real* only, is invalid. Phillips v. Carson, i, 552.

8. He who claims as heir, must prove the death of the ancestor, who is presumed to live till he be one hundred years old. Sassman v. Aimé and Wife, i, 721.

9. An heir cannot set aside his ancestor's deed on the ground that it was made in fraud of his creditors. Terrel's Heirs v. Cropper, i, 733.

10. Although the heirs renounce the inheritance, a creditor cannot, without obtaining letters of curatorship, stand in judgment and oppose the rights or actions of another. Vienne v. Boissier, ii, 107.

11. Property within the state must be distributed, according to its laws, unless it be shown that the court is bound to give effect to those of another country. Bryan and Wife v. Moore's Heirs, ii, 168.

12. In a suit by heirs against the representative of their ancestor, the judgment should sever the share of each heir. Varion's Heirs v. Rousant's Syndics, ii, 292.

13. If a widow renounces her rights under a will in the idea that she is entitled to one half of it in her own right, and it afterwards appears she was in error as to the extent of her claim, the renunciation will not bind her. Tanner v. Robert, iii, 530.

14. Collateral kindred claiming an estate, are bound to show the lineal heirs have ceased to exist. Owens v. Mitchell, iii, 704; Bernardine v. L'Espinasse, iii, 761.

15. A child must collate the value of the hire of slaves lent to him by his father, to enable him to procure others. Hamilton v. Hamilton et al., iii, 783.

16. But not that of one sent to attend the child as a domestic. Ibid.

17. In a donation to one of the spouses in a contract of marriage, the posterity of the donee, not proceeding from the marriage, can not take. Doucet v. Broussard et al., iii, 806.

18. That person is to take as heir, who is such at the opening of the succession. Ibid.

19. An executor who qualified in another state, and removes to this state the property of the estate, is suable in the district court. He never was an executor here, but one who has been executor elsewhere. The property which is claimed from him was not the testator's when it was brought into this state, but that of the heirs. Singletary et al. v. Singletary, iv, 194.

20. Creditors of a succession cannot sue the heirs, while an action in which the same matters are involved, is pending between the curator and the defendants. Barbineau's Heirs v. Castille et al., iv, 204.

21. Until the curator of a succession makes a demand of the heirs of the effects belonging to it, they are not in fault in retaining them. Ibid.

22. Privileged or mortgagee creditor is not obliged to discuss the undivided property of a succession. Delahoussaye v. Delahoussaye et al., iv, 209.

23. Representation for the purpose of inheritance, does not extend to the children of cousins of the deceased. Civil Code, 803. Ratcliff et al. v. Ratcliff et al., iv, 263.

24. In a case where there was a conditional judgment, that the defendant should have ninety days to procure evidence and establish any set-offs he might have, and no use made of the condition within the time, it is too late for the heirs in a subsequent trial to inquire into this matter. Dangerfield's Executors v. Thurston's Heirs, iv, 499.

25. If a woman marries a second time having children by the first marriage, she cannot inherit from them in case of the decease of any. The survivor or survivors are heirs. But if they and their forced heirs die before the mother, the property so inherited by them belongs to her. Leblanc v. Landry, iv, 391.

26. Collateral kindred claiming as heirs must establish the death of relatives in ascending line. Hooter's Heirs v. Tippet, ii, 330.

27. A forced surrender cannot be ordered of the estate of a deceased person; it must be administered under the authority of the court of probates. Dupuy et al. v. Greffin's Executor, ii, 432.

28. The provisions of the Civil Code, 68, art. 54, 56, apply as well to successions opened before its passage and unsettled, as to those opened afterwards. Agaisse et al. v. Guedron et al., ii, 599.

29. Whether a foreigner can be admitted as a beneficiary heir? Quære. Lecesne v. Cottin, ii, 713.

30. A curator may demand the succession of his intestate's son, who died in his father's lifetime: the right of intestate was vested by law and required only to be exercised by the apprehension or possession of the property of the estate; it required no formal acceptance. If it did, the succession is accepted by the present suit. Bradford's Curator v. Beauchamp, iii, N. S. 473.

31. The net proceeds of an estate, are the amount of the inventory, after deducting the debts of insolvent debtors, articles which prove of no value, and its passive debts. Sanders v. Harding's Heirs, iii, 454.

SURETY.

The surety may be sued jointly with the principal though he pray the discussion of the property of his principal. Bernard et al. v. Curtis et al., i, 241.

2. If judgment be obtained against surety, execution shall be suspended until it be ascertained by the sale of the property of the principal debtor, how much the surety may have to pay. *Ibid.*

3. If a man puts his name on the back of a note not negotiable, the presumption is that he meant thereby to become surety for the payor. In such a case his liability does not depend on the fulfilment of the formalities by which the endorser of a negotiable paper becomes liable; and the payor may recover from such a surety, although he may have neglected to see the principal debtor, or through negligence suffered some advantage to be lost, whereby the surety is placed in a worse condition. Cooley *v.* Lawrence, i, 309.

4. The surety to an attachment bond is bound, though it should appear that at the time it was subscribed, no such bond was required by law to obtain an attachment. Lartigue *v.* Baldwin, i, 356.

5. A letter from defendant to plaintiffs, borne by M'Leary, saying "Capt. M'Leary being unacquainted at New Orleans, will be indebted to your politeness in affording him such assistance as his present situation requires, and a bill on his father for the funds he may need will be honored forthwith," is not a mere recommendation and advice, but an application for money on behalf of M'Leary. Amory *et al. v.* Boyd, i, 394.

6. If a curator die without accounting, and his representatives fail to do so, his surety is liable to be sued on the bond. Denys *v.* Armitage, i, 425.

7. Plaintiff need not sue the principal before he resorts to the surety. Curtis *v.* Martin i, 439; Delazerry *v.* Blanque's Syndics, i, 506.

8. The surety in a bond, in which it is stated that the principal has been appointed as auctioneer, is estopped from denying that he was. Duchamp *et al. v.* Nicholson, ii, 775.

9. The sureties of an auctioneer are bound for the payment of the amount of the goods sold, after the date of the bond, although they were delivered to him before. *Ibid.*

10. In whatever manner he may appear to have bound himself, he shall be bound. *Ibid.*

11. A surety in a custom-house bond is bound to reimburse his part, to the co-surety, who has paid the whole amount, although the goods were delivered and sold by the latter. Lloyd *et al. v.* Martin, i, 582.

12. If a person recommending his friend as trustworthy, says the debt will be paid and if not, he will be responsible, a recovery may be had against him on his friend's note posterior to the promise. Herries *v.* Canfield *et al.,* i, 746.

13. The surety wishing to avail himself of the plea of discussion, must point out property. *Ibid.*

14. A surety on a twelve months' bond on a *fi. fa.,* under the act of 1817, is immediately liable, though his principal died since its execution. Bynum *v.* Jackson, ii, 115.

15. The court may order a change of surety so as to enable the actual surety to testify. Butler *v.* De Hart, ii, 429.

16. The party who is bound under an order of court to give surety, must give persons residing within the state, and answerable to the process of her courts. Potter *v.* Richardson, ii, 455.

17. If a suit be brought against the principal and his sureties, and he fail in the meanwhile, judgment may well be taken against the sureties. Kuhn *et al. v.* Abat *et al.,* ii, 630.

18. The sureties of an auctioneer are liable for the value of goods, sold by him and a person whom he has associated to his business. *Ibid.*

19. The sureties on a sheriff's bond are liable, although it be not recorded. Whitehurst *v.* Hickey *et al.,* iii, 169.

20. Surety on a note has not the same liability with an endorser. Guidrey *v.* Vives, iii, 190.

21. On a suit against the sureties to a marshal's bond for fees collected, it is no defence that the plaintiff's claim against the United States is unimpaired. Dick *v.* Reynolds's Heirs *et al.,* iii, 378.

22. The surety on an injunction bond cannot resist payment on the ground that the plaintiff did not record his judgment. Elliott *v.* Cox, iii, 543.

23. Married women cannot, under any circumstances, become sureties for their husbands. M'Micken *v.* Smith and Wife, iii, 605; Hughes *v.* Harrison, iv, 229.

24. If A B fetch defendant to the counting-house of plaintiff (the latter having previously refused A B a loan,) and defendant, on coming there told plaintiff that A B was an honest man; that he might be trusted with safety to whatever amount he might wish, for that he was an honest man, and that he would pay; and that, if the defendant had the money himself, he would lend it to A B; and plaintiff on this statement accept A B's bill, who speedily becomes insolvent and fails to pay back the amount of this draft, yet is not defendant liable to plaintiff for the loss. Lobre *v.* Pointz, iii, 612.

25. A woman cannot be surety. The provisions of the Spanish law prohibiting it are not repealed by the Civil Code. Lacroix *v.* Coquet, iii, 644.

26. The surety is affected by notice of the assignment of the debt given to the principal. Reeves *et al. v.* Burton *et al.*, iii, 841.

27. A creditor may recover from the surety, although the former told the latter, the debtor was good, and no injury would result to the surety. Ford v. Miles, iii, 879.

28. The surety on a twelvemonths' bond cannot compel the obligor to proceed against the land sold, if the obligee's wife has obtained an injunction, which he unsuccessfully attempted to have dissolved. Louisiana Code, art. 3016. Dejean's Syndics *v.* Martin's Heirs, iv, 204.

29. If an absolute sale be made to a surety, for his indemnification, the legal title is in him, until he be relieved from the suretyship. Casson *v.* Louisiana State Bank, iv, 241.

30. Where there are several joint debtors, the surety has a right to call on each of them for the whole amount of his obligation. Representatives of Dickey *v.* Rogers, iv, 362.

31. The creditor who has a surety is not obliged to sue the principal. Moore *v.* Broussard, iv, 514.

32. The sureties on a sheriff's bond, are liable for the taxes on suits. Police Jury *v.* Bullit *et al.*, iv, 533.

33. The surety, on an attachment bond, is not liable, when the principal had a cause of action, but fails to recover, on account of some irregularity in the proceedings, posterior to the bond. Garretson *et al. v.* Zacharie, iv, 591.

TAXES.

1. The treasurer may withhold from a person, to whom the legislature has made an allowance, the amount of his taxes, for which the collector has reported him as a defaulter to the treasurer. Flower *et al. v.* Arnaud, iii, 232.

2. According to our laws on the subject of taxation, it is necessary that an assessment should be made in the manner pointed out therein, and transmitted to the collectors of taxes, before they can proceed to make their collections. Nancarrow *v.* Weathersbee, iii, 866.

3. The power of summarily enforcing payment of a tax, cannot be exercised in regard to other taxes. Police Jury *v.* Bullit *et al.*, iv, 533.

4. A sheriff, sued for the taxes he was bound to collect, must show he failed in doing so, after having used proper diligence. *Ibid.*

5. The state is not bound to show the amount of taxes actually collected. *Ibid.*

6. A tax levied on the stock in trade of an insurance company, extends to capital secured as well as paid in. The La. Ins. Co. *v.* Morgan *et al.*, iv, 643.

7. The oath of the president and directors is not conclusive as to the amount of stock. *Ibid.*

8. The act of 1813, imposing a tax on stock, does not require the president and directors of stock companies *all* to swear to their declarations: the affidavit of either or one suffices. La. State Ins. Co. *v.* Morgan *et al.*, iv, 663.

TERRITORY OF ORLEANS.

1. The inhabitants of the Territory became citizens of Louisiana and of the United States by the admission of the country as one of the United States. Desbois's Case, i, 57.

2. Congress have power to govern the territories of the United States, and may establish territorial legislatures. The State *v.* New Orleans Navigation Company, ii, 303.

3. The governor and legislative council of the Orleans territory had power to grant the charter of the New Orleans Navigation Company. The charter is not affected by any law of congress, anterior or posterior to its date. *Ibid.*

THIRD PERSONS.

1. Third parties to an act, are those who are not parties to an instrument by which their interest in the thing conveyed, is affected. Trudeau *et al. v.* Smith's Syndics, ii, 367.

2. Plaintiffs having failed in their case, both parties go out of court, and the claim of a third party to the property attached can not be investigated, his pretensions to the same not being contradictory with those of any party. Mackee *et al. v.* Cairnes, ii, 754.

3. A creditor has no right to interfere in a suit between his debtor and a third party. Brown & Sons *v.* Saul *et al.*, iii, 343.

4. A third party cannot intervene in a suit to plead peremptory exceptions on behalf of the defendants. Clamegeran *v.* Bucks & Hendrick *et al.*, iii, 366.

5. Third parties are not bound by the recitals in an act of sale. Delahoussaye *v.* Delahoussage *et al.*, iii, 209.

TRESPASS.

1. The seizure of real estate on a *fieri facias* divests the defendant of the legal pos. session, and whomsoever the sheriff puts into possession is not a trespasser as regards the person divested. Prevost and Wife *v.* Hennen, i, 362.

2. A justice and constable, who proceed in a case after a prohibition, and a person who aids the constable, are trespassers. Seré *v.* Armitage *et al.,* i, 750.

3. A void authority will not justify a trespass though the party acting under it is in good faith. *Ibid.*

4. The party who succeeds on the question of title, in a suit for land, may be obliged to pay damages for an illegal and forcible entry. Larche *v.* Jackson, i, 755.

5. Trespassers cannot avert a judgment for damages by compensation or reconvention. Innis *v.* Ware, ii, 544.

6. No man can protect himself upon a trespass by averring himself agent of another, unless that other had authority to do the act. Peet *et al. v.* Morgan, iii, 780.

7. An officer, sued as a trespasser, in a sale on a *fieri facias* may cite the party by whose directions he acted, and who gave a bond of indemnity. Thompson *v.* Chaveau *et al.,* iv, 15.

8. A trespasser cannot allege that the plaintiff has a title which is voidable. Kernion *v.* Guenon, ii, 197.

9. Trespassers cannot call in warranty those under whose authority they acted. Tourné *et al. v.* Lee *et al.* iv, 615.

TRUST.

1. The code in abolishing substitutions, did not abolish naked trusts uncoupled with an interest, which were to be executed immediately. Marthurin *v.* Livaudais, iii, 551.

2. Where trustees are appointed in a country governed by the common law, to receive interest on a bond and pay it over to a *cestui que trust*, and the obligor fails, the trustees have authority to lend the money out to others. Morgan *et al. v.* Their Creditors, iii, 894.

UNDERTAKERS AND WORKMEN.

1. Carpenter repairing a ship for a fixed price, loses his materials and labor if the ship be destroyed before the work is finished. Seguin *v.* Debon, i, 77.

2. The workman who proffers a plan stipulates that it is feasible. Orleans Navigation Company *v.* Boutte, i, 46.

3. Material-men and workmen, employed by the undertaker of a building, have no privilege of their own; but may avail themselves of it. Nolte *et al. v.* Their Creditors, iii, 794.

4. This claim is not postponed to the reimbursement of advances not stipulated for *Ibid.*

5. Neither of them acquires a preference over the other by a seizure. *Ibid.*

6. Artisans have no right to protect more tools from seizure on a *fieri facias* than those which are necessary to their livelihood. Parker *v.* Starkweather, iv, 264.

7. A person undertaking to superintend a distillery and sugar plantation comes under an implied covenant, to possess and display the necessary skill to conduct such business. Garahan *v.* Weeks, iv, 482.

8. If a party agrees to go to New York, and report himself as ready to commence work in the capacity of an engineer, for building one or more steam engines, and to attend to the casting, erecting and putting up said engines, in complete operation, his claim for compensation is not that of an overseer, but that of a workman, which is prescribed by the lapse of one year. Louisiana Code, art. 3499. Nichols *v.* Hanse *et al.,* iv, 596.

9. And an agreement, that he will be guided by the defendants, does not affect their claim for damages, if the work be not performed in a skilful and workmanlike manner. *Ibid.*

UNITED STATES MARSHAL AND OTHER OFFICERS.

1. The marshal of the United States is suable in a state court for a trespass committed under color of an authority under a process issued out of a court of the United States. Dunn and Wife *v.* Vail, i, 577; Johnson's Executor *v.* Wall *et al.,* ii, 530.

2. An injured person may bring suit, in his own name, on a marshal's bond. Hernandez *et al. v.* Montgomery, ii, 697.

3. It is a breach of the condition of the bond, not to have the proceeds of the sale of a vessel ordered to be sold, ready, &c. *Ibid.*

WALLS.

He who builds first in the city, towns and suburbs of the territory, in a place which is not surrounded by walls, may rest one half of his wall on the land of his neighbour. Larche *v.* Jackson, i, 51.

WAR.

The march of French troops into Spain, in 1813, was an act of war against Spain.—Pouts *v.* Louisiana State Insurance Company, iii, 236.

WARRANTY.

Damages on warranty are not confined to the price of the thing. Findley *v.* Breedlove *et al.*, iii, 244.

WATER COURSES.

1. Erecting works on a stream of water, by which a mill previously placed there is prevented working, is illegal. Boatner *v.* Henderson *et al.*, iii, 500.

2. And it is immaterial whether the obstruction is created by preventing the stream from descending, or by throwing the water back on the old mill, so that it cannot work. *Ibid.*

WOMAN.

1. A woman could not, previous to the passage of the Louisiana Code, bind herself as surety, though she gave to her engagement the form of an endorsement on a note.—Louisiana State Bank *v.* Rowell, iv, 266.

2. And she may give parol evidence that she was in fact surety though the instrument on the face of it creates a higher obligation. *Ibid.*

3. A woman cannot be curatrix to an absentee. Carraby *v.* Carraby, iv, 318.

4. *Semble,* a wife, to be preferred to the presumptive heir, under article 50, Civil Code, must have the qualification of the masculine gender? *Ibid.*

THE END.